# HISTORIC HOUSES CASTLES & GARDENS

## OPEN TO THE PUBLIC

## 1989

*Editor:* Sheila Alcock

Published by British Leisure Publications, Windsor Court.
East Grinstead House, East Grinstead, West Sussex RH19 1XA
Telephone (0342) 326972    Telex 95127 INFSER G

BRITISH
Leisure
PUBLICATIONS

Warwick Castle
The finest mediaeval castle in England
Open every day
(except Christmas Day)

HISTORIC HOUSES CASTLES & GARDENS in Great Britain & Ireland

# INTRODUCTION

This Guide to Historic Houses, Castles and Gardens includes most of the habitable properties open to the public; monuments and properties in the care of English Heritage are shown in a special section.

The introductory article this year is by John Forgie, who describes the tremendous variety of properties in the care of the National Trust for Scotland, and on page 22, the aims and aspirations of the Heritage Education Trust are discussed by Martyn Dyer.

Arley Hall Gardens were the winners of the Historic Houses Association/Christies Garden of the Year Award, and are featured on our title page. More information about the award can be found on page 8.

Gardens open by courtesy of the owners in aid of the National Gardens Scheme and Scotland's Garden Scheme, or the Gardeners' Charities, are included where these gardens are open on several occasions during the summer months. Guided tours are organised at many houses and these denoted by a symbol. Connoisseur days are becoming more widely featured by House owners, but are not generally guided. All admission charges quoted are subject to change without notice. All dates are inclusive, i.e. May to September, Weds, means first Wednesday in May to last Wednesday in September. Opening times and dates apply to 1989 only.

# CONTENTS



Symbols shown in text:

△ Guided tours Ⓔ Educational services recognised by Heritage Education Trust ♿ Majority of the property is accessible by wheelchairs Ⓢ The property is a recipient of the Sandford Award.

Cover picture: Hill of Tarvit
by kind permission of The National Trust for Scotland.

Title Page picture: Arley Hall Gardens,
winner – Christie's/HHA Garden of the Year award.

 ISBN No: 0 948056 12 6.

Woburn Abbey
Showplace of England
For details see Bedfordshire section

ARUNDEL CASTLE

Family home of the Dukes of Norfolk

For details see West Sussex section

So much to do at Chatsworth
for full details see under Derbyshire

# Come to RAGLEY HALL a day out with a difference

Ragley Hall, designed by Robert Hooke in 1680 and the home of the Seymour family for over 300 years.

The Great Hall, designed in 1750 by James Gibbs.

The South Staircase Hall with magnificent mural 'The Temptation', painted by Graham Rust between 1969 and 1983.

Queen Jane Seymour.

The Marquess and Marchioness of Hertford invite you to spend an enjoyable day at Ragley Hall, one of the finest Palladian houses in England, set in 400 acres of landscaped parkland, woodland and garden.

Experience the grandeur and history of the Hall and the fun of the Adventure Wood and other outdoor attractions ...all in one visit!

The Adventure Wood – very popular with children.

For more details see Warwickshire section or telephone Ragley Hall on Alcester (0789) 762090

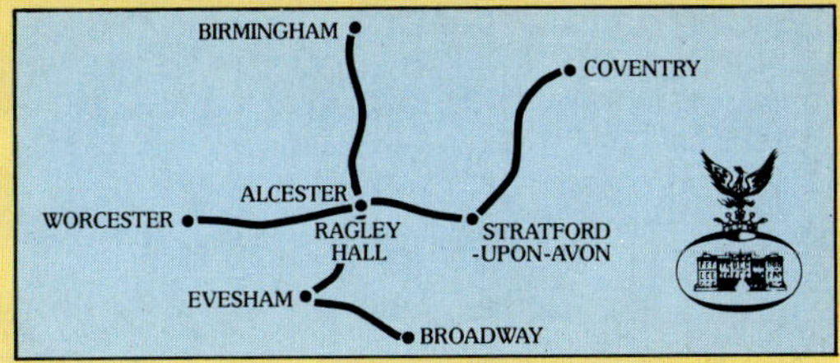


Ragley Hall is on the Alcester to Evesham road, only 15 minutes' drive from Stratford.

# The Country's Strangest Landlord

by John Forgie

Where can you go to compare the life-style of a lord with that of a Glasgow seamstress or the skill of a weaver with that of a printer? For those touring in Scotland, the answer is not hard to find. Such differing lifestyles, together with many other diverse attractions, are all to be found at various properties of the National Trust for Scotland.

Often described as "the country's strangest landlord", the Trust owns over a 100 properties dotted throughout the country – from Threave Garden, in the south, to Fair Isle, in the north. There is a rich scattering of castles and gardens, birthplaces of famous people, thousands of acres of beautiful countryside, a clutch of islands, several battlesites – and so much more.

At many of its properties there are visitor centres where modern interpretation facilities add to the interest of the visitor. Shops and restaurants cater for the further enjoyment of a visit to a property. Children are not forgotten and at a number of the Trust's locations there are special guidebooks and adventure play areas for children. The Trust encourages family visits and even offers a special category for membership which gives free admittance to all its properties for an entire family. Details of this scheme may be obtained from the head office of the National Trust for Scotland at 5 Charlotte Square, Edinburgh.

But what a wide spectrum of interest is reflected in the properties and activities of the Trust – a completely separate organisation from the National Trust in England, Wales and Northern Ireland. Driving north across the border, near the busy A74 and only 20 miles north of Carlisle, in the little village of Ecclefechan is the birthplace of Thomas Carlyle, the great 19th-century historian, essayist, social reformer and prophet. Or if gardens are your bent, head west towards the shimmering waters of the Solway Firth and you come to the beautiful gardens at Threave, near Castle Douglas. Here too is the Trust's School of Gardening where resident students qualify for a place in the professional world of horticulture.

Anyone with a taste for castles, has a choice of nine in differing shapes and sizes and in various parts of Scotland. To combine a short sea voyage with a visit to a castle, take the ferry from the Ayrshire port of Ardrossan. Fifty-five minutes later you will be standing on the pier on the beautiful Isle of Arran, looking across the bay to the red-sandstone bulk of Brodick Castle. The magnificence of the scenario, with the spectacular background of mountain peaks and glens, is only matched by the splendour of the interior of the castle.

On display is a superb collection of silver, paintings and furnishings, many of the items being part of William Beckford's great collection which in its time would have rivalled the great Burrell Collection in Glasgow. The castle rooms are set out as they were when it was the home of the Duke and Duchess of Montrose. The rich furnishings of the first floor

*Glenfinnan Monument.*

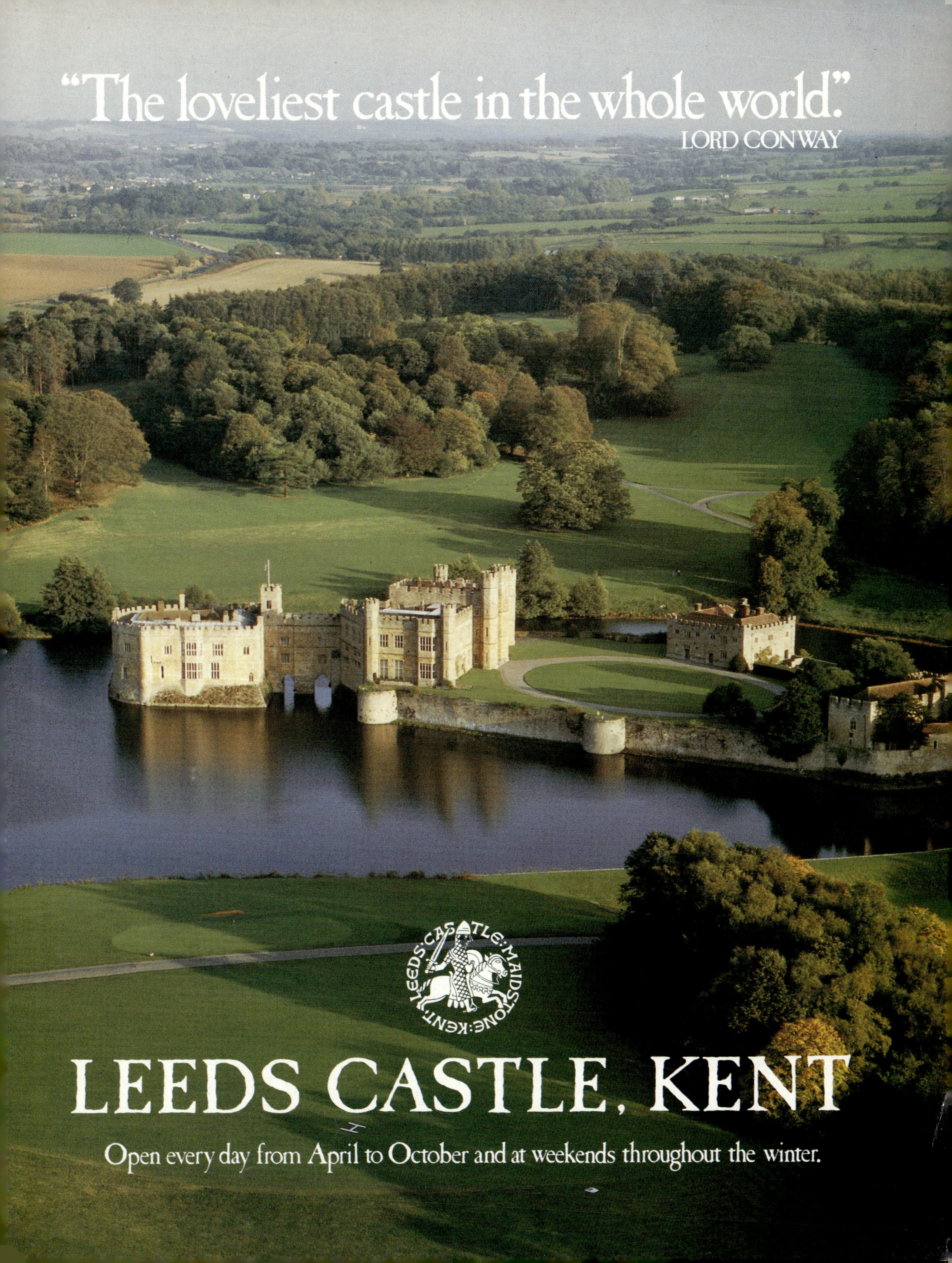
"The loveliest castle in the whole world."
LORD CONWAY
LEEDS CASTLE · MAIDSTONE · KENT
LEEDS CASTLE, KENT
Open every day from April to October and at weekends throughout the winter.

rooms contrast with the busy clutter of the Victorian kitchen on the ground floor.

Outside, children can enjoy themselves for hours in an imaginative adventure playground while their parents wander through 60 acres of gardens ablaze with colour and world-famous for their rhododendrons. Visitors may have a cup of tea or a meal in the restaurant, buy good quality souvenirs in the castle shop and then have the prospect of the pleasant sail back to mainland Scotland.

"Spend a day-out with the family at a Trust property" proclaims one of the organisation's publicity leaflets and at Brodick or at many other properties, like Culzean Castle and Country Park further down the Ayrshire coast, or in the north-east at magnificent Crathes Castle and gardens near Aberdeen, or over in the west at lovely Inverewe Garden, that is what many holidaymakers and local residents alike enjoy doing.

Apart from birthplaces, castles and gardens, the Trust offers an experience of Scotland's industrial heritage. Amid the rolling and luxurious farmland of East Lothian, near Dunbar, is Preston Mill, the oldest, mechanically working, water-driven meal mill. Here the gush of water through the mill lade heralds the squeak and rumble of the old machinery as it gathers momentum to grind the grain into flour. Or in the Border country, at Innerleithen, the Trust is painstakingly restoring an almost 150-year-old printing works – a time capsule of the industry where the skills and machines of yester-year are being revived.

Gardens have already been mentioned, and Inverewe in particular, and for the horticulturist or, as the old song says – "people who have gardens . . ." – twenty-two major gardens beckon the Trust's visitors. From a city garden – Branklyn in Perth – to Inverewe, fringed by the Atlantic Ocean there are spectacles to delight both the expert gardener or simply those

*Brodick Castle, Arran. Ancient seat of the Dukes of Hamilton, and more recently of the late Mary, Duchess of Montrose, built on a fortress site since Viking days. Part of present castle dates from 13th century; it was extended in 1652 and 1844. The contents include silver, porcelain, and paintings from the collections of the Dukes of Hamilton, William Beckford and the Earls of Rochford. Sporting pictures and trophies.*

*Smail's Printing works.*

who enjoy being in beautiful and restful surroundings. In the far north-west, at Inverewe, 125 years ago there was a barren peninsula but importantly it was warmed by the Gulf Stream (or as children are now taught – the North Atlantic Drift). To this lonely place came a man of vision, Osgood Mackenzie. He began planting the peninsula in 1862 and created one of the finest gardens in Scotland now in the care of the Trust and visited annually by some 120,000 people.

A recent newspaper article was headed, "Who Cares for the Countryside?". One of the answers has to be the National Trust for Scotland because it has in its care over 100,000 acres of mountains, glens, moorland and islands. The rugged cliffs at St Abbs Head contrast with frowning peaks in Glen Coe or the towering magnificence of the Torridon mountains in Wester Ross. Access to the Trust's countryside is free and encouraged. Rangers are on hand to explain the country code which visitors are encouraged to follow so that the countryside which is in trust for the nation is not despoiled. Buildings are more tangible in preservation terms but the Trust also exercises careful stewardship of its many countryside properties.

The Trust casts a wide net in its interpretive work and it brings the past alive at its historic sites – at Bannockburn, dominated by the great equestrian statue of Robert the Bruce, King of Scots; by the banks of Loch Shiel at Glenfinnan, where Bonnie Prince Charles raised by his Jacobite standard; at the now peaceful Pass of Killiecrankie, in Perthshire, where 330 years ago much blood was spilt; or in the evocative

Blenheim Palace
Home of the 11th Duke of Marlborough, birthplace of Sir Winston Churchill.
Open daily 10.30 am–5.30 pm (last admission 4.45 pm) mid March to 31st October 1989.
Visit Blenheim Palace; A wonderful way to spend the day.
The inclusive ticket lets you park your car, Tour the Palace with it's magnificent State Rooms, view the Churchill Exhibition, walk in the beautiful Gardens and Arboretum, relax in the peaceful Parkland, enjoy a trip on the Lake, ride on the Train, take the children to the Butterfly House and Adventure Play Area, browse in the Gift Shops and Garden Centre, and use the Water Terrace or Garden Restaurants.
All at Blenheim Palace—one of Britain's most magnificent and accessible Historic Houses.
Charity Cricket Match, Lord Taveners XI v Oxford University XI Spring Bank Holiday Sunday.
Administrator, Blenheim Palace, Woodstock, Oxford OX7 1PX (Tel: 0993-811325).
The right to close the Palace and Park without notice is reserved.

atmosphere at Culloden, near Inverness, where in 1746 was fought the last major battle on mainland Britain.

At Trust properties throughout Scotland there is so much to see and so much to do. The Trust's Ranger service offers a wide selection of guided walks throughout the summer. Walks to hear the dawn chorus, "wellie" walks for children, garden, mountain and naturalist walks are all part of the outdoor programme.

So much to do and so much to see and all provided by Scotland's leading conservation organisation whose dedicated staff take a special pride in helping to preserve the best of the country's past for future generations.

**A designated charity, the Trust depends largely on the strength of its ever-expanding membership to provide finance to maintain its momentum. Founded in 1931 by 11 far-seeing conservationists, it now has a membership of over 160,000.**

**Details and a free leaflet about its many properties, as well as application forms for membership, can be obtained at any property or by writing to The National Trust for Scotland, 5 Charlotte Square, Edinburgh EH2 4DU.**

*Equestrian statue of King Robert the Bruce at Bannockburn.*

*Carlyle's Birthplace. The Arched House in which Thomas Carlyle was born, 4 Dec. 1795. House was built by his father and uncle, both master masons. Contains collection of his belongings and MSS letters. Visitors in 1973, 1,911. Handed over in 1935 by Trustees of Carlyle's House Memorial Fund.*

# FOUR HISTORIC FAMILY HOMES
## within easy reach of London

### STRATFIELD SAYE HOUSE

Family home of the Dukes of Wellington.
For details see Hampshire section.

### HATFIELD HOUSE

Family home of the Marquess of Salisbury.
For details see Hertfordshire section.

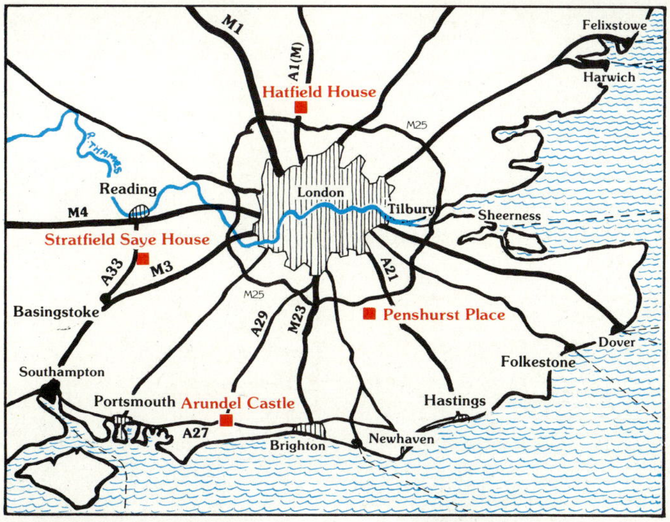


### ARUNDEL CASTLE

Ancestral home of the Dukes of Norfolk.
For details see West Sussex section.

### PENSHURST PLACE

Family home of William Sidney, Vicount De L'Isle, VC, KG. For details see Kent section.

## THE GARDENS AT

# HATFIELD HOUSE Hertfordshire

"There are nearly 14 acres of formal and informal gardens dating back to the late 15th century. From 1609 to 1611 John Tradescant the Elder laid out and planted the gardens for Robert Cecil, the builder of the House. Today the gardens, much embellished in the last years, contain many of the same plants growing in knot gardens typical of the period, arranged in the court of the 15th century Palace where Queen Elizabeth I spent much of her childhood. There are herb and sweet gardens, a parterre of herbaceous plants and roses, fountains, statuary and a foot maze or labyrinth, the whole enclosed in ancient rose-brick walls, topiaried yews, holly and pleached limes.

A wilderness garden, planted with forest and ornamental trees, blossoms in the spring with crabs, cherries, magnolias and rhododendrons underplanted with many flowers and bulbs, the whole providing colour and interest (for there are many rare and unusual plants) for all seasons."

*"Photographs by Mick Hales, Garry Rogers and Jeremy Whitaker."*

"I feel at home here as I gaze down and respond to the feeling of total delight which it gives me . . ." Sir Roy Strong

"Hatfield's gardens are the most completely beautiful and fit for their purpose of any great house in England." "Tradescant" of the RHS Journal.

# Belvoir Castle

## HOME OF THE DUKE AND DUCHESS OF RUTLAND

A CASTLE IN THE GRAND STYLE commanding a magnificent view over the Vale of Belvoir ("beautiful view"). The name dates back to the famous Norman Castle that stood on this same site.
The Castle was rebuilt in 1816 after a catastrophic fire and owes much to the inspiration of Elizabeth the 5th Duchess of Rutland. There are many notable art treasures and interesting military relics.

## THE GARDENS

The Statue gardens contain many beautiful 17th Century sculptures. There are flowers in bloom throughout most of the season.

## MEDIEVAL JOUSTING

The world famous Medieval Jousting Tournaments on the Castle terrace attract 25,000 visitors annually.

## JOUSTING DATES 1989

Sunday and Monday May 28th and 29th
Sunday June 25th, Sunday July 30th
Sunday and Monday August 27th and 28th
Sunday September 10th

These exciting professionally staged tournaments are a must for overseas visitors. NO EXTRA CHARGE.

## FLOWER FESTIVAL

September 14th, 15th, 16th and 17th. Flowers in most rooms, decorations by the North Midlands area of NAFAS.

## SCHOOL VISITS

Guided tours, talks and special projects are all devised to capture a child's imagination.

## CONFERENCE/FILMING

A magnificent backdrop for conferences, banquets, film and TV location.

## FILMS

Location of the film "Little Lord Fauntleroy" with Alec Guinness. Steven Spielberg's "Young Sherlock Holmes" and "Hazard of Hearts" from the novel by Barbara Cartland.

## ADMISSION PRICES

£2.60 adults. £1.50 children. Group rates: 30+ adults £2.00, 30+ Snr. citizens and School Parties £1.50. All Coach Tours and Excursions £2.00. No additional charges, free parking.

## PRIVATE PARTIES

Can be arranged by appointment when the House is otherwise closed.
For opening details, please see under Belvoir Castle, Leicestershire.
For Free Colour Leaflet with all opening hours, group rates, catering tariffs and any other information—please contact: Jimmy Durrands, Controller, The Estate Office, Belvoir Castle, FREEPOST, Grantham, Lincs. NG31 6BR (no stamp needed) or telephone Grantham 0476 870262.

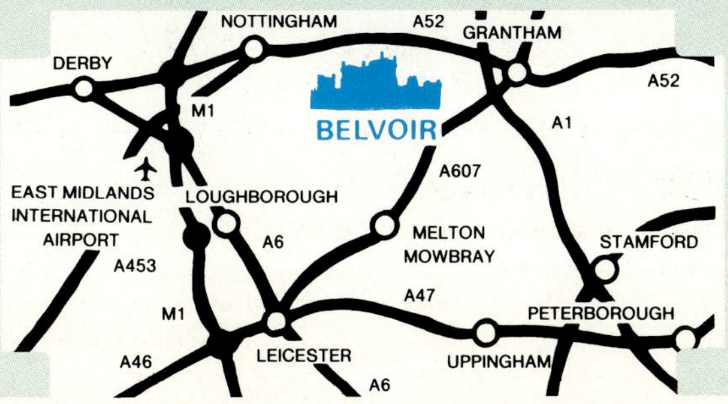

# The Royal Palaces.
# Easy to get to, hard to leave.

London has so many interesting sights that it's hard to know where to begin.

But if you're interested in the Kings and Queens of England, we would like to suggest four royal palaces you really shouldn't overlook.

*Kensington Palace*

Our first suggestion is the Kensington Palace State Apartments.

Bought by William III from the Earl of Nottingham for £14,000 in 1689, the Palace became William and Mary's London home and is still used as a royal residence today.

Visit the State Apartments, view the superb ceilings by William Kent, marvel at the fine wall tapestries and admire the impressive collection of seventeenth century paintings.

You can also stand in the room where Queen Victoria is reputed to have been born and in the Court Dress Collection you can even get a close look at the wedding dress of HRH The Princess of Wales.

*The Tower of London*

The next recommendation isn't so much one sight, as many.

The Tower of London is a complete day out in itself.

It has been a royal palace as well as a fortress and prison during its 900 year history.

Visit the Bloody Tower where the little princes met their fate.

Stand on Tower Green, the site of the execution block where two of Henry's wives met theirs.

Walk along the wall or inspect everything from a suit of armour to an oar from the "Mary Rose" in the Royal Armouries.

And don't leave without first gazing upon the Crown Jewels in all their glory, guarded as ever by the Yeomen Warders.

*The Banqueting House*

While the Tower of London is famous for its treasures, Whitehall possesses one little known gem.

It is the Banqueting House, directly opposite Horse Guards Parade and all that remains of the Whitehall Palace.

Designed by Inigo Jones, it was Charles I who commissioned Rubens to paint the splendid ceiling as a tribute to his father, James I.

Unhappily for Charles, his last glimpse of the ceiling was from the scaffold outside, on the day of his execution.

*Hampton Court Palace*

Last, but not least, is Hampton Court Palace.

Built by Thomas Wolsey – later Cardinal Wolsey – the Palace quickly became Henry VIII's favourite royal residence.

Indeed, Hampton Court Palace has played host to four centuries of history up to Queen Victoria's reign when the State Apartments were opened to the public.

You'll want to see where they still play "real" tennis, pass the time of day with the Astronomical Clock made for Henry VIII by Nicholas Oursian in 1540, and get lost in the maze.

You can also walk around the beautiful gardens just as the Kings and Queens of England once did.

So there you have it.

Four very different sights of London not to be missed. Each one an experience you'll always treasure.

And all of them so easy to get to.

HOW TO GET THERE:

*Kensington Palace.*
Nearest Tube: High Street Kensington (District & Circle), Queensway (Central). Nearest Bus route: 9, 49, 52, 52a, C1. All year Mon-Sat 09.00-17.00. Sun 13.00-17.00. Closed 24-26 Dec, 1 Jan, Good Friday.

*The Tower of London.*
Nearest Tube: Tower Hill (District & Circle). Nearest Bus route: 15, 42, 56, 70, 78, 188, 278. Mar-Oct Mon-Sat 09.30-17.00. Sun 14.00-17.00. Nov-Feb Mon-Sat 09.30-16.00. Closed Sun. Closed 24-26 Dec, 1 Jan, Good Friday. Jewel House closed Feb.

*The Banqueting House.*
Nearest Tube: Charing Cross (Bakerloo, Jubilee, Northern), Westminster (District & Circle). Nearest Bus route: 3, 9, 11, 12, 24, 29, 53, 70, 72, 77a, 88, 109, 177, 184, 196. All year Tues-Sat 10.00-17.00. Sun 14.00-17.00. Closed 24-26 Dec, 1 Jan, Good Friday and at short notice for government functions.

*Hampton Court Palace.*
Nearest Rail Station: Hampton Court (from Waterloo). Nearest Bus routes: 111, 131, 216, 267. Apr-Sept Mon-Sat 09.30-18.00. Sun 11.00-18.00. Oct-Mar Mon-Sat 09.30-17.00. Sun 14.00-17.00. Last admissions half an hour before closing. Closed 24-26 Dec, 1 Jan.

Department of the Environment

**ROYAL PARKS & PALACES**

**An experience you'll always treasure.**

# HERITAGE EDUCATION TRUST

## Sainsbury Family Trust Supports Heritage Education

### BIG GRANT TO HET

The Headley Trust, one of the Sainsbury Family Trusts is to support the work of the Heritage Education Trust (HET) with an award of **£22,500.00** spread over the next three years. The money will be used to help a new HET initiative entitled **"Education Through Heritage and the Arts".**

The aim of the project is to encourage all the creative and performing arts subjects to draw upon the resources of the heritage for inspiration and the enrichment of their curriculum and in turn to use their creativity and skills as a means of presenting and promoting a further understanding of historic buildings, their contents, surroundings and history as well as of their place in the economy of the country and current social role.

Participating schools will be asked to stage a series of regional events to demonstrate how they have done this. From these regional responses three schools will be selected by HET as finalists to appear in an historic prestige venue in London in 1992.

**"Education Through Heritage and the Arts"** will be promoted nationwide by HET as part of its on-going strategy of encouraging more and more schools to use the unique resources of our heritage as part of their curriculum, persuading more and more owners to co-operate with schools by setting up educational services and facilities on site and of finding original and practical ways and means of creating opportunities within the Heritage for the talent which exists in our schools

*Girls from Sydenham School (ILEA) presented dances choreographed by Alison Pooley at the Banqueting House, Whitehall, on 12 November 1987. It was part of the HET event **Under a Rubens Ceiling** which led to the Headley Trust grant in support of the new project **Education Through Heritage and the Arts.***

Kettering Evening Telegraph

*The Rt. Hon. Kenneth Baker, M.P., Secretary of State for Education and Science was the Guest of Honour at the launch of HET's new journal, NIMROD, at Lamport Hall, Northants, Friday 6th May 1988. The Minister accepted the invitation from pupils of Bective Middle School to join them in their seventeenth century Snake Dance on the lawns. Northamptonshire Schools also demonstrated drama, computers, music, graphics design and display as part of their programme in Heritage Education.*

to present and interpret historic buildings to each other and to the wider visiting public.

The project will be of interest to owners and administrators of properties and to anyone working in the educational field who values the heritage and wishes to see its resources used to enhance the school curriculum. Full details are now available and enquiries are invited from those in responsible positions in properties, Chief Education Officers, Heads of Schools and Departments, advisers, teachers and parent governors. **See below for address.**

**Wigan Pier Hosts 1988 Sandford Awards Ceremony**

The Earl of Caithness, Minister for the Environment, was the Guest of Honour at the 1988 Presentation Ceremony for the 1987 Sandford Award winners. Wigan Pier, was the first museum venue chosen by the Trust to stage its main prestige event of the year. In choosing Wigan the Trust wished to mark not only the achievements of the Education Service at the Pier but also the strong support given by Wigan Metropolitan and its Education Department to the concept of Heritage Education. The Department has seconded a team of three teachers led by **Marilyn Sumner** to direct Heritage Education at Wigan Pier, backed directly by **Kevin Hampson**, Director of Education and his assistant, **David Davies**.

*Some of Captain Coram's Northamptonshire Kids.*

The formal presentation ceremony at Wigan was set in a day long programme of events with full schools participation throughout. At the end of the formal proceedings the Minister spent over an hour touring the Wigan Pier Heritage Centre where the various exhibits also included a comprehensive exhibition of educational work from thirty past winners of the Sandford Award. This exhibition then went on tour first to the Wiend Centre and then to the Derby Room in the Wigan Metropolitan area before being sent south to Northampton for exhibition at the Third Biennial Conference of the Heritage Education Trust. There it was displayed over the three days of the conference – Wednesday 14th–Friday 16th September 1988, after which it began a six months tour of Teachers' Centres throughout the county of Northampton.

*Commander Michael Saunders Watson, Vice-Chairman of the Heritage Education Trust, and David Mann, Managing Director of the Northamptonshire Enterprise Agency, after a performance of* **Captain Coram's Kids** *given by choirs of Rushden Whitefriars Junior School and Montagu Secondary School at the 1988 National Conference of HET held at Nene College Northants. The Agency sponsored the performance which was attended by the composer, Michael Hurd (second from the left). Also in the picture are the choirs' teachers Judith Tomkin and Barry Clark and Martyn Dyer.* **Captain Coram's Kids** *was originally commissioned by HET and sponsored by British Leisure Publications as part of the programme, Under a Rubens Ceiling in the Banqueting House Whitehall.*

Kettering Evening Telegraph

*Mr. Baker with David Hill, Senior Inspector, Northamptonshire County Council and Brenda Briggs, Head of Art and Design at Bective School who trained the dance group.*

**Northamptonshire Enterprise Agency and the Trusts' Northants '88 Programme**

Throughout 1988 the Heritage Education Trust mounted a comprehensive programme in Northampton culminating in the Third National Conference referred to above at Nene College. The Trust's efforts were supported by a grant of **£1,000** from the Northamptonshire Enterprise Agency.

A new feature of the Trust's Third Conference was a display by Northamptonshire schools relating to work done over the year in schools using the heritage resources available in the county. Northamptonshire leads the rest of the nation with no less than four Sandford Award winning properties within its boundaries. In order to encourage further development of work in Heritage Education in the county the Heritage Education Trust has allocated **£300** of its Northamptonshire Enterprise Agency grant to three prizes of **£100** each, to be made to the three Northamptonshire schools, one in each of the age groups **under 9, 9–13, and 13+** which demonstrate the most imaginative use of the educational resources of the four Sandford Award winning properties in Northampton.

For full details of **"Education Through Heritage and the Arts"** project and of the Heritage Education Trust address your enquiry to **Martyn Dyer, Chief Executive, Heritage Education Trust, St. Mary's College, Strawberry Hill, TW1 4SX or telephone 01-892 0051 ext. 202 9.30am to 2.30pm Mondays to Thursdays inclusive or telephone answer service (24 hours) at other times on same number.**

# Sandford Award Winners

## Complete List, 1978—1988

The following properties received Sandford Awards in the years in brackets after their names. Two dates indicate that the property has been reviewed and received a second Sandford Award under the system of Quinquennial Review introduced by the Heritage Education Trust in 1986.

Any property which wishes to retain its listing must apply for review of its educational services and facilities five years after the date of its last award.

The closing date for initial applications and quinquennial review is 31st March.

AVONCROFT MUSEUM OF BUILDINGS, Bromsgrove, Worcs (**1988**)
BEAULIEU ABBEY, Nr. Lyndhurst, Hampshire (**1978**) (**1986**)
BEDE MONASTERY MUSEUM, Jarrow, Tyne and Wear (**1988**)
BICKLEIGH CASTLE, Nr. Tiverton, Devon (**1983**) (**1988**)
BLENHEIM PALACE, Woodstock, Oxfordshire (**1982**) (**1987**)
BOLLING HALL, Bradford, West Yorkshire (**1978**) (**1987**)
THE BOAT MUSEUM, Ellesmere Port, South Wirral (**1986**)
BOUGHTON HOUSE, Kettering, Northants (**1988**)
BUCKFAST ABBEY, Buckfastleigh, Devon (**1985**)
CANTERBURY CATHEDRAL, Canterbury, Kent (**1988**)
CASTLE MUSEUM, York (**1987**)
CASTLE WARD, County Down, Northern Ireland (**1980**) (**1987**)
CATHEDRAL & ABBEY CHURCH OF SAINT ALBAN St. Albans, Herts (**1986**)
CHATTERLEY WHITFIELD MINING MUSEUM, Tunstall, Stoke-on-Trent (**1988**)
COMBE SYDENHAM, Nr. Taunton, Somerset (**1984**)
CROXTETH HALL and COUNTRY PARK, Liverpool, Merseyside (**1980**)
CULZEAN CASTLE and COUNTRY PARK, Ayrshire, Scotland (**1984**)
DODDINGTON HALL, Doddington, Lincolnshire (**1978**) (**1986**)
GAINSBOROUGH OLD HALL, Gainsborough, Lincolnshire (**1988**)
GEORGIAN HOUSE, Edinburgh, Lothian Region (**1978**)
HAGLEY HALL, Nr. Stourbridge, West Midlands (**1981**)
HAREWOOD HOUSE, Leeds, West Yorkshire (**1979**)
HOLDENBY HOUSE, Northampton, Northamptonshire (**1985**)
HOLKER HALL, Cark in Cartmel, Cumbria (**1982**) (**1988**)
HOPETOUN HOUSE, South Queensferry, Lothian Region (**1983**)
HORNSEA MUSEUM, North Humberside (**1987**)
IXWORTH ABBEY, Nr. Bury St. Edmunds, Suffolk (**1982**)
LAMPORT HALL, Northampton, Northamptonshire (**1985**)
LEIGHTON HALL, Carnforth, Lancashire (**1982**)
MACCLESFIELD MUSEUMS, Macclesfield (**1988**)
MARGAM PARK, Nr. Port Talbot, West Glamorgan (**1981**) (**1986**)
MOSELEY OLD HALL, Wolverhampton, West Midlands (**1983**)
OAKWELL HALL COUNTRY PARK, Birstall, West Yorkshire (**1988**)
PENHOW CASTLE, Nr. Newport, Gwent (**1980**) (**1986**)
QUARRY BANK MILL, Styal, Cheshire (**1987**)
RANGER'S HOUSE, Blackheath, London (**1979**) (**1987**)
ROCKINGHAM CASTLE, Nr. Corby, Northamptonshire (**1980**) (**1987**)
SHELDON MANOR, Wiltshire (**1985**)
THE SHUGBOROUGH ESTATE, Stafford (**1987**)
TATTON PARK, Knutsford, Cheshire (**1979**) (**1987**)
TOWER OF LONDON, Tower Bridge, London (**1978**) (**1986**)
WIGAN PIER, Lancashire (**1987**)
WIGHTWICK, MANOR, Wolverhampton, West Midlands (**1986**)
WIMPOLE HALL, Nr. Cambridge (**1988**)
YORK MINISTER, York (**1984**)

## 1988 RESULTS

**Full Sandford Awards**

AVONCROFT MUSEUM OF BUILDINGS
THE BEDE MONASTERY MUSEUM
BOUGHTON HOUSE
CANTERBURY CATHEDRAL
CHATTERLEY WHITFIELD MINING MUSEUM
GAINSBOROUGH OLD HALL
MACCLESFIELD MUSEUMS
OAKWELL HALL COUNTRY PARK
WIMPOLE HALL

**Highly Commended**

BENINGBROUGH HALL,
Shipton by Beningbrough, Yorkshire

**Quinquennial Review**

At quinquennial review a successful applicant will receive either a second Sandford Award indicating that educational services and facilities have been developed and improved since the date of the last award, or continued listing indicating that the educational services and facilities have been maintained at their original level of excellence.

| | |
|---|---|
| **BICKLEIGH CASTLE** | **Sandford Award** |
| **HOLKER HALL** | **Sandford Award** |
| **GEORGIAN HOUSE** | **Listing continued** |

Full details of the Sandford Award, and the work of the Heritage Education Trust will be supplied on request. The following are available: Brochure setting out the main aims of the Trust SAE; Sandford Award Application Form SAE; Criteria used in judging properties for a Sandford Award SAE; Details of Educational Consultancy Service for owners and administrators considering setting up educational services (SAE would be appreciated); 1984 Course Papers £2.50 post free; Heritage Education Handbook £3.95 post free.

NIMROD, the quarterly journal of the Heritage Education Trust is sent free to all those on the mailing list – Registration fee £2.50.

All cheques should be made payable to the **Heritage Education Trust** and all enquiries and requests addressed to: **Martyn Dyer, Chief Executive, Heritage Education Trust, St. Mary's College, Strawberry Hill, TW1 4SX. Tel: 01-892 0051, ext 202.**

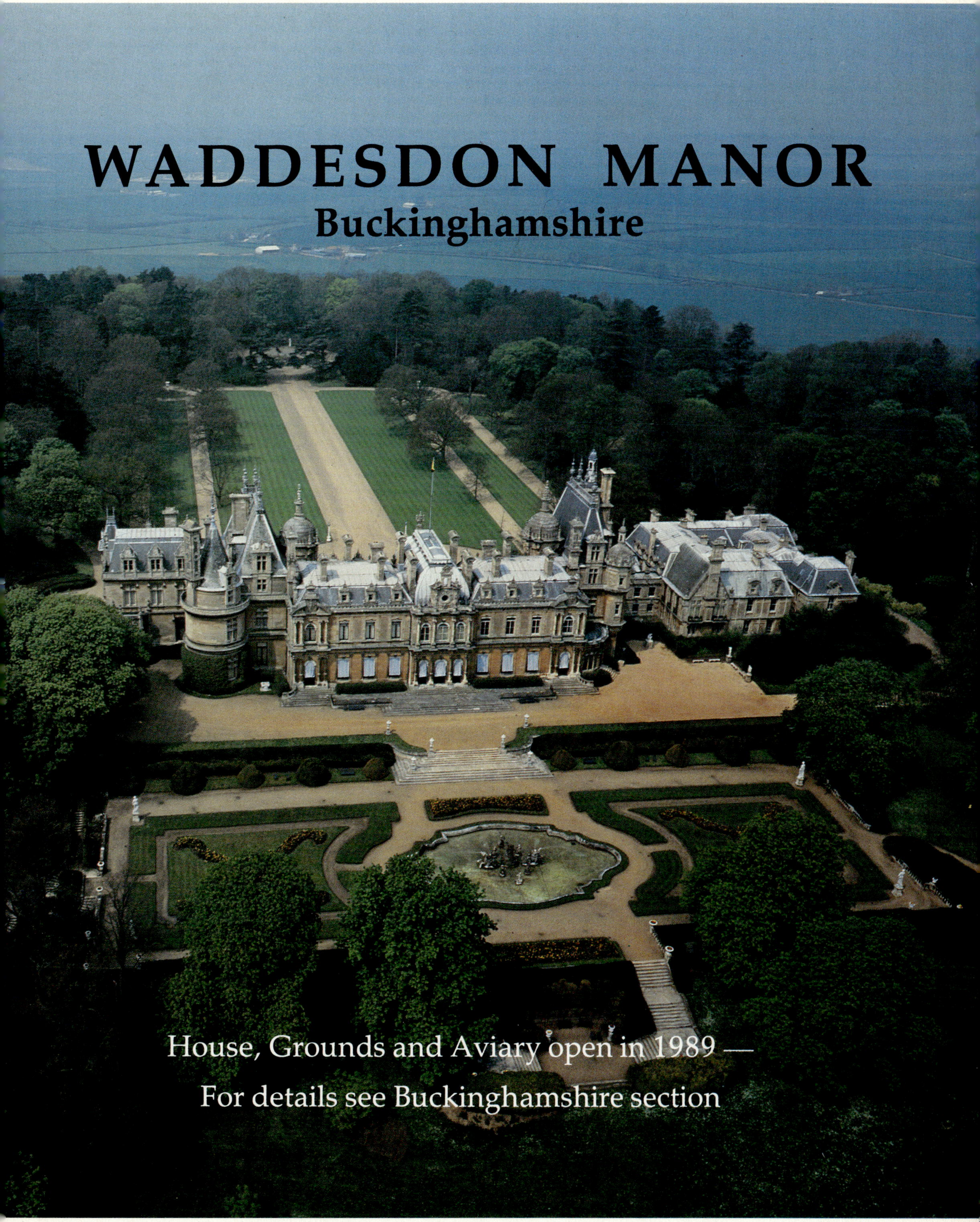
WADDESDON MANOR
Buckinghamshire
House, Grounds and Aviary open in 1989 —
For details see Buckinghamshire section

Avebury Stone Circles – Wiltshire

Rochester Castle – Kent

Whitby Abbey – North Yorkshire

# Explore the past. and protect

Formed by Act of Parliament in 1984, English Heritage has been given the vital role of protecting the rich and varied heritage of our country.

We strive to ensure that the treasures of our past are maintained for future generations, while making them available for you to enjoy today.

Not only do we assist others to protect historic properties, but our direct responsibility covers over 350 properties in nearly every English county, from Devon across to Kent, Northumberland down to the Isles of Scilly. The range of these properties is unrivalled and stretches over some 5,500 years of fascinating history.

Stonehenge, the famous prehistoric site; Hadrian's Wall, one of the great Roman endeavours; Kenilworth, an extensive medieval castle; the beautiful ruins of Rievaulx Abbey and even Queen Victoria's own seaside villa – Osborne House.

Just a few of our many properties. To find out more about these and other

*The Gardens at Belsay – Northumberland*

*Osborne House – Isle of Wight*

*Lindisfarne Priory – Northumberland*

# Alton Towers

## 19TH CENTURY GARDEN SPLENDOUR IN HISTORIC SETTING

We pride ourselves on a specially warm welcome to more than two million guests every year. Former home to the Earls of Shrewsbury, our 500 acre estate embraces the Gothic ruins of the Talbot family mansion, splendid grounds and landscaped gardens - open all year. 19th Century monuments, follies and fine conservatory cunningly evoke memories of the past. Careful concern for our historic setting and the surrounding countryside has governed the design and development of the rides and attractions for which we are famous. Guests enjoy a successful harmony of past and present with shopping and a wide variety of catering outlets to enhance the day.

Pay once only to enjoy all that Alton Towers has to offer. Main season from March 18 to November 5. Special reductions for groups, senior citizens and young people under 16. Children under 4 FREE. Disabled facilities. Afternoon tickets half price after 2.30 p.m. Grounds and gardens open all year. Much reduced Winter rates November 6 to mid March.

Step into the unique world of leisure at Alton Towers. You'll have the best day out ever!

ALTON TOWERS LTD
Alton, North Staffordshire
ST10 4DB Tel: (0538) 702200

# Historic Houses Castles & Gardens

## in Great Britain and Ireland

△ Denotes guided tours of the House
♿ Denotes the major part of the property is suitable for wheelchairs
Ⓔ Denotes educational services recognised by the Heritage Education Trust
Ⓢ Denotes that all property is a recipient of the Sandford Award

## AVON

### BARSTAPLE HOUSE (TRINITY ALMSHOUSES)

**Bristol** *map G4*
Telephone: Bristol (0272) 265777 (Warden)
*(Bristol Municipal Charities)*

Victorian almshouse with garden courtyard.

**Location:** Old Market Street, Bristol; ½ m from City centre on A420.
*Station: Bristol Temple Meads (¾ m).*
**Opening Times:** GARDEN & EXTERIOR OF BUILDINGS ONLY. All the year—Weekdays 10–4. Adm free. *The Almshouse is occupied mainly by elderly residents & their rights for privacy should be respected.*

### BECKFORD'S TOWER

**Bath** *map G4*
Telephone: Bath (0225) 336228
*(The Beckford Tower Trust)*

Built 1827 by William Beckford of Fonthill. A Beckford Museum (first floor); fine views from Belvedere (156 steps).

**Location:** 2 m from Bath Spa Station via Lansdown Road.
*Station: Bath Spa (2 m).*
**Opening Times:** Apr 2 to Oct 30—Sats, Suns & Bank Hol Mons 2–5. Adm £1p, Chd & OAPs 50p. *Parties other days by arrangement.*

### BLAISE CASTLE HOUSE MUSEUM

**Henbury** *map G4*
Telephone: Bristol (0272) 506789
*(City of Bristol)*

18th century house set in landscaped park; containing collections illustrating everyday life of the last 300 years.

**Location:** 4 m NW of central Bristol.
*Station: Sea Mills (2 m).*
**Opening Times:** All the year—Sats to Weds 10–1, 2–5. *Closed Thurs & Fris; Christmas Day, Boxing Day, New Year's Day & Good Friday.* Adm free.
**Refreshments:** Tea bar (in park).

### CLAVERTON MANOR

**nr Bath** *map G4* △
Telephone: Bath (0225) 60503
*(The American Museum in Britain)*

A Greek Revival house high above the valley of the Avon. Completely furnished rooms, 17th, 18th and 19th century brought from the U.S.A.

**Location:** 2½ m from Bath Station via Bathwick Hill; 3¾ m SE of Bath via Warminster Road (A36) & Claverton village.
*Station: Bath Spa (2½ m).*
**Opening Times:** Mar 24–Oct 29—Daily (except Mons) 2–5; Bank Hols Sun and Mon 12–5. *Mornings and winter months on application only.* School parties by previous arrangement, except Jan. Educational Tel 63538. Adm (1988) House & Grounds £3, Chd £2, and Senior Citizens £2.50. Grounds only £1. Parties of children not admitted during normal opening hours. *Pre-arranged parties over 30 at reduced rate.* Gardens open throughout the season (*except Mon*) 12–6.
**Refreshments:** Tea with American cookies (*Gingerbread cooked in 18th century oven*).

### CLEVEDON COURT, The National Trust

**nr Clevedon** *map F4*

A 14th century manor house incorporating a 12th century tower and a 13th century hall with terraced 18th century garden; rare shrubs and plants. The home of the Elton family. Important collections of Nailsea glass and Eltonware.

**Location:** 1½ m E of Clevedon on the Bristol Road B3130.
*Station: Yatton (3 m).*
**Opening Times:** Mar 26 to Sept 28—Weds, Thurs & Suns, also Bank Hol Mons 2.30–5.30 (last adm 5).
Adm £2, Chd £1 (children under 17 must be accompanied by an adult). No dogs. Unsuitable for wheelchairs & coaches.
**Refreshments:** Teas at the house.

### DYRHAM PARK, The National Trust

**nr Bristol and Bath** *map G4* ♿
Telephone: Abson 2501

Late 17th century house in a splendid deer park. The Blathwayt furniture and Dutch paintings in a fine series of panelled rooms.

**Location:** 12 m E of Bristol approach from Bath/Stroud Road (A46), 2 m S of Tormarton interchange with M4, 8 m N of Bath.
**Opening Times:** Park—Daily 12–6 (or dusk if earlier).
House & Garden: Mar 25 to Oct 29—Daily (except Thurs & Fris) 2–6. Last adm 5.30. Adm House, Gardens & Park £3, Chd £1.50. *Pre-booked parties of 15 or more £2.* Park only 80p, Chd 40p. Dogs in park on leads, please. Wheelchairs provided.
**Refreshments:** Teas in the Orangery.

### GEORGIAN HOUSE

**Bristol** *map G4*
Telephone: Bristol (0272) 299771 ext 237
*(City of Bristol)*

A merchant's town house, completed in 1791. Furnished in the style of the period, both 'above' and 'below' stairs.

**Location:** 7 Great George St., Bristol 1.
*Station: Bristol Temple Meads (¾ m).*
**Opening Times:** All the year—Mon to Sat 10–1, 2–5. *Closed Christmas Day, Boxing Day, New Year's Day, Good Friday. May 1 & Spring Bank Hol Mon.* Adm free.

### HORTON COURT, The National Trust

**Horton** *map G4* ♿

A Cotswold manor house restored and altered in the 19th century. 12th century hall and late Perpendicular ambulatory in garden only shown.

**Location:** 3 m NE of Chipping Sodbury, ¼ m N of Horton, 1 m W of Bath/Stroud Road (A46).
**Opening Times:** Hall & Ambulatory only: Mar 25 to Oct 28—Weds & Sats 2–6 (or sunset if earlier).
*Other times by written appointment with the tenant.* Adm 80p. *No reduction for parties or children.* No dogs. Unsuitable for coaches. Wheelchairs—ambulatory only.

## LITTLE SODBURY MANOR

**Chipping Sodbury** *map G4*
Telephone: Chipping Sodbury 312232
*(Mr & Mrs Gerald Harford)*

Medieval House with fine Great Hall. There are Tudor, Jacobean and Queen Anne additions.

**Location:** 2½ m from Chipping Sodbury off A46.
**Opening Times:** Apr to Sept—By appointment only. Adm £2.
**Refreshments:** Teas on request.

## THE MANOR HOUSE

**Walton-in-Gordano** *map F4*
Telephone: Clevedon (0272) 872067
*(Mr & Mrs Simon Wills)*

Four acres—mainly shrubs and fine trees, bulbs, alpines and herbaceous plants, mostly labelled.

**Location:** W of Bristol; via B3124 from Clevedon to Portishead; driveway on left before 1st houses in Walton-in-Gordano.
*Station: Yatton (6 m).*
**Opening Times:** GARDEN ONLY: Apr 12 to Sept 14 every Wed & Thurs 10–4. Suns Apr 30, May 28, Aug 27, 2–6; Mons May 1 & 29, Aug 28, 2–6. Open by appointment all year. Adm 75p, accompanied Chd free. Plants for sale. No dogs. Coaches by appointment only. In aid of National Gardens Scheme and St. Peter's Hospice.

## NUMBER ONE, ROYAL CRESCENT

**Bath** *map G4*
Telephone: Bath (0225) 28126
*(Bath Preservation Trust)*

A Georgian Town House at the eastern end of Bath's most magnificent crescent; redecorated and furnished to show the visitor how it might have appeared in the late 18th century.

**Location:** Bath.
**Opening Times:** Mar to end Oct: Tues to Sat 11–5; Sun 2–5. Bank Hol Mon (last adm 4.30). Nov & Dec: Sat, Sun 11–3 (last adm 2.30). Adm £1.50, Chd, OAPs & Students 80p. Museum shop.

## ORCHARD HOUSE

**Claverton** *map G4*
*(Rear Adm & Mrs Hugh Tracy)*

Plantsman's garden of 2½ acres in which owners have tried to combine botanical interest with attractive and informal layout. Collections of foliage plants, herbs, alpines, ground-cover and silver plants; rock gardens, herbaceous borders, lawns, shrubs, views.

**Location:** 3½ m from centre of Bath via A36 (Warminster) road; turn off at signpost for American museum; or ½ m down hill from American Museum, Claverton.
*Station: Bath Spa (2½ m).*
**Opening Times:** GARDEN ONLY. Weds Apr 26, May 3, 10, 17, 24, 31; June 7, 14. Adm 80p, Chd 30p. *In aid of National Gardens Scheme & King George's Fund for Sailors.* No dogs. Plants for sale. Small (wholesale) nursery.

## PEAR TREE HOUSE

**Litton BA3 4PP** *map G4*
Telephone: Chewton Mendip (076121) 220
*(Mr & Mrs John Southwell)*

Three acres landscaped into several gardens of distinctive character. Many unusual trees and shrubs; collection of acers; special collection of hollies (about 100 varieties); clematis (over 50 varieties). Ponds with moisture gardens. Pinetum. Featured on 'Gardeners World'. Picnic area. Permanent exhibition of watercolours.

**Location:** Litton, 8 miles N of Wells on B3114 off A39.
**Opening Times:** GARDEN ONLY June 17, 18. Oct 7, 8 for National Garden Scheme; also Sat and Mon from June 19 to Sep 11. Other times by appointment. Adm 75p. Open 11–6. Parties by arrangement. Car parking free in adjoining field. Suitable for disabled persons, no wheelchairs available.
**Refreshments:** Home-made teas on National Garden Scheme days and for parties; at other times tea/coffee available.

## RED LODGE

**Bristol** *map G4*
Telephone: Bristol (0272) 299771 ext 236
*(City of Bristol)*

Late 16th century house with period panelling and plasterwork; some rooms altered c.1730. Furnished in the style of both periods.

**Location:** Park Row, Bristol 1.
*Station: Bristol Temple Meads (¾ m).*
**Opening Times:** All the year—Mon to Sat 10–1, 2–5. *Closed Christmas Day, Boxing Day, New Year's Day, Good Friday, May 1 & Spring Bank Hol Mon.* Adm free.

## VINE HOUSE

**Henbury, Bristol** *map G4*
Telephone: Bristol (0272) 503573
*(Professor & Mrs T. F. Hewer)*

Two acres. Trees, shrubs, small water garden; bulbs; naturalised garden landscape.

**Location:** 4 m NW of Bristol centre next to 'Salutation' Public House.
*Stations: Bristol Parkway; Bristol Temple Meads each about 4 m from Henbury.*
**Opening Times:** GARDENS ONLY. Suns & Mons Mar 26 & 27, May 28 & 29, 2–7. Also open by appointment throughout the year. Adm 60p, Chd & OAPs 30p. Dogs on leads. *In aid of National Gardens Scheme & 'Friends of Blaise'.*

# BEDFORDSHIRE

**Bushmead Priory** – see English Heritage Section.

## CECIL HIGGINS ART GALLERY & MUSEUM

**Castle Close, Bedford MK40 3NY** *map J6* ♿
Telephone: Bedford (0234) 211222
*(Gallery jointly owned and administered by the North Bedfordshire Borough Council and the Trustees of the Cecil Higgins Art Gallery)*

Award-winning re-created Victorian Mansion, original home of Cecil Higgins. Rooms displayed to give 'lived-in' atmosphere, including bedroom with furniture designed by William Burges (1827–1881). Adjoining gallery with outstanding collections of ceramics, glass and watercolours. Situated in gardens leading down to the river embankment.

# NUMBER 1 ROYAL CRESCENT

**BATH**

*ADMISSION – SEE EDITORIAL REFERENCE*

# THE CECIL HIGGINS ART GALLERY & MUSEUM

**BEDFORD**

Re-created Victorian Mansion which has won many awards. Rooms displayed to give 'lived-in' atmosphere, including bedroom with furniture designed by William Burges (1827–1881). Situated in pleasant gardens.

# LUTON HOO

## WERNHER COLLECTION

**LUTON BEDFORDSHIRE**

*ADMISSION – SEE EDITORIAL REFERENCE*

# CHICKSANDS PRIORY

**near Shefford, Bedfordshire**

Founded by Payne de Beauchamp and his wife Countess Rohese, for Nuns and Canons of the English Order of Gilbertines circa 1150.

**Enjoy even more of Bedfordshire.**

**Explore the English Heritage Supplement on the Red Pages.**

**English Heritage**

**Location:** Centre of Bedford, just off The Embankment.
*Station: Bedford Midland (1/2 m).*
*Bus Station: (1/2 m).*
**Opening Times:** Tues–Frid 12.30–5, Sat 11–5, Sun 2–5. *Closed Mons (except Bank Hol Mons), Christmas Day, Boxing Day, Good Fri.*
Adm free. Group bookings and refreshments by prior arrangement. Facilities for the disabled. Trains from London (St. Pancras), and King's Cross Thameslink – fast trains 36 mins. National Express. United Counties 131/132 Bedford/Milton Keynes – Buckingham – Bicester – Oxford, 128/129 Northampton – Bedford – Cambridge and Express Service from London.

### CHICKSANDS PRIORY

**Shefford** *map K5*
Telephone: Biggleswade 315674
*(Ministry of Defence Property Administered by RAF Commander. Friends of Priory licensed to open Priory to public and redecorate interior)*

Chicksands Priory was founded by Payne De Beauchamp and his wife Countess Rohese for Nuns and Canons of the English Order of Gilbertines c 1150. Dissolved and surrendered 1538, it was sold by Henry VIII for £810 11s 8d to the Snowe family 1540. Acquired by the Osborne family in 1576, it so remained their family home until sold to The Crown, 1936. 13th and 15th century monastic remains survive with architectural work by Isaac Ware (1740) and James Wyatt (1813). Stained glass, Chinese wallpaper, Coade statuary have been uncovered since the Anglo-American Group of Friends opened the building to the public, 1975. The 18th century Venetian Prayer Book purchased by Sir Danvers Osborn, 3rd Baronet, is shown in the refurbished Private Chapel. Ghosts of former inhabitants are said to haunt the building; a plaque boasts of a walled up Nun within the cloisters and remains of monastic residents are buried in the still landscaped gardens. Game larder, Orangery and grapevines are on show exclusive of guided tour of the interior, which takes approximately 45 minutes. Past visitors to Chicksands include St Thomas Becket, King James I, HRH Princess Alice, Duchess of Gloucester, the Duke of Bedford, Terence, Cardinal Cooke. Following intensive external restoration by the Ministry of Defence, The Friends are decorating and restoring the interior.

**Location:** 1¼ miles from Shefford. Entrances on A507 Shefford to Ampthill Road and on A600 Shefford to Bedford Road.
**Opening Times:** 1st & 3rd Suns of Month Apr to Oct 2–5; last tour 4.30. Guided tours only. No adm charge—donations for interior decoration requested. Parties by appointment only. Car Parking. Unsuitable for wheelchairs.
**Refreshments:** Light refreshments at Priory. Nearest hotels at Biggleswade, Bedford & Hitchin, all being 7 miles from Chicksands.

### LUTON HOO

**Luton** *map K5*
Telephone: Luton (0582) 22955
*(The Wernher Family)*

Exterior commenced by Robert Adam, 1767. Interior remodelled in the French style early in this century. Magnificent art collection includes Fabergé jewels and unique porcelain collection. Park landscaped by 'Capability' Brown.

**Location:** Entrance at Park Street Gates Luton 30 m N of London via M1 (exit 10, junction A1081 – formerly A6). Railway & Bus Stations 3 m.
*Station: Luton (2½ m).*
**Opening Times:** House & Gardens. Easter then Apr 15 to Oct 15, 1988. Open daily 2–5.45; closed Mons *except Bank Hols*; last adm 5; £3, Chd £1.50. Reduced rates for parties by prior arrangement (minimum 30 adults). No dogs admitted to House or Gardens.

### STAGSDEN BIRD GARDENS

**Stagsden** *map J5*
Telephone: Oakley (023 02) 2745

A large Bird Zoo and breeding establishment for birds with over 1300 specimens in approximately 150 species. Also a collection of shrub roses.

**Location:** 5 m W of Bedford, 7 m N of A422. Turn N at Stagsden Church.
**Opening Times:** Every day of the year 11–6 (or dusk if earlier). Adm £1.50, Chd (4–15 inc.) 70p, OAPs £1.30.

### THE SWISS GARDEN

**Old Warden, nr Biggleswade** *map K5* ♿
Telephone: Bedford (0234) 228330
*(Bedfordshire County Council)*

An unusual Romantic landscaped garden dating from the early 19th century, containing original buildings, ironwork and other features together with many interesting plants and trees, some of great rarity. Attractive lakeside picnic area in adjoining woodlands.

**Location:** 2½ m W of Biggleswade, adjoining Biggleswade/Old Warden Road; approximately 2 m W of A1.
*Station: Biggleswade (3 m).*
**Opening Times:** Apr to Oct—Weds, Thurs, Sats, Suns (but closed the last Sun in each month), & Bank Holidays. Mons 2–6 (last admission 5.15). Adm (1988 rates) 60p, Chd (5–16) and OAPS 30p. Special rates for School parties & group visits by prior arrangement. Wheelchair access by special arrangement. Lakeside picnic area open at all times. Public lavatory (facilities for disabled).
**Refreshments:** Cafeteria at adjoining Shuttleworth Aeroplane Collection.

### WOBURN ABBEY

**Woburn** *map J5*
Telephone: Woburn (0525) 290666; Catering (0525) 290662; Antiques Centre (0525) 290350
*(The Marquess of Tavistock and Trustees of the Bedford Estates)*

Home of the Dukes of Bedford for over 300 years. Rebuilt by Henry Flitcroft mid-18th century, and added to by Henry Holland in early 19th century. 3000 acre deer park landscaped by Humphry Repton. Very important and extensive art collection.

**Location:** In Woburn 8½ m NW of Dunstable on A418. 42 m from London off M1 at junction with A5120, exit 12 or 13.
*Station: Ridgmont (3 m).*
**Opening Times:** House and Gardens. Dec 31 to Mar 19—Sats & Suns only. House 11–4.45; Park 10.30–3.45. Mar 20 to Oct 29—Daily. House: Weekdays 11–5.45; Suns 11–6.15. Park: Weekdays 10–4.45; Suns 10–5.45. *Last adm to House 45 mins before closing time every day.* House Adm £4, Chd (7–16) £1.50, OAPs £3.
*Party rates are available.*
*Free car park.*
**Refreshments:** Flying Duchess Pavilion Coffee Shop, Restaurants for pre-booked parties.

### WREST PARK HOUSE AND GARDENS

**Silsoe** *map J5*
Telephone: (0525) 60718
*(English Heritage)*

Here is a history of English gardening in the grand manner from 1700–1850, which would not, of course, be complete without some designs by 'Capability' Brown. Every whim of fashion is represented, whether it be for a Chinese bridge, artificial lake, classical temple or rustic ruin. The present house was built about 1839 by the Earl de Grey, whose family had lorded it over the Manor of Wrest for 600 years. The State Rooms and gardens are open to the public.

**Location:** ¾ m (1 km) east of Silcoe.
**Opening Times:** Good Friday to Sept 30, weekends and Bank Hols only 10–6. Adm £1.10, OAPs 80p, Chd 55p.

## BERKSHIRE

### BASILDON PARK, The National Trust

**nr Pangbourne** *map J4*
Telephone: Pangbourne (07357) 3040

Classical house built 1776. Unusual Octagon room; fine plasterwork; important paintings and furniture, Garden and Woodland walks.

**Location:** 7 m NW of Reading between Pangbourne and Streatley on A329.
*Stations: Pangbourne (2½ m); Goring and Streatley (3 m).*
**Opening Times:** Mar 25 to end Oct—Weds to Sats 2–6; Suns & Bank Hol Mons 12–6. *Last adm to house half-hour before closing.* Adm House & Grounds £2. Grounds only £1, Chd half price. Reductions (except Suns and Bank Hol Mons) to House & Grounds for parties of 15 or more (Booking essential). *Closed Mons (except Bank Hols), Tues & Weds following Bank Hols and Good Friday.* Shop. Dogs in grounds only on leads. House unsuitable for wheelchairs.
**Refreshments:** Tea room in house accessible to wheelchairs.

### FROGMORE GARDENS

**Windsor** *map J4*
*(Her Majesty The Queen)*

Beautifully landscaped gardens with trees, shrubs and lake.

**Location:** Entrance to garden through Long Walk Gate. *(Visitors are requested kindly to refrain from entering grounds of the Home Park).*
*Stations: Windsor & Eton Central; Windsor & Eton Riverside (both 20 mins walk).*
**Opening Times:** GARDEN ONLY. Open on Wed May 3 & Thurs May 4: 10.30–7 (last adm 6.30). Adm £1, accompanied Chd free. No dogs. Free car park. Coaches by appointment only (apply to National Gardens Scheme, 57 Lower Belgrave Street, London SW1W 0LR. Tel: 01-730 0359, stating whether am or pm pass is required). The Royal Mausoleum also open on above 2 days, adm free. (In addition Mausoleum open Wed May 24: 11–4, but *not* the gardens).
**Refreshments:** Tent at car park—May 4 & 5.

MAPLEDURHAM HOUSE—SEE UNDER OXFORDSHIRE

### LITTLECOTE

**Hungerford** *map H4*
Telephone: (0488) 84000

An impressive Tudor Manor House, built between 1490 and 1520. Colonel Alexander Popham garrisoned his private army here during the Civil War. The magnificent Great Hall contains a 30ft Shovel Board table (possibly the longest in the world), and the unique collection of Cromwellian armour belonging to the Royal Armouries. The grounds include a working rare breeds farm, Tudor style rose gardens, and a 'period village' with craftsmen and shopkeepers in Tudor costume. Visitors can also enjoy daily falconry displays and jousting tournaments. Important Roman excavations and Orpheus mosaic.

**Location:** 4 m S of M4 (junction 14) nr. Hungerford. B4193 W to Chilton Foliat and Swindon, into village of Chilton Foliat, then 1 m out of village and follow signposting.
**Opening Times:** Mar 19 to Oct 1: Daily from 10 am.
**Refreshments:** Tavern, licensed restaurant, picnic area.

**HERITAGE EDUCATION TRUST**

**HET**

has now published the first

**HERITAGE EDUCATION HANDBOOK**

Edited by Martyn Dyer

Sandford Award winning properties assessed.
Theory practice and development of Heritage Education explained.
Work of the Trust described
Heritage Groups listed
Illustrated

Price **£3.95**

May be ordered through branches of W.H. Smith or direct from

**Heritage Education Trust,**
**St. Mary's College,**
**Strawberry Hill, TW1 4SX**
**01 892 0051 x202**

# STAGSDEN BIRD GARDENS

**STAGSDEN, BEDFORD**

A specialist Bird Garden and Breeding Centre in a country setting featuring cranes (including rare white-naped cranes), flamingos, birds of prey, pheasants, waterfowl and old breeds of poultry. Owl complex, talking mynahs and parrots. Free car park and picnic area. Off the A428/A422 roads. Open daily from 11 am. Admission: Adults £1.50. OAP's £1.30. Children 70p. Tel: Oakley 2745.

# THE SWISS GARDEN

*ADMISSION – SEE EDITORIAL REFERENCE*

# WOBURN ABBEY

**BEDFORDSHIRE**

The Deer Park has lots of wild life, including nine species of deer, roaming freely. One of these, the Pere David, descended from the Imperial Herd of China, was saved from extinction at Woburn and is now the largest breeding herd of this specie in the world. In 1985 twenty-two Pere David were given by the Family to the People's Republic of China with the hope that the specie may become re-established in its natural habitat. The Marquess of Tavistock visited Beijing (Peking) to release the herd at Nan Haizi, the former Imperial hunting ground outside Beijing (Peking). Happily the deer have already bred, and as further consolidation, the Family gave another 15 Pere David to the Republic in 1987.

The Abbey contains one of the most important private art collections in the world, including paintings by Canaletto, Van Dyck, Cuyp, Teniers, Rembrandt, Gainsborough, Reynolds, Velazques and many other famous artists. French and English 18th century furniture, silver and the fabulous Sèvres dinner service presented to the 4th Duke by Louis XV of France.

The tour of the Abbey covers three floors, including the Crypt and it is regretted that wheelchairs can only be accommodated in the House by prior arrangement.

The 40 shop Antiques Centre is probably the most unusual such centre outside London – the shop fronts having been rescued from demolition sites in various parts of Britain. Shipping can be arranged on a world-wide basis.

All catering is operated by ourselves with banqueting, conferences and receptions our speciality, in the beautiful setting of the Sculpture Gallery, overlooking the private gardens. There is a Pottery and Garden Centre, and summer weekend events are arranged.

Extensive picnic areas with ample coach and car parking. Gift shops. Pottery and a Garden & Camping Equipment Centre.

# BASILDON PARK

**Near PANGBOURNE, BERKSHIRE**

*THE NATIONAL TRUST*

*ADMISSION – SEE EDITORIAL REFERENCE*

### THE OLD RECTORY
**Burghfield** *map J4*
*(Mr & Mrs R. R. Merton)*

Garden of horticultural interest; roses, hellebores, lilies, many rare and unusual plants from China and Japan; old-fashioned cottage plants; autumn colour.

**Location:** 5½ m SW of Reading, between M4 junctions 11 & 12.
*Stations: Reading and Mortimer (3½ m).*
**Opening Times:** GARDEN ONLY. Weds: Feb 22, March 29, April 26, May 31, June 28, July 26, Aug 30, Sept 27, Oct 25, 11–4. Adm 50p, Chd 10p. *In aid of National Gardens Scheme.* (Share to Save the Children & BB & O NCCPG). Plants & produce for sale. No dogs.

### SAVILL GARDEN
**Windsor Great Park** *map J4*
*(Crown Property)*

Mainly a woodland garden of 35 acres together with a formal area of roses and herbaceous plants, all of which offer great interest and beauty at every season of the year.

**Location:** To be approached from A30 via Wick Road & Wick Lane, Englefield Green.
*Station: Egham (3 m).*
**Opening Times:** Open daily 10–6. *Closed for a short period at Christmas.* Adm £1.80, OAPs £1.60. Parties of 20 and over £1.60, accompanied Chd (under 16) free.

### SWALLOWFIELD PARK
**Swallowfield** *map J4*
*(Country Houses Association Ltd)*

Built by the Second Earl of Clarendon in 1678.

**Location:** In the village of Swallowfield 6 m SE of Reading.
**Opening Times:** May to September—Weds & Thurs 2–5. Adm £1, Chd 50p.
Free car park. No dogs admitted.

### VALLEY GARDENS
**Windsor Great Park** *map J4*
*(Crown Property)*

Extensive woodland gardens of 400 acres which include a large heather garden offering beauty and charm at all seasons of the year.

**Location:** To be approached from Wick Road off A30 (1 m walk).
*Station: Egham (3 m).*
**Opening Times:** Open daily from sunrise to sunset. Adm free to pedestrians. Car park adjoining gardens. £1.50 per car (£2 in Apr & May).

### WINDSOR CASTLE
**Windsor** *map J4*
Telephone: Windsor (0753) 868286
*(Official residence of H.M. The Queen)*

Perhaps the largest fortress of its kind in the world, Windsor Castle has belonged to the Sovereigns of England for over 900 years, and is by far, the oldest residence still in regular use. The Castle has the following areas open to the public:–
**State Apartments** (except when HM The Queen in official residence).
**Queen Mary's Dolls' House.**
**Exhibition of Drawings.**
**Exhibition of The Queen's Presents and Royal Carriages.**

**Location:** 3m off J6 of M4.
**Opening Times: The Curfew Tower:** Tues to Sat 11–1, 2–4. *Closed Sun and Mon.* Adm 20p, Chd (accompanied) 10p. **St. George's Chapel:** Summer: weekdays 10.45–4, Sun 2–4. Winter: 10.45–3.45, Sun 2–3.45. *Closed in Jan (except for services) and occasionally at other times for special services.* Adm £1.50, Chd (5–16) and retirement pensioners 60p. **Albert Memorial Chapel:** Weekdays: 10–1, 2–3.45. *Closed Sun.* **Castle precincts:** open daily from 10–4.15, or 10–7.15 (depending on time of year. Adm free. **State Apartments:** Jan 4 to Mar 12 and Oct 23 to Dec 10: Mon to Sat 10.30–3, *Closed Sun.* May 1 to June 5, and June 26 to Oct 22: Mon to Sat 10.30–5, Sun 1.30–5. Adm £1.80, Chd 80p. **Queen Mary's Dolls' House and Exhibition of Old Master Drawings:** Jan 4 to Mar 27, Oct 23 to Dec 31: Mon to Sat 10.30–3, *Closed Sun;* Mar 28 to Oct 22: Mon to Sat 10.30–5, Sun 1.30–5. *Closed Apr 3, 10, 17, 24, June 13, Dec 24–27.* Adm 80p, Chd 40p. **Exhibition of the Queen's Presents and Royal Carriages:** Jan 24 to Mar 27, and Oct 23 to Dec 31: Mon to Sat 10.30–3. *Closed Sun;* Mar 28 to Oct 22: Mon to Sat 10.30–5, Sun 10.30–3. Adm 80p, Chd 40p. *Closed Good Friday, Apr 3, 10, 17, 24 and Dec 24–27.* **Group Discounts:** deom Nov 1 to Mar 31 a discount of 20% is available for parties of 15 or more who have pre-booked and pre-paid. This applies to the following: The State Apartments, Exhibition of Old Master Drawings, Exhibition of the Queen's Presents and Royal Carriages, Queen Mary's Dolls' House.
*Whilst there is every intention to adhere to the above schedule this cannot be guaranteed as Windsor Castle is always subject to closure, sometimes at short notice. All enquiries (about Chapel only): Tel: Windsor 65538.*
**Refreshments:** Castle Hotel (opposite).

## BUCKINGHAMSHIRE

### ASCOTT, The National Trust
**Wing** *map J5* △
Telephone: Aylesbury (0296) 688242

Anthony de Rothschild collection of fine pictures. French and Chippendale furniture, exceptional Oriental porcelain containing examples of the Ming, K'ang Hsi and Chun ware of the Sung dynasty. Gardens contain unusual trees, flower borders, topiary sundial, naturalised bulbs and water lilies.

**Location:** ½ m E of Wing; 2 m SW of Leighton Buzzard, on the S side of Aylesbury/Leighton Buzzard Road (A418).
*Station: Leighton Buzzard (2 m).*
**Opening Times:** House & Gardens. July 18–Sept 17, Tues to Suns 2–6. Bank Hol Mon Aug 28, closed Tues Aug 29. Garden only: Apr to July 13 and Sept 21, 24, 28; every Thurs and last Sun in each month 2–6. Last adm 5.30. Adm House & Gardens £2.60, Chd £1.80; Gardens only £1.60, Chd 80p. *No reduction for parties.* Dogs on leads, in car park only. Wheelchair access to ground floor and part of garden only. Enquiries: Estate Manager.
NB Owing to large number of visitors, entry is by timed ticket. Occasionally there will be considerable delays in gaining admission to the House.

### CHENIES MANOR HOUSE
**Chenies** *map J5*
Telephone: Little Chalfont 2888
*(Lt Col & Mrs MacLeod Matthews)*

Charming 15th/16th century Manor House and garden in picturesque village.

**Location:** Off A404 between Amersham & Rickmansworth (M25 – junction 18).
*Station: Chorleywood (1½ m).*
**Opening Times:** First week in April to end of Oct Weds and Thurs 2–5. Also open Bank Hol Mons May 29 & Aug 28, 2–6. Adm £2.10, Chd (under 14) half-price. Gardens only £1. Parties throughout the year by prior arrangement—min charge £40. Free parking. No dogs.
**Refreshments:** Home-made teas.

### CHICHELEY HALL
**Newport Pagnell** *map J5*
Telephone: North Crawley (023 065) 252
*(Trustees of the Hon Nicholas Beatty)*

Beautiful Baroque house and gardens built 1719–1723. Fine panelling. Naval pictures and mementoes of Admiral Lord Beatty. Sir John Chester's unique Hidden Library.

**Location:** 2 m E of Newport Pagnell; 11 m W of Bedford on A422.
**Opening Times:** Mar 24 to May 30, and Aug 6 to Sept 24. Suns and Bank Holiday Mons 2.30–6. Last tour 5. Day or evening parties, with or without meals, by appointment at any time throughout the summer. Adm £2.20, Chd £1, parties (over 20) £1.60.

### CHILTERN OPEN AIR MUSEUM
**Newland Park, Gorelands Lane nr Chalfont St Giles** *map J4*
Telephone: Chalfont St Giles (024 07) 71117
*(Chiltern Open Air Museum Ltd)*

A museum of historic buildings, rescued from demolition and re-erected in Newland Park. Barns, Granaries, Stables, Forge, Toll House plus an Iron Age House. Woodland Nature Trail.

**Location:** Between Chalfont St Peter and Chalfont St Giles; 4½ m Amersham, 8 m Watford, 6 m Beaconsfield; 2 m A413 at Chalfont St Peter, 4 m from junction 17 on the M25 via Maple Cross and the Chalfonts.
*Station: Chorleywood (2 m via footpath).*
**Opening Times:** Mar 26 to end Oct—Weds, Suns & Bank Hols 2–6, Wed to Sun incl July 1 to Sept 10. Parties & School parties by arrangement weekdays all year round. Adm £1.50, OAPs £1, Chd under 16yrs £1, under 5 free.
**Refreshments:** Home-made teas.

### CLAYDON HOUSE, The National Trust
**Middle Claydon, nr Winslow** *map J5* ♿
Telephone: Steeple Claydon (029673) 349

Built mid 18th century as an addition to an earlier house. The stone-faced West front contains a series of magnificent and unique rococo state-rooms including Florence Nightingale Museum, her bedroom and sitting room.

**Location:** Nr the village of Middle Claydon, 13m NW of Aylesbury, 3½ m SW of Winslow.
**Opening Times:** Mar 25 to end of Oct—Sat to Wed 2–6, Bank Hol Mons 1–6. Last adm 5.30. *Closed Thurs & Fris (inc Good Friday).* Adm £2, Chd £1. Parties write to Custodian. Dogs in car park only. Wheelchairs provided.
**Refreshments:** Available at house.

### CLIVEDEN, The National Trust
**Maidenhead (1851)** *map J4* △
Telephone: Burnham (06286) 5069

Gardens contain temples by Giacomo Leoni. Box parterre, fountain, formal walks; amphitheatre, water garden, rose garden, herbaceous borders. Views of Thames.

**Location:** 3 m upstream from Maidenhead; 2 m N of Taplow on Hedsor Road (B476). Main entrance opposite Feathers Inn.
*Stations: Taplow (3 m) (not Suns); Maidenhead (4¼ m).*

**THE HOME OF GOOD PLANTS AND TRULY A GARDEN FOR ALL SEASONS.**

# *The* Savill Garden

**IN WINDSOR GREAT PARK**

*Clearly signposted from Ascot, Egham and Windsor.*

*Ample Free Car/Coach parking adjoining the garden in Wick Lane, Englefield Green.*

**The Garden is open daily throughout the year from 10 am to 6 pm or sunset if earlier. (Closed December 25–28)**
Admission: Adults £1.80, Senior Citizens £1.60, Parties of 20 or more £1.60.
Accompanied children under the age of 16 free. (Large groups of children by arrangement)
Licensed Self Service Restaurant.
Also our well stocked Plant/Gift Shop is open throughout the season.

# Chiltern Open Air Museum

**NEWLAND PARK, CHALFONT ST GILES**
**BUCKINGHAMSHIRE**
**Tel: (02407) 71117**

Historic Chiltern buildings, rescued and re-erected in the beautiful grounds of Newland Park. Farm Buildings, a Forge, Toll House, and Furniture Factory. Plus an Iron Age House. Woodland Nature Trail.

Open Easter Sunday to end October, Wednesdays, Sundays and Bank Holidays 2pm-6pm. Wednesday-Sunday inclusive in July and August

Free Car Park | Teas | Picnic Area

# CHENIES MANOR

**CHENIES**
**BUCKINGHAMSHIRE**

15/16th century Manor House with fortified tower. Original home of the Earls of Bedford, visited by Henry VIII and Elizabeth I. Home of the MacLeod Matthews family. Contains contemporary tapestries and furniture. Early examples of English brickwork, hiding places, 'secret passages'. Surrounded by beautiful gardens—sunken garden, 'white' garden, physic garden, penitential maze, 13th century undercroft, 14th century well and collection of recovered items.

Interesting kitchen garden.

Collection of antique dolls.

Special exhibitions throughout open period.

Flower drying and arrangements.

OPEN: First week in April to end of October, Wednesdays and Thursdays, 2 to 5 pm, also Bank Holiday Mondays May 29 and August 28.

Open, by prior arrangement, for parties throughout the year.

No dogs, no indoor photography. Wheelchair access to garden only.

Free parking.

Gift shop in old forge.

Teas with home-made cakes.

Herbs for sale.

*Home of the Hon. Nicholas Beatty*

# Chicheley Hall

**near Newport Pagnell, Buckinghamshire**

Chicheley Hall, still a lived-in family home, is an exceptionally fine early Georgian House built 1719-1723 by Francis Smith of Warwick. Here is some of the most notable brickwork to be found in any house of the period, with the four sides of the house displaying a carefully graduated crescendo of architectural effect.
The interior has a striking Palladian Hall designed by Flitcroft and beautiful panelled rooms including Sir John Chester's ingenious hidden library. The rooms are furnished with fine period furniture and pictures.
The BEATTY NAVAL MUSEUM at Chicheley contains many fascinating momentoes of Admiral Earl Beatty and World War I at sea. The gardens contain a formal three-sided canal designed in 1700 by George London who also worked at Hampton Court. Recently renovated 18th century dovecote. Tea Room and Gift Shop.
OPEN: 24 March–30 May & 6 Aug–24 Sept. SUNDAYS & PUBLIC HOLIDAY MONDAYS, 2.30 to 6 pm. Last tour 5 pm. Day or evening parties, with or without meals, by appointment, at any time throughout summer. Adm. £2.20, Chd £1, Parties ( over 20) £1.60.
Tel: North Crawley (023 065) 252.

## BUCKINGHAMSHIRE – *continued*

**Opening Times:** Grounds: Mar to Dec—Daily 11–6 or sunset if earlier. *Closed Jan & Feb.* House: Apr 2 to Oct 29, Thurs & Suns 3–6 (last adm 5.30). Adm Grounds £2.40. House 80p extra (timed ticket), Chd half price. *Parties must give advance notice. No dogs in House or in gardens, elsewhere only on lead.* Wheelchairs (available) in parts of garden & house. Shop: Good Friday to end Oct, Weds to Suns (incl Good Friday) & Bank Hol Mons 1–5.30.
**Refreshments:** Light lunches, coffee, teas in Orangery Restaurant Good Friday to end Oct (Weds to Suns).

### COWPER & NEWTON MUSEUM
**Olney** *map J6*
Telephone: Bedford (0234) 711516

Personal belongings of William Cowper and Rev. John Newton. Bobbin lace and items of local interest.

**Location:** Market Place, Olney; N of Newport Pagnell via A509.
**Opening Times:** Easter—Oct 31: Tues to Sats 10–12, 2–5. Open Bank Hol Mons. Limited winter opening. Adm £1.

### DORNEY COURT
**nr Windsor** *map J4*
Telephone: Burnham (062 86) 4638 (please note from early 1989 tel. no. will be (0628) 604638)
*(Mr & Mrs Peregrine Palmer)*

Beautiful Tudor pink brick and timber Manor House which has been in the family for over 450 years. Superb collection of furniture and paintings.

**Location:** 2 m W of Eton & Windsor in village of Dorney on B3026.
*Stations: Burnham (2 m).*
**Opening Times:** Easter weekend Fri to Mon then Suns & Bank Hol Mons to second Sun in Oct; also Mons & Tues in June, July, Aug & Sept; 2–5.30. Adm £2.30, Chd over 9 £1. 10% discount for National Trust members and OAPs on Mons & Tues *(excluding Bank Holidays).* Parties at other times by arrangement.
**Refreshments:** Home-made cream teas.

### HUGHENDEN MANOR, The National Trust
**High Wycombe** *map J4* ♿
Telephone: High Wycombe (0494) 32580

Home of Benjamin Disraeli, Earl of Beaconsfield (1847-1881). Small formal garden.

**Location:** 1½ m N of High Wycombe on W side Gt Missenden Road (A4128).
*Station: High Wycombe (2 m).*
**Opening Times:** House & Garden. Mar 4–Mar 19—Sats & Suns only 2–6 (or sunset if earlier), Easter Sat to end of Oct—Weds to Sats 2–6; Suns & Bank Hol Mons 12–6. *Closed Good Friday.* Adm £2, Chd half price. Shop open mid-March to end Oct as House and pre-Christmas. *Parties must book in advance.* Dogs in Park & car park only. Wheelchair provided. Parties Weds to Fris only if booked in advance.

### MILTON COTTAGE
**Chalfont St Giles** *map J5* ♿
Telephone: Chalfont St Giles 2313
*(Milton's Cottage Trust)*

The Cottage where John Milton completed 'Paradise Lost' and began 'Paradise Regained', contains many Milton relics and a library including first and early editions. Preserved as it was in 1665. Charming Cottage Garden.

**Location:** ½ m W of A413; on B4442 to Beaconsfield.
*Station: Seer Green (2½ m).*
**Opening Times:** Mar to Oct—Tues to Sats 10–1, 2–6; Suns 2–6. Spring & Summer Bank Hol Mons 10–1, 2–6. *Closed Mons (except Bank Hols) & Jan, Feb, Nov & Dec.* Adm £1, Chd (under 15) 40p, Parties of 20 or more 80p.

### NETHER WINCHENDON HOUSE
**Aylesbury** *map J5* △ ♿
Telephone: Haddenham 290101
(Mrs John Spencer Bernard)
Correspondence to Administrator, R.V. Spencer Bernard Esq.

Tudor manor house with 18th century additions. Home of Sir Francis Bernard, Governor of New Jersey and Massachusetts, 1760.

**Location:** 1 m N of A418 Aylesbury/Thame Road, nr village of Lower Winchendon, 6 m SW Aylesbury.
*Station: Aylesbury (7½ m).*
**Opening Times:** May to Aug: Thurs 2.30–5.30. Bank Hol weekends (i.e. Sat, Sun, Mon) 2.30–5.30; first weekend in June (Sat & Sun) 2.30–5.30; Second weekend in Aug (Sat & Sun) 2.30–5.30. Parties at any time of year by written appointment. Adm £1.50, Chd (under 12) £1; OAPs £1 (Thurs only).

### PRINCES RISBOROUGH MANOR HOUSE, The National Trust
**Princes Risborough** *map J5* ♿

17th century red-brick house with Jacobean oak staircase.

**Location:** Opposite church off market square in town centre.
*Station: Princes Risborough (1 m).*
**Opening Times:** Open by written appointment only—Weds 2.30–4.30. Last adm 4. Two rooms only shown. Adm £1, Chd 50p. No reductions for parties. No dogs. Wheelchair access.

### STOWE (Stowe School)
**Buckingham** *map J5*

Famous 18th century house formerly the home of the Duke of Buckingham. Garden and garden buildings by Bridgeman, Kent, Gibbs, Vanburgh and 'Capability' Brown.

**Location:** 4 m N of Buckingham town.
**Opening Times:** Grounds, Garden Buildings & Main State Rooms: Mar 24 to Apr 16 and July 9 to Aug 28. Daily from 12. Adm £1.40, Chd & OAPs £1.
**Refreshments:** Light refreshments.

### WADDESDON MANOR, The National Trust
**nr Aylesbury** *map J5* △ ♿
Telephone: Aylesbury (0296) 651211 or 651282

Built 1874–89 for Baron Ferdinand de Rothschild in the style of a French Renaissance château and bequeathed to the National Trust by Mr James A. de Rothschild in 1957. Rooms with 18th century French panelling furnished with French royal furniture, Sèvres and Meissen porcelain, and Savonnerie carpets. Dutch, Flemish and Italian paintings, and portraits by Gainsborough, Reynolds and Romney. Other rooms contain French 17th and 18th century drawings, also lace, buttons and fans, and an exhibition of ladies' clothes of c.1865, together with personal mementoes and pastimes of the family. In the Bachelors' Wing, open on Fridays only (except Good Friday), are 15th, 16th and 17th century works of art and European small arms. Extensive grounds with 18th century style aviary and small herd of Japanese Sika deer. Fine trees and views. Play area for young children.

# The National Trust in BUCKINGHAMSHIRE

## CLIVEDEN

## WEST WYCOMBE PARK

## HUGHENDEN MANOR

## CLAYDON

*ADMISSION–SEE EDITORIAL REFERENCE*

**Location:** At W end of Waddesdon village; 6 m NW of Aylesbury on Bicester Road (A41).
*Station: Aylesbury (6 m).*
*Buses: Red Rover 1, 15, 16, from Aylesbury. (Tel: Aylesbury 28686).*
**Opening Times:** Mar 15 to Oct 22. House: Weds to Suns 1–5 (open until 6 on Sat & Sun in May to Sept). Bachelors' Wing open Fris (except Good Friday). Grounds & aviary: Weds to Sats from 1, Suns from 11.30. Good Friday and Bank Hol Mons House and Grounds 11–6. *Completely closed Weds following Bank Hol Mons.* Adm House, grounds & aviary £3. Bachelors' Wing £1 extra. Chd 10–17 years, half price; Chd under 10 not admitted to house. Grounds & aviary only, £1.50; Chd from 5–17 half price; Chd under 5 free. Parties by arrangement (no reduction except pre-booked parties of OAPs Weds, Thurs Sats). Private morning guided tours by arrangement, £7.50. Free car park. Shops with books, gifts, plants and flowers. Dogs in grounds only, excluding aviary and children's play area. Wheelchairs provided on request. *No photography indoors.*
**Shops:** Two shops during the summer season, special Christmas shop Oct 27 to Dec 23, Fri, Sat & Sun 12–5. Free entry and free parking.
**Refreshments:** Light lunches and afternoon teas available.

### WEST WYCOMBE PARK (1750), The National Trust
**West Wycombe** *map J4* △
Telephone: High Wycombe (0494) 24411

Palladian house with frescoes and painted ceilings. 18th century landscape garden with lake and various classical temples, including the newly reconstructed Temple of Venus.

**Location:** At W end of West Wycombe, S of Oxford Road (A40), 2½ m W High Wycombe.
*Station: High Wycombe (2½ m).*
**Opening Times: Grounds only:** Apr & May Mons to Thurs 2-6, and Easter, May Day and Spring Bank Hols. Sun & Mon 2–6. *Closed* Good Friday. **House & Grounds:** June, July & Aug, Suns to Thurs inc Summer Bank Hol Mon 2–6 (last adm 5.15). Adm House & Grounds £2.60; Grounds only £1.60, Chd half price. *No reduction for parties.* Dogs in car park only. House unsuitable for wheelchairs.

### WINSLOW HALL
**Winslow** *map J5* △
Telephone: (029 671) 2323
*(Sir Edward & Lady Tomkins)*

Built 1698–1702. Almost certainly designed by Sir Christopher Wren. Has survived without major structural alteration and retains most of its original features. Modernized and redecorated by the present owners. Good eighteenth century furniture, mostly English. Some fine pictures, clocks and carpets. Several examples of Chinese art, notably of the Tang period. Beautiful gardens with many unusual trees and shrubs.

**Location:** At entrance to Winslow on the Aylesbury road (A413).
**Opening Times:** Visits by appointment.
**Refreshments:** Catering by arrangement.

### WOTTON HOUSE
**nr Aylesbury** *map J5*
*(Administrator Mrs Patrick Brunner)*

Built 1704, on the same plan as Buckingham House, which later became Buckingham Palace Interior remodelled by Sir John Soane 1820. Wrought iron by Tijou and Thomas Robinson. 'Capability' Brown landscape 1757-1760.

**Location:** In Wotton Underwood 2 m S of A41 midway between Aylesbury and Bicester.
**Opening Times:** Aug to end of Sept—Weds. Tours 2 and 3 (last tour). Small parties by arrangement.

## CAMBRIDGESHIRE

### ANGLESEY ABBEY, The National Trust
**nr Cambridge** *map K6* ♿
Telephone: Cambridge (0223) 811200

The Abbey, founded in the reign of Henry I, was later converted to an Elizabethan manor. Contains Fairhaven collection of art treasures. About 100 acres of grounds, including flower borders, trees, avenues, unique garden statuary and a working water mill that grinds corn.

**Location:** In village of Lode 6 m NE of Cambridge on B1102.
*Station: Cambridge (6 m).*
**Opening Times:** HOUSE & GARDEN. Mar 25 to Oct 15—Wed to Sun & Bank Hol Mons 1.30–5.30. *Closed Good Friday.* Adm £3.50. Pre-booked parties of 15 or more £2.50 (Weds, Thurs & Fris only).
GARDENS ONLY. Mar 25 to July 2, Wed to Sun & Bank Holiday Mons 12–5.30; July 3–Oct 15 daily 12 noon–5.30. Adm £1.50, Chd (with adult) half price. No dogs. Indoor photography by permission only. Wheelchair access (house difficult); chairs provided. Free car park & picnic area. Shop *(closed Mons & Tues).*
Lode Mill: Mar 25 to Oct 15—Sat, Suns & Bank Hol Mons 1.30–5.30.
**Refreshments:** Restaurant open same days as House, 12–5, lunches and teas. Table licence.

**Denny Abbey** – See English Heritage Section.

### DOCWRA'S MANOR
**Shepreth** *map K6*
Telephone: (0763) 60235, 61473 or 61557
*(Mrs John Raven)*

Two acres of choice plants in a series of enclosed gardens.

**Location:** Opposite War Memorial in centre of Shepreth village; ½ m W of Cambridge –Royston Rd (A10) bus stops at gate.
*Station: Shepreth.*
**Opening Times:** GARDEN ONLY. Suns Apr 2, May 7, June 4, July 2, Aug 6, Sept 3, Oct 1, 2–6, also Bank Holiday Mons Mar 27, May 1, May 29, Aug 28 10–5; Mar 15–Oct 13: every Wed & Fri 10–5. Adm £1, accompanied Chd free. Proceeds for garden upkeep. Also Suns May 14, June 11, 2–7 *in aid of National Gardens Scheme.* Also open by appointment. Plants for sale. No dogs.
**Refreshments:** Teas Suns May 14, June 11.

# The National Trust in CAMBRIDGESHIRE

## ANGLESEY ABBEY

## PECKOVER HOUSE

## WIMPOLE HALL

*ADMISSION – SEE EDITORIAL REFERENCE*

## ELTON HALL NR PETERBOROUGH

Elton Hall, 'spanning 5 centuries', has been the home of the Proby family since the reign of Charles II. Their passion for collecting is reflected in the remarkable contents to be seen today; an excellent library including Henry VIII's Prayer Book, excellent furniture and outstanding paintings by Gainsborough, Reynolds, Constable, Alma Tadama, Millais and other fine artists. Gardens under restoration, rose garden replanted in 1984, new herbaceous borders.

**Enjoy even more of Cambridgeshire.**

**Explore the English Heritage Supplement on the Red Pages.**

English Heritage

### ELTON HALL
**nr Peterborough** *map J6*
*(Mr & Mrs William Proby)*

The Proby family have lived at Elton Hall for over 3 centuries. This romantic and gracious house with its mixture of medieval, gothic and classical styles contains excellent pictures and furniture and one of the finest collections of books in private hands. Rose garden restored and new herbaceous borders.
**Location:** On A605, 5 m W of Peterborough.
**Opening Times:** Every Wed June 1 to Sept 30; Every Sun July 1 to Sept 30. Guided tours. Bank Hols: Easter Sun & Mon, Mar 26, 27; May Sun & Mon, Apr 30, May 1; Whit Sun & Mon, May 28, 29; Aug Sun & Mon, Aug 27, 28. Open 2–5. Parties other days by appointment. Prices on application. Adults: £2.40, Chd £1.20. Free parking.
**Refreshments:** Home-made teas. Suppers and lunches by arrangement. Shop.

### ISLAND HALL
**Godmanchester** *map K6*
*(Mr Christopher & The Hon Mrs Vane Percy)*

A mid 18th century Mansion, of architectural importance with fine panelled rooms, in a tranquil riverside setting, with an ornamental island forming part of the gardens.
**Location:** In centre of Godmanchester next to the car park. 1 m S of Huntingdon (A1); 15 m NW of Cambridge (A604).
*Station: Huntingdon (1 m).*
**Opening Times:** June 11–Sept 17 Suns only 2.30–5.30. Parties particularly welcome May–Sept by appointment. Party rate £1.50 groups over 30. Adm House and Grounds £2, Chd £1 (grounds only). Grounds only £1.
**Refreshments:** Teas.

### KIMBOLTON CASTLE
**Kimbolton** *map K6*
*(Governors of Kimbolton School)*

Tudor manor house associated with Katherine of Aragon, completely remodelled by Vanbrugh (1708-20); courtyard c. 1694. Fine murals by Pellegrini in chapel, boudoir and on staircase. Gatehouse by Robert Adam.
**Location:** 8 m NW of St Neots on A45; 14 m N of Bedford.
*Station: St Neots (9 m).*
**Opening Times:** Easter Sun & Mon; Spring Bank Hol Sun & Mon; Summer Bank Hol Mon; also July 23 to Aug 27 – Suns only: 2–6. Adm 75p Chd & OAPs 30p.

**Longthorpe Tower** – See English Heritage Section.

### PECKOVER HOUSE AND GARDEN, The National Trust
**Wisbech** *map K7* △ ♿
Telephone: Wisbech 583463

Important example of early 18th century domestic architecture. Fine rococo decoration. Interesting Victorian garden contains rare trees, flower borders, roses. Under glass are orange trees. Georgian stables.
**Location:** Centre of Wisbech town on N bank of River Nene (B1441).
*Station: March (9½ m).*
**Opening Times:** Principal Rooms & Gardens: Mar 25 to Oct 15; Sat, Sun & Mon. 2–5.30. Adm £1.50, Chld 75p. Party rate £1. No dogs. Wheelchairs garden only.
**Refreshments:** In the Old Kitchen.

### PRIOR CRAUDEN'S CHAPEL
**The College, Ely** *map K6*
Telephone: (0353) 662837
*(The Bursar, The King's School)*

Built as a private chapel in 1324/1325 for Prior Crauden, the Prior of the Mediaeval Benedictine Monastery from 1321 to 1341. Recently restored to show glimpses of coloured walls, painted glass and wall paintings. In 1649 Cromwell's Commissioners planned to destroy the Chapel, but it was saved by being turned into a dwelling house for two hundred years, until a restoration in 1850. Now on view to the public and used for services by the King's School, Ely.
**Location:** In the precincts of Ely Cathedral.
**Opening Times:** Mon to Fri 9–5, excluding statutory and Bank Hols. Adm free. Parking in Cathedral Car Park. Not suitable for disabled visitors.
**Refreshments:** Lamb Hotel, and restaurants in City of Ely.

### UNIVERSITY BOTANIC GARDEN
**Cambridge** *map K6*
*(Cambridge University)*

Fine specimen trees and shrubs. Founded 1761.
**Location:** In Cambridge, 1 m S of City Centre.
*Station: Cambridge (½ m).*
**Opening Times:** All the year—Daily 8–6 (dusk in winter).
Adm free, weekdays (Suns, May to Sept only 2.30–6.30). *Open to ticketholders only, Suns at other times throughout year.* Picnic area.

### WIMPOLE HALL, The National Trust
**nr Cambridge** *map K5* Ⓢ
Telephone: Cambridge (0223) 207257

An architecturally refined house of aristocratic proportions, sumptuous 18th and 19th century staterooms, set in a beautifully undulating park devised by the best of the landscape architects. Exhibition at Stable Block.
**Location:** 8 m SW of Cambridge; signposted off A603 at New Wimpole.
*Stations: Shepreth (5 m) (not Suns); Royston (7 m).*
**Opening Times:** House, Garden & Park. Mar 25 to Oct 29—Daily except Mons & Fris 1–5, Bank Hol Mon 11–5. Adm: £3.50 Chld £1.75. Pre-booked parties of 15 or more £2.50 (Tues to Thurs only). Joint ticket Hall & Farm £4.50. Picnic area. Shop. Dogs allowed in park only on leads. Wheelchair access, 3 chairs provided.
**Refreshments:** Lunches & teas in the Dining Room 12–5. Table licence. Light refreshments at stable block.

### WIMPOLE HOME FARM, The National Trust
**nr Cambridge** *map K5*

An historic farm, faithfully restored by the National Trust, set in 350 acres of beautiful parkland. Approved Rare Breeds Centre. Children's corner. Agricultural museum. Adventure playground. Shop. Film loft.
**Location:** 8 m S of Cambridge; signposted off A603 at New Wimpole.
*Stations: Shepreth (5 m); Royston (7 m).*
**Opening Times:** Mar 25 to Oct 29—Daily (except Mons & Fris) (open Bank Hol Mon) 10.30–5. (Mar, Apr and Oct: 11–4). Adm £2.50, NT members £1, Chd £1, parties (pre-booked) £2. Joint ticket for Hall and Farm £4.50.
**Refreshments:** Lunches & teas at Wimpole Hall. Snacks at Home Farm.

## CHESHIRE

### ADLINGTON HALL
**Macclesfield** *map G8*
Telephone: Prestbury 829206
*(Charles Legh, Esq.)*

Great Hall dates from about 1450, Elizabethan half-timbered 'black and white' portion 1581.
**Location:** 5 m N of Macclesfield on the Stockport/Macclesfield Road (A523).
*Station: Adlington (½ m).*
**Opening Times:** Good Friday to Oct 1—Suns & Bank Hols; also Aug—Weds & Sats 2–5.30. Adm £1.75, Chd 85p. *Special parties by arrangement other days (over 25 people £1.25).*
**Refreshments:** At the Hall.

### ARLEY HALL AND GARDENS
**nr Northwich** *map G8*
Telephone: Arley (056 585) 353
*(The Hon M L W Flower)*

Victorian country house and private Chapel (c 1840). Gardens of great variety and charm—topiary, rhododendrons, azaleas, herbaceous border, shrub roses, walled gardens, herb garden, woodland garden and woodland walk.
**Location:** 5 m N of Northwich; 6 m W of Knutsford; 7 m S of Warrington; 5 m off M6 at junction 19 & 20; 5 m off M56 at junction 9 & 10.
**Opening Times:** Mar 24 to Oct 8—Tues to Suns & Bank Hol Mons Gardens 2–6 (June, July & Aug 12–6). Hall 2–5.30 throughout. Last adm Hall 5, Gardens 5.30. 1988 charges not available at time of going to press. Special rates, opening hours and catering for organised parties by appointment.
**Refreshments:** In converted Tudor Barn.

### BEESTON CASTLE
*map F8*
Telephone: (0829) 260464
*(English Heritage)*

Built on an isolated crag, Beeston Castle is visible for miles around. The view across the Cheshire plain extends to the Pennines in the east and westwards to Wales. Begun about 1220 by Ranulf de Blundeville, the castle was further fortified by Edward I. The ditch alone can have been no small task, as it is hewn from the solid rock. There is an exhibition on the history of the castle in the museum.
**Location:** 2 m (3.2 km) west of Bunbury. 11m (18 km) south east of Chester. OS map ref SJ537593.
**Opening Times:** Good Friday to Sept 30, 10–6; Oct 1 to Maundy Thurs, daily 10–4. *Closed* Mon, Dec 24–26 and Jan 1. Adm £1.30, OAPs £1, Chd 65p.

### BRAMALL HALL
**Bramhall, Stockport** *map G8*
Telephone: 061-485 3708
*(Metropolitan Borough of Stockport)*

Bramall Hall is one of the most splendid of Cheshire's black and white timber framed houses. The oldest parts date back to the fourteenth century, and there are many interesting features from later centuries. The magnificent 16th century wall paintings are some of the finest in the North West, and the Elizabethan withdrawing room has a fine plaster ceiling and overmantel. The Victorian additions are in the most romantic spirit and include attractive wrought iron fittings. Special events and concerts are arranged throughout the year. The Hall stands in a landscaped park with streams, lakes and woods. Shop.

# ISLAND HALL

**GODMANCHESTER, CAMBRIDGESHIRE**

On the banks of the Great Ouse, overlooking the Island from which it takes its name, this beautiful house, very much a family home, contains lovely rooms with fine period detail and interesting possessions relating to the owners ancestors since their first occupation of the house in 1800.

*ADMISSION – SEE EDITORIAL REFERENCE*

# ADLINGTON HALL

**near MACCLESFIELD, Cheshire (off A523)**

*'Country Life' photograph*

Adlington Hall is a Cheshire Manor and has been the home of the Leghs since 1315. The Great Hall was built between 1450 and 1505, the Elizabethan 'Black & White' in 1581 and the Georgian South Front in 1757. The Bernard Smith Organ was installed c. 1670.

A 'Shell Cottage', Yew Walk and Lime Avenue are features of the gardens.

Open Good Friday to October 1—Sundays and Bank Holidays (also Wednesdays and Saturdays during August) from 2 to 5.30pm.

Admission £1.75. Children 85p. Car Park free.

Home-made teas and refreshments.

Organised Parties on other days by arrangement (over 25 people £1.25). Gift shop.

Enquiries to The Guide. Telephone Prestbury 829206.

# ARLEY HALL AND GARDENS

**Near Gt. Budworth, Northwich, Cheshire**

*the home of the Hon Michael and Mrs Flower*

*Arley Hall* *Lawrence Sands, Northwich Photograph*

Arley Hall lies at the centre of an estate owned by one family for over 500 years. The present Hall, built about 1840 in the 'Victorian Jacobean' style, contains fine plaster work, oak panelling, furniture and interesting pictures. The Gardens, winners of the Christie's and Historic Houses Association Garden of the Year Award, provide great variety of style and design. The magnificent twin herbaceous borders are amongst the first to be planted in England. Other features include an unusual avenue of Ilex trees trimmed to the shape of giant cylinders, fine yew hedges, walled gardens, azaleas, rhododendrons and a newly developed woodland garden leading to a woodland walk.

There is a gift shop, plants are for sale and teas are served in a converted Tudor Barn.

A cabinet maker, potter and blacksmith have workshops at Arley.

Enquiries: The Administrator, Arley Hall & Gardens, Northwich, Cheshire CW9 6NP

Telephone: Arley (056 585) 353.

*ADMISSION – SEE EDITORIAL REFERENCE*

# BRAMALL HALL

**BRAMHALL PARK, BRAMHALL, STOCKPORT**

*ADMISSION – SEE EDITORIAL REFERENCE*

**Location:** 4 m S of Stockport; off A5102.
*Station: Cheadle Hulme (½ m).*
**Opening Times:** Apr–Sept daily 1–5; Oct–Jan 1: Tues–Sun 1–4; Jan 2–Jan 31: *Closed* Feb–Mar: Tues–Sun 1–4. Adm £1.50, Chd 75p (subject to alteration for special events). Parking and gardens free and open at all times. Guided tours of the Hall every afternoon. Day and evening tours for parties by arrangement.
**Refreshments:** The Stables cafe serves lunches and teas, and is available for functions. Cafe open Apr–Sept daily 11–4.30. Oct–Dec: Tues–Sun 11–4; Jan: Sat & Sun 11–4; Feb–Mar: Sun 11–4.

## CAPESTHORNE
**Macclesfield** *map G8*
Telephone: Chelford 861221 or 861439
*(Lt Col Sir Walter Bromley-Davenport)*

Recent research has revealed that Francis and William Smith of Warwick were almost certainly the original architects of this Jacobean style house built in 1722. Later alterations were made by Blore and Salvin. Pictures, furniture, Capesthorne collection of vases, family muniments and Americana.

**Location:** 7 m S of Wilmslow, on Manchester/London Road (A34); 6½ m N of Congleton, Junction 18 (M6).
*Station: Chelford (3 m).*
**Opening Times:** Park, Gardens and Chapel 12–6, Hall 2–5. April—Suns; May & Sept—Sats, Suns & Weds; June, July & Aug—Tues, Weds, Thurs, Sats & Suns. Open Good Fri and all Bank Hols. Adm Park, Gardens & Chapel £1.20, Chd (5–16 years) 50p, Park, Gardens, Chapel & Hall £2.40, Chd £1. Budget Family ticket £6. Visitors to Gardens, Caravanners etc, may visit the Hall by paying the excess of £1.20, Chd 50p, at the desk in the Hall entrance. Chd under 5 years accompanied by an adult free. Coach and Car Park free. Dogs are allowed in the Park area only. Organised parties are welcome daily (except Mons and Fris) by appointment (please send for booking form and coloured brochure). Special reductions for parties of 20 or more at £1.70 per person to Hall, Park, Gardens & Chapel. Evening parties are also welcome from May to July (by appointment). Evening party rate £2 per person, minimum number 20.
**Refreshments:** Garden Restaurant & Bromley room.

## CHOLMONDELEY CASTLE GARDENS
**Malpas** *map F7*
Telephone: Cholmondeley (082 922) 383 or 203
*(The Marquess of Cholmondeley)*

Lakeside picnic area, rare breeds of farm animals, and romantically landscaped gardens full of variety. Ancient private chapel in Park. Evening service 6.30 every third sun in month.

**Location:** Off A41 Chester/Whitchurch Road and A49 Whitchurch/Tarporley Road.
**Opening Times:** GARDEN & FARM ONLY. Easter Sun to Sept 24—Suns & Bank Hols only 12–5.30. Adm £1.50, OAPs £1, Chd 50p. Enquiries to: The Secretary, Cholmondeley Castle, Malpas, Cheshire. Gift Shop, Plants for sale. (House not open to public.)
**Refreshments:** Tea room.

## DORFOLD HALL
**Nantwich** *map G7* △
Telephone: Nantwich (0270) 625245
*(R. C. Roundell, Esq.)*

Jacobean country house built 1616. Beautiful plaster ceilings and panelling. Attractive gardens. Guided tours.

**Location:** 1 m W of Nantwich on A534 Nantwich/Wrexham Road.
*Station: Nantwich (1½ m).*
**Opening Times:** Apr to Oct—Tues & Bank Hol Mons 2–5. Adm £2, Chd £1. *At other times by appointment only.*

## DUNHAM MASSEY, The National Trust
**Altrincham** *map G8*
Telephone: 061-941 1025

Fine 18th century house with Georgian and Edwardian interiors. Huguenot silver collection, fine furniture and family portraits. Extensive gardens recently restored, woodlands, deer park and water mill.

**Location:** 3 m SW of Altrincham off A56; junction 19 off M6; junction 7 off M56.
**Opening Times:** Mar 25 to Oct 29—Daily (except Fris). Garden, restaurant & shop 12–5.30 (Suns & Bank Hol Mons 11–5.30). House 1–5 (Suns & Bank Hol Mons 12–5). Last adm 4.30. Guided evening tours by arrangement at an extra charge. Car park £2 (refundable on house entry). Coaches free. Adm: House and Garden £3, Chd £1.50. Family ticket £8. Reduced rates for pre-booked parties. Dogs in park only on lead. Wheelchairs provided—access to shop, garden and park. Limited access to house. Information from the Administrator, Dunham Massey Hall, Altrincham, Cheshire. WA14 4SJ.
**Refreshments:** Lunches & teas available. Also open for booked parties, functions etc – by arrangement. Tel: 061-941 2815. Restaurant and shop also open Nov to Dec 17, Thur to Sun 12–4, and Jan 6 to Mar 25 1990, Sat and Sun 12–4.

## GAWSWORTH HALL
**Macclesfield** *map G8*
Telephone: North Rode (0260) 223456
*(Mr & Mrs Timothy Richards)*

Tudor half-timbered manor house with tilting ground. Former home of Mary Fitton, Maid of Honour at the Court of Queen Elizabeth I, and the supposed 'dark lady' of Shakespeare's sonnets. Pictures, sculpture and furniture. Open air theatre with covered grand stand – June/July/August.

**Location:** 3 m S of Macclesfield on the Congleton/Macclesfield Road (A536).
**Opening Times:** Mar 26 to Oct 9–Daily 2–6. Adm £2.20, Chd £1.10. *Evening parties by arrangement.* Free car park.
**Refreshments:** In the Pavilion

## HANDFORTH HALL
**Handforth, nr Wilmslow** *map G8*
*(Dr J. C. Douglas)*

Small 16th century half-timbered manor house. Fine Jacobean staircase. Collection of oak furniture.

**Location:** ½ m E of Handforth on B5358.
*Station: Handforth (few mins walk).*
**Opening Times:** June to Sept by written appointment only.

## HARE HILL GARDEN, The National Trust
**Over Alderley, nr Macclesfield** *map G8*

Walled garden with pergola, rhododendrons and azaleas; parkland.

**Location:** Between Alderley Edge and Prestbury off B5087 at Greyhound Road. Link path to Alderley Edge.
*Stations: Alderley Edge (3½ m); Prestbury (2½ m).*
**Opening Times:** GARDEN ONLY. Easter Sun to end of Oct—Weds, Thurs, Sats, Suns and Bank Hol Mons 10–5.30. Special opening for rhododendrons and azaleas May 22 to June 9, daily 10–5.30. Adm £1. Parties by appointment in writing to the Head Gardener, Garden Lodge. Unsuitable for school parties. Wheelchair access – some assistance needed.

# CAPESTHORNE

**near MACCLESFIELD, CHESHIRE**

Capesthorne is the home of the Bromley-Davenport family where they and their ancestors have lived since Domesday times. Adjoining the house is a beautiful little Georgian chapel. The gardens and dining rooms overlook a chain of lakes. Arboretum, nature trail and delightful woodland walk.

OPEN
Park, Gardens and Chapel 12 noon until 6 pm. Hall 2 to 5 pm. April to September inclusive. April—Sundays only. May & September—Wednesdays, Saturdays, Sundays. June, July, August—Tuesdays, Wednesdays, Thursdays, Saturdays, Sundays and all Bank Holidays.

ADMISSION CHARGES
Park/Gardens/Chapel etc. Adults £1.20. Children (5–16) 50p. Park/Gardens/Chapel and Hall Adults £2.40. Children (5–16) £1.
Budget Family Ticket £6.00.

Visitors to Gardens, Caravanners etc. may visit the Hall by paying the excess of £1.20. Adult and 50p Children at the desk in the hall entrance. Children under 5 accompanied by an adult free. Coach and Car Park free. Dogs are allowed in the Park area only. Touring caravan park.

Enquiries to Administrator, Capesthorne, Macclesfield, Cheshire, SK11 9JY.
Telephone: Chelford 861221 or 861439.

# CHOLMONDELEY CASTLE GARDENS

**MALPAS, CHESHIRE**

*Home of The Marquess and Marchioness of Cholmondeley*

Lakeside picnic area, rare breeds of farm animals, and romantically landscaped gardens full of variety.

Ancient Private Chapel in the Park.
Evening Services 6.30pm every third Sunday in month.

Open SUNDAYS and BANK HOLIDAYS ONLY from EASTER SUNDAY to September 24th 12 noon to 5.30 pm.

Weekday visits accepted by prior arrangement.
Reduced rate for coach parties.

Admission: £1.50 Adults
£1.00 OAPs
50p Children

Tea Room and Gift Shop.
Plants for Sale.

Situated off Whitchurch/Tarporley Road and Chester/Whitchurch Road.

All enquiries: The Secretary, Cholmondeley Castle, Malpas, Cheshire.
Telephone: Cholmondeley (082 922) 383 or 203.

THE HOUSE IS NOT OPEN TO THE PUBLIC

# THE PALACE ON THE EDGE OF THE PEAKS

As a young man Alfred Shaughnessy, creator of the Upstairs Downstairs T.V. Series, was a frequent house guest at Lyme. You, too, can now experience the atmosphere of an Edwardian Country House by stepping into this magnificent mansion.

Staff reconstruct the life of the servants of Lyme, whilst introducing visitors to the magnificent treasures. Here you can see beautiful Grinling Gibbons woodcarvings, Mortlake tapestries and a collection of clocks which includes no less than three examples by Thomas Thompion.

Surrounded by magnificent Victorian gardens Lyme Hall is set in 1300 acres of park containing Red and Fallow deer.

## LITTLE MORETON HALL, The National Trust

**Congleton CW12 4SD** *map G7* ♿
Telephone: Congleton (0260) 272018

Begun in the 15th century, one of the most perfect examples of a timber-framed moated manor house in the country. Remarkable carved gables. The recently discovered and restored 16th century wall paintings are on view. Attractive knot garden.

**Location:** 4 m SW of Congleton off Newcastle-under-Lyme/Congleton Road (A34).
**Opening Times:** Mar & Oct—Sats & Suns 1.30-5.30. Easter Mon 11.30–5.30. *Closed* Good Friday. Apr to end Sept; 1.30–5.30 every day except Tues. Bank Holiday 11.30–5.30, last adm 5. School parties: Apr to end Sept mornings only not Tues by prior arrangement with Administrator (sae please). Guided tours usually each afternoon. Adm weekends & Bank Hols £2.50; weekdays £2; Family ticket £6, reduced rate for pre-booked parties. Dogs in car park and grass area in front of Hall only. Wheelchairs provided. Shop.
**Refreshments:** Light lunches and home made teas from 1.30.

## LYME PARK, The National Trust (Cared for by Stockport Metropolitan Borough Council)

**Disley** *map G8* △
Telephone: Disley (0663) 62023

An Elizabethan House with 18th and 19th century alterations, particularly by Giacomo Leoni in the 1730's. A lively visitor centre evokes the atmosphere of Edwardian Lyme.
Formal gardens, including a spectacular Dutch Garden. Over 1,300 acres of Parkland and Moorland, set on edge of the Peak District and populated with herds of Red and Fallow Deer.

**Opening Times:** HALL: Mar 24–Apr 9, daily free flow 2–5 (last entry 4.15). Apr 9–Apr 30, Sun only free flow 2–5 (last entry 4.15). May 1–June 29 Tues, Weds, Thurs, Sat, Sun plus Bank Holiday, weekdays guided tours hourly 2–4. Sat guided tours half hourly 2–4.30. Sun free flow 2–5 (last entry 4.15). May 27–June 11, free flow 2–5 (last entry 4.15). July 1–Aug 31, Tues, Weds, Thurs, Sat, Sun plus Bank Holiday, free flow 2–5 (last entry 4.15). Sept 2–Oct 1, Tues, Weds, Thurs, Sat, Sun, weekdays guided tours hourly 2–4. Sat guided tours half hourly 2–4.30. Sun free flow 2–5 (last entry 4.15). Oct 8–Dec 10, Sun only guided tours half hourly 2–4.30. SHOP: open as Hall, 1 hour before to ½ hour after Hall times. Special bookings when Hall is closed by arrangement with the Manager. Adm for car, including occupants: Park and Gardens incl. N.T. £2.50. Park, Gardens and Hall £6.00 (N.T. £2.50). GARDENS: Mar 24–Sept 30, daily 11–6. Oct 1–Apr 1 1990, 11–4. *Closed* Christmas Day & Boxing Day. INFORMATION CENTRE: Open Sat Mar 18–Oct 1 and Oct School Holiday, daily 10–6. Oct–Mar 1990 (inclusive) 11–4.
**Refreshments:** Kiosk – weekends and school holidays and June, July, Aug, daily from 11. Servants Hall Tea Room: dates as Hall, from midday.
**Other Activities:** Pitch and putt course, fishing and horse riding permits, children's adventure playground, orienteering course (open all year), nature trail. Function facilities. 1989 Events – See events leaflet. Guided walks and Chapel services throughout the year. For further information contact The Manager, address above, or Tel: Disley (0663) 62023.

## NESS GARDENS

**Wirral** *map F8* ♿
Telephone: 051-336 2135
*(Liverpool University Botanic Gardens)*

Finest collection of rhododendrons and azaleas in the NW. Superb specimen trees and shrubs. Large rock, water, heather and terrace gardens. Visitor centre with slide shows, indoor exhibitions and shop.

**Location:** Between Neston and Burton; NW of Chester off A540.
*Station: Neston (1½ m).*
**Opening Times:** All the year—Daily 9 to sunset. *Closed Christmas Day.* Adm £1.80, Chd & OAPs £1, Family ticket £4. Picnic area.
**Refreshments:** Tea room facilities Mar–Sept (party catering by prior arrangement).

## NETHER ALDERLEY MILL, The National Trust

**Nether Alderley** *map G8*
Telephone: Wilmslow (0625) 523012

15th century corn-mill in use until 1939 and now restored; tandem overshot water wheels. Flour ground occasionally for demonstration.

**Location:** 1½ m S of Alderley Edge on E side of A34.
*Station: Alderley Edge (2 m).*
**Opening Times:** Easter Sunday to June 30 & Oct—Weds, Suns & Bank Hol Mons 2–5.30. *Closed* Good Friday. July, Aug & Sept—Daily (except Mons but open Bank Hol Mons) 2–5.30. Adm £1.10, Chd 50p. No dogs. Unsuitable for disabled or visually handicapped. Parties by prior arrangement with Mrs Pamela Ferguson, 7 Oak Cottages, Styal, Wilmslow.

## NORTON PRIORY MUSEUM

**Runcorn** *map F8*
Telephone: Runcorn (092 85) 69895
*(Norton Priory Museum Trust)*

The beautiful woodland gardens covering 16 acres contain the 12th century undercroft and excavated remains of the Priory. Displays of mediaeval tiles, stonework, ceramics etc. Shop, picnic area, refreshments.

**Location:** From M56 (junction 11) turn towards Warrington and follow Norton Priory Road signs.
**Opening Times:** Mar to Oct—Sats, Suns & Bank Hols 12–6; Mons to Fris 12–5. Nov to Feb—Daily 12–4. *Closed* Dec 24, 25 & 26. Special arrangements for groups. Adm £1.20, Chd, Students & OAPs 60p.

## PEOVER HALL

**Over Peover, Knutsford** *map G8*
Telephone: Lower Peover 2135
*(Randle Brooks)*

House dates from 1585. Fine Caroline stables. Mainwaring Chapel. 18th century landscaped park. Large garden with Topiary work, also Walled and Herb gardens.

**Location:** 4 m S of Knutsford off A50 at Whipping Stocks Inn.
**Opening Times:** Beginning of May to end of Sept (except Bank Holidays). House, Stables & Gardens—Mons 2.30–5. Adm £1.80, Chd 90p. Thurs Stables & Gardens Only 2–5. Adm £1. Enquiries: N. Brooks, Peover Hall Farm.
**Refreshments:** Teas in the Stables on Mons.

## QUARRY BANK MILL, The National Trust & Quarry Bank Mill Trust Ltd

**Styal** *map G8* Ⓢ
Telephone: Wilmslow (0625) 527468

Award-winning working museum of the cotton industry housed in a 200-year-old spinning mill. Skilled demonstrators operate vintage machinery showing cotton processes from carding and spinning to weaving on Lancashire looms. Displays on water power, the lifestyle of the mill-owning Greg family plus the millworkers' world at home and at work in the 19th century. Giant 1850 waterwheel restored to working order. Renovated Apprentice House. The millworkers' village of Styal and the mill are set in the 250 acre Styal County Park. Museum of the Year 1984. A winner of the Sandford Award for Heritage Education 1987.

Cheshire Life photograph

## NESS GARDENS

**S. WIRRAL, CHESHIRE**

*University of Liverpool Botanic Gardens*

Extensive Garden with sweeping lawns and fine specimen trees and shrubs including some original specimens introduced by George Forrest. Rock, water, heather and terrace Gardens, Herbaceous borders, Rose collection and Herb Garden. Views across the Dee Estuary to the Clwyd Hills.

Visitor Centre with slide show and indoor exhibitions. Picnic area. Tea room facilities March–Sept. Gift shop.

Open daily, except Christmas Day, 9 am to sunset.

Admission: Adults £1.80. Children & OAPs £1. Family Ticket £4.

Working demonstrations from waterwheel to woven cloth.
Experience the mill worker's world at

## Quarry Bank Mill

Open daily 11 am *(closed Mon Oct–May).*
The Shop sells cotton goods woven in the Mill.
Restaurant.
Pre-booked parties welcome.
Near Manchester Airport – from M56 take exit 5 (2 miles).

Styal is a National Trust property

Restored **Apprentice House**

Enquiries (0625) 527468

## PEOVER HALL **KNUTSFORD, CHESHIRE**

Elizabethan House dated 1585
Fine Carolean Stables
Extensive gardens
Fine Topiary work
Mainwaring Chapel
18th Century Landscape Park

Opening beginning of May to end of September, Mondays (but not Bank Holidays) House, Stables and Gardens 2.30 to 5.00 pm. Thursdays—Stables and Gardens only.

Parties by arrangement also on other days of the week.

Teas in the Stables on Mondays.

## NORTON PRIORY

### MUSEUM and GARDENS

**Runcorn, Cheshire**

Beautiful woodland gardens contain the 12th century undercroft and excavated remains of the Priory. Displays of medieval tiles, stonework, ceramics. Shop, refreshments, picnic area. Open daily.

Tel: Runcorn (092 85) 69895

## Tatton Park

The complete Country Estate

*alive with history*

- **FINE GEORGIAN MANSION** with original furnishings "upstairs and downstairs".
- **MAGNIFICENT GARDENS** among England's "top ten".
- **15th CENTURY OLD HALL** the Tatton of ages past, touching all the senses.
- **A 1930's HOME FARM** the heart of the estate.
- All set in a thousand acres of deer park and meres in the rolling Cheshire countryside.

Park and gardens open daily (except Christmas Day). Mansion, Home Farm and Old Hall open April to October.

Just off M6 (Junction 19) and M56 at Knutsford, Cheshire with ample car and coach parking, restaurant, high class gift shop and garden sales.

For details of discounted group rates and programme of events contact: Secretary, Tatton Park, Knutsford, Cheshire WA16 6QN
Telephone: Knutsford (0565) 54822

## CHESHIRE – *continued*

**Location:** 1½ m N of Wilmslow off B5166.
*Stations: Styal (½ m) (not Suns); Wilmslow (1½ m).*
**Opening Times:** Oct–Mar 11–4 Tues–Sun, April/May 11–5 Tues–Sun, June–Sept 11–5 daily. Open Bank Holidays. Mill and Apprentice House: £3.75, Chd £2.75. Mill only: £2.75, Chd £2. Apprentice House only £1.50, Chd £1.25. Family tickets: Mill & Apprentice House £12; Mill only £8. Apprentice House only £5. NT members free. Car park £1 per vehicle. (NT members may park free of charge). Parties should apply for details of special rates and booking form at least 4 weeks in advance. Disabled visitors asked to telephone before visit. No coach parties Suns or Bank Holidays.
**Sandford Award for Heritage Education.**
**Refreshments:** Licensed restaurant. Mill shop.

### RODE HALL
**Scholar Green, Stoke-on-Trent** *map G7*
Telephone: Alsager 3237
*(Sir Richard Baker Wilbraham Bt.)*

18th century country house with Georgian stable block. Later alterations by L. Wyatt and Darcy Braddell.

**Location:** 5 m SW of Congleton between A34 & A50.
*Station: Alsager (2¼ m).*
**Opening Times: Closed in 1989 for repairs.**
**Refreshments:** Bleeding Wolf Restaurant, Scholar Green.

### TATTON PARK, The National Trust (financed and managed by Cheshire County Council)
**Knutsford** *map G8* ♿ Ⓢ
Telephone: Knutsford (0565) 54822

Seat of the late Lord Egerton of Tatton. Fine Georgian mansion by Samuel and Lewis Wyatt, beautifully furnished and decorated. Family museum. Restored 15th century Old Hall. 1930s working Farm. Magnificently varied 50 acre garden, showhouse, fernery, waterfowl, 1,000 acre deer park, two large meres, swimming, sailing, fishing, riding. Medieval village trail. Historical nature trail. Gift shop and Garden sales.

**Location:** 2 m N of Knutsford; 3½ m off M6 (exit 19); 4 m S of M56 (exit 7) fully signposted. A556 Chester Rd, or A50 from Stoke on Trent.
*Station: Knutsford (2 m).*
**Opening Times:** PARK AND GARDENS open all year (except Christmas Day). MANSION open daily—Easter to Oct 31. House (Suns & Public hols in brackets): Easter to mid-May & Sept/Oct: Park 11–6 (10–6); Garden 11.30–5 (10.30–5.30); Mansion 1–4 (1–5); Old Hall 12–4 (12–5); Farm 12–4 (12–4). Mid-May to Aug: Park 10.30–7 (10–7); Garden 11–5.30 (10.30–6); Mansion 1–4 (1–5); July/Aug 1–5 (12–5); Old Hall 12–4 (12–5); July/Aug 12–5 (12–5); Farm 11–4 (11–4). Nov to Apr 1: Park 11–dusk (11–dusk); Garden 1–4 (12–4). *Everything closed June 20 & 21.* Farm closed but open Suns in Nov & Mar 1–4 (Old Hall closed). Exits remain open for 1 hour after adm times. Adm Mansion £1.35; Garden £1; Old Hall £1; Farm 95p. Reduction for parties of 12 or more weekdays on application only. Park: cars £1.20 (incl NT members), coaches free. Knutsford Gate car park: cars 60p (incl NT members). Information from: Secretary, Tatton Park, Knutsford. Send sae for full calendar of events.
**Refreshments:** Restaurant.

### WOODHEY CHAPEL
**Faddiley, nr Nantwich** *map G7*
Telephone: Faddiley (027 074) 215
*(The Trustees of Woodhey Chapel)*

'The Chapel in the Fields.' A small private chapel, recently restored, dating from 1699.

**Location:** 1 m SW of Faddiley off A534 Nantwich/Wrexham Road.
**Opening Times:** Apr to Oct—Sats & Bank Hol Mons 2–5. Adm 50p, Chd 25p. At other times by appointment.

## CLEVELAND

**Gisborough Priory** – See English Heritage Section.

### ORMESBY HALL, The National Trust
**nr Middlesbrough** *map H11* △

Mid-18th century house. Contemporary plasterwork. Small garden.

**Location:** 3 m SE of Middlesbrough.
*Station: Marton (1½ m) (not Suns April, Sept & Oct).*
**Opening Times:** Easter to end Oct, Mar 24–27: 2–5.30. Apr and Oct, Wed and Sun: 2–5.30. May–Sept, Weds, Thurs and Sun: 2–5.30. Adm £1, Chd (accompanied) 50p. *Pre-booked parties of 15 or over 80p each adult, 30p Chd.* No dogs (except guide dogs). Wheelchair access to ground floor only. Small shop.

## CORNWALL

### ANTONY HOUSE, The National Trust
**Torpoint** *map E2* △
Telephone: Plymouth (0752) 812191

The home of Mr. Richard Carew Pole. Built for Sir William Carew 1711-1721. Unaltered Queen Anne house, panelled rooms. Fine furniture. Extensive garden.

**Location:** 5 m W of Plymouth via Torpoint car ferry. 2 m NW of Torpoint, N of A374.
**Opening Times:** Mar 27 to end of Oct—Tues, Weds & Thurs; also Bank Hol Mons and Suns in June, July and Aug 2–6 (last adm 5.30). Adm £2.40, Chd £1.20. Pre-arranged parties £1.80, Chd 90p. No dogs. Unsuitable for wheelchairs. Shop.

### ANTONY WOODLAND GARDEN
**Torpoint** *map E2* △
*(Carew Pole Garden Trust)*

A woodland garden extending to over 50 acres bordering the Lynher Estuary, an area designated as one of Outstanding Natural Beauty and a Site of Special Scientific Interest. Established in the late 18th century with the assistance of Humphrey Repton, the gardens feature extensive woodland and riverside walks with over 300 types of Camellias and a wide variety of Magnolias, Rhododendrons, Hydrangeas, Azaleas and other flowering shrubs together with many fine specimen indigenous and exotic hardwood and softwood trees.

**Location:** 5 m W of Plymouth via Torpoint Car Ferry. 2 m NW of Torpoint off A374.
**Opening Times:** Mar 15–May 31 and Sept 15–Oct 31, Mon–Fri 11.30–5.30. Suns 2.30–5.30. *Closed* Sats. Special openings in aid of Charities by arrangement. Adm £1, Chd 50p. Car parking available. No dogs allowed.

**Chysauster Ancient Village** – See English Heritage Section.

### COTEHELE HOUSE, The National Trust
**Calstock** *map E2* ♿
Telephone: Liskeard 50434. Restaurant 50652.

Fine mediaeval house former home of Earls of Mount Edgcumbe. Armour, furniture, tapestries. Terrace garden falling to the sheltered valley, ponds, stream, unusual shrubs. Memorial Watermill and Cotehele Quay museum.

# ORMESBY HALL

**Near MIDDLESBROUGH**

*THE NATIONAL TRUST*

*ADMISSION – SEE EDITORIAL REFERENCE*

# GODOLPHIN HOUSE

**near HELSTON, CORNWALL**

A former home of the Earls of Godolphin and the birthplace of Queen Anne's famous Lord High Treasurer—Sidney, first Earl of Godolphin. Parts of the house are of early Tudor date and additions were made in Elizabethan and Carolean times. The unique front was completed shortly before the Civil War and rests on massive columns of local granite. The fine 'Kings Room' is traditionally said to have been occupied by Charles II (then Prince of Wales) at the time of his escape from Pendennis Castle to the Scilly Islands. Pictures include 'The Godolphin Arabian' by John Wootton.

May & June—Thursdays 2 to 5 pm; July & September—Tuesdays & Thursdays 2 to 5 pm; August—Tuesdays 2 to 5 pm. Thursdays 10 am to 1 pm & 2 to 5 pm. Also open Bank Holiday Mondays. Admission £1.50, Children 50p. (1989 prices). Parties by arrangement all year round.

# PRIDEAUX PLACE

**PADSTOW**

Guided tours of this delightful 16th century Elizabethan house, set in extensive grounds with 20 acres of Deer Park above the fishing port of Padstow, include visits to the dining room, morning room, drawing room, reading room, library and the great chamber which features an embossed plaster ceiling dating from about 1585.

Gift shop, tea room, exhibitions, concerts etc.

*ADMISSION – SEE EDITORIAL REFERENCE*

**Enjoy even more of Cornwall.**

**Explore the English Heritage Supplement on the Red Pages.**

**English Heritage**

# CORNWALL – *continued*

**Location:** On W bank of the Tamar, 1 m W of Calstock by footpath, (6 m by road). 8 m SW of Tavistock; 14 m from Plymouth via Tamar Bridge.
*Station: Calstock (1½ m) (not Suns).*
**Opening Times:** Mar 24 to end of Oct—Garden, Mill and Quay every day, House every day *except Friday*, but open Good Friday 11–6 (last adm 5.30) 11–5 in Oct. Closes dusk if earlier. Nov to Mar—Garden open daily during daylight. Adm House, Gardens, Cotehele Mill and Quay £3.50, Chd £1.75. Gardens, Cotehele Mill and Quay £1.60 Chd 80p. *Reduced fee of £2.80, Chd £1.40 for pre-booked coach parties. Organisers should book visits & arrange for meals beforehand with the Administrator.* DOGS IN WOOD ONLY – on lead. Wheelchairs provided; house only accessible. Shop.
**Refreshments:** Available.

## GLENDURGAN GARDEN, The National Trust
**Helford River** *map C1*

A valley garden of great beauty with fine trees and shrubs, overlooking estuary. Giant's Stride and maze much enjoyed by children.

**Location:** 4 m SW of Falmouth ½ m SW of Mawnan Smith on road to Helford Passage.
**Opening Times:** Mar 1 to end of Oct—Mons, Weds & Fris (except Good Friday) 10.30–5.30 (last adm 4.30). Adm £1.60, Chd 80p. *No reduction for parties.* No dogs. Unsuitable for wheelchairs.

## GODOLPHIN HOUSE
**Helston** *map C1*
*(Mrs. Schofield)*

Tudor house. Colonnaded front added 1635. A former house of the Earls of Godolphin.

**Location:** 5 m NW of Helston; between villages of Townshend and Godolphin Cross.
**Opening Times:** Bank Hol Mons; May & June—Thurs 2–5. July & Sept—Tues 2–5, Thurs 2–5, Aug—Tues 2–5, Thurs 10–1, 2–5. Adm £1.50, Chd 50p (1988 rates, 1989 charges not known at time of going to press). Open at other times for pre-booked parties & all year round for arranged parties.

## LANHYDROCK, The National Trust
**nr Bodmin** *map D2* ♿
Telephone: Bodmin 73320. Restaurant 74331.

The great house of Cornwall, with 36 rooms open to the public. 17th century long gallery. Fine plaster ceilings. Family portraits 17th to 20th centuries. The extensive kitchen and servants' quarters (1883) are also shown. Formal garden with clipped yews, and parterre, laid out in 1857. Rhododendrons, magnolias, rare trees and shrubs. Woodland garden and parkland setting.

**Location:** 2½ m SE of Bodmin on Bodmin/Lostwithiel Road (B3268).
*Station: Bodmin Parkway (1¾ m by signposted carriage-drive to house; 3 m by road).*
**Opening Times:** House, Garden and Grounds – Mar 24 to end of Oct—Daily except Mon (*open Bank Holiday Mons*) 11–6 (last adm 5.30) 11–5 in Oct. Nov to end of Mar—Garden and Grounds – open daily during daylight hours. Adm £3.50, Chd £1.75; Garden only £1.60, Chd 80p. Pre-booked parties £2.80, Chd £1.40. *Organisers should book visits & arrange for meals beforehand with The Administrator.* Dogs in park only on leads. Wheelchairs provided. Shop (also open Nov & Dec).
**Refreshments:** Teas in restaurant at House; snacks in stable block (last adm 5.30).

**Launceston Castle** – See English Heritage Section.

## LONG CROSS VICTORIAN GARDENS
**nr Port Isaac** *map D2*
Telephone: Port Isaac (0208) 880243

Late Victorian gardens set amidst majestic pines with panoramic sea views.

**Location:** Just off B3314 between Port Isaac & Port Quin, Trelights & St Endellion: 7 m NE of Wadebridge.
**Opening Times:** Easter to Oct—Daily 11 to dusk. Children's playground; family room. Adm free. *Collection box in aid of MacMillan Nurses.*
**Refreshments:** Beer Garden, coffee & refreshments, cream teas.

## MOUNT EDGCUMBE HOUSE & COUNTRY PARK
**nr Plymouth** *map E2*
Telephone: Plymouth (0752) 822236
*(City of Plymouth & Cornwall County Council)*

Stretching along 10 miles of spectacular coastline from Plymouth to Whitsand Bay, the Park contains one of only three Grade I Historic Gardens in Cornwall. The first landscape park in Cornwall, it was designed 240 years ago with wonderful woodland walks and views and includes a deer park and Formal Gardens in the Italian, French and English styles. It is the site for the collection of International Camellia Society. Mount Edgcumbe House, a restored Tudor mansion with the Earls Garden surrounding it was the home of the Edgcumbe family for 400 years and has recently been refurbished and redecorated to reflect the late 18th century.

**Location:** On Rame Peninsula, 12 m from Torpoint or from Trerulefoot (A38) via A374 to Antony or Crafthole, and B3247 to Mount Edgcumbe, or by Cremyll (pedestrian) Ferry from Plymouth (Stonehouse) to Park entrance.
**Opening Times:** Country Park, including Landscaped Park and Formal Gardens open every day, all year round. Free. House and Earls Garden open Mar 24 to Oct 31 11–5.30 Wed to Sun and Bank Hol Mons. Adm £2 adult, Chd £1, concessions £1.50 including pre-booked parties of 10 or more. Visitor Centre and Shop selling guides and souvenirs open Mar 24 to Oct 31 every day.
**Refreshments:** Lunches, teas and light refreshments available in the Orangery Restaurant/Cafe, Mar 24 to Oct 31, Reservations and enquiries telephone Plymouth (0752) 822586.

## PENCARROW HOUSE AND GARDEN
**Bodmin** *map D2* ♿
Telephone: St Mabyn (020 884) 369
*(The Molesworth – St Aubyn Family)*

Georgian mansion. Fine collection of 18th century paintings. English, French and Oriental furniture and china. 50 acres of formal gardens and woodland, ancient British encampment and lake. Noted specimen conifer collection.

**Location:** 4 m NW of Bodmin off A389 & B3266 at Washaway.
**Opening Times:** House, Tearooms and Craft Centre Easter to Oct 15—Every day *(except Fri and Sat)* 1.30–5 (Bank Hol Mon and from June 1 to Sept 10 from 11). Gardens open daily. Adm (1988 rates) House and gardens: £2.30. Gardens only: 60p. Chd £1.10. Gardens only: 30p. Guided tours. Car park and toilet facilities for disabled. Dogs very welcome in grounds. *Special arrangements for pre-booked* coach parties. Plant shop. Picnic area. Small children's play area, and pets corner. Self pick soft fruit in season.
**Refreshments:** Light lunches and cream teas.

## PENDENNIS CASTLE
**Falmouth** *map C1*
Telephone: (0326) 316594
*(Cornwall English Heritage)*

Henry VIII's reply to the Pope's crusade against him was to fortify his coastline. Two castles guarded the Fal Estuary, Pendennis and St Mawes. Built high on a promontory, Pendennis saw action in the Civil War when 'Jack-for-the-King' Arundell held the castle for five terrible months. It continued in military use until 1946. Also see Museum exhibition, 1588 gundeck tableau.

**Location:** Pendennis Head 1 m (1.6 km) south east of Falmouth.
**Opening Times:** Good Friday to Sept 30, daily 10–6; Oct 1 to Maundy Thurs, daily 10–4. *Closed* Mons, Dec 24–26, Jan 1. Adm £1.30, OAPs £1, Chd 65p.

## PRIDEAUX PLACE
**Padstow** *map D2*
Telephone: (0841) 532945
*(The Prideaux-Brune family)*

An Elizabethan Mansion House set in extensive grounds including 20 acres of deer park. Guided tours through this family home include a visit to the Great Chamber with its interesting embossed plaster ceiling dating from 1585.

**Location:** 7 m from Wadebridge.
**Opening Times:** House, shop, tearoom – Good Fri for two weeks then Spring Bank Hol to end of Sept, Sun to Thurs inclusive, 1.30–5.30. Adm House & grounds £2. Grounds only 50p. Chd half price. Special party rates. Open all the year round by written appointment. Large public car park on A389 nearby. Enquiries to the Administrator, Prideaux Place, Padstow PL28 8RP. Tel: (0841) 532945.

**Restormel Castle** – See English Heritage Section.

**St Mawes Castle** – See English Heritage Section.

## ST MICHAEL'S MOUNT, The National Trust
**Marazion, nr Penzance** *map C1* △
Telephone: Penzance 710507

Home of Lord St Levan. Mediaeval and early 17th century with considerable alterations and additions in 18th and 19th century.

**Location:** ½ m from the shore at Marazion (A394), connected by causeway. 3 m E Penzance.

**Opening Times:** Mar 24 to end of Oct: Mons to Fri 10.30–5.45. Nov to end of Mar: Guided tours as tide, weather and circumstances permit. *NB: ferry boats do not operate a regular service during this period).* Adm £2.50, Chd £1.25, Family ticket £7. Shop and restaurant—Mar 24 to end of Oct, daily. No dogs. Unsuitable for wheelchairs.

### TINTAGEL CASTLE

*map D2*
Telephone: (0840) 770328
*(English Heritage)*

Amazing that anything has survived on this wild, windswept coast. Yet fragments of Earl Reginald's great hall, built about 1145, and Earl Richard's 13th century wall and iron gate still stand in this incomparable landscape. No wonder that King Arthur and his Knights were thought to have dwelt here. Site exhibition.

**Location:** ½ m (0.8 km) north west of Tintagel. OS map ref SX048891.
**Opening Times:** Good Friday to Sept 30, daily 10–6; Oct 1 to Maundy Thurs, daily 10–4, *closed* Mons, Dec 24–26, Jan 1. Adm 1.30, OAPs £1, Chd 65p.

### TINTAGEL – THE OLD POST OFFICE, The National Trust

**Tintagel** *map D2* ♿

A miniature 14th century manor house with large hall.

**Location:** Nos 3 & 4 in the centre of Tintagel.
**Opening Times:** Mar 24 to end of Oct—Daily 11–6 (or sunset if earlier). (Oct closed 5). Adm £1, Chd 50p. *No reduction for parties.* No dogs. Wheelchair access. Shop.

### TRELISSICK GARDEN, The National Trust

**nr Truro** *map C1* ♿
Telephone: Truro 862090

Large shrub garden. Beautiful wooded park overlooking the river Fal. Woodland walks. Particularly rich in rhododendrons, camellias and hydrangeas.

**Location:** 4 m S of Truro on both sides of B3289 overlooking King Harry Ferry.
**Opening Times:** Gardens only: Mar 1 to end of Oct—Mons to Sats 11–6 (or sunset if earlier), Suns 1–6 (or sunset if earlier), 11–5 in Mar and Oct. Entrance on road to King Harry Passage. Adm £1.90, Chd 95p. *No reduction for parties.* Shop, with special plants section. New Art and Craft gallery. Dogs in woodland walk and park only, on leads. Wheelchairs provided.
**Refreshments:** In the barn.

### TRELOWARREN HOUSE & CHAPEL

**Mawgan-in-Meneage, Helston** *map C1* △
Telephone: Mawgan (032 622) 366
*(Sir John Vyvyan, Bt.)*

Home of the Vyvyan family since 1427 part of the house dates from early Tudor times. The Chapel, part of which is pre-Reformation, and the 17th century part of the house are leased to the Trelowarren Fellowship, an Ecumenical Christian Charity.

**Location:** 6 m S of Helston off B3293 to St Keverne.
**Opening Times:** House & Chapel. Open from Mar 27 to end Oct—Weds & Bank Hol Mons, also open Suns July 30–Aug 27. Always 2.30–5. Conducted tours. Adm £1, Chd 50p (under 12 years free), includes entry to various exhibitions of paintings. Concerts are held in Chapel and Chapel Services every Sun during the holiday season. Organised tours by arrangement. Ground floor only suitable for disabled.

### TRENGWAINTON GARDEN, The National Trust
**Penzance** *map C1* ♿

Large shrub and woodland garden. Fine views. A series of walled gardens contain rare sub-tropical plants.

**Location:** 2 m NW of Penzance ½ m W of Heamoor on Morvah Road (B3312).
*Station: Penzance (2 m).*
**Opening Times:** Mar 1 to Oct—Weds, Thurs, Fris, Sats & Bank Hol Mons 11–6, 11–5 in Mar and Oct. Adm £1.50, Chd 75p. *No reduction for parties.* No dogs. Wheelchair access.

### TRERICE, The National Trust
**St Newlyn East (1571)** *map C2* ♿
Telephone: Newquay 875404

A small Elizabethan house, fine furniture, plaster ceilings and fireplaces, in a recently planted garden. A small museum in the Barn traces the development of the lawn mower.

**Location:** 3 m SE of Newquay A392 & A3058 (turn right at Kestle Mill).
*Station: Quintrel Downs (1½ m).*
**Opening Times:** Mar 24 to end of Oct—Daily 11–6 (last adm 5.30), 11–5 in Oct. Adm £2.60, Chd £1.30. *Reduced rate of £2, Chd £1 for pre-booked parties.* No dogs. Wheelchairs available; access to house only. Shop.
**Refreshments:** In the barn 11–6 (last adm 5.30). *Parties must book.*

### TREWITHEN HOUSE AND GARDENS
**Probus, nr Truro** *map D1*
Telephone: St Austell (0726) 882418/882764

The name means 'House of the trees' which truly describes this fine early Georgian house in its splendid setting of wood and parkland. The house has been described by Christopher Hussey in *Country Life* magazine as **'one of the outstanding West Country houses of the 18th century'**. The origins of the house go back to the 17th century, but it was the architect Thomas Edwards of Greenwich who was responsible for the fine building we see today. Bought by Philip Hawkins in 1715, who commissioned the substantial rebuilding, it was completed only some 40 years later. The house has been lived in and cared for by the same family for over 250 years. Some of the magnolias and rhododendron species in the Garden are well known throughout the world. Plants and shrubs, of which many are exported, are for sale. These Gardens are particularly spectacular between March and the end of June, and again the Autumn, although there is much to see throughout the year. There is a 25 minute video of the House and Gardens.

**Location:** On A390 between Probus and Grampound, adjoining County Demonstration Gardens.
**Opening Times:** Gardens: Open Mar 1 to Sept 30, Mon to Sat 10–4.30. *Closed* Sun. Free car parking. Plants for sale. Dogs on leads. Adm Gardens: Mar–June £1.50, Chd (under 15) 75p: July to Sept £1.20, Chd (under 15) 60p. House: £2 per person. There are guided tours around this charming house on Mons & Tues (2–4.30) Apr to July & August Bank Holiday Monday. Parties by arrangement please.

## CUMBRIA

### ABBOT HALL ART GALLERY & MUSEUM OF LAKELAND LIFE & INDUSTRY
**Kirkland, Kendal** *map F10* ♿
Telephone: Kendal (0539) 22464
*(Lake District Art Gallery & Museum Trust)*

Impressive Georgian House; comprehensive collections of portraits by George Romney and Daniel Gardner, Lake District landscapes and furniture by Gillows of Lancaster displayed in elegant 18th C. rooms; lively temporary exhibition programme; craft shop selling work by leading artist-craftsmen. Adjacent Museum of Lakeland Life & Industry recaptures unique flavour of everyday life in Lake District: everything from hip baths to sheep dips; Arthur Ransome room; first Museum of the Year. Also visit award winning Kendal Museum of Natural History & Archaeology, Station Road.

**Location:** Off Kirkland nr Kendal Parish Church. From M6 exit 36.
*Station: Oxenholme (1½ m); Kendal (¾ m).*
**Opening Times:** All the year – daily except Dec 25, 26, Jan 1 and Good Friday. Mon–Fri 10.30–5, Sat & Sun 2–5, (Spring Bank Holiday – Oct 31; Sat 10.30–5). Adm charge; concessions for OAPs, Chd, Students and families. Lift for disabled (Mon–Fri only).
**Refreshments:** Coffee shop (in season).

### ACORN BANK GARDEN, The National Trust
**Temple Sowerby, Penrith** *map F11*

This 2½ acre garden is protected by fine oaks under which grow a vast display of daffodils. Inside walls are two orchards with medlar, mulberry, cherries, quince and apples. Surrounding the orchards are mixed borders with herbaceous plants and many flowering shrubs and climbing roses. The adjacent herb garden has the largest collection of culinary, medicinal and narcotic herbs in the north. The red sandstone house is let to the Sue Ryder Foundation and is open on application.

**Location:** Just N of Temple Sowerby, 6 m E of Penrith on A66.
**Opening Times:** GARDEN ONLY. Easter to end October—Daily 10–6. Adm 80p, Chd 40p. No reduction for parties. No dogs. Wheelchair access to parts of garden only. Small shop. Plant sales.

### BRANTWOOD
**Coniston** *map F10*
Telephone: (0966) 41396
*(Brantwood Educational Trust)*

The home of John Ruskin from 1872–1900. Large collection of pictures by Ruskin and his associates. Ruskin's coach, boat, furniture and other associated items. Ruskin's woodland gardens are currently being restored. There is a delightful nature walk around the 250 acre estate.

**Location:** 2½ m from Coniston. Historic House signs at Coniston, Head of Coniston Water & Hawkshead.
**Opening Times:** Open all year. Mid-Mar to mid-Nov—Daily 11–5.30. Winter season—Weds to Suns 11–4. Adm House, Wainwright Exhibition & Nature Walks £2, Chd 90p; Family Ticket (2 adults and children) £5.25, Nature trails only 50p, Chd 25p. Steam Yacht Gondola sails regularly from Coniston Pier. Free car park. Parking for disabled near house. Toilets (incl for disabled). Lakeland Guild Craft Gallery and shop.
**Refreshments:** Tea room/coffee; light meals available.

**Brough Castle** – See English Heritage Section.

**Brougham Castle** – See English Heritage Section.

### CARLISLE CASTLE
**Carlisle** *map F11*
Telephone: (0228) 31777
*(English Heritage)*

Twenty-six years after the Battle of Hastings. Carlisle remained unconquered. In 1092 William II marched north, took the city and ordered the building of a stronghold above the River Eden. Since William's time the castle has survived 800 years of fierce and bloody attacks, extensive rebuilding and continuous military occupation. A massive Norman keep contains an exhibition on the history of the castle. D'Ireby Tower now open to the public, containing furnishings to authentic medieval design, an exhibition and shop.

**Location:** North of town centre. O.S. map NY 397563
**Open:** Good Friday to Sept 30, daily 10–6; Oct 1 to Maundy Thurs, daily 10–4. *Closed* Mons, Dec 24–26, Jan 1. Adm £1.30, OAPs £1, Chd 65p.

### CASTLETOWN HOUSE
**Rockcliffe, Carlisle** *map F11*
Telephone: Rockcliffe (0228 74) 205
*(Giles Mounsey-Heysham, Esq.)*

Georgian Country House set in attractive gardens and grounds. Fine ceilings. Naval pictures, furnishings and model engines.

**Location:** 5 m NW of Carlisle on Solway coast, 1 m W of Rockcliffe village and 2 m W of A74.
**Opening Times:** HOUSE ONLY. Apr to Sept—Weds & Bank Hol Mons 2–5. Other times & parties by prior arrangement. Adm £1.50, Chd (accompanied) & OAPs £1.
**Refreshments:** Hotels & refreshments in Carlisle.

### DALEMAIN
**nr Penrith** *map F11*
Telephone: Pooley Bridge (085 36) 450
*(Mr & Mrs Bryce McCosh)*

Medieval, Tudor and early Georgian house and gardens lived in by the same family for over 300 years. Fine furniture and portraits. Countryside museum and picnic areas, Agricultural Museum, Westmorland and Cumberland Yeomanry Museum and Adventure Playground, Fell Pony Museum. Interesting garden as portrayed in various publications. Plant Centre.

**Location:** 3 m from Penrith on A592. Turn off M6 exit 40 onto A66 (A592) to Ullswater.
**Opening Times:** Easter Sun—Mid Oct daily except Fris and Sats, 11.15–5. Adm charged. Car park and picnic area free. Shop.
**Refreshments:** Coffee from 11.15. Bar lunches 12–2.30. Home made teas from 2.30 pm.

**Furness Abbey** – See English Heritage Section.

**Hadrian's Roman Wall** – See English Heritage Section.

### HOLKER HALL
**Cark-in-Cartmel, nr Grange-over-Sands**
*map F10* △ ♿ Ⓢ
Telephone: Flookburgh (044 853) 328
*(Mr & Mrs Hugh Cavendish)*

Former home of the Dukes of Devonshire and still lived in by members of the family. 120 acre Deer Park, formal and woodland gardens. Exhibitions including **The Lakeland Motor Museum,** a fine collection of over 80 historic vehicles, tel (044 853) 509. Victorian, Edwardian and Wartime Kitchens Exhibition from the Zanussi Collection.

**Location:** ½ m N of Cark-in-Cartmel on B5278 from Haverthwaite; 4 m W Grange-over-Sands.
**Opening Times:** House, Gardens & Motor Museum. Easter Sun to last Sun in Oct—Daily (ex Sat) 10.30–4.30. Park open until 6. *Thurs evenings until 9 for booked groups of 20 or more.* Group rates for parties of 20 or more. Free Coach and Car Park. Gift Shop.
**Refreshments:** Clock Tower Cafe serving salads, sandwiches, home made cakes and pastries, beverages including wine and beer. *Group catering by prior arrangement.*

### HUTTON-IN-THE-FOREST
**Penrith** *map F11*
Telephone: Skelton (085 34) 449
*(Lord Inglewood)*

One of the ancient manors in the Forest of Inglewood, and the home of Lord Inglewood's family since the beginning of the 17th century. The House stands in magnificent gardens and woodland.

**Location:** 6 m NW of Penrith on B5305 Wigton Road (from M6 exit 41).
**Opening Times:** Bank Hol Suns & Mons also Thurs, Fris and Suns from June 1–Oct 1. Grounds open every day 11–5. Private parties by arrangement any day from Apr 1. Adm: House & Grounds: £2, Chd (accompanied) free of charge. Grounds only: £1.00.
**Refreshments:** Fresh home-made teas available in the cloisters when house open.

### 19/20 IRISH STREET
**Whitehaven** *map E11* ♿
Telephone: Whitehaven (0946) 3111, Ext 287
*(Copeland Borough Council)*

1840-50 Italianate design, possibly by S. Smirke. Stuccoed 3-storey building now occupied by the Council Offices.

**Location:** In town centre.
*Station: Whitehaven.*
**Opening Times:** All the year during office hours. For details & appointments telephone Mr J. A. Pomfret. Ground floor only suitable for disabled.
**Refreshments:** Hotels and restaurants in town centre.

**Lanercost Priory** – See English Heritage Section.

### LEVENS HALL
**Kendal** *map F10* ♿
Telephone: Sedgwick (053 95) 60321
*(C. H. Bagot, Esq.)*

Elizabethan family home with fine plaster-work, panelling, paintings and Jacobean furniture. World famous topiary garden laid out in 1692.

**Location:** 5 m S of Kendal on the Milnthorpe Road (A6); Exit 36 from M6.
**Opening Times:** Easter Sunday to Sept 30. House, Garden, Gift Shop, Tearooms, Plants for sale, Play Area and Picnic Area. Suns, Mons, Tues, Weds & Thurs 11–5. Steam Collection 2–5. Closed Fris & Sats. Adm House & Garden £2.60, Garden £1.40. Groups and OAPs: House and Garden £2.10; Garden £1.25. Chd half price. Regret House not suitable for wheelchairs.
**Refreshments:** Home-made light Lunches and teas.

### MIREHOUSE
**Keswick** *map F11* ♿
Telephone: Keswick (076 87) 72287
*(Mr & Mrs Spedding)*

Seventeenth century Manor House with 19th century additions. Portraits and manuscripts of Francis Bacon and many literary friends of the Spedding family including Tennyson, Wordsworth, Southey. Walk through grounds to Bassenthwaite Lake. Adventure Playgrounds. Norman Lakeside Church of St. Bega.

**Location:** 4½ m N of Keswick on A591 (Keswick to Carlisle Road).
**Opening Times:** Apr to Oct – Lakeside Walk, Adventure Playgrounds—Daily 10.30–5.30. House—Suns, Weds & Bank Hol Mons 2–5. Parties welcome at other times by appointment.
**Refreshments:** Old Sawmill Tearoom open daily 10.30–5.30; specialises in salad & sandwiches made to order, home baking. Parties please book (Tel: Keswick (07687) 74317).

### MUNCASTER CASTLE
**Ravenglass** *map F10* △
*(Mrs P. Gordon-Duff-Pennington)*

Seat of the Pennington family since 13th century. Famed rhododendron and azalea gardens. Superb views over Esk Valley (Ruskin's Gateway to Paradise).

**Location:** 1 m SE of Ravenglass village on A595 (entrance ½ m W of Church).
*Station: Ravenglass (¼ m).*
**Opening Times:** Grounds and Bird Garden; Good Friday to Sept 30—Daily (except Mons but open Bank Hols) 12–5. Castle; Good Friday to Sept 30—Daily (except Mons but open Bank Hols) 1.30–4.30 (last adm). Adm Grounds only £1.25, Chd 90p; Inclusive Ticket £2.50, Chd £1.25. Special party rates.

### NAWORTH CASTLE
**Brampton** *map F11*
Telephone: Brampton (069 77) 2692 (Curator)
*(The Earl of Carlisle MC)*

Set amid rugged Hadrian's Wall country this historic Border fortress (referred to several times in Sir Walter Scott's novels) is neither ruin nor museum, but a lived-in family home. Its Great Hall is breathtaking with huge heraldic beasts and eight Gobelin tapestries, which are one of the most important collections in the country. Also woodland walk, dungeon, garde robes and original fish, White Knight, griffin, etc. from 'Alice Through the Looking Glass' as well as work by Salvin, Burne Jones and Philip Webb.

**Location:** 12 m from Carlisle, 2 m from Brampton, just off the A69 to Newcastle.
**Opening Times:** Easter Sun & Mon, thereafter Weds and Suns to Sept 30; also Sats in July and Aug and Bank Hols. Adm £1.50, Chd/OAPs 75p. Parties by arrangement on other days. Free car park. Not suitable for disabled.

### RYDAL MOUNT
**Ambleside** *map F10*
Telephone: Ambleside (05394) 33002
*(Mrs Mary Henderson—nee Wordsworth)*

Wordsworth home from 1813–1850. Family portraits and furniture, many of the poet's personal possessions, and first editions of his works. The garden which was designed by Wordsworth has been described as one of the most interesting small gardens to be found anywhere in England. Two long terraces, many rare trees and shrubs. Extends to 4½ acres.

**Location:** Off A591, 1½ m from Ambleside, 2½ m from Grasmere.
**Opening Times:** Mar 1 to Oct 31—Daily 9.30–5. Nov 1 to Mar 1—10–4. *(Closed Tues in winter).* Adm House & Gardens £1.50, Chd 50p. Parties, £1. See Lake District National Park Visitor Centre for out of season package.

# HUTTON-IN-THE-FOREST

**PENRITH, CUMBRIA**

A 17th century house built around a medieval pele tower with 18th and 19th century additions. Fine English furniture and pictures, ceramics and tapestries. Outstanding gardens and grounds with terraces, walled garden, dovecote, lake and woodland walk through magnificent specimen trees.

HOUSE open Bank Hol Suns and Mons, also Thurs, Fris and Suns from 1–4pm, June 1st – Oct 1st.
GROUNDS open every day 11–5pm.
Private parties from April 1st by prior arrangement.

# NAWORTH CASTLE

Set serenely amid the rugged Border countryside Naworth Castle stands today as a token of permanence in a turbulent world. Within sight of the Scottish border and Hadrian's Wall, battles and skirmishes have taken place around it but Naworth has remained the family home of the Earls of Carlisle and their ancestors for seven centuries. Its supreme glory is the Great Hall, hung with tapestries, with its four heraldic beasts and superb roof and fireplace —still used by the Earl and Countess for present-day entertaining.

# RYDAL MOUNT

**AMBLESIDE, CUMBRIA**

*ADMISSION – SEE EDITORIAL REFERENCE*

# LEVENS HALL

**near KENDAL, CUMBRIA**

This magnificent Elizabethan home of the Bagot family, with its famous topiary garden (c.1692) is a must for visitors to the Lake District.

The garden is unique in age and appearance, beautifully maintained in its original design with colourful bedding and herbaceous borders.

The house contains a superb collection of Jacobean furniture, fine plaster ceilings, panelling, paintings and needlework, including the earliest English patchwork (c.1708).

A collection of working model steam engines showing the development of steam power from 1820 to 1920, with full-sized traction engines in steam on Sundays and Bank Holiday Mondays.

Home-made light lunches and teas.

Gift Shop. Plants for Sale. Play and Picnic areas.

Open Easter Sunday to 30th September Sundays to Thursdays 11 am to 5 pm.

Steam Collection 2 pm to 5 pm.

Groups welcomed.

For information Telephone: (05395) 60321

*Lucy Sclater photograph.*

# MUNCASTER CASTLE

**RAVENGLASS, CUMBRIA**

Write or phone for Party Bookings and details of events during the season to: MUNCASTER CASTLE, RAVENGLASS, CUMBRIA. Tel: RAVENGLASS 614 or 203.

This magnificent Castle with its famous rhododendron gardens and superb views of Eskdale dates from early 14th century, although the Pele tower is built on Roman foundations. There is an excellent collection of family portraits, tapestry and porcelain, but its outstanding feature is the large collection of 16th and 17th century furniture in beautiful condition. The octagonal library is one of Salvins finest works and contains over 6,000 books. It is a very special family home.

The gardens offer a variety of walks which can all offer some of the finest views in England.

Open daily except Mondays but open all Bank Holidays: GOOD FRIDAY to SEPTEMBER 30.

GROUNDS: 12 noon to 5 pm.

CASTLE: 1.30 am to 4.30 pm (last admission).

BEARS COMMANDO COURSE: BRITISH OWL BREEDING AND RELEASE STATION: GIFT SHOP: LUNCHES: TEAS: LIGHT REFRESHMENTS: TABLE LICENCE.

*Access is from A595, 1½ miles east of Ravenglass. Free Car Park opposite Main Gates.*

## SIZERGH CASTLE AND GARDEN, The National Trust

**Kendal** *map F10*
Telephone: Sedgwick (05295) 60070

The 14th century Pele tower (the oldest part of the castle) rises to 60 feet, contains some original windows, floors and fireplaces; 15th century Great Hall, extended in later centuries; 16th century wings; fine panelling and ceilings; contents include French and English furniture, china, family portraits, Stuart portraits and relics; extensive garden includes 2/3 acre limestone rock garden, the largest owned by the Trust with large collection of Japanese maples, dwarf conifers, hardy ferns and many perennials and bulbs; water garden; herbaceous borders; wild flower banks; fine autumn colour.

**Location:** 3½ m S of Kendal NW of A6/A591 interchange; 2 m from Levens Hall.
**Opening Times:** Castle & Garden; Mar 26 to Oct 30—Suns, Mons, Weds & Thurs; 2–6 (last admission 5.30). Garden & Shop open from 12.30 same days. Adm £2.00 (House and Garden), Chd half-price. Garden only: £1, Chld 50p. Parties by arrangement with The Administrator, Sizergh Castle, Tel: Sedgwick 60070. Please send sae. Shop. No dogs. Wheelchairs (one provided) in garden only.

**Stott Park Bobbin Mill** – See English Heritage Section.

## TOWNEND, The National Trust

**Troutbeck** *map F10*
Telephone: Ambleside (05394) 32628

17th century Lakeland farmhouse with original furnishings including much woodcarving in traditional style. Home of the Browne family for 300 years, and last remaining glimpse into the old farming way of life.

**Location:** At S end of Troutbeck village, 3 m SE of Ambleside.
**Opening Times:** Mar 24–Nov 5. Daily (except Mons & Sats but open Bank Hol Mons) 2–6 or dusk if earlier). Last adm 5.30. Adm £1.50, Chd 75p. *No reductions for parties. No dogs. No coaches.* Unsuitable for wheelchairs.

## WORDSWORTH HOUSE, The National Trust

**Cockermouth** *map F11* △
Telephone: Cockermouth (0900) 824805

North country Georgian House built in 1745, birthplace of the poet Wordsworth, furnished in the style of his time, with some of his belongings. The pleasant garden is referred to in his 'Prelude'. Static and audio-visual displays.

**Location:** In Main Street.
**Opening Times:** Mar 24–Nov 5—Mons to Sats (except Thurs) 11–5; Suns 2–5 (last admission 4.30). Adm £1.50, Chd 75p. Reductions for pre-booked parties except on Suns. No dogs. Shop open daily in summer & Nov to Dec 24 (except Thurs & Suns) 10–4.30. Unsuitable for wheelchairs.
**Refreshments:** Light refreshments & lunches in the old kitchen (licensed).

# DERBYSHIRE

## BOLSOVER CASTLE

*map H8*
Telephone: (0246) 823349
*(English Heritage)*

Castle in name only, the present mansion was built during the 17th century by Sir Charles Cavendish and his son William on the site of a 12th century castle. The Little Castle, separate and self-contained, is a delightful romantic folly decorated in Jacobean style.

**Location:** Bolsover 6 m east of Chesterfield on A632. OS map ref SK471707.
**Opening Times:** Good Friday to Sept 30, daily 10–6; Oct 1 to Maundy Thurs, daily 10–4. *Closed* Mons, Dec 24–26, Jan 1. Adm £1.30, OAPs £1, Chd 65p.

## CALKE ABBEY AND PARK, The National Trust

**nr Derby** *map H7*
Telephone: Melbourne (033 16) 3822

Calke Abbey was built 1701-1703. Visitor route includes the Caricature room, Saloon, Drawing room and Butler's Pantry. Information Room, carriage and display in Stable Block. Calke Park is a fine landscaped setting (approx. 750 acres). Park accessible via Ticknall entrance only. (One-way system in operation).

**Location:** 9m S of Derby on A514 at Ticknall between Swadlincote and Melbourne.
**Opening Times:** Mar 25–end Oct: Sat–Wed including Bank Holiday Mon. *Closed* Good Friday. 1–5.30 (last adm 5). Admission by time of ticket only. Parties **must** book in advance with the Administrator. Adm £3.50, Chd £1.70.

## CHATSWORTH

**Bakewell** *map H8*
Telephone: Baslow (024 688) 2204
*(Chatsworth House Trust)*

Built by Talman for 1st Duke of Devonshire between 1687 and 1707. Splendid collection of pictures, drawings, books and furniture. Garden with elaborate waterworks surrounded by a great park. CHATSWORTH'S TEMPLE OF FLORA, a botanical exhibition in the Sculpture Gallery. **Regret House impossible for wheelchairs, but they are most welcome in the garden.**

**Location:** ½ m E of village of Edensor on A623, 4 m E of Bakewell, 16 m from junction 29, M1. Signposted via Chesterfield.
**Opening Times:** HOUSE & GARDEN. Mar 22 to Oct 29—Daily 11.30–4.30. FARMYARD & ADVENTURE PLAYGROUND. Mar 22 to Oct 1—Daily 10.30–4.30. Adm charges not available at time of going to press. Gift shops. Baby Room. All details subject to confirmation.
**Refreshments:** Home-made refreshments. Coach Drivers' Rest Room.

## HADDON HALL

**Bakewell** *map H8*
Telephone: Bakewell 2855
*(His Grace the Duke of Rutland)*

Fine example of medieval and manorial home containing priceless tapestries, wood carvings and wall paintings. Delightful terraced garden noted for wall and bed roses, and many old fashioned flowers.

**Location:** 2 m SE Bakewell & 6½ m N of Matlock on Buxton/Matlock Road (A6).
**Opening Times:** Mar 24 to Oct 1—Tues–Sun, 11–6. *Closed Mons except Bank Hols, also closed Suns in July and Aug except Bank Hol weekends.* Adm £2.60, Chd £1.50; Party rate £2, OAPs £2.
**Refreshments:** Morning coffee, lunches, afternoon teas at Stables Restaurant.

## HARDWICK HALL, The National Trust

**Nr Chesterfield** *map H8*
Telephone: Chesterfield (0246) 850430

Built 1591–1597 by "Bess of Hardwick". Notable furniture, needlework, tapestries. Gardens with yew hedges and borders of shrubs and flowers. Extensive collection of herbs. Information Centre in Country Park.

**Location:** 2 m S of Chesterfield/Mansfield Road (A617) 6½ m NW of Mansfield and 9½ m SE of Chesterfield. Approach from M1 exit 29.
**Opening Times:** House & Garden. Mar 25 to Sept 17. House—Weds, Thurs, Sats, Suns & Bank Hol Mons 1–5.30 (or sunset if earlier). Last adm to Hall 5 pm. Garden open daily to end Oct, 12–5.30. *Closed Good Friday.* Adm: House & Garden £4, Chd £2; Garden only £1.50, Chd 70p. *No reduction for parties (including schools). School parties must book.* Car park (gates close 6.30). Dogs in park only, on leads. Wheelchairs in garden only. *Enquiries to The National Trust, Hardwick Hall, Doe Lea, nr Chesterfield, Derbys. Access to Hall may be limited at peak periods.*
**Refreshments:** In the Great Kitchen of Hall 2.30–5. Lunches 12–2 (last orders 15 mins before closing) on days when hall is open.

## KEDLESTON HALL

**Derby** *map H7*
Telephone: Derby (0332) 842191

One of the best examples of neo-classical architecture in the country. Robert Adam designed the late 18th century house for Sir Nathaniel Curzon. Fine collection of furniture, tapestries and portraits. Landscaped park includes further examples of Adam's work.

**Location:** 4 m NW of Derby on Derby/Hulland Road via the Derby Ring Road Queensway.
**Opening Times:** House, park and garden: Mar 25 to end Oct, Sats to Wed including Bank Holiday Mons. Park: from 11. Gardens and tea room: 12–5. House and Shop: 1–5.30 (last adm 5). £3, Chld £1.50. Coach parties welcome on days when the property is open, but **must** book well in advance in writing to the Administrator. 1989 events – details from Administrator.

## LEA GARDENS

**Lea, nr Matlock** *map H8* ♿
*(Mr & Mrs Tye)*

A rare collection of rhododendrons, azaleas, alpines and conifers in a lovely woodland setting.

**Location:** 5 m SE of Matlock off A6.
*Station: Whatstandwell (2¾ m).*
**Opening Times:** GARDEN ONLY. Mar 20 to July 31—Daily 10–7. Adm: Season ticket £1.50, Chd 50p. *Donation to National Gardens Scheme.* Coaches by appointment only. Plants for sale.
**Refreshments:** Light lunches, teas, home baking.

## LOSEHILL HALL

**Castleton** *map H8*
Telephone: Hope Valley (0433) 20373
*(Peak National Park Centre)*

Victorian Hall with formal garden, parkland and Victorian woodlands. Organises holidays, talks, guided visits to local historic houses and gardens.

**Location:** ½ m E of Castleton Village on A625 towards Hope. Turn left after leaving Castleton before Losehill Caravan Site.
*Station: Hope (2 m).*

# BRANTWOOD

CONISTON, CUMBRIA

The home of John Ruskin, from 1872-1900. Brantwood is the most beautifully situated house in the Lake District, with the best lake and mountain views in England. The house contains a fine collection of Ruskin drawings and watercolours. There is a delightful nature walk around the Brantwood Estate. Also the Lakeland Guild Craft Gallery, the Wainwright Exhibition (the famous walker and artist), and a well stocked bookshop. Excellent tea room with delicious cakes. Steam yacht 'Gondola' sails regularly to Brantwood from Coniston Pier.

*ADMISSION – SEE EDITORIAL REFERENCE*

BAKEWELL DERBYSHIRE

# HADDON HALL

One of our few remaining 12th century Manor Houses perfectly preserved. Noted for its tapestries, wood carvings and decorations. Haddon, The Derbyshire Seat of the Duke of Rutland, is totally unspoiled. It stands on a wooded hillside overlooking the fast flowing River Wye.

The Gardens.—Beautifully terraced gardens dating from the Middle Ages are famous for roses and other old fashioned flowers and herbs.

Excellent self service Restaurant/Tea Rooms.

Banqueting, Conference and Clay Pigeon facilities available in the Hall and Park.

Open April-September, daily, except Mondays, and Sundays in July and August.

Enquiries to: The Comptroller, Haddon Hall Bakewell, Derbyshire DE4 1LA. Tel: (062981) 2855.

# LOSEHILL HALL

GREAT HOUSES and GARDENS

**7 DAY HOLIDAYS IN THE PEAK DISTRICT**

VISITS INCLUDE CHATSWORTH, HADDON AND HARDWICK HALLS

SPECIAL TOURS ARRANGED WITH GARDENERS

OTHER HOLIDAYS INCLUDE (2, 5 and 7 Days) VILLAGES AND CHURCHES, EXPLORING THE PEAK DISTRICT, PHOTOGRAPHY AND NATURE WALKS.

*PRICES ON APPLICATION*

Further details (sae please) from: Peter Townsend, Principal, Peak National Park Centre, Losehill Hall, Castleton, Derbyshire, S30 2WB.

Enjoy even more of Derbyshire.

Explore the English Heritage Supplement on the Red Pages.

English Heritage

**Opening Times:** Holidays on the theme of Great Houses and Gardens for individuals and families, Mar 25–Mar 31, July 29–Aug 5, Aug 5–Aug 12. Visits to Chatsworth, Haddon, Hardwick, Kedleston, etc. Special residential holidays are organised for private parties. Booked parties only, guided day visits of Losehill Hall with talk about Peak National Park. Prices on application.
**Refreshments:** Teas for booked parties. Full accommodation for holidays.

### OLD HOUSE MUSEUM
**Bakewell** *map H8*
*(Bakewell & District Historical Society)*

An early Tudor house with original wattle & daub screen and open chamber. Costumes and Victorian kitchen, children's toys, craftsmen's tools and lacework.

**Location:** Above the church in Bakewell. ¼ m from centre.
**Opening Times:** HOUSE ONLY. Mar 24 to Oct 31—Daily 2–5. Parties in morning or evening by appointment (Telephone Bakewell (062 981) 3647. Adm 75p, Chd 35p.

**Peveril Castle** – See English Heritage Section.

### SUDBURY HALL, The National Trust
**nr Derby** *map H7* Ⓢ
Telephone: Sudbury (028 378) 305

A 17th century brick built house. Contains plasterwork ceilings. Laguerre murals staircase carved by Pierce and overmantel by Grinling Gibbons. Museum of childhood.

**Location:** At Sudbury, 6 m E of Uttoxeter off A50 Road.
**Opening Times:** Mar 25 to end of Oct—Weds to Suns and Bank Holiday Mons 1–5.30 (last adm 5). Adm £2.50, Chd £1.20. Pre-booked parties special rates. Museum small adm charge. Shop. Dogs in grounds only, on lead. Wheelchairs in garden only. 1989 events – details from the Administrator.
**Refreshments:** Light lunches & teas in Coach House, same open days as property, 12.30–5.30.

### WINSTER MARKET HOUSE, The National Trust
**nr Matlock** *map H8*
Telephone: Thorpe Cloud (033 529) 245

A stone market house of the late 17th or early 18th century in main street of Winster.

**Location:** 4 m W of Matlock on S side of B5057.
**Opening Times:** Afternoons most summer weekends. Adm free. Shop and Information Centre. No dogs. Unsuitable for wheelchairs.

## DEVON

### A LA RONDE
**Exmouth** *map F2* △ ♿
Telephone: Exmouth (0395) 265514
*(Mrs Ursula Tudor Perkins)*

A unique sixteen sided house designed in 1795 by the Misses Jane and Mary Parminter. Almost unchanged and still owned by the same family, it combines contrived 18th century fashions with total practicability. Parkland. Panoramic views of sea and estuary; Shell Gallery, Gothic grottos.

**Location:** 2 m N of Exmouth on A376.
*Station: Lympstone (1¼ m).*
**Opening Times:** Good Friday–Oct 31: Daily 10–6, Sun 2–7. Coaches—day & evening visits by appointment.
**Refreshments:** Devon cream teas (in old kitchen). Summer & Winter meals, functions etc. on request.

### ARLINGTON COURT, The National Trust
**Barnstaple** *map E3* ♿
Telephone: Shirwell (027 182) 296

Regency house furnished with the collections of the late Miss Rosalie Chichester; including shells, pewter and model ships. Display of horse-drawn vehicles in the stables. Good trees. Victorian formal garden.

**Location:** 8 m NE of Barnstaple on E side of A39.
**Opening Times:** Nov to Mar 24: Garden & park open daily during daylight hours. House, Carriage Collection, Stables, Shop: Good Friday to end of Oct—Daily (except Sats but open Sats of Bank Hol Weekends) 11–6, 11–5 during Oct. (Last adm ½ hour before closing.) Garden & Park: Good Friday to Oct—Daily 11–6. Open Good Friday. Adm: House & Carriage Collection £3, Chd £1.50. Gardens, Ground & Stables £1.60, Chd half-price. *Reduced fee of £2.30 for parties of 15 or more on application to the Administrator. Parties who do not pre-book will be charged full rate.* Shop. Dogs in grounds only, on leads. Wheelchairs provided. Carriage rides.
**Refreshments:** Licensed restaurant at the House: Mar 24 to end of Oct—days and times as for House.

### BICKHAM HOUSE
**Roborough** *map E2*
*(The Lord Roborough)*

Shrub garden; camellias, rhododendrons, azaleas, cherries, bulbs, trees. Lovely views.

**Location:** 8 m N of Plymouth on Roborough Down turn for Maristow.
**Opening Times:** GARDEN ONLY: Suns Mar 26–June 4 incl, and Sun June 18, Mons Mar 27, May 1, 29, 2–6. Adm 50p. *In aid of National Gardens Scheme. No dogs.*
**Refreshments:** Home-made teas, parties catered for by appointment up to the end of June.

### BICKLEIGH CASTLE
**nr Tiverton** *map E3* △ ♿ Ⓢ
Telephone: Bickleigh (088 45) 363
*(Mr & Mrs O. N. Boxall)*

Medieval romantic home of the heirs of the Earls of Devon. Great Hall. Armoury Guard Room, Stuart farmhouse, Elizabethan bedroom. 11th century Chapel. Tower Museum and spy & escape gadgets, Exhibition showing Bickleigh Castle's connection with Tudor maritime history and the Mary Rose, also a feature on the "Titanic". Moated Gardens.

**Location:** 4 m S of Tiverton A396. At Bickleigh Bridge take A3072 and follow signs.
**Opening Times:** Easter Week (Good Fri to Fri) then Weds, Suns & Bank Hol Mons to Spring Bank Hol; then to early Oct—Daily (except Sats) 2–5. *Parties of 20 or more by prior appointment only (preferably at times other than above) at reduced rates.* Adm £2, Chd half-price (1988 prices). Free coach & car park. Souvenir shops.
**Refreshments:** Tea in the thatched Barn.

### BOWDEN HOUSE
**Totnes** *map E2* △
Telephone: Totnes (0803) 863664
*(Mr & Mrs C V Petersen)*

Dating back to the 9th century Bowden became the residence of the De Broase family, builders of 13th century Totnes Castle. Parts of the house date from this period. An Elizabethan mansion was created in 1510 with a Queen Anne facade added in 1704. The Grand Hall is decorated in Neo-classical Baroque style.

**Location:** 1 m from centre of Totnes, follow Historic House signs.
*Station: Totnes (1 m).*
**Opening Times:** Open from first Tues in Apr to last Thurs in Oct, Tues, Weds and Thurs, plus Suns and Mons during July and Aug, and Bank Holidays. Grounds, cafe, Photographic Museum open 12 noon. House: guided tours from 2 (1.30 in high season). Last tour 4.30. **Tours given in Georgian costume.** Adm £2, reduction for chd. Photographic Museum £1 extra. Reductions for chd.
**Refreshments:** Licensed café, cream teas, ploughmans lunches served by wenches (open 12–5). **Picnic and play area.**

### BRADLEY MANOR, The National Trust
**Newton Abbot** *map E2*

Small, roughcast 15th century manor house with perpendicular chapel, set in woodland and meadows.

**Location:** W end of town, 7½ m NW of Torquay opp Old Totnes Road Junction. On W side of A381.
*Station: Newton Abbot (1½ m).*
**Opening Times:** Apr 1 to end of Sept—Weds 2–5; also Thurs, Apr 6 & 13, Sept 21 & 28. Adm £1.50, Chd half-price. *No reduction for parties.* Parties of 15 or more must book in writing. No indoor photography. No access for coaches—Lodge gates too narrow. No dogs. Unsuitable for disabled or visually handicapped.

### BUCKLAND ABBEY, Jointly managed by The National Trust, and Plymouth City Council
**Yelverton** *map E2*
Telephone: Yelverton (082 285) 3607

13th century Cistercian monastery bought by Sir Richard Grenville in 1541, altered by his grandson Sir Richard Grenville, of the 'Revenge', in 1576. Home of Drake from 1581 and still contains many relics of the great seaman, including Drake's drum. Exhibition to illustrate the Abbey's history. Restored buildings, including the monk's guesthouse and 18th century farm buildings. Great Barn.

**Location:** 11 m N of Plymouth 6 m S of Tavistock between the Tavistock/Plymouth Road (A386) & River Tavy.
**Opening Times:** Good Friday to end Oct: daily 11–6, 11–5 during Oct. Last admissions ½ hour before closing time. Nov to Mar 1990: Weds, Sats and Suns 2–5. Adm £2.80. Chd half price. Reduced rate for parties (£2); school parties £1.20 on application to the Administrator. Parties who do not pre-book will be charged at full rate. Dogs in grounds only on leads. Shop.
**Refreshments:** Licensed Restaurant serving home-made lunches and teas as well as warming coffee. Good Friday to end Oct; 11 to ½ hour before closing; Nov–Mar 1990 11–5.

### THE BULL HOUSE
**Pilton, Barnstaple** *map E3*
*(Mr M.L. Corney)*

Text book example of small late mediaeval mansion almost unaltered. Former Prior's House and Guest Lodging of Pilton Priory. Great hall, solar, parlour, guest chambers etc. with moulded oak roofs, ceilings, panelling and stone arches.

**Location:** ½ m N of Barnstaple, off A39, beside Pilton churchyard.
**Opening Times:** Apr to Oct by appointment. Adm £1.25 adults only.

## BOWDEN HOUSE
**Totnes, S. Devon**

Bowden dates back to the 9th century although it became well known as the residence of the De Broase family, builders of the 13th century Totnes Castle we see today. Parts of the house date from this period. John Giles, who was the richest man in Devon, created a large Elizabethan Mansion in 1510. The Trist family in 1704 added the Queen Anne facade. The Grand Hall is decorated in Neo-classical Baroque style; the Great Hall is adorned with 18th and 19th century muskets, 18 early 16th century bread ovens etc. The House was opened for the first time in 1984. Bowden is a 'lived-in' Historic House, 1 mile from Totnes, with the Family and guides giving guided tours in Georgian costume. Visit the British Photographic Museum adjacent to Bowden House.

## BICKLEIGH CASTLE
**nr TIVERTON, DEVON**

The home of Alward mentioned in Domesday, the sons of the Earls of Devon in the 15th century and the Carews during the Civil War, the intriguing history of Bickleigh Castle spans nine centuries. The 11th century Chapel, the Armoury containing Cromwellian arms and armour, the Guard Room with tudor furniture and pictures, the Great Hall, Elizabethan Bedroom, and the Stuart Farmhouse all are shown. The Tower can be climbed for extensive views of the wooded Exe Valley and the attractive gardens are moated.

- **Museum of 19th century domestic and agricultural objects and toys. Children may ride the period Rocking Horses.**
- **Exhibition showing Bickleigh Castle's connection with Maritime history, including the "Mary Rose" and the "Titanic".**
- **World War II original spy and escape gadgets M16, SOE, SAS.**
- **Heritage Education Trust Sandford Award Winner.**
- **A Royalist stronghold with 900 years of history and architecture: full of interest for all the family.**

Shop. Cream Teas in the thatched Barn. Free Coach/Car park.
Tel: Bickleigh (088 45) 363.

*ADMISSION–SEE EDITORIAL REFERENCE*

## TIVERTON CASTLE
**DEVON**

Discover English history in a Castle in continued occupation for nearly 900 years.

Important Civil War arms and armour collection. Entrances to secret passageway extending throughout the town. Medieval Gatehouse and tower. Romantic ruins of towers, walls and chapel destroyed in English Civil War siege. Notable Campbell clock collection. Fine furniture and pictures. Famous Victorian murder mystery exhibit. New World Tapestry.

*ADMISSION – SEE EDITORIAL REFERENCE*

## CADHAY

**Ottery St Mary** *map F2* △
Telephone: Ottery St Mary 2432
*(Lady William-Powlett)*

Cadhay is approached by an avenue of lime-trees, and stands in a pleasant listed garden, with herbaceous borders and yew hedges, with excellent views over the original mediaeval fish ponds. Cadhay is first mentioned in the reign of Edward I, and was held by a de Cadehaye. The main part of the house was built about 1550 by John Haydon who had married the de Cadhay heiress. He retained the Great Hall of an earlier house, of which the fine timber roof (about 1420) can be seen. An Elizabethan Long Gallery was added by John's successor at the end of the 16th century, thereby forming a unique and lovely courtyard. Some Georgian alterations were made in the mid 18th century. The house is viewed by conducted tour. Photography is permitted outside.

**Location:** 1 m NW of Ottery St Mary on B3176.
*Station: Feniton (2½ m) (not Suns).*
**Opening Times:** Spring (May 28 & 29) & Summer (Aug 27 & 28) Bank Hol Suns & Mons; also Tues, Weds & Thurs in July & Aug: 2–6 (last adm 5.30). Adm £2, Chd 50p. *Parties by arrangement.*

## CASTLE DROGO, The National Trust

**nr Chagford** *map E2* ♿
Telephone: Chagford (064 73) 3306

Granite castle designed by Sir Edwin Lutyens, standing at over 900ft overlooking the wooded gorge of the River Teign. Terraced garden and miles of splendid walks.

**Location:** 4 m NE of Chagford; 6 m S of A30.
**Opening Times:** Good Friday to end of Oct—Daily 11–6, 11–5 during Oct (last adm ½ hour before closing). Adm £2.80; Grounds only £1.30. Chd half-price. *Reduced rates for parties* (£2) *on application to the Administrator. Parties who do not pre-book will be charged at full rate.* No dogs except guide dogs. Wheelchairs provided. Shop. The restored croquet lawn is open. Equipment for hire from the Administrator.
**Refreshments:** Coffee, light lunches (licensed) & teas at the castle 11–½ hour before closing.

## COLETON FISHACRE GARDEN, The National Trust

**Coleton** *map E2* ♿
Telephone: Kingswear (080 425) 466

18 acre garden in a stream-fed valley. Garden created by Lady Dorothy D'Oyly Carte between 1925 and 1940; planted with wide variety of uncommon trees and exotic shrubs.

**Location:** 2 m from Kingswear; take Lower Ferry Road, turn off at tollhouse & follow 'Garden Open' signs.
**Opening Times:** Good Friday to end Oct—Weds, Fris & Suns 11–6. Adm £1.50, Chd half price. Pre-booked parties £1.10. Limited wheelchair access.

## COMPTON CASTLE, The National Trust

**nr Paignton** *map E2*
Telephone: Kingskerswell (080 47) 2112

Fortified manor house. Great Hall (restored), Solar, Kitchen, Chapel and rose garden.

**Location:** 1 m N of Marldon off A381.
**Opening Times:** Easter Mon to end of Oct—Mons, Weds & Thurs 10–12.15, 2–5 (last adm 30 mins before closing). Adm £1.50, Chd half-price. Parties £1.20—*organisers should please notify the Secretary.* No dogs except guide dogs. Additional parking and refreshments at Castle Barton, opposite entrance.

## DARTMOUTH CASTLE

**Dartmouth** *map E2*
Telephone: (08043) 3588
*(English Heritage)*

Boldly guarding the narrow entrance to the Dart Estuary, this castle was among the first in England to be built for artillery. Construction began in 1481 on the site of an earlier castle. 1861 Battery with fully equipped guns opening 1989.

**Location:** 1 m (1.6km) south east of Dartmouth.
**Opening Times:** Good Friday to Sept 30, daily 10–6; Oct 1 to Maundy Thurs, daily 10–4. *Closed* Mons, Dec 24–26, Jan 1. Adm £1.10, OAPs 80p, Chd 55p.

## FERNWOOD

**Ottery St Mary** *map F2*
*(Mr & Mrs H Hollinrake)*

2 acre woodland garden; wide selection of flowering shrubs, conifers and bulbs giving colour over a long period; species and hybrid rhododendrons and azaleas.

**Location:** 1½ m W of Ottery St Mary; ¼ m down Toadpit lane (off B3174).
**Opening Times:** GARDEN ONLY. Apr 1 to Sept 30—Daily, all day. *In aid of National Gardens Scheme.* No dogs. Adm 50p, accompanied chd free.

## FLETE

**Ermington, Ivybridge** *map E2*
*(Country Houses Association Ltd)*

Built around an Elizabethan manor.

**Location:** 11 m E of Plymouth.
**Opening Times:** May to Sept—Weds & Thurs, 2–5. Adm £1, Chd 50p. Free car park. No dogs admitted.

## FURSDON HOUSE

**Cadbury, Thorverton** *map E3* △
Telephone: Exeter (0392) 860860
*(E D Fursdon, Esq)*

Georgian fronted manor house, home of the Fursdon family who have lived here for over 700 years in unbroken male succession. Regency Library, family portraits, costumes and mementos. House set in farmland with superb views across estate. Informal garden undergoing restoration. Primarily a family home.

**Location:** 9 m N of Exeter, 6 m SW of Tiverton; ¾ m off A3072 Tiverton/Crediton Road.
**Opening Times:** Easter – Sat to Mon incl. May to Sept 30: Thurs, Bank Holidays and the Suns immediately preceding Bank Hol Mon 2–5 each open day. Parties by arrangement please. Adm House & Grounds £1.90, Chd under 16 £1; under 10, free.
**Refreshments:** Tea room (open days). Food available at Inns in Bickleigh (2 m) & Thorverton (2 m).

## THE GARDEN HOUSE

**Buckland Monachorum, Yelverton** *map E2*
Telephone: Yelverton 854769
*(The Fortescue Charitable Trust)*

8 acre garden of interest throughout the year and including a 2 acre walled garden that is one of the finest in the country. Fine collections of herbaceous and woody plants.

**Location:** 5 m S of Tavistock; from Yelverton on A386 turn W; 10 m N Plymouth.
**Opening Times:** GARDENS ONLY. Apr 1 to Sept 30—Daily 12–5. Adm £1, Chd 50p. *In aid of National Gardens' Scheme.* No dogs. Coaches & parties by appointment. Car park. Unusual plants for sale.

## HARTLAND ABBEY

**Bideford, North Devon** *map D3*
Telephone: Hartland 559
*(Sir Hugh Stucley, Bt.)*

The Abbey was founded soon after 1157. Much of the house has been rebuilt through various periods. The original cloisters have been used in the basement. There is a Queen Anne wing built in 1705 and further alterations to the front of the house were completed in 1779. Since the dissolution of the monasteries the house has descended to the present day through a series of marriages and has never been sold. It contains a unique collection of documents dating from AD1160 and pictures, furniture and porcelain collected over many generations. Either side of the house are shrub gardens containing mostly rhododendrons, azaleas and camellias. The house is set in an area of outstanding natural beauty.

**Location:** NW Devon (Hartland Point); 15 m from Bideford; 5 m approx from A39.
**Opening Times:** May to Sept incl—Weds 2–5.30. Bank Hols (Easter to Summer) Suns & Mons 2–5.30. Adm £2, Chd £1. Parties welcomed £1.75. Ample car parking close to house.
**Refreshments:** Cream teas provided at house.

## HEMERDON HOUSE

**Plympton, Plymouth** *map E2* ♿
Telephone: Plymouth (0752) 223816 (Office hours);
337350 (weekend & evenings)
*(J H G Woollcombe, Esq)*

Regency house containing West country paintings and prints, with appropriate furniture and a Library.

**Location:** 2 m from Plympton.
**Opening Times:** May – 22 days including Bank Holidays and Aug – 8 days including Bank Holiday 2–5.30. For opening dates please contact the Administrator. Adm £1.50.

## KILLERTON, The National Trust

**nr Exeter** *map F2* ♿
Telephone: Exeter (0392) 881345

Late 18th century house in a beautiful setting containing the Paulise de Bush Collection of Costume. Lovely throughout the year, with flowers from early spring, and splendid late autumn colours. 19th century Chapel and Ice House. Estate exhibition in Stables. Paths lead up the hill to the Dolbury, an isolated hill with an Iron Age hill fort site.

**Location:** 7 m NE of Exeter on W side of Exeter Cullompton (B3181—formerly A38); from M5 s'bound exit 28/B3181; from M5 n'bound exit 29 via Broadclyst & B3181.
**Opening Times:** House: Good Friday to end of Oct—Daily 11–6, 11–5 during Oct (last adm ½ hour before closing). Park: All the year during daylight hours. Adm. House and Garden £2.80 (tickets available at Stable Block), Chd half-price; Garden only £1.50. *Reduced rates for parties* (£2) *on application to the Administrator. Parties who do not pre-book will be charged at full rate.* The Conference Room may be booked for meetings, etc. Applications (in writing) to: The Administrator, Killerton House, Broadclyst, Exeter, Devon. Shop in Stables. Dogs in Park only. Wheelchairs provided. Motorised buggy for disabled visitors to tour the garden.
**Refreshments:** Licensed restaurant at House, entrance from garden—tickets necessary, available in Stables. Light refreshments and ice cream in Coach House, home baked bread and pastries for sale and to take away.

## KIRKHAM HOUSE

**Paignton** *map E2*
Telephone: (0803) 522775
*(English Heritage)*

This well-preserved house near the church is an interesting example of 15th century architecture. It was probably the home of a prosperous merchant. Display of modern furniture.

**Location:** Kirkham Street, Paignton.
**Opening Times:** Good Friday to Sept 30, daily 10–6. Adm 80p, OAPs 60p, Chd 40p.

# The National Trust in DEVON and CORNWALL

## CASTLE DROGO

## COTEHELE

## KILLERTON

## LANHYDROCK

## SALTRAM

## TRERICE

*ADMISSION — SEE EDITORIAL REFERENCE*

### KNIGHTSHAYES COURT, The National Trust

**nr Tiverton** *map E3* ♿
Telephone: Tiverton (0884) 254665

One of the finest gardens in Devon with specimen trees, rare shrubs, spring bulbs, summer flowering borders; of interest at all seasons. House by William Burges, begun in 1869, decorated by J D Crace.

**Location:** 2 m N of Tiverton; turn off A396 (Bampton/Tiverton Road) at Bolham.
**Opening Times:** Good Friday to end of Oct—Garden daily 11–6, 11–5 during Oct. House – daily except Fri (but open Good Friday) 1.30–6, 1.30–5 during Oct (last adm ½ hour before closing). *Nov and Dec: Sun 2–4; pre-arranged parties only.* Adm £2.90, Chd £1.45. Garden & Grounds only £1.70. *Reduced rates for parties (£2.20) on application to the Administrator. Parties who do not pre-book will be charged at full rate.* Shop. Plants available at garden shop. Dogs in park only on leads. Wheelchairs provided.
**Refreshments:** Licensed restaurant for coffee, lunches and teas 11–½ hour before closing, daily. Picnic area in car park.

### MARWOOD HILL

**nr Barnstaple** *map E3*
*(Dr J A Smart)*

Extensive collection of camellias under glass and in the open, daffodils, rhododendrons, rare flowering shrubs: rock and alpine garden, rose garden, waterside planting. Bog garden. 18 acre garden with 3 small lakes. Australian native plants. Many clematis.

**Location:** 4 m N of Barnstaple; opposite church in Marwood.
**Opening Times:** GARDENS ONLY. All the year—Daily (except Christmas Day) dawn to dusk. Adm £1, Chd 10p. *In aid of National Gardens Scheme.* Plants for sale. Dogs allowed, on leads only.
**Refreshments:** Teas. Apr to Sept, Suns & Bank Hols, or by prior arrangement for parties.

**Okehampton Castle** – See English Heritage Section.

### OVERBECKS MUSEUM & GARDEN, The National Trust

**Sharpitor, Salcombe** *map E2*
Telephone: Salcombe (054 884) 2893

6 acres of garden with rare and tender plants and beautiful views eastwards over Salcombe Bay. Part of house forms museum of local interest and of particular interest to children.

**Location:** 1½ m SW of Salcombe signposted from Malborough & Salcombe.
**Opening Times:** Gardens. All the year—Daily 10–8, or sunset if earlier. Museum: Good Friday to Oct 31—Daily 11–5. Last adm ½ hour before closing. Adm Museum & Garden £1.70, Chd half-price. Garden only £1.30. *No reduction for parties.* Dogs allowed in gardens & conservatory only on leads, not in Museum. Shop. Picnicking allowed in gardens. Not suitable for coaches.

### POWDERHAM CASTLE

**nr Exeter** *map F2*
*(The Earl and Countess of Devon)*

Medieval castle built c 1390 by Sir Philip Courtenay, ancestor of the present Earl of Devon. Damaged in the Civil War and restored and altered in 18th and 19th centuries. Music Room by Wyatt. Park stocked with deer. A family home.

**Location:** 8 m SW of Exeter off A379 to Dawlish.
*Station: Starcross 1½ m.*

**Opening Times:** May 28–Sept 14—Suns–Thurs 2–5.30 (last adm 5). Closed Fris & Sats. Extended tour: Tues, Wed, Thurs. For information please contact: The Administrator Tel. Starcross (0626) 890 243. Teas, souvenirs. Good free parking. Dogs admitted to shaded car park only.

### ROSEMOOR GARDEN

**Great Torrington** *map E3*
*(The Royal Horticultural Society)*

Important plantsman's garden of eight acres which has recently been given by Lady Anne Palmer to the RHS and is being enlarged to 40 acres; rhododendrons (species and hybrid), ornamental trees and shrubs, dwarf conifer collection, species and old-fashioned roses, scree and alpine beds, arboretum. Nursery selling rare plants.

**Location:** 1 m SE of Great Torrington on B3220 to Exeter.
**Opening Times:** Daily 8–7 or dusk. Nursery open 8–5. Adm £1.50, Chd 50p. Parties of over 20 persons £1.35 each. In aid of National Gardens Scheme on Jun 17 & Jul 23.
**Refreshments:** Teas Suns, Weds and to order.

### SALTRAM HOUSE, The National Trust

**Plymouth** *map E2* ♿
Telephone: Plymouth (0752) 336546

A George II house, built around and incorporating remnants of a late Tudor mansion, in a landscaped park. Two exceptional rooms by Robert Adam. Furniture, pictures, fine plasterwork and woodwork. Great Kitchen. Beautiful garden with Orangery. Octagonal summer-house, rare shrubs and trees. Shop in stables.

**Location:** 2 m W of Plympton 3½ m E of Plymouth city centre, between A38 & A379 main roads.
**Opening Times:** Nov to end of Mar. Garden open daily 11–6. Good Friday to end Oct. House: Suns–Thurs, Good Friday and Bank Hol, Sats 12.30–6, 12.30–5 during Oct; Kitchen, Shop & Art Gallery 11–6, 11–5 during Oct; Garden 11–6 (open daily). Last adm ½ hour before closing. Adm £3.20, Chd half-price; Garden only £1.20. *Reductions for parties (£2.40) at certain times of day by prior arrangement for visits/meals with the Administrator.* The Chapel may be booked for meetings, etc. Applications (in writing) to: The Administrator, Saltram House, Plympton, Plymouth. Dogs in grounds only. Wheelchairs provided.
**Refreshments:** Licensed restaurant in House (entrance from Garden); Suns–Thurs & Bank Hols 11–6, 11–5 during Oct (last adm ½ hour before closing). Light refreshments at Coach House near car park during peak periods.

### SAND

**Sidbury, nr Sidmouth** *map F2* △
*(Lt Col P V Huyshe)*

Lived in Manor house owned by Huyshe family since 1560, rebuilt 1592–4, situated in unspoilt valley. Screens passage, panelling, family documents, heraldry. Also **Sand Lodge** roof structure of late 15th century Hall House.

**Location:** ¾ m NE of Sidbury; 400 yds from A375, Grid ref 146925.
**Opening Times:** Suns & Mons—Mar 26, 27; May 28, 29, July 30, 31, Aug 27, 28 2–5.30. Last tour 4.45. Adm £1.50, Chd & Students 20p. Sand Lodge and outside of Sand by written appointment, £1.
**Refreshments:** Light teas in house, cream teas in Sidbury (free car parking).

### TAPELEY PARK

**Instow** *map E3* △ ♿
Telephone: Instow (0271) 860528
*(H T C Christie Esq.)*

A fine historic house, basically William and Mary but with later neo-classic façades by John Belcher. Standing in one of the most beautiful settings in North Devon, with magnificent views over the Taw and Torridge estuary. Italian gardens with many rare plants, lily ponds, woodland walks with lakes, walled kitchen garden, ice house, shell house, peacocks, rare breed sheep, picnic areas.

**Location:** Between Barnstaple & Bideford on A39; 1 m SW of Instow.
**Opening Times:** Easter to Oct (Gardens open all year, during daylight hours only) 10–6, daily except Sat. House tours regularly through day provided minimum of 10 adults. Adm Gardens: £1.50, Chd 50p; House: (extra) £1.50, Chd 50p. Reduced rates for coaches.
**Refreshments:** The Queen Anne Dairy is open all day for light lunch, cream tea & other refreshments.

### TIVERTON CASTLE

**Tiverton** *map E3*
Telephone: (0884) 253200 or 01-727 4854
*(Mr and Mrs A.K. Gordon)*

Originally a Royal Castle built in 1106, then a Tudor palace and Civil War fortress, now enclosing a private house. Important Civil War Armoury. Medieval gatehouse and towers. Entrances to secret passageways extending throughout the town. Romantic ruins of towers, walls and chapel. Famous Victorian murder mystery exhibit. New World Tapestry. Fine furniture and pictures.

**Location:** Next to St. Peter's Church. The Castle is well signposted in Tiverton.
**Opening Times:** Good Friday to last Sun in Sept—Suns to Thurs 2.30–5.30. Adm £1.80, Chd under 7 free, 7–16 £1. OAPs and students £1.25. Party bookings at special rates. Free parking inside. Coach parties by appointment only.
**Refreshments:** Devon cream teas during Summer. Light lunches, evening parties by appointment.

### TORRE ABBEY

**Torquay** *map E2*
Telephone: Torquay (0803) 23593
*(Torbay Borough Council)*

12th century monastery converted into a private residence after the Dissolution in 1539. Extensively remodelled in the early 18th century and currently undergoing complete renovation and restoration. Contains furnished period rooms, family chapel, extensive collection of paintings and other works of art, and the Dame Agatha Christie memorial room, containing many mementos of the Torquay born authoress. Over 20 rooms now open to the public including those in the newly restored South-West wing. Ruins of medieval Abbey also on show, including the remains of the Abbey Church, excavated in 1987/8. Formal gardens containing tropical palm house, summer bedding, rockeries and spring bulbs.

**Location:** On Torquay Sea front.
*Station: Torquay (¼ m).*
**Opening Times:** HOUSE: Apr to Oct—Daily 10–5 (last adm 4.30). Other times by appointment. Adm (1988 rates) 75p, OAPs 40p, Chd Free (if accompanied).
GARDENS: All the year—Daily. Adm free.

**Totnes Castle** – See English Heritage Section.

### UGBROOKE HOUSE

**Chudleigh** *map E2*
Telephone: Chudleigh (0626) 852179

The original house and church were built about 1200 and redesigned by Robert Adam. The Clifford family live in the house, and the rooms are in constant use. Ugbrooke contains fine furniture and paintings, beautiful embroideries and uniforms. The grounds by Capability Brown provide delightful walks and a pleasant picnic area. Afternoon snacks and teas are served in the Wyvern Cafe in the original 18th century stable block. Also on display is a fine collection of maps dating back to the 18th century and a unique collection of Indian weaponry captured during the Indian mutiny. Items of nostalgia include: letters and photographs. Lakeside walks.

**Location:** Chudleigh
**Opening Times:** May 27 to Aug 28, Sat, Sun and Bank Hols only. GROUNDS – 1–5. Guided tours of House at 2.15 and 3.45. Adm £2.80, Chd (5–16) £1.30, Groups (over 20) £2.30.
**Refreshments:** Snacks & afternoon teas at the Wyvern Café, 1.30–5.

### WOODSIDE

**Barnstaple** *map E3*
Telephone: Barnstaple (0271) 43095
*(Mr & Mrs Mervyn Feesey)*

2 acre plantsman's garden, south sloping, raised beds. Collection of ornamental grasses, bamboos, sedges and other monocots; unusual and rare dwarf shrubs and plants; troughs; variegated and peat-loving shrubs and conifers; New Zealand collection.

**Location:** N outskirts of Barnstaple; off A39 to Lynton (400 yds. beyond Fire Station).
*Station: Barnstaple Junction (1 m).*
**Opening Times:** GARDEN ONLY. Sat May 20, Suns June 18, July 16; 2–6. Adm 75p, Chd 25p. *In aid of National Gardens Scheme.* Other days by appointment.

# DORSET

### ABBOTSBURY–SWANNERY & SUB-TROPICAL GARDENS

**Abbotsbury, nr Weymouth** *map G2* △
Telephone: Abbotsbury (030 587) 387
*(Strangways Estates)*

Owned by the Strangways family since 1541 it received a Conservation award in 1975. The Swannery—unique colony of mute swans; 17th century duck decoy; reed bed walk. Sub-Tropical Gardens—20 acres of woodland and walled gardens containing tender and exotic plants growing outdoors. Peacocks.

**Location:** On B3157 Weymouth/Bridport Road; may be approached from A35 at Winterbourne Abbas.
**Opening Times:** The Swannery mid May to mid Sept 9.30–4.30. The Gardens mid Mar to mid Sept 10–6.
**Refreshments:** Tea garden at sub-tropical gardens.

### ATHELHAMPTON

**Athelhampton** *map G2* △ ♿
Telephone: Puddletown (0305) 848363
*(Lady Cooke)*

One of the finest medieval houses in England. 10 acres of formal and landscape gardens.

**Location:** ½ m E of Puddletown on Dorchester/Bournemouth Road (A35); 5 m NE of Dorchester.
**Opening Times:** Easter to Oct 15, 2–6 on Weds, Thurs & Suns; Good Fri & Bank Hols; also Mons & Tues in Aug: 2–6. Entrance and Garden: £1.25, House £1.25 extra. (Chd free of charge in gardens). Special rate for pre-booked parties £2 incl. Dogs admitted only to shaded car park.
**Refreshments:** Tea at the House.

## CHETTLE HOUSE
**Chettle, Blandford** *map G3*
Telephone: Chettle (0258 89) 209
*(J. P. C. Bourke)*

One of the finest examples of a Queen Anne House in the English Baroque style by Thomas Archer. Set in 5 acres of garden with many unusual herbaceous plants and shrubs. Fine Art Gallery and vineyard.

**Location:** 6 m NE of Blandford on A354 & 1 mile W.
**Opening Times:** Adm £1. Car and Coach park. Wheelchairs garden only. Apr–Oct daily (except Tues) 10.30–5.30. Plant Centre specialising in unusual herbaceous plants. No dogs.
**Refreshments:** Many pubs within 2 miles. Picnic area available, teas weekends.

## CLOUDS HILL, The National Trust
**nr Wool** *map G2*

The cottage home of T E Lawrence (Lawrence of Arabia) after the first World War; contains his furniture and other relics.

**Location:** 1 m N of Bovington Camp, 1½ m E of Waddock crossroads (B3390), 9 m E of Dorchester.
**Opening Times:** Apr to end Sept—Weds, Thurs, Fris (inc Good Friday) Suns & Bank Hol Mons 2–5. Oct to Mar—Suns only 1–4. Adm £1.50. *No reduction for children or parties.* No photography. Unsuitable for wheelchairs & coaches.

## COMPTON HOUSE
**nr Sherborne** *map G3*
Telephone: Yeovil (0935) 74608
*(Worldwide Butterflies Ltd)*

16th century Manor House with 19th century Tudor style front. Set in tranquil surroundings with lawns and 13th century church, an historic building with a difference: here butterflies are bred and visitors see all stages of their development. Tropical Jungle, Breeding Hall, Palm House. Other display areas include the new Butterfly House, vintage tractors and fire-engine. House still lived in. Visitors also see the Lullingstone Silk Farm which produced the silk for two coronations, the wedding of the Prince and Princess of Wales and other Royal occasions.

**Location:** On A30 dual carriageway, midway between Sherborne & Yeovil.
*Station: Yeovil Pen Mill (2 m), Sherborne (3 m) (Waterloo line).*
**Opening Times:** Apr 1 to Oct 30—Daily 10–5. **Visitors should telephone to check the current times and dates in advance of visit.** Adm charges not available at time of going to press. *The gardens of the house are now open to visitors and it is possible to see some of the fine outbuildings which are gradually to be restored.*
**Refreshments:** Oliver's Coffee House and Restaurant in the house, overlooking the garden.

## CORFE CASTLE, The National Trust
**nr Wareham** *map G2*
Telephone: Corfe Castle 480921

Ruins of former royal castle, sieged and 'slighted' by Parliamentary forces in 1646.

**Location:** In the village of Corfe Castle: on A351 Wareham-Swanage road.
**Opening Times:** Feb 11 to Nov 5: every day 10–4.30pm or sunset if earlier. Nov 5 to Feb 10: Sat and Sun (weather permitting) 12–4pm (or sunset if earlier). Adm: Adults £1.60, Chd 80p, parties (15 or more) £1.20. Not suitable for wheelchairs. N.T. Shop and refreshments.

## CRANBORNE MANOR GARDENS
*map H3*
Telephone: Cranborne 248
*(The Viscount and Viscountess Cranborne)*

Walled gardens, yew hedges and lawns; wild garden with spring bulbs, herb garden, Jacobean mount garden, flowering cherries and collection of old-fashioned and specie roses. Gardens originally laid out by John Tradescant.

**Location:** 18 m N of Bournemouth, B3078; 16 m S of Salisbury, A354, B3081.
**Opening Times:** GARDENS ONLY. Apr to Sept—Weds 9–5. Free car park. GARDEN CENTRE open Tues–Sats 9–5, Suns 2–5 (not Jan & Feb). *Closed* Mons except Bank Holidays. Something for every gardener, but specialising in old-fashioned and specie roses, herbs, ornamental pots and Italian statuary and garden furniture.

## DEANS COURT
**Wimborne** *map H3* ♿
*(Sir Michael & Lady Hanham)*

Partly wild garden, specimen trees, interesting birds, organic kitchen garden.

**Location:** 2 m walk South from Wimborne Minster & Square; nr free car parks in town.
**Opening Times:** GARDEN. Bank Hols Mar 27, May 1 and 29, Aug 28, 10–6; Suns Mar 26, Apr 30, May 28, June 25, July 23, Aug 27, Sept 24. 2–6. Thurs in Apr, May, June, July & Sept, 2–6. Adm £1, Chd 50p. No dogs or unaccompanied children. *Special arrangements and car park for disabled on application at gate.* Parties by prior **written** appointment. Organically-grown produce for sale. Vegetable sanctuary. GARDEN HERITAGE WEEK APR 29 TO MAY 7. Telephone Tourist Information Office Wimborne (0202) 886116 for details of special daily events.
**Refreshments:** Wholefood teas on all Suns and Bank Hols, & Thurs in June & July. Coffee on Bank Hol morning.

## EDMONDSHAM HOUSE AND GARDENS
**Nr. Wimborne** *map H3*
Telephone: Cranborne (072 54) 207
*(Mrs J. E. Smith)*

A family home since the 16th century, and a fine blend of Tudor and Georgian architecture, with a Victorian stable block and dairy, interesting furniture, lace and other exhibits. The Gardens include an old-fashioned walled garden, cultivated organically, with an excellent display of spring bulbs, shrubs, lawns and herbaceous border.

**Location:** Between Cranborne and Verwood, off the B3081.
**Opening Times:** HOUSE AND GARDENS: Easter Sun 2.30–5. Bank Holiday Mon and Wed in Apr 2.30–5. Parties and individuals by arrangement at other times. Adm £1.20, Chd 60p. GARDENS: Apr, May, June and Oct: Wed–Sat incl. 10–12, and at other times when the owner is at home. Adm 60p, Chd 30p.

**Fiddleford Mill House** – See English Heritage Section.

## FORDE ABBEY AND GARDENS
**nr Chard** *map F3* △
Telephone: (0460) 20231
*(Trustees of Forde Abbey)*

Cromwellian Country House created out of a 12th century Cistercian Monastery. Famous Mortlake tapestries. 25 acres of outstanding gardens.

**Location:** 1 m E of Chard Junction, 4 m SE of Chard. 7 m W of Crewkerne.
**Opening Times:** GARDENS AND PLANT CENTRE: open daily throughout the year 10.30–4.30; HOUSE: Easter–Mid Oct. Suns, Weds & Bank Hol Mons, 2–5.30. Adm £2.50; Gardens only £1.50, Chld free.
**Refreshments:** Tea room open mid-day.

## HARDY'S COTTAGE, The National Trust
**Higher Bockhampton** *map G2* ♿
Telephone: Dorchester 62366

Birthplace of Thomas Hardy 1840–1928. A thatched cottage, built by his grandfather; little altered.

**Location:** 3 m NE of Dorchester; ½ m S of Blandford Road (A35).
**Opening Times:** Interior: by prior appointment with the custodian. Adm to interior £1.50. Garden: between Easter–Oct 30 (except Tues am) from 11–6 or sunset if earlier. Exterior and garden free. Approached by 10 mins walk from car park via woods. Wheelchairs, garden only.

## HIGHBURY
**West Moors** *map H3*
Telephone: Ferndown 874372
*(Mr & Mrs Stanley Cherry)*

Half acre garden in mature setting; many rare and unusual plants and shrubs. Specialist collections. Botanical and horticultural interest with everything labelled.

**Location:** 8 m N of Bournemouth. In Woodside Road off B3072, Bournemouth/Verwood (last Road N end of village).
**Opening Times:** GARDEN ONLY. Apr 2 to Sept 3—Suns & Bank Hol Mons 2–6. Parties other days by appointment. Adm 45p, Chd 25p. *In aid of National Gardens Scheme.* No dogs.
**Refreshments:** Teas in the orchard when fine.

## KINGSTON LACY, The National Trust
**nr Wimborne Minster** *map G3*
Telephone: Wimborne 883402

17th century House designed by Sir Roger Pratt but with considerable alterations by Sir Charles Barry in the 19th century. Important Italian and English paintings collected by W.J. Bankes. Set in 250 acres of wooded park.

**Location:** on B3082—Wimborne–Blandford Road, 1½ m W of Wimborne.
**Opening Times:** Mar 25 to Oct 29—Sats to Weds incl. HOUSE: 1–5. PARKS AND GARDEN: 12–6 (last adm half-hour before closing). Guided Tours Sat 10–12 by written appointment only. Adm: HOUSE & GARDEN: £3.50, Chd £1.80, Guided Tours £5. PARK & GARDEN ONLY: £1, Chd 50p. House not suitable for wheelchairs. One wheelchair available for use in Garden. Guide dogs admitted to grounds. Parties by arrangement **only. Timed Tickets.**
**Refreshments:** Lunches and cream teas. National Trust Shop.

## MAPPERTON
**Beaminster** *map G3*
Telephone: (0308) 862645
*(Mr J. Montagu)*

Terraced and hillside gardens with daffodils, formal borders and specimen shrubs and trees. Modern orangery in classical style, 17th century stone fish ponds and summer house. Tudor manor house, enlarged under Charles II. Magnificent views.

**Location:** 1 m off B3163, 2 m off B3066.
**Opening Times:** Mar 15–Oct 31, Sun–Fri 2–6. Adm £1.20, under 18 and OAPs 60p, under 5 free. House also open to group tours by appointment, prices as for gardens.

# ATHELHAMPTON

**DORSET**

*Surrounded by one of the Great Gardens of England*

Five centuries of history in a family house built in 1485 on the site of King Athelston's Palace. Great Hall with unique roof, oriel window, heraldic glass and linenfold panelling. Enjoy the fine furniture in the Tudor Great Chamber, 18th century Dining Room, State Bedroom, Wine Cellar and exhibition room. 12 architectural and water gardens with rare plants and trees encircled by the River Piddle. 15th century dovecote.

OPENING TIMES
Easter - 15th October

2 to 6pm on Wednesdays, Thursdays and Sundays. Good Friday and Bank Holidays: also Mondays and Tuesdays during August. Children free of charge in gardens. House & gardens £2.50, pre-booked parties minimum 20 £2.00. Dogs admitted only to shaded car park.

Antique shop.

Home made cream teas.

Telephone: (0305) 848363.

# ABBOTSBURY

**DORSET**

From St. Catherine's Chapel on its hill above the old village, the panoramic view includes the world-famous swannery and the unique sub-tropical gardens.

*ADMISSION – SEE EDITORIAL REFERENCE*

# CRANBORNE MANOR GARDENS

**CRANBORNE, WIMBORNE, DORSET**

*One of the "Great Gardens of Great Britain"*

These beautiful and historic gardens, laid out in the 17th century by John Tradescant, and much embellished and enlarged in the 20th century, feature several gardens surrounded by walls and yew hedges—enclosing a White garden, Herb, Mount and Knot garden planted with Elizabethan flowers. There are also Water and Wild gardens. Visitors will find many interesting plants, fine trees and avenues.

GARDEN CENTRE

Specialising in rare and uncommon plants, Italian pots and statuary, old fashioned and specie roses, herbs, etc. Large Gift Shop.

# FORDE ABBEY AND GARDENS

**CHARD – SOMERSET TEL: 0460 20231**

Forde Abbey was founded in 1138 as a Cistercian Monastery and was 'modernised' in 1500 by Abbot Chard whose Great Hall and Tower remain. In 1640 the Abbey was converted into a Country House, whose magnificent interior is untouched, and includes a series of unique plaster ceilings and an outstanding set of Raphael Tapestries.
Today the Abbey, surrounded by 30 acres of Gardens and Lakes, on the bank of the River Axe is the home of the Roper family.
Tea room in Monks Kitchen.

THE GARDENS

30 Acres of outstanding gardens, first landscaped in the early 18th century. Herbaceous borders, bog garden, arboretum.
Open daily throughout the year.
Rare and unusual plants for sale in kitchen garden.
Free: Car park.
Free: Entry to plant centre.
Free: Accompanied children under 15.

FORDE ABBEY FRUIT GARDENS

Pick your own fruit. Mid-June to Mid-August. Extensive car park with refreshments set in delightful countryside.
Open daily 9am–7pm.
Tel: 0460 21206

## MELBURY HOUSE
**nr Yeovil** *map G3*
*(The Lady Teresa Agnew)*

Large garden; very fine arboretum; shrubs and lakeside walk; beautiful deer park.

**Location:** 13 m N of Dorchester.
*Station: Chetnole (2 m).*
**Opening Times:** GARDEN ONLY. Thurs June 15 & 22; July 6 & 20, Aug 31, Sept 7 (for St John's Ambulance). Adm will be charged. Teas and plants available. *In aid of the National Gardens Scheme and the MacMillan Trust.*

## MILTON ABBEY
**Milton Abbas, nr Blandford** *map G3*
*(The Council of Milton Abbey School Ltd)*

A fine Abbey Church (Salisbury Diocese) partially completed 15th century on site of 10th century Abbey. Georgian Gothic Mansion (Milton Abbey School). Architect Sir William Chambers, with ceilings and decorations by James Wyatt. Incorporates Abbots Hall, completed 1498, with fine hammerbeam roof and carved screen.

**Location:** 7 m SW of Blandford, just N of A354 from Winterborne Whitechurch or Milborne St Andrew.
**Opening Times:** HOUSE & GROUNDS. Mar 24–Apr 2 and July 16–Sept 3 inc.—Daily 10–6.30. Adm 60p, Chd free. ABBEY CHURCH: Throughout the year. Free except for above dates.
**Refreshments:** Available when House is open in summer only.

## MINTERNE
**Dorchester** *map G3*
Telephone: Cerne Abbas (03003) 370
*(The Lord Digby)*

Important rhododendron and shrub garden, many fine and rare trees, landscaped in the 18th century with lakes, cascades and streams.

**Location:** On A352 2 m N of Cerne Abbas; 10 m N of Dorchester, 9 m S of Sherborne.
**Opening Times:** Apr 1 to Oct 31—Daily 10–7. Adm £1, accom chd free. Free car park.

## PARNHAM
**Beaminster** *map G3*
Telephone: Beaminster (0308) 862204
*(Mr & Mrs John Makepeace)*

An Elizabethan manor, restored by Nash and surrounded by gardens landscaped by Inigo Thomas, extensively replanted over recent years by Jennie Makepeace. In the workshop, furniture designed by John Makepeace is made for public and private collections.

**Location:** On A3066, 1 m S of Beaminster; 5 m N of Bridport.
**Opening Times:** Good Friday Mar 24 to Sun Oct 29—Weds, Suns & Bank Hols 10–5. Group visits on these and other days by prior arrangement only. Adm Principal rooms, gardens, workshops, car parks, picnic areas: £2.50, Chd (10–15) £1.20; under 10, free.
**Refreshments:** Light lunches, teas etc in licensed 17th century buttery.

**Portland Castle** – See English Heritage Section.

## PRIEST'S HOUSE MUSEUM AND GARDEN
**23 High Street, Wimborne Minster** *map H3*
Telephone: Wimborne 882533
*(Mrs K. Callow, Curator)*

A partly Tudor house, with beautiful, large walled garden, in the town centre.

**Location:** Centre of Wimborne Minster.
**Opening Times:** Easter Mon to Sept 30: Daily 10.30–4.30, Sun 2–4.30, also open for short Christmas period 2–4.30, please telephone for details. Small charge includes admission to garden.

## PURSE CAUNDLE MANOR
**nr Sherborne** *map G3*
Telephone: Milborne Port 250400
*(Michael de Pelet, Esq)*

Interesting 15th/16th century Manor House. Lived in as a family home. Great Hall with minstrel gallery; Winter Parlour; Solar with oriel; bedchambers; garden.

**Location:** 4 m E of Sherborne; ¼ m S of A30.
**Opening Times:** Easter Mon to Sept 28, Thurs, Suns & Bank Hols, 2–5. Coaches welcomed by appointment. Adm £1.50, Chd 50p. Free car park.
**Refreshments:** Home-made cream teas by prior arrangement.

## RUSSELL-COTES ART GALLERY & MUSEUM
**Bournemouth** *map H2*
*(Bournemouth Corporation)*

Victorian House designed by Fogerty in 1894 as the East Cliff Hall.

**Location:** Russell-Cotes Road, East Cliff, Bournemouth.
*Station: Bournemouth (¾ m).*
**Opening Times:** All the year—Weekdays 10–5.30. Gardens open June 1 to Sept 30. Adm 50p, Chd 10p (under 5 free).

## SANDFORD ORCAS MANOR HOUSE
**Sandford Orcas, Sherborne** *map G3*
Telephone: Corton Denham (096 322) 206
*(Sir Mervyn Medlycott, Bt)*

Tudor Manor House in remarkable original state of preservation, with gatehouse, spiral staircases, and Tudor and Jacobean panelling. Fine collections of 14th–17th C. stained glass, Queen Anne and Chippendale furniture, Elizabethan and Georgian needlework, and 17th C. Dutch paintings. Mature terraced gardens, with topiary, and herb garden.

**Location:** 2½ m N of Sherborne, ent. next to Church.
**Opening Times:** Easter Mon 10–6 then May to Sept—Suns 2–6 & Mons 10–6. Adm £1.20, Chd 60p. Pre-booked parties (of 10 or more) at reduced rates on other days if preferred.

## SHERBORNE CASTLE
**Sherborne** *map G3*
Telephone: Sherborne (0935) 813182
*(Simon Wingfield Digby, Esq)*

16th century mansion in continuous occupation of the Digby family since 1617.

**Location:** 5 m E of Yeovil off A30 to S.
*Station: Sherborne (few mins walk).*
**Opening Times:** Easter Sat to end of Sept—Thurs, Sats, Suns & Bank Hol Mons 2–6. Grounds open 12 noon Sats, Suns and Bank Hol Mons and Thurs 1.30. Adm charges available on request by telephone. *Special terms & days for parties by arrangement.* Gift shop.
**Refreshments:** Tea at the house.

# PARNHAM and MAKEPEACE

## *Craftsmanship for the future*

In the heart of peaceful West Dorset stands an impressive Tudor house. Home and inspiration to designer and furniture-maker John Makepeace, Parnham is a place which demonstrates excellence, enterprise and innovation in wood. Its formal and intimate gardens provide an idyllic dimension to the vitality and creativity of the furniture workshops and of the School for Craftsmen in Wood. At Parnham, the collaborative efforts of those working with John Makepeace have created an exciting experience of true craftsmanship. Exhibitions by leading artists and craftsmen and live performances make Parnham complete as an artistic entity.

Connoisseurs from around the world come to Parnham to purchase or commission work by a Master in the creative tradition of English furniture-making. John Makepeace's workshop regularly produces fine furniture for public, corporate and private collections.

Parnham is open to visitors from 10 a.m. to 5 p.m. on Wednesdays, Sundays and Bank Holidays from Easter to October inclusive.

**Parnham House, Beaminster, Dorset, DT8 3NA. Telephone (0308) 862204**

*On the A3066, one mile south of Beaminster, five miles north of Bridport.*

# RUSSELL-COTES ART GALLERY & MUSEUM

**BOURNEMOUTH, DORSET**

The Russell-Cotes Museum designed in 1894 by Fogerty as a villa for Sir Merton Russell-Cotes, is a remarkable example of a late Victorian Residence. The interior is decorated in the Italian manner and there is a fine collection of paintings and other works of art.

# SHERBORNE CASTLE

**SHERBORNE, DORSET**

*Family home of Mr Simon Wingfield Digby*

Built by Sir Walter Raleigh in 1594 and enlarged in 1625 by Sir John Digby, 1st Earl of Bristol. Home of the Digby family since 1617, the house contains fine furniture, porcelain and pictures by Vandyck, Gainsborough, Reynolds, Lely, Kneller and other famous artists. Twenty acres of lawns and pleasure grounds planned by "Capability Brown" around the newly restored 50 acre lake are open to the public.

One of the two castles in the ancient and attractive town of Sherborne.

*ADMISSION – SEE EDITORIAL REFERENCE*

# SMEDMORE HOUSE

**DORSET**

Smedmore has remained in the same family since 1620, when Sir William Clavell "built a little newe house and beautified it with pleasant gardens". Walls and trees now protect these gardens, creating a favourable climate for tender and specialist plants, shrubs and climbers. The contents of the house include objects connected with a Russian Empress, Nelson, Napoleon and William of Orange. The setting in unspoilt country between the Purbeck Hills and the sea is superb, and there are spectacular views along the last few miles of the approach road.

*ADMISSION and OTHER INFORMATION – SEE EDITORIAL REFERENCE*

# DORSET – *continued*

**Sherborne Old Castle** – See English Heritage Section.

### SMEDMORE
**Kimmeridge** *map G2* ♿
Telephone: Corfe Castle 480717
*(Major and Mrs John Mansel)*

17th/18th century manor house, still lived in by the family who built it. Plenty to see including 18th century marquetry furniture, Dresden china, antique dolls, Nelson letters. Walled gardens, interesting shrubs, fuchsias and hydrangeas.

**Location:** 7 m S of Wareham.
**Opening Times:** June 7 to Sept 13—Weds 2.15–5.30 (last adm 5). Also Sun, Aug 27, 2.15–5.30. Adm House & Gardens £1.50, Chd 75p. Gardens only 75p, Chd free. Organised parties Weds afternoons during same period by arrangement. Written guides in French, German & Dutch.
**Refreshments:** Tea at Kimmeridge (1 m).

### WOLFETON HOUSE
**Dorchester** *map G2*
Telephone: (0305) 63500
*(Capt. N. T. L. Thimbleby)*

Outstanding medieval and Elizabethan manor house with magnificent wood and stone work, fireplaces and ceilings; Great Hall and stairs; parlour, dining room, Chapel and Cider House.

**Location:** 1½ m from Dorchester on Yeovil road (A37); indicated by Historic House signs.
*Stations: Dorchester South and West 1¾ m.*
**Opening Times:** May to Sept—Tues, Fris and Bank Hol Mons 2–6. At other times throughout the year, parties by arrangement. Adm charges not available at time of going to press.
**Refreshments:** Ploughman's lunches, teas and evening meals for parties, by prior arrangement. Cider for sale.

# DURHAM

### AUCKLAND CASTLE
**Bishop Auckland** *map H11*
Telephone: Bishop Auckland (0388) 609766
*(The Church Commissioners)*

Historic home of the Bishops of Durham with parts dating from 12th century. Very fine private Chapel remodelled by Bishop Cosin from 1660. 14th century Hall, gothicised by James Wyatt in 1795. Also large public park and unusual 18th century deerhouse.

**Location:** In Bishop Auckland, at the end of Market Place.
*Station: Bishop Auckland.*
**Opening Times:** Castle and Chapel: May 15 to Sept 29—Suns & Weds 2–5. Chapel only Thurs 10–12. Adm 75p, Chd 30p, OAPs 50p. Park: Daylight hours throughout the year.

**Barnard Castle** – See English Heritage Section.

### BOTANIC GARDEN, UNIVERSITY OF DURHAM
**Durham** *map H11*
Telephone: (091) 3742671
*(University of Durham)*

18 acres of trees and shrubs, set in mature woodland.

**Location:** Take the Durham turn off at A167 at Cock o' the North Roundabout. 1 m from Durham, along Hollingside Lane.
**Opening Times:** All year including Bank Holidays 10–4.30. Parties welcome, guided tours charged. Attractive Visitor Centre. Free parking. Not suitable for disabled.

### DURHAM CASTLE
**Durham** *map H11* △
*(The University of Durham)*

The Norman castle of the prince bishops has been used by Durham University since 1832.

**Location:** In the centre of the city (adjoining Cathedral).
*Station: Durham (½ m).*
**Opening Times:** All the year; first three weeks in Apr then July, Aug & Sept—Weekdays 10–12, 2–4.30. Other months—Mons, Weds & Sats 2–4. Adm 95p, Chd 45p.

**Finchale Priory** – See English Heritage Section.

### RABY CASTLE
**Staindrop, Darlington** *map G11* ♿
Telephone: Staindrop (0833) 60202
*(The Lord Barnard, T.D.)*

Principally 14th century, alterations made 1765 and mid-19th century. Fine pictures and furniture. Collection of horse-drawn carriages and fire engines. Large walled Gardens.

**Location:** 1 m N of Staindrop village, on the Barnard Castle/Bishop Auckland Road (A688).
**Opening Times:** Easter weekend (Sat–Wed) then Apr 29 to June 30, Weds & Suns; July 1 to Sept 30, daily (except Sats); May, Spring and Aug Bank Hols, Sat–Tues; Castle 1–5; Park & Gardens 11–5.30. Adm Castle, Gardens & Carriage collection £2, Chd & Senior Citizens £1.20; Park, Gardens & Carriages only 80p, Chd & Senior Citizens 60p. Separate adm charge for Bulmer's Tower when open. Special terms for parties over 25 people on above and other days by arrangement (Tel Curator). Picnic area.
**Refreshments:** Tea at the Stables.

### ROKEBY PARK
**nr Barnard Castle**

Palladian House built by Sir Thomas Robinson in 1735. Fine rooms, furniture and pictures (including exceptional collection of 18th century needlework pictures by Anne Morritt).

**Opening Times:** May 1, then each Mon from May 29 to Sept 11, each Tues from July 18 to Sept 12, and each Thur from Aug 3–Aug 31, 2–5 (last adm 4.30). Parties of 25 or more will also be admitted on other days if a written appointment is made with the Curator.

# ESSEX

### AUDLEY END HOUSE AND PARK
*map K5*
Telephone: (0799) 22399
*(English Heritage)*

James I is said to have remarked that Audley End was too large for a king but not for his Lord Treasurer, Sir Thomas Howard, who built it. The house was so large in fact that early in the 18th century about half of it was demolished as being unmanageable, but this still leaves a very substantial mansion. The interior contains rooms decorated by Robert Adam, a magnificent Jacobean Great Hall, a picturesque 'Gothick' chapel and a suite of rooms decorated in the revived Jacobean style of the early 19th century.

**Location:** ¾ m (1 km) west of Saffron Walden off B1383. OS map ref TL525382.
**Opening Times:** Good Friday to Sept 30, daily 1–6. Park and garden open 12 noon. Last admission 1 hr before closing. Adm £3, OAPs £2, Chd £1.50.

### BELCHAMP HALL
**Belchamp Walter, Sudbury** *map L5*
Telephone: Sudbury (0787) 72744
*(M. M. J. Raymond, Esq)*

Queen Anne period house with period furniture and 17th and 18th century family portraits. Gardens.

**Location:** 5 m SW of Sudbury.
**Opening Times:** By appointment only. May to Sept—Tues & Thurs and Easter, Spring & Summer Bank Hol Mons 2.30–6. Adm £1.40, Chd 70p. Reduction for parties.

### BETH CHATTO GARDENS
**Elmstead Market** *map L5*
*(Mrs Beth Chatto)*

5-acre garden, attractively landscaped with many unusual plants in wide range of conditions.

**Location:** 4 m E of Colchester on A133 Colchester/Clacton Road.
*Station: Colchester.*
**Opening Times:** GARDEN ONLY. All the year—Mons to Sats 9–5 Mar to Oct. Mon–Fri 9–4 Nov to Feb. *Closed Suns & Bank Hols also Sats Nov 4 to end of Feb.* Adm £1, Chd free. *In aid of National Gardens Scheme.* Adjacent nursery also open. *Parties by arrangement.* No dogs please.

### CASTLE HOUSE
**Dedham** *map L5* ♿
Telephone: (0206) 322127

Home of the late Sir Alfred Munnings. KCVO, President of the Royal Academy 1944-1949. The house and studios contain many paintings, drawings, sketches and other works.

**Location:** ¾ m Dedham village, 7 m NE Colchester 2 m E of Ipswich Road (A12).
**Opening Times:** Apr 30 to Oct 1—Weds, Suns & Bank Hol Mons, also Thurs & Sats in Aug, 2–5. Adm £1.50, Chd 25p, OAPs 75p.

### GOSFIELD HALL
**Halstead** *map L5*
*(Country Houses Association Ltd).*

Very fine Tudor gallery.

**Location:** 2½ m SW of Halstead on Braintree/Haverhill Road (A131).
**Opening Times:** May to Sept—Weds & Thurs 2–5. Adm £1, Chd 50p. Free car park. No dogs admitted.

# SANDFORD ORCAS MANOR HOUSE

**DORSET**

Tudor house in golden Hamhill stone, almost unaltered since it was built c1550. Visitors are given a personal conducted tour by the owner, in whose family this house has been since 1736.

*ADMISSION – SEE EDITORIAL REFERENCE*

# WOLFETON

**DORSET**

*The home of Captain & Mrs Thimbleby*

A beautiful and romantic Tudor house with Elizabethan additions, fine stonework, interior woodcarvings and plaster ceilings; the medieval gatehouse, French in appearance, has two unmatched and far older towers.

# AUCKLAND CASTLE

**BISHOP AUCKLAND, CO. DURHAM**

*THE CHURCH COMMISSIONERS*

Steeped in the history of the ancient and important See of Durham, the Castle has been the home of successive bishops since 1183. The medieval Chapel, the size of a parish church, has recently been splendidly restored, and the State Rooms include a Gothick Throne Room lined with the portraits of past bishops.

Bishop Auckland is 11 miles South-West of Durham via A167 & A688.

*ADMISSION – SEE EDITORIAL REFERENCE*

# ROKEBY PARK

**Nr BARNARD CASTLE**

*ADMISSION – SEE EDITORIAL REFERENCE*

# RABY CASTLE

**STAINDROP, CO. DURHAM**

The Castle is one of the largest 14th century Castles in Britain and was built by the Nevills although one of the towers probably dates back to the 11th century. Interior mainly 18th and 19th century; medieval Kitchen and Servants' Hall.

There are some fine pictures of the English, Dutch and Flemish Schools and good period furniture. Collection of horse drawn carriages.

The large walled Gardens are also open to the public.

*ADMISSION – SEE EDITORIAL REFERENCE*

## HEDINGHAM CASTLE
**Castle Hedingham, nr Halstead** *map L5*
Telephone: Hedingham (0787) 60261 or 60804
*(The Hon Thomas & Mrs Lindsay)*

Home of the famous medieval family the de Veres, Earls of Oxford. Besieged by King John and visited by King Henry VII and Queen Elizabeth I. Visitors can see the Garrison Chamber, the Banqueting Hall with Minstrel's Gallery and the beautiful Tudor bridge built in 1496.

**Location:** On B1058 4 m N of Halstead, turn off A604; 9 m N of Braintree; 30 m SE of Cambridge.
**Opening Times:** Easter Weekend & May to end of Oct—Daily 10–5. Parties & schools welcome all year round by appointment with the Curator. Adm £2, Chd £1.
**Refreshments:** Light refreshments.

## HYDE HALL
**Rettendon** *map L5*
*(Hyde Hall Garden Trust)*

Varied collection of trees and shrubs, spring bulbs, roses and ornamental greenhouse plants.

**Location:** 7 m SE of Chelmsford (off A130).
**Opening Times:** GARDEN ONLY. Suns, Weds and Bank Holidays 11–6 from Easter to Oct 29. Adm £1, Chd 25p. *In aid of National Gardens Scheme & other charities.* Plant stall. Dogs on leads allowed.
**Refreshments:** Light refreshments available.

## LAYER MARNEY TOWER
**nr Colchester** *map L5*
Telephone: Colchester 330202
*(Major & Mrs Gerald Charrington)*

1520 Tudor brick house with eight-storey gate tower. Terracotta dolphin cresting and windows. Formal yew hedges, rose bushes and lawns. Adjoining church contains three effigy tombs of the Marneys and original St Christopher wall painting.

**Location:** 3 m from Tiptree, 1 m S of B1022. Colchester/Maldon Road.
**Opening Times:** Apr 1 to Sept 30—Suns & Thurs 2–6; Bank Hols 11–6; also Tues 2–6 during July & Aug. Adm £1.25, Chd 50p. *Parties other days by prior arrangement.*

## THE MAGNOLIAS
**18, St John's Avenue, Brentwood CM14 5DF** *map L4*
Telephone: Brentwood 220019
*(Mr & Mrs R. A. Hammond)*

It is hoped that the small front garden doesn't put the potential visitor off as the back garden seems to go on and on. Cleverly laid out paths lead the visitor up and down, maximising the half acre informal plantsman's garden. The ground is intensively planted with a wide variety of trees, shrubs, climbers, herbaceous groundcover and bulbs. Here can be seen good collections of Acer, Magnolia, Rhododendron, Camellia, Pieris, Hosta and ferns plus the N.C.C.P.G. National Collection of Arisaema. There are seven ponds including one in a green house, some with Koi Carp.

**Location:** 1 m from Brentwood High Street (A1023). At Wilsons Corner turn S down A128; after 300 yds turn right at traffic lights; over railway bridge: St. John's Ave 3rd on right.
**Opening Times:** Weds Apr, May and June 2–5; Suns Mar 26, Apr 2, 16, 30, May 14, 28, June 11, 25, 10–5. Adm 70p, Chd 30p. Parties by appointment. Not suitable for disabled.
**Refreshments:** Teas.

## OLIVERS
**Olivers Lane, Colchester** *map L5*
Telephone: (0206) 330575
*(Mr & Mrs D. Edwards)*

Twenty acres of landscaped gardens slope down from redbrick, mainly Georgian house (not open). Fine trees and shrubs including rhododendrons and azaleas, underplanted with Spring bulbs. Three lakes and stream with bluebells and primulas. Yew hedges back mixed shrub and herbaceous borders with a wide variety of planting. Shrub roses. Eighteenth century dovecote.

**Location:** 3 m SW of Colchester between B1022 and B1026. Olivers Lane is a turning off Gosbeck's Road.
**Opening Times:** Sat & Sun May 6 & 7. All Weds in May 2–6. Adm £1, Chd free. Parties by appointment any time of year. Ample car parking. Suitable for disabled, no wheelchairs available. Plants for sale.
**Refreshments:** Teas at house in May. From June–Oct, strawberry cream teas at adjoining pick-your-own orchard.

## PARK FARM (GARDEN)
**Great Waltham** *map L5*
Telephone: (0245) 360871
*(Mrs Jill Cowley & Mr Derek Bracey)*

Young garden still to be completed on farmyard site. Two acres of bulbs, herbaceous plants and especially roses planted in separate rooms formed by new hedges. There is also a newly-constructed pond garden.

**Location:** A131 to Braintree from Chelmsford: on Little Waltham Bypass turn W to Chatham Hall Lane: Park Farm ½ m on left hand side.
**Opening Times:** Every Sun in May, June and July 2–6; Mon evenings 6 pm–dusk. Adm 60p, Chd 30p. Parties by arrangement. Not suitable for disabled.
**Refreshments:** Teas provided in Victorian Dairy.

## PAYCOCKE'S, The National Trust
**Coggeshall (1500)** *map L5*

Richly ornamented merchant's house, dating from about 1500. Special display of local lace. Delightful garden leading down to small river.

**Location:** On A120; S side of West St. Coggeshall next to Fleece Inn; 5½ m E of Braintree.
*Station: Kelvedon (2½ m).*
**Opening Times:** Mar 25 to Oct 6—Tues, Thurs, Suns and Bank Hol Mons 2–5.30. Adm £1.10, Chd (accompanied) half-price. *Parties exceeding six should make prior arrangements with the tenant.* No reduction for parties. No dogs.
**Refreshments:** In Coggeshall.

**Priors Hall Barn, Widdington** – See English Heritage Section.

## ST. OSYTH PRIORY
**St. Osyth** *map L5*
*Telephone: (0255) 820492*
*(Somerset de Chair)*

Great gatehouse c 1475, "unexcelled in any monastic remains in the country", *Country Life.* A unique group of buildings dating from the 13th, 15th 16th, 18th and 19th centuries, surrounding a wide quadrangle like an Oxford or Cambridge college. Gardens include Rose garden, Topiary garden, Water Garden etc. Art collection in Georgian wing includes world-famous paintings George Stubbs ARA.

**Location:** 65 miles from London via A12, A120; A133 12 miles from Colchester; 8 miles from Frinton.
**Opening Times: Easter weekend. Then May 1–Sept 30.** Gardens and Ancient Monuments open 10–5. Art Collection 10.30–12.30, 2.30–4.30. Adm £2, Chld 50p, OAPs £1. Parties by arrangement. Free car parking. Gardens suitable for disabled persons. Gardens overlook but do not include deer park on the estuary of the River Colne. Contact Mrs Colby tel (0255) 820242.
**Refreshments:** In village 100 yards from entrance.

## SALING HALL
**Great Saling, nr Braintree** *map L5*
*(Mr & Mrs Hugh Johnson)*

12 acre garden; wall garden dated 1698; small park with fine trees, extensive new collection of unusual plants with emphasis on trees; water gardens.

**Location:** 6 m NW of Braintree; mid-way between Braintree & Dunmow (A120); turn off N at Saling Oak Inn.
**Opening Times:** GARDEN ONLY. Weds in May, June & July 2–5. Suns May 28, and July 9, 2–6. *Parties other days by arrangement.* Adm £1, accompanied Chd free. No dogs please. *In aid of National Gardens Scheme & Village Church Fund.*

## SHALOM HALL
**Layer Breton, nr Colchester** *map L5*
*(Lady Phoebe Hillingdon)*

19th century house containing a collection of 17th and 18th century French furniture and porcelain and portraits by famous English artists including Thomas Gainsborough, Sir Joshua Reynolds etc.

**Location:** 7 m SW of Colchester; 2 m from A12.
**Opening Times:** Aug—Mon to Fri 10–1, 2.30–5.30. Adm free.

**Tilbury Fort** – See English Heritage Section.

# SIR ALFRED MUNNINGS, KCVO

**(1878–1959)**

## HOME, PAINTINGS, STUDIOS & GARDENS

## CASTLE HOUSE

**DEDHAM, ESSEX**

Exhibition of paintings, drawings, sketches and other works by this famous East Anglian artist (President of the Royal Academy 1944–1949) in the delightful setting of his home.

Open April 30 to October 1 Wednesdays, Sundays and Bank Holiday Mondays: also Thursdays and Saturdays in August: 2 to 5 pm. Admission £1.50, Children 25p, OAPs, 75p. Private parties by arrangement.

Free Car Park.

Tel. Colchester 322127.

# LAYER MARNEY TOWER

**Nr COLCHESTER, ESSEX**

*'BTA' photograph*

Lord Marney's Tudor masterpiece of 1520. The highest Tudor gatehouse in the country, flanked by 4 turrets each 8 stories. Terracotta windows and cresting to the turrets of Italian form. Excellent views of the Essex countryside and Blackwater Estuary from the tower. Adjoining church contains three effigy tombs of the Marneys and original St. Christopher wall painting.

*ADMISSION – SEE EDITORIAL REFERENCE*

*Oil painting by Julian Barrow.*

# ST. OSYTH PRIORY

**ESSEX**

*The home of Mr Somerset and the Lady Juliet de Chair.*

The Great Gate House ('unexcelled by any monastic remains in the Country' – *Country Life*) was built 20 years before Christopher Columbus sailed. Here Peacocks stroll on shady lawns, surrounded by buildings half as old as England's history.

London 65 miles, Colchester 12 miles, Frinton 8 miles.

Admission £2 Adults
£1 O.A.P.'s
50p Children

# Explore the past, enjoy the present and protect the future in Essex.

Turn to our Red Page listing at the back and find out more about the exciting range of English Heritage properties throughout the country.

Audley End House

**English Heritage**

# GLOUCESTERSHIRE

## ARLINGTON MILL
**Bibury** *map H5*
Telephone: Bibury 368
*(Mrs D. C. W. Verey)*

Large 17th century Mill. Old Mill machinery. Country Museum. Very pretty village. Arts & Crafts furniture. Changing exhibitions contemporary art, craft displays at weekends. Old breeds of farm animals, and picnic area.

**Location:** 7 m NE of Cirencester on the Cirencester to Burford Road (A433).
**Opening Times:** Mar to Oct—Daily 10.30–7 or dusk if earlier. Also open weekends in winter. Adm £1.50, OAPs £1.20, Chd 60p. Family ticket (2 adults, 2–4 Chd) £3.60. Season ticket £5. Museum shop.
**Refreshments:** Swan Hotel, Bibury.

## BARNSLEY HOUSE GARDEN
**Barnsley, nr Cirencester** *map H5* ♿
Telephone: Bibury 281
*(Mrs D. C. W. Verey)*

Garden laid out 1770, trees planted 1840. Re-planned 1960. Many spring bulbs. Laburnum avenue (early June). Lime walk, herbaceous and shrub borders. Ground cover. Knot garden. Autumn colour. Gothic summerhouse 1770. Classical temple 1780. House 1697 (not open). Vegetable garden laid out as decorative potager.

**Location:** 4 m NE of Cirencester on Cirencester to Burford Road (A433).
**Opening Times:** GARDEN ONLY. All the year—Mon–Sat 10–6 (or dusk if earlier); Adm (Mar to Nov inc) £1.50, OAPs £1. Season tickets £4. Guided Parties minimum charge £50 VAT. Dec to Feb free. Plants for sale.
**Refreshments:** Lunch and supper – The Village Pub, Barnsley. Tea – Bibury & Cirencester.

## BATSFORD ARBORETUM
**Moreton-in-Marsh** *map H5*
Telephone: Blockley (0386) 700409 or Moreton (0608) 50722.
*(The Batsford Foundation)*

Over 1000 species of different trees set in fifty acres of delightful Cotswold countryside overlooking the Vale of Evenlode, with a unique collection of exotic shrubs and bronze statues from the Orient.

**Location:** 1½ m NW of Moreton-in-Marsh on A44 to Evesham. Turn right into Park drive prior to Bourton-on-the-Hill.
*Station: Moreton-in-Marsh (2½ m).*
**Opening Times:** Garden only: Apr 1 to Oct 31—every day 10–5. Adm £1.50, Chd & OAPs 75p *(1987 rates)*. Parties by arrangement. Free parking. Garden Centre open all year round 9–5.30 (Suns 10–5).
**Refreshments:** Tea room for coffee, light lunches and teas (Apr to Oct except Mons). Picnic area.

## BERKELEY CASTLE
**nr Bristol** *map G4* △
Telephone: Dursley (0453) 810332
*(Mr & Mrs R. J. Berkeley)*

One of the most historic castles, over 800 years old, and still lived in by the Berkeleys. Scene of the murder of Edward II (1327).

**Location:** S of the town of Berkeley, midway between Bristol and Gloucester, just off A38.
**Opening Times:** Apr—Daily (exc Mons) 2–5, May to Aug—Tues to Sats 11–5, Suns 2–5; *closed Mons.* Sept—Daily (exc Mons) 2–5; Oct—Suns only 2–4.30, also Bank Hol Mons 11–5. Grounds open until 6 pm (5.30 in Oct) also Bank Hol Mons 11–5. Admission charges not available at time of going to press. *Reduced terms for pre-arranged parties of 25 or over—apply Custodian.*
**Refreshments:** Light lunches (May to Aug) and teas at Castle.

**Blackfriars** – See English Heritage Section.

## CHAVENAGE
**Tetbury** *map G4*
Telephone: Tetbury 52329
*(David Lowsley-Williams, Esq)*

Elizabethan House (1576) with Cromwellian associations. 16th and 17th century furniture and tapestries. Family Chapel and medieval barn. Personally conducted tours.

**Location:** 2 m N of Tetbury signposted off A46 B4014.
**Opening Times:** Easter Sun & Mon then May to Sept—Thurs, Suns & Bank Hols 2–5. Adm £2, Chd half-price. Parties by appointment as above and also on other dates and times.

## CHEDWORTH ROMAN VILLA, The National Trust
**Yanworth, nr Cheltenham.** *map H5* ♿
Telephone: Withington 256

The best exposed Romano-British villa in Britain. It was built about AD120 and extended and occupied until about AD400. There are good fourth century mosaics in the bath suits and triclinium (dining room). The villa was excavated in 1864, and a museum has a good range of household objects.

**Location:** 3 m NW of Fossebridge on Cirencester–Northleach road (A429).
**Opening Times:** Mar to end Oct: Tues to Sun & Bank Hol Mon 10–5.30. Last admissions 5. *Closed* Good Friday. Nov to 10 Dec: Wed to Sun 11–4. Feb: pre-booked parties only, subject to weather conditions. Adm £1.80, Chd 90p. Parties by prior written arrangement only. Disabled – all parts accessible but some with difficulty. Disabled WC.

**Hailes Abbey** – See English Heritage Section.

## HARDWICKE COURT
**nr Gloucester** *map G5*
Telephone: (0452) 720212
*(C.G.M. Lloyd-Baker)*

Late Georgian house designed by Robert Smirke, built 1816–1817. Entrance hall, drawing room, library and dining room open. Gardens under course of restoration.

**Location:** 5 m S of Gloucester on A38 (between M5 access 12 S only and 13).
**Opening Times:** Easter Mon to End Sept – Mons only 2–4. Other times by prior written appointment. Adm £1. Parking for cars only. Not suitable for disabled.

## HIDCOTE MANOR GARDEN, The National Trust
**Hidcote Bartrim, nr Chipping Campden** *map H5* ♿
Telephone: Mickleton 333

One of the most beautiful English gardens.

**Location:** 4 m NE of Chipping Campden, 1 m E of A46 off B4081.
**Opening Times:** Mar 25 to end of Oct—Daily (except Tues & Fris) 11–8 (last adm 7 or one hour before sunset) (*closed* Good Fri). Adm £2.90, (£3.20 on Sun and Bank Hol Mon) Chd £1.45. *Parties by prior written arrangement only.* No dogs. Liable to serious overcrowding on Bank Holiday Weekends and fine Sundays. Wheelchair access to part of garden only, wheelchairs provided.
**Refreshments:** Coffee, light lunches & cream teas 11–5.

## KIFTSGATE COURT
**nr Chipping Campden** *map H5*
*(Mr & Mrs J. G. Chambers)*

Garden with many unusual shrubs and plants including tree paeonies, abutilons etc, specie and old fashioned roses.

**Location:** 3 m NE of Chipping Campden 1 m E of A46 and B4081.
**Opening Times:** GARDENS ONLY. Apr 1 to Sept 30—Weds, Thurs & Suns 2–6; also Bank Hols 2–6. Adm £1.70, Chd 70p. Coaches by appointment only. *Unusual plants for sale on open days.*
**Refreshments:** Whit Sun to Sept 1.

## LITTLE DEAN HALL
**Littledean** *map G5*
*(D. E. & D. M. Macer-Wright, Esq.)*

Little Dean or correctly Dean Hall gets its name from the Dene family, Lords of Dene from 1080–1327. The oldest part of the Hall can be seen in the cellar where the remains of a sunken floored open hall of Saxon type has been identified, surviving to over mid wall height and dating from the 11th century. Present knowledge indicates Dean Hall is the oldest lived in house in England. The Jacobean front includes panelled rooms and carved chimney pieces. Civil War connections. Historical and museum displays covering over 2000 years of history. In the grounds are terraced lawns, remarkable trees some over 500 years old, water garden with ornamental fish, temple and outstanding views. The restored and reconstructed remains of the largest

# BERKELEY CASTLE GLOUCESTERSHIRE

The Castle and Gardens are open to the public: April—Daily (except Mondays) 2 to 5 pm. May to August—Weekdays (except Mondays) 11 am to 5 pm; Sundays 2 to 5 pm. September—Daily (except Mondays) 2 to 5 pm. October—Sundays only 2 to 4.30 pm. Also Bank Holiday Mondays 11am to 5 pm.

Refreshments, light lunches and afternoon teas available.
Luncheons, to order only, for parties of 20 or more persons in separate room. Free Coach and Car Park. Dogs not allowed.

*Charge for admission:* Not available at time of going to press.

For further information apply to the Custodian. Berkeley Castle, Glos. (stamped addressed envelope please). Telephone 0453 810332.

Built in 1153, the castle stands in a state of perfect preservation. This, the oldest inhabited castle in England, has everything one expects to find in such an historic building.

Here is the massive Norman Keep, Dungeon, Great Hall and Kitchen, and the cell which was the SCENE OF THE MURDER OF KING EDWARD II.

The State Apartments contain a magnificent collection of furniture, rare paintings and tapestries. Part of the world-famous Berkeley silver is also on display. The lovely Elizabethan Terraced Gardens, with an ancient bowling alley, overlook the watermeadows, the Kennels of the Berkeley Hounds and beyond, the Deer Park with its Red and Fallow Deer, Butterfly House. Picnic area adjacent to coach and car parks.

*ENGLANDS MOST FAMOUS HISTORIC HOME*

# LITTLEDEAN HALL

**GLOUCESTERSHIRE**

*© Eric Crichton Field Magazine*

Reflecting 900 years of architectural history.

*ADMISSION – SEE EDITORIAL REFERENCE*

# KIFTSGATE COURT

**MICKLETON, NR CHIPPING CAMPDEN**

*Mark Ellidge photograph*

A magnificently situated house with fine views and trees. The Garden (adjacent to Hidcote Manor National Trust Garden) was made by Mrs J. B. Muir between 1920 and 1950 and is carried on by her daughter, Mrs D. H. Binny and grand-daughter, Mrs J. G. Chambers.
There are many unusual shrubs and plants in the garden, also the original Rose Filipes Kiftsgate which we claim to be the largest rose in England. Plants from the garden for sale each open day.

**Enjoy even more of Gloucestershire.**

**Explore the English Heritage Supplement on the Red Pages.**

**English Heritage**

Roman water shrine known in Britain are unique. This is believed by Dr. Anne Ross to have been the cult shrine of Sabrina, goddess of the Severn. The panorama walk to the Old Castle of Dene provides the finest view in Gloucestershire over the famous Severn horseshoe bend.

**Location:** 12 W of Gloucester; 2 m E of Cinderford; 400 yds from A4151 on Littledean/ Newnham-on-Severn Road, turn at King's Head.
**Opening Times:** Gardens & House. Good Friday to Oct—Daily 10.30–6. Adm £2, Chd (5–16) £1. Dogs on lead. Picnic grounds.
**Refreshments:** Lunches at Littledean House Hotel.

### LYDNEY PARK
**Lydney** *map G5*
Telephone: (Office) Dean (0594 42844)
*(Viscount Bledisloe)*

Extensive Woodland Garden with lakes and a wide selection of fine shrubs and trees. Museums and Roman Temple Site. Deer Park (picnics). Country shop.

**Location:** ½ m W of Lydney on A48 (Gloucester to Chepstow).
**Opening Times:** Easter Sun and Mon; every Sun, Wed and Bank Hol from Apr 23 to June 11, but every day from Sun May 28 to Sun June 4, 11–6. Dogs on lead. **Coaches and parties** on Open Days and on other days by appointment (minimum 25). Easter to mid June; thereafter to end Sept for Temple Site and Museum only.
**Refreshments:** Teas in house (house not otherwise open).

### MISARDEN PARK GARDENS
**Miserden, Stroud** *map G5*
Telephone: Miserden 303
*(Major M T N H Wills)*

The garden has a timeless quality of a typically English Garden. A particular feature is the extensive yew topiary. To the south of the house is a wide Terrace laid with York paving. Sir Edward Lutyens Wing contains a Loggia overhung with Wisteria and on a lower terrace against the wing is a magnificent Magnolia 'Soulangeana'. On the south lawn are two flights of finely detailed grass steps. West of the main lawn are a series of terraced lawns leading to the Nurseries. To the east of these lawns is a broad grass walk lined by two substantial and very colourful herbaceous borders and beyond this is a traditional rose garden. There are many fine specimen trees throughout the garden and the bulbs in variety and blossom in the Spring are other particular features. The garden stands high overlooking the wooded 'Golden Valley'.

**Location:** Miserden 7 m from Gloucester, Cheltenham, Stroud & Cirencester; 3 m off A417 (signed).
**Opening Times:** Every Wed & Thurs from Mar 29 to Sept 28, 10–4.30. Adm £1 (includes guide), Chd (accompanied) free. Reductions for parties by appointment. Car parking provided. Suitable for disabled. No wheelchairs available. Nurseries adjacent to garden open daily (except Mons) throughout the year.
**Refreshments:** Carpenters Arms in village serves good meals.

### NEWARK PARK, The National Trust
**Wotton under Edge** *map G4*
Telephone: Dursley 842644

Elizabethan Hunting Lodge built on cliff edge, modified in 1790's by James Wyatt and rehabilitated by present tenant. Woodland garden.

**Location:** 1½ m E of Wotton under Edge, 1½ m S of junction of A4135 and B4058.
**Opening Times:** Apr, May, Aug & Sept; Weds & Thurs 2–5. Adm £1, Chd 50p. Parties by prior written arrangement only. No reductions. Not suitable for coaches or wheelchairs. No dogs.

### PAINSWICK ROCOCO GARDEN
**Painswick** *map G5*
Telephone: Painswick 813204
*(Lord & Lady Dickinson)*

This beautiful six acre garden, set in a hidden combe, is a rare and complete survivor of the brief eighteenth century taste for the Rococo in garden design.

**Location:** ½ m from Painswick on B4073.
**Opening Times:** GARDEN ONLY: **Snowdrops Feb 1 to Feb 28, Wed to Suns.** Easter Fri to Mon; May to Sept—Weds to Suns incl, Bank Hols 11–5. Groups: (minimum 15) by arrangement all the year. Dogs on leads. Adm £1.50, Chd 75p.
**Refreshments:** In licensed restaurant, morning coffees and home made light lunches and afternoon teas. Present Collection shop.

### RODMARTON MANOR GARDEN
**Cirencester** *map G4*
Telephone: (028584) 219
*(Mrs Anthony Biddulph)*

Cotswold House (not open except chapel), designed by Earnest Barnsley. Featured in Country Life, RHS Journal, Stately Gardens of Britain, The English Garden in Over Time (Brown), and English Gardens (Peter Coats). English Topiary Gardens – Ethne Clarke. Vita Sackville West admired its long, cool facade looking over an enchanting garden. Terrace and leisure garden. Herbaceous borders – long vistas. Hornbeam avenue. Beech, Holly and Yew hedges. Topiary. Many 'rooms'. A series of gardens, many enclosed with hedges. A present day garden in keeping with the traditional house, and with many weed suppressing plantings such as hostas, potentillas, and lavender planted in paving.

**Location:** 6½ m Cirencester, 20 m M4 via Cricklade by-pass. 4 m Tetbury.
**Opening Times:** Open daily every Thurs from 2–5, Mar 1 to Aug 31. For further open days which have not yet been decided, please see the NGS 'Yellow Book'. Adm £1. No special reductions. Car park. Suitable for disabled persons (wheelchairs not available).
**Refreshments:** Teas can be provided if booked in advance.

### RYELANDS HOUSE
**Taynton** *map G5*
*(Captain & Mrs Eldred Wilson)*

Fascinating sunken garden of 1½ acres with great variety of plants, many rare and unusual, in beautiful unspoilt country setting. Country walk to see abundance of wild flowers and spectacular views; landscaped lake in woodlands.

**Location:** 8 m NW of Gloucester; on B4216 halfway between Huntley (A40) & Newent (B4215).
**Opening Times:** Suns, Apr 2, 9, 16, 23, 30; Mon May 1; Suns June 11, 18, 25; July 16, 23, Sun Aug 27, Mon Aug 28. Adm £1.25. All dates 2–6. Parties by appointment. In aid of National Gardens Scheme. Dogs welcome on walk. Plants for sale.
**Refreshments:** Home made teas Suns and Bank Hol Mons.

### SEZINCOTE
**Moreton-in-Marsh** *map H5*
*(Mr & Mrs D. Peake)*

Oriental water garden by Repton and Daniell with trees of unusual size. House in 'Indian' style inspiration of Royal Pavilion, Brighton.

**Location:** 1½ m W of Moreton-in-Marsh on A44 to Evesham; turn left by lodge before Bourton-on-the-Hill.
**Opening Times:** GARDEN. Thurs, Fris & Bank Hol Mons 2–6 (or dusk if earlier) throughout year, except Dec. Adm £1.60, Chd 50p. No dogs. HOUSE May, June, July & Sept, Thurs & Fris 2.30–6. Parties by appointment. Adm House & Garden £2.75.
**Refreshments:** Hotels & restaurant in Moreton-in-Marsh.

# The National Trust in GLOUCESTERSHIRE

## SNOWSHILL MANOR
**nr. Broadway**

## CHEDWORTH ROMAN VILLA
**nr. Cheltenham**

## WESTBURY COURT GARDEN
**Westbury-on-Severn**

## HIDCOTE MANOR GARDEN
**nr. Chipping Campden**

## NEWARK PARK
**Wotton under Edge**

## LYDNEY PARK GARDENS

**GLOUCESTERSHIRE**

Extensive Rhododendron, Azalea and Flowering Shrub Gardens in Lakeland Valley. Museum and famous Roman Site. Fine views across the Severn. Teas and Picnics.

*ADMISSION – SEE EDITORIAL REFERENCE*

## STANWAY HOUSE

**GLOUCESTERSHIRE**

This jewel of Cotswold Manor houses is very much a home rather than a museum and the centre of a working landed estate which has changed hands once in 1272 years. The mellow Jacobean architecture, the typical squire's family portraits, the exquisite Gatehouse, the old Brewery, mediaeval Tithe Barn, the extensive gardens, arboretum pleasure grounds and formal landscape contribute to the timeless charm of what Arthur Negus considered one of the most beautiful and romantic houses in England.

### SNOWSHILL MANOR, The National Trust
**nr Broadway** *map H5* ♿
Telephone: Broadway 852410

A Tudor house with c1700 facade; 21 rooms containing interesting collection of craftsmanship, including musical instruments, clocks, toys, bicycles and Japanese armour, with small formal garden.

**Location:** 3 m SW of Broadway, 4 m W of junction A44 & A424.
**Opening Times:** Easter Sat to Mon 11–1, 2–6. Apr & Oct: Sat & Sun 11–1, 2–5. May to end Sept: Wed to Sun & Bank Hol Mon 11–1, 2–6. Last admissions to house ½ hour before closing. *Closed Good Friday.* Adm £2.80, Chd £1.40. Parties by prior written arrangement only. No dogs. Liable to serious overcrowding on Bank Holiday weekends. Disabled – limited access to house (ground floor) and part of garden.

### STANWAY HOUSE
**nr Broadway** *map H5*
Telephone: Stanton 469
*(Lord Neidpath)*

**Location:** 1 m off A46 Cheltenham/Broadway road; on B4077 Toddington/Stow-on-the-Wold road; M5 junction 9.
**Opening Times:** June, July and Aug—Tues and Thurs 2–5. Adm £1.75, OAPs £1.50, Chd 75p.
**Refreshments:** Teas in Old Bakehouse in village (Stanton 204).

### SUDELEY CASTLE
**Winchcombe** *map G5* △
Telephone: Cheltenham (0242) 602308
*(The Lady Ashcombe)*

Beautiful 12th century home of Queen Katherine Parr, rich in Tudor history. Art treasures include Constable, Rubens and Van Dyck. Lovely gardens with historic Elizabethan garden as main highlight. Falconry exhibition with Flying Displays each Tues, Wed and Thurs from May to Aug (see inside back cover). Traditional Craft Exhibition, incorporating craftsmen at work.

**Location:** 6 m NE of Cheltenham on A46. Access A40, A438, M5 (at Tewkesbury turn off).
**Opening Times:** Apr to Oct—Daily (inc Bank Hols) 12–5. Grounds open from 11. All inclusive adm £3.25, Chd £1.75. Special rates for OAPs and parties. Ample free car parking. (Guides in major rooms. Guided tours available in Apr, Sept & Oct by prior arrangement.) Educational material relating to Civil War and the Tudors, available for school parties on request. *Closed Nov–Mar inclusive.*
**Refreshments:** The Old Kitchen Restaurant is open daily from 11–5 for coffees, buffet lunches and afternoon teas.

### WESTBURY COURT GARDEN, The National Trust
**Westbury-on-Severn** *map G5* ♿
Telephone: Westbury-on-Severn 461

A formal Dutch water-garden with canals and yew hedges, laid out between 1696 and 1705; the earliest of its kind remaining in England.

**Location:** 9 m SW of Gloucester on A48.
**Opening Times:** Mar 25 to Oct (*closed* Good Fri)—Weds to Suns & Bank Hol Mons 11–6. Adm £1.20, Chd 60p. Parties by prior written arrangement only. Picnic area. No dogs. Wheelchairs provided.

### WHITTINGTON COURT
**Whittington, nr Cheltenham Gl54 4HF** *map G5*
Telephone: (0242) 820218.
*(Mrs R. J. Charleston)*

Small Elizabethan stone-built manor house with family possessions.

**Location:** 4½ m E of Cheltenham on A40.
**Opening Times:** Mar 25 to Apr 9: Aug 14 to 28. Daily 2–5. Adm £1.50, OAPs £1, Chd 50p. Open to parties by arrangement.

## GREATER MANCHESTER

### FLETCHER MOSS MUSEUM AND ART GALLERY
**Didsbury** *map G8*
Telephone: 061-236 9422 enquiries
*(Manchester City Art Galleries)*

A late Georgian and early Victorian parsonage set in pleasant gardens. A local heritage centre displaying works by artists related to the North West.

**Location:** 5 m S of City centre on main Wilmslow Road.
**Opening Times:** Open Apr to Sept. Please telephone to check times before visit. Adm free.

### HALL I' TH' WOOD
**Bolton** *map G9*
Telephone: Bolton (0204) 51159
*(Bolton Metropolitan Borough)*

Dating from latter half of the 15th century and furnished throughout in the appropriate period. The Hall, built in the post and plaster style, dates from 1483, a further extension was added in 1591, the last addition being made in 1648. Home of Samuel Crompton in 1779 when he invented the Spinning Mule. House contains Crompton relics.

**Location:** In Green Way, off Crompton Way; 2 m NE of town centre off A58 (Crompton Way); signposted. Hall i' th' Wood (½ m).
*Station: Bolton (2½ m); Bromley Cross (1¼ m). Hall i' th' Wood (½ m).*
**Opening Times:** Apr to Sept: Tues to Sat 11–5; Sun 2–5. *Closed* Mons except Bank Holidays. Oct to Mar: *Closed* to general public. Open to pre-booked parties and evening party tours.

### HEATON HALL
**Heaton Park, Prestwich** *map G8*
Telephone: 061-236 9422 enquiries
*(Manchester City Art Galleries)*

Former home of the Earls of Wilton and designed by James Wyatt in 1772 the Hall has a unique decorated interior. Described by Pevsner as one of the finest country houses of its period in the country.

**Location:** 6 m N of City centre.
*Station: Heaton Park (½ m).*
**Opening Times:** Open Apr to Sept, including Bank Holidays. Please telephone to check times before visit. Adm free.

### PLATT HALL
**Platt Fields, Rusholme** *map G8*
Telephone: 061-224 5217
*(Manchester City Art Galleries)*

A Georgian country house of the 1760's, designed by John Carr of York and Timothy Lightoler for the Worsleys, it is now the internationally famous Gallery of English Costume, showing the changing styles in clothes and accessories from the 17th century to the present day.

**Location:** In Platt Fields, Rusholme 2 m S of City on Wilmslow Road.
*Station: Levenshulme.*
**Opening Times:** Open all year. Please telephone to check times before visit. Adm free.
**Refreshments:** Teas in the park.

### SMITHILLS HALL
**Bolton** *map G8*
Telephone: Bolton (0204) 41265
*(Bolton Metropolitan Borough)*

Dating from the 14th century with later additions. Great Hall with open roof. Fine linenfold panelling. 16th and 17th century furnishings. Grounds contain nature trail and trailside museum.

**Location:** Off Smithills Dean Road; 1½ m NW of town centre off A58 (Moss Bank Way); signposted.
*Station: Bolton.*
**Opening Times:** Apr to Sept: Tues to Sat 11–5, Sun 2–5. *Closed* Mons except Bank Holidays. Oct to Mar: *Closed* to general public. Open to pre-booked educational parties and to evening party tours.

### WYTHENSHAWE HALL
**Northenden** *map G8*
Telephone: 061-236 9422
*(Manchester City Art Galleries)*

A timber framed country house which was the home of the Tatton family for over 500 years. 17th century furniture, oil paintings and rare, recently discovered Tudor wall paintings.

**Location:** 7 m S of City centre in Wythenshawe Park, on the Altrincham/Stockport Road.
**Opening Times:** Open Apr to Sept. Please telephone to check times before visit. Adm free.
**Refreshments:** Teas at the Hall.

## HAMPSHIRE

### ALRESFORD HOUSE
**Alresford** *map J3*
Telephone: (096 273) 2843
*(Mr & Mrs P Constable Maxwell)*

Georgian country house built by Admiral Lord Rodney 1750.

**Location:** 8 m E of Winchester off A31 Winchester/Alton Road.
**Opening Times:** All Aug, parties at other times by arrangement, Wed to Sun 2.30–6. Adm £1.50. Fruit & vegetables—'Pick Your Own' throughout the summer. Catering facilities available for parties, receptions, etc by arrangement.
**Refreshments:** Teas in walled garden throughout August.

## HALL I'TH' WOOD MUSEUM

**Greenway, off Crompton Way, Bolton**

Dating from the latter half of the 15th century and furnished throughout in the appropriate period. The Hall itself, built in the post and plaster styles, dates from 1483, a further extension was added in 1591 in the form of a north west wing, the last addition being made in 1648 during the Civil War. Home of Samuel Crompton in 1779 when he invented the Spinning Mule. House contains Crompton relics.

## SMITHILLS HALL MUSEUM

**off Smithills Dean Road, Bolton**

One of the oldest manor houses in Lancashire, a house has stood on this site since the 14th century. The oldest part of Smithills, the Great Hall, has an open timber roof. Smithills has grown piece by piece over the centuries and such irregularly planned buildings, with the cluster of gables at the west end, gives the hall its present day picturesque effect. Furnished in the styles of the 16th and 17th centuries. Withdrawing room contains linenfold panelling. Grounds contain a nature trail and trailside museum which is open to the public between Easter and October.

## CITY OF MANCHESTER HEATON HALL

'The finest house of its period in Lancashire and one of the finest in the country' (Pevsner). Designed for the Earl of Wilton by James Wyatt in 1772, the house has sumptuous decorated interiors and commands panoramic views of Manchester. Heaton Hall was Wyatt's first country house commission and a principal example of his classical style. Contents include a range of magnificent state rooms with plasterwork by J. B. Maini, one of the few surviving Etruscan rooms with decorations by Biagio Rebecca, library with fittings by Gillows of Lancaster, an organ built by Samuel Green (1790), furniture, paintings and sculpture of the period.

Open April – September, including Bank Holidays. Please telephone before visit for latest information on opening times, 061-236 9422. Admission free.

## AVINGTON PARK

**WINCHESTER**

Red brick house in the Wren tradition with facilities available for filming or still photography.
The Library is also available for Wedding Receptions, Conferences etc.
Enquiries to the Secretary, Avington Park, Winchester, Hants. Tel.: Itchen Abbas (0962 78) 202.

*ADMISSION–SEE EDITORIAL REFERENCE*

### AVINGTON PARK
**Winchester** *map H3* △
Telephone: 0962-78 202
*(Mr and Mrs J B Hickson)*

William Cobbett wrote of Avington that it was 'one of the prettiest places in the County' and indeed it is true today. Avington Park, where Charles II and George IV both stayed at various times, is an old house enlarged in 1670 by the addition of two wings and a classical Portico surmounted by three Statues. The State Rooms on view include the Ballroom with its magnificent ceiling, the Red Drawing Room, Library etc. Avington Church, one of the most perfect Georgian Churches in Hampshire, is in the grounds close by and may be visited.
The facilities are available for filming or still photography.
The Library is also available for Wedding Receptions, Conferences etc.

**Location:** 4 m NE of Winchester, just S of B3047 in Itchen Abbas.
**Opening Times:** May to Sept—Sats, Suns & Bank Hols 2.30–5.30 (last tour begins 5). *Occasionally closed Sats or Suns for wedding receptions.* Adm £1.50, Chd (under 10) 75p. *Other times for large parties by prior arrangement.*
**Refreshments:** Tea at the House *(Suns & Bank Hols only).*

### BEAULIEU
**Beaulieu** *map H3* Ⓢ
Telephone: Beaulieu (0590) 612345
*(The Lord Montagu of Beaulieu)*

Palace House and Gardens; Beaulieu Abbey and Exhibition of Monastic Life; The National Motor Museum featuring more than 200 exhibits including motor cars, commercial vehicles and motorcycles; 'Wheels' – a fantastic ride on 'space age' pods through 100 years of motoring from 1895 to the present day. Monorail, veteran bus and miniature veteran car rides, 'Transporama' – an audio-visual presentation of the history of motoring; model railway, radio-controlled cars, mini racing car and motorcycle rides. Daily cavalcades of historic vehicles during peak summer season and many other events throughout the year.

**Location:** In Beaulieu 7 m SE of Lyndhurst; 14 m S of Southampton; 6 m NE of Lymington.
**Opening Times:** All facilities open throughout the year. May to Sept—Daily 10–6; Oct to May—Daily 10–5. *Closed Christmas Day.* Inclusive adm charge. Reduced rates for Children & OAPs. *Parties at special rates.*
**Refreshments:** Lunches and teas at licensed Brabazon Restaurant.

### BISHOP'S WALTHAM PALACE
*map J3*
Telephone: (048 93) 2460
*(English Heritage)*

The Bishops of Winchester held Waltham since Saxon times, but they did not build here until about 1135. Heavily fortified, this was more castle than palace, and was dismantled by Henry II. Most of the present remains are from the spacious 15th century palace with its walled garden, all within this vast moated site. Forfeited by the bishops at the Reformation, the palace was reduced to a ruin in the Civil War, when it was held for the King against Parliament.

**Location:** Bishop's Waltham. OS map ref SU552173.
**Opening Times:** Good Friday to Sept 30, daily 10–6; Oct 1 to Maundy Thurs, daily 10–4. *Closed* Mons, Dec 24–26, Jan 1. *Closed* all day Mon & Tues am in winter. Adm £1.10, OAPs 80p, Chd 55p.

### BRAMDEAN HOUSE
**Bramdean, nr Alresford** *map J3*
Telephone: 096 279 214
*(Mrs H. Wakefield)*

Carpets of Spring bulbs. Walled garden with famous herbaceous borders, working kitchen garden and large collection of unusual plants.

**Location:** Bramdean. On A272 midway between Winchester & Petersfield.
**Opening Times:** Suns Mar 26, Apr 16, May 21, July 16, Aug 20, Mon Mar 27 2–5. Adm £1, Chd free. Car park. Not suitable for disabled.

### BREAMORE HOUSE
**nr Fordingbridge** *map H3* △
Telephone: Downton (0725) 22468
*(Sir Westrow Hulse, Bt)*

Elizabethan Manor House (1583) with fine collection of paintings, tapestries, furniture. Countryside Museum. Carriage Museum.

**Location:** 3 m N of Fordingbridge off the main Bournemouth Road (A338) 8 m S of Salisbury.
**Opening Times:** Mar 25, 26, 27; Apr—Tues, Weds, Suns; May, June, July & Sept—Tues, Weds, Thurs, Sats, Suns and all Bank Hols; Aug—Daily, 2–5.30. Adm: Combined ticket £3, Chd £1.50. Reduced rates for parties & OAPs. *Other times by appointment.*
**Refreshments:** Home-made Teas. Food available. Bat and Ball, Breamore.

### BROADLANDS
**Romsey** *map H3*
Telephone: Romsey (0794) 516878
*(Lord and Lady Romsey)*

Famous in recent times as the home of Lord Mountbatten, Broadlands was also the country residence of Lord Palmerston, the great Victorian Prime Minister. Fine example of Palladian architecture set in Capability Brown parkland by the banks of the River Test. Visitors may view interior of house containing many fine works of art including "The Iron Forge" by Joseph Wright of Derby, several Van Dycks and furniture by Ince and Mayhew. Visitors may also relive Lord Mountbatten's life and times in the Mountbatten Exhibition and audio-visual display housed in William and Mary stable block.

**Location:** 8 m N of Southampton (A3057); entrance from by-pass immediately S of Romsey (A31).
*Station: Romsey (1 m).*
**Opening Times:** Mar 23 to Oct 1. Daily 10–4. *Closed* Mons, except Bank Hols, until Aug. Adm £3.95, Chd 12–16 £2.25, Chd under 12 accompanied by parent/guardian free, OAPs £2.95. Disabled £2.95, Students £2.95. Reduced rates for parties of 15 or more. Free coach and car park.
**Refreshments:** Self-service restaurant. Kiosk in picnic area.

**Calshot Castle** – See English Heritage Section.

### EXBURY GARDENS
**nr Southampton** *map H3*
*(E L de Rothschild, Esq)*

Unique 200 acre woodland garden created by Lionel de Rothschild, with a superb display of Rhododendrons, Azaleas, Camellias, Magnolias, other fascinating flora and new plantings. Well stocked Plant Centre and Gift Shop, artist's studio, licensed tea rooms.

**Location:** Exbury village, 15 m SW of Southampton close to New Forest. Turn S off B3054 between Beaulieu & Dibden Purlieu.
**Opening Times:** Daily Mar 18 to July 9, 10–5.30. Adm; early and late season discounts – please telephone. **Spring:** main flowering season £2.20, OAPs, Parties & Chd (12–15) £1.70; Bank Hol weekends and May weekends all charges 50p more. **Autumn:** Sept 9 to Oct 22. Adm OAPs £1, all others £1.50. **Plant Centre:** Daily Feb 25 to Dec 21. 10–5.30 or dusk if earlier.
**Refreshments:** Tearooms. Ample parking. Toilets.

**Fort Brockhurst** – See English Heritage Section.

## FURZEY GARDENS

**Minstead, nr Lyndhurst** *map H3* ♿
Telephone: Southampton (0703) 812464

Lovely gardens in nearly eight acres of peaceful glades. There are many main attractions including Heathers throughout the year and Azaleas, Rhododendrons, Bluebells, Peonies and Irises in season, plus many other attractive plants to extend the beauty.

**Location:** Southampton 10 m, Ringwood 8 m, Lyndhurst 3½ m.
**Opening Times:** All the year—Daily 10–5. *Closes at dusk in winter.* Adm Mar–Oct £1.75, Chd (5-14 years) 90p; Nov–Feb £1, Chd (5-14 years) 50p.
**Refreshments:** Trusty Servant; Honeysuckle Restaurant.

## GREATHAM MILL

**Greatham, nr Liss** *map J3*
Telephone: Blackmoor 219
*(Mrs Frances Pumphrey)*

Attractive garden of 1½ acres bordered by small river and intersected by Mill waterways. Many unusual plants. Also nursery garden with plants for sale.

**Location:** 5 m from Petersfield. Take A325 towards Farnham and turn L to B3006. After 500 yds fork L into NTR lane to garden.
**Opening Times:** Suns & Bank Hols Apr 16 to Sept 24, 2–7. Adm £1, Chd free. Parties by arrangement on weekdays. Ample car parking space on grass. Coaches must disembark and park at lane head, 200 yds from garden. Not suitable for disabled persons. On Suns and Bank Hols follow yellow signs from Greatham.
**Refreshments:** None at garden, Queens Hotel and Teashop in Selborne, 2½ miles.

## THE HAWK CONSERVANCY

**Weyhill** *map H4*
Telephone: Weyhill 2252
*(R., H. and A. Smith)*

The Hawk Conservancy is a specialist centre for birds of prey from all over the world, created in a wild garden setting on the edge of Salisbury plain. Using traditional methods to train our birds, Hawks, Falcons, Eagles and Owls are flown daily at 12 noon, 2, 3, and 4 (weather permitting), and this really is a unique opportunity to appreciate the beauty and splendour of the birds in flight. At these demonstration times you will have the chance to hold a Bird of Prey and to take photographs.

**Location:** 4 miles west of Andover, just off the A303.
**Opening Times:** Open daily from Mar 1 to last Sun in Oct 10.30–last adm 4 (Spring and Autumn) 5 (Summer). Adm not available at time of going to press. Reduction for pre-booked parties of 20 and over. Large free car park. Suitable for disabled persons but no toilets for disabled.
**Refreshments:** Cafe offering a wide variety of snacks and hot and cold meals.

## HIGHCLERE CASTLE

**nr Newbury RG15 9RN** *map H4*
Telephone: (0635) 253210
*(The Earl of Carnarvon KCVO, KBE)*

Highclere Castle is the ultimate in high Victorian exuberance. Designed by Charles Barry in the 1830s at the same time as he was building the Houses of Parliament, this soaring pinnacled mansion provided the perfect social setting for the 3rd Earl of Carnarvon, one of the great hosts of Queen Victoria's reign. Several prominent Victorian architects, including Barry, George Gilbert Scott and Thomas Allom, are responsible for the extravagant interiors in styles which range from church Gothic through Moorish flamboyance and rococo revival to the solid masculinity in the long library. Old master paintings mix with portraits by Van Dyck and 18th Century painters. Napoleon's desk and chair rescued from St. Helena sits with other 18th and 19th Century furniture.
The 5th Earl of Carnarvon, passionate archaeologist and Egyptologist, was the discoverer of the tomb of Tutankhamun and a special display shows some of his early finds in Egypt which had laid hidden for over 60 years and have only recently been rediscovered.
GARDENS – The parkland with its massive cedars was designed by Capability Brown. The walled gardens also date from the earlier house at Highclere but the dark yew walks are entirely Victorian in character. The glass Orangery and Fernery add an exotic flavour and an impression of the complexity of the gardens at their peak. Walking through to the Secret Garden, the walled walks unexpectedly open up into a curving, densely planted herbaceous garden laid out in this Century with ornamental trees and flowering plants and shrubs.

**Location:** 4½ m S of Newbury on A34, junction 13 of M4 about 2 m from Newbury. M3. Basingstoke junction about 15 m. Heathrow via M4 1 hour. Rail from London (Paddington station) 1 hour. Taxi W. Martin (0635) 253561 from Newbury.
**Opening Times:** Sun July 2 – Sun Oct 1 1989, 2–6 (last entry 5). Adm £3, OAP/Chd (under 16) £2. Special reductions for parties of 50 or more by application. Car park and picnic area adjacent to Castle. Suitable for disabled persons on ground floor only. One wheelchair available. Visitors can buy original items in Castle Gift Shop and visit the Plant Centre only a short distance away in the Park.
**Refreshments:** Traditional country cream teas, ices, soft drinks, etc.

## THE HILLIER GARDENS AND ARBORETUM

**Ampfield, nr Romsey** *map H3*
*(Hampshire County Council)*

Begun by the famous nurseryman Sir Harold Hillier in 1953, and gifted to Hampshire County Council in 1977, the Gardens and Arboretum now extend to some 160 acres and contain the largest collection of different hardy plants in the British Isles. With this diversity in plants, the Gardens provide something of interest throughout the seasons, from the magnificent floral displays in the spring, followed by the pastel shades of summer which become overwhelmed by the riot of autumnal hues in October to the highly scented winter flowering Witch Hazels.

**Location:** 3 m north east of Romsey, off A31.
**Opening Times:** Mon to Fri 10–5 (all year round). Sats, Suns and Bank Hols 1–6 (Mar to mid Nov). Adm £1.50, Chd (under 16 years) Free on weekdays, 50p at weekends and Bank Holidays. Groups over 30 £1.20. Regret NO DOGS.
**Refreshments:** Attractive picnic area.

## HINTON AMPNER, The National Trust

**nr Alresford** *map J3* ♿

The house was remodelled in the Georgian style in 1934 by Ralph Dutton but decimated by fire in 1960. Rebuilt and re-furnished with fine regency furniture, pictures and porcelain. The gardens juxtapose formality of design and informality of planting, producing delightful walks and unexpected vistas.

**Location:** 1 m W of Bramdean Village on A272; 8 m E of Winchester.

# The National Trust in HAMPSHIRE

## THE VYNE
**SHERBORNE ST JOHN**

## HINTON AMPNER
**Nr ALRESFORD**

## MOTTISFONT ABBEY
**Nr ROMSEY**

*ADMISSION – SEE EDITORIAL REFERENCE*

## THE HAWK CONSERVANCY
**Nr. ANDOVER**

The Hawk Conservancy is a specialist centre for birds of prey from all over the world, created in a wild garden setting on the edge of Salisbury Plain. Using traditional methods to train our birds, Hawks, Falcons, Eagles and Owls are flown daily at 12 noon, 2pm, 3pm and 4pm (weather permitting), and this really is a unique opportunity to appreciate the beauty and splendour of the birds in flight. At these demonstration times you will have the chance to hold a Bird of Prey and to take photographs.

*ADMISSION – SEE EDITORIAL REFERENCE*

## THE OATES MEMORIAL LIBRARY AND MUSEUM AND GILBERT WHITE MUSEUM
**SELBORNE, ALTON, HAMPSHIRE**

The Wakes, home of The Rev. Gilbert White, author of The Natural History of Selborne

- Historic house and 5-acre garden
- Gilbert White Museum
- Oates Memorial Museum

Come and enjoy a day out in Selborne

**Opening Times:** Mar 24 to end Sept. Garden: Wed to Sun 1.30–5.30. House: Wed only 1.30–5.30 (last adm 5). Admission: Garden £1.30, House £1 extra. Children half-price. No dogs. Most of garden accessible by wheelchair. Party reductions (£1.50 House & Garden) Wed only by prior booking with Southern Region Office, Polesden Lacey, Dorking, Surrey. (Tel: Dorking (0372) 53401.)
**Refreshments:** Teas.

## HOUGHTON LODGE
**Stockbridge** *map H3* ♿
*(Captain & Mrs M W Busk)*

Starred Grade II in the Register of Parks and Gardens of Special Historic Interest in England. From the terrace of this 18th century 'cottage orne' the lawns lead down to the River Test with fine views over the unspoilt valley. Rare chalkcob walls surround the Kitchen Garden. Extensive greenhouses and vinery. Over 100 varieties of fuchsia. 18th century Folly.

**Location:** 1½ m S of A30 at Stockbridge on minor road to Houghton village.
**Opening Times:** GARDEN ONLY. Mar to Aug inclusive—Weds & Thurs, Easter Sun & Mon and Bank Hols in May, and Sun Sept 3 2–5 or by appointment. Adm £1, Chd 50p. *No dogs.* Plants & produce for sale every weekday.

**Hurst Castle** – See English Heritage Section.

## JANE AUSTEN'S HOUSE
**Chawton** *map J3*
*(Jane Austen Memorial Trust)*

Jane Austen's home with many interesting personal relics of herself and her family.

**Location:** 1 m SW of Alton off A31 and B3006, sign post Chawton.
*Station: Alton (1¾ m).*
**Opening Times:** Daily Apr–Oct; Nov, Dec & Mar: Weds to Suns. Jan & Feb: Sats & Suns only, 11–4.30. *Closed Christmas Day & Boxing Day.* Adm £1, Chd (under 14) 50p.

## JENKYN PLACE
**Bentley** *map J3*
*(Mr & Mrs G E Coke)*

Beautifully designed garden with large collection of rare plants, roses, double herbaceous borders.

**Location:** In Bentley 400 yds N of cross roads (sign to Crondall). Signposted on A31.
*Station: Bentley (1 m).*
**Opening Times:** GARDEN ONLY. Apr 13 to Sept 10—Thurs, Fris, Sats, Suns & Bank Hol Mons 2–6. Coaches only by prior arrangement. Adm £1.50, Chd (5–15) half price. Open on certain Suns in aid of the National Gardens Scheme. No dogs. Car park free.

## MACPENNY'S
**Bransgore, nr Christchurch** *map H3*
Telephone: Bransgore (0425) 72348
*(Tim Lowndes, Esq)*

Large woodland garden. Nurseries, camellias, rhododendrons, azaleas, heathers.

**Location:** 4 m NE of Christchurch; 1½ m W of A35.
**Opening Times:** Garden and nurseries open all year daily (except Christmas Hols). Mons to Sats 9–5; Suns 2–5. *Collecting box in aid of National Gardens Scheme.*

**Medieval Wine Merchants House** – See English Heritage Section.

## MOTTISFONT ABBEY, The National Trust
**Mottisfont** *map H3* △ ♿
Telephone: Lockerley 40757

Originally a 12th century Augustinian Priory. South front 18th century. Drawing room by Rex Whistler. Fine lawns and trees. Walled garden with Trust's collection of old fashioned roses.

**Location:** 4½ m NW Romsey ¾ m W of A3057.
*Station: Dunbridge (¾ m).*
**Opening Times:** Apr to end Sept: GROUNDS (including Rose Garden) daily except Fri and Sat, 2–6 (last adm 5); ROSE GARDEN only also open 7–9 Tues, Wed, Thurs and Sun during rose season (check with property before making special visit) (last adm 8.30). HOUSE: (Whistler Room and Cellarium only) Weds 2–6. Adm: Grounds £1.50; Chd half-price. Whistler Room & Cellarium 40p extra, Chd half-price; no reduction for parties. Owing to difficulties with opening arrangements, it is not always possible to view rooms in the house (please check in advance). Visits to the house are by guided parties. Numbers are restricted and access may not be possible for all at peak times. Timed tickets should be obtained at entrance kiosk on arrival. Shop. Dogs in car park only. Wheelchairs—grounds and cellarium only. Special parking area for disabled people, please ask at kiosk on arrival.

**Netley Abbey** – See English Heritage Section.

## OATES MEMORIAL LIBRARY AND MUSEUM AND THE GILBERT WHITE MUSEUM
**Selborne** *map J3*
Telephone: Selborne 275
*(Rev Gilbert White, 1720–1793)*

'The Wakes', home of the Rev Gilbert White, pioneer English naturalist and author of *The Natural History of Selborne*, a classic published nearly 200 years ago and still in print. Historic house, two furnished rooms and museum displays on Gilbert White and Selborne, together with 5 acres of historic garden, the subject of White's *Garden Kalendar.* Also including The Oates Memorial Museum with exhibitions on Frank Oates, 19th century explorer and naturalist in southern Africa and Capt Lawrence Oates of Antarctic fame.

**Location:** In Selborne.
**Opening Times:** Mar 23 to Oct 30, Wed to Sun 11–5.30. (Last adm 5). *Closed* Nov to Feb, also Mon & Tues, except Bank Holidays. Parties by arrangement. Adm £1, Chd (under 16) 50p, OAPs 75p (1988 rates). Special rates for parties booked in advance. Parking nearby.
**Refreshments:** available nearby.

## THE PILGRIMS' HALL
**Winchester** *map H3*
*(The Dean & Chapter, Winchester Cathedral)*

Late 13th century hall with fine hammer-beam roof.

**Location:** In the Cathedral Close.
*Station: Winchester (5 mins walk).*
**Opening Times:** All the year—Daily (except when booked for private meetings, functions, etc). *Parties must give notice in advance.* Adm free.

**Portchester Castle** – See English Heritage Section.

## SANDHAM MEMORIAL CHAPEL, The National Trust
**Burghclere, nr Newbury** *map H4* ♿
Telephone: Burghclere 394 or 292

Walls covered with paintings by Stanley Spencer depicting war scenes in Salonica.

**Location:** In village of Burghclere 4 m S of Newbury ½ m E of A34.
**Opening Times:** All the year—Daily 11–6 (or dusk if earlier). Open Good Friday, but closed Christmas Day & New Year's Day. Adm 70p, Chd half-price. Parties must book. No reduction for parties. No dogs. Wheelchair access.

## SPINNERS
**Boldre** *map H3*
Telephone: Lymington 73347
*(Mr & Mrs P G G Chappell)*

Garden entirely made by owners; azaleas, rhododendrons interplanted with primulas, blue poppies and other choice woodland and ground cover plants.

**Location:** 1½ m N of Lymington.
*Station: Lymington Town (2 m).*
**Opening Times:** GARDEN ONLY. Apr 22 to Sept 1—Daily 10–6. Other times by appointment. Large nursery for choice and rare plants open all the year. Adm 75p. *For National Gardens Scheme on certain days. No dogs.* Many rare plants for sale.

## HIGHCLERE CASTLE

Home of the Earl and Countess of Carnarvon,
Victorian splendour at its very best.
Created by Sir Charles Barry, builder of the Houses of Parliament, with grounds by Capability Brown.
Stunning interiors include Napoleon's chair, collections of old masters and finds from ancient Egypt, and a unique chance to see how life was lived below stairs.

Open each week
**Wednesday to Sunday** inclusive
from 2pm to 6pm
July 2nd to October 1st
(including August Bank Holiday Monday)
Admission £3
Children under 16/OAP's £2

**4 miles south of Newbury, off the A34 road to Winchester**
**Well signed**

Visitor enquiries
Telephone: 0635 253210

Country Teas

Garden centre/Picnic area

# JENKYN PLACE GARDEN

**Bentley, Hants**

*ADMISSION – SEE EDITORIAL REFERENCE*

# JANE AUSTEN'S HOUSE

**CHAWTON, near Alton, Hants.**

Jane Austen's home in Chawton, near Alton, contains many interesting personal relics of the famous authoress. It was the scene of the composition of "Mansfield Park", "Emma" and "Persuasion": and of the revision of "Sense and Sensibility", "Pride and Prejudice" and "Northanger Abbey".
The house is one mile from Alton. Open daily April to October: November, December and March Wednesday to Sunday: January and February Saturday and Sunday only. Closed Christmas Day and Boxing day. Hours of opening 11am to 4.30pm.
Entrance fee £1 Adults and 50p for Children under 14.

# STRATFIELD SAYE HOUSE

**A personal insight into the private life of the first Duke of Wellington**

THE HOUSE
Rebuilt in the reign of Charles I, replacing an older residence, the house has been the home of the Dukes of Wellington since it was presented to the Great Duke in 1817. It contains a unique collection of paintings, prints, furniture, effects and personal belongings of this most famous soldier and statesman.

THE EXHIBITION
The Wellington Exhibition re-creates many scenes from the life of the Great Duke and the battle of Waterloo. 'The Last Journey', a special display, features the Duke's magnificent Funeral Carriage.

THE GROUNDS
Include a wildfowl sanctuary, gardens and Copenhagen's Grave. A licensed restaurant and gift shop are provided to complete your enjoyment.

Open daily (except Fridays) from 1st May to last Sunday in September, 11.30 am to 5.00 pm.

Situated on the Hampshire/Berkshire borders, signposted off A33 equidistant Reading/Basingstoke, close to M4 and M3.
For further details please write to: The Wellington Office, Stratfield Saye, Reading, RG7 2BT. Tel: Basingstoke (0256) 882882.

### STRATFIELD SAYE HOUSE
**Reading** *map J4* ♿
Telephone: Basingstoke (0256) 882882
*(The Duke of Wellington)*

This Stuart house is filled with the Great Duke's possessions and personality. Wellington Exhibition. State Coach. Great Duke's Funeral Carriage. Grounds, gardens, wildfowl sanctuary and Copenhagen's grave.

**Location:** 1 m W of A33 between Reading & Basingstoke (turn off at Wellington Arms Hotel); signposted. Close to M3 & M4.
**Opening Times:** House and Gardens; open daily (except Fris) from May 1 to last Sun in Sept 11.30–5. Wellington Country Park (3 m from House)—Nature trails, adventure playgrounds, animals, boating, windsurfing, fishing, deer park miniature steam railway. National Dairy Museum, Thames Valley Time Trail—Mar to Oct daily 10–5. Nov–Feb Sats & Suns only. Adm charges House: £3, Chd £1.50. Park: £2, Chd £1. Combined House and Park: £3.60, Chd £1.70.
**Refreshments:** Tea and snacks, licensed restaurant.

**Titchfield Abbey** – See English Heritage Section.

### THE VYNE, The National Trust
**Basingstoke** *map J4* ♿
Telephone: Basingstoke 881337

An important early 16th century house with classic portico added 1654. Tudor panelling, 18th century ornamented staircase. Extensive lawns, lake, trees, herbaceous border.

**Location:** 4 m N of Basingstoke between Bramley & Sherborne St John (1½ m from each).
*Station: Bramley (2½ m).*
**Opening Times:** Mar 24 to Oct 15—Tues, Weds, Thurs, Sats & Suns 1.30–5.30. Open Bank Hol Mons 11–5.30. Last adm 5. *Closed Tues, following Bank Hol Mons.* Adm HOUSE AND GARDEN: Suns & Bank Hol Mons £2.60, other open days £2.30. GARDEN ONLY: £1.30/£1.10. Chd half price. *Reduced rates for pre-booked parties Tues, Weds & Thurs only.* Shop. Dogs in car park only. Wheelchair provided.
**Refreshments:** Light lunches and teas in the Old Brewhouse (12.30–5.30).

### WEST GREEN HOUSE, The National Trust
**Hartley Wintney** *map J4*

Small early 18th century house of great charm in a delightful garden.

**Location:** 1 m W of Hartley Wintney, 1 m N of A30; 10 m NE of Basingstoke.
*Station: Winchfield (2 m).*
**Opening Times:** Mar 26–end Sept. Garden: Wed, Thurs & Sun 2–6; House: (three rooms and staircase) *by written appointment only Wed 2–6.*. Adm Garden only £1.30, House 50p extra, Chd half price. No reductions for parties. Apply: Lord McAlpine of West Green, 40 Bernard Street, London WC1N 1LG. Last adm 5.30.

**Wolvesey Abbey** – See English Heritage Section.

## HEREFORD & WORCESTER

### ABBERLEY HALL
**nr Worcester** *map G6*
Telephone: (0299) 896634 (office hours only)
*(Mrs Atkinson)*

Five principal rooms show ornate decoration of mid-Victorian period.

**Location:** 12 m NW of Worcester on A443.
**Opening Times:** HOUSE ONLY. May 29; July 18–21 and 24–28; Aug 1–4, 7–11, 14–18, 21–25, 28; 1.30–4.30. Adm £1. Unsuitable for wheelchairs. No dogs.

### AVONCROFT MUSEUM OF BUILDINGS
**Stoke Heath, Bromsgrove** *map G6* Ⓢ
Telephone: Bromsgrove 31886 or 31363
*(Council of Management)*

An open-air Museum containing buildings of great interest and variety. Exhibits include a working windmill, a 15th century timber-framed house, a cockpit theatre, two great 14th century roofs, a 1946 prefab and an ice house and earth closet from the 18th century. New exhibit – a toll house.

**Location:** At Stoke Heath 2 m S of Bromsgrove off A38 between junctions 4 & 5 of M5 and 3½ m S of M42 junction 1.
**Opening Times:** Mar & Nov 11–4.30, closed Mons & Fris; Apr, May, Sept & Oct 11–5.30, *closed Mons;* June, July & Aug daily 11–5.30. Open Bank Holidays. *Closed Dec to Feb.* Adm £2, Chd £1, OAPs £1.20. Parties at reduced rates by arrangement. Free car park & picnic site.
**Refreshments:** Available at Museum tea room. Souvenir and Bookshop.

### BERNITHAN COURT
**Llangarron** *map G5*
Telephone: Llangarron 477
*(M.J. Richardson)*

William & Mary house built for Hoskyns family in 1692: some surviving panelling, fine staircase, walled gardens.

**Location:** 4 m Ross on Wye, 1½ m from A40 Ross–Monmouth road.
**Opening Times:** By prior appointment, telephone Mrs James (0989 84) 477. Adm £1.

### BERRINGTON HALL, The National Trust
**Leominster** *map F6* △ ♿
Telephone: Leominster 5721

Built 1778–1781 by Henry Holland, the architect of Carlton House. Painted and plaster ceilings. "Capability" Brown laid out the park.

**Location:** 3 m N Leominster W of A49.
**Opening Times:** Easter Sat–Mon: 2–6; Apr and Oct Sat & Sun 2–5; May to end of Sept—Weds to Suns & Bank Hol Mons 2–6. Grounds & tea room open from 12.30. Adm £1.80, Chd half-price. Parties by prior written arrangement only. Joint ticket with Croft Castle £3.20, Chd half-price; Parties by prior written arrangement only; this refers to joint ticket with Croft Castle. No dogs. Wheelchairs provided. Wheelchair access grounds only. Indoor photography by prior written arrangement only. Last admission 30 mins before closing.
**Refreshments:** Tea room at Hall.

### BREDON SPRINGS
**Ashton-under-Hill, nr Evesham** *map G5*
*(Ronald Sidwell, Esq)*

1¾ acre garden. Large plant collection in natural setting.

**Location:** 6 m SW of Evesham, turn off A435; in Ashton turn right then 1st left.
**Opening Times:** GARDEN ONLY. Apr 1 to Oct 29—Sats, Suns, Weds, Thurs, Bank Hol Mon & Tues, 10–dusk. Adm 50p (Chd free). *In aid of National Gardens Scheme.* Coach parties alight at church—6 mins walk through churchyard and over 2 fields. Limited parking at house. Plants for sale. Dogs welcome.

### BROBURY GARDEN & GALLERY
**Brobury, nr Hereford** *map F6*
Telephone: Moccas (09817) 229
*(Eugene Okarma, Esq)*

6 acres of garden around a 100 years' old house on the banks of the River Wye. Spacious lawns, rock gardens, terraces, herbaceous borders; mature conifers. The Gallery specialises in old prints and 19th and 20th century watercolours.

**Location:** 11 m W of Hereford, off A438; signposted Brobury Bredwardine.
**Opening Times:** GARDEN. June 1 to Sept 30—Mons to Sats 9–4.30. Adm £1, Chd 50p. GALLERY: Open all the year—Mons to Sats 9–4.30 (closes at 4 in winter). Adm free.

### BURFORD HOUSE GARDENS
**Tenbury Wells** *map G6*
Telephone: (0584) 810777
*(Treasures of Tenbury Ltd.)*

The gardens at Burford were created by John Treasure over a period of 35 years and are filled with a wealth of rare and interesting plants many of which are grown by the adjoining world famous nursery which bears his name.

**Location:** 1 m W of Tenbury Wells on the A456.
**Opening Times:** Mar 18 to Oct 22, Mon to Sat 11–5, Sun 2–5. At other times by prior arrangement. Adm £1.95, Chd 80p. Parties of 25 or more by prior arrangement – Adm £1.60 each. No wheelchairs available.
**Refreshments:** Tea Rooms situated near entrance, serving morning coffee, light lunches and teas with locally baked cakes and scones.

### BURTON COURT
**Eardisland** *map F6* ♿
Telephone: Pembridge 231
*(Lt-Cmdr & Mrs R. M. Simpson)*

14th century Great Hall. European and Oriental Costume. Working model fairground.

**Location:** 5 m W of Leominster between A44 & A4112.
**Opening Times:** Spring Bank Hol to end Sep—Weds, Thurs, Sats, Suns & Bank Hol Mons 2.30–6. Adm £1.25, Chd 60p. Coach parties £1.
**Refreshments:** Coach parties catered for. Teas.

### CLACK'S FARM
**Boreley, Ombersley, Droitwich** *map G6*
Telephone: Worcester (0905) 620250
*(Mr & Mrs Arthur Billitt)*

Well known to television viewers, featured in BBC2 'Gardener's World' programmes from 1969 till 1981 and more recently in Central T.V. 'Gardening Time' programmes. A 2½ acre garden created from zero since 1965 without any paid labour, Arthur and Riet Billitt are the caring gardeners. The ornamental garden with its shrubs and trees, plus its alpine and peat areas, is supplemented during the season with many different bedding plants and is at all times colourful. There is also a water garden with small and medium sized pools. The television area with its 8 amateur greenhouses of varying sizes demonstrate how the home gardener can grow melons, cucumbers, tomatoes, houseplants, etc. There are demonstration plots for growing vegetables, soft fruit and tree fruits, with the emphasis on varieties of quality and with flavour. The demonstration rose gardens illustrate the control of pest and diseases on a number of old and new varieties. The two patio areas show the use of container growing and a display of hanging baskets. On open days there are experts available to answer your questions.

# National Trust in HEREFORD & WORCESTER

## BERRINGTON HALL
**Leominster**

## CROFT CASTLE
**nr. Leominster**

## HANBURY HALL
**nr. Droitwich**

## GREYFRIARS
**Worcester**

## AVONCROFT
### MUSEUM OF BUILDINGS

Covering seven centuries of history – buildings rescued and restored on 15 acres of Worcestershire countryside.

See the new additions, visit the gift shop. Also refreshments, picnic area, free coach and car park. Open daily throughout the season.

For details of events, opening times and party bookings –

Telephone (0527) 31886/31363

**AVONCROFT MUSEUM OF BUILDINGS**
Stoke Heath Bromsgrove Worcestershire B60 4JR
Midway between M5 juncs 4 and 5 off the A38 Bromsgrove Bypass
and 3½ miles south of the M42 junction 1.

## BROBURY GARDEN & GALLERY
**BROBURY, HEREFORDSHIRE**

Six acres of gardens around a 100 year old house built on the banks of the River Wye. Spacious lawns, rock gardens, terraces and herbaceous borders laid out to feature splendid views and a wide variety of mature conifers.

The Gallery specialises in old prints, from simple topographical views to Rembrandt etchings. Many thousands in stock arranged for easy viewing. Also large collection of 19th and 20th century watercolours.

*ADMISSION – SEE EDITORIAL REFERENCE*

**Location:** 8 miles from Worcester and Kidderminster. A449 Worcester–Kidderminster Road, turn into Woodfield Lane, then follow signs.
**Opening Times:** Sat & Sun May 13 and 14, June 10 and 11, June 17 and 18 (Special Fuchsia Week-end), July 8 and 9, Aug 12 and 13, Sept 9 and 10. By previous arrangement only, coach parties at any time during the season. Adm 50p, Chd 25p. Parties £1 per person including coffee or tea and biscuits. *In aid of National Gardens Scheme*, R.N.L.I., Stars Organisation for Spastics, Horticultural Therapy, and The Blue Cross. Car park free (room for 500 cars). Suitable for disabled persons, no wheelchairs available.
**Refreshments:** Several pubs/restaurants in Ombersley (3 miles), The Mitre Oak, Crossway Green, on the A449 (2½ miles). Clack's Farm itself has a tea garden serving coffee, tea, soft drinks, etc. and biscuits (no food available).

### THE COMMANDERY
**Sidbury** *map G6*
Telephone: Worcester (0905) 355071

Founded late in the 11th century as the Hospital of St. Wulstan, the Commandery became in 1545 the country home of the Wylde family. During their 200 year stay, Charles II came here and held his Council of War before the Battle of Worcester.
The building itself dates mainly from 1500 – an excellent Tudor construction where Monks once ministered to the sick and poor. Mediaeval wall paintings of the saints can still be seen in the room where dying patients were laid. The Great Hall has a superb hammer-beam roof and a minstrels gallery.
**Location:** Centre of Worcester.
**Opening Times:** Mon to Sat 10.30–5, Sun 2–5. Adm £1.50, Chd/OAPs 75p (1988 rates).
**Refreshments:** Snacks, lunches, cream teas available at the canalside tearooms.

### CROFT CASTLE, The National Trust
**nr Leominster** *map F6* ♿
Telephone: Yarpole 246

Welsh Border castle mentioned in Domesday. Inhabited by the Croft family for 900 years. Fine 18th century Gothic interior. Extensive wooded parkland.
**Location:** 5 m NW of Leominster just N of B4362 signposted from Ludlow Road (A49).
**Opening Times:** Easter Sat, Sun & Mon: 2–6; Apr & Oct Sat & Sun 2–5; May to Sept—Weds to Suns & Bank Hol Mons 2–6. Adm £1.80, Chd 90p; Parties by prior written arrangement. Joint ticket with Berrington Hall £3.20, Chd £1.60; Parties by prior written arrangement. Access for disabled to ground floor and part of grounds. Wheelchairs provided. Last admission 30 mins before closing.

### CWMMAU FARMHOUSE, BRILLEY, The National Trust
**Whitney-on-Wye** *map F5*

Early 17th century timber-framed and stone tiled farmhouse.
**Location:** 4 m SW of Kington between A4111 and A438. Approached by a long narrow lane.
**Opening Times:** Easter, Spring, May & Summer Bank Hol weekends only—Sats, Suns & Mons 2–6. *At other times by prior written appointment with the tenant Mr S M Joyce.* Adm £1.10, Chd 55p. *No reduction for parties.* No dogs. Unsuitable for wheelchairs & coaches. Picnics only by prior arrangement with the tenant.

### DINMORE MANOR
**nr Hereford** *map F5* ♿
*(R.G. Murray)*

14th century Chapel also cloisters, "Music Room" and rock garden.
**Location:** 6 m N of Hereford on Leominster Road (A49).
**Opening Times:** All the year—Daily (except Christmas Day & Boxing Day) 2–6. Adm £1.50, OAPs 75p, children under 14 admitted free when accompanied. *Garden, Chapel & Music Room only open.*
**Refreshments:** Occasional teas served during summer. Also café at Dinmore Hill, Little Chef 2 m N on A49.

### EASTGROVE COTTAGE GARDEN NURSERY
**Sankyns Green, Little Witley** *map G6*
Telephone: (0299) 896389
*(Mr & Mrs J. Malcolm Skinner)*

A peaceful old world country flower garden displaying a specialist collection of hardy plants maintained by the owners since 1970. This cottage garden is sensitively arranged with great emphasis laid on colour and form, and with the 17th century cottage and timber framed barn, it blends into the unspoiled country of meadow and woodland. The owners are on hand to offer advice and a wide range of good quality and unusual plants are grown at the nursery.
**Location:** Near Shrawley—4 m SW of Stourport; 8 m NW of Worcester on road between Shrawley (on B4196) and Great Witley (on A443).
**Opening Times:** Open Daily, afternoons—Apr 1 to Oct 30, 2–5; except Tues & Weds; *closed throughout Aug.* Adm 80p, Chd 20p in aid of National Garden Scheme. Parties by arrangement – mornings & evenings. Suitable for disabled (wheelchairs not provided).

### EASTNOR CASTLE
**nr Ledbury** *map G5*
Telephone: Ledbury (0531) 2305

Excellent specimen of 19th century castellated architecture containing armour, pictures, etc. Arboretum, extensive park with red deer.
**Location:** 5 m from M50 (exit 2) 2 m E of Ledbury on Hereford/Tewkesbury Road A438.
*Station: Ledbury (2 m).*
**Opening Times:** Bank Hol Mons. May 21 to Sept 17: Suns. July and Aug: Weds and Thurs. 2.15–5.30. Parties by appointment on any day, Easter to Sept. Adm £2, Chd & OAPs £1. Reduced rates for parties of 20 or more.
**Refreshments:** At the castle.

### EYTON OLD HALL
**nr Leominster**
Telephone: (0568) 2418
*(Ronald Rolf)*

Early Victorian House with Regency additions. Gardens approached by 300 yard drive, with lawns and woodland. Special display of spring flowering bulbs.
**Location:** Village of Eyton 2 m NW Leominster, Herefordshire.
**Opening Times:** By appointment only between the period of Easter to mid Sept. Adm charges will be given on telephoned appointment.

**Goodrich Castle** – See English Heritage Section.

## THE GREYFRIARS, The National Trust

**Worcester** *map G6* △
Telephone: Worcester 23571

A richly timber-framed house built c. 1480, sympathetically furnished with tapestries, crewel work hangings etc.

**Location:** In Friar Street, Worcester.
*Station: Worcester, Foregate Street (½ m).*
**Opening Times:** Mar 27 to Oct—Weds & Thurs and Bank Holiday Mons 2–6. Other times adult parties by written application only. Adm £1.10, Chd 55p. Parties of children (inc schools) not admitted. No dogs. Unsuitable for wheelchairs.

## HANBURY HALL, The National Trust

**nr Droitwich** *map G6* ♿
Telephone: Hanbury 214

Wren style red brick house c. 1700 built for a wealthy lawyer. Outstanding painted ceilings and staircase by Sir James Thornhill. The Watney Collection of porcelain; Orangery c. 1730.

**Location:** 3½ m E of Droitwich, 1 m N of B4090.
**Opening Times:** Easter Sat, Sun, Mon 2–6. Mar 29–31, 2–5. Apr and Oct, Sat, Sun 2–5. May to end Sept, Wed to Sun and Bank Holiday Mon 2–6. Adm £1.90, Chd 95p. *Parties by prior written arrangement only.* Evening visits for pre-booked parties, 7.30–9.30, third Wed each month. Full price for evening visits (including National Trust members). Shop. No dogs. Wheelchairs provided. Braille guidebook available. Last admission 30 mins before closing.
**Refreshments:** Teas in the house.

## HARTLEBURY CASTLE

**nr Kidderminster** *map G6*
Telephone: Hartlebury (0299) 250410
*(The Church Commissioners)*

Historic home of the Bishops of Worcester for over 1,000 years. Fortified in 13th century, rebuilt after sacking in the Civil War and Gothicised in 18th century. State Rooms include medieval Great Hall, Hurd Library and Saloon. Fine plaster-work and interesting portraits. Also County Museum in North Wing.

**Location:** In village of Hartlebury, 5 m S of Kidderminster, 10 m N of Worcester off A449.
**Opening Times: State Rooms** Easter Sunday to Sept 4—First Sun in every month. Every Wed Easter to end of August Bank Hol Sun & Mon 2–4. Adm 60p, Chd 25p, OAPs 25p. Guided tours for parties of 30 or more on weekdays by arrangement. **County Museum** Mar to Nov—Mons to Fris 2–5. Suns 2–6. Bank Hols 11–5. Closed Good Friday. Adm 40p, OAPS, Students & Chd 20p. Family tickets (2 adults and up to 3 children) £1 (all 1987 rates). School parties free. Picnic area.
**Refreshments:** Available.

## HARVINGTON HALL

**nr Kidderminster** *map G6*
Telephone: Chaddesley Corbett (056 283) 267
*(The Roman Catholic Archdiocese of Birmingham)*

Moated medieval and Elizabethan manor-house containing secret hiding-places and rare wall-paintings. Georgian Chapel in garden with 18th century altar, rails and organ. Harvington Festival 14, 15 & 16 July 1989. Other events throughout the summer.

**Location:** 3 m SE of Kidderminster, ½ m from the junction of A448 and A450 at Mustow Green.
**Opening Times:** Mar 1 to Oct 31 daily except Good Friday, 11.30–5.30. *Closed Nov to Feb except by appointment.* Adm £1.75, Chd 80p, OAPs £1.25. (Correct at time of going to press.) Parties by arrangement with the custodian. Free car parking.
**Refreshments:** Licensed restaurant in the medieval wing overlooking the moat, open Easter to end Sept daily, except Mons and Fris and on Suns in Oct. Light refreshments in the dairy on other afternoons. Bookings taken for Sunday lunch and evening functions.

## HELLEN'S

**Much Marcle** *map G6* △
*(The Pennington-Mellor-Munthe Trust)*

Manorial house lived in since 1292. Visited by Black Prince and Bloody Mary.

**Location:** In village of Much Marcle on Ledbury/Ross Road. Entrance opp church.
**Opening Times:** Easter to Oct 1—Weds, Sats & Suns 2–6 (guided tours each hour). *Other times by written appointment with the Custodian).* Adm £2, Chd (must be accompanied by adult) 75p.
**Refreshments:** Teas by prior arrangement.

## HERGEST CROFT GARDENS

**Kington** *map F5*
Telephone: Kington (0544) 230160
*(W L & R A Banks, Esq)*

50 acres of trees, shrubs and many other plants from all over the temperate world. Excellent autumn colour, a working kitchen garden and fine herbaceous borders.

**Location:** On outskirts W of Kington off Rhayader Road (A44) *(signposted to Hergest Croft at W end of bypass).*
**Opening Times:** Daily—Apr 30 to Oct 29, 1.30–6.30. Adm £1.40, Chd 70p. Reduced rates for pre-booked parties of over 20 by appointment at any time.
**Refreshments:** Home-made teas on most Suns and for parties of over 20 by arrangement.

## HILL COURT GARDENS & GARDEN CENTRE

**Homm Green, Ross on Wye** *map G5* ♿
Telephone: Ross 763123
*(Mr J C Rowley)*

Set in the beautiful grounds of a William and Mary Mansion. An avenue of white limes line the drive up to the house, gardens, and garden centre. The two and a half acres of ornamental gardens include an 18th century Yew Walk, colourful herbaceous borders, water garden with gazebo, rose gardens and monthly shrub borders. Set in one of the walled gardens these borders are designed to assist the visitors in their choice of shrubs for their own gardens throughout the year. The garden centre offers the gardener excellent choice in plants and products, professional advice from horticulturally trained staff, a relaxing environment and the pleasure of strolling through the gardens too. There is a tea garden serving light lunches and afternoon teas within another of the lovely walled gardens.

**Location:** B4228 from Ross on Wye, fork right at the Prince of Wales public house, drive for 2½ miles.
**Opening Times:** Open daily 9.30–5.30, open all Bank Holidays. Adm free. All parties by appointment only, particularly coach parties. Ample car parking. Suitable for disabled, although shingled ground does sometimes cause problems.
**Refreshments:** A delightful tea garden set in one of the walled gardens with indoor and patio seating. Open Spring & Summer season, weekends only during early Spring season. Light lunches and afternoon teas available, all cakes homemade. Special group bookings possible. The house is not open to the public.

### HOW CAPLE COURT GARDENS
**How Caple** *map G5*
Telephone: How Caple 626
*(Mr & Mrs P L Lee)*

11 acres overlooking the river Wye. Formal terraced Edwardian gardens, extensive plantings of mature trees and shrubs, water features and a sunken Florentine garden undergoing restoration. Norman church with 16th century Diptych. Specialist nursery plants for sale. Fabrics shop.

**Location:** B4224, Ross on Wye (4½ m) to Hereford (9 m).
**Opening Times:** April to Nov Mons to Sats 9.30–4.30. May to Oct also Suns 10–5. Adm £1.50, Chld 75p. Parties by appointment. Car parking. Toilets.
**Refreshments:** Afternoon teas available Suns & Bank Hols.

### KENTCHURCH COURT
**Hereford** *map F5*
Telephone: Golden Valley 240228
*(J E S Lucas-Scudamore, Esq)*

Fortified border manor house altered by Nash. Gateway and part of the original 14th century house still survives. Pictures and Grinling Gibbons carving. Owen Glendower's tower.

**Location:** Off B4347, 3 m SE of Pontrilas; 12 m Monmouth; 14 m Hereford; 14 m Abergavenny, on left bank River Monnow.
**Opening Times:** May to Sept. *Parties only by appointment.* Adm £2, Chd £1.
**Refreshments:** At Kentchurch Court by appointment.

### LITTLE MALVERN COURT
**nr Great Malvern** *map G5*
Telephone: Malvern (0684) 892988
*(Mr and Mrs T M Berington)*

14th century Prior's Hall once attached to 12th-century Benedictine Priory, and principal rooms in Victorian addition by Hansom. Family and European paintings and furniture. Collection of 18th and 19th century needlework. Home of the Berington family by descent since the Dissolution.

**Location:** 3 m S of Great Malvern on Upton-on-Severn Road (A4104).
**Opening Times:** Apr 12 to July 13—Weds and Thurs 2.30–5.00. Parties by prior arrangement. Adm £1.60, Chd 80p. No concession for OAPs. Parties at other times £2 by arrangement per head. Unsuitable for wheelchairs. Garden open only in aid of National Gardens Scheme Sun Apr 9, June 25. Adm £1.

### LOWER BROCKHAMPTON, The National Trust
**Bromyard** *map G6* ♿
Telephone: Bromyard 88099

Small half-timbered manor house c. 1400 with unusual detached 15th century gate house and ruins of 12th century chapel.

**Location:** 2 m E of Bromyard N of A44 Bromyard/Worcester Road.
**Opening Times:** Medieval Hall and Parlour only: Mar 25 to end of Sept (closed Good Fri)—Weds, Thurs, Fris, Sats, Suns & Bank Hol Mons 10–1, 2–6. Oct – Wed to Sun 10–1, 2–4. Other months by previous written appointment only. Adm £1, Chd 50p; Parties by prior written arrangement only. N.B. Hall reached by rough narrow road through 1½ m woods & farmland. No dogs in Hall. Wheelchair access.

### MOCCAS COURT
**Moccas** *map F5*
Telephone: Moccas (098 17) 381
*(R T G Chester-Master, Esq)*

Designed by Adam, built by Keck in 1775 and has been in the ownership of the Cornewalls, and the present owner, for three centuries. The House stands in 'Capability' Brown parkland on the south bank of the River Wye.

**Location:** 13 m W of Hereford by River Wye. 1 m off B4352.
**Opening Times:** House & Gardens. Apr to Sept—Thurs 2–6. Adm £1.20. Picnics in garden allowed.
**Refreshments:** Food and drink available at the Red Lion Hotel, Bredwardine, by pre-booking only.

**Mortimer's Cross Water Mill** – See English Heritage Section.

### THE PRIORY
**Kemerton** *map G5*
*(Mr & The Hon Mrs Peter Healing)*

4 acre garden; main features are long herbaceous borders planned in colour groups; stream and sunken garden; many interesting and unusual plants and shrubs.

**Location:** NE of Tewkesbury, turn off A435 (Evesham/Cheltenham) at Beckford.
**Opening Times:** GARDEN ONLY. May to Sept—Thurs; also Suns May 21, June 18, July 9, Aug 6, 27 & Sept 10: 2–7. Adm £1. Accompanied chd free. *In aid of National Gardens Scheme & other charities.* Plants for sale.

### SPETCHLEY PARK
**Worcester** *map G5*
*(Mr & Mrs R J Berkeley)*

This garden, extending over nearly 30 acres, is a plantsman's delight, and it contains many fine trees and rare shrubs and plants. Particularly beautiful in April, May and June but also a show of colour throughout the summer. The park contains Red and Fallow Deer.

**Location:** 3 m E of Worcester on Stratford-upon-Avon Road (A422).
**Opening Times:** Gardens & Garden Centre: Mar 24 to Sept 30—Daily (except Sats) 11–5; Suns 2–5; Bank Hol Mons 11–5. Adm £1.40, Chd 70p. Regret no dogs. Plants and shrubs for sale. House not open.
**Refreshments:** Tea in the garden *(Suns & Bank Hols).*

### STONE HOUSE COTTAGE GARDENS
**Kidderminster** *map G6* ♿
Telephone: Kidderminster 69902
*(Major & The Hon Mrs Arbuthnott)*

Sheltered wall garden with towers. Rare wall shrubs and climbers also interesting herbaceous plants, all labelled. Adjacent Nursery.

**Location:** 2 m SE of Kidderminster on A448 to Bromsgrove; next to Stone Church. *Station: Kidderminster (2 m).*
**Opening Times:** GARDEN & NURSERY ONLY. Mar to Nov: Weds, Thurs, Fris, Sats 10–6; Suns, May and June, 2–6. Adm £1, accompanied Chd free. Coaches by appointment only. *In aid of National Gardens Scheme and Mother Teresa.*
**Refreshments:** Food & drink available at Harvington Hall.

### THE WEIR, The National Trust
**Swainshill, nr Hereford** *map F5*

Spring garden with fine views of the river Wye and the Welsh and Monmouthshire hills from the cliff garden walks.

**Location:** 5 m W of Hereford on A438.
**Opening Times:** Mar to Oct—Wed to Sun & Bank Hol Mon 2–6. (*Closed* Good Fri). Adm 50p. No reduction for parties. No coach parties. No dogs. Unsuitable for wheelchairs or visually handicapped.

### WORCESTER CATHEDRAL
**Worcester** *map G6* △ ♿
Telephone: Worcester (0905) 28854
*(The Dean and Chapter of Worcester)*

Beside the River Severn opposite the Malvern Hills. Built between 1084 and 1375. Norman Crypt and Chapter House. Early English Quire, Perpendicular Tower. Monastic buildings include refrectory (now College Hall and open on request during August), cloisters, remains of guesten hall and dormitories. Tombs of King John and Prince Arthur. Cloister herb garden, Elgar memorial window, misericords. Edgar Tower gatehouse.

**Location:** Centre of Worcester. Main roads Oxford and Stratford to Wales. 3 m junction 7 (M5).
**Opening Times:** Every day 7.30–6 (June to early Sept, 7.30–7). Choral Evensong daily (except Thurs and school hols). Tower open on Sats and Public Hols. Appointments for parties and coach groups. No admission charge but donations accepted. Parties: suggested minimum donation of £2 (Chd 50p) per head for guided tours. No cathedral car parking—City centre parking. Disabled visitors most welcome—some steps, but help and wheelchair available. Bookstall, shop and toilets, including toilet for disabled.
**Refreshments:** Light refreshment in Cloister Tea Room. Special arrangements made for parties.

# HERTFORDSHIRE

### ASHRIDGE
**Berkhamsted** *map J5*
Telephone: Little Gaddesden (044 284) 3491
*(Governors of Ashridge Management College)*

Early Gothic revival. Begun 1808 by James Wyatt for 7th Earl of Bridgewater. 13th century Crypt. Tudor barn. Gardens landscaped by Repton.

**Location:** 3½ m N of Berkhamsted (A41), 1 m S of Little Gaddesden.
**Opening Times:** Gardens open Apr to Oct—Sats & Suns 2–6. Adm £1, Chd/OAPs 50p. House fully open some weekends & partially on others during the summer; please telephone for further information. Adm House & Garden £2, Chd/OAPs £1.

### BENINGTON LORDSHIP GARDENS
**nr Stevenage** *map K5*
Telephone: Benington (043 885) 668
*(Mr & Mrs C. H. A. Bott)*

Terraced hill-top garden overlooking lakes. Includes old and modern roses, Victorian folly, Spring rock and water garden. Spectacular herbaceous borders. Woodland walk and Norman defences. Interesting all the year.

**Location:** 4 m E of Stevenage in village of Benington between Walkern (B1037) & Watton-at-Stone (A602).
**Opening Times:** GARDEN ONLY. Easter Mon, Spring and Summer Bank Hols 12–5, and every Wed May to end Oct 12–5. Suns Apr 24, May 8, 15, 22 and every Sun June, July and Aug to 7th, other days shown 2–5. Parties please book. Open by appointment for parties all the year. Adm £1.20 Weds and Suns, accompanied Chd free, 12–18 60p. No facilities for wheelchairs or disabled. *No dogs please.*
**Refreshments:** Teas (Suns and Bank Holidays only).

## HARTLEBURY CASTLE

**NEAR KIDDERMINSTER, WORCESTERSHIRE**

*THE CHURCH COMMISSIONERS*

The red sandstone Castle has been the seat of the Bishops of Worcester since 850. Notable features of the State Rooms include the rococo decoration of the Saloon and a remarkable collection of episcopal portraits.

*ADMISSION – SEE EDITORIAL REFERENCE*

## HARVINGTON HALL

**KIDDERMINSTER**

*ADMISSION – SEE EDITORIAL REFERENCE*

## HELLEN'S

**MUCH MARCLE, HEREFORDSHIRE**

Ancient manorial house of brick and stone, begun 1292. Contains 'Great Hall' with stone table at which Black Prince dined and bedroom prepared for Queen 'Bloody Mary' in 1554. Much original furnishings and 19th century carriages.

Easter to October 1. Visitors are guided at each hour 2 to 6 pm Wednesdays, Saturdays and Sundays or by special appointment with the Custodian in writing. Admission £2 Children 75p (must be accompanied by an adult). Teas by previous arrangement.

## THE HILL COURT GARDEN

**ROSS-ON-WYE**

*ADMISSION – SEE EDITORIAL REFERENCE*

## MOCCAS COURT

**HEREFORDSHIRE**

Set in parkland laid out by Capability Brown, the house stands in a superb position on the south bank of the River Wye, between Hereford and Hay. It was built for Sir George Cornewall in 1775 by Anthony Keck to designs by Robert Adam and is noted for the oval staircase hall and a circular drawing room which retains the original wallpaper and plaster work. The property still belongs to Sir George's descendants and contains an interesting collection of furniture and family portraits.

*ADMISSION – SEE EDITORIAL REFERENCE*

## WORCESTER CATHEDRAL

**WORCESTER**

*ADMISSION – SEE EDITORIAL REFERENCE*

## SPETCHLEY PARK

**WORCESTER**

*Home of Mr and Mrs R.J. Berkeley*

*ADMISSION – SEE EDITORIAL REFERENCE*

## BENINGTON LORDSHIP GARDENS

**NR STEVENAGE, HERTFORDSHIRE**

*Photograph: A.F. Kersting*

Laid out in 1906 around a Norman castle this hilltop garden has changed little and is very 'English'. Full of atmosphere the entrance is through a magnificent neo-Norman gate house. Sweeping lawns stretch downhill towards lakes and parkland. A broad terrace cuts across the lawn and leads to a Spring rock/water garden, double herbaceous borders outstanding in mid-Summer, kitchen garden and plant centre. There are also masses of old and modern roses and many unusual plants with interest all the year.

*ADMISSION – SEE EDITORIAL REFERENCE*

## HERTFORDSHIRE – *continued*

### CAPEL MANOR

**nr Enfield** *map K5*
Telephone: Lea Valley (0992) 763849
*(London Borough of Enfield)*

The extensive grounds of this Horticultural College offer a comprehensive collection of hardy outdoor and glasshouse plants. Many fine trees including one of the largest surviving Copper Beeches in the country. Shrub borders containing old fashioned Roses, herbaceous plants. Attractive bedding schemes. Large rock and water garden. 17th century garden containing culinary, aromatic and medicinal plants. Also knot hedges and contemporary plants. 5 acre trials and demonstration garden. Facilities for physically handicapped persons. A sensory garden for the blind is just one of the many theme gardens which are on show for the public to enjoy.

**Location:** 2½ m NE of Enfield; ¼ m W of A10 at Bullsmoor Lane traffic lights; junction 25/M25/A10.S ¼ m W off A10 traffic lights.
*Station: Turkey Street (1¼ m).*
**Opening Times:** Apr to Oct—Mons to Fris 10–4.30, Sat & Sun 10–5.30. Adm £1, under 18 & OAPs 50p. Several Open weekends throughout the year. Adm £1.50, under 18 & OAPs 75p. Special rates for season tickets and coach parties or visiting groups. Further details on request from the Resources Officer, Capel Manor, Bullsmoor Lane, Waltham Cross, Herts. EN7 5HR.

### THE GARDENS OF THE ROSE

**Chiswell Green, St Albans** *map K5* ♿
Telephone: St Albans (0727) 50461
*(Royal National Rose Society)*

The Showgrounds of the R.N.R.S. containing some 30,000 roses of over 1,650 different varieties.

**Location:** Off B4630 (formerly A412) St Albans/Watford Road.
*Stations: St Alban's City (2 m).*
**Opening Times:** Mid-June to Oct—Mons to Sats 9–5; Suns & Bank Holidays 10–6. Adm £1.80, Chd (under 16) free. British Rose Festival—July 8 & 9, increased admission charge. Facilities for the disabled.
**Refreshments:** Licensed cafeteria.

### GORHAMBURY

**St Albans** *map K5* △
Telephone: St Albans (0727) 54051
*(The Earl of Verulam)*

Mansion built 1777-84 in modified classical style by Sir Robert Taylor. 16th century enamelled glass and historic portraits.

**Location:** 2 m W of St Albans. Entrance off A4147.
**Opening Times:** May to Sept—Thurs 2–5. Adm £2, Chd & OAPs £1. Guided tours only. Parties by prior arrangement.

### HATFIELD HOUSE

**Hatfield** *map K5* △
*(The Marquess of Salisbury)*

Noble Jacobean house and Tudor palace, childhood home of Queen Elizabeth I. House built by Robert Cecil, first Earl of Salisbury in 1611. Fine portraits, furniture and relics of Queen Elizabeth I. Fine gardens and large park. TWO EXHIBITIONS FOR 1989. THE TONY DUROSE VEHICLE COLLECTION—*A splendid display of veteran, vintage, classic and specialist vehicles together with a large variety of accessories and vehicle memorabilia spanning more than 60 years. Open one hour before the House plus the NATIONAL COLLECTION OF MODEL SOLDIERS.*

**Location:** In Hatfield, 21 m N of London. Close to M1 & A1(M).
*Station: Hatfield (opposite house).*
**Opening Times:** House & West Gardens. Mar 25 to Oct 8—Daily (except Mons but open on all Bank Hol Mons). *Closed Good Friday.* Hours—Weekdays 12–5 (guided tours); Suns 1.30–5; Bank Hols 11–5 (Suns & Bank Hols no guided tours—guides in each room). Adm £3.20, Chd £2.25. Reductions for pre-booked parties of 20 or more. Coach & car park free. A guided tour of State rooms (weekdays) takes 1 hr. Dogs not adm to House or Gardens. Park & West Gardens: Mar 25 to Oct 8. Park—Daily 10.30–8; West Gardens open at House times (also Mons 2–5). *Closed Good Friday.* Park, East & West Gardens: Mons only (except Bank Hols)—Park 10.30–8; Gardens 2–5.
**Refreshments:** Available in adjacent restaurant—cafeteria. ELIZABETHAN BANQUETING IN THE OLD PALACE THROUGHOUT THE YEAR.

### HUNSDON HOUSE

**Hunsdon** *map K5*
Telephone: Estate Office: (0920) 871445

A house was first built on the site in 1447 and later used as a hunting lodge by Henry VIII and nursery for the Tudor Princesses and Edward VI. It was greatly altered in the early 19th C. Today the grounds and mainly Victorian house are the subject of a continuing programme of conservation and restoration.

**Opening Times:** HOUSE: open by written appointment. GARDEN: open in June, Mon–Fri 10–2 only. Adm HOUSE: £1.50; GARDEN: 50p. Parties (Max 20) by written appointment. Free car parking close to house. Most of the guided tour suitable for disabled persons (no wheelchairs available).
**Refreshments:** No refreshments available, but full catering facilities at Briggens House Hotel, 1 mile away.

# KNEBWORTH·HO

HERTFORDSHIRE

*HISTORIC HOME OF THE LYTTON FAMILY SINCE 1490*

**Knebworth House,** built between 1500 and 1540, was transformed 150 years ago by romantic Victorian novelist, **Sir Edward Bulwer-Lytton** into a spectacular high gothic fantasy. Behind the pinnacled exterior, the house retains features of all periods — a magnificent Jacobean Banqueting Hall, the 1843 State Drawing Room designed by **John Crace** and the Edwardian White Drawing Room by **Sir Edwin Lutyens.** There is a fine collection of furniture and portraits. **Charles Dickens** performed private theatricals in the house and **Winston Churchill** sat at his easel and painted. Knebworth was the home of **Constance Lytton,** the suffragette, and of **Robert Lytton,** Viceroy of India. The beautiful formal gardens, simplified early this century by Lutyens, contain a unique quincunx pattern herb garden designed for Knebworth by **Gertrude Jekyll.** The house stands in 250 acres of beautiful parkland with red deer, sika and fallow herds. Knebworth above all is a much loved family home.

THRONE OF MAHARAJAH OF MYSORE

## *DELHI DURBAR EXHIBITION*

A unique Exhibition of Viceregal India and the British Raj, commemorating the Great Durbar of 1877 when Queen Victoria was proclaimed Empress of India by the Viceroy, Robert 1st Earl of Lytton — The Exhibition and audio-visual display tell the story of two generations of family involvement in India's dramatic history.

LORD LYTTON AS VICEROY 1877

**Plus children's adventure playground and wild west fort**
**Opening times and admission details — see editorial reference**
**WITHIN EASY REACH OF LONDON**
**DIRECT ACCESS FROM A1(M) MOTORWAY AT JUNCTION 7 (Stevenage South)**
**Telephone: Stevenage (0438) 812661**

## ...RTH HOUSE
**...h** *map K5*
...ne: Stevenage 812661
*(...ord Cobbold)*

...ly home of the Lyttons since 1490, it was transformed 150 years ago by the ...ectacular high gothic decoration of Sir Edward Bulwer-Lytton the Victorian ...ovelist and statesman. Lutyens gardens currently being restored and include a Jekyll herb garden. Delhi Durbar Exhibition. Large adventure playground with Fort Knebworth.

**Location:** 28 m N of London. Own direct access off A1(M) Junction 7 (Stevenage South A602).
*Stations: Stevenage (2 m).*
**Opening Times:** HOUSE, GARDENS AND PARK, weekends, Bank Hols and School Hols from Mar 22 to May 21; then daily (except Mons) May 27 to Sept 10, plus weekends only to Oct 1 (subject to special events). Open Park: 11–5.30; House & Gardens 12–5. House, Garden and Park: £3.30, Chd/OAPs £2.80; Park only: £1.80. (No reductions for Chd/OAPs.) Reductions for pre-booked parties of 20 or more (Mar 22 to Oct 1). Coach and Car Park free. Dogs admitted to Park only on leads. Telephone above number for further details.
**Refreshments:** Catering in 16th century Tythe Barns, Tel: Stevenage 813825.

## MOOR PARK MANSION
**nr Rickmansworth** *map J4*
Telephone: Rickmansworth (0923) 776611
*(Three Rivers District Council)*

Palladian house reconstructed in 1720 by Sir James Thornhill and Giacomo Leoni incorporating house built in 1678/79 for James, Duke of Monmouth. Magnificent interior decorations by Verrio, Sleker and others. Club House of Moor Park Golf Club. Being restored by the District Council.

**Location:** 1 m SE of Rickmansworth.
*Stations: Rickmansworth or Moor Park.*
**Opening Times:** All the year—Mons to Fris 10–4; Sats 10–12 noon. *Restricted viewing may be necessary on occasions.* Visitors are requested to report to reception. Adm free. Descriptive leaflet available. Guided tours during summer months. Information from Information Centre or Prestel page 28800741.

## SHAW'S CORNER, The National Trust
**Ayot St Lawrence, Nr Welwyn** *map K5*
Telephone: Stevenage (0438) 820307

Home of George Bernard Shaw from 1906–1950. The rooms downstairs remain as in his lifetime. Upstairs rooms (Shaw's bedroom and bathroom) open on weekdays.

**Location:** SW end of village of Ayot St Lawrence. 3 m NW Welwyn; 2 m NE of Wheathampstead.
**Opening Times:** Mar 25 to end Oct—Wed to Sat 2–6; Suns & Bank Hol Mons 12–6. *Closed Good Friday & Mons & Tues.* Group visits by written appointment only. Mar to Nov. Last adm 5.30. Adm £1.80, Chd 90p. Parties must book. *On busy days adm may be by timed ticket.* Dogs in car park only. Unsuitable for wheelchairs.

## ST. PAUL'S WALDEN BURY
**Whitwell, nr Hitchin** *map K5*
*(Simon Bowes Lyon)*

Formal woodland garden with temples, statues, lake, ponds. Laid out about 1730, covering about 40 acres. There are also rhododendron and flower gardens.

**Location:** 5 m S of Hitchin; ½ m N of Whitwell on B651.
**Opening Times:** GARDEN ONLY. Telephone Whitwell 229 or 218 for information on dates. Adm £1, Chd and OAPs 50p. *Opened in aid of National Gardens Scheme and other charities.*
**Refreshments:** Tea at the garden on open days.

# HUMBERSIDE

## BLAYDES HOUSE
**Hull** *map J9*
Telephone: Hull (0482) 26406
*(The Georgian Society for East Yorkshire)*

Mid-Georgian merchants house, fine staircase and panelled rooms. Restored by the Society in 1974-5.

**Location:** 6 High Street, Hull.
*Station: Hull.*
**Opening Times:** Staircase, Blaydes and Partners' Rooms—all the year Mons to Fris (except Bank Hols) 10.30–1, 2–4. By appointment only with Blackmore Son & Co, Chartered Architects at Blaydes House. Adm 50p.

## BURNBY HALL GARDENS
**Pocklington** *map J9* ♿
Telephone: Pocklington (0759 30) 2068
*(Stewart's Burnby Hall Gardens & Museum Trust)*

Large gardens with 2 lakes. Finest display of hardy water lilies in Europe – 45 varieties, designated Supplementary National Collection. Museum housing Stewart Collection—sporting trophies, ethnic material. Picnic area.

**Location:** 13 m E of York on A1079.
**Opening Times:** Easter to mid Oct—daily 10–6. Adm 80p, Chd (under 5) free, (5–16) 30p, OAPs & Parties 60p. Free coach and car park. Disabled facilities.
**Refreshments:** Teas in the garden.

## BURTON AGNES HALL
**nr Bridlington** *map J10*
Telephone: Burton Agnes (0262 89) 324
*(Preservation Trust Ltd)*

One of the least altered of Elizabethan country houses. Fine collection of old and French impressionist paintings, carved ceilings and overmantels.

**Location:** In village of Burton Agnes, 6 m SW of Bridlington on Driffield/Bridlington Road (A166).
**Opening Times:** Mar 24 to Oct 31—Daily 11–5. Hall and Gardens: Adm £1.75, Chd & OAPs £1.25. *The management reserves the right to close the house or part thereof without prior notice; adm charges will be adjusted on such days.*
**Refreshments:** Licensed cafeteria. Teas, light lunches & refreshments. Gift shop. Toilet for the disabled.

## BURTON CONSTABLE
**nr Hull** *map K9*
Telephone: (0964) 562400
*(J Chichester Constable, Esq)*

Magnificent Elizabethan House, built c1570. Outstanding collection of furniture, pictures and works of art. Unique collection of eighteenth century scientific instruments. Carriage display in stables, parkland by 'Capability' Brown.

**Location:** At Burton Constable; 1½ m N of Sproatley; 7½ m NE of Hull (A165); 10 m SE of Beverley (A1035).
**Opening Times:** Apr 1 to Sept 30. Apr, May, June & Sept – Suns & Bank Holiday Mons only 1–5.30: July & Aug – Suns to Thurs inclusive 1–5.30. Grounds open at noon. Parties at any time by arrangement. For further details write to: The Administrator, Burton Constable Hall, Hull, HU11 4LN, or Tel: (0964) 562400.
**Refreshments:** Cafeteria. Gift shop.

## CARLTON TOWERS
**Goole** *map J9* △
Telephone: (0405) 861662
*(Duke of Norfolk)*

The most complete Victorian Gothic House, still a family home and includes beautiful china, silver, carved woodwork, etc and a Priest's Hiding Hole.

**Location:** 20 m S of York; 6 m S of Selby and 1 m N of Snaith (A1041) and 6 m from M62 exits 34 & 36.
*Station: Snaith (1 m).*
**Opening Times:** Easter Sat to Tues incl; Early May Bank Hol Sun & Mon; Spring Bank Hol Sat to Tues incl; Aug Bank Hol Sat to Tues incl. All Suns from the beginning of May to end of Sept. House open 1–5 (last adm 4.30), Parkland and Rose Garden, 12.15–6. Adm £2, Chd £1, OAPs £1.50. Party bookings on any day, by appointment (minimum of 20); a guided tour given from beginning of May to end of Sept and also on Thurs evenings, £2 per person. Enquiries to The Comptroller, Carlton Towers, Nr Goole.
**Refreshments:** Tea room (open 12.30–5.30).

# SHAW'S CORNER

**HERTFORDSHIRE**

*THE NATIONAL TRUST*

*ADMISSION – SEE EDITORIAL REFERENCE*

# THE GARDENS OF THE ROSE

**CHISWELL GREEN, ST. ALBANS**

**The Showgrounds of the ROYAL NATIONAL ROSE SOCIETY**

Open mid June to October, Monday to Saturday 9 am to 5 pm. Sunday 10 am to 6 pm. Admission £1.80. Children (under 16) free. Licensed cafeteria. Facilities for the disabled. British Rose Festival July 8 & 9 Increased admission charges.

# BURTON AGNES HALL

**near BRIDLINGTON, Humberside**

*Described by 'Everybody's' as a Yorkshire Treasure House*

*'Country Life' photograph*

Burton Agnes Hall, built AD 1598-1610, is filled with treasures collected during four centuries. Antique furniture, Elizabethan carved ceilings, oriental china and the largest private collection in the North of French Impressionist and Modern paintings—Renoir, Pissaro, Corot, Utrillo, Gauguin, Augustus John, etc.

Open to the public daily from March 24 to October 31, 1989. Admittance to Hall and Gardens £1.75. Children & OAPs £1.25 Hours of opening 11 am to 5 pm. Licensed Cafeteria, Teas, light lunches and refreshments served. Guides and guide books are available and there is a free car park within a few yards of the Hall. Bus service 200 yards from Hall. Bridlington 6 miles, Scarborough 18 miles, York 34 miles. Toilets for the Disabled.

For further particulars apply: Estate Office, Burton Agnes, Driffield, East Yorkshire. Tel: Burton Agnes (0262 89) 324.

# CARLTON TOWERS

**(Yorkshire Home of The Duke of Norfolk)**

The most complete Victorian Gothic House, still a family home and includes beautiful china, silver, carved woodwork, etc and a Priest's Hiding Hole.

OPEN: Easter Sat to Tues inclusive; Early May Bank Holiday Sunday & Monday; Spring Bank Holiday Saturday to Tuesday inclusive; August Bank Holiday Saturday to Tuesday inclusive.

ALL SUNDAYS from the beginning of MAY to SEPTEMBER. House open from 1 to 5 pm (last admission 4.30); Parkland Rose Garden from 12.15 to 6 pm. Adults £2, OAPs £1.50, Children £1.

**PARTY BOOKINGS ON ANY DAY,** by appointment (minimum of 20 visitors) when a guided tour will be given from beginning of MAY to end of SEPTEMBER, and also on THURSDAY EVENINGS £2.00 per person.

Situated 20 miles S of York, 6 miles S of Selby and 1 mile N of Snaith (A1041) and 6 miles from M62, exits 34 & 36. Enquiries (0405) 861662, or in writing to The Comptroller, Carlton Towers, Nr Goole.

## THE CHARTERHOUSE

**Hull** *map J9*
Telephone: (0482) 20026
*(Charterhouse Trustees)*

God's House Hospital, commonly called The Charterhouse, was founded in 1384 by Michael de la Pole, Earl of Suffolk. The Charterhouse is an almshouse which provides accommodation for the elderly, and visitors are requested not to enter areas other than the Chapel and Gardens.

**Location:** Charterhouse Lane, Hull.
**Opening Times:** CHAPEL & GARDENS open daily during July and on Good Friday, Easter Day, Easter Monday, Spring and Summer Bank Holidays 10–8. No adm charge but prior notice should be given for parties of 10 or more. Children should be accompanied by an adult. Dogs not permitted. Limited car parking available.
**Refreshments:** Facilities in nearby City centre.

## ELSHAM HALL COUNTRY PARK

**Brigg** *map J8* △ ♿
Telephone: Barnetby 688698
*(Capt J Elwes, DL)*

Beautiful English park with lakes and wild gardens. Waterfowl and giant Carp. Domestic animals, Chinese Muntjac Deer and Bird garden. Nature trails. Adventure playground. Arts and Craft Centre, Granary Tearooms, Wrawby Moor Art Gallery, Blacksmith (weekends only). Caravan Club site. Wild Butterfly Garden. Six National Awards for Catering and Conservation.

**Location:** 4 m from Brigg on Barton-on-Humber Road A15.
*Stations: Elsham (1½ m); Barnetby (2½ m); Kirmington Airport 3½ m.*
**Opening Times:** PARK. Easter to Oct—Mons to Sats 11–5.30; Suns & Bank Hols 11–6.30. *Park closes 8 pm or dusk.* Oct to Easter—Suns & Bank Hols only 11–4 or dusk. Park closes early in bad weather. Closed Good Friday & Christmas Day. Admission: Price subject to review. Please telephone for Party bookings and winter discount. Schools party discount and Guided Natural History Trails available on request.
**Refreshments:** The Granary Tea Room—lunches & fresh teas daily in summer & Suns & Bank Hols in winter. Parties by arrangement. Special menus available. Winter conferences and wedding catering. Coach parties welcome by arrangement with Administrator.

## EPWORTH

**The Old Rectory** *map J8* △
Telephone: Epworth (0427) 872268
*(Trustees of the World Methodist Council)*

Built 1709. Restored 1957. Childhood home of John & Charles Wesley, oldest Methodist shrine.

**Location:** In Epworth, 3 m N of Haxey on A161, 18 m E of Doncaster M180 exit 2.
**Opening Times:** Mar to Oct—Weekdays 10–12, 2–4; Suns 2–4. Adm £1, Chd 50p. A/V presentation. Coaches by arrangement only. Accommodation by arrangement.
**Refreshments:** At the House *by arrangement only.*

## THE GUILDHALL

**Beverley** *map J9*
Telephone: 0482 882255
*(East Yorkshire Borough of Beverley Borough Council)*

The Guildhall, Beverley, established in 1500, in original medieval house, rebuilt 1762, when served as Town Hall. Currently used as the Mayor's Parlour. Houses Magistrates' Room, formerly Council Chamber, containing 15th century furniture and 16th century pewter collection. Also Mayor's Parlour, built 1830 and used as Council Chamber until 1896 when Court Room altered to accommodate meetings. Exhibits of civic regalia, ancient charters, records, paintings and mayoral historic items. Court-room reveals medieval wall, a particularly beautiful all-seeing figure of Justice riding the clouds; an outstanding example of work of Italian stuccoist Cortese; also town's and Kings Arms, executed by Cortese.

**Location:** In Town Centre, off pedestrianised zone, Register Square.
**Opening Times:** Easter to Oct on Tues 10–4.30. Also Bank Holidays 10–4.30. Adm free. Parties welcomed by appointment – small charge applies only on days other than Tues. Car parking very limited. Free car parks in near vicinity. Ground floor only suitable for disabled.
**Refreshments:** Facilities in near proximity.

## MAISTER HOUSE, The National Trust

**Hull** *map J9*
Telephone: Hull (0482) 24114

Rebuilt 1744 with a superb staircase-hall designed in the Palladian manner.

**Location:** 160 High Street, Hull.
*Station: Hull (¾ m).*
**Opening Times:** Staircase and entrance hall only. All the year—Mons to Fris 10–4. *Closed Bank Hols.* Adm by guide book 50p. No dogs. Unsuitable for wheelchairs & parties.

## NORMANBY HALL AND COUNTRY PARK

**Scunthorpe** *map J9*
Telephone: Scunthorpe (0724) 720215
*(Scunthorpe Borough Council)*

A Regency mansion set in 350 acres of beautiful parkland and gardens. Normanby Hall was designed by Sir Robert Smirke (architect of the British Museum) and completed in 1830. It is now leased from the Sheffield family, formerly Dukes of Buckingham and owners of Buckingham Palace, and has been decorated and furnished in period by Scunthorpe Museums and Art Gallery. The spacious Country Park surrounding the Hall provides interest for all the family, with herds of red and fallow deer, wild and exotic birds, lakeside and woodland nature trails, a Craft and Countryside Centre, picnic areas, riding stables and a golf club. The Normanby Park Farming Museum is due to open in 1989.

**Location:** 4 m N of Scunthorpe on B1430, turn right at Normanby village. Car Park off Thealby Lane.
**Opening Times:** HALL: Easter to Oct—Mons to Fris 11–5, Suns 2–5, Nov to Mar—by appointment only. *Closed Sats all year.* Adm 65p, Chd/OAPs 35p. (1988 rates.) Wheelchairs—ground floor only. Guided tours and parties by appointment.
PARK: Open during daylight hours, daily throughout the year.
**Refreshments:** Café in grounds, summer only.

## SEWERBY HALL

**Bridlington** *map K10*
*(Borough of East Yorkshire)*

Built 1714–20 by John Greame with additions 1803. Gardens of great botanical interest.

**Location:** In Bridlington on the cliffs, 2 m NE from centre town.
*Stations: Bridlington (2½ m); Bempton (2 m).*
**Opening Times:** Park open all year—Daily 9–dusk. Art Gallery open Easter to Sept—Suns to Fris 10–12.30, 1.30–6; Sats 1.30–6. Provisional adm £1, Chd 50p (including zoo and art gallery). Pay and Display car park.
**Refreshments:** Self-service snack bar in the Hall (summer season only).

## SLEDMERE HOUSE

**Driffield** *map J10*
*(Sir Tatton Sykes, Bart)*

A Georgian house begun in 1751 with important additions attributed to Samuel Wyatt in conjunction with Sir Christopher Sykes, containing superb library 100ft long. The entire building was burnt to the ground in 1911 and splendidly restored with an Edwardian feeling for space by York architect Walter Brierley during the first world war. The latter copied Joseph Rose's fine ceilings and inserted a magnificent Turkish room. The House contains much of its original furniture and paintings. An unusual feature is the great organ, which is frequently played on open days. Capability Brown Park. 18th century walled rose garden. Main garden under reconstruction.

**Location:** 24 m E of York on main York/Bridlington Road; 8 m NW of Driffield at junction of B1251 & B1253.
**Opening Times:** Easter weekend, all Suns in Apr; Apr 30 to Oct 1—Daily (except Mons and Fris); open all Bank Hols; 1.30–5.30 (last adm 5). Adm £2, Chd £1, OAPs and Coach Parties £1.70; grounds only £1, Chd 60p. Private parties arranged by appointment only on Weds evenings. Free Car Park and Coach Parks. Illustrated brochure from The House Secretary, Sledmere House, Driffield, East Yorkshire.
**Refreshments:** Self service restaurant. Licensed restaurant for booked meals, Driffield (0377) 86208.

**Thornton Abbey** – See English Heritage Section.

## WILBERFORCE HOUSE

**Hull** *map J9*
Telephone: Hull (0482) 222737
*(Hull City Council)*

17th century mansion. Birthplace of William Wilberforce, the slave emancipator.

**Location:** 25 High Street, Hull.
*Station: Hull.*
**Opening Times:** All the year—Weekdays 10–5; Suns 1.30–4.30. *Closed Good Friday, Christmas Day, Boxing Day & New Year's Day.* Adm free.

## *Historic* BEVERLEY

**NORTH HUMBERSIDE**

Beverley's Heritage spans a period of 1300 years which is reflected in its fine old buildings and outstanding Market Square, in particular, in Register Square, is the

### GUILDHALL

Bought by the Council for use as a Town Hall in 1500 and extended in 1762, containing the Mayor's Parlour and the Tourist Information Centre. Doric portico leads to 18th century Courtroom and Magistrates' Room. Fine collection of civic regalia, charters, period furniture and other exhibits. Notable features – medieval wall and outstanding work of Italian stuccoist Cortese in beautiful ceiling depicting all-seeing figure of Justice.

Open Tuesdays, Bank Holidays 10 am – 4.30 pm and by appointment on other days.

For further details: Tourist Officer, TIC, The Guildhall, Register Square, Beverley, HU17 9AU (Open Daily) Telephone 0482 867430.

BEVERLEY

Heritage Centre of East Yorkshire

## NORMANBY HALL

**SCUNTHORPE, HUMBERSIDE**

*ADMISSION – SEE EDITORIAL REFERENCE*

## ELSHAM HALL COUNTRY PARK

**BRIGG, South Humberside**

Elsham Country Park is set in the magnificent lakeside gardens of Elsham Hall and surrounding the three lakes is a superb collection of shrubs noted for their rich display of spring flowers and blossom. The Elsham Estate covers over 400 acres of woodland through which run long nature trails and other recreational activities.

Other attractions: Elsham Craft Centre, Wrawby Moor Art Gallery, Walled garden with rare breeds of livestock, poultry and Longwool Sheep, Hazel Coppice Bird Garden—rare native and foreign birds. Carp lake—giant carp to hand feed. The Monks Wood Arboretum. Wild Butterfly Garden with Walkway, Sculpture Trail. Adventure Playground. Award winning Granary Tearooms (also for functions and catering).

Your support will help us to help you!

## SEWERBY HALL

**Two miles north of Bridlington**

An 18th century mansion with museum and art gallery in a dramatic setting overlooking Bridlington Bay. The 50 acres of gardens of great beauty and botanical interest include fine old English Walled Garden and small zoo and aviary. Museum includes Amy Johnson Trophy Room dedicated to the pioneer woman aviator.

Refreshments. Ample parking (Pay & Display).

*ADMISSION–SEE EDITORIAL REFERENCE*

## SLEDMERE HOUSE

**DRIFFIELD, HUMBERSIDE**

*ADMISSION – SEE EDITORIAL REFERENCE*

## WILBERFORCE HOUSE, HULL

17th century Merchant's house, now a local history museum with period furniture, Hull silver, costume, dolls, toys and adjoining chemists' shop. New displays were opened in 1983 to commemorate the 150th Anniversary of the Death of William Wilberforce, born in the house in 1759. Secluded gardens. Open weekdays 10am to 5pm; Sundays 1.30 tp 4.30pm.

*Closed Good Friday, Christmas Day, Boxing Day, and New Year's Day. Admission Free.*

# ISLE OF WIGHT

**Appledurcombe House** – See English Heritage Section.

**Carisbrooke Castle** – See English Heritage Section.

### THE NEEDLES OLD BATTERY, The National Trust
**West Highdown, Totland Bay** *map H2*
Telephone: Isle of Wight 754772

A former Palmerstonian fort built in 1862, 250 ft above sea level; 200 ft tunnel to spectacular view of the Needles. Exhibition on history of the Needles Headland.

**Location:** West Highdown, Totland Bay.
**Opening Times:** Mar 24 to Nov 5—Daily, except Fris & Sats but open Good Fri & Easter Sat; also Fris & Sats in July & Aug; 10.30–5 (last admission 4.30). Adm £1, Chd 50p. No reduction for parties.

### NEWTOWN OLD TOWN HALL, The National Trust
**Newtown** *map H2*

18th century building of brick and stone. One of the buildings surviving from the island's former ancient borough.

**Location:** In Newtown, midway between Newport and Yarmouth.
**Opening Times:** Mar 24 to end Sept: Mons, Weds & Suns 2–5; July & Aug daily except Fri & Sat 2–5 (last adm 4.45). Also open Good Friday & Easter Saturday. *Closed Oct to end March.* Adm 50p, Chd 25p. No reduction for parties. No dogs. Unsuitable for wheelchairs.

### NUNWELL HOUSE AND GARDENS
**Brading** *map J2*
Telephone: Isle of Wight (0983) 407240
*(Colonel & Mrs J A Aylmer)*

Nunwell with its historic connections with King Charles I is set in beautiful gardens and parkland with channel views. A finely furnished family house with Jacobean and Georgian wings. Home Guard museum and family military collection.

**Location:** 1 m from Brading, turning off A3055; 3 m S of Ryde.
*Station: Brading.*
**Opening Times:** House and Gardens: May Bank Holidays Apr 30 to May 1, and May 28, 29, Sun July 9 to Thurs Sept 28, Suns to Thurs 10–5. Adm £1.80, Chd 60p. Gardens only: June 1 to June 30 – 1.30–5. Adm £1, Chd 50p. *Closed* Fri and Sats. Coach and School parties welcome all year by appointment. No dogs.
**Refreshments:** Light refreshments when House open; large parties book catering in advance.

### OSBORNE HOUSE
**East Cowes** *map H3*
Telephone: (0983) 200022
*(English Heritage)*

This was Queen Victoria's seaside residence built at her own expense, in 1845. The Prince Consort played a prominent part in the design of the house—it was his version of an Italian villa—and the work was carried out by Thomas Cubitt, the famous London builder. The Queen died here in 1901 and her private apartments have been preserved more or less unaltered. Crowded with furniture and bric-a-brac they epitomise the style we call 'Victorian'. Also see Queen's bathing machine.

**Location:** 1 m SE of East Cowes. OS map ref SZ 516948.
*Station: Ferry terminal East Cowes (1 m).*
**Opening Times:** Good Friday to Sept 30, daily 10–6; Oct 1–31, daily 10–5. Last Adm 1 hour before closing. Adm £3, OAPs £2, Chd £1.50.

**Yarmouth Castle** – See English Heritage Section.

# KENT

### BEDGEBURY NATIONAL PINETUM
**nr Goudhurst** *map L3*
Telephone: (0580) 211044
*(Forestry Commission Research Station)*

Has the most comprehensive collection of conifers in Europe. Conifers from all continents are planted in generic groups within 160 acres. Landscaped with grass avenues, paths, stream valleys, ridges and a lake. Rhododendrons, azaleas, maples and uncommon oak species add colour in spring and autumn.

**Location:** On B2079, 1 m from A21 London to Hastings travelling towards Goudhurst.
**Opening Times:** Daily 10 till dusk. Adm charge. Visitor centre: open Easter to Sept. Car parking. Difficult for wheelchairs.
**Refreshments:** In nearby villages.

### BELMONT
**nr Eastling, Faversham** *map L4*
Telephone: 079 589 202
*(Harris (Belmont) Charity)*

Belmont was built in the late 18th century to the design of Samuel Wyatt, in a splendid elevated position having commanding views over the attractive and unspoilt countryside. It has been the family seat of the Harris family since it was acquired in 1801 by General George Harris, the victor of Seringapatam. The Mansion remains in its original state and contains the finest collection of clocks in any English country house open to the public, superbly presented in an ideal setting.

**Location:** 3½ m SSW of Faversham.
**Opening Times:** Easter to end of Sept. Suns, 10–5, Gardens and Park only. Adm £1. Tues, Thurs, Sat and Bank Holiday Mons, Grounds, Mansion and Clock Museum. Visit by telephone appointment only in guided parties. Adm to Mansion and Clock Museum £3, Chd half price. Car parking. To book, contact Curator, Telephone 079-589-202.

### BENENDEN WALLED GARDEN
**nr Cranbrook** *map L3*
Telephone: Cranbrook (0580) 240749
*(Richard & Diane Cotter)*

An 18th century walled garden with large collection of old fashioned, fragrant plants, specie salvias and herbs. Picnic lawn. Ladies garden, Gourmet garden, plants for sale. No dogs in garden. Richard & Diane Cotter are available for illustrated lectures.

**Location:** Benenden, nr Cranbrook, Kent. In the grounds of Benenden School, entrance on Benenden to Sissinghurst Road 1 mile from Benenden cross road.
**Opening Times:** Mar 18 to Apr 17, May 27 to June 1, July 9 to Sept 6, 10–Dusk. Adm £1, OAP 75p, Disabled 75p, Chld under 16 free. Parties of 10 or more 75p by appointment. Conducted tours can be arranged. Hard standing and grass car park areas. No coaches in school grounds. Suitable for disabled persons.
**Refreshments:** Morning coffee, light lunches, cream teas.

# BENENDEN WALLED GARDEN

**BENENDEN, CRANBROOK, KENT**

*ADMISSION – SEE EDITORIAL REFERENCE*

# BELMONT

**KENT**

*ADMISSION – SEE EDITORIAL REFERENCE*

# BOUGHTON MONCHELSEA PLACE

**near MAIDSTONE, KENT**

Battlemented Elizabethan Manor of Kentish ragstone built in 1567, with interesting Regency alterations. Dramatically situated with breathtaking view over its own landscaped park, in which fallow deer have roamed for at least 300 years, and beyond it to the whole Weald of Kent. Its beautiful interior is still that of an intimate and inhabited 'home' to which successive generations have added new treasures. Dress display. Ancient vehicles and early farm implements. Manor records. Walled flower gardens with interesting plants. Tudor Kitchen and Garden Tea Rooms.
Good Friday to early October on Saturdays, Sundays and Bank Holidays (also Wednesdays in July and August). 2.15 to 6 pm.
Parties welcome any day, at special rates, but only by previous arrangement.
Telephone Maidstone 43120. Free Car Park.

# CHILHAM CASTLE GARDENS

**CANTERBURY, KENT**

For the lover of gardens, trees and fine views. For the excitement of medieval jousting (on Sundays) and the grace of flying birds of prey and a peaceful lakeside walk.

# CHIDDINGSTONE CASTLE

**NEAR EDENBRIDGE, KENT**

Wet or fine Chiddingstone Castle is enthralling. Set in 30 acres of parkland with lake and caves and glorious views over the Weald, it is an important example of romantic late Georgian passion for the Middle Ages. In 1805 the former 17th century mansion (of which some internal features remain) was remodelled by William Atkinson in the 'Castle Style' which he was then also employing at Scone Palace. It was the home of the late Denys Eyre Bower who left it to the Nation. It is now administered by a private charitable trust and its sole support is the income from visitors.

Inside the Castle is a treasure house. Royal Stuart and Jacobite relics bring history to life (Lely's 'Nell Gwyn', Samuel Cooper's 'Charles II'), Japanese swords and lacquer enchant the eye; Egyptian antiquities, fine furniture, Georgian barrel organs playing 18th century dance music. All this and more were the life time collections of that remarkable connoisseur Denys Bower whose last wish was that the others should continue to enjoy them as he had.

*ADMISSION – SEE EDITORIAL REFERENCE*

## BLACK CHARLES

**nr Sevenoaks** *map K4*
Telephone: Hildenborough (0732) 833036
*(Mr & Mrs Hugh Gamon)*

Charming 14th century home of John de Blakecherl and his family. A hall house with beautiful panelling, fireplaces and many other interesting features.

**Location:** 3 m S of Sevenoaks off A21; 1 m E in the village of Underriver.
**Opening Times:** Open to groups by appointment (minimum of 10).

## BOUGHTON MONCHELSEA PLACE

**nr Maidstone** *map L4* △
Telephone: Maidstone (0622) 43120
*(M B Winch, Esq)*

Grey stone, battlemented Elizabethan manor house with breathtaking views over the 18th century landscaped park with fallow deer.

**Location:** On B2163. In village of Boughton Monchelsea 5 m S of Maidstone. Turn off Maidstone/Hastings Road (A229) at Linton.
**Opening Times:** Good Fri to early Oct—Sats, Suns & Bank Hols (also Weds during July & Aug) 2.15–6. House & Grounds Adm £1.80, Chd £1. Grounds only Adm £1, Chd 50p (1989 prices). *Parties welcome any day, at special rates, but only by previous engagement.*
**Refreshments:** Tea rooms at the House. For parties lunch & supper can be ordered in advance.

## CHARTWELL, The National Trust

**Westerham** *map K4* ♿
Telephone: Edenbridge 866368

The home for many years of Sir Winston Churchill.

**Location:** 2 m S of Westerham off B2026.
**Opening Times:** House. Mar to end Nov: Mar 1–22, & Nov—Sats, Suns & Weds only 11–4; Mar 25 to end Oct—Tues, Weds, Thurs 12–5; Sats, Suns & Bank Hol Mons 11–5. Closed Good Fri and Tues following Bank Hol. All Tues mornings (except after Bank Hols) reserved for pre-booked parties and guided tours.
Garden & Studio: Mar 25 to end Oct—Same times as house. Adm House & Garden £3, Chd £1.50. Garden only £1.20, Chd 60p. Studio 40p extra (Chd no reduction). Pre-booked parties, Tues mornings only, £2.50, Chd £1.30. Guided tours for parties (15 or more) Tues mornings only. Write to the Administrator, Chartwell, Westerham, Kent. Car Park. Lavatory for disabled.
**Refreshments:** Restaurant open from Mar 25 to end Oct—10.30–5 (Mar 1–22 & Nov: 10.30–4) on days when house is open. Self-service, licensed (no spirits).

## CHIDDINGSTONE CASTLE

**nr Edenbridge** *map K4* ♿
Telephone: Penshurst (0892) 870347
*(Trustees of the Denys Eyre Bower Bequest)*

Royal Stuart and Jacobite collection; superb Japanese lacquer and swords; Egyptian antiquities, displayed in gracious country house setting.

**Location:** In Chiddingstone off Edenbridge-Tonbridge road B2027 at Bough Beech Turning. *Bus Service:* Tunbridge Wells–Edenbridge via Bough Beech.
*Station: Penshurst (2½ m).*
**Opening Times:** Mar 26 to Oct 31 – All public holidays. Mar and Apr – Suns and Easter holiday. May 1 to Sept 30 – Weds to Suns, also Tues from mid June to mid Sept. Oct – Weds and weekends only. Hours: weekdays 2–5.30, Suns and Public Holidays 11.30–5.30. Other times also available for booked parties. Adm £2.50, chld 5–15 £1.30, under 5 free. Booked parties of 20 and over £2.25. Coarse fishing in lake in season £6 daily (one onlooker permitted per fisherman £2.50).
**Refreshments:** Home-made teas, organised by Friends of Chiddingstone Castle. Catering for parties by arrangement. Shop. The courtyard wing of the Castle may be hired for conferences, dinners, weddings etc. A useful stopping place for parties going to and from Gatwick airport.

## CHILHAM CASTLE GARDENS

**nr Canterbury** *map L4*
Telephone: Canterbury 730319
*(Viscount Massereene & Ferrard DL)*

25 acre garden with formal terraces first made by Tradescant when the Jacobean house was built by the side of the old Norman Castle Keep Informal lake garden. Magnificent views and many fine trees. Park reputedly laid out by Capability Brown. Birds of Prey on display and flying free, afternoons daily except Mon and Fri. Gift shop. Jousting display Sundays & Bank Holidays. Medieval banquets, dinners, wedding receptions in Gothic Hall.

**Location:** In Chilham village, 6 m W of Canterbury (A252); 8 m NE of Ashford (A28); 22 m NW of Dover, Faversham turn off M2.
*Station: Chilham (1 m).*
**Opening Times:** Apr to mid-Oct—Daily (inc Bank Hols). Open from 11 am. Adm weekdays £2, Sun £3, Chd half-price (1987 rates). Free parking. Coaches welcome. Special rates for parties on application.
**Refreshments:** Jacobean tea room.

## COBHAM HALL

**nr Rochester** *map L4*
Telephone: Shorne 3371
*(Westwood Educational Trust Ltd)*

Charming mixture of Gothic and Renaissance architecture in 50 acres of grounds. Fine example of work of James Wyatt. Now a girls' public school.

**Location:** 4 m W of Rochester on Watling Street & Rochester Way (B2009 off A2). 27 m from London.
*Station: Sole Street (1½ m).*
**Opening Times:** Easter, Mar 23, 24, 26, 27, 29, 30; Apr 5, 6; July 16, 19, 20, 30; Aug 6, 9, 10, 13, 16, 17, 20, 23, 24, 28, 30, 31. 2–5.30 (last tour 5). Adm £1.50 Chd & OAPs 75p, disabled 30p. No reduction for parties.
**Refreshments:** Teas and light refreshments, enquiries (0474 82) 3371.

## CRITTENDEN HOUSE

**Matfield** *map L3*
*(B P Tompsett, Esq)*

Garden completely planned and planted since 1956 on labour-saving lines. Spring shrubs, roses, lilies, foliage, waterside planting of ponds in old iron workings. Of interest from the early Spring bulbs to Autumn colour.

**Location:** 5 m SE of Tonbridge off B2160.
**Opening Times:** GARDENS ONLY. Sun, Mon, Mar 26, 27; Sun Apr 30; Mon May 1 *National Gardens Scheme;* Sun May 7; Sun, Mon, May 28, 29, RSPCA; Sun June 11 2–6. Adm £1, Chd 20p. Cars free.

**Deal & Walmer Castles –** See English Heritage Section.

# The National Trust in KENT

## QUEBEC HOUSE
WESTERHAM

## CHARTWELL
Nr. WESTERHAM

## KNOLE
SEVENOAKS

## IGHTHAM MOTE
IVY HATCH, SEVENOAKS

## SCOTNEY CASTLE GARDEN
LAMBERHURST, KENT

## SMALLHYTHE PLACE
THE ELLEN TERRY MEMORIAL MUSEUM
TENTERDEN

*ADMISSION – SEE EDITORIAL REFERENCE*

## DODDINGTON PLACE GARDENS

**nr Sittingbourne ME9 0BB** *map L4*
Telephone: Doddington (079585) 385
*(Mr Richard and The Hon. Mrs Oldfield)*

10 acres of landscaped gardens set in the grounds of a large Victorian house built by Charles Trollope in 1860. A Wellingtonia avenue dates from that period. The rest of the garden was laid out in the early 1900s by a forebear of the present owner. The main features are a large rock garden with a series of pools, a formal sunk garden and terraces, and wide lawns with fine trees bordered by yew hedges. A woodland rhododendron and azalea garden was added in the 1960s. There are excellent views over the Syndale valley and surrounding countryside.

**Location:** 4 m from A2 and A20. 5 m from Faversham. 6 m from Sittingbourne. 12 m from Canterbury.
**Opening Times:** Weds and Bank Holiday Mons, May to Sept 11–6. Adm £1, Chd 25p. 20% discount for groups of more than 20 by prior arrangement. Car parking free. Suitable for disabled (no wheelchairs available). Present shop.
**Refreshments:** Restaurant serving morning coffee, light lunches, afternoon teas; supper parties by arrangement.

## DOVER CASTLE

*map M4*
Telephone: (0304) 201628
*(English Heritage)*

Castle Hill dominates the shortest passage between Britain and the Continent, and has been the scene of military activity from the Iron Age to the present day. Here is extensive proof from every age of man's ingenuity in devising ways to repel invaders. Dover Castle had its narrowest escape in 1216 when—in an heroic siege—it just managed to hold out against the French. There is much to see, including the underground works, the Roman lighthouse (now the bell tower of a fine Saxon church) and the great keep itself and a spectacular exhibition 'All the Queen's Men'.

**Location:** East side of Dover. OS map ref TR326416.
**Opening Times:** Good Friday to Sept 30, daily 10–6; Oct 1 to Maundy Thurs, daily 10–4. *Closed* Dec 24–26, Jan 1. Adm £2.50, OAPs £1.80, Chd £1.30.
**Refreshments:** in the Keep Yard.

## DOWN HOUSE

**Downe** *map K4* ♿
Telephone: Farnborough (0689) 59119
*(Royal College of Surgeons of England)*

The home of Charles Darwin for 40 years—now his memorial and museum. House, garden and Sandwalk Wood.

**Location:** In Downe, 5½ m S of Bromley off A233.
**Opening Times:** Mar 1 to following Jan 31—Daily (except Mons & Fris but open Bank Hol Mons) 1–6. Last adm 5.30. Adm £1.50, Chd 30p, OAPs 75p. *Closed Dec 24–26 & Feb.*

**Dymchurch Martello Tower** – See English Heritage Section.

## EMMETTS GARDEN, The National Trust

**nr Brasted** *map K4* ♿
Telephone: Ide Hill 429

Hillside shrub garden of 5 acres. Lovely spring and autumn colours, formal garden and roses. Further areas of garden being restored and re-planted.

**Location:** 1½ m S of A25 on Sundridge/Ide Hill Road.
**Opening Times:** GARDEN ONLY. Mar 24 to end Oct—Wed to Sun, Good Fri, Bank Hol Mon 2–6. Last adm 5. Adm £1.50, Chd 80p. Pre-booked parties: £1.10, Chd 60p (15 or more). Dogs admitted on lead. Wheelchair access to level parts of garden only. Tearoom.

## FINCHCOCKS

**Goudhurst** *map L3*
Telephone: Goudhurst (0580) 211702
*(Mr & Mrs Richard Burnett)*

Early 18th century house containing historic keyboard instruments.

**Location:** 1½ m W of Goudhurst, 10 m E of Tunbridge Wells off A262.
**Opening Times:** Mar 26 to Sept 24—Suns; also Bank Hol Mons & Weds to Suns in Aug: 2–6. Demonstrations & Music on instruments of the collection on Open Days. Adm £3.20, Chd £1.80. Family ticket £7.50. Free parking.
**Refreshments:** Teas available.

## GADS HILL PLACE

**Rochester** *map L4*
*(Gads Hill Place School Ltd)*

Grade 1 listed building, built 1780. Home of Charles Dickens from 1858 to 1870.

**Location:** On A226; 3 m from Rochester; 4 m from Gravesend.
*Station: Higham (1 m).*
**Opening Times:** By prior appointment only. Apply to the Bursar, Gads Hill Place School, Higham, Rochester. Adm free.
**Refreshments:** Food & Drink available at Sir John Falstaff Hotel opposite House.

## GODINTON PARK

**Ashford** *map L4* △
*(Alan Wyndham Green, Esq)*

House belongs mostly to Jacobean times, interior contains wealth of panelling and carving, portraits, furniture and china. Formal gardens.

**Location:** 1½ m W of Ashford off Maidstone Road at Potter's Corner (A20).
*Station: Ashford (2 m).*
**Opening Times:** Easter Sat, Sun & Mon; then June to Sept—Suns & Bank Hols only 2–5. Adm House & Gardens £1.50, Chd (under 16) 70p. Weekdays by appointment only. Parties of 20 or more £1.20 per person.

## GOODNESTONE PARK

**nr Canterbury** *map M4*
*(The Lord & Lady FitzWalter)*

Large garden. Old walled rose garden. Fine trees; good views. Connections with Jane Austen.

**Location:** 8 m SE of Canterbury; 4 m E of A2; ¼ m SE of B2046; S of A257.
*Station: Adisham (2 m).*
**Opening Times:** GARDEN ONLY. Apr 10 to July 14, Mons to Fris 11–5; Aug 21 to Sept 29, Mons to Fris 11–5 (including Bank Hols); also Suns—Apr 16, 23, May 21 and every Sun to July 9, and Aug 27 2–6. *Closed Sats.* Adm £1.30, Chd (under 12) 20p, OAP £1.10. Disabled in wheelchairs 90p. Parties over 25 £1. **No dogs.**
**Refreshments:** Teas Suns only *but not in April.*

## GREAT COMP

**nr Borough Green** *map L4*
Telephone: Borough Green 882669
*(The Great Comp Charitable Trust)*

Outstanding garden of seven acres, very wide variety of trees, shrubs, heathers and herbaceous plants. Old brick walls, much new stone work, paving and ornaments.

**Location:** 2 m E of Borough Green B2016 off A20. First right at Comp crossroads ½ m on left.
*Station: Borough Green & Wrotham (1½ m).*
**Opening Times:** GARDEN ONLY. Apr 1 to Oct 31—Daily 11–6. *Parties by prior arrangement.* Adm £1.50, Chd 70p. *No dogs.*
**Refreshments:** Tea for parties by arrangement.

## GREAT MAYTHAM HALL

**Rolvenden** *map L3*
*(Country Houses Association Ltd)*

Built in 1910 by Sir Edwin Lutyens.

**Location:** ½ m W of Rolvenden village.
**Opening Times:** May to Sept—Weds & Thurs 2–5. Adm £1, Chd 50p. Free car park. No dogs admitted.

## HAXTED MILL & MUSEUM

**Haxted, nr. Edenbridge** *map K4*
Telephone: Curator, Summer months Edenbridge (0732) 862914. Mr. D.G. Neville. Dorking (0306) 887979 during winter months.

Working Water Mill & Museum.

**Location:** 1½ m W of Edenbridge beside road joining B2029 at Lingfield Common with B2026 at Edenbridge.
**Opening Times:** April to May: Sat, Sun & Bank Hols, 12–5; June to end Sept: daily including Sun. Guides parties at any time by prior appointment. Adm £1.50, Chd 75p, OAPs £1. Reductions for parties booked in advance.
**Refreshments:** Licensed restaurant open daily *except Mon.*

# FINCHCOCKS Goudhurst Kent

Finchcocks, dated 1725, is a fine example of Georgian baroque architecture, noted for its fine brickwork, with a front elevation attributed to Thomas Archer. It is set in beautiful gardens and parkland near the village of Goudhurst. The house contains a magnificent collection of historic keyboard instruments which are restored to full playing condition, and provides a unique setting where visitors can hear music performed on the instruments for which it was written. Demonstration tours and music whenever the house is open.

Open Days: Easter to end of September, Sundays only: Bank Holiday Mondays and daily in August except for Mondays and Tuesdays. 2 to 6 pm. Teas.

Open by appointment for groups on other days from April to October, with musical tours and special catering. Fully licensed restaurant.

Festival of concerts in September. Fairs in May & October. Also lectures, courses, master classes and children's events. Full details send sae.

# GODINTON PARK

**ASHFORD, KENT**

The existing house belongs mostly to Jacobean times though there are records of another house being here in the 15th century. The interior of Godinton contains a wealth of very fine panelling and carving, particularly in the Hall and on the Staircase.

The house contains interesting portraits and much fine furniture and china. The gardens were originally laid out in the 18th century and were further extended and improved in the 19th century by Sir Reginald Blomfield with topiary work and formal gardens giving a spacious setting to the house.

The house is open to visitors by permission of Mr Alan Wyndham Green, the present owner.

# GOODNESTONE PARK GARDENS

**KENT**

*ADMISSION – SEE EDITORIAL REFERENCE*

# HAXTED MILL & MUSEUM

**HAXTED, EDENBRIDGE, KENT**

An ancient working Watermill and dynamic Museum of functioning Mill machinery combining to provide a unique illustration of the history, development and uses of water power throughout the centuries. The galleries contain artifacts and working models relating to all aspects of milling. There are special attractions for children – including a den of Lions and Tigers with their Cubs. Home-made cream teas and meals are available in the Licensed Restaurant.

# GREAT COMP GARDEN

**NR BOROUGH GREEN, KENT**

*Colorline Photographic photographs*

The garden of seven acres made, and until 1982 maintained, by Mr and Mrs R. Cameron, with virtually no assistance is now, after 32 years, fully developed. In a setting of well maintained lawns the design contains paving, old brick walls, new stone walls, 'ruins', terraces, ornaments and a Chilstone temple, informal woodland glades and winding paths and many heathers. A wide variety of trees, shrubs and herbaceous plants includes many which are rarely seen. Good autumn colour. Unusual plants for sale. Festival and other events in September, S.A.E. to R. Cameron, Great Comp, Borough Green, Sevenoaks, Kent.

## HEVER CASTLE & GARDENS
**nr Edenbridge** *map K4*
Telephone: Edenbridge (0732) 865224; Fax (0732) 866796
*(Broadland Properties Limited)*

Enchanting 13th century double-moated castle, childhood home of Queen Anne Boleyn, set in magnificent gardens of 30 acres. The gardens feature fine topiary including a maze, the magnificent Italian garden with statuary and sculpture dating back 2000 years, and the 35 acre lake alongside which visitors can walk and picnic. The Castle was restored and filled with treasures by William Waldorf Astor in 1903.

**Location:** Mid-way between London and S coast, between Sevenoaks and East Grinstead, 3 m SE Edenbridge off B2026. M25—junction 6, 20 mins. M23—junction 10, 20 mins.
*Station: Hever (1 m walk, taxis available), Edenbridge Town (3 m).*
**Opening Times:** CASTLE & GARDENS open daily—Mar 21–Nov 5. GARDENS: 11–6 (last entry 5pm). CASTLE: opens 12 noon. Dogs on leads gardens only. Adventure playground. Facilities for disabled visitors. Special pre-booked private tours available all year. Special rate for groups.
**Refreshments:** Large self-service cafeteria (licensed). Picnics welcome.

## IGHTHAM MOTE, The National Trust
**Ivy Hatch** *map K4*
Telephone: Plaxtol 810378

One of the most complete remaining examples of a medieval moated manor house.

**Location:** 3 m S of Ightham, off A227, 4½ m E of Sevenoaks off A25.
**Opening Times:** Mar 24 to end Oct—Mons, Weds, Thurs, Fris 12–5.30; Suns and Bank Hol Mons 11–5.30 (last adm 5); pre-booked tours 11–12 weekdays. Open Good Friday. Adm £2.50, Chd £1.20. Parties: £2.20, Chd £1.
**Refreshments:** Tea bar in car park.

## KNOLE, The National Trust
**Sevenoaks** *map K4* △
Telephone: Sevenoaks 450608

One of the largest private houses in England, dating mainly from 15th century, with splendid Jacobean interior and fine collection of 17th century furniture.

**Location:** At the Tonbridge end of Sevenoaks, just E of A225; 25 m from London.
*Station: Sevenoaks (1½ m)*
**Opening Times:** Mar 24 to end of Oct—Weds to Sats (inc Good Fri) & Bank Hol Mons 11–5; Suns 2–5. Last Adm 4. Guided tours Tues only, for pre-booked parties of 25 or more. Garden: May to Sept, first Wed in every month. Adm: £2.50 (£3 Fri – extra rooms shown). Chd £1.30 (£1.50 Fri). Garden only: 50p. Pre-booked parties of 25 or more £1.80, Chd £1. Wheelchairs park and gardens only. Parking £5 (£5.50 Fri) includes one admission.

## LADHAM HOUSE
**Goudhurst** *map L3*
*(Betty, Lady Jessel)*

10 acres of rolling lawns, fine specimen trees, rhododendrons, azaleas, camellias, shrubs and magnolias. Newly planted arboretum. Spectacular twin mixed borders. Fountain garden and bog garden. Fine view. Re-planted and tidied up since the hurricane.

**Location:** 11 m E of Tunbridge Wells off A262 on NE of village.
**Opening Times:** GARDEN ONLY. Suns May 7, 14: 11–6. Sun July 9: 11–6. *Open other times by appointment and for coaches:* Adm £1, Chd (under 12) 50p. *In aid of National Gardens Scheme.* Free parking.

## LEEDS CASTLE
**nr Maidstone** *map L4*
Telephone: Maidstone (0622) 765400. Telex: 965737
*(Leeds Castle Foundation)*

Fairytale Castle of the medieval Queens of England. Built in the middle of a lake in romantic setting of landscaped parkland. Dating back to 9th century, rebuilt in 1119 as a Norman fortress, it was later converted to a royal palace by Henry VIII. Superb collection of medieval furnishings, tapestries and Impressionist paintings. Museum of medieval Dog Collars. Water and woodland garden. Culpeper flower garden, Greenhouses, Vineyard. Duckery, new Aviaries, Maze and Grotto. 9 hole public golf course open daily all year. Castle gift shop and plant shop. Regret no dogs.

**Location:** 4 m E of Maidstone; access on B2163 A20 at junction 8 of the M20.
*Station: Bearsted or Hollingbourne (2 m). Inclusive rail/admission tickets from British Rail.*
**Opening Times:** Mar 24 to Oct 31—Daily 11–5*. Nov to Mar—Sats & Suns only 12–4* (*last admission to grounds). Winter—Sunday Lunches with tours of Castle. Special events programme. Kentish Evening Dinners every Saturday throughout year. Reduced prices for Chd (under 16) Students & OAPs, also for Groups and School Parties who are welcomed at any time all year round, by appointment. Picnic area. Car park. Passenger trailer takes elderly visitors from car park to Castle. Facilities for the disabled.
*NB The Trustees reserve the right to close all or parts of the Castle for Government seminars. Closed July 1 & Nov 4 for Open Air Concert & Fireworks Display.*
**Refreshments:** Lunch and refreshments available in licensed restaurants and the Park Gate Inn.

## LULLINGSTONE CASTLE
**Eynsford** *map L4*
Telephone: Farningham (0322) 862114
*(Guy Hart Dyke, Esq)*

Family portraits, armour, Henry VII gateway. Church.

**Location:** In the Darenth valley via Eynsford on A225.
*Station: Eynsford (½ m).*
**Opening Times:** CASTLE & GROUNDS. Apr to Oct, Sats, Suns, Bank Hols 2–6. Adm £2.50, Chd £1, OAPs £2. Weds, Thurs & Fris 2–6 by arrangement. No dogs. Free car parking. Telephone for enquiries or bookings.
**Refreshments:** At the gate house on Sun and for booked parties only.

**Lullingstone Roman Villa** – See English Heritage Section.

## LYMPNE CASTLE
**nr Hythe** *map M3*
Telephone: Hythe (0303) 67571
*(Harry Margary, Esq)*

14th century building restored in 1905. Once owned by the Archdeacons of Canterbury. Terraced gardens with magnificent views out to sea and across Romney Marshes to Fairlight.

**Location:** 3 m NW of Hythe off B2067, 8m W of Folkestone.
*Station: Sandling (2½ m).*
**Opening Times:** May to Sept & Bank Hol weekends—Daily 10.30–6. *Open most days Easter to May 31, but please check, and to parties by appointment.* Adm £1.25, Chd 30p.

**Maison Dieu, Ospringe** – See English Heritage Section.

**Milton Chantry, Gravesend** – See English Heritage Section.

# LEEDS CASTLE

**Nr. MAIDSTONE KENT**

Leeds Castle stands as one of the most beautiful and ancient Castles in the Kingdom, rising from its two small islands in the middle of a lake and surrounded by 500 acres of magnificent parkland and gardens.

Dating back to the 9th century and rebuilt by the Normans in 1119. Leeds Castle was then a Royal Palace for over 3 centuries. It now contains a superb collection of mediaeval furnishings, French and English furniture, tapestries and Impressionist art.

You can wander through woodland and water gardens, where peacocks and swans roam free. Through the aviaries with rare tropical birds and the Culpeper Garden full of old fashioned flowers and fragrance. See a fascinating underground grotto at the centre of the new maze. Or play our 9-hole golf course.

Now owned by the Leeds Castle Foundation, a private Charitable Trust, the Castle is also used as a high level residential conference centre.

**Special Events**

**Easter Egg Hunt**
Saturday 25th to Monday 27th March
**Country Fayre**
Saturday 29th April to Monday 1st May
**Festival of English Wines**
Saturday 27th to Monday 29th May
**International Balloon Fiesta**
Saturday 10th and Sunday 11th June
**Open Air Concert** (Advance ticket sales only)
Saturday 1st July
**Jazz at Leeds**
24th – 26th August.
**Flower Festival**
Friday 22nd to Sunday 24th September
**Firework Display**
Saturday 4th November
**Kentish Evening Dinners**
Saturdays all year round (by reservation)
**Sunday lunches**
November to March (by reservation)

*Enquiries and reservations to:-*

**Leeds Castle, Maidstone,**
**Kent ME17 1PL**
**Tel: Maidstone (0622) 765400**
**Telex: 965737**
**Fax: (0622) 35616**

# LYMPNE CASTLE

**KENT**

Romantic medieval castle with an earlier Roman, Saxon and Norman history. It was rebuilt about 1360. 300 ft above the well-known Roman Shore Fort—Stutfall Castle. Four miles from the ancient Cinque Port of Hythe, it commands a tremendous view across Romney Marshes to Fairlight over the great sweep of the coast from Dover to Dungeness and across the sea to France.

*ADMISSION – SEE EDITORIAL REFERENCE*

# OWL HOUSE GARDENS

**LAMBERHURST, KENT**

*Property of Maureen, Marchioness of Dufferin & Ava and setting for her 16th Century 'Owlers on Smugglers' Haunt.*

13 acres of romantic gardens surround this former wool smugglers' cottage, with spring flowers, roses, rare flowering shrubs, ornamental fruit trees. Expansive lawns lead to leafy woodland walks graced by English and Turkish oaks, elm, birch and beech trees. Rhododendrons, azaleas, camillias encircle peaceful informal sunken water gardens. Gardens open daily, 11 to 6 pm all year, including Bank Holiday weekends. Dogs on lead. Free car park. Coach parties welcome.
Admission: Adults £1.50. Children 75p. (All proceeds towards Lady Dufferin's Charity, Maureen's Oast House for Arthritics.)

## The National Trust

**Welcomes**

## Disabled Visitors

Almost every National Trust property advertised and listed in this Guide has a great deal to offer visitors with disabilities. Please telephone the property you wish to visit for full details – or for a comprehensive booklet on facilities and access at National Trust properties send an adhesive label, stamped with minimum postage to:

**Dept HHG**
**Facilities for Disabled Visitors**
**The National Trust**
**36 Queen Anne's Gate**
**London SW1H 9AS**

# LULLINGSTONE CASTLE

**EYNSFORD, KENT**

Lullingstone Castle, historic family mansion, frequented by Henry VIII and Queen Anne, still lived in by descendants of the original owners who built it nearly 500 years ago.

*ADMISSION – SEE EDITORIAL REFERENCE*

# MOUNT EPHRAIM GARDENS

**HERNHILL, Nr FAVERSHAM, KENT**

Mount Ephraim has been the Dawes home for 300 years but the present gardens were laid out around 1912. By the end of the Second World War they were badly overgrown and it has taken many years to reclaim them. With some simplifications their old beauty and serenity have been restored. The site is magnificent, with views over the Thames estuary and rose terraces sloping down to a small lake and woodland area. There are many fine trees, a topiary garden, a herbaceous border and an extensive Japanese rock garden with a series of pools and a diversity of plants and shrubs. A new vineyard is an added attraction.

## MOUNT EPHRAIM
**Hernhill, nr Faversham** *map L4*
Telephone: Canterbury (0227) 751310 or 751496.
*(Mrs M N Dawes & Mr & Mrs E S Dawes)*

Terraced garden, with beautiful views, leading to small lake. Herbaceous border, topiary, extensive Japanese rock garden. Small woodland area with rhododendrons. Wide variety of plants and shrubs. Fine trees. Rose terraces.
**Location:** 6 m W of Canterbury, 3 m E of Faversham; ½ m N of A2 at Boughton.
**Opening Times:** GARDENS ONLY. May, June, Aug & Sept 2–6. Adm £1.25, Chd 25p. Parties by prior arrangement.
**Refreshments:** Teas available. Suns only.

## NEW COLLEGE OF COBHAM
**Cobham** *map L4* ♿
Telephone: Meopham (0474) 814280
*(Presidents of the New College of Cobham)*

Almshouses based on medieval chantry built 1362, part rebuilt 1598. Originally endowed by Sir John de Cobham and descendants.
**Location:** 4 m W of Rochester; 4 m SE of Gravesend; 1½ m from junction Shorne/ Cobham (A2). In Cobham rear of Church of Mary Magdalene.
*Station: Sole St (1 m).*
**Opening Times:** Apr to Sept—Daily (except Thurs) 10–7. Oct to Mar—Mons, Tues, Weds, Sats & Suns 10–4.
**Refreshments:** Afternoon teas by prior arrangement.

## NORTHBOURNE COURT GARDENS
**Deal** *map M4*
Telephone: (0304) 611281
*(The Lord Northbourne)*

Northbourne Court is on the site of a palace which belonged to Eadbald, son of Ethelbert Saxon King of Kent. In 618 he gave it to the monks of St Augustines Abbey who used the produce from the farms and fish ponds for the support of the poor. After the dissolution it reverted to the crown and finally King James I gave it to Sir Edwyn Sandys. Sir Edwyn built a large house facing three tiers of terraces, which were probably built by Edwin Saunders. These terraces and their high flanking walls are still standing and provide the principal architectural feature of the gardens. The terrace forms a mount which is a rarely surviving characteristic of Tudor Gardens. These gardens are planted with a wide range of old fashioned and grey foliage plants on chalk soil to provide interest and colour all year round.
**Location:** A256 (Dover to Sandwich). Turn right towards Deal/Mongeham and continue for approximately 2 m.
**Opening Times:** Suns May 28, June 11, 25, July 9, 23, Aug 13, 27, Sept 17: 2–6. Weds May 31 to Aug 30: 2–5. Adm £1.40, Chd/OAP 50p (reductions for parties) in aid of National Gardens Scheme. Plenty of car/coach parking nearby. Limited access for disabled persons (no wheelchairs available).
**Refreshments:** Pub in village serves good food. Otherwise contact C James on (0304) 611281.

## OWL HOUSE GARDENS
**Lamberhurst** *map L3*
*(Maureen, Marchioness of Dufferin & Ava)*

16th century half-timbered, tile-hung wool smuggler's cottage. Beautiful gardens, magnificent roses, daffodils, rhododendrons. Woodland walks.
**Location:** 8 m SE of Tunbridge Wells; 1 m from Lamberhurst off A21.
**Opening Times:** GARDENS ONLY. All the year—daily and weekends including all Bank Hol weekends 11–6. Adm £1.50, Chd 75p. (Proceeds towards Lady Dufferin's charity, Maureen's Oast House for Arthritics.) Dogs on lead. Free parking. Coach parties welcome.

## OWLETTS, The National Trust
**Cobham** *map L4*

A red-brick Carolean house with contemporary staircase and plasterwork ceiling. Small gardens.
**Location:** 1 m S of A2 at W end of village, at junction of roads from Dartford & Sole Street.
*Station: Sole Street (1 m).*
**Opening Times:** Mar 29 to end of Sept—Weds & Thurs 2–5 (last adm 4.30). Adm 60p. *No reduction for parties or children. No indoor photography. No dogs.* Wheelchair access to ground floor only.

## PENSHURST PLACE
**Tunbridge Wells** *map K4* △
Telephone: Penshurst (0892) 870307
*(The Rt Hon Viscount De L'Isle, VC, KG)*

The early house, including the Great Hall, dates from 1340. There were later additions but the whole house conforms to the English Gothic style in which it was begun.
**Location:** In Penshurst village on B2176, W of Tonbridge & Tunbridge Wells.
*Station: Penshurst (2 m).*
**Opening Times:** Penshurst Place is open every afternoon (except Mons) from Apr 1 to Oct 1. Open Bank Hol Mons & Easter Bank Hols.
Grounds 12.30–6. House 1–5.30 (last entry to House is 5). Reduced adm rates for groups, OAPs and Chd. Free car park for visitors. No dogs admitted.
**Refreshments:** Light luncheons and teas available in Endeavour Restaurant.

## PORT LYMPNE ZOO PARK, MANSION & GARDENS
**Lympne, Hythe** *map M3*
Telephone: Hythe (0303) 264646
*(John Aspinall, Esq)*

Described as the "last historic house built this century", Port Lympne encompasses the essence of Roman villas and the English country house. Overlooking the Channel and set in ornamental gardens, the interior of the house features a Moorish patio, marble columns, an intriguing hall floor plus the exquisitely painted Tent Room by Rex Whistler and another, South Asian in concept, currently being painted by wildlife artist Spencer Roberts. Wildlife Art Gallery, exhibitions of photography and bronzes. 270 acre zoo park. Safari trailer. Gift shop. Picnic areas.
**Location:** 3 m W of Hythe; 6 m W of Folkestone; 7 m SE of Ashford off A20.
**Opening Times:** All the year—Daily. Summer 10–5*; Winter 10–one hour before dusk* (*last admissions). *Closed Christmas Day.* Reduced prices for OAPs and Chld 4–14 (3 and under free). Special party rates. Free car park.
**Refreshments:** Cafeteria.

## QUEBEC HOUSE, The National Trust
**Westerham** *map K4*
Telephone: Westerham 62206

Probably early 16th century in origin, now mainly 17th century. Mementos of General Wolfe, and colourful exhibition about the Battle of Quebec.
**Location:** At junction of Edenbridge & Sevenoaks Roads (A25 & B2026).
**Opening Times:** Mar 24 to end of Oct—Daily (except Thurs & Sats), inc Good Fri and Bank Holiday Mon 2–6. Last adm 5.30. Adm £1.40, Chd 70p. *Pre-booked parties £1, Chd 50p.* No dogs. Unsuitable for wheelchairs.

## QUEX HOUSE, QUEX PARK
**Birchington** *map M4*
Telephone: Thanet (0843) 42168
*(Powell-Cotton Museum Trustees)*

Wander through the period rooms of P.H.G. Powell-Cotton's lovely Regency mansion, with its superb woodcarving and panelling, beautiful plasterwork and air of mellow maturity. The rooms are arranged much as they were in his lifetime and contain fine 17th and 18th century English furniture and many family treasures. The unique Chinese Imperial porcelain collection however, has been moved to a gallery in the Powell-Cotton Museum, built adjoining the mansion; this purpose-built museum now extends to nine large galleries; here Powell-Cotton created huge dioramas showing 500 African and Asian animals, all mounted by Rowland Ward, in scenes re-creating their natural habitats. He assembled the finest collection of African ethnography collected on 28 expeditions, and displayed it at Quex, together with a superb weapons collection, local archaeology, bygones and the wonderful oriental Fine arts. This year, the porcelain has been re-displayed and a full catalogue has been published much of it in full colour.
**Location:** In Birchington, ½ m S of Birchington Square (signposted). SW of Margate; 13 m E of Canterbury.
*Station: Birchington (1 m).*
**Opening Times:** Apr 1 to Sept 30—Weds, Thurs & Suns (also Fris in Aug): 2.15–6. *Open Bank Hols in summer.* Adm £1.50, Chd £1 (last entry 5). Parties on other days by arrangement. Ground floor rooms & museum only, suitable for disabled.
**Refreshments:** Tea room, light refreshments.

**Reculver Towers and Roman Fort** – See English Heritage Section.

**Richborough Castle** – See English Heritage Section.

## RIVERHILL HOUSE
**Sevenoaks** *map K4* △
Telephone: Sevenoaks (0732) 452557/458802
*(John Rogers Esq)*

Small country house, home of the Rogers family since 1840. Panelled rooms, portraits and interesting memorabilia. An historic garden with rare trees and shrubs. Fine collection of mature trees. Sheltered terraces and rhododendrons and azaleas in woodland setting. Good hydrangeas. Ancient trackway known as "Harold's Road".
**Location:** 2 m S of Sevenoaks on road to Tonbridge (A225).
*Station: Sevenoaks (2 m).*
**Opening Times:** Easter to end of Aug. GARDEN every Sun in above period, also Sats & Mons of all Bank Hol weekends, 12–6. Picnics allowed. No dogs. Adm £1, Chd 30p. HOUSE **only** open Sat, Sun & Mon of Bank Hol weekends. Adults only inside. Adm £2, 2–5. Party bookings for House and Garden or Garden only (20 upwards) any day except Bank Hol weekends from Easter until Oct 18.
**Refreshments:** Home-made teas in the Old Stable from 2.30. Catering for booked parties—Ploughman's Lunches and Teas—by arrangement. All enquiries to Mrs Rogers.

## ROCHESTER CASTLE
**Rochester** *map L4*
Telephone: (0634) 402276
*(English Heritage)*

Large 11th century castle partly founded on the Roman city wall, with a splendid keep of c. 1130, the tallest in England.
**Location:** By Rochester Bridge (A2).
**Opening Times:** Good Friday to Sept 30, daily 10–6; Oct 1 to Maundy Thurs, daily 10–4. *Closed* Mons, Dec 24–26, Jan 1. Adm £1.10, OAPs 80p, Chd 55p.

# PENSHURST PLACE KENT

William Sidney, Lord De L'Isle, welcomes you to Penshurst Place, one of Britain's outstanding Stately Homes.

- ⋆ Magnificent house with fine state rooms and famous medieval Great Hall.
- ⋆ Ten acre walled garden with hedged enclosures.
- ⋆ Farm Museum.
- ⋆ Park, Venture Playground with Tuck Shop and Nature Trail.
- ⋆ Self-service restaurant for lunches and teas.

Open: 12.30 – 6 pm. Tuesday through Sunday plus Bank Holiday Mondays from 1 April – October. Open Easter Bank Holiday. Free car and coach parking. No dogs admitted except Guide Dogs. Special rates for groups and senior citizens. Private and educational tours by arrangement. Home Park available for outdoor functions. Medieval Sunderland Room can be reserved for luncheons, dinners, conferences and wedding receptions.

FOR OPENING DETAILS SEE ENTRY UNDER KENT. For all enquiries and for Party Bookings please contact: The Administrator, Penshurst Place, Penshurst, Tonbridge, Kent, TN11 8DG. Telephone: Penshurst (0892) 870307.

# RIVERHILL HOUSE

**Sevenoaks**

Ragstone house built in 1714 and added to by John Rogers in 1842. Riverhill enjoys a favoured position and has a very protected hillside garden with extensive views over the Weald of Kent. It is unsuitable for the disabled.

GARDEN: Open every Sunday from Easter to end of August also the Saturday and Monday of Bank Holiday weekends.

HOUSE: Open ONLY at Bank Holiday weekends.

*See editorial reference for complete details.*

# QUEX HOUSE

**QUEX PARK, BIRCHINGTON PARK**

*Family home of P.H.G. Powell-Cotton, great Victorian explorer and collector.

*Purpose built nine-gallery Museum of international acclaim with superb displays.

*Peaceful mature gardens in lovely wooded parkland.

*For days of opening please see editorial entry.*

# PORT LYMPNE

**Kent**

Built for Sir Philip Sassoon between 1911 and 1913, Port Lympne is set in 15 acres of beautiful terraced gardens. The principal architect was Sir Herbert Baker who designed New Delhi. No expense was spared to create a totally luxurious summer pleasance. It became famous for its weekend parties with guests who included the Prince of Wales and Mrs Simpson, Bernard Shaw, Lawrence of Arabia, Lloyd George, Charles Chaplin, Stanley Baldwin, Winston Churchill and Mountbatten. Bought and restored by Mr John Aspinall in 1973, it is now open to the public together with its 270 acre Zoo Park.

# SQUERRYES COURT

**Westerham, Kent**

William and Mary Manor House built in 1681. Home of the Warde family who have lived there since 1735. Previously owned by the Earl of Jersey.

This mellow, red brick house contains many fine pictures, furniture, tapestries and china collected by the Warde family in the 18th century.

Relics of General Wolfe, who was a childhood friend of General George Warde, are also on view.

Landscaped grounds in a parkland setting include lake, rhododendrons, azaleas and a formal garden.

Home-made teas at weekends and for booked parties.

*ADMISSION – SEE EDITORIAL REFERENCE UNDER KENT.*

*Jeremy Whitaker photograph*

**St Augustine's Abbey** – See English Heritage Section.

### ST JOHN'S JERUSALEM GARDEN, The National Trust
**Dartford** *map L4* ♿

Large garden, moated by River Darent. The house, the main walls of which formed the church of a Commandery of the Knights Hospitallers, was altered in later centuries. Only the former chapel and the garden are open to the public.

**Location:** 3 m S of Dartford at Sutton-at-Hone on E side of A225.
*Station: Farningham Road (¾ m).*
**Opening Times:** GARDEN & FORMER CHAPEL ONLY. Mar 29 to end Oct—Weds 2–6 (last adm 5.30). Adm 40p. *No reduction for parties or children. No dogs.* Wheelchair access to garden only.

### SALTWOOD CASTLE
**nr Hythe** *map M3*
Telephone: Hythe (0303) 67190 (Secretary)
*(The Hon Alan Clark, MP & Mrs Clark)*

Norman castle, subject of quarrel between Thomas à Becket and Henry II. Grounds and parts of Castle including battlement walk, undercroft, armoury.

**Location:** 2 m NW of Hythe; from A20 turn S at sign to Saltwood.
*Station: Sandling (1½ m).*
**Opening Times:** *Saltwood Castle is closed to the general public in 1989.* Private parties of 20 or more can be accommodated *(on weekdays only)* following an appointment confirmed in writing.

### SCOTNEY CASTLE GARDEN, The National Trust
**Lamberhurst** *map L3* ♿
Telephone: Lamberhurst (0892) 890651

Romantic landscape garden framing moated castle.

**Location:** 1½ m SE of Lamberhurst (A21).
**Opening Times:** Garden: Mar 25 to Nov 12—Weds to Fris 11–6 or sunset if earlier *(closed Good Fri)*; Sats, Suns & Bank Hol Mons 2–6 or sunset if earlier. Last adm half-hour before closing. Old Castle: May to end Aug—days & times as for Garden. Adm £2, Chd £1. Parties by prior appointment £1.60. *No reduction on Sats, Suns or Bank Hol Mons. No dogs.* Shop. Wheelchairs available. (Steep entrance to garden.)

### SISSINGHURST CASTLE GARDEN, The National Trust
**Sissinghurst** *map L3*
Telephone: Cranbrook 712850

The famous garden created by the late Vita Sackville-West and Sir Harold Nicolson between the surviving parts of an Elizabethan mansion.

**Location:** 2 m NE of Cranbrook; 1 m E of Sissinghurst village (A262).
**Opening Times:** Mar 24 to Oct 15—Tues to Fris 1–6.30; Sats, Suns & Good Fri 10–6.30. (Last adm 6.) *Closed Mons, incl Bank Hol Mons.* The garden may be over-crowded at around 3pm. Visitors may be asked to wait. Adm Tues to Sats £3, Suns £3.50; Chd £1.50, Suns £1.80. Parties by appointment only; reductions on weekdays only. No dogs. Shop. No picnics in garden. Adm to wheelchair visitors is restricted to 2 at any one time.
**Refreshments:** In the Granary Restaurant. Mar 24 to Oct 15—Tues to Fri 12–6, Sat & Sun 10–6. Closed Mons.

### SMALLHYTHE PLACE, The National Trust
**Tenterden** *map L3*
Telephone: Tenterden 2334

The Ellen Terry Memorial Museum. Half-timbered 16th century yeoman's home. Mementoes of Dame Ellen Terry, Mrs Siddons, etc.

**Location:** 2½ m S of Tenterden on E side of Rye Road (B2082).
**Opening Times:** Mar 24 to end of Oct—Daily (except Thurs & Fris) 2–6 or dusk if earlier. Open Good Fri. Last adm half-hour before closing. Adm £1.40, Chd 70p. *Parties should give advance notice—no reduction. No parties in August.* No indoor photography. No dogs. Unsuitable for wheelchairs. Can only take 25 at a time in house.
**Refreshments:** Tea available at The Spinning Wheel & the Tudor Rose, Tenterden.

### SPRIVERS GARDEN, Mrs G C Dibben (The National Trust)
**Horsmonden** *map L3*

Garden with some unusual plants and shrubs, herbaceous borders, architectural temples and ornaments. Parts of the garden under restoration and replanting. Small collection of Waterfowl. Woodland walks and avenues being re-opened and planted.

**Location:** 3 m N of Lamberhurst on B2162; 10 m SE of Tonbridge.
**Opening Times:** May to Sept 27—Weds only 2–5.30 (last adm 5). Adm 70p. No reductions for parties or Chd. No dogs. Wheelchair access. No lavatories.

### SQUERRYES COURT
**Westerham** *map K4*
Telephone: Westerham (0959) 62345 or 63118
*(J St A Warde, Esq)*

William and Mary manor house. Period furniture, paintings, tapestries and china. Objects of interest connected with General Wolfe. Attractive grounds with lake, fine display of spring bulbs, rhododendrons and azaleas.

**Location:** Western outsirts of Westerham on A25.
**Opening Times:** Mar Suns and Bank Hol only 2–6. Apr–Sept, Weds, Sats, Suns and Bank Hol Mons 2–6 pm (last adm 5.30). Adm House & Grounds £2.20, Chd (under 14) £1.20; Grounds only £1.20, Chd (under 14) 60p. Parties over 20 (any day except Suns) by arrangement at reduced rates. Dogs on leads in grounds only. Free parking at house.
**Refreshments:** Homemade teas at weekends & for booked parties.

### STONEACRE, The National Trust
**Otham** *map L4*

A half-timbered small manor house, c. 1480. Small garden.

**Location:** In Otham, 3 m SE of Maidstone; 1 m S of A20.
*Station: Bearsted (2 m).*
**Opening Times:** Apr to end Oct—Weds & Sats 2–6 (last adm 5). Adm £1, Chd 50p. No reduction for parties. No dogs. Unsuitable for wheelchairs. Narrow access road.

**Upnor Castle** – See English Heritage Section.

### WALMER CASTLE
**Walmer** *map M4*
Telephone: (0304) 364288
*(English Heritage)*

One of the coastal castles built by Henry VIII and the official residence of The Lords Warden of The Cinque Ports, including the Duke of Wellington who died at Walmer and whose furnished rooms have been preserved unaltered. (The original 'Wellington Boot' may be seen here).

**Location:** On coast at Walmer 2 m S of Deal off the Dover/Deal Road.
*Station: Walmer (1½ m).*
**Opening Times:** Good Friday to Sept 30, daily 10–6; Oct 1 to Maundy Thurs, daily 10–4. *Closed Mons, Dec 24–26, Jan 1 and when Lord Warden of the Cinque Ports is in residence.* Adm £1.60, OAPs £1.20, Chd 80p.

## LANCASHIRE

### ASHTON MEMORIAL
**Williamson Park, Lancaster** *map F9*
Telephone: (0524) 33318
*(Lancaster City Council)*

Described by Sir Nikolaus Pevsner as 'The Grandest Monument in England', the Ashton Memorial stands in a superb site overlooking the city. The design is in the style of the Edwardian revival of the English Baroque, typical of the late Wren, Vanbrugh and Hawksmoor 200 years earlier. Architect John Belcher RA, PRIBA. The Old Palm House, near the Ashton Memorial, has been restored and transformed into a Butterfly House for rare and exotic tropical butterflies. A British Butterfly House will be opening early in 1989.

**Opening Times:** Open all year except Christmas Day, Boxing Day and New Year's Day. Winter opening 10–3. Summer opening 10–5. Adm charge. Party rate available for prior bookings.

### ASTLEY HALL
**Chorley** *map G9*
*(Chorley Borough Council (1922))*

Elizabethan house reconstructed in 1666. Furniture, pottery, tapestries, pictures.

**Location:** 2 m NW town centre on A6 (footpath access only to Hall ¾ m) or A581 (car access, turn right after 1½ m—signposted).
**Opening Times:** All the year Apr to Sept—Daily 12–5.30; Oct to Mar—Mons to Fris 12–3.30; Sats 10–3.30; Suns 11–3.30. Adm 75p, Chd (accompanied by adult) 35p, Chd (unaccompanied) OAPs & registered unemployed 50p. (Prices subject to review in Apr 1989.) Reduced rates for parties. Large free car park.
**Refreshments:** At the Hall (summer months).

### BROWSHOLME HALL
**nr Clitheroe** *map G9* △
Telephone: Stoneyhurst 330

Home of the Parker family, Bowbearers of the Forest of Bowland. Tudor with Elizabethan front, Queen Anne Wing and Regency additions. Portraits furniture and antiquities. Guided tours by members of the family.

**Location:** 5 m NW of Clitheroe; off B6243; Bashall Eaves—Whitewell signposted.
**Opening Times:** Easter Sat, Sun & Mon and following Sat & Sun. Late May Bank Hol weekend. Every Sat in June, July & Aug. Summer Bank Hol & preceding week 2–5. Reductions for booked parties at other times by appointment with Mrs Parker, Tel. as above.

# SALTWOOD CASTLE KENT

One of the finest Norman Castles in private ownership. Famous 'Battlement Walk' rings the Inner Bailey. Medieval Undercroft, torture chamber. Dungeon where Thorpe the Lollard was imprisoned for sixteen years. Ruined 13th century chapel.

Formerly lived in by the wicked Sir Ralph de Broc, murderer of Thomas à Becket and more recently by Lord Clark of Civilization fame, part of whose art collection is housed in the Keep which is open to private parties by appointment.

Special VIP tours conducted by members of the family, including sherry in the Great Library, for pre-booked parties at extra charge.

Tea-shop exclusively home-made with produce from the estate.

*NB Saltwood Castle is closed to the general public in 1989. Private parties of 20 or more can be accommodated (weekdays only) following an appointment confirmed in writing.*

*'Aerofilms Ltd' photograph*

# ASHTON MEMORIAL

**WILLIAMSON PARK LANCASTER**

"The grandest monument in England"

*Sir Nikolaus Pevsner*

*ADMISSION – SEE EDITORIAL REFERENCE*

# CHINGLE HALL

**Nr PRESTON**

Small moated Manor House

Earliest domestic brick built structure in the British Isles 1260

Archeological excavation in progress

Birthplace of St John Wall (1620–1679)

Site of foundation meeting of modern Ecumenical movement

The most haunted house in the British Isles

*ADMISSION – SEE EDITORIAL REFERENCE*

# HOGHTON TOWER

**Lancashire**

*5 miles east of Preston on A675; M6 Exit 28, M61 Exit 8*

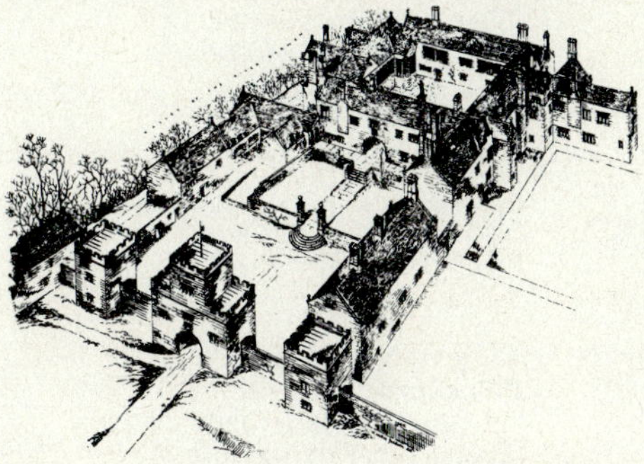

Historic Hoghton Tower. Dramatic 16th century Fortified Hilltop Mansion. The seat of Sir Bernard de Hoghton, Bt. As seen in 'The Roots of England' and 'Lancashire Witches' on BBC TV. Spend a few hours in this delightful historic mansion where, in the magnificent Banqueting Hall James I knighted the loin of beef in 1617. Permanent exhibition and Dolls Houses and historic Hoghton Documents. Underground passages, dungeons, and Lancashire witches kitchen. Gift Shop. Tea Rooms. Special catering for private parties and functions. Exciting events throughout the year. Open Easter Saturday, Sunday and Monday; every Sunday until the end of October: Saturdays and Sundays July and August; all Bank Holidays. 2 pm to 5 pm. Admission £2. Children 50p. School parties, children 50p. Private visits welcome, minimum 25 at any time throughout the week. Apply Administrator, Hoghton Tower, Preston PR5 0SH. Tel: (0254) 852986.

# ASTLEY HALL

**LANCASHIRE**

*ADMISSION – SEE EDITORIAL REFERENCE*

## CHINGLE HALL

**Goosnargh** *map F9*
Telephone: (0772) 861082

Built by Adam de Singleton in 1260 almost certainly on a Viking or earlier site adjacent to the Viking village of Goosnargh, the Hall is the earliest surviving brick built house in the British Isles; this small moated Manor House is currently an undisturbed enigma but now subject to 5 areas of serious ongoing Research: **Archaeological:** Excavation in progress, moat and drawbridge being reconstructed. **Architectural:** Subject of several renovations its Great Hall is Viking beamed (circa 700 AD). **Historical:** Part of the running skirmish of the Battle of Preston occurred on the grounds, etc. **Religious:** A Reformation Mass Centre (undiscovered by Lord Birley in 1580). Hides by Nicholas Owen (Martyred). Birthplace of St. John Wall (Martyred) Franciscan. Modern Ecumenical movement founded in a meeting between Bishop Hoskins Abrahall and Cardinal Heenan in 1962 on re-discovery of the Chingle Cross. Catholic Shrine. **Paranormal:** Reputed to be one of the most haunted houses in the British Isles monks among other sightings and manifestations. Garden, play area, picnic area.

**Location:** Leave M6 at Junction 32 on to M55 to Blackpool, leave M55 at Junction 1 on to A6 to Garstang. Turn right at first set of traffic lights, continue for 2 miles, turn right at Whittingham/Goosnargh signpost.
**Opening Times:** Open all year. (Booked parties only between Dec 20 and Jan 31.) Tour (1 hour) – Adults £2.50, Students and OAPs £2, Chd (7–12) £1.50. Coaches (day or evening) by appointment.
**Refreshments:** Available. Stay the night in St John Wall's or the Priest's Room, by prior arrangement only for paranormal and charity 'sit ins'. Telephone above no. for details.

## GAWTHORPE HALL, The National Trust

**Padiham** *map G9*
Telephone: Padiham (0282) 78511

House built in 1600-1605, restored by Barry in 1850; Barry's designs newly re-created in principal rooms. Display of Rachel Kay-Shuttleworth textile collections, private study by arrangement. Major display of late 17th century portraits on loan from the National Portrait Gallery. Estate building, recently restored, houses a broad programme of craft and management courses.

**Location:** On E outskirts of Padiham (¾ m drive to house is on N of A671).
*Station: Rose Grove (2 m).*
**Opening Times:** Mar 24 to end Oct. HALL: Tues, Weds, Thurs, Sats & Suns, 2–6, last adm 5.30. Open Good Fri & Bank Holiday Mons. GARDEN: Open daily all year 10–6. GALLERY and SHOP: Daily Feb to Dec 20, 10.30–12.30, 2–5 (Sat & Sun 2–5). Adm House and Garden: £1.50, Chd 75p. Reductions for pre-booked parties of 15 or more (except Bank Holidays). No dogs. Access for disabled: Ground floor of Hall, Shop & Gallery. W.C.
**Refreshments:** Refectory in Estate Building open as shop, but 11–5 weekdays.

## HOGHTON TOWER

**nr Preston** *map F9*
Telephone: Hoghton (025 485) 2986
*(Sir Bernard de Hoghton, Bt)*

Dramatic 16th century fortified hill-top mansion with the magnificent Banqueting Hall where James I knighted the 'Loin of Beef' in 1617. Permanent collection of dolls' houses. Walled gardens and Old English Rose Garden.

**Location:** 5 m E of Preston on A675.
*Station: Pleasington (2¾ m).*
**Opening Times:** Easter Sat, Sun & Mon, then Suns to end of Oct, also Sats in July & Aug & all Bank Hols: 2–5. Adm £2, Chd 50p. School parties—Chd 50p. Private visits welcome (minimum 25 persons) at any time throughout week. Apply Administrator, Hoghton Tower, Preston PR5 0SH. Souvenir & Craft Shop.
**Refreshments:** Tea rooms.

## JUDGES' LODGINGS – GILLOW AND TOWN HOUSE MUSEUM AND MUSEUM OF CHILDHOOD

**Lancaster** *map F9*
Telephone: (0524) 32808
*(Lancashire County Council)*

17th century town house, built by Thomas Covell, Keeper of the Castle during the notorious Pendle Witches Trial. Used as a lodging for visiting judges from 1826 to 1975. Period rooms, Gillow furniture, turn of the century classroom, children's dolls, toys and games from 18th century to present day.

**Location:** Church Street, Lancaster
*Station: Lancaster Castle.*
**Opening Times:** Apr to Oct: Mon to Sat 2–5. Also mornings in July to Sept 10–1. **Gillow and Town House Museum & Museum of Childhood:** Open Good Fri to Oct 31.

## LEIGHTON HALL

**Carnforth** *map F10* △ Ⓢ
Telephone: 0524 734474
*(Mr & Mrs R. G. Reynolds)*

Mid 12th century House rebuilt in the late 18th century with a neo Gothic façade added in 1800. Home of the Gillow family containing early and prototype Gillow furniture. Extensive grounds and garden. **Displays with trained eagles and falcons at 3.30 pm unless raining.**

**Location:** 2 m W of A6 through Yealand Conyers; signposted from M6, exit 35 junction with A6.
*Stations: Silverdale (1½ m, bridlepath only); Carnforth (2½ m).*
**Opening Times:** May to Sept—Suns, Bank Hol Mons & Tues to Fris 2–5 (last tour of House 4.30). Other times by appointment for parties of 25 or more. Special Educational Programme for Schools—mornings from 10 am. Adm House & Grounds £2, Chd £1.10 – family ticket 2nd child free. Teachers with schools free. Inquiries: Mrs Reynolds at the Hall. Schools Programme—Mr A Oswald Tel: 0524 701353. Disabled visitors welcome.
**Refreshments:** Teas at the Hall. Salad lunches/high teas for booked parties.

## MARTHOLME

**Great Harwood, Blackburn** *map G9*
*(Mr & Mrs T H Codling)*

Screens passage and service wing of medieval manor house altered 1577 with 17th century additions. Gatehouse built 1561, restored 1969.

**Location:** 2 m from Great Harwood off A680 to Whalley.
**Opening Times:** Exterior: all the year—Fri & Sat. Interior: by appointment only. Adm: Exterior: £1. Interior: £2.

## MEOLS HALL

**Southport** *map F9*
*(R. F. Hesketh Esq.)*

A 17th century house, with subsequent additions, containing an interesting collection of pictures, furniture, china, etc.

**Location:** 1 m N of Southport; 16 m SW of Preston; 20 m N of Liverpool; near A565 & A570.
*Stations: Southport (1¾ m); Meols Cop (1 m).*
**Opening Times:** Mon May 29: 2–5; Aug 1–31: 2–5. Adm £1, Chd (accompanied by adult) free.

## RUFFORD OLD HALL, The National Trust

**Rufford, nr Ormskirk** *map F9*
Telephone: Rufford (0704) 821254

One of the finest buildings of the 15th century in Lancashire. The Great Hall is remarkable for its ornate hammer-beam roof and unique screen. Fine collections of 17th century oak furniture and 16th century arms and armour and tapestries.

**Location:** 7 m N of Ormskirk at N end of Rufford village on E side of A59.
*Stations: Rufford (½ m) (not Suns); Burscough Bridge (2½ m).*
**Opening Times:** Mar 24 to Nov 5—Daily (except Fris) 1–5, Suns 2–5. Last adm 4.30. Garden, Cafe and shop: open 11–5 on same days, Suns 2–5. Adm Hall & Garden £1.50, Chd 75p. Reduced rate for parties of 15 or more by arrangement. Access for disabled garden only. Guide dogs.
**Refreshments:** At the Hall (parties should book).

## SAMLESBURY HALL

**nr Preston** *map G9*
*(Samlesbury Hall Trust)*

14th century Manor House owned and administered by private trust.

**Location:** On A677; 6 m E of Preston; 5 m W of Blackburn.
**Opening Times:** All the year—Tues to Suns 11.30–5 (summer), 11.30–4 (winter). *Closed Mons.* Adm £2, Chd (under 16) 80p. Coach & organised parties by appointment Tues to Fris only. Ongoing sales of antiques and collectors' items. Also various craft, at work and other exhibitions.
**Refreshments:** Tea-room open 12–4 (coffee etc).

## TOWNELEY HALL ART GALLERY & MUSEUM and MUSEUM OF LOCAL CRAFTS & INDUSTRIES

**Burnley** *map G9*
Telephone: Burnley 24213
*(Burnley Borough Council)*

House dates from 14th century with 16th, 17th and 19th century modifications. Fine entrance hall.

**Location:** ½ m SE of Burnley on the Burnley/Todmorden Road (A671).
*Station: Burnley Central (1¾ m).*
**Opening Times:** All the year—Mons to Fris 10–5, Suns 12–5. *Closed Sats throughout year.* Adm free. *Closed Christmas–New Year.*
**Refreshments:** At café in grounds.

## TURTON TOWER

**Blackburn** *map G9*
Telephone: Bolton (0204) 852203
*(Lancashire County Council)*

15th century pele tower with Elizabethan farmhouse attached, standing in 8 acres of grounds. Owned by Humphrey Chetham of Manchester in the Civil War. Period furnishings, paintings, weaponry and local history room.

**Location:** Chapeltown Road, Turton. 5 m N of Bolton on B6391.
*Station: Bromley Cross.*
**Opening Times:** Gardens open throughout the year—Adm. Tower Mar, Apr, Oct: Sat to Wed 2–5; May to Sept: Mon to Fri 10–12, 1–5, Sat & Sun 1–5. Nov and Feb: Suns 2–5; Dec & Jan: *Closed.* Adm 70p, OAPs 50p, Chd 35p. Family ticket £1.70.

# LEICESTERSHIRE

**Ashby de la Zouch Castle** – See English Heritage Section.

## BELGRAVE HALL
**Leicester (1709-13)** *map J7* ♿
Telephone: Leicester (0533) 554100
*(Leicestershire Museums, Art Galleries & Records Service)*

A small Queen Anne house and garden with furniture of 18th and early 19th century.
**Location:** Off Thurcaston Road, Belgrave 2 m from City centre on Loughborough Road (A6).
*Station: Leicester (2½ m).*
**Opening Times:** All the year—Weekdays 10–5.30; Suns 2–5.30. Adm free. *Closed Good Friday, Christmas Day & Boxing Day.*

## BELVOIR CASTLE
**nr Grantham** *map J7*
Telephone: Grantham (0476) 870262
*(His Grace the Duke of Rutland)*

Seat of the Dukes of Rutland since Henry VIII's time, rebuilt by Wyatt 1816. Notable pictures, furniture, objets d'art. Special Events most Sundays.
**Location:** 7 m WSW of Grantham, between A607 (to Melton Mowbray) and A52 (to Nottingham).
**Opening Times:** Mar 18 to Oct 8—Tues, Weds, Thurs & Sats 11–6; Suns 11–7; Bank Hol Mons only 11–7; Good Friday and also Fri during June, July, Aug, Sept 11–6; also Sats & Suns only in Oct, 11–6. Last adm 40 mins before closing. Adm £2.60, Chd £1.50. *No extra charges in Castle.* Parties of 30 or more OAPs £1.50 (organiser free); 30 or more adults £2; 30 or more School children £1.50 (accompanying teachers free). All Coach Excursion passengers £2. No dogs.
**Refreshments:** Café at Castle.

## BOSWORTH BATTLEFIELD VISITOR CENTRE & COUNTRY PARK
**Market Bosworth** *map H6* ♿
Telephone: Market Bosworth (0455) 290429
*(Leicestershire County Council)*

Site of the famous Battle of Bosworth Field (1485) with extensive Visitor Centre including exhibitions, models, film theatre, book and gift shops and cafeteria; and outdoor interpretation of the Battle. Series of special mediaeval attractions during summer months.
**Location:** 15 m W of Leicester; 2 m S of Market Bosworth (sign posted off A5, A447, A444 and B585).
**Opening Times:** BATTLEFIELD VISITOR CENTRE. Mar 22 to Oct 31—Mons to Sats 2–5.30; Suns and Bank Hols 1–6. July 1 to Aug 31: open from 11a.m. Admission £1.20, Chd (under 16 years) and OAPs 80p. (Special charges apply on main Special Event days.) Parties at any time by appointment at reduced rates. COUNTRY PARK & BATTLE TRAILS: All year during daylight hours.
**Refreshments:** Bosworth Buttery Cafeteria.

## GUILDHALL
**Leicester** *map J7* ♿
Telephone: Leicester (0533) 554100
*(Leicestershire Museums, Art Galleries & Records Service)*

A medieval timber building dating from 14th to 17th centuries. Mayor's Parlour, Library and old police cells.
**Location:** Guildhall Lane.
*Station: Leicester.*
**Opening Times:** All the year—Weekdays 10–5.30; Suns 2–5.30. Adm free. *Closed Good Friday, Christmas Day & Boxing Day.*

**Kirby Muxloe Castle** – See English Heritage Section.

## LYDDINGTON BEDE HOUSE
*map J6*
Telephone: (057 282) 2438
*(English Heritage)*

The building is the only surviving part of a grand medieval palace of the Bishops of Lincoln. After the Reformation it passed to Thomas, Lord Burghley, who turned it into an almshouse. It was used as such until the present century.
**Location:** In Lyddington 6m (9.6 km) north of Corby. OS map ref SP875970.
**Opening Times:** Good Friday to Sept 30 – daily 10–6. Adm 80p, OAPs 60p, Chd 40p.

## MANOR HOUSE
**Donington le Heath** *map H7*
Telephone: Coalville (0530) 31259
*(Leicestershire Museums, Art Galleries & Records Service)*

Early 14th century Manor house with furniture. Herb garden.
**Location:** 1 m SW of Coalville; 13 m NW of Leicester off A50; 4 m from M1 at exit 22.
**Opening Times:** Mar 22 to Oct 1 Bank Hol Mons & Tues 2–6. Adm free.
**Refreshments:** Cream teas available in the Barn.

## OAKHAM CASTLE
**Oakham** *map J7* ♿
Telephone: Oakham (0572) 3654
*(Leicestershire Museums, Art Galleries & Records Service)*

Late 12th century Norman hall with collection of horseshoes given by peers of the realm.
**Location:** N of Market Place nr town centre. Off A605.
*Station: Oakham (5 mins walk).*
**Opening Times:** Grounds. Apr to Oct—Daily 10–5.30. Nov to Mar—Daily 10–4. Castle, Apr to Oct—Suns 2–5.30; Tues to Sats & Bank Hols 10–1, 2–5.30; Nov to Mar—as above but closing at 4. Adm free. *Closed Good Friday, Christmas Day & Boxing Day.*

ROCKINGHAM CASTLE—SEE UNDER NORTHANTS.

## STANFORD HALL
**Lutterworth** *map J6* △
Telephone: Rugby (0788) 860250
*(The Lady Braye)*

A William and Mary House built in the 1690's containing a fine collection of pictures (including the Stuart Collection), antique furniture and family costumes dating from Queen Elizabeth I's time. There is a full-size replica of the 1898 Flying Machine of Percy Pilcher who is officially recognised as England's Pioneer Aviator. He experimented at Stanford where he was killed whilst flying in 1899. The Motorcycle Museum contains an outstanding collection of Vintage and historic motorcycles. Walled Rose Garden leading to Old Forge. Nature Trail. Craft Centre most Sundays.
**Location:** 7½ m NE of Rugby; 3½ m from A5; 6 m from M1 at exit 18; 5 m from M1 at exit 20; 6 m from M6 at exit 1; 1¼ m from B5414 at Swinford.
**Opening Times:** Easter Sat to end of Sept—Thurs, Sats & Suns also Bank Hol Mons & Tues following 2.30–6. Adm House & Grounds, etc, £2.10, Chd £1. Grounds, Rose Garden, Flying Machine, Old Forge, Craft Centre (most Suns) £1.10, Chd 50p. Parties of 20 or more (min £36) £1.80, Chd 80p. OAP parties of 20 or more £1.70. School parties of 20 or more (one teacher adm free) £1.80, Chd 80p. Adm prices subject to increase on occasional Event Days. Motor cycle Museum £1, Chd 25p.
NB On Bank Hols and Event Days open 12–6 (House 2.30).
**Refreshments:** Home-made teas. Light lunches most Suns. Lunches, High Tea or Suppers for pre-booked parties any day during season.

## WYGSTON'S HOUSE
**Leicester** *map J7*
Telephone: Leicester (0533) 554100
*(Leicestershire Museums, Art Galleries & Records Service)*

Museums of Costume (1769-1924) in a medieval house with Georgian additions. Shop reconstructions.
**Location:** Applegate St Nicholas Circle nr City centre.
*Station: Leicester.*
**Opening Times:** All the year—Weekdays 10–5.30; Suns 2–5.30. Adm free. *Closed Good Friday, Christmas Day & Boxing Day.*

# LEICESTERSHIRE'S HERITAGE

Belgrave Hall, from the gardens.

The Manor House, Donington-le-Heath.

Horseshoes in Oakham Castle.

**Belgrave Hall,** Leicester. A furnished Queen Anne house and garden on the outskirts of the town.

**Oakham Castle,** Oakham. A late 12th century Norman hall, with the famous display of horseshoes presented by peers of the realm.

**The Manor House,** Donington-le-Heath. A superb example of an early 14th century first floor hall house.

Admission – see Editorial Reference

Leicestershire Museums, Arts and Records Services

# STANFORD HALL

**Lutterworth, Leicestershire**

*Seat of the Cave family, ancestors of Lady Braye, since 1430.*

A beautiful William and Mary house set in a fine Park on the River Avon.

*ADMISSION—SEE EDITORIAL REFERENCE*

# LINCOLNSHIRE

## BELTON HOUSE, The National Trust

**nr Grantham** *map J7* Ⓢ
Telephone: Grantham (0476) 66116

The crowning achievement of Restoration country house architecture, built 1684–1688 for Sir John Brownlow, heir to the fortunes of a successful Elizabethan lawyer; alterations by James Wyatt 1777, plasterwork ceilings by Edward Goudge, fine wood carvings of the Grinling Gibbons school. Family portraits, furniture, tapestries, Speaker Cust's silver and silver-gilt, Duke of Windsor memorabilia. Formal gardens, orangery by Jeffrey Wyattville, 17th century stables, magnificent landscape park. Extensive Adventure Playground for children.

**Location:** 3 m NE of Grantham on A607 Grantham/Lincoln Road; easily accessible from A1.
**Opening Times:** Mar 25 to end of Oct—Weds to Suns & Bank Hol Mons 1–5.30. Closed Good Friday. Gardens open 12. Parkland opens daily with free access on foot (may be closed for special events). Last adm 5. Adm House £3. Party rate £2.40. School parties contact the Administrator for details. 1989 Events—details from the Administrator.
**Refreshments:** Counter service licensed restaurant open 12–5.30 for lunches and teas.

**Bishop's Palace** – See English Heritage Section.

BELVOIR CASTLE – SEE UNDER LEICESTERSHIRE

## BURGHLEY HOUSE

**Stamford** *map J7* △
Telephone: Stamford (0780) 52451
*(Burghley House Trustees)*

The finest example of later Elizabethan architecture in England. Eighteen State rooms open containing fine furniture, porcelain, silver and the largest private collection of Italian art. Also magnificent painted ceilings by Verrio and Laguerre. Special exhibition for 1989 of the large collection of clocks and timepieces, many of which will be exhibited for the first time. The deer park is open to the public at no extra charge.

**Location:** 1 m SE of Stamford just off A1.
*Station: Stamford (1m).*
**Opening Times:** Good Friday to Oct 1—Daily 11–5. Good Friday 2–5. *Closed Sept 9.* Adm £3, Chld £1.70. Party rates available.
**Refreshments:** Lunches and teas in the Orangery. Enquiries for party rates & menus tel: (0780) 52451.

## DODDINGTON HALL

**Doddington** *map J8* △ Ⓢ
Telephone: Lincoln (0522) 694308
*(Mr & Mrs A. G. Jarvis)*

Elizabethan mansion, furniture. Spring bulbs, rose garden; Schools project.

**Location:** 5 m W of Lincoln on the B1190 & signposted off the A46 Lincoln by-pass.
**Opening Times:** Easter Mon then May to Sept—Weds, Suns & Bank Hol Mons 2–6. Adm £2.50, Chd £1.25. Party rates £2.25, Chd £1.25. Gardens only: £1.25, Chd 60p. Minimum charge per booked party, 20 people, £45.

## FULBECK HALL

**Grantham** *map J7*
Telephone: Loveden (0400) 72205
*(Mrs M. Fry)*

Home of the Fane family since 1632. House mainly 18th century – older service wing, later additions to main block. Family collection furniture, pictures and items from India and the Far East. 11 acres garden. Plants for sale. Nature trail with free leaflet.

**Location:** On A607. Lincoln 14 m, Grantham 11 m. 1 m S of A17.
**Opening Times:** Easter and May Bank Holiday Mons. Daily from Aug 3 to Aug 29 incl. 2–5. Adm £2, OAPs, £1.50, Chd 50p. Members HHA Free. Parties by agreement. Car parking free. Suitable for disabled persons (no wheelchairs available).
**Refreshments:** None at house. Village pub does lunches and dinners. Coffee shop at local craft centre.

## GRANTHAM HOUSE, The National Trust

**Grantham** *map J7*

Dating from 1380 but extensively altered and added to throughout the centuries. Ground floor only open to the public. The grounds run down to the river.

**Location:** In Castlegate, immediately E of Grantham Church.
*Station: Grantham (1 m).*
**Opening Times:** Apr to end of Sept, Weds only—2–5 by written appointment only with Maj-Gen Sir Brian Wyldbore-Smith, Grantham House, Castlegate, Grantham NG1 6SS. Adm £1, Chd 50p. No reduction for parties. No dogs. Unsuitable for wheelchairs. No lavatories.

## GRIMSTHORPE CASTLE AND GARDENS

**Bourne** *map J7*
*(Grimsthorpe & Drummond Castle Trust)*

The home of the Willoughby de Eresby family since 1516. Examples of early 13th century architecture, the Tudor period of the reign of Henry VIII and work by Sir John Vanbrugh. State Rooms and Picture Galleries open to the Public.

**Location:** 4 m NW of Bourne on A151 Colsterworth/Bourne Road, SE of Grantham.
**Opening Times:** Castle, Garden & Grounds—July 30 to Sept 3—daily except Mons & Fris, but including Aug 28—2–6. Adm £2.30, Students £1, Chd under 5 free. Nature Trails.
**Refreshments:** Afternoon teas.

## GUNBY HALL, The National Trust

**Burgh-le-Marsh** *map K8*

Built by Sir William Massingberd in 1700. Reynolds' portraits, contemporary wainscoting. Ground floor only open to the public. Walled gardens full of flowers and roses.

**Location:** 2½ m NW of Burgh-le-Marsh; 7 m W of Skegness on S side of A158.
**Opening Times:** House & Garden. Mar 25 to end of Sept—Thurs 2–6; Tues, Weds & Fris by prior written appointment only to J. D. Wrisdale, Esq., Gunby Hall, nr Spilsby, Lincs. Gardens only also on Weds 2–6. Adm House & Gardens £1.30, Chd 60p. Garden only: 90p, Chd 40p. No reduction for parties. Dogs in garden only, on leads. Wheelchairs in garden only.

# DODDINGTON HALL

***A SUPERB ELIZABETHAN MANSION SET IN ROMANTIC GARDENS***

This lovely house was completed in 1600 during the reign of Queen Elizabeth I. Its fascinating contents reflect continuous occupation by four families over nearly 400 years, and the Hall is still a family home.

Delicious meals in the licensed Garden Restaurant are available from 12 noon on open days. For information ring (0522) 690980.

**Schools Project.** Doddington Hall has twice received the Sandford Award for Heritage Education, and is a pioneer in the imaginative use of historic houses as a teaching resource. For information ring (0522) 694308.

*ADMISSION – SEE EDITORIAL REFERENCE*

# FULBECK HALL

**LINCOLNSHIRE**
**between Grantham & Lincoln**

Occupied by the same family since 1632, with alterations and additions by nearly every generation. This is a friendly lived-in house, full of interest, where you will receive a personal welcome. Links with the first Duke of Wellington.

*ADMISSION – SEE EDITORIAL REFERENCE*

# GAINSBOROUGH OLD HALL

**Parnell Street, Gainsborough. Tel: 0427-2669**

MAGNIFICENT MEDIEVAL MANOR HOUSE

Open Mondays–Saturdays 10am–5pm (all year) Sundays 2pm–5pm (Easter to October only)
Closed Christmas Day, Boxing Day, New Year's Day & Good Friday.

LINCOLNSHIRE COUNTY COUNCIL
Recreational Services Department

ENGLISH
HERITAGE

# LINCOLN CASTLE

**LINCOLN**

ADMISSION—SEE EDITORIAL REFERENCE

**Enjoy even more of Lincolnshire.**

**Explore the English Heritage Supplement on the Red Pages.**

**English Heritage**

## LINCOLN CASTLE
**Castle Hill** *map J8*
Telephone: Lincoln (0522) 511068
*(Recreational Services Dept, Lincolnshire County Council)*

Visitors can enjoy the impressive walls, towers and gatehouses that enclose beautiful and peaceful lawns and gardens. There are fine views of Lincoln and the surrounding countryside from the walls, and particularly from the Observatory Tower. The Castle, built in 1068, also houses a unique Victorian Prison Chapel which is open to visitors. During the summer the Castle is the ideal setting for a wide range of special events, including historical reconstructions, jousting tournaments, rallies and concerts. Further details regarding this year's special events can be obtained from the Manager, Lincoln Castle, or Recreational Services Department, Lincolnshire County Council, Telephone Lincoln (0522) 552222.

**Location:** Above Hill, Lincoln.
**Opening Times:** Open Bank Hols, except Christmas, British Summer Time: Mons to Sats 9.30–5.30, Suns 11–5.30. Winter Time: Mons to Sats 9.30–4, *Closed Suns.* Adm 50p concessionary 30p. Reduced rates for parties of 20 or more. No public car parking inside Castle, adequate parking in car parks close to walls. Suitable for disabled persons but not on walls and towers. The Castle has a well stocked gift shop and is close to Lincoln Cathedral and other museums run by the Recreational Services Department.
**Refreshments:** Available at Castle. Picknicking is encouraged within the grounds.

## MARSTON HALL
**Grantham** *map J7*
Telephone: Loveden (0400) 50225
*(Rev Henry Thorold, FSA)*

16th century manor house. Interesting pictures and furniture. Held by Thorolds since 14th century. Ancient garden with notable trees. Gothick gazebo.

**Location:** 6 m NW of Grantham; 1½ m off A1.
**Opening Times:** Open on certain Sundays for local charities (details to be announced in local press) and at other times by appointment. Adm House & Garden £1.

## THE OLD HALL
**Gainsborough** *map J8* △ Ⓢ
Telephone: 0427 2669.
*(Lincolnshire County Council and English Heritage)*

An unspoilt 15th century timber framed manor house, built between 1460 and 1480 by Thomas Burgh. Superb medieval kitchen and great hall. Kitchen displayed to portray its use in 1483, on the eve of Richard III's visit. Henry VIII held court here in 1541. Manor house sold to William Hickman in 1597 who allowed the early Dissenters to worship here. They were later the core of the Mayflower Pilgrims. John Wesley preached at the Hall several times. 17th and 18th century Hickman portraits and furniture. Medieval, Tudor, and Stuart room settings. Displays on Richard III, Henry VIII's Lincolnshire, and the history of the building. Soundalive sound tour. Regular living history events, and school re-enactments.

**Location:** In centre of Gainsborough.
*Stations: Gainsborough Lea Road and Gainsborough Central.*
**Opening Times:** All the year—Mons to Sats 10–5; Suns (Easter to Oct) 2–5. *Closed Christmas Day, Boxing Day, New Year's Day & Good Friday.* Adm charge. Organised parties welcome outside normal opening hours.
**Refreshments:** Tea shop open daily. Meals by arrangement. We look forward to seeing you!

**Sibsey Trader Mill** – See English Heritage Section.

## SPRINGFIELDS GARDENS
**Spalding** *map K7* ♿
Telephone: Spalding (0775) 4843
*(Springfields Horticultural Society)*

Centre of the British Bulb Industry. 25 acres of landscaped gardens with over 1,000,000 Spring flowers in bloom. In Summer over 5,000 roses together with 250,000 bedding plants. Glasshouses etc. SPECIAL ATTRACTIONS – FLOWER PARADE WEEKEND MAY 6, 7, 8. COUNTRY FAIR MAY 6, 7. GARDENER'S AND FLOWER ARRANGER'S WEEKEND AUGUST 12, 13.

**Location:** 1½ m from centre of Spalding on A151.
*Station: Spalding (2 m).*
**Opening Times:** Apr 1 to Sept 30—Daily 10–6. Adm £1.80. Special events £2. Reduction of 15% for pre-booked parties of 30 and over. Shops. Free Wheelchairs, etc.
**Refreshments:** Cafeteria/tea shop. Licensed Restaurant open all year.

## TATTERSHALL CASTLE, The National Trust
**Lincoln** *map K8*
Telephone: Coningsby (0526) 42543

The Keep is one of the finest examples of a fortified brick dwelling, although built more for show than defence, c. 1440, for Ralph Cromwell. Museum and shop in Guardhouse.

**Location:** 12 m NE of Sleaford on Louth Road (A153); 3½ m SE of Woodhall Spa.
**Opening Times:** Daily—Mar 25 to end of Oct, 10.30–6. Nov to Apr 1990: 12 noon–4.30 *Closed Christmas Day & Boxing Day.* Adm £1.50, Chd 70p. Parties of 15 or more £1.50, Chd 70p. Dogs in grounds only, on leads. Wheelchair access.
**Refreshments:** Fortescue Arms Hotel, Tattershall.

## WOOLSTHORPE MANOR, The National Trust
**nr Grantham** *map J7*
Telephone: Grantham (0476) 860338

17th century farm house, birthplace of Sir Isaac Newton. Traditionally it was under an apple tree in this garden that Newton was struck with the theory of gravity.

**Location:** 7 m S of Grantham, ½ m NW of Colsterworth; 1 m W of A1 (not to be confused with Woolsthorpe, nr Belvoir).
**Opening Times:** Mar 25 to end of Oct—Weds to Suns 1–5.30, last adm 5. *Closed Mons and Tues* (except Bank Hol Mons). Adm £1.50, Chd £1.40. No reduction for parties. *Closed Good Friday.* No dogs. Wheelchair access to garden & ground floor only. Parking for coaches limited to one at a time—please book.
*NB In the interests of preservation numbers admitted to rooms at any one time must be limited; liable to affect peak weekends & Bank Hols.*

# LONDON

## APSLEY HOUSE
**Wellington Museum** *map K4* ♿
Telephone: 01-499 5676
*(Trustees of the Victoria & Albert Museum)*

Built 1771–8, the Iron Duke's London Palace housing his famous collection of paintings, porcelain, silver and personal relics.

**Location:** At 149 Piccadilly, Hyde Park Corner.
**Opening Times:** All the year—Daily (except Mons) 11–5. Open Bank Hol Mons (except May 1). Adm £2, Chd (under 16), OAPs £1. *Closed Good Friday also Christmas Eve, Christmas Day, Boxing Day and New Year's Day.*
**Refreshments:** Coffee shop and new basement gallery opening '89.

## ASHBURNHAM HOUSE
**Westminster** *map K4*
Telephone: 01-222 3116
*(Westminster School)*

Closed for major renovation work during 1988.

## BANQUETING HOUSE
**Whitehall** *map K4*
Telephone: 01-930 4179
*(Department of Environment)*

Built 1619–22 to design of Inigo Jones. Painted ceilings by Rubens. Used for Court ceremonies, masques and banquets, and as s chapel from 1724 to 1890.

**Location:** Whitehall SW1A 2ER
**Opening Times:** Open all year, Tues to Sat 10–5, Sun 2–5, *except Jan 1, Dec 24–26, Good Friday and Mons.* Adm 80p, OAPs 60p, Chd 40p (under 5, free). 10% discount for parties of 11 or more. Applications for free educational visits. Parking in NCP Car Park, Trafalgar Square. Unsuitable for disabled persons; no wheelchairs available.

# Burghley House Stamford

**THE LARGEST AND GRANDEST HOUSE OF THE ELIZABETHAN AGE**

Home of the Cecils for over 400 years.
Built in 1587 by William Cecil, first Lord Burghley and Lord High Treasurer to Queen Elizabeth I and occupied by his descendants ever since. Eighteen treasure filled State Rooms are on view including the Heaven Room – the finest painted room in England. Of special interest are the silver fireplaces, needlework, painted ceilings, medieval kitchen with over 260 copper utensils, and one of the largest private art collections in Britain. The house is set in a Deer Park landscaped by 'Capability' Brown. Home of the famous Burghley House Trials.

Easily reached – just 1 mile from the Great North Road (A1) at Stamford.

Refreshments available in the Orangery.

Open daily from Good Friday to October 1 (not September 9) 11 am to 5 pm; Good Friday 2 to 5 pm.

For further information and details of special party rates and menus contact: The Manager, telephone Stamford (0780) 52451.

### THE BLEWCOAT SCHOOL, The National Trust
**Westminster** *map K4*
Telephone: 01-222 2877

Built in 1709 at the expense of William Green, a local brewer, to provide an education for poor children; in use as a school until 1926, the building was bought by the Trust in 1954; it was restored in 1975 and now houses a National Trust shop and information centre.

**Location:** No 23 Caxton Street, Westminster, SW1.
*Stations: Victoria ¼ m; Underground St James's Park (Circle and District Lines) less than 100 yards.*
**Opening Times:** All year, Mon to Fri 10–5.30; late night shopping Thurs until 7. *Closed Bank Holiday Mondays, Dec 25–31, Jan 1 & 2 and Good Friday.* Adm free.

### BOSTON MANOR
**Brentford** *map K4*
Telephone: 01-570 7728 ext 3974
*(London Borough of Hounslow)*

Jacobean house (1622) with elaborate plaster ceiling in the State Room which also contains a fireplace and mantelpiece dating from 1623. Original oak staircase. The house is set in a small park.

**Location:** In Boston Manor Road.
**Opening Times:** May 20 to Sept 23—Sat afternoons only 2–4.30. Adm free.

### BURGH HOUSE
**Hampstead** *map K4* ♿
Telephone: 01-431 0144
*(Burgh House Trust)*

Built 1703. Now used for art exhibitions, concerts. Hampstead Museum. Terrace Garden.

**Location:** New End Sq E of Hampstead Underground Station.
*Station: Hampstead (Underground). Hampstead Heath (BR North London Link).*
**Opening Times:** Weds to Suns 12–5; Bank Hol Mons 2–5. Adm free.
**Refreshments:** Coffee, lunches and Teas. Licensed Buttery (for bookings Tel: 01-431 2516).

### CARLYLE'S HOUSE, The National Trust
**Chelsea** *map K4*
Telephone: 01-352 7087

Home of Thomas and Jane Carlyle 1834/1881. *Note: Certain rooms have no electric light, visitors wishing to make a close study of the interior should avoid dull days.*

**Location:** At 24 Cheyne Row, Chelsea SW3 (off Cheyne Walk on Chelsea Embankment).
*Stations: Sloane Sq (Underground 1 m); Clapham Junction (BR 1½ m).*
**Opening Times:** Mar 25 to end of Oct—Weds to Suns & Bank Hol Mons 11–5. Last adm 4.30. *Closed Good Friday.* Adm £1.60, Chd 80p. No reduction for parties, which should not exceed 20. No dogs. Unsuitable for wheelchairs.

**Chapter House and Pyx Chamber, Westminster Abbey** – See English Heritage Section.

### CHELSEA PHYSIC GARDEN
**Chelsea** *map K4*

The second oldest Botanic garden in the country, founded 1673 and only recently opened to the public, comprises 4 acres densely packed with c. 5,000 plants, many rare and unusual.

**Location:** 66 Royal Hospital Road, Chelsea; nr junction of Royal Hospital Road & Chelsea Embankment; entry via Swan Walk.
*Station: Sloane Square (Underground).*
**Opening Times:** Apr 2 to Oct 22—Suns and Weds, 2–5. Also Tues 23 to Fri May 26 (Chelsea Flower Show Week) 12–5. Adm (1988 prices) £1.50, Chd & students (with cards) £1. Open at other times for groups by appointment. No dogs. Garden accessible for disabled & wheelchairs. Parking in street Suns, other days across Albert Bridge in Battersea Park, free.

### CHISWICK HOUSE
**Chiswick** *map K4*
Telephone: 01-995 0508
*(English Heritage)*

Architect and patron of the arts, the third Earl of Burlington set a fashion with this Italian-style villa, built to house his library and art collections. The gardens were landscaped by William Kent.

**Location:** Burlington Lane (½ m) NE of Chiswick Station.
**Opening Times:** Good Friday to Sept 30, daily 10–6; Oct 1 to Maundy Thurs, daily 10–4. *Closed* Dec 24, 25, Adm £1.30, OAPs £1, Chd 65p.

### COLLEGE OF ARMS
**City of London EC4V 4BT** *map K4* △
Telephone: 01-248 2762
*(The Corporation of Kings, Heralds & Pursuivants of Arms)*

Mansion built in 1670s to house the English Officers of Arms and their records, and the panelled Earl Marshal's Court.

**Location:** On N side of Queen Victoria Street; S of St Paul's Cathedral.
**Opening Times:** EARL MARSHAL'S COURT ONLY. Open all the year (except Public holidays & on State & special occasions) Mons to Fris 10–4. Group visits (up to 10) by arrangement only. RECORD ROOM open for tours (groups of up to 20) by special arrangement in advance with the Registrar. Adm free (parties by negotiation). *No coaches, parking, indoor photography or dogs.* Shop—books, souvenirs.

### DE MORGAN FOUNDATION
**Old Battersea House** *map K4*
Telephone: 01-788 1341
*(De Morgan Foundation)*

A substantial part of the De Morgan Foundation collection of ceramics by William De Morgan and paintings and drawings by Evelyn De Morgan (nee Pickering), her uncle Roddam Spencer Stanhope, J. M. Strudwick and Cadogan Cowper are displayed in the ground floor rooms of elegantly restored Old Battersea House – a Wren building. The setting is that of a privately occupied house. The guided tour usually includes a visit to nearby old Battersea Church.

**Location:** Vicarage Crescent, Battersea.
**Opening Times:** Admission by appointment only – usually Weds afternoons. Adm 50p, optional catalogue £1. No special reductions. Parties – maximum 30 (split into two groups of 15). Car parking in Vicarage Crescent. Suitable for disabled, (no special facilities for wheelchairs) front steps are the only obstacle. Adm by writing in advance to agent.
**Refreshments:** No catering at house. Many facilities in Battersea/Wandsworth.

# DULWICH COLLEGE

'Dating from 1866 onwards, the present buildings of Dulwich College provide a versatile mixture of classical, medieval and contemporary styles, to suit all occasions from dynamic conferences to convivial dinners.'

# FULHAM PALACE

**BISHOPS AVENUE, SW6**

London Borough of Hammersmith and Fulham

Palace of the Bishops of London from 704–1973. Present buildings date from 15th century. Tudor Courtyard and Great Hall, 18th century Bishops Study, 19th century Drawing Room and Chapel by Butterfield. The grounds, formerly enclosed by a mile long moat, include rare trees and a herb garden. Recent archaeological excavations have revealed remains of the former medieval palace, a Romano-British settlement and stone-age occupation dating back more than 5,000 years. Reputed site of 9th century Viking camp. Scene of persecutions during the Reformation. Site of foundation of Episcopalian Church of America. Royal visitors include, James I, Elizabeth I, Charles I, George III and Oliver Cromwell. One of England's most historic Houses.
Grounds open daily – no charge.

*ADMISSION – SEE EDITORIAL REFERENCE*

# FENTON HOUSE

**HAMPSTEAD**

# CARLYLE'S HOUSE

**24 CHEYNE ROW, CHELSEA SW3**

*ADMISSION — SEE EDITORIAL REFERENCE*

## THE DICKENS HOUSE, WC1N 2LF
*map K4*
Telephone: 01-405 2127
*(The Trustees of the Dickens House)*

House occupied by Dickens and his family 1837-39. Relics displayed include manuscripts, furniture, autographs, portraits, letters and first editions.

**Location:** 48 Doughty Street, near Grays Inn Road/Guilford Street.
**Opening Times:** All the year—Mons to Sats 10–5. *Closed Suns, Bank & Public Hols.* Adm £1.50, Students £1, Chd 75p; Families £3 (subject to alteration). Parties by appointment. Ground floor only (2 rooms) suitable for disabled—reduced adm charge.
For further details see advertisement.

## DULWICH COLLEGE
**Dulwich** *map K4*
Telephone: 01-693 3737

Founded in 1619 Dulwich College is uniquely fortunate in its position, combining the green and spacious surroundings of its estate and excellent communications with Central London. The College offers a new and unusual venue for conferences, receptions, product launches, theatre rehearsals, concerts and filming.

**Location:** The College grounds are bordered by the South Circular A205, and provide parking for up to 500 cars. West Dulwich main line station is a leisurely ten minute walk from the grounds.
**Opening Times:** The College is open throughout the year although some facilities are limited during normal school terms. You are cordially invited to see Dulwich College at first hand by telephoning the Bursar's Office (01) 693 3737, for an appointment and any further information you require.
**Refreshments:** Full catering facilities are available for groups from 20 to 600.

## FENTON HOUSE, The National Trust
**Hampstead** *map K4*
Telephone: 01-435 3471

Collection of porcelain, pottery and Benton Fletcher collection of early keyboard musical instruments.

**Location:** On W side of Hampstead Grove, 300 yards N of Hampstead.
*Stations: Hampstead (Underground 300 yards); Hampstead Heath (BR 1 m).*
**Opening Times:** Mar 4–19—Sat & Sun only 2–6; Easter Sat to end Oct—Sats to Weds (inc Bank Hol Mons) 11–6. Last adm 5 pm. *Closed Good Friday.* Adm £2, Chd half price. *Reduction for parties on application to Custodian.* No dogs. Unsuitable for wheelchairs.

## FULHAM PALACE
**Fulham** *map K4*
Telephone: 01-736 5821, 01-385 3723
*(London Borough of Hammersmith and Fulham)*

Former residence of the Bishops of London since the 8th century. Buildings now date from 15th century and stand on the site of a Roman Settlement.

**Location:** In Bishop's Ave, ½ m N of Putney Bridge.
**Opening Times:** Tours of principal rooms and grounds are conducted by the Fulham Archaeological Rescue Group on certain Sunday afternoons throughout the year at 2pm in winter and 2.30pm in summer. Adm £1.50, includes historical notes and tea and biscuits, Chd 75p. **Grounds** open daily as usual, adm free.

## HALL PLACE
**Bexley** *map K4*
*(Bexley London Borough Council)*

Historic mansion (1540). Outstanding Rose, Rock, Water, Herb, Peat gardens and Floral bedding displays, Conservatories, Parkland, Topiary designed in the form of the Queen's Beasts.

**Location:** Near the junction of A2 and A223.
*Station: Bexley (½ m).*
**Opening Times:** MANSION. Weekdays 10–5; Suns 2–6 (except from Nov to Mar). Museum & other exhibitions. PARK & GROUNDS. Daily during daylight throughout the year. Adm free.
**Refreshments:** At café.

## HAM HOUSE
**Richmond** *map K4* ♿
Telephone: 01-940 1950
*(Administered by the Trustees of the Victoria and Albert Museum on behalf of The National Trust)*

17th century house with superb Charles II and Early Georgian furnishings. Portrait gallery.

**Location:** On S bank of River Thames opposite Twickenham 1 m S of Richmond.
*Stations: Kingston (2 m); Richmond (2 m).*
**Opening Times:** All the year—Daily (except Mons), 11–5. Open Bank Hol Mons (except May 1). Adm £2, Chd (under 16) & OAPs £1, Children under 12 must be accompanied by an adult. Grounds free. *Closed Good Friday, Christmas Eve, Christmas Day, Boxing Day, New Year's Day & May 1.*
**Refreshments:** In Orangery (summer months).

## HAMPTON COURT PALACE
**Hampton Court** *map K4*
*(Dept of the Environment)*

The splendour of Cardinal Wolsey's country house began in 1514, surpassed that of many a royal palace, so it is not surprising that Henry VIII at first coveted and then obtained it prior to Wolsey's fall from power. Henry enlarged it; Charles I lived in it as King and as prisoner; Charles II repaired it; and William and Mary largely rebuilt it to a design by Sir Christopher Wren. The beauty of Wren's buildings is combined with some of the finest Tudor architecture in Britain.

**Note:** This historic property is in the care of the Department of the Environment.
**Location:** North side of Thames by Hampton Court Bridge.
**Opening Times:** State Apartments open Apr to Sept—Mons to Sats 9.30–6, Suns 11–6; Oct to Mar—Mons to Sats 9.30–5, Suns 2–5. Last admissions half an hour before closing time. *Closed Dec 24–26, Jan 1.* Great Kitchens and Cellars. Tudor Tennis Court. Apr to Sept only, times as above. Mantegna Paintings Gallery, as above, except in winter when closing time is either 5 or half an hour before dusk.
Gardens: Great Vine, King's Privy Garden, Great Fountains Gardens, Tudor and Elizabethan Knot Gardens, Broad Walk and Wilderness are open, free of charge, every day until dusk (9).
Maze: open daily, Mar to Oct, 10–5. Inquiries: 01-977 8441.
**Refreshments:** In the Grounds.

## HIGHGATE CEMETERY
**Highgate** *map K4* △
Telephone: 01-340 1834
*(Highgate Cemetery Charity)*

**The Western Cemetery:** burial place of Jacob Bronowski, Michael Faraday and the Dickens family and many famous Victorians. A place of tranquility set in managed woodland with rare wild flowers and bizarre buildings.
**The Eastern Cemetery:** burial place of George Eliot, Ralph Richardson and Karl Marx is open for unrestricted access every day of the year but closed during funerals and on Christmas Day. 10–4 Nov to Mar; 10–5 Apr to Oct. Donations requested at sales point where there are numerous publications.

**Location:** Swains Lane, Highgate.
*Station: (Underground) Archway.*
**Opening Times:** (Western Cemetery only) – Guided tours are essential and held every hour (10–4) each weekend of the year. Special tours for groups by appointment at any time (s.a.e. please). Midweek tours planned for 12, 2 and 4 from Apr to Oct only. Generous donations, please, to help Friends of Highgate Cemetery (Charity No. 282220) who are responsible for management.
Special arrangements for photography and other facilities on application.

## HOGARTH'S HOUSE
**Chiswick** *map K4* △
Telephone: 01-994 6757
*(London Borough of Hounslow)*

The artist's country house for 15 years containing many prints and some relics associated with the artist.

**Location:** In Hogarth Lane, Great West Road, Chiswick W4 2QN (200 yards Chiswick House).
*Stations: Chiswick (½ m) (Southern Region); Turnham Green (1 m) (District Line).*
**Opening Times:** Apr to Sept—Mons to Sats 11–6; Suns 2–6. Oct to Mar—Mons to Sats 11–4; Suns 2–4. *Closed Tues, Good Friday, Sept 4–17, last 3 weeks in Dec & New Year's Day.*

## KEATS HOUSE
**Wentworth Place, Keats Grove, Hampstead NW3 2RR** *map K4*
Telephone: 01-435 2062
*(London Borough of Camden)*

Built in 1815-16 and completely restored in 1974-75. Poet John Keats wrote his famous odes here.

**Location:** S end of Hampstead Heath nr South End Green.
*Station: (BR Hampstead Heath). Underground: Belsize Park or Hampstead. Bus: 24, 46, 168, C11 (alight South End Green). 268 (alight Downshire Hill).*
**Opening Times:** All the year—Apr to Oct: Mon–Fri 2–6, Sat 10–5, Sun and Bank Holiday 2–5. Nov to Mar: Mon–Fri 1–5, Sat 10–5, Sun 2–5. Adm free. *These times are not confirmed. You are advised to telephone for up-to-date information before your visit. Closed Christmas Day, Boxing Day, New Year's Day, Good Friday, Easter Eve & May 4.*

## KENSINGTON PALACE
**Kensington** *map K4*
*(Dept of the Environment)*

Bought by William III, 1689. Altered and added to by Wren and later alterations. Court Dress Collection.

**Location:** W side of Kensington Gardens.
*Station: (Underground) Kensington High Street (½ m).*
**Opening Times:** Open all year Mon–Sat 9–5; Sun 1–5. *Closed* Good Friday, Dec 24–26, Jan 1. Enquiries 01-937 9561.

## KENWOOD, THE IVEAGH BEQUEST
**Hampstead** *map K4*
Telephone: 01-348 1286
*(English Heritage)*

Adam mansion, once the seat of Lord Mansfield. The Iveagh Bequest of Old Master and British paintings, including works by Rembrandt, Vermeer, Hals, Gainsborough, Turner and Reynolds. Fine collection of neo-classical furniture.

# HIGHGATE CEMETERY

*ADMISSION – SEE EDITORIAL REFERENCE*

# HOGARTH'S HOUSE

**CHISWICK**

**LONDON BOROUGH OF HOUNSLOW**

The artist's country house for 15 years.
Hogarth Lane, Great West Road, Chiswick W4 2QN
(200 yards from Chiswick House)
Telephone: 01-994 6757

# KEATS HOUSE

**KEATS GROVE, LONDON**

*London Borough of Camden*

Keats House was built in 1815–1816 as Wentworth Place, a pair of semi-detached houses. John Keats, the poet, lived here from 1818 to 1820; here he wrote *'Ode to a Nightingale'* and met Fanny Brawne, to whom he became engaged. Keats' early death in Italy prevented the marriage.
Keats House was completely restored in 1974–1975. It houses letters, books and other personal relics of the poet and his fiancée.

**Telephone: 01-435 2062.**

Leighton House Museum from the Garden

# LEIGHTON HOUSE MUSEUM

*(See Editorial Entry)*

Royal Borough of Kensington Libraries and Arts Service

The Arab Hall

# LINLEY SAMBOURNE HOUSE

**18 STAFFORD TERRACE, LONDON W8**

The home of Linley Sambourne (1844–1910). Chief political cartoonist at PUNCH. A unique survival of a town house reflecting artistic taste of the late 19th century. The original decorations and furnishings have been preserved by three generations of the family, together with many of Sambourne's own cartoons and photographs, and those of other artists and cartoonists of the period.

# THE OCTAGON

## ORLEANS HOUSE GALLERY

**RIVERSIDE, TWICKENHAM**

**LONDON BOROUGH OF RICHMOND UPON THAMES**

*Russells photograph*

The magnificent Octagon built by James Gibbs in c. 1720 for James Johnston, Joint Secretary of State for Scotland under William III. An outstanding example of baroque architecture. The adjacent wing has been converted into an art gallery and the whole is situated in an attractive woodland garden.

*ADMISSION – SEE EDITORIAL REFERENCE*

# PITSHANGER MANOR MUSEUM

Built 1800–04 by Sir John Soane (1753–1837) as his family home.
Changing Exhibitions.

*ADMISSION – SEE EDITORIAL REFERENCE*

**Location:** Hampstead Lane, NW3.
*Station: Archway or Golders Green Underground (Northern Line), then Bus 210.*
**Opening Times:** Good Friday to Sept 30, daily 10–6; Oct 1 to Maundy Thurs, daily 10–4. *Closed* Dec 24, 25. Adm free.
**Refreshments:** At the Coach House.

## KEW GARDENS

**Kew** *map K4* ♿
*(Royal Botanic Gardens)*

300 acres in extent containing living collection of over 50,000 different plant species. Greenhouses. Museums.

**Location:** On south bank of Thames at Kew 1 m from Richmond.
*Station: Kew Gardens (½ m).*
**Opening Times:** All the year—Daily, open at 9.30. *Closed Christmas Day & New Year's Day.* Museums open from 9.30. Closing times vary according to season but not later than 4.30 Mons to Sats & 5.30 Suns. Adm 50p (adults, Chd 10 yrs & over, prams & invalid vehicles). Invalid chairs may be obtained free of charge at the Main Gate. Accompanied children under 10 yrs. adm free (1987 times & rates). Organised school parties issued with free entry vouchers on prior application.
**Refreshments:** At Pavilion (Mar–Nov); at Tea Bar (all year).

## KEW PALACE (Dutch House)

**Kew** *map K4*

Built 1631 Dutch style. Souvenirs of George III.

**Location:** In Kew Gardens on S bank of Thames.
*Station: Kew Bridge (¾ m). Underground Kew Gardens (¼ m).*
**Opening Times:** Apr to Sept—Daily 11–5.30. Adm 80p, Chd (under 16) & OAPs 40p (1987 rates).
**Refreshments:** In Kew Gardens *(summer months)*

## LEIGHTON HOUSE MUSEUM

**12 Holland Park Road** *map K4*
Telephone: 01-602 3316
*(Royal Borough of Kensington and Chelsea)*

Adjacent to Holland Park in Kensington lies the Artists' Colony, a group of remarkable Studio Houses, built by some of the leading figures of the Victorian art world. Leighton House Museum was the first of these to be built, and is today a museum of high Victorian art. The opulent fantasy of Frederick Lord Leighton, President of the Royal Academy, the house was designed by George Aitchison. Leighton lived here from 1866 until his death in 1896. His unique collection of Islamic tiles is displayed in the walls of the Arab Hall, and the Victorian interiors, now being restored to their original splendour, are hung with paintings by Leighton, Millais, Watts, Burne-Jones and others. Fine 'New Sculpture' by Leighton, Brock and Thornycroft is displayed in the house and garden. The study collection of Leighton drawings may be seen by appointment. Temporary exhibitions of modern and historic art throughout the year.

**Location:** Kensington.
**Opening Times:** All year. Mon–Sat 11–5 *(During exhibitions 11–6)* **Garden:** Apr–Sept *(Closed Bank Holidays).* Parties by arrangement with the Curator. Chd under 16 must be accompanied by an adult.

## LINLEY SAMBOURNE HOUSE, W8

*map K4*
Telephone: 01-994 1019
*(The Victorian Society)*

The home of Linley Sambourne (1844–1910), chief political cartoonist at 'Punch'. A unique survival of a late Victorian town house. The original decorations and furnishings have been preserved together with many of Sambourne's own cartoons and photographs, as well as works by other artists of the period.

**Location:** 18 Stafford Terrace.
*Station: (Underground) Kensington High Street.*
**Opening Times:** 1 Mar to 31 Oct—Weds 10–4, Suns 2–5. Parties at other times by prior arrangement. Apply to The Victorian Society, 1 Priory Gardens, London W4. Adm £2.

## LITTLE HOLLAND HOUSE

**Carshalton** *map K4*
*(London Borough of Sutton)*

The home of Frank Dickinson (1874–1961), follower of the Arts and Crafts movement: artist, designer and craftsman in wood and metal who built the house himself to his own design and in pursuance of his philosophy and theories. Features his interior design, painting, hand-made furniture and other craft objects.

**Location:** 40 Beeches Avenue, Carshalton. On B278 (off A232).
*Station: Carshalton Beeches.*
**Opening Times:** Mar to Oct—first Sun in the month plus Bank Hol Suns & Mons in that period 12–6. Adm free.

## MARBLE HILL HOUSE

**Twickenham** *map K4*
Telephone: 01-892 5115
*(English Heritage)*

A complete example of an English Palladian villa. Early Georgian paintings and furniture.

**Location:** Richmond Road.
*Stations: St Margaret's (½ m); Twickenham (1 m); Richmond (2 m).*
**Opening Times:** Good Friday to Sept 30, daily 10–6; Oct 1 to Maundy Thurs, daily 10–4. *Closed* Dec 24, 25. Adm free.
**Refreshments:** In Stable Block.

## MARLBOROUGH HOUSE

**Pall Mall**

Will be closed indefinitely for repairs.

## MUSEUM OF GARDEN HISTORY

**Lambeth** *map K4*
Telephone: 01-373 4030 (between 7 and 9 am)
and 01-261 1891 (between 11 and 3)
*(The Tradescant Trust)*

The former church of St Mary-at-Lambeth has been converted into the first museum of its kind in the world. The tomb of John Tradescant, gardener to Charles I, lies in the churchyard where the Tradescant Garden has been created, planted with species shrubs and flowers of the period. Lectures, exhibitions, shop.

**Location:** At the gates of Lambeth Palace.
*Station: Waterloo or Victoria, then 507 Red Arrow bus, alight Lambeth Palace.*
**Opening Times:** Mons to Fris 11–3; Suns 10.30–5. At other times by appointment. *Closed from second Sun in Dec to first Sun in Mar.* Further information from: The Tradescant Trust, 74 Coleherne Court, London SW5 0EF. Adm free. Donation requested.
**Refreshments:** Tea, coffee, light lunches; parties catered for if pre-booked.

## THE OCTAGON, ORLEANS HOUSE GALLERY

**Riverside Twickenham** *map K4* ♿
Telephone: 01-892 0221
*(London Borough of Richmond upon Thames)*

The magnificent Octagon built by James Gibbs circa 1720. An outstanding example of the baroque, with adjacent art gallery situated in attractive woodland garden.

**Location:** Access from Richmond Road (A305).
*Stations: St Margaret's (½ m); Twickenham (½ m).*
**Opening Times:** Tues to Sats 1–5.30 (Oct to Mar, 1–4.30); Suns 2–5.30 (Oct to Mar, 2–4.30). Easter, Spring, Summer Bank Hols 2–5.30. *Closed Christmas.* Adm free.

## THE OLD PALACE

**Old Palace Road, Croydon** *map K4* △
Telephone: 01-680 5877
*(Old Palace School (Croydon) Ltd)*

Seat of Archbishops of Canterbury since 871. 15th century Banqueting Hall and Guardroom. Tudor Chapel, Norman undercroft.

**Location:** In central Croydon. Adjacent to Parish Church. A212 & A213.
*Stations: East Croydon or West Croydon (few mins walk).*
**Opening Times:** Conducted Tours Only. Doors open 2, all tours commence promptly at 2.30. Mon Apr 3 – Sat Apr 8; Tues May 30 – Fri June 2; Mon July 17 – Sat July 22; Mon July 24 – Sat July 29. Adm £2, Chd & OAPs £1.25, this includes home made tea served in the Undercroft. Car park. Souvenir shop. Parties catered for, apply Bursar. Unsuitable for wheelchairs.

## OLD ROYAL OBSERVATORY

**Greenwich** *map K4*
*(National Maritime Museum)*

Part of the National Maritime Museum it includes Flamsteed House, designed by Sir Christopher Wren, the Meridian Building and the Greenwich Planetarium.

**Location:** In Greenwich Park, N side of Blackheath.
*Station: Maze Hill (short walk).*
**Opening Times:** Weekdays—summer 10–6; winter 10–5. Suns—summer 2–6; winter 2–5. *Closed Good Friday, Christmas Eve, Christmas Day, Boxing Day, New Year's Day & May Day Bank Holiday.* Adm charge.
**Refreshments:** In Park cafeteria and museum main buildings.

## OSTERLEY PARK HOUSE

**Osterley** *map K4* △ ©
Telephone: 01-560 3918
*(Administered by the Trustees of the Victoria & Albert Museum on behalf of The National Trust)*

Splendid State Rooms furnished by Robert Adam, including a Gobelins Tapestry Room. Garden houses and Tudor stable block.

**Location:** ½ m N of Great West road (turn off at traffic lights, Thornbury Road, near Osterley Station).
*Stations: Syon Lane (½ m); Brentford (1¾ m).*
**Opening Times:** House: all year daily (except Mons) 11–5, Open Bank Holiday Mons (except May 1), closed Good Friday, Dec 24–28 and Jan 1. Adm £2, Chd (under 16) & OAPs £1. Chd under 12 must be accompanied by an adult. Park: open daily 10–8 (or sunset if earlier). Adm free.
**Refreshments:** In the Stables (summer months).

HISTORIC HOUSES ADMINISTERED BY THE TRUSTEES OF THE

**VICTORIA & ALBERT MUSEUM**

ON BEHALF OF THE NATIONAL TRUST

## Osterley Park House

Osterley, Middlesex

An Elizabethan mansion transformed into an 18th century villa. Elegant neo-classical interior decoration designed by Robert Adam for the banker Robert Child. The state apartment comprises a Gobelins tapestry ante-room, a bedroom with embroidered velvet bed, and a dressing room decorated in the "Etruscan" style.

The house is set in a landscaped park with an Elizabethan stable block.

## Apsley House

London W1

Sometimes called "Number 1, London," Apsley House was the home of the first Duke of Wellington, famous for his success in the Peninsular War and at the Battle of Waterloo (1815). Apsley House, designed by Robert Adam from 1771 to 1778, was bought by the Duke from his brother Marquis Wellesley in 1817. In 1818 the architect Benjamin Dean Wyatt was employed to alter the house and from 1828 to 1830 he added the Waterloo Gallery. Apsley House contains many Wellington relics, porcelain from Sèvres, Berlin and Meissen, magnificent silver such as the Portuguese centrepiece and the Waterloo shield.

The house is the most splendid surviving London palace of the early 19th century. Its culmination is the Waterloo Gallery, the supreme example of the revived Louis XIV style, hung with Wellington's superb paintings, many from the Spanish royal collection and including works by Velasquez, Van Dyck, Correggio, Murillo and Goya.

## Ham House

Richmond

Ham House dates from the early 17th century but was enlarged and enriched by the Duke and Duchess of Lauderdale in the 1670s. The house contains most of the paintings and furniture which so impressed John Evelyn 300 years ago, as well as fine Georgian furnishings introduced by the Earls of Dysart.

The formal gardens have recently been returned to their 17th century plan.

### PITSHANGER MANOR MUSEUM
**Mattock Lane, Ealing W5** *map K4*
Telephone: 01-579 2424 ext 42683
*(London Borough of Ealing)*

Set in an attractive park, Pitshanger Manor was built 1800-04 by the architect Sir John Soane (1753-1837) as his family home. The house incorporates a wing of the late 1760s by George Dance. The interiors are being restored. *Please enquire in advance as to which of these rooms are open to the public.* A Victorian room holds a changing and extensive display of Martinware pottery including a unique chimney-piece of 1891. Exhibitions are held from time to time. Adm free. Parties by arrangement in advance. Limited disabled access – further details available on request.

**Location:** ⅓ m from Ealing Broadway Tube Station (Central and District Lines). On the A3001 (Ealing Green). No parking.
**Opening Times:** Tues to Sat 10–5. *Closed Sun & Mon. Also closed Christmas, Easter and New Year.*
**Refreshments:** Tea and coffee vending machine.

### RANGER'S HOUSE
**Blackheath** *map K4* Ⓢ
Telephone: 01-853 0035
*(English Heritage)*

A Gallery of English Portraits in the 4th Earl of Chesterfield's house, from the Elizabethan to the Georgian period. Dolmetsch Collection of musical instruments in period rooms on newly restored first floor.

**Location:** Chesterfield Walk, SE10.
*Stations: Greenwich or Blackheath (15 mins walk).*
**Opening Times:** Good Friday to Sept 30, daily 10–6; Oct 1 to Maundy Thurs, daily 10–4. *Closed* Dec 24, 25. Adm free.

### ROYAL GEOGRAPHICAL SOCIETY
**Kensington Gore** *map K4*

Map Room open to public 10–5 weekdays, only for serious enquiries about maps preferably by appointment with Map Curator.

### ST JOHN'S GATE
**Clerkenwell** *map K4* △
Telephone: 01-253 6644, Ext 35
*(The Order of St John)*

Headquarters of the Order in England, the 16th gatehouse contains the most comprehensive collection of items relating to the Order of St John outside Malta.

**Location:** In St John's Lane, EC1M 4DA.
*Station: (Underground) Farringdon.*
**Opening Times:** MUSEUM. Tues, Fris 10–6; Sats 10–4. Tours of the building, including the Grand Priory Church and Norman crypt, 11 & 2.30 on these days.

### SIR JOHN SOANE'S MUSEUM
**13 Lincoln's Inn Fields, WC2A 3BP map K4**
Telephone: 01-405 2107

Built by Sir John Soane, RA, in 1812–13 as his private residence. Contains his collection of antiquities and works of art. Tues to Sat 10–5 (lecture tours Sat 2.30, maximum 22 people, no groups). Groups welcome at other times, but must book in advance. Also library and architectural drawings collection: access by appointment. *Closed* Bank Holidays.

### SOUTHSIDE HOUSE
**Wimbledon Common** *map K4* △
*(Pennington–Mellor–Munthe Trust)*

The Kemeys-Pennington-Mellor-Munthe family built the house after the great plague of London in 1665 and still live here. Furniture and pictures of the 17th to 19th centuries; vanity case of Anne Boleyn; sword used in a fatal duel of 1608. Home of Hilda Pennington-Mellor, English wife of Axel Munthe, the Swedish doctor and philanthropist.

**Location:** On S side of Wimbledon Common, opposite 'Crooked Billet' Inn.
*Stations: Wimbledon (1 m); Raynes Park (1 m).*
**Opening Times:** Oct 1 to May 31, '89—Tues, Thurs & Sat 2–5. Guided tours each hour. Adm £2, Chd £1 (must be accompanied by adult). Other times by written appointment only to the Curator. *The house is closed for Christmas & Easter.*

### SYON HOUSE
**Brentford** *map K4* △
Telephone: 01-560 0881/3
*(His Grace the Duke of Northumberland)*

Noted for its magnificent Adam interior and furnishings, famous picture collection, and historical associations dating back to 1415, 'Capability' Brown landscape.

**Location:** On N bank of Thames between Brentford & Isleworth.
*Stations: Brentford (BR 1 m); Syon Lane (BR 1 m).*
**Opening Times:** Apr 1 to Sept 29—Daily (except Fris & Sats) 12–5. Last adm 4.15. Also Suns in Oct, 12–5. Adm charges not available at time of going to press.

### SYON PARK GARDENS
**Brentford** *map K4*
Telephone: 01-560 0881/3
*(His Grace the Duke of Northumberland)*

Includes the Great Conservatory by Dr Fowler. Within the Estate is the London Butterfly House and the British Heritage Motor Museum (telephone details below); also the Syon Art Centre.

**Location:** On N bank of Thames between Brentford & Isleworth.
*Stations: Brentford (1 m); Syon Lane (¾ m).*
**Opening Times:** All the year—Mar to Oct—Daily 10–6. Oct to Feb—Daily 10–dusk; Last adm 1 hour before closing. *Closed Christmas Day & Boxing Day.* Adm charges not available at time of going to press. Winter—reduced rates. Free car park. Telephone 01-560 0881/3.
London Butterfly House—opening times & adm charges: Telephone 01-560 7272.
British Heritage Motor Museum—opening times & adm charges: Telephone 01-560 1378.
Syon Art Centre—free admission: Telephone 01-568 6021
**Refreshments:** Light refreshments and meals in Bars & Restaurant. Telephone 01-568 0778/9.

### TOWER OF LONDON
**Tower Bridge** *map K4* Ⓢ
*(Dept of the Environment)*

Dating from Norman times. Historical relics, armouries, dungeons. Crown jewels.

**Location:** On N bank of Thames above Tower Bridge.
*Stations: London Bridge (¾ m); Fenchurch Street (¼ m); Cannon Street (½ m) (Mons to Fris); Liverpool St (¾ m); Moorgate (1 m). (Underground) Tower Hill.*
**Opening Times:** All the year. Mar to Oct—Weekdays 9.30–5, Suns 2–5; Nov to Feb—Weekdays 9.30–4. *Closed Suns Nov to Feb also Good Fri, Dec 24, 25, 26 & Jan 1.* Adm charge. Enquiries 01-709 0765.

### THE TRAVELLERS' CLUB
**Pall Mall** *map K4*
Telephone: 01-930 8688 *(by prior appointment)*

Built in 1829-33 by Sir Charles Barry. (Roof restored in 1986).
**Location: 106 Pall Mall.**
*Station: Piccadilly Circus Underground.*
**Opening Times:** By prior appointment Mon and Fri only (except from 5th to 30th January when inclusive of Tues to Thurs) from 10–12 and 2–5. *Closed Bank Hols, Aug and Christmas.* Adm £5.

### WHITEHALL
**Cheam** *map K4*
Telephone: 01-643 1236
*(London Borough of Sutton)*

Timber-framed house built c 1500. Features exposed sections of original fabric; and displays including medieval Cheam pottery; Nonsuch Palace; timber-framed buildings; and Cheam School.

**Location:** 1 Malden Road; on A2043 nr Cheam village crossroads; just N of junction with A232.
*Station: Cheam (¼ m).*
**Opening Times:** Apr to Sept—Tues to Fris. Sun 2–5.30. Sat 10–5.30. Oct to Mar—Wed, Thurs, Sun 2–5.30. Sat 10–5.30. Also open Bank Holiday Mons 2–5.30. *Closed Dec 24 to Jan 2 incl.* Adm 50p, (under 18 years, 25p). Party bookings & guided tour facilities.
**Refreshments:** Home-made Refreshments.

# LITTLE HOLLAND HOUSE

**40 BEECHES AVENUE, CARSHALTON, SURREY**

*The Living Room and part of the Sitting Room*

The home of Frank Dickinson (1874–1961), follower of the Arts and Crafts movement; artist, designer and craftsman in wood and metal who built the house himself to his own design and in the pursuance of his philosophy and theories. Features his interior design, painting, hand-made furniture and other craft objects. Admission free. Guide book and other publications available.

# ST. JOHN'S GATE

**The Museum & Library of the Order of St. John**

**CLERKENWELL, LONDON EC1M 4DA**

*Original Drawing by Maria Grazyana Lee*

St. John's Gate, formerly the southern entrance to the Priory of the Knights of St. John houses the most comprehensive collection of items relating to the Order of St. John outside Malta. Together with the nearby Priory Church and 12th century Crypt it now forms the headquarters of the modern Order of St. John, whose charitable foundations include St. John Ambulance and the Ophthalmic Hospital in Jerusalem. The collection includes Maltese silver, Italian furniture, paintings, coins and pharmacy jars.

*ADMISSION – SEE EDITORIAL REFERENCE*

# SYON HOUSE

**BRENTFORD, Middlesex**

Set on the bank of the Thames and on the road to Hampton Court this historic seat of the Duke of Northumberland is noted not only for its association with some of the fascinating characters and stirring historical events of the last five-and-a-half centuries, but also for its elegant furniture and interesting pictures within the magnificent setting of one of Robert Adam's masterpieces of decoration.

Pedestrian entrances: Brent Lea, London Road, Brentford and Park Road, Isleworth.

Motorists: Park Road, Isleworth, only. Free Car Park. Restaurant.

Enquiries to the Supervisor, Syon House, Brentford. Telephone: 01-560 0881.

'You feel as if you're almost in the middle of a jewel box' – Basil Taylor, BBC4

*ADMISSION – SEE EDITORIAL REFERENCE*

# SOUTHSIDE HOUSE

**WIMBLEDON COMMON**

*The Kemeys – Pennington – Mellor – Munthe family*

Built by Robert Pennington as a refuge from the plague in London after his small son perished in 1665, the façade and entrance hall show Dutch baroque influence—admired by Pennington during exile in Holland with Charles II.

Contents include family portraits from 1580 onwards; relics of the Pennington-Mellor's 'dear infamous relative' Philip, the last Duke of Wharton (member of the 'Hell Fire Club') and of the family's 'Scarlet Pimpernel' son, John Pennington, from the French Revolution; also the vanity case of Anne Boleyn (whose sister married into the family). A music room was prepared mid-18th century for Frederick, Prince of Wales (the silver box with comfits for his sore throat is still on view).

Past visitors include Nelson, Lady Hamilton, Byron and Axel Munthe who wrote part of his 'Story of San Michele' here.

# WHITEHALL

**CHEAM, SURREY**

This unique timber-framed, continuous-jettied house dates back to about 1500. Originally built as a farmhouse, Whitehall, with its many additions, has associations with Henry VIII's Nonsuch Palace, the English Civil War and Cheam School. The latter became famous for its many royal, aristocratic and otherwise distinguished pupils. Whitehall now features revealed sections of original fabric and displays including Medieval Cheam Pottery, Nonsuch Palace, Timber-framed Buildings and Cheam School.

Refreshments and appropriate publications available.

# MERSEYSIDE

### BLUECOAT CHAMBERS
**Liverpool** *map F8*
Telephone: 051-709 5297
*(Bluecoat Arts Centre)*

Fine Queen Anne building, cobbled quadrangle, garden courtyard, gallery, concert hall, artists studios.

**Location:** School Lane, in the City centre.
*Station: Liverpool Lime Street (½ m).*
**Opening Times:** Mons to Sats 10–5. Adm free.
**Refreshments:** Coffee shop, Bistro and Bar.

### CROXTETH HALL & COUNTRY PARK
**Liverpool** *map F8* ♿ Ⓢ
Telephone: 051-228 5311

500 acre Country Park centred on the ancestral home of the Molyneux family, Earls of Sefton. Hall rooms with character figures on the theme of an Edwardian houseparty. Victorian Home Farm and Walled Garden both with quality interpretive displays; superb collection of farm animals (Approved Rare Breeds Centre). Miniature Railway. Special events and attractions most weekends. Picnic areas and play areas.

**Location:** 5 m NE of Liverpool City Centre; signposted from A580 & A5088 (ring road).
**Opening Times:** Parkland open daily throughout the year, adm free. Hall, Farm & Garden open 11–5 daily in main season, please telephone to check exact dates. Inclusive admission to Hall, Farm & Gardens; £2, Chd/OAPs £1 (provisional prices). Reduced rates for parties. Wheelchair access to Farm, Garden and Café but to ground floor only in Hall.
**Refreshments:** 'The Old Riding School' cafe during season.

### SPEKE HALL, The National Trust
**Liverpool** *map F8* △ ♿
Telephone: 051-427 7231

Richly half-timbered Elizabethan house around a courtyard; features include Great Hall, Priest holes; Jacobean plasterwork and Victorian restoration and decoration. Attractive gardens and extensive woodlands.

**Location:** On N bank of Mersey 8 m from City centre.
*Station: Garston (2 m); Hunts Cross (2 m).*
**Opening Times:** Mar 25 to Nov 5—daily except Mons, but open Bank Holiday Mons; Tues to Sat 1–5.30; Sun and Bank Holiday Mons 1–6, *closed Good Fri.* Nov 11 to Dec 17—Sats & Suns 1–5. Adm £1.80. Discount for parties. Guided tours and school visits by prior arrangement with Administrator.
**Refreshments:** Tea room and shop.

# NORFOLK

### AUGUSTINE STEWARD'S HOUSE
**Norwich** *map M7*
Telephone: (0603) 619056
*(Norwich City Council)*

Fine timber framed 16th century merchant's house built for Augustine Steward, Sheriff, Mayor and elected member of Parliament who was one of the most interesting historical figures in the Norwich largely responsible for the revival of the city in the 1530s. He also owned the house in Elm Hill which is now Strangers Club. Now converted to a restaurant.

**Location:** 14 Tombland, Norwich.
**Opening Times:** Tues – Sat 12–2, 7–9.30. Car parks in central Norwich.

### BACON HOUSE
**Norwich** *map M7*
*(Norwich City Council)*

Fifteenth century merchant's house with 16th and 17th century additions now converted into housing, office, club and shop.

**Location:** 31 Colegate, Norwich.
**Opening Times:** Shop at shop hours. Club by prior arrangement with the Secretary, City Club, Bacon House, Colegate, Tel: (0603) 625057. Car parks in central Norwich.
**Refreshments:** Restaurants and cafes in central Norwich.

### BEESTON HALL
**Beeston St Lawrence** *map M7*
Telephone: (0692) 630771
*(Sir Ronald & Lady Preston)*

18th century 'Gothick' country house with Georgian interiors in picturesque setting.

**Location:** 2½ m NE of Wroxham on S side of A1151; 11 m NE of Norwich.
*Station: Wroxham (2¾ m). Also accessible from Broads at Neatishead.*
**Opening Times:** Principal Rooms, Gardens, Wine Cellars and Woodland Walks. Mar 26 to Sept 17—Fris & Suns, also Bank Hols 2–5.30, Aug also Weds. Adm £1.80, Chd (accompanied by adult) 60p, OAPs £1.50. Parties by arrangement. Free car park.
**Refreshments:** Teas and light refreshments in the Orangery.

**Berney Arms Windmill** – See English Heritage Section.

### BLICKLING HALL, The National Trust
**Aylsham** *map M7* ♿
Telephone: Aylsham 733084

Great Jacobean house, altered 1765-70. State rooms include Peter the Great Room with fine Russian tapestry, Long Gallery with exceptional ceiling and State bedroom. Textile conservation workshop open to visitors Tues only 2–4. The Formal Garden design dates from 1729. Temple and Orangery, park and lake.

**Location:** 1½ m NW of Aylsham on N side of B1354 (which is 15 m N of Norwich on A140).
**Opening Times:** Hall & Gardens—Mar 25 to Oct 29 daily except Mons and Thurs 1–5; Closed Good Fri. Open Bank Hol Mons. Adm House and Garden: £3.50, Chd (with adult) £1.75. Pre-booked parties £3. Free car park. Shop. Dogs in Park & Picnic area only, on leads. Wheelchair access—2 provided. Lift to first floor.
**Refreshments:** Teas, coffee and lunches. Shop. Open 12–5. (*Parties by arrangement; table licence*). Picnic area in walled orchard. Restaurant, shop and garden open daily in July & Aug, 12–5.
NB Free access to the South Front, shop and restaurant when Hall is open.

### BRIDEWELL MUSEUM
**Norwich** *map M7*
Telephone: (0603) 667228
*(Norwich City Council/Norfolk Museums Service)*

A merchant's house dating from the 15th century, the Bridewell was for 250 years a prison for beggars and tramps. The wall facing St. Andrews Church has been described as the finest flint walling in England. Now a museum, the displays illustrate the trades and industries of Norwich during the past two hundred years.

**Location:** In Bridewell Alley, off Bedford Street, Norwich.
**Opening Times:** Mon to Sat 10–5. *Closed Bank Hols.* Adm winter 20p, Chd 10p, concession 15p. Summer (Spring Bank Hol to end Sept) 40p, Chd 10p, concession 20p. Parties by prior arrangement. Car parking in city centre car parks.
**Refreshments:** Restaurants and cafes in the centre of Norwich.

### BRITON'S ARMS
**Norwich** *map M7* ♿
Telephone: (0603) 623367
*(Norwich City Council/Briton's Arms Coffee House and Restaurant)*

A 15th century three storey timber framed building with a decorative arcaded upper floor, it was originally a house for the radical and intellectual group of religious women known as the Béguines. Now a restaurant/coffee house.

**Location:** 9 Elm Hill, Norwich.
**Opening Times:** Open as restaurant: Mon to Sat 10–5. *Closed Suns & Bank Hols.* Parties by prior arrangement. Car parking in city centre car parks. Suitable for disabled persons.

**Castle Acre Priory and Castle** – See English Heritage Section.

**Castle Rising** – See English Heritage Section.

### CHURCHMAN HOUSE
**Norwich** *map M7* ♿
*(Norwich City Council)*

Built in the mid-18th century this is one of the best provincial houses of its period with fine interior plasterwork, wall paintings and fireplaces.

**Location:** At junction of St. Giles and Betnel Street, Norwich.
**Opening Times:** For information apply to the Tourist Information Centre, Guildhall. Parties by prior arrangement. Car parking in city centre car parks. Suitable for disabled persons.
**Refreshments:** Restaurants and cafes in central Norwich.

### NO 18 COLEGATE
**Norwich** *map M7*
Telephone: (0603) 610734
*(Norwich City Council/The Broads Authority)*

Early 18th century house of seven bays, with good plasterwork ceiling inside, now offices.

**Location:** 18 Colgate, Norwich.
**Opening Times:** By prior arrangement with the Broads Authority. Car parking in city centre car parks.
**Restaurants:** Restaurants and cafes in the centre of Norwich.

### DRAGON HALL (THE OLD BARGE)
**Norwich** *map M7* ♿
Telephone: (0603) 663922
*(Norwich City Council)*

A magnificent large timber framed merchant's hall built about 1480 with a rear wing converted into a house about 1700. In the 15th century part of the building was occupied by Anne Boleyn's grandfather. It is to be used as a Heritage Centre for the study of Norwich.

**Location:** 115-123 King Street, Norwich.
**Opening Times:** Mons – Thurs 10–4. Car parking in city centre car parks. Suitable for disabled persons.
**Refreshments:** Restaurants and cafes in central Norwich.

## NORFOLK – *continued*

### ELM HILL
**Norwich** *map M7* ♿
*(Norwich City Council)*

A narrow cobbled street of mainly timber framed buildings all of which belong to the City Council. Purchased in the early part of the century for the purpose of slum clearance, from which they were saved, the street is an early example of a conservation scheme.

**Location:** Elm Hill, Norwich.
**Opening Times:** Interiors of shops and restaurants at normal commercial hours. Car parking in car parks in central Norwich. Suitable for disabled persons.
**Refreshments:** Briton's Arms (see separate entry).

### FELBRIGG HALL, The National Trust
**nr Cromer** *map M7* ♿
Telephone: West Runton 444

17th century country house with Georgian interiors set in a fine wooded park. Important 18th century Library and Orangery, Traditional walled garden. Woodland and Lakeside walks.

**Location:** 2 m SW of Cromer on S side of A148.
*Station: Cromer (2¼ m).*
**Opening Times:** Hall & Gardens—Mar 25 to Oct 29—Daily (*except* Tues and Fris) open Bank Hol Mons 1.30–5.30. Gardens 11–5.30. Adm £3, Chd (with adult) £1.50. Gardens only £1. Pre-booked parties of 15 or more £2.50. Shop. No dogs. Wheelchair access, 2 provided. Picnic area.
**Refreshments:** From 12 noon, teas & lunches in old kitchen. Table licence.

### Grime Graves – See English Heritage Section.

### HOLKHAM HALL
**Wells** *map L7*
Telephone: Fakenham (0328) 710227

Fine Palladian mansion. Pictures, Tapestries, Statuary, Furnishings. Nessfield laid out the formal garden.

**Location:** 2m W of Wells; S of the Wells/Hunstanton Road (A149).
**Opening Times:** Daily (except Fri/Sat) from May 28 to end Sept 1.30–5, also Spring and Summer Bank Holiday Mons 11.30–5. Adm £1.70, Chd (5–15) 50p, OAPs £1.30. Adm to Park: Cars 50p, Motorcycles 25p, Coaches & Pedestrians free. Pre-paid coach parties of 20 or more 10% reduction.
**Refreshments:** Served in tea rooms.

### HOUGHTON HALL
**Kings Lynn** *map L7* ♿
Telephone: East Rudham 569
*(The Marquess of Cholmondeley)*

18th century mansion built for Sir Robert Walpole. State rooms, pictures and china. Pleasure grounds. Shetland ponies. Heavy horses on show in the stables. Private collection of model soldiers and militaria.

**Location:** 13 m E of King's Lynn; 10 m W of Fakenham off A148.
**Opening Times:** Easter Sun (Mar 26) to Sept 24—Suns, Thurs & Bank Hols. HOUSE opens 1–5.30. Last adm 5. Gates, Picnic Area. Children's Playground, stables and Model Soldier & Militaria Collection opens Suns, Thurs & Bank Hols 12.30–5. Adm £2.50, OAPs £2, Chd £1 (under 5 free). No additional charges except for special events which will be advertised. Reduction of 10% for pre-booked parties of 20 or more. Car park near House, toilets & lift to State floor for the disabled. Free parking for coaches & cars.
**Refreshments:** Tea room.

### LAZAR HOUSE (BRANCH LIBRARY)
**Norwich** *map M7* ♿
Telephone: (0603) 45452
*(Norwich City Council/Norfolk County Libraries)*

A Norman Leper Hospital later used as an almshouse, the building was restored in 1906 and is now a branch library.

**Location:** 219 Sprowston Road, Norwich.
**Opening Times:** Telephone librarian for current opening hours. Parties by appointment with the librarian. Car parking. Suitable for disabled persons.
**Refreshments:** Cafe opposite on Sprowston Road.

### MANNINGTON HALL GARDENS
**Saxthorpe, Norfolk** *map L7*
Telephone: Saxthorpe (026 387) 284
*(Hon Robin & Mrs Walpole)*

15th century moated house and Saxon church ruin set in attractive gardens. Outstanding rose gardens. Extensive walks and trails around the estate.

**Location:** 2 m N of Saxthorpe, nr B1149; 18 m NW of Norwich. 9 m from coast.
**Opening Times:** GARDEN. Easter Sun 12–5 then Apr to Dec, 12–5 or dusk if earlier. Also Weds, Thurs & Fris June to Aug, 11–6. Adm £1.50, Chd (accompanied children under 16) free, Senior Citizens/Students £1. House open by prior appointment only.
**Refreshments:** Coffee, salad lunches and home-made teas.

### NORWICH CASTLE
**Norwich** *map M7* ♿
Telephone: (0603) 611277 ext 279
*(Norwich City Council/Norfolk Museums Service)*

Norwich Castle houses one of the finest regional museums in Britain. The castle keep built by the Normans between 1100 and 1130 contains displays of medieval objects and an exhibition illustrating Norfolk's links with Europe. Galleries displaying art (the Norwich School) natural history, archaelogy and ceramics.

**Location:** In the centre of Norwich.
**Opening Times:** Mon to Sat 10–5, Suns 2–5, Bank Hols 10–5, *closed Christmas Day.* Adm winter 35p, Chd 10p, concession 20p, Spring Bank Hol to end Sept 70p, Chd 10p, concession 30p. Car parking in central Norwich. Suitable for disabled persons. Wheelchairs available. Museum shop.
**Refreshments:** Coffees, lunches and teas in Museum cafeteria.

### Old Merchants House and the Row III Houses – See English Heritage Section.

### OXBURGH HALL, The National Trust
**Swaffham** *map L7* ♿
Telephone: Gooderstone 258

Late 15th century moated house. Outstanding gatehouse tower. Needlework by Mary Queen of Scots. Unique French parterre laid out circa 1845. Woodland walk and traditional herbaceous garden. Chapel with fine altar piece.

**Location:** 7 m SW of Swaffham on S side of Stoke Ferry Road.
**Opening Times:** Gatehouse, Principal Rooms & Gardens: Mar 25, 26, 27; Sats and Suns in Apr. May 1 to Sept 30—Daily (except Thurs and Fris) 1.30–5.30. Bank Hol Mons 11–5.30. Oct: Sat and Sun 1.30–5.30. Adm £2.50, Chd (with adult) £1.25. Pre-booked parties of 15 or more £1.80. Shop. No dogs. Wheelchair access, 2 provided.
**Refreshments:** In Old Kitchen. Light lunches and teas 12–5.

# HOLKHAM HALL

**WELLS, NORFOLK**

18th century Palladian Home of Coke of Norfolk was erected in 1734. Open to visitors daily (except Fri/Sat) from May 28th to end September 1.30 to 5.00p.m., and Spring and Summer Bank Holiday Mondays 11.30a.m. to 5.00p.m. On view, the Marble Hall and State Rooms containing the extensive collection of Pictures, Tapestries, Statuary and Furnishings. Only entry to Park, Almhouse Gates, Holkham Village.
Charge for admission to view Hall: Adults £1.70, Children (5-15) 50p. OAPs £1.30. Admission to Park: Cars 50p, Motor Cycles 25p, Coaches and Pedestrians free. Pre-paid Coach Parties of 20 or more 10% reduction.

Also on View
The Holkham Studio Pottery
Bygones at Holkham, Agricultural and Domestic Bygones incorporating Craft Demonstrations, Steam Days and Engineerium. Garden Centre

# RAINTHORPE HALL

**NORFOLK**

Rainthorpe Hall has appeared in several Television productions. In both 1982 and 1987 it was used for 'Tales of the Unexpected'. It served as the principal location for the six hour murder mystery 'Cover Her Face', which was shown in England in 1985 and in the United States in 1987. Its drive and gates were used in 'The Black Tower' in 1986, and it was the scene of the Hunt Ball in 'Menace Unseen', a three-hour drama shown in 1988.

**Your number one choice**

# DISCOVER NORW1CH

## BRITAIN'S HISTORIC SECOND CITY

## *For a range of attractions second to none*

**Norwich City Council is the owner of many fine historic buildings. The City's museums are all located in buildings of outstanding interest.**

**Other important buildings owned by the City and open to the public are: The Guildhall · The Stuart and Suckling Halls · St. Andrew's and Blackfriars' Halls · The Lazar House · The Subscription Library · Shops and restaurants in Elm Hill, Bedford Street, Princes Street and Tombland.**

**For details see the Editorial Reference.**

**Norwich also has two magnificent Cathedrals, and the largest collection of mediaeval churches in Europe (31). For detailed information about these please contact the Tourist Information Centre, telephone Norwich (0603) 666071.**

**Norwich City Council**
Tourist Information Centre
**Guildhall, Gaol Hill, Norwich, NR2 1NF**
**Telephone: (0603) 666071**

**N.A.T.A.**
For information about opportunities in tourism and leisure contact
The Norwich Area Tourism Agency, Director: Paul Simons, Guildhall, Gaol Hill, Norwich NR2 1NF. Telephone (0603) 622233 Ext 2932
Sponsored by Norwich and Norfolk Chamber of Commerce and Industry – English Tourist Board – Norwich City Council – Norfolk County Council – Broadland and South Norfolk District Councils – Norwich and District Hoteliers Association – East Anglia Tourist Board

# WELLE MANOR HALL, UPWELL, NORFOLK

A rare example of a fortified prebendary manor house some parts of which date back to 1202. Welle Manor offers also for the visitors interest, its herborium, selenium spa, craft museums and collection of Lafayette photographs and equipment. In the grounds a collection of historic horse drawn vehicles and agricultural equipment. Welle Manor is the home of Norfolk punch. The hall is open all year by appointment for groups and offers a special tour first Sunday of every month. Entrance fee £1.00. Wholesome refreshments available.

TELEPHONE: WISBECH (0945) 773333

# WALSINGHAM ABBEY

**NORFOLK**

*East Window (Priory Church)*

The Grounds contain the remains of the Augustinian Priory, founded in 1153 on a site next to the Holy House, the shrine of Our Lady, built in 1061. The Grounds are open to the public from 2 to 5 pm. April: Weds; May, June, July & Sept: Weds, Sats & Suns; Aug: Mons, Weds, Fris, Sats & Suns. Also Bank Holidays from Easter to Sept.

Walsingham is a picturesque village containing fine examples of 15th–18th century architecture with half-timbered houses and medieval pump-house. Ruins of Franciscan Friary, Court House Museum. Anglican Shrine, R.C. Slipper Chapel and new Chapel 1 m to the south.
Accommodation and Catering available in the village.

## RAINTHORPE HALL & GARDENS

**Flordon, nr Norwich** *map M6* △ ♿
*(George Hastings, Esq.)*

Rebuilt in 1503 after a fire, and modernised during the reign of Elizabeth, Rainthorpe Hall is one of the very few half-timbered houses of its period in East Anglia. Its chimney breasts are placed in the French manner, at either end of the Great Hall – a pattern rare in this country. It is set in large gardens, with a conservation lake.

**Location:** 1 m SSW of Newton Flotman (A140) on Flordon Road, 8 m S of Norwich.
**Opening Times:** GARDENS. May to Sept—Suns & Bank Hol Mons 2–5.30. Adm £1, Chd 50p, OAPs 50p. Car park free. Plants on sale. House open by appointment. Gardens only suitable for disabled.

## RAVENINGHAM HALL GARDENS

**Norwich NR14 6NS** *map M6*
Telephone: (050846) 206
*(Sir Nicholas Bacon Bt.)*

An extensive garden laid out at the turn of the century surrounding original Georgian house. In the last thirty years there has been considerable designing and planting of new areas including unusual shrubs, plants and old roses, all in the traditional manner. In recent years the large and important Nursery Garden has grown to include many rare and exotic plants that can be seen in the Garden. Catalogue 3 ×18p stamp (refundable on orders over £10).

**Location:** 4 m from Beccles off the B1136 between Beccles and Loddon.
**Opening Times:** NURSERY: 9–3 weekdays and at weekends only if Garden is open. GARDEN: 2–5.30 Mar 26, 27; Apr 9, 23, 30; May 1, 21, 28, 29; June 11, 25; July 9, 23; Aug 13, 27, 28; Sept 10 in aid of local Charities. The house is not open. Adm £1, chd free. Car park free. Suitable for disabled persons.
**Refreshments:** Home made teas served on Garden Open Days only.

## ST. ANDREWS AND BLACKFRIARS' HALLS

**Norwich** *map M7* ♿
Telephone: (0603) 628477
*(Norwich City Council/Timothy Aldous Manager)*

A medieval friary built in the 14th and 15th centuries which has been in the ownership of the City of Norwich since the Reformation. The two halls (former nave and choir of the friars' church) contain part of the extensive collection of civic portraits dating back to the 16th century. With its cloister and other monastic buildings it represents the finest and most complete friary complex in England.

**Location:** St. Andrews Street, Norwich.
**Opening Times:** Mon to Sat 10–5 (the halls are sometimes booked for functions). Adm free. Parties by prior arrangement with the Manager. Car parking in city centre car parks. Suitable for disabled persons.
**Refreshments:** Crypt coffee bar Mon to Sat 10–4.

## ST. PETER HUNGATE MUSEUM

**Norwich** *map M7* ♿
Telephone: (0603) 611277 ext 279
*(Norwich City Council/Norfolk Museums Service)*

One of the city's large collection of medieval churches St. Peter Hungate is largely 15th century with fine hammer beam roof and painted glass. Now a museum of church art and brass-rubbing centre.

**Location:** Princes Street, Norwich.
**Opening Times:** Mon to Sat 10–5, *closed Bank Hols.* Adm free. Parties by prior arrangement. Car parking in city centre car parks. Suitable for disabled.
**Refreshments:** Restaurants and cafes in central Norwich.

## SANDRINGHAM HOUSE & GROUNDS

**Sandringham** *map L7*
Telephone: King's Lynn (0553) 772675
*(Her Majesty the Queen)*

House, Grounds and Museum open. *House, Grounds and Museum are NOT open when HM The Queen or any member of the Royal Family is in residence.*

**Location:** 8 m NE of King's Lynn (off A149).
**Opening Times:** House & Grounds. Mar 26 to Sept 28—Mons, Tues, Weds & Thurs 11–4.45 (Grounds 10.30–5), Suns 12–4.45 (Grounds 11.30–5). House only closed July 17 to Aug 5 inc. House and Grounds closed July 21 to Aug 2 inc. House & Grounds: £2, Chd £1.20, OAP £1.50. Grounds only: £1.50, Chd 80p, OAP £1.10. No reductions for coach parties. Free coach and car parks. Please check July closing dates with estate office.

## STRANGERS' HALL MUSEUM

**Norwich** *map M7*
Telephone: (0603) 611277 ext 279
*(Norwich City Council/Norfolk Museums Service)*

A medieval house built around a courtyard with Great Hall, stone vaulted undercroft and interesting 17th and 18th-century additions. The rooms are furnished in styles from the 16th century onwards with exhibits of domestic life.

**Location:** Charing Cross, Norwich.
**Opening Times:** Mon to Sat 10–5, *closed Bank Hols.* Adm winter 20p, Chd 10p, concession 15p; Spring Bank Hol to end Sept 40p, Chd 10p, concession 20p. Parties by prior arrangement. Car parking in city centre car parks.
**Refreshments:** Restaurants and cafes in the centre of Norwich.

## STUART HOUSE AND SUCKLING HALLS (CINEMA CITY)

**Norwich** *map M7* ♿
Telephone: (0603) 622047
*(Norwich City Council/Norfolk & Norwich Film Society)*

Former medieval Hall House, of which the Great Hall with its early scissor truss roof and the brick vaulted services rooms remain. Now a cinema.

**Location:** St. Andrews Street, Norwich.
**Opening Times:** Weekdays from noon onwards. Adm free. Parties apply to the Administrator, Cinema City. Car parking in city centre car parks. Suitable for disabled persons.
**Refreshments:** Restaurants and cafes in Norwich.

## THE SUBSCRIPTION LIBRARY/ADVICE ARCADE

**Norwich** *map M7* ♿
Telephone: (0603) 622233
*(Norwich City Council)*

The subscription library was built in 1837. Newly restored and open as an Advice Arcade it retains its late 19th century interior with bookshelves and reading room which are entered through a fine replica of a Greek temple.

**Location:** Guildhall Hill, Norwich.
**Opening Times:** Mon to Sat 10–5. Parties apply to Arcade Manager. Car parking in city centre car parks. Suitable for disabled persons.
**Refreshments:** Restaurants and cafes in central Norwich.

## SWANINGTON MANOR GARDENS

**Swannington, nr Norwich** *map L7* ♿
Telephone: Norwich 860700
*(Mr & Mrs Richard Winch)*

East Anglia's most romantic garden. Peaceful 4 acre garden framed by 300-year old yew and box topiary hedge. 17th century house (not open). Fine herbaceous borders with many labelled unusual plants. Colourful 50-yard shrub and herbaceous border. Stream. Woodland walk. Outstanding knot and herb garden. Orchids and greenhouses. Many other interesting features.

**Location:** 10 m NW of Norwich; turn off Norwich–Fakenham Rd (A1067) at Attlebridge.
**Opening Times:** Easter to End Sept—Weds and Bank Hol Mons 11–6. Adm £1.50, Chd 50p. Parties, by prior arrangement, at special rates. Free parking. Suitable for disabled persons.
**Refreshments:** Licensed restaurant. Morning coffee, home-made light lunches and afternoon teas.
**The Present Shop:** One of the most exciting present shops in the country, prices range from very little to indulgent. Everything pretty. Interesting selection of plants for sale.

## TRINITY HOSPITAL

**Castle Rising** *map L7*
*(Trustees)*

Nine 17th century brick and tile Almhouses with court, chapel and treasury.

**Location:** 4 m NE of King's Lynn on A149.
**Opening Times:** All the year—Tues, Thurs & Sats. Summer: 10–12, 2–6. Winter: 10–12, 2–4. Adm free.

## WALSINGHAM ABBEY

**Walsingham** *map L7*
Telephone: Walsingham 259
*(Walsingham Estate Company)*

Augustinian Priory and crypt.

**Location:** On B1105 midway between Wells and Fakenham.
**Opening Times:** Grounds open 2–5; Apr—Weds; May to July & Sept—Weds, Sats & Suns; Aug—Mons, Weds, Fris, Sats & Suns. Also Bank Hols, Easter to Sept. *Other times by arrangement with Estate Office.* Adm 50p, Chd & OAPs 25p.
**Refreshments:** Available in the village including Black Lion Hotel; Knight's Gate Hotel and the Old Bakehouse.

## WELLE MANOR HALL

**Upwell, PE14 9AB**
Telephone: (0945) 773333

Home of Norfolk Punch, the ancient herbal drink, Welle Manor Hall is a rare example of a fortified prebendary manor house, some parts of which date back to 1202. Visitors can see the Hall, the herborium, selenium spa, craft museum, collection of Lafayette photographs and equipment, assembly of historic horse-drawn vehicles, and collection of agricultural implements.

**Location:** 5 m SE of Wisbech on A1101 next to Church of Upwell, St Peter, in Upwell.

**Opening Times:** All year by appointment for groups. Special tour on the first Sun of each month. Adm £1.

**Refreshments:** Wholesome organic refreshments available.

# NORTHAMPTONSHIRE

## ALTHORP
**Northampton** *map J6* △
*(The Earl Spencer)*

Built by Sir John Spencer in 1508, altered by Henry Holland in 1790 and entirely redecorated in 1982. Splendid interior containing pictures of many European schools; French furniture; large collection of porcelain. Rooms open in rotation.
NB—*Please respect times when house and grounds are closed. No early arrivals except by appointment.*

**Location:** 6 m NW of Northampton on Northampton/Rugby Road (A428); 6 m from M1 exit 16.
**Opening Times:** Sept to June: HOUSE 1–5; July to Aug: HOUSE 11–6, Bank Holidays 11–6. Open all year daily except Christmas Day. Weds – Connoisseurs day throughout the year (extra rooms, longer tour). Adm House and Grounds: £2.75, groups of 8 or more £2.50, Chd £1.75. Connoisseurs day £3.75, Chd £2. Jan, Feb, Mar £2.50. Grounds and Lake only: Adm 50p, Chd 25p. Coach parking fees £10 in advance please, booking essential. Groups of more than 8 people during Jan and Feb £1.50. Cars free. Wine shop & Gift shop. Private morning visits by arrangement at extra cost. Weddings, 21st Birthdays, business or private lunches and dinners our speciality. Ploughman's Platters in Stables Restaurant for groups. For booking (enclosing sae) write to: The Countess Spencer, Althorp, Northampton NN7 4HG. *Information & prices are subject to alteration without notice as details submitted well in advance of printing.*
**Refreshments:** Tea room; home-made cakes & scones available at counter.
NB—*For security reasons House & Grounds may be closed without notice; Coach parties will be informed.* House unsuitable for small children and frail & disabled people.

## AYNHOE PARK
**Aynho** *map H5*
*(Country Houses Association Ltd)*

17th century mansion. Alteration by Soane.

**Location:** 6 m SE of Banbury on main London/Birmingham Road.
**Opening Times:** May to Sept—Weds & Thurs 2–5. Adm £1, Chd 50p. Free car park. No dogs admitted.

## BOUGHTON HOUSE
**Kettering** *map J6* △ ♿ Ⓢ
Telephone: Kettering (0536) 515731 & 82248
*(His Grace the Duke of Buccleuch & Queensberry KT and the Living Landscape Trust)*

15th century monastic building enlarged between 1530 and 1695 around 7 courtyards. Celebrated art treasures; lovely grounds, exciting adventure woodland play area and nature trail.

**Location:** 3 m N of Kettering on A43 at Geddington; 75 m from London by A1 or M1.
**Opening Times:** House and grounds: July 29–Aug 31. Daily, grounds 12–6; House 2–5. Adm House & Grounds £2.50, (Students, OAPs, Chd £2). Staterooms by prior booking £1 supplement. Grounds (excluding gardens) Apr 29–Oct 1—Daily except Fris, 12–5. Adm 80p, Chd 60p. Stable Yard, Tea Room, Gift Shop and Plant Stall open with House and at most weekends/public holidays. Exhibitions and lecture rooms in Stable Block. Museum and Educational groups by appointment at other times.
**Refreshments:** Teas in restored Stables during Aug and on some other occasions.

## CANONS ASHBY HOUSE, The National Trust
**Canons Ashby** *map H5*
Telephone: Blakesley (0327) 860044

The home of the Dryden family since the 16th century; a manor house c. 1580 and altered for the last time in 1710; Elizabethan wall paintings and outstanding Jacobean plasterwork; formal garden with terraces, walls and gatepiers of 1710: medieval Priory Church, privately owned since the Reformation. 70 acre park.

**Location:** On B4525 Northampton/Banbury Road.
**Opening Times:** Mar 25 to end of Oct—Weds to Suns & Bank Hol Mons 1–5.30. *Closed Good Friday.* Adm £2.50, Chd £1.20. Parking for cars & coaches which must pre-book (discount for parties). Dogs on leads, in Home Paddock only. 1989 events – details from the Administrator.
**Refreshments:** Tea room open as House.

## COTON MANOR GARDENS
*map J6* ♿
Telephone: Northampton (0604) 740219
*(Commander & Mrs H. Pasley-Tyler)*

An outstanding old English Garden of exceptional charm and beauty. Enchanted by flamingoes, wildfowl and tropical birds at large in the water gardens.

**Location:** 10 m N of Northampton & 11 m SE of Rugby. Follow tourist signs on A428 and A50.
**Opening Times:** Easter to end of Sept: Suns and Bank Hol Mons, also Weds in July & Aug, 2–6. Unusual plants for sale.
**Refreshments:** Home-made teas.

## DEENE PARK
**nr Corby** *map J6* △ ♿
Telephone: Bulwick 278 or 361 (office hours)
*(Edmund Brudenell, Esq.)*

Mainly 16th century house of great architectural importance and historical interest. Large lake, park, extensive gardens with old fashioned roses, rare trees and shrubs.

**Location:** 8 m NW of Oundle; 6 m NE of Corby on Kettering/Stamford Road (A43).
**Opening Times:** Easter, Spring & Summer Bank Hol Suns & Mons, also every Sun in June, July & Aug 2–5. Adm charges not available at time of going to press. Upstairs rooms now usually on view. *Special guided tours to parties of 20 or more may be arranged on application to the House Keeper.*

## DELAPRE ABBEY
**nr Northampton** *map J6*
*(Northamptonshire Borough Council)*

House rebuilt or added to 16th to 19th centuries. Converted for use as The County Record Office.

**Location:** On London Road (A508) 1 m due S of centre of Northampton.
*Station: Northampton (1 m).*
**Opening Times:** All the year—Thurs 2.30–5 (closes 4.30 Oct to Apr). Adm free 'public rooms and passages only'.

# BOUGHTON HOUSE

**NR KETTERING, NORTHAMPTONSHIRE**

*Home of The Duke of Buccleuch and Queensberry K.T., and his Montagu ancestors since 1528.*

A 500 year old Tudor monastic building gradually enlarged around 7 courtyards until the French style addition of 1695. Outstanding collection of 17/18th century French and English furniture, tapestries, 16th century carpets, porcelain painted ceilings—notable works by El Greco, Murillo, Caracci and 40 Van Dyck sketches—celebrated Armoury and Ceremonial Coach. Exhibition and Lecture rooms in Stables block with audio/visual facilities.

Beautiful parkland with avenues and lake—picnic area—gift shop—exciting adventure woodland play area.

OPEN: House and grounds July 29–Aug 31 Daily, Grounds 12–6 pm. House 2-5 pm. Grounds excluding gardens Apr 29–Oct 1 Daily except Fridays 12-5 pm. Admission 80p. Stable Yard, Tea Room, Gift Shop, Plant Stall open with House at most weekends and public holidays.

Off A43 through Geddington, 3 m North of Kettering. Northampton 17 m. Leicester 26 m, Peterborough 32 m Coventry 44 m. Cambridge 45 m. London 70 minutes by train.

For details of our specialist one, three or five day Art Courses run in conjunction with Sotheby's and for our Schools Education Facilities, please telephone the Living Landscape Trust at Kettering (0536) 515731 or 82248.

*"A vision of Louis XIV's Versailles transported to England"*

# DEENE PARK

**NORTHAMPTONSHIRE**

Deene, which has belonged to the Brudenell family since 1514, is a 16th and 17th century transformation of a mediaeval manor house with extensive 19th century additions.

It is still the 'elegant habitation of the Brudenells' as William Camden described it in the 16th century and was the home of the Earl of Cardigan who led the Charge of the Light Brigade.

Its special appeal lies in its indefinable atmosphere of a home cherished by the same family for over four centuries.

*ADMISSION – SEE EDITORIAL REFERENCE*

# HOLDENBY HOUSE GARDENS

**NORTHAMPTONSHIRE**

*Home of James Lowther Esq.*

Once the largest house in Elizabethan England Holdenby secured its place in history, when it became the prison of Charles I during the Civil War.

Today Holdenby's Falconry Centre and collection of rare farm animals complement the beauty and history of the grounds with their Elizabethan and fragrant borders. As buzzards and other birds of prey capture the attention in the sky above, donkey and train rides and a 'cuddle farm' ensure an enjoyable day for the children on the ground.

The house, with it's museum of rare pianos is open by appointment.

## HINWICK HOUSE

**nr Wellingborough** *map J6* △
Telephone: Rushden (0933) 53624
*(R. M. Orlebar)*

A Queen Anne house of excellent architecture. Pictures by Van Dyck; Lely, Kneller etc. Lace, tapestries and needlework. Furniture, china, objets d'art. 'A Century of Fashion' clothes from 1840 to 1940 on permanent display. Restaurant and Banqueting facilities for 100 people available. Medieval banquets held monthly. For details contact the Secretary.

**Location:** 3½ m S of Rushden, 6 m SE of Wellingborough; 3 m from A6 at Wymington.
**Opening Times:** Mar 26 and 27; Apr 30; May 1, May 2–20, 28 and 29; Aug 27 & 28, 2–4.30 (last tour). Otherwise by appointment. Adm £2. Parties welcome throughout year.
**Refreshments:** Home-made teas and other catering facilities by arrangement, for parties over 20, otherwise a fully licensed restaurant is available for lunch and dinner. Known as the Flemish House Restaurant, it is situated in the wing of the House.

## HOLDENBY HOUSE GARDENS

**Northampton** *map J6*
Telephone: Northampton (0604) 770786 or 770241
*(James Lowther, Esq.)*

Once the largest house in Elizabethan England, subsequently the prison of Charles I in the Civil War. Original garden remains. Elizabethan garden, fragrant and silver borders. Rare farm animals, falconry centre. Donkeys and train rides. Museum. Pottery.

**Location:** 7 m NW of Northampton, off A428 & A50; 7 m from M1 exit 18.
**Opening Times:** GARDENS. Apr to Sept—Suns & Bank Hol Mons 2–6; also Thurs July & Aug, 2–6. Adm Gardens: £1.75, Chd 80p. House and Gardens: £2.75, Chd £1. HOUSE. Open by arrangement to pre-booked parties Mons to Fris Adm £2.50, Chd £1. Enquire for special rates for school parties. Plant & Souvenir shop.
**Refreshments:** Home-made teas in Victorian Kitchen.

## KIRBY HALL

*map J6*
Telephone: (0533) 203230
*(English Heritage)*

Richness and variety of architectural detail distinguish this Elizabethan country house from others. Begun by Sir Humphrey Stafford in 1570, it was completed by Sir Christopher Hatton, a talented courtier to Queen Elizabeth. The fourth Sir Christopher Hatton devoted his energies to the garden. His death in 1706 marked the end of the Hall's golden age.

**Location:** 2 m (3.2 km) north of Corby. OS map ref SP926927.
**Opening Times:** Good Friday to Sept 30, daily 10–6; Oct 1 to Maundy Thurs, daily 10–4. *Closed* Mons, Dec 24–26, Jan 1. Adm 80p, OAPs 60p, Chd 40p.

## LAMPORT HALL

**Northampton** *map J6* Ⓢ
*(Lamport Hall Trust)*

The home of the Isham family from 1560 to 1976. Present house mainly 17th and 18th century. Site of one of the oldest alpine gardens in Britain, which housed the first garden gnomes – introduced by Sir Charles Isham around 1850.

**Location:** 8 m N of Northampton on A508 to Market Harborough.
**Opening Times:** House & Gardens. Easter to end of Sept—Suns & Bank Hol Mons 2.15–5.15. Also Thurs in July & Aug, 2.15–5.15. School & private parties any time by appointment. Adm £2.20, OAPs £1.70, Chd £1. Free car park. No dogs please.
**Refreshments:** Teas at the house.

## LILFORD PARK

**nr Oundle, Northants** *map J6*
Telephone: Clopton (08015) 648
*(J. M. Dishington, Esq.)*

Country park with extensive aviaries, children's farm, childrens's play area, gift/craft shop. Picnic areas.

**Location:** On A605 mid-way between Oundle and Thrapston. AA signposted.
**Opening Times:** Open daily Easter to Oct 10–6 (or dusk). Adm £1.50, Chd 75p. Party discounts by arrangement. Sorry no dogs.
**Refreshments:** Cafeteria.

## LYVEDEN NEW BIELD, The National Trust

**Oundle** *map J6*
Telephone: Benefield (083 25) 358

The shell of an unusual Renaissance building erected about 1600 by Sir Thomas Tresham to symbolize the Passion. He died before the building could be completed and his son was then imprisoned in connection with the Gunpowder Plot. A viewing platform allows visitors to look from the East Window.

**Location:** 4 m SW of Oundle via A427. 3 m E of Brigstock (A6116) (½ m walk from roadside parking).
**Opening Times:** All the year— Daily. *Property approached via two fields. Parties by arrangement with Custodian, Lyveden New Bield Cottage, nr Oundle, Northants.* Adm 80p, Chd 40p. *No parking for coaches but which may drop & return to pick up passengers.* Dogs admitted on leads. Unsuitable for disabled or visually handicapped.

## PRIEST'S HOUSE, The National Trust

**Easton-on-the-Hill** *map J7*
Telephone: Stamford (0780) 62506

Pre-Reformation priest's house given to the National Trust by The Peterborough Society. Contains a small museum of village bygones.

**Location:** 2 m SW of Stamford off A43.
*Station: Stamford (2 m).*
**Opening Times:** Access only by prior appointment with Mr. R. Chapman, Glebe Cottage, 45 West St., Easton-on-the-Hill, nr Stamford. Adm free. No dogs. Unsuitable for disabled or visually handicapped & Coaches.

## ROCKINGHAM CASTLE

**nr Corby** *map J6* △ Ⓢ
Telephone: Corby (0536) 770240
*(Commander Michael Saunders Watson)*

Royal Castle till 1530, since then home of the Watson family. Spans 900 years of English life and culture set amid lovely gardens and fine views.

**Location:** 2 m N of Corby; 9 m from Market Harborough; 14 m from Stamford on A427; 8 m from Kettering on A6003.
**Opening Times:** Easter Sun to Sept 30—Suns & Thurs also Bank Hol Mons & Tues following and Tues during Aug: 1.30–5.30. Adm £2.50, Chd £1.30. Gardens only £1.30. OAPs £2. *Any other day by previous appointment for parties.*
**Refreshments:** Teas—home-made at Castle.

## RUSHTON HALL

**Rushton, nr Kettering** *map J6*
*(Royal National Institute for the Blind)*

Dates from c. 1500, with earlier wing and later additions.

**Location:** 4 m NW of Kettering, off A6003.
**Opening Times:** Grounds & exterior of premises only (with a limited inspection of the interior) by prior appointment with the Head Teacher.

**Rushton Triangular Lodge** – See English Heritage Section.

## SOUTHWICK HALL

**nr Oundle** *map J6*
Telephone: Oundle (0832) 74064
*(Christopher Capron, Esq.)*

Manor house, retaining medieval building dating from 1300, with Tudor re-building and 18th century additions. Exhibitions:– Victorian and Edwardian life; musical instrument workshop; collections of agricultural and carpentry tools, named bricks and local archaeological finds and fossils.

**Location:** 3 m N of Oundle 4 m E of Bulwick.
**Opening Times:** Bank Holidays, Sun & Mon (Mar 26, 27; Apr 30 & May 1; May 28, 29; Aug 27, 28). Weds from May 3 to Aug 23: 2–5. Adm £2, Chd £1, OAPs £1.30. Parties at other times by arrangement with Secretary at Southwick Hall, Peterborough PE8 5BL.
**Refreshments:** Teas available.

# ROCKINGHAM CASTLE

'Arnescote' as in BBC TV's 'By the Sword Divided'

*'The castelle of Rockingham standeth upon the toppee of an hill right stately.'*

The house itself is memorable not so much as representing any particular period, but rather a procession of periods. The dominant influence in the building is Tudor within the Norman walls, but practically every century since the 11th has left its mark in the form of architecture, furniture, or works of art. There is a particularly fine collection of English 18th, 19th and 20th century paintings, and Charles Dickens, a frequent visitor, was so captivated by Rockingham that he used it as a model for Chesney Wold in Bleak House.

2 miles from Corby, Northamptonshire.

Home of Commander and Mrs Michael Saunders Watson

*'A royal residence for 500 years'.*

Rockingham Castle was built by William the Conqueror on the site of an earlier fortification and was used by the early Kings of England until the 16th century when it was granted by Henry VIII to Edward Watson whose family still live there today.

The Castle stands in 12 acres of formal and wild garden and commands a splendid view of five counties. Particular features are the 400 years old elephant hedge and the rose garden marking the foundations of the old keep.

See also
Special Exhibition
Gardens for a Castle 1100–1980

*ADMISSION – SEE EDITORIAL REFERENCE*

# LAMPORT HALL

**NORTHAMPTON**

Lamport Hall was the home of the Isham family from 1560 to 1976. The South West front is a rare example of the work of John Webb, pupil and son-in-law of Inigo Jones and was built in 1655 (during the Commonwealth) with wings added in 1732 and 1740.
There is a High Room with a plaster ceiling by John Woolston, an outstanding library and a fine collection of portraits, tranquil gardens and teas in the house.
Now run by the Lamport Hall Trust, school visits and private openings are especially encouraged and a programme of drama, music, art and craft events is staged in the summer—details from the Director. For admission times please see the entry under Northamptonshire.

*ADMISSION – SEE EDITORIAL REFERENCE*

# SOUTHWICK HALL

**Nr OUNDLE, NORTHAMPTONSHIRE**

*Photograph—Royal Commission on Historical Monuments (England)*

A FAMILY HOME SINCE 1300—the oldest parts of the present house date from 1300, since when it has been in continuous occupation as a home by three families: Knyvetts, Lynnes and now Caprons.

*ADMISSION – SEE EDITORIAL REFERENCE*

## SULGRAVE MANOR

Open to the public
**Every day except Wednesday**
**from March 1 to December 31**
April to September inclusive
10.30 am to 1 pm & 2 to 5.30 pm
Other months
10.30 am to 1 pm & 2 to 4 pm
**Will be open February for Groups by appointment.**

ADMISSION: Adults £2.00, Schoolchildren 1.00
includes access to House & Gardens, Guided Tour
Free parking for Cars & Coaches

Light Refeshments and Shop available

Refreshments at 'Thatched House Hotel'
(opposite the Manor House)

Telephones:
Manor House — Sulgrave (029 576) 205
Hotel — Sulgrave (029 576) 232

# SULGRAVE MANOR

**BANBURY, OXON OX17 2SD**

## THE WASHINGTON ANCESTRAL HOME

The Washington ownership dates from 1539 when Lawrence Washington purchased the land upon the Dissolution by Henry VIII, of St. Andrew's Priory, Northampton. The House was completed in 1558 (the year Elizabeth I came to the throne of England) and was lived in by descendants of the Washington family for 120 years.

Today it is an excellent example of a small Manor House, typical of a wealthy man's home and gardens in Elizabethan times, restored and refurbished with scholarly care and attention to detail which makes a visit both a delight and an education.

**'A perfect illustration of how a house should be shown to the public' is how Nigel Nicholson describes it in his 'Great Houses of Britain'.**

SULGRAVE MANOR has been open to the public since 1921 when it was established as a 'Token of Friendship' between the people of Britain and the United States. It is now held in trust for the peoples of both nations, the trustees being the American Ambassador in London, the British Ambassador in Washington and the Regent of Mount Vernon, Virginia. Endowed by the National Society of Colonial Dames of America.

The village of Sulgrave is situated 1 mile off the Northampton road (B4525), 7 miles NE of Banbury, 28 miles SE of Stratford upon Avon, 30 miles N of Oxford and 70 miles NW of London.

### STOKE PARK PAVILIONS
**Towcester** *map J5*
*(A. S. Chancellor, Esq)*

Two pavilions and colonnade. Built in 1630 by Inigo Jones.

**Location:** Stoke Bruerne village; 7 m S of Northampton just W of Stony/Northampton Road A508.
**Opening Times:** June, July & Aug—Sats, Suns & Bank Hols 2–6. *Exterior only on view.* Adm £1. Car park free.

### SULGRAVE MANOR
**Banbury** *map H5* △
Telephone: Sulgrave (029 576) 205
*(The Sulgrave Manor Board)*

English home of ancestors of George Washington. The house was completed in 1558 and was lived in by descendants of the Washington family for 120 years.

**Location:** Sulgrave Village is off Banbury/Northampton Road (B4525); 7 m NE of Banbury; 28 m SE of Stratford-upon-Avon; 30 m N of Oxford; 70 m NW of London.
**Opening Times:** Mar to Dec 31—Daily (except Weds); Apr to Sept (inc) 10.30–1, 2–5.30. Other months 10.30–1, 2–4. *Closed Christmas Day, Boxing Day, and all January.* February: Groups only by appointment. Adm £2, Chd £1. Free car & coach parking.
**Refreshments:** At Thatched House Hotel opposite, Tel Sulgrave (029 576) 232.

## NORTHUMBERLAND

### ALNWICK CASTLE
**Alnwick** *map H12*
Telephone: Alnwick (0665) 510777
*(His Grace the Duke of Northumberland, KG)*

Important example of medieval fortification restored by Salvin, dating to 12th century. Including the Keep, Armoury, Guard Chamber, Library and other principal apartments, Dungeon, State Coach and Museum of British and Roman antiquities. Pictures by Titian, Canaletto, Van Dyck, and other famous artists.

**Location:** In the town of Alnwick, 30 m N of Newcastle off the A1.
**Opening Times:** May–Sept—Daily (except Sats but open Bank Holiday weekends including Sats) 1–5. No admission after 4.30. Adm £2, Chd (under 16) £1, OAPs £1.70. (Organised Party Rates by arrangement.) Free Parking. *No dogs.*

**Aydon Castle** – See English Heritage Section.

### BAMBURGH CASTLE
**Bamburgh** *map H13* △
Telephone: Bamburgh 208

Fine 12th century Norman Keep. Remainder of castle considerably restored.

**Location:** Coastal – 16 m N of Alnwick 6 m from Belford; 3 m from Seahouses.
**Opening Times:** Easter to last Sun of Oct—Daily (incl Suns) open at 1; Adm £1.70, Chd 60p (1988 prices). *Parties may be booked out of normal hours.* For closing times enquire The Custodian.
**Refreshments:** Clock Tower tea rooms.

### BELSAY HALL CASTLE AND GARDENS
*map G12*
Telephone: (066 181) 636
*(English Heritage)*

XIX century Neo-Classical mansion lies at the entrance to 30 acres of exciting gardens, which in turn lead on to the XIV century castle and ruined manor. Important collections of rare and exotic flowering trees grow in the meandering, deep ravines of the "picturesque" Quarry Gardens. Massed plantings of rhododendrons. Large heather garden. Spring bulbs. Exhibition of Belsay's architectural and landscape history in stable block.

**Location:** 14 m (22.4 km) north west of Newcastle upon Tyne. OS map ref NZ088785.
**Opening Times:** Good Friday to Sept 30, daily 10–6; Oct 1 to Maundy Thurs, daily 10–4. *Closed* Mons, Dec 24–26, Jan 1. Adm £1.60, OAPs £1.20, Chd 80p.

**Berwick Barracks** – See English Heritage Section.

**Brinkburn Priory** – See English Heritage Section.

**Chesters Fort** – See English Heritage Section.

**Corbridge Roman Site** – See English Heritage Section.

### CRAGSIDE HOUSE & COUNTRY PARK, The National Trust
**Rothbury** *map G12* ♿
Telephone: Rothbury (0669) 20333

The House was designed by Richard Norman Shaw for the first Lord Armstrong and built between 1864-95. It contains much of its original furniture and Pre-Raphaelite paintings. It was the first house in the world to be lit by electricity generated by water power. The Country Park is famous for its rhododendrons, magnificent trees and the beauty of the lakes. New in 1988 'The Power Circuit', a three mile circular walk including the restored Ram & Power Houses with their hydraulic and hydroelectric machinery.

**Location:** ½ m E of Rothbury; 30 m N of Newcastle-upon-Tyne. Entrance off Rothbury/Alnwick Road B6341; 1 m N of Rothbury at Debdon Burn Gate.
**Opening Times:** COUNTRY PARK, ARMSTRONG ENERGY CENTRE & POWER CIRCUIT: Mar 24 to Oct 30 daily (*closed* Mon) but open Bank Holiday Mon. Easter to end Oct: 10.30–7 (or dusk if earlier). Nov to Easter: 10.30–4, Sat and Sun. HOUSE: Mar 24 to Oct 30 daily 1–5.30 (*closed* Mon) but open Bank Holiday Mon. Last adm 5. In Apr and Oct on selected days only, guided tours may be available. Adm House & Country Park, Museum & Power Circuit £3; Country Park £1.50. Parties £2.50; Country Park £1.20. Parties by prior arrangement only with the Administrator. Armstrong Energy Centre & shop in Visitor centre. Dogs in Country Park only. Wheelchair access to House—lift available (wheelchairs provided). Toilets for disabled. Fishing.
**Refreshments:** Restaurant in Visitor Centre. Telephone Rothbury (0669) 20134

**Dunstanburgh Castle** – See English Heritage Section.

### GEORGE STEPHENSON'S BIRTHPLACE, The National Trust
**Wylam** *map G11*
Telephone: Wylam (06614) 3457

A small stone cottage built c. 1750. The birthplace, in 1781, of the inventor.

**Location:** 8 m W of Newcastle 1½ m S of A69 at Wylam-on-Tyne.
*Station:* Wylam (½ m).
**Opening Times:** Mar 24 to Oct 30—Weds, Sats & Suns (open Good Friday & Bank Holiday Mon) 1–5.30 (last adm 5). Other times of the year by appointment only with the tenant. Adm 60p, Chd 30p. Parking facilities 500 yards from cottage by War Memorial in village. No dogs. Wheelchair access.
NB Access to cottage by foot and bicycle only.

**Hadrian's Roman Wall** – See English Heritage Section.

**Housesteads Roman Fort** – See English Heritage Section.

### HOWICK GARDENS
**Alnwick** *map H12*
*(Howick Trustees Ltd)*

Lovely flower, shrub and rhododendron gardens.

**Location:** 6 m NE of Alnwick, nr Howick village.
**Opening Times:** Apr to Sept—Daily 2–7. Adm £1, Chd 50p.

### LINDISFARNE CASTLE, The National Trust
**Holy Island** *map G13*
Telephone: Berwick (0289) 89244

Built about 1550. Sympathetically restored as a comfortable house by Lutyens in 1903.

**Location:** 5 m E of Beal across causeway.
**Opening Times:** Mar 24 to Sept 30—Daily (closed Fris, open Good Fri) 1–5.30; Oct—Weds, Sats & Suns 1–5.30. Last adm 4.30. Adm June, July Aug: £2.50. Other times £1.50. No party rate. No dogs in Castle. Unsuitable for wheelchairs.

**Lindisfarne Priory** – See English Heritage Section.

### MELDON PARK
**Morpeth** *map G12* ♿
*(M. J. B. Cookson, Esq.)*

Built in 1832 for the Cookson family and occupied by them up to the present time. Main ground floor rooms only open to the public. Different coloured rhododendrons, especially in the wild garden.

**Location:** 7 m W of Morpeth on B6343 Morpeth/Hartburn Road; NW of Newcastle-upon-Tyne.
**Opening Times:** House & Grounds—May 20 to June 18, and Aug 19, 20, 21: daily from 2–5.
**Refreshments:** Light snacks weekends only.

**Norham Castle** – See English Heritage Section.

### PRESTON TOWER
**Chathill** *map H13*
*(Major T. H. Baker-Cresswell)*

One of the few survivors of 78 Pele Towers listed in 1415. The tunnel vaulted rooms remain unaltered and provide a realistic picture of the grim way of life under the constant threat of 'Border Reivers'. Two rooms are furnished in contemporary style and there are displays of historic and local information.

**Location:** 7 m N of Alnwick; 1 m E from A1. Follow Historic Property signs.
*Station: Chathill (1 m).*
**Opening Times:** All year—Daily during daylight hours. Adm £1, Chd 50p. Free car park. No dogs (except those left in car).

# ALNWICK CASTLE

**NORTHUMBERLAND**

*Home of the Duke of Northumberland*

Including the Keep, Armoury, Guard Chamber, Library and other principal apartments, Dungeon, State Coach and Museum of British and Roman Antiquities. Pictures by Titian, Canaletto, Van Dyck and other famous Artists, fine furniture, Meissen china and various historical heirlooms.

OPEN TO VISITORS
29th April to 6th October 1989 (Daily except Saturdays)
(Open Saturdays Bank Holiday Weekends only)
1 pm to 5 pm (No Admission after 4.30 pm)
Admission: Adults – £2, O.A.P's – £1.70, children under 16 – £1
(Organised Party Rates: By Arrangement)
Free Parking
Enquiries to The Supervisor, Estates Office, Alnwick Castle, Alnwick. Telephone Alnwick 510777

# MELDON PARK

**MORPETH, NORTHUMBERLAND**

Meldon Park was built by John Dobson, the famous North East architect, in 1832 for the Cookson family and since that date it has been occupied by them up to the present time except for the duration of the last war.

The public are admitted to the main ground floor rooms which are renowned for the spacious view of the local rolling countryside. Early June the grounds are highlighted by many different coloured flowering rhododendrons, especially those in the wild garden.

Light refreshments are on sale weekends only. Car park – free: and there are facilities for the disabled.

# BAMBURGH CASTLE

## AND ARMSTRONG MUSEUM

The home of Lady Armstrong

The Norman Keep has stood for eight centuries and its setting upon The Crag, which is referred to as a Royal Centre by A.D. 547, is certainly one of the most dramatic of all Castles in Britain.

**Featuring:**
- **Magnificent Seascapes including Holy Island and the Farne Islands, and Landscapes extending to the Cheviot Hills.**
- **Public Rooms with exhibition of porcelain, china, paintings, furniture and items of interest.**
- **The Armoury, including loan collections from H.M. Tower of London, The John George Joicey Museum, Newcastle-upon-Tyne, and others.**
- **Fine Paintings including some from the Duke of Cambridge's collection.**

Open to the Public from Maundy Thursday to the last Sunday in October.
— Concessionary Rates for Parties in or out of Season —
Restaurant – Tea Room in the Castle Clock Tower
**Operators** – All at one stop. Tour. Food. Cloakrooms. Free Coach Parking at Entrance to Walled Castle.
CUSTODIAN – TEL: BAMBURGH (066 84) 208

# PRESTON TOWER

**NORTHUMBERLAND**

*ADMISSION – SEE EDITORIAL REFERENCE*

# SEATON DELAVAL HALL

**Northumberland**

*The Home of Lord Hastings*

The house was designed by Sir John Vanbrugh in his most theatrical manner for Admiral George Delaval and built between 1718–1728. Built on a small budget it is ducal magnificence in miniature. Relatively small, the house gives the impression of being vast, which is of course what was intended. It is the theatre again – Vanbrugh the playwright using stones, columns and pediments instead of words. It comprises a centre block between two arcaded and pedimented wings, the centre block being gutted by fire in 1822 and for many years stood a gaunt ruin, but it was partially restored in 1862–63 and again in 1959–62. The East Wing contains very fine stables and in the grounds are extensive gardens and statues.

*ADMISSION – SEE EDITORIAL REFERENCE*

**Enjoy even more of Northumberland.**

**Explore the English Heritage Supplement on the Red Pages.**

**English Heritage**

## NORTHUMBERLAND – *continued*

**Prudhoe Castle** – See English Heritage Section.

### SEATON DELAVAL HALL
**Whitley Bay** *map H12*
Telephone: Tyneside (091) 2373040/2371493
*(The Lord Hastings)*

Splendid English baroque house, regarded by many as Sir John Vanbrugh's masterpiece. An early 18th century feat of architecture, comprising a centre block between two arcaded and pedimented wings.

**Location:** ½ m from coast at Seaton Sluice, and between Blyth and Whitley Bay (A190). (Northumbria Bus from Newcastle 363, 364.)
**Opening Times:** May 1–Sept 30: Wed, Sun, and Bank Holidays 2–6. Adm £1, Chd (accompanied by adult) 50p, OAPs 50p.
**Refreshments:** Lunch and refreshments available at Astley Arms (½ m) on coast.

**Vindolanda Fort & Roman Milestone** – See English Heritage Section.

### WALLINGTON HOUSE, WALLED GARDEN and GROUNDS, The National Trust
**Cambo** *map G12* ♿
Telephone: Scots Gap (067 074) 283 (House)

Built 1688, altered 18th century. Central Hall added in 19th century, decorated by William Bell Scott, Ruskin and others. Fine porcelain, furniture and pictures in series of rooms including a late Victorian nursery and dolls' houses. Museum. Coach display in West Coach House. Woodlands, lakes, walled terraced garden and conservatory with magnificent fuchsias.

**Location:** Access from N, 12 m W of Morpeth on B6343. Access from S, A696 from Newcastle; 6 m NW of Belsay B6342 to Cambo.
**Opening Times: HOUSE:** Mar 24 to Oct 30, daily 1–5.30. *Closed* Tues. In Apr and Oct on selected days only guided tours may be available. **WALLED GARDEN:** Open all year daily. Easter to end of Sept 10–7 (or dusk if earlier). Oct: 10–6; Nov to Easter 10–4. **GROUNDS:** Open all year during daylight hours. Adm House and Grounds £2.80, Grounds only £1. Party rate £2.40, Chd 70p. No dogs in house; on leads in walled garden. Shop & Information Centre. Wheelchairs provided. *Parties by prior arrangement with the administrators.*
**Refreshments:** Available at Clock Tower Restaurant. Telephone Scots Gap (067 074) 274.

**Warkworth Castle** – See English Heritage Section.

**Warkworth Hermitage** – See English Heritage Section.

# NOTTINGHAMSHIRE

### CARLTON HALL
**Carlton-on-Trent** *map J8* △
*(Trustees of G H Vere-Laurie dec'd)*

George III house built c.1765 by Joseph Pocklington of Newark, banker, 1736–1817. Beautiful drawing room. Magnificent ancient cedar in grounds. Stables attributed to Carr of York.

**Location:** 7 m N of Newark just off A1.
**Opening Times:** Any day, telephone (0636) 821421 to be certain of being shown round. Adm House and Garden £1.50.

### CLIFTON HALL
**Clifton Village, nr Nottingham** *map H7*
*(Trent Polytechnic)*

This recently restored Georgian mansion forms part of Trent Polytechnic and houses the School of Education.

**Location:** Just outside the village, 5 m SW from Nottingham on A453.
**Opening Times:** Open weekdays, except public holidays. Application for parties to visit the Hall should be made to The Assistant Director (Administration). Trent Polytechnic, Burton Street, Nottingham.

### CLUMBER PARK, The National Trust
**nr Worksop** *map J8* ♿
Telephone: Worksop (0909) 476592

4,000 acre landscaped park with lake and woods. Classical bridge, temples, lawned Lincoln Terrace and pleasure grounds. Kitchen garden exhibition.

**Location:** Clumber Park 4½ m SE of Worksop; 6½ m SW of East Retford.
**Opening Times:** Open daily all year. The Estate Office, Gardens Cottage, Clumber Park, Worksop, Notts S80 3AZ. Vehicle parking charges. Dogs admitted. Shop. Cycle hire. Fishing bank. Tricycles, tandems, wheelchairs & special fishing platform for disabled.
**Refreshments:** Cafeteria open all year daily. Licensed restaurant for lunches daily, evening meals available for pre-booked parties. Telephone: Worksop 484122.

### HOLME PIERREPONT HALL
**Radcliffe-on-Trent, nr Nottingham** *map J7* △
*(Mr & Mrs Robin Brackenbury)*

Medieval brick manor house. Historic Courtyard garden with box parterre, 1875. Regional 17th, 18th, 19th and 20th century furniture, china and pictures. Quiet and free from crowds. Jacob sheep. Shop with Jacob wool products.

**Location:** 5 m SE from centre of Nottingham off A52 approach past National Water Sports Centre and continue for 1½ m.
**Opening Times:** Easter Sun, Mon & Tues; May Bank Holiday & Spring & Summer Bank Hol Mons & Tues; June, July & Aug—Suns, Tues, Thurs & Fris 2–6. Adm £1.80, Chd 75p, *subject to alteration. Parties by appointment throughout year.*
**Refreshments:** Home made teas. Other refreshments by arrangement.

### NEWSTEAD ABBEY
**Linby** *map H7*
Telephone: Mansfield (0623) 793557
*(Nottingham City Council)*

The medieval Priory of Newstead was converted into the Byron family house in the 16th century and restored in the 1820s. It was the home of the poet Byron in the early 19th century and now contains his possessions, furniture, pictures, letters, manuscripts and first editions. Furniture and possessions of the later 19th century owners are also to be seen. The house stands in over 300 acres of beautiful parkland with lakes, waterfalls, a Japanese water garden, rock and rose gardens, a subtropical garden and a Monk's stew pond.

**Location:** 11 m N of Nottingham on the Mansfield Road (A60).
*Station: Nottingham, then by Trent bus no. 63 from Victoria Centre.*
**Opening Times:** House: open Good Friday to Sept 30—Daily 11.30–6 (last adm 5). Adm £1.20, Chd 20p, OAPs & UB40 holders 40p (1988). Also Oct 1 to Easter by arrangement. Gardens open all year—Daily 10–dusk. Grounds & Gardens Adm 85p, Chd 40p (1988). Charges subject to revision.
**Refreshments:** Tea at tearoom in the grounds. Telephone (0623) 797392.

### PAPPLEWICK HALL
**Near Nottingham** *map H7*
Telephone: (0602) 633491
*(Dr R. B. Godwin-Austen)*

Fine Adam house built 1784 with park and woodland garden.

**Location:** 6 m N of Nottingham, 2 m from exit 27 M1.
**Opening Times:** By appointment only, all year.

### THRUMPTON HALL
**Nottingham** *map H7* △
Telephone: Nottingham 830333
*(George FitzRoy Seymour, Esq)*

Jacobean. Magnificent carved staircase. Fine pictures and furniture. Lived in and shown by owners.

**Location:** 7 m S of Nottingham; 3 m E of M1 at junction 24; 1 m from A453.
**Opening Times:** By appointment for parties of 20 or more persons. Adm House & Gardens £2, Chd £1. Minimum charge of £40. Open all year including evenings.
**Refreshments:** By prior arrangement.

## NOTTINGHAMSHIRE – *continued*

### WOLLATON HALL

**Nottingham** *map H7*
Telephone: Nottingham 281333
*(City of Nottingham)*

Fine example of late Elizabethan Renaissance architecture. Natural History Museum – one of the finest in the country.
**Location:** 2½ m W of City centre.
*Station: Nottingham (2¾ m).*
**Opening Times:** All the year. Apr to Sept—Weekdays 10–7, Suns 2–5; Oct to Mar—Weekdays 10–dusk, Suns 1.30–4.30. Adm free (small charge Suns & Bank Hols). *Conducted tours by arrangement 50p, Chd 20p (subject to alteration). Closed Christmas Day.*
**Refreshments:** Tea at refreshment pavilion *(Apr to Sept).*

## OXFORDSHIRE

### ARDINGTON HOUSE

**nr Wantage** *map H4*
Telephone: (0235) 833244
*(D. C. N. Baring, Esq.)*

Early 18th century of grey brick with red brick facings. Hall with Imperial staircase, panelled dining room with painted ceiling. Magnificent cedar trees.
**Location:** 12 m S of Oxford; 12 m N of Newbury; 2½ m E of Wantage.
*Station: Didcot (8 m).*
**Opening Times:** May to Sept—Mons & all Bank Hols 2.30–4.30. Parties of 10 or more welcomed any day by appointment. Adm House & Grounds £1.50.
**Refreshments:** Coffee & Teas by arrangement.

### ASHDOWN HOUSE, The National Trust

**nr Lambourn** *map H4* △

17th century house built by 1st Lord Craven and by him 'consecrated' to Elizabeth, Queen of Bohemia; great staircase rising from hall to attic; portraits of the Winter Queen's family; access to roof, fine views; box parterre and lawns. Avenues and woodland walks.
**Location:** 2¼ m S of Ashbury; 3½ m N of Lambourn on W side of B4000.
**Opening Times:** Hall, stairway & roof only (fine views). Apr to end Oct—Weds & Sats 2–6. Guided tours only: at 2.15, 3.15, 4.15 and 5.15, from front door. *Closed* Easter and Bank Holiday Mon. Adm Grounds, hall, stairway & roof £1.20, Chd half-price. **Woodlands** open all year—Sats to Thurs, dawn to dusk, adm free. No reduction for parties (which should pre-book in writing). No dogs allowed in house or grounds. Wheelchair access to garden only.

### BLENHEIM PALACE

**Woodstock** *map H5* △ Ⓢ
Telephone: Woodstock (0993) 811325 (24 hrs)
*(His Grace the Duke of Marlborough)*

Masterpiece of Sir John Vanbrugh in the classical style. Fine collection of pictures and tapestries. Gardens and park designed by Vanbrugh and Queen Anne's gardener, Henry Wise. Later construction was carried out by 'Capability' Brown, who also created the famous Blenheim lake. Exhibition of Churchilliana and Sir Winston Churchill's birth room. Churchill paintings on exhibition. Also Blenheim Butterfly House, Garden Centre (open throughout the year), Adventure Playground, Garden Restaurant, Motor Launch and Train. All inclusive ticket.
**Location:** SW end of Woodstock which lies 8 m N of Oxford (A34).
**Opening Times:** mid-Mar to Oct 31—Daily 10.30–5.30 (last adm 4.45). Special prices & times apply on Spring Bank Holiday Sunday when the Lord Taverners Charity Cricket Match takes place. *Reduced rates for parties.* Educational service for school parties—Palace, Farm, Forestry, Horticulture & Nature Trail. Adm charges not available at time of going to press.
**Refreshments:** Licensed Restaurant & self service cafeteria at the Palace. Self Service restaurant at the Garden Centre.

### BOTANIC GARDENS

**Oxford** *map H5*
*(University of Oxford)*

Oldest botanic garden in Britain, founded 1621.
**Location:** High Street.
*Station: Oxford (1 m).*
**Opening Times:** All the year—9–5, (closes 4.30 winter). Adm free. *Closed Good Fri and Christmas day.*

### BROOK COTTAGE

**Alkerton** *map H5*
Telephone: Edge Hill (029 587) 303 or 590
*(Mr & Mrs David Hodges)*

4 acre landscaped garden, mostly formed since 1964, surrounding 17th century house. Wide variety of trees, shrubs and plants of all kinds; water garden; one-colour borders; collection of shrub roses; many clematis. Interesting throughout season.
**Location:** 6 m NW of Banbury; ½ m A422 (Banbury/Stratford-upon-Avon). In Alkerton take lane opposite war memorial then right fork.
**Opening Times:** GARDEN ONLY. Apr 1–Oct 31, Mon–Fri 10–6. Adm £1, Chd free. Evenings and weekends by appointment. *In aid of National Gardens Scheme.*
**Refreshments:** For parties by prior arrangement.

### BROUGHTON CASTLE

**Banbury** *map H5*
Telephone: Banbury (0295) 62624
*(The Lord Saye & Sele)*

A moated Tudor mansion with early 14th century nucleus. 16th and 18th century plaster ceilings and 16th century chimney pieces.
**Location:** 2 m SW of Banbury on the Shipston-on-Stour Road (B4035).
**Opening Times:** May 18 to Sept 14—Weds & Suns 2–5; also Thurs in July & Aug 2–5; Bank Hol Suns & Bank Hol Mons including Easter 2–5. Adm £2, Chd £1, OAPs/Students £1.60. Groups on other days throughout the year by appointment (reduced rates).
**Refreshments:** Buffet teas on open days; by arrangement for groups.

# BROUGHTON CASTLE

**2 miles SW of BANBURY**

The home of Lord and Lady Saye and Sele and owned by the family for 600 years. Moated mediaeval Castle greatly enlarged in 1550. Fine panelling and fireplaces, splendid plaster ceilings and good period furniture. Interesting Civil War connections including the secret meeting room of the parliamentary leaders.

OPEN 18th May–14th September
Wednesdays and Sundays.
Also Thursdays in July and August
and Bank Holiday Sundays
and Bank Holiday Mondays (including Easter)
2.00–5.00pm

GROUPS ON OTHER DAYS THROUGHOUT THE YEAR BY APPOINTMENT

# GREYS COURT

**HENLEY-ON-THAMES**

*THE NATIONAL TRUST*

*ADMISSION – SEE EDITORIAL REFERENCE*

# KINGSTON HOUSE

**KINGSTON BAGPUIZE, OXFORDSHIRE**

*The Home of Lord and Lady Tweedsmuir*

ADMISSION – SEE EDITORIAL REFERENCE

**Enjoy even more of Oxfordshire.**

**Explore the English Heritage Supplement on the Red Pages.**

**English Heritage**

## BUSCOT OLD PARSONAGE, The National Trust
**nr Lechlade** *map H4*

Built in 1703 of Cotswold stone and stone tiles. On the banks of the Thames. Small garden.

**Location:** 2 m SE of Lechlade; 4 m NW of Faringdon on A417.
**Opening Times:** Mar 29 to end Oct—Weds 2–6, by appointment in writing with the tenant. Adm £1. *No parties.* No dogs. No WCs. Unsuitable for wheelchairs.

## BUSCOT PARK, The National Trust
**nr Faringdon** *map H4* △
Telephone: Faringdon (0367) 20786 (not weekends)

Built 1780. Fine paintings and furniture. Burne-Jones room. Attractive garden walks, lake.

**Location:** 3 m NW Faringdon on Lechlade/Faringdon road (A417).
**Opening Times:** Mar 22 to end Sept (incl Good Fri, Easter Sat & Sun)—Weds, Thurs & Fris 2–6; and every 2nd and 4th Sat and each Sun immediately following 2–6. *Last admission to house 5.30.* Adm House & Grounds £2.50, Chd £1.25. Grounds only £1.50, Chd 75p. *No dogs. No indoor photography.* Unsuitable for wheelchairs.

## CHASTLETON HOUSE
**Nr Moreton-in-Marsh** *map H5* △
Telephone: Barton-on-Heath (0608 74) 355
(Mrs Clutton-Brock)

Jacobean Manor House c. 1603. Original Panelling, furniture, tapestries, embroideries. Topiary garden c. 1700.

**Location:** 4 m from Moreton-in-Marsh off A44 Chipping Norton to Moreton-in-Marsh road; 5 m from Stow-on-the-Wold off A436 Stow to Chipping Norton road.
**Opening Times:** Good Friday to Sun Oct 1 incl. Fri, Sat, Sun & Bank Hol Mon 2–5. Parties be previous arrangement all year round. Adm £2.50, Chd £1.50. Reductions for parties over 20 in number. Limited free parking. Guided Tours only.

## DITCHLEY PARK
**Enstone** *map H5*
Telephone: Enstone (060 872) 346
*(Ditchley Foundation)*

Third in size and date amongst the great 18th century mansions of Oxfordshire. Designed by Gibbs, decoration of Great Hall by Kent.

**Location:** 1½ m W of A34 at Kiddington; 2 m from Charlbury (B4437).
*Station: Charlbury (2 m).*
**Opening Times:** It is unlikely that there will be a set open period in 1989, but private parties will be welcome by special arrangement Mons–Thurs afternoons until early July.

## THE GREAT BARN, The National Trust
**Great Coxwell** *map H4*

13th century, stone built, stone tiled roof, exceptionally interesting timber roof construction. Magnificent proportions.

**Location:** 2 m SW of Faringdon between A420 & B4019.
**Opening Times:** All year daily at reasonable hours. Adm 50p. Dogs on leads admitted. Wheelchair access.

## GREYS COURT, The National Trust
**Henley-on-Thames** *map J4* ♿
Telephone: Rotherfield Greys (04917) 529

Beautiful gardens, medieval ruins, a Tudor donkey wheel for raising well water and a 16th century house containing interesting 18th century plasterwork and furniture. The 'Archbishop's' Maze was open for the first time in 1982.

**Location:** At Rotherfield Greys NW of Henley-on-Thames on the road to Peppard A423.
**Opening Times:** House: Mar 27 to end Sept—Mons, Weds, Fris 2–6. Garden: Mar 25 to end of Sept—Mons to Sats 2–6. Last admissions half-hour before closing. Adm House & Garden £2.40. Garden only £1.60, Chd half-price. Parties must book in advance. No reduction for parties. *Closed Good Friday.* Dogs in car park only. Wheelchairs provided.
**Refreshments:** Teas (Mar 27, and May—Weds & Sats; June to end Sept—Mons, Weds, Fris & Sats); also for booked parties at other times by arrangement.

## HISTORIC HOUSE & MUSEUM, FAWLEY COURT
**Henley-on-Thames** *map J4*
*(Marian Fathers)*

Designed by Sir Christopher Wren, built 1684 as a family residence. The house, decorated by Grinling Gibbons, is situated in a beautiful park designed by "Capability" Brown. The Museum contains documents of the Polish kings and memorabilia of the Polish Army.

**Location:** 1 m N of Henley-on-Thames via A4155 to Marlow.
*Station: Henley-on-Thames (1½ m).*
**Opening Times:** Mar to Nov: Weds, Thurs, Suns 2–5. *Closed Easter and Whitsuntide weeks.* Adm £2, Chd £1, OAPs £1.50. Car park. No dogs. Dec, Feb: open to groups by pre-booked appointment.
**Refreshments:** Tea, coffee & home-made cakes available July & Aug.

## KINGSTON HOUSE
**Kingston Bagpuize** *map H4* △ ♿
Telephone: (0865) 820259
*(Lady Tweedsmuir)*

A superb Charles II manor house surrounded by parkland, a large garden and attractive 17th century stable buildings. The house has a magnificent cantilevered staircase and well-proportioned panelled rooms with fine furniture and pictures. The large and interesting garden contains beautiful trees, lawns, a woodland garden, herbaceous and shrub borders and many lovely bulbs.

**Location:** 5½ m W of Abingdon at junction of A415 & A420.
**Opening Times:** May, June, and Sept – Weds and Suns, also May and Aug Bank Hols 2.30–5.30. Adm House and Gardens: £2, OAPs, £1.50, Chd £1. Garden only: 50p. Group rates on request. (Chd under 5 free adm to Gardens, not admitted to House). Groups welcome by appointment. Wheelchairs garden only. No dogs. Gifts, books, plants for sale. Car parking.
**Refreshments:** Teas.

## KINGSTONE LISLE PARK
**nr Wantage** *map H4*
Telephone: Uffington (036 782) 223
*(Mrs Leopold Lonsdale)*

Handsome house with dramatic flying staircase. Fine furnishings and beautiful gardens.

**Location:** 5 m W of Wantage on B4507.
**Opening Times:** Easter to Sept 9—Thurs & Bank Hol weekends (Sats, Suns & Mons): 2–5. Parties at other times by arrangement. Adm £2.20, Chd 80p. Parties and OAPs £2.
**Refreshments:** Teas by arrangement and at Bank Holidays.

# DITCHLEY PARK

**OXFORDSHIRE**

*Property of the Ditchley Foundation Ltd.*

*Photograph by Vernon Brooke of Oxford*

Third in size and date of the great 18th century houses of Oxfordshire. Ditchley is famous for its splendid interior decoration (William Kent and Henry Flitcroft). For three and a half centuries the home of the Lee family and their descendants—with whom Robert E. Lee was directly connected—Ditchley was the weekend Headquarters of Sir Winston Churchill during the last War. It has now been restored furnished and equipped as an Anglo - American Conference Centre.

*Open by special arrangement until early July.*

# THE MANOR HOUSE AND GARDENS

**STANTON HARCOURT, OXFORDSHIRE**

*9 miles West of Oxford, 5 Miles SE of Witney on B4449*

Unique mediaeval buildings in tranquil surroundings – Old Kitchen, (Alexander) Pope's Tower and Domestic Chapel. House maintained as family home, containing a fine collection of pictures, silver, furniture and porcelain.

12 acres of garden with Great Fish Pond and Stew Ponds.

*The Old Kitchen*

# KINGSTONE LISLE PARK

**Nr Wantage, Oxon**

This central part of this house was built in 1677 but most of the ingenious and dramatic interior dates from 1812. A notable feature is the fascinating procession of spaces comprising the hall, in part of which the renowned staircase rises. This staircase, two flights of which are flying, is such that it can connect the most unexpected levels.

The house is furnished with good furniture, pictures, glass and tapestry work. The extensive gardens have outstanding charm and beauty, displaying a succession of colour and interest throughout the year.

# MAPLEDURHAM

**4 miles west of Reading on the north bank of the River Thames**

MAPLEDURHAM HOUSE

Elizabethan Mansion built by Sir Michael Blount in 1588, now the home of his descendants Mr John and Lady Anne Eyston and their family. It stands on the bank of the Thames and is set in an unspoilt village of great charm, with its church, almshouses and watermill. This romantic house was frequently visited by Alexander Pope, and among the portraits are those of the beautiful sisters, Martha and Teresa Blount, to whom he dedicated much of his poetry. Great oak staircases, moulded ceilings of late Tudor plasterwork, fine collection of pictures and family portraits of 16th, 17th and 18th centuries. The family chapel built in 1797 by special licence is decorated in Strawberry Hill Gothick.

OPEN: Easter Sunday to the end of September on Saturdays, Sundays and Public Holidays.

HOUSE: 2.30 to 5.30 pm.

WATERMILL & COUNTRY PARK PICNIC AREA: Watermill open 1.00 to 5 pm Saturday, Sunday and Bank Holidays Easter to September. Also open 2 to 4 pm Sundays from October to April.

COUNTRY PARK: 12 to 7 pm, as above, also weekdays in July and August.
N.B. Weekday opening in July and August is provisional at this stage.

GUIDED PARTY VISITS of House and Watermill: Tuesday, Wednesday and Thursday afternoons by appointment only. Reduced Rates for Parties

Shop for gifts, flour and other Watermill produce.

Home made cream/afternoon teas available.

Visit Mapledurham by river. A passenger boat leaves Reading from Caversham Promenade at 2 pm each day the House is open. This boat can also be hired for party visits.

**For all enquiries and details of prices please contact: The Estate Office, Mapledurham House, Reading RG4 7TR. Telephone (0734) 723350/723277**

MAPLEDURHAM WATERMILL

The picturesque Corn and Grist Mill in the grounds of Mapledurham House, dates from the 15th century. Visitors will often be able to see flour being ground by the old millstones in the traditional Oxfordshire manner. The wooden machinery powered by an undershot waterwheel also built of wood, is a unique working example of a Thames watermill. Its two pairs of millstones are set up to produce wholewheat flour which may be purchased in the shop.

## MAPLEDURHAM HOUSE
**nr Reading** *map J4*
Telephone: Reading (0734) 723350 or 723277
*(J J Eyston and Lady Anne Eyston)*

Late 16th century Elizabethan home of the Blount Family. Original moulded ceilings, great oak staircase, fine collection of paintings and private chapel. Unique setting in grounds running down to the Thames. 15th century Watermill nearby is now restored and operating.

**Location:** 4 m NW of Reading on North Bank of Thames. Signposted off Caversham/ Woodcote Road on A4074. Boats from Caversham Bridge 2pm on open days. (Caversham Bridge is ½ m from Reading Station).
**Opening Times:** House. Easter Sun to end of Sept—Sats, Suns & Bank Hols 2.30–5.30. Last admission 5. Midweek party visits, see advertisement for details. Watermill and Country Park/Picnic area—see advertisement for details.
**Refreshments:** Tea room serving home made afternoon/cream teas.

## MILTON MANOR HOUSE
**nr Abingdon** *map H4* △ ♿
Telephone: Abingdon (0235) 831287 or 831871
*(Mrs Majorie Mockler)*

17th century house with Georgian wings. Traditionally designed by Inigo Jones. Walled garden & pleasure grounds.

**Location:** In Milton village 4 m S of Abingdon; 1 m from Sutton Courtney on B4016; A34, signpost Milton.
**Opening Times:** Easter Sat to Oct 30—Sats & Suns and all Bank Hols: 2–5.30. Adm £1.50, Chd 60p. Free car park. *Coach parties welcome by arrangement at reduced rates. Candlelight tours in the evening by arrangement.*
**Refreshments:** By arrangement.

## MINSTER LOVELL HALL AND DOVECOTE
*map H5*
Telephone: (0993) 775315
(English Heritage)

Originally a 15th century manor house, the hall was built around a courtyard. The medieval dovecote, complete with nesting boxes, has recently been restored. When the hall was dismantled in the 18th century, a skeleton was found in the cellars. This is thought to have been the Yorkist Lord Lovell who disappeared after the Battle of Bosworth 1485, where he fought on the losing side.

**Location:** 2½ m (4 km) north west of Witney. OS map ref SP324114.
**Opening Times:** Good Friday to Sept 30, daily 10–6; Oct 1 to Maundy Thurs, daily 10–4. *Closed* Mons, Dec 24–26, Jan 1. Adm 80p, OAPs 60p, Chd 40p.

**North Leigh Roman Villa** – See English Heritage Section.

## NUFFIELD PLACE
**Nettlebed** *map J4*
Telephone: (0491) 641224
*(Nuffield College, Friends of Nuffield Place)*

The home from 1933–1963 of Lord Nuffield, founder of Morris Motors, Nuffield Place is a rare survival of a complete upper-middle class home of the 1930s. Built in 1914, the house was enlarged in 1933 for Lord Nuffield. Several rooms are still decorated in the '30s style, and all rooms contain furnishings acquired by Lord and Lady Nuffield when they took up residence. Clocks, rugs and some tapestries are of fine quality. Some of the furniture is antique but much was custom made by Cecil A. Halliday of Oxford, and is of skilled craftsmanship. The gardens, with mature trees, stone walls and rockery, were laid out during and just after the First World War. Lady Nuffield's Wolseley car is also on display.

**Location:** Approximately 7 m from Henley-on-Thames, just off A423 to Oxford.
**Opening Times:** May to Sept, every 2nd and 4th Sun 2–5. Adm £1.50, Chd 50p. Parties by arrangement. Ground floor and garden suitable for the disabled.
**Refreshments:** Teas.

## PUSEY HOUSE GARDENS
**nr Faringdon** *map H4* ♿
Telephone: Buckland 222
*(Pusey Garden Trust)*

Herbaceous borders, walled gardens, water garden, large collection of shrubs and roses. Many fine trees.

**Location:** 5 m E of Faringdon, ½ m S off A420; 12 m W of Oxford.
**Opening Times:** Mar 25 to Oct 29—Tues, Weds, Thurs, Sats & Suns; also Bank Hol Mons: 2–6. Adm £2 (children under 11 free). Parties please book, £1.50 per person. Car park free. Plants for sale.
**Refreshments:** Teas available.

## ROUSHAM HOUSE
**Steeple Aston** *map H5* △
Telephone: Steeple Aston (0869) 47110
*(C Cottrell-Dormer, Esq)*

17th century country house with landscape garden by William Kent. Portraits, miniatures.

**Location:** 12 m N of Oxford off Banbury Road (A423) at Hopcrofts Holt Hotel (1 m). *Station: Heyford (1 m).*
**Opening Times:** Apr to Sept inclusive—Weds, Suns & Bank Hols 2–4.30. Gardens only, everyday 10–4.30. No children under 15. No dogs. *Parties by arrangement on other days.*

**Rycote Chapel** – See English Heritage Section.

## STANTON HARCOURT MANOR
**Stanton Harcourt** *map H5* ♿
*(Mr Crispin & The Hon Mrs Gascoigne)*

Unique medieval buildings in tranquil surroundings—Old Kitchen, Pope's Tower and Domestic Chapel. House contains fine collection of pictures, furniture, silver and porcelain.

**Location:** 9 m W of Oxford; 5 m SE of Witney; on B4449, between Eynsham & Standlake.
**Opening Times:** House & Gardens. Mar 26, 27; Apr 6, 9, 27, 30; May 1; (Artists & Craftsmen at work), 11, 14, 25, 28, 29; June 8, 11, 22, 25; July 6, 9, 20, 23; Aug 3, 6, 24, 27, 28; Sept 7, 10, 21, 24: 2–6. **House & Garden** £2, Chd (12 and under) £1. **Garden only** £1, Chd (12 and under) 50p. Large parties and coaches by prior arrangement. Disabled visitors welcome. Home container-grown shrubs & pot plants for sale.
**Refreshments:** Teas on Suns and Bank Hols in aid of Parish Church.

## STONOR PARK
**nr Henley-on-Thames** *map J4*
Telephone: Turville Heath (049 163) 587
*(Lord & Lady Camoys)*

Ancient home of the Stonor family and centre of Catholicism. Fine furniture and important sculpture. Magnificent setting.

**Location:** On B480; 5 m N of Henley-on-Thames, 5 m S of Watlington.
**Opening Times:** Apr—Suns & Bank Hol Mons only; May to Sept—Weds, Thurs, Suns & Bank Hol Mons, Sats (Aug); 2–5.30 (last adm to house 5); (but *closed Sun June 25.*) Bank Hol Mons 11–5.30. Parties by prior arrangement any Tues, Weds, Thurs (morning or afternoon) and Sun (afternoon only). Adm (1988) £2, OAPs £1.70, Chd (under 14) in family parties free. Party rates on application.

## WATERPERRY GARDENS
**nr Wheatley** *map J5*
Telephone: Ickford (084 47) 226 and 254

Church of Saxon origin and historical interest in grounds. Famous old glass, brasses and woodwork. Many interesting plants. Shrub, Herbaceous and Alpine Nurseries. Glasshouses and comprehensive Fruit Section.

**Location:** 8 m E of Oxford. 2 m from Wheatley off old A40. Well signposted locally with Tourist Board 'Rose' symbol.
**Opening Times:** All the year. Daily—Apr to Sept 10–5.30 (weekdays); 10–6 (weekends); Oct to Mar 10–4.30 *(Teashop closes 30 mins earlier).* Closed for Christmas and New Year Hols. Open only to visitors to ART IN ACTION July 13–16. Adm to Ornamental Gardens & Nurseries Mar to Oct £1.20, Nov to Feb no charge. Parties and coaches at all times by appointment only. High quality Plant Centre and Garden Shop, telephone: Ickford (084 47) 226. *In aid of National Gardens' Scheme & Gardeners' Sun, June 11 & Aug 13.*
**Refreshments:** Teashop.

# PUSEY HOUSE GARDENS

**near FARINGDON, OXFORDSHIRE**

The garden at Pusey House affords a wide variety of attractions. The herbaceous borders and the roses are outstanding in midsummer, the shrubberies are full of interesting and unusual plants and the lake is fringed with a water garden filled with many varieties of primula and other waterside plants. There are exceptionally fine trees, many of which are particularly effective with their autumn colouring.

ADMISSION – SEE EDITORIAL REFERENCE

# STONOR

**HOME OF LORD AND LADY CAMOYS AND THE STONOR FAMILY FOR OVER EIGHT HUNDRED YEARS**

Set in beautiful wooded Chiltern Hills with commanding views of the surrounding Deer Park.

House of considerable architectural interest – built over many centuries from c. 1190.

Site of prehistoric stone circle – now re-created within the grounds.

Family home containing fine family portraits and rare items of furniture, paintings, drawings, tapestries, sculptures and bronzes from Britain, Europe and America.

Centre of Catholicism throughout the Recusancy Period with its own medieval Chapel where mass is still celebrated today.

Sanctuary for St. Edmund Campion in 1581. An exhibition features his life and work.

Peaceful hillside gardens overlooking the house.

Souvenir gift shop and afternoon tea room serving home made cakes.

Parties welcome, lunches available by prior arrangement.

**Nr HENLEY ON THAMES, OXFORDSHIRE**

# WATERPERRY GARDENS

**NR WHEATLEY, OXFORDSHIRE**

The peaceful gardens at Waterperry feature a magnificent herbaceous border, shrub and heather borders, alpine and rock gardens, and a new formal garden. Together with stately trees, a river to walk by and a quiet Saxon Church to visit – all set in 83 acres of unspoilt Oxfordshire – the long established herbaceous and alpine nurseries provide year round interest. For the experienced gardener, the novice, or those who have no garden of their own, here is a chance to share, enjoy and admire the order and beauty of careful cultivation.

Garden Shop and Plant Centre with exceptionally wide range of plants, shrubs and fruit produced in the nurseries for sale. Expert care and training is shown in all stages of development. Pots, tubs and sundries also available.
The Teashop provides a delicious selection of home-made food, tea, coffee, fruit juices, etc. Light lunches, morning coffee, teas with scones and cream, cakes, etc. Wine licence.

Open all year from 10 am. Closed for Christmas and New Year Holidays. Open only to visitors to ART IN ACTION between 13th and 16th July.

*ADMISSION – See Editorial Reference*

# SHROPSHIRE

## ACTON ROUND HALL
**Bridgnorth** *map G6*
*(H L Kennedy, Esq)*

Built in 1714 for Sir Whitmore Acton by the Smith Brothers of Warwick and abandoned from 1717–1918, the house remains little altered from its original state.

**Location:** 6 m W of Bridgnorth; 15 m SE of Shrewsbury.
**Opening Times:** May, June, July Aug—Thurs 2.30–5.30. Adm £1.50.

## ADCOTE
**Little Ness, nr Shrewsbury** *map F7*
Telephone: (0939) 260202
*(Adcote School Educational Trust Ltd)*

"Adcote is the most controlled, coherent and masterly of the big country houses designed by Norman Shaw" (Mark Girouard, 'Country Life' Oct 1970).

**Location:** 7 m NW of Shrewsbury off A5.
**Opening Times:** Apr 11 to July 6 (except May 26–29); 2–5. Re-open Sept 1–30, 2–5. Other days throughout the year by appointment. Adm free but the Governors reserve the right to make a charge.

## ATTINGHAM PARK, The National Trust
**nr Shrewsbury SY4 4TP** *map G7* ♿
Telephone: Upton Magna (0743 77) 203

Designed in 1785 by George Steuart for the 1st Lord Berwick. Elegant classical interior decoration. Famous painted boudoir. Nash Picture Gallery. Fine collection of Regency Silver. Park landscape designed by Humphry Repton, 1797. Extensive deer park.

**Location:** At Atcham; 4 m SE of Shrewsbury, on N side of Telford Road (A5).
**Opening Times:** Mar 25 to end of Sept—Sats to Weds 2–5.30; Bank Hol Mons 11.30–5.30. Last adm 5. Closed Good Friday. Oct—Sats & Suns 2–5.30. Adm House & Grounds £2.20, Chd £1.10. Deer Park & Grounds only 70p. Family ticket £5.50. Pre-booked parties, including evening opening, by arrangement. Dogs in grounds only (not in deer park). Wheelchair provided. Shop. Mother and Baby room.
**Refreshments:** Home-made teas (parties must pre-book). Lunches Sun only 12.30–2. Light buffet meals by arrangement with The Administrator.

## BENTHALL HALL, The National Trust
**Broseley TF12 5RX** *map G6*
Telephone: Telford (0952) 882159

16th century stone house with mullioned windows. Interior improved in 17th century. Fine oak staircase and plaster ceilings. Interesting small garden.

**Location:** 1 m NW of Broseley; 4 m NE of Much Wenlock; 6 m S of Wellington, (B4375).
**Opening Times:** Easter Sun to end Sept—Tues, Weds, Suns and Bank Hol Mons 2–6 (last adm 5.30). Adm £1.60, Chd 80p. Garden only 80p. *No reduction for parties.* No dogs. Wheelchair access.

## BOSCOBEL HOUSE
**Shifnal** *map G6*
Telephone: (0902) 850244
*(English Heritage)*

When John Giffard built his tall, gabled, timber-framed hunting lodge in the 17th century, he little knew that it would become a refuge for the future King Charles II after his defeat at Worcester in 1651. It is now fully re-furnished with historic tapestries, oil paintings and items of antique furniture. The Victorians called Boscobel 'the showhouse' and today it is furnished as they thought it would have appeared at the time when Charles II hid in the priest's hole and took refuge in the oak tree in the gounds. New exhibition, shop and tea room.

**Location:** 8 m NW of Wolverhampton; 3¾ m N of Albrighton. O.S. map ref SJ 837083.
**Opening Times:** Good Friday to Sept 30, daily 10–6; Oct 1 to Maundy Thurs, daily 10–4. *Closed* Mons, Dec 24–26, Jan 1. Adm £1.80, OAPs £1.40, Chd 90p.

**Buildwas Abbey** – See English Heritage Section.

## CARDING MILL VALLEY & LONG MYND, The National Trust
**Church Stretton** *map F6*
Telephone: Church Stretton 722631

Chalet Pavilion in the magnificent scenery of Carding Mill Valley.

**Location:** 15 m S of Shrewsbury; W of Church Stretton Valley & A49.
*Station: Church Stretton (1 m).*
**Opening Times:** Moorland open all year. Chalet Pavilion Information Centre, Shop & Café: Mar 25 to end of Sept and weekends in Oct: Mon–Sat 12.30–5.30 (*closed* Fris Mar 31 to end June, and in Sept); Sun and Bank Holiday Mon 10.30–6. Open for booked parties & special functions. Adm free. Car park charge in Carding Mill Valley. Coaches free. Dogs allowed if kept under control.
**Refreshments:** Snacks, light lunches, teas, etc at Chalet Pavilion (Dogs not allowed in Pavilion).

## CASTLE GATES LIBRARY
**Shrewsbury** *map F7*
Telephone: Shrewsbury 241487

Former premises of Shrewsbury Grammar School, from 16th and 17th centuries. Now used as a public library. Also houses Shropshire's Local Studies Library. Granted a Civic Trust award for a recent restoration scheme.

**Opening Times:** Public part of the building Mon–Fri 9.30–6. Thurs 9.30–1. Sats 9.30–5. Private areas by prior appointment only.

## CONDOVER HALL
**nr Shrewsbury** *map F6*
*(Royal National Institute for the Blind)*

"E" shaped building, an excellent example of masons' craft of the late 16th century.

**Location:** 5 m S of Shrewsbury; 1½ m from A49.
**Opening Times:** Grounds & exterior of premises (with a limited inspection of the interior) Aug only, by prior appointment.

## DUDMASTON, The National Trust
**Quatt, Bridgnorth** *map G6* ♿
Telephone: Quatt 780866

Late 17th century house; collections of Dutch flower paintings, modern art, botanical paintings and family history. Extensive grounds, woodlands and lakeside garden.

**Location:** 4 m SE of Bridgnorth on A442.
**Opening Times:** Easter Sun to end of Sept—Weds & Suns 2.30–6 (last adm 5.30); also Thurs afternoons special opening for pre-booked parties only 2.30–6. Adm House & Garden £2.20, Family £5.50. Garden only £1. Parties must book in advance. Dogs in garden only, on leads. Shop.
**Refreshments:** Home-made teas 3–5.30.

**Haughmond Abbey** – See English Heritage Section.

## HODNET HALL GARDENS
**nr Market Drayton** *map G7* ♿
Telephone: (063 084) 202
*(Mr & the Hon Mrs Heber Percy)*

The colourful jewel in Shropshire's crown. From the glorious daffodils of Spring to the magnificent roses of Summer, each season brings fresh delights to these award winning gardens. Over 60 acres of magnificent forest trees, sweeping lawns and tranquil pools ensure plentiful wildlife and brilliant natural colour within this beautiful setting.

**Location:** 12 m NE of Shrewsbury; 5½ m SW of Market Drayton, at junction of A53 to A442; M6 18½ m (junction 15) leading to A53 or M54 (junction 3).
**Opening Times:** Apr 1 to end of Sept—Weekdays 2–5; Suns & Bank Hols 12–5.30. Adm £1.80, OAPs £1.25, Chd £1. *Reduced rates for organised parties of 25 or over.* Season tickets on application. Free car & coach park. Dogs allowed, but must be kept on leads.
**Refreshments:** Tearooms open daily 2–5. *Parties to pre-book (menu on request). Gift shop, kitchen garden sales.*

## THE LAWNS
**Broseley, nr Much Wenlock** *map G6*
Telephone: Telford (0952) 882557
*(Michael & Molly Berthoud – The Lawns Preservation Trust)*

Historic Georgian house where the industrial revolution began. Former home of John Wilkinson, ironmaster, and of John Rose, founder of Coalport. Extensive collections of English pottery and porcelain, 'Cabinet of a Thousand Cups', exhibition of tea and tea wares. Magnificent kitchen. Gardens of 1 acre. Picnic area.

**Location:** Just off B4373 Bridgnorth/Ironbridge road 6 m N of Bridgnorth.
*Station: Telford (5 m).*
**Opening Times:** Apr to Sept – Weds to Suns (& Bank Hols) 2–6. Guided tours on the hour. Last tour 5pm. Adm £2. No reductions. Booked parties for tours, lectures, seminars, MOST WELCOME AT ALL TIMES. Send s.a.e. for full details of 'Learning at Leisure' visits. No dogs, no stilettos. Unsuitable for wheelchairs.
**Refreshments:** Home made teas 2–5.30. Pre-booked party lunches, teas, suppers by arrangement.

**Lilleshall Abbey** – See English Heritage Section.

## LUDFORD HOUSE
**Ludlow SY8 1PJ** *map F6*
*(Mr and Mrs D. F. A. Nicholson)*

House dating back to 12th century.

**Location:** ½ m S of Ludlow, B4361 road.
**Opening Times:** Grounds and exterior by written permission, with limited inspection of interior. Adm £2. Unsuitable for disabled.
**Refreshments:** Hotels and Restaurants in Ludlow available.

## MAWLEY HALL
**Cleobury Mortimer** *map G6*
*(Galliers Trustees)*

18th century house attributed to Smith of Warwick. Notable contemporary plasterwork & panelling.

**Location:** 1 m S of Cleobury Mortimer (A4117); 7 m W of Bewdley.
**Opening Times:** By written appointment to Administrator. Adm £2.

# The National Trust

## ATTINGHAM PARK

Designed in 1785 – remarkable interior decoration, painted boudoir, Regency silver collection. Landscaped deer park.

## BENTHALL HALL

16th century stone house with mullioned windows. Interior improved in 17th century. Fine oak staircase and plaster ceilings. Interesting small garden.

## DUDMASTON

Late 17th century house and collections of Dutch flower paintings, modern art, botanical paintings and family history. Extensive grounds, woodlands and lakeside garden.

*ADMISSION – SEE EDITORIAL REFERENCE*

# Explore the past, enjoy the present and protect the future in Shropshire.

Turn to our Red Page listing at the back and find out more about the exciting range of English Heritage properties throughout the country.

Buildwas Abbey

**English Heritage**

### SHIPTON HALL
**Much Wenlock** *map G6*
*(J N R N Bishop, Esq)*

Delightful Elizabethan stone manor and Georgian stable block. Interesting Georgian Roccoco and Gothic plasterwork by T. F. Pritchard. Stone walled garden, medieval dovecote and Parish Church, dating from late Saxon period.

**Location:** In Shipton; 6 m SW of Much Wenlock junction B4376 & B4368.
**Opening Times:** May to Sept—Thurs also Suns in July & Aug—Bank Hols (except Christmas and New Year) Suns and Mons: 2.30–5.30. Other times by appointment for parties of 20 or more. Adm £1.20, Chd 60p. Special rate for parties of 20 plus.
**Refreshments:** Teas/buffets by prior arrangement.

### STOKESAY CASTLE
**Craven Arms** *map F6*
Telephone: Craven Arms (0588) 672544
*(Sir Philip & Lady Magnus-Allcroft)*

Finest example of a moated and fortified manor house, dating from the 13th century.

**Location:** 8 m from Ludlow; ¾ m S of Craven Arms on 3rd class Road off A49.
*Station: Craven Arms (1 m).*
**Opening Times:** First Wed in March—Daily (except Tues) 10–5; Apr to Sept—Daily (except Tues) 10–6; Oct—Daily (except Tues) 10–5; Nov—Weekends only 10–dusk. Mons to Fris party bookings only. Last adm half an hour before closing. *Closed Dec, Jan & Feb.* Adm £1, Chd (under 15) 50p. Party bookings in advance. Toilets. Car park. Enquiries to The Custodian, Stokesay Castle, Craven Arms, Shropshire SY7 9AH.
**Refreshments:** In castle courtyard.

### TYN-Y-RHOS HALL AND SHRINE OF ST. GEORGE (Greek Orthodox)
**Weston Rhyn, nr Oswestry** *map F7* △ ♿
Telephone: Chirk (0691) 777898
*(Brother Demetrius)*

Mansion with historic Welsh Royal connections. Featured on HTV Dec 1982. Morning prayers, Sun 11 am.

**Location:** 2½ m from Weston Rhyn, near Bron-y-Garth (off A5).
*Station: Chirk (1½ m).*
**Opening Times:** Suns May to end Sept 2.30–5.30. Adm £1, Chd 50p.

### UPTON CRESSETT HALL
**Bridgnorth** *map G6*
Telephone: Morville 307
*(William Cash, Esq)*

Elizabethan Manor House and magnificent Gatehouse in beautiful countryside by Norman church. Unusually fine medieval timber work and interesting brick and plaster work; 14th century Great Hall.

**Location:** 4 m W of Bridgnorth; 18 m SE of Shrewsbury off A458.
**Opening Times:** May to Sept—Thurs 2.30–5. Adm £1, Chd 50p. *Parties at other times throughout the year by appointment.*
**Refreshments:** Teas & light refreshments by prior arrangement.

### WENLOCK PRIORY
**Much Wenlock** *map G6*
Telephone: (0952) 727466
*(English Heritage)*

The long history of Wenlock stretches back to the 7th century, although nothing visible remains of the religious house founded by St Milburge. After the Norman Conquest, a Cluniac priory was established, which came to be regarded as alien during the Hundred Years' War with France. Decorative arcading from the 12th century chapter house survives and some unusual features in the later, rebuilt church.

**Location:** In Much Wenlock.
**Opening Times:** Good Friday to Sept 30, daily 10–6; Oct 1 to Maundy Thurs, daily 10–4. *Closed* Mons, Dec 24–26, Jan 1. Adm 80p, OAPs 60p, Chd 40p.

### WESTON PARK
**nr Shifnal** *map G7*
Telephone: Weston-under-Lizard 207
*(The Earl of Bradford)*

Built 1671 by Lady Wilbraham and contains a superb art collection. Miniature Railway, Adventure Playground, Museum, Aquarium, Nature Trails, Countryside Pottery and Pets Corner.

**Location:** Entrance from A5 at Weston-under-Lizard, 6 m W of Junction 12, M6 (Gailey); 3 m N of Junction 3, M54 (Tong).
**Opening Times:** House & Park. Apr 2 to May 31—weekends; Bank Hols, Easter week, Spring Bank Hol week, June 6 to July 24—Daily (except Mons & Fris); July 25–Sept 4—Daily then weekends only until Sept 25. Park 11–7. Last admission 5. Adm Grounds, Aquarium, Museum, Adventure Playground, Pottery, Pets Corner £1.80, Chd & OAPs £1.30. House extra. Special rates for pre-booked parties and school visits. Entry charges may be adjusted on certain days for special events. Free coach and car park. Dogs (on leads) admitted to Park.
**Refreshments:** In the Old Stables licensed bar and cafeteria. Restaurant service for pre-booked parties.

### WILDERHOPE MANOR, The National Trust
**Wenlock Edge** *map G6* ♿
Telephone: Longville 363

Elizabethan manor house with 17th century plaster ceilings. House now run as a Youth Hostel.

**Location:** 7 m SW of Much Wenlock; ½ m S of B4371.
**Opening Times:** Mar 25 to end of Sept—Weds & Sats 2–4.30; Oct to Mar—Sats only 2–4.30. Adm £1, Chd 50p. *No reduction for parties. No dogs.*

**Wroxeter (Viroconium) Roman City** – See English Heritage Section.

## SOMERSET

### BARFORD PARK
**Enmore** *map F3*
Telephone: Spaxton (027 867) 269
*(Mr & Mrs Michael Stancomb)*

Queen Anne house set in park with fine trees; formal garden, water garden and woodland garden.

**Location:** 5 m W of Bridgwater.
**Opening Times:** June 1 to Sept 16—Weds, Thurs and Bank Hol weekends 2–6, or other times by appointment. Please telephone above number. Adm charges not available at the time of going to press.

### BARRINGTON COURT, The National Trust
**Ilminster** *map F3* △
Telephone: South Petherton 41480

One of the finest examples of 1920's creativity – thanks to Col. Lyle whose family still live there. A model estate and farm buildings complex, a series of beautiful gardens influenced by Gertrude Jekyll, and a large kitchen garden all designed to support the large Tudor manor house leased by Mr. Lyle to Stuart Interiors, the furniture reproducers. Most recently an estate trail over 200 acres and a farm exhibition centre.

**Location:** In Barrington village, 5 m NE of Ilminster, off A303, 6 m S of Curry Rivel on A378 between Taunton and Langport. (0460) 40601/52242.
**Opening Times:** Court and Garden: Mar 25 to Nov 5, Sats to Weds 11–5.30. Adm Gardens £2.50 (parties of 15 or more £2, Chd £1). Coaches by appointment only. Picnic area. Shop (not NT). Children's play area. No dogs. Wheelchair access. Plant sales.
**Refreshments:** Cream teas, lunches & suppers by arrangement.

# THE LAWNS

**SHROPSHIRE**

Neither a museum nor a stately home. Two hundred years of English pottery and porcelain displayed in period room settings in a private family house steeped in local history. An unforgettable experience.

Where plants and trees flourish and quietness reigns.

- Tea rooms (with animal trophy display)
- Gift shop
- Kitchen Garden sales
- Free car park
- Sixty acres of beautiful gardens to admire.

OPEN 1st April to End of Sept. Weekdays 2p.m.-5p.m. Sun., Bank Holiday Mon. 12 noon to 6p.m.

Hodnet Hall is 12 miles N.E. of Shrewsbury on the A53. Exit M6 at Junction 15.

(Parties catered for – ring Mrs Hensby 063 084 202)

GARDEN OF THE YEAR AWARD 1986

Christies/Historic Houses Association

# WESTON PARK

**Shropshire**

This historic mansion, set in a thousand acres of 'Capability' Brown landscape, was built by Lady Wilbraham in 1671 and has been the seat of the Earls of Bradford for nearly 300 years. The house is one of the finest examples of the restoration period and contains a superb collection of pictures, including works of the English, Flemish and Italian schools with notable examples by Holbein, Van Dyck, Bassano, Reynolds, Gainsborough, Hoppner and Lely. Beautiful furniture, books, china, tapestries by Gobelin and Aubusson and many other objects de vertu combine to make Weston a treasure house of delight.

As well as buildings of architectural interest, such as the Temple of Diana by James Paine, the grounds offer a great variety of walks through woodland gardens and alongside tranquil lakes.

Other attractions include a miniature railway, aquarium, pottery, woodland adventure playground, pets corner and toddlers playground, museum of bygones, fallow deer and rare breeds of sheep.

Enquiries to Mrs Christine Lakeland, Administrator, Weston Park, Nr. Shifnal, Shropshire TF11 8LE.
Telephone: Weston-under-Lizard (095 276) 207.

# The National Trust in SOMERSET

## MONTACUTE HOUSE

## DUNSTER CASTLE

*ADMISSION – SEE EDITORIAL REFERENCE*

## BARRINGTON COURT GARDENS

**Barrington** *map F3*
Telephone: (0460) 40601/52242
*(Paul Johnson – Estate Manager)*

Superb walled gardens – influenced by Gertrude Jekyll. Colonel A.A. Lyle took over the lease of the property in 1920. The gardens are renowned for their lilies and irises and also boast the oldest working Victorian Kitchen Garden in the south-west, comprising of nectarines, peaches, gages, plums, apples and pears as well as asparagus, artichoke, sea kale and celeriac. All produce is available for sale throughout the year. Barrington Court Estate totals some 1000 acres of farmland and woodland situated in a fertile belt of south Somerset and incorporates 7 farms and dairies.

**Location:** 3 m N of Ilminster off B3168, 25 minutes from M5 (Taunton), 10 minutes from A303.
**Opening Times:** Open from Good Friday to end Oct: Aug: daily 11–5.30. Apr, May, June, July, Sept and Oct: Sat, Sun, Mon, Tues, Wed 11–5.30. Adm £2.50, Chd £1. Season tickets £10 (for the whole family for as many visits as wished). Parties welcome. Large area of car parking for coaches. Suitable for disabled persons (no wheelchairs available). Garden Centre, Shop, Children's Corner, Nature and Farm Trail, Farm Exhibition.
**Refreshments:** Licensed restaurant (party bookings for lunches and early evening suppers). Picnic and play area. Strode House offers bed and breakfast.

## THE BISHOP'S PALACE

**Wells** *map G3*
Telephone: Wells (0749) 78691
*(The Church Commissioners)*

The fortified and moated Palace comprises Jocelin's Hall (early 13th century), the Bishop's Chapel and the ruins of the Banqueting Hall (both late 13th century) and the Bishop's Residence (15th century). The grounds which include the wells from which Wells derives its name, provide a beautiful setting for gardens of herbaceous plants, roses, shrubs, mature trees and the Jubilee Arboretum. On the Moat are waterfowl and swans.

**Location:** City of Wells, at end of Market Place (enter through Bishop's Eye).
**Opening Times:** Palace, Chapel and Grounds. Easter to end of Oct—Bank Holiday Mons, Thurs & Suns; Aug—Daily: 2–6; May, June, July & Sept also Weds 11–6. Last admission 5.30. Adm £1.75, Chd 30p. Party rates by appointment.
**Refreshments:** Available in Undercroft.

## BRYMPTON d'EVERCY

**nr Yeovil** *map G3*
Telephone: Yeovil (0935) 862528
*(Charles E B Clive-Ponsonby-Fane, JP)*

Mansion house with 17th century South front and Tudor West front. State Rooms, extensive gardens and Vineyard, Priest House, museum, licensed Distillery, painting and photographic exhibitions. Estate produce, wine and cider. 14th century Parish Church alongside.

**Location:** Just W of Yeovil. Follow signs off A30 or A3088.
**Opening Times:** Easter weekend (Fri to Mon incl) then May 1 to Sept 28—Daily (except Thurs & Fris) 2–6. *Further details from Brympton Estate Office, Yeovil.* DISCOUNT RATES FOR OAPs, NATIONAL TRUST MEMBERS—EVERY TUES & WEDS.
**Refreshments:** Freshly made cream teas in Old Stables.

## THE CHURCH HOUSE

**Crowcombe** *map F3*
*(The Charity Commissioners)*

Historic 15th century stone building with graceful open timber roof.

**Location:** Opposite Crowcombe Church; off A358 Taunton/Minehead Road.
**Opening Times:** May 23 to Sept 23—Mons to Fris 2.30–4.30. Adm free.

## CLAPTON COURT GARDENS

**Crewkerne** *map F3* ♿
Telephone: Crewkerne (0460) 73220
*(Capt S J Loder)*

One of the most beautiful and interesting gardens in the West Country with many rare and unusual trees and shrubs of botanical interest in immaculate formal gardens and fascinating Woodland Garden. The 10 acres includes Terraces, Rose Garden, Rockery and Water Garden. A garden worth visiting at all seasons from springtime bulbs to autumn colours. Plant Centre offering high quality and unusual container shrubs, plants, alpines, etc also specialising in fuchsias and over 220 varieties of pelargoniums. Recently featured on BBC Gardener's World and in Country Life.

**Location:** 3 m S of Crewkerne on B3165.
**Opening Times:** GARDENS ONLY. Feb to Nov inclusive—Mons to Fris 10.30–5; Suns 2–5. *Closed Sats (except Easter Sat & all Sats in May 2–5).* Adm £2, OAPs £1.60, Chd 30p. Special rates for pre-booked coach & private parties *(not Suns prior to June).* PLANT CENTRE Feb to Nov inclusive—times as for Gardens above. *No dogs in garden. Free car parking.*
**Refreshments:** Home-made cream teas and light lunches Apr to Sept, times as garden. Meals by arrangement for parties. Licensed.

**Cleeve Abbey** – See English Heritage Section.

## COLERIDGE COTTAGE, The National Trust

**Nether Stowey, nr. Bridgwater** *map F3*
Telephone: Nether Stowey 732662

Home of S T Coleridge from 1797–1800, where he wrote 'The Ancient Mariner'.

**Location:** At W end of village on S side of A39; 8 m W of Bridgwater.
**Opening Times:** PARLOUR AND READING ROOM ONLY. Mar 26 to Sept 28—Tues to Thurs & Suns 2–5. *Closed Good Fri.* Adm £1, Chd 50p. *No reduction for parties.* Parties are asked to notify the tenant beforehand. *Adm in winter by written application to the tenant.* No dogs. Unsuitable for wheelchairs & coaches.
**Refreshments:** In village.

## COMBE SYDENHAM COUNTRY PARK

**Monksilver** *map F3* Ⓢ
Telephone: Stogumber (0984) 56284
*(Mr and Mrs W. Theed)*

Built in 1580 on the site of a monastic settlement and home of Elizabeth Sydenham, wife of Sir Francis Drake. The Cannon Ball associated with their wedding can still be seen in the Great Hall. The Court Room has now been beautifully restored, and onsite work is continuing including the old Corn Mill. Elizabethan-style gardens, Country Park walks and Deer Park. Fly fishing available on valley ponds. Children's play area. Speciality smoked trout/pate. Gift Shop, tea room, free car/coach park.

**Location:** 5 m N of Wiveliscombe; 3 m S of Watchet on B3188.
*Station: Stogumber (2½ m) (West Somerset Railway).*
**Opening Times:** Mar 20 to Nov 3. COUNTRY PARK 11–6. Mar, Apr, May and Oct closing 5 pm. Sun Special admission ticket. Sat morning Gift Shop and Fish sales only. HALL: Last entry to Hall two hours before closing time. House and Garden closed every Sat and Sun throughout the year. School parties welcomed by arrangement throughout the year for activity days. (Winner 1984 Sandford Award for Heritage Education).

## CRICKET ST. THOMAS

**Chard** *map F3*
Telephone: (0460 30) 755

Estate of Cricket St. Thomas recorded in Domesday Book of 1087. Today it is a wildlife and leisure park of outstanding natural beauty. Animals and birds from all over the world, many leading a free natural life. Visitors can also enjoy the Tropical Aviary, Countrylife Museum, the Heavy Horse Centre, Craft Workshops, lakeside walks, woodland railway and children's Adventure Playground. Film location for BBC TV series 'To The Manor Born'.

**Location:** 4 m E of Chard on A30. Nearest M5 junction No. 25.
**Opening Times:** All year round. Daily from 10 am.
**Refreshments:** Licensed restaurant, tearooms, picnic area.

## DODINGTON HALL

**nr. Nether Stowey, Bridgwater** *map F3*
Telephone: Holford (0278 74) 400
*(Lady Gass, occupier P. Birkett)*

Small Tudor Manor House on the lower slopes of the Quantock Hills. Great hall with oak roof. Plasterwork. Carved stone fireplace. Display of cowboy and horse equipment. Terraced garden with many varieties of roses.

**Location:** ½ m from A39. 11 m from Bridgwater; 7 m from Williton.
**Opening Times:** May, June, July & Aug, Mon 11–5. Adm – donations to Dodington Church. Groups by arrangement. Parking for 15 cars. Unsuitable for disabled.
**Refreshments:** None at house. Hotels and restaurants in Nether Stowey and Holford.

## DUNSTER CASTLE, The National Trust

**nr. Minehead** *map F3* ♿
Telephone: Dunster 821314

Castle dating from 13th century, remodelled by Anthony Salvin in 19th century. Fine 17th century staircase and plaster ceilings. Terraced Gardens.

**Location:** In Dunster, 3 m SE of Minehead on A396.
*Station: Dunster (West Somerset Railway) (¾ m).*
**Opening Times:** Mar 26 to end of Sept—Sun to Thurs 11–5. Oct—Sun to Thurs 2–4. Last adm half-hour before closing. Adm £3, Chd £1.50. Parties of 15 or more by written appointment with the Administrator, £2. Garden and grounds open daily Apr to May and Sept—Sun to Thurs 11–5; Oct—Sun to Thurs 2–4; June to Aug —Daily 11–5. Adm £1.50, Chd 50p. Dogs in park only. Shop. Wheelchair access.
**Refreshments:** Luttrell Arms, Dunster, and village tearooms (not N.T.). National Trust Shop.

## EAST LAMBROOK MANOR GARDEN

**South Petherton** *map F3*
Telephone: South Petherton (0460) 40328
*(Mr & Mrs Andrew Norton)*

The garden, created by the late Margery Fish, surrounds the mediaeval house which dates from about 1470. The many books written by Mrs Fish and her extensive lecturing popularised this first of the Cottage style gardens which is now the pattern of many. It is both a traditional English garden and an important collection of unusual and now rare plants. Registered as a grade one garden it is maintained as a living and developing memorial to its creator. The Margery Fish Nursery offers a wide range of plants propagated from the garden.

**Location:** Off A303 2 m N of South Petherton.
**Opening Times:** Mon–Sat 9–5 and Bank Hols. *Closed Christmas and New Year.* Adm £1.20 *National Gardens Scheme.* Parties by arrangement only. Car parking limited.

BARRINGTON COURT
GARDENS

# FOR A WONDERFUL DAY OUT

Visit one of the National Trusts first properties... Beautifully restored and enriched by the Lyle family in the 1920's.

**Now one of Somersets Finest Estates**

Superb Walled Gardens – Influenced by Gertrude Jekyll lilly – Iris – White – Kitchen Garden

Fascinating Buildings–
See how the model estate and farm buildings of the 1920's blend in with the magnifincently restored Tudor Manor House

Enjoy the elegance of the layout
–Full avenues of chestnut trees, moats and parkland
–Nature and Farm Trail – Farm Exhibitions

Licensed Restaurant, Garden Centre, Shop, Picnic and Play Areas and Childrens Corner.

**OPENING TIMES**

Open 11 a.m. to 5.30 p.m. Saturday, Sunday, Monday, Tuesday and Wednesday from Good Friday to end October AND Seven days a week August

3 miles north of Ilminster off B3168
25 minutes from the M5 (Taunton)
10 minutes from A303

**BARRINGTON ILMINSTER SOMERSET**
**Tel (0460 – 40601/52242)**

## BARFORD PARK

**ENMORE, Nr BRIDGWATER**

Set in a large garden and looking out across a ha-ha to a park dotted with fine trees, it presents a scene of peaceful domesticity, a miniature country seat, on a scale appropriate today. The well-proportioned rooms, with contemporary furniture, are all in daily family use. The walled flower garden is in full view from the house and the woodland and water gardens and archery glade with their handsome trees form a perfect setting for the stone and red-brick Queen Anne building.

*ADMISSION—SEE EDITORIAL REFERENCE*

## THE BISHOP'S PALACE, WELLS

*THE CHURCH COMMISSIONERS*

'The most memorable of all bishops' palaces in England. It combines high architectural interest with exquisite beauty of setting.' (Pevsner)

*ADMISSION – SEE EDITORIAL REFERENCE*

## Brympton d'Evercy

**YEOVIL**

*WINNER BTA "HERITAGE AWARD"*

'I know no other houses of which the whole impression is more lovely and none that summarises so exquisitely English Country Life' – Christopher Hussey.

## HATCH COURT

**HATCH BEAUCHAMP, Nr Taunton**

A fine Bath stone mansion in the Palladian style, designed in 1755 by Thomas Prowse of Axbridge. Curved wings, magnificent stone staircase and much of the internal decoration carried out around 1800. The house has a good collection of pictures, 17th and 18th century furniture and unusual semicircular china room. The medieval parish church of St. John the Baptist is situated nearby.

*ADMISSION – SEE EDITORIAL REFERENCE*

**Farleigh Hungerford Castle** – See English Heritage Section.

## GAULDEN MANOR

**Tolland, nr Taunton** *map F3* △
Telephone: Lydeard St Lawrence (09847) 213
*(Mr & Mrs James LeGendre Starkie)*

Small historic red sandstone Manor House of great charm. A real lived-in home. Past Somerset seat of the Turberville family, immortalised by Thomas Hardy. Great Hall has magnificent plaster ceiling and oak screen to room known as the Chapel. Fine antique furniture. Interesting grounds include bog garden with primulas and other moisture loving plants. Herb garden.

**Location:** 9 m NW of Taunton; 1 m E of Tolland Church. Gaulden Manor signposted from A358 Taunton/Williton Rd just N of Bishops Lydeard and from B3188 Wivelscombe/Watchet Rd (cars only). Nearest village Lydeard St Lawrence (1½ m).
**Opening Times:** Apr 30 to June 30—Suns & Thurs; July 1 to Sept 10—Suns, Weds & Thurs, also Easter Sun and Mon and all Bank Hols: 2–6 (last adm 5.30). House & Garden Adm (1988 rates) £2, Chd (under 14) 80p. Garden only 80p. *Parties on other days by prior arrangement. Mornings, afternoons or evenings & out of season.* Shop—books, rare and unusual plants.
**Refreshments:** Teas in Garden Tearoom, on Sun, Bank Holidays and Parties.

**Glastonbury Tribunal** – See English Heritage Section.

## HADSPEN HOUSE

**Castle Cary** *map G3*
*(N.A. Hobhouse)*

8 acre garden on a south-facing slope, containing many unusual plants in an 18th century setting, having a Rare Plant and Old Fashioned Rose Nursery.

**Location:** 2 m SE of Castle Cary on A371 to Wincanton.
**Opening Times:** GARDEN ONLY. open all year daily, 9–6 (evenings by request). Adm £1, Chd 50p. *In aid of National Gardens Scheme. Nursery open Apr 1 to Oct 31 closed Mons except Bank Holidays.*
**Refreshments:** Teas—Sats, Suns & Bank Holidays 2–6, or for groups by request.

## HATCH COURT

**Hatch Beauchamp** *map F3* △
Telephone: Hatch Beauchamp (0823) 480208
*(Commander & Mrs Barry Nation)*

A Palladian style Georgian house in Bath stone with superb views of Somerset. A house of great elegance and charm. Small Canadian Military Museum. China room. Deer park.

**Location:** 6 m SE of Taunton midway between Taunton & Ilminster off A358.
**Opening Times:** July 6 to Sept 14—Thurs 2.30–5.30, last tour 4.30 *(no coaches)*. Also open Bank Holiday Monday afternoon. Adm £2. Coaches & organised parties by prior appointment only—May to Oct *(except Thurs when House is open)*. Special rates for organised parties. Members of HHA free.
**Refreshments:** By arrangement. Cups of tea & biscuits available Thurs.
Hatch Inn & Farthings Restaurant.

## HESTERCOMBE HOUSE AND GARDENS

**Cheddon Fitzpaine, Taunton** *map F3*
Telephone: (0823) 87222
*(Somerset County Council Fire Brigade Headquarters)*

Appearance of present house dates from 1870's with magnificent hallway and wooden staircase, when in ownership of Lord Portman. Main attraction is the historic multi-level garden laid out at the turn of this century by Sir Edwin Lutyens with planting by Miss Gertrude Jekyll. Restoration by County Council over last ten years to portray garden in its original form. Attractive stonework, a long Pergola supported by stone pillars and a magnificent Orangery on the east side of the garden. Best seen in the months of June, July and early Aug. Lovely views across the vale of Taunton Deane.

**Location:** 4 m NE of Taunton town centre.
**Opening Times:** All year—Mon to Fri 12–5. Plus last Suns June and July. Donations of £1 requested for garden restoration. Parties welcome – including coach parties. Ample free car parking. Parts of garden suitable for disabled (toilets for disabled).
**Refreshments:** Only on the Open Suns mentioned above.

## KENTSFORD HOUSE

**Watchet** *map F3*
*(Mrs Wyndham. Occupier: Mr H Dibble)*

House open **only** by written appointment with Mr H. Dibble.

**Opening Times:** Gardens: Tues and Bank Hols Mar 27–Sept 19. Donations towards renovation of fabric.

## KING JOHN'S HUNTING LODGE, The National Trust

**Axbridge** *map F4*

Early Tudor merchant's house extensively restored in 1971. Museum of local history and archaeology.

**Location:** On corner of the Square.
**Opening Times:** Mar 24 to end Sept—Daily 2–5. Adm free. No dogs, including Guide dogs. Unsuitable for wheelchairs.
**Refreshments:** In Axbridge.

## LYTES CARY MANOR, The National Trust

**nr Ilchester** *map G3*

Mediaeval manor house with chapel; fine furnishings; formal garden.

**Location:** On W side of Fosse Way (A37); 2½ m NE of Ilchester signposted on bypass (A303).
**Opening Times:** Mar 25 to Oct 28—Weds & Sats 2–6 (last adm 5.30). Adm £2, Chd £1. *Dogs in garden only, on leads.* No lavatories. NB. Large coaches cannot pass gate piers.
**Refreshments:** Refreshments and National Trust Shop at Montacute.

## MAUNSEL HOUSE

**North Newton, nr Bridgwater** *map F3*
Telephone: (0278) 663413
*(Sir Benjamin Slade Bt.)*

Home of Sir Benjamin & Lady Slade. Ancestral seat of the Slade family under extensive restoration. Part of the house built before Conquest, most of house built around a Hall erected in 1420. Geoffrey Chaucer was a frequent visitor and guest. He wrote part of the Canterbury Tales whilst staying at the house. Also the ancestral home of Madeline Slade (Mira Behn) devotee to the great Indian leader Mahatma Gandhi. In AD 1086 (Domesday) the Manor was called 'Maunsel' being derived from the French meaning 'sleave of land' and was granted to Count Eustace of Boulogne, Kinsman of William the Conqueror. At the time of Henry II, William de Erleigh granted Maunsel to Philip Arbalistarius as a dowry to his daughter Mabel on payment of two pigs every Whitsuntide at his Court of Durston. His son Philip married the daughter of Sir Hugh D'Auderville and assumed the surname of Maunsel. Philip de Maunsel became progenitor of the family with the surname 'Maunsell' and 'Mansel'. The estate passed to the Bacon family of Norfolk and then to the Slade family.

**Location:** Bridgwater 4 m, Bristol 20 m, Taunton 7 m, junction 24 M5, turn left North Petherton 1½ m North Newton, ½ m S St. Michael Church.
**Opening Times:** Apr 1 to Sept 30: Sun & Mon 2.30–5.30. Tues to Sat by appointment only. Adm House and Grounds £2, Chd £1. Coach parties by arrangement. Parties welcome by arrangement – mornings available. Receptions and banqueting by arrangement. Free car parking. Picnic & Barbecue area £1, Chd 50p. Children's adventure play area. *Dogs on leads allowed in grounds only.* Fishing – bring own tackle £1. Boating – bring own boat £1.

## MIDELNEY MANOR

**Drayton, nr Langport** *map F3* △
*(Mr John Cely Trevilian)*

16th to 18th century Manor House. Originally island manor of Abbots of Muchelney and property of Trevilian family since 1500. 17th century Falcons Mews. Gardens; Woodland walks; Heronry.

**Location:** Signposted from A378 at Bell Hotel; Curry Rivel & from B3168 Hambridge/Curry Rivel Road & in Drayton.
**Opening Times:** May 1 to Sept 21: Thurs and all Bank Holiday Mons 2.30–5.30 (last tour 4.30). Adm £2, Chd £1. Display of falcon flying Sat Aug 12, 2–5.30. **House not open.** Coach parties and teas by appointment.

## MILTON LODGE GARDENS

**Wells** *map G4*
Telephone: (0749) 72168
*(Mr & Mrs David Tudway Quilter)*

Mature alkaline terraced garden of great charm dating from 1909. Replanned 1962 with mixed shrubs and herbaceous plants, old fashioned roses and ground cover; numerous climbers; old established yew hedges. Fine trees in garden and in separate 7 acre arboretum on opposite side of Old Bristol Road.

**Location:** ½ m N of Wells. From A39 Bristol–Wells turn N up Old Bristol Road; free car park first gate on left.
**Opening Times:** GARDEN AND ARBORETUM ONLY: Weds and Suns in May, June and July 2–6. Adm £1, Chd 50p in aid of National Gardens Scheme and the Somerset Red Cross. Parties by appointment throughout the year. No dogs.
**Refreshments:** Teas available Suns only.

## MONTACUTE HOUSE, The National Trust

**Yeovil** *map G3*
Telephone: Martock 823289

Magnificent Elizabethan house of Ham Hill stone begun in the 1590s by Sir Edward Phelips. Fine heraldic glass, tapestries, panelling and furniture. National Portrait Gallery Exhibitions of Elizabethan and Jacobean portraits. Fine formal garden and park.

**Location:** In Montacute village 4 m W of Yeovil on S side of A3088; 3 m S of A303 nr Ilchester.
**Opening Times:** House: Mar 25 to Nov 5: Daily (except Tues) 12.30–5.30. Last adm 5 (or sunset if earlier). *Closed Good Fri. Parties by written appointment with the Administrator.* Garden & Park: All the year—Daily 12–5.30 (or sunset if earlier). Adm House, Garden & Park £3, Chd £1.50; Parties of 15 or more £2. Garden & Park only: Oct to May 60p; June to Sept £1, Chd half-price. Dogs in park only. Wheelchairs in garden only.
**Refreshments:** Light lunches & teas (Apr to end Oct noon–5.30). *Parties catered for by arrangement with the Administrator. National Trust Shop.*

**Muchelney Abbey** – See English Heritage Section.

# CLAPTON COURT GARDENS

One of Somerset's great gardens with an amazing collection of unusual trees, shrubs and plants in beautiful park-like setting. Interesting at all seasons.

ADMISSION – SEE EDITORIAL REFERENCE

# COMBE SYDENHAM HALL

**SOMERSET**

*ADMISSION – SEE EDITORIAL REFERENCE*

# MAUNSEL HOUSE

**Nr BRIDGWATER, SOMERSET**

*ADMISSION*
*SEE EDITORIAL REFERENCE*

# GAULDEN MANOR

**TOLLAND, Nr Taunton, Somerset**

Red sandstone Manor house of great charm. A real lived-in home. Past seat of the Turberville family immortalised by Thomas Hardy. The Great Hall has a magnificent plaster ceiling. Grounds include Bog and Herb gardens. Herbs and other unusual plants for sale.

*ADMISSION – SEE EDITORIAL REFERENCE*

# MIDELNEY MANOR

**DRAYTON, Nr LANGPORT**

16th to 18th century Manor House originally island manor of Abbots of Muchelney and home of Trevilian family since 1500. 17th century Falcon's Mews, Gardens, Heronry.

*ADMISSION – SEE EDITORIAL REFERENCE*

## POUNDISFORD PARK

**Pitminster, nr Taunton** *map F3* △ ♿
Telephone: Blagdon Hill (082342) 244
*(Mr & Mrs R Vivian-Neal)*

Delightful 'lived-in' 16th Century house on an intimate scale with 18th Century additions, set in the former Deer Park of Taunton Castle. Particularly fine Elizabethan plaster ceilings, good furniture, china, glass, family pictures, costumes and needlework. Windowed gallery to hall. Garden contains some interesting plants and a fine brick Gazebo. Rare surviving detached Great Kitchen (now a restaurant).

**Location:** 3½ m S of Taunton on Trull/Pitminster Road; ½ m W of B3170 Taunton/Honiton Road. Coaches should approach via Staplehay (signposted), from Taunton–Blagdon Hill road only.
**Opening Times:** HOUSE & GARDEN: July 6 to Sept 14—Thurs & Aug Bank Hol Mons: 11–5. Parties by appointment only, throughout the year. Adm £1.90, Chd (10–16) £1, (under 10 accompanied by adult, free). Parties pre-booked 15 or more £1.60. Disabled to Ground Floor & Garden £1. Guided tours by owners.
**Refreshments:** For groups – Lunches, Teas & Dinners in the Well House Restaurant (the Tudor Kitchen) by prior appointment only. Tel Blagdon Hill (082342) 566.

## PRIEST'S HOUSE, The National Trust

**Muchelney** *map F3* △
Telephone: (0458) 250672

Late medieval house, originally the residence of the secular priests who served the parish church. The Tenant shows his own collection of furniture and paintings.

**Location:** 1 m S of Langport.
**Opening Times:** All year by appointment with: The Tenant. Priest's House, Muchelney, nr Langport. Adm £1. *No reduction for parties or children.* No dogs. Unsuitable for wheelchairs.

## STOKE-SUB-HAMDON PRIORY, The National Trust

**nr Montacute** *map G3* ♿

Complex of buildings begun in 14th century for the priests of the chantry chapel of St Nicholas (destroyed).

**Location:** Between A303 & A3088; 2 m W of Montacute between Yeovil & Ilminster.
**Opening Times:** All the year—Daily 10–6 (or sunset if earlier). Adm free. *Great Hall only open to the public.* No dogs.

## STOWELL HILL

**Templecombe** *map G3*
*(Mr & Mrs Robert McCreery)*

Spring bulbs; collecton of flowering shrubs, including rhododendrons, azaleas, magnolias, etc Japanese Cherries.

**Location:** 5 m S of Wincanton, turn at Stowell ½ m from Templecombe on A357.
**Opening Times:** GARDEN ONLY. Suns May 7, 14, 21, 28. 2–6. Adm 75p, Chd 20p. *In aid of National Gardens Scheme.* No dogs.
**Refreshments:** Tea available.

## TINTINHULL HOUSE GARDEN, The National Trust

**nr. Yeovil** *map G3* △ ♿

Modern formal garden with borders and ponds surrounding 17th century house (house not open).

**Location:** 5 m NW of Yeovil; ½ m S of A303 on outskirts Tintinhull village.
**Opening Times:** Mar 25 to Sept 30—Weds, Thurs & Sats, also Bank Hol Mons 2–6 (last adm 5.30). Adm £2. *No reductions for parties or children.* Coach parties by written arrangement with the tenant. No dogs. Wheelchairs provided—garden only accessible.
**Refreshments:** Refreshments and National Trust Shop at Montacute.

# STAFFORDSHIRE

## ALTON TOWERS

**Alton ST10 4DB** *map H7*
Telephone: (0538) 702200

Former estate of the Earls of Shrewsbury set in 500 acres. Gardens developed from 1814. Splendid rock and rose gardens, tree lined valley slopes, pathways bordered by rhododendrons. Woodland walks. Well preserved ruins of Gothic Talbot family mansion. 19th century garden follies including replicas of the To Ho Pagoda of Canton and Choragic Monument of Lysicrates. Fine conservatory.

**Location:** 12 m Stoke-on-Trent.
**Opening Times:** Grounds and gardens open all year. Main season with rides and attractions: Mar 18 to Nov 5. Adm – discounts for groups, young people, and senior citizens. Chd under 4 FREE. Afternoon tickets half price after 2.30 pm. Much reduced rates in Winter season: Nov 6 to mid Mar. Disabled facilities. Special Events Calendar all year.
**Refreshments:** Wide choice of fast food to à la carte. Catering and banqueting facilities.

## ANCIENT HIGH HOUSE

**Stafford** *map G7*

Largest timber framed town house in England, dating from 1595. Heritage Exhibition and Tourist Information Centre.

**Location:** Off junction 13 – A449 to Stafford and junction 14 – A5103 to Stafford off M6.
**Opening Times:** House and Exhibition Centre: Mon to Fri 9–5; Sat 10–3. Adm £1, Chd/OAPs 50p, reduced rate for parties. Tourist Information Centre: Mon to Fri 9–5; Sat 10–3. No car park.

## CHILLINGTON HALL

**nr Wolverhampton** *map G7* △
Telephone: Brewood 850236
*(Mr & Mrs Peter Giffard)*

Georgian house. Part 1724 (Francis Smith); part 1785 (Sir John Soane). Fine saloon. Grounds and lake by 'Capability' Brown. Extensive woodland walks.

**Location:** 4 m SW of A5 at Gailey; 2 m Brewood; 8 m NW of Wolverhampton; 14 m S of Stafford. Best approach is from A449 (Junction 2, M54) through Coven and follow signposts towards Codsall (no entry at Codsall Wood).
**Opening Times:** May to Sept 14—Thurs (also Suns in Aug) 2.30–5.30. Open Easter Sun & Suns preceding May and late Spring Bank Holidays 2.30–5.30. Adm £1.40; Grounds only 70p. Chd half-price. *Parties other days by arrangement.*

## ANCIENT HIGH HOUSE

Largest timber-framed town house in England dating from 1595 and constructed of local oak.

Building now houses the area's Tourist Information Centre; Heritage and Exhibition facilities, including local archaeological inds from Stafford Castle and the town centre; video theatre and shop.

**Opening Times**
**Tourist Information Centre:**
9 am to 5 pm Mondays to Fridays
10 am to 3 pm Saturdays

**Heritage/Exhibition Centre:**
9 am to 5 pm Mondays to Fridays
10 am to 3 pm Saturdays

**Admission:**
Adults £1
Children 50p

**Telephone:**
**Stafford 40204**

# HANCH HALL

**LICHFIELD, STAFFORDSHIRE**

*'Tyler's Barn' in Granada TV's serial 'After the War'*

The house, listed as a building of outstanding architectural interest, is an unusual combination of architecture from Tudor to early Victorian which gives each room a fresh interest. Fine strapwork staircase, armorial window mentioned in Samuel Pepys Diary. 15th century timbers. Observation Tower giving extensive views of the estate. Elizabethan Cellars with escape tunnel. Period furniture including a four-poster bed associated with Percy Bysshe Shelley. Doll Museum. Needlework Museum. Collections of teapots, early parchments, sea shells. Exhibitions of costumery. 19th century Christening gowns, waxworks and 'Postmen through the Ages'. Now exhibits Lichield D.C. museum items.

Visitors receive a one hour guided tour through 20 rooms of this privately owned family home and are welcomed by Mr and Mrs Douglas Milton-Haynes and their family who have, without inheritance, taken up the challenge of restoring this historic mansion. **Evening visits** for groups arranged at any time. Featured by Central T.V., Location for 1989 T.V. serials 'After the War' and 'Boon III' Landscaped gardens, lawns and partly wild grounds and pools. Free roaming peacocks, pheasants, guinea-fowl, geese, ducks. Swans and Wildfowl Sanctuary on Trout Pool. Award winning 40ft high model of Lichfield-Cathedral-In-The-Trees.

*ADMISSION – SEE EDITORIAL REFERENCE*

# CHILLINGTON HALL

**Codsall Wood**
**Nr. Wolverhampton**
**Staffordshire**

Chillington is the home of the Giffard family for over 800 years. Visit Soane's 18th century house and stroll quietly in the park or walk for 4 miles through woodlands around 'Capability' Brown's lake with its temples and bridges and Sham House. Dogs allowed in grounds if kept on leads.

WELCOME TO

# ECCLESHALL CASTLE

**STAFFORD**

WILLIAM AND MARY SANDSTONE MANSION HOUSE SET IN 20 ACRES OF WOODED GROUNDS INCLUDING THE NEWLY RESTORED CASTLE RUINS. SITUATED ON A519, BETWEEN M6 JUNCTIONS 14 AND 15.

# Shugborough

**ANCESTRAL HOME OF LORD LICHFIELD MILFORD, STAFFORDSHIRE**

18TH CENTURY MANSION HOUSE · STAFFORDSHIRE COUNTY MUSEUM · WORKING RARE BREEDS FARM · RESTORED MILL · BEAUTIFUL FORMAL GARDENS AND PARKLAND WITH HISTORIC NEO-CLASSICAL MONUMENTS · TEA ROOMS · SHOP AND PICNIC AREAS.

*FOR OPENING TIMES AND ADMISSION CHARGES SEE EDITORIAL REFERENCE*

## DOROTHY CLIVE GARDEN
**Willoughbridge** *map G7*
*(Willoughbridge Garden Trust)*

7 acre woodland and rhododendron garden; shrub roses, water garden and a large scree in a fine landscape setting.

**Location:** 9 m SW Newcastle-under-Lyme. On A51 between junctions with A525 & A53, 1 m E of Woore.
**Opening Times:** Garden only. Mar 24 to Oct 31—Daily: Suns and Bank Holidays 12–5.30. Sats and weekdays 2–5. Adm £1, Chd 25p. Large car park.

## ECCLESHALL CASTLE
**Eccleshall, Stafford** *map G7*
Telephone: Eccleshall (0785) 850250
*(Mr & Mrs Mark Carter)*

William and Mary Mansion House containing fine collections of porcelain, paintings and furniture. Extensive grounds containing part of the original 14th century castle. Nature Trail, Souvenir shop.

**Location:** 400 yards N of Eccleshall on A519; 6 m NW of Junct 14 on M6, 9 m SW of Junct 15 on M6.
**Opening Times:** Easter to Oct 1 from 2–5.30 on Suns, Bank Holidays and Tues following. Also Thurs from June 1 and Tues in Aug. Adm House and Grounds: £2, Chd £1. Family (2 adults & up to 3 Chd) £5.50. Grounds only £1, Chd 50p. Parties (over 20) welcome by appointment at any reasonable time at reduced rates. Reduced rates also available on Tues and Thurs for OAPs and National Trust Members.
**Refreshments:** Home-made cream teas are available in the Hogarth Restaurant. Full catering service for booked parties.

## HANCH HALL
**Lichfield** *map H7* △
Telephone: Armitage (0543) 490308
*(Mr & Mrs Douglas Milton-Haynes)*

Original mansion built in reign of Edward I. Seat of the Aston family until end of the 16th century then the Ormes, staunch supporters of Charles I. Home of General William Dyott from 1817, then Sir Charles Forster later in the 19th century. The present house, which is lived in as a family home, exhibits Tudor, Jacobean, Queen Anne and Georgian architecture. Wealth of oak panelling; Observation Tower; interesting collections. Landscaped gardens, trout pool, waterfowl. Tiny Chapel in grounds. Nature trail.
NB. *The owners reserve the right to change days and hours of opening and to close all or parts of the Hall without prior notice.*

**Location:** 4 m NW of Lichfield on Uttoxeter Road (B5014).
**Opening Times:** Mar 26 to Oct 1—Suns & Bank Hol Mons & Tues following 2–6; June, July, Aug & Sept—Tues, Weds, Thurs & Sats 2–6 (last tour of House 5). Parties of 20 or more, daily, mornings, afternoons or evenings by arrangement. Adm House & Gardens £2.50, Chd £1.30. Reduction for parties of 20 or more. Free car park. Gift & Bric-a-brac shop. Lengthy tour of the house not really suitable for small children. *Regret no dogs. No stiletto heels in the house.* Candlelight evenings first week in Dec. For further information contact Mrs Milton-Haynes.
**Refreshments:** Tea & home baking in 17th century Stable Block. Hot or cold meals by arrangement.

## MOSELEY OLD HALL, The National Trust
**Wolverhampton** *map G6* △ Ⓢ ♿
Telephone: Wolverhampton (0902) 782808

A 17th century formal garden surrounds this mainly Elizabethan house where Charles II hid after the battle of Worcester.

**Location:** 4 m N of Wolverhampton mid-way between A449 & A460 Roads. Off M6 at Shareshill then via A460. Traffic from S via. M6 and M54 take junction 1 to Wolverhampton and Moseley is signposted after ½ m. Coaches via. A460 to avoid low bridge.
**Opening Times:** Mar 11–Oct 29. Mar 11–Apr 30 Sat & Sun 2–6; May 1–Jul 12 Wed, Sat & Sun 2–6; Jul 15–Sept 6 Sat–Wed 2–6; Sept 9–27 Wed, Sat & Sun 2–6; Sept 30–Oct 29 Sat & Sun 2–6. Bank Holiday Mon & Tues following (except May 2) 2–6. *Closed Good Friday.* Pre-booked parties at other times including evening tours. Adm £2, Chd half price. Family ticket £5.50. Parties £1.70, evening parties £2. Educational facilities. Wheelchair access ground floor only.
**Refreshments:** Home-made teas from 2.30. Lunches, dinners, candlelit suppers by arrangement. Licensed.

## PILLATON OLD HALL
**Penkridge** *map G7* ♿
Telephone: Penkridge (078 571) 2200
*(Mr R. W. & The Hon Mrs Perceval)*

15th century gatehouse wing and chapel.

**Location:** 1 m E of Penkridge on Cannock Road (B5012); turn right at Pillaton Hall Farm.
**Opening Times:** Open by appointment. Adm 50p.

## SHUGBOROUGH, The National Trust
**Stafford** *map G7* Ⓢ ♿
Telephone: Little Haywood (0889) 881388
*(Administered by Staffordshire County Council)*

Seat of the Earls of Lichfield. Architecture by James Stuart and Samuel Wyatt. Rococo plasterwork by Vassalli. Extensive parkland with neo-classical monuments. Beautiful formal gardens with Chinese house, Victorian terraces and rose-garden. Guided garden and woodland walks.

**Location:** 6 m E of Stafford on A513, entrance at Milford. 10 mins drive from M6, junction 13.
**Opening Times:** House, Museum, Farm, Working Mill & Gardens. Mar 24 to Sept 30—open daily incl. Bank Hol Mons 11–5. Winter opening – Oct 1 to Dec 24—open daily incl. Bank Hol Mons 11–4. Site open all year round to booked parties from 10.30. Adm: House £1.50, (reduced rate £1). Museum £1.50 (reduced rate £1). Farm £1.50 (reduced rate £1). All-in-ticket (House, Museum & Farm) £4 (reduced rate £2). Coach parties: All-in-ticket £2 or £1 per site. (Adm prices subject to change.) Reduced rates available for chd, OAPs and registered unemployed. Chd (under 5) free. NT members free entry to house. Parties can be booked in for guided tours at all sites. School parties can be booked in for guided tours at each site, 60p per head per site, incl. of guide. School All-in-tickets £1.50 per head. When special events are held charges may vary. Guide dogs admitted to House and Museum but not other dogs. Site access for parking, picnic area, parkland, garden and woodland trails £1 per vehicle. Coaches free. National Trust shop and toilets.
**Refreshments:** Tea-rooms restaurant.

## TAMWORTH CASTLE
**Tamworth** *map H7*
Telephone: Tamworth 311222, Ext 389.
Weekends only Tamworth 63563
*(Tamworth Borough Council)*

Norman Keep and tower with Tudor and Jacobean additions. Houses a museum.

**Location:** In Tamworth; 15 m NE of Birmingham.
*Station: Tamworth (¾ m).*
**Opening Times:** All the year—Weekdays (except Fris) 10–5, Suns 2–5. Open Bank Hols. *Closed Fris and Christmas Eve, Christmas Day & Boxing Day.* Adm £1, OAPs and unaccompanied Chd 55p; accompanied Chd 25p.


**Wall (Letocetum) Roman Site** – See English Heritage Section.

WESTON PARK—SEE UNDER SHROPSHIRE


## WHITMORE HALL
**Whitmore, nr Newcastle-under-Lyme** *map G7*
Telephone: (0782) 680478
*(Mr G. Cavenagh-Mainwaring)*

Carolinian Manor House, owner's family home for over 800 years. Family portraits dating back to 1624. Outstanding Tudor Stable Block.

**Location:** Four miles from Newcastle-under-Lyme on the A53 Road to Market Drayton.
**Opening Times:** Open 2–5.30 every Tues & Weds, May to Aug inclusive (last tour 5). Adm £1.50. *No reduction for parties. Free car parking. Not suitable for disabled. No wheelchairs available.*
**Refreshments:** Mainwaring Arms Inn, Whitmore & also at Whitmore Art Gallery & Tea rooms, Whitmore.

# SUFFOLK


BELCHAMP HALL—SEE UNDER ESSEX


## BLAKENHAM WOODLAND GARDEN
**Little Blakenham, nr Ipswich** *map L6*
*(Lord Blakenham)*

5 acre wood with many rare trees and shrubs. Lovely throughout the year, with bluebells, camellias and magnolias followed by azaleas, rhododendrons, roses, hydrangeas and fine autumn colouring.

**Location:** 4 m NW of Ipswich. The garden is signposted from Little Blakenham which is 1 m off the old A1100 now called B1113.
**Opening Times:** Apr to Sept—Weds, Thurs, Suns and Bank Hols 1–5. Adm £1. Free car-park. No dogs.

## CHRISTCHURCH MANSION
**Ipswich** *map M5*
Telephone: Ipswich (0473) 53246
*(The Borough of Ipswich)*

Extensive Tudor town house in park. Furnished period rooms, 16th to 19th century; outstanding decorative art collections of china, glass etc. Attached art gallery includes work by Gainsborough, Constable and other Suffolk artists up to the present day. Temporary art exhibition programme.

**Location:** In Christchurch Park, near centre of Ipswich.
*Station: Ipswich (1¼ m).*
**Opening Times:** All the year—Mons to Sats 10–5 *(dusk in winter)*; Suns 2.30–4.30 *(dusk in winter)*. Open Bank Hols. *Closed Dec 24, 25 & 26 and Good Fri.* Adm free.

## The National Trust

# MOSELEY OLD HALL

**WOLVERHAMPTON**

A 17th century formal garden surrounds this mainly Elizabethan house where Charles II hid after the battle of Worcester.

*ADMISSION – SEE EDITORIAL REFERENCE*

# TAMWORTH CASTLE

**STAFFORDSHIRE**

Built in the 1180s, Tamworth's sandstone castle is one of the country's few remaining Norman motte and bailey castles with a shell-keep. Fine mid 15th century timber-framed Great Hall, panelled Jacobean rooms with period furniture and a local history museum.

*ADMISSION – SEE EDITORIAL REFERENCE*

# EUSTON HALL

**SUFFOLK**

*ON A1088 3 MILES SOUTH OF THETFORD*

Euston Hall—Home of the Duke of Grafton. The 18th century house contains a famous collection of paintings including works by Stubbs, Van Dyck, Lely and Kneller. The pleasure grounds were laid out by John Evelyn and William Kent. Garden and nearby 17th century parish church in the Wren style. Teas and shop in Old Kitchen.

OPEN: Thursdays, June 1 to September 28 and last Sunday in June (25th). 2.30 to 5.30 pm.
ADMISSION: Adults £2, OAPs £1.20
Schoolchildren 50p. Parties of 12 or more £1 per head.
For further details apply:
Estate Office, Euston, Thetford, Norfolk.
Tel. Thetford (0842) 66366.

# HELMINGHAM HALL GARDENS

**Between IPSWICH and DEBENHAM**

Home of the Tollemache family since 1480, when it was built, to the present day—probably the last and finest house of the Tudor period, surrounded by a wide moat with drawbridge raised every night. A superb garden and immaculate kitchen garden with lovely herbaceous borders and walks extending for several acres, set in 400 acres of ancient deer park with large herds of Red and Fallow deer. English Heritage Grade I Garden.

*ADMISSION – SEE EDITORIAL REFERENCE*

### EUSTON HALL
**Thetford** *map L6*
*(The Duke of Grafton)*

18th century house. Fine collection of paintings, including Stubbs, Van Dyck, Kneller and Lely. Pleasure grounds by John Evelyn and William Kent. Gardens and 17th century parish church in Wren style.

**Location:** A1088; 3 m S Thetford.
**Opening Times:** June 1 to Sept 28—Thurs only 2.30–5.30. Also Sun June 25, 2.30–5.30. Adm £2, Chd 50p, OAPs £1.20. Parties of 12 or more £1 per head.
**Refreshments:** Teas and shop in Old Kitchen. Picnic area.

### FRAMLINGHAM CASTLE
*map M6*
Telephone: (0728) 723330
*(English Heritage)*

The present massive walls and their 13 towers were built by Roger Bigod, second Earl of Norfolk, on a site given to his father by Henry I. The ornamental brick chimneys were added in Tudor times when the arch of the entrance gateway was rebuilt. In 1636 the castle passed to Pembroke College, Cambridge, and in later years the great hall was converted to a poor-house and many of the buildings inside the walls were demolished. It was here, in 1553, that Mary Tudor learned she had become Queen of England.

**Location:** North side of Framlingham. OS map ref TM287637.
**Opening Times:** Good Friday to Sept 30, daily 10–6; Oct 1 to Maundy Thurs, daily 10–4. *Closed* Mons, Dec 24–26, Jan 1. Adm £1.10, OAPs 80p, Chd 55p.

### GAINSBOROUGH'S HOUSE
**Sudbury** *map L5*
Telephone: Sudbury (0787) 72958
*(Gainsborough's House Society)*

Thomas Gainsborough's birthplace. Pictures and furniture associated with the artist and the 18th century. Exhibitions of historic and contemporary art throughout the year. Contemporary craft gallery. Print workshop; garden.

**Location:** 46 Gainsborough Street, Sudbury.
*Station: Sudbury (¼ m).*
**Opening Times:** Open all the year. Easter to Sept—Tues to Sats 10–5; Sun & Bank Hol Mons 2–5; Oct to Maundy Thursday—Tues to Sats 10–4; Sun and Bank Hol Mons 2–4. *Closed Mons, Good Fri & between Christmas & New Year.* Adm £1, Students/Chd/OAPs 50p.

### GUILDHALL, The National Trust
**Lavenham** *map L6*

Early 16th century timber-framed Tudor building; originally hall of Guild of Corpus Christi. Display of local history and industry including a unique exhibition of 700 years of the woollen cloth trade. Delightful small garden.

**Location:** Market Place Lavenham, Sudbury.
**Opening Times:** Mar 25 to Nov 4—Daily 11–1, 2–5.30. Closed Good Fri. Adm £1.50, Chd 75p. Parties £1.20, please book with sae to Custodian in charge. School parties 50p by prior arrangement. Shop.
**Refreshments:** Coffee, light lunches and teas.

### HAUGHLEY PARK
**nr Stowmarket** *map L6*
*(Mr & Mrs A J Williams)*

Jacobean manor house. Gardens and woods, fine trees and shrubs.

**Location:** 4 m W of Stowmarket signed on A45 nr Wetherden (not Haughley).
**Opening Times:** May to Sept—Tues 3–6. Adm £1.50, Chd 50p.

### HELMINGHAM HALL GARDENS
**Ipswich** *map M6*
*(The Lord & Lady Tollemache)*

The House was completed in 1510 by the Tollemache family and is surrounded by a wide moat with drawbridges which are raised every night. The large park contains herds of Red and Fallow deer and Highland Cattle and the gardens, which date with the house, are renowned for their herbaceous borders and old fashioned roses. English Heritage Grade I Garden.

**Location:** 9 m N of Ipswich on B1077.
**Opening Times:** GARDENS ONLY. Apr 30 to Oct 1—Suns only 2–6. Adm £1.30, Chd 80p, OAPs £1. Safari rides 70p, Chd 50p. Craft shop. *House not open to the public.*
**Refreshments:** Cream teas. Home-grown plants and produce for sale.

### ICKWORTH, The National Trust
**nr Bury St Edmunds** *map L6* ♿
Telephone: Horringer 270

The house, begun c. 1794, was not completed until 1830. Contents of this architectural curiosity include late Regency and 18th century French furniture, magnificent silver, pictures. Formal gardens, herbaceous borders, orangery. 18th century walks in woodland and around the lake. 35 minute taped guide available.

**Location:** 3 m SW of Bury St Edmunds on W side of A143.
**Opening Times:** Rotunda, Corridors & Garden. Mar 25, 26, 27; Apr: Sat & Suns. May 1 to Sept 30: Daily (except Mons & Thurs): 1.30–5.30. Oct: Sat and Sun 1.30–5.30. Open Bank Hol Mons: 1.30–5.30. Adm £3, Chd £1.50. Access to Park, Garden, Restaurant and Shop £1. Parties £2.50. Park open daily. Dogs in park only, on leads. Wheelchair access, one provided; special car park for disabled. Shop.
**Refreshments:** Lunch & tea in old Servants' Hall. Table licence, restaurant opens 12 noon.

### IPSWICH MUSEUM
**Ipswich** *map M6*
Telephone: Ipswich (0473) 213761/2
*(Ipswich Borough Council)*

Geology and natural history of Suffolk; Mankind galleries covering Africa, Asia, America and the Pacific. 'Romans in Suffolk' gallery showing local archaeology. Temporary exhibitions in attached gallery.

**Location:** High Street, in town centre.
*Station: Ipswich.*
**Opening Times:** Mons to Sats 10–5. Temporary exhibition programme. Adm free.

### IXWORTH ABBEY
**nr Bury St Edmunds** *map L6* △ Ⓢ
*(John Rowe, Esq)*

House contains 12th century monastic buildings with 15th to 19th century additions. 13th century Undercroft and 15th century Priors Lodging recently restored.

**Location:** 6 m NE of Bury St Edmunds; 8 m SE of Thetford; at junction of A143 & A1088.
**Opening Times:** May 1 to June 6: weekdays only 2–4. Also Spring and Summer Bank Holidays 2–4. Adm £2.20, Chd over 5 £1. Guided visits only.
**Refreshments:** Meals by prior arrangement only.

### KENTWELL HALL
**Long Melford** *map L6*
*(J. Patrick Phillips, QC)*

Red brick Tudor E-plan mansion surrounded by a broad moat. Exterior little altered. Interior being refurbished. Ancient moats and interconnecting gardens. 15th century Moat House, rare breed farm animals, brick paved Maze and costume display.

**Location:** Entrance on W of A134, N of Green in Long Melford; 3 m N of Sudbury.
**Opening Times:** Easter: Good Fri to Thurs following. Easter to June 17—Suns only. July 10 to Sept 30—Weds to Suns 2–6; Bank Hol Sats, Suns & Mons 11–6. Adm £2.40, Chd (5–15) £1.40, OAPs £2.10. Bank Holidays: £3.50, Chd (5–15) £2, OAPs, £3. June 18 to July 19, annual Re-Creation of Tudor Life – weekdays, prebooked school parties only; general public at weekends: 11–5 (special admission charges). Reduction of 20% for prebooked parties over 20 on open days, also groups at other times by arrangement. No dogs.
**Refreshments:** Teas in the Hall 2–6. Also lunches over Bank Hols.

### LITTLE HALL
**Lavenham** *map L6*
*(Suffolk Preservation Society)*

15th century "hall" house, rooms furnished with Gayer Anderson collection of furniture, pictures, china, books, etc.

**Location:** E side Lavenham Market Place.
**Opening Times:** Easter to mid-Oct—Sats, Suns & Bank Hols 2.30–6. *Groups by appointment tel: (0787) 247179.* Adm 80p, Chd 40p.

# ICKWORTH

**SUFFOLK**

*THE NATIONAL TRUST*

*ADMISSION — SEE EDITORIAL REFERENCE*

## GAINSBOROUGH'S HOUSE

**Sudbury, Suffolk**

*Garden Front (partly late 18c)*

The only birthplace of a great artist open to the public in Britain. Fine collection of work by Thomas Gainsborough in Georgian weaver's house; temporary historic and contemporary exhibitions; craft gallery; print workshop; charming town garden containing mulberry tree planted in 1600s.

*ADMISSION – SEE EDITORIAL REFERENCE*

There's more than meets the eye . . .

to

Ipswich Museums and Galleries

*Discover the rest at:*

**IPSWICH MUSEUM and the HIGH ST. EXHIBITION GALLERY**
High Street, Ipswich, Suffolk.
Geology and natural history of Suffolk; Mankind galleries covering Africa, Asia, America and the Pacific. 'Romans in Suffolk' gallery showing local archaeology. Temporary exhibitions in attached gallery.

**CHRISTCHURCH MANSION and the WOLSEY ART GALLERY**
Christchurch Park, Ipswich, Suffolk
Period rooms, decorative and fine arts

*For further information telephone:*
Ipswich (0473) 213761

**IPSWICH BOROUGH COUNCIL**

# KENTWELL HALL

LONG MELFORD

**BTA HERITAGE AWARD WINNER**

***A magnificent mellow redbrick Tudor Manor House surrounded by a broad moat. Tranquil, timeless atmosphere and a real family home. Extensive gardens. Farm with timber-framed buildings and rare breed farm animals.***

DIARY OF EVENTS 1989

| | |
|---|---|
| Easter W/E: | **Great Easter Egg Hunt Quiz** |
| Mayday W/E: | **Maypole and Country Dancing** |
| Spring BH W/E: | **Re-Creation of Tudor Life** |
| June 4: | **Sheep Shearing Sunday** |
| June 18 - July 9: | **Kentwell 1605** – Major Re-Creation of Everyday Tudor Domestic Life. Open to Schools only on weekdays, to the public on Sats & Suns |
| July 28 & 29: | **Open Air Theatre** – Shakespeare's "Cymbeline" |
| August BH W/E: | **Re-Creation of Tudor Life** |
| September 30 & October 1: | **Michaelmas Craft Market** |

ADMISSION - SEE EDITORIAL REFERENCE

### MELFORD HALL, The National Trust
**nr Sudbury** *map L5* ♿

Built between 1554 and 1578 by Sir William Cordell, contains fine pictures, furniture and Chinese porcelain. Interesting garden and gazebo. Beatrix Potter display.

**Location:** In Long Melford on E side of A134; 3 m N of Sudbury.
**Opening Times:** Principal Rooms & Gardens. Mar: 25, 26, 27; Apr Sat and Sun; May 1 to Sept 30: Wed, Thurs, Sat, Sun, Bank Holidays 2–6. Oct: Sat and Sun 2–6. Adm £2, Chd (with adult) £1. Pre-booked parties of 15 or more £1.60, Weds & Thurs only. No dogs. Wheelchair access, one provided.
**Refreshments:** In Long Melford.

### NETHER HALL
**Cavendish, nr Sudbury** *map L5*
*(B T Ambrose, Esq)*

Listed 15th century Manor House situated in the centre of scenic Stour Valley village, beside its churchyard and famous village green. Surrounded by its own vineyards producing prize-winning Estate white wines.

**Location:** 12 m S of Bury St Edmunds; beside A1092.
**Opening Times:** Open daily for tours & wine tasting 11–4. Adm £2, Chd (accompanied) free, OAPs £1.50. Parties by appointment.
**Refreshments:** Widely available in village.

**Orford Castle** – See English Heritage Section.

### OTLEY HALL
**nr Ipswich** *map M6* △
*(Mr and Mrs J G Mosesson)*

15th century Moated Hall (Grade 1) and Gardens. Home for 250 years of the Gosnold family. Fine timbers, herring-bone brick, pargetting. Historical associations.

**Location:** 10 m N of Ipswich, via B1077/B1078; ¼ m NE of Otley village.
**Opening Times:** Easter Sun & Mon (Mar 26 and 27); Spring Bank Hol Sun & Mon (May 28 and 29); Summer Bank Hol Sun & Mon (Aug 27 and 28): 2–6. Open by appointment to parties, special interest groups, etc. Guided tours. Lectures available on associated history, architectural background, etc. Adm £2.75, Chd (with adult) £1.75.
**Refreshments:** Tea & light refreshments, buffet meals available by arrangement.

### THE PRIORY
**Lavenham** *map L6*
Telephone: Lavenham (0787) 247417
*(Mr & Mrs A Casey)*

Through the ages the home of Benedictine monks, medieval clothiers, an Elizabethan rector, and now of the Casey family, who rescued the house from a derelict ruin. Beautiful timber-framed building (Grade 1) with stimulating interior design blending old and new, enhanced by paintings, drawings and stained glass by Ervin Bossanyi (1891–1975). Lovely herb garden of unique design. Work still continues on parts of the building. On display is an exhibition of photographs illustrating the restoration.

**Location:** In Water Street, Lavenham; 10 m S of Bury St Edmunds.
**Opening Times:** Apr to end Oct—Daily 10.30–5.30. Adm £2, Chd £1. Open by appointment for groups all year, morning, afternoon or evening, please telephone above number. Guided tours can emphasise timber framed buildings and their restoration, history of the house and the area, the Bossanyi collection, interior decor – according to your interests. For winter bookings, there is central heating and log fires!
**Refreshments:** Coffee, lunches and teas served in the Refectory. Gift shop. Selection of unusual gifts and woven tapestries.

**Saxtead Green Post Mill** – See English Heritage Section.

### SOMERLEYTON HALL
**nr Lowestoft** *map M6*
*(The Lord & Lady Somerleyton)*

Early 19th century mansion on which no expense was spared. Beautiful gardens, famous maze, miniature railway (on most days).

**Location:** 5 m NW Lowestoft off B1074; 7 m Yarmouth (A143).
*Station: Somerleyton (1½ m).*
**Opening Times:** House, Maze and Gardens open 1989 – Easter Sun to Jun 1, Thurs, Suns and Bank Holidays. June 1 to Oct 1, Suns, Mons, Tues, Weds & Thurs—2–5.30. Adm £2.50, Chd £1.20, OAPs £2.

### THE SUE RYDER FOUNDATION MUSEUM
**Sue Ryder Home, Cavendish** *map L5*
Telephone: Glemsford (0787) 280252
*(The Sue Ryder Foundation)*

This small Museum is set in beautiful surroundings. It depicts the remarkable story of how the Foundation was established, its work today and its hopes for the future.

**Location:** On A1092 Long Melford–Cambridge. (Long Melford 4 m: Sudbury 8 m: Bury St Edmund's 16 m: Cambridge 29 m).
**Opening Times:** Daily—Mon–Sat 10–5.30; Sun 10–11, 12.15–5.30. Parties welcome. For special bookings, please write to:– The Sue Ryder Foundation, Cavendish, Suffolk CO10 8AY.
**Refreshments:** Coffee shop providing lunches and light meals also gift shop.

### WINGFIELD COLLEGE
**Nr Eye** *map M6* △
Telephone: Stradbroke (037 984) 505
*(Ian Chance, Esq)*

Founded in 1362 on the 13th century site of the Manor House by Sir John de Wingfield, a close friend of the Black Prince. Magnificent Medieval Great Hall. Surrendered to Henry VIII in 1542 and seized by Cromwell's Parliament in 1549. Mixed period interiors with 18th century neo-classical façade. Walled gardens. Teas. Celebrated Arts and Music Season. Adjacent church with tombs of College founder and Benefactors, The Dukes of Suffolk.

**Location:** Signposted off B1118; 7 m SE of Diss.
**Opening Times:** Easter Sat to Sept 25—Sats, Suns & Bank Hols 2–6.
**Refreshments:** Home-made teas.

## SURREY

### ALBURY PARK
**Albury, Guildford** *map J4*
*(Country Houses Association Ltd)*

Country mansion by Pugin.

**Location:** 1½ m E of Albury.
*Stations: Chilworth (2 m); Gomshall (2 m); Clandon (2 m)*
**Opening Times:** May to Sept—Weds & Thurs 2–5. Adm £1, Chd 50p. Free car park. No dogs admitted.

### ASGILL HOUSE
**Richmond** *map K4*
*(Asgill House Trust Ltd)*

Palladian villa designed by Sir Robert Taylor.

**Location:** Richmond, Surrey
**Opening Times:** By written application. Unsuitable for disabled. Car parking on street only.

### CHILWORTH MANOR
**nr Guildford** *map J4*
*(Lady Heald)*

Garden laid out in 17th century on site of 11th century monastery, 18th century walled garden, spring flowers, flowering shrubs, herbaceous border, 11th century stewponds. House open. Floral arrangements.

**Location:** 3¾ m SE of Guildford off A248 in Chilworth Village turn at Blacksmith Lane.
*Station: Chilworth (¾ m).*
**Opening Times:** GARDEN ONLY: Sats to Weds incl—Apr 8–12; May 13–17; June 17–21; July 15–19; Aug 5–Aug 9. Other times by appointment. Car park open 12.30 for picnics. Adm Garden £1, House (Sats & Suns only) 50p, accompanied Chd free. Cars free. In aid of National Gardens Scheme. Floral decorations.
**Refreshments:** Tea at the house, Sats & Suns only.

### CLANDON PARK, The National Trust
**nr Guildford** *map J4* ♿
Telephone: Guildford 222482

A Palladian house built 1731–35 by Giacomo Leoni. Fine plasterwork. Collection of furniture, pictures and porcelain. Museum of the Queen's Royal Surrey Regiment. Garden with parterre, grotto and Maori house.

**Location:** At West Clandon 3 m E Guildford on A247; S of A3 & N of A246.
*Station: Clandon (1 m).*
**Opening Times:** Mar 24 to Oct 15—Daily (except Thurs & Fris) 1.30–5.30 (last adm 5). Open Bank Hol Mons and preceding Suns 11–5.30; open Good Friday. Parties & guided tours by arrangement with the Administrator *(no reduced rate at weekends & Bank Hols)*. Adm House & Museum £2.30, Chd £1.10. Shop. Picnic area. Dogs in car park & picnic area only, on leads. Wheelchairs provided.
**Refreshments:** Restaurant in house 12.30–2 & 3.15–5.30. Prior booking advisable for luncheon, Tel Guildford 222502.

### CLAREMONT
**Esher** *map K4*
Telephone: Esher (0372) 67841
*(The Claremont Fan Court Foundation Ltd)*

Excellent example of Palladian style; built 1772 by "Capability" Brown for Clive of India; Henry Holland and John Soane responsible for the interior decoration. It is now a co-educational school run by Christian Scientists.

**Location:** ½ m SW from Esher on Esher/Cobham Road A307, turning before entrance to NT Claremont Landscape Garden.
*Stations: Claygate (1½ m); Esher (2 m) (not Suns).*
**Opening Times:** Feb to Nov—First complete weekend (Sats & Suns) in each month 2–5. Adm £1, Chd/OAPs 50p. Reduced rates for parties. Souvenirs.
**Refreshments:** Not available.

## Somerleyton Hall GARDENS AND MAZE Nr. Lowestoft

*The home of Lord and Lady Somerleyton*

Somerleyton Hall is an extravagantly splendid early Victorian mansion built around a Tudor and Jacobean shell, epitomising an era of self confident expansion. No expense was spared in the building or the fittings. Stone was brought from Caen and Aubigny and the magnificent carved stonework created by John Thomas (who worked on the Houses of Parliament) has recently been fully restored.

In the State rooms there are paintings by Landseer, Wright of Derby and Stanfield, together with fine wood carving by Willcox of Warwick and from the earlier house, Grinling Gibbons.

Twelve acres of gardens surround the Hall with magnificent specimen trees, azaleas, rhododendrons and splendid statuary. There are handsome glass houses designed by Paxton. The most notable feature is the MAZE, planted in 1846, which ranks among the finest in this country.

The stable tower clock by Vulliamy made in 1847 is the original mode for a great clock to serve as the Tower Clock in the new Houses of Parliament, now world famous as Big Ben.

A quarter mile long MINIATURE RAILWAY carries passengers at the edge of the park, on most days.

Tea in the Winter Garden Tea Room. Free car parking. No dogs allowed.

*ADMISSION – SEE EDITORIAL REFERENCE*

## The Priory

### Lavenham, Suffolk.

**Open daily 10.30-5.30**
**April to end October.**
**For details see editorial reference.**

## THE SUE RYDER FOUNDATION MUSEUM

**SUE RYDER HOME, CAVENDISH, SUFFOLK**

This small Museum is set in beautiful surroundings. It depicts the remarkable story of how the Foundation was established, its work today and its hopes for the future. Location: On A1092 Long Melford—Cambridge. (Long Melford 4 miles: Sudbury 8 miles: Bury St. Edmunds 16 miles: Cambridge 29 miles). Open daily: Mondays to Saturdays 10 am to 5.30 pm. Sundays 10 to 11 am; 12.15 to 5.30 pm. GIFT SHOP also COFFEE SHOP providing lunches and light meals. Parties welcome. For special bookings, please write to:– The Sue Ryder Foundation, Cavendish, Suffolk CO10 8AY. Tel: Glemsford (0787) 280252.

## DETILLENS

**LIMPSFIELD, SURREY**

A medieval Manor House built in 1450 with a vast Crown Post and Tie Beam in the old Hall. The Georgian front was added in 1725. The contents include superb items of furniture, china, militaria and the largest collection of Orders and Decorations of Chivalry in the UK. Another attraction is the Butchers Slaughter House in the grounds which is laid out as a Museum of Country Crafts and Implements especially of local interest.

## FARNHAM CASTLE

**FARNHAM, SURREY**

*THE CHURCH COMMISSIONERS*

Formerly the seat of the Bishops of Winchester, the Castle was built by Henry of Blois in the 12th century. Its features include the Renaissance brickwork of Waynflete's Tower and the 17th century Chapel.

*ADMISSION – SEE EDITORIAL REFERENCE*

## CLAREMONT LANDSCAPE GARDEN, The National Trust

**Esher** *map K4* ♿

The earliest surviving English landscape garden, recently restored. Begun by Vanbrugh and Bridgemen before 1720, extended and naturalized by Kent. Lake, island with pavilion, grotto and turf amphitheatre, viewpoints and avenues. House not National Trust property.

**Location:** ½ m SE of Esher on E side of A307. NB: no access from A3 by-pass.
*Stations: Esher (2 m) (not Suns); Hersham (2 m); Hinchley Wood (2½ m).*
**Opening Times:** All the year. May to end of Sept—Daily 9–7 (or sunset if earlier). Oct to end of Apr—Daily 9–5 (last adm half hour before closing). *Closed Christmas Day & New Year's Day.* Adm Sun £1.30; Mon to Sat £1 (Chd half price). Guided tours (minimum 15 persons) £1 plus admission price by prior booking, telephone Bookham 53401. Wheelchairs provided. No reduction for parties. Dogs admitted on leads. Shop.
**Refreshments:** New tea room open Mar: Sat & Sun 11–4; Apr to end Oct: Tues–Sun from 11. Nov to Dec 17: Tues–Sun from 1 pm.

## COVERWOOD LAKES

**Peaslake Road, Ewhurst** *map K4*
Telephone: (0306) 731103
*(Mr & Mrs C G Metson)*

Landscaped water and cottage gardens in lovely setting between Holmbury Hill to the north and Pitch Hill to the south. Rhododendrons, azaleas, primulas, fine trees – both mature and young. Four small lakes and bog garden. Herd of pedigree Poll Hereford cattle and flock of mule sheep in the adjoining farm (Mr Nigel Metson). Garden is included in the Collins Book of British Gardens by George Plumptre and 'Gardens Open Today' – a guide to gardens open to the public through the National Gardens Scheme. It is shortly to be featured in the American publication 'Architectural Digest'.

**Location:** ½ m from Peaslake village. 8 m from Guildford. 8 m from Dorking (A25). 3 m from A25.
**Opening Times:** GARDEN ONLY: Suns Apr 30, May 14, 21, 28, 2–6.30. Adm £1, Chd (5 to 16) 50p. GARDEN AND FARM: May, Wed 31, Sun June 4, 11, 2–6.30. Adm £1.50 Chd (5 to 16) 50p. Chd under 5 free. Special reductions for large parties if arrangements made prior to visit. Plenty of free parking space. No dogs please. Suitable for disabled persons (no wheelchairs available). Open for NGS on May 21 & 28, 2–6.30.
**Refreshments:** Teas and home-made cakes available. Nearest hotel is the Hurtwood, (THF) at Peaslake village (½ m away from garden).

## DETILLENS

**Limpsfield** *map K4*
Telephone: Oxted (0883) 713342
*(Mr & Mrs D G Neville)*

Mid 15th century Wealden House, fine inglenooks, firebacks and panelling. 2½ acres of walled gardens with duck pond.

**Location:** Centre Limpsfield village opposite Bull Inn off A25.
*Station: Oxted (1 m).*
**Opening Times:** May to June—Sats; July to Sept—Weds & Sats: 2–5. *Bank Hols during above periods.* Guided tours at other times by prior arrangement. Adm £2, Chd £1.

## FARNHAM CASTLE

**Farnham** *map J4* △
*(The Church Commissioners)*

Bishop's Palace built in Norman times with Tudor and Jacobean additions. Fine Great Hall re-modelled at the Restoration.

**Location:** ½ m N of Town Centre on A287.
*Station: Farnham.*
**Opening Times:** Castle—All year Weds 2–4. Parties at other times by arrangement. Adm 70p, Chd and Students 35p. Reductions for parties. All visitors are given guided tours. Centrally heated in winter.

**Farnham Castle Keep** – See English Heritage Section.

## FEATHERCOMBE GARDENS

**Hambledon** *map J3* ♿
*(Miss Parker)*

Wide views, flowering shrubs, heathers.

**Location:** S of Godalming 2 m from Milford Station on Hambledon Road, turn to Feathercombe off road between Hydestyle crossroads and Merry Harriers pub.
**Opening Times:** GARDENS ONLY. Bank Hol Suns & Mons, Apr 30, May 1, 28, 29. 2–6. Adm 60p, Chd 10p. Picnic area. Plants for sale.

## GREATHED MANOR

**Lingfield** *map K4*
*(Country Houses Association Ltd)*

Victorian Manor house.

**Location:** On the outskirts of the village of Dormansland; 5 m SE of Lingfield.
*Stations: Dormans (1½ m); Lingfield (1½ m).*
**Opening Times:** May to Sept—Weds & Thurs 2–5. Adm £1, Chd 50p. Free car park. No dogs admitted.

## GUILDFORD HOUSE GALLERY

**Guildford** *map J4* ♿
Telephone: (0483) 444741
*(Guildford Borough Council)*

17th century town house now an art gallery. Original fine carved staircase, plaster ceilings and wrought iron window fittings. Temporary exhibitions include historical and modern paintings of local and national importance, photography and craftwork.

**Location:** 155 High Street, town centre; off A3 (1½ m).
*Station: Guildford (½ m).*
**Opening Times:** Mons to Fris 10.30–4.50, Sats 10.30–4.15. *Closed when staging exhibition.* Adm free. Suitable for disabled (ground floor).
**Refreshments:** Hotels & Restaurants in the town.

## HASCOMBE COURT

**Hascombe, Nr Godalming** *map J4*
Telephone: (048 632) 254
*(Mr & Mrs M E Pinto)*

Jekyll influences but mainly designed by Percy Cane. Herbaceous border, rhododendron garden, views, Japanese/rock garden with stream, specimen trees.

**Location:** 2½ m from Godalming off the B2130
**Opening Times:** Apr 17, May 29, July 30, Aug 28 2–6. Adm £1, Chd 10p (in aid of the National Gardens Scheme). Parties by arrangement. Car park.
**Refreshments:** White Horse Pub, Hascombe; Winkworth Arboretum.

## HATCHLANDS, The National Trust

**East Clandon** *map K4* ♿
Telephone: Guildford 222787

Built by Admiral Boscawen in 18th century, interior by Robert Adam, with later modifications. Boscawen exhibition. Garden.

**Location:** E of East Clandon on N side of Leatherhead/Guildford Road (A246).
*Station: Clandon (2 m).*
**Opening Times:** Mar 26 to Oct 15—Tues, Weds, Thurs, Suns & Bank Hol Mons only 2–6 (no admission after 5.30). Adm £2, Chd half price. Pre-booked parties £1.50 (Tues, Weds & Thurs only). No dogs. Wheelchair access to ground floor and part of the garden.
**Refreshments:** Teas.

LITTLE HOLLAND HOUSE, CHEAM—SEE UNDER LONDON

## LOSELEY HOUSE

**Guildford** *map J4* ♿ △
Telephone: Guildford (0483) 571881
*(J R More-Molyneux, Esq)*

Elizabethan mansion built 1562. Panelling, furniture, paintings, ceilings. Farm tours.

**Location:** 2½ m SW of Guildford (take B3000 off A3 through Compton); 1½ m N of Godalming (off A3100).
*Station: Farncombe (2 m).*
**Opening Times:** May 29 to Sept 30—Weds, Thurs, Fris & Sats 2–5; also Summer Bank Hol Mon 2–5. Adm £2.80, Chd £1.50. Parties of 20 and over £2.20 per person. School parties £1.30 per person. Farm shop. Farm Tours when house is open; at other times, booked parties only.
**Refreshments:** Home produce, wholefood lunches and teas.

## PAINSHILL PARK

**Portsmouth Road, Cobham** *map K4*
Telephone: (0932) 68113
*(Painshill Park Trust)*

Painshill, contemporary with Stourhead & Stowe, is one of Europe's finest eighteenth century landscape gardens. It was created by The Hon Charles Hamilton, plantsman, painter and brilliantly gifted designer, between 1738 and 1773. He transformed barren heathland into ornamental pleasure grounds and parkland of dramatic beauty and contrasting scenery, dominated by a 14 acre meandering lake fed from the river by an immense waterwheel. Garden buildings and features adorned the Park, including a magnificent Grotto, Temple, ruined Abbey, Chinese Bridge, castellated Tower, and a Mausoleum. Well maintained for 200 years in private ownership, the Park was neglected after 1948 and sank into dereliction. In 1981 the Painshill Park Trust, a registered charity, was formed to restore the gardens to their original splendour, raising the extensive funds needed for such an ambitious project. Already, after nearly 10 years, the Trust has made enormous progress, and this masterpiece is re-emerging from the wilderness.

**Location:** W of Cobham on A245. 200 yards E of A3/A245. Roundabout.
**Opening Times:** Apr 15 to Oct 14: Sats 1–6 (last ticket 5). Adm £2, Chd and OAPs £1.50. Pre-booked parties (min. 15) Sun to Fri, excl. Mon. School parties particularly welcome by arrangement with Painshill Park Education Trust. Please ring (0932) 64674 for information and bookings. Much of Park accessible for disabled (no wheelchairs available). Limited facilities and parking. NO DOGS PLEASE.
**Refreshments:** Light refreshments available.

## PINEWOOD HOUSE

**Heath House Road, Woking** *map J4*
Telephone: Brookwood (048 67) 3241
*(Mr & Mrs J van Zwanenberg)*

Four acres of garden. Stream and small lakes – ½ acre of wild garden. Large walled garden – new house built in Roman style, villa also open with oval hall and conservatory.

**Location:** Woking 4 m, Guildford 5 m. On A322 Guildford to Bagshot road, turning into Heath House Road.
**Opening Times:** Parties of not more than 25 by appointment Apr, May, June and July. Adm £1. Car parking in drive, courtyard and road. Suitable for disabled persons; ramps for wheelchairs, wide doors to W.C. (no wheelchairs available). Plants for sale. A.R.C.C. stall.
**Refreshments:** Home made teas by arrangement.

## POLESDEN LACEY, The National Trust

**nr Dorking** *map K4* ♿
Telephone: Bookham 58203 or 52048

Originally a Regency villa altered in Edwardian period. Greville collection of pictures, tapestries, furniture. 18th century garden extended 1906, with herbaceous borders, rose garden, clipped hedges, lawns, beeches. Views.

**Location:** 3 m NW of Dorking, reached via Great Bookham (A246) & then road leading S (1½ m).
*Stations: Boxhill or Bookham (both 2½ m).*
**Opening Times:** Mar & Nov—Sats & Suns 1.30–4.30; Apr to end of Oct—Weds to Suns 1.30–5.30. Last adm half hour before closing. Open Good Friday. Open Bank Hol Mons & preceding Suns 11–5.30. Garden open daily all year, 11–sunset. No dogs in formal gardens. Adm Garden only Apr to end Oct £1.20, Nov to end Mar £1. House: Sun & Bank Holiday Mon £1.80 extra. Other open days £1.30 extra. Chd half-price. *Party reductions on Weds, Thurs & Fris only by prior arrangement with the Administrator.* Wheelchairs admitted & provided. Shop open at same times as restaurant.
**Refreshments:** Licensed Restaurant in the grounds; Mar—Sat & Sun only 11–2.30 & 3–5; Apr to end Oct—Weds to Suns & Bank Hol Mons 11–2.30 & 3–6; Nov to mid-Dec—Weds to Suns 11–2.30 & 3–5. Tel Bookham 56190.

## PYRFORD COURT

**nr Woking** *map J4*
Telephone: Woking (048 62) 65880
*(Mr & Mrs C. Laikin)*

Twenty acres of wild and formal gardens, azaleas, wisteria, rhododendrons, pink marble fountain, venetian bridge.

**Location:** 2 m E of Woking, B367 junction with Upshott Lane, M25 (exit 10) on to A3 towards Guildford, off to Ripley signposted Pyrford.
**Opening Times:** Suns May 21, 28, 2–6.30. Sun, Oct 22 12–4. Adults £1, Chd 50p. Open in aid of National Gardens Scheme. For details of operas/concerts and other events in the house please phone above number.
**Refreshments:** Tea and home made cakes.

## RAMSTER

**Chiddingfold** *map J3*
Telephone: (0428) 4422
*(Mr & Mrs Paul Gunn)*

Mature 20 acre woodland garden of exceptional interest. Laid out by Gauntlett Nurseries of Chiddingfold in early 1900's. Fine rhododendrons, azaleas, camellias, magnolias, trees and shrubs in lovely setting.

**Location:** On A283 1½ m S of Chiddingfold.
**Opening Times:** GARDEN ONLY. Apr 22 to June 11—Daily 2–6. Adm £1, Chd 20p. Parties by arrangement. *Share to National Gardens Scheme.*
**Refreshments:** Teas Sats, Suns & Bank Hol Mons in May only.

### VANN
**Hambledon** *map J3*
Telephone: Wormley (042 879) 3413
*(Mr & Mrs M. B. Caröe)*

16th to 20th century house surrounded by 5 acre 'paradise' garden. Water garden by Gertrude Jekyll 1911.

**Location:** 6 m S of Godalming; A283 to Chiddingfold; turn off at green, signposted Vann Lane at P.O.
*Station: Witley (2 m).*
**Opening Times:** GARDENS ONLY: Apr 17–22, May 2–6, 22–27, June 19–24, 10–6. Suns—Apr 16, May 21, June 18, Bank Holiday Mon May 1, 2–7 and by prior appointment Easter–Sept (Tel: Wormley 3413). Plant and vegetable stall. Party bookings and guided tours with morning coffee, lunches or home made teas in house by arrangement. Adm £1, Chd 20p. In aid of National Gardens Scheme and Hambledon Charities.
**Refreshments:** Home made teas in house, Apr 16, Bank Hol Mon May 1, May 21 and June 18 only.

WHITEHALL, CHEAM—SEE UNDER LONDON

### WINKWORTH ARBORETUM, The National Trust
**nr Godalming** *map J3* ♿

99 acres of trees and shrubs planted mainly for Spring and Autumn colour. Two lakes, fine views.

**Location:** 2 m SE of Godalming on E side of B2130.
*Station: Godalming (2 m).*
**Opening Times:** Open all the year during daylight hours. Adm £1, Chd 50p. No reduction for parties. *Coach parties please book to ensure parking space and refreshments.* Bookings Tearoom Concessionaire, The Homestead, Cottage Lane, Thorncombe Street, Bramley, Guildford GU5 0LT. Dogs must be kept under control. Wheelchair access.
**Refreshments:** Apr to end of Oct—Tues, Weds, Thurs, Fris, Sats, Suns & Bank Hol Mons 2–6 or dusk if earlier. *Closed Tues following Bank Hols.* Also open weekends and some other fine days in Mar.

### WISLEY GARDEN
**Wisley** *map K4* ♿
*(The Royal Horticultural Society)*

British gardening at its best in all aspects. 250 acres of glorious garden. The wooded slopes with massed rhododendrons and azaleas, the wild daffodils of the alpine meadow, the calm of the pinetum, the gaiety of the herbaceous border, the banked mounds of heathers, the new alpine house, the panorama of the rock garden, the model fruit and vegetable gardens and the range of greenhouse displays are there waiting for you to enjoy them and to learn from them.

**Location:** In Wisley just off M25 Junction 10, on A3. London 22 m, Guildford 7 m.
**Opening Times:** All the year—Mons to Sats 10–7 (or sunset if earlier). *Sundays – members & their guests only. Closed Christmas Day.* Adm £2.50, Chd £1. A reduction for parties – tickets for parties must be obtained 14 days in advance of visit. Dogs not admitted other than guide dogs. Information centre, Shop & Plant sales centre.
**Refreshments:** Licensed restaurant in garden (Jan 7 to mid Dec) & licensed cafeteria.

## EAST SUSSEX

### ALFRISTON CLERGY HOUSE, The National Trust
**Alfriston, nr Seaford** *map K3*
Telephone: Alfriston (0323) 870001

Bought in 1896, the first building acquired by the Trust. Possibly a parish priest's house, c. 1350.

**Location:** 4 m NE of Seaford just E of B2108; adjoining The Tye & St Andrew's Church.
*Station: Berwick (2½ m).*
**Opening Times:** Exhibition Room, Medieval Hall, two other rooms & Garden. Mar 24 to end Oct—Daily 11–6 (or sunset if earlier). Last adm half-hour before closing. Adm 80p, Chd 40p. Pre-booked parties 60p. Shop (open until Christmas). No dogs. Unsuitable for wheelchairs.

### BATEMAN'S, The National Trust
**Burwash** *map L3* △
Telephone: Burwash 882302

Built 1634. Rudyard Kipling lived here. Water-mill restored by the National Trust. Attractive garden, yew hedges, lawns, daffodils and wild garden.

**Location:** ½ m S of Burwash on the Lewes/Etchingham Road (A265).
**Opening Times:** Mar 24 to end of Oct—Daily (except Thurs & Fris but open Good Fri) 11–6. Last adm 5. Adm House, Mill & Garden £2.50, Chd £1.30, weekends & Bank Hols £2.80, Chd £1.40. Pre-booked parties £2.20., Chd £1.10, weekends and Bank Holidays £2.50, Chd £1.30. No dogs.
**Refreshments:** Tea room: coffees, light lunches and teas, open as House.

### BATTLE ABBEY
*map L3*
Telephone: (04246) 3792
*(English Heritage)*

The Battle of Hastings, 1066—the best-known date in English history. Battle Abbey was built by William the Conqueror as a thanksgiving for his victory, with the high altar on the spot where King Harold died. The church has yet to be fully excavated, but visitors may walk over the battlefield, and see the remains of many of the domestic buildings of the monastery and watch a film on the battle.

**Location:** Battle. OS map ref TQ749157.
**Opening Times:** Good Friday to Sept 30, daily 10–6; Oct 1 to Maundy Thurs, daily 10–4. *Closed* Dec 24–26, Jan 1. Adm £1.60, OAPs £1.20, Chd 80p.

**Bayham Abbey** – See English Heritage Section.

### BEECHES FARM
**nr Uckfield** *map L3* △
*(Mrs Vera Thomas)*

16th century tile hung farm house. Lawns, yew trees, borders, sunken garden, roses, fine views.

**Location:** Off A2102, Buckham Hill 1½ m W Uckfield (on Isfield Road).
*Station: Uckfield (1½ m).*
**Opening Times:** All the year—Daily 10–5. Adm Gardens 25p. House (by appointment) 75p. Suns May 7, July 9 & Nov 26. *In aid of National Gardens' Scheme,* and on June 11 *Winged Fellowship.*

### BODIAM CASTLE, The National Trust
**nr Robertsbridge** *map L3* ♿
Telephone: Staplecross (058 083) 436

Built 1385–9, one of the best preserved examples of medieval moated military architecture.

**Location:** 3 m S of Hawkhurst; 1 m E of A229.
**Opening Times:** Mar 24 to Oct 31 incl. Good Fri. Daily 10–6 (or sunset if earlier). Nov to Mar 23—Mons to Sats only. 10–sunset. Last adm half-hour before closing. *Closed Dec 25 to 28.* Adm £1.30, Chd 70p. *Parties of 15 or more by prior arrangement £1, Chd 50p.* Car park free to members. Museum. Audio visual. Shop. Dogs admitted except in shop & museum. Wheelchair access.
**Refreshments:** Tea room, Mar 24 to end Oct.

### BRICKWALL HOUSE
**Northiam, Rye** *map L3*
Telephone: Northiam (07974) 2494 or Curator, Rye 223329
*(Frewen Educational Trust)*

Home of the Frewen family since 1666. 17th century drawing room with superb 17th century plaster ceilings, and family portraits spanning 400 years of history. Grand staircase. Chess garden and arboretum.

**Location:** 7 m NW of Rye on B2088.
**Opening Times:** Apr to end Sept—Sats and Bank Holiday Mons 2–5; Adm £1, OAPs half price. Open at other times by prior arrangement with the curator.

## CHARLESTON FARMHOUSE
**Firle, nr Lewes** *map K3*
Telephone: Ripe (032 183) 265
*(The Charleston Trust)*

17/18th century farmhouse, the home of Vanessa and Clive Bell and Duncan Grant from 1916 until Grant's death in 1978. House and contents decorated by the artists; traditional flint-walled flower garden of the period.

**Location:** 6 m E of Lewes, on A27, between Firle and Selmeston.
*Station: Lewes 6 m; Berwick 3 m.*
**Opening Times:** Mar 25, 26, 27; Apr 1 to Oct 29—Weds, Thurs, Sats (Guided Tours) and Suns and Bank Hol Mons (unguided), 2–6 (last adm 5). Kitchen open Thurs only. Adm £3; car park 50p (no parking charge midweek Apr, May, Oct). Coaches by prior appointment only. Numbers in the House will be limited; no dogs. Student/OAP/UB40 concessions midweek throughout the season, also weekends Apr, May, Oct. Contact Charleston Office at Farmhouse.

## COBBLERS GARDEN
**Crowborough** *map K3*
*(Mr & Mrs Martin Furniss)*

2 acre garden on sloping site designed and planted by owners since 1968 in informal manner for all-season colour; large range of herbaceous and shrub species; water garden. Featured in RHS Journal, Mar 1978 and two BBC television programmes Aug 1978, 'Country Life' and 'Homes & Gardens' 1981.

**Location:** At Crowborough Cross (A26) turn on to B2100 (signposted Crowborough station & Rotherfield); at 2nd crossroads turn right into Tollwood Road.
*Station: Crowborough (1 m).*
**Opening Times:** GARDEN ONLY—Suns May 21, 28; June 11, 18, 25; July 9, 16, 23; Aug 6, 13. Times 2.30–5.30. Adm £1, Chd 50p. *In aid of National Gardens Scheme and The National Trust.* No dogs please. Plants for sale.
**Refreshments:** Home made teas.

## FILCHING MANOR
**Jevington Road, Wannock, nr. Polegate** *map L3*
Telephone: (03212) 7838/7124
*(Paul Foulkes-Halbard)*

A magnificent example of medieval construction, with central hall open to the roof, the Buttery, (now the drawing room), minstrels' gallery considered to be unique. The oak panelling between the hall and the drawing room represents the earliest type known. An underground passage runs from the cellars to a considerable distance, and is probably an ancient escape hole. The Manor is set in 28 acres of Sussex downland and formal gardens. A special feature of the Manor is the unique and exclusive collection of some of the rarest sports and racing cars in the world, including the 1937 world record breaking Bluebird, piloted by Sir Malcolm Campbell. Antiquities, arms and armour can also be seen in an historic Manor house which is also very much a family home.

**Location:** 1¼ m from A22 at Polegate Crossroads. 5 m N of Eastbourne.
**Opening Times:** Mar to Oct, Thurs to Sun 10.30–4.30, also Bank Holidays. Open at other times by prior appointment. Adm £2, Chd/OAPs £1. Reductions for parties of 10 or more, £1 per person. **Parties must book in advance.** Suitable for disabled, and special toilet facilities for the disabled.
**Refreshments:** Light refreshments.

## FIRLE PLACE
**nr Lewes** *map K3* △
Telephone: Glynde (079 159) 335
*(Viscount Gage)*

Important collection of Italian, Dutch and English pictures. Notable Sèvres porcelain, French and English furniture and objects of American interest.

**Location:** 5 m SE of Lewes on the Lewes/Eastbourne Road (A27).
*Station: Glynde (1½ m) or Lewes (5 m, taxis available).*
**Opening Times:** June, July, Aug & Sept—Weds, Thurs & Suns. Also Easter, May, Spring & Summer Bank Hol Suns & Mons: 2 last tickets 5. First Wed in month longer, unguided Connoisseurs' tour of House. Pre-booked group parties of 25 on Open Days (except first Wed in month) at reduced rate. Special exclusive viewings at other times of year for parties over 30 by arrangement. *Party bookings in writing to Showing Secretary, Firle Place, Nr Lewes, East Sussex BN8 6LP (079 159) 335.*
**Refreshments:** Cold buffet luncheon 12.30–2; Sussex cream teas from 3. Shop and contemporary pictures exhibition. Car park adjacent to house.

## GLYNDE PLACE
**nr Lewes** *map K3* △
Telephone: Glynde (079 159) 337
*(Viscount Hampden)*

Beautiful example of 16th century architecture. Pictures, bronzes, historical documents.

**Location:** 4 m SE of Lewes on Eastbourne/Lewes Road (A27) or A265.
*Station: Glynde (½ m).*
**Opening Times:** June 1 to Sept 29—Weds & Thurs and first and last Sun of each month 2.15–5.30 (last adm 5). Open Easter Sun & Mon and Bank Hols. House open for guided tours by prior arrangement (25 or more £1.80 per person). Adm £2.20, Chd £1. Garden only 75p (rebate on entry into house). Free parking.
**Refreshments:** Home-baked teas in Coach House (parties to book in advance).

## GREAT DIXTER
**Northiam** *map L3* △
Telephone: (07974) 3160
*(Quentin Lloyd, Esq)*

15th century half-timbered manor house in a Lutyens designed garden.

**Location:** ½ m N of Northiam; 8 m NW of Rye; 12 m N of Hastings. Just off A28.
**Opening Times:** Good Friday Mar 24 to Sun Oct 15—Daily except Mons (but open all Bank Hol Mons) also weekends Oct 21, 22, 28, 29; open 2 until last adm at 5. Gardens open at 11 on May 27, 28, 29. Suns in July & Aug, also Aug 28. Adm House & Gardens £2.25, Chd 50p. Gardens only £1.50, Chd 25p. Concessions to OAPs and NT members on Fris £1.90 – House and Gardens. Adult guided garden tour for groups £2.75 (minimum charge £19), ask for details. No dogs.
**Refreshments:** Locally, ask for list.

## HAREMERE HALL
**Etchingham** *map L3*
Telephone: Etchingham 245
*(Jacqueline, Lady Killearn)*

Early 17th century Manor House with Minstrel staircase, panelled Great Hall, carved doors and Flemish fireplace. Period furniture. Collections of rugs, ornaments, pottery, plate from Middle and Far East. Terraced gardens.

**Location:** On A265 between Etchingham & Hurst Green; N of Battle.
*Station: Etchingham (5 mins walk).*

# The National Trust in EAST SUSSEX

## BODIAM CASTLE

NEAR ROBERTSBRIDGE

## SHEFFIELD PARK GARDEN

## ALFRISTON CLERGY HOUSE

## BATEMAN'S

BURWASH

*ADMISSION — SEE EDITORIAL REFERENCE*

## FIRLE PLACE

near Lewes, East Sussex

Home of the Gage family since the 15th century. The original Tudor house was largely altered about 1730.

The House contains an important collection of European and English Old Masters. The pictures are further enhanced with French and English furniture by famous craftsmen. Also a quantity of Sèvres china of the finest quality. All these are largely derived from the Cowper collection and can be seen in a lovely spacious family setting.

*Duncan McNeil photograph*

House is set in parkland under the South Downs. 55 miles from London by road. Hourly rail service Victoria to Lewes takes 64 minutes, thence by taxi (5 miles).

Through General Gage, Commander-in-Chief of the British forces at the beginning of the War of Independence, and his wife Margaret Kemble of New Jersey there are items of particular interest to visitors from the USA.

OPENING TIMES

June to September: Wednesdays, Thursdays and Sundays: Connoisseurs unguided tours 1st Wednesday of month; Easter, May, Spring and Summer Bank Holiday Sundays and Mondays. Open 2 to 5 pm (last admission). Exclusive private viewing for groups 30+ on application. Prices under review at time of going to press.

**Opening Times:** GARDENS—Daily from Easter to Oct 31. SHIRE HORSE FARM—Daily (not Mons except Bank Hols) from Easter to Oct 31 (demonstrations at 11 & 3). HOUSE open to public Bank Hol weekends 2–5—otherwise to parties of 25 or more by appointment. Hall, Grounds & Gardens £2.50; Gardens only 70p. Party, Chd, OAPs discounts. Registered with English Tourist Board. 5 star accommodation, 4-poster beds, etc, by arrangement with House Manager—brochure and tariff on request.
**Refreshments:** Luncheon & tea for parties by appointment. Guests for Glyndebourne Opera Festival and Christmas breaks a speciality.

## KIDBROOKE PARK WITH REPTON GROUNDS

**Forest Row** *map K3*
*(The Council of Michael Hall School)*

Sandstone house and stables built in 1730s with later alterations.

**Location:** 1 m SW of Forest Row, off A22, 4 m S of East Grinstead.
**Opening Times:** Spring Bank Hol Mon (May 30) then Aug—Daily (inc Bank Hol Mon), 9–6. Application for admission to the Bursar.

## LAMB HOUSE, The National Trust

**Rye** *map L3*

Georgian house with garden. Home of Henry James from 1898 to 1916.

**Location:** In West Street facing W end of church.
*Station: Rye (½ m).*
**Opening Times:** House (Hall & 3 rooms only) & Garden. Apr to end of Oct—Weds & Sats 2–6 (last admission 5.30). Adm £1. No reduction for children or parties. No dogs. Unsuitable for wheelchairs. No lavatories.

## MICHELHAM PRIORY

**nr Hailsham** *map L3* △ ♿
*(Sussex Archaeological Society)*

Founded in 1229 this Augustinian Priory is surrounded by one of the largest moats in England. Elizabethan wing and 14th century gatehouse. Special exhibitions and events. Tudor barn. Working Watermill restored, grinding wholemeal flour.

**Location:** ½ m E of Upper Dicker just off London/Eastbourne Road (A22); 10 m N of Eastbourne.
**Opening Times:** Mar 25 to Oct 31—Daily 11–5.30. Adm (inc Watermill) £2, OAPs £1.80, Chd (5–16) £1. Reduction for parties booked in advance. *No dogs. 1989:* Sussex Crafts & Small Industries Aug 2–6. Festival of Music & Art and Activities week in Aug & many other events.
**Refreshments:** At licensed restaurants in Grounds.

## MONKS HOUSE, The National Trust

**Rodmell** *map K3*

A small village house and garden. The home of Virginia and Leonard Woolf from 1919 until his death in 1969. House administered and largely maintained by tenants.

**Location:** 3 m SE of Lewes, off C7 in Rodmell village.
*Station: Southease (1 m).*
**Opening Times:** Mar 25 to end Apr and Oct—Weds & Sats 2–5; May to end Sept—Weds & Sats 2–6 (last adm ½ hour before closing time). Adm £1.20. No reduction for children or parties. No dogs. Unsuitable for wheelchairs. Maximum of 15 people in house at any one time. Narrow access road.

## NEWICK PARK

**Lewes** *map K5*
Telephone: (082 572) 3633
*(Viscount Brentford)*

Originally an Elizabethan ironmasters house c.1580 this lovely country house is predominantly Georgian (Grade II listed). Home of Viscount Brentford, with some fine furniture and porcelain. The house is open for functions and conferences. Set in 240 acres of farm and parkland. 12 acres of garden (Grade II listed) over Tudor mine workings include specimen ferns, trees and extensive collection of camellias, azaleas and rhododendrons. Beautiful spring flowers, many species over 100 years old. Other interesting features are 19th century ice house, walled garden with herb nursery. Elizabethan hammer ponds, lakeside walk. National collection of candelabra and sikkimensis primulas.

**Location:** Lewes 7 m to S, 1 m A272, Haywards Heath 7 m to W, 1 m A275, Uckfield 5 m to E, 3 m A22.
**Opening Times:** GARDENS: Mar 15–Oct 31, 10.30–6; Adm £1, OAPs 75p, Chd 25p. Reductions for parties 75p per head (4 or more). Car parking for 50 cars, room for up to 6 coaches. Suitable for disabled persons (no wheelchairs).
**Refreshments:** For garden visitors: teas, lunches (by arrangement). House: available for functions, special parties, day and residential conferences, promotional events.

**Pevensey Castle** – See English Heritage Section.

## PRESTON MANOR

**Brighton** *map K3*
Telephone: (0273) 603005
*(Borough of Brighton)*

Georgian house with Edwardian additions. Contains a notable collection of fine furniture, silver, porcelain and pictures. Servants' quarters now open.

**Location:** On main Brighton to London Road at Preston Park.
*Station: Preston Park.*
**Opening Times:** All the year—Tues–Sun 10–5. Closed Mons (except Bank Hols) Good Fri, Christmas & Boxing Day. Admission charge. *Reduced rates for parties, families, Chd and OAPs.* Garden free. Parties by arrangement.

## ROYAL PAVILION

**Brighton** *map K3* ♿
Telephone: (0273) 603005

Spectacular seaside palace of the Prince Regent, transformed by John Nash (1815–1822) into one of the most dazzlingly exotic buildings in the British Isles. Interiors furnished in the Chinese style.

**Location:** In centre of Brighton (Old Steine).
*Station: Brighton (¾ m).*
**Opening Times:** All the year—Daily 10–5 (June to Sept 10–6). *Closed Christmas Day & Boxing Day.* Admission charge. *Reduced rates for parties, families, children and OAPs.* Ground floor accessible for the disabled.
**Refreshments:** Tearoom.

# MICHELHAM PRIORY

**Upper Dicker, near HAILSHAM, EAST SUSSEX**

*(Sussex Archaeological Society)*

Augustinian Priory founded 1229 on an earlier island site, became a Tudor farmhouse in the 16th century. Owned by the Sackville family 1603–1897. Beautiful grounds enclosed by a medieval moat. Imposing 14th century Gate House. Period Furniture. Tapestries. Sussex Ironwork, Stained Glass, Musical Instruments Collection, Doll's House. Forge and Wheelwright's Shop. Wagons. Art Exhibitions in Great Barn. Sussex Craft Shop. Working Watermill grinding wholemeal flour. 'Physic' Garden. Picnic area and childrens playground.

Open March 25th to October 31st
DAILY 11 am to 5.30 pm
Tel. Hailsham (0323) 844224

MORNING COFFEES,
FARMHOUSE
LUNCHEONS
and SUSSEX TEAS
served daily

Also buffet service available during peak periods.

*Special Events 1989*

SUSSEX CRAFTS
AND
SMALL INDUSTRIES
EXHIBITION
August 2nd to 6th

FESTIVAL OF MUSIC AND
ART AND ACTIVITIES WEEK

Many other events.

# HAREMERE HALL

**ETCHINGHAM, EAST SUSSEX**

The history of the Manor of Haremere dates from the 12th Century when there is mention of Miles de Haremere. The present house, home of Jacqueline Lady Killearn – widow of Baron Killearn of Killearn, former Ambassador to Egypt, was built in 1616 and has many original fireplaces. It is full of 17th and 18th Century panelling, whilst the twisted balusters on the main staircase date from 1682, the time when improvements were first made to the house. Subsequent alterations mostly date from the 19th Century. The west wing, which is the oldest part of the house, has two small stained glass windows which bear the dates 1509 ad 1603 and which were probably taken from an earlier house on the site.

# NEWICK PARK

**Newick, E. Sussex**

*ADMISSION – SEE EDITORIAL REFERENCE*

# Brighton

## The Royal Pavilion

*The most fantastic palace in Europe   Open Daily 10am–5pm   Why not also visit . . .*

## Preston Manor

A charming Edwardian Manor House which through it's notable collection of furniture, pictures and memorabilia powerfully evokes the feeling of the period. Fascinating servants quarters now open.

**For further information telephone 0273 603005**

## SHEFFIELD PARK GARDEN, The National Trust

**nr Uckfield** *map K3* ♿
Telephone: Danehill 790655

Large garden with series of lakes linked by cascades; great variety of unusual shrubs.

**Location:** Midway between East Grinstead & Lewes on E side of A275; 5 m NW of Uckfield.
**Opening Times:** Mar 25 to Nov 5—Tues to Sats (closed Good Fri) 11–6 or sunset if earlier; Suns and Bank Hol Mons 2–6 or sunset if earlier. Suns during Oct & Nov: 1–sunset. Last adm one hour before closing. *Closed Tues following Bank Hol Mons.* Liable to overcrowding Suns & Bank Hols. Adm May, Oct & Nov £2.80, Chd £1.40; Mar, Apr & June to Sept £2.20, Chd £1.10. Pre-booked parties £2.10 & £1.60 according to season. *No reduction for parties on Sats, Suns & Bank Hols.* No dogs. Shop. Wheelchairs available.

# WEST SUSSEX

## ARUNDEL CASTLE

**Arundel** *map J3* ♿
Telephone: Arundel 883136
*(Arundel Castle Trustees Ltd.)*

This great castle, situated in magnificent grounds overlooking the River Arun, was built at the end of the 11th century by Roger de Montgomery, Earl of Arundel. It has been the seat of the Dukes of Norfolk and their ancestors for over seven hundred years. Badly damaged in 1643, the castle was restored by the 8th, 11th and 15th Dukes in the 18th and 19th centuries. Fine furniture, tapestries, clocks and portraits by Van Dyck, Gainsborough, Reynolds, Mytens, Lawrence etc. Fitzalan Chapel. Host to Arundel Festival at the end of August each year, which attracts international artists.

**Location:** In Arundel 9 m W of Worthing: 10 m E of Chichester. Entrance for cars and pedestrians: Lower Lodge Mill Road.
*Station: Arundel (¾ m).*
**Opening Times:** Mar 24 to Oct 27—Suns to Fris 1–5 (during June, July & Aug and all Bank Hols 12–5). Last adm any day 4 pm. *The Castle is NOT open on Sats.* Adm charges not available at time of going to press. No dogs. *Special rates for organised parties.*

## BERRI COURT

**Yapton** *map J3*
Telephone: (0243) 551 663
(Mr & Mrs J. C. Turner)

3-acre garden of wide interest, trees, flowering shrubs, heathers, eucalyptus, daffodils, shrub roses, hydrangeas.

**Location:** Centre of Yapton village.
*Station: Barnham (1¾ m).*
**Opening Times:** Suns, Mons, Apr 16, 17, May 14, 15, June 25, 26, Oct 22, 23. 2–4. Adm 70p, Chd 30p. In aid of National Gardens Scheme. Dogs on leads.

## BORDE HILL GARDEN

**Haywards Heath** *map K3*
Telephone: Haywards Heath (0444) 450326

Large garden with woods and parkland of exceptional beauty. Rare trees and shrubs, herbaceous borders and fine views. Woodland Walk, water feature, new lake.

**Location:** 1½ m N of Haywards Heath on Balcombe Road. Brighton 17 m; Gatwick 10 m.
*Station: Haywards Heath (1½ m).*
**Opening Times:** Open daily from Good Friday to last weekend in Oct 10–6. Adm £1.50, Chd 50p: parties of 20 or more £1. Parking free. Picnic area. Interesting plants for sale. Dogs allowed on lead.
**Refreshments:** Licensed—morning coffee, snacks, afternoon tea; full meals by arrangement.

## CHICHESTER CATHEDRAL

**West Street** *map J3*
Telephone: Chichester 782595
*(The Dean & Chapter of Chichester)*

In the heart of the city, this fine Cathedral has been a centre of Christian worship and community life for 900 years. Site of Shrine of St Richard of Chichester; Romanesque stone carvings; works by Sutherland, Feibusch, Procktor, Chagall, Skelton, Piper, and new Anglo/German tapestry. Treasury. Cloister. Refectory. Shop. Vicars' close and hall.

**Location:** Centre of city; British Rail; A27, A286.
**Opening Times:** All year 7.10–7 (6 in winter). Choral Evensong daily (except Weds) during term time; occasionally visiting choirs at other times. Ministry of welcome operates. Guided tours must be booked. No dogs except guide dogs. Wheelchair access (one wheelchair available on application to Vergers). Adm free: suggested donations Adults £1, Chd 20p. Parking in city car parks.
**Refreshments:** Refectory off Cathedral Cloisters with lavatory facilities (including those for the disabled).

## COATES MANOR

**nr Fittleworth** *map J3*
*(Mrs G. H. Thorp)*

One acre garden, mainly shrubs and foliage of special interest.

**Location:** ½ m S of Fittleworth; SE of Petworth; turn off B2138 signposted 'Coates'.
**Opening Times:** GARDEN ONLY. Sun, Mon & Tues June 18, 19 & 20, 11–6. Adm 75p, Chd 20p. Also by appointment. *In aid of National Gardens Scheme.*
**Refreshments:** Tea & cakes.

## DANNY

**Hurstpierpoint** *map K3*
*(Country Houses Association Ltd)*

Elizabethan E-shaped house, dating from 1593.

**Location:** Between Hassocks and Hurstpierpoint.
*Station: Hassocks (1 m).*
**Opening Times:** May to Sept—Weds & Thurs 2–5. Adm £1, Chd 50p. Free car park. No dogs admitted.

## DENMANS

**Fontwell** *map J3* ♿
Telephone: Eastergate (024 368) 2808
*(Mrs J. H. Robinson)*

Unique 20th century walled garden extravagantly planted for overall, all-year interest in form, colour and texture; areas of glass for tender species. John Brookes School of Garden Design at Clock House, short courses throughout the season.

**Location:** Between Arundel and Chichester; turn off A27 into Denmans Lane (W of Fontwell racecourse).
*Station: Barnham (2 m).*
**Opening Times:** Tues Mar 21 to Sun Oct 29, 10–5—Daily except Mons. Coaches by appointment. Adm £1.60, Chd £1, OAPs £1.40. Groups of 15 or more £1.30. Plant centre. The Country Shop. No dogs. National Gardens Scheme.
**Refreshments:** Teas shop open 11–5.

## DUCKYLS

**Sharpthorne** *map K3*
Telephone: (0342) 810352
*(Mr & Mrs Michael Taylor)*

Twelve acre terraced and woodland garden being gradually restored with collection of azaleas, rhododendrons, camellias; woodland walk, fine views, interesting primroses and auricula.

**Location:** B2028 S Sharpthorne. 3 m East Grinstead.
**Opening Times:** Sun Apr 16, Tues Apr 18, 25, May 2, 9, Sun May 14, Tues May 16, 23, 30. Adm £1, Chd 25p. *In aid of National Gardens Scheme.* Parties by arrangement. Car park. Suitable for disabled persons.
**Refreshments:** Teas etc. at house. White Hart Inn, Ardingly Road, Cat Inn, West Hoathly.

## GOODWOOD HOUSE

**Chichester** *map J3*
Telephone: Chichester (0243) 774107
*(Duke of Richmond)*

Bought by the first Duke of Richmond (son of King Charles II and a French female spy!) and home of the Dukes of Richmond ever since, Goodwood House is filled with the treasures collected by all nine Dukes. They include Canalettos, snuff boxes, tapestries, family portraits by Van Dyck, Kneller, Lely, Reynolds, etc; French commodes (!) and Sevres porcelain bought by the Third Duke when (a very bad) British Ambassador at Versailles. There are royal relics. Napoleonic booty and the bits and pieces inevitable after a family has stayed put for 300 years. Chambers, then Wyatt, enlarged the House to hold these Collections. Country Park near the Racecourse on crest of South Downs. Pleasure flights available from the Goodwood Aerodrome together with flying instruction to top standards. Dressage Championships (National & International) and other events in Goodwood Park. Glorious Goodwood Racecourse.

**Location:** 3½ m NE of Chichester, approach roads A285 & A286, A27. Aerodrome 1 m from House.
**Opening Times:** Easter Sun & Mon then Apr 30 to Oct 2—Suns & Mons (except June 18, 25, July 9 and event days); also Tues, Weds & Thurs in Aug, 2–5. Large free car park for visitors to House during open hours; House suitable for wheelchairs (no steps); a wheelchair available; Goodwood souvenirs and prints for sale. For all information & group rates contact the House Secretary, Goodwood House, Chichester, West Sussex.
**Refreshments:** Teas in the State Supper Room for pre-booked parties (min 20); unbooked teas for individuals and families on days when no evening function, or tea and biscuits at The Goodwood Park Hotel Golf and Country Club at the Park Gate (east).

## HAMMERWOOD PARK

**nr East Grinstead** *map K3* △
Telephone: Cowden (0342) 850594 or Woldingham (088 385) 2366
*(David Pinnegar, Esq)*

Set in 37 acres on the edge of the Ashdown Forest the house was built in 1792 by Latrobe, the architect of The White House and The Capitol, Washington D.C., U.S.A. Although this was his first work it was forgotten for many years. Extensive restoration works have been completed and won numerous awards. Hammerwood Park houses a copy of the Elgin Marbles, various changing exhibitions and the largest private dress collection in the South East. Guided tours, cream teas and musical evenings bring the house to life.

**Location:** 3½ m E of East Grinstead on A264 to Tunbridge Wells; 1 m W of Holtye.
**Opening Times:** Easter Mon to end of Sept—Weds, Sats & Bank Hol Mons 2–5.30. Coaches by appointment only. Adm House and Park £2. Additional tours on Weds – 2 pm Garden restoration, £2. 3.30 Dress Collection, £2.

## HEASELANDS

**Haywards Heath** *map K3*
*(Mrs Ernest Kleinwort)*

Over 30 acres of garden with flowering shrubs and trees; water gardens; woodland; small collection of waterfowl.

**Location:** 1 m SW of Haywards Heath Hospital on A273 to Burgess Hill.
*Station: Haywards Heath (1½ m).*
**Opening Times:** GARDEN ONLY. Weds—May 10, 17 & 24; Suns—May 14, 21 & 28, also Sun July 23, 2–6. Parties by arrangement for Autumn colour. Adm £1.20, Chd 30p. Cars free. *In aid of National Gardens Scheme and World Wildlife.* Coaches by appointment. No dogs.
**Refreshments:** At the house.

## THE HIGH BEECHES GARDENS

**Handcross** *map K3*
Telephone: Handcross (0444) 400589
*(The High Beeches Conservation Trust)*

Sixteen acres of enchanting woodland valley gardens, planted with Magnolias, Camellias, Rhododendrons and Azelias, set among sheets of Daffodils and Bluebells in Spring. In Autumn, this is one of the most brilliant gardens for leaf colour, superbly landscaped with Maples, Liquidambers, Amelanchiers and Nyssas. Gentians, Primulas and Iris are naturalised, with Royal Fern and Gunnera in the Water Gardens. There is also three acres of native Wild Flower Meadow, with many species attractive to butterflies.

**Location:** 1 m E of A23 at Handcross On B2110.
**Opening Times:** GARDENS ONLY. Easter Mon to Jun 17 and Sept 18 to Oct 29—daily 1–5 *except Weds and Suns.* Special event with plant stall and bazaar on Sun Oct 29, 10–5. Bank Hols also 10–5. Adm £1.50, accompanied Chd free. Guided tour for parties by appointment all year. Landscaped picnic area, toilets and barn shelter. Free car park. No dogs.
**Refreshments:** Home-made teas and snacks on Spring Bank Hols and Oct 29 only.

## LEONARDSLEE GARDENS

**Horsham** *map K3*
*(The Loder Family)*
**Centenary Year 1889–1989**

Extensive spring-flowering shrub garden, listed Grade I, in a valley filled with Rhododendrons, Azaleas and magnificent trees by a series of beautiful lakes. Striking Autumn Tints. Wallabies and Sika Deer. Rock Garden and Wishing Well.

**Location:** In Lower Beeding, 4½ m SE of Horsham at junction of A279 & A281; 3 m SW of Handcross at bottom of M23.
**Opening Times:** Spring: Apr 15 to June 18—Daily 10–6. Summer: July, Aug & Sept—Weekends only 12–6. Autumn: Oct—Weekends 10–5. Adm May £2.50 (*50p surcharge on May 14, 21, 28 & 29*), Apr, June & Oct £2, July, Aug & Sept: £1.50, Chd £1. Coaches welcome by arrangement. Tel: Lower Beeding (040 376) 212. *No dogs please.* Large selection of plants for sale.
**Refreshments:** New cafeteria; salad bar and teas.

## MALT HOUSE

**Chithurst, nr Midhurst** *map J3*
Telephone: Rogate (073 080)433
*(Mr & Mrs Graham Ferguson)*

Approximately 4 acres; flowering shrubs including exceptional rhododendrons and azaleas, leading to 60 acres of lovely woodland walks.

**Location:** 3½ m W of Midhurst via A272, turn N to Chithurst cont 1½ m; or via A3, 2 m S of Liphook turn SE to Milland and Chithurst.
**Opening Times:** GARDEN ONLY. Suns—Apr 23 to May 28; Bank Hol Mons; May 1 & 29, 2–6. Adm 80p, Chd 40p. *In aid of National Gardens Scheme.* Also open by appointment for parties. Plants for sale.
**Refreshments:** Tea and biscuits.

## NEW HALL

**Small Dole, Henfield** *map K3*
Telephone: Henfield (0273) 492546
*(Mr & Mrs J. N. Carreck)*

16th to 18th Century manor house of Henfield, originally owned by the Bishops of Chichester and exhibiting Georgian design and woodwork. A large collection of historic phonographs and gramophones is demonstrated with famous voices of the past from 1888 onward, and other bygones. Also Elizabethan walled garden with bee shelters, Georgian coach house, barn, courtyard and dairy wing. In 3½ acres of gardens with many old trees.

**Location:** 2 m S of Henfield, off A2037, 4½ m N of Shoreham.
**Opening Times:** Apr to Oct 11–1, 2.30–5.30. Adm £1.50, Chd 75p. Please telephone beforehand.
**Refreshments:** In Henfield High Street.

## NEWTIMBER PLACE

**Newtimber** *map K3*
Telephone: Hurstpierpoint (0273) 833104
*(His Honour Judge & Mrs John Clay)*

Moated house—Etruscan style wall paintings.

**Location:** 1 m N of Pyecombe 7 m N of Brighton off London Road (A23).
**Opening Times:** May to Aug—Thurs 2–5. Adm £1.

## NYMANS GARDEN, The National Trust

**Handcross** *map K3* ♿
Telephone: Handcross 400321 or 400002

Extensive garden, partly enclosed by walls, with exceptional collection of rare trees, shrubs and plants, herbaceous borders, bulbs. Exhibition on the history of the garden.

**Location:** At Handcross just off London/Brighton M23/A23.
**Opening Times:** Garden only. Mar 24 to Nov 5—Daily (except Mons & Fris) 11–7 or sunset if earlier. Open Bank Hol Mons. Last adm 1 hour before closing. Adm £2. Chd half price. Parties of 15 or more by prior arrangement with Head Gardener. No dogs. Wheelchair provided. Shop.
**Refreshments:** Teas.

## PARHAM HOUSE AND GARDENS

**Pulborough** *map J3*
Telephone: Storrington (090 66) 2021

Peaceful Elizabethan House with fine gardens, standing in the heart of a Deer Park at the foot of the South Downs.

**Location:** A283 Storrington/Pulborough road.
**Opening Times:** Easter Sun to first Sun in Oct. Suns, Weds, Thurs & Bank Hols 2–6. Gardens 1–6 (last adm 5.30). Adm House & Gardens £2.50, Chd £1.50, OAPs £2. Gardens only £1, Chd 75p (1988 prices). Guided parties for house (£50 min) by prior appointment, Wed & Thurs mornings. Bookings and all enquiries to Administrator. Church. Shop. Picnic enclosure. Dogs on lead in garden only. Arrangements can be made for wheelchair users to see ground floor of house, gardens easily accessible.
**Refreshments:** In Big Kitchen from 3.

## PETWORTH HOUSE, The National Trust

**Petworth** *map J3* ♿
Telephone: Petworth 42207

Rebuilt 1688-96 by the 6th Duke of Somerset. Later reconstruction by Salvin, in large and beautiful deer park, landscaped by 'Capability' Brown and painted by Turner. 14th century chapel. Important collection of paintings, sculpture and furniture.

**Location:** In centre of Petworth 5½ m E of Midhurst.
**Opening Times:** Mar 24 to Nov 5—Tues, Weds, Thurs, Sats, Suns, Bank Hol Mons and Good Friday 1–5 (last adm 4.30). Adm £2.70, Chd £1.35. Pre-booked parties of 15 or more welcome on Weds, Thurs & Sats only, £2. No dogs in House or Pleasure Grounds. Car park for visitors to House during open hours, 800 yds. Shop. Wheelchairs provided. No prams or pushchairs in showrooms.
Deer Park open daily all year—9–sunset, adm free. Car park for Park only on A283, 1½ m N of Petworth. Dogs must be kept under control.
**Refreshments:** Light lunches and teas in House on open days, 1–5.

## ST MARY'S

**Bramber** *map K3*
Telephone: Steyning 816205
*(Peter Thorogood Esq)*

The foundations of St Mary's go back to the 12 century when land at Bramber was granted to the Knights Templar. The present house (c 1470) was re-fashioned by William Waynflete, Bishop of Winchester, founder of Magdalen College, Oxford, and is classified as "the best late 15th century timber-framing in Sussex". Fine panelled rooms, including unique 'Painted Room' decorated for Elizabeth I's visit. The 'King's Room' has connections with Charles II's escape to France in 1651. Also other Royal and historic associations. Rare 16th century painted wall-leather, splendid carved oak fireplaces, massive 'dragon-beam' in the 'Warden's Room', superb marquetry decoration and strapwork doors. Furniture, pictures, manuscripts. Library contains largest private collection of first editions and illustrated books by celebrated 19th century comic poet and artist, Thomas Hood. Victorian Music room, with elaborate medieval Gothic stone fireplaces, added in 1896 by Hon. Algernon Bourke, son of the Earl of Mayo. Sherlock Holmes connection during ownership (1903–13) of Alfred Musgrave. Ring for details of Summer Festival of Music & Drama, May to October.

**Location:** 10 m NW of Brighton in village of Bramber on A283.
*Station: Shoreham-by-Sea (4 m). Trains from London (Victoria).*
**Opening Times:** Easter Mon to last Sun in Oct—Suns 10–6, Mons & Thurs 2–6, Bank Hol Mons 10–6. Adm £2, OAP £1.80, Chd £1. **Coach party bookings** Mons to Sat by prior arrangement. Reduced rates for parties £1.80 (20 or over). Free coach and car parking in grounds.
**Refreshments:** Light lunches Suns and Bank Hols. Morning coffee, homemade afternoon tea in the Music Room. Catering for parties including "Palm Court" teas by arrangement.

## STANDEN, The National Trust

**East Grinstead** *map K3*
Telephone: East Grinstead (0342) 23029

Built 1894 by Philip Webb. William Morris wallpapers and textiles. Period furniture, paintings. Hillside garden with fine views across Medway Valley.

**Location:** 1½ m S of East Grinstead signposted from the Turners Hill road (B2110).
*Station: East Grinstead (2 m).*

# GOODWOOD HOUSE

Astounding collections of pictures – Canaletto's first London paintings, Van Dyck, Lely, Reynolds and Stubbs; furniture and porcelain; Gobelins Tapestries and fascinating small items – the emerald ring given by Charles II to Louise de Querouaille; Napoleon's breakfast plate from the morning of Waterloo – even Queen Victoria's Coronation cushion and her Faberge walking stick.

*ADMISSION – SEE EDITORIAL REFERENCE*

# HAMMERWOOD PARK

**near East Grinstead, Sussex**

*ADMISSION – SEE EDITORIAL REFERENCE*

# LEONARDSLEE GARDENS

**Lower Beeding, Nr. Horsham, West Sussex**

(3 miles SW of Handcross at bottom of M23)

**Centenary 1889–1989**

Rhododendrons, Azaleas
Views, Reflections
Lakes, Waterfalls
Wallabies, Deer
Rock Garden, Wishing Well

Grade I listed garden in extensive valley with series of lakes providing spectacular views and marvellous reflections. Famous for its Rhododendrons (Rh. Loderi was bred here). New cafeteria for snacks & teas. Coach parties welcome by appointment at any time. Large selection of plants for sale.

*ADMISSION – SEE EDITORIAL REFERENCE*

# THE HIGH BEECHES

*ADMISSION – SEE EDITORIAL REFERENCE*

# WEALD & DOWNLAND OPEN AIR MUSEUM

**SINGLETON, CHICHESTER, WEST SUSSEX**

The Museum is rescuing and re-erecting historic Buildings from South-East England. The Collection illustrates the history of vernacular architecture in the Weald and Downland area. Exhibits include Medieval Farmhouses, a Tudor Market Hall, a 16th century Treadwheel. Farm Buildings including two 18th century Barns and a Granary, a Blacksmith's Forge, Plumber's and Carpenter's Workshops, a Charcoal Burner's Camp and a Village School. During 1989 a History of Farming Exhibition and Medieval Farmstead centred on the Bayleaf House (above) will be opened.

# WEST SUSSEX – *continued*

**Opening Times:** Mar 24 to Nov 5—Weds, Thurs, Fris, Sats & Suns 1.30–5.30 (last adm 5). Adm £2.40. Garden only, open from 1, £1.20. Chd half-price. Pre-booked parties £1.80 Weds, Thurs & Fris only; telephone Administrator. *Dogs admitted to car park & woodland walks only.* Wheelchairs provided; disabled drivers may park near house with prior permission from administrator. Shop.
**Refreshments:** Light lunches and teas served from 1–5.30.

## STANSTED PARK
**Rowlands Castle** *map J3*
Telephone: 0705 412265
*(Stansted Park Foundation)*

This Neo-Wren house with its ancient chapel and walled gardens and arboretum is surrounded by an enchanting forest through which runs the longest beech avenue in the South of England. John Keats describes the interior of the chapel in his Eve of St. Mark. Organically grown produce will be sold in the garden shop. Cricket matches are played in front of the house on most Sundays throughout the season.

**Location:** Rowlands Castle, 4 m by road; 2 m walking through forest; Westbourne 3 m; Havant 5 m and Chichester 8 m.
*Station: Rowlands Castle (2 m).*
**Opening Times:** Easter Sun and Mon; Apr 30 to Sept 26—Suns, Mons & Tues only 2–6, last entries 5.30. Bus parties by arrangement only. Ample free car parking. Grounds, Chapel, Theatre Museum, Shop and tearoom only suitable for disabled at present. Adm £2, Chd 80p, OAPs £1.40. Party rate (by prior arrangement) £1.40, Chd 60p. Grounds, Chapel and tearoom and shop only £1, Chd 50p, OAPs 80p.
**Refreshments:** Home made cream teas served in cricket pavilion.

## UPPARK, The National Trust
**South Harting, nr Petersfield** *map J3* △ ♿
Telephone: Harting 317 or 458

Romantic house (1690) high on the Downs. Interior decoration and furnishings virtually unaltered since 1750. Victorian kitchen with original fittings. Queen Anne dolls' house. Small garden landscaped by Humphrey Repton.

**Location:** 5 m SE of Petersfield entrance on E side of South Harting/Emsworth road (B2146).
**Opening Times:** Mar 26 to end of Sept—Weds, Thurs, Suns & Bank Hol Mons 2–6. Last adm 5.30. Adm Sun & Bank Hol Mons £2.50, other open days £2, Chd half price. *Weds & Thurs £1.70 for pre-booked parties of 15 or more by arrangement with Administrator.* Shop. No dogs. Wheelchairs provided.
**Refreshments:** Teas.

## THE UPPER LODGE
**Stopham, nr Pulborough** *map J3*
*(J. W. Harrington, Esq)*

Garden with rhododendrons and azaleas; wide range of shrubs for acid soil.

**Location:** ½ m N of Stopham Bridge on A283 Pulborough to Petworth.
*Station: Pulborough (1 m).*
**Opening Times:** Mar: Fri 24, Sun 26, Mon 27. Apr: Suns 2, 9, 16, 30 (2–5). May: Suns 7, 14, 21, 28, Bank Hol Mons May 1, 29, (2–6). No dogs. Plants for sale. *In aid of the National Gardens Scheme.*

## WAKEHURST PLACE GARDEN, The National Trust
**nr Ardingly** *map K3* ♿
Telephone: Ardingly (0444) 892701
*(Administered by Royal Botanic Gardens, Kew)*

A wealth of exotic plant species including many fine specimens of trees and shrubs. Picturesque watercourse linking several ponds and lakes. Heath garden and rock walk.

**Location:** 1½ m NW of Ardingly on B2028.
**Opening Times:** All the year—Daily Jan, Nov & Dec, 10–4; Feb & Oct, 10–5; Mar, 10–6; Apr to end of Sept, 10–7. Last adm ½ hour before closing. *Closed Christmas Day & New Year's Day.* Adm £1.50, Chd (under 16) 60p. Parties £1. Chd (under 16) 40p. No dogs. Wheelchairs provided. Exhibition in Mansion. Book shop open all year.
**Refreshments:** Light refreshments.

## THE WEALD AND DOWNLAND OPEN AIR MUSEUM
**Singleton, nr Chichester** *map J3*
Telephone: Singleton (024 363) 348

A collection of historic buildings saved from destruction, including medieval houses, farm buildings, working watermill. 40 acres of park and woodland.

**Location:** 6 m N of Chichester on A286 just S of Singleton.
**Opening Times:** Mar 19 to Oct 31—Daily 11–5. Nov 1 to Mar 18—Weds, Suns and Bank Hols only 11–4. Adm £2.50, Chd £1.25, OAPs £1.80. Parties by arrangement. (Group rates available.)
**Refreshments:** Light refreshments during main season.

## WEST DEAN GARDENS
**nr Chichester** *map J3*
*(The Edward James Foundation)*

35 acres of informal gardens, fine specimen trees; 300ft pergola; gazebo; borders; wild garden: picnic and play area. Walled garden with Victorian glasshouses containing a collection of lawnmowers and a garden history exhibition.

**Location:** 6 m N of Chichester on A286, nr Weald & Downland Open Air Museum.
**Opening Times:** Easter to Sept—Daily 11–6 (last adm 5). Adm £1.40, Chd 65p, OAPs £1.20. Parties by arrangement £1 per person. Garden shop with a wide range of container grown plants for sale. Coach & car parking. No dogs.
**Refreshments:** Available, outdoor sitting only.

# TYNE & WEAR

## GIBSIDE CHAPEL & AVENUE, The National Trust
**Gibside** *map H11*
Telephone: Consett (0207) 542255

Built to James Paine's design soon after 1760. Outstanding example of Georgian architecture approached along a terrace with an oak avenue.

**Location:** 6 m SW of Gateshead; 20 m NW of Durham between Rowlands Gill and Burnopfield.
**Opening Times:** Mar 24 to end Oct—Weds, Sats, Suns, Good Fri & Bank Hol Mons 1–5.30. Other times by appointment with the Custodian. Adm to car park, Avenue & Chapel £1, Chd 50p. *Parties please notify Custodian in advance 80p.* Dogs on terrace only, on leads.

# ST. MARY'S

**Bramber**

**c. 1470**

Magnificent Grade I medieval house, classified as "the best late 15th century timber-framing in Sussex". Rare 16th century painted wall-leather. Fine panelled rooms, including the unique trompe l'oeil 'Painted Room', decorated for the visit of Queen Elizabeth I. Furniture, marquetry, books, manuscripts. Charming garden with Topiary.

*ADMISSION – SEE EDITORIAL REFERENCE*

# STANSTED PARK

**Bordering Hants and Sussex**

Stansted Park
(The Earl of Bessborough)

This Neo-Wren house with its ancient chapel, theatre museum and old walled gardens is surrounded by an enchanting forest.

*ADMISSION – SEE EDITORIAL REFERENCE*

# The National Trust in TYNE & WEAR

# WASHINGTON OLD HALL

*ADMISSION – SEE EDITORIAL REFERENCE*

**Hylton Castle** – See English Heritage Section.

**Tynemouth Castle and Priory** – See English Heritage Section.

### WASHINGTON OLD HALL, The National Trust
**Washington** *map H11* ♿
Telephone: Washington (091) 4166879
*(Leased by Sunderland Borough Council)*

Jacobean manor house incorporating portions of 12th century house of the Washington family.

**Location:** In Washington on E side of Ave; 5 m W of Sunderland (2 m from A1); S of Tyne Tunnel, follow signs for Washington New Town District 4 & then village.
**Opening Times:** Mar 24 to Sept 30—Daily (except Fri, but open Good Friday) 11–5; Oct—Weds, Sats & Suns 11–5 (last adm 4.30). Adm £1.50; Chd 50p. *Parties of 15 or more £1 each, by prior arrangement only with the Custodian.* Shop. Dogs in garden only, on leads. Wheelchair access.

## WARWICKSHIRE

### ARBURY HALL
**Nuneaton** *map H6* △
Telephone: Nuneaton (0203) 382804 or Fillongley (0676) 40529
*(The Rt Hon the Viscount Daventry)*

George Eliot's 'Cheverel Manor 16th century Elizabethan House, gothicized late 18th century, pictures, period furniture etc. Park and landscape gardens.

**Location:** 2 m SW of Nuneaton off B4102. RAC direction signs.
**Opening Times:** Suns from Easter Sun to end of Sept. Bank Hol Mons. Tues & Weds in July & Aug. Gardens 2–6, Hall 2–5.30 (last adm 5). Adm Hall and Gardens £2.50 Chd £1.20, Gardens & Park £1.20, Chd 60p. Organised parties any day (25 or over) special terms by prior arrangement with Administrator. School parties also welcome. Free car park.
**Refreshments:** Available on all open days. Set meals arranged for parties.

### BADDESLEY CLINTON, The National Trust
**Solihull** *map H6* ♿
Telephone: Lapworth (056 43) 3294

A romantically sited medieval moated manor house, with 120 acres, dating back to the 14th century and little changed since 1634.

**Location:** ¾ m W of A41 Warwick to Birmingham Road, nr Chadwick End; 7½ m NW of Warwick; 13 m SE of Birmingham.
*Station: Lapworth (2 m) (not Suns).*
**Opening Times:** Mar 18 to end of Sept–Weds to Suns & Bank Hol Mons 2–6. *Closed Good Fri;* Oct—Weds to Suns 12.30–4.30. Adm £2.30, Chd £1.15, Last admissions 30 mins before closing. Family tickets £6.50 (2 adults and up to 3 chd). Coach parties by prior arrangement only. No prams or pushchairs in the house. No dogs. Wheelchair provided. Shop.
*NB: Timed tickets are issued for entry into the house.*
**Refreshments:** Lunches from 12.30 and teas.

### CHARLECOTE PARK, The National Trust
**Warwick** *map H6* △ ♿
Telephone: Stratford-upon-Avon (0789) 840277

Originally built by the Lucy family, 1550s. Refurbished 1830s in Elizabethan Revival style. Deer park.

**Location:** 5 m E of Stratford-upon-Avon on the N side of B4086.
**Opening Times:** Mar 25 to Oct—Daily (except Mon & Thurs) 11–6 (open Bank Hol Mons 11–6). Closed Good Fri. Last adm one hour before closing. Evening visits for pre-booked parties second Weds each month, 7.30–9.30. Full price for evening visits (including NT members). School parties by prior arrangement only. Adm £2.60, Chd £1.30. Parties by prior written arrangement only. Family tickets £7.20. No dogs. Wheelchairs provided. Shop.
**Refreshments:** Refreshments in Orangery.

### COUGHTON COURT, The National Trust
**Alcester** *map H6*
Telephone: Alcester (0789) 762435

Central gatehouse 1509. Two mid-Elizabethan half-timbered wings. Jacobite relics. The home of the Throckmorton family since 1409.

**Location:** 2 m N of Alcester just E of A435.
**Opening Times:** Apr—Sats, Suns & Easter Mon to Thurs 2–6; May to Sept—Daily except Mon & Fri, but open Bank Hol Mons 2–6; Oct—Sats & Suns 2–5. Adm £1.80, Chd 90p. Parties by prior arrangement. Shop. Limited access for wheelchairs. Dogs on leads in grounds.
**Refreshments:** Tea at the House.

### FARNBOROUGH HALL, The National Trust
**nr Banbury** *map H5*
*(The National Trust)*

Mid 18th century house incorporates fine plasterworks and ancient sculpture. ¾ mile terrace walk feature temples and obelisk, but the splendid panoramic views are soon to be marred by M40.

**Location:** 6 m N of Banbury; ½ m W of A423.
**Opening Times:** April to end of Sept—Weds, Sats & May Day Bank Hol Sun & Mon 2–6. Adm House, Grounds & Terrace Walk £1.50. Terrace Walk 50p. (Thurs and Fris) 2–6 (But closed Good Friday). Chd half-price. *No reduction for parties.* Parties by prior written arrangement only. Dogs in grounds only, on leads. No indoor photography. NB: The tenants are responsible for the showing arrangements.

### THE GRAMMAR SCHOOL
**Church Street, Stratford-upon-Avon** *map H6* △ ♿

Present-day schoolboys assist your visit to this picturesque half-timbered Guildhall (1417) which includes Shakespeare's schoolroom.

**Location:** Church Street, Stratford-upon-Avon between the Guild Chapel and almshouses.
**Opening Times:** Easter and summer school holidays daily 2–6. Times may be changed – details from the Guild School Association. Adm charge.

### HONINGTON HALL
**Shipston-on-Stour** *map M5*
Telephone: Shipston-on-Stour (0608) 61434
*(Sir John Wiggin, Bart.)*

Originally built by the Parker family in 1680. Contains fine 18th century plasterwork.

**Location:** 10 m S of Stratford-on-Avon; ½ m E of A34.
**Opening Times:** June, July, Aug—Weds & Bank Hol Mons 2.30–5. Parties at other times by appointment. Adm £1.50, Chd 50p.

### KENILWORTH CASTLE
*map H6*
Telephone: (0926) 52078
*(English Heritage)*

One of the grandest ruins in England, this castle was made famous by Sir Walter Scott. Gone now is the great lake that once surrounded it, but still standing is the huge Noman keep with walls nearly 20ft (6m) thick in places. Inside the encircling walls built by King John are the remains of John of Gaunt's chapel and great hall, the Earl of Leicester's stables and gatehouse. The most splendid royal occasion took place in 1575 when Queen Elizabeth I was entertained lavishly by the Earl with music and dancing, fireworks and hunting, for 19 days.

**Location:** West side of Kenilworth. OS map ref SP278723.
**Opening Times:** Good Friday to Sept 30, daily 10–6; Oct 1 to Maundy Thurs, daily 10–4. *Closed* Mons, Dec 24–26, Jan 1. Adm £1.10, OAPs 80p, Chd 55p.

# The National Trust in WARWICKSHIRE

## COUGHTON COURT
ALCESTER

## UPTON HOUSE
EDGE HILL

## CHARLECOTE PARK
STRATFORD-ON-AVON

## PACKWOOD HOUSE
HOCKLEY HEATH

## FARNBOROUGH HALL
nr BANBURY

## BADDESLEY CLINTON
SOLIHULL

*ADMISSION – SEE EDITORIAL REFERENCE*

## LORD LEYCESTER HOSPITAL

**Warwick** *map H6* △
Telephone: Warwick (0926) 492797
*(The Governors of Lord Leycester Hospital)*

In 1100 the chapel of St. James was built over the West Gate of Warwick and became the centre for the Guilds established by Royal Charter in 1383. In 1571 Robert Dudley, Earl of Leycester, founded his Hospital for twelve 'poor' persons in the buildings of the Guilds, which had been dispersed in 1546. The Hospital has been run ever since for retired or disabled ex-Servicemen and their wives. The buildings have been recently restored to their original condition including the Great Hall of King James' the Guildhall (museum), the Chaplain's Hall (Queen's Own Hussars Regimental Museum) and the Brethren's Kitchen.

**Location:** W gate of Warwick (A46).
*Station: Warwick (¾ m).*
**Opening Times:** All the year—Mons to Sats 10–5.30 (summer) 10–4 (winter). Gate closes 15 mins earlier. *Closed Suns, Good Fri & Christmas Day.* Adm £1.50, Chd (under 14) 50p, OAPs and students £1. Free car park.
**Refreshments:** Tea (Easter to Oct). Lunches (for booked parties).

## PACKWOOD HOUSE, The National Trust

**Hockley Heath** *map H6*
Telephone: Lapworth (056 43) 2024

Elizabethan house with mid-17th century additions. Tapestry, needlework, Carolean formal garden, and yew garden of c. 1650 representing the Sermon on the Mount.

**Location:** 2 m E of Hockley Heath (which is on A34) 11 m SE of Birmingham.
*Stations: Lapworth (1½ m); Dorridge (2 m).*
**Opening Times:** Mar 25 to end of Sept—Weds to Suns & Bank Hol Mons 2–6. *Closed Good Friday.* Oct—Wed to Suns 12.30–4 (last adm ½ hr before closing). Adm £1.90, Chd 95p. Family tickets £5.50 (2 adults and up to 3 chd). Parties by prior written arrangement only. No dogs. No prams in House. Wheelchair access to part of garden & ground floor (difficult).

## RAGLEY HALL

**Alcester** *map H6*
Telephone: Alcester (0789) 762090 or 762455
*(The Marquess of Hertford)*

Built in 1680. Fine paintings, china, furniture and works of art and mural 'The Temptation'. Gardens, park and lake. Adventure wood, Farm and woodland walks and lakeside picnic places.

**Location:** 2 m SW of Alcester on Birmingham/Alcester/Evesham Road (A435); 8 m from Stratford-upon-Avon.
**Opening Times:** HOUSE, GARDEN & PARK: Mar 25 to Oct 1—Daily except Mons and Fris, always open Bank Hol Mons.
GARDEN & PARK, with Adventure Wood and Farm and woodland walk, and lakeside picnic places. Mar, Apr, May & Sept 12–5.30; June, July & Aug 10–6. Licensed Terrace tearooms 12–5. Restaurant for booked parties only.
HOUSE: 12–5.
ADMISSION: HOUSE, GARDEN & PARK, (includes Adventure Wood and Farm and woodland walks) £2.90, Chd £1.90.
GARDEN & PARK ONLY, including Adventure Wood and Farm and woodland walks £1.90, Chd 90p. Coach parties of 30 and over & OAPs £2.40.
Free car park. Dogs welcome on leads in Park and on Country Trail, not in House, Garden or Adventure Wood.
**Refreshments:** Licensed Terrace tearooms and Restaurant open daily except Mons and Fris, 12 noon–5. Restaurant for booked parties only serving lunches & teas.
**Advance Bookings:** (at any time of the year). Coach parties welcome by arrangement. Lunches and teas – parties please write for menus. The Great Hall is available for functions throughout the year. Private dinner parties for any number between 2–150 can be arranged. For further information please contact: The Marquess of Hertford, Ragley Hall, Alcester, Worcestershire. Telephone: Alcester (STD 0789) 762090 or 762455.

## THE SHAKESPEARE BIRTHPLACE TRUST PROPERTIES

All the properties are open daily except on Good Friday morning, Christmas Eve, Christmas Day, Boxing Day and the morning of Jan 1st. For those needing transport there is a regular guided bus tour service during the summer months connecting the town properties with Anne Hathaway's Cottage and Mary Arden's House.

## SHAKESPEARE'S BIRTHPLACE

**Stratford-upon-Avon** *map H6* △ ♿

The half-timbered house where Shakespeare was born, containing many rare Shakespearian exhibits, also BBC Television Shakespeare Costume Exhibition.

**Location:** Henley Street.
**Opening Times:** Apr to Oct—Weekdays 9–6 (9–5 Oct); Suns 10–6 (10–5 Oct); Nov to Mar—Weekdays 9–4.30; Suns 1.30–4.30. Adm £1.70, Chd 70p. Adm incl Exhibition £1.90, Chd 80p.

## ANNE HATHAWAY'S COTTAGE

**Stratford-upon-Avon** *map H6* △

The picturesque thatched home of Anne Hathaway before her marriage to Shakespeare.

**Location:** Shottery (1 m).
**Opening Times:** Apr to Oct—Weekdays 9–6 (9–5 Oct); Suns 10–6 (10–5 Oct); Nov to Mar—Weekdays 9–4.30; Suns 1.30–4.30. Adm £1.60, Chd 60p.

## HALL'S CROFT

**Stratford-upon-Avon** *map H6* △ ♿

A fine Tudor house complete with period furniture and walled garden where Shakespeare's daughter Susanna and Dr John Hall lived.

**Location:** Old Town.
**Opening Times:** Apr to Oct—Weekdays 9–6 (9–5 Oct); Suns 10–6 (10–5 Oct); Nov to Mar—Weekdays only 9–4.30. Adm £1.10, Chd 50p.

## MARY ARDEN'S HOUSE and THE SHAKESPEARE COUNTRYSIDE MUSEUM

**Stratford-upon-Avon** *map H6* △ ♿

The Tudor farmhouse where Shakespeare's mother lived, with a farming and Shakespeare countryside museum now extended to include the adjoining Glebe Farm. Interesting dovecote. Rural Crafts.

**Location:** Wilmcote (3 m).
**Opening Times:** Apr to Oct—Weekdays 9–6 (9–5 Oct); Suns 10–6 (10–5 Oct); Nov to Mar—Weekdays only 9–4.30. Adm £1.60, Chd 70p.

# ARBURY HALL AND LANDSCAPE GARDENS

**Nuneaton, Warwickshire**

*The Home of Lord and Lady Daventry*

Arbury has been the home of the Newdegate family since the 16th century. For a country house the Gothic architecture is unique, the original Elizabethan house being Gothicized by Sir Roger Newdigate between 1750 and 1800 under the direction of Sanderson Miller, Henry Keene and Couchman of Warwick. Beautiful plaster ceilings, pictures and fine specimens of period furniture, china and glass. Fine stable block with central doorway by Wren. Arbury Hall is situated in very large grounds and is about one mile from any main road. Excellent carriage drives lined with trees.

Further details from:
The Administrator, Arbury Hall, Nuneaton,
Warwickshire CV10 7PT.
Telephone: Nuneaton (0203) 382804.

*ADMISSION – SEE EDITORIAL REFERENCE*

# WARWICK CASTLE

**WARWICK**

The finest mediaeval castle in England and most visited stately home in Great Britain stands on a steep rock cliff dominating the River Avon at Warwick. The site was originally fortified by William the Conqueror in 1068.

Remarkably well preserved the castle is a very fine example of 14th century fortification and contains an outstanding collection of arms and armour (1,000 items) as well as magnificently appointed State Rooms full of historic treasures including a splendid collection of paintings by various masters.

Set in 100 acres of parkland landscaped by Brown where peacocks roam freely. Plus a delightful Victorian Rose Garden reconstructed from the original designs of Robert Marnock in 1864.

AWARD WINNING FEATURE

'A Royal Weekend Party—1898' by Madame Tussauds. Re-created in 12 rooms of the former Private Apartments featuring 29 wax portrait figures.
A unique attraction at no extra charge.

OPENING TIMES

March 1 to October 31
10 am to 5.30 pm.
November 1 to February 28
10 am to 4.30 pm.
Open every day except Christmas Day.

Licensed restaurant and cafeteria in the Castle serving meals, teas and refreshments. Medieval Banquets.

Car Park available.

Enquiries to:
General Manager,
Warwick Castle,
Warwick CV34 4QU.
Tel: Warwick 495421.

# LORD LEYCESTER HOSPITAL

**WARWICK**

*FOR ADMISSION – SEE EDITORIAL REFERENCE*

BADDESLEY CLINTON – SEE UNDER WARWICKSHIRE

### NEW PLACE/NASH'S HOUSE

**Stratford-upon-Avon** *map H6* △ ♿

Foundations of Shakespeare's last home, preserved in an Elizabethan garden setting with Nash's House adjoining which is furnished in period style.

**Location:** Chapel Street.
**Opening Times:** Apr to Oct—Weekdays 9–6 (9–5 Oct); Suns 10–6 (10–5 Oct); Nov to Mar—Weekdays only 9–4.30. Adm £1.10, Chd 50p.

Inclusive ticket admitting to all five properties and also the BBC Television Shakespeare costume exhibition £5, Chd £2.
*School party permit including the BBC Television Shakespeare costume exhibition £1.50. (One member of staff to each 10 children is admitted free.)*
*Inclusive adm permit for Colleges & University student parties including the BBC Television Shakespeare costume exhibition £2.40. (One member of staff to each 10 students is admitted free.) In both cases, additional adults £5.*
Last adm 20 mins before the advertised closing time at all the properties.

### STONELEIGH ABBEY

**Kenilworth** *map H6*
Telephone: 0926 52116
*(Lord and Lady Leigh)*

The Georgian Mansion, originally a Cistercian Abbey, has now been restored following the disastrous fire in 1960. The North and West Wing State rooms and part of the South wing are now open to visitors. Children's playground, miniature steam railway (Suns and Bank Hols only). Souvenir shop, picnic areas, monks stew ponds, woodland walks. Nature Trail.

**Location:** 3 m E of Kenilworth; 6 m S of Coventry; 5 m N of Leamington Spa; 6 m NE of Warwick; 1½ m S of Stoneleigh village via B4115 and A444.
**Opening Times:** Details from: The Administrator, Stoneleigh Abbey, Kenilworth, Warwickshire. Tel: (0926) 52116.
**Refreshments:** Licensed facilities available.

### UPTON HOUSE, The National Trust

**Edge Hill** *map H5* ♿
Telephone: Edge Hill 266

Fine collection paintings, porcelain. Tapestries. Beautiful terraced gardens.

**Location:** 1 m S of Edge Hill; 7 m NW of Banbury on the Stratford Road (A422).
**Opening Times:** Mar 25 to end Apr, and Oct: Sat, Sun & Easter Mon 2–6. May to Sept: Sat to Wed 2–6. Last adm to House 5.30. Adm House & Grounds £2.20, Chd £1.10. Parties (except weekends & Bank Hols) by prior arrangement with the Administrator. No indoor photography. Dogs in garden only, on leads. Wheelchairs provided. Wheelchair access ground floor only.

### WARWICK CASTLE

**Warwick** *map H6* △
Telephone: Warwick (0926) 495421

One of the finest medieval castles, standing on a steep rock cliff beside the River Avon, 8 miles from Stratford. The present castle is a fine example of 14th century fortification with towers and dungeons open to visitors all the year round. The State Rooms contain a magnificent collection of pictures by Rubens, Van Dyck and other Masters. Surrounded by acres of parkland landscaped by 'Capability' Brown, gardens where peacocks roam freely and a river island.

**Location:** In the centre of Warwick.
*Stations: Warwick (½ m); Leamington Spa (2 m).*
**Opening Times:** Open daily (except Christmas Day) all year. Mar 1 to Oct 31—Daily 10–5.30. Nov 1 to Feb 28—Daily 10–4.30. Adm charges not available at time of going to press. Car park.
**Refreshments:** Licensed restaurant & cafeteria in the Castle. Medieval Banquets.

## WEST MIDLANDS

### ASTON HALL

**Birmingham** *map H6* △
Telephone: 021-327 0062
*(Birmingham Metropolitan District Council)*

A fine Jacobean house built 1618–35 with many rooms furnished as period settings. A branch of Birmingham Museums and Art Gallery.

**Location:** 2½ m from centre of city. Entrance for coaches at Frederick Road; entrance for cars at Witton Lane.
*Station: Aston (¾ m).*
**Opening Times:** Mar 18–Oct 29— Daily 2–5. Adm free. School parties can arrange to visit throughout the year.

### BLAKESLEY HALL

**Birmingham** *map M6*
Telephone: 021-783 2193
*(Birmingham Metropolitan District Council)*

A timber-framed yeoman's farmhouse c. 1575 carefully furnished to an inventory of 1684. Also contains displays on timber building methods and 17th century pottery from a single excavation. A branch of Birmingham Museums and Art Gallery.

**Location:** 3 m from city centre; entrance in Blakesley Road.
*Stations: Stechford (¾ m); Birmingham New Street. Buses: 16 & 17, 11 on Outer Circle.*
**Opening Times:** Mar 18 to Oct 29—Daily 2–5. Adm free. School parties can arrange to visit throughout the year.

### HAGLEY HALL

**nr Stourbridge** *map G6* Ⓢ
Telephone: Hagley (0562) 882408
*(The Viscount & Viscountess Cobham)*

The last of the great Palladian Houses, designed by Sanderson Miller and completed in 1760. Superb Italian plasterwork and the fine Lyttelton collection of 18th century paintings and furniture.

**Location:** Just off A456 Birmingham to Kidderminster; 12 m from Birmingham within easy reach M5 (exit 3 or 4), M6 or M42.
*Stations: Hagley (1 m) (not Suns); Stourbridge Junction (2 m).*
**Opening Times:** Jan 2 to Feb 28: daily except Sats. Mar 26, 27, May 28, 29, Aug 27, 28, 2–5. For further details, please telephone Hagley (0562) 882408.
**Refreshments:** Tea available in the House.

### WIGHTWICK MANOR, The National Trust

**Wolverhampton** *map G6* △ Ⓢ
Telephone: (0902) 761108

Strongly influenced by William Morris the interiors of this late 19th century house include Morris wallpapers and fabrics, Kempe glass, de Morgan ware and a connoisseurs' collection of pre-Raphaelite paintings. Victorian/Edwardian gardens, terraces & pools.

**Location:** 3 m W of Wolverhampton, up Wightwick Bank (A454).
**Opening Times:** All year (except Feb)—Thurs, Sats, Bank Hol Suns & Mons 2.30–5.30. Also open for pre-booked parties only May to end Sept—Weds 2.30–5.30 and Weds & Thurs evenings. Pre-booked school & student tours Weds & Thurs mornings & afternoons. *Closed Dec 25, 26, Jan 1, 2.* Adm £2.50 Sat afternoons £3, (extra rooms shown *but not Bank Hol weekends*). Chd half price. Students £1.50. Gardens only £1. *Parties must book in advance (no reductions).* Photography by permission only. Dogs in garden only, on leads.

# ASTON HALL

BIRMINGHAM

* Home of the Holte family for 200 years.
* James Watt the younger lived there.
* Outstanding Jacobean plasterwork, panelling and great staircase.
* Long Gallery.
* Paintings, tapestry and furniture of 17-19th centuries.
* Summer events, bi-ennial Candlelight evenings.
* Pre-booked parties by arrangement.
* Admission is free.

OPEN - SEE EDITORIAL REFERENCE
Information: 021-235 2834 or 021-327 0062 in season

Birmingham

# BLAKESLEY HALL

YARDLEY, BIRMINGHAM

* Built for Richard Smalbroke, a leading merchant in late 16th century Birmingham.
* Original wall paintings and diminutive Long Gallery.
* From Boulting Hall to Buttery, the house is furnished in accordance with the 1684 inventory, yielding a unique insight into the lifestyle and domestic surroundings of the family in Stuart times.
* 18th century country pottery display.
* In walking distance of Yardley village (Medieval Church, Trust School, Georgian cottages).
* Pre-booked parties by arrangement.
* Summer events.
* Admission is free.

OPEN - SEE EDITORIAL REFERENCE
Information: 021-235 2834 or 021-783 2193 in season

Birmingham

Near Stourbridge **HAGLEY HALL** West Midlands

The ruined castle, built in 1740 from stones from Halesowen Abbey.

Home of Viscount and Viscountess Cobham, Hagley Hall was designed by Sanderson Miller for George 1st Lord Lyttelton.

- Teas in the House.
- Receptions and private dinner parties by arrangement throughout the year.
- Open for prebooked parties by arrangement.

Opening dates: Please telephone Hagley (0562) 882408 for details on opening times in 1988.

**Enquiries: The Secretary, Hagley Hall, Near Stourbridge, West Midlands. Telephone Hagley (0562) 882408.**

The House contains the finest examples of Italian Rococo plaster work by Francesco Vassali and a unique collection of 18th Century furniture and family portraits including works by Van Dyck, Reynolds and Lely.

# WILTSHIRE

## AVEBURY MANOR & GARDENS
**Avebury SN8 1RF** *map H4*
Telephone: (06723) 203

Avebury Manor a fine Elizabethan manor house, original oak panelled rooms and plasterwork ceilings, fine oak furniture and early paintings fill the house. The attic rooms have been chosen to take you back in time where you will find wax figures of William Sharrington, Sir John Stawell and Sir Richard Holford, late owners of the house. Additional attractions include Sir John Stawell's armoury, supplied by the Royal Armouries, H.M. Tower of London. Replica jewellery and dress of the Elizabethan period. An exhibition of torture instruments and the story of torture and punishment. Within the grounds you will find an Elizabethan market square full of craft shops. See and hear minstrels, jugglers, strolling players, jesters, Lords and Ladies, and become part of Elizabethan life. With all the colour and pageantry of this by-gone age. There are also daily falconry demonstrations, a large adventure play-ground, nature and adventure trails, topiary, rose and herb gardens, rose centre and gift shop together with 16th century dovecote and wishing well.

**Location:** 1½ m from A4 London–Bath road; 9 m from Junc. 15, Swindon exit M4. 6 m from Marlborough.
**Opening Times:** Open daily from Easter to Oct 10–6. All enquiries Estate's Office, Avebury Manor (06723) 203. 1989 Educational group reductions. Groups welcomed – special rates. Car and coach parking within Manor grounds, plus extra parking in Avebury. Suitable for disabled persons (no wheelchairs available).
**Refreshments:** Restaurant for 60+ and tea rooms for 40+. Banqueting services (banquets, receptions, conferences and corporate hospitality). All enquiries Estate's Office, Avebury Manor.

**Avebury Museum** – See English Heritage Section.

## BOWOOD HOUSE & GARDENS
**Calne** *map G4* ♿
Telephone: Calne (0249) 812102
*(The Earl of Shelburne)*

100 acre garden containing many exotic trees, 40 acre lake, waterfall, cave, and Doric Temple, arboretum, pinetum, rose garden and Italian garden. 60 acres of rhododendrons, (flowering season mid-May to June). Interesting rooms in the house include Robert Adam's Library, Dr Joseph Priestley's Laboratory, the Chapel, and a series of Exhibition Rooms featuring classical sculpture, costumes, furniture, Indiana and family jewellery. Important collection of drawings and water colours by English Masters.

**Location:** 2½ m W of Calne; 5 m SE of Chippenham. Immediately off A4; 8 m S of M4.
**Opening Times:** House, Gardens & Grounds (entrance off A4 at Derry Hill village between Calne & Chippenham). End Mar to mid Oct—Daily incl Bank Hols 11–6. Rhododendron Walks (entrance off A342 at Kennels Lodge) mid-May to mid-June (depending on season) 11–6. Adm rates and information apply Estate Office, Bowood Estate, Calne, Wiltshire. Free car park. No dogs.
**Refreshments:** Licensed restaurant & Garden Tearoom. Children's Adventure Play-ground in Pleasure Grounds.

## BROADLEAS GARDENS (Charitable Trust)
**Devizes** *map G4*
Telephone: Devizes 2035
*(Lady Anne Cowdray)*

A garden with rare and unusual plants and trees. Rhododendrons, magnolias and interesting perennials and ground cover.

**Location:** 1½ m SW of Devizes on A360
**Opening Times:** Apr 1 to Oct 31—Suns, Weds & Thurs 2–6. Adm £1, Chd (under 12) half-price. Parties by arrangement. Own plants propagated for sale.
**Refreshments:** Home-made teas by prior arrangement only.

## CHALCOT HOUSE
**Westbury** *map G4*
*(Mr & Mrs Anthony Rudd)*

Small 16th century Palladian Manor.

**Location:** 2 m W of Westbury on A3098 to Frome.
*Station: Dilton Marsh (1½ m).*
**Opening Times:** Aug—Daily 2–5. Adm £1.50 including brochure. *Parties at other times by arrangement.*
**Refreshments:** By arrangement.

## CHARLTON PARK HOUSE
**Malmesbury** *map G4*
*(The Earl of Suffolk and Berkshire)*

Jacobean/Georgian mansion, built for the Earls of Suffolk, 1607, altered by Matthew Brettingham the Younger, c. 1770.

**Location:** 1½ m NE Malmesbury. Entry only by signed entrance on A429, Malmesbury/Cirencester Road. No access from Charlton village.
**Opening Times:** May to Oct, Mon & Thurs 2–4. Viewing of Great Hall, Staircase and saloon. Adm £1, Chd/OAPs 50p. Car parking limited. Unsuitable for wheelchairs. No dogs. No picnicking.

## CORSHAM COURT
**Chippenham** *map G4* ♿
Telephone: Corsham (0249) 712214
*(The Lord Methuen)*

Elizabethan (1582) and Georgian (1760–70) house, fine 18th century furniture. British, Spanish, Italian and Flemish Old Masters. Park and gardens laid out by "Capability" Brown and Humphrey Repton.

**Location:** In Corsham 4 m W of Chippenham off the Bath Road (A4).
**Opening Times:** Staterooms. Jan 1 to Nov 30—Daily except Mons and Fris 2–4.30 (From Good Friday to Sept 30, 2–6 (including Fri and Bank Hols); *Closed* Dec. Last adm 5.30. Other times by appointment. Parties welcome. Adm (incl gardens) £2.50, Chd £1.20; Parties of 20 or more by arrangement. Gardens only £1.20, Chd 60p.
**Refreshments:** Methuen Arms, Corsham *(parties by prior arrangement).*

# AVEBURY MANOR

**Original oak panelling**

**Plasterwork ceilings**

**Topiary**

**Rose centre**

Enter the Elizabethan Experience

AVEBURY MANOR

**Sir John Stawell's Armoury**

**Minstrels Jugglers**

**Strolling players**

**Elizabethan market square**

**Walled rose and herb gardens Adventure playground Falconry demonstrations**

**16th century Dovecote and much much more**

## AVEBURY MANOR, WILTSHIRE

**All Enquiries Telephone: (06723) 203**

"Do please let this one scene fasten upon your memory. Whatever memories of England you carry away, let this be uppermost. For this, to me, is England." *R.C. Hutchinson, novelist.*

*FOR ADMISSION DETAILS – SEE EDITORIAL REFERENCE*

## THE COURTS GARDEN, The National Trust

**Holt** *map G4* ♿
Telephone: North Trowbridge (0225) 782340

7 acre garden of mystery—of interest to amateur and botanist. Borders, lily pond and arboretum carpeted with wild flowers.

**Location:** 2½ m E of Bradford-on-Avon on S side of B3107; 3 m N of Trowbridge. *Station: Bradford-on-Avon (2½ m).*
**Opening Times:** GARDEN ONLY. Mar 24 to Oct 29—Daily (except Sat), 2–5. Adm £1, Chd free (if accompanied). Other times by appointment; please telephone the Head Gardener. House not open. No dogs. Wheelchair access.

## FITZ HOUSE GARDEN

**Teffont Magna** *map H3*
*(Major & Mrs Mordaunt-Hare)*

Lovely hillside terraced gardens frame a listed group of beautiful ancient stone buildings in one of Wiltshire's prettiest villages. 16th/17th century House (not shown) admired by Nikolaus Pevsner in his Wiltshire Guide. The gardens, bordered by yew and beech hedges and a stream, are a haven of tranquillity, planted with spring bulbs and blossom, azaleas, roses and clematis of all types, honeysuckles, vines and mixed borders. Something of interest throughout the season including much new planting during the last three years. Many scented plants.

**Location:** On B3089 Barford St Martin (A30) to Mere Road (A303) in the village; 10 m W of Salisbury on direct route Wilton House-Stourhead.
**Opening Times:** GARDEN ONLY: Easter Sun to end Sept: Suns 2–6; also Sats May 20 and June 17 for the National Gardens Scheme. No dogs. No coaches.

## GREAT CHALFIELD MANOR, The National Trust

**nr. Melksham** *map G4*

15th century moated manor house restored in the 20th century. Set across a moat between Parish Church and stables.

**Location:** 2½ m NE Bradford-on-Avon via B3109, signposted in Holt village.
**Opening Times:** Apr to Oct—Tues to Thurs 12–1, 2–5 (tours start 12.15, 2.15, 3, 3.45, 4.30). Adm £2. *Historical & other Societies by written arrangement. No reductions for parties or children.* No dogs. Unsuitable for wheelchairs.
**Refreshments:** Swan Hotel, Bradford-on-Avon; Kings Arms, Melksham.

## HAMPTWORTH LODGE

**Landford, Salisbury SP5 2EA** *map H3*
Telephone: Romsey (0794) 390215
*(Mr N. Anderson)*

Reproduction Jacobean Manor.

**Location:** 10 m SE of Salisbury on the C44 road between Redlynch and Landford, which is a link road joining the A36 Salisbury–Southampton and the A338 Salisbury–Bournemouth.
**Opening Times:** House and garden open daily, except Suns, June 1 to July 5 1989, 2.15–5. Conducted parties 2.30 and 3.45. Adm £3, OAPs and Chd 11–18 £2, under 11 free. No special arrangements for parties, but about 15 is the maximum. Car parking. Suitable for disabled ground floor only.
**Refreshments:** Nearest Hotel is in Salisbury. No refreshments at house.

## HEALE GARDENS AND PLANT CENTRE

**Woodford, Salisbury** *map H3* ♿
Telephone: Middle Woodford (072 273) 504
*(Major David & Lady Anne Rasch)*

Winner of Christie's/HHA Garden of the Year 1984 award. Early Carolean manor house where King Charles II hid during his escape. The garden provides an interesting and varied collection of plants, shrub, musk and other roses, growing in the formal setting of clipped hedges and mellow stonework, at their best in June and July. Particularly attractive in Spring and Autumn is the water garden, planted with Magnolia and Acers, surrounding an authentic Japanese Tea House and Nikko Bridge. Many of these plants are for sale in the plant centre.

**Location:** 4 m N of Salisbury on the Woodford Valley road between A345 and A360.
**Opening Times:** Garden: Mons to Sats and first Sun of the month and Bank Hols from Easter to Autumn 11–5. **Plant Centre and Shop open throughout the year.** Tours of the house for parties over 20 by arrangement with Lady Anne Rasch.
**Refreshments:** Lunches & Teas in the House for parties over 20 by arrangement.

## IFORD MANOR

**Bradford-on-Avon** *map G4*
Telephone: Bradford-on-Avon (02216) 3146 or 2840
*(Mrs Cartwright-Hignett)*

Iford Manor, a Tudor house with an 18th century façade, stands beside a medieval bridge over the River Frome. Once a busy centre of the woollen trade, it is now surrounded by a peaceful terraced garden of unique character. Designed in the Italian style, it was the home of Harold Peto, the Edwardian landscape architect. There are pools, statues, a colonnade, antique carvings, cloisters and many plants of botanical interest.

**Location:** 7 m SE of Bath on A36, signpost Iford 1 m; or from Bradford-on-Avon and Trowbridge via Westwood.
**Opening Times:** GARDENS ONLY. Weds and Suns in May, June, July & Aug 2–5. Also Summer Bank Hols. Adm £1, Chd & OAPs 70p. At other times by appointment. Coaches by appointment only. Dogs on leads. Free car parking.
**Refreshments:** On the premises, Sun only.

## THE KING'S HOUSE

**Salisbury** *map H3* ♿
Telephone: Salisbury (0722) 332151
*(Salisbury & South Wiltshire Museum)*

The King's House is a Grade 1 listed building dating from the 13th century and is one of the finest houses in the Cathedral Close. It is also the home of the award-winning Salisbury and South Wiltshire Museum with highly-praised galleries on Stonehenge, Early Man, Old Sarum and Salisbury (with its famous Giant and Hob Nob), the Pitt Rivers collection, pictures, ceramics, a pre-N.H.S. surgery and the new Wedgwood room. Temporary exhibitions and lectures throughout the year. Winner – Special Judges' Award, Museum of the Year Award 1985. Winner – Certificate of Distinction, BTA 'Come to Britain' Trophy 1986. **Costume gallery opening 1989**.

**Location:** In Salisbury Cathedral Close opposite the west door.
*Station: Salisbury.*
**Opening Times:** House & Museum. Apr to Sept—Mons to Sats 10–5; Oct to Mar—Mons to Sats 10–4; Suns in July & Aug 2–5. Closed Christmas. Adm £1.50, Chd 50p, OAPs/Students/Unemployed £1. Gift shop.
**Refreshments:** Apr to Sept. Party bookings all year.

# Visit magnificent Bowood

## The home of the Earl of Shelburne

Bowood is an outstanding example of 18th century architecture, set in a magnificent park which is itself a classical example of English landscaping created by Capability Brown between 1763 and 1766.

Historical rooms inside the house include Robert Adam's own famous Library and the Laboratory where Dr. Joseph Priestley discovered oxygen gas in 1774. In the Sculpture Gallery are assembled fine marbles and tapestries, and part of the Lansdowne collection of paintings hangs in the Orangery.

The house also contains fascinating collections of Indiana, silver and family jewellery, and important watercolours and drawings by English masters.

The Orangery

The pleasure grounds extend to some hundred acres, and visitors can enjoy walks around the magnificent lake to view the Doric Temple, and the delightful water Cascade. Over 200 kinds of trees and shrubs are included in the Arboretum.

From mid-May to mid-June, thousands of rhododendron blooms are a breathtaking separate attraction.

For children under 12, there is a giant Adventure Playground. There is also a Garden Centre, and a licensed Restaurant serving home cooked meals, and a Garden Tearoom for snacks. There are facilities for the disabled, and coaches are welcome. Dogs are not permitted.

**BOWOOD HOUSE & GARDENS.** OPEN END MARCH – MID OCTOBER daily 11am to 6pm including Bank Holidays. Garden Centre open all year round 9am to 5pm.
Admission prices and party rates upon application to the House Aministrator, telephone Calne (0249) 812102. Reductions for parties of 20 and over.
Entrance: Off the A4 in Derry Hill Village, midway between Calne and Chippenham.

**RHODODENDRON WALKS:** OPEN MID-MAY TO MID-JUNE daily 11am to 6pm. Admission prices upon application to the House Administrator, telephone Calne (0249) 812102. (No reduced rate for party bookings). Entrance: Off the A342 Chippenham to Devizes road midway between Derry Hill and Sandy Lane villages.

The Management reserves the right to alter catering facilities depending on adverse weather conditions or visitor demand.

**BOWOOD · CALNE · WILTSHIRE** Telephone (0249) 812102

**Entrance off A4 in Derry Hill Village, midway between Calne and Chippenham.**

### LACOCK ABBEY, The National Trust
**nr Chippenham** *map G4* △
Telephone: Lacock 227

13th century abbey converted into a house in 1540, with 18th century "Gothick" alterations for the Talbot family whose home it still is. The medieval cloisters, the brewery and the house are also open to the public. Fine trees.

**Location:** In the village of Lacock; 3 m N of Melksham; 3 m S of Chippenham just E of A350.
**Opening Times:** House & Grounds. Mar 25 to Nov 5—Daily (except Tues) 2–6. Last adm 5.30. *Closed Good Fri.* Nov to Mar—Historical and other societies by written arrangement. Grounds only: open Mar to Nov 5—Daily 2–6. Adm House & Grounds £2.50, Chd £1.30. Parties of 15 or more £1.70. Grounds and Cloisters only £1, Chd 50p. *No dogs.* Lavatory for the disabled. Wheelchairs in grounds, village & museum only.

### LONGLEAT HOUSE
**Warminster** *map G3* △
Telephone:
Longleat House: Maiden Bradley (098 53) 551
Safari Park: Maiden Bradley (098 53) 328
Caravan Club site: Maiden Bradley (098 53) 663
*(The Marquess of Bath)*

Longleat House, built by Sir John Thynne in 1580, and still owned and lived in by the same family, was the first truly magnificent Elizabethan House to be built in the Italian Renaissance style. Longleat was also the first Stately Home to be opened to the public in 1949, it is still actively run by the 6th Marquess of Bath and other members of the Thynne family, thus keeping Longleat alive with their presence. Throughout its existence, ancestors have commissioned alterations within the House; ceilings by Italian craftsmen, rooms and corridors by Wyatville, additional libraries to house the vast collection of rare books and of course, the beautiful parkland landscaped by Lancelot 'Capability' Brown. In 1966, Lord Bath, in conjunction with Jimmy Chipperfield established the first drive through wild animals reserve outside Africa and it remains the model for Safari Parks throughout the world. Many other attractions have since been opened, making Longleat a full day's entertainment for all the family. Attractions include, Victorian Kitchens, Lord Bath's Bygones, Dolls Houses, Dr. Who Exhibition, Butterfly Garden, Railway, World's Largest Maze, Pets Corner, Safari Boat Ride, Lord Bath's V.I.P. Vehicle Exhibition. 'Adventure Castle' for children. New for 1989 – 1.25 scale model of Longleat House; in the Safari Park, 'Mayura' the only white tiger in Britain.

**Opening Times:** Longleat House open all year – Daily (Except Christmas Day) incl. Suns Easter to September 10–6, remainder of year 10–4. Safari Park every day from mid Mar to end Oct, 10–6. (Last cars admitted 5.30 or sunset if earlier.) All other attractions every day from Easter–Oct 30, 11–6 – for Maze, Railway & Adventure Castle last entry 5.30. School Parties welcome at all times of the year – reduced rates for Parties booking in advance. Helicopter landing facilities provided advance notice given.
**Refreshments:** At the Old Cellar Cafe at the House and in the Restaurant Complex.

### LUCKINGTON COURT
**Luckington** *map G4*
Telephone: Malmesbury 840 205
*(The Hon Mrs Trevor Horn)*

Mainly Queen Anne with magnificent group of ancient buildings. Beautiful mainly formal garden with fine collection of ornamental trees and shrubs.

**Location:** 6 m W of Malmesbury on B4040 Bristol Road.
**Opening Times:** All the Year—Weds 2–6. Outside only, 50p. Inside view by appointment 3 weeks in advance, £1. Open Sun, May 14, 2.30–6. *Collection box for National Gardens' Scheme.*
**Refreshments:** Teas in garden or house (in aid of Luckington Parish Church). May 14 only.

### LYDIARD MANSION
**Lydiard Park, Swindon** *map H4* △ ♿
*(Borough of Thamesdown)*

Dating from medieval times, reconstructed 1743–49. Outstanding mid-Georgian decoration.

**Location:** 5 m W of Swindon just N of A420; signpost Lydiard Park.
**Opening Times:** Weekdays 10–1, 2–5.30; Suns 2–5.30. Adm free, but children under 14 must be accompanied by an adult.

### MOMPESSON HOUSE, The National Trust
**Salisbury** *map H3*

Fine Queen Anne town house, furnished as the home of a Georgian gentleman; walled garden.

**Location:** In Cathedral Close on N side of Choristers' Green.
*Station: Salisbury (½ m).*
**Opening Times:** Mar 25 to Oct 29—Mons, Tues, Weds, Sats & Suns 12.30–6 (or dusk if earlier). Adm £1.50, Chd 70p. *No reduction for parties.* No dogs.

### NEWHOUSE
**Redlynch** *map H3*
Telephone: Downton 20055
*(Mr & Mrs George Jeffreys)*

Brick Jacobean "Trinity" house, c. 1619, with two Georgian wings. Contents include costume collection, Nelson relics and "Hare" picture.

**Location:** 9 m S of Salisbury; 3 m from Downton, off B3080.
**Opening Times:** Bank Hol Mons May 1, 29 & Aug 28; Suns in May to Sept inclusive 2–5.30. Adm £1.50, Chd (under 15) 70p.
**Refreshments:** In stable yard June to Sept inclusive.

**Old Sarum** –See English Heritage Section.

**Old Wardour Castle** – See English Heritage Section.

### PHILIPPS HOUSE, The National Trust
**Dinton** *map G3* ♿
Telephone: Teffont 208

Classical house completed in 1816 by Sir Jeffry Wyattville for the Wyndham family.

**Location:** 9 m W of Salisbury; on N side of B3089.
**Opening Times:** By prior appointment only with the Warden. Adm £1. *No reduction for parties or children.* House leased to YWCA for residential conferences. No dogs.

### PYTHOUSE
**Tisbury** *map G3*
*(Country Houses Association Ltd)*

Palladian style Georgian mansion.

**Location:** 2½ m W of Tisbury; 4½ m N of Shaftesbury.
*Station: Tisbury (2½ m).*
**Opening Times:** May to Sept—Weds & Thurs 2–5. Adm £1, Chd 50p. Free car park. No dogs admitted.

### SHELDON MANOR
**Chippenham** *map G4* Ⓢ ♿
Telephone: Chippenham (0249) 653120
*(Major Martin Gibbs, DL, JP)*

Plantagenet Manor House, lived in as a family home for 700 years. 13th century porch, 15th century detached chapel.

**Location:** 1½ m W of Chippenham, signposted from A420; eastbound traffic also signposted from A4, E of Corsham (2½ m). M4 exit 17 4 m.
*Station: Chippenham (2½ m).*
**Opening Times:** Sun, Mar 26 to Sun, Sept 30—Thurs, Suns & Bank Hols 12.30–6. Gardens open 12.30 for lunches. House open at 2. Other times by arrangement for parties (for whom home-cooked meals can be provided). Majority of property suitable for wheelchairs.
**Refreshments:** Home-made lunches & cream teas. Coaches welcome by appointment.

### STONEHENGE
*map H3*
*(English Heritage)*

Built between 2800 and 1100 BC, this is Britain's most famous ancient monument and one of the world's most astonishing engineering feats. Many of the stones, some weighing 4 tons each, were brought from the Preseli Mountains in Wales to Salisbury Plain, there to be erected by human muscle power.

**Location:** 2 m (3.2 km) west of Amesbury. OS map ref SU123422.
**Opening Times:** Good Friday to Sept 30, daily 10–6; Oct 1 to Maundy Thurs, daily 10–4. *Closed* Dec 24–26, Jan 1. Adm £1.60, OAPs £1.20, Chd 80p.

### STOURHEAD, The National Trust
**Stourton, nr Mere** *map G3* △ ♿
Telephone: Bourton (0747) 840348

The world famous garden was laid out 1741–80; its lakes, temples and rare trees forming a landscape of breath-taking beauty throughout the year. Palladian House designed in 1722 by Colen Campbell. Furniture by Thomas Chippendale the Younger.

**Location:** 3 m NW of Mere (A303) in the village of Stourton off the Frome/Mere Road (B3092).
**Opening Times:** HOUSE: Apr & Oct—Sats to Weds 2–6 (or sunset if earlier); May to end Sept—Sat to Thurs 2–6 (or sunset if earlier). *Other times by written arrangement with the Administrator.* Adm £2.50, Chd £1.30. Parties of 15 or more £1.70. GARDENS: All the year—Daily 8–7 (or dusk if earlier). Adm £2, Chd £1. Parties of 15 or more £1.60 (half-price Dec to Feb) May and June £2.50, Chd £1.30, Parties £1.70. Dogs in gardens Oct to end of Feb only. Wheelchairs provided—access to gardens only.
**Refreshments:** Accommodation, Spread Eagle Inn at Garden entrance, (0747) 840587. National Trust Shop.

### TOTTENHAM HOUSE
**Savernake Forest, Marlborough** *map H4*
Telephone: Marlborough 870331
*(The Trustees of the Savernake Estate)*

Tottenham House, built by the Marquess of Ailesbury, was originally designed by Burlington and built in the early 18th century. About one hundred years later the house was completely rebuilt by Thomas Cundy although some evidence of Burlington's work still remains. The house is let to Hawtreys Preparatory School.

**Location:** 3 m A4; 6 m Marlborough.
**Opening Times:** HOUSE ONLY. Open in School holidays—Jan 2–6 1–4pm; Mar 20–24, and 27–31, Apr 3–7, Aug 28–Sept 1, 4–8: 2–5pm. Adm £1, Chd (under 14) 50p. No reductions. There are steps to the front door (although there is assistance permanently available), thereafter every room open to the public is on one floor, and the property could not strictly be described as unsuitable for the disabled. Car park.
**Refreshments:** Savernake Forest Hotel ½ m.

### WESTWOOD MANOR, The National Trust
**nr. Bradford-on-Avon** *map G4* △

15th century stone manor house altered in the late 16th century. Fine furnishings. Gardens of clipped yew. Administered for the National Trust by a tenant.

**Location:** Beside Westwood Church 1½ m SW of Bradford-on-Avon off Frome Road (B3109).
*Stations: Avoncliff (1 m); Bradford-on-Avon (1½ m).*
**Opening Times:** Mar 26 to Sept 25—Mons & Suns 2–5. Adm £2. *Other times parties of 15 or more by written application to the tenant. No reduction for parties or children. No photography.* No dogs. Unsuitable for wheelchairs.

### WILTON HOUSE
**Salisbury** *map H3* △
*(The Earl of Pembroke)*

Superb 17th Century state rooms by Inigo Jones (c. 1650) and later James Wyatt (1810). World famous collection of paintings and other treasures. Exhibitions of 7,000 model soldiers set in Diorama scenes, also 'The Pembroke Palace dolls house' and historical tableau of dolls and toys through the ages. Miniature model railway and Adventure Playground. Notable fine cedar trees and Palladian Bridge. Restricted viewing of Double and Single Cube rooms due to restoration. Video of these rooms will be shown. Some exterior restoration work. 14th century Washern Grange, the Holbein Porch and Hunting room may be seen by appointment. Garden Centre.

**Location:** In town of Wilton, 3 m W of Salisbury on A30. Trains from Waterloo and many other southern and western region stations to Salisbury. Buses from Salisbury Centre every 10 mins.
*Station: Salisbury 2½ m. Buses every 10 mins. from Salisbury.*
**Opening Times:** HOUSE and GROUNDS: Mar 24 to Oct 15—Tues to Sats & Bank Hol Mons 11–6; Suns 1–6. Last adm to House & Grounds 5.15. Adm House & Grounds £2.40, OAPs, Students and parties (20 or over) £2, Chd (under 16) £1.80. Adm to HOUSE, GROUNDS and EXHIBITIONS: £3.40, OAPs, Students and parties £2.90, Chd (under 16) £2.50. GROUNDS ONLY: £1.30, Chd 90p. GROUNDS/EXHIBITIONS: £2.30, Chd £1.60. Free car park. No dogs, except guide dogs for the blind.
**Refreshments:** Licensed Restaurant—self-service.

# NORTH YORKSHIRE

**Aldborough Roman Town –** See English Heritage Section.

### ALLERTON PARK
**nr. Knaresborough** *map H9* △
Telephone: (0423) 330927
*(The Gerald Arthur Rolph Foundation for Historic Preservation and Education)*

The grandest of the surviving Gothic revival stately homes. Its Great Hall and Dining Room are considered amongst the finest carved wood rooms in England. Allerton Park is the ancestral home of Lord Mowbray (c. 1283), Segrave (c. 1283) and Stourton (c. 1448), the premier Baron in England. House designed by George Martin, some interior rooms by Benjamin Baud. Temple of Victory built by Frederick, Duke of York (brother to King George IV) in 18c. The setting for Sherlock Holmes film 'The Sign of Four'. Private collection of mechanical music machines and luxury antique motor cars.

**Location:** 14½ m W of York; ¼ m E of A1 on York Road (A59); 4½ m W of Knaresborough, 6 m N of Wetherby; 7 m S of Boroughbridge; 14 m N of Leeds.
**Opening Times:** Easter Sun to end Sept – Suns and Bank Holiday Mons 12–5. Adm House and Grounds £2.50. Students, OAPs and Parties (25 and over) £2. Chd (under 16) with adult £1.50. School Groups £1 each. Free car parking. No dogs, except guide dogs for the blind. Other days by appointment for parties of 25 or more. Enquiries to: Mr. Farr, Administrator, Allerton Park, nr. Knaresborough, N. Yorkshire HG5 0SE. Tel: (0423) 330927.
**Refreshments:** By request.

### BENINGBROUGH HALL
**nr York** *map H9* △ ♿
Telephone: York (0904) 470666
*(The National Trust)*

This handsome Georgian house has been completely restored and in the principal rooms are 100 famous portraits on loan from the National Portrait Gallery. Victorian laundry, potting shed and exhibitions. Garden and Adventure Playground.

**Location:** 8 m NW of York; 3 m W of Shipton (A19); 2 m SE Linton-on-Ouse; follow signposted route.
**Opening Times:** Easter to end Oct; Mar 24–30, 12–6. Apr weekends 12–6, School groups & parties on weekdays by prior appointment. May to Oct—Tues, Weds, Thurs, Sats, Suns & Bank Hol Mons 12–6, last adm 5.30. Adm House & Garden £2.50, Chd (accompanied) £1.20. Family ticket (2 adults, 2 Chd) £6.20. Parties £2, Chd £1. Garden & Exhibitions £1.70, Chd (accompanied) 80p. Picnic area. Shop. No dogs. Wheelchairs provided.
**Refreshments:** The Restaurant serves homemade hot & cold lunches, teas, special suppers. Wheelchair access. Picnic area. Kiosk. Special functions catered for, details from the Administrator.

### BOLTON CASTLE
**nr Leyburn** *map G10*
Telephone: (0969) 23981/23674
*(The Hon. Harry Orde-Powlett)*

One of Britain's best preserved medieval castles now in the first stages of redecoration and refurbishment with period tapestries, arms and suits of armour, a manuscript room and tableaux depicting everyday life in the fifteenth and sixteenth centuries.

**Location:** Situated within the Yorkshire Dales National Park, 5 m W of Leyburn, 10 m E of Hawes, road signs from the A684.
**Opening Times:** Daily, Mar to end Oct: 10–5; Nov to Mar – tours by special arrangement. Party visits welcomed: groups of 25 and over, 10 per cent discount and one person free. Car park. Modern toilet facilities.
**Refreshments:** Tea room with homemade light refreshments. Under cover.

# WILTON HOUSE

**The home of the Earl of Pembroke**

*ADMISSION – SEE EDITORIAL REFERENCE*

# SHELDON MANOR

**CHIPPENHAM**

There has been a house here since early Platagenet times. The present Great Porch and Parvise above, dating from 1282, were built by Sir Geoffrey Gascelyn, Lord of the Manor and Hundred of Chippenham and were 700 years old in 1982. Sheldon is the sole survivor of a vanished medieval village.

Succeeding generations and other families, notably the Hungerfords, have added to the beautiful house, its forecourt and surrounding buildings. All the house is lived in and it is shown by the family. There are good collections of early oak furniture, Nailsea glass, porcelain and Persian saddle bags.

*"It embodies my ideal of England"*
*Hugh Montgomery-Massingberd*

There are beautiful informal terraced gardens with ancient yew trees, water, interesting trees and shrubs, connoisseur collection of old-fashioned roses.

Home-made lunches and cream teas served in the Barn or on the lawn. Visitors to Sheldon will find the food "a major consideration".

"In nominating an eating place with an 'intimate' atmosphere I could do no better than to recommend Sheldon", Hugh Montgomery-Massingberd, Weekend Telegraph, July 11th, 1987.

## NORTH YORKSHIRE – *continued*

**Byland Abbey** – See English Heritage Section.

### CASTLE HOWARD
**York** *map J10*
Telephone: Coneysthorpe (065 384) 333
*(The Hon. Simon Howard)*

Designed by Vanbrugh 1699–1726 for the 3rd Earl of Carlisle assisted by Hawksmoor, who designed the Mausoleum. Fine collection of pictures, statuary and furniture. Beautiful park and grounds. Costume Galleries covering 18th to 20th centuries in the Stable Court. Displays changed every year.

**Location:** 15 m NE of York; 3 m off A64; 6 m W of Malton; 38 m Leeds; 36 m Harrogate; 22 m Scarborough; 50 m Hull.
**Opening Times:** Mar 20 to end Oct—Daily. House and Costume Galleries are open 11–4.30. Plant centre, rose gardens, grounds and cafeteria open 10. Adm charges not available at time of going to press. *Special terms for adult booked parties.*
**Refreshments:** Cafeteria. Licensed restaurant available for advance bookings.

### CLIFFORD'S TOWER, YORK
*map H9*
Telephone: (0904) 646940
(English Heritage)

York Castle, like the city itself, has had a long and turbulent history. Clifford's Tower was built on an earlier motte (or mound) in the 13th century. The tower is named after a Lancastrian leader from the Wars of the Roses, Sir Robert Clifford, who was defeated in 1322, and his body hung in chains from the tower.

**Location:** Near Castle Museum. OS map ref SE605515.
**Opening Times:** Good Friday to Sept 30, daily 10–6; Oct 1 to Maundy Thurs, daily 10–4. *Closed* Dec 24–26, Jan 1. Adm 80p, OAPs 60p, Chd 40p.

### CONSTABLE BURTON HALL
**Leyburn** *map H10*
Telephone: Bedale 50428
*(M. C. A. Wyvill, Esq.)*

Extensive borders, interesting alpines, large informal garden. John Carr house completed in 1768.

**Location:** On A684, between Leyburn (3 m) & Bedale; A1 (7 m).
**Opening Times:** Gardens. May 1 to Aug 1—Daily 9–6. Adm 50p (1987 charge), collecting box.
House: opening dates & adm charges not available at time of going to press. Party rates by arrangement.

### DUNCOMBE PARK
**Helmsley** *map H10*
*(The Rt. Hon. Lord Feversham)*

Two 18th century Temples. Landscaped Gardens.

**Location:** 1 m W of Helmsley.
**Opening Times:** Gardens only. May to Aug—Weds 10–4. Adm £1. *Apply to Tourist Information Centre, Helmsley Market Place. No access for cars.*

**Easby Abbey** – See English Heritage Section.

### EBBERSTON HALL
**Scarborough** *map J10*
*(W. de Wend Fenton, Esq.)*

Palladian Villa of 1718 designed by the architect Colin Campbell. Water gardens attributed to William Benson and Switzer. Elaborate woodwork and cornices comparable to Castle Howard and Beningbrough.

**Location:** 11 m W of Scarborough on A170 Scarborough/Pickering Road.
**Opening Times:** Easter to Oct 1—Daily 10–6. Adm £1.50.

### FAIRFAX HOUSE
**Castlegate, York** *map H9*
Telephone: (0904) 655543
*(York Civic Trust)*

18th century townhouse, exceptional decoration and contents.

**Location:** next to Clifford's Tower and the Castle Museum.
*Station: York (½ m)*
**Opening Times:** Mar 1 to Jan 1—Mons, Tues, Weds, Thurs & Sats 11–5; Suns 1.30–5. *Closed* Fri. Last adm 4.30. Adm £2, Chd 75p, Pre-booked parties (15 or more) £1.25, Chd 50p. Evening visits by arrangement. Gift and Antique Shop.

### FOUNTAINS ABBEY & STUDLEY ROYAL, The National Trust
**Ripon** *map H10* ♿

Ruins of Cistercian monastery. Ornamental gardens laid out by John Aislabie, 1720. Exhibition and video film in Fountains Hall. Awarded World Heritage status.

**Location:** 2m W of Ripon; 9 m W of Harrogate; NW of A61.
**Opening Times:** DEER PARK. Open all year during daylight hours, adm free. ABBEY & GARDENS. Jan, Feb, Mar, Nov & Dec—Daily except Christmas Eve, Christmas Day and Fri in Jan, Nov & Dec 10–5 or dusk if earlier. Apr, May, June & Sept 10–7; July & Aug 10–8; Oct 10–6 or dusk if earlier. FOUNTAINS HALL. Apr to Sept, 11–6; Oct to Mar, 1–4. Adm £1.90, Chd 90p. Family ticket £4.70 (2 Adults/2 Chd). Parties (up to 40) £1.50, Chd 70p. Parties of 40 and more (Mon to Fri) £1.30, Chd 60p. Car parking: Cars 70p, Motorcycles 30p. Coaches (Mon to Fri) no charge, Sat & Sun £3. *Closed Christmas Eve & Christmas Day.*
**Refreshments:** Light lunches, sandwiches, cakes, soup, tea, coffee, cold drinks available Studley Cafe, Studley Park. Open Jan to end March, 11–5; Apr to Oct, 10–5.30; Oct to Jan, 11–5. Fountains Cafe open Apr to Oct 10–5.30. Nov and Dec: weekends only 11–5. Wheelchair access. Picnics can be taken anywhere on Estate. Dogs on leashes only. Studley Royal Shop—Tel: (0765) 4246. Open all year Jan to end Mar, 11–5. Apr to Oct, 10–6 and Oct to Dec, 11–5. Abbey Stores – open Apr – Oct 10–5.

### GEORGIAN THEATRE ROYAL
**Richmond** *map H10*
Telephone: (0748) 3021
*(The Georgian Theatre (Richmond) Trust Ltd.)*

Built in 1788. Historically very important being country's oldest theatre in original form. Beautiful intimate interior; also Theatre Museum.

**Location:** 4 m from Scotch Corner (A1) on the A6108.
**Opening Times:** Theatre & Museum—Easter weekend, then May to Sept—Daily 2.30–5; also Sats & Bank Hol Mons 10.30–1. Adm charge. Party rates on application. Intermittent season of Plays, Recitals, etc. *Theatre may be viewed during winter months; apply in writing to the Manager.*

# BOLTON CASTLE

NEAR LEYBURN, NORTH YORKSHIRE

Historical tableaux, manuscripts, arms and suits of armour, period tapestries.

Halls and chambers, monk's cell, dungeon, armourer's forge, ale house, threshing floor, accessible battlements.

Open 10am to 5pm every day March to end October, November to March – tours by special arrangement. Party visits welcome. Undercover tea room with homemade light refreshments. Car parking.

A medieval experience

# FAIRFAX HOUSE

CASTLEGATE YORK

A richly decorated interior, completed in 1762 to the design of John Carr and described as the finest example of its type in England.

It is now the permanent home of a unique collection of Georgian furniture, clocks and carpets. In addition, important loans of paintings and porcelain together with an exhibition on Georgian life in York, make it an experience not to be missed.

ADMISSION
SEE EDITORIAL REFERENCE

# Explore the past, enjoy the present and protect the future in North Yorkshire.

Turn to our Red Page listing at the back and find out more about the exciting range of English Heritage properties throughout the country.

Rievaulx Abbey

English Heritage

### GILLING CASTLE
**Helmsley** *map H10*
*(Ampleforth Abbey Trustees)*

Original Norman keep with 16th and 18th century additions.

**Location:** In Gilling East, 18 m N of York.
**Opening Times:** All the year (except Christmas Day, Boxing Day and New Year's Day)—Mon to Fri 10–12, 2–4. Adm free to Hall and Great Chamber only. Gardens—July to Sept. Adm 50p.

### HARLOW CAR GARDENS
**Harrogate** *map H9*
*(The Northern Horticultural Society)*

60 acres of ornamental gardens and woodlands.

**Location:** 1½ m from centre of Harrogate, Otley Road B6162.
*Station: Harrogate (1½ m).*
**Opening Times:** All the year—Daily 9–7.30 (or dusk if earlier). Adm charge. Free car park. Cafe. Shop and plant sales.

**Helmsley Castle** – See English Heritage Section.

### HOVINGHAM HALL
**York** *map J10*
*(Sir Marcus & Lady Worsley)*

Palladian house designed c. 1760 by Thomas Worsley. Unique Riding School, magnificent yew hedges, dovecot, private cricket ground. Family portraits.

**Location:** 20 m N of York on Malton/Helmsley Road (B1257).
**Opening Times:** Open for parties of 15 or more **by written appointment only**—Apr 18 to Sept 28, Tues, Weds & Thurs 11–7. Adm £2, Chd £1.
**Refreshments:** At the Hall by arrangement. Meals at The Worsley Arms, Hovingham.

**Kirkham Priory** – See English Heritage Section.

### MARKENFIELD HALL
**Ripon** *map H10*
*(The Lord Grantley, MC)*

Fine example of English manor house 14th, 15th & 16th century buildings surrounded by moat.

**Location:** 3 m S of Ripon off the Ripon/Harrogate Road (A61). Access is up a road marked 'Public Bridleway Hell Wath Lane'.
**Opening Times:** Apr to Oct—Mons 10–12.30, 2.15–5. Adm 50p, Chd (accompanied by adult) free. Exterior only outside courtyard and moat all other days in May—times as above. Adm free.

### MERCHANT ADVENTURERS' HALL
**Fossgate or Piccadilly, York** *map H9* ♿
Telephone: (0904) 654818
*(The Governor and Company of Merchant Adventurers)*

One of the finest surviving medieval gild halls in Europe.

**Location:** Next to Clifford's Tower, the Castle Museum and Fairfax House.
*Station: York (½ m).*
**Opening Times:** Mid-Mar to early Nov—Daily 8.30–5; early Nov to mid-Mar—Daily (except Sun) 8.30–3.30. Adm £1, OAPs 80p, Chd 50p. Suitable for the disabled, including lavatory for disabled. No car parking, except in city of York.

**Middleham Castle** – See English Heritage Section.

**Mount Grace Priory** – See English Heritage Section.

### NEWBURGH PRIORY
**Coxwold** *map H10*
Telephone: Coxwold (034 76) 435
*(Sir George Wombwell Bt)*

Originally 12th century Augustinian Priory with 16th, 17th and 18th century alterations and additions. Rare water garden and collection of rock and alpine plants. Walled garden.

**Location:** 5 m from Easingwold off A19, 9 m from Thirsk.
**Opening Times:** May 10 to Aug 30—Weds and Suns, Easter Mon and Aug Bank Hol Mon. House open 2.30–4.45. Grounds 2–6. Adm House & Grounds £1.70, Chd 80p. Grounds only 70p, Chd 30p. *Other days for parties of 25 or more by appointment with the Administrator.*
**Refreshments:** In the Old Priory Kitchens.

## NEWBURGH PRIORY
**COXWOLD, YORK**

One of the North's most interesting Historic Houses. Originally built in 1145 with alterations in 1568 and 1720–1760, the Priory has been the home of one family and its descendants since 1538. The house contains the tomb of Oliver Cromwell (his third daughter, Mary, was married to Viscount Fauconberg—owner 1647 1700). In the grounds there is a really beautiful Water Garden full of rare alpines, plants and rhododendrons. Afternoon tea is served in the original kitchen.

*ADMISSION—SEE EDITORIAL REFERENCE*

## EBBERSTON HALL
**Scarborough**

*ADMISSION – SEE EDITORIAL REFERENCE*

## MERCHANT ADVENTURERS' HALL
**YORK**

The Great Hall of the York Merchants' Gild was built in the 1350s. In it the Merchants transacted their business and held their feasts, as their successors still do today. Gild banners and Merchants' portraits hang on the walls, and there is a good collection of early furniture.

Below the Great Hall is a Hospital where they cared for the poor, and also their private Chapel.

# The National Trust in YORKSHIRE

FOUNTAINS ABBEY
& STUDLEY ROYAL

TREASURER'S
HOUSE

RIEVAULX TERRACE
AND TEMPLES

NUNNINGTON
HALL

EAST RIDDLESDEN
HALL

BENINGBROUGH
HALL

*ADMISSION — SEE EDITORIAL REFERENCE*

## NEWBY HALL & GARDENS

**Ripon** *map H10* ♿
Telephone: (0423) 322583
*(R. E. J. Compton, Esq.)*

One of the most famous Adam houses beautifully redecorated, contains superb Gobelins tapestries, fine collection of antique sculpture and furniture. 25 acres of glorious Gardens. Miniature Railway through the Gardens and Adventure Gardens for children. Woodland discovery walk. Steam boat on Suns. Gift shop. Plant stall. Picnic area.

**Location:** 4 m SE of Ripon on Boroughbridge Road (B6265). 3 m W of A1; 14 m Harrogate; 20 m York; 35 m Leeds; 32 m Skipton.
**Opening Times:** Mar 24 to Oct 29—Daily except Mons (but open Bank Hol Mons). House open until Oct 1 from 12–5. Garden open until Oct 29, 11–5.30 last adm 5 pm. Adm charges not available at time of going to press. Enquiries to: Opening Administrator, The Estate Office, Newby Hall, Ripon HG4 5AE.
**Refreshments:** Licensed Restaurant for lunches & teas in the Garden Restaurant.

## NORTON CONYERS

**Ripon HG4 5EH** *map H10* △ ♿
Telephone: Melmerby (076 584) 333
*(Sir James Graham, Bt)*

This late medieval house with Jacobean and Georgian additions has belonged to the Grahams since 1624. James I, Charles I and James II stayed here. Family pictures, furniture and wedding dresses. Relics of Charlotte Brontë who paid a visit in 1839, the house is one of the originals of Thornfield Hall in 'Jane Eyre', and a family legend was reputedly the inspiration for the mad Mrs Rochester.

**Location:** 3½ m NW of Ripon nr Wath; 1½ m from A1.
**Opening Times:** Suns from June 4 to Sept 17, also all Bank Holiday Suns & Mons, and daily from July 29 to Aug 5, 2–5.30. Any time for booked parties; inquiries to Beatrice, Lady Graham at above address. Adm £1.50, Chd (4–14) 70p, OAPs £1, parties of 15 or more £1. Small gift shop, free parking. Dogs (excluding guide dogs) in grounds only. Visitors are requested not to wear stiletto heels.
Interesting **Small Garden Centre** in the 18th century walled garden, specialising in unusual hardy plants. Open all year Mons to Fris 9–5; Sats & Suns Apr 1 to Oct 1, 2–5.30.
**Refreshments:** Bank holiday and charity openings. Also for booked parties by request.

## NUNNINGTON HALL

**nr Helmsley** *map J10*
Telephone: Nunnington 283
*(The National Trust)*

Sixteenth century manor house with fine panelled hall and staircase. Carlisle Collection of Miniature Rooms on display.

**Location:** In Ryedale; 4½ m SE of Helmsley; 1½ m N of B1257.
**Opening Times:** Easter to end Oct. Closed Good Fri. Open Bank Hol Mons 12–6. Mar 25–30, and Apr weekends only 2–6; May, June, Sept & Oct—Tues, Weds, Thurs, Sats & Suns 2–6; July & Aug—Tues, Weds, Thurs & Sats 2–6; Suns 12–6. Last admission 5.30. School Parties on weekdays by arrangement with administrator. Adm £1.80, Chd 90p, Parties £1.50, Chd 70p. Access to Ground Floor and tearoom only for Wheelchairs. Lavatory for disabled at rear of house. Access to main gardens via ramp. Guide dogs permitted. Dogs in car park only.
**Refreshments:** Afternoon teas available at all times when house is open 2–5.30 in indoor tearooms or tea garden. Lunches July & Aug. Shop.

**Pickering Castle** – See English Heritage Section.

**Richmond Castle** – See English Heritage Section.

**Rievaulx Abbey** – See English Heritage Section.

## RIEVAULX TERRACE, The National Trust

**Helmsley** *map H10* ♿
Telephone: Bilsdale 340

Beautiful half mile long grass terrace with views of Rievaulx Abbey. Two 18th century Temples and permanent exhibition.

**Location:** 2½ m NW of Helmsley on Stokesley Road (B1257).
**Opening Times:** Good Friday to Oct 29—Daily 10.30–6 (last adm 5.30). Ionic Temple closed 1–2. Adm £1.30, Chd 60p, Parties £1.10, Chd 50p. All dogs on leash. Battery operated 'Runabout' available.
**Refreshments:** Teas available at Nunnington Hall, 7 m E.

## RIPLEY CASTLE

**Ripley** *map H9*
Telephone: Harrogate (0423) 770152
*(Sir Thomas Ingilby Bt)*

Has been the home of the Ingilby family since early 14th century. Main gateway dates from reign of Edward IV. Extensive gardens.

**Location:** In Ripley 3½ m N Harrogate; 7½ m from Ripon.
**Opening Times:** Castle: Apr, May and Oct—Sats & Suns, 11.30–4.30; June to Oct (incl)—Daily except Mons and Fri 11.30–4.30. Good Friday and all Bank Holidays in season 11–4.30. Booked parties: Groups can visit the castle on any day during the year, by prior appointment. Gardens only: Daily Apr 1 to Oct.
**Refreshments:** Licensed restaurant (The Butlers Pantry) in village: Tearoom in castle courtyard, serving home-made teas.

**Scarborough Castle** – See English Heritage Section.

## SHANDY HALL

**Coxwold** *map H10*
Telephone: Coxwold 465
*(The Laurence Sterne Trust)*

Exceptional medieval house altered and added to in 17th and 18th centuries but little changed since Laurence Sterne wrote *'A Sentimental Journey'* and most of *'Tristram Shandy'* there. Walled garden with unusual plants.

**Location:** 20 m from York via A19; 6 m from A19 at Easingwold; 8 m from Thirsk; 13 m from A1 at Dishforth.
**Opening Times:** June to Sept—Weds 2–4.30. Suns 2.30–4.30. *Any other day or time all year by appointment with Hon Curators.* Adm £1.50, Chd (accompanied) half-price. Book & handicrafts shop. Plants for sale.
**Refreshments:** Close by in village.

## SHERIFF HUTTON PARK

**Sheriff Hutton, York YO6 1RH** *map J10*
Telephone: Sheriff Hutton (034 77) 442
*(The East 15 Acting School Limited)*

Grade I historic house, originally King James I's Royal Hunting Lodge. Open to public are 3 rooms of significant importance and main staircase; they include 2 magnificent Jacobean plaster ceilings and a beautiful screens passage. Extensive grounds with routed walkways, picnic areas, lily pond, lake, statues. Croquet introduced here mid 19th Century by Leonard Thompson whose rules were published by Cordeaux & Ernest 1864.

**Location:** Park entrance clearly signposted ¼ m S of Sheriff Hutton village centre, at junction York and Flaxton/Lilling roads.
**Opening Times:** Apr 1 to Oct 31, daily except Mon 10–6. Winter weekends by appointment only. Adm £1, Chd/OAPs 50p, under 5 free. Group adm 12 – £10, 16 – £13, 50 – £40. Family ticket £2. Adequate free car parking. Section of grounds traversible in wheelchair by request, lift to ground floor rooms in Hall (no wheelchairs available). Sheriff Hutton Park is the venue of the Galtres Theatre Company and productions are frequently presented here and open to tourists. In 1989 numerous performances will be staged in the Company's new Greek-style amphitheatre by the lakeside.
**Refreshments:** Picnic venues and tearoom provided; hotel next door.

## SION HILL HALL

**Kirby Wiske, nr Thirsk** *map H10*
Telephone: Thirsk (0845) 587206
*(The H W Mawer Trust)*

Neo-Georgian country house by Walter Brierley, with fine collection of furniture, paintings and porcelain from most periods. R.I.B.A. Architectural Award Winner.

**Location:** 6 m S of Northallerton, 4 m W of Thirsk, ½ m off A167 signpost Kirby Wiske.
**Opening Times:** Last Sun in month May–Sept incl. 2–4.30, other times organised groups only by arrangement with the Curator. Adm £2, Chd under 12 free if accompanied. Free parking for cars or coaches.
**Refreshments:** Teas on open Suns only at Village Hall.

# SHERIFF HUTTON PARK

**SHERIFF HUTTON, YORK YO6 1RH**

Sheriff Hutton Park is a fine red-brick mansion standing in well wooded grounds which command pleasant views of the neighbouring castle, and on clear days, a distant prospect of York Minster. From the outside it displays the good proportions and distinctive charm of a Queen Anne style country house, but within, the visitor will find a variety of unspoilt Jacobean and early-Georgian rooms. The former survive from the Great Lodge built by Sir Arthur Ingram between 1619 and 1624; while the latter date from the alterations made about 1730 by Leonard Thompson. The garden also preserves many Jacobean features, including some delightful statues and heraldic beasts carved by local decorative artists.
**The Royal Hunting Lodge.** In the early 17th century Sheriff Hutton and all the surrounding countryside was part of the immense Forest of Galtres. The whole area was a royal hunting reserve controlled by officers of the Crown who were responsible for maintaining the game and seeing that the local inhabitants did not kill the deer, steal wood; or keep swine within the bounds of the forest. Sheriff Hutton itself consisted of a small village; a derelict castle (not lived in since the reign of Henry VIII), and a large deer park which contained the royal hunting lodge or 'Launde House' as it is referred to in documents.

# FOR THE COMPLETE FAMILY DAY OUT VISIT

# Newby Hall and Gardens

*Winner of the 1986 Christies/HHA Garden of the Year Award*
*Winner of the 1983 BTA Heritage Award*

Newby Hall, the lived-in home of Mr and Mrs Robin Compton. Set in one of the loveliest gardens in England, this famous Adam house contains many unique treasures.

Newby Hall and Gardens offer unparalleled opportunities for all the family to have an exciting and peaceful day out.

**NEWBY HALL & GARDENS – the *Complete* family day out!**

BEAUTIFUL LIVED-IN HALL · AWARD WINNING GARDENS · 10¼" GAUGE TRAIN · STEAM BOAT ON SUNDAY · ADVENTURE GARDENS · WOODLAND DISCOVERY WALK · PLANT STALL · GIFT SHOP · LICENSED GARDEN RESTAURANT · PICNIC AREA · FREE CAR PARKING

Newby Hall and Gardens
Open daily from 24 March to 30 October *(house closes 1 October)*
daily except Mondays *(but including Bank Holidays)*

Gardens and licensed restaurant open 11.00 am · Hall open 12.00 noon
For further details write to the Estate Office, Newby Hall, Ripon, North Yorkshire HG4 5AE or telephone (0423) 322583

# NORTON CONYERS

**BEDFORD**

*Photograph: Simon Warner, Keighley*

Norton Conyers has something special to offer. Many visitors have remarked on its friendly atmosphere. The main rooms, with their pictures and furniture, reflect over 360 years of occupation by the same family. The furniture includes a very rare 16th century marble-topped table, the pictures, a pair of Romney portraits and a famous Ferneley, "The Quorn Hunt", painted in 1822. On the first floor, the room and the bed traditionally used by the Duke of York, later James II, and his Duchess during their visit in 1679 are on view to the public.

*ADMISSION DETAILS – SEE EDITORIAL REFERENCE*

**SIR THOMAS AND LADY INGILBY**

invite you to

# VISIT RIPLEY CASTLE

If you are visiting this area for a few days, don't miss this fascinating and beautiful castle, just three miles north of Harrogate and half an hour from York. Let us tell you about our 660 years of history and show you some of the remarkable items that our ancestors left behind. It will be a richly rewarding and thoroughly entertaining experience for you. Come and see the Priest's secret hiding place and Civil War armour in the 1555 tower. You won't regret it.

**THE LAURENCE STERNE TRUST**

# SHANDY HALL

**COXWOLD, NORTH YORKSHIRE**

*The medieval house where the modern novel was born*

Here in 1760–67 the witty and eccentric parson Laurence Sterne wrote *Tristram Shandy* and *A Sentimental Journey*, 'novels that jump clean out of the 18th century into the 20th', influencing Dickens, Goethe, Tolstoy, Balzac, Proust, Melville, Joyce, Virginia Woolf, and other great writers. Shandy Hall was built as a timber-framed open-hall in the mid-15th century, modernised in the 17th, curiously added to by Sterne in the 18th. It survives much as he knew it, almost as full of surprises and odd digressions as his novels, most of which he wrote in his little book-lined study. Not a museum but a lived-in house where you are sure of a personal welcome. Surrounded by a walled garden full of old-fashioned roses and cottage-garden plants.

*ADMISSION – SEE EDITORIAL REFERENCE*

# SUTTON PARK

**York**

*ADMISSION – SEE EDITORIAL REFERENCE*

# THORP PERROW

**Near SNAPE, NORTH YORKSHIRE**

Thorpe Perrow, the North Country home of Sir John and Lady Ropner, contains within its 60 acres of landscaped grounds an arboretum—a fine collection of over 2,000 species of trees and shrubs, including some of the largest and rarest in England. The grounds are now open to the general public, and have rapidly become a popular focal point in the North of England.

Thorp Perrow is open from the end of March until the end of October. This is a pleasant outing that may be enjoyed by all members of the family, who may wander at will amidst these magnificent surroundings. There is a free car park and picnic area, and the entrance to Thorp Perrow Arboretum can be found on the Well to Bedale Road (near Snape) north of Ripon.

### SKIPTON CASTLE
**Skipton** *map G9* △
Telephone: Skipton (0756) 2442

First-time visitors are delighted to discover that this most popular Yorkshire castle is still complete and fully roofed. Skipton Castle's massive mediaeval towers and beautiful Conduit Court featured on TV in 'Treasure Hunt'.

**Location:** Head of High Street.
*Railway Station: (½ m).*
*Bus Station: (town centre).*
**Opening Times:** Every day, except Christmas Day. Adm £1.60; under-18's half price; under-5's free! Everyone under 18 gets a Skipton Castle Explorer's badge. Guides are available for pre-booked parties; otherwise, illustrated Tour Sheets in English, French, German or Japanese are provided. Party visits are welcomed: School parties 80p each including accompanying adults; 10% discount for other parties of 15 or more. Large coach and car park nearby, off High Street.

### STOCKELD PARK
**Wetherby** *map H9*
Telephone: Wetherby (0937) 66101
*(Mr & Mrs P. G. F. Grant)*

Small country mansion, one of the finest examples of the work of James Paine, built in the Palladian style 1758–63. Main feature is the central hall and staircase. Attractive grounds and gardens.

**Location:** 3 m N of Wetherby; 7 m SE of Harrogate on A661.
**Opening Times:** July 1 to 30 1989, daily (*except Mons*) 2.30–5.30. Other times by appointment. Adm charges not available at time of going to press.
**Refreshments:** Teas at weekends only.

### SUTTON PARK
**Sutton-on-the-Forest** *map H10*
Telephone: 0347 810249
*(Mrs Sheffield)*

Most welcoming early Georgian house, the home of Mrs Nancy Sheffield, built in 1730. Historical contents include Chippendale, Sheraton and French furniture, decorative plasterwork by Cortese, fine paintings and porcelain, with fresh flower arrangements in every room. Very beautiful landscaped gardens and parkland created by Capability Brown. Georgian Ice House, Woodland/Daffodil Walks, Nature Trail and Gift Shop.

**Location:** 8 m N of York; on the B1363 York/Helmsley road. Also signposted from the A19 York/Thirsk road in the Easingwold area.
**Opening Times:** GARDENS: open daily from Easter to Oct 1 (*except Sat*) from 11–5.30. HOUSE AND GARDENS: open all Easter weekend, Apr: Suns only from 1.30; May to Sept 12: Sun, Tues and Bank Holiday Mons from 1.30. Adm charges not available at time of going to press. Booked parties of 20 or more welcome every day. Contact: The Secretary, Sutton Park, Sutton-on-the-Forest, York, YO6 1DP. Tel: (0347) 810249.
**Refreshments:** Tea room/restaurant.

### THORP PERROW ARBORETUM
**nr Snape** *map H10*
*(Sir John & Lady Ropner)*

60 acres of landscaped grounds containing an arboretum of over 2,000 species of trees and shrubs, including some of the largest and rarest in England.

**Location:** N of Ripon on the Well/Bedale Road.
**Opening Times:** End of Mar to end of Oct. Adm £1, Chd under 12 & OAPs 50p. Free car park. Picnic area.

### TREASURER'S HOUSE, The National Trust
**York** *map H9*
Telephone: York (0904) 624247

Large 17th century house of great interest. Fine furniture and paintings. Exhibition.

**Location:** Behind York Minster.
*Station: York (½ m).*
**Opening Times:** Good Friday to Oct 29—Daily 10.30–5. Last adm 4.30. Guided tours by arrangement. Adm £1.50, Chd 70p, Parties £1.30, Chd 60p. Wheelchair access—part of ground floor only. No car parking facilities. Dogs not allowed, except for guide dogs. Shop.
**Refreshments:** Available in licensed tea rooms serving morning coffee, light lunches, teas. Open for pre-booked parties during and outside normal opening hours and for private functions. Tel: York 646757.

**Whitby Abbey** – See English Heritage Section.

# SOUTH YORKSHIRE

### CANNON HALL
**Cawthorne** *map H8*
Telephone: Barnsley 790270
*(Barnsley Metropolitan Borough Council)*

18th century house by Carr of York. Collections of fine furniture, paintings, glassware, pewter and pottery. Also the Regimental Museum of the 13th/18th Royal Hussars. 70 acres of parkland.

**Location:** 5 m W of Barnsley on A635; 1 m NW of Cawthorne.
**Opening Times:** All the year—Weekdays 10.30–5; Suns 2.30–5. Adm free. *Closed Christmas Day, Boxing Day, December 27, New Year's Day & Good Friday.*

**Comisbrough Castle** – See English Heritage Section.

**Monk Bretton Priory** – See English Heritage Section.

**Roche Abbey** – See English Heritage Section.

### SHEFFIELD BOTANIC GARDENS
**Clarkehouse Rd, Sheffield** *map H8*
*(Sheffield City Council)*

Begun as a private venture in 1833, transferred to the Town Trust in 1898, and to Sheffield Corporation 1951. Demonstration gardens, conservation area and garden, and garden and chalet for the disabled, together with the Paxton Pavilion complex, which includes aviary, aquarium and half hardy house.

**Location:** 1 m from centre of Sheffield.
**Opening Times:** Daily all year. Admission free.

### THE SUE RYDER HOME, HICKLETON HALL
**nr Doncaster** *map H8*
*(The Sue Ryder Foundation)*

This Home cares for 50 physically handicapped and others who are homeless and unable to cope on their own.

**Location:** 6 m NW of Doncaster; on A635 Doncaster/Barnsley Road (behind Hickleton Church).
**Opening Times:** Individuals wishing to visit the Home may do so, Mons to Fris 2–4 without prior appointment. Please report your arrival to the Office in the main entrance.
**Refreshments:** Hotels & Restaurants in Doncaster.

# WEST YORKSHIRE

### ACKWORTH SCHOOL
**Pontefract** *map H9*
Telephone: Hemsworth (0977) 611401
*(Co-educational Boarding School Society of Friends)*

Georgian building (1750)—only remaining building of London Foundling Hospital.

**Location:** 3½ m S of Pontefract on A628.
**Opening Times:** During School vacations—Monday to Fri 10–4 (by appointment). Adm: voluntary donation.

### BOLLING HALL
**Bradford** *map H9* Ⓢ
Telephone: Bradford 723057
*(Bradford Metro Council)*

Furnished Manor House built between the 15th and 18th centuries.

**Location:** Bowling Hall Road, Bradford BD4 7LP
**Opening Times:** All the year—Daily (except Mons but open Bank Hol Mons) Oct to Mar 10–5. Apr to Sept 10–6. *Closed Christmas Day, Boxing Day & Good Friday.* Adm free (Public Museum).

### BRAMHAM PARK
**Wetherby** *map H9*
Telephone: Boston Spa (0937) 844265
*(Mr & Mrs George Lane Fox)*

The house was created during the first half of the 18th century and affords a rare opportunity to enjoy a beautiful Queen Anne mansion containing fine furniture, pictures and porcelain—set in magnificent grounds with ornamental ponds, cascades, tall beech hedges and loggias of various shapes—unique in the British Isles for its grand vistas design stretching out into woodlands of cedar, copper beech, lime and Spanish chestnut interspersed with wild rhododendron thickets.

**Location:** 5 m S of Wetherby on the Great North Road (A1).
**Opening Times:** GROUNDS ONLY. Easter weekend, May Day, Spring Bank Hol weekend. HOUSE & GROUNDS. June 11 to Aug 31—Suns, Tues, Weds & Thurs also Bank Hol Mon (Aug 28) 1.15–5.30. Last adm 5 pm. For adm charges concessionary rates contact The Estate Office, Bramham Park, Wetherby, W. Yorks LS23 6ND. BRAMHAM HORSE TRIALS—June 1–4, 1989.

# *Come & explore* Skipton Castle

This finely preserved mediaeval castle – seen on TV in 'Treasure Hunt' – is open throughout the year.
*Explorer's Badge* **free** *for all under-18s.*

## THE SUE RYDER HOME HICKLETON HALL

**Nr DONCASTER**

This Home cares for 50 physically handicapped and others who are homeless and unable to cope on their own.

Individuals wishing to visit the Sue Ryder Home may do so on any afternoon between the hours of 2 and 4 pm, Monday to Friday, without prior appointment.

Please call at the office in the Entrance on arrival.

## BOLLING HALL

**BRADFORD**

Bolling Hall is one of the oldest houses in Bradford and its varied interiors and furnishings reflect its long history. A medieval tower opens into a traditional kitchen, the central hall has huge stained glass windows, the bedrooms display wonderful 17th Century furniture which compliments the architecture, and the wing altered in the 18th Century provides a contrast with its lighter decoration and furnishings. There are fine displays of historical material evoking the splendour of times past.

Open daily October to March 10 am to 5 pm. April to September 10 am to 6 pm. Admission free. Closed Mondays (except Bank Holidays).
Bowling Hall Road, Bradford BD4 7LP. Tel: 723057.

## BRAMHAM PARK

**WETHERBY, WEST YORKSHIRE**

Magnificent Queen Anne Mansion

66 acres of gardens unique in the British Isles. Inspired by Andre Le Notre who created Versailles.

Pleasure Grounds—bounded by two massive beech avenues with rides radiating from temples and an obelisk.

Location—5 miles South of Wetherby just off the A1.

*ADMISSION – SEE EDITORIAL REFERENCE*

## HERITAGE EDUCATION TRUST

**HET**
has now published the first
**HERITAGE EDUCATION HANDBOOK**
Edited by Martyn Dyer

Sandford Award winning properties assessed.
Theory practice and development of Heritage Education explained.
Work of the Trust described
Heritage Groups listed
Illustrated

Price **£3.95**

May be ordered through branches of W.H. Smith or direct from
**Heritage Education Trust,**
**St. Mary's College, Strawberry Hill, TW1 4SX**
**01 892 0051 x202**

## Enjoy even more of South Yorkshire.

## Explore the English Heritage Supplement on the Red Pages.

English Heritage

## BRONTË PARSONAGE
**Haworth** *map G9*
Telephone: Haworth 42323
*(The Brontë Society)*

Georgian Parsonage, containing many relics of the Brontë family, including furniture, clothes, manuscripts and drawings. Small formal garden.

**Location:** 4 m SW of Keighley on A6033 at Haworth.
**Opening Times:** All the year—Daily Apr to Sept, 11–5.30; Oct to Mar, 11–4.30. Adm Good Fri–Aug 31 inclusive, £1, OAPs & Students 50p, Chd 25p; all other times, 60p, OAPs & Students 30p, Chd 25p. *Closed Dec 24, 25 and 26 and Feb 1 to 21 incl.*

## EAST RIDDLESDEN HALL, The National Trust
**Keighley** *map H9* ♿

17th century manor house. Magnificent tithe barn. Small formal garden.

**Location:** 1 m NE of Keighley on S side of A650, on N bank of Aire.
*Station: Keighley (1½ m).*
**Opening Times:** Easter to end Oct: Mar 24–31: 2–5.30. Apr—Weekends only 2–5.30. School groups and parties on weekdays by prior arrangement. May, June, Sept & Oct, Wed–Sun and Bank Holiday Mons 2–5.30; July & Aug, Weds to Suns & Bank Hol Mons 12–5.30 (last adm 5). Tearoom open 2–5. Adm £1.50, Chd 70p, Parties £1.30, Chd 60p. Dogs, with the exception of guide dogs, allowed in grounds only and must be on leash. Only ground floor and garden accessible for disabled visitors. Shop and Information Centre. Large camera bags are not allowed in house – photography by permission only.
**Refreshments:** Afternoon teas and refreshments in Bothy Tearoom adjacent to house (on first floor), special arrangements for disabled visitors contact Administrator.

## HAREWOOD HOUSE AND BIRD GARDEN
**Leeds** *map H9* Ⓢ
Telephone: (0532) 886225
*(The Earl of Harewood)*

18th century house designed by John Carr and Robert Adam and still the home of the Lascelles family. As well as superb ceilings, plasterwork and Chippendale furniture it contains fine English and Italian paintings and Sevres and Chinese porcelain. In the grounds, landscaped by 'Capability' Brown, are lakeside and woodland walks, displays of roses and rhododendrons and a herbaceous border running the length of the Terrace.

**Location:** 7 m S of Harrogate; 8 m N of Leeds on Leeds/Harrogate road; Junction A61/659 at Harewood village; 5 m from A1 at Wetherby 22m from York.
**Opening Times:** HOUSE, GROUNDS, BIRD GARDEN AND ALL FACILITIES—Easter to Oct 31 daily. Gates open 10 House open 11. Limited opening Nov, Feb and Mar—Suns. Concession rates for Coach parties, school parties welcome at all times. Adm charges and details of Summer and Weekend Events—including Car Rallies and Leeds Championship Dog Show available from Gerald Long, Visitors Information, Estate Office, Harewood, Leeds LS17 9LQ. State Dining Room (max 48) available.
**Refreshments:** Cafeteria; Restaurant; also Courtyard Functions Suite for Conference/Product launches throughout the year.

## LEDSTON HALL
**nr Castleford** *map H9*
*(G. H. H. Wheler, Esq.)*

17th century mansion with some earlier work.

**Location:** 2 m N of Castleford off A656.
*Station: Castleford (2¾ m).*
*Opening Times:* Exterior only. May, June, July and Aug—Mon to Fri 9–4. Other days by appointment.
**Refreshments:** Chequers Inn, Ledsham (1 m).

## LOTHERTON HALL
**Aberford** *map H9*
*(Leeds Metro District Council)*

Edwardian house with attractive gardens. Gascoigne collection of pictures and furniture.

**Location:** 1 m E of A1 at Aberford on the Towton Road (B1217).
**Opening Times:** All the year—Tues to Sun 10.30–6.15 (or dusk if earlier); Thurs from May to September 10.30–8.30. *Closed Mons except Bank Hol Mons.* Adm 75p, Chd & OAPs 30p. Students free. Season ticket £3.15 (includes Temple Newsam, see below).

## MANOR HOUSE
**Ilkley** *map H9*
Telephone: Ilkley 600066
*(Bradford Metro Council)*

Small 16th/17th century Manor built on part of the site of a Roman fort. Lively exhibition programme.

**Location:** Castle Yard, Ilkley.
*Station: Ilkley.*
**Opening Times:** All year—Daily (except Mons but open Bank Hol Mons) Oct to Mar 10–5. Apr to Sept 10–6. *Closed Christmas Day, Boxing Day & Good Friday.* Adm free (Public Museum).

## NOSTELL PRIORY, The National Trust
**Wakefield** *map H9* ♿
Telephone: Wakefield 863892

Built for Sir Rowland Winn by Paine; a wing added in 1766 by Robert Adam. State rooms contain pictures and famous Chippendale furniture made especially for the house.

**Location:** 6 m SE of Wakefield, on N side of A638.
*Station: Fitzwilliam (1½ m).*
**Opening Times:** Mar 25–28, Apr, May, June, Sept & Oct—Sats 12–5, Suns 11–5; July & Aug—Daily (except Fris) 12–5, Sun 11–5. Bank Hol Openings: Easter Bank Hol—Mon & Tues; May Bank Hol—Mon; Spring Bank Hol—Mon & Tues; Aug Bank Hol—Mon: Mons 11–5, Tues 12–5. Adm House & Grounds £2.40, Chd £1.20; Party rate (30 or more) £2, Chd £1. Grounds only £1.30, Chd 60p; Parking free. Pre-booked parties welcome outside normal published opening times. However, on these occasions, a charge will be made to National Trust members. *Dogs in grounds on leashes, not in house (except guide dogs). Lift available for disabled.*
**Refreshments:** Lunches and afternoon teas available in stable tea rooms (not NT).

## OAKWELL HALL and COUNTRY PARK
**Birstall** *map H8* Ⓢ
Telephone: Batley 474926
*(Kirklees Metro Council)*

Elizabethan moated manor house (1583) with Civil War and Brontë connections. It was 'Fieldhead' of Charlotte Brontë's novel 'Shirley'. The Hall was completely refurbished in 1988 and is now displayed as a seventeenth century gentleman's house. The Hall is surrounded by period gardens and 87 acres of country park. Features include a wildlife garden, arboretum, countryside information centre, equestrian arena and adventure playground. New facilities include a visitor complex with interpretive centre, craft workshops, converted barn for indoor events and shop. SANDFORD AWARD 1989.

**Location:** Birstall, Batley.
**Opening Times:** Open all year – Mons to Sats 10–5; Suns 1–5. Adm free.
**Refreshments:** Tea room.

## SHIBDEN HALL & FOLK MUSEUM
**Halifax** *map G9*
Telephone: Halifax (0422) 52246
*(Calderdale Metropolitan Borough Council)*

15th century timber-framed house.

**Location:** ¼ m SE of Halifax on the Halifax/Hipperholme Road (A58).
**Opening Times:** Apr to Sept—Mons to Sats 10–6, Suns 2–5. Oct, Nov & Mar—Mons to Sats 10–5, Suns 2–5. Feb—Suns only 2–5. *Closed December to January.* Adm Summer 60p, Chd 30p; Low season 50p, Chd 25p. *Conducted tours after normal hours* (Fee payable).
**Refreshments:** At the Hall.

## TEMPLE NEWSAM
**Leeds** *map H9*
*(Leeds Metro District Council)*

Tudor-Jacobean house, birthplace of Lord Darnley, with collection of pictures and furniture.

**Location:** 5 m E of Leeds; 1 m S of A63 (nr junction with A642).
*Station: Cross Gates (1¾ m).*
**Opening Times:** All the year—Tues to Sun 10.30–6.15 (or dusk if earlier); Weds from May to Sept 10.30–8.30. *Closed Mons except Bank Hol Mons.* Adm 75p, Chd & OAPs 30p. Students free. Season tickets £3.15 (includes Lotherton Hall, see above).

# BRONTË PARSONAGE MUSEUM

**HAWORTH, KEIGHLEY, WEST YORKSHIRE**

Once the home of the famous Brontë family this Georgian Parsonage has rooms furnished as in the Brontës' day with displays of their personal treasures. See where the writers of Jane Eyre and Wuthering Heights lived.
**Become a member of the Brontë Society and enjoy the many privileges this offers. Write for details.**

*Re-discover*

# OAKWELL HALL

Open Monday – Saturday 10.00 am – 5.00 pm
Sunday 1.00 pm – 5.00 pm
Oakwell Hall Country Park
Nutter Lane, Birstall
Telephone Batley : 0924 – 474926
Free car park

*A great trip out for all the family*

# *Harewood House. Home of the Earl & Countess of Harewood.*

*Set in a landscape designed by Capability Brown, Harewood House is one of the most magnificent houses anywhere in England.*

*Here you can see paintings by the great masters, the elaborate interiors by Robert Adam, Sevrès porcelain and furniture by Thomas Chippendale.*

*The best of English landscape and design.*

*In the new Tropical Houses at Harewood you can experience the atmosphere of a rain forest and see tropical birds and plants that are under threat in the wild.*

*A Freedom Ticket admits you to the House, the Exhibition Hall, the Bird Garden and Tropical Houses, the terraces, the lakeside walks and the adventure playground.*

*Harewood House is just north of Leeds on the A61. Gates open at 10am every day from Easter to the 31st October.*

*Telephone (0532) 886225 (24 hours) for more details.*

*Harewood House*

# LOTHERTON HALL

**ABERFORD, near LEEDS, West Yorkshire**

Lotherton Hall was built round an earlier house dating from the mid-eighteenth century. The extensions to the east were completed in 1896 and those to the west in 1903. The Hall, with its art collection, park and gardens, was given to the City of Leeds by Sir Alvary and Lady Gascoigne in 1968 and opened as a country house museum in 1969. The Gascoigne collection, which contains pictures, furniture, silver and porcelain of the 17th and 18th centuries, as well as works of a later period, includes a magnificent portrait by Pompeo Batoni and an impressive group of silver race cups ranging in date from 1776 to 1842. The first floor and costume galleries were opened in 1970 and the oriental gallery in 1975. There is also a Museum shop and audio visual room.

# SHIBDEN HALL

**HALIFAX**

**WEST YORKSHIRE FOLK MUSEUM**

An early 15th century half-timbered house with later additions, furnished with 17th and 18th century material. The 17th century barn and outbuildings are equipped with early agricultural implements and craft workshops, the museum is set in a large park and surrounded by terrace gardens. Snack bar facilities. Admission: Summer—Adults 60p, Children 30p. Low Season—Adults 50p, Children 25p.

*ADMISSION – SEE EDITORIAL REFERENCE*

# WALES

## CLWYD

### BODELWYDDAN CASTLE
**Bodelwyddan LL18 5YA** *map F8*
Telephone: (0745) 583539
*(Clwyd County Council)*

Bodelwyddan Castle has been authentically restored as a Victorian Country House and contains a major collection of portraits and photography on permanent loan from the National Portrait Gallery. The collection includes works by many eminent Victorian Portraitists such as G. F. Watts, William Holman Hunt, John Singer Sargeant, Sir Edwin Landseer and Sir Thomas Lawrence. The portraits are complemented by furniture from the Victoria & Albert Museum and sculptures from the Royal Academy. The Castle is situated in beautiful countryside and is a member of the National Garden Scheme. The extensive formal gardens have been restored and many original features have been retained. For children, there is an adventure woodland and a funland play area.

**Location:** Just off the A55 near St. Asaph (opposite the Marble Church).
**Opening Times:** To Mar 19, 1989: Thurs to Sun 11–3. Mar 21 to Oct 1 1989: Open daily except Mons (but open Bank Holiday Mons) 11–5; from Oct 5, details on application. Adm £2, Chd £1, Family group £5.60 (2 Adults 3 Chd), OAPs/Unemployed £1.50, Students £1. Discount rates available for groups of 20 or more. Ample car parking. Suitable for disabled persons (no wheelchairs available). Gift Shop, Picnic area, Woodland walk.
**Refreshments:** Victorian Tea Room, Pavilion Restaurant, Cafeteria.

### BODRHYDDAN HALL
**Rhuddlan, nr Rhyl** *map F8* △
*(Col the Lord Langford)*

17th century manor house of historic interest. Famous portraits, armour, furniture. Extensive garden, Arboretum and picnic area.

**Location:** 4 m SE of Rhyl, midway between Rhuddlan & Dyserth.
**Opening Times:** June to Sept—Tues & Thurs 2–5.30. Adm £1, Chd 50p. *Special terms for parties.*
**Refreshments:** At the hall. Picnic areas.

### CHIRK CASTLE, The National Trust
**nr Wrexham** *map F7*
Telephone: Chirk 777701

Built 1310; a unique, unaltered example of a border castle of Edward I's time, inhabited continuously for 660 years. Interesting portraits, tapestries etc. Gardens.

**Location:** ½ m from Chirk (on A5 trunk road) then 1½ m private driveway; 20 m NW of Shrewsbury 7 m SE of Llangollen.
*Station: Chirk (2 m).*
**Opening Times:** Mar 24 to Sept 29—Daily except Mons & Sats 12–5, Gardens open 12–6. (Open Bank Holiday Mons 12–5). Sept 30 to Oct 29—Sats and Suns only 12–5, Gardens open 12–6. (Last adm to Castle 4.30, Gardens 5.30.) Adm £2.30, Chd £1.15, Family £5.75. Pre-booked parties of 20 or more £1.85. Shop. No dogs. Very limited access for wheelchairs.
**Refreshments:** Tea rooms (light lunches & teas).

### ERDDIG, The National Trust
**nr Wrexham** *map F7* ♿
Telephone: Wrexham (0978) 355314

Late 17th century house with 18th century additions and containing much of the original furniture, set in a garden restored to 18th century formal design and containing varieties of fruit known to have been grown there during that period. Range of domestic outbuildings include laundry, bakehouse, sawmill and smithy, all in working order; the extensive restoration work on house and garden is now complete. Visitor Centre containing early farm implements.

**Location:** 2 m S of Wrexham off A525.
*Stations: Wrexham Central (1¾ m); Wrexham General (2½ m), includes 1 m driveway to House.*
**Opening Times:** Mar 24 to June 30: Daily except Thurs & Fri (open Good Friday) 11–6; House open 12–5; (last adm House 4, Gardens 5.30). July 1 to Sept 1: Daily except Fri 11–6. House open 12–5; (last adm House 4, Gardens 5.30). Sept 2 to Oct 22: Daily except Thurs and Fri 11–6; House open 12–5; (last adm House 4, Gardens 5.30). School and Youth Groups by arrangement. Adm £3, Chd £1.50, Family £7.50. Pre-booked groups of 20+ £2.40.
*NB: Certain rooms have no electric light; visitors wishing to make a close study of pictures & textiles should avoid dull days early & late in season. Due to extreme fragility the Tapestry & Chinese Rooms will be open only on Weds & Sats.*
**Refreshments:** Light lunches & teas.

### EWLOE CASTLE
**nr Hawarden** *map F8*
*(Cadw: Welsh Historic Monuments)*

Native Welsh castle with typical round and aspidal towers.

**Location:** 1 m NW of Hawarden.

### GYRN CASTLE
**Llanasa, Holywell** *map F8*
Telephone: (074 56) 3500
*(Sir Geoffrey Bates, BT, MC)*

Dating, in part, from 1700; castellated 1820. Large picture gallery, panelled entrance hall. Pleasant woodland walks.

**Location:** 26 m W of Chester (off A55); 4 m SE of Prestatyn.
**Opening Times:** All the year—by appointment. Adm £1.50, parties welcome.
**Refreshments:** By arrangement.

### PLAS TEG
**Pontblyddyn, Nr Mold** *map F7*
Telephone: (0352) 771335
*(Mrs C Bayley)*

Built in 1610, one of the finest buildings of its kind, at each corner there are projecting towers with corbelled eaves, and a ogee-shaped roof supporting wooden copulas and finials, this is of architectural interest. As you enter this fine Jacobean mansion (recently restored to its former glory) notice the remarkable carved oak staircase, with massive newels, moulded finials and pendants. Enjoy a relaxed atmosphere as you discover rooms with influences from Europe, India and the Orient, four poster beds dating back to 1627, wall hangings, rare baths especially an 1815 coal fired bath with shower, plus a delight of rare carpets, wall brackets, fine furniture and china. Plas Teg can also cater for banquets, conferences, concerts and weddings. The long gallery is available for temporary exhibitions. We now have a collection of Parrots and Macaws on view, not forgetting Martin the Toucan.

**Location:** 1¾ m N of Caergwrle on the Wrexham-Mold Road (A541).
**Opening Times:** Daily including Bank Holidays, closed Tues 11–6, Sun 12–6. Adm £2, Chd £1. Parties of over 20 pre-booked 10% off. Car park. Unsuitable for wheelchairs except ground floor. No dogs in the house.
**Refreshments:** Teas, coffee, cake etc.

### RHUDDLAN CASTLE
**Rhuddlan** *map E8*
*(Cadw: Welsh Historic Monuments)*

Begun by Edward I in 1277; concentric castle of simple design.
**Location:** In Rhuddlan.

### VALLE CRUCIS ABBEY
**Llangollen** *map F7*
*(Cadw: Welsh Historic Monuments)*

Impressive 13th century Abbey, still with its own fishpond.
**Location:** On Horseshoe Pass, 1 m N of Llangollen.

## DYFED

### CARREG CENNEN CASTLE
**Trapp** *map E5*
*(Cadw: Welsh Historic Monuments)*

A 13th century castle dramatically perched on a limestone crag.
**Location:** Signposted from Trapp Village near Llandeilo.

### CILGERRAN CASTLE
**Cilgerran** *map E5*
*(Cadw: Welsh Historic Monuments)*

A 13th century castle which has been a favourite subject for painters since the 18th century.
**Location:** 3 m from Cilgerran itself along River Tefi.

### COLBY LODGE GARDEN, The National Trust
**Amroth** *map D5*
Telephone: Llandeilo 822800

Formal and woodland gardens; walks through a secluded valley along open and wooded pathways with rhododendrons and azaleas. Mr and Mrs A. Scourfield Lewis kindly allow access to the Walled Garden during normal visiting hours.
**Location:** NE of Tenby off A477; E of junction A477/A478.
*Station: Kilgetty (2½ m).*
**Opening Times:** Daily all year during daylight hours. Adm free.

### KIDWELLY CASTLE
**Kidwelly** *map D5*
*(Cadw: Welsh Historic Monuments)*

A very substantial castle possessing a notable chapel built out over the river bank.
**Location:** In Kidwelly.

### LAMPHEY PALACE
**Lamphey** *map D4*
*(Cadw: Welsh Historic Monuments)*

Substantial remains of the medieval Bishops of St David's country residence.
**Location:** 2½ m E of Pembroke on A4139.

### LLAWHADEN CASTLE
**Llawhaden** *map D5*
*(Cadw: Welsh Historic Monuments)*

Built to protect the Church's estates in West Wales.
**Location:** Llawhaden, off A40(T).

### PICTON CASTLE
**Haverfordwest** *map D5*
*(The Picton Castle Trust)*

A scheduled ancient monument, but also a beautiful home, occupied continuously since the 15th century by the Philipps family who are still in residence.
**Location:** 4 m SE of Haverfordwest S of A40 via the Rhos.
**Opening Times:** CASTLE: Easter Sun & Mon, and following Bank Hols. Also every Sun & Thurs from mid-July to mid-Sept: 2–5. GROUNDS: Easter Sat to Sept 30—Daily 10.30–5, except Mon. GRAHAM SUTHERLAND GALLERY: dates and times of opening under review. Craft Shop. Free car park. Charges not available at time of going to press.
**Refreshments:** Tea shop. *Closed* Mon.

### ST DAVIDS BISHOPS PALACE
**St Davids** *map C5*
*(Cadw: Welsh Historic Monuments)*

A most impressive mediaeval Bishop's Palace within the Cathedral Close.
**Location:** In the centre of St Davids.

### STRATA FLORIDA ABBEY
**Strata Florida** *map E6*
*(Cadw: Welsh Historic Monuments)*

A remote, 13th century Cistercian site in a lovely setting.
**Location:** Up minor road, 2 m from Pontrhydfendigaid.

### TALLEY ABBEY
**Talley** *map E5*
*(Cadw: Welsh Historic Monuments)*

A small 12th century monastic site founded for the Premonstratensian Order.
**Location:** ¼ m from Talley Village.

### TUDOR MERCHANT'S HOUSE, The National Trust
**Tenby** *map D4*

An example of a merchant's house of the 15th century.
**Location:** Quay Hill, Tenby.
*Station: Tenby (8 mins walk) (not Suns, except June-Aug).*
**Opening Times:** Easter Sun to end Sept, Mon–Fri 10–1 & 2.30–6. *Closed Sat.* Open Sun 2–6. Last adm 5.45. Adult £1, Chd 50p. No dogs. Unsuitable for wheelchairs.

## MID GLAMORGAN

### COITY CASTLE
**Coity** *map E4*
*(Cadw: Welsh Historic Monuments)*

A typical Norman stronghold guarding a fertile area of the Vale of Glamorgan.
**Location:** Coity Village, nr Bridgend (on M4).

## SOUTH GLAMORGAN

### CAERPHILLY CASTLE
**Caerphilly** *map F4*
*(Cadw: Welsh Historic Monuments)*

Second largest castle area in Europe.
**Location:** In Caerphilly; 6 m N of Cardiff.

### CARDIFF CASTLE
**Cardiff** *map F4* △
*(Cardiff City Council)*

Begun 1090 on remains of Roman Fort. Rich interior decorations. Location for Cardiff Searchlight Tattoo.
**Location:** In centre of Cardiff city.
*Station: Cardiff Centre (½ m).*

### CASTELL COCH
**Tongwynlais** *map F4*
*(Cadw: Welsh Historic Monuments)*

13th century castle, restored on original lines for the Marquess of Bute in 19th century and made habitable. Unique Neo Gothic decorations.
**Location:** 6 m N of Cardiff off Pontypridd Road by village of Tongwynlais.

## WEST GLAMORGAN

### NEATH ABBEY
**Neath** *map E4*
*(Cadw: Welsh Historic Monuments)*

In the 16th century the 'fairest building in Wales'.
**Location:** In Neath.

### WEOBLEY CASTLE
**Weobley** *map E4*
*(Cadw: Welsh Historic Monuments)*

A fortified mediaeval manor house.
**Location:** Minor road from Llanrhidian, Gower Peninsula.

## GWENT

### CAERLEON ROMAN FORTRESS BATHS AND AMPHITHEATRE
**Caerleon** *map F4*
*(Cadw: Welsh Historic Monuments)*

The only excavated Legionary baths in Europe; in a town still boasting many other Roman remains.
**Location:** Caerleon 2 m N of Newport, off M4 junction 25.

### CHEPSTOW CASTLE
**Chepstow** *map G4*
*(Cadw: Welsh Historic Monuments)*

Great Tower dates from late 11th century.
**Location:** On W bank of the Wye, near Chepstow Bridge.

### PENHOW CASTLE
**Nr Newport** Ⓢ
Telephone: Penhow (0633) 400800 and bookings/enquiries (0633) 400555
*(Stephen Weeks Esq.)*

**Location:** On A48, midway between Chepstow and Newport. M4 junctions 22 or 24.
**Opening Times:** Good Fri to end of Sept – Weds to Suns inclusive and Bank Holidays, 10–6 (last adm 5). Winter opening: Wed only, 10–5. Adm £2.25, Chd and concessions £1.15. Family tickets (2 2): £5.50. *Price includes Soundalive Walkman Tour.* 'Candlelit Tours' by appointment and on summer Weds at 7. Inn, craft centre, gift shop, accommodation, events, restaurant. Please call the Administrator for full information on educational and out-of-hours visits. The Penhow Castle Visitor Centre is open all year round.

### RAGLAN CASTLE
**Raglan** *map F5*
*(Cadw: Welsh Historic Monuments)*

A most impressive 15th century castle: possibly the last truly mediaeval castle.
**Location:** N of Raglan, signposted from A40 Raglan by-pass.

### TINTERN ABBEY
**Tintern** *map G4*
*(Cadw: Welsh Historic Monuments)*

One of Britain's most complete Cistercian Abbeys, the Abbey Church is inspiringly beautiful.
**Location:** In Tintern.

### TREDEGAR HOUSE
**Newport** *map F4*
Telephone: Newport (0633) 815880
*(Newport Borough Council)*

One wing of the 16th century house survives, but Tredegar House owes its character to lavish 17th century rebuilding in brick. The Country Park includes gardens, lake (boating and coarse fishing), adventure play farm, carriage rides and craft workshops.

**Location:** SW of Newport; signposted from M4 junction 28, A48.
*Station: Newport (2¾ m).*
**Opening Times:** COUNTRY PARK. Daily 6.15–Sunset. HOUSE & ATTRACTIONS. Good Fri to last Sun in Sept. Weds to Suns & Public Hols. House Tours every ½ hour from 12.30–4.30. House open at other times by appointment. Adm (1988 rates) £1.80, Chd/OAPs £1. Family £4. Carriage Rides £1, Chd 50p. Boats £1.50 per ½ hour. Fishing £1, Chd 50p during season. Touring Caravans £2–£4, Tents £1.20–£4. Coach & school parties welcome if booked in advance.
**Refreshments:** Lunch & teas at the Old Brewhouse Bar & Tea Room.

### WHITE CASTLE
**Llantilio Crossenny** *map F5*
*(Cadw: Welsh Historic Monuments)*

One of the border castles of the Norman Marcher Lords.
**Location:** Minor roads, signposted from B4521 & B4233.

## GWYNEDD

### ABERCONWY HOUSE, The National Trust
**Conwy** *map E8*
Telephone: Conwy (049259) 2246

Town house that dates from 14th century, now housing the Conwy Exhibition, depicting the life of the borough from Roman times to the present day.
**Location:** In the town at junction of Castle Street & High Street.
*Station: Llandudno Junction (¾ m).*
**Opening Times:** Mar 24 to Nov 5—Daily (except Tues) 11–5.30 (last admission 5.15); Adm 80p, Chd 40p, Family £2. Pre-booked parties 60p. Shop.

### BEAUMARIS CASTLE
**Beaumaris** *map E8*
*(Cadw: Welsh Historic Monuments)*

Last of great castles of the Edwardian conquest.
**Location:** In Beaumaris.

### BODNANT GARDEN, The National Trust
**Tal-y-Cafn** *map E8* ♿
Telephone: Tyn-y-Groes (0492) 650460

Begun in 1875 by Henry Pochin. Amongst the finest gardens in the country. Magnificent collections of rhododendrons, camellias, magnolias and conifers.
**Location:** 8 m S of Llandudno & Colwyn Bay on A470; Entrance along Eglwysbach Road.
*Station: Tal-y-Cafn (1½ m).*
**Opening Times:** Mar 18 to Oct 31—Daily 10–5 (last adm 4.30). Adm £2, Chd £1. Pre-booked parties of 20 or more £1.80. Free car park. *No dogs (except guide dogs for the blind).* Wheelchairs provided but garden is steep & difficult. Braille guide.
**Refreshments:** Tea at car park Kiosk.

### BRYN BRAS CASTLE
**Llanrug** *map E8*
Telephone: Llanberis 870 210
*(Mr & Mrs N E Gray-Parry)*

The Castle, Grade II* listed, was built in c.1830 in the Romanesque style on an earlier structure built before 1750. There are fine examples of stained glass, panelling, interesting ceilings and richly carved furniture in this romantic castle, which was built by a Welshman, and is still a Welsh family home. The extensive and tranquil Victorian gardens of natural beauty, with much wild life, gradually merge into the foothills of Snowdon. They include peaceful lawns, walled Knot Garden, stream and pools, woodland walks and a ¼ mile mountain walk with magnificent panoramic views of Snowdon, Anglesey and the sea.
**Location:** 4½ m E of Caernarfon; 3½ m NW of Llanberis; ½ m off A4086.
**Opening Times:** Spring Bank Hol to mid-July & Sept—Daily (except Sats) 1–5. Mid-July to end Aug—Daily (except Sats) 10.30–5. Adm £1.50, Chd 75p. *25% reduction for parties.* Free car park. Picnic area. No dogs.
**Refreshments:** Home made Welsh teas (including Bara Brith) in charming tea room & the tea garden. Castle Apartments for holidays available all year.

### CAERNARFON CASTLE
**Caernarfon** *map D8*
*(Cadw: Welsh Historic Monuments)*

The most important of Edward I's castles.
**Location:** In Caernarfon.

### COCHWILLAN OLD HALL
**Talybont, Bangor** *map E8*
Telephone: Bangor 364608
*(R. C. H. Douglas Pennant, Esq)*

Fine example of medieval architecture (restored 1971).
**Location:** 3½ m Bangor; 1 m Talybont village off A55.
**Opening Times:** Open by appointment.

### CONWY CASTLE
**Conwy** *map E8*
*(Cadw: Welsh Historic Monuments)*

Built by Edward I to command Conwy ferry.
**Location:** In Conwy.

### CRICCIETH CASTLE
**Criccieth** *map D7*
*(Cadw: Welsh Historic Monuments)*

Native Welsh castle dating mainly first half 13th century.
**Location:** In Criccieth.

### CYMER ABBEY
**Cymer** *map E7*
*(Cadw: Welsh Historic Monuments)*

A small Cistercian foundation on the banks of the Mawddach.
**Location:** 2 m NW of Dolgellau on A494.

### DINORWIC SLATE QUARRY WORKSHOPS/MUSEUM
**Llanberis** *map E7*
*(Cadw: Welsh Historic Monuments)*

Perfectly preserved Victorian slate workshops with interpretive displays provided by the National Museum of Wales.
**Location:** nr Llanberis.

### GWYDIR UCHAF CHAPEL
**Llanrwst** *map E7*
*(Cadw: Welsh Historic Monuments)*

A 17th century private chapel with elaborately painted ceilings and walls.
**Location:** On Forestry Commission land S of Llanrwst.

### HARLECH CASTLE
**Harlech** *map D7*
*(Cadw: Welsh Historic Monuments)*

Built 1283–9 by Edward I. Concentric plan.
**Location:** In Harlech.

### PENRHYN CASTLE, The National Trust
**Bangor** *map E8* ♿
Telephone: (0243) 353084

The 19th century Castle is a unique and outstanding example of neo-Norman architecture. The garden and grounds have exotic and rare trees and shrubs. There is an Industrial Railway Museum and exhibition of dolls. Victorian formal garden. Superb views of mountains and Menai Strait.
**Location:** 3 m E of Bangor, on A5122.
*Station: Bangor (3 m).*
**Opening Times:** Mar 24 to Nov 5—Daily except Tues 11–6. Please note: Castle and Museums 12–5, July & Aug 11–5 (except Tues), last adm 30 mins prior to closing. Adm £2.50, Chd £1.25, Family £6.25, Groups £2.
**Refreshments:** Light lunches & teas at Castle.

### PLAS MAWR
**Conwy** *map E8*
*(Royal Cambrian Academy of Art)*

Built by Robert Wynne 1577–80.
**Location:** High Street Conwy.
*Station: Conwy (200 yards).*
**Opening Times:** Nov, Feb & Mar—Weds to Suns 10–4; Apr to Sept—All week 10–6; Oct—All week 10–4. *Closed Dec & Jan.* Adm 75p, Chd 25p, OAPs/Students 50p.

### PLAS NEWYDD, The National Trust
**Isle of Anglesey** *map D8* ♿
Telephone: Llanfairpwll (0248) 714795

18th century house by James Wyatt in unspoilt position adjacent to Menai Strait. Magnificent views to Snowdonia. Fine spring garden. Rex Whistler exhibition and mural painting. Military museum.
**Location:** 1 m SW of Llanfairpwll on A4080 to Brynsiencyn; turn off A5 to Llanfairpwll at W end of Britannia Bridge.
*Station: Llanfairpwll (1¾ m).*
**Opening Times:** Mar 24 to Oct 1—Daily except Sats 12–5. Shop, tearoom and gardens only 11–5. (July & Aug 11–5 except Sat). Shop, tearoom and gardens only 11–5. Last adm 4.30. Oct 6 to Nov 5, Fri and Sun only 12–5 (last adm 4.30). Adm £2.20, Chd £1.10, Family £5.50, Group £1.80.
**Refreshments:** Tea rooms (light lunches & teas).

### TY MAWR WYBRNANT, The National Trust
**nr. Penmachno** *map E7*
Telephone: Penmachno (069 03) 213

The birthplace of Bishop William Morgan. (c. 1541–1604), the first translator of the Bible into Welsh.
**Location:** At the head of the little valley of Wybrnant, 3½ m SW of Betws-y-Coed; 2 m W of Penmachno.
**Opening Times:** Mar 24 to Oct 1 daily excluding Mon and Sat (open Bank Holiday Mons) 12–5. Last adm 15 mins before closing. Oct 6 to Nov 5: Fri and Sun only 12–4. Adm £1, Chd 50p, Family £2.50.

# POWYS

### GREGYNOG
**Newtown** *map F6*
Telephone: (068 687) 224
*(The University of Wales)*

A Victorian mansion, in 750 acres of wooded parkland with extensive gardens, including one of the most striking displays of rhododendrons in Wales; the Western red cedar 'Zebrina' is probably the biggest tree of this variety in the U.K. Many walks in the grounds. The Hall has an exceptionally fine carved parlour of 1636, retained when the old hall was rebuilt in the 1840s. The works of art still remaining from the collections of the Davies sisters include two Rodin bronzes. On show also are books by the Gregynog Press, one of the best-known private presses of the 1920s and 30s, and by the present Gwasg Gregynog, where fine printing is still carried on. This is a working Press and visitors can only be accepted occasionally by prior appointment. Accommodation is sometimes available in the Hall, depending on the nature and size of the resident conference.
**Location:** Near the village of Tregynon, 5 m N of Newtown, off B4389.
**Opening Times:** Gardens always open. Hall: Jun 5–Sept 30, Mon to Sat. *Guided tours only at 11 and 3,* adm £1.50, including morning coffee or afternoon tea. Chd under 15 half price. Parties by arrangement. Free car parking. Suitable for disabled persons (no wheelchairs provided). Hall and Gardens may very exceptionally have to be closed for a day.

### POWIS CASTLE, The National Trust
**Welshpool** *map F6* ♿
Telephone: Welshpool (0938) 4336

The medieval stronghold of the Welsh princes of Upper Powys, the home of the Herbert family since 1587. Clive of India Museum. Fine plaster work, murals, furniture, paintings and tapestry. Historic terraced garden; herbaceous borders, rare trees and shrubs.
**Location:** 1 m S of Welshpool on A483; Pedestrian access from High Street (A490); Cars enter road to Newtown (A483); 1 m.
*Stations: Welshpool (1¼ m); Welshpool Raven Square (1¼ m); BR service Aug only.*
**Opening Times:** Mar 24 to June 30: Wed to Sun 12–5 (open Bank Holiday Mon). NB *closed Apr 20 & 21.* July 1 to Aug 31: daily except Mon 11–6 (open Bank Holiday Mon). Sept 1 to Nov 5: Wed to Sun 12–5, last adm 30 mins prior to closing. Nov 6 to Apr 8 1990, Sun only 2–4.30. Gardens, Clive Museum and tearoom open.
**Refreshments:** Tea rooms (light lunches & teas).

### TREBINSHWN HOUSE
**nr Brecon** *map F5*
*(Robin Watson, Esq)*

A medium sized 16th century manor house which underwent extensive restoration in 1800. Fine courtyard and walled garden.
**Location:** 7 m SE of Brecon; 1½ m from Bwlch & A40; 4 m from Llangorse (B4560).
**Opening Times:** May 1 to Aug 31—Mons & Tues 10–5. Adm charge not available at time of going to press.
**Refreshments:** Red Lion Hotel, Llangorse (4 m).

### TRETOWER COURT & CASTLE
**Crickhowell** *map F5*
*(Cadw: Welsh Historic Monuments)*

One of the finest medieval houses in Wales.
**Location:** 3½ m NW Crickhowell between A40 & A479 Roads.

# IRELAND (REPUBLIC OF)

### ANNES GROVE GARDENS

**Castletownroche** *map (i)V*
Telephone: 022-26145
*(Mr & Mrs Patrick Grove Annesley)*

Extensive Robinsonian woodland and riverside gardens with notable collection of rhododendrons and other exotica. Edwardian flower garden.

**Location:** 1 m N of Castletownroche, signposted from N72 Fermoy/Killarney road.
**Opening Times:** Apr 1 to Sept 30—Mons to Fris 10–5; Suns 1–6; Sats by appointment only. Guided tours for pre-booked groups. Adm £1.80, Chd/OAPs £1, disabled free. Free car park, adjacent picnic site.
**Refreshments:** Lunches and teas for pre-booked groups by arrangement.

### BANTRY HOUSE

**Bantry Co. Cork** *map (i)X*
Telephone: (027) 50047
*(Mr & Mrs Egerton Shelswell-White)*

Partly-Georgian mansion standing at edge of Bantry Bay, with beautiful views. Seat of family of White, formerly Earls of Bantry. Unique collection of tapestries, furniture etc. Terraces and Statuary in the Italian style in grounds.

**Location:** In outskirts of Bantry (½ m); 56 m SW of Cork.
**Opening Times:** Open all year–Daily 9–6 *(open until 8 on most summer evenings).* Adm House & Grounds £2, Chd (up to 14) accompanied by parents, free, OAPs/ Students £1. Parties of 20 or more £1.50. Craft shop.
**Refreshments:** Tea room. Bed and Breakfast. Lunch/dinner in main dining room for groups of 10–30. (Advance Booking.)

### BIRR CASTLE DEMESNE

**Co Offaly** *map (iii)Y*
Telephone: (353509) 20056

Over 100 acres of gardens, rivers with waterfalls, lake and lake walks, terraces and parkland, scenically laid out and planted with most important collection of plants, many introduced directly from the wild. The Park contains the nineteenth century's largest telescope. Facilities include exhibition gallery, educationally explained tree trail, picnic and play area, coffee shop and tourist office.

**Opening Times:** Jan to Apr and Oct to Dec: Adm £2, Chd £1. Exhibition season (May to Sept): Adm £2.40, Chd £1.20; Group rates £2, Chd £1. (Admission free to all subscribing Friends of the Demesne.) Open daily throughout the year: 9–1 and 2–6 (or dusk in winter).
**Refreshments:** Morning coffee, lunch, afternoon teas.

### BLARNEY CASTLE AND BLARNEY HOUSE

**Blarney, Co. Cork** *map (i)X* ♿
*(Sir Richard Colthurst, Bart)*

**Blarney Castle and Rock Close.** Situated 5 miles from Cork City, the Castle is famous for its Stone which has the traditional power of conferring eloquence on all who kiss it. The word "Blarney" has found its way into the English language and has been described as conferring upon anyone who kisses it "a cajoling tongue and the art of flattery, or of telling lies with unblushing effrontery". The battlements crowning the fine intact keep are typically Irish in form and set in the walls below the battlements is the Stone. To kiss it one has to lean backwards out from the parapet walk. Adjacent to the Castle is the Rock Close, said to have Druidic connections and containing the gardens laid out by the Jefferies family in 1759 and now containing many old specimens and much new planting of shrubs, trees and beds, amongst the fine old limestone rocks scattered in 25 acres. **Blarney House & Gardens:** 200 yards from the Castle is Blarney House and Gardens, a fine Scottish Baronial type house, with distinguished corner turrets and bartizans with conical roofs and now restored inside with fine rooms and stairwell. Outside, the formal gardens and fine view of Blarney Lake together with the walk down to it and between the House and the Castle a large area of new planting, with shrubs, trees, beds and walks.

**Location:** 7 m from Cork City. 9 m from Cork Airport; 9 m from Ringaskiddy Port.
**Opening Times: Blarney Castle & Rock Close:** Mon to Sat, May, 9–7. June/July, 9–8.30. Aug, Sept, 9–7.30. Oct–Apr, 9–sundown. Sun, Summer 9.30–5.30. Winter 9.30–sundown. **Blarney House & Gardens:** June–mid Sept Mons to Sat only 12–6. (Last adm 30 mins before stated closing times.) Adm **Blarney Castle and Rock:** IR £2.30, Chd IR £1, OAPs and Students IR £1.50. **Blarney House & Gardens:** IR £2, Chd IR £1, OAPs and Students IR £1.50. Car and Coach Parking.
**Refreshments:** Sweet and soft drink kiosk; three hotels, three public houses; tea houses.

### BUNRATTY CASTLE & FOLK PARK

**Bunratty, Co. Clare** *map (ii)X*
Telephone: (061) 361511
*(Shannon Free Airport Development Company)*

Bunratty Castle, built in 1469, is the most complete and authentic example of a Mediaeval Castle in Ireland. Its furniture, tapestries and works of art are displayed to give the visitor an idea of the furnishings and arrangement of a Castle of the late 16th or early 17th century. The Folk Park, in the grounds of the Castle, contains typical rural dwellings recreated and furnished to reflect life in Ireland at the turn of the century. The Park also features the complete reconstruction of a 19th century Irish village street, including craft shops, post office and general stores. **Bunratty House** (1805) has also been restored and furnished.

**Location:** 7 m from Shannon International Airport—N18 on Map.
**Opening Times:** Daily—9–5.30 (last adm 4.30). Adm: Bunratty Castle and Folk Park £3.10, Chd £1.60. Special group rates and family tickets. Car Parking. Suitable for disabled persons in Folk Park only.
**Refreshments:** Tea room in grounds of Folk Park, providing tea, coffee, scones, etc. Mediaeval Banquets and Entertainment nightly in Bunratty.

### CARRIGGLAS MANOR

**Longford** *map (iv)Y*
Telephone: Ireland (043) 45165
*(Mr & Mrs Lefroy)*

Tudor Gothic Revival House with beautifully furnished interiors. Fine Georgian stableyard by James Gandon with costume museum. Tea room & shop. Woodland Garden.

**Location:** 3 m from Longford on T15/R194 Ballinalee/Granard Road. 2 m N of main N4 Route on signed turn-off avoiding Longford Town congestion.
**Opening Times: House, Stableyard, Costume Museum, Tea Room & Shop.** June 2 to Sept 10, daily except Wed & Thurs 12.30–4.30 (Aug 5.30). Pre-booked parties at other times by arrangement. Hourly House Tours – Last Tour 3.30 (Aug 4.30). Adm £2, Chd £1, Adult Group rate £1.50, Chd Group rate 75p.
**Refreshments:** Tea room, light lunches & afternoon teas. Hotels, pubs etc. in Longford (3m). Dinner, Bed & Breakfast available IR£75 per person. Pre-booking absolutely essential.

## CASTLE MATRIX
**Rathkeale, Co. Limerick**
Telephone: (069) 64284

This Norman tower was built upon a Celtic Santuary from which the original name *Matres* was derived: later Anglicized to *Matrix*. Constructed in 1440 by the 7th Earl of Desmond who along with his father are the earliest recorded Norman poets in the Irish language. Here in 1580, Raleigh and Spenser first met and began their lifelong friendship.

**Location:** 18 m SW of Limerick City on the main Killarney road; the castle is at the SW edge of Rathkeale village.
**Opening Times:** May 15 to Sept 15, Sats to Tues 1–5. Open at other times by prior arrangement. Adm £2, Chd £1. Spit-roasted mediaeval banquets available to groups by arrangement.
**Refreshments:** Teas and luncheons available to groups by arrangement.

## CASTLETOWN HOUSE
**Celbridge, Co. Kildare** *map (iii)Z*
*(Castletown Foundation)*

Built in 1722, the finest Georgian country house in Ireland.

**Location:** 12 m W of Dublin.
**Opening Times:** Open daily all year. Mon to Fri 10–5; Suns and Bank Hols 2–6. Adm £2.50, Chd 90p. Group rates available.
**Refreshments:** At the House at weekends.

## CLONALIS HOUSE
**Castlerea, Co. Roscommon**
Telephone: (0907) 20014

Clonalis is the ancestral home of the O'Conor's of Connaught, descendants of the last High Kings of Ireland and traditional kings of Connaught. The Gaelic history of the family is recorded through the collection of archives, documentation and portraits in the house.

**Location:** Situated to the W of Castlerea town.
**Opening Times:** June 18 to Sept 7 – Daily 11–5.30. May to June 18 – Sats and Suns only 2–5.30. Other times by arrangement. Craft shop.
**Refreshments:** Tea room.

## THE CRAGGAUNOWEN PROJECT
**Craggaunowen, Quin, Co. Clare** *map (ii)X*
Telephone: 061-61511
*(Shannon Free Airport Development Company)*

The Craggaunowen project is pleasantly situated in the wooded farmland of County Clare. The site consists of a mediaeval Tower House containing a display of furniture and art objects, including some rare Irish pieces. There are two iron-age dwellings – a lake dwelling and a ring fort – and the leather boat 'Brendan' sailed by Tim Severin from Ireland to Newfoundland. In the summer months experiments and displays are conducted on the techniques associated with milling, pottery making and weaving in the iron age.

**Location:** 6 km E of Quin, 4 km N of Sixmilebridge. 24 km NW of Limerick.
**Opening Times:** May to Sept 10–6. Adm £2.30, Chd £1.35, Adult Groups £2, Student Groups £1. Car parking. Access to all exhibits for disabled.
**Refreshments:** Teas, home made scones.

## CRATLOE WOODS HOUSE
**Cratloe, Co. Clare** *map (ii)X*
Telephone: Ireland (061) 87306
*(Mr & Mrs J.G. Brickenden)*

Cratloe Woods House is one of the few roofed examples of a Longhouse to survive. The Longhouse is a singularly Irish type of building. Exhibition of works of art and curios. Craft shop. Display of horse drawn farm machinery.

**Location:** 5 m from Limerick and 10 m from Shannon Airport on the Limerick-Shannon and Ennis dual carriageway.
**Opening Times:** June 1–Mid Sept – daily 2–6 except Suns. Adm £1.50, Chd 80p. Parties and special reductions by arrangement. Car park. Suitable for disabled persons.
**Refreshments:** Afternoon Teas.

## DAMER HOUSE – ROSCREA HERITAGE CENTRE
**Roscrea, Co. Tipperary**
Telephone: (0505) 21850
*(William Hayes, Administrator)*

An important early 18th century house situated in the courtyard of the 13th century Roscrea Castle, a polygonal fortification with gate-tower, corner turrets and curtain wall. The centrepiece of the house is the richly carved stairway. The house and attached 19th century Georgian annexe contain exhibitions relating mainly to the history of the Midlands. Computerised ancestral research service is available.

**Location:** Castle Street, centre of town, on main Dublin–Limerick road, close to Round Tower and 12th century Romanesque church gable.
**Opening Times:** May to Sept, Mon to Fri 10–5, Sat 11–5, Sun 2–5. Oct to Apr, Mon to Fri 10–5. Adm including guided tour of castle and house £1.75, OAPs and Students £1, Parties £1.50, Family £3.75.
**Refreshments:** Coffee Shop serving teas, coffees, sandwiches, scones, etc.

## DUNGUAIRE CASTLE
**Kinvara, Co. Galway**
Telephone: (091) 37108

Dunguaire was the stronghold of Guaire, King of Connaught in the 7th century. The 15th century Dunguaire Castle, now beautifully restored overlooks Galway Bay and gives an insight into the lifestyles of those that lived there. Dunguaire features mediaeval banquets nightly, May to September.

**Location:** The Castle is on the Ennis/Galway road.
**Opening Times:** Open daily Apr (from Easter) to Sept 30, 10–5. Adm £1.60, Chd 90p. Special Group rates. Souvenir Shop.
**Refreshments:** Tea room. Snacks.

## DUNLECKNEY MANOR
**Bagenalstown, Co. Carlow**
Telephone: (0503) 21932

Built c. 1835 by Daniel Robertson incorporating original Manor of 1610. Dunleckney is perhaps the finest example of early 19th century Tudor Gothic architecture in Ireland. Magnificent stairwell and fine oak and walnut panelling throughout the house.

**Location:** ½ m N Bagenalstown. 60 m S Dublin. 8 m S Carlow.
**Opening Times:** June to Sept 2–6. Otherwise by appointment. Adm £1.50, Chd 50p.

## DUNLOE CASTLE HOTEL GARDENS
**Beaufort, Killarney, Co. Kerry**
Telephone: (064) 44111

The gardens at Dunloe Castle contain an extensive and interesting collection of plants, several of which are rarely, if at all, found elsewhere in Ireland. Each season brings its own specialities, camelias and rhododendron in spring, magnolias and sun roses in summer, Irish heaths and richly tinted leaves in autumn, are just a few of the many attractions. This combination of wild grandeur and garden exotica is situated in a setting of incomparable views of mountains and lakes.

**Location:** Situated adjacent to the Deluxe 140 bedroomed Hotel Dunloe Castle, off the main Killarney/Killorglin road, on the route to the Gap of Dunloe, approximately 8 km from Killarney.
**Opening Times:** May 1 to end Sept. Adm free. Catalogue of plants and trees available at hotel reception.
**Refreshments:** Available at Hotel Dunloe Castle.

## DUNKATHEL
**Glanmire, Co. Cork** *map (i)X*
*(Mrs Geoffrey Russell)*

Classic Ducart style Georgian House with fine furniture and a superb Bath Stone Staircase. The Beatrice Gubbins water colour collection is on view and an Orchestrion dating from 1880 may be heard by visitors.

**Location:** 3½ m from Cork on the Waterford Road.
**Opening Times:** May 1 to Oct 31—Weds–Suns 2–6. Adm IR £1.50, Chd IR 50p. Parties at other times by arrangement.
**Refreshments:** Afternoon teas available.

## EMO COURT
**Portlaoise, Co. Leix** *map (iii)Y*
Telephone: Ireland (0502) 26110
*(C.D. Cholmeley-Harrison)*

Outstanding neo-classical house by James Gandon completed in 1796. Extensive gardens containing a wealth of specimen trees & flowering shrubs, spectacular in spring and autumn.

**Location:** Portlaoise 6 m on N7.
**Opening Times:** Apr to end Oct. GARDENS – daily 2.30–5.30 (last entry). Adm £1.50, Students & OAPs £1. HOUSE – Mon 2–6, Adm £2.50 *(no reductions and no children)*. Free car park. Suitable for disabled persons.
**Refreshments:** Montague Hotel 1½ m – on N7.

## FERNHILL GARDEN
**Sandyford** *map (iii)Z*
Telephone: Ireland (01) 956000
*(Mrs Sally Walker)*

A Garden for all seasons, 200 years old in Robinsonian style with over 4,000 species and varieties of trees, shrubs and plants. Dogs not allowed.

**Location:** 7 m S centre Dublin on the Enniskerry Rd, or 4 m inland from Dun Laoghaire. N11.
**Opening Times:** Mar 1–Oct 31, Tues–Sat 11–5, Suns 2–5, Bank Holidays 11–5. Adm £2; OAPs, Chd over 5, Students £1; Parties (20) £1.50.
**Refreshments:** Stepeside & Dundrum.

## FOTA
**Fota Island, Carrigtwohill, Co. Cork** *map (i)Y* ♿
Telephone: Cork (021) 812555
*(Richard Wood)*

Regency mansion with fine neo-classical and French Revival rooms, contains an important collection of Irish period landscapes. Furnished with Irish 18th and 19th century pieces. Also world famous arboretum and 70 acre wildlife park. **European Museum of the Year Award Winner.**

**Location:** 10 m E of Cork City, on Cobh Road, off main Waterford Road.
*Station: Fota.*
**Opening Times:** Mar 17 to end Oct—Mons to Sats 11–6, Suns 2–6. Remainder of year, Suns & Bank Hols 2–6. Parties any time by prior arrangement with the Administrator. Adm £2, Chd 50p, OAPs, Students & Unemployed £1. Disabled free (ground floor only suitable).
**Refreshments:** Light teas available. Lunches and dinners organised for groups by prior arrangement. Coffee shop in Wildlife Park. Restaurants and Hotels in Cobh (4 m).

## GLIN CASTLE
**Glin** *map (ii)X*
Telephone: Ireland (068) 34173/34112
*(The Knight of Glin and Madam Fitz-Gerald)*

A Georgian Gothic castle with a series of battlemented folly lodges on lands held by the Knights of Glin for over 700 years. The interiors possess elaborate neo-classical plaster ceilings, a flying grand staircase and a notable collection of 18th century Irish mahogany furniture, family portraits and Irish landscapes. Formal gardens.

**Location:** On N69 32 m W of Limerick and 3 m E of Tarbert.
**Opening Times:** May 1 to May 31, 10–12, 2–4, and at other times groups by arrangement. Adm IR £2, Chd IR £1, groups IR £1.50. Car Parking. Suitable for disabled persons.
**Refreshments:** At the Glin Castle Gate Shop in one of the Gothic lodges on main road. Proprietress Joan Stack Tel. (068) 34188. Open Apr–Oct inclusive.

## HOWTH CASTLE GARDENS
**Howth** *map (iii)Z*
Telephone: Ireland (01) 322624
*(Howth Estate Co)*

Howth Castle Rhododendron Gardens. A natural woodland garden with over 2000 different species and Hybrids. Best May/June. The Irish Transport Museum is also in the Grounds.

**Location:** 9 m E of Dublin.
**Opening Times:** Daily except Christmas Day, dawn to sunset. Adm – Easter to July 1 IR £1, (£1.10). Rest of year free, parties over 15, discount of 10%. Parking for 180 cars.
**Refreshments:** Deer Park Hotel adjoins Gardens and car park.

## IRISH LIFE VIKING ADVENTURE
**St. Audoen's Church, High Street, Dublin 8**
Telephone: Dublin 797104

An authentic reconstruction of a street in Dublin in the year 988 brought to life by characters. They play the part of the typical merchant or house builder or other inhabitants that one would have met a thousand years ago. Visit these people in their houses, see how they live and experience the sounds and smells of Viking Dublin.

**Location:** Dublin City.
**Opening Times:** Daily 9–4 (last admission). Adm £2.75, Chd (under 14) £2 (under 5 free), Students/OAPs £2.25. Group rates for 20+.

## THE JAMES JOYCE TOWER
**Sandycove** *map (iii)Z*
Telephone: Ireland (01) 809265/808571
*(Dublin and East Tourism)*

Martello Tower built in 1804 as part of defence system against threatened Napoleonic invasion. Lived in briefly by James Joyce in 1904, and made the setting for the opening of his famous novel *Ulysses*. Opened as the James Joyce Museum in 1962. First and rare editions, personal possessions and other Joyce memorabilia, various military fittings preserved. Commanding view of Dublin Bay. Books of Joycean and Irish interest, posters, cards etc. on sale. Occasional evening lectures, slide shows etc.

**Location:** 1¼ m SE of Dun Laoghaire, Turn L from Sandycove Road along Sandycove Avenue to Sandycove Harbour and footpath to the Tower.
**Opening Times:** Apr 1 to Oct 31 (including Bank Holidays), Mon–Sat 10–1, 2–5, Suns 2.30–6. Rest of the year by appointment. Tel. Ireland (01) 808571. Adm £1.20, Students and OAPs 90p, Chd 60p. Parties (20+) 80p, School parties negotiable. Guided tours for parties by arrangement in advance. Suitable for disabled persons on ground floor only.
**Refreshments:** Fitzgerald's Pub, Sandycove: Wishbone Restaurant, Glasthule: Carney Arms Hotel, Dun Laoghaire: Royal Marine Hotel, Dun Laoghaire.

## JAPANESE GARDENS
**Tully** *map (iii)Y*
Telephone: (045) 21617
*(Irish National Stud)*

Created between 1906–1910, the Japanese Gardens symbolise the Life of Man from the Cave of Birth to the Gateway to Eternity. Special features include the Tea House, Red Bridge and some very old bonsai trees.

**Location:** Co. Kildare 1 m from Kildare Town and 5 m from Newbridge.
**Opening Times:** Easter to Oct 31 – Mon to Fri 10–5, Suns 2–5.30, Sat and Bank Holidays 10–5.30. Adm £1.50, Students and OAPs £1, Chd 80p. Family (2 adults and 2 children) £4. Groups (25) £1.40. Unsuitable for the disabled. Entrance to The Irish National Stud is at the same gate.
**Refreshments:** Tea, coffee, soup, salads, sandwiches etc. Groups can be catered for with some notice.

## THE JOHN F. KENNEDY ARBORETUM
**New Ross** *map (ii)Z*
Telephone: (051) 88171
*(The State/Forest Service)*

A comprehensive, scientifically laid-out arboretum with plant collections arranged in botanical circuits. Incorporated are forest plots and areas devoted to plant research. Reception building with display panel, Lecture Hall with A/V. Special collections of conifers, rhododendrons etc. A road gives access to a view point (890 ft) from which six counties may be seen.

**Location:** 12 km (7½ m) S of New Ross on R733.
**Opening Times:** Daily all year, except Christmas Day and Good Friday. May to Aug 10–8; Apr & Sept 10–6.30; Oct to Mar 10–5. Charge for car parking – Car £1.80 (IR £2), Season ticket £7.20 (IR £8), Coach £7.20 (IR £8), Minibus £3.60 (IR £4). Suitable for the disabled.
**Refreshments:** Cafe/Shop (May to Sept and weekends Apr). Tea, coffee, soup, sandwiches, salads etc. Five counties Hotel, New Ross 11km (7 m), Horse & Hound, lounge bar, Ballynabola 10km (6 m).

## JOHNSTOWN CASTLE
**Wexford** *map (ii)Z* ♿
*(An Foras Taluntais (Land-use & Grassland Research Centre))*

Grounds and gardens only. Many acres of well laid out grounds, with artificial lakes and fine collection of ornamental trees and shrubs. Agricultural museum.

**Location:** 5 m SW of Wexford.
**Opening Times:** All the year—Daily 9–5. Guidebook available at Castle. Adm to be decided.
**Refreshments:** Coffee shop during July & Aug.

FREE
HITHA LEAFLET
AVAILABLE

# Ireland

**Historic Irish Tourist Houses & Gardens Association Ltd. (H.I.T.H.A.)**

Under the auspices of Bord Failte (Irish Tourist Board) to promote
Houses, Castles and Gardens open to the public.

**3a Castle Street, Dalkey, Co. Dublin. Tel: 859323**

*More than 50 properties in Ireland including those listed on these pages.*

ANNES GROVE GARDENS

DUNGUAIRE CASTLE

BIRR CASTLE DEMESNE

DUNKATHEL

BUNRATTY CASTLE

EMO COURT

CLONALIS HOUSE

FOTA HOUSE

CRAGGAUNOWEN PROJECT

JAPANESE GARDENS

KNAPPOGUE CASTLE

MUCKROSS HOUSE

KYLEMORE ABBEY

NEWBRIDGE HOUSE

LISMORE CASTLE

POWERSCOURT GARDENS

LOUGH GUR

POWERSCOURT TOWNHOUSE

MALAHIDE CASTLE

MOUNT USHER

HITHA

FREE
HITHA LEAFLET
AVAILABLE

## KILLRUDDERY HOUSE & GARDENS
**Bray, Co. Wicklow**
Telephone: (01) 863405

Home of the Earl and Countess of Meath. The Garden and Park is the only surviving 17th century layout in Ireland. The House is fully furnished with an interesting period collection.

**Location:** 23 km S of Dublin. The main entrance 2 km beyond Bray on the Greystones road.
**Opening Times:** May, June and Sept daily 1–5. Open at other times and dates for groups by prior arrangement. Adm House: £2.50, Chd £1.50, Gardens only: £1, Chd 50p.

## KNAPPOGUE CASTLE
**Quin, Co. Clare** *map (ii)X*
Telephone: (061) 71103
*(Mr and Mrs M E Andrews)*

Knappogue Castle is one of the forty-two Castles built by the great McNamara Tribe which ruled over the territory of Clancullen from the 5th to the mid-15th centuries. The Castle has undergone extensive restoration work with its furnishings giving an authentic 15th century atmosphere. Craftshop.

**Location:** Quin—R469 on Map.
**Opening Times:** Easter to Sept 30 9.30–5.30. Adm £1.90, Chd £1.15, Special Group rates. Car Parking. Mediaeval Banquets and Entertainment twice nightly at 5.45 and 8.45 from May 1 to Oct 31. Souvenir shop in beautifully restored courtyard.

## KYLEMORE ABBEY
**Kylemore, Connemara** *map (iii)W*
Telephone: (095) 41146, or shops (095) 41113.

The only home of the Benedictine Nuns in Ireland. The Castle was acquired by the Nuns in 1920, and a precious heirloom was preserved, both for and on behalf of the people of Ireland, and visitors from all over the world. Built by Mr Mitchell Henry, MP for County Galway, and a native of Manchester. The Abbey is set amidst the lakes and mountains of Connemara in an area of outstanding beauty.

**Location:** 50 m from Galway city, between Galway and Clifden, near Letterfrack.
**Opening Times:** The grounds and part of the Abbey are open daily, Mar to Nov 10–6. Adm free. Pottery, gift and craft shop.
**Refreshments:** Light lunches, teas and snacks.

## LISMORE CASTLE
**Lismore, Co. Waterford** *map (ii)Y*
Telephone: Dungarvan (058) 54424
*(Trustees of the Lismore Estates)*

Beautifully situated walled and woodland gardens, containing a fine collection of camellias, magnolias and other shrubs. There is a remarkable yew walk.

**Location:** In town of Lismore; 45 m W of Waterford; 35 m NE of Cork.
**Opening Times:** GARDENS ONLY. May 8 to Sept 8—Daily (except Sats) 1.45–4.45. Adm £1, Chd (under 16) 50p. Reduced rates for parties.

## LISSADELL
**Sligo** *map (iv)X*
*(Josslyn Gore-Booth, Esq)*

The finest Greek-revival country house in Ireland. Splendid views of the surrounding countryside. The home of Countess Markievicz.

**Location:** 8 m NW of Sligo overlooking Sligo Bay.
**Opening Times:** Easter week then May 1 to Sept 30—Weekdays 2–5.15. Last tour 4.30. *Closed Suns.* Adm £1.50.

## LOUGH GUR VISITOR CENTRE
**Lough Gur** *map (ii)X*
Telephone: (061) 85186

Lough Gur Visitor Centre is modelled on Neolithic circular and rectangular houses and illustrates the story of man and his landscape through audio-visuals, artifacts and replicas of materials found in this historic place.

**Location:** Lough Gur – 16 m SE of Limerick City on the road to Kilmallock.
**Opening Times:** May 1 to Sept 30 – daily 10–6. Adm IR £1.50 (includes free cup of tea), Chd/Students 75p. Group rates available. Car parking free. Unsuitable for the disabled.

## MALAHIDE CASTLE
**Malahide** *map (iii)Z*
Telephone: 452655/452371
*(Ann Chambers, Administrator)*

One of Ireland's oldest and most historic castles containing a unique collection of Irish period furniture and Irish historical portraits, most of which are on permanent loan from the National Gallery of Ireland. In the adjacent gardens there are in excess of 5000 species and varieties of shrubs.

**Location:** 8 m from centre of Dublin.
**Opening Times:** Open all year Mon–Fri 10–12.45 & 2–5; Apr to Oct Sats 11–6; Suns and Bank Holidays 2–6; Nov–Mar Sats, Suns, Bank Holidays 2–5. Adm £2.15, OAPs & Students £1.50, Chd £1.15, Family £6. Parties £1.85, OAPs & Students £1.30, Chd £1. Bus & public car park. Unsuitable for the disabled.
**Refreshments:** Restaurant open in Castle during opening hours. Private evening banquets on request for groups; Local Hotel, Grand Hotel, Malahide, Co. Dublin.

## MOUNT USHER GARDENS
**Ashford** *map (iii)Z*
Telephone: (0404) 40205
*(Mrs Madelaine Jay)*

The Gardens extend along the Vartry river in beautiful County Wicklow. They are laid out in the informal 'Robinsonian' style comprising rare plants, shrubs and trees, collected from many parts of the world.

**Location:** Ashford, 1 m from Wicklow on Dublin-Bray-Wexford Road.
**Opening Times:** Mar 17 to Oct 31, open daily including Suns and Bank Holidays 10.30–6. Adm IR £2, OAPs, Chd, Students IR £1.50. Groups (20) IR £1.50, OAPs, Chd, Students IR £1.20. Car parking. Suitable for the disabled. No wheelchairs provided. Shopping courtyard.
**Refreshments:** Tea room at entrance, snacks, light lunches. Hunters Hotel 1 m.

## MUCKROSS HOUSE AND GARDENS
**Killarney, Co. Kerry**
Telephone: (064) 31440

Muckross House is a 19th century manor house, beautifully situated close to Muckross Lake, second largest of Killarney's three lakes. The house has many items of historic interest including locally carved period furniture, prints, maps and items which illustrate a traditional way of life of the people of Kerry. Skilled craftworkers at Muckross House carry on some of the traditional crafts of Kerry as their predecessors did in bygone days. The gardens, informal in design, are noted for their fine collection of rhododendrons and azaleas, extensive water gardens and an outstanding rock garden on natural limestone.

**Location:** 6 km (3.5 m) from Killarney on the Kenmare road.
**Opening Times:** Open all year. Mar 17 to June 30 daily 9–6. July 1 to Aug 31 daily 9–7. Sept 1 to Oct 31 daily 9–6; Rest of year daily, except Mons when the house is closed 11–5. Free car park, suitable for buses. Adm IR £2, Chd IR £1, group rates for 20+ IR £1.50. Free adm to the gardens.
**Refreshments:** Tea Room located in the old coach-house, serving teas, coffees, soup, sandwiches, pastries, minerals, etc.

## NATIONAL BOTANIC GARDENS
**Glasnevin, Dublin 9** *map (iii)Z*
*(Department of Agriculture)*

Founded 1795. 47 acres in extent containing 25,000 different living plant species and varieties. Flowering shrubs. Dwarf conifers. Orchids. Herbarium, 500,000 specimens.

**Location:** 2 m from city centre.
**Opening Times:** All the year—Daily (except Christmas Day); Weekdays 9–6 (summer); 10–4.30 (winter). Sundays 11–6 (summer); 11–4.30 (winter). Conservatories. Mons to Fris 9–12.45, 2.15–5 (summer); 10–12.45, 2.15–4.15 (winter). Sats 9–12.15, 2.15–5.45 (summer); 10–12.15, 2.15–4.15 (winter). Suns 2–5.45 (summer); 2–4.15 (winter). Adm free.

## NEWBRIDGE HOUSE
**Donabate** *map (iii)Z*
Telephone: Dublin 436534/5
*(Ann Chambers, Administrator)*

Newbridge House is an 18th century mansion in its own magnificent parkland of 300 acres. The Great Drawing room, in its original state, is one of the finest Georgian interiors in Ireland. Kitchen and laundry capture the 'below stairs' atmosphere of the big house, and the courtyard, with its coach house and various workshops, connect the past with the present.

**Location:** 12 m from the centre of Dublin.
**Opening Times:** Apr to Oct – Mon–Fri 10–12.45 & 2–5. Suns & Bank Holidays 2–6. Nov to Mar – Suns & Bank Holidays 2–5. Adm £2, OAPS & Students £1.50, Chd £1.10, Family ticket £5.95. Parties £1.75, OAPs & Students £1.25, Chd 90p. Bus & public car parks. Unsuitable for the disabled.
**Refreshments:** Coffee Shop serving teas, coffees, cakes, sandwiches.

## POWERSCOURT GARDENS & WATERFALL
**Enniskerry, Co. Wicklow** *map (iii)Z* ♿
Telephone: Dublin 867676/7/8

Powerscourt is owned by the Slazenger family and has been welcoming visitors for more than 50 years. Powerscourt is a magnificent example of an artistocratic garden laid out with taste and imagination. The breathtaking location nestling under the Great Sugar Loaf, the beauty of its Italian and Japanese Gardens, the splendid statuary and the incomparable iron work make it a fairytale demesne. The Waterfall is 398 feet high, which makes it one of the most spectacular in Ireland. Restaurant, souvenir gift and craft shop and children's play areas, garden centre and house-plant shop.

**Location:** ¼ mile Enniskerry, 12 miles S of Dublin.
**Opening Times:** Gardens: Mar 1 to Oct 31—Daily 9–5.30. Garden Centre open all year. Waterfall open all year 10.30–7. Closes dusk wintertime. Guided tours for specialist groups on request. Adm charges Gardens: £1.90, Chd 95p; Waterfall: £1, Chd 50p. Group reductions, season tickets. Property suitable for disabled persons. Wheelchair available.
**Refreshments:** Gardens: small restaurant (50 people) serving lunches, teas etc. Waterfall: Teas, light lunches available in high season.

## POWERSCOURT TOWNHOUSE CENTRE
**59 South William Street, Dublin 2**
Telephone: Dublin 687477

Built in 1771 for Richard Wingfield – Third Viscount Lord Powerscourt. Designed by Robert Mack and contains fine plasterwork by James McCullagh and Michael Stapleton.

**Location:** 59 South William Street, Dublin 2.
**Opening Times:** Open daily 9.30–5.30. *Closed* Bank Holidays. Adm free. Wheelchair access to three floors.

## RIVERSTOWN HOUSE
**Glanmire, Co. Cork**

The House was originally built in 1602. It became the seat of Doctor Jemmett Brown, Bishop of Cork, who rebuilt it in 1745 with fine plasterwork by the Francini brothers.

**Location:** 6 km from Cork City on the Cork/Dublin road.
**Opening Times:** May to Aug, Thurs to Sat. At other times by appointment. Adm £1.50.

## ROTHE HOUSE
**Kilkenny**
Telephone: (056) 22893

Rothe House is a 16th century merchant house built by the Rothe family. It is being restored by Kilkenny Archaeological Society and contains the Society's Museum with costumes, pictures, and artifacts of Kilkenny interest. The house is a charming Tudor style composition built around two courtyards.

**Location:** Centre of Kilkenny city, 75 m from Dublin.
**Opening Times:** Apr to Oct 10.30–12.30, 2–5. Mon to Sat and Sun 3–5. Nov to Mar 3–5, Sat and Sun. Adm £1, Chd 30p, OAPs/Students 50p, group rate adults 60p.
**Refreshments:** Coffee shop serving teas, coffee and snacks during summer period.

## THE ROYAL HOSPITAL
**Kilmainham** *map (iii)Z*
Telephone: (01) 718666

Founded in 1680 by the Duke of Ormond as a hospice for pensioner soldiers, the Royal Hospital Kilmainham is the earliest surviving public building in the country. Recently restored, it is now the National Centre for Culture and the Arts.

**Location:** Situated 2 m W of Dublin city; 300 metres from Heuston Station.
**Opening Times:** For information please tel: (031) 718666. Adm: Tues free; Wed to Fri £1, Chd 50p, Family ticket (2 adults plus children) £3; Sat, Sun £2, Chd 50p, Family ticket £4. OAPs free.
**Refreshments:** Sunday Brunch: adults £6, Chd £3 each.

## RUSSBOROUGH
**Blessington, Co. Wicklow** *map (iii)Z*
Telephone: (045) 65239
*(Alfred Beit Foundation)*

Palladian house in romantic setting in the Wicklow mountains, built 1740–50 and housing the Beit Art Collection.

**Location:** 20 m SW of Dublin; 2 m SW of Blessington on N81.
**Opening Times:** Easter to Oct 31: Easter to May 31, and Sept to Oct 31: Suns and Bank Holidays only 2–5.30. June 1 to Aug 31: daily 2–5.30. Adm £2.50, Chd (accompanied) 50p. Chd (over 12 accompanied) £1, Student/OAP £1.50. Upstairs – £1, Chd (accompanied) free. Shop. Children's playground. Extensive wooded parkland. Adjacent lakeside amenity and picnic area.
**Refreshments:** Tea room.

## SLANE CASTLE
**Slane** *map (iv)Z*
Telephone: Drogheda (041) 24207
*(The Earl of Mount Charles)*

Dramatic 18th century Castle on river Boyne, featuring work of James Wyatt, Francis Johnston, James Gandon and Capability Brown, with fine pictures and furniture.

**Location:** 29 m from Dublin. 8 m from Navan. 9 m from Drogheda. Slane village on N2. Castle entrance on N51 (to Navan).
**Opening Times:** Mar 17 to Oct 30 – Suns and Bank Holiday Mons 2–6. Adm £1.65, Students & OAPs 50p, Family Rate £3.50, Parties (20) £1.25. Car park for 100. Suitable for the disabled, no wheelchairs available.
**Refreshments:** Steak bar/restaurant fully licensed. Open Wed–Sun 12–10.30pm.

## THOOR BALLYLEE
**Gort** *map (iii)X*
Telephone: (091) 31436
*(Senator Michael Yeats)*

16th Century Norman Tower with thatched cottage attached. Summer home of W.B. Yeats for 12 years 1917–1929. Location of inspiration of the 'Tower' and 'Winding Stair' poems.

**Location:** 4 m from Gort Town. 1 m from N18 Galway/Gort road. 1 m from N66 Gort/Loughrea road.
**Opening Times:** Open daily June–Sept 10–6. Large car park suitable for buses. Unsuitable for the disabled. Bus groups and large parties given lecture.
**Refreshments:** Tea room in grounds of Tower supplying tea, coffee, minerals, pastries, biscuits etc.

## TIMOLEAGUE CASTLE GARDENS
**Bandon** *map (i)X*
Telephone: (023) 46116 or (021) 831512
*(Mr N.R.E. Travers)*

Seven acres of old fashioned gardens in a beautiful and historic setting. Palm trees and other frost-tender shrubs flourish in the mild climate of this beautiful part of West Cork.

**Location:** Adjoining Timoleague village, Bandon 8 m.
**Opening Times:** GARDEN ONLY Easter Weekend, then daily mid May to mid Sept 12–6. Adm £1.08 (IR £1.20), Chd 56p (IR 60p). Parties by arrangement. Car park. Suitable for the disabled.
**Refreshments:** At local hotels.

# IRELAND (NORTHERN)

**ARDRESS HOUSE, The National Trust**
**Co Armagh** *map (v)Z* △ ♿
Telephone: Annaghmore 851236

17th century country house with fine plasterwork. Small garden, agricultural display in farmyard. Woodland play area.

**Location:** 7 m W of Portadown on Portadown/Moy Road (B28); 2 m from Loughgall intersection on M1.
**Opening Times:** Easter: Mar 24 to Apr 2: daily 12–6. Apr and May: Sat, Sun & Bank Holidays 12–6. June, July and Aug: daily except Tues 12–6. Sept: Sat and Sun 12–6. Booked parties by arrangement throughout the season. Adm House: £1, Parties 75p (outside normal hours £1.20). Farmyard: 50p, Parties 40p. Parking 50p. Wheelchairs admitted. Picnic areas.
**Refreshments:** Picnic teas available on summer Suns.

**THE ARGORY, The National Trust**
**Co Armagh** *map (v)Y* △ ♿
Telephone: Moy 84753

295 acre estate with neo-classical house, built c. 1820.

**Location:** 4 m from Moy on Derrycaw Road; 3 m from Coalisland intersection.
**Opening Times:** Easter: Mar 24 to Apr 2: daily 12–6. Apr and May: Sat, Sun and Bank Holidays 12–6. June, July and Aug: daily except Tues 12–6. Sept: Sat and Sun 12–6. Adm £1.25, Chd 65p, Parties £1, Chd 35p, (parties outside normal hours £1.50). Parking 50p. Dogs in grounds only on leads. Wheelchairs provided – access to ground floor only.
**Refreshments:** Tea room Apr, May and Sept: Sat, Sun and Bank Holidays 2–6; open all Easter week. June to Aug: daily except Tues 2–6.

**CASTLE COOLE, The National Trust**
**Co Fermanagh** *map (iv)Y* △
Telephone: Enniskillen 22690

Magnificent 18th century mansion by James Wyatt with plasterwork by Joseph Rose.

**Location:** 1½ m SE of Enniskillen on Belfast/Clogher/Enniskillen Road (A4).
**Opening Times:** The estate is open from dawn to dusk free of charge from Apr 1 to Sept 30. Picnickers welcome. House open Easter: Mar 24 to Apr 2: daily 12–6. Apr and May: Sat, Sun and Bank Holidays 12–6. June, July and Aug: daily except Tues 12–6. Sept: Sat and Sun 12–6. Adm House: £1.50, parties £1.25 (outside normal hours £2). Parking 50p.

**CASTLE WARD, The National Trust**
**Co Down** *map (v)Z* △ ♿ Ⓢ
Telephone: Strangford 204

Built by the first Lord Bangor in 1765 in a beautiful setting. Laundry museum. Wildfowl collection on lake. Strangford Lough Information Centre in converted barn on edge of shore.

**Location:** 7 m NE of Downpatrick; 1½ m W of Strangford village (A25).
**Opening Times:** Easter: Mar 24 to Apr 2: daily 12–6. Apr: Sat and Sun 12–6. May: Wed to Sun and Bank Holiday Mons 12–6. June, July and Aug: daily except Tues 12–6. Sept and Oct: Sat and Sun 12–6. Estate and grounds open all year dawn to one hour after dusk. (Charge for car park only.) Adm House: £1.25, parties £1 (outside normal opening hours £1.50). Parking £2.50 (£1 when house and other facilities are closed). Wheelchairs access (3 provided).
**Refreshments:** Refreshments available. Open as house.

**DOWNHILL CASTLE, The National Trust**
**Londonderry** *map (v)Y* ♿

Built by the Earl of Bristol, Bishop of Derry, in 1783 with Mussenden Temple, the Bishop's Gate, the Black Glen and the Bishop's Fish Pond.

**Location:** 5 m W of Coleraine on Coleraine/Downhill Road (A2).
*Station: Castlerock.*
**Opening Times: Temple:** Apr to end Sept: daily 12–6. Glen and grounds always open. Grounds free at all times. Glen open free at all times. Dogs admitted. Limited wheelchair access.

**FLORENCE COURT, The National Trust**
**Co Fermanagh** *map (iv)Y* △ ♿
Telephone: Florence Court 249

Important 18th century house built by John Cole. Excellent rococo plasterwork. Pleasure Gardens.

**Location:** 8 m SW of Enniskillen via A4 and A32; 1 m W of Florence Court village.
**Opening Times:** Easter: Mar 24 to Apr 2: daily 12–6. Apr to end Sept: daily except Tues 12–6. Last adm 5.15. Grounds open all year round, 10am to one hour before dusk. Adm £1.50, Chd 75p. Parties £1.25 (outside normal opening hours £2). Parking 50p. Dogs in pleasure gardens only, on leads. Wheelchair access—ground floor only.
**Refreshments:** Tearoom open as house.

**GRAY'S PRINTING PRESS, The National Trust**
**Strabane, Co Tyrone** *map (v)Y*

The shop was in existence in 18th century. It has close links with Scots-Irish tradition in America.

**Location:** In Main Street, Strabane.
**Opening Times:** Press: Mar 24 to end of Sept—Daily (except Thurs & Suns) 12–6. Shop (not N.T.): Every day except Thurs, Suns & public hols, 9–1 and 2–5.30. Adm 50p, Chd 25p.

**HEZLETT HOUSE, The National Trust**
**Co Londonderry** *map (v)Y* △
Telephone: Castlerock 848567

Thatched cottage of particular importance because of the unusual cruck/truss construction of the roof.

**Location:** 4 m W of Coleraine on Coleraine/Downhill Coast Road (A2).
**Opening Times:** Easter: Mar 24 to Apr 2: daily 12–6. Apr to June: Sat, Sun and Bank Holidays 12–6. July and Aug: daily except Tues 12–6. Sept: Sat and Sun 12–6. Adm 50p, Chd 25p, Parties outside normal hours 60p. No dogs. Unsuitable for wheelchairs.

**MOUNT STEWART HOUSE, GARDEN AND TEMPLE, The National Trust**
**Co Down** *map (v)Z* △ ♿
Telephone: Greyabbey 387

Interesting house with important associations with Lord Castlereagh. Gardens designed by Lady Edith, Marchioness of Londonderry. Fine topiary work, flowering shrubs and rhododendrons. Temple of the Winds, modelled on that at Athens, built 1783.

**Location:** On E shore of Strangford Lough; 5 m SE of Newtownards; 15 m E of Belfast (A20).
**Opening Times: House & Temple:** Easter: Mar 24 to Apr 2: daily 12–6. Apr: Sat and Sun 12–6. May: Wed to Sun 12–6. June to end Aug: daily except Tues 12–6. Sept: Sat and Sun 12–6. **Garden:** Mar 17, then Mar 24 to Apr 2: 12–6. Apr: Sat and Sun 12–6. May: Wed to Sun 12–6. June to end Aug: daily except Tues 12–6. Sept and Oct: daily except Tues 12–6. Adm House, Garden and Temple £2. Parties £1.50 (outside normal hours £1.75). Garden and Temple £1.50. Parties £1 (outside normal hours £1.50). Dogs in garden only, on leads. Wheelchairs provided. Booked parties by arrangement throughout the season. Open Bank Hols falling on a Monday.
**Refreshments:** Tea room open as house.

**ROWALLANE GARDEN, The National Trust**
**Saintfield, Co Down** *map (v)Z* ♿
Telephone: Saintfield 510131

Beautiful gardens containing large collection of plants, chiefly trees and shrubs. Of particular interest in spring and autumn.

**Location:** 11 m SE of Belfast; 1 m S of Saintfield on the W of the Downpatrick Road (A7).
**Opening Times:** Easter (inc. Good Friday) and Apr: daily 12–6. May and June: daily 12–9. July to end Sept: daily 12–6. Oct to end Mar: Mon to Fri 12–4.30. *Closed* Dec 25 and 26, Jan 1. Open all Bank Holidays. Adm Apr to end Oct £1. Parties 80p. Nov to end Mar 50p. Parties 35p. Outside normal opening hours £1.20. Dogs admitted on leads, to indicated areas. Wheelchair access (1 provided).
**Refreshments:** Tea room, Apr to Sept: daily 2–6.

**SPRINGHILL, The National Trust**
**Moneymore, Co Londonderry** *map (v)Z* △ ♿
Telephone: Moneymore 48210

House dating from 17th century. Magnificent oak staircase and interesting furniture & paintings. Costume museum. Cottar's kitchen.

**Location:** On Moneymore/Coagh Road (1 m from Moneymore).
**Opening Times:** Easter: Mar 24 to Apr 2: daily 12–6. Apr and May: Sat, Sun and Bank Holidays 12–6. June to end Aug: daily except Tues 12–6. Sept: Sat and Sun 12–6. Adm £1.25. Parties £1 (outside normal opening hours £1.50). Dogs in grounds only, on leads. Wheelchair access to ground floor & museum.
**Refreshments:** Light refreshments and shop in Servants Hall. Lunches, high teas & dinners at Manor House, Main Street, Moneymore. Tel Moneymore 48206.

**TEMPLETOWN MAUSOLEUM, The National Trust**
**Co Antrim** *map (v)Z*

Built 1783 by Robert Adam.

**Location:** Castle Upton Graveyard, Templepatrick (A6).
**Opening Times:** All year during daylight hours. Adm free. Dogs admitted. Access difficult for wheelchairs.

**WELLBROOK BEETLING MILL, The National Trust**
**Cookstown, Co Tyrone** *map (v)Y*

A water-powered mill built in 18th century with 19th century modifications.

**Location:** 3 m from Cookstown on Cookstown/Omagh Road.
**Opening Times:** Easter: Mar 24 to Apr 2: daily 12–6. Apr and May: Sat, Sun and Bank Holidays 12–6. June to end Aug: daily except Tues 12–6. Sept: Sat and Sun 12–6. Adm 50p, Chd 25p. Parties 50p (outside normal opening hours 60p). No dogs. Unsuitable for wheelchairs.

# The National Trust Northern Ireland Properties

For further information about properties in the care of the National Trust in Northern Ireland apply to The National Trust, Rowallane, Saintfield, Co. Down. Telephone: Saintfield 510721.

## SPRINGHILL

**MONEYMORE, CO. LONDONDERRY**

## CASTLE WARD

**STRANG FORD, CO. DOWN**

## MOUNT STEWART HOUSE & GARDEN

**GREYABBEY, CO. DOWN**

## CASTLE COOLE

**ENNISKILLEN, CO. FERMANAGH**

## ARDRESS

**CO. ARMAGH**

## ROWALLANE GARDEN

**SAINTFIELD, CO. DOWN**

*ADMISSION DETAILS — SEE EDITORIAL REFERENCE*

# SCOTLAND

## BORDERS REGION

### ABBOTSFORD HOUSE
**Melrose** *map 13F* ♿
*(Mrs P Maxwell-Scott)*

The home of Sir Walter Scott, containing many historical relics collected by him.

**Location:** 3 m W of Melrose just S of A72; 5 m E of Selkirk.
**Opening Times:** 3rd Mon of Mar to Oct 31—Daily 10–5; Suns 2–5. *Cars with wheelchairs or disabled visitors enter by private entrance.* Gift shop.
**Refreshments:** Teashop.

### AYTON CASTLE
**Eyemouth** *map G13*
Telephone: (089 07) 81212

Victorian castle in red sandstone.

**Location:** 7 m N of Berwick-upon-Tweed on A1.
**Opening Times:** May to Sept—Suns 2–5 or by appointment. Adm £1, Chd (under 15) free.

### BOWHILL
**nr Selkirk** *map F13* △ ♿
Telephone: Selkirk (0750) 20732
*(His Grace the Duke of Buccleuch & Queensberry KT)*

Border home of the Scotts of Buccleuch. Famous paintings include 8 Guardis, Canaletto's Whitehall, Claudes, Gainsboroughs, Reynolds and Raeburns. Superb French furniture and porcelain. Monmouth, Sir Walter Scott and Queen Victoria relics. For details of our specialist courses, run in conjunction with Sotheby's please tel: Buccleuch Heritage Trust Selkirk (0750) 20732. Restored Victorian kitchen. Audio-Visual programme. Lecture Theatre. Exciting Adventure Woodland Play Area. Walks to historic Newark Castle and by lochs and rivers along nature trails.

**Location:** 3 m W of Selkirk on A708 Moffat-St. Mary's Loch road. Edinburgh, Carlisle, Newcastle approx 1½ hours by road.
**Opening Times:** House open July 1 to July 31—Daily 1–4.30 (Suns 2–6). Grounds (includes Adventure Woodland Play Area, Nature Trails)—July 1 to July 31—Daily 12–5 (Suns 2–6). Last entry 45 mins before closing time. Riding Centre and Pony Trekking (0750) 20192 open all day all year. Adm House & Grounds £2.50. Parties over 20 £1.75. Grounds only £1. Wheelchair users and Chd (under 5) free. Free car & coach parking. Open by appointment at additional times for museums and specialist or educational groups.
**Refreshments:** Gift shop and licensed tea room open daily during 'House open' period.

### DAWYCK BOTANIC GARDEN
**nr Peebles** *map 13F*
*(Royal Botanic Garden, Edinburgh)*

Impressive woodland garden.

**Location:** 8 m SW of Peebles; 28 m S of Edinburgh.
**Opening Times:** Apr to Oct—Daily 10–6. Adm 30p. No animals.

### DRYBURGH ABBEY
**Dryburgh** *map 13F*
*(Secretary of State for Scotland)*

Sir Walter Scott and Field Marshal Earl Haig are buried in this 12th century Abbey.

**Location:** 5 m SE of Melrose, nr St Boswells.
**Opening Times:** Apr 1 to Sept 30—Weekdays 9.30–7; Suns 2–7; Oct 1 to Mar 31—Weekdays 9.30–4; Suns 2–4. *Closed Dec 25, 26 & Jan 1 & 2).* Adm £1, Chd & OAPs 50p.

### FLOORS CASTLE
**Kelso** *map G13*
Telephone: Kelso (0573) 23333
*(The Duke of Roxburghe)*

Built in 1721 by William Adam and later added to by Playfair. Magnificent tapestries, fine French and English furniture, paintings, porcelain.

**Location:** N of Kelso.
**Opening Times:** Easter Sun & Mon Mar 26, 27 and from Apr 30 to Sept 28—Suns to Thurs (incl Bank Hol Mons); July and Aug: also open Fris. Grounds, Gardens and Castle—10.30–5.30 (last adm to Castle 4.45). Oct: Sun and Wed, 10.30–4. The Castle will open on Fris during Apr, May, June & Sept to coach parties by appointment only. Closed Sats. Adm £2.20, Chd (aged 8 and over) £1.50, OAPs £2; Family ticket £6. Party rates on request from The Factor, Roxburghe Estate Office, Kelso, Roxburghshire. Garden Centre and coffee shop open seven days.
**Refreshments:** Licensed restaurant, gift shop and coffee shop.

### HERMITAGE CASTLE
**Liddlesdale** *map F12*
*(Secretary of State for Scotland)*

Here in 1566, Queen Mary visited her wounded lover Bothwell.

**Location:** In Liddlesdale; 5½ m NE of Newcastleton.
**Opening Times:** Apr 1 to Sept 30—Weekdays 9.30–7, Suns 2–7; Oct 1 to Mar 31—Weekends only. *Closed Dec 25, 26; Jan 1, 2.* Adm 60p, Chd & OAPs 30p.

### THE HIRSEL GROUNDS & DUNDOCK WOOD
**Coldstream** *map G13*
Telephone: Coldstream (0890) 2834

Snowdrops, aconites and daffodils in Spring in grounds. Fantastic rhododendrons and azaleas May/June Dundock wood and grounds. Marvellous Autumn colouring. Picnic areas. Parking. Homestead museum, Craft Centre and workshops.

**Opening Times:** All reasonable daylight hours throughout the year. Adm by donation.
**Refreshments:** In main season.

### JEDBURGH ABBEY
**Jedburgh** *map F13*
*(Secretary of State for Scotland)*

Founded by David I this Augustinian Abbey is remarkably complete. Recent excavations are now open to the public. New Visitor Centre.

**Location:** In Jedburgh.
**Opening Times:** Apr to Sept—Weekdays 9.30–7; Suns 2–7; Oct to Mar—Weekdays 9.30–4; Suns 2–4. Adm £1, Chd & OAPs 50p.

### KAILZIE GARDENS
**nr Peebles** *map F13* ♿
*(Mrs A M Richard)*

Beautifully situated private gardens re-created in the last 20 years. Magnificent spring show of snowdrops and daffodils; mature timber. Herbaceous borders, shrub and floral beds in old walled garden. Formal rose garden. Greenhouse. Wild Garden and Burnside walk with Primulas, Meconopsis and Rhododendrons. A garden for all seasons.

**Location:** 2½ m SE from Peebles on B7062.
**Opening Times:** Fri Mar 24 to Sun Oct 8—Daily 11–5.30. Adm £1, Chd 45p. Car park. Picnic area. Shop. Art Gallery. Owls. Waterfowl pond. Plants for sale when available.
**Refreshments:** Licensed tea room; lunches & teas.

### MANDERSTON
**Duns** *map G12*
Telephone: Duns (0361) 83450
*(Mr and Mrs Adrian Palmer)*

The finest Edwardian house in the classical style in Britain. Remarkable picturesque group of farm and dairy buildings; gardens.

**Location:** 2 m E of Duns on A6105; 14 m W of Berwick upon Tweed.
**Opening Times:** May 11 to Sept 24—Thurs & Suns also Bank Hol Mons May 29 & Aug 28, 2–5.30. Adm charges not available at time of going to press. Parties at any time. Gift shop.
**Refreshments:** Cream Teas.

### MELLERSTAIN
**Gordon** *map G13*
Telephone: Gordon (057 381) 225
*(The Earl of Haddington)*

Scotland's famous Adam mansion. Beautifully decorated and furnished interiors. Terraced gardens and lake. Gift shop.

**Location:** 9 m NE of Melrose; 7 m NW of Kelso; 37 m SE of Edinburgh.
**Opening Times:** Easter weekend (Mar 24–27) then May 1 to Sept 30—Daily (except Sats) 12.30–5. Last adm to House 4.30. Adm charges not available at time of going to press. Free parking. *Special terms for organised parties by appointment, apply Curator.*
**Refreshments:** Tea rooms.

### MELROSE ABBEY
**Melrose** *map F13*
*(Secretary of State for Scotland)*

Beautiful Cistercian Abbey founded by David I.

**Location:** In Melrose.
**Opening Times:** Apr 1 to Sept 30—Weekdays 9.30–7, Suns 2–7; Oct 1 to Mar 31—Weekdays 9.30–4, Suns 2–4. *Closed Dec 25, 26; Jan 1, 2.* Adm £1.00, Chd & OAPs 50p.

### MERTOUN GARDENS
**St Boswells** *map F13*
Telephone: St Boswells 23236
*(His Grace the Duke of Sutherland)*

20 acres of beautiful grounds with delightful walks and river views. Fine trees, herbaceous plants and flowering shrubs. Walled garden and well-preserved circular dovecot.

**Location:** 2 m NE of St Boswells on the B6404.
**Opening Times:** Garden only. Sats and Suns, Mons on Bank Holidays only—Apr to Sept 2–6 (last entry 5.30). Parties by arrangement. Adm 80p, Chd 30p, OAPs 30p. No dogs. Car parking.
**Refreshments:** Dryburgh Abbey Hotel, Buccleuch Arms Hotel, St Boswells.

## ABBOTSFORD HOUSE

**MELROSE**

*ADMISSION – SEE EDITORIAL REFERENCE*

## BOWHILL NEAR SELKIRK

Edinburgh 42 miles,
Berwick 43,
Carlisle 56,
Glasgow 75.

Opening dates 1989.
House and Grounds
1 July – 13 August daily.

Grounds only: 29 April – 28 August daily except Fridays.

See line entry for times and admission charges.

Free car and coach parking.

For details of our specialist one, three or five day Arts Courses run in conjunction with Sotheby's. please telephone Buccleuch Heritage Trust (0750) 20732.

## FLOORS CASTLE

**KELSO, ROXBURGHSHIRE, SCOTLAND**

The Grand Tour of Scotland

*SCOTLAND'S LARGEST INHABITED CASTLE*

Home of the Duke and Duchess of Roxburghe. Situated in the beautiful and historic border country and overlooking the River Tweed, the town of Kelso and the ruins of Roxburgh Caslte.

Open Easter Sunday & Monday, 26th & 27th March, and from 30th April to 28th September Sunday to Thursday inclusive, except during the months of July and August when it will be open Sunday to Friday inclusive 10.30 a.m. to 5.30 p.m. (last admission to Castle 4.45 p.m.) Gift shop and Licensed restaurant. Party rates on request from: **Roxburghe Estate Offices, Kelso, Roxburghshire. Telephone: 0573 23333.**

## HERMITAGE CASTLE

**Admission – See editorial reference.**

## Manderston Duns Berwickshire

*'The Swansong of the Great Classical House'*

The swan-song of the great classical house. Georgian in its taste but with all the elaborate domestic arrangements designed for Edwardian convenience and comfort.
Superb classical yet luxurious rooms and the only silver staircase in the world, in a house on which the architect was ordered to spare no expense. The extensive 'downstairs' domestic quarters are equally some of the grandest of their type.
Outside the grandeur is continued. See the most splendid stables and picturesque marble dairy. Acres of formal and woodland garden and lakeside walks.

### NEIDPATH CASTLE
**Peebles** *map F13*
Telephone: Aberlady (087 57) 201
*(Lady Elizabeth Benson)*

Medieval castle updated in the 17th century, situated on a bluff above the River Tweed. Pit prison, well hewn out of solid rock and fine views.

**Location:** 1 m W of Peebles on A72.
**Opening Times:** Mar 23 to Apr 2; Apr 29 to Oct 8—Mons to Sats 10–1, 2–5; Suns 1–5 Adm £1, Chd 50p, OAPs 50p. Parties at reduced rates—enquiries to The Factor, Estates Office, Longniddry, East Lothian EH32 0PY.
**Refreshments:** Hotels in Peebles.

### PRIORWOOD GARDEN
**Melrose** *map F13*
Telephone: Melrose (089 682) 2555
*(The National Trust for Scotland)*

Garden featuring flowers suitable for drying. Shop and Trust visitor centre.

**Location:** In Melrose.
**Opening Times:** Mar 24 to Apr 27, Nov 1 to Dec 24: Mon–Sat 10–1, 2–5.30. Apr 28 to June 30, Oct 1 to 31: Mon–Sat 10–5.30, Sun 1.30–5.30. July 1 to Sept 30: Mon–Sat 10–6, Sun 1.30–5.30. Adm by donation.

### ROBERT SMAIL'S PRINTING WORKS
**Tweeddale** *map F13*
*(The National Trust for Scotland)*

The buildings contain vintage working machinery, including a 100-year-old press which was originally driven by water wheels. The Victorian office is on display complete with its acid-etched plate-glass windows and examples of historic items printed in the works.

**Location:** In Innerleithen High Street, 30 m S of Edinburgh.
**Opening Times:** Mar 24 to Dec 24, Mon–Sat (except Tues) 10–5. Adm free.

### SMAILHOLM TOWER
**nr Smailholm** *map F13*
*(Historic Buildings and Monuments)*

Simple tower house displaying a collection of costume figures and tapestries relating to Sir Walter Scotts' 'Minstrelsy of the Scottish Borders'.

**Location:** nr Smailholm Village 6 m NW of Kelso.
**Opening Times:** Apr 1 to Sept 30—Weekdays 9.30–7, Suns 2–7. Oct 1 to Mar 31, *closed*. Adm 60p, Chd & OAPs 30p.

### THIRLESTANE CASTLE
**Lauder, Berwickshire** *map F13*
Telephone: Lauder (05782) 430

Described as one of the oldest and finest Castles in Scotland, Thirlestane has its roots in an original 13th century fort overlooking the Leader Valley. The main keep was built in 1590 by the Maitland family who have lived in the Castle for over 400 years; it was extended in 1670 and again in 1840. The Restoration Period plasterwork ceilings are considered to be the finest in existence. The family nurseries now house a collection of over 7,000 historic toys and children are encouraged to dress up. Visitors see the old kitchens, pantries and laundries as well as the Country Life Exhibitions portraying day to day life in the Borders through the centuries. Grounds, picnic garden, woodland walk, free car park, gift shop.

**Location:** 28 m S of Edinburgh off A68 – follow signs on all main approach roads.
**Opening Times:** Easter Sun and Mon, May, June and Sept – Wed, Thur and Sun only. July and Aug – daily except Sat. Castle 2–5. Grounds 12–6. Adm £2, Chd/OAPs and party rate £1.50, family ticket (parents and children only) £5. Booked party tours any time by arrangement.
**Refreshments:** Tea room.

### TRAQUAIR
**Innerleithen** *map F13* △
Telephone: Innerleithen (0896) 830323
*(P. Maxwell Stuart of Traquair)*

A house full of beauty, romance and mystery. Rich in associations with Mary Queen of Scots, the Jacobites and Catholic persecution. Priest's room with secret stairs. The Bear gates have remained closed since 1745. The present Laird brews his world famous Traquair House Ale in the 18th century Brew House. Extensive grounds and newly planted maze.

**Location:** 1 m from Innerleithen; 6 m from Peebles; 29 m from Edinburgh at junction of B709 & B7062 (40 minutes by road from Edinburgh Turnhouse Airport, 1½ hours from Glasgow).
**Opening Times:** Easter Sat, Sun & Mon. Suns and Mons in May, then daily from May 27 to Sept 30, 1.30–5.30; (July and Aug only 10.30–5.30). Last adm 5. Grounds: May to Sept: 10.30–5.30. Gift Shop, Antique Shop.
**Refreshments:** Home cooking at the 1745 Cottage Tea Room from 12.30.

# *Six of the best*

A warm welcome
is extended to visitors to the six properties illustrated on this page
and to the many others which are owned by the National Trust for Scotland,
all of which are described in the Scotland section of this publication.

◀ INVEREWE GARDEN

Cradled in the magnificent mountains of Wester Ross, the world-famous garden is an oasis of fertility on a Highland peninsula.

FALKLAND PALACE AND GARDEN ▶

A Royal palace, in the Kingdom of Fife, once the country residence of the Stuart kings and queens when they hunted deer and wild boar.

◀ CULZEAN CASTLE & COUNTRY PARK

Perched on an Ayrshire cliff beside the Firth of Clyde, the castle is an outstanding example of the skill of Robert Adam, the famous architect.

CULLODEN BATTLEFIELD AND VISITOR CENTRE ▶

Scene of the last great battle fought on the soil of mainland Britain in 1746, when government forces defeated Prince Charles Edward Stuart, near Inverness.

◀ FYVIE CASTLE

A superb castle, north-west of Aberdeen, dating from the 13th century, it contains a magnificent collection of paintings and furniture.

THE GEORGIAN HOUSE ▶

A splendid example of a Georgian New Town house, appropriately furnished as it might have been in the time of the first occupants.

For full details
of over 100 properties
cared for by the National Trust for Scotland, send £1 for our attractively illustrated guide to
The National Trust for Scotland 5 Charlotte Square, Edinburgh EH2 4DU.

**National Trust for Scotland**

# CENTRAL REGION

### CASTLE CAMPBELL
**Dollar** *map E14*
*(Secretary of State for Scotland)*

15th century oblong tower with later additions, set in a steep sided glen. Sometimes known as "Castle Gloom".

**Location:** 1 m N of Dollar; on N slope of Ochil Hills at head of Dollar Glen.
**Opening Times:** Apr 1 to Sept 30—Weekdays 9.30–7, Suns 2–7; Oct 1 to Mar 31—Weekdays 9.30–4, Suns 2–4. *(Closed Thurs pm & Fris in winter, also Dec 25, 26; Jan 1, 2).* Adm 60p, Chd & OAPs 30p.

### LINLITHGOW PALACE
**Linlithgow** *map E14*
*(Secretary of State for Scotland)*

Birthplace of Mary Queen of Scots.

**Location:** In Linlithgow.
*Station: Linlithgow (½ m).*
**Opening Times:** Apr 1 to Sept 30—Daily 9.30–7 (Suns 2–7). Oct 1 to Mar 31—Daily 9.30–4 (Suns 2–4). *Closed Dec 25, 26, Jan 1 & 2.* Adm £1, Chd & OAPs 50p.

### STIRLING CASTLE
**Stirling** *map E14*
*(Secretary of State for Scotland)*

Royal Castle on a great basalt rock dominating the surrounding countryside.

**Location:** In Stirling.
*Station: Stirling (¾ m).*
**Opening Times:** Apr 1 to Sept 30—Weekdays 9.30–6.00. Suns 10.30–5.30. Oct 1 to Mar 31—Weekdays 9.30–5.05. Suns 12.30–4.20. *Closed Dec 25, 26; Jan 1, 2 and 3.* Adm £1.50, Chd & OAPs 75p, Family £4. Last ticket sold 45 mins before closing time.

# DUMFRIES & GALLOWAY

### ARBIGLAND GARDENS
**Kirkbean** *map E11*
*(Captain J B Blackett)*

Woodland, formal and water gardens arranged round a secluded bay. The garden where Admiral Paul Jones worked as a boy.

**Location:** 15 m SW of Dumfries on A710.
**Opening Times:** Gardens: May to Sept incl—Tues, Thurs & Suns 2–6. House and Gardens: May 20–28, 1989: 2–6; Aug 19–27, 1989: 2–6. Adm £1, Chd 50p. Toddlers free. Car park free. Picnic area by sandy beach. Dogs on leads please. Produce Shop.
**Refreshments:** Tea room. Hotels in Dumfries or Southerness (2 m).

### BROUGHTON HOUSE
**High Street, Kirkcudbright** *map E11*
Telephone: (0557) 30437
*(The Hornel Trust)*

Home of the artist E. A. Hornel 1864–1933. Mainly 18th century. Fine furniture, Scottish paintings. George III–Victorian samplers. Special exhibitions: The Artist in his Studio: House Laundry 1920's. Superb town garden and Japanese garden.

**Location:** 12 High Street, Kirkcudbright DG6 4JX.
**Opening Times:** Easter to Oct 14: weekdays 11–1, 2–5, Sun 2–5. *Closed* Tues. Adm 60p, OAPs/Chd half price. Conducted tours for parties available. Car parking nearby in town park. Suitable for disabled persons (no wheelchairs available).
**Refreshments:** Many in Kirkcudbright.

### CAERLAVEROCK CASTLE
**nr Dumfries** *map E11*
*(Secretary of State for Scotland)*

One of the finest examples of early classical Renaissance building in Scotland and chief seat of the Maxwell family.

**Location:** 8 m SSE of Dumfries on the Glencaple Road (B725).
**Opening Times:** Apr 1 to Sept 30—Weekdays 9.30–7, Suns 2–7; Oct 1 to Mar 31—Weekdays 9.30–4, Suns 2–4. Adm 60p, Chd & OAPs 30p.

### CARLYLE'S BIRTHPLACE
**Ecclefechan** *map F12*
Telephone: Ecclefechan (057 63) 666
*(The National Trust for Scotland)*

Thomas Carlyle was born here in 1795. Mementoes and MSS.

**Location:** 5 m SE of Lockerbie on the Lockerbie/Carlisle Road (A74).
**Opening Times:** Mar 24 to Oct 31—daily 12–5. Adm 90p, Chd 45p (under 5 free). OAPs & Students (on production of their cards) adm at half the standard rate. Adult parties 70p, school parties 35p.
**Refreshments:** Ecclefechan Hotel.

### CASTLE KENNEDY GARDENS
**Stranraer** *map D11* ♿
Telephone: Stranraer (0776) 2024
*(The Earl and Countess of Stair)*

Beautiful gardens laid out on a peninsula between two lochs, Rhododendrons, azaleas, magnolias, embothriums and many other plants from overseas.

**Location:** 3 m E of Stranraer on A75; Stranraer/Dumfries Road (entrance by Castle Kennedy Lodge only).
**Opening Times:** Apr to Sept—Daily 10–5. Adm £1.50, Chd (under 16) 50p, OAPs £1. Party rates on application. Free parking. Plant Centre.
**Refreshments:** Light refreshments only. Hotels Eynhallow, Castle Kennedy & Stranraer.

### DRUMLANRIG CASTLE AND COUNTRY PARK
**nr Thornhill** *map E12* △ ♿
Telephone: Thornhill (0848) 30248
*(Home of the Duke of Buccleuch & Queensberry KT)*

Magnificent pink sandstone castle with outstanding art treasures – Leonardo, Rembrandt, Hobein – beautiful silverware, superb furniture and porcelain, Bonnie Prince Charlie's relics. Extensive grounds and woodland includes gardens, exciting adventure woodland play area, nature trails and picnic sites. Tearoom and giftshop. Working craft centre, lecture room and cycle hire.

**Location:** 18 m N of Dumfries; 3 m N of Thornhill off A76; 16 m from A74 at Elvanfoot; approx 1½ hrs by road from Edinburgh, Glasgow & Carlisle.
**Opening Times:** Castle and Grounds – Sat, Apr 29 to Sun Aug 20. Daily *(except Thurs)* 11–5. Sun 2–6. Grounds and Adventure Woodland only – open daily through season and until Sept 30. Adm Castle and Grounds £2.50. Grounds only £1. Chd under 16, Castle and Grounds £1 (under 5 free). Discounts for groups of 20 or over, OAPs and students.
**Refreshments:** Lunches, Afternoon Teas and snacks at above times.

### LOGAN BOTANIC GARDEN
**Port Logan** *map D11*
*(Royal Botanic Garden, Edinburgh)*

A wide collection of plants from the warm temperate regions of the world.

**Location:** 10 m S of Stranraer.
**Opening Times:** Apr to Oct—Daily 10–6. Adm 60p, Chd/OAPs 30p. No animals.
**Refreshments:** Teas available.

### SWEETHEART ABBEY
**New Abbey** *map E11*
*(Secretary of State for Scotland)*

Cistercian monastery famous for the touching and romantic circumstances of its foundation by Lady Dervorgilla.

**Location:** 7 m S of Dumfries on coast road (A710).
**Opening Times:** Apr 1 to Sept 30—Weekdays 9.30–7, Suns 2–7; Oct 1 to Mar 31—Weekdays 9.30–4, Suns 2–4. Adm 60p, Chd & OAPs 30p.

### THREAVE GARDEN
**nr Castle Douglas** *map E11* ♿
Telephone: Castle Douglas (0556) 2575
*(The National Trust for Scotland)*

The Trust's School of Gardening. Gardens now among the major tourist attractions of SW Scotland. Visitor centre.

**Location:** 1 m W of Castle Douglas off A75.
**Opening Times:** GARDENS. All the year—Daily 9-sunset. WALLED GARDEN & GLASSHOUSES—Daily 9–5. Visitor Centre. Shop Mar 24 to Oct 31—daily 9–6, tearoom Mar 24 weekend to Oct 31 daily 10–5. Adm £2, Chd £1. Adult parties £1.60, Schools 80p, Chd under 5 years free. OAPs & Students (on production of their cards) adm at half the standard adult rate.

# FIFE REGION

### ABERDOUR CASTLE
**Aberdour** *map F14*
*(Secretary of State for Scotland)*

A 14th century tower with the remains of a terraced garden and bowling green. There is also a splendid dovecot and panoramic views across the Firth of Forth.

**Location:** At Aberdour.
**Opening Times:** Apr 1 to Sept 30—Daily 9.30–7 (Suns 2–7); Oct 1 to Mar 31—Daily 9.30–4 (Suns 2–4). *Closed Thurs pm and Fri in winter, also Dec 25, 26; Jan 1, 2.* Adm 60p, Chd & OAPs 30p.

# CASTLE CAMPBELL

**Admission – See editorial reference.**

# ARBIGLAND GARDENS

**Kirkbean, Dumfries**

Built in the 18th century, on land that long ago belonged to the Murrays, the house is set amongst woodland, formal and water gardens arranged round a secluded bay in the Solway Firth.
The garden in which John Paul Jones, regarded by history as the father of the United States Navy, worked as a boy. Birthplace of Dr James Craik, Washington's Physician.

# DRUMLANRIG CASTLE

## AND COUNTRY PARK

**NR THORNHILL, DUMFRIESSHIRE**

*Home of the Duke of Buccleuch and Queensberry KT.*

Beautiful pink sandstone castle in picturesque woodland setting. Magnificent collection of paintings, porcelain and silverware. Extensive grounds and gardens. Nature Trails, Guided Walks, Tea Room, Gift Shop, Working Craft Centre, Lecture Room, Cycle Hire, Picnic Sites. EXCITING ADVENTURE WOODLAND PLAY AREA.

Open 1989: Castle Daily (except Thursday) 29th April to 20th August.
Grounds and Adventure Playground open Daily 29th April to 30th September.

# CASTLE KENNEDY GARDENS

**STRANRAER : WIGTOWNSHIRE**

CASTLE KENNEDY GARDENS

OPEN DAILY

APRIL to SEPTEMBER

10 a.m. - 5 p.m.

*The Gardens are situated on a peninsula between two lochs and are nationally famous for their rhododendrons, azaleas, magnolias and embothriums. They are set in extensive grounds and offer a range of interesting and varied walks.*

**PLANT CENTRE. Light Refreshments Available.**

Situated 3 miles east of Stranraer on the A75 Stranraer - Dumfries Road.
For further information contact:
Stair Estates, Estates Office, Rephad, Stranraer.
Phone 0776 - 2024.

# CAERLAVEROCK CASTLE

**Admission – See editorial reference.**

# ABERDOUR CASTLE

**Admission – See editorial reference.**

# FIFE REGION – *continued*

### BALCARRES
**Colinsburgh** *map F14*
Telephone: 033334 206
*(Balcarres Trust)*

16th century house with 19th century additions by Burn and Bryce. Woodland and terraced garden.

**Location:** ½ m N of Colinsburgh.
**Opening Times:** WOODLANDS AND LOWER GARDEN: Feb 20–Mar 7; Apr 3–29; May 18–July 17; (Daily except Suns). WEST GARDEN: June 30–July 15 (Daily except Suns) 2–5. Adm £1.50, OAPs & Chd £1. *House not open except by written appointment* and May 1–17 (except Suns). Adm £2. Car park. Suitable for disabled persons, no wheelchairs provided.

### BALGONIE CASTLE
**By Markinch** *map F14*
Telephone: (0592) 750119
*(The Laird and Lady of Balgonie and Eddergoll)*

One of the finest late 14th century Ashlar built towers in Scotland. Once more a family home after being abandoned for 160 years. Consisting of five floors with the two lower ones being vaulted. Around the large courtyard are buildings from 1496 to 1702. The gatehouse also contains a prison. 17th century home of Sir Alexander Leslie, the Lord General of the Covenanting Army of Scotland. He was later created the 1st Earl of Leven. During the Jacobite rising of 1715, the castle was garrisoned by Rob Roy McGregor. The present owners have a long-term project for total restoration for public and educational usage. They are also professional leather carvers and tapestry weavers. A wild-life garden has been established between the castle and the River Leven.

**Location:** B921 2 m E of Glenrothes; 4 m N of Kirkcaldy.
**Opening Times:** Tours through the tower 2–5 all year round. Otherwise by appointment. Studios and courtyard open daily all year round. Adm £1, Chd/OAPs special reductions. Parties by prior booking. Car parking. Property suitable for disabled persons in courtyard and ground floors only.
**Refreshments:** Picnic area only.

### CULROSS PALACE
**Fife** *map E14*
*(Secretary of State for Scotland)*

Built between 1597 and 1611. Contains very fine series of paintings on wooden walls and ceilings.

**Location:** In the village of Culross on the Firth of Forth between Kincardine and Dunfermline (A985).
**Opening Times:** Apr 1 to Sept 30—Weekdays 9.30–7 (Suns 2–7); Oct 1 to Mar 31—Weekdays 9.30–4 (Suns 2–4). *Closed Dec 25 & 26; Jan 1 & 2.* Adm £1, Chd & OAPs 50p.
**Refreshments:** Dundonald Arms, Culross.

### FALKLAND PALACE & GARDEN
**Fife** *map F14* △
Telephone: Falkland (033 757) 397
*(Her Majesty the Queen. Hereditary Constable, Capt & Keeper: Ninian Crichton Stuart. Deputy Keeper: The National Trust for Scotland)*

Attractive 16th century royal palace, favourite retreat of Stuart kings and queens. Gardens now laid out to the original Royal plans. Town Hall, Visitor Centre, Exhibition and Shop.

**Location:** In Falkland, 11 m N of Kirkcaldy on A912.
**Opening Times:** Mar 24 to Sept 30—Mons to Sats 10–6; Suns 2–6. Oct 1 to 29—Sats 10–6; Suns 2–6. Last tour of Palace 5. Adm Palace & Gardens £2.10, Chd £1.05. Adult parties £1.70. Schools 85p. Gardens only £1.30, Chd 65p (under 5 free). OAPs & Students (on production of their cards) adm at half the standard adult rate. Visitor centre and Trust shop.
**Refreshments:** Bruce Arms, Falkland.

### HILL OF TARVIT
**nr Cupar** *map F14*
Telephone: Cupar (0334) 53127
*(The National Trust for Scotland)*

Mansion house remodelled 1906. Collection of furniture, tapestries, porcelain and paintings. Gardens.

**Location:** 2½ m SW of Cupar A916.
*Station: Cupar (2½ m).*
**Opening Times:** House: Mar 24 to Mar 27 daily 2–6. Apr 28 to Sept 30; also weekends Apr 1 to Apr 23, Oct 1 to Oct 29 (last tour 5.30). Gardens & grounds all year. 10–sunset. Adm House & Gardens £2, Chd £1. Adult parties (20 or more) £1.60. Schools 80p. Gardens only £1, Chd 50p. Chd under 5 free, OAPs & Students (on production of their cards) adm at half the standard adult rate.

### KELLIE CASTLE AND GARDEN
**Fife** *map F14* ♿
Telephone: Arncroach (033 38) 271
*(The National Trust for Scotland)*

Fine example of 16th-17th century domestic architecture of lowland countries of Scotland.

**Location:** 3 m NNW of Pittenweem on B9171.
**Opening Times:** CASTLE and GARDEN: Mar 24 to Mar 27—Daily, Apr 28 to Sept 30—Daily 2–6. Last tour 5.30, also weekends Oct 1 to Oct 29, and Apr 1 to Apr 27. GARDENS: All the year—Daily 10–sunset. Adm £2, Chd £1. Adult parties (20 or more) £1.60. Schools 80p. Gardens only 80p, Chd (accompanied by adult) 40p (under 5 free). OAPs & Students (on production of their cards) adm at half the standard adult rate. *Gardens only suitable for disabled.*

### THE TOWN HOUSE & THE STUDY
**Culross** *map E14*
Telephone: Newmills (0383) 880359
*(The National Trust for Scotland)*

Outstanding survival of Scottish 17th century burgh architecture carefully restored to 20th century living standards.

**Location:** 12 m W of Forth Road Bridge, off A985.
**Opening Times:** Town House (with visual presentation) open Mar 24 to Mar 27, and Apr 28 to Oct 1 daily 11–1, 2–5. Adm 60p, Chd 30p. The Study open Apr 1 to 23, Jun 1 to Aug 31 and Oct 7 to 29, Sat and Sun 2–4. Other times by appointment only. Adm 40p, Chd 20p. Joint ticket—adults £1, Chd 50p. Students (on production of their cards) adm at half the standard adult rate.

# GRAMPIAN REGION

### BALMORAL CASTLE
**nr Ballater** *map F16*
*(Her Majesty the Queen)*

Grounds and Exhition open.

**Location:** 8 m W of Ballater on A93.
**Opening Times:** Gardens and Exhibition open during May, June & July—Daily (except Suns) 10–5. Adm (1987 rates) £1.20, OAPs £1, Chd free. Donation to charities. Pony trekking.
**Refreshments:** Refreshment room at Balmoral.

### BALVENIE CASTLE
**Dufftown** *map F17*
*(Secretary of State for Scotland)*

A 13th century castle visited by Mary Queen of Scots in 1562.

**Location:** At Dufftown.
**Opening Times:** Apr 1 to Sept 30—Daily 9.30–7 (Suns 2–7). *Closed Oct to Mar.* Adm 60p, Chd & OAPs 30p.

### BRAEMAR CASTLE
**Braemar** *map E16* △
Telephone: Braemar (033 83) 219 – *out of season* 224
*(Captain A A C Farquharson of Invercauld)*

Romantic 17th century castle, originally of the Earls of Mar of architectural and historical interest. A fully furnished private residence of surprising charm.

**Location:** ½ m NE of Braemar on A93.
**Opening Times:** May to early Oct—Daily 10–6. Adm £1.30, Chd 65p. Special rates for groups and OAPs. Free car and bus park.

## BRODIE CASTLE
**nr Nairn Moray** *map E17* ♿
Telephone: Brodie (030 94) 371
*(The National Trust for Scotland)*

Ancient seat of the Brodies, burned in 1645 and largely rebuilt, with 17th/19th century additions. Fine furniture, porcelain and paintings.

**Location:** Off A96 between Nairn & Foress.
**Opening Times:** Mar 24 to Sept 30: Mons to Sats 11–6; Suns 2–6 (last tour 5.15). Also open weekends only Oct 1 to Oct 22, Sat 11–6, Sun 2–6. Grounds open all year 9.30–sunset. Adm £2.10, Chd £1.05 (under 5 free). Adult parties £1.70, Schools 85p. OAPs & Students (on production of their cards) adm at half the standard adult rate. Grounds by donation.

## CASTLE FRASER
**Sauchen** *map G16*
Telephone: Sauchen (033 03) 463
*(The National Trust for Scotland)*

One of the most spectacular of the Castles of Mar. Z-plan castle begun in 1575 and completed in 1636.

**Location:** 3 m S of Kemnay off B993; 16 m W of Aberdeen.
**Opening Times:** Apr 28 to Oct 1—Daily 2–6 (last tour 5.15). Adm £2.10, Chd £1.05. Adult parties £1.70, Schools 85p. Chd under 5 years free. OAPs & Students (on production of their cards) adm at half the standard adult rate. Garden & grounds open all year, 9.30–sunset, adm by donation. Picnic area.

## CRAIGIEVAR CASTLE
**Lumphanan** *map F16*
Telephone: Lumphanan (033 98) 83635
*(The National Trust for Scotland)*

Exceptional tower house. Structurally unchanged since its completion in 1626.

**Location:** 6 m S of Alford on A980; 26 m W of Aberdeen.
**Opening Times:** Apr 28 to June 30, Sept 1 to Oct 1—Daily 2–6. July 1 to Aug 31, daily 11–6 (last tour 5.15). Parties of 12 or more at other times by arrangement. Adm £2.10, Chd £1.05. Adult parties £1.70, Schools 85p. Chd under 5 years free. OAPs & Students (on production of their cards) adm at half the standard adult rate. Grounds open all year 9.30–sunset. Adm by donation. *It is recommended that all coach parties should book in advance.*

## CRATHES CASTLE & GARDEN
**Banchory** *map G16* △ ♿
Telephone: Crathes (033 044) 525
*(The National Trust for Scotland)*

Fine 16th century baronial castle. Remarkable early painted ceilings. Beautiful gardens.

**Location:** 3 m E of Banchory on A93; 15 m W of Aberdeen.
**Opening Times:** CASTLE & VISITOR CENTRE: Mar 24 to Mar 27, weekends: Apr **only** (Apr 1 to 23). Apr 28 to Oct 31—Daily 11–6; (last tour 5.15). Adm Castle & Grounds £2.20, Chd £1.10. Garden & Grounds £2, Chd £1. Combined ticket (Castle, Garden & Grounds) £2.80, Chd £1.40, Adult parties £2.20, Schools £1.10. Booked parties also accepted on weekdays in Apr and Oct. GARDENS & GROUNDS. All the year—Daily 9.30–sunset. Chd under 5 years free. OAPs & Students (on production of their cards) adm at half the standard adult rate. Visitor Centre.
**Refreshments:** Shop and Restaurant.

## DRUM CASTLE
**nr Aberdeen** *map G16*
Telephone: Drumoak (033 08) 204
*(The National Trust for Scotland)*

The oldest part of the historic Castle, the great square tower—one of the three oldest tower houses in Scotland—dates from the late 13th century. Charming mansion added in 1619.

**Location:** 10 m W of Aberdeen, off A93.
**Opening Times:** Apr 28 to Oct 1—Daily 2–6 (last tour 5.15). Adm Castle £2.10, Chd £1.05. Adult parties £1.70, Schools 85p. Chd under 5 years free. OAPs & Students (on production of their cards) adm at half the standard adult rate. Grounds open all year 9.30–sunset. Adm by donation.

## DUFF HOUSE
**Banff** *map F17*
*(Secretary of State for Scotland)*

18th century mansion designed by William Adam.

**Location:** ½ m S of Banff.
**Opening Times:** Apr 1 to Sept 30—Weekdays 9.30–7, Suns 2–7. Oct 1 to Mar 31—apply keykeeper. Adm 60p, Chd & OAPs 30p.

## ELGIN CATHEDRAL
**Elgin** *map F17*
*(Secretary of State for Scotland)*

Probably Scotland's most beautiful cathedral with certainly the finest chapter house.

**Location:** In Elgin.
**Opening Times:** Apr 1 to Sept 30—Daily 9.30–7, Suns 2–7; Oct 1 to Mar 31—Daily 9.30–4. Suns 2–4. *Closed Dec 25, 26; Jan 1, 2.* Adm 60p, Chd & OAPs 30p.

## FASQUE
**Fettercairn** *map G16*
Telephone: Fettercairn (056 14) 201
*(The Gladstone Family)*

1809 Home of the Gladstone family with a full complement of furnishings and domestic articles little changed for 160 years.

**Location:** 1 m N of Fettercairn on the B974 Cairn O Mount pass road; 34 m Aberdeen and Dundee; 17 m Stonehaven; 12 m Montrose; 18 m Banchory.
**Opening Times:** House open May 1 to end of Sept every day except Fris 1.30–5.30 with last entry at 5 pm. Adults £2, Chd 90p. Parties £1.75 over 25 pre-booked. Evening opening for parties by arrangement.

## FYVIE CASTLE
**Fyvie** *map G17*
Telephone: Fyvie (065 16) 266
*(The National Trust of Scotland)*

The oldest part of the castle dates from the 13th century and its five great towers are the monuments to the five families who owned the castle. The building contains the finest wheel stair in Scotland and a magnificent collection of paintings.

**Location:** Off A947, 8 m SE of Turriff.
**Opening Times:** Apr 28 to May 25—Daily 2–6; May 26 to Oct 1—Daily 11–6 (last tour 5.15). Adm Castle: £2.10, Chd £1.05, Adult parties £1.70, Schools 85p. Parkland free. Chd (under 5) free. OAPs & Students (on production of their cards) adm at half the standard adult rate. Permanent exhibition – Castles of Mar.

### HADDO HOUSE
**nr Methlick** *map G17* △ ♿
Telephone: Tarves (065 15) 440
*(The National Trust for Scotland)*

Georgian house designed in 1731 by William Adam. Home of the Gordons of Haddo for over 500 years. Terraced gardens.
**Location:** 4 m N of Pitmedden; 19 m N of Aberdeen (A981 & B999).
**Opening Times:** Mar 24 to Mar 27; Apr 28 to Oct 31 daily 2–6. Apr 2 to Apr 23, Suns only 2–6 (last tour 5.15). Adm £2.10, Chd £1.05 (under 5 free). Adult parties £1.70, Schools 85p. OAPs & Students (on production of their cards) adm at half the standard adult rate. Gardens & grounds open all year 9.30–sunset, adm by donation. Wheelchair access. Permanent exhibition, shop and Restaurant open Mar 24 to 27, and Apr 28 to Oct 31 daily 11–6.
**Refreshments:** Restaurant.

### HUNTLY CASTLE
**Huntly** *map F17*
*(Secretary of State for Scotland)*

A magnificent ruin of an architectural and heraldic house built in the 16th and 17th centuries.
**Location:** In Huntly.
**Opening Times:** Apr 1 to Sept 30—Daily 9.30–7, Suns 2–7; Oct 1 to Mar 31—Daily 9.30–4, Suns 2–4. *Closed Dec 25, 26; Jan 1, 2.* Adm 60p, Chd & OAPs 30p.

### KILDRUMMY CASTLE GARDEN
**Donside** *map F16* ♿
Telephone: Kildrummy (09755) 71264 or 71277
*(Kildrummy Castle Garden Trust)*

Approximately 10 acres of garden with shrubs, heaths, gentians, rhododendrons, lilies etc. Alpine and water garden dominated by ruins of 13th century castle. Walks, play area and video room.
**Location:** On A97 off A944 10 m W of Alford; 15 m S of Huntly; 35 m W of Aberdeen.
**Opening Times:** GARDENS ONLY. Apr to Oct—Daily 10–5. Adm £1 (1988 rates). Car park inside hotel main entrance free. Coach park inside hotel trade entrance free. Plants for sale. Wheelchairs.
**Refreshments:** At Kildrummy Castle Hotel in the grounds (please make reservations) Kildrummy (09755) 71288. The Kildrummy Inn, Kildrummy (09755) 71227.

### LEITH HALL AND GARDEN
**Kennethmont** *map F17* ♿
Telephone: Kennethmont (046 43) 216
*(The National Trust for Scotland)*

Home of the Leith family from 1650. Jacobite relics, and major exhibition of family's military collection. Charming garden.
**Location:** 1 m W of Kennethmont on B9002; 34 m NW of Aberdeen.
**Opening Times:** Apr 28 to Oct 1—Daily 2–6 (last tour 5.15). Gardens and Grounds all the year—Daily 9.30–sunset. Adm House and garden £2.10, Chd £1.05 (under 5 free). Adult parties £1.70, Schools 85p. OAPs & Students (on production of their cards) adm at half the standard adult rate. Admission to gardens & grounds by donation. Picnic area.

### MUCHALLS CASTLE
**Stonehaven** *map G16* △
*(Mr & Mrs Maurice A Simpson)*

Early 17th century elaborate plaster work ceilings and fireplaces. Built by Burnetts of Leys, 1619.
**Location:** 5 m N Stonehaven; 9 m S Aberdeen; ¾ m off Aberdeen/Stonehaven Road (A92).
**Opening Times:** July and Aug, Sun and Tues 2.30–4.30. Other times by written application only. Adm 60p, Chd/OAPs 20p.

### PITMEDDEN
**Udny** *map G16* ♿
Telephone: Udny (065 13) 2445
*(The National Trust for Scotland)*

Reconstructed 17th century garden with floral designs, fountains and sundials. Display on the evolution of the formal garden. Museum of Farming Life.
**Location:** 14 m N of Aberdeen on A920.
**Opening Times:** Garden & grounds open all year—Daily 9.30–sunset. Museum, Visitor Centre & other facilities—Apr 28 to Oct 1—Daily 11–6 (last adm 5.15). Adm Garden & Museum (May to Sept) £1.70, Chd 85p (under 5 free). Adult parties £1.40, Schools 70p. Adm Garden only £1, Chd 50p. OAPs & Students (on production of their cards) adm at half the standard adult rate. No dogs in garden please. *House not open.*

## HIGHLANDS REGION

### ARDTORNISH
**Lochaline, Morvern** *map C15*
*(Mrs John Raven)*

Garden of interesting mature conifers, rhododendrons and deciduous trees and shrubs set amidst magnificent scenery. ½ m from Kinlochaline Castle (open by donation) 14th century tower house on the river Aline.
**Location:** Off A82; 41 m SW of Fort William via A82, Corran Ferry & A884.
**Opening Times:** Apr 1 to Oct 31—Daily 10–6. Adm (by collecting box for garden upkeep) £1, Chd (under 16) free. Also Sun May 28 *in aid of the Scottish Gardens Scheme & Morvern Parish Church* when teas are provided.
**Refreshments:** Sun May 28—teas in main house, otherwise self catering accommodation available by the week.

### CAWDOR CASTLE
**nr Inverness** *map E17*
Telephone: Cawdor (066 77)615 Telex 75225
*(The Earl of Cawdor, FRICS)*

The 14th century Keep, fortified in the 15th century and impressive additions, mainly 17th century, form a massive fortress. Gardens, nature trails and splendid grounds. Shakespearian memories of Macbeth. The most romantic castle in the Highlands.
**Location:** S of Nairn on B9090 between Inverness and Nairn.
**Opening Times:** May 1 to Oct 1—Daily 10–5.30 (last adm 5). Adm £2.60, Chd (aged 5–15) £1.40, OAPs and disabled £2.10. Parties of 20 or more adults £2.40; 20 or more children £1.15. Family ticket (2 adults and up to 5 children) £7.50. Gardens & grounds only £1.30. Free coach & car park. Gift shop. Picnic area. Pitch & Putt course. Putting Green, Nature Trails. No dogs allowed in Castle or Grounds.
**Refreshments:** Licensed restaurant (self-service); Snack bar.

## DUNROBIN CASTLE

**Golspie** *map E16*
*(The Countess of Sutherland)*

One of Scotland's oldest inhabited houses. Historic home of the Sutherland family. Furniture, paintings and plate. Exhibits of local and general interest. Victorian Museum in grounds.

**Location:** ½ m NE of Golspie on A9.
*Station: Golspie (2 m).*
**Opening Times:** June 1 to Sept 15—Mons to Sats 10.30–5.30; Suns 1–5.30. Last adm half hour before closing. Coaches welcome all year by appointment. Adm £2.20, Chd £1.10. Parties (12 or more) £2, Chd £1. OAPs £1.40. Family ticket £5.50 (incl Guide Book).
**Refreshments:** Tearoom.

## DUNVEGAN CASTLE

**Isle of Skye** *map B17* △
*(John MacLeod of MacLeod)*

Dating from the 13th century and continuously inhabited by the Chiefs of MacLeod. Fairy flag.

**Location:** Dunvegan village (1 m); 23 m W of Portree on the Isle of Skye.
**Opening Times:** Mar 24 to Sept 30: 10–5; Oct 2 to Oct 28: 11–4.30; Nov to Mar: by appointment; Suns: garden, grounds, craft shop and restaurant open, castle – closed. Adm £2.80, Chd £1.50. Parties – special rates on application.

## EILEAN DONAN CASTLE

**Wester Ross** *map C16* △
Telephone: Dornie (059 985) 202
*(J D H MacRae, Esq)*

13th century Castle. Jacobite relics—mostly with Clan connections.

**Location:** In Dornie, Kyle of Lochalsh; 8 m E of Kyle on A87.
**Opening Times:** Apr to Sept 30—Daily (inc Suns) 10–12.30, 2–6. Adm £1.

## FORT GEORGE

**Ardersier** *map E17*
*(Secretary of State for Scotland)*

One of the most outstanding military fortifications virtually unaltered from the 18th century. Re-creations of 18th & 19th century barrack rooms. Seafield collection of arms.

**Location:** At Ardersier. 11 m NE of Inverness.
**Opening Times:** Apr 1 to Sept 30—Daily 9.30–7, Suns 2–7; Oct 1 to Mar 31—Daily 9.30–4, Suns 2–4. *Closed Dec 25, 26; Jan 1, 2.* Adm £1.50, Chd & OAPs 75p. Family £4.

## HUGH MILLER'S COTTAGE

**Cromarty** *map E17*
Telephone: Cromarty (038 17) 245
*(The National Trust for Scotland)*

Birthplace (10 Oct 1802) of Hugh Miller, stonemason, eminent geologist, editor and writer. Furnished thatched cottage built c 1711 for his grandfather contains an interesting exhibition on his life and work. Captioned video programme.

**Location:** In Cromarty 22m from Invernes A832.
**Opening Times:** Mar 24 to Mar 27 and Apr 28 to Oct 1—Mons to Sats 10–12, 1–5; Suns 2–5. Adm 90p, Chd 45p (under 5 free). OAPs & Students (on production of their cards) adm at half the standard adult rate.

## INVEREWE

**Poolewe, Wester Ross** *map C17* ♿
Telephone: Poolewe 229 (Information Centre)
*(The National Trust for Scotland)*

Remarkable garden created by the late Osgood Mackenzie. Rare and sub-tropical plants.

**Location:** 7 m from Gairloch; 85 m W of Inverness, A832.
**Opening Times:** Garden open all the year—Daily 9.30–sunset. Visitor Centre: Mar 24 to May 4 & Sept 4 to Oct 22—Mons to Sats 10–5; Suns 12–5. May 5 to Sept 3—Mons to Sats 9.30–6.30; Suns 12–6. Adm £2, Chd £1. Cruise and adult parties £1.60, Chd 80p. Chd under 5 years free. OAPs & Students (on production of their cards) adm at half the standard adult rate. Ranger Naturalist Service.
**Refreshments:** (Licensed) restaurant in garden (Apr 1 to May 4 and Sept 5 to Oct 15—Mons to Sats 10.30–4.30, Suns 12–4.30. May 5 to Sept 4—Mons to Sats 10–5, Suns 12–5). Poolewe (044 586) 200.

## URQUHART CASTLE

**Loch Ness** *map D16*
*(Secretary of State of Scotland)*

Remains of one of the largest Castles in Scotland

**Location:** On W shore of Loch Ness 1½ m SE of Drumnadrochit.
**Opening Times:** Apr 1 to Sept 30—Weekdays 9.30–7, Suns 2–7; Oct 1 to Mar 31—Weekdays 9.30–4, Suns 2–4. *Closed Dec 25, 26; Jan 1, 2.* Adm £1, Chd & OAPs 50p.

# LOTHIAN REGION

### AMISFIELD MAINS
**nr Haddington** *map F14*
Telephone: Aberlady (08757) 201
*(Lord Wemyss Trust)*

Georgian farmhouse with "Gothick" Barn and Cottage.

**Location:** Between Haddington & East Linton on A1 Edinburgh/Dunbar Road.
**Opening Times:** Exteriors only. By appointment, Wemyss & March Estates, Estate Office, Longniddry, East Lothian EH32 0PY.

### BEANSTON
**nr Haddington** *map F14*
Telephone: Aberlady (08757) 201
*(Lord Wemyss Trust)*

Georgian farmhouse with Georgian Orangery.

**Location:** Between Haddington & East Linton on A1 Edinburgh/Dunbar Road.
**Opening Times:** Exteriors only. By appointment, Wemyss & March Estates, Estate Office, Longniddry, East Lothian EH32 0PY.

### DALKEITH PARK
**nr Edinburgh** *map F13*
Telephone: Edinburgh (031-663) 5684
*(The Buccleuch Estates)*

Woodland and riverside walks in extensive grounds of Dalkeith Palace. Tunnel walk, and beautiful Adam Bridge, Nature trails and Exciting Adventure Woodland Play Area. Attractive Barbeque Area.

**Location:** 7 m S of Edinburgh City Centre from E end of Dalkeith High Street, off A68.
**Opening Times:** Mar 25 to Oct 30—Daily 11–6; Nov—Sats & Suns only. Adm £1 (Chd in parties of over 20, 70p). Educational facilities. Free car park & coach parking.

### DALMENY HOUSE
**South Queensferry** *map F14* △ ♿
Telephone: (031 331) 1888
*(The Earl of Rosebery)*

Rosebery Collection of paintings; Napoleonic and other historical items. Mentmore collection of superb French furniture, Goya tapestries and porcelain.

**Location:** 3 m E of South Queensferry; 7 m W of Edinburgh; on B924 (off A90).
*Station: Dalmeny (2 m).*
**Public Transport:** From St. Andrew Sq. Bus Station to Chapel Gate (1 m from house).
**Opening Times:** May 1 to Sept 28—Suns to Thurs 2–5.30. Conducted tours. Adm £1.90, Chd & Students £1.30, OAPs £1.50. Special party rate £1.60 (minimum 20). Special parties at other times throughout the year by arrangement with the Administrator.
**Refreshments:** Tea.

### DIRLETON CASTLE & GARDEN
**Dirleton** *map F14*
*(Secretary of State for Scotland)*

Well preserved 13th century castle, attractive gardens.

**Location:** In the village of Dirleton on Edinburgh/North Berwick Road (A198).
*Station: North Berwick (2 m).*
**Opening Times:** Apr 1 to Sept 30—Weekdays 9.30–7, Suns 2–7; Oct 1 to Mar 31—Weekdays 9.30–4, Suns 2–4. *Closed Dec 25 & 26; Jan 1 & 2.* Adm £1, Chd & OAPs 50p.

### EDINBURGH CASTLE
**Edinburgh** *map F14*
*(Historic Buildings and Monuments)*

Ancient fortress of great importance. St Margaret's Chapel has Norman features.

**Location:** Castlehill, Edinburgh.
**Opening Times:** Apr 1 to Sept 30—Weekdays 9.30–5.50, Suns 11–5.50; Oct 1 to Mar 31—Weekdays 9.30–5.05, Suns 12.30–4.20. Last tickets sold 45 mins before closing. *Castle closed Dec 25, 26; Jan 1, 2 & 3.* Adm £2.20, Chd & OAPs £1.10, Family £5.

### THE GEORGIAN HOUSE
**No. 7 Charlotte Square, Edinburgh** *map F14* Ⓢ
Telephone: 031-225 2160
*(The National Trust for Scotland)*

The north side of Charlotte Square is classed as Robert Adam's masterpiece of urban architecture. The main floors of No. 7 are open as a typical Georgian House. Audio-visual shows.

**Location:** In Edinburgh city centre.
**Opening Times:** Mar 24 to Oct 31—Mons to Sats 10–5, Suns 2–5. *Last admission ½ hour before closing time.* Adm incl Audio-Visual, £1.70, Chd 85p (under 5 free). Adult parties £1.40, schools 70p. OAPs/Students (on production of their cards) adm at half the standard adult rate.

## EDINBURGH CASTLE

**Admission – See editorial reference.**

## DALKEITH PARK
**Nr EDINBURGH**

*Dalkeith House from the Nature Trail*

Nature Trails and Exciting Adventure Woodland Play Area. Attractive Barbecue Area. Woodland and riverside walks in the beautiful grounds of Dalkeith Palace. Tunnel Walk. Adam Bridge. Educational packs and special facilities for School parties with Ranger Service. Information Centre. Light Refreshments.

Open daily—March 25 to October 30; Saturdays & Sundays only in November, 11 am to 6 pm. Access from East end Dalkeith High Street, 3 miles from Edinburgh City Boundary off A68.

## Dalmeny House
**South Queensferry·Edinburgh**

**Home of the Earl and Countess of Rosebery**

Magnificently set in beautiful parkland on the shores of the Firth of Forth, 7 miles from Edinburgh. Designed in 1814 by William Wilkins, the first Gothic Revival house in Scotland.

**The Rothschild Collection.** Superb French 18th century furniture, tapestries, porcelain and paintings from Mentmore, the English home of the Earl of Rosebery.
**The Napoleon Room.** Paintings and furniture associated with the Emperor Napoleon and the Duke of Wellington's campaign chair.

**The Rosebery Collection.** Prime Minister the 5th Earl of Rosebery's important collection of political portraits by Reynolds, Gainsborough, Raeburn and Lawrence. Early Scottish portraits and furniture. Goya Tapestries. Exhibition of Adam and other architectural designs. Rose and Primrose racing colours and momentos of the Mentmore stud that produced 7 Derby winners.

**Woodland Shore Walk.** 4½ mile walk from South Queensferry to the ferry at Cramond open (except on Fridays) all year round.
**House open.** May 1 - Sept 28, Suns - Thurs, 2-5.30.

## GLADSTONE'S LAND

**Edinburgh** *map F14*
Telephone: 031-226 5856
*(The National Trust for Scotland)*

Built 1620 and shortly afterwards occupied by Thomas Gledstanes. Remarkable painted wooden ceilings; furnished as typical 'Old Town' house of the period.

**Location:** 483 Lawnmarket, Edinburgh.
**Opening Times:** Mar 24 to Oct 31—Mons to Sats 10–5, Suns 2–5. *Last admission ½ hour before closing time.* Adm £1.60, Chd 80p (under 5 free). Adult parties £1.30, schools 65p. OAPs/Students (on production of their cards) adm at half the standard adult rate.

## GOSFORD HOUSE

**East Lothian** *map F14*
Telephone: Aberlady (08757) 201
*(Lord Wemyss Trust)*

Robert Adam Mansion, central block surviving; striking maritime situation. Original wings replaced 1890; South wing contains celebrated Marble Hall, fine collection of paintings etc. Part of Adam block burnt 1940, re-roofed 1987. Policies laid out with ornamental water. Grey Lag Geese and other wildfowl breeding.

**Location:** On A198 between Aberlady & Longniddry; NW of Haddington.
*Station: Longniddry (2 m).*
**Opening Times:** June and July— Weds, Sats & Suns 2–5. Adm £1, Chd 50p, OAPs 75p. Wemyss & March Estates, Longniddry, East Lothian EH32 0PY.
**Refreshments:** Hotels in Aberlady.

## HAMILTON HOUSE

**Prestonpans** *map F14*
Telephone: 031-336 2157
*(The National Trust for Scotland)*

Built in 1628 by John Hamilton, a prosperous Edinburgh burgess.

**Location:** 8½ m E of Edinburgh on A198.
*Station: Prestonpans.*
**Opening Times:** By prior arrangement.

## HARELAW FARMHOUSE

**nr Longniddry**
Telephone: Aberlady (08757) 201
*(Lord Wemyss' Trust)*

Harelaw Farmhouse. An early 19th Century 2-storey farmhouse built in the old fashioned way, as an integral part of the steading, which is also distinguished by a dovecote over the entrance arch surmounted by a windvane.

**Location:** Between Longniddry and Drem on the B1377.
**Opening Times:** Exteriors only. By appointment, Wemyss and March Estates, Estate Office, Longniddry, East Lothian EH32 0PY.

## HOPETOUN HOUSE

**South Queensferry, nr Edinburgh** *map E14* Ⓢ
Telephone: 031 331 2451
*(Hopetoun House Preservation Trust)*

Home of the Marquess of Linlithgow. Fine example of 18th century Adam architecture. Magnificent reception rooms, pictures, antiques.

**Location:** 2 m from Forth Road Bridge nr South Queensferry off A904.
**Opening Times:** Easter, then Sat Apr 29 to Sun Oct 1. Daily 11–5.30. Adm House and Grounds: £2.50. Special concessions for students, children and OAPs, also for groups of 20 or more, and family group. Free parking. Gift shop. Deerpark. Picnic areas. Free Ranger service. Magnificent views of the Forth and the Bridges. The house is also available for special private evening functions. Enquiries to Administrator's Office 031-331 2451.
**Refreshments:** Licensed restaurant and snack bar.

## THE HOUSE OF THE BINNS

**by Linlithgow** *map E14* △
Telephone: Philipstoun (050 683) 4255
*(The National Trust for Scotland)*

Historic home of the Dalyells. Fine plaster ceilings. Interesting pictures. Panoramic viewpoint.

**Location:** 3½ m E of Linlithgow on Queensferry Road (A904).
**Opening Times:** Mar 25 to Mar 27 daily 2–5; Apr 29 to Oct 1—Daily (except Fris) 2–5 (last adm 4.30). Parkland open 10–7. Adm £2, Chd £1 (under 5 free). Adult parties £1.60, Schools 80p, OAPS/Students (on production of their cards) adm at half the standard adult rate. *Members of the Royal Scots Dragoon Guards (in uniform) admitted free.*

## INVERESK LODGE AND GARDEN

**Inveresk** *map F13*
*(The National Trust for Scotland)*

New garden, with large selection of plants.

**Location:** In Inveresk village; 6 m E of Edinburgh off A1.
**Opening Times:** GARDEN ONLY. All year—Mons to Fris 10–4.30; Suns 2–5. Adm 50p, Chd (with adult) 25p, under 5 free, OAPs/Students (on production of their cards) adm at half the standard adult rate. Honesty Box.

## KINNEIL HOUSE

**nr Bo'ness** *map E14*
*(Secretary of State for Scotland)*

Stately home of the Dukes of Hamilton.

**Location:** To the west of Bo'ness.
**Opening Times:** Apr 1 to Sept 30—Daily 9.30–7, Suns 2–7; Oct 1 to Mar 31—Daily 9.30–4, Suns 2–4. *Closed every Tues pm & Fris in winter. Dec 25, 26; Jan 1, 2.* Adm 60p, Chd & OAPs 30p.

## LAMB'S HOUSE

**Leith** *map F13*
Telephone: 031-554 3131
*(The National Trust for Scotland)*

Residence and warehouse of prosperous merchant of late 16th or early 17th century. Renovated 18th century. Now old people's day centre.

**Location:** In Leith.
**Opening Times:** Mons to Fris—Daily 9–5. *(Except Christmas/New Year.)*

## LAURISTON CASTLE

**Edinburgh** *map F14* △
*(City of Edinburgh District Council)*

A beautifully furnished Edwardian home, associated with John Law (1671–1729) founder of first bank in France.

**Location:** Cramond Road South, Davidsons Mains, 4½ m from GPO, Edinburgh.
**Opening Times:** Castle. All the year. Apr to Oct—Daily (except Fris) 11–1, 2–5; Nov to Mar—Sats & Suns only 2–4. Adm £1, Chd 50p. Guided tours only (last tour 40 mins before closing time). Grounds—Daily 9–dusk.

## LENNOXLOVE

**Haddington** *map F13*
Telephone: Haddington (062 082) 3720
*(His Grace the Duke of Hamilton)*

Formerly Lethington Tower, ancient home of the Maitlands. The Lime Avenue, known as Politician's Walk, was laid out by William Maitland, Secretary to Mary Queen of Scots.

**Location:** 1½ m S of Haddington on B6369; 18 m E of Edinburgh off A1.
**Opening Times:** Easter weekend, then May to Sept—Weds, Sats & Suns 2–5. At other times by appointment (minimum of 10 people); apply to Estate Office, Lennoxlove, Haddington. Adm £2, Chd £1. Pre-booked parties of 10 or more £1.50, Chd 50p. Price includes guided tour of House, entry to gardens and parking.

## MALLENY GARDEN

**Balerno** *map F13* ♿
*(The National Trust for Scotland)*

A delightfully personal garden with a particularly good collection of shrub roses. National Bonsai Collection for Scotland.

**Location:** In Balerno, off A70.
**Opening Times:** GARDEN ONLY. All the year—Daily 10–sunset. Adm £1, Chd 50p (under 5 free). OAPs/Students (on production of their cards) adm at half the standard adult rate. No dogs in garden please.

## NIDDRY CASTLE

**Winchburgh** *map E13*
Telephone: Winchburgh 890 753
*(Peter and Janet Wright)*

Late 15th century Scottish Castle, built by the Seton family. Following her escape from Loch Leven, Mary Queen of Scots was given brief shelter at Niddry by the 5th Lord Seton in 1568. Early in the 18th century Niddry Castle was abandoned and lay in ruins for over 250 years. It is now being restored over a seven year period (1984–91) by Peter and Janet Wright. Niddry is a scheduled ancient monument and the subject of a conservation agreement with the National Trust for Scotland.

**Location:** By Winchburgh. Turn off A89 1 m West Newbridge – 1 m, or turn off B9080 in Winchburgh – 1 m.
**Opening Times:** Open Wed and Sun only, May to Sept incl 10–4.30. Adm by donation. Parties by arrangement. Car parking is available, adjacent to the Castle. Not suitable for disabled. Outdoor footwear and clothing advisable. For safety reasons children must be adequately supervised.

## PALACE OF HOLYROODHOUSE

**Edinburgh** *map E14*
Telephone: 031-556 7371
*(Royal Palace)*

The Official Residence of H.M. The Queen in Scotland. The ridge, known as the Royal Mile, that slopes downwards from Edinburgh Castle, comes to a majestic conclusion at Holyroodhouse, where Palace and Abbey stand against the spectacular backdrop of Salisbury Crag. Throughout history, Holyrood has been the scene of turbulent and extraordinary events, yet the Palace retains a modern appeal to a Royal residence still in regular use.

**Location:** Central Edinburgh.
**Opening Times:** Summer season: Mar 27 to May 9, June 1 to June 12, July 7 to Oct 23: fully open – adm £1.60, Chd/Students/OAPs 80p. May 10 to July 5, 6: partly open – adm £1, Chd/Students/OAPs 50p. *Closed May 16 to May 31, and June 13 to July 4.* Winter season: Jan 5 to Mar 26, and Oct 23 to Dec 31: fully open – adm £1.60, Chd/Students/OAPs 80p. *Closed Dec 26 and 27.* All visitors are conducted by Palace Wardens in groups leaving at about 10 minute intervals. From Nov to Mar pre-paid

# GOSFORD HOUSE

**EAST LOTHIAN**

'Seaside Situation: 1800 (Adam) and 1890, Marble Hall, Picture Collection, Ornamental Waters, Wildfowl.

*ADMISSION – SEE EDITORIAL REFERENCE*

# HOPETOUN HOUSE

**SOUTH QUEENSFERRY, NR. EDINBURGH**

*(Home of the Marquess of Linlithgow)*

Begun in 1699 by architect Sir William Bruce, the house was enlarged by William Adam from 1721, and survives today not only as one of his greatest personal achievements, but also as an important monument to the Scottish Enlightenment.

The rooms contain fine furniture, paintings, carpets and tapestries. Visit the State Apartments, Museum, Gift Shop, Restaurant/Snack Bar. Enjoy the Deer Park, Nature Trail and Picnic Area. Free Ranger Service. Fine views of the Forth and the Bridges. Open daily 11-5.30 (last admission 4.45 pm). Easter weekend and then Sat 29 April until Sun 1 October 1989.

Enquiries The Administrator 031-331 2451.

# LAURISTON CASTLE

**A late-16th century tower-house with extensive 19th century additions, the castle stands in attractive grounds overlooking the Firth of Forth. In the interior it is preserved as an Edwardian middle-class country house. It contains period and reproduction furniture and impressive collections of Derbyshire Blue John, Crossley wool mosaics and objets d'art. There is a free car park. Visitors are given a guided tour of about 40 minutes duration.**

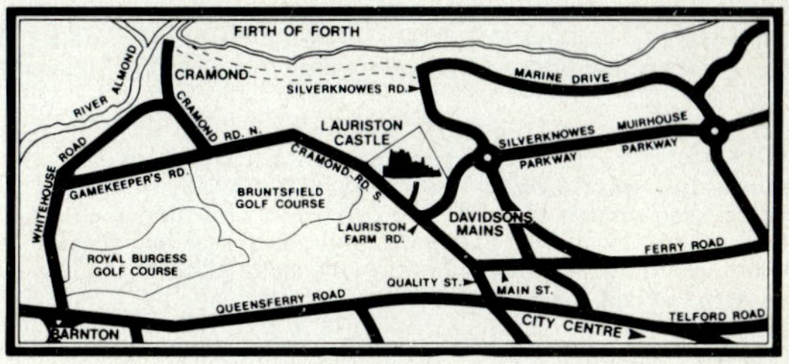


**OPEN**

April to October, Daily (except Friday) 11am-1pm, 2-5pm (last tour begins at approximately 4.20pm) November to March, Saturdays and Sundays only 2-4pm (last tour begins at approximately 3.20pm). Telephone 031-336 2060.

**ADMISSION CHARGES**

Adults: £1. Children, O.A.P.'s, UB40's and Benefit Recipients 50p.
Admission to the grounds is free.

**City of Edinburgh District Council, Department of Recreation. Improving Services – Creating Jobs!**

# LENNOXLOVE

**HADDINGTON, EAST LOTHIAN**

*A. F. Kersting photograph*

Lennoxlove, home of the Duke of Hamilton, is a house with a three-fold interest; its historic architecture, the association of its proprietors with the Royal House of Stewart and the famous Hamilton Palace collection of works of art, including the Casket and Death Mask of Mary Queen of Scots.

*ADMISSION – SEE EDITORIAL REFERENCE*

# NIDDRY CASTLE

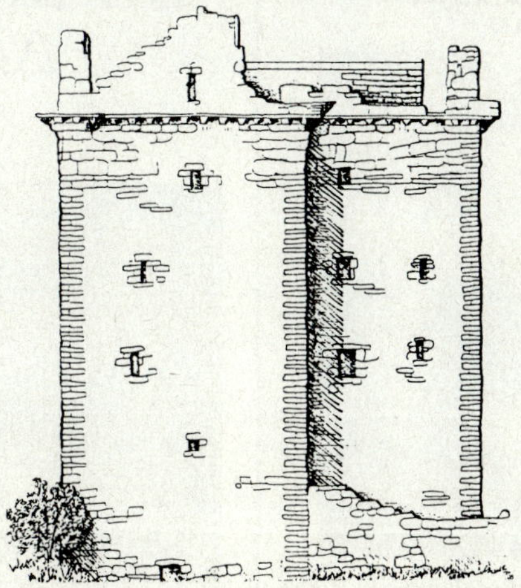

A west elevation of Niddry as it may look after restoration.

*ADMISSION – SEE EDITORIAL REFERENCE*

# STEVENSON HOUSE

**NEAR HADDINGTON**

Dating from 13th century when it belonged to the Cistercian Nunnery at Haddington.

The present house dates mainly from the 16th century with 18th century additions.

groups of 15 or more receive a 20% discount, and accompanied school parties are admitted free Mon to Fri; in both cases, prior application must be made. Special interest tours can sometimes be arranged, particularly during off-season. *The Palace and Abbey may sometimes be closed at short notice.*
**Refreshments:** Tea room outside Main Gate.

### PRESTON MILL
**East Linton** *map F14*
Telephone: East Linton (0620) 860426
*(The National Trust for Scotland)*

The oldest (16th century) of its kind still working and only survivor of many on the banks of the Tyne. Popular with artists. Renovated machinery.

**Location:** 5½ m W of Dunbar, off A1.
**Opening Times:** Preston Mill and Phantassie Doo'cot: Mar 24 to Sept 30—Mons to Sats 10–1, 2–5; Oct 1–31—Mons to Sats 10–1, 2–4.30, Suns 2–4.30; Nov 1 to Nov 30—Sats 10–12.30 and 2–4.30, Sun 2–4.30. Adm £1.10, Chd 55p (under 5 free). OAPs/Students (on production of their cards) adm at half the standard adult rate. Adult parties 90p, school parties 45p.

### ROYAL BOTANIC GARDEN
**Edinburgh** *map F14*
*(Royal Botanic Garden, Edinburgh)*

Founded 17th century. Beautiful rock garden. Exhibition Plant Houses.

**Location:** Inverleith Row, Edinburgh.
**Opening Times:** All the year. Mar to Oct (during BST)—Weekdays 9–one hour before sunset, Suns 1–one hour before sunset. Remainder of year—Weekdays 9–sunset, Suns 11–sunset. *Closed Christmas Day & New Year's Day.* Planthouses and Exhibition Hall—Weekdays 10–5, Suns 11–5. Adm free.
**Refreshments:** Tea in the garden *(Apr to Sept).*

### STEVENSON HOUSE
**Haddington** *map F13*
Telephone: Haddington (062 082) 3376 Mrs. J. C. H. Dunlop
*(Trustees of the Brown Dunlop Country Houses Trust)*

A family home for four centuries, of charm and interest and dating from the 13th century when it belonged to the Cistercian Nunnery at Haddington, but partially destroyed on several occasions, and finally made uninhabitable in 1544. Restored about 1560 and the present house dates mainly from this period, with later additions in the 18th century.

**Location:** 20 m approx from Edinburgh; 1½ m approx from A1; 2 m approx from Haddington. (See Historic House direction signs on A1 in Haddington.)
**Opening Times:** July to mid-Aug—Thurs, Sats & Suns 2–5. Guided tours 2.30–4. Other times by arrangement. Adm £1.50, OAP 75p, Chd (under 14) 75p. Special arrangement parties welcome. Car parking. Suitable for wheelchairs in garden only.
**Refreshments:** Appointment parties morning coffee etc at Stevenson. Nearest hotels and restaurants are in Haddington, i.e. 2 m from Stevenson.

### TANTALLON CASTLE
**nr North Berwick** *map F14*
*(Secretary of State for Scotland)*

Famous 14th century stronghold of the Douglases occupies a magnificent situation on the rocky coast of the Firth of Forth.

**Location:** On the coast approx 3 m E of North Berwick.
**Opening Times:** Apr 1 to Sept 30—Weekdays 9.30–7, Suns 2–7; Oct 1 to Mar 31—Weekdays 9.30–4, Suns 2–4. *Closed Weds & Thurs am in winter, and Dec 25, 26; Jan 1, 2.* Adm £1, Chd & OAPs 50p.

### WINTON HOUSE
**Pencaitland** *map F13* △
Telephone: Pencaitland (0875) 340 222
*(Sir David & Lady Ogilvy)*

Built 1620. Famous twisted stone chimneys and beautiful plaster ceilings in honour of Charles I's visit. Enlarged 1800. Fine pictures and furniture. Terraced gardens.

**Location:** Drive entrances with wrought-iron gates and lodges in Pencaitland (A6093) and towards New Winton village on B6355. Tranent (A1) 3 m, by B6355; Haddington (A1) by A6093 6 m; Pathhead (A68) 6 m by A6093.
**Opening Times:** Restricted to groups of ten or more (and others very specially interested) at any time by prior arrangement with the owner. Adm (Party rate) House *(personally conducted tour)* grounds and car park £1.50.
**Refreshments:** Tea and biscuits can be arranged in the house, or Old Smiddy Inn, Pencaitland (1 m).

## STRATHCLYDE REGION

### ACHAMORE GARDENS
**Isle of Gigha** *map C13*
Telephone: Gigha Hotel 05835 254
*(D W N Landale, Esq)*

50 acre woodland garden of great botanical interest, with world famous Gigha collection of rhododendrons, azaleas, and camellias.

**Location:** Isle of Gigha. Ferry from Tayinloan on A82, 17 miles south of Tarbert.
**Opening Times:** Garden only, all year round—9 to sunset. Adm £2 (1988 rate). Dogs on leads allowed. Plants sold.
**Refreshments:** Gigha Hotel. Boathouse Bar.

### BACHELORS' CLUB
**Tarbolton** *map D13*
Telephone: Tarbolton (0292) 541 or 940
*(The National Trust for Scotland)*

17th century thatched house where Burns and his friends formed their club in 1780. Period furnishings.

**Location:** In Tarbolton village 7½ m NE of Ayr (off A758).
**Opening Times:** Mar 24 to Oct 31—Daily 12–5. Adm 90p, Chd 45p (under 5 free). OAPs/Students (on production of their cards) adm at half the standard adult rate. Adult parties 70p, school parties 35p. *Other times by appointment.*

### BALLOCH CASTLE COUNTRY PARK
**Balloch** *map D14*
Telephone: Alexandria (0389) 58216
*(Dumbarton District Council)*

200 acres. Situated beside Loch Lomond contains many conifers, rhododendrons and other shrubs. Walled garden. Fairy Glen. Castle Visitor Centre, site of old castle and moat. Nature trail and countryside ranger service. Guided walks in summer.

**Location:** Balloch, Dumbartonshire.
*Station: Balloch (¾ m).*
**Opening Times:** All the year—Daily 10 to dusk. Adm free. Car parks.

## BELLAHOUSTON PARK
**Glasgow** *map D13*
*(City of Glasgow District Council)*

171 acres. Sunk, wall and rock gardens. Dry ski-slope. Athletic and indoor sports centre.
**Location:** Paisley Road West.
*Station: Cardonald (1¼ m).*
**Opening Times:** All the year—Daily 8 to dusk. Adm free.

## BENMORE YOUNGER BOTANIC GARDEN
**nr Dunoon** *map D14*
*(Royal Botanic Garden, Edinburgh)*

A woodland garden on a grand scale.
**Location:** 7 m NW of Dunoon (off A815).
**Opening Times:** Daily—Apr to Oct 10–6. Adm 60p, Chd/OAPs 30p.
**Refreshments:** Tea at main entrance.

## BLAIRQUHAN CASTLE AND GARDENS
**Straiton, Maybole, Ayrshire** *map D12*
Telephone: Straiton (065 57) 239
*(James Hunter Blair)*

Magnificent Regency castellated mansion approached by a 3 m private drive beside the river Girvan. Walled gardens and pinetum. Plants and trees for sale. Picture gallery.
**Location:** 14 m S of Ayr; off A77. Entrance Lodge is on B7045 ½ m S of Kirkmichael.
**Opening Times:** Aug 1 to Aug 31 *(not Mons)*. Adm £2.50, Chd £1.50, OAPs £2. Parties by arrangement at any time of year. Car parking. Wheelchairs—around gardens and principal floor of the castle.
**Refreshments:** Tea in castle.

## BOTANIC GARDENS
**Glasgow** *map D13*
*(City of Glasgow District Council)*

Covering 40 acres. Extensive botanical collections, tropical plants, herb and systematic gardens.
**Location:** Great Western Road.
**Opening Times:** All the year—Daily (incl Suns) 7–dusk. Kibble Palace 10–4.45 (winter 10–4.15). Main range of glasshouses 1–4.45 (winter 1–4.15). Suns all year 12–4.45, (winter 12–4.15). Adm free.

## BOTHWELL CASTLE
**Bothwell** *map E13*
*(Secretary of State for Scotland)*

The largest and finest 13th century Stone Castle in Scotland.
**Location:** At Bothwell but approached from Uddingston.
**Opening Times:** Apr 1 to Sept 30—Weekdays 9.30–7, Suns 2–7; Oct 1 to Mar 31—Weekdays 9.30–4. *(Closed Thurs pm and Fris in winter)*, Suns 2–4. *Closed Dec 25, 26; Jan 1, 2.* Adm 60p, Chd & OAPs 30p.



## BRODICK CASTLE, GARDEN AND COUNTRY PARK
**Isle of Arran** *map C13* ♿
Telephone: Brodick (0770) 2202
*(The National Trust for Scotland)*

Historic home of the Dukes of Hamilton. The castle dates in part from the 13th century. Paintings, furniture, objets d'art. Formal and woodland gardens, noted for rhododendrons. Country park.
**Location:** 1½ m N of Brodick pierhead on the Isle of Arran.
*Station: Ardrossan Harbour and Claonaig in Kintyre (& hence by Caledonian MacBrayne ferry).*
Ferry enquiries to Caledonian MacBrayne. Tel. Gourock (0475) 33755.
**Opening Times:** CASTLE. Mar 24–27: 1–5; Mar 28 to Apr 27 Mon, Wed, Sat 1–5; Apr 28 to Oct 1: daily 1–5; Oct 2 to Oct 14: Mon, Wed, Sat 1–5. (*Last tour* 4.30). Tea room. COUNTRY PARK & GARDEN. All the year—Daily 9.30–sunset. Adm Castle & Gardens £2.10, Chd £1.05; Parties £1.70, Chd 85p. Gardens only £1.30, Chd 65p, Chd under 5 free, OAPs/Students (on production of their cards) adm at half the standard adult rate. Car park free. Shop.
**Refreshments:** Tea at the Castle.

## BURNS COTTAGE
**Alloway** *map D12*
*(Trustees of Burns Monument)*

Thatched cottage in which Robert Burns was born, 1759. Museum with Burns' relics.
**Location:** 1½ m SW of Ayr.
*Station: Ayr (1½ m).*
**Opening Times:** Open all year round—June to Aug 9–7, Suns 10–7; Apr to May, Sept to Oct 10–5, Suns 2–5. During winter 10–4 *(closed Suns)*. Adm Cottage & Monument £1.20, Chd & OAPs 60p, includes entry to Burns Monument.
**Refreshments:** Tea at cottage in Summer.

## CRARAE GLEN GARDEN
**Crarae, Inveraray** *map C14*
Telephone: (0546) 86607/86614
*(Crarae Garden Charitable Trust)*

50 acres of trees, shrubs and plants in natural surroundings with waterfalls and magnificent panoramic views over Loch Fyne.
**Location:** 10 m SW of Inverary on A83 to Lochgilphead (14 m).
**Opening Times:** Daily throughout the year – summer 9–6, winter during daylight hours. Adm fixed charge, Chd up to age 5 free. Car parking free. Visitor centre, crafts, tea/coffee. Plants for sale Apr–Oct 10–4.30.

## CULZEAN CASTLE, GARDEN AND COUNTRY PARK
**Maybole** *map D12* △ ♿ Ⓢ
Telephone: Kirkoswald (065 56) 269
*(The National Trust for Scotland)*

One of the finest Adam houses in Scotland. Spacious policies and gardens. Adventure playground.
**Location:** 12 m SW of Ayr just off A719.
**Opening Times:** CASTLE. Mar 24 to Mar 31: 10–6; Apr 1 to Apr 27: 10–5; Apr 28 to Aug 31: 10–6; Sept 1 to Oct 31: 10–5. Last adm ½ hour before closing. Adm £2.10, Chd £1.05 (under 5 free). Adult parties £1.70, Schools 85p. OAPs/Students (on production of their cards) adm at half the standard adult rate. House not suitable for wheelchairs.
CULZEAN COUNTRY PARK *(Charges under review). (NTS and Kyle & Carrick; Cunninghame; Cummock & Doon Valley District Councils & Strathclyde Region)*—open all year. Adm free to members. Cars £3.50, mini buses & caravans £5, Coaches £15, charges Apr 1 to Oct only, vehicles (except school coaches) free at other times. Open all year, daily 9–sunset. Visitor Centre, Shop and Tourist Information Centre. Visitor Centre, Shop and Tourist Information Centre Mar 24–31, Apr, Sept and Oct: 10–5; May to Aug: 10–6. Ranger-Naturalist service.
**Refreshments:** Restaurant, Apr 1 to Apr 30 and Sept 1 to Oct 31, daily 10.30–5; May 1 to Aug 31, daily 10.30–6.

## DUMBARTON CASTLE
**Dumbarton** *map D13*
*(Secretary of State for Scotland)*

Sited on a volcanic rock overlooking the Firth of Clyde.
**Location:** At Dumbarton.
**Opening Times:** Apr 1 to Sept 30—Daily 9.30–7, Suns 2–7; Oct 1 to Mar 31—Daily 9.30–4, Suns 2–4. *Closed Dec 25, 26; Jan 1, 2.* Adm 60p, Chd & OAPs 30p.

## FINLAYSTONE HOUSE AND GARDENS
**Langbank** *map D13*
Telephone: Langbank 285
*(Mrs G MacMillan)*

Formerly home of fifteen Earls of Glencairn; now the home of the chief of Clan MacMillan. Exhibitions of international dolls, flower books and prints, and Celtic art. Woodlands, with picnic/play areas. Ranger service.
**Location:** On A8 between Langbank & Port Glasgow; 20 minutes W of Glasgow on S bank of the Clyde.
*Station: Longbank (1¼ m).*
**Opening Times:** Beautiful gardens and woods open ALL THE YEAR. Adm 90p, Chd 60p. House: Apr to Aug—Suns 2.30–4.30, **and** by appointment any time. Pre-booked groups welcome.
**Refreshments:** Home-baked afternoon teas Sats & Suns in summer in Old Laundry.

# STRATHCLYDE REGION – *continued*

## GREENBANK GARDEN

**Glasgow** *map D13* ♿
Telephone: 041-639 3281
*(The National Trust for Scotland)*

Walled garden, woodland walk and policies. Wide range of plants, flowers and shrubs. Garden for disabled. Regular garden walks and events. Best seen Apr–Oct. Attractive series of gardens, extending to 2½ acres, surrounding Georgian house (not open to the public).

**Location:** Flenders Road, near Clarkston Toll.
Station: Clarkston (1¼ m).
**Opening Times:** Garden. All the year—Daily 9.30–sunset. Adm £1.10, Chd (accompanied by adult) 55p; Chd party 45p. Adult parties 90p. Chd under 5 free, OAPs/Students (on production of their cards) adm at half the standard adult rate. *House closed.*

## THE HILL HOUSE

**Helensburgh** *map D14*
Telephone: (0436) 3900
*(The National Trust for Scotland)*

Overlooking the estuary of the River Clyde the house is considered to be the finest example of the domestic architecture of Charles Rennie Mackintosh. Commissioned in 1902 and completed in 1904 for the Glasgow publisher Walter W Blackie. Audio-visual programme on life of Charles Rennie Mackintosh.

**Location:** In Upper Colquhoun Street, Helensburgh; NW of Glasgow via A814.
**Opening Times:** Open all year (except Christmas and New Year Hols)—Daily 1–5 (last adm 4.30). Adm £1.70, Chd 85p. Adult parties £1.40, schools 70p.

## HUTCHESONS' HALL

**Glasgow** *map DE13*
Telephone: 041-552 8391
*(The National Trust for Scotland)*

Described as one of the most elegant buildings in Glasgow's city centre, the Hall was built in 1802–5 to a design by David Hamilton.

**Location:** 158 Ingram Street, nr SE corner of George Square.
**Opening Times:** Visitor Centre: open all year, Mons–Fris 9–5. Shop: Mons–Sats 10–4. Entry free.

## INVERARAY CASTLE

**Inveraray** *map D14*
Telephone: Inveraray (0499) 2203.
*(The Trustees of the 10th Duke of Argyll)*

Since 15th century the headquarters of the Clan Campbell. Present castle built 18th century by Roger Morris and Robert Mylne.

**Location:** ¾ m NE of Inveraray on Loch Fyne 58 m NW of Glasgow.
**Opening Times:** First Sat in Apr to second Sun in Oct. Apr, May, June, Sept & Oct: daily (except Fri) 10–1, 2–6. Sun 1–6. (During June, the Castle will remain open at lunch time.) July & Aug: daily 10–6, Sun 1–6. Last admission 12.30 & 5.30. **Note: The Castle will be closed Aug 9–15 1989 inclusive.** Gardens open by appointment, woodland walk open all year. Craft shop. *Enquiries:* The Factor, Dept HH, Cherry Park, Inveraray, Argyll. Telephone: (0499) 2203.
**Refreshments:** Tearoom.

## KELBURN COUNTRY CENTRE AND KELBURN CASTLE

**Largs** *map D13*
Telephone: Fairlie (0475) 568685
*(The Home and Park of the Earls of Glasgow on the Firth of Clyde.)*

Waterfalls, gardens, famous trees, spectacular walks and views. Adventure course, Commando Assault course, pet's corner, children's stockade, pony trekking. Shop, exhibitions.

**Location:** On the A78 between Largs and Fairlie in Ayrshire.
*Station: Largs (2 m).*
**Opening Times: Kelburn Country Centre:** Open with all facilities daily 10–6 from Good Friday to mid-Oct. Adm £1.80, Chd/OAPs £1.20. Reductions for booked parties. Dogs admitted on leads. **Winter opening:** Grounds only mid-Oct to Apr 12. Adm £1 and 60p. **Kelburn Castle:** Open to visitors from Sat Apr 22 to Sun May 29 only. Closed at all other times, except to special parties by prior arrangement. Adm £1.50 per person excluding admission to Kelburn Country Centre.
**Refreshments:** Licensed cafe, lunches, snacks, home baking, ice cream parlour, picnic areas. Open from Good Friday to mid-Oct.

## LINN PARK

**Glasgow** *map D13*
*(City of Glasgow District Council)*

212 acres pine and deciduous woodlands with enchanting riverside walks. Nature centre. Nature trail and Children's Zoo.

**Location:** Clarkston Road; Netherlee Road; Simshill Road, Linnview Avenue.
*Station: Minrend (¾ m).*
**Opening Times:** All the year—Daily 8 to dusk. Adm free. Car park at golf course & Netherlee Road.

## PENKILL CASTLE

**Girvan** *map D12* △
Telephone: Old Dailly (046 587) 261
*(Elton A Eckstrand, JD.)*

15th century Castle, impressive later additions. Fine furniture, tapestries and paintings. Favourite haunt of the Pre-Raphaelites, an inspiration to Dante Gabriel Rossetti and his sister Christina and other well known visitors.

**Location:** 2½ m E of Girvan on B734 Barr Road (off A77 Stranraer/Ayr Road).
*Station: Girvan (2½ m).*
**Opening Times:** By appointment. Guided tour with coffee and cakes in Banqueting Hall £5.50 incl. For details of other programmes contact Administrator.

## POLLOK HOUSE & PARK

**Glasgow** *map D13* ♿
Telephone: 041-632 0274
*(City of Glasgow District Council)*

Built 1747–52, additions by Sir Rowand Anderson 1890–1908. Contains Stirling Maxwell collection of Spanish and other European paintings; displays of furniture, ceramics, glass and silver. Nearby in Pollok Park is the Burrell Collection, winner of 1985 Museum of the Year Award and numerous other awards. Opening times as Pollok House.

**Location:** 3½ m from City Centre.
*Station: Pollokshaws West (1 m).*
**Opening Times:** All the year—Weekdays 10–5, Suns 2–5. Adm free. *Closed Christmas Day & New Year's Day.*
**Refreshments:** Tea room (reservations Tel 041-649 7547).

## ROSS HALL PARK

**Glasgow** *map D13*
*(City of Glasgow District Council)*

33 acres. Majestic trees by River Cart. Extensive heather and rock gardens, with water features, nature trails.

**Location:** Crookston Road SW.
**Opening Times:** All the year—Daily 8–dusk. Adm free.

## SOUTER JOHNNIE'S COTTAGE

**Kirkoswald** *map D12*
Telephone: Kirkoswald (065 56) 603
*(The National Trust for Scotland)*

Thatched home of the original Souter in Burns' "Tam o' Shanter", Burns' relics. Life-sized stone figures of the Souter, Tam, the Innkeeper and his wife, in garden.

**Location:** In Kirkoswald village 4 m W of Maybole on A77.
**Opening Times:** Mar 24 to Oct 31—Daily 12–5 (or by appointment) Adm 90p, Chd 45p. Adult parties 70p, Schools 35p, (under 5 free) OAPs/Students (on production of their cards) adm at half the standard adult rate.

## THE TENEMENT HOUSE

**Glasgow** *map D13*
Telephone: (041) 333 0183
*(The National Trust of Scotland)*

A restored first floor flat in a Victorian tenement building, built 1892, presents a picture of social significance.

**Location:** No 145 Buccleuch Street, Garnethill (N of Charing Cross).
**Opening Times:** Jan 7 to Mar 19 – Sat and Suns 2–4; Mar 24 to Oct 31 – Daily 2–5; Nov 4 to Dec 17 – Sat and Suns 2–4. Weekday morning visits by educational & other groups (no more than 15) to be arranged by advance booking only. Adm £1.10, Chd 55p; Adult parties 90p, school parties 45p.

## TOROSAY CASTLE AND GARDENS

**Craignure, Isle of Mull** *map C15*
Telephone: Craignure (068 02) 421
*(Mr Christopher James)*

Early Victorian house by David Bryce with 11 acres of unexpected terraced gardens laid out by Sir Robert Lorimer with 18th century Italian statues by Antonio Bonazza.

**Location:** 1½ m SE of Craignure by A849, by Forest Walk or by Steam Railway.
**Opening Times:** Castle. May 1 to Sept 30—Daily 10.30–5.30 (last adm 5). Late Apr and early Oct according to Easter and weather. Gardens. All the year during daylight hours. *Parties to Castle at other times by appointment only.* Adm Castle not available at time of going to press. Gardens only £1.50, Chd (between 5–16), OAPs/Students 75p (by Honesty box when Castle closed). Car park free. Dogs on leads in Garden only. Gardens and tearooms only suitable for wheelchairs. Local craft shop.
**Refreshments:** Home baked teas in Castle.

## VICTORIA PARK

**Glasgow** *map D13*
*(City of Glasgow District Council)*

Fossilised tree stumps, 300 million years old, in Fossil Grove Building. 58 acres. Extensive carpet bedding depicting centennial events.

**Location:** Victoria Park Drive North.
**Opening Times:** Park: All the year—Daily 8–dusk. Fossil Grove Building: Mon–Fri 8–4, Sat & Sun pm only. Adm free.

## WEAVER'S COTTAGE

**Kilbarchan** *map D13*
*(The National Trust for Scotland)*

Typical cottage of 18th century handloom weaver: looms, weaving equipment, domestic utensils.

**Location:** In Kilbarchan village; 8 m SW of Glasgow off A737.
*Station: Johnstone (2½ m).*
**Opening Times:** Mar 25 to May 25 and Sept 2 to Oct 31 – Tues, Thurs, Sats & Suns 2–5; May 26 to Aug 31 – daily 2–5 (last tour 4.30). Adm 90p, Chd 45p (under 5 free); Adult parties 70p; Chd party 35p, OAPs/Students (on production of their cards) adm at half the standard adult rate. Video programme.

## ACHAMORE GARDENS

**ISLE OF GIGHA, ARGYLL**

An exotic woodland garden covering fifty acres created by the late Sir James Horlick, who endowed his world-renowned collection of rhododendrons, azaleas and camellias to the National Trust for Scotland. Situated on the lovely Island of Gigha only 3 miles off Kintyre.

## INVERARAY CASTLE

**ARGYLL**

*Home of the Duke and Duchess of Argyll*

Since the early 15th century Inveraray has been the Headquarters of the Clan Campbell. The present Castle was built in the third quarter of the 18th century by Roger Morris and Robert Mylne. The Great Hall and Armoury, the State Rooms, Tapestries, Pictures and 18th century Furniture and old kitchen are shown.

Bus and Car Park free.

Shop and Tea Room.

ADMISSION—SEE EDITORIAL REFERENCE

## KELBURN CASTLE AND COUNTRY CENTRE

**Fairlie, Nr Largs, Ayrshire**

Kelburn has been the home of the Earls of Glasgow since the creation of the title in 1703, but has been the seat of the Boyle family for over 800 years. The Kelburn Glen is one of the most romantic in Scotland, dropping 700 ft by way of many waterfalls and deep gorges. There is a Walled Garden full of unusual shrubs peculiar to the West Coast of Scotland, a New Zealand Garden created by the 7th Countess in 1898, a small formal Garden designed by the 3rd Earl in the 1760s for his four children, and two unique sundials. There are some very remarkable trees, including the largest Monterey Pine in Scotland, the thousand-year old Yews, and the amazing Weeping Larch. Kelburn Castle is fully lived in, and open for only one month of the year, but it makes an impressive background to many walks and views.

## PENKILL CASTLE

**GIRVAN, AYRSHIRE**

'Penkill, one scarcely need desire aught more exquisite in the world.'
Christina Rossetti.

**HERITAGE EDUCATION TRUST**

**HET**

has now published the first

**HERITAGE EDUCATION HANDBOOK**

Edited by Martyn Dyer

Sandford Award winning properties assessed.
Theory practice and development of Heritage Education explained.
Work of the Trust described
Heritage Groups listed
Illustrated

Price **£3.95**

May be ordered through branches of W.H. Smith or direct from

**Heritage Education Trust,**
**St. Mary's College,**
**Strawberry Hill, TW1 4SX**
**01 892 0051 x202**

## POLLOK HOUSE GLASGOW

Original house built 1747–52, additions by Sir Rowand Anderson 1890–1908. Contains Stirling Maxwell collection of Spanish and other paintings and displays of European decorative arts.

Nearby in Pollok Park is the Burrell Collection winner of the 1985 Museum of the Year Award.

Open all the year: Weekdays 10 am to 5 pm, Sundays 2 to 5 pm.

CLOSED CHRISTMAS DAY AND NEW YEAR'S DAY

# TAYSIDE REGION

## ANGUS FOLK MUSEUM
**Glamis** *map F15*
*(The National Trust for Scotland)*

Row of 19th century cottages with stone-slabbed roofs, restored by the Trust. Adapted to display the Angus Folk Collection, one of the finest in the country.

**Location:** In Glamis village; 12 m N of Dundee A94.
**Opening Times:** Mar 24 to Mar 27, Apr 28 to May 25 and Sept 1 to Oct 1—Daily 12–5; May 26 to Aug 31—Daily 11.30–5.30 (last adm ½ hour before closing). Adm £1.20, Chd 60p (under 5 free). Adult parties £1, Schools 50p. OAPs/Students (on production of their cards) adm at half the standard adult rate.

## BARRIE'S BIRTHPLACE
**Kirriemuir** *map F15*
Telephone: Kirriemuir (0575) 72646
*(The National Trust for Scotland)*

Contains mementoes of Sir James Barrie. Peter Pan display and A/V programme.

**Location:** No 9 Brechin Road, in Kirriemuir.
**Opening Times:** Mar 24 to Mar 27, Apr 28 to Oct 1—Mons to Sats 11–5.30, Suns 2–5.30 (last tour 5). Adm 90p, Chd 45p (under 5 free). OAPs/Students (on production of their cards) adm at half the standard adult rate. Adult parties 70p, schools 35p.
**Refreshments:** Airlie Arms Hotel.

## BLAIR CASTLE
**Blair Atholl** *map E15*
Telephone: (079 681) 207
*(His Grace the Duke of Atholl)*

13th century home of The Duke of Atholl, Blair Castle is Scotland's most visited Historic House and has 32 rooms of infinite variety displaying beautiful furniture, fine collection of paintings, Arms and Armour, china, lace and embroidery, children's games and Jacobite relics. The Duke of Atholl has Europe's only official private army – The Atholl Highlanders.

**Location:** 8 m NW of Pitlochry off A9.
*Station: Blair Atholl (1½ m).*
**Opening Times:** Open Mar 23 to Oct 29 Mon to Sat 2–6, Sun (June to Sept) 12–6, Suns (Apr, May & Oct) 2–6. Last adm 5. Adm £2.50, Chd £1.50, reductions for pre-booked groups. Family tickets available. Picnic areas, Deer Park, Nature trails, pony trekking, free car and coach parking. Gift shop. Children's Guide Book. Up to 2,000 visitors a day can be accommodated.
**Refreshments:** Self Service Restaurant. Catering for pre-booked groups of up to 200 in separate rooms with waitress service can be provided. Further details available from The Administrator, Tel: 079 681 207. Fax: 079 681 487.

## BRANKLYN GARDEN
**Perth** *map E14*
Telephone: Perth (0738) 25535
*(The National Trust for Scotland)*

One of the finest gardens of its size in Britain (2 acres).

**Location:** 1½ m E of Perth on Dundee Road (A85).
**Opening Times:** Mar 1 to Oct 31—Daily 9.30–sunset. Adm £1.10, Chd 55p (under 5 free) OAPs/Students (on production of their cards) adm at half the standard adult rate. Adult parties 90p, schools 45p.

## CASTLE MENZIES
**Weem** *map E15*
*(Menzies Clan Society)*

Magnificant example of a 16th century fortified house, seat of the Chiefs of Clan Menzies, situated in the beautiful valley of the Tay. It was involved in the turbulent history of the Central Highlands and here "Bonnie Prince Charlie" rested on his way to Culloden in 1746.

**Location:** 1½ m from Aberfeldy on B846.
**Opening Times:** Apr to Sept—Weekdays 10.30–5, Suns 2–5. Adm £1.50, Chd 50p, OAPs 75p. Reductions for parties by prior arrangement.

## DRUMMOND CASTLE GARDENS
**Muthill** *map E14*
*(The Grimsthorpe & Drummond Castle Trust Ltd)*

Gardens only are open.

**Location:** 3 m S of Crieff, W off Crieff/Muthill Road (A822)—East Lodge.
**Opening Times:** May to Aug—Daily 2–6 (last admission 5); Sept—Weds & Suns 2–6. Adm £1.20, Chd/OAPs 60p. Free car park. *Gardens only are open to the public, according to the Rules in force.*

## EDZELL CASTLE & GARDENS
**Edzell** *map F15*
*(Secretary of State for Scotland)*

16th century castle. Unique renaissance garden. New Visitor Centre.

**Location:** 1 m W of Edzell; 6 m N of Brechin off B996.
**Opening Times:** Apr 1 to Sept 30—Weekdays 9.30–7, Suns 2–7; Oct 1 to Mar 31—Weekdays (*except Tues and Thurs morning*) 9.30–4, Suns 2–4. *Closed Dec 25 & 26; Jan 1 & 2.* Adm 60p, Chd & OAPs 30p.

## GLAMIS CASTLE
**Glamis** *map 15*
*(Mary, Countess of Strathmore and Kinghorne)*

Family home of the Earls of Strathmore and Kinghorne and a royal residence since 1372. Childhood home of H.M. Queen Elizabeth The Queen Mother and birthplace of H.R.H. The Princess Margaret. Legendary setting of Shakespeare's play 'Macbeth'. Five-storey L shaped tower block dating from 13th century, remodelled 1606, containing magnificent rooms with wide range of historic pictures, furniture, porcelain etc.

**Location:** Glamis.
**Opening Times:** Good Friday to Easter Monday, then Apr 29 to Oct 16—daily 12–5.30 (last tour 4.45). Adm £2.50, reductions for Chd, OAPs and groups. Ample bus and car parking. Picnic area, Shops, Garden and Nature Trail.
**Refreshments:** Licensed Restaurant at the Castle.

## HOUSE OF DUN
**Nr Montrose** *map G15*
Telephone: (067481) 264
*(The National Trust for Scotland)*

Modest size Palladian house overlooking the Montrose Basin, built in 1730 for David Erskine, Lord Dun, to designs by William Adam. Exuberant plasterwork in the saloon.

**Location:** 3 m W of Montrose.
**Opening Times:** Apr 28 to Oct 29 (last tour of House ½ hr before closing). House, courtyard and tea room 11–5.30. Grounds open all year. Adm £2.10, Chd £1.05, Adult parties £1.70, schools 85p.

## HUNTINGTOWER CASTLE
**nr Perth** *map E14*
*(Secretary of State for Scotland)*

Two fine and complete towers in which are excellent painted ceilings.

**Location:** 2 m W of Perth.
**Opening Times:** Apr 1 to Sept 30—Daily 9.30–7, Suns 2–7; Oct 1 to Mar 31—Daily 9.30–4, Suns 2–4. *Closed Dec 25, 26; Jan 1, 2.* Adm 60p, Chd & OAPs 30p.

## SCONE PALACE
**Perth** *map E15*
Telephone: Perth (0738) 52300
*(Rt Hon the Earl of Mansfield)*

This medieval palace was Gothicised for the third Earl of Mansfield in the early 19th century. Superb collections of French furniture, china, ivories, clocks, Vernis Martin vases and objets d'art.

**Location:** 2 m NE of Perth on the Braemer Road (A93).
*Station: Perth (2½ m).*
**Opening Times:** Mar 24 to Oct 16—Mons to Sats 9.30–5, Suns 1.30–5 (July and Aug 10–5). Adm £2.70. Special rates for booked parties. Free car park. Shops. Picnic park. Playground. Winter tours by special arrangment.
**Refreshments:** Coffee shop. Old Kitchen Restaurant (licensed). Home baking. State Room dinners.

# CASTLE MENZIES

PERTHSHIRE

Magnificent example of a 16th century fortified house, seat of the Chiefs of Clan Menzies. Situated in the beautiful valley of Tay. It was involved in the turbulent history of the Central Highlands, and here 'Bonnie Prince Charlie' rested on his way to Culloden in 1746.

# EDZELL CASTLE AND GARDENS

Admission – See editorial reference.

# DRUMMOND CASTLE GARDENS

MUTHILL, PERTHSHIRE

The Gardens of Drummond Castle were originally laid out about 1630 by John Drummond, 2nd Earl of Perth. In about 1830, the parterre was Italianized and embellished with fine figures and statues from Italy. Probably one of the most interesting pieces of statuary is the Sundial, designed and built by John Mylne, Master Mason to King Charles I.

## The National Trust

Welcomes

## Disabled Visitors

Almost every National Trust property advertised and listed in this Guide has a great deal to offer visitors with disabilities. Please telephone the property you wish to visit for full details – or for a comprehensive booklet on facilities and access at National Trust properties send an adhesive label, stamped with minimum postage to:

**Dept HHG**
**Facilities for Disabled Visitors**
**The National Trust**
**36 Queen Anne's Gate**
**London SW1H 9AS**

The Grand Tour of Scotland

# SCONE PALACE

PERTH

Scone Palace was home to the Stone of Scone or Destiny for nearly 500 years and was the crowning place of 40 kings of Scotland. Scone was first the capital of the Pictish kings then capital city of Kenneth MacAlpen, first king of Scots. Scone has been home of the Murray family for 400 years and the present palace is the third to stand on this ancient site. On view in the state rooms are superb collections of French furniture, clocks, china, ivories, 16th century needlework and a unique collection of Vernis Martin vases. The extensive grounds include a woodland garden, a Pinetum which has one of the finest collections of rare conifers including the original Douglas Fir.

# GLAMIS CASTLE

The Grand Tour of Scotland

ANGUS

Glamis Castle is the family home of the Earls of Strathmore and Kinghorne and a Royal residence since 1372. It is the childhood home of H.M. Queen Elizabeth The Queen Mother, the birthplace of H.R.H. The Princess Margaret and the legendary setting for Shakespeare's play 'Macbeth'.

# UNIVERSITY OF CAMBRIDGE

NOTE: Admission to *Colleges* means to the Courts, not to the staircases and students' rooms. All opening times are subject to closing for College functions, etc., on occasional days. *Halls* normally close for lunch (12–2) and many are not open during the afternoon. *Chapels* are closed during services. *Libraries* are not usually open, special arrangements are noted. *Gardens* do not usually include the Fellows' garden. *Figures* denote the date of foundation, and existing buildings are often of later date. *Daylight hours*—some Colleges may not open until 9.30 am or later and usually close before 6 pm—many as early as 4.30 pm.

All parties exceeding 10 persons wishing to tour the colleges between Easter and October are required to be escorted by a Cambridge registered Guide. All enquiries should be made to the Tourist Information Centre, Wheeler Street, Cambridge CB2 3QB.

**Terms:** *Lent:* Mid-January to Mid-March. *Easter:* 21nd April to 12th June. *Michaelmas:* 2nd week October to 1st week December. Examination Period closures which differ from one college to another, now begin in early April and extend to late June. Notices are usually displayed. Important: Before entering any college, please call at the Porter's Lodge. This applies both to individual visitors and guided parties.

| *Address of College and Entrance Gate* | *Opening Arrangements* |
|---|---|
| **Christ's College** (1505). St. Andrew's Street (Porter's Lodge) | *College:* Daily, all day. Closed May 1 to mid-June. *Chapel:* Term—Daily, all day. *Hall:* Weekdays 10–1. *Library:* By appointment with Librarian. *Fellows' Garden:* Weekdays 10.30–12.30, 2–4. (Closed Bank Hols & Easter Week and May 1 to mid-June). |
| **Clare College** (1326). Trinity Lane CB2 1TL | *Hall:* Mons to Sats 9–12 (usually). *Chapel:* Daily during term time except Apr 10–June 18. Otherwise by prior arrangement with the Dean. *Library:* By prior arrangement with the Librarian. *Gardens:* Mons to Fris 2–4.45 (usually). (Closed Bank Hols & weekends). |
| **Corpus Christi College** (1352). Trumpington Street (Porter's Lodge) | Opening times shown at Porter's Lodge. |
| **Downing College** (1800). Regent Street (Porter's Lodge) | *College & Gardens:* Daily, daylight hours. *Chapel:* Term—Daily, all day. Vacation—By appointment. *Hall:* Closed to the public. *Library:* By arrangement only. |
| **Emmanuel College** (1584). St. Andrew's Street (Porter's Lodge) | *College:* Daily 9–6. *Hall & Chapel:* Daily, except when in use. *Library:* Only by prior application to Librarian. *Gardens & Paddock:* Daily 9–6 or dusk if earlier. *Fellows' Garden:* Not open to visitors. (Closed for annual holidays, variable). |
| **Gonville & Caius College** (1348). Trinity Street (Porter's Lodge) | *College & Chapel:* Daily, daylight hours. *Library:* By appointment with Librarian. (Closed to all guided parties) Closed for short periods each day: times shown at Porter's Lodge. |
| **Jesus College** (1496). Jesus Lane (Porter's Lodge) | *College:* Daily 9–5.30. *Chapel:* Apply Porter's Lodge. *Hall:* Closed to the public. |
| **King's College** (1441). King's Parade (Porter's Lodge) | *College:* Daily until 6. Limited access mid-Apr to mid-June. *Library:* Scholars, on application to librarian. *Chapel:* Term—Weekdays 9.30–3.45. Suns 2–3, 4.45–5.45. Summer Vacation—Weekdays 9.30–5.45. Suns 10.30–5.45 and subject to closure at other times for rehearsals etc. *Dining Hall:* Closed to the public. Entire college closed Aug 8, 9, Dec 26 to Jan 3 1989. |
| **Magdalene College** (1542). Magdalene Street (Porter's Lodge) | *College & Chapel:* Daily 9–6.30 (May & June 11.30–5.30). *Hall:* Daily during term 9.30–12.30 (May & June 11.30–5.30). *Library—Pepys':* No groups except by prior arrangement. Jan 13 to Mar 14 & Oct 6 to Dec 5: Weekdays 2.30–3.30. Apr 21 to Aug 31: Weekdays 11.30–12.30, 2.30–3.30. *Gardens:* Daily 1–6.30 (May & June 1–5.30). |
| **Newnham College** (1871). Sidgwick Avenue | *College & Gardens:* Daily during daylight hours. Apply Porter's Lodge. (College and gardens closed May 1–July and Aug.) |
| **Pembroke College** (1347). Trumpington Street | Opening times shown at Porter's Lodge. *Library:* By appointment with Librarian. |
| **Peterhouse** (1284). Trumpington Street (Porter's Lodge) | *Chapel:* Daily. *Hall:* Mornings only during term. Guided parties of not more than 12, daily 1–5. |
| **Queens' College** (1448). Silver Street (Porter's Lodge). Visitor's entrance, Queen's Lane | Open daily 1.45–4.30 & also 10.15–12.45 during July, Aug & Sept & for guided parties of not more than 20. Adm charge. |
| **St. Catharine's College** (1473). Trumpington Street (Porter's Lodge) | *College & Chapel:* Daily, during daylight hours. (Closed May & June). *Hall:* Closed to the public. |
| **St. John's College** (1511). St. John's Street (Porter's Lodge) | *College:* Daily until 5.30. (Closed May & June). *Chapel:* Apply Porter's Lodge. *Hall:* Closed to the public. |
| **Sidney Sussex College** (1596). Sidney Street (Porter's Lodge) | *College:* Daily, during daylight hours. *Hall & Chapel:* Apply Porter's Lodge. |
| **Trinity College** (1546). Trinity Street (Porter's Lodge) | Opening times shown at Porter's Great Gate, Lodge. |
| **Trinity Hall** (1350). Trinity Lane | *College, Chapel & Gardens:* Daily, during daylight hours. *Library:* Apply beforehand to College Librarian. |

# UNIVERSITY OF OXFORD

NOTE: Admission to *Colleges* means to the quadrangles, not to the staircases and students' rooms. All opening times are subject to closing for College functions, etc., on occasional days. *Halls* normally close for lunch during term (12–2). *Chapel* usually closed during services. *Libraries* are not usually open, special arrangements are noted. *Gardens* do not usually include the Fellows' garden. *Figures* denote the date of foundation, and existing buildings are often of later date.

**Terms:** *Hilary:* Mid-January to Mid-March. *Trinity:* 3rd week April to late June. *Michaelmas:* Mid-October to 1st week December.

| *Address of College and Entrance Gate* | *Opening Arrangements* |
|---|---|
| **All Souls College** (1438). High Street (Porter's Lodge) | *College:* Daily 2–5. |
| **Balliol College** (1263). Broad Street (Porter's Lodge) | *Hall, Chapel & Gardens:* Daily 10–5 (summer), 10–dusk (winter). Parties limited to 25. |
| **Brasenose College** (1509). Radcliffe Square (Porter on duty) | *Hall, Chapel & Gardens:* Daily 10–5 (summer), 10–dusk (winter). *Library:* By special request only. |
| **Christ Church** (1546). St. Aldate's (Meadow Gate) | *Cathedral:* Daily 9–4.30 (winter), 9–5.30 (summer). *Hall:* Oct to Mar: Daily 9.30–12, 2–4.30. Apr to Sept: Daily 9.30–12, 2–6. Adm 60p. *Picture Gallery:* Weekdays 10.30–1, 2–4.30. Adm 40p. *Meadow:* Daily 7–dusk. |
| **Corpus Christi College** (1516). Merton Street (Porter's Lodge) | *College, Chapel & Gardens:* Terms — Daily 2–4. Vacations — Daily 10–4. |
| **Exeter College** (1314). Turl Street (Porter's Lodge) | *College & Chapel, Fellows' Garden:* Term — Daily 2–5. Vacations — Daily 9–7. |
| **Hertford College** (1284, 1740 & 1874). Catte Street (Porter's Lodge) | *College, Hall & Chapel:* Daily 10–6. (Closed for a week at Christmas and Easter). |
| **Jesus College** (1571). Turl Street (Gate in Turl Street) | *College, Hall & Chapel:* Daily 2.30–4.30. *Library:* Special permission of Librarian. (Closed Christmas and Easter holidays). |
| **Keble College** (1868). Parks Road (Porter's Lodge) | *College & Chapel:* Daily 10–7 (or dusk if earlier). |
| **Lady Margaret Hall** (1878). Norham Gardens (Porter's Lodge) | *College Gardens:* Daily 2–6 (or dusk if earlier). |
| **Lincoln College** (1427). Turl Street (Porter's Lodge) | *College, Hall & Chapel:* Weekdays 2–5. Suns 11–5. *Wesley Room:* On application to Porter's Lodge. *All Saints Library:* Tues & Thurs 2.30–4.30. |
| **Magdalen College** (1458). High Street (Front Lodge) | *College, Chapel, Deer Park & Water Walks:* Daily 2–6.15. Parties limited to 25. |
| **Mansfield College** (1886). Mansfield Road (Porter's Lodge) | *College:* Open May, June & July, Mon to Sat 9–5. Interior of Chapel and Library may be viewed by prior appointment, please enquire at Porter's Lodge. |
| **Merton** (1264). Merton Street (Porter's Lodge) | *Chapel & Quadrangles:* Mons to Fris 2–4 (Mar 2 to Oct 31: closes at 5). Sats & Suns 10–4 (Mar 2 to Oct 31: closes at 5). *Old Library and Max Beerbohm Room:* Mons to Sats 2–4. Adm 40p. Apply Verger's Office (closed Dec 25 to Feb 12). |
| **New College** (1379). New College Lane | *College, Hall, Chapel & Gardens:* Term — Daily 2–5. Vacation — Daily 11–5. |
| **Nuffield College** (1937). New Road (Porter's Lodge) | *College only:* Daily 9–7. |
| **Oriel College** (1326). Oriel Square (Main Gate) | *College:* Daily 2–5. (Closed Christmas & Easter holidays & mid-Aug to mid-Sept). |
| **Pembroke College** (1624). St. Aldate's (Porter's Lodge) | *College, Hall, Chapel & Gardens:* Term — Daily 2–6.30. Vacation — Daily 9.30–6.30. (Closed Christmas and Easter holidays & occasionally in Aug). |
| **The Queen's College** (1340). High Street (Porter's Lodge) | *Hall, Chapel, Quadrangles & Garden:* Daily 2–5. |
| **St. Edmund Hall** (1270). Queen's Lane (at the Lodge) | *College, Old Hall, Chapel & Garden:* Daily, daylight hours. *Crypt of St. Peter in the East:* On application to Porter. |
| **St. John's College** (1555). St. Giles' (Porter's Lodge) | *College & Garden:* Term & Vacation — Daily 1–5 (or dusk if earlier). Guided parties must obtain permission from the Lodge). *Hall & Chapel:* Summer — 2.30–4.30 (Apply Porter). (Closed during conferences & College functions). |
| **Trinity College** (1554). Broad Street (Main Gate) | *Hall, Chapel & Garden:* Daily 2–5.30 (summer). 2–dusk (winter). (Opening hrs may vary – visitors should check in advance.) |
| **University College** (1249). High Street (Porter's Lodge) | *College, Hall & Chapel:* Term — 2–4. Apply Porter. |
| **Wadham College** (1610). Parks Road (Porter's Lodge) | *College, Hall, Chapel & Gardens:* Daily 1–4.30. Hall: Apply Lodge. |
| **Worcester College** (1714). Worcester Street (Porter's Lodge) | *College & Gardens:* Term — Daily 2–6. Vacation — Daily 9–12, 2–6. *Hall & Chapel:* Apply Lodge. |

Visitors and especially guided parties should always call at the Porter's Lodge before entering any College.

**GUIDED WALKING TOURS OF THE COLLEGES AND CITY OF OXFORD** Tours, conducted by the Oxford Guild of Guides Lectures, are offered by the Oxford Information Centre, morning for much of the year, afternoon tours daily. For tour times please ring (0865) 726871.

Tours are offered for groups in English, French, German, Spanish, Russian, Japanese, Greek and Serbo-Croat.

The most popular tour for groups, Oxford Past and Present, can be arranged at any time. The following special interest tours are available in the afternoon only: Alice in Oxford; Literary Figures in Oxford; American Roots in Oxford; Oxford Gardens; Modern Architecture in Oxford; Architecture in Oxford (medieval, 17th century and modern); Oxford in the Civil War and 17th century.

Further details are available from The Deputy Information Officer tel (0865) 726871.

# Supplementary List of Properties Open by Appointment Only

The list of Houses in England, Wales and Scotland printed here are those which are usually open 'by appointment only' with the Owner, or open infrequently during the summer months. These are in addition to the Houses and Gardens which are open regularly and are fully classified starting on page 33. Where it is necessary to write for an appointment to view, see code *(WA)*. * Indicates that these Houses are also classified and more details are shown under the respective 'County' headings.

The majority of these properties have received a grant from the Minister of Housing and Local Government for urgent repairs, given on the advice of the Historic Buildings Councils. Public buildings, almshouses, tithe barns, business premises in receipt of grants are not usually included, neither are properties where the architectural features can be viewed from the street.

## ENGLAND

### AVON

| *House* | *Owner (with address if different from first column)* |
|---|---|
| **The Refectory, The Vicarage,** nr Bristol | Rev R. Salmon *Yatton* (0934) 833126 |
| **Eastwood Manor Farm,** East Harptree | Mr A. J. Gay |
| **Partis College,** Bath | The Bursar *Bath* (0225) 21532 |
| **Woodspring Priory,** Kewstoke | The Landmark Trust, Shottesbrooke, nr Maidenhead, Berks *Open daily* |

### BEDFORDSHIRE

| *House* | *Owner (with address if different from first column)* |
|---|---|
| **Avenue House,** Ampthill | Mr S. Houfe *(WA)* |
| **The Temple,** Southill Park, Biggleswade | The Estate Office *(WA)* |
| **Warden Abbey,** nr Biggleswade | The Landmark Trust, Shottesbrooke, nr Maidenhead, Berks *(WA)* |

### BERKSHIRE

| *House* | *Owner (with address if different from first column)* |
|---|---|
| **High Chimneys,** Hurst, Reading | Mr & Mrs H. Farrar *(WA)* |
| **St Gabriel's School,** Sandleford Priory, Newbury | The Headmistress *Newbury* 40663 |

### BUCKINGHAMSHIRE

| *House* | *Owner (with address if different from first column)* |
|---|---|
| **Bisham Abbey,** nr Marlow | *Viewing by appointment only.* The Director, The Sports Council, Bisham Abbey *Marlow* (062 84) 76911 |
| **Brudenell House,** Quainton | Dr H. Beric Wright *(WA) 1 week's notice* |
| **Church of the Assumption,** Hardmead, Newport Pagnell | Friends of Friendless Churches *For key apply to H. Tranter, Manor Cottage, Hardmead, by letter or telephone* *North Crawley* 257 |
| **Iver Grove,** Shreding Green, Iver | Mr & Mrs T. Stoppard *(WA)* |
| **Remnantz,** West St. Marlow *(WA)* to | A. Wethered Esq., Brampton House, 100 High St. Marlow SL7 1AQ |
| **Repton's Subway Facade,** Digby's Walk, Gayhurst | Mr J. H. Beverley, The Bath House, Gayhurst. *(WA)* or *Goldington* 564 |

### CAMBRIDGE

| *House* | *Owner (with address if different from first column)* |
|---|---|
| **Chantry (The),** Ely | Mrs T. A. N. Bristol *(WA)* |
| **Church of St John The Baptist,** Papworth St Agnes | Friends of Friendless Churches *For key apply to M. Knox, Avebury House, Papworth St Agnes, Cambs by letter or telephone* *Huntingdon* 830522 |
| **The King's School,** Ely, Monastic Barn. | Bursar's Office, The King's School, Ely. *(WA)* (0353) 662837 |
| **Leverington Hall,** Wisbech | Professor A. Barton *(WA)* |
| **The Lynch Lodge,** Alwalton, nr Peterborough | The Landmark Trust *(WA)* |
| **The Post Mill,** Six Mile Bottom | The Trustees of the Six Mile Bottom Trust, The Estate Office, Six Mile Bottom, Newmarket, Suffolk *(WA)* |

### CHESHIRE

| *House* | *Owner (with address if different from first column)* |
|---|---|
| **Bewsey Old Hall,** Warrington | The Administrator *(WA)* |
| **Charles Roe House,** Chestergate, Macclesfield | McMillan Martin Ltd *(WA)* |
| **Crown Hotel,** Nantwich | Prop P. J. Martin |
| **Shotwick Hall,** Shotwick | Mr R. B. Gardner, 'Wychen', 17 St Mary's Rd, Leatherhead, Surrey *By appointment only with the tenants: Mr & Mrs G. A. T. Holland* (0244) 880228 |
| **Tudor House,** Lower Bridge St, Chester | *Chester* 20095 |

### CLEVELAND

| *House* | *Owner (with address if different from first column)* |
|---|---|
| **St Cuthbert's Church & Turner Mausoleum,** Kirkleatham | Kirkleatham Parochial Church Council<br>Mr R. S. Ramsdsale, Church Warden (0642) 475198<br>Miss L. Clish, Church Warden (0642) 483195 |

### CORNWALL

| *House* | *Owner (with address if different from first column)* |
|---|---|
| **College (The),** Week St Mary | The Landmark Trust, Shottesbrooke, nr Maidenhead, Berks *(WA)* |
| **Town Hall,** Camelford | Camelford Town Trust |
| **Trecarrel Manor,** Trebullett, Launceston *(Hall & Chapel restored)* | *Telephone application only to Mr N. H. Burden* *Coads Green* 82286 |

### CUMBRIA

| *House* | *Owner (with address if different from first column)* |
|---|---|
| **Preston Patrick Hall,** Milnthorpe | Mrs J. D. Armitage *Crooklands* 200 |
| **Whitehall,** Mealsgate, Carlisle | Mrs S. Parkin-Moore, 40 Woodsome Rd, London NW5 *(WA)* |

### DERBYSHIRE

| *House* | *Owner (with address if different from first column)* |
|---|---|
| **Elvaston Castle,** nr Derby | Derbyshire County Council *Derby* 571342 |
| **The Mansion** Church St, Ashbourne | *Garden, Hall and Drawing Room by appointment only with the Headmaster* (0335) 43685 |
| **North Lees Hall,** Outseats, Hathersage, By Sheffield | At present being converted to holiday flats. 3–4 open days annually. *(WA)* Vivat Trust, 35 King St., Bristol |
| **10 North Street,** Cromford | The Landmark Trust, Shottesbrooke, nr Maidenhead, Berks *(WA)* |
| **The Pavilion,** Swarkestone, nr Ticknall | The Landmark Trust *(WA)* |

### DEVON

| *House* | *Owner (with address if different from first column)* |
|---|---|
| **Bindon Manor,** Axmouth | Sir John and Lady Loveridge *(WA)* |
| **Bowringsleigh,** Kingbridge | Mr M. C. Manisty *(WA)* |
| **Endsleigh House,** Milton Abbot, nr Tavistock | Endsleigh Fishing Club Ltd, Apr to Sept *Milton Abbot* (082 287) 248 |
| **Hareston House,** Brixton | Mr & Mrs K. T. Basset *Mons, May to Sept* *Plymouth* 880 426 |
| **Library (The),** Stevenstone, nr Torrington | The Landmark Trust, Shottesbrooke, nr Maidenhead, Berks *(WA)* |
| **Sanders,** Lettaford | The Landmark Trust, Shottesbrooke, nr Maidenhead, Berks *(WA)* |
| **Shell House (The),** Endsleigh Milton Abbot, nr Tavistock | Endsleigh Fishing Club Ltd *April to Sept* *Milton Abbot* 248 |
| **Shute Barton,** nr Axminster | The National Trust *By appointment only with the Tenants* *Axminster* 33682 |
| **Shute Gatehouse,** Shute Barton, nr Axminster | The Landmark Trust, Shottesbrooke, nr Maidenhead, Berks *(WA)* |
| **Ugbrooke Park,** Chudleigh | Captain The Lord Clifford *Chudleigh* 852179 |
| **Wortham Manor,** Lifton | The Landmark Trust, Shottesbrooke, nr Maidenhead, Berks *(WA)* |

### DORSET

| *House* | *Owner (with address if different from first column)* |
|---|---|
| **Bloxworth House,** Bloxworth | Mr T. A. Dulake *(WA)* |
| **Clenston Manor,** Winterborne Clenston, Blandford Forum | Mr & Mrs M. Best (0258) 880681 |
| **Moignes Court,** Owermoigne | Mr A. M. Cree *(WA)* |
| **Woodsford Castle,** Woodsford | The Landmark Trust, Shottesbrooke, nr Maidenhead, Berks *(WA)* |

### DURHAM

| *House* | *Owner (with address if different from first column)* |
|---|---|
| **The Buildings in The Square** | Lady Gilbertson, 1 The Square, Greta Bridge, Barnard Castle *(WA)* |

### ESSEX

| *House* | *Owner (with address if different from first column)* |
|---|---|
| **Blake Hall Battle of Britain Museum and Gardens,** Chipping Ongar | Mr R. Capel Cure *Parties catered for. Telephone the Adminstrator:* *Chipping Ongar* 362502 |
| **Colville Hall,** White Roding, Essex | Mr C. A. Webster *(WA)* *(Listed Grade II *Barn only)* |
| **Great Priory Farm,** Panfield, Braintree | Miss Lucy Tabor. Weekends only, by telephoned appointment *Braintree* 24590 |
| **Guildhall (The),** Great Waltham | Mr J. J. Tufnell |
| **Old All Saints,** Langdon Hills | Mr R. Mill *Basildon* 414146 |
| **Rainham Hall,** Rainham | The National Trust (tenant Mr Ian Botes) (WA) |
| **Rayne Hall,** Rayne, Braintree | Mr and Mrs R. J. Pertwee *(WA)* |
| **Round House (The),** Havering-atte-Bower, Romford | Mr M. E. W. Heap *Romford* 28136 |

### GLOUCESTERSHIRE

| *House* | *Owner (with address if different from first column)* |
|---|---|
| **Abbey Gateway (The),** Tewkesbury | The Abbey Lawn Trust *Key may be obtained from Abbey Sacristan* |
| **Ashleworth Court,** nr Gloucester | Mr H. J. Chamberlayne *Parties only* *Hartpury* 241 |
| **Ashleworth Manor,** Ashleworth | Dr and Mrs Jeremy Barnes *(WA)* |
| **Bearland House,** Gloucester | The Administrator *(WA)* |
| **Castle Godwyn,** Painswick | Mr & Mrs John Milne *(WA)* |
| **Chaceley Hall,** nr Tewkesbury | Mr W. H. Lane *Tirley* 205 |
| **Cheltenham College** (Thirlestaine House), Cheltenham | The Secretary to the Council, Bursar's Office, The College *Cheltenham* 513540 |
| **Cottage (The),** Stanley Pontlarge, Winchcombe | Mrs S. M. Rolt *(WA)* |
| **Daneway House,** Sapperton | Sir Anthony Denny, Bt *(WA)* |
| **Frampton Court & Gothic Orangery,** Frampton-on-Severn, Gloucester | Frampton Court Estate *Apply to Mrs Clifford* *Gloucester* (0452) 740267 |
| **Frampton Manor,** Frampton-on-Severn, Gloucestershire | Mr & Mrs R. Clifford *(WA)* |
| **Matson House,** Gloucester | The Bursar, Selwyn School *During School holidays only* *Gloucester* 26572 |
| **Minchinhampton Market House,** Stroud | Mr B. E. Lucas *Brimscombe* 883241 |
| **Old Vicarage (The),** Church Stanway | 'Lord Weymyss' Trust; Apply to Stanway House, Stanway, Cheltenham *Stanton* 469 |
| **St Margaret's Church,** London Rd, Gloucester | Gloucester Municipal Charities *Services Suns 3 pm. Other times by appointment with Warden* *Gloucester* 23316 |
| **Stroud Subscription Rooms,** Stroud | Stroud District Council, Technical Services Department, Old Town Hall, The Shambles, High St, Stroud *Stroud* 4999 |
| **Tyndale Monument** North Nibley | Tyndale Monument Charity, 26 Long St, Dursley<br>P. N. Bayley *Dursley* 2357<br>Key available as per notice as foot of Wood Lane. |

Where it is necessary to write for an appointment to view, see code *(WA)*

## GREATER MANCHESTER

| *House* | *Owner (with address if different from first column)* |
|---|---|
| **Chetham's Hospital & Library**, Manchester M3 1SB | The Feoffees of Chetham's Hospital & Library 061-834 9644 |
| **Slade Hall**, Slade Lane, Manchester M13 0QP | Manchester and District Housing Assn. *(WA)* |

## HAMPSHIRE

| *House* | *Owner (with address if different from first column)* |
|---|---|
| **Chesil Theatre** (formerly St Peter Chesil Church) | Winchester Dramatic Society *Winchester* 67086 |
| **Houghton Lodge**, Stockbridge | *(WA)* Captain and Mrs M. W. Busk. |
| **Manor Farm House**, Hambledon | Mr S. B. Mason |
| **Marsh Court**, Stockbridge | Headmaster, Marsh Court School *Andover* 810503 |
| **Moyles Court**, Ringwood | Manor House School Trust Ltd *Ringwood* 472856 |

## HEREFORD & WORCESTER

| *House* | *Owner (with address if different from first column)* |
|---|---|
| **Britannia House**, The Tything, Worcester | The Alice Ottley School *(WA) Apply to The Headmistress* |
| **Church House**, Evesham | The Trustees of the Walker Hall & Church House |
| **Grafton Manor**, Bromsgrove | Mr J. W. Morris *Bromsgrove* 31525 |
| **Huddington Court**, nr Droitwich | Professor Hugh D. Edmondson *(WA)* |
| **Ley (The)**, Weobley | Lt Col Sir Richard Verdin, Stoke Hall, Nantwich *Wettenhall* 284 |
| **Newhouse Farm**, Goodrich, Ross-on-Wye | The Administrator *(WA)* |
| **Old Palace (The)**, Worcester | The Dean & Chapter of Worcester *(WA) Apply to Diocesan Secretary, Old Palace, Deansway, Worcester WR1 2JE* |
| **Shelwick Court**, nr Hereford | The Landmark Trust *(WA)* |

## HERTFORDSHIRE

| *House* | *Owner (with address if different from first column)* |
|---|---|
| **Homewood**, Park Lane, Knebworth | Mr & Mrs Pollock-Hill (WA) |
| **Manor House**, Little Gaddesden, Berkhamsted | Mr A. Graham-Stewart *(WA)* |
| **Woodhall Park**, Watton-at-Stone, Hertford | The Abel Smith Trustees *Apply to The Headmaster, Heath Mount School* *Ware* 830230 |

## KENT

| *House* | *Owner (with address if different from first column)* |
|---|---|
| **Barming Place**, Maidstone | Mr J. Peter & Dr Rosalind Bearcroft *Maidstone* 27844 |
| **Foord Almshouses**, Rochester | *(WA)* The Clerk to the Trustees Easter to Sept 30 2–5 except Mon & Thurs. Adm £1, Chd 50p |
| **6 Market Place**, Faversham | Mr J. B. Kerr *(WA)* |
| **Mersham-le-Hatch**, nr Ashford | Lord Brabourne *Apply to tenant – The Directors, Caldecott Community* *Ashford (Kent)* 23954 |
| **Nurstead Court**, Meopham | Mrs S. M. H. Edmeades-Stearns *Meopham* 812121 |
| **Old College of All Saints**, Kent Music Centre, Maidstone | *Apply to Area Director* *Maidstone* 690404 |
| **Starkey Castle**, Wouldham, Rochester | Mr & Mrs Gerald Davies *Medway* 681600 |
| **Yaldham Manor**, Wrotham | Mr & Mrs John Mourier Lade, Yaldham Manor, Kemsing, Sevenoaks, Kent TN15 6NN (postal address) *(WA)* |

## LANCASHIRE

| *House* | *Owner (with address if different from first column)* |
|---|---|
| **Music Room (The)**, Lancaster | The Landmark Trust, Shottesbrooke, nr Maidenhead, Berks *Open daily, times displayed* |
| **Parrox Hall**, Preesall, Fleetwood FY6 0JU | *(WA)* Mrs C. V. Elletson (0253) 810245 |

## LEICESTERSHIRE

| *House* | *Owner (with address if different from first column)* |
|---|---|
| **The Forecourt**, Burley on the Hill, nr Oakham, Rutland. | *Open Good Fri, Easter Mon, May Day, Spring Bank Hol, Summer Bank Hol, Aug 1–25. House itself not open to the public.* |
| **Moat House (The)**, Appleby Magna | Mr H. S. Hall *Measham* 70301 |
| **Old Grammar School**, Market Harborough | The Market Harborough Exhibition Foundation, 12 Hillcrest Avenue, Market Harborough (0858) 63201 |
| **Staunton Harold Hall**, nr. Ashby de la Zouch | Ryder-Cheshire Mission for the Relief of Suffering Exhibition. Coffee shop and beautiful gardens open to the public *Melbourne* 862798 |

## LINCOLNSHIRE

| *House* | *Owner (with address if different from first column)* |
|---|---|
| **Bede Houses**, Tattershall | *Access for exterior viewing noon to sunset daily* |
| **The Chateau**, Gate Burton, nr Gainsborough | The Landmark Trust *(WA)* |
| **East Lighthouse**, Sutton Bridge, Spalding PE12 9YT | Exterior viewing of House and wildfowl ponds year round. Cdr. M. D. Joel RN. *(WA)* for interior |
| **Fulbeck Manor**, Grantham | Mr J. F. Fane *(WA)* |
| **Harlaxton Manor**, Grantham | University of Evansville *(WA)* |
| **House of Correction**, Folkingham | The Landmark Trust, Shottesbrooke, Maidenhead SL6 3SW *(WA)* |
| **The Norman Manor House**, Boothby Pagnell | Lady Netherthorpe *(WA)* |
| **Pelham Mausoleum**, Limber, Grimsby | The Earl of Yarborough, Brocklesby Park, Habrough, Lincs |
| **Scrivelsby Court**, nr Horncastle | Lt Col J. L. M. Dymoke, M.B.E., D.L. *(WA)* |

## LONDON

| *House* | *Owner (with address if different from first column)* |
|---|---|
| **All Hallows Vicarage**, Tottenham, N17 | Rev R. Pearson 01-808 2470 |
| **69 Brick Lane**, E1 | *(WA)* |
| **24 The Butts**, Brentford | Mrs Sally Mills *(WA)* |
| **192, 194, 196, 198, 202, 204–224 Cable Street**, E1 | *(WA)* |
| **11–13 Cavendish Square**, W1 | Heythrop College *(WA)* |
| **Celia and Phillip, Blairman Houses**, Elder St, E1 | *(WA)* |
| **Charlton House**, Charlton, SE7 | London Borough of Greenwich *Apply to Manager* 01-856 3951 |
| **Charterhouse**, Charterhouse Square, EC1 | The Governors of Charterhouse *(WA) April 1 to July 31 – every Wed 2.45 pm* |
| **14/15 Clapton Square**, E5 | *(WA)* |
| **88/190 The Crescent**, Hertford Rd, N9 | *(WA)* |
| **17/27 Folgate Street**, E1 | *(WA)* |
| **36 Hanbury Street**, E1 | *(WA)* |
| **Heathgate House**, 66 Crooms Hill, Greenwich, SE10 8HN | Rev Mother Superior, Ursuline Convent 01-858 0779 |
| **House of St Barnabas-in-Soho**, 1 Greek St, W1V 6NQ | The Administrator and the Organising Guide to the House *(WA)* |
| **140, 142, 166, 168 Homerton High Street**, E5 | *(WA)* |
| **69/83 Paragon Road**, E5 | *(WA)* |
| **Permanent Exhibition of Judicial & Legal Costume**, Law Courts, Strand, WC2 | The Administrator *Adm free whenever building open* |
| **Red House**, Red House Lane, Bexleyheath | Mr & Mrs Hollamby *(WA only, with SAE) First Sat & Sun in month 2.30–4.30 pm* |
| **Rutland House**, Park Place, St James St, SW1 1LR | Royal Over-Seas League *Open 3–5 Spring Bank Holiday and August 1–31* |
| **Wesley's House**, 47 City Rd, EC1 | The Trustees of Wesley's Chapel *Open weekdays 10 am–4 pm* 01-253 2262 |

## MERSEYSIDE

| *House* | *Owner (with address if different from first column)* |
|---|---|
| **The Turner Home**, Dingle Head, Liverpool L8 9RN | *By appointment only with the Officer in Charge* 051-727 4177 |

## NORFOLK

| *House* | *Owner (with address if different from first column)* |
|---|---|
| **All Saints' Church**, Barmer | Norfolk Churches Trust Ltd – Keyholder – No 4 The Cottages on main road near the church. |
| **All Saints' Church**, Cockthorpe | Norfolk Churches Trust Ltd – Keyholder – Mrs Case at the farmhouse opposite the church. |
| **All Saints' Church**, Hargham | Norfolk Churches Trust Ltd – Keyholder – Mrs Clifford Amos, Station Road, Attleborough |
| **All Saints' Church**, Rackheath | Norfolk Churches Trust Ltd – Open |
| **All Saints' Church**, Snetterton | Norfolk Churches Trust Ltd – Keyholder – Mrs Clifford Amos, Station Road, Attleborough or Captain & Mrs Law, The Old Rectory, West of church. |
| **19-21 Bedford St**, Norwich. | *Open times as restaurant and shops. Norwich City Council* |
| **Billingford Mill**, nr Scole | Norfolk County Council *Norwich* 611122, Ext 5224 |
| **6 The Close**, Norwich | The Dean & Chapter of Norwich Cathedral *(WA) Apply to Tenant-Subud Norwich* |
| **2 The Close**, Norwich | |
| **3–4 The Close**, Norwich | |
| **27 The Close**, Norwich | |
| **32 The Close**, Norwich | |
| **34 The Close**, Norwich | Cathedral Steward's Office, Messrs Percy Howes & Co. 3 The Close, Norwich *(WA)* |
| **35 The Close**, Norwich | |
| **56 The Close (The Deanery)**, Norwich | |
| **64 The Close**, Norwich | |
| **73 The Close**, Norwich | |
| **Denver Mill**, off A10 | Norfolk County Council *Norwich* 611122, Ext 5224 |
| **Ditchingham Hall**, Ditchingham, Bungay | The Rt Hon Earl Ferrers |
| **Earlham Hall**, University of East Anglia, Norwich. | *By appointment with the School of Law, University of East Anglia.* (0603) 56161 |
| **Fishermen's Hospital**, Great Yarmouth | J. E. C. Lamb, FIH, Clerk to the Trustees *Great Yarmouth* 856609 |
| **Gowthorpe Manor**, Swardeston | Mrs Watkinson to Oct 1989 (0508) 470398, then *Mulbarton* 70216 |
| **Hales Hall**, Loddon | Mr & Mrs T. Read *(WA)* (050 846) 395 |
| **Hoveton House**, Wroxham | Mr J. C. C. Blofeld Open only to parties booked by prior appointment in writing, and not individuals. |
| **Lattice House**, King's Lynn | Mr and Mrs T. Duckett *(WA) Kings Lynn* (0553) 777292 |
| **Little Cressingham Mill**, Watton | Norfolk County Council *Norwich 611122 ext 5224* |
| **Little Hautbois Hall**, nr Norwich | Mrs Duffield *Buxton* 333 |
| **Manor House (The)**, Great Cressingham | Mrs F. Chapman *(WA)* |
| **Manor House (The)**, 54 Bracondale, Norwich | Mr P.B. Macqueen. Small parties welcome *(WA)* |
| **Music House (The)** at Wensum Lodge, King Street, Norwich | The Warden Norwich 666021/2 |
| **The Old Princes Inn Restaurant**, 20 Princes St, Norwich | *Open times as restaurant* (0603) 621043 |
| **Old Vicarage (The)**, Methwold, Thetford IP26 4NR | Mr & Mrs H. C. Dance (WA) |
| **St Andrew's Church**, Frenze | Norfolk Churches Trust Ltd – Keyholder – Mrs Alston at the farmhouse opposite or ask at adjacent cottage |
| **St Margaret's Church**, Moreton-on-the-Hill | Norfolk Churches Trust Ltd – Keyholder – Lady Prince-Smith at The Hall, NE of church |
| **St Mary's Church**, Bagthorpe | Norfolk Churches Trust Ltd – Open |
| **St Mary's Church**, Dunton | Norfolk Churches Trust Ltd – Open. Key of tower at Burwood Hall |
| **St Peter's Church**, West Rudham | Norfolk Churches Trust Ltd – Keyholder – Lord & Lady Romney, Wensum Farm or Mrs Walker, Pockthorpe Cottages, West Rudham |
| **Stracey Arms Mill**, nr Acle (A47) | Norfolk County Council *Norwich* 611122, Ext 5224 |
| **The Strangers' Club**, 22, 24 Elm Hill, Norwich | *By appointment with the Steward* (0603) 623814 |
| **Thoresby College**, Queen Street, King's Lynn | King's Lynn Preservation Trust *(WA)* |
| **Wilby Hall**, Quidenham | Mr & Mrs C. Warner *(WA)* |
| **Wiveton Hall**, Holt | D. MacCarthy *(WA)* |

Where it is necessary to write for an appointment to view, see code *(WA)*

## NORTHAMPTONSHIRE

| *House* | *Owner (with address if different from first column)* |
|---|---|
| **Astwell Castle**, nr Brackley | Mr Graham Pidgeon *(WA)* |
| **Courteenhall**, Northampton | Sir Hereward Wake, Bt. M.C. *(WA)* |
| **Drayton House**, Lowick, Kettering | L. G. Stopford Sackville *(WA)* |
| **Menagerie (The)**, Horton, Northampton | Mr Gervase Jackson-Stops *(WA)* |
| **Monastery (The)**, Shutlanger | Mr & Mrs R. G. Wigley *(WA)* |
| **Paine's Cottage**, Oundle | Mr R. O. Barber *(WA)* |

## NORTHUMBERLAND

| *House* | *Owner (with address if different from first column)* |
|---|---|
| **Capheaton Hall**, Newcastle upon Tyne | Exterior only. Mr J. Browne-Swinburne *(WA)* |
| **Craster Tower**, Alnwick | Lt Col J. M. Craster, Miss M. D. Craster, Mr F. Sharratt *(WA)* |
| **Elsdon Tower**, Elsdon | Mr G. N. Taylor *Otterburn* 20688 |
| **Harnham Hall**, Belsay | Mr J. Wake |
| **Netherwitton Hall**, Morpeth | Mr J. C. R. Trevelyon *(WA)* |

## NOTTINGHAMSHIRE

| *House* | *Owner (with address if different from first column)* |
|---|---|
| **Flintham Hall**, nr Newark | Mr M. T. Hildyard *(WA)* |
| **Winkburn Hall**, nr Southwell | Mr R. Craven-Smith-Milnes (0636) 86465 |
| **Worksop Priory Church and Gatehouse** | The Parish Office *Worksop* 472180 |

## OXFORDSHIRE

| *House* | *Owner (with address if different from first column)* |
|---|---|
| **39/43 The Causeway**, Steventon | Mr & Mrs H. C. Dance, The Old Vicarage, Methwold, Thetford, Norfolk IP26 4NR *(WA)* |
| **Cogges Priory**, Witney | The Oxford Diocesan Parsonages Board *(WA) Apply to The Incumbent, c/o Oxford Diocesan Parsonages Board, Church House, North Hinksey, Oxford* |
| **26/7 Cornmarket Street,** and **26 Ship Street**, Oxford | Shop on ground and first floors open during normal trading hours shop basement by written appt. Laura Ashley Ltd., Braywick House, Braywick Rd., Maidenhead SL6 1DW. 2nd floor by written appt. Home Bursar, Jesus College, Oxford OX1 3DW. |
| **Cote House**, Aston | Mrs David Anderson *(WA)* |
| **85 High Street**, Banbury | Mrs E. Zwirn, Mr H. Cohen & Mrs S. Sherwood (Bennett's Estates (London) Ltd) *(WA)* |
| **Hope House**, Woodstock | Mrs D. M. Money *(WA)* |
| **Manor (The)**, Chalgrove | Mr & Mrs Paul L. Jacques *(WA)* |
| **Monarch's Court House**, Benson | Mr R. S. Hine *(WA)* |
| **Ripon College**, Cuddesdon | The Principal *(WA)* |

## SHROPSHIRE

| *House* | *Owner (with address if different from first column)* |
|---|---|
| **Cronkhill House**, nr. Crosshouses, Shrewsbury. | The National Trust. House designed c.1803 by John Nash *(WA)* Mrs L. Motley (tenant) |
| **Guildhall, The**, Dogpole, Shrewsbury | Shrewsbury & Atcham Borough Council *(WA)* |
| **Hatton Grange**, Shifnal | Mrs P. Afia, Mon and Fri only May 1–Aug 10 *(WA)* |
| **Moat House, The**, Longnor, Shrewsbury SY5 7PP | Mr C.P. Richards (074 373) 434 |
| **Morville Hall**, nr Bridgnorth | The National Trust (tenant Mr J. K. Norbury) *(WA)* |
| **Rowleys House and Mansion**, Barker St, Shrewsbury | Shrewsbury & Atcham Borough Council *Open daily except winter Suns* |
| **Stanwardine Hall**, Cockshutt, Ellesmere | Mr D. J. Bridge *Cockshutt* 212 |

## SOMERSET

| *House* | *Owner (with address if different from first column)* |
|---|---|
| **Cothelstone Manor and Gatehouse**, Cothelstone, Taunton | Mrs E. Warmington, Cothelstone House Estate, Cothelstone Manor, Cothelstone *(WA)* |
| **Manor Farm**, Meare, Wells | Mrs I. M. Bull (tenant Mr C. J. Look) |
| **Old Drug Store (The)**, Axbridge | Mr & Mrs K. E. J. D. Schofield *(WA)* |
| **Old Hall (The)**, Croscombe | The Landmark Trust, Shottesbrooke, nr Maidenhead, Berks *(WA)* |
| **Manor House (Elizabethan)**, Crowcombe | The Manager *(WA)* |
| **The Priest's House**, Holcombe Rogus, nr Wellington | The Landmark Trust *(WA)* |
| **Stogursey Castle**, Stogursey, nr Bridgwater | The Landmark Trust *(WA)* |
| **West Coker Manor**, West Coker BA22 9BJ | Mr & Mrs Derek Maclaren. Open during August. (093 586) 2646 |
| **Whitelackington Manor**, Ilminster | Dillington Estate Office, Ilminster *(WA)* |

## STAFFORDSHIRE

| *House* | *Owner (with address if different from first column)* |
|---|---|
| **Broughton Hall**, Eccleshall | The Administrator *(WA)* |
| **The Great Hall in Keele Hall**, Keele | Registrar, University of Keele *(WA)* |
| **Old Hall Gatehouse (The)**, Mavesyn Ridware | Mr R. M. Eades *Armitage* 490312 |
| **Park Hall**, Leigh | Mr E. J. Knobbs *(WA)* |
| **Tixall Gatehouse**, Tixall | The Landmark Trust, Shottesbrooke, nr Maidenhead, Berks *(WA)* |

## SUFFOLK

| *House* | *Owner (with address if different from first column)* |
|---|---|
| **Deanery (The)**, Hadleigh | The Dean of Bocking *Hadleigh* 822218 |
| **Hall (The)**, Great Bricett, nr Ipswich | Mr & Mrs R. B. Cooper *(WA)* |
| **Hengrave Hall**, Bury St Edmunds | The Warden, Hengrave Hall Centre, Bury St Edmunds *(WA) Bury St. Edmunds* 701561 |
| **Moat Hall**, Parham, nr Woodbridge | Mr J. W. Gray *Wickham Market* 746317 |
| **Newbourne Hall**, nr Woodbridge | John Somerville Esq *(WA)* |
| **New Inn (The)**, Peasenhall | The Landmark Trust, Shottesbrooke, nr Maidenhead, Berks *Great Hall open daily* |
| **Worlingham Hall**, Beccles | Viscount Colville of Culross *(WA)* |

## SURREY

| *House* | *Owner (with address if different from first column)* |
|---|---|
| **Crossways Farm**, Abinger Hammer | Mr C. T. Hughes (tenant) *(WA)* |
| **St. Mary's Homes**, Church Lane, Godstone | Open Oct to Mar 10–4; Apr to Sept 10–6 (0883) 842385 |
| **Sunbury Court**, Sunbury-on-Thames, Middx | The Salvation Army *Sunbury* 782196 |

## EAST SUSSEX

| *House* | *Owner (with address if different from first column)* |
|---|---|
| **Ashdown House**, nr Forest Row | The Headmaster, Ashdown House School *Forest Row* 2574 |
| **Laughton Tower**, nr Lewes | The Landmark Trust, Shottesbrooke, nr Maidenhead, Berks *(WA)* |

## WEST SUSSEX

| *House* | *Owner (with address if different from first column)* |
|---|---|
| **Chantry Green House**, Steyning | Mr & Mrs G. H. Recknell *Steyning* 81-2239 |
| **Chapel (The), Bishop's Palace**, Chichester | Church Commissioners, The Palace, Chichester *(WA)* **only** *to The Chaplain* |
| **Christ's Hospital**, Horsham | School buildings open by appointment with School Secretary (0403) 52547 |

## TYNE & WEAR

| *House* | *Owner (with address if different from first column)* |
|---|---|
| **Gibside Banqueting House**, nr Whickham | The Landmark Trust, Shottesbrooke, nr Maidenhead, Berks *(WA)* |

## WARWICKSHIRE

| *House* | *Owner (with address if different from first column)* |
|---|---|
| **Binswood Hall**, Binswood Ave, Leamington Spa | North Leamington School *(WA) to Head of Hall* |
| **Foxcote**, Shipston-on-Stour | Mr C. B. Holman *(WA)* |
| **Nicholas Chamberlain's Almshouses**, Bedworth | The Warden (0203) 312225 |
| **Northgate**, Warwick | Mr R. E. Phillips *(WA)* |
| **St Leonard's Church**, Wroxall | T. W. Alsop, Bursar, Wroxall Abbey School, Warwick CV35 7NB *(WA)* |
| **War Memorial Town Hall**, Alcester | The Secretary, Mr J. W. Roberts, 10 Haselor Close, Alcester B49 6QD *Alcester* (0789) 762101 *or* Mr J. Adams (762648) |

## WILTSHIRE

| *House* | *Owner (with address if different from first column)* |
|---|---|
| ***Abbey House (The)**, Malmesbury | Sister-in-Charge (066 82) 2212 |
| **Chinese Summerhouse**, Amesbury Abbey, Amesbury | Visitors are requested to keep to the paths indicated. For open days Tel: (0980) 22957 |
| **Farley Hospital**, Farley | The Warden *Farley* 231 |
| **Grove (The)**, Corsham | Trustees of Corsham Estate *(WA)* |
| **Little Clarendon**, Dinton | The National Trust (Sq Leader A. C. Southward) *(WA)* |
| **Milton Manor**, Pewsey | Mrs Rupert Gentle (0672) 63344 |
| **Old Bishop's Palace**, 1 The Close, Salisbury | The Bursar, The Cathedral School *Salisbury* 22652 |
| **Old Manor House (The)**, 5 Whitehead Lane, Bradford on Avon | Mr John Teed *(WA)* |
| **Orpins House**, Church Street, Bradford-on-Avon | Mr J. Vernon Burchell *(WA)* |
| **Porch House (The)**, Potterne, nr Devizes | *(WA)* |
| **Roche Old Court**, Winterslow | Major H. B. Trevor Cox *(WA)* |

## NORTH YORKSHIRE

| *House* | *Owner (with address if different from first column)* |
|---|---|
| **Allerton Park**, nr Knaresborough | Michael Farr, Administrator (0423) 330632 |
| **Beamsley Hospital**, nr Skipton | The Landmark Trust, Shottesbrooke, Maidenhead, SL6 3SW *(WA)* |
| **Broughton Hall**, Skipton | H. R. Tempest Esq *Skipton* 2267 |
| **Busby Hall**, Carlton-in-Cleveland | Mr G. A. Marwood *(WA)* |
| **Cawood Castle**, nr Selby | The Landmark Trust, Shottesbrooke, Maidenhead, SL6 3SW *(WA)* |
| **Chapel and Coach House**, Aske, Richmond | *Open daily during August 11 am–6 pm* |
| **The Church of Our Lady and Saint Everilda**, Everingham | *View by appointment. Donations.* Key at Rockby Hse, Everingham (0696) 73202 |
| **Culloden Tower (The)**, Richmond | The Landmark Trust, Shottesbrooke, nr Maidenhead, Berks *(WA)* |
| **The Dovecote**, Forcett Hall, Forcett, nr Richmond | External viewing from road through Forcett (B6274) Internal viewing – apply Mrs P. E. Heathcote, Forcett Hall, Forcett, Richmond (0325) 718226 |
| **Home Farm House**, Old Scriven, Knaresborough | Mr G. T. Reece *(WA)* |
| **Moulton Hall**, nr Richmond | The National Trust (tenant the Hon. J. D. Eccles) *(WA)* |
| **Old Rectory (The)**, Foston, nr York | Mrs R. F. Wormald *(WA)* |

## WEST YORKSHIRE

| *House* | *Owner (with address if different from first column)* |
|---|---|
| **Fulneck Boys' School**, Pudsey | I. D. Cleland, B.A., M.Phil., Headmaster *(WA) Open during school holidays only* |
| **Grand Theatre & Opera House (The)**, Leeds | Warren Smith, General Manager (0532) 456014 |
| **Horbury Hall**, Horbury, nr Wakefield | D. J. H. Michelmore Esq (0924) 277552 |
| **Old Hall (The)**, Calverley, nr Pudsey, Leeds | The Landmark Trust, Shottesbrooke, nr Maidenhead, Berks *(WA)* |
| **Town Hall**, Leeds | Leeds City Council *Leeds* 462352 |
| **Weston Hall**, nr Otley | Lt Col H. V. Dawson *(WA)* |

# WALES

## CLWYD

| House | Owner (with address if different from first column) |
|---|---|
| **Fferm**, Pontblyddyn, Mold | Dr M. C. Jones-Mortimer *Apply to tenant* *Pontybodkin* 770371 |
| **Gatehouse at Gilar Farm**, Pentrefoclas | Mr P. J. Warbourton-Lee *(WA)* |
| **Gwrch Castle**, Abergele | Miss J. Donald Abergele (0745) 825007 |
| **Halghton Hall**, Bangor-on-Dee, Wrexham | Mr J. D. Lewis *(WA)* |
| **Lindisfarne College**, Wynnstay Hall, Ruabon | The Headmaster (0978) 810407 |
| **Nerquis Hall**, Mold | Mr A. W. Furse *(WA)* |
| **Pen Isa'r Glascoed**, Bodelwyddan | Mr M. E. Harrop *St Asaph* 583501 |
| **Plas Uchaf**, Llangar | The Landmark Trust, Shottesbrooke, nr Maidenhead, Berks *(WA)* |

## DYFED

| House | Owner (with address if different from first column) |
|---|---|
| **French Mill**, Carew | Mr Anthony Trollope-Bellew *April to Sept* |
| **Old Hall (The)**, Monkton, Pembroke | The Landmark Trust, Shottesbrooke, nr Maidenhead, Berks *(WA)* |
| **St David's University College**, Lampeter | Principal: Professor Brian Morris *Lampeter* 422-351 |
| **Taliaris Park**, Llandeilo | Mr J. H. Spencer-Williams *(WA)* |
| **West Blockhouse**, Dale, Haverfordwest | The Landmark Trust, Shottesbrooke, Maidenhead SL6 3SW *(WA)* |

## GWENT

| House | Owner (with address if different from first column) |
|---|---|
| **Blackbrook House**, Skenfrith | Mr G. F. W. Buckland *Skenfrith* 238 |
| **Castle Hill House**, Monmouth | Mr T. Baxter-Wright *(WA)* |
| **Clytha Castle**, nr Abergavenny | The Landmark Trust, Shottesbrooke, nr Maidenhead, Berks *(WA)* |
| **Cwrt Porth Hir**, Llanover | Coldbrook & Llanover Estate *(WA)* |
| **Great Cil-Lwch**, Llantilio Crossenny | Mr J. F. Ingledew *(WA)* |
| **Kemys House**, Kemys Inferior, Caerleon | Mr I. S. Burge *(WA)* |
| **Overmonnow House** (formerly Vicarage), Monmouth | Mr J. R. Pangbourne *(WA)* |
| **3/4 Priory Street**, Monmouth | Mr H. R. Ludwig *(WA)* |
| **St James House**, Monmouth | The Governors of Monmouth School: The Haberdashers Co *(WA)* |
| **Treowen**, Wonastow, Monmouth | Mr R. H. Wheelock *Dingestow* 224 |

## GWYNEDD

| House | Owner (with address if different from first column) |
|---|---|
| **Bath Tower (The)**, Caernarfon | The Landmark Trust, Shottesbrooke, nr Maidenhead, Berks *(WA)* |
| **Cymryd**, Conwy | Miss D. E. Glynne *(WA)* |
| **Dolaugwyn**, Towyn | Mrs S. Tudor *(WA)* |
| **Nannau**, Llanfachreth, nr Dolgellau | Mr P. Vernon *(WA)* |
| **Penmynydd**, Alms Houses, Llanfairpwll | Rev G. M. Hughes *(Hon Secretary)* *(WA)* |
| **Plas Coch**, Llanedwen, Llanfairpwll | Mrs N. Donald *Llanfairpwll* (0248) 714272 |
| **Royal Welsh Yacht Club**, Porth Yr Aur, Caernarfon | T. W. Williams, D.F.C., 64 High St, Llanberis *Llanberis* 331 |

## MID GLAMORGAN

| House | Owner (with address if different from first column) |
|---|---|
| **Llancaiach Fawr**, Nelson | Rhymney Valley District Council *Apply to Public Relations Officer* *Hengoed* 815588 |

## POWYS

| House | Owner (with address if different from first column) |
|---|---|
| **Abercamlais**, Brecon | Mrs J. C. R. Ballance *(WA)* |
| **Abercynrig**, Llanfrynach | Mr W. R. Lloyd, Abercynrig, Brecon, Powys LD3 7AQ *(WA)* |
| **1 Buckingham Place**, Brecon | Mrs Meeres *(WA)* |
| **3 Buckingham Place**, Brecon | Mr & Mrs A. Whiley *(WA)* |
| **Maesmawr Hall Hotel**, Caersws | Mr & Mrs J. Kendal (068 684) 255 |
| **Newton Farm**, Brecon | Mrs Ballance *(WA) to Mr D. L. Evans, tenant* |
| **Pen-Y-Lan**, Meifod | Mr S. R. J. Meade *Meifod* 202 |
| **Plasau Duon**, Clatter | Mr C. Breese |
| **Plas Llangattock**, Crickhowell | Mr J. P. C. Sankey-Barker *Crickhowell* 810484 |
| **Rhydycarw**, Trefeglwys, Caersws | Mr M. Breese-Davies *Trefeglwys* 363 |
| **Ydderw**, Llyswen | Mr D. P. Eckley *(WA)* |

## SOUTH GLAMORGAN

| House | Owner (with address if different from first column) |
|---|---|
| **Fonmon Castle**, Barry | Sir Brooke Boothby, Bt *Rhoose* (0446) 710206 |
| **Great House (The)**, Llantwit Major | Mr C. Baxter Jones *Llantwit Major* 2483 |

## WEST GLAMORGAN

| House | Owner (with address if different from first column) |
|---|---|
| **Penrice Castle**, Penrice, Reynoldston, Gower, Swansea | Mr C. Methuen-Campbell *(WA)* |

# SCOTLAND

## BORDERS REGION

| House | Owner (with address if different from first column) |
|---|---|
| **Darnick Tower**, Melrose | Mrs T. H. Wilson *Melrose* 2735 |
| **Old Gala House**, Galashiels | Ettrick & Lauderdale District Council *Open Apr to Oct daily except Tues* *Galashiels* 2611 |
| **Sir Walter Scott's Courtroom**, Selkirk | Ettrick & Lauderdale District Council *Open weekdays in July & Aug. Other times by appt.* *Selkirk* 20096 |
| **Wedderlie House**, Gordon TD3 6NW | Mrs J. R. L. Campbell *Westruther* 223 |

## CENTRAL REGION

| House | Owner (with address if different from first column) |
|---|---|
| **Bardowie Castle**, by Milngavie | Mr R. T. Allen *Balmore* 366 |
| **Castlecary Castle**, by Bonnybridge, Stirlingshire | Mr Hugo B. Millar *(WA)* |
| **Gargunnock House**, by Stirling | Miss V. H. C. Stirling, C.B.E. *(WA)* |
| **Old Tolbooth Building**, Stirling | Stirling District Council, Municipal Buildings, Corn Exchange Rd *Stirling* 79000 |
| **Pineapple (The)**, Dunmore, Airth | The Landmark Trust, Shottesbrooke, nr Maidenhead, Berks *(WA)* |
| **Touch House**, by Stirling | Mr P. B. Buchanan *(WA)* |

## DUMFRIES & GALLOWAY REGION

| House | Owner (with address if different from first column) |
|---|---|
| **Bonshaw Tower**, Kirtlebridge, nr Annan | Dr J. B. Irving *View by appointment* *Kirtlebridge* 256 |
| **Carnsalloch House**, Kirkton, nr Dumfries | The Leonard Cheshire Foundation *Dumfries* 54924 |
| **Craigdarroch House**, Moniaive | Major and Mrs H. F. Stanley *Moniaive* 202 |
| **Kirkconnell House**, New Abbey, nr Dumfries | Mr F. Maxwell Witham *New Abbey* 276 |
| **Tolbooth**, Royal Burgh of Sanquhar | Mr T. A. Johnston *Sanquhar* 303 |

## FIFE REGION

| House | Owner (with address if different from first column) |
|---|---|
| **Bath Castle**, Bogside, nr Oakley | Mr Angus Mitchell, 20 Regent Terrace, Edinburgh EH7 5BS 031-556 7671 |
| **Castle (The)**, Elie | Miss Scott-Moncrieff *(WA)* |

## GRAMPIAN REGION

| House | Owner (with address if different from first column) |
|---|---|
| **Balbithan House**, Kintore | Mrs M. McMurtrie *Kintore* 32282 |
| **Balfluig Castle** | Mr Mark Tennant, 30 Abbey Gardens, London NW8 9AT *(WA)* |
| **Barra Castle**, Old Meldrum | Dr & Mrs Andrew Bogdan *(WA)* |
| **Castle of Fiddes**, Stonehaven | Dr M. Weir *Drumlithie* 213 |
| **Corsindae House**, Sauchen | Mr Laurence Fyffe *(WA)* |
| **Craig Castle**, Lumsden | Mrs C. G. M. Barlas of Craig *Lumsden* 202 |
| **Craigston Castle**, Turriff | Bruce Urquhart of Craigston *Temporarily closed due to urgent repairs* *King Edward* (08885) 228 |
| **Drumminor Castle**, Rhynie | Mr A. D. Forbes *(WA)* |
| **Gordonstoun School**, Elgin *(Round Square only)* | The Headmaster, Gordonstoun School *(WA)* |
| **Grandhome House**, nr Aberdeen | D. R. Paton Esq *Aberdeen* 72 2202 |
| **Kintore Town House**, Kintore | Gordon District Council *Inverurie* 20981 |
| **Phesdo House**, Laurencekirk | Mr J. M. Thomson *(WA)* |
| **Pluscarden Abbey**, Elgin | The Abbot *Dallas* 257 |

## HIGHLAND REGION

| House | Owner (with address if different from first column) |
|---|---|
| **Embo House**, Dornoch | Mr John G. Mackintosh *Dornoch* 810260 |

## LOTHIAN REGION

| House | Owner (with address if different from first column) |
|---|---|
| **Arniston House**, Gorebridge | Mr & Mrs A. R. Dundas-Bekker *(WA)* |
| **Cakemuir**, Tynehead | Mr M. M. Scott *(WA)* |
| **Castle Gogar**, Edinburgh | Lady Steel-Maitland *Corstorphine* 1234 |
| **Ford House**, Ford | F. P. Tindall, O.B.E. *(WA)* |
| **108–110 Grassmarket**, Edinburgh | Mr & Mrs Paul Coutts *(WA)* |
| **Linnhouse**, nr Livingston | Mr H. J. Spurway *(WA)* |
| **Newbattle Abbey College**, Dalkeith | The Principal 031-663 1921 |
| **Northfield House**, Prestonpans | Mr W. Schomberg Scott *(WA)* |
| **Peffermill House**, Peffermill Rd, Edinburgh EH16 5UX | Nicholas Groves-Raines, Architects 031-661 7172/3 |
| **Penicuik House**, Penicuik | Sir John Clerk, Bt *(WA)* |
| **Preston Hall**, Pathhead | Major J. H. Callander *(WA)* |
| **Roseburn House**, Murrayfield | Miss M. E. Sturgeon *(WA)* |
| **Forth Road Bridge**, South Queensferry | The Bridgemaster 031-319 1699 |
| **Town House**, Haddington | East Lothian District Council *Access at all reasonable times* |

## SHETLAND ISLANDS AREA

| House | Owner (with address if different from first column) |
|---|---|
| **Lodberrie (The)**, Lerwick | Mr Thomas Moncrieff |

## STRATHCLYDE REGION

| House | Owner (with address if different from first column) |
|---|---|
| **Barcaldine Castle**, Benderloch | Morton, Fraser & Milligan, W. S., 19 York Place, Edinburgh EH1 3EL (Trustees of Sir A. W. D. Campbell) *(WA)* |
| **Craufurdland Castle**, Kilmarnock | J. P. Houison Craufurd Esq (056 06) 402 |
| **Duntrune Castle**, Lochgilphead | Robin Malcolm of Poltalloch *(WA)* |
| **Kelburn Castle**, Fairlie | The Earl of Glasgow *(WA)* |
| **New Lanark**, Lanark | New Lanark Conservation Trust, Mill No. 3, New Lanark Mills, Lanark ML11 9DB (0555) 61345 |
| **Place of Paisley (The)**, Paisley | Paisley Abbey, Kirk Session *(WA) Apply to Minister* |
| **Saddell Castle**, nr Campbeltown | The Landmark Trust, Shottesbrooke, nr Maidenhead, Berks *(WA)* |
| **Tangy Mill**, nr Campbeltown | The Landmark Trust, Shottesbrooke, nr Maidenhead, Berks *(WA)* |
| **Tannahill's Cottage**, Queen St, Paisley | Secretary, Paisley Burns Club 041-887 7500 |

## TAYSIDE REGION

| House | Owner (with address if different from first column) |
|---|---|
| **Ardblair Castle**, Blairgowrie | Laurence P. K. Blair Oliphant *Blairgowrie* 3155 |
| **Craig House**, Montrose | Charles F. R. Hoste *Montrose* 72239 |
| **Kinross House**, Kinross *(Garden only)* | Sir David Montgomery, Bt *(WA)* |
| **Michael Bruce's Cottage**, Kinnesswood | The Caretaker |
| **The Pavilion**, Gleneagles, Auchterarder PH3 1PJ | J. Martin Haldane Esq. *(WA)* |
| **Tulliebole Castle**, Crook of Devon | The Lord Moncreiff *By appointment only* *Fossoway* 236 |

# WE'VE BEEN *visited by* THE SCOTS, *the PICTS,* THE ROMANS, *the* SAXONS, THE *NORMANS,* *the* VIKINGS, & *the ENGLISH.*

*Historic Scotland have 330 properties from Skara Brae on Orkney to Jedburgh Abbey in the Borders.*

*Some dating back to 3000 BC.*

*Throughout the centuries, these time honoured stones haven't been short of visitors, though on occasion, friendship was sadly lacking.*

*To preserve our castles, palaces, gardens and abbeys for future visitors, we need friends.*

*Friends, who'll visit them and cherish them.*

*For as little as £10 each year you can become a Friend of the Scottish Monuments. (A family ticket is only £15, senior citizens £5.)*

*For this sum, you'll have a full year's free entry to all our sites and, in your first year, half price entry to English Heritage and Welsh Cadw sites too. Free entry in your second year.*

*And a free Directory packed with information and maps plus a regular newsletter to keep you in touch with all our activities.*

*For further details on becoming a Friend of the Scottish Monuments contact us at the address below or ask at any manned monument.*

*Nowadays, Scots, Picts, Romans, Saxons, Normans, Vikings and English are more than welcome.*

EDINBURGH CASTLE
*Standing proudly on a rock that has been a fortress since time immemorial.*

STIRLING CASTLE
*Dominates the surrounding area from its 250ft rock and once housed Wallace, Bruce, Mary Queen of Scots.*

FORT GEORGE
*11 miles NE of Inverness, by the village of Ardersier. Begun in 1748 following the battle of Culloden.*

JEDBURGH ABBEY
*Founded by David I dating from c. 1118, perhaps the finest of the four great Border Abbeys.*

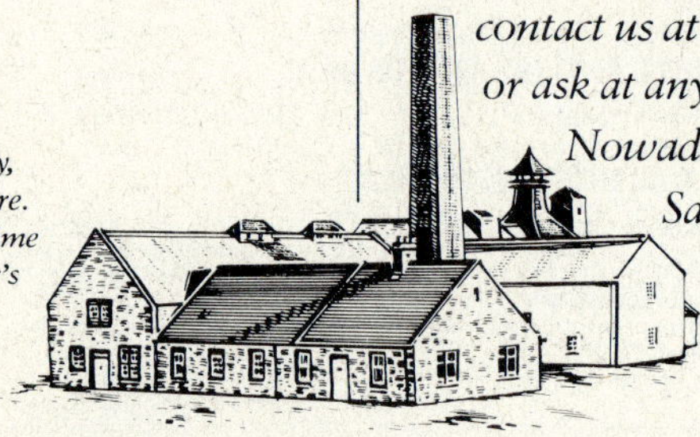

DALLAS DHU DISTILLERY
*Dallas Dhu Distillery, near Forres, Morayshire. A perfectly preserved time capsule of the distiller's craft.*

## NOW WE *could use some* *FRIENDS*

## HISTORIC SCOTLAND

*Five thousand years of history. All yours for less than £1 per month.*

*Historic Scotland, 20 Brandon Street, Edinburgh EH3 5RA. Tel: 031-244 3099. (Monday-Friday 9am-5pm.)*

# English Heritage

## YOUR GATEWAY TO HISTORIC ENGLAND

English Heritage cares for over 350 historic properties throughout England – prehistoric and Roman remains, castles and monasteries, houses and gardens, and much more. These are the tangible reminders of England's past, and fundamental elements in our landscape, literature and art.

This supplement describes a careful selection of these properties. From the austere life of a medieval fortress to the elegance of a stately home, from the rugged prospect of Hadrian's Wall to the tranquillity of a Cistercian monastery, English Heritage has something to offer everyone.

## BEDFORDSHIRE

### BUSHMEAD PRIORY

*map K6*
Telephone: (023 062) 614

The priory was a small house for Augustinian canons and founded in about 1195. The remains consist of the 13th century canon's refectory occupying one side of the former cloister. The timber-framed roof is a rare example of an almost complete crown-post construction of about 1250. The refectory contains wall-paintings and interesting stained glass.

**Location:** 4 m west of A1 at St Neots. OS map ref TL115607.
**Opening Times:** Open Good Friday to Sept 30 10–6, weekends only. Adm 80p, OAPs 60p, Chd 40p.

### WREST PARK HOUSE AND GARDENS

*map K5*
Telephone: (0525) 60718

Here is a history of English gardening in the grand manner from 1700–1850, which would not, of course, be complete without some designs by 'Capability' Brown. Every whim of fashion is represented, whether it be for a Chinese bridge, artificial lake, classical temple or rustic ruin. The present house was built about 1839 by the Earl de Grey, whose family had been Lord of the Manor of Wrest for 600 years. The State Rooms and gardens are open to the public.

**Location:** ¾ m (1 km) east of Silsoe off A6. OS map ref TL093356.
**Open:** Good Friday to Sept 30, 10–6 weekends and Bank Holidays only. Adm £1.10, OAPs 80p, Chd 55p.

## CAMBRIDGESHIRE

### DENNY ABBEY

*map K6*
Telephone: (022 024) 489

After a brief life as a Benedictine priory, the abbey passed to the Knights Templar who used it as a hospital for their sick and aged members. In 1308 the Order was suppressed and the inmates arrested. The abbey remained empty until 1339 when the widowed Countess of Pembroke acquired it and moved the Franciscan nuns from her Abbey at Waterbeach to Denny. Most of the monastic buildings were demolished in the 16th century, but there are remnants of the 12th century church and 14th century additions.

**Location:** 6 m (9.7 km) north of Cambridge on A10. OS map ref TL495684.
**Opening Times:** Good Friday to Sept 30, daily 10–6; Oct 1 to Maundy Thursday, Sun only 10–4. *Closed Christmas and New Year.* Adm 80p, OAPs 60p, Chd 40p.

WREST PARK HOUSE AND GARDENS

## CAMBRIDGESHIRE – *continued*

### LONGTHORPE TOWER

*map K6*
Telephone: (0733) 268482

This three-storey tower, added to an existing fortified manor house about 1300, is remarkable for the richness and completeness of its early 14th century wall-paintings. These were discovered less than 40 years ago under layers of limewash and distemper, and depict scenes from the Bible and of life in the East Anglian countryside; the most complete set of such paintings of the period in England.

**Location:** 2 m (3.2 km) west of Peterborough on A47. OS map ref TL163983.
**Opening Times:** Good Friday to Sept 30, daily 10–6; Oct 1 to Maundy Thursday, daily 10–4. *Closed Mons, Christmas and New Year.* Adm 80p, OAPs 60p, Chd 40p.

## CHESHIRE ⌗

### BEESTON CASTLE

*map F8*
Telephone: (0829) 260464

Built on an isolated crag, Beeston Castle is visible for miles around. The view across the Cheshire plain extends to the Pennines in the east and westwards to Wales. Begun about 1220 by Ranulf de Blundeville, the castle was further fortified by Edward I. The ditch alone can have been no small task, as it is hewn from the solid rock. There is an exhibition on the history of the castle in the museum.

**Location:** 2 m (3.2 km) west of Bunbury. 11m (18 km) south east of Chester. OS map ref SJ537593.
**Opening Times:** Good Friday to Sept 30, daily 10–6; Oct 1 to Maundy Thursday, daily 10–4. *Closed Mons, Christmas and New Year.* Adm £1.30, OAPs £1, Chd 65p.

## CLEVELAND ⌗

### GISBOROUGH PRIORY

*map H11*
Telephone: (0287) 38301

Founded in the 12th century for Augustinian canons by Robert de Brus, the priory was among the richest and most magnificent in the north. The remains include an impressive gatehouse, and the wonderful east wall, an important example of early Gothic architecture.

**Location:** Guisborough, next to the parish church. OS map ref NZ618163.
**Opening Times:** Good Friday to Sept 30, daily 10–6; Oct 1 to Maundy Thursday, daily 10–4. *Closed Mons, Christmas and New Year.* Adm 55p, OAPs 40p, Chd 25p.

## CORNWALL ⌗

### CHYSAUSTER ANCIENT VILLAGE

*map C1*
Telephone: (0736) 61889

Halfway up a hillside, through a stone passage, lie the stone houses erected by our prehistoric ancestors. By the time the Romans came the village had already existed for two centuries. Each house, built around a courtyard, had its own terrace. Were these the earliest gardens?

**Location:** 2½ m (3.5 km) north west of Gulval, near Penzance. OS map ref SW473350.
**Opening Times:** Good Friday to Sept 30, daily 10–6; Oct 1 to Maundy Thursday, daily 10–4. *Closed Mons, Christmas and New Year.* Adm 80p, OAPs 60p, Chd 40p.

### LAUNCESTON CASTLE

*map D2*
Telephone: (0566) 2365

The impressive round keep stands high on its grassy mound within a circular wall. Inside, a tall cylindrical tower soars from the centre. The space between tower and keep was roofed. Like Launceston itself, the castle was important in the Middle Ages. Small site museum.

**Location:** Launceston. OS map ref SX330846.
**Opening Times:** Good Friday to Sept 30, daily 10–6; Oct 1 to Maundy Thursday, daily 10–4. *Closed Mons, Christmas and New Year.* Adm 80p, OAPs 60p, Chd 40p.

### PENDENNIS CASTLE

*map C1*
Telephone: (0326) 316594

Henry VIII's reply to the Pope's threatened crusade against him was to fortify his coastline. Two castles guarded the Fal Estuary, Pendennis and St Mawes. Built high on a promontory, Pendennis saw action in the Civil War when 'Jack-for-the-King' Arundell held the castle for five terrible months. It continued in military use until 1946. Also, see museum, exhibition, 1588 gun deck tableau.

**Location:** Pendennis Head 1 m (1.6 km) south east of Falmouth. OS map ref SW824318.
**Opening Times:** Good Friday to Sept 30, daily 10–6; Oct 1 to Maundy Thursday, daily 10–4. *Closed Mons, Christmas and New Year.* Adm £1.30, OAPs £1, Chd 65p.

### RESTORMEL CASTLE

*map D2*
Telephone: (0208) 872687

Crowning a hill overlooking the River Fowey, the castle rises steeply above a dry but deep, wide moat. The outer 12th century wall is a perfect circle. Domestic buildings were later added inside and a rectangular chapel outside.

**Location:** 1½ m (2.4 km) north of Lostwithiel. OS map ref SX104614.
**Opening Times:** Good Friday to Sept 30, daily 10–6; Oct 1 to Maundy Thursday, daily 10–4. *Closed Mons, Christmas and New Year.* Adm 80p, OAPs 60p, Chd 40p.

### ST MAWES CASTLE

*map C1*
Telephone: (0326) 270526

Shaped like a clover leaf, this small 16th century castle, still intact, nestles among rock plants and tropical shrubs. During the Civil War the Governor capitulated without gunfire or bloodshed, unlike Pendennis on the opposite shore.

**Location:** St Mawes. OS map ref SW842328.
**Opening Times:** Good Friday to Sept 30, daily 10–6; Oct 1 to Maundy Thursday, daily 10–4. *Closed Mons, Christmas and New Year.* Adm 80p, OAPs 60p, Chd 40p.

### TINTAGEL CASTLE

*map D2*
Telephone: (0840) 770328

Amazing that anything has survived on this wild, windswept coast. Yet fragments of Earl Reginald's great hall, built about 1145, and Earl Richard's 13th century wall and iron gate still stand in this incomparable landscape. No wonder that King Arthur and his Knights were thought to have dwelt here. Site exhibition.

**Location:** ½ m (0.8 km) north west of Tintagel. OS map ref SX048891.
**Opening Times:** Good Friday to Sept 30, daily 10–6; Oct 1 to Maundy Thursday, daily 10–4. *Closed Mons, Christmas and New Year.* Adm £1.30, OAPs £1, Chd 65p.

DENNY ABBEY

GISBOROUGH PRIORY

# CUMBRIA ⌗

## BROUGH CASTLE
*map G11*
Telephone: (093 04) 219

The importance of Brough-under-Stainmore, lying between Carlisle and York, did not escape the Romans. So it is hardly surprising that the Normans built a stronghold on the site of that derelict Roman fort. The Scots destroyed it in 1174 and the present castle is a product of the rebuilding that followed. Until 1204 Brough was a royal castle; then King John granted it to Robert de Vipont, ancestor of the Lords Clifford. Part of the 11th century wall remains and much of the 17th century repair work carried out by that energetic restorer of castles, Lady Anne Clifford.

**Location:** 8 m (13 km) south east of Appleby. OS map ref NY791141.
**Opening Times:** Good Friday to Sept 30, daily 10–6; Oct 1 to Maundy Thursday, daily 10–4. *Closed Mons, Christmas and New Year.* Adm 55p, OAPs 40p, Chd 25p.

## BROUGHAM CASTLE
*map F11*
Telephone: (0768) 62488

The oldest part of the surviving building, the keep, was constructed in Henry II's reign after the Scots had relinquished their hold on the north west of England. The keep, later heightened, and its gatehouses formed an impregnable fortress, while also providing a lordly residence of spacious proportions.

**Location:** 1½ m (2.4 km) east of Penrith. OS map ref NY537290.
**Opening Times:** Good Friday to Sept 30, daily 10–6; Oct 1 to Maundy Thursday, daily 10–4. *Closed Mons, Christmas and New Year.* Adm 80p, OAPs 60p, Chd 40p.

## CARLISLE CASTLE
*map F11*
Telephone: (0228) 31777

Twenty-six years after the Battle of Hastings, Carlisle remained unconquered. In 1092 William II marched north, took the city and ordered the building of a stronghold above the River Eden. Since William's time the castle has survived 800 years of fierce and bloody attacks, extensive rebuilding and continuous military occupation. A massive Norman keep contains an exhibition on the history of the castle.

**Location:** North of town centre. OS map ref NY397563.
**Opening Times:** Good Friday to Sept 30, daily 10–6; Oct 1 to Maundy Thursday, daily 10–4. *Closed Mons, Christmas and New Year.* Adm £1.30, OAPs £1, Chd 65p.

## FURNESS ABBEY
*map F10*
Telephone: (0229) 23420

At the time of its suppression in 1537, the abbey was one of the wealthiest monasteries in the land. Founded in 1124 by King Stephen, the abbey belonged at first to the Order of Savigny, then to the Cistercians. Ruined buildings of red sandstone evoke a vision of past splendour. Magnificent still are the canopied seats in the presbytery and the Chapter House. Exhibition in the museum at the entrance.

**Location:** 1½ m (2.4 km) north of Barrow-in-Furness. OS map ref SD218717.
**Opening Times:** Good Friday to Sept 30, daily 10–6; Oct 1 to Maundy Thursday, daily 10–4. *Closed Mons, Christmas and New Year.* Adm £1.10, OAPs 80p, Chd 55p.

## HADRIAN'S WALL
*map G12*

Snaking across the north of England, from Bowness to Wallsend, is Hadrian's remarkable wall, built to demarcate the frontier of Britain and the northernmost limit of the Roman Empire at the time. With true Roman precision, a milecastle was constructed at every mile and two observation turrets between each milecastle, many sections have withstood the ravages of time. At strategic points great forts were built to garrison 500 or 1000 men. English Heritage has a well-preserved milecastle at Harrow's Scar, near Gilsland, and several turrets in the Brampton area, the best at Banks East.

(See also Northumberland Section)

## LANERCOST PRIORY
*map F11*
Telephone: (069 77) 3030

Just south of Hadrian's Wall, in the wooded valley of the River Irthing, stands this noble Augustinian priory founded by Robert de Vaux in the 12th century. Centrepiece is the priory church, 800 years old, and the nave is still a parish church. English Heritage has the cloistral area and the ruined East End of the church.

**Location:** 2 m (3.2 km) north east of Brampton. OS map ref NY556637.
**Opening Times:** Good Friday to Sept 30, daily 10–6. Adm 55p, OAPs 40p, Chd 25p.

## STOTT PARK BOBBIN MILL
*map F10*
Telephone: (0448) 31087

The Victorian mill buildings forming Stott Park are virtually the same today as they were 150 years ago. The bobbin mill developed from man's ability to harness the power of the fast-flowing Lakeland streams to run machinery and also from the abundance of local coppice wood. Restored as a working industrial monument, much of the machinery still remains, including a turbine and steam engine.

**Location:** On unclassified road north of the village of Finsthwaite, 2 m (3.2 km) north of A590 Kendal/Barrow-in-Furness Road at Newby Bridge (near east bank of Lake Windermere). OS map ref SD373883.
**Opening Times:** Good Friday to Oct 31, daily 10–6 (or dusk if earlier). Adm £1.30, OAPs £1, Chd 65p.

# DERBYSHIRE ⌗

## BOLSOVER CASTLE
*map H8*
Telephone: (0246) 823349

Castle in name only, the present mansion was built during the 17th century by Sir Charles Cavendish and his son William on the site of a 12th century castle. The Little Castle, separate and self-contained, is a delightful romantic folly decorated in Jacobean style.

**Location:** Bolsover 6 m east of Chesterfield on A632. OS map ref SK471707.
**Opening Times:** Good Friday to Sept 30, daily 10–6; Oct 1 to Maundy Thursday, daily 10–4. *Closed Mons, Christmas and New Year.* Adm £1.30, OAPs £1, Chd 65p.

## PEVERIL CASTLE
*map H8*
Telephone: (0433) 20613

The castle was built to control Peak Forest, where lead had been mined since prehistoric times. William the Conqueror thought so highly of this metal—and of the silver that could be extracted from it—that he entrusted the forest to one of his most esteemed knights, William Peveril.

**Location:** In Castleton on A625, 15 m west of Sheffield. OS map ref SK150827.
**Opening Times:** Good Friday to Sept 30, daily 10–6; Oct 1 to Maundy Thursday, daily 10–4. *Closed Mons, Christmas and New Year.* Adm 80p, OAPs 60p, Chd 40p.

LANERCOST PRIORY

BOLSOVER CASTLE

# DEVON

## DARTMOUTH CASTLE
*map E2*
Telephone: (080 43) 3588

Boldly guarding the narrow entrance to the Dart Estuary, this castle was among the first in England to be built for artillery. Construction began in 1481 on the site of an earlier castle. Also see 1861 battery with fully equipped guns opening summer 1989.

**Location:** 1 m (1.6 km) south east of Dartmouth. OS map ref SX887503.
**Opening Times:** Good Friday to Sept 30, daily 10–6; Oct 1 to Maundy Thursday, daily 10–4. *Closed Mons, Christmas and New Year.* Adm £1.10, OAPs 80p, Chd 55p.

## KIRKHAM HOUSE
*map E2*
Telephone: (0803) 522775

This well-preserved house near the church is an interesting example of 15th century architecture. It was probably the home of a prosperous merchant. Display of modern furniture.

**Location:** Kirkham Street, Paignton. OS map ref SX885610.
**Opening Times:** Good Friday to Sept 30, daily 10–6. Adm 80p, OAPs 60p, Chd 40p.

## OKEHAMPTON CASTLE
*map E2*
Telephone: (0837) 2844

Rebellion broke out in the south west after the Battle of Hastings and a stronghold was built here to subdue it. The castle passed from Baldwin FitzGilbert to Robert de Courtenay in 1172 and remained with this family, off and on, for 3½ centuries. The last Courtenay to own it, the Marquis of Exeter, was beheaded in 1538 and the castle dismantled.

**Location:** 1 m (1.6 km) south west of Okehampton. OS map ref SX584942.
**Opening Times:** Good Friday to Sept 30, daily 10–6; Oct 1 to Maundy Thursday, daily 10–4. *Closed Mons, Christmas and New Year.* Adm 80p, OAPs 60p, Chd 40p.

## TOTNES CASTLE
*map E2*
Telephone: (0803) 864406

The Normans also built a stronghold here to overawe the townspeople. But they surrendered without a blow, as they did again in the Civil War. The remains date largely from the 14th century, although the huge earth mound on which the castle rests is Norman.

**Location:** Totnes. OS map ref SX800605.
**Opening Times:** Good Friday to Sept 30, daily 10–6; Oct 1 to Maundy Thursday, daily 10–4. *Closed Mons, Christmas and New Year.* Adm 80p, OAPs 60p, Chd 40p.

# DORSET

## FIDDLEFORD MILL HOUSE
*map G3*

14th century house, altered in the early 16th century, comprising a hall and solar block, both with elaborate roofs.

**Location:** 1 m (1.6 km) east of Sturminster Newton off A357. OS map ref ST801136.
**Opening Times:** Good Friday to Sept 30, daily 10–6. Adm 80p, OAPs 60p, Chd 40p.

## PORTLAND CASTLE
*map G2*
Telephone: (0305) 820539

Built in the middle of the 16th century on the northern shore of the Isle of Portland, the castle was part of Henry VIII's coastal defences and is little altered. Unusually shaped, like a segment of a circle, it was seized by Royalists in the Civil War, changing hands twice before yielding to Parliament in 1646.

**Location:** Overlooking Portland Harbour, adjacent to RN helicopter base. OS map ref SY684743.
**Opening Times:** Good Friday to Sept 30, daily 10–6. Adm 80p, OAPs 60p, Chd 40p.

## SHERBORNE OLD CASTLE
*map G3*
Telephone: (0935) 812730

The powerful and wealthy Bishop Roger de Caen built the castle in the early 12th century, but by 1135 it had been seized by the Crown. In 1592 the castle passed to Sir Walter Raleigh who built Sherborne Lodge in the grounds. The buildings were largely demolished after the Civil War, but a gatehouse, some graceful arcading and decorative windows survive.

**Location:** ½ m (0.8 km) east of Sherborne. OS map ref ST647167.
**Opening Times:** Good Friday to Sept 30, daily 10–6; Oct 1 to Maundy Thursday, daily 10–4. *Closed Mons, Christmas and New Year.* Adm 80p, OAPs 60p, Chd 40p.

# COUNTY DURHAM

## BARNARD CASTLE
*map G11*
Telephone: (0833) 38212

Named after its founder, Bernard de Baliol, the castle overlooks the River Tees from a craggy cliff-top. Its ownership was disputed by the Bishops of Durham, one of whom seized it in 1296. He added a magnificent hall and refortified the castle. Part of the castle has recently been excavated to discover more of its complex building history.

**Location:** In Barnard Castle. OS map ref NZ049165.
**Opening Times:** Good Friday to Sept 30, daily 10–6; Oct 1 to Maundy Thursday, daily 10–4. *Closed Mons, Christmas and New Year.* Adm 80p, OAPs 60p, Chd 40p.

## FINCHALE PRIORY
*map H11*
Telephone: (0385) 63828

This 13th century priory was built around the tomb of St Godric, who founded a hermitage here in 1110. St Godric led an adventurous life as a travelling pedlar, then a sailor, until a vision summoned him to Finchale. His stone tomb can still be seen in the chapel, but the coffin is now empty.

**Location:** 5½ m (9 km) north of Durham. OS map ref NZ297471.
**Opening Times:** Good Friday to Sept 30, daily 10–6; Oct 1 to Maundy Thursday, daily 10–4. *Closed Mons, Christmas and New Year.* Adm 80p, OAPs 60p, Chd 40p.

# ESSEX

## AUDLEY END HOUSE AND PARK
*map K5*
Telephone: (0799) 22399

James I is said to have remarked that Audley End was too large for a king but not for his Lord Treasurer, Sir Thomas Howard, who built it. The house was so large in fact that early in the 18th century about half of it was demolished as being unmanageable, but this still leaves a very substantial mansion. The interior contains rooms decorated by Robert Adam, a magnificent Jacobean Great Hall, a picturesque 'Gothick' chapel and a suite of rooms decorated in the revived Jacobean style of the early 19th century.

**Location:** ¾ m (1 km) west of Saffron Walden off B1383. OS map ref TL525382.
**Opening Times:** Good Friday to Sept 30, daily 1–6. Park and Gardens open at 12 noon. Last admissions one hour before closing. Adm £3, OAPs £2, Chd £1.50.

## PRIOR'S HALL BARN, WIDDINGTON
*map K5*
Telephone: (0799) 41047

One of the finest surviving medieval barns in south-east England, this is typical of aisled barns and representative of a group of such structures centred on north-west Essex. It displays a number of unusual features and has been restored where necessary with seasoned English oak and new roof tiles made in Sussex.

**Location:** 2 m (3.2 km) south east of Newport, Essex. OS map ref TL538319.
**Opening Times:** Good Friday to Sept 30, 10–6 weekends and Bank Holidays only. Adm 55p, OAPs 40p, Chd 25p.

## TILBURY FORT
*map L4*
Telephone: (037 52) 78489

After an audacious raid up the Thames by the Dutch in 1667, Charles II commissioned plans for a defensive fort at Tilbury, on the site of Henry VIII's smaller

AUDLEY END HOUSE & PARK

fortification. It took 13 years to build but never saw the action for which it was designed. In the First World War a German Zeppelin was gunned down from the parade ground. Entry is now from the landward side across two restored bridges. In 1988 Tilbury Fort will celebrate Queen Elizabeth I's visit to rally her troops against the Armada threat. An Armada centre will be open Apr–Sept.

**Location:** ½ m (0.8 km) south east of Tilbury. OS map ref TQ651754.
**Opening Times:** Good Friday to Sept 30, daily 10–6; Oct 1 to Maundy Thursday, daily 10–4. *Closed Mons, Christmas and New Year.* Adm £1.10, OAPs 80p, Chd 55p.

# GLOUCESTERSHIRE ⌗

## BLACKFRIARS, GLOUCESTER

*map G5*
Telephone: (0452) 27685

The Black Friars of St Dominic were welcomed enthusiastically as they spread across Europe at the beginning of the 13th century. In England houses were set up for them in Oxford, London and, in 1239, Gloucester. No less a notability than King Henry III donated oak for the roofs of the Gloucester Black Friary, some of which are still almost complete. The friary buildings were inevitably changed in the 16th century when they were bought by a local alderman.

**Location:** Ladybellegate Street. OS map ref SO830186.
**Opening Times:** Good Friday to Sept 30, daily 10–6. Adm 80p, OAPs 60p, Chd 40p.

## HAILES ABBEY

*map G5*
Telephone: (0242) 602398

His life in danger at sea, Richard, Earl of Cornwall, vowed he would found a religious house if he lived. In 1245 his brother, King Henry III, gave him the manor of Hailes so that he could keep his pledge. After its establishment Richard's son, Edmund, presented the Cistercian monks of the abbey with a phial said to contain the Blood of Christ and from then until the Dissolution Hailes became a magnet for pilgrims. Extensive ruins survive and there is an excellent museum.

**Location:** 2 m (3.2 km) north east of Winchcombe. OS map ref SP050300.
**Opening Times:** Good Friday to Sept 30, daily 10–6; Oct 1 to Maundy Thursday, daily 10–4. *Closed Mons, Christmas and New Year.* Adm £1.10, OAPs 80p, Chd 55p.

# HAMPSHIRE ⌗

## BISHOP'S WALTHAM PALACE

*map J3*
Telephone: (048 93) 2460

The Bishops of Winchester held Waltham since Saxon times, but they did not build here until about 1135. Heavily fortified, this was more castle than palace, and was dismantled by Henry II. Most of the present remains are from the spacious 15th century palace with its walled garden, all within this vast moated site. Forfeited by the bishops at the Reformation, the palace was reduced to a ruin in the Civil War, when it was held for the King against Parliament.

**Location:** Bishop's Waltham. OS map ref SU552173.
**Opening Times:** Good Friday to Sept 30, daily 10–6; Oct 1 to Maundy Thursday, daily 10–4. *Closed Mons, Christmas and New Year.* Adm £1.10, OAPs 80p, Chd 55p.

## CALSHOT CASTLE

*map H3*
Telephone: (0703) 892023

Part of the chain of Henry VIII's coastal defences against the Catholic powers of Europe. Completed in 1540 and still virtually intact, the Castle has played an important role in England's defence from the 16th Century until World War II. From 1912 to the mid 1950's it formed part of a flying boat base, initially a Royal Naval Air station, then RAF Calshot. Site exhibition in restored WWI barrack room.

**Location:** On Spit 2 m (3.2 km) south west of Fawley off B5053, 15 m (24 km) south east of Southampton. OS map 196, ref SU488025.
**Opening Times:** Good Friday to Sept 30, daily 10–6. Adm £1.10, OAPs 80p, Chd 55p.

## FORT BROCKHURST

*map J3*
Telephone: (070 17) 81059

One of five forts known as the Gosport Advanced Line, Brockhurst was built in the mid-19th century to protect Portsmouth Dockyard. The traditional star shape was abandoned for a polygonal plan. Norman castles had become obsolete with the use of gunpowder, but some features were retained. Brockhurst has a moat and a drawbridge. It also has a keep, traditionally the point of last defence. There is an exhibition on the history of Portsmouth's defences.

**Location:** Off the A32 in Elson on the north side of Gosport. OS map ref SU596020.
**Opening Times:** Good Friday to Sept 30, daily 10–6; Oct 1 to Maundy Thursday, daily 10–4. *Closed Mons, Christmas and New Year.* Adm £1.10, OAPs 80p, Chd 55p.

## HURST CASTLE

*map H2*
Telephone: (0590) 2344

Built by Henry VIII to defend the Solent, Hurst Castle was completed in 1544, and had a garrison of 23 men. During the Civil War it was occupied by Parliamentary forces and Charles I was imprisoned here for a short time. A longer incarceration was that of an unfortunate priest called Atkinson, who was a prisoner here for 29 years in the 18th century. The castle was considerably modernised in the mid-19th century, under the fear of a French invasion, and was still useful in the Second World War.

**Location:** Approach by ferry from Keyhaven. OS map ref SZ319898.
**Opening Times:** Good Friday to Sept 30, daily 10–6; Oct 1 to Maundy Thursday, weekends only 10–4. *Closed Christmas and New Year.* Adm £1.10, OAPs 80p, Chd 55p.

## MEDIEVAL WINE MERCHANTS HOUSE

**map H3**
Telephone: (0892) 48166

A medieval merchant's house, built in the 1290s is now fully restored to its 14th century appearance. On the ground floor is the restored medieval shop stocked with traditional wines and other produce. The house is furnished with medieval reproductions based on contemporary illustrations.

**Location:** In Southampton City centre between Castle Way and Town Quay.
**Opening Times:** Good Friday to Sept 30, daily 10–6; Oct 1 to Maundy Thursday, daily 10–4. *Closed Mons, Christmas and New Year.* Adm £1.10, OAPs 80p, Chd 55p.

## NETLEY ABBEY

**map H3**
Telephone: (0703) 453076

Extensive picturesque remains of a Cistercian abbey on the east bank of the Southampton Water. Netley Abbey was founded in 1239 by monks from Beaulieu. Remains include the church and cloister buildings.

**Location:** In Netley, 7 m SE of Southampton, facing Southampton Water.
**Opening Times:** Good Friday to Sept 30, daily 10–6; Oct 1 to Maundy Thursday, weekends only 10–4. *Closed Christmas and New Year.* Adm 80p, OAPs 60p, Chd 40p.

## PORTCHESTER CASTLE

*map J3*
Telephone: (0705) 378291

A Roman fortress, a Norman castle and a Romanesque church share this same site on the north shore of Portsmouth harbour. The outer walls were built in the 3rd century when Britain was the vulnerable north-west frontier of a declining Roman Empire. Today they are among the finest Roman remains in northern Europe. Eight centuries —and very little repair work—later, the walls were sound enough to encompass a royal castle. Portchester was popular with the medieval monarchs but by the 15th century royal money was being spent on Portsmouth instead. The last official use of the castle was as a prison for French seamen during the Napoleonic wars.

**Location:** South side of Portchester. OS map ref SU625046.
**Opening Times:** Good Friday to Sept 30, daily 10–6; Oct 1 to Maundy Thursday, daily 10–4. *Closed Mons, Christmas and New Year.* Adm £1.10, OAPs 80p, Chd 55p.

## TITCHFIELD ABBEY

*map J3*
Telephone: (0329) 43016

Founded in 1232 for the Premonstratensian Order or 'White Canons'. Several royal visits are recorded in the Middle Ages. On its dissolution in 1537, the abbey was converted into a mansion for the Earl of Southampton. The third earl is best known as Shakespeare's patron. Much of the Tudor building was demolished in the 18th century, to reveal the 13th century stonework.

**Location:** ½ m (0.8 km) north of Titchfield. OS map ref SU541067.
**Opening Times:** Good Friday to Sept 30, daily 10–6. Adm 80p, OAPs 60p, Chd 40p.

**PORTCHESTER CASTLE**

## HAMPSHIRE – *continued*

### WOLVESEY: OLD BISHOP'S PALACE
*map H3*
Telephone: (0962) 54766

Ruins of an extensive palace of the Bishops of Winchester, built round a quadrangular courtyard.

**Location:** ¼ m (0.5 km) south east of Winchester Cathedral, next to the Bishop's Palace. OS map ref SU484291.
**Opening Times:** Good Friday to Sept 30, daily 10–6. Adm 80p, OAPs 60p, Chd 40p.

## HEREFORD & WORCESTER ⌗

### GOODRICH CASTLE
*map G5*
Telephone: (0600) 890538

The castle was built to command the ancient crossing of the Wye by the Gloucester/Caerleon road. Among the extensive remains of the original castle the keep survives, which largely dates from the late 13th century. For almost 300 years from the mid-14th century it was held by the Earls of Shrewsbury.

**Location:** 3 m (4.8 km) south west of Ross-on-Wye. OS map ref SO579199.
**Opening Times:** Good Friday to Sept 30, daily 10–6; Oct 1 to Maundy Thursday, daily 10–4. *Closed Mons, Christmas and New Year.* Adm £1.10, OAPs 80p, Chd 55p.

### MORTIMER'S CROSS WATER MILL, LUCTON
*map F6*

Erected in the 18th century, this small and compact watermill was still in use in the 1940s. The outer housing is of sandstone rubble and the mechanism, which could be worked by one man, is located on three floors.

**Location:** 4½ m (7.2 km) north west of Leominster. OS map ref SO426637.
**Opening Times:** Apr 1 to Sept 30, Thurs, Suns and Bank Holidays only 2–6. Adm 55p, OAPs 40p, Chd 25p.

## HUMBERSIDE ⌗

### THORNTON ABBEY
*map J9*
Telephone: (0469) 40357

The great crenellated gatehouse demonstrates that Thornton was one of the richer monasteries of the Augustinian Order. It was founded about 1139 by William le Gros, Earl of Albemarle, who is buried here. The dissolution of the monastery in the 16th century gave rise to a macabre legend—that the remains of a monk had been found walled up in a room, seated at a table with a book, pen and ink.

**Location:** 2 m (3.2 km) north east of Thornton Curtis. OS map ref TA115190.
**Opening Times:** Good Friday to Sept 30, daily 10–6; Oct 1 to Mar 23, weekends only 10–4. Adm 80p, OAPs 60p, Chd 40p.

## ISLE OF WIGHT ⌗

### APPULDURCOMBE HOUSE
*map J2*
Telephone: (0983) 852484

The only house in the 'grand manner' on the Island, Appuldurcombe (pronounced 'Applercombe') was a status symbol and not a home. Sir Robert Worsley started the house in 1701 but ran out of money. The east façade, a beautiful example of English baroque, dates from this year. The house was not completed until the end of the century. The house is now an empty shell but still stands in its fine park, moulded by 'Capability' Brown.

**Location:** ½ m (0.8 km) west of Wroxall. OS map ref SZ543800.
**Opening Times:** Good Friday to Sept 30, daily 10–6; Oct 1 to Maundy Thursday, daily 10–4. *Closed Mons, Christmas and New Year.* Adm 80p, OAPs 60p, Chd 40p.

### CARISBROOKE CASTLE
*map H2*
Telephone: (0983) 522107

Here are seven acres of castle and earthworks to explore. The oldest parts of the castle are 12th century, but the great mound—71 steps high—bore a wooden castle before that, and there are fragments of Roman wall at its base. Fortified against the French, then the Spaniards, the castle is best known as the prison of Charles I in 1647/8. A bold escape plan failed when the King became wedged between the bars of the great chamber window. The castle contains the island's museum.

**Location:** 1¼ m (2 km) south west of Newport. OS map ref SZ486877.
**Opening Times:** Good Friday to Sept 30, daily 10–6; Oct 1 to Maundy Thursday, daily 10–4. *Closed Mons, Christmas and New Year.* Adm £2.20, OAPs £1.65, Chd £1.10.

### OSBORNE HOUSE
*map H3*
Telephone: (0983) 200022

This was Queen Victoria's seaside residence built at her own expense, in 1845. The Prince Consort played a prominent part in the design of the house—it was his version of an Italian villa—and the work was carried out by Thomas Cubitt, the famous London builder. The Queen died here in 1901 and her private apartments have been preserved more or less unaltered. Crowded with furniture and bric-a-brac they epitomise the style we call 'Victorian'. Also see the Queen's bathing machine.

**Location:** 1 m (1.6 km) south east of Cowes. OS map ref SZ516948.
**Opening Times:** Good Friday to Sept 30, daily 10–6; Oct 1 to Oct 31, daily 10–5. Last admissions are one hour before closing. Adm £3, OAPs £2, Chd £1.50.

### YARMOUTH CASTLE
*map H2*
Telephone: (0983) 760678

Part of the coastal defences of Henry VIII, Yarmouth embodied the very latest fashion in military engineering. Completed in 1547, it is square in plan, and washed on two sides by the sea. During the Civil War the island was strongly royalist and throughout the Commonwealth Cromwell kept a large garrison here. When Sir Robert Holmes was appointed Captain of the Island in 1667, the castle was already outmoded and ineffective. He reduced it in size, filled in the moat and built himself a house—now the hotel—on the site.

**Location:** Yarmouth. OS map ref SZ354898.
**Opening Times:** Good Friday to Sept 30, daily 10–6. Adm 80p, OAPs 60p, Chd 40p.

## KENT ⌗

### DEAL AND WALMER CASTLES
*map M4*
Telephone: Deal Castle (0304) 372762 or
Walmer Castle (0304) 364288

When Henry VIII divorced Catherine of Aragon he defied the Pope and broke with

THORNTON ABBEY

CARISBROOKE CASTLE

Catholic Europe. Deal and Walmer were built under the threat of a 'crusade' against Henry—an invasion which never came. Deal contains an exhibition on the coastal defences of Henry VIII. At Walmer the atmosphere is country house rather than martial, for this has long been the official residence of the Lords Warden of the Cinque Ports. One of the best remembered is the Duke of Wellington (the original 'Wellington boot' may be seen here), and one of the best loved, Queen Elizabeth the Queen Mother.

**Location:** Deal Castle is near the town centre. OS map ref TR378521.
**Opening Times: Deal:** Good Friday to Sept 30, daily 10–6; Oct 1 to Maundy Thursday, daily 10–4. *Closed Mons, Christmas and New Year.* Adm £1.10, OAPs 80p, Chd 55p.

**Location:** Walmer is south of Deal. OS map ref TR378501.
**Opening Times: Walmer:** Good Friday to Sept 30, daily 10–6; Oct 1 to Maundy Thursday, daily 10–4. *Closed Mons, Christmas and New Year and when Lord Warden is in residence.* Adm £1.60, OAPs £1.20, Chd 80p.

## DOVER CASTLE

*map M4*
Telephone: (0304) 201628

Castle Hill dominates the shortest passage between Britain and the Continent, and has been the scene of military activity from the Iron Age to the present day. Here is extensive proof from every age of man's ingenuity in devising ways to repel invaders. Dover Castle had its narrowest escape in 1216 when—in a heroic siege—it just managed to hold out against the French. There is much to see, including the underground works, the Roman lighthouse (now the bell tower of a fine Saxon church) and the great keep itself and a spectacular exhibition "All the Queen's Men".

**Location:** East side of Dover. OS map ref TR326416.
**Opening Times:** Good Friday to Sept 30, daily 10–6; Oct 1 to Maundy Thursday, daily 10–4. *Closed Christmas and New Year.* Adm £2.50, OAPs £1.80, Chd £1.30. Refreshments in the Keep Yard.

## DYMCHURCH MARTELLO TOWER (No 24)

*map M3*
Telephone: 0303 873684

Seventy-four Martello towers were built along the coast between 1805 and 1812. The 24 lb gun on the roof was to resist a Napoleonic invasion. To further confound the French there was no doorway at ground level—entry was by a movable external ladder to the first floor.

**Location:** Dymchurch. OS map ref TR102294.
**Opening Times:** Good Friday to Sept 30, daily 10–6. Adm 80p, OAPs 60p, Chd 40p.

## LULLINGSTONE ROMAN VILLA

*map K4*
Telephone: (0322) 863467
(Closed for refurbishment in 1989.)

The ancient Romans understood the art of gracious living. In this country villa they walked on mosaic floors, dined off fine tableware and commissioned elaborate wall paintings to decorate one of the earliest churches in Britain. The museum gives a remarkable picture of what it was like to be wealthy in the 2nd, 3rd and 4th centuries.

**Location:** ½ m (0.8 km) south west of Eynsford. OS map ref TQ529651.
**Opening Times:** *Good Friday to Sept 30, daily 10–6; Oct 1 to Maundy Thursday, daily 10–4. Closed Mons, Christmas and New Year.* Tel: 01-211 8828 for details. Adm £1.30, OAPs £1, Chd 65p.

## MAISON DIEU, OSPRINGE

*map L4*
Telephone: (0795) 76204

Maison Dieu (God's House) was the medieval name for a hospital. A hospital was also part hotel, and Maison Dieu gave shelter to travellers, from the poorest pilgrim to the King himself. Only fragments of the medieval building survive, but some fine 16th century beamed ceilings may be seen, and a collection of Roman burial objects—pottery, glass and jewellery.

**Location:** ½ m (0.8 km) west of Faversham. OS map ref TR002608.
**Opening Times:** Good Friday to Sept 30, weekends only 10–6. Adm 80p, OAPs 60p, Chd 40p.

## MILTON CHANTRY, GRAVESEND

*map L4*
Telephone: (0474) 21520

In the 14th century priests prayed here for the souls of the de Valence and Montechais families, and the building also housed the chapel of a leper hospital. After the Reformation, the building was used as a house, barracks, tavern and museum.

**Location:** Adjacent to the Fort in Milton. OS map ref TQ652743.
**Opening Times:** Good Friday to Sept 30, daily 10–6. Adm 55p, OAPs 40p, Chd 25p.

## RECULVER TOWERS AND ROMAN FORT

*map M4*
Telephone: (022 73) 66444

Some of the Roman walls remain—after seventeen centuries. But more striking are the twin towers, 'The Reculvers'. Long after most of the Saxon and Norman church was demolished the Towers have been preserved as a famous landmark and guide to sailors.

**Location:** 3 miles (4.8 km) east of Herne Bay. OS map ref TR228694.
**Opening Times:** Good Friday to Sept 30, daily 10–6. Adm 80p, OAPs 60p, Chd 40p.

## RICHBOROUGH CASTLE

*map M4*
Telephone: (0304) 612013

The sea has deserted Richborough, but as Rutupiae it was well-known in Roman times as a seaport. It was here that the conquering Roman army landed in AD 43. The massive stone walls were built in the 3rd century to combat the ferocious attacks of Saxon sea-raiders.

**Location:** 1½ m (2.4 km) north of Sandwich. OS map ref TR324602.
**Opening Times:** Good Friday to Sept 30, daily 10–6; Oct 1 to Maundy Thursday, daily 10–4. *Closed Mons, Christmas and New Year.* Adm 80p, OAPs 60p, Chd 40p.

## ROCHESTER CASTLE

*map L4*
Telephone: (0634) 402276

The great square keep of Rochester Castle has resisted destruction for 900 years. Besieged many times, it held out in 1215 for two months against King John. Battering the castle from huge stone-throwing engines, the King finally breached the keep by mining under it and setting fire to the pit props with the fat of 40 pigs.

**Location:** Just south of Rochester Bridge. OS map ref TQ742686.
**Opening Times:** Good Friday to Sept 30, daily 10–6; Oct 1 to Maundy Thursday, daily 10–4. *Closed Mons, Christmas and New Year.* Adm £1.10, OAPs 80p, Chd 55p.

**OSBORNE HOUSE**

**DEAL AND WALMER CASTLES**

## KENT – *continued*

### ST AUGUSTINE'S ABBEY
*map M4*
Telephone: (0227) 67343

This was founded in 598 by St Augustine, the first Archibishop of Canterbury. The excavated finds from this early building are rare memorials of the Anglo-Saxon church. The remains we see today are from the later Norman church, its well-preserved crypt, and the medieval monastery.

**Location:** Canterbury, near the Cathedral. OS map ref TR154578.
**Opening Times:** Good Friday to Sept 30, daily 10–6; Oct 1 to Maundy Thursday, daily 10–4. *Closed Mons, Christmas and New Year.* Adm 80p, OAPs 60p, Chd 40p.

### TEMPLE MANOR, ROCHESTER
*map L4*
Telephone: (0634) 718743

Once part of a large medieval farm the Manor was built in 1240 by the Knights Templar, an order of celibate soldiers, founded to protect the Holy Land. This surviving building was probably used to house distinguished visitors.

**Location:** ½ m (0.8 km) south west of Rochester Bridge. OS map ref TQ733686.
**Opening Times:** Good Friday to Sept 30, daily 10–6. Adm 55p, OAPs 40p, Chd 25p.

### UPNOR CASTLE
*map L4*
Telephone: (0634) 718742

The Castle was built in 1559 on the orders of Elizabeth I, to protect her warships moored in the Medway alongside the new dockyards at Chatham. Within a century the castle was out of date, and was used as a magazine for gunpowder and munitions.

**Location:** 1¾ m (2.8 km) north east of Strood. OS map ref TQ758706.
**Opening Times:** Good Friday to Sept 30, daily 10–6. Adm 80p, OAPs 60p, Chd 40p.

## LEICESTERSHIRE ⌗

### ASHBY DE LA ZOUCH CASTLE
*map H7*
Telephone: (0530) 413343

In 1464 Edward IV granted the Norman manor house of Ashby to his Lord Chamberlain, Lord Hastings, who built the impressive four-storey tower. His enjoyment of it was short-lived, alas, for in 1483 he was beheaded by Richard III. His successors fared better and among royal visitors were Henry VII, Mary Queen of Scots, James I and Charles I. In 1649 the tower was partially destroyed by Parliamentary forces.

**Location:** In Ashby de la Zouch. OS map ref SK363167.
**Opening Times:** Good Friday to Sept 30, daily 10–6; Oct 1 to Maundy Thursday, daily 10–4. *Closed Mons, Christmas and New Year.* Adm 80p, OAPs 60p, Chd 40p.

### KIRBY MUXLOE CASTLE
*map H7*
Telephone: (0533) 663230

William, Lord Hastings, was a very wealthy man, so he was able to indulge his passion for building. He developed his moated brick mansion from a fortified manor house, but it was never completed. A striking feature is the patterned brickwork, clearly visible on the gatehouse walls.

**DOVER CASTLE**

**Location:** 4 m (6.4 km) west of Leicester. OS map ref SK524046.
**Opening Times:** Good Friday to Sept 30, daily 10–6; Oct 1 to Maundy Thursday, daily 10–4. *Closed Mons, Christmas and New Year.* Adm 80p, OAPs 60p, Chd 40p.

### LYDDINGTON BEDE HOUSE
*map J6*
Telephone: (057 282) 2438

The building is the only surviving part of a grand medieval palace of the Bishops of Lincoln. After the Reformation it passed to Thomas, Lord Burghley, who turned it into an almshouse. It was used as such until the present century.

**Location:** In Lyddington 6m (9.6 km) north of Corby. OS map ref SP875970.
**Opening Times:** Good Friday to Sept 30, daily 10–6. Adm 80p, OAPs 60p, Chd 40p.

## LINCOLNSHIRE ⌗

### GAINSBOROUGH OLD HALL
**map J8**
Telephone: (0427) 2669

The Hall is one of the largest and most complete late medieval houses in the country, built by Sir Thomas de Burgh. It houses a variety of historical items, furniture and several exhibitions including one about Richard III.

**Location:** In Gainsborough, opposite the Library.
**Opening Times:** Easter Saturday to Oct 31, Mon to Sat 10–5, Suns 2–5; Nov 1 to Maundy Thursday, Mon to Sat 10–5. *Closed Good Friday, Christmas and New Year.* Adm 75p, Chd 45p.

### LINCOLN: BISHOP'S PALACE
*map J8*
Telephone: (0522) 27468

When James I visited Lincoln in 1617 the palace was a ruin. It was not until the 1880s that it was partially restored by Bishop King. Excavations have revealed most of the medieval layout which largely dates from the 12th, 13th and 15th centuries.

**Location:** South side of Lincoln cathedral. OS map ref SK981717.
**Opening Times:** Good Friday to Sept 30, daily 10–6. Adm 55p, OAPs 40p, Chd 25p.

### SIBSEY TRADER MILL
*map K7*
Telephone: (0205) 750036

Near the Stone Bridge Drain stands this cornmill, built in 1877 on the site of an older mill. One of the last to be erected in Lincolnshire, it is notable for having six sails. The Trader Mill was still working in 1953. It has since been completely restored.

**Location:** ¾ m (1 km) west of Sibsey, north west of Boston. Os map ref TF345511.
**Opening Times:** Good Friday to Sept 30, daily 10–6. Adm 55p, OAPs 40p, Chd 25p.

## LONDON ⌗

### CHAPTER HOUSE AND PYX CHAMBER WESTMINSTER ABBEY
*map K4*

Described as 'incomparable' when it was finished in 1253, with some of the finest of English medieval sculpture, the chapter house was one of the largest in England and could seat 80 monks around its walls. It was converted to a record office in the 16th century, but by 1740 the roof had decayed and been removed. Restoration of the whole building took place in 1865 and again after it was bombed in 1941. The 11th century Pyx Chamber now houses the Abbey Treasures. A joint ticket admits to the Abbey Museum.

**Location:** East side of the abbey cloister.
**Opening Times:** Good Friday to Sept 30, daily 10–6; Oct 1 to Maundy Thursday, daily 10–4. *Closed Christmas and New Year.* Adm £1.50, OAPs 75p, Chd 40p.

### CHISWICK HOUSE
*map K4*
Telephone: 01-995 0508

Architect and patron of the arts, the third Earl of Burlington set a fashion with this Italian-style villa, built to house his library and art collections. The gardens were originally landscaped by William Kent.

**Location:** Burlington Lane, ½ m (0.8 km) north east of Chiswick Station.
**Opening Times:** Good Friday to Sept 30, daily 10–6; Oct 1 to Maundy Thursday, daily 10–4. *Closed Christmas.* Adm £1.30, OAPs £1, Chd 65p.

### KENWOOD, THE IVEAGH BEQUEST
**map K4**
Telephone: 01-348 1286/7

Adam mansion, once the seat of Lord Mansfield. The Iveagh Bequest of Old Master and British paintings, including works by Rembrandt, Vermeer, Hals, Gainsborough, Turner and Reynolds. Fine collection of neo-classical furniture.

**Location:** Hampstead Lane, NW3.
*Station: Archway or Golders Green Underground (Northern Line), then Bus 210.*
**Opening Times:** Good Friday to Sept 30, daily 10–6; Oct 1 to Maundy Thursday, daily 10–4. *Closed Christmas.* Adm Free.
**Refreshments:** At the Coach House.

## MARBLE HILL HOUSE
**map K4**
Telephone: 01-892 5115

A complete example of an English Palladian villa. Early Georgian paintings and furniture.

**Location:** Richmond Road; 11m from Charing Cross.
*Stations: St. Margaret's (½ m); Twickenham (1 m); Richmond (2 m).*
**Opening Times:** Good Friday to Sept 30, daily 10–6; Oct 1 to Maundy Thursday, daily 10–4. *Closed Christmas.* Adm Free.
**Refreshments:** In Stable Block.

## RANGER'S HOUSE
**map K4**
Telephone: 01-853 0035

A Gallery of English Portraits in the 4th Earl of Chesterfield's house, from the Elizabethan to the Georgian period. Dolmetsch Collection of musical instruments in period rooms on newly restored first floor.

**Location:** Chesterfield Walk, SE10; 8 m Charing Cross.
*Stations: Greenwich or Blackheath (15 mins walk).*
**Opening Times:** Good Friday to Sept 30, daily 10–6; Oct 1 to Maundy Thursday, daily 10–4. *Closed Christmas.* Adm Free.

# NORFOLK ⌗

## BERNEY ARMS WINDMILL
*map M7*
Telephone: (0493) 200605

At one time the Norfolk and Suffolk marshes were drained entirely by wind-power, a function carried out by this 'tower' mill after it was no longer used for its original purpose of grinding cement clinker. The Mill has seven floors, making it the highest marsh-mill in the area and a landmark for miles around. The whole of the mechanism is in working order.

**Location:** North bank of River Yare, 3½ m (5.6 km) north east of Reedham. OS map ref TG465051. Accessible only by boat, or ½ m walk.
**Opening Times:** Good Friday to Sept 30, daily 10–6. Adm 80p, OAPs 60p, Chd 40p.

## CASTLE ACRE—PRIORY AND CASTLE
*map L7*
Telephone: (076 05) 394

William de Warenne and his wife were so impressed with the great Abbey of Cluny in Burgundy that they determined to found the Order in England. This they did—at Lewes. The priory at Castle Acre was probably established by their son and it survived, not without friction, until 1537 when it was surrendered to Henry VIII. The gaunt ruins span seven centuries and include a 16th century gatehouse, a church of mixed origins and a prior's lodging almost fit to be lived in. The castle, at the other end of the village started as an undefended Norman manor house but later evolved into a conventional keep. Ruins of this keep and outer earthworks can be seen.

**Location:** 3½ m (5.6 km) north of Swaffham. OS map ref TF814148.
**Opening Times:** Good Friday to Sept 30, daily 10–6; Oct 1 to Maundy Thursday, daily 10–4. *Closed Mons, Christmas and New Year.* Adm £1.10, OAPs 80p, Chd 55p.

## CASTLE RISING CASTLE
*map K7*
Telephone: (055 387) 330

The long and distinguished history of Castle Rising began in 1138. It was then that William de Albini started to build a grand castle to mark the upturn in his fortunes which followed his marriage to Henry I's widow. Later owners were no less notable and included Isabella 'the She-Wolf of France', wife of Edward II, the Black Prince, Prince Hal and the Howard Dukes of Norfolk. The 12th century keep, reached through a handsome, decorated doorway, was—and is—the finest building in the castle. Outside, there is a gatehouse of the same date and the remains of a church.

**Location:** 4 m (6.4 km) north of King's Lynn. OS map ref TF666246.
**Opening Times:** Good Friday to Sept 30, daily 10–6; Oct 1 to Maundy Thursday, daily 10–4. *Closed Mons, Christmas and New Year.* Adm 80p, OAPs 60p, Chd 40p.

## GRIME'S GRAVES
*map L6*
Telephone: (0842) 810656

This is an intricate network of pits and shafts sunk by our neolithic ancestors some 4000 years ago. The purpose of all this industriousness was to find flints for the world's first farmers—flints to make axes to fell trees so that the cleared ground could be sown with seed. Between 700 and 800 pits were dug, some of them to a depth of 30 or 40ft (9–12m). Two of the 16 excavated shafts have been left open; they give an idea of those early miners' working conditions.

**Location:** 2¾ m (4.4 km) north east of Brandon. OS map ref TL818898.
**Opening Times:** Good Friday to Sept 30, daily 10–6; Oct 1 to Maundy Thursday, daily 10–4. *Closed Mons, Christmas and New Year.* Adm 80p, OAPs 60p, Chd 40p.

## OLD MERCHANTS' HOUSE AND THE ROW 111 HOUSES, GREAT YARMOUTH
*map M7*
Telephone: (0493) 857900

Herrings brought prosperity to the town in the mid-16th century and it expanded rapidly to house the growing population. Buildings of wood and reed-thatch were replaced by houses with brick and flint walls, tiled roofs and windows with leaded lights. These distinctive houses were pleasant places to live in until 19th century developers crowded them out. Soon they became cramped, ill lit and insanitary, a decline that was hastened by bombing in the Second World War. Fortunately, two fine examples survive with their fittings.

**Location:** Off South Quay. OS map ref TG525072.
**Opening Times:** Good Friday to Sept 30, daily 10–6. Adm 55p, OAPs 40p, Chd 25p.

# NORTHAMPTONSHIRE ⌗

## KIRBY HALL
*map J6*
Telephone: (0533) 663230

Richness and variety of architectural detail distinguish this Elizabethan country house from others. Begun by Sir Humphrey Stafford in 1570, it was completed by Sir Christopher Hatton, a talented courtier to Queen Elizabeth. The fourth Sir Christopher Hatton devoted his energies to the garden. His death in 1706 marked the end of the Hall's golden age.

**Location:** 2 m (3.2 km) north of Corby. OS map ref SP926927.
**Opening Times:** Good Friday to Sept 30, daily 10–6; Oct 1 to Maundy Thursday, daily 10–4. *Closed Mons, Christmas and New Year.* Adm 80p, OAPs 60p, Chd 40p.

LYDDINGTON BEDE HOUSE

CHISWICK HOUSE

### RUSHTON TRIANGULAR LODGE

*map J6*
Telephone: (0536) 710761

Three walls with three windows and three gables to each . . . three storeys topped by a three-sided chimney. What is the reason for this triangular theme? The building is the brainchild of Sir Thomas Tresham and every detail is symbolical of the Holy Trinity and the Mass. Tresham's religious beliefs, unpopular in Elizabethan England, earned him many years' imprisonment. The lodge, begun on his return home in 1593, was finished four years later.

**Location:** ¾ m (1 km) west of Rushton; 4 m (6.4 km) north west of Kettering. OS map ref SP830831.
**Opening Times:** Good Friday to Sept 30, daily 10–6. Adm 80p, OAPs 60p, Chd 40p.

## NORTHUMBERLAND

### AYDON CASTLE

*map G11*
Telephone: (043 471) 2450

Built as a manor house at the end of the 13th century, Aydon Castle fortified almost immediately afterwards as a result of the insecurity of the borders with Scotland. Captured by the Scots in 1315, it was pillaged and burned, and seized again by English rebels two years later. It has survived as a result of its conversion to a farmhouse in the 17th century.

**Location:** 1 m (1.6 km) north east of Corbridge, on minor road off B6321 or A68. OS map 87, ref NZ002663.
**Opening Times:** Good Friday to Sept 30, daily 10–6. Adm £1.10, OAPs 80p, Chd 55p.

### BELSAY HALL CASTLE AND GARDENS

*map G12*
Telephone: (066 181) 636

"XIX century Neo-Classical mansion lies at the entrance to 30 acres of exciting gardens, which in turn lead on to the XIV century castle and ruined manor. Important collections of rare and exotic flowering trees grow in the meandering, deep ravines of the "picturesque" Quarry Gardens. Massed plantings of rhododendrons. Large heather garden. Spring bulbs. Exhibition of Belsay's architectural and landscape history in stable block."

**Location:** 14 m (22.4 km) north west of Newcastle upon Tyne. OS map ref NZ088785.
**Opening Times:** Good Friday to Sept 30, daily 10–6; Oct 1 to Maundy Thursday, daily 10–4. *Closed Mons, Christmas and New Year.* Adm £1.60, OAPs £1.20, Chd 80p.

### BERWICK BARRACKS

*map G13*
Telephone: (0289) 304493

The barracks were designed in 1717 to accommodate 36 officers and 600 men, first being occupied in 1721. The buildings consist of three blocks of accommodation around a square, the fourth side having a splendidly decorated gatehouse. The barracks' new exhibition, the award winning 'Beat of Drum' traces the history of the British infantryman from 1660 to the end of the 19th century. The regimental museum of the King's Own Scottish Borderers and Borough Museum of Berwick on Tweed are also housed here.

**Location:** On the Parade, off Church St, Berwick town centre.
**Opening Times:** Good Friday to Sept 30, daily 10–6; Oct 1 to Maundy Thursday, daily 10–4. *Closed Mons, Christmas and New Year.* Adm £1.30, OAPs £1, Chd 65p.

### BRINKBURN PRIORY

*map G12*
Telephone: (066 570) 628

The priory church stands within a loop of the River Coquet, in beautiful surroundings. Founded about 1130, the priory suffered badly from Scottish raids. In the last century the church was carefully restored by the Newcastle architect, Thomas Austin, and is still in occasional use. It is a fine example of early Gothic architecture.

**Location:** 5 m (8 km) east of Rothbury. OS map ref NZ116984.
**Opening Times:** Good Friday to Sept 30, daily 10–6. Adm 80p, OAPs 60p, Chd 40p.

### CHESTERS FORT

*map G12*
Telephone: (043 481) 379

An impressive bath-house, buildings of great interest inside the fort, the remains of the bridge carrying Hadrian's Wall across the Tyne, a museum full of Roman inscriptions and sculptures, all set in one of the most beautiful valleys in Northumberland—these are among the attractions of Chesters, once garrisoned by a regiment of Roman cavalry.

**Location:** ½ m (0.8 km) south west of Chollerford. OS map NY913702.
**Opening Times:** Good Friday to Sept 30, daily 10–6; Oct 1 to Maundy Thursday, daily 10–4. *Closed Mons, Christmas and New Year.* Adm £1.30, OAPs £1, Chd 65p.

### CORBRIDGE ROMAN SITE

*map G11*
Telephone: (043 471) 2349

For nearly a century this was the site of a sequence of Roman forts, since Corbridge was an important junction of roads to Scotland, York and Carlisle. It developed into a prosperous town and supply base for Hadrian's Wall, with shops, temples, houses, granaries and an elaborate fountain. Among the rich collection of finds in the museum is a remarkable fountainhead—the Corbridge Lion.

**Location:** ½ m (0.8 km) north west of Corbridge. OS map ref NY983649.
**Opening Times:** Good Friday to Sept 30, daily 10–6; Oct 1 to Maundy Thursday, daily 10–4. *Closed Mons, Christmas and New Year.* Adm £1.30, OAPs £1, Chd 65p.

### DUNSTANBURGH CASTLE

*map H13*
Telephone: (066 576) 231

Isolated and unspoilt, the ruins stand on a large, rocky cliff top rising steeply from the sea. Begun by Thomas, Earl of Lancaster, in 1313, the castle was attacked by the Scots and besieged during the Wars of the Roses. The keep gatehouse is still impressive and the south wall an enduring memorial to the workmanship of Earl Thomas's masons.

**Location:** 8 m (13 km) north east of Alnwick. OS map ref NU258220.
**Opening Times:** Good Friday to Sept 30, daily 10–6; Oct 1 to Maundy Thursday, daily 10–4. *Closed Mons, Christmas and New Year.* Adm 80p OAPs 60p, Chd 40p.

### HADRIAN'S ROMAN WALL IN NORTHUMBERLAND AND TYNE AND WEAR

*map G12*

The wall runs from Bowness to Wallsend-on-Tyne, a distance of 73 miles (117 km). Although parts of the wall have been lost over the centuries, fine sections remain at Walltown Crags, Cawfields, Sewingshields and Heddon-on-the-Wall. At Denton, near Newcastle, there is a well-preserved turret, and there are others at Brunton, where the wall is still 7ft (2m) high, at Sewingshields and Black Carts. These turrets, or observation towers, punctuated the wall at every third of a Roman mile between milecastles, good examples of which may be seen at Cawfields and Sewingshields. At Benwell and Carrawburgh there are Roman temples; at Chesterholm a milestone and the great fort Vindolanda, for which there is an admission fee. Other sites may be visited free of charge.

RUSHTON TRIANGULAR LODGE

BRINKBURN PRIORY

**Locations:** OS map references. Heddon-on-the-Wall NZ136669; Planetrees Farm, Chollerford NY928696; Brunton Turret, Chollerford NY921698; Chesters Bridge Abutment, Chollerford NY913701; Black Carts NY884713; Carrawburgh, Temple of Mithras NY869713; Sewingshields, Haydon Bridge NY813702; Chesterholm, Vindolanda Roman Fort and Milestone NY771664; Winshields Milecastle, Bardon Mill NY745676; Cawfields Milecastle NY726669; Walltown Crags, Greenhead NY674664; Benwell Condercum NZ215646; Benwell Roman Temple NZ217646; Denton Hall Turret NZ198655 and West Denton NZ195656.

## HOUSESTEADS ROMAN FORT

*map G12*
Telephone: (049 84) 363

This is the best-preserved Roman troop-base on Hadrian's Wall. In the museum, a model shows the layout of barracks, headquarters buildings, commandant's house and granaries. Also displayed are relics from the fort and the settlement that grew up outside the walls in the 3rd and 4th centuries.

**Location:** 2¾ m (4.4 km) north east of Bardon Mill. OS map ref NY790687.
**Opening Times:** Good Friday to Sept 30, daily 10–6; Oct 1 to Maundy Thursday, daily 10–4. *Closed Mons, Christmas and New Year.* Adm £1.30, OAPs £1, Chd 65p.

## LINDISFARNE PRIORY

*map G13*
Telephone: (028 989) 200

Roofless and ruined, the priory is still supremely beautiful, its graceful arches and decorated doorways commemorating the craftsmanship of their Norman builders. This has been sacred soil since 634 when the missionary Bishop Aidan was sent from Iona, to spread Christianity through northern England. New visitor centre with exhibition and shop.

**Location:** On Holy Island, which can be reached at low tide across a causeway. Tide tables are posted at each end of the causeway. OS map ref NU126418.
**Opening Times:** Good Friday to Sept 30, daily 10–6; Oct 1 to Maundy Thursday, daily 10–4. *Closed Mons, Christmas and New Year.* Adm £1.10, OAPs 80p, Chd 55p.

## NORHAM CASTLE

*map G13*
Telephone: (028 982) 329

Built in the 12th century by the Bishop of Durham, this massive castle stands on a site of great natural strength. It withstood repeated attacks in the 13th and 14th centuries and was thought to be impregnable. But in 1513 it was stormed by the forces of James IV and partially destroyed. Although later rebuilt, the castle lost its importance as a defensive stronghold by the end of the 16th century.

**Location:** 8 m (13 km) south west of Berwick. OS map ref NT907476.
**Opening Times:** Good Friday to Sept 30, daily 10–6; Oct 1 to Maundy Thursday, daily 10–4. *Closed Mons, Christmas and New Year.* Adm 80p, OAPs 60p, Chd 40p.

## PRUDHOE CASTLE

*map G11*
Telephone: (0661) 32303

Extensive remains of 12th century castle with gatehouse, curtain wall and keep enclosed within surrounding earthworks. In the 19th century a house was built within the ruins, now containing an exhibition on the history of the castle.

**Location:** In Prudhoe, on minor road off A695. OS map ref NZ092634.
**Opening Times:** Good Friday to Sept 30, daily 10–6; Oct 1 to Maundy Thursday, daily 10–4. *Closed Mons, Christmas and New Year.* Adm £1.10, OAPs 80p, Chd 55p.

## WARKWORTH CASTLE

*map H12*
Telephone: (0665) 711423

From 1332 the history of Warkworth was the history of the Percy family. In 1399 this became the history of England, when the third Percy lord of Warkworth and his son Harry Hotspur put Henry IV on the throne. Three scenes from Shakespeare's Henry IV Part 1 are set at Warkworth. Norman in origin, the castle has some very fine medieval masonry. The keep was restored and made habitable in the 19th century.

**Location:** 7½ m (12 km) south of Alnwick. OS map ref NU247057.
**Opening Times:** Good Friday to Sept 30, daily 10–6; Oct 1 to Maundy Thursday, daily 10–4. *Closed Mons, Christmas and New Year.* Adm 80p, OAPs 60p, Chd 40p.

## WARKWORTH HERMITAGE

*map H12*
Telephone: (0665) 711423

The hermitage and chapel of Holy Trinity is situated in a peaceful, retired place, overshadowed and surrounded by trees upon the left bank of the River Coquet half a mile above the castle, in that part of the manor of Warkworth anciently called Sunderland Park. It can be approached by boat up the river from the landing place below the castle or by a pleasant footpath through woods and meadows up the right bank and across by ferry from the upper boat landing.

**Location:** 7½ m (12 km) south of Alnwick.
**Opening Times:** Good Friday to Sept 30, open 10–6 weekends only. Adm 55p, OAPs 40p, Chd 25p.

LINDISFARNE PRIORY

WARKWORTH CASTLE

# OXFORDSHIRE ⌗

## MINSTER LOVELL HALL AND DOVECOTE

*map H5*
Telephone: (0993) 775315

Originally a 15th century manor house, the hall was built around a courtyard. The medieval dovecote, complete with nesting boxes, has recently been restored. When the hall was dismantled in the 18th century, a skeleton was found in the cellars. This is thought to have been the Yorkist Lord Lovell who disappeared after the Battle of Bosworth 1485, where he fought on the losing side.

**Location:** 2½ m (4 km) north west of Witney. OS map ref SP324114.
**Opening Times:** Good Friday to Sept 30, daily 10–6; Oct 1 to Maundy Thursday, daily 10–4. *Closed Mons, Christmas and New Year.* Adm 80p, OAPs 60p, Chd 40p.

## NORTH LEIGH ROMAN VILLA

*map H5*
Telephone: (0993) 881830

This was the home of a 'county' family in the 4th century. Farming was clearly profitable on this good arable land, with Akeman Street nearby to transport the produce to the Roman centres at St Albans and Cirencester. Excavations have revealed an elaborate courtyard villa with over sixty rooms. The site has suffered in the past from souvenir hunters, but it is clear that the villa was equipped with an enviable range of 'comforts' in the form of underfloor heating, painted walls, mosaic tile floors and an elaborate system of hot and cold bath houses.

**Location:** 4¼ m (6.8 km) south east of Charlbury. OS map ref SP397154.
**Opening Times:** Good Friday to Sept 30, daily 10–6. Adm 55p, OAPs 40p, Chd 25p.

## RYCOTE CHAPEL

*map J5*
Telephone: (084 47) 346

It was at the great mansion of Rycote that Sir Henry Norreys entertained that most peripatetic monarch, Elizabeth I. The house has long since disappeared, but the private chapel survives in its entirety. Founded in 1449 by Richard Quatremayne, the chapel still has the original font and some of the early seating. But the superb interior is mainly the work of 17th century craftsmen, and because it has escaped any restoration, it is of outstanding interest.

**Location:** 3 m (4.8 km) west of Thame. OS map ref SP667046.
**Opening Times:** Good Friday to Sept 30, daily 10–6; Oct 1 to Maundy Thursday, daily 10–4. *Closed Mons, Christmas and New Year.* Adm 80p, OAPs 60p, Chd 40p.

# SHROPSHIRE ⌗

## BOSCOBEL HOUSE

*map G6*
Telephone: (090 28) 50244

When John Giffard built his tall, gabled, timber-framed hunting lodge in the 17th century, he little knew that it would become a refuge for the future King Charles II after his defeat at Worcester in 1651. In the grounds stands the offspring of the famous oak that sheltered Charles from Cromwell and his search parties. Although still recognisable from contemporary engravings, the house has been much altered over the centuries.

**Location:** 8 m (12 km) north west of Wolverhampton; 3¾ m (6 km) north of Albrighton. OS map ref SJ837083.
**Opening Times:** Good Friday to Sept 30, daily 10–6; Oct 1 to Maundy Thursday, daily 10–4. *Closed Mons, Christmas and New Year.* Adm £1.80, OAPs £1.40, Chd 90p.

RYCOTE CHAPEL

## BUILDWAS ABBEY

*map G7*
Telephone: (095 245) 3274

Founded in 1135 as an offshoot of Furness Abbey in Cumbria, the abbey belonged briefly to the Savignac Order, then to the Cistercians. Building continued throughout the 12th century and, once completed, the abbey changed little until the Dissolution. The church is almost complete, except for the roof, and the well-preserved west front typifies the austere style favoured by the Cistercians.

**Location:** 3¼ m (5.2 km) north east of Much Wenlock. OS map ref SJ642044.
**Opening Times:** Good Friday to Sept 30, daily 10–6; Oct 1 to Maundy Thursday, daily 10–4. *Closed Mons, Christmas and New Year.* Adm 80p, OAPs 60p, Chd 40p.

## HAUGHMOND ABBEY

*map F7*
Telephone: (074 377) 661

William FitzAlan re-established this house for Augustinian canons in 1135. It was rebuilt when FitzAlan became abbot, and further changes and additions were made over the centuries. In 1539 the church was demolished and the abbot's lodging, great hall and kitchens were converted into a private house. Some fine Norman doorways and 14th century statues repay a visit.

**Location:** 3½ m (5.6 km) north east of Shrewsbury. OS map ref SJ542152.
**Opening Times:** Good Friday to Sept 30, daily 10–6; Oct 1 to Maundy Thursday, daily 10–4. *Closed Mons, Christmas and New Year.* Adm 80p, OAPs 60p, Chd 40p.

## LILLESHALL ABBEY

*map G7*
Telephone: (0952) 604431

But for its conversion into a fortified stronghold during the Civil War, more might have survived of this medieval Augustinian abbey. As it is, the sandstone remains of the 12th century church and two well-proportioned doorways, one richly carved and decorated, give tantalising glimpses of past magnificence.

**Location:** 4½ m (7.2 km) south of Newport. OS map ref SJ738142.
**Opening Times:** Good Friday to Sept 30, daily 10–6. Adm 80p, OAPs 60p, Chd 40p.

## STOKESAY CASTLE

*map F6*
Telephone: (05882) 2544

One of the finest fortified manor houses in England and little altered since it was built by Laurence de Ludlow in the late 13th century. The gatehouse was rebuilt in the early 17th century in spectacular ornamental style. There is a fine Great Hall with a suite of rooms at each end, a separate defensible tower and a timber fire surround in solar.

**Location:** 1 m (1.6km) S of Craven Arms off A49. OS map ref. 137, ref SO 436817.
**Opening Times:** Mar 2 to Oct 31, daily (except Tues) 10–6 (5 in Mar & Oct); Nov 1–30, 10–dusk weekends only. Mons to Fris party bookings only,. Last adm half an hour before closing. *Closed Dec, Jan & Feb.* Adm £1, Chd (under 15) 50p. Party bookings in advance. Toilets. Car park. Enquiries to The Custodian, Stokesay Castle, Craven Arms, Shropshire SY7 9AH.

## WENLOCK PRIORY

*map G6*
Telephone: (0954) 727466

The long history of Wenlock stretches back to the 7th century, although nothing visible remains of the religious house founded by St Milburge. After the Norman Conquest, a Cluniac priory was established, which came to be regarded as alien during the Hundred Years' War with France. Decorative arcading from the 12th century chapter house survives and some unusual features in the later, rebuilt church.

**Location:** In Much Wenlock. OS map ref SJ625001.
**Opening Times:** Good Friday to Sept 30, daily 10–6; Oct 1 to Maundy Thursday, daily 10–4. *Closed Mons, Christmas and New Year.* Adm 80p, OAPs 60p, Chd 40p.

## WROXETER (VIROCONIUM) ROMAN CITY

*map G6*
Telephone: (074 375) 330

Viroconium was the fourth largest city in Roman Britain and the largest to escape modern development. Deep beneath the exposed walls of the market-hall excavations are revealing a legionary fortress of the first century; while nearby the timber buildings of later settlers are being examined. The most impressive feature is the huge wall dividing the exercise yard from the baths.

**Location:** 5½ m (8.8 km) south east of Shrewsbury. OS map ref SJ568088.
**Opening Times:** Good Friday to Sept 30, daily 10–6; Oct 1 to Maundy Thursday, daily 10–4. *Closed Mons, Christmas and New Year.* Adm 80p, OAPs 60p, Chd 40p.

# SOMERSET ⌗

## CLEEVE ABBEY

*map F3*
Telephone: (0984) 40377

Although little remains of the church, some of the buildings surrounding the cloister of this Cistercian abbey are remarkably complete. A timber roof of outstanding workmanship survives in the 15th century dining hall; also preserved are fragments of pavements, tiles and wall paintings of earlier date.

**Location:** Washford. OS map ref ST047407.
**Opening Times:** Good Friday to Sept 30, daily 10–6; Oct 1 to Maundy Thursday, daily 10–4. *Closed Mons, Christmas and New Year.* Adm £1.10, OAPs 80p, Chd 55p.

### FARLEIGH HUNGERFORD CASTLE
*map G4*
Telephone: (02214) 4026

Sir Thomas de Hungerford, Speaker of the House of Commons, fortified the original manor house without permission; he was later pardoned. His mailed effigy, surrounded by the tombs of other Hungerfords, lies in the chapel, a place to stir the imagination.

**Location:** Farleigh Hungerford 3½ m (5.6 km) west of Trowbridge. OS map ref ST801577.
**Opening Times:** Good Friday to Sept 30, daily 10–6; Oct 1 to Maundy Thursday, daily 10–4. *Closed Mons, Christmas and New Year..* Adm 80p, OAPs 60p, Chd 40p.

### GLASTONBURY TRIBUNAL
*map G3*
Telephone: (0458) 32949

Justice was administered here by the Abbot of Glastonbury until the Dissolution. Later a kitchen was added and the building converted to a private house. It is well preserved, with decorative details from three centuries.

**Location:** High Street. OS map ref ST499390.
**Opening Times:** Good Friday to Sept 30, daily 10–6; Oct 1 to Maundy Thursday, daily 10–4. *Closed Mons, Christmas and New Year.* Adm 80p, OAPs 60p, Chd 40p.

### MUCHELNEY ABBEY
*map F3*
Telephone: (0458) 250664

This was one of the oldest abbeys in Somerset. The church has now vanished but the abbot's house is remarkably intact. Up a stairway of great beauty, the parlour adds flesh to the story that the monks lived well. Two lions smile down from pillars over an ornate fireplace; a wooden settle runs the length of a wall lit by magnificent windows; all are well preserved despite later use as a farmhouse.

**Location:** 2 m (3.2 km) south of Langport. OS map ref ST428248.
**Opening Times:** Good Friday to Sept 30, daily 10–6. Adm 80p, OAPs 60p, Chd 40p.

## STAFFORDSHIRE ⌗

### WALL (LETOCETUM) ROMAN SITE
*map H7*
Telephone: (0543) 480768

Much of the business of Imperial Rome depended on official couriers who travelled the comprehensive road network. Posting stations were built for them at regular intervals. At Wall, on Watling Street, traces of the hostel and a large part of the bath-house survive.

**Location:** 2 m (3.2 km) south west of Lichfield. OS map ref SK099067.
**Opening Times:** Good Friday to Sept 30, daily 10–6; Oct 1 to Maundy Thursday, daily 10–4. *Closed Mons, Christmas and New Year.* Adm 80p, OAPs 60p, Chd 40p.

## SUFFOLK ⌗

### FRAMLINGHAM CASTLE
*map M6*
Telephone: (0728) 723330

The present massive walls and their 13 towers were built by Roger Bigod, second Earl of Norfolk, on a site given to his father by Henry I. The ornamental brick chimneys were added in Tudor times when the arch of the entrance gateway was rebuilt. In 1636 the castle passed to Pembroke College, Cambridge, and in later years the great hall was converted to a poor-house and many of the buildings inside the walls were demolished. It was here, in 1553, that Mary Tudor learned she had become Queen of England.

**Location:** North side of Framlingham. OS map ref TM287637.
**Opening Times:** Good Friday to Sept 30, daily 10–6; Oct 1 to Maundy Thursday, daily 10–4. *Closed Mons, Christmas and New Year.* Adm £1.10, OAPs 80p, Chd 55p.

### ORFORD CASTLE
*map M6*
Telephone: (039 44) 50472

No sooner had Henry II built this castle on the Suffolk coast than rebellion broke out (in 1173). The castle's powerful presence helped to uphold the King's authority and it continued to be an important royal residence for more than 100 years. In 1280 it was granted to the Earl of Norfolk for his lifetime, and from then on it remained in private hands. The design was very advanced for its time, and the keep, much of which remains, is unique in England. The outer wall of the castle, the last section of which collapsed in 1841, was punctuated by rectangular towers, an innovation that provided excellent cover for the defenders.

**Location:** In Orford. OS map ref TM419499.
**Opening Times:** Good Friday to Sept 30, daily 10–6; Oct 1 to Maundy Thursday, daily 10–4. *Closed Mons, Christmas and New Year.* Adm 80p, OAPs 60p, Chd 40p.

### SAXTEAD GREEN POST MILL
*map M6*
Telephone: (0728) 82346

In the 13th century Framlingham was a thriving farming community, whose wealth derived from cereals, particularly wheat. This corn-mill, one of the finest in the world, probably dates from 1287 and produced flour until the First World War. The upper part of the mill, containing the machinery, was rotated by a track-mounted fantail. This ensured that the sails always faced square into the wind.

**Location:** 2 m (3.2 km) west of Framlingham. OS map ref TM253645.
**Opening Times:** Good Friday to Sept 30, daily 10–6, *closed Sun.* Adm 80p, OAPs 60p, Chd 40p.

## SURREY ⌗

### FARNHAM CASTLE KEEP
*map J4*
Telephone: (0252) 713393

Farnham formed part of the estate of the Bishops of Winchester long before the Norman Conquest. And there was still a bishop in residence until 1955—an impressive tenancy. But why should the massive keep be built *around* the mound of earth, and not on top of it? Your guess is as good as the archaeologists'!

**Location:** Farnham. OS map ref SU839474.
**Opening Times:** Good Friday to Sept 30, daily 10–6. Adm 80p, OAPs 60p, Chd 40p.

GLASTONBURY TRIBUNAL

FARLEIGH HUNGERFORD CASTLE

ORFORD CASTLE

# SUSSEX (EAST)

## BATTLE ABBEY

*map L3*
Telephone: (04 246) 3792

The Battle of Hastings, 1066—the best-known date in English history. Battle Abbey was built by William the Conqueror as a thanksgiving for his victory, with the high altar on the spot where King Harold died. The church has yet to be fully excavated, but visitors may walk over the battlefield, and see the remains of many of the domestic buildings of the monastery and watch a film on the battle.

**Location:** Battle. OS map ref TQ749157.
**Opening Times:** Good Friday to Sept 30, daily 10–6; Oct 1 to Maundy Thursday, daily 10–4. *Closed Mons, Christmas and New Year.* Adm £1.60, OAPs £1.20, Chd 80p.

## BAYHAM ABBEY

*map L3*
Telephone: (0892) 890381

Built by monks in the 13th century, the abbey owes its survival not to historical or archaeological interest, but to its being a picturesque ruin. By the 18th century the building was in a desperate condition, but then came the Gothic revival and the structure was repaired and landscaped to provide a romantic vista for the nearby Dower House.

**Location:** 1¾ m (2.8 km) west of Lamberhurst. OS map ref TQ651366.
**Opening Times:** Good Friday to Sept 30, daily 10–6. Adm 80p, OAPs 60p, Chd 40p.

## PEVENSEY CASTLE

*map L3*
Telephone: (0323) 762604

The walls that enclose this 10-acre site are from the 4th century Roman fort, Anderida. The inner castle, with its great keep, is medieval. With the fall of France in 1940, Pevensey was put into service again, after centuries of neglect.

**Location:** Pevensey. OS map ref TQ645048.
**Opening Times:** Good Friday to Sept 30, daily 10–6; Oct 1 to Maundy Thursday, daily 10–4. *Closed Mons, Christmas and New Year.* Adm £1.10, OAPs 80p, Chd 55p.

# TYNE & WEAR

## HYLTON CASTLE

*map H11*
Telephone: (0783) 495048

Heraldic shields and carved figures adorn this splendid castle, shaped like an enormous gatehouse and designed more for comfort than defence. Sir William Hylton built it about 1400 but it was much altered in the 1860s and transformed into a suburban villa. These later additions have now been removed.

**Location:** 3¾ m (6 km) west of Sunderland. OS map ref NZ358588.
**Opening Times:** Good Friday to Sept 30, daily 10–6; Oct 1 to Maundy Thursday, daily 10–4. *Closed Mons, Christmas and New Year.* Adm 55p, OAPs 40p, Chd 25p.

## TYNEMOUTH CASTLE AND PRIORY

*map H12*
Telephone: 091-257 1090

Two saints were buried within the walls of this Benedictine priory, established in the 11th century on the site of an earlier abandoned monastery. Two walls of the presbytery still tower to their full height and the 15th century chantry chapel has a splendid collection of roof bosses. A fortified gatehouse was added during the Border wars, which persuaded Henry VIII to retain the priory as a royal castle after the Dissolution. The headland remained in use for coastal defence until 1956, one battery is not open to the public.

**Location:** Tynemouth. OS map ref NZ374695.
**Opening Times:** Good Friday to Sept 30, daily 10–6; Oct 1 to Maundy Thursday, daily 10–4. *Closed Mons, Christmas and New Year.* Adm 80p, OAPs 60p, Chd 40p.

# WARWICKSHIRE

## KENILWORTH CASTLE

*map H6*
Telephone: (0926) 52078

One of the grandest ruins in England, this castle was made famous by Sir Walter Scott. Gone now is the great lake that once surrounded it, but still standing is the huge Norman keep with walls nearly 20ft (6m) thick in places. Inside the encircling walls built by King John are the remains of John of Gaunt's chapel and great hall, and the Earl of Leicester's stables and gatehouse. The most splendid royal occasion took place in 1575 when Queen Elizabeth I was entertained lavishly by the Earl with music and dancing, fireworks and hunting, for 19 days.

**Location:** West side of Kenilworth. OS map ref SP278723.
**Opening Times:** Good Friday to Sept 30, daily 10–6; Oct 1 to Maundy Thursday, daily 10–4. *Closed Mons, Christmas and New Year.* Adm £1.10, OAPs 80p, Chd 55p.

# WILTSHIRE

## AVEBURY MUSEUM

*map H4*
Telephone: (0672) 3250

No one knows quite why our ancient ancestors built Silbury Hill or the Sanctuary. But fortunately some of their tools, pottery and weapons have survived and are housed in the museum, which lies at the heart of Britain's earliest beginnings.

**Location:** In Avebury, 7 m (11.2 km) west of Marlborough. OS map ref SU100700.
**Opening Times:** Good Friday to Sept 30, daily 10–6; Oct 1 to Maundy Thursday, daily 10–4. *Closed Mons, Christmas and New Year.* Adm 80p, OAPs 60p, Chd 40p.

## OLD SARUM

*map H3*
Telephone: (0722) 335398

On the summit of a hill north of Salisbury, huge ramparts and earth mounds are silhouetted against the skyline. Ancient Britons fortified the hill-top which was later inhabited by Romans, Saxons and Normans. Parts of an 11th century castle remain and the foundations of two successive cathedrals are marked on the grass.

**Location:** 2 m (3.2 km) north of Salisbury. OS map ref SU138327.
**Opening Times:** Good Friday to Sept 30, daily 10–6; Oct 1 to Maundy Thursday, daily 10–4. *Closed Mons, Christmas and New Year.* Adm 80p, OAPs 60p, Chd 40p.

## OLD WARDOUR CASTLE

*map G3*
Telephone: (0747) 870487

The ruins stand in a romantic lakeside setting as a result of landscaping and planting in the 18th century. French in style and designed more for living than defence, the

BATTLE ABBEY

OLD WARDOUR CASTLE

castle was built in 1393 by the fifth Lord Lovel, a campaigner in France. It was badly damaged in the Civil War and never repaired. The 18th century Banqueting House contains a small display about the 'Capability' Brown landscape.

**Location:** 2 m (3.2 km) south of Tisbury. OS map ref ST939263.
**Opening Times:** Good Friday to Sept 30, daily 10–6; Oct 1 to Maundy Thursday, 10–4 weekends only. *Closed Christmas and New Year.* Adm 80p, OAPs 60p, Chd 40p.

### STONEHENGE
*map H3*

Built between 2800 and 1100 BC, this is Britain's most famous ancient monument and one of the world's most astonishing engineering feats. Many of the stones, some weighing 4 tons each, were brought from the Preseli Mountains in Wales to Salisbury Plain, there to be erected by human muscle power.

**Location:** 2 m (3.2 km) west of Amesbury. OS map ref SU123422.
**Opening Times:** Good Friday to Sept 30, daily 10–6; Oct 1 to Maundy Thursday, daily 10–4. *Closed Mons, Christmas and New Year.* Adm £1.60, OAPs £1.20, Chd 80p.

## YORKSHIRE (NORTH) ⌗

### ALDBOROUGH ROMAN TOWN
*map H10*
Telephone: (090 12) 2768

The little village of Aldborough lies within the bounds of what was once the rich Roman city Isurium Brigantum. Aldborough has even retained part of the Roman street plan—a regular grid with a central open space, once the forum. Part of the Roman town walls survive, and two mosaic pavements may be seen in their original positions. A remarkable collection of Roman objects is on display in the Museum.

**Location:** ¾ m (1 km) east of Boroughbridge. OS map ref SE405667.
**Opening Times:** Good Friday to Sept 30, daily 10–6; Oct 1 to Maundy Thursday, daily 10–4. *Closed Mons, Christmas and New Year.* Adm 80p, OAPs 60p, Chd 40p.

### BYLAND ABBEY
*map H10*
Telephone: (034) 76614

Built in the shadow of the Hambleton Hills, this 12th century Cistercian monastery is still magnificent, both in size and workmanship. The area of the cloister, for example, is larger than either Fountains or Rievaulx Abbeys. Some of the carved stone details are particularly fine, and sections of medieval green and yellow glazed tile floor may be seen.

**Location:** 1 m (1.6 km) north east of Coxwold. OS map ref SE549789.
**Opening Times:** Good Friday to Sept 30, daily 10–6; Oct 1 to Maundy Thursday, daily 10–4. *Closed Mons, Christmas and New Year.* Adm 80p, OAPs 60p, Chd 40p.

### CLIFFORD'S TOWER, YORK
*map H9*
Telephone: (0904) 646940

York Castle, like the city itself, has had a long and turbulent history. Clifford's Tower was built on an earlier motte (or mound) in the 13th century. The tower is named after a Lancastrian leader from the Wars of the Roses, Sir Robert Clifford, who was defeated in 1322, and his body hung in chains from the tower.

**Location:** Near Castle Museum. OS map ref SE605515.
**Opening Times:** Good Friday to Sept 30, daily 10–6; Oct 1 to Maundy Thursday, daily 10–4. *Closed Christmas and New Year.* Adm 80p, OAPs 60p, Chd 40p.

### EASBY ABBEY
*map H10*
Telephone: (0748) 5224

Founded in 1155 by the wealthy Scrope family, Easby was a monastery of the white-robed Premonstratensian Order. The gatehouse looks much as it did in the 14th century a staircase on the outer wall led to the upper floor where the abbot held his court. Some fine canopied choir stalls taken from Easby when it dissolved may be seen in Richmond parish church, a mile of pleasant riverside walk away.

**Location:** 1 m (1.6 km) east of Richmond. OS map ref NZ185003.
**Opening Times:** Good Friday to Sept 30, daily 10–6; Oct 1 to Maundy Thursday, daily 10–4. *Closed Mons, Christmas and New Year.* Adm 80p, OAPs 60p, Chd 40p.

### HELMSLEY CASTLE
*map H10*
Telephone: (0439) 70442

Even in its ruined state, Helmsley Castle is spectacular. Begun by Walter Espec shortly after the Norman Conquest, the huge earthworks—now softened to green valleys—are all that remain of this early castle. The oldest stonework is 12th century. Like many English castles, Helmsley rendered indefensible during the Civil War, when it belonged to the notorious George Villiers, Duke of Buckingham. It was abandoned as a great house when its owners built nearby Duncombe Park.

**Location:** Helmsley. OS map ref SE611836.
**Opening Times:** Good Friday to Sept 30, daily 10–6; Oct 1 to Maundy Thursday, daily 10–4. *Closed Mons, Christmas and New Year.* Adm £1.10, OAPs 80p, Chd 55p.

### KIRKHAM PRIORY
*map J10*
Telephone: (065 381) 768

The patrons of this monastery, the Lords of Helmsley, are still much in evidence. Their coats of arms adorn the gatehouse, and four family graves have survived amid

BYLAND ABBEY

STONEHENGE

the ruins of the Church. Built for the monks the Augustinian Order, or Black Canons, Kirkham was founded early in the 12th century by Walter Espec, who also founded Rievaulx Abbey.

**Location:** 5 m (8 km) south west of Malton. OS map ref SE735657.
**Opening Times:** Good Friday to Sept 30, daily 10–6; Oct 1 to Maundy Thursday, daily 10–4. *Closed Mons, Christmas and New Year.* Adm 80p, OAPs 60p, Chd 40p.

## MIDDLEHAM CASTLE
*map H10*
Telephone: (0969) 23899

The great days of Middleham were in the 14th and 15th centuries, when it was the stronghold of the mighty Neville family. After the death of Richard Neville—'Warwick the Kingmaker'—in 1471, the castle was forfeited to the Crown. The dominant feature of the castle is the great keep, one of the largest in England.

**Location:** 2 m (3.2 km) south of Leyburn. OS map ref SE128875.
**Opening Times:** Good Friday to Sept 30, daily 10–6; Oct 1 to Maundy Thursday, daily 10–4. *Closed Mons, Christmas and New Year.* Adm 80p, OAPs 60p, Chd 40p.

## MOUNT GRACE PRIORY
*map H10*
Telephone: (0609) 83249

These 14th century ruins provide a rare opportunity to study the plan of a Carthusian monastery, or 'charterhouse'. The Carthusian monks lived like hermits—in seclusion not only from the world, but from each other. They met together only in chapel, and for religious feasts. Every monk had his own cell—21 in all—a tiny two-storey house with its own garden and workshop. And each cell had running water—a remarkable luxury in the Middle Ages.

**Location:** 7 miles (11.3 km) north east of Northallerton. OS map ref SE453982.
**Opening Times:** Good Friday to Sept 30, daily 10–6; Oct 1 to Maundy Thursday, daily 10–4. *Closed Mons, Christmas and New Year.* Adm £1.10, OAPs 80p, Chd 55p.

## PICKERING CASTLE
*map J10*
Telephone: (0751) 74989

Most of the medieval kings visited Pickering Castle. They came to hunt deer and wild boar in the neighbouring forest. It was a sport of which they were inordinately fond, and the royal forests were zealously guarded. Romantics may like to speculate as to why Rosamund's Tower has been linked with 'Fair Rosamund', mistress of Henry II. They should, however, be aware that the tower was built in 1323, a century after the lady died.

**Location:** Pickering. OS map ref SE800845.
**Opening Times:** Good Friday to Sept 30, daily 10–6; Oct 1 to Maundy Thursday, daily 10–4. *Closed Mons, Christmas and New Year.* Adm £1.10, OAPs 80p, Chd 55p.

## RICHMOND CASTLE
*map H10*
Telephone: (0748) 2493

Surrounded on three sides by high moorland, Richmond Castle is in a strongly defensible position. However, the castle has seen little active service, which accounts for the remarkable amount of early Norman stonework that has survived. Built by Alan the Red, shortly after 1066, the castle went with the title 'Duke of Richmond' and has had many royal and powerful owners.

**Location:** Richmond. OS map ref NZ174006.
**Opening Times:** Good Friday to Sept 30, daily 10–6; Oct 1 to Maundy Thursday, daily 10–4. *Closed Mons, Christmas and New Year.* Adm £1.30 OAPs £1, Chd 65p.

## RIEVAULX ABBEY
*map H10*
Telephone: (043 96) 228

The fluctuating fortunes of the abbey may be read from the ruins. Within two decades of its foundation in 1131, Rievaulx—the first Cistercian monastery in the north—was vast, with 140 monks and 500 lay brothers. A costly building programme followed, and it is little wonder that by the 13th century the monastery was heavily in debt, and buildings were being reduced in size. By the Dissolution in the 16th century, there were only 22 monks. The church is a beautiful example of early English Gothic. New visitor centre with exhibition and shop.

**Location:** 3 miles (4.8 km) north west of Helmsley. OS map ref SE577849.
**Opening Times:** Good Friday to Sept 30, daily 10–6; Oct 1 to Maundy Thursday, daily 10–4. *Closed Mons, Christmas and New Year.* Adm £1.30, OAPs £1, Chd 65p.

## SCARBOROUGH CASTLE
*map J10*
Telephone: (072 3) 72451

Standing on the massive headland between the North and South Bays, the castle commands magnificent views. There was a prehistoric settlement here, and a Roman signal station, but the first mention of the castle is in the 12th century, when it was seized by Henry II. During the Civil War the castle was besieged and changed hands several times. A hundred years later it was still in use to detain political prisoners—notably George Fox, founder of the Society of Friends (Quakers).

**Location:** East of town centre. OS map ref TA050893.
**Opening Times:** Good Friday to Sept 30, daily 10–6; Oct 1 to Maundy Thursday, daily 10–4. *Closed Mons, Christmas and New Year.* Adm £1.10, OAPs 80p, Chd 55p.

## WHITBY ABBEY
*map J10*
Telephone: (0947) 603568

Founded in 655 and presided over by an abbess, Whitby was a double monastery for both men and women—a feature of the Anglo-Saxon church. This early history has been chronicled by the Venerable Bede, who tells us that here the poet Caedmon lived and worked. Destroyed by invading Danes in 857, the monastery was refounded after the Norman Conquest, but its exposed cliff-top site continued to invite attack by sea pirates. The building remains are from the later Benedictine monastery.

**Location:** Whitby. OS map ref NZ904115.
**Opening Times:** Good Friday to Sept 30, daily 10–6; Oct 1 to Maundy Thursday, daily 10–4. *Closed Mons, Christmas and New Year.* Adm 80p, OAPs 60p, Chd 40p.

# YORKSHIRE (SOUTH) ⌗

## CONISBROUGH CASTLE
*map H8*
Telephone: (070 986) 3329

Sir Walter Scott's novel 'Ivanhoe' made Conisbrough Castle famous. The magnificent keep—still largely intact—is one of the finest examples of 12th century building in England. Sited by the River Don, the castle we see today was probably the work of Hamelin Plantagenet, illegitimate half-brother of Henry II.

**Location:** 4½ m (7.2 km) south west of Doncaster. OS map ref SK515989.
**Opening Times:** Good Friday to Sept 30, daily 10–6; Oct 1 to Maundy Thursday, daily 10–4. *Closed Mons, Christmas and New Year.* Adm £1.10, OAPs 80p, Chd 55p.

## MONK BRETTON PRIORY
*map H9*
Telephone: (0226) 20489

The monastery was founded about 1154, initially for monks of the Cluniac Order. The priory was involved in violent arguments with another Cluniac monastery at Pontefract, and more than once an armed force was sent to occupy Monk Bretton. Their differences were only resolved by Monk Bretton leaving the Order to become a Benedictine house. The remains show the layout of the monastery. One of the best-preserved buildings is the 14th century prior's lodging, which stands three storeys high.

**Location:** 2 m (3.2 km) north east of Barnsley. OS map ref SE373065.
**Opening Times:** Good Friday to Sept 30, daily 10–6; Oct 1 to Maundy Thursday, daily 10–4. *Closed Mons, Christmas and New Year.* Adm 55p, OAPs 40p, Chd 25p.

## ROCHE ABBEY
*map H8*
Telephone: (0709) 812739

Most medieval monasteries are near running water, since the monks were more fastidious about sanitation than their contemporaries. The two founders of Roche gave land on either side of a stream, and parts of the building bridge the water. Founded in 1147 for monks of the Cistercian Order, the name 'Roche' derives from its rocky site. Sadly, the only part of the abbey's history of which we know any detail, is the Dissolution. When the monks left, the monastery was plundered and the carved wood from the church burnt in order to melt the lead taken from the roof.

**Location:** 1½ m (2.4 km) south of Maltby. OS map ref SK544898.
**Opening Times:** Good Friday to Sept 30, daily 10–6; Oct 1 to Maundy Thursday, 10–4 weekends only. *Closed Christmas and New Year.* Adm 80p, OAPs 60p, Chd 40p.

ROCHE ABBEY

# Index to Houses, Castles and Gardens

# Properties New to 1989 Edition
(*Shown in main index*)

Alton Towers, *Alton, Staffs.*
Avebury Manor and Gardens, *Avebury, Wilts.*

Banqueting House, *London*
Barrington Court Gardens, *Ilminster, Somerset*
Belmont, *Nr. Faversham, Kent*
Bodelwyddan Castle, *Clwyd, Wales*
Bolton Castle, *Nr. Leyburn, North Yorks*
Bowringsleigh, *Kingbridge, Devon*
Bramdean House, *Bramdean, Hants.*
Brobury Garden and Gallery, *Nr. Hereford*
Broughton House, *Kirkcudbright, Dumfries and Galloway*
Burford House Gardens, *Tenbury Wells, Hereford & Worcs.*

Castle Matrix, *Rathkeale, Republic of Ireland*
Chedworth Roman Villa, *Yanworth, Gloucs.*
Chichester Cathedral, *Chichester, West Sussex*
Chinese Summerhouse, *Amesbury, Wilts.*
Clonalis House, *Castlerea, Co Roscommon*
Cronkhill House, *Shrewsbury, Shropshire*

Damer House, Roscrea Heritage Centre, *Co. Tipperary*
De Morgan Foundation, *London*
Doddington Place Gardens, *Nr. Sittingbourne, Kent*
Dulwich College, *London*
Dunguaire Castle, *Co. Galway*
Dunleckney Manor, *Co. Carlow*
Dunloe Castle Hotel Gardens, *Killarney*

East Lighthouse, *nr. Spalding, Lincs.*
Eyton Old Hall, *nr. Leominster, Hereford & Worcs.*

Filching Manor, *nr. Polegate, East Sussex*
Foord Almshouses, *Rochester, Kent*

Glamis Castle, *Glamis, Tayside*
Greatham Mill, *Greatham, Hants.*

Hamptworth Lodge, *nr. Salisbury, Wilts.*
Highclere Castle, *nr. Newbury*
Holkham Hall, *Wells, Somerset*

Irish Life Viking Adventure, *Dublin*

Kilruddery House and Gardens, *Co Wicklow*
King's School, *Ely, Cambs.*

Lincoln Bishop's Palace, *Lincoln*
Little Dean Hall, *Littledean, Gloucestershire*
Ludford House, *Ludlow, Shropshire*

Magnolias, (The), *Brentwood, Essex*
Muckross House and Gardens, *Killarney*

Northbourne Court Gardens, *Deal, Kent*

Olivers, *Colchester, Essex*

Painshill Park, *Cobham, Surrey*
Park Farm Garden, *Great Waltham, Essex*
Parrox Hall, *Fleetwood, Lancs.*
Pear Tree House, *Litton, Avon*
Powerscourt Townhouse Centre, *Dublin*
Prior Crauden's Chapel, *Ely, Cambs.*

Raveningham Hall Gardens, *Norwich, Norfolk*
Riverstown House, *Co Cork*
Robert Smail's Printing Works, *Tweeddale*
Rodmarton Manor Garden, *Cirencester, Glos.*
Rothe House, *Kilkenny*

St Mary's House, *Godstone, Surrey*
Sheriff Hutton Park, *York*
Snowshill Manor, *Broadway, Glos.*
Stockeld Park, *Wetherby, Yorks.*

Whittington Court, *Whittington, Glos.*
Winton House, *Pencaitland*
Wiveton Hall, *Holt, Norfolk*
Woodsford Castle, *Woodsford, Dorset*
Wortham Manor, *Lifton, Devon*

Typesetting by Composing Operations Ltd., Tunbridge Wells, Kent. Printed by William Clowes Limited, Beccles and London

# Page Index

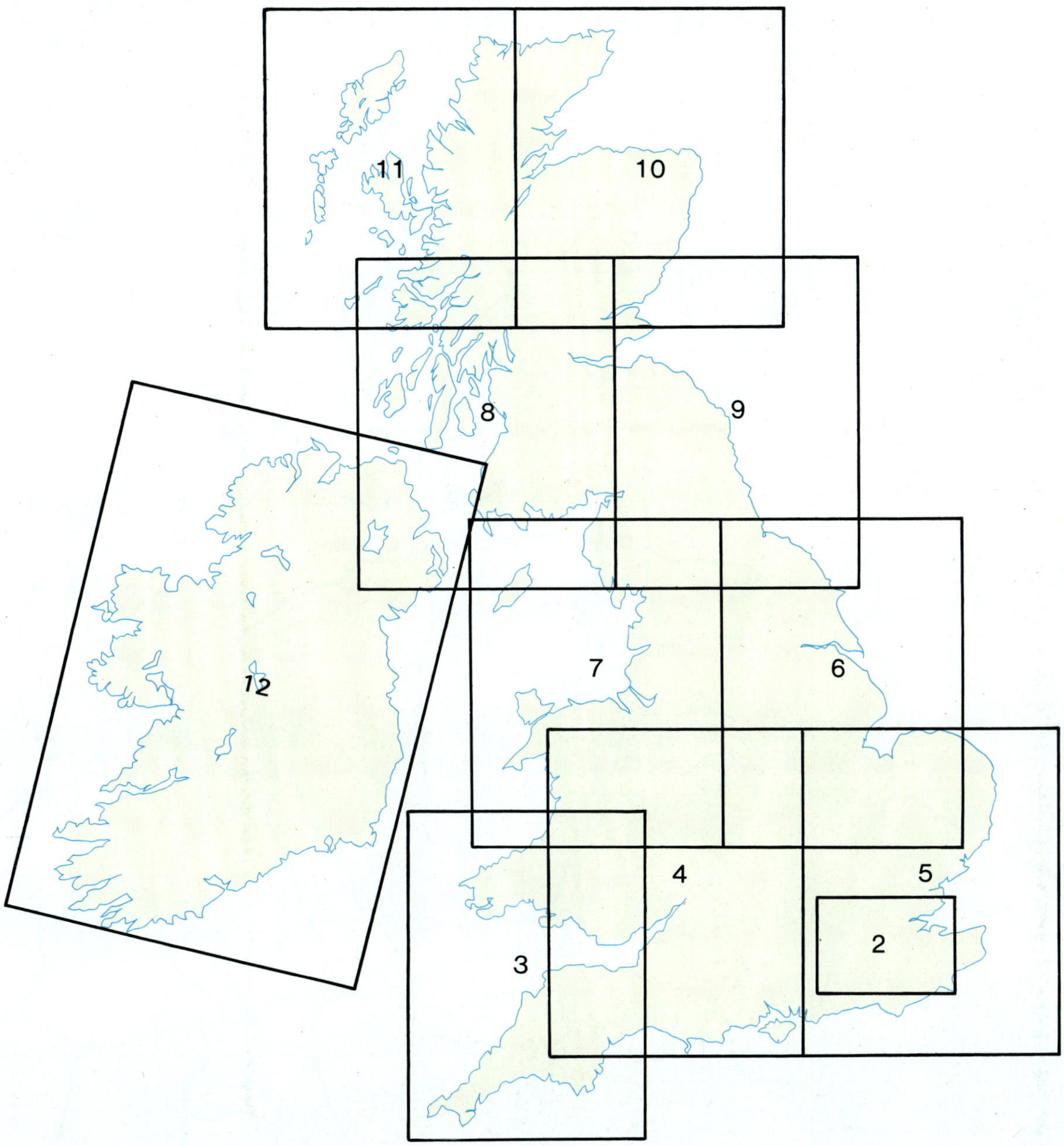


## Legend

| | |
|---|---|
| Motorway | **House with or without garden** |
| Motorway Intersections | **Castle with or without garden** |
| Primary route | **Garden** |
| Major Roads | **Property in the care of English Heritage** *(see supplement)* |

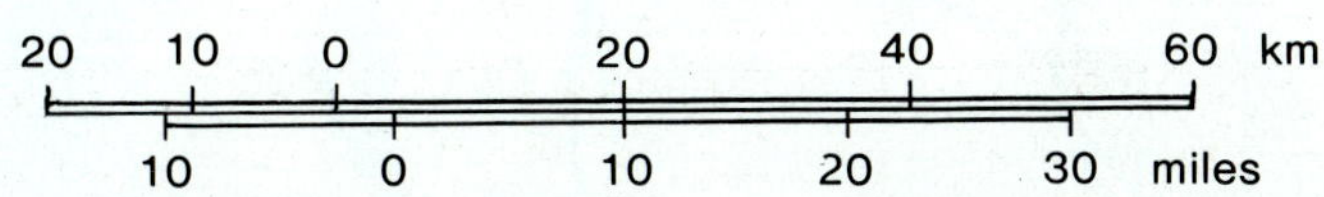






PRINTED IN ENGLAND BY COOK, HAMMOND & KELL LTD.

1 Apsley House
2 Rutland House
3 Lancaster House
4 The Blewcoat School
5 Leighton House Museum
6 Sir John Soane's Museum
7 Sir John's Gate
8 College of Arms
9 Celia and Philip Blairman Houses
17/27 Folgate Street
29 Fournier Street
36 Hanbury Street
10 Royal Geographical Society
11 Travellers' Club
BUCKINGHAMSHIRE
HERTFORDSHIRE
ESSEX
BERKSHIRE
GREATER LONDON
SURREY
KENT
WEST SUSSEX
EAST SUSSEX
River Thames
Hyde Hall
The Magnolias
Capel Manor Institute of Horticultural & Field Studies
88/190 The Crescent
14/15 Clapton Square
Homerton High St
69 Brick Lane
Cable Street
Tower of London
Museum of Garden History
Chelsea Physic Garden
Dulwich College
The Old Palace
Little Holland House
The Banqueting House
Whitehall
Hampton Court Palace
Windsor Castle
Syon Park Gardens
Kew Palace
Kenwood
Highgate Cemetery
Keats House
Old Royal Observatory
Ranger's House
Milton Chantry
Gads Hill Place
Upnor Castle
Temple Manor
Cobham Hall
Owletts
New College of Cobham
St. John's Jerusalem Garden
Eynsford Castle
Lullingstone Castle
Lullingstone Roman Villa
Down House
Quebec House
Emmetts Garden
Squerryes Court
Chartwell
Knole
Ightham Mote
Old Soar Manor
Great Comp
Riverhill House
Black Charles
Leeds Castle
Stoneacre
Boughton Monchelsea Place
Doddington Place
Belmont Park
Chilham Castle Gardens
Godington Park
Sissinghurst Castle Garden
Benenden Walled Garden
Great Maytham Hall
Hole Park
Smallhythe Place
Great Dixter
Brickwall House
Lamb House
Bodiam Castle
Bateman's
Haremere Hall
Battle Abbey
Michelham Priory
Glynde Place
Hever Castle
Chiddingstone Castle
Penshurst Place
Hall Place Gardens
Haxted Mill
Greathed Manor
Crittenden House
Sprivers Garden
Finchcocks
Ladham House
Scotney Castle Garden
The Owl House
Bayham Abbey
Hammerwood Park
Standen
Sackville College
The Spring Hill Wildfowl Park
Kidbrooke Park
Duckyls
Wakehurst Place Garden
The High Beeches
Nymans Garden
Sheffield Park
Sheffield Park Garden
Newick Park
Beeches Farm
Horsted Place Gardens
Borde Hill Garden
Heaselands
Leonardslee
Christ's Hospital
New Hall
Newtimber Place
Danny
St. Mary's
Parham
Coates Manor
Upper Lodge
Petworth House
Malt House
West Dean Gardens
The Weald and Downland Open Air Museum
Ramster
Vann
Feathercombe Gardens
Winkworth Arboretum
Hascombe Court
Coverwood Lakes
Loseley House
Chilworth Manor
Albury Park
Guildford House
Clandon Park
Hatchlands
Polesden Lacey
Pinewood House
Pyrford Court
Wisley Garden
Painshill Park
Claremont
Claremont Landscape Garden
Farnham Castle
Jenkyn Place
Savill Garden
Valley Gardens
Frogmore Gardens
Dorney Court
Cliveden
Hughenden Manor
West Wycombe Park (1750)
Spindrift
Chiltern Open Air Museum
Milton Cottage
Chenies Manor House
Moor Park Mansion
The Gardens of the Rose
2

DYFED
WEST GLAMORGAN
MID GLAMORGAN
SOUTH GLAMORGAN
GWENT
DEVON
CORNWALL
SOMERSET
Aberaeron
Cardigan
Cilgerran Castle
Newcastle Emlyn
Newport
Fishguard
St. Davids Bishops Palace
St. David's
Llawhaden Castle
Haverfordwest
Picton Castle
Milford Haven
Pembroke Dock
Pembroke
Lamphey Palace
Tudor Merchant's House
Tenby
Colby Lodge Garden
Pendine
St. Clears
Carmarthen
Kidwelly Castle
Kidwelly
Carmarthen Bay
Weobley Castle
Port Eynon
The Mumbles
Swansea
Pontardulais
Pontardawe
Neath Abbey
Neath
Port Talbot
Maesteg
Porthcawl
Coity Castle
Bridgend
Cowbridge
Barry
Penarth
Cardiff
Cardiff Castle
Castell Coch
Caerphilly
Caerphilly Castle
Pontypridd
Rhondda
Mountain Ash
Aberdare
Hirwaun
Merthyr Tydfil
Ebbw Vale
Tredegar
Blaenavon
Abertillery
Pontypool
Bargoed
Newbridge
Risca
Cwmbran
Caerleon
Caerleon Roman Fortress
Newport
Tredegar House
Abergavenny
White Castle
Brynmawr
Tretower Court & Castle
Brecon
Trebinshwn House
Sennybridge
Llandovery
Llandeilo
Carreg Cennen Castle
Ammanford
Llanwrda
Talley Abbey
Lampeter
Tregaron
Strata Florida Abbey
Aberystwyth
Ponterwyd
Llangurig
Rhayader
Llanbadarn Fynydd
Llandrindod Wells
Builth Wells
Llanwrtyd Wells
R Wye
R Teifi
R Tywi
R Usk
R Neath
R Taff
R Lugg
Clun
Knighton
New Radnor
Kington
Hergest Croft Gardens
Brilley, Cwmmau Farmhouse
Brobury Garden & Gallery
Moccas Court
Pontrilas
Weston-Super-Mare
Burnham-on-Sea
Ilfracombe
Lynton
Minehead
Dunster
Dunster Castle
Cleeve Abbey
Williton
Kentsford House
Dodington Hall
Coleridge Cottage
Combe Sydenham Hall
Gaulden Manor
Bridgwater
Barford Park
Hestercombe House and Gardens
The Church House
Taunton
Wiveliscombe
Dulverton
Arlington Court
The Bull House
Marwood Hill
Woodside
Barnstaple
Braunton
Northam
Bideford
Tapeley Park
Hartland Abbey
South Molton
R Barle
Bampton
Knightshayes Court
Tiverton
Tiverton Castle
Wellington
Poundisford Park
Barrington Court Gardens
Hatch Court
Ilminster
Chard
Bickleigh Castle
Cullompton
Rosemoor Garden Charitable Trust
R Torridge
Stratton
Bude
Holsworthy
R Tamar
Crediton
Fursdon House
Killerton
Exeter
Honiton
R Otter
Axminster
Cadhay
Fernwood
Sand
Lyme Regis
Sidmouth
Okehampton
Okehampton Castle
Castle Drogo
Moretonhampstead
Powderham Castle
A La Ronde
Exmouth
Ugbrooke House
Dawlish
Teignmouth
Newton Abbot
Bradley Manor
Torquay
Torre Abbey
Torbay
Compton Castle
Paignton
Kirkham House
Brixham
Kingswear
Coleton Fishacre Garden
Dartmouth Castle
Dartmouth
Totnes
Totnes Castle
Bowden House
Ashburton
Two Bridges
R Dart
R Avon
R Plym
Kingsbridge
Salcombe
Overbecks Museum & Garden
Modbury
Flete
Hemerdon House
Saltram House
Plymouth
Royal Citadel
Bickham House
Buckland Abbey
Tavistock
The Garden House
Cotehele House
Callington
Liskeard
Saltash
Antony House
Antony Woodland Gardens
Torpoint
Mount Edgcumbe House & Country Park
Looe
Fowey
R Fowey
Launceston Castle
Launceston
Camelford
The Old Post Office
Tintagel Castle
Long Cross Victorian Gardens
Padstow
Prideaux Place
Wadebridge
Pencarrow House & Gardens
Bodmin
Lanhydrock
Restormel Castle
Lostwithiel
St. Austell
Newquay
Trerice
Trewithen
Truro
Trelissick Garden
Redruth
Camborne
St. Ives
Hayle
Chysauster Ancient Village
Godolphin House
St. Just
Trengwainton Garden
Penzance
St. Michael's Mount
Mounts Bay
Lands End
Helston
Penryn
Falmouth
St. Mawes Castle
Pendennis Castle
Glendurgan Garden
Trelowarren House & Chapel
Lizard
C
D
E
F
1
2
3
4
5

CLWYD
GWYNEDD
POWYS
SHROPSHIRE
STAFFORDSHIRE
WEST MIDLANDS
WARWICKSHIRE
HEREFORD AND WORCESTER
GLOUCESTERSHIRE
OXFORDSHIRE
GWENT
MID GLAMORGAN
WEST GLAMORGAN
SOUTH GLAMORGAN
WILTSHIRE
BERKSHIRE
SOMERSET
DEVON
DORSET
HAMPSHIRE
LEICESTERSHIRE
NORTHAMPTONSHIRE
7
6
5
4
3
E
F
G
H
See Inset on Page 5
Capel Curig
Betws-y-Coed
Ty Mawr
Blaenau Ffestiniog
Ffestiniog
Penrhyndeudraeth
Harlech Castle
Harlech
Cymmer Abbey
Barmouth
Dolgellau
Dinas Mawddwy
Llwyngwril
Machynlleth
Aberdyfi
Ponterwyd
Aberystwyth
Strata Florida Abbey
Tregaron
Lampeter
Talley Abbey
Llanwrda
Llandeilo
Carreg Cennen Castle
Ammanford
Pontardulais
Swansea
Neath Abbey
Neath
Port Talbot
The Mumbles
Porthcawl
Bridgend
Coity Castle
Cowbridge
Cardiff
Castell Coch
Caerphilly Castle
Barry
Penarth
Merthyr Tydfil
Pontypridd
Rhondda
Maesteg
Aberdare
Mountain Ash
Hirwaun
Ebbw Vale
Tredegar
Abertillery
Blaenavon
Pontypool
Newbridge
Risca
Cwmbran
Caerleon Roman Fortress
Newport
Tredegar House
Brecon
Trebinshwn House
Tretower Court & Castle
Abergavenny
White Castle
Raglan Castle
Monmouth
Tintern Abbey
Chepstow
Sennybridge
Llandovery
Builth Wells
Llanwrtyd Wells
Llandrindod Wells
Rhayader
Llangurig
Llanbadarn Fynydd
Newtown
Gregynog
Llanfair Caereinion
Welshpool
Powis Castle
Trelydan Hall
Oswestry
Tyn-Y-Rhos Hall
Chirk Castle
Llangollen
Corwen
Valle Crucis Abbey
Rhosllanerchrugog
Ruabon
Wrexham
Erddig
Overton
Ellesmere
Whitchurch
Whittington
Adcote
Shrewsbury
Rowleys House and Mansion
Condover Hall
Haughmond Abbey
Castle Gates
Attingham Park
Wroxeter (Viroconium) Roman City
Wenlock Priory
Buildwas Abbey
Benthall Hall
Carding Mill Valley & Long Mynd
Church Stretton
Shipton Hall
Wilderhope Manor
Lydham
Clun
Knighton
Stokesay Castle
Ludlow
Ludford House
Burford House Gardens
Woofferton
Croft Castle
Berrington Hall
Mortimer's Cross Mill
Leominster
Lower Brockhampton
Kington
New Radnor
Hergest Croft Gardens
Brilley, Cwmmau Farmhouse
Dinmore Manor
Hereford
The Weir
Brobury Garden & Gallery
Moccas Court
Hellen's
How Caple Court Gardens
Kentchurch Court
Bernithan Court
Ross-on-Wye
Hill Court Gardens
Goodrich Castle
Pontrilas
Ledbury
Eastnor Castle
Great Malvern
Little Malvern Court
Worcester
The Greyfriars
Worcester Cathedral
The Commandery
Spetchley Park
Pershore
Bredon Springs
The Priory
Tewkesbury
Ryelands House
Gloucester
Blackfriars
Westbury Court Garden
Painswick Rococo Garden
Hardwicke Court
Little Dean Hall
Blakeney
Lydney Park
Berkeley Castle
Misarden Park Gardens
Stroud
Tyndale Monument
Cirencester
Cheltenham
Sudeley Castle
Winchcombe
Hailes Abbey
Stanway House
Snowshill Manor
Broadway Tower
Broadway
Evesham
Chedworth Roman Villa
Barnsley House Garden
Arlington Mill
Northleach
Burford
Minster Lovell Hall and Dovecote
Witney
North Leigh Roman Villa
Blenheim Palace
University of Oxford Buildings
Oxford
Kiddington
Stanton Harcourt Manor
Buscot Park
Buscot Old Parsonage
Lechlade
Kingston House
Pusey House Gardens
Faringdon
Abingdon
Milton Manor House
Wallingford
Nuffield Place
Kingstone Lisle Park
Wantage
Ardington House
Ashdown House
Swindon
Lydiard Mansion
Wootton Bassett
Marlborough
Littlecote House
Hungerford
Newbury
Avebury Manor
Avebury Museum
Calne
Bowood House & Gardens
Chippenham
Sheldon Manor
Corsham Court
Lacock Abbey
Bath
Great Chalfield Manor
Bradford on Avon
Melksham
Devizes
Broadleas
Trowbridge
The Courts Garden
Westwood Manor
Farleigh Castle
Chalcot House
Westbury
Frome
Longleat House
Warminster
Stourhead
Shepton Mallet
Radstock
Bristol
Clevedon Court
Clevedon
Weston-Super-Mare
Burnham-on-Sea
King John's Hunting Lodge
Milton Lodge Gardens
The Bishop's Palace
Wells
Glastonbury Tribunal
Glastonbury
Street
Minehead
Dunster Castle
Dodington Hall
Kentsford House
Cleeve Abbey
Combe Sydenham Hall
Coleridge Cottage
Bridgwater
Barford Park
Gaulden Manor
Wiveliscombe
Dulverton
Taunton
Hestercombe House and Gardens
Maunsel House
Poundisford Park
Barrington Court Gardens
Hatch Court
Barrington Court
Ilminster
Muchelney Abbey
Priest's House
Lytes Cary Manor
Ilchester
Stoke-Sub-Hamdon Priory
Tintinhull House
Montacute House
Yeovil
Brympton d'Evercy
East Lambrook Manor
Hadspen House
Wincanton
Stowell Hill
Sandford Orcas Manor House
Sherborne Old Castle
Sherborne Castle
Purse Caundle Manor
Melbury House
Shaftesbury
Fiddleford Mill House
Pythouse
Old Wardour Castle
Chard
Cricket St Thomas
Crewkerne
Forde Abbey
Clapton Court
Parnham House and Garden
Mapperton
Minterne
Bridport
Axminster
Honiton
Lyme Regis
Lyme Bay
Abbotsbury – Swannery & Sub-Tropical Gardens
Wolfeton House
Hardy's Cottage
Athelhampton
Clouds Hill
Dorchester
Puddletown
Weymouth
Portland Castle
Portsmouth
Blandford Forum
Milton Abbey
Kingston Lacy House
Wimborne
Deans Court
Priest's House Museum
Wareham
Corfe Castle
Swanage
Smedmore
Bere Regis
Poole
Compton Acres Gardens
Bournemouth
Russell-Cotes Art Gallery & Museum
Christchurch
Cranborne Manor Gardens
Edmondsham House and Gardens
Fordingbridge
Breamore House
Salisbury
Wilton House
Wilton
Philipps House
Old Sarum
Stonehenge
Amesbury
Heale House
Stockbridge
Houghton Lodge
Mottisfont Abbey
Romsey
Broadlands
Hillier Arboretum
Winchester
The Pilgrims' Hall
Avington Park
Southampton
Medieval Merchants House
Netley Abbey
Titchfield Abbey
Fort Brockhurst
Fareham
Gosport
Beaulieu
Exbury Gardens
Lyndhurst
Lymington
Spinners
Macpenny's
Hurst Castle
The Needles Old Battery
Yarmouth Castle
Newport
Newtown Old Town Hall
Carisbrooke Castle
Appuldurcombe House
Osborne House
Cowes
Andover
The Hawk Conservancy
Highclere Castle
Sandham Memorial Chapel
Basingstoke
Upavon
Tottenham House
Burbage
Ilfracombe
Lynton
Arlington Court
Marwood Hill
The Bull House
Woodside
Barnstaple
South Molton
Knightshayes Court
Bampton
Tiverton
Tiverton Castle
Rosemoor Garden Charitable Trust
Bickleigh Castle
Cullompton
Killerton
Crediton
Fursdon House
Exeter
Fernwood
Cadhay
Sand
Sidmouth
A La Ronde
Powderham Castle
Exmouth
Dawlish
Teignmouth
Okehampton
Okehampton Castle
Castle Drogo
Moretonhampstead
Ugbrooke House
Two Bridges
Ashburton
Newton Abbot
Bradley
Stoke-on-Trent
Newcastle-under-Lyme
Crewe
Nantwich
Dorfold Hall
Cholmondeley Castle Gardens
Churche's Mansion
Woodhey Chapel
Rode Hall
Dorothy Clive Garden
Whitmore Hall
Market Drayton
Hodnet Hall Gardens
Eccleshall Castle
Stafford
Shugborough
Ancient High House
Rugeley
Cannock
Penkridge
Weston Park
Boscobel House
Newport
Lilleshall Abbey
Telford
Chillington Hall
Moseley Old Hall
Wolverhampton
Wightwick Manor
Bridgnorth
Dudmaston
Upton Cressett Hall
Acton Round Hall
The Lawns
Dudley
Stourbridge
Hagley Hall
Kidderminster
Bewdley
Harvington Hall
Stone House Cottage Gardens
Hanbury Hall
Bromsgrove
Avoncroft Museum of Buildings
Clack's Farm
Redditch
Eastgrove Cottage
Abberley Hall
Stourport-on-Severn
Tenbury Wells
Mawley Hall
Birmingham
Aston Hall
Blakesley Hall
Solihull
Sutton Coldfield
Walsall
Brownhills
Lichfield
Wall (Letocetum) Roman Site
Tamworth
Tamworth Castle
Hanch Hall
Atherstone
Nuneaton
Arbury Hall
Coventry
Coventry Cathedral
Kenilworth
Kenilworth Castle
Stoneleigh Abbey
Lord Leycester Hospital
Warwick Castle
Warwick
Royal Leamington Spa
Binswood Hall
St. Mary's Church
Packwood House
Baddesley Clinton
Henley-in-Arden
Mary Arden's House
Coughton Court
Alcester
Ragley Hall
Anne Hathaway's Cottage
Shakespeare's Birthplace Trust Properties
The Grammar School
Charlecote Park
Stratford-upon-Avon
Ettington
Farnborough Hall
Upton House
Honington Hall
Brook Cottage
Banbury
Broughton Castle
Hidcote Manor Garden
Kiftsgate Court
Batsford Park Arboretum
Moreton-in-Marsh
Sezincote Garden
Chastleton House
Chipping Norton
Ditchley Park
Stow-on-the-Wold
Rousham House
Aynhoe Park
Deddington
Bicester
Canon's Ashby House
Sulgrave Manor
Brackley
Rugby
Stanford Hall
Lutterworth
Coton Manor Gardens
Holdenby House
Daventry
Hinckley
Leicester
Kirby Muxloe Castle
Battlefield of Bosworth Project
Wygston's House
Coalville
Ashby De La Zouch Castle
Ashby-de-la-Zouch
Manor House
Calke Abbey
Swadlincote
Burton-upon-Trent
Sudbury Hall
Uttoxeter
Derby
Kedleston Hall
All Saints
Long Eaton
Ilkeston
Heanor
Belper
Ripley
Eastwood
Nottingham
Wollaton Hall
Thrumpton Hall
Whatton Garden
Loughborough
Prestwold Hall
The Mansion House
Alton Towers
Ashbourne
Cheadle
Papplewick Hall
Hucknall
R Severn
R Wye
R Dee
R Dyfi
R Teifi
R Tywi
R Usk
R Neath
R Taff
R Lugg
R Avon
R Thames
R Kennet
R Test
R Stour
R Exe
R Otter
R Axe
R Barle
R Brue
R Wylye
R Mersey

NORWICH
1 Bacon House
2 Bridewell Museum
3 Briton's Arms
4 Churchman House
5 18 Colegate
6 Dragon Hall
7 Augustine Steward's House
8 Elm Hill
9 Lazar House
10 Norwich Castle
11 St. Andrew's and Blackfriars Hall
12 St. Peter Hungate Museum
13 Strangers Hall Museum
14 Atuart House and Suckling Halls
15 Subscription Library
See Inset on Page 2
BRISTOL AND BATH
NORFOLK
SUFFOLK
ESSEX
KENT
SURREY
EAST SUSSEX
WEST SUSSEX
CAMBRIDGESHIRE
LONDON
GREATER LONDON
NORWICH
GREAT YARMOUTH
LOWESTOFT
IPSWICH
CAMBRIDGE
PETERBOROUGH
COLCHESTER
CHELMSFORD
SOUTHEND-ON-SEA
CANTERBURY
MARGATE
RAMSGATE
BRIGHTON
EASTBOURNE
HASTINGS
BRISTOL
BATH
The Wash
7
6
5
4
J
K
L
M
G

Logan Botanic Garden
Drummore
Port William
Whithorn
Ramsey
Peel
Douglas
Port Erin
Castletown
10
9
8
7
6
D
E
F
G
Maryport
Workington
Whitehaven
Egremont
Wordsworth House
Cockermouth
Mirehouse
Keswick
Bassenthwaite Lake
Derwent Water
Crummock Water
Wast Water
19/20 Irish Street
CUMBRIA
Hutton-in-the-Forest
Penrith
Brougham Castle
Acorn Bank
Dalemain
Patterdale
Appleby in Westmorland
Brough Castle
Brough
Barnard Castle
Kirkby Stephen
Tebay
Rydal Mount
Ambleside
Stagshaw
Townend
Brantwood
Muncaster Castle
Ravenglass
Graythwaite Hall
Stott Park Bobbin Mill
Newby Bridge
Broughton in Furness
Kendal
Abbot Hall Art Gallery & Museum of Lakeland Life & Industry
Levens Hall
Sizergh Castle
Sedbergh
Hawes
Bolton Castle
Millom
Ulverston
Holker Hall
Furness Abbey
Dalton-in-Furness
Conishead Priory
BARROW-IN-FURNESS
Leighton Hall
Kirkby Lonsdale
NORT
R Wear
R Eden
R Lune
R Wharfe
Settle
MORECAMBE
Heysham
Ashton Memorial
Judges' Lodgings
Lancaster
Skipton Castle
Skipton
Fleetwood
Gisburn
Broughton Hall
BARNOLDSWICK
LANCASHIRE
Cleveleys
Thornton
Browsholme Hall
Clitheroe
Colne
Barrowford
Bronte Parsonage
BLACKPOOL
Longridge
Martholme
Whalley
Padiham
Gawthorpe Hall
Burnley
Towneley Hall Art Gallery & Museum & Museum of Local Crafts & Industries
Hoghton Tower
Gt. Harwood
Accrington
Lytham St. Anne's
Kirkham
PRESTON
Samlesbury Hall
BLACKBURN
Bacup
Todmorden
Meols Hall
Leyland
Astley Hall
Darwen
Rawtenstall
Turton Tower
SOUTHPORT
CHORLEY
Rufford Old Hall
Hall i' th' Wood
BOLTON
BURY
ROCHDALE
Smithills Hall
Formby
Ormskirk
WIGAN
FARNWORTH
MIDDLETON
OLDHAM
SKELMERSDALE
HINDLEY
Heaton Hall
MANCHESTER
CROSBY
ST. HELENS
LEIGH
SALFORD
Wallasey
Croxteth Hall & Country Park
PRESCOT
Platt Hall
Wythenshawe Hall
Fletcher Moss
HYDE
STOCKPORT
MERSEYSIDE
Hoylake
BIRKENHEAD
LIVERPOOL
Speke Hall
WARRINGTON
Dunham Massey
Quarry Bank Mill
Altrincham
Bramall Hall
Norton Priory Museum
WIDNES
RUNCORN
Handforth Hall
Adlington Hall
Arley Hall and Gardens
KNUTSFORD
Tatton Park
Wilmslow
Nether Alderley Mill
Hare Hill Garden
NESTON
Ness Gardens
ELLESMERE PORT
NORTHWICH
Peover Hall
Macclesfield
Capesthorne
Gawsworth Hall
CHESTER
Flint
Holywell
CONNAH'S QUAY
Ewloe Castle
Hawarden
Mold
Middlewich
WINSFORD
SANDBACH
Congleton
Tarporley
Beeston Castle
Little Moreton Hall
Leek
Woodhey Chapel
Cholmondeley Castle Gardens
Nantwich
Dorfold Hall
CREWE
Churche's Mansion
Rode Hall
NEWCASTLE-UNDER-LYME
STOKE-ON-TRENT
Wrexham
Erddig
Whitchurch
Dorothy Clive Garden
Whitmore House
Market Drayton
STAFFORDSHIRE
Hodnet Hall Gardens
Eccleshall Castle
Ancient High House
Overton
Ellesmere
Whittington
Adcote
Newport
Lilleshall Abbey
Haughmond Abbey
Penkridge
Weston Park
Boscobel House
SHREWSBURY
Castle Gates
Attingham Park
Wellington
TELFORD
Chillington Hall
Rowleys House and Mansion
Condover Hall
Wroxeter (Viroconium) Roman City
Buildwas Abbey
Moseley Old Hall
Wenlock Priory
Ironbridge
Benthall Hall
The Lawns
WOLVERHAMPTON
Wightwick Manor
Wilderhope Manor
Acton Round Hall
Upton Cresset Hall
Bridgnorth
Dudmaston
DUDLEY
STOURBRIDGE
Hagley Hall
Carding Mill Valley & Long Mynd
Church Stretton
Shipton Hall
SHROPSHIRE
Lydham
Stokesay Castle
Clun
KIDDERMINSTER
Stone House Cottage Gardens
Bewdley
Harvington Hall
Hartlebury Castle
BROMSGROVE
Mawley Hall
STOURPORT-ON-SEVERN
Ludlow
Ludford House
Burford House Gardens
Woofferton
Avoncroft Museum of Buildings
Jack's Fo..
Tenbury Wells
Eastgrove Cottage
Abberley
Croft Castle
Berrington Hall
Mortimer's Cross Mill
Leominster
Lower Brockhampton
Worcester Cathedral
WORCESTER
The Greyfriars
The Commandery
Knighton
Kington
Llandrindod Wells
Rhayader
R Wye
Llanbadarn Fynydd
Newtown
R Severn
Gregynog
Llanfair Caereinion
Welshpool
Powis Castle
Trelydan Hall
POWYS
Machynlleth
Dinas Mawddwy
Aberdyfi
R Dyfi
Llwyngwril
Cardigan Bay
Ponterwyd
Llangurig
Aberystwyth
Strata Florida Abbey
Tregaron
Aberaeron
Barmouth
Dolgellau
Cymmer Abbey
Harlech Castle
Harlech
GWYNEDD
Bala
Corwen
Llangollen
Valle Crucis Abbey
Ruabon
Chirk Castle
Chirk
Tyn-Y-Rhos Hall
Oswestry
Rhosllanerchrugog
Plas Teg
CLWYD
Ruthin
Denbigh
Denbigh Castle
R Clwyd
Bodelwyddan Castle
Rhuddlan Castle
Bodrhyddan Hall
Rhyl
Gyrn Castle
PRESTATYN
Colwyn Bay
Abergele
LLANDUDNO
Plas Mawr
Aberconwy House
Conwy
Conwy Castle
Bodnant Garden
Cochwillan Old Hall
Llanrwst
Gwydir Uchaf Chapel
Betws-y-Coed
Capel Curig
Ty Mawr
Blaenau Ffestiniog
Ffestiniog
Penrhyndeudraeth
Porthmadog
Criccieth Castle
Pwllheli
Nefyn
Abersoch
Amlwch
HOLYHEAD
Llangefni
Llanfairfechan
Beaumaris Castle
Penrhyn Castle
Bangor
Plas Newydd
Caernarfon
Caernarfon Castle (1283-1322)
Bryn Bras Castle
Dinorwic Slate Quarry museum
R Dee
R Mersey
R Ribble

HARTLEPOOL
CLEVELAND
REDCAR
BILLINGHAM
Saltburn-by-the-Sea
Stockton-on-Tees
MIDDLESBROUGH
Ormesby Hall
Guisborough Priory
Whitby Abbey
Whitby
DARLINGTON
R Esk
Stokesley
Mount Grace Priory
Northallerton
Scalby
Scarborough
Scarborough Castle
Rievaulx Abbey
Rievaulx Terrace
Gilling Castle
Pickering Castle
Ebberston Hall
Sion Hill Hall
Duncombe Park
Helmsley Castle
Nunnington Hall
Pickering
Filey
Norton Conyers
Byland Abbey
Newburgh Priory
Shandy Hall
Hovingham Hall
YORKSHIRE
Newby Hall
RIPON
Boroughbridge
Easingwold
Castle Howard
Malton
Norton
Sewerby Hall
Bridlington
Markenfield Hall
Aldborough Roman Town
Sutton Park
Sheriff Hutton Park
Kirkham Priory
Sledmere House
Burton Agnes Hall
Gt Driffield
Beningbrough Hall
KNARESBOROUGH
HARROGATE
Treasurer's House
Fairfax House
YORK
Merchant Adventurer's Hall
Clifford's Tower
Burnby Hall Gardens
Pocklington
R Hull
Hornsea
Stockeld Park
Wetherby
Bramham Park
HUMBERSIDE
Guildhall, Beverley
Beverley
Harewood House & Bird Garden
WEST YORKSHIRE
Tadcaster
Lotherton Hall
R Ouse
Selby
Burton Constable
Wilberforce House
Maister House
KINGSTON UPON HULL
Blaydes House
The Charterhouse
Withernsea
LEEDS
Temple Newsam
Ledston Hall
CASTLEFORD
Howden
Goole
R Aire
Humber
New Holland
Patrington
Oakwell Hall
Batley
Nostell Priory
Ackworth School
Carlton Towers
Barton upon Humber
Dewsbury
Wakefield
PONTEFRACT
Thornton Abbey
Immingham
Thorne
Normanby Hall
SCUNTHORPE
GRIMSBY
Cleethorpes
Hatfield
M62
M180
Brigg
Cannon Hall
Barnsley
Monk Bretton Priory
The Sue Ryder Home, Hickleton Hall
Elsham Hall Country Park
Epworth
Caistor
Wombwell
Doncaster
Mexborough
R Trent
Conisbrough Castle
Bawtry
The Old Hall Gainsborough
Market Rasen
Rotherham
Louth
Mablethorpe
SOUTH YORKSHIRE
SHEFFIELD
Sheffield Botanic Gardens
Maltby
Roche Abbey
Worksop
E.Retford
Wragby
Peveril Castle
Clumber Park
Lincoln Castle
Harrington Hall
Chesterfield
Bolsover
Bolsover Castle
Doddington Hall
LINCOLN
Bishop's Palace
Horncastle
Chatsworth
Haddon Hall
Ollerton
Carlton Hall
LINCOLNSHIRE
Gunby Hall
Skegness
Rowsley
SUTTON IN ASHFIELD
Hardwick Hall
Bede Houses
MANSFIELD
Matlock
Winster Market House
Lea Rhododendron Gardens
Newark-on-Trent
Tattershall Castle (1440)
R Witham
Sibsey Trader Mill
KIRKBY IN ASHFIELD
Newstead Abbey
Papplewick Hall
Ripley
HUCKNALL
Fulbeck Hall
Sleaford
Boston
The Wash
Hunstanton
Holkham Hall
Wells-next-the-Sea
Blakeney
Cromer
The Mansion House
BELPER
HEANOR
NOTTINGHAM
Clifton Hall
Marston Hall
Belton House
Swineshead
Walsingham Abbey
Holt
Felbrigg Hall
Kedleston Hall
ILKESTON
Wollaton Hall
Holme Pierrepont Hall
Grantham
Sutterton
Sandringham House & Grounds
Fakenham
DERBY
All Saints
Belvoir Castle
Grantham House
Donington
Trinity Hospital
Houghton Hall
Mannington Hall Gardens
Blickling Hall
Aylsham
Sudbury Hall
LONG EATON
Thrumpton Hall
R Glen
Castle Rising
Spalding
Holbeach
Grimsthorpe Castle
Swannington Manor Gardens
R Bure
BURTON-UPON-TRENT
NOTTINGHAMSHIRE
Woolsthorpe Manor
Springfield Gardens
Long Sutton
King's Lynn
NORFOLK
Calke Abbey
Whatton Garden
Prestwold Hall
Melton Mowbray
Bourne
Castle Acre Priory and Castle
East Dereham
SWADLINCOTE
Ashby De La Zouch Castle
Loughborough
R Welland
Wisbech
Peckover House
Market Deeping
LEICESTERSHIRE
Coalville
Little Cressingham Mill
Swaffham
NORWICH
Manor House
Oakham Castle
Oakham
Downham Market
Oxburgh Hall
Wymondham
Tamworth Castle
Wygston's House
Belgrave Hall
Priest's House
Stamford
Guyhirn
Welle Manor Hall
Kirby Muxloe Castle
Guildhall
Burghley House
Duddington
Thorney
Stoke Ferry
Tamworth
LEICESTER
Longthorpe Tower
R Nene
March
Attleborough
Rainthorpe Hall & Gardens
Battlefield of Bosworth Project
Uppingham
Lyddington Bedehouse
Wansford
PETERBOROUGH
Whittlesey
Atherstone
Kirby Hall
Deene Park
Elton Hall
Mundford
Grime's Graves
SUTTON COLDFIELD
HINCKLEY
Rockingham Castle
CORBY
Southwick Hall
NUNEATON
Arbury Hall
Langton Hall
Oundle
Chatteris
Littleport
Brandon
Thetford
Market Harborough
Rushton Triangular Lodge
Lyveden New Bield
Ramsey
BEDWORTH
Lutterworth
Boughton House
Elford Park
Ely
Prior Crauden's Chapel
Diss
Coventry Cathedral
COVENTRY
Stanford Hall
Husbands Bosworth
Rushton Hall
Thrapston
Euston Hall
Wingfield Castle
Wingfield College
Kettering
Mildenhall
Ixworth Abbey
Ixworth
Kenilworth Castle
KENILWORTH
RUGBY
Lamport Hall
Huntingdon
Godmanchester Island Hall
Stoneleigh Abbey
Coton Manor Gardens
Wellingborough
Denny Abbey
CAMBRIDGESHIRE
Lord Leycester Hospital
ROYAL LEAMINGTON SPA
Binswood Hall
Holdenby House Gardens
Higham Ferrers
Kimbolton Castle
Anglesey Abbey
Newmarket
Bury St. Edmunds
Haughley Park
Post Mill
Warwick Castle
St. Mary's Church
Daventry
Althorp
Hinwick House
Ickworth
Stowmarket
Helmingham Hall
Shakespeare's Birthplace
NORTHAMPTON
Delapre Abbey
St. Neots
University of Cambridge
University Botanic Garden
CAMBRIDGE
SUFFOLK
Otley Hall
Bushmead Priory
Kentwell Hall
Blakenham Woodland Garden
Ipswich Museum
Anne Hathaway's Cottage
Stratford-upon-Avon
NORTHAMPTONSHIRE
Cowper & Newton Museum
BEDFORD
Cecil Higgins Art Gallery
Nether Hall
Melford Hall
H
J
K
L
10
9
8
7
6
NORWICH
1 Bacon House
2 Bridewell Museum
3 Briton's Arms
4 Churchman House
5 18 Colegate
6 Dragon Hall
7 Augustine Steward's House
8 Elm Hill
9 Lazar House
10 Norwich Castle
11 St. Andrew's and Blackfriars Hall
12 St. Peter Hungate Museum
13 Strangers Hall Museum
14 Atuart House and Suckling Halls
15 Subscription Library

Fort William
Corpach
Acharacle
Loch Shiel
Corran
Kinlochleven
Glencoe
Loch Sunart
Tobermory
Ardtornish
Lochaline
Portnacroish
Salen
Bridge of Orchy
Craignure
Torosay Castle and Gardens
Connel
Oban
Taynuilt
Tyndrum
Fionnphort
Bunessan
Kilninver
Kilmelford
Inveraray Castle
Inveraray
Loch Awe
Crianlarich
Ardlui
Tarbet
Kilmartin
Furnace
Crarae Woodland Garden
Loch Fyne
Ardlussa
Garelochead
Luss
Loch Lomond
Benmore
The Hill House
HELENSBURGH
Balloch Castle Country Park
ALEXANDRIA
Finlaystone House and Gardens
PORT GLASGOW
Dumbarton
Dumbarton Castle
Dunoon
Greenock
Tighnabruaich
Port Askaig
Feolin Ferry
Craighouse
Bridgend
Tarbert
Rothesay
Largs
Kelburn Castle and Country Centre
Clachan
Achmore
STRATHCLYDE
Lochranza
Brodick Castle, Garden and Country Park
Brodick
Lamlash
Blackwaterfoot
Port Ellen
Glenbarr
Campbeltown
ARDROSSAN
SALTCOATS
Kilwinning
Irvine
Kilmarnock
Galston
TROON
Bachelors' Club
Mauchline
PRESTWICK
Ayr
R Ayr
Burns Cottage
Culzean Castle, Garden and Country Park
Maybole
Scouter Johnnie's Cottage
Blairquhan Castle & Gardens
Girvan
Penkill Castle
R Stinchar
Ballantrae
Barrhill
Bargrennan
Kirkcolm
Cairnryan
Stranraer
Castle Kennedy Gardens
Glenluce
Portpatrick
Sandhead
Logan Botanic Garden
Drummore
Port William
Whithorn
Wigtown
Newton Stewart
New Galloway
DUMFRIES AND GALLOWAY
Carsphairn
Dalmellington
New Cumnock
Cumnock
Muirkirk
Sanquhar
R Nith
Drumlanrig Castle
Thornhill
Moniaive
Maxwelton House
Dumfries
Crocketford
Sweetheart Abbey
Caerlaverock Castle
Castle Douglas
Threave Garden
Dalbeattie
Arbigland Gardens
Broughton House
Kirkcudbright
R Dee
Solway Firth
Maryport
Wordsworth House
Workington
Whitehaven
19/20 Irish Street
Egremont
Moffat
Blair Castle
Blair Atholl
R Tummel
Pitlochry
Kirkmichael
Bridge of Cally
Blairgowrie
Aberfeldy
Castle Menzies
Kenmore
Loch Tay
Killin
Dunkeld
Amulree
Scone Palace
Huntingtower Castle
Lochearnhead
Crieff
Comrie
Drummond Castle Gardens
R Earn
Auchterarder
Callander
Greenloaning
Doune
Dunblane
Menstrie Castle
Castle Campbell
Tillicoultry
Aberfoyle
R Forth
CENTRAL
Stirling
Stirling Castle
Alloa
Cowdenbeath
DUNFERMLINE
The Town House & The Study
Culross Palace
Kinneil House
BO'NESS
Hopetoun House
Larbert
Falkirk
GRANGEMOUTH
Linlithgow Palace
LINLITHGOW
The House of the Binns
Niddry Castle
KILSYTH
KIRKINTILLOCH
Cumbernauld
BATHGATE
MILNGAVIE
Glasgow Cathedral
The Tenement House
Victoria Park
Botanic Gardens
GLASGOW
Paisley
Bellahouston Park
JOHNSTONE
Ross Hall Park
Weaver's Cottage
Linn Park
Greenbank Garden
Hutchesons' Hall
AIRDRIE
COATBRIDGE
Armadale
WHITBURN
BARRHEAD
Pollok House & Park
Bothwell Castle
HAMILTON
MOTHERWELL
WISHAW
Beith
EAST KILBRIDE
Carluke
Carnwath
Strathaven
Lanark
R Clyde
Biggar
DOUGLAS
Kailzie
Dawyck
Lough Neagh
R Bann
Belfast Lough
Ramsey
15
14
13
12
11
B
C
D
E

EDINBURGH
Dalmeny House
Lauriston Castle
Granton
Lamb's House
Leith
Royal Botanic Garden
Cramond Bridge
The Georgian House
Palace of Holyroodhouse
Portobello
Hamilton House
Edinburgh Castle
Gladstone's Land
Musselborough
Corstorphine
Morningside
Craig millar
Inveresk Lodge
Suntrap
Colinton
Liberton
River Esk
Dalkeith Park
Fairmilehead
Water of Leith
Dalkeith
Lasswade
Malleny Garden
Loanhead
Edzell Castle & Gardens
Brechin
House of Dun
Montrose
Forfar
Glamis Castle
Arbroath
Carnoustie
Newport-on-Tay
ST. ANDREWS
Hill of Tarvit
FIFE
Balcarres
Kellie Castle
Kirkton of Largo
Leven
METHIL
BUCKHAVEN
KIRKCALDY
Firth of Forth
Dirleton Castle & Gardens
Tantallon Castle
Gosford House
Amisfield Mains
Beanston
Dunbar
Preston Mill
LOTHIAN
See Inset
Haddington
Lennoxlove
Stevenson House
Cockburnspath
Ayton Castle
Ayton
Manderston
Duns
Berwick Barracks
Berwick upon Tweed
Norham Castle
Lindisfarne Priory
Lindisfarne Castle
Thirlestane Castle
Lauder
Greenlaw
Hirsel Grounds & Dundock Wood
Coldstream
Stow
Mellerstain
Robert Smalls Printing Works
Galashiels
Mertoun Gardens
Floors Castle
Kelso
Priorwood Garden
Abbotsford House
Smailholm Tower
Melrose
Melrose Abbey
Dryburgh Abbey
Bamburgh Castle
Belford
Bowhill
Selkirk
R Tweed
BORDERS
Wooler
Preston Tower
Dunstanburgh Castle
Howick Gardens
Jedburgh Abbey
Jedburgh
HAWICK
Alnwick Castle
Alnwick
Warkworth Hermitage
Warkworth Castle
Amble
R Teviot
R Coquet
Cragside House & Country Park
Brinkburn Priory
Felton
NORTHUMBERLAND
Kielder Reservoir
Ashington
Newbiggin by the Sea
Hermitage Castle
Wallington House, Garden & Grounds
Meldon Park
Morpeth
Bedlington
BLYTH
Langholm
Seaton Delaval Hall
Canonbie
Belsay Hall
Whitley Bay
Tynemouth Castle and Priory
TYNEMOUTH
Hadrian's Wall
Chesters Fort
Housesteads Roman Fort
George Stephenson's Cottage
NEWCASTLE UPON TYNE
Corbridge Roman Site
Longtown
R Lyne
Chesterholm
Haydon Bridge
Corbridge
Gateshead
SOUTH SHIELDS
Lanercost Priory
Naworth Castle
Haltwhistle
Hexham
Prudhoe
Prudhoe Castle
TYNE AND WEAR
Castletown House
Brampton
R S Tyne
R Tyne
Gibside Chapel & Avenue
Washington Old Hall
SUNDERLAND
WASHINGTON
Hylton Castle
Carlisle Castle
CARLISLE
Carlisle Cathedral
CHESTER-LE-STREET
Consett
SEAHAM
Finchale Priory
Houghton-le-Spring
Alston
Easington
PETERLEE
Durham Castle
Durham University Botanic Gardens
DURHAM
SPENNYMOOR
Hutton-in-the-Forest
R Wear
HARTLEPOOL
Brougham Castle
Auckland Castle
Sedgefield
CLEVELAND
BISHOP AUCKLAND
Mirehouse
Penrith
Acorn Bank
REDCAR
West Auckland
BILLINGHAM
Saltburn-by-the-Sea
Dalemain
Raby Castle
Stockton-on-Tees
Loftus
Appleby in Westmorland
MIDDLESBROUGH
Ormesby Hall
Gisborough
Guisborough Priory
R Eden
Barnard Castle
Brough Castle
Brough
Barnard Castle
Rokeby Park
Whitby Abbey
Whitby
Patterdale
DARLINGTON
Bowes
1 The Square, Greta Bridge
CUMBRIA
Stokesley
R Esk
Kirkby Stephen
Rydal Mount
Ambleside
Stagshaw
Tebay
Scotch Corner
Georgian Theatre
Easby Abbey
Richmond Castle
Richmond
Mount Grace Priory
Townend
R Duddon
Northallerton
Scalby
Abbot Hall Art Gallery & Museum of Lakeland Life & Industry
Kendal
Sedbergh
Bolton Castle
Leyburn
Constable Burton Hall
Rievaulx Abbey
Rievaulx Terrace
Scarborough
Scarborough Castle
Graythwaite
Stott Park Bobbin
Levens Hall
Sizergh Castle
Middleham Castle
Bedale Hall
Sion Hill
Thorp Perrow Arboretum
Helmsley
Gilling Castle
Helmsley Castle
Duncombe Park
Pickering
Pickering Castle
Nunnington Hall
Filey
Thirsk
15
14
13
12
11
F
G
H
J

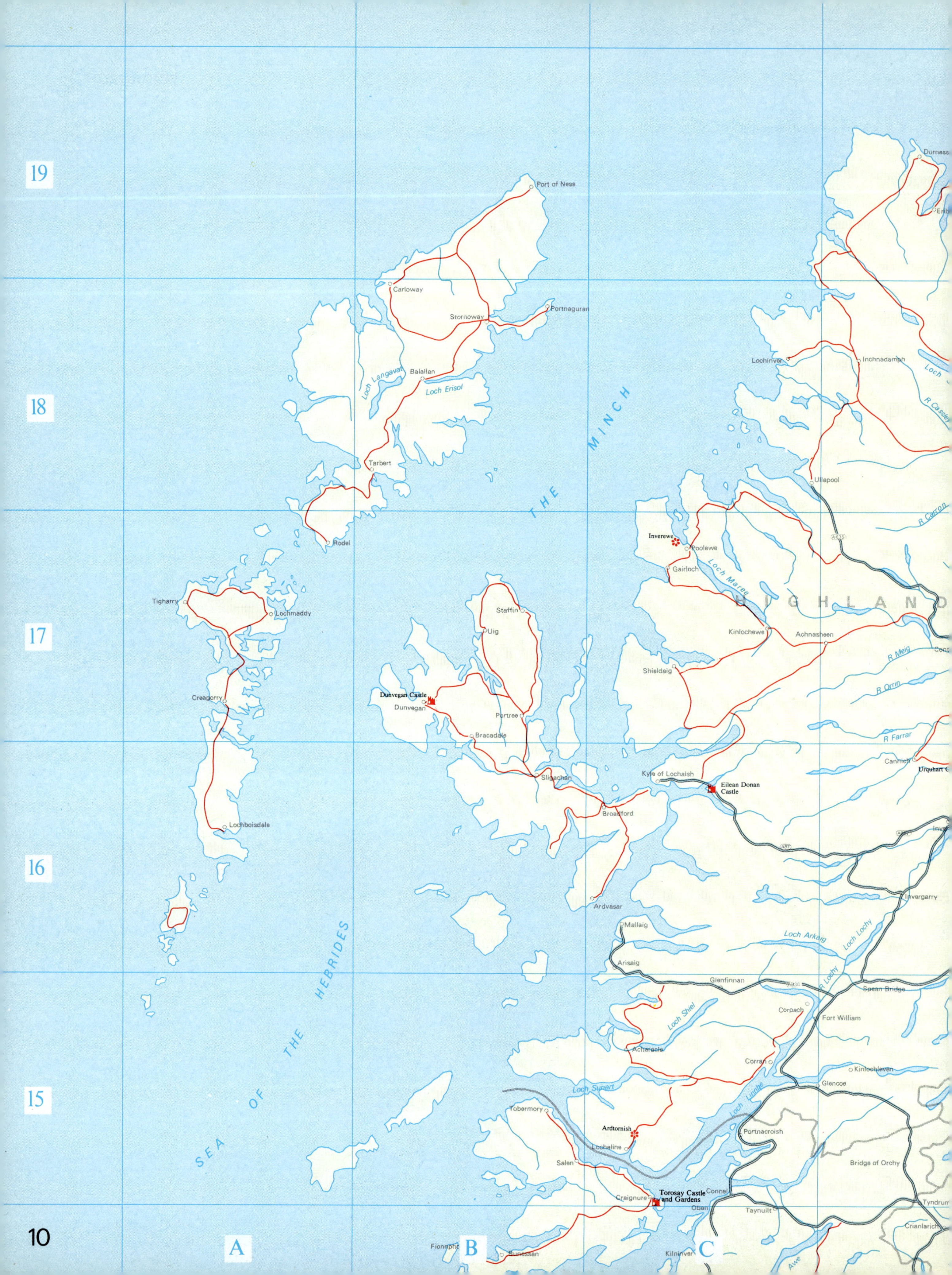
19
18
17
16
15
A
B
C
Port of Ness
Carloway
Stornoway
Portnaguran
Balallan
Loch Langavat
Loch Erisol
Tarbert
Rodel
THE MINCH
Tigharry
Lochmaddy
Creagorry
Lochboisdale
SEA OF THE HEBRIDES
Staffin
Uig
Dunvegan Castle
Dunvegan
Portree
Bracadale
Sligachan
Broadford
Ardvasar
Kyle of Lochalsh
Eilean Donan Castle
Durness
Lochinver
Inchnadamph
R Cassley
Ullapool
R Carron
A835
Inverewe
Poolewe
Gairloch
Loch Maree
HIGHLAND
Kinlochewe
Achnasheen
R Meig
R Orrin
R Farrar
Shieldaig
Cannich
Urquhart
A87
Invergarry
Mallaig
Arisaig
Loch Arkaig
Loch Lochy
R Lochy
Glenfinnan
A830
Spean Bridge
Corpach
Fort William
Loch Shiel
Acharacle
Corran
Kinlochleven
Glencoe
Loch Sunart
Loch Linnhe
Tobermory
Ardtornish
Lochaline
Portnacroish
Salen
Bridge of Orchy
Connel
Torosay Castle and Gardens
Craignure
Oban
Taynuilt
Tyndrum
Crianlarich
Fionnphort
Bunessan
Kilninver
Awe

# NORTH AMERICA

# *in focus*



*Paul Guinness*

Hodder & Stoughton
LONDON SYDNEY AUCKLAND TORONTO

# Acknowledgements

The publisher would like to thank the following for their permission to reproduce copyright material:

Associated Press for 'The land of a million millionaires' (5.1 Figure 1); The Canadian Business Review and the Conference Board of Canada for a figure from *The Canadian Business Review*, Autumn 1985 (11.3 Figure 6); Coal Age and the Mining Information Services for a figure from *Coal Age*, May 1985 (7.4 Figure 5); The Congressional Quarterly Inc for the chart 'Medicaid Enrollment Trends' 11 May 1985 (5.3 Figure 5); The Economist for a figure from *The Economist* 20 October 1984 (9.2 Figure 6), a figure from *The Economist* 14 May 1983 (11.3 Figure 1), a figure from *The Economist* 2 March 1985 (11.3 Figure 2),

*For Mary, Courtenay and Christopher.*

*British Library Cataloguing in Publication Data*

Guinness, Paul
North America in Focus
1. North America. Human geographical features – For schools
I. Title
304.2'097

[redacted]



Typeset by Photo·graphics, Honiton, Devon

Printed for Hodder and Stoughton Educational a division of Hodder and Stoughton Limited, Mill Road, Dunton Green, Sevenoaks, Kent by Colorcraft Ltd.

'Renewable energy' *The Economist* 24 May 1986 (8.7 Figure 5), 'Back to the City' *The Economist* 8 June 1985 (7.1 Figure 3), 'Go South' *The Economist* 23 May 1981 (5.2 Figure 4), a figure from *The Economist* 19 May 1984 (9.6 Figure 2), 'Some Issues in Californian Agriculture' *The Economist* 2 March 1987 (10.5 Figure 5), a figure from *The Economist* 19 April 1986 (9.2 Figure 6) and a figure from *The Economist* 24 May 1980 (8.5 Figure 4); EDN for a figure from *EDN* © 1988 Cahners Publishing Company, a Division of Reed Publishing USA (8.3 Figure 2); Fortune and Time Life for the chart 'Where to live and prosper' (9.4 Figure 3) and the 'Listing of the 20 largest industrial corporations in the world' from Fortune 31 July 1989 (9.7 Figure 1); The City of Houston for a map from the Houston Downtown Data Book Update 1982 (6.4 Figure 1); McGraw Hill for a map from *Geography of Crime and Justine* by Harries (5.4 Figure 4); Methuen & Co for the figure from *An Atlas of North American Affairs* by Adams, Mills and Rogers 1979 (10.2 Figure 2); the Metropolitan Planning Department of Toronto for the figure 'Retailing in Regional Municipalities and Metropolitan Toronto 1983' (6.6 Figure 1); Ministry of Tourism and Recreation, Ontario (12.1 Figures 1 and 2); Penn Well Publishing Co for the extract from *Oil and Gas Journal* 28 January 1985 (8.2 Figure 4);
[redacted] Books Ltd for 2 diagrams from
[redacted] World Population History by
[redacted] McEvedy and Richard Jones
[redacted] in Books 1978) © Colin McEvedy
[redacted] chard Jones 1978 (2 Figure 1); Power
[redacted] stern mining and reclamation'
[redacted] ed from *Electrical World* May 1981
[redacted] gure 3) and a figure from *Electrical World* July 1986 (9.3 Figure 2); Routledge and Methuen & Co for four figures from *Post Industrial America* by D. Clarke (6.2 Figure 2, 9.1 Figure 2i, 9.2 Figure 2, 9.4 Figure 1); The Times Newspapers Ltd for 'Britons top European immigrant list in US' reprinted from *The Times* 6 November 1985 (4.1 Figure 6) and 'Despair grows in the grain belt' reprinted from *The Times* 6 November 1985 (10.1 Figure 4); The City of Toronto Planning & Development Department for use of the planning district map (12.2 Figure 5); The City of Vancouver for 'Where core workers live' from Quarterly Review 1984 (6.3 Figure 2).

The publisher would like to thank the following for their permission to reproduce photographs in this book:

D. Atherton (12.4 Figure 2); P. Atherton (6.7 Figure 3); Barnaby's Picture Library (1 Figure 7, 2 Figure 2, 3 Figure 3, 6.4 Figure 2, 7.4 Figure 4, 7.5 Figure 4, 7.6 Figure 4, 8.7 Figure 4, 9.1 Figure 3, 10.4 Figure 2, 11.2 Figure 5); British Petroleum Company Ltd (7.3 Fig 2, 8.2 Figures 1 and 3); Canada House, London (1 Figure 4, 7.4 Figure 5, 8.4 Figure 3, 8.7 Figure 1, 9.3 Figure 4, 9.8 Figure 5, 11.1 Figure 6, 11.2 Figures 2 and 4, 12.2 Figures 3 and 6); Canadian National Railways (7.2 Figure 2); J. Allan Cash Ltd (7.3 Figure 4, 7.6 Figure 6, 8.3 Figure 5, 9.1 Figure 4, 9.6 Figure 3, 9.6 Figure 5, 10.1 Figure 1 (b)); Communications Partnership Ltd (7.1 Figure 5, 7.2 Figure 3); Edmonton Economic Development Authority (8.1 Figure 6); Dr. D.J.A. Evans (10.3 Figure 1) (12.3 Figure 6); Ford Motor Company (9.7 Figure 2, 9.7 Figure 5); General Motors (9.2 Figure 6); Dr. K. Hoggart (6.2 Figure 4, 6.5 Figure 6); Hutchinson Library (5.1 Figure 3, 6.5 Figure 5, 7.6 Figure 2, 7.3 Figure 1, 7.5 Figure 2, 8.6 Figure 3, 10.1 Figure 1 (c), 10.2 Figures 2 and 4, 11.1 Figure 3, 12.4 Figure 5, 12.5 Figures 1, 3 and 6); L. Kimpton (3 Figure 2, 5.5 Figure 4, 10.5 Figure 4, 11.4 Figure 4); Magnum Picture Library (4.4 Figure 4, 5.1 Figure 4); Ontario House, London (6.1 Figure 4); Popperfoto (5.5 Figure 2); Port Authority of New York (7.2 Figure 1); Quadrant (7.7 Figures 3, 4 and 5); Quebec House, London (8.4 Figures 2 and 5); Rex Features Ltd. (5.5 Figure 5); Texaco Inc. (6.2 Figure 5); Topham Picture Library (3 Figures 5 and 6, 4.1 Figure 4, 5.4 Figure 6, 8.1 Figure 4, 8.5 Figure 1, 9.2 Figure 2, 9.6 Figure 4, 10.5 Figure 3); Tourism British Columbia (6.3 Figures 6 and 7); USDA – Soil Conservation Service (8.3 Figure 3, 10.1 Figure 1(a), 10.3 Figure 1, 10.4 Figure 4, 11.3 Figure 3); US Department of Energy (8.6 Figure 1); Dr. A.M. Warnes (4.3 Figure 5).

Every effort has been made to trace and acknowledge correctly all copyright holders, but if any have been overlooked the publishers will be pleased to make the necessary arrangements at the first opportunity.

# Contents

# 1. Introducing North America

## Pacific to Atlantic, Arctic to Gulf

Canada and the USA are the second and fourth largest countries in the world in land area. However, their combined size is still less than that of the Soviet Union (Figure 1).

| *Country* | *Area in millions of km²* |
|---|---|
| USSR | 22.4 |
| Canada | 10.0 |
| China | 9.6 |
| USA | 9.4 |
| Brazil | 8.5 |
| Australia | 7.7 |

**Fig 1 The six countries in the world with the largest land areas. Compare them with the United Kingdom which has an area of only 244 000 km².**

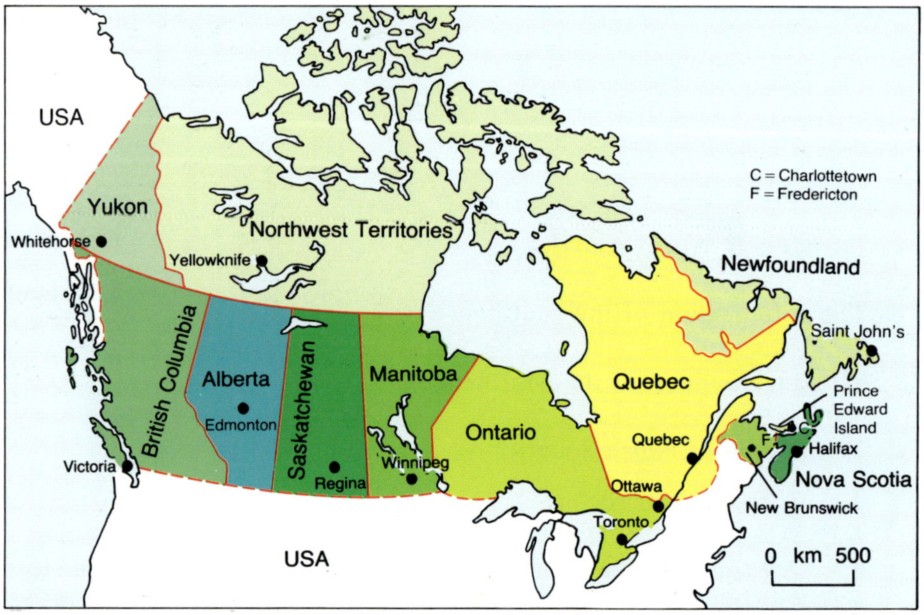


**Fig 2 Canada's provinces and territories with their capitals. Fredericton is the capital of New Brunswick and Charlottetown of Prince Edward Island. The capitals are not always the largest settlements in each region.**

Canada (Figure 2) crosses six of the world's 24 time zones. Its greatest east–west expanse is 5200 kilometres. The greatest north–south distance is 4600 kilometres, from the border with the USA to the northern tip of Ellesmere Island. The country is more than 40 times as big as the United Kingdom. Canada is the only nation in the world to be bounded by three oceans, the Pacific, Atlantic and Arctic.

The USA–Canada border in the west is at latitude 49°N. It then follows the Great Lakes and the mid-point of the St Lawrence river. Further east, the border runs south of the St Lawrence until it reaches the Atlantic Ocean.

In the south of the USA the Florida Keys extend below 25°N, very close to the Tropic of Cancer. Forty-eight of the 50 states are in this one large block of land. The two 'isolated' states are Alaska and Hawaii.

**Fig 3 The main features of the relief and drainage of North America. The continent has a great variety of spectacular landscapes.**

**Fig 4 Arctic Islands.**

"Good-bye God, I'm going to Canada."
*Anonymous remark attributed to a little girl on crossing the Canada–US border in the 1930s, later altered by the Toronto Board of Trade to, "Good! By God, I'm going to Canada!"*

**Fig 5 The images that Americans and Canadians hold of each other's countries are interesting. In the past Americans have often thought of Canada as a rather uninteresting place to live. Canadians have always found this puzzling.**

**Fig 6 States and divisions of the USA. The two isolated states of Alaska and Hawaii are included in the Pacific division.**

**Fig 7 Florida Keys.**

**Fig 8 Niagara Falls.**

"Geography has made us neighbors, history has made us friends. Economics has made us partners. And necessity has made us allies."
*President John F. Kennedy*

**Fig 9 Part of a speech by President John F Kennedy to the Canadian Parliament in 1962.**

## Canada

Canada is a federation of ten provinces and two territories. Ottawa in south-east Ontario is the capital city. Under Canada's system of government the provinces make many major decisions for themselves, particularly in education, local government, direct taxation, property and civil rights. In the north the huge Yukon and Northwest Territories have very small populations and are directly ruled by the federal government in Ottawa. They may become provinces at some time in the future with the agreement of the federal government and the existing provinces. For a country with such a large land area Canada has a small population of only 25 million.

## The USA

The USA has 50 states and a federal district (the District of Columbia) in which the national capital city, Washington, is located. Like Canada's provinces the USA's states have considerable decision-making powers. They also vary a great deal in size. The largest is Alaska (1 518 776 square kilometres) while the smallest is Rhode Island (3144 square kilometres). In general, the largest states in area are in the west.

To make regional patterns clearer, the 50 states are often grouped into nine divisions (Figure 6). Much of the data in this book refers to these divisions.

# 2. The colonisation of the continent

## The first North Americans

About 10 000 BC, Siberian mammoth hunters crossed the Bering Strait between north-east Asia and Alaska in search of food. These were the first people to inhabit the Americas (north, central and south America). Their descendants are the Indians and Inuits (Eskimos) of today.

By AD 1, the areas now covered by the USA and Canada had a population of about 300 000 people. This rose to 500 000 in AD 1000. The Norse people landed on the Labrador coast about this time. They were the first Europeans to reach North America. They were few in number. It is thought that their community died out after just a few generations.

Between AD 1000 and AD 1500 the population of North America doubled (Figure 1). However, from 1500 onwards the continent was influenced by a new and powerful source: sustained migration from many different countries, mainly European.

## The Europeans arrive

In 1492 Christopher Columbus landed in the West Indies. This was the beginning of the modern age of settlement in the Americas. Soon other explorers sailed west to the New World. Among them was Amerigo Vespucci whose name was used to describe the new lands.

The Spanish explored much of the south and west of what is now the USA. Settlement was limited but missionaries did establish the sites of some of today's large cities, including San Francisco (1775) and Los Angeles (1781). French exploration was centred around the St Lawrence river, the Great Lakes and the Mississippi river as far south as New Orleans. The fur trade was the basis of the French presence.

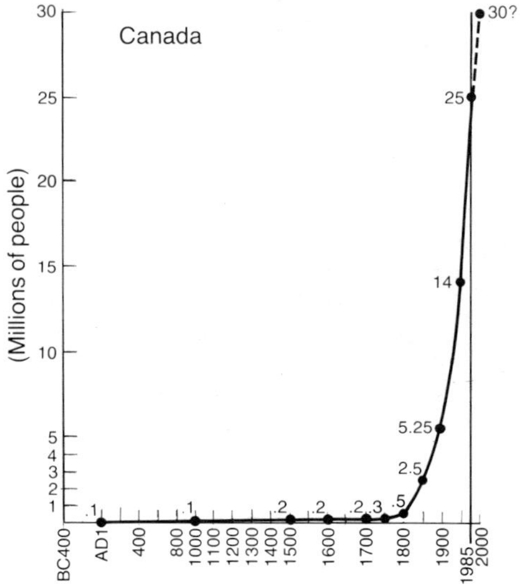


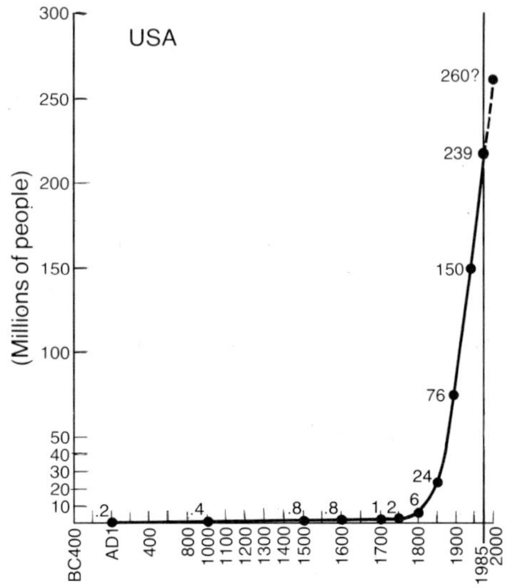


**Fig 1 Population growth in a) Canada b) USA**

The first permanent English settlement was established in 1607 at Jamestown, Virginia. Soon many more settlements developed on, and inland from, the Atlantic coastline. Along the east coast, colonies were established under the control of England although people were also arriving from many other European countries.

**Fig 2 The War of Independence was a bloody conflict between the colonies and Britain. The outcome was a major defeat for Britain.**

As settlement spread inland, a series of conflicts arose with the Indians, the French and the Spanish.

As the 18th century progressed, relations between the thirteen colonies and Britain became strained. The colonies felt that British rule did not allow them enough freedom. The worsening relationship led to the War of Independence (1776–83). The Declaration of Independence on July 4th 1776 is still seen as the most important day in the history of the USA (Figure 2).

## The USA grows rapidly

Under the peace treaty of 1783 Britain recognised the independence of the thirteen states. It was also agreed that the new nation should have all the land westward to the Mississippi. In the next century the USA was to expand even more as the frontier (the area settled by people of European origin) moved towards the Pacific Ocean (Figure 3).

- The Louisiana Purchase 1803; the USA paid $15 million to France for over 2.6 million km$^2$ of land and gained control of the central river system.
- Florida was purchased from Spain in 1819.

- Texas was accepted as a state in 1845. Between 1836 and 1845 Texas had been an independent nation, after throwing off Mexican rule.
- In 1846 the USA gained the Oregon Territory by treaty with Britain.
- In 1848 a large part of the southwest was ceded (given) to the USA by Mexico after a brief war.
- The Gadsden purchase completed US territory in the southwest in 1853.
- In 1867 Alaska was purchased from Russia for $7 million.
- Hawaii joined the USA at its own request in 1898.

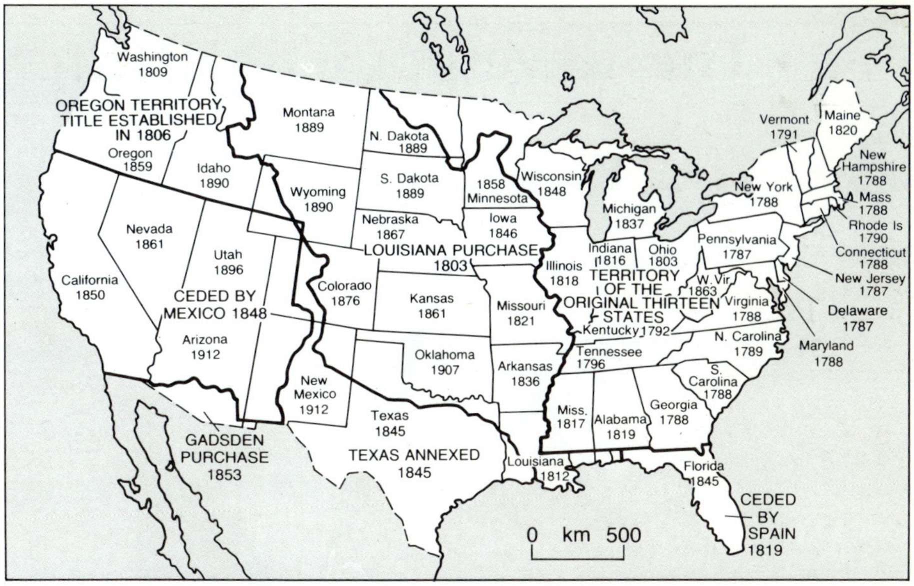


**Fig 3 Territorial expansion of the USA.**

Before European settlement most of the Indian population lived in the eastern part of what was to become the USA. As the frontier pushed forward the Indians were removed from these lands and forced to live on reservations (areas of land set aside for the use of Indian peoples only). Most Indian reservations are on poor quality land in the west.

## Canada becomes a nation

The Canadian story is really one of accepting the land that was left after claims by the USA following the War of Independence, the War of 1812 (between the USA and the British in Canada) and the 1846 Oregon agreement. Canada became a self-governing dominion in 1867 under the British North America Act. The four original provinces were Ontario, Quebec, Nova Scotia and New Brunswick.

Canada gained the huge land area owned by the Hudson's Bay Company in 1869. Manitoba became a province in 1870, British Columbia in 1871 and Prince Edward Island in 1873. Alberta and Saskatchewan joined the federation in 1905. Newfoundland became the tenth province in 1949.

**Fig 4 Centre of population – 1790 to 1980. Imagine a flat, weightless and rigid map of the USA. If on each date shown, weights representing the location of each person were placed on it, the map would balance at the 'centre of population'.**

**Q1**
Look at Figure 1.
**(a)** Write down the population of the USA and Canada every 100 years from 1500 onward.
**(b)** When was the fastest period of growth for each country?

**Q2**
**(a)** In the USA, which territories became states in (i) the 18th century? (ii) 19th century? (iii) 20th century?
**(b)** Which do you think was the USA's most important territorial gain as it expanded westward? Why?

**Q3**
Look at Figure 4.
**(a)** Where was the 'centre of population' in the USA in 1800?
**(b)** How far westward had it moved by (i) 1850? (ii) 1900? (iii) 1950? (iv) 1980?

**Q4**
As the frontier moved westward the Indians suffered great hardship. Their lands were taken from them and they were forced to move to reservations. Find out what you can about the life of the Indians during this time.

# 3. The development of the continent

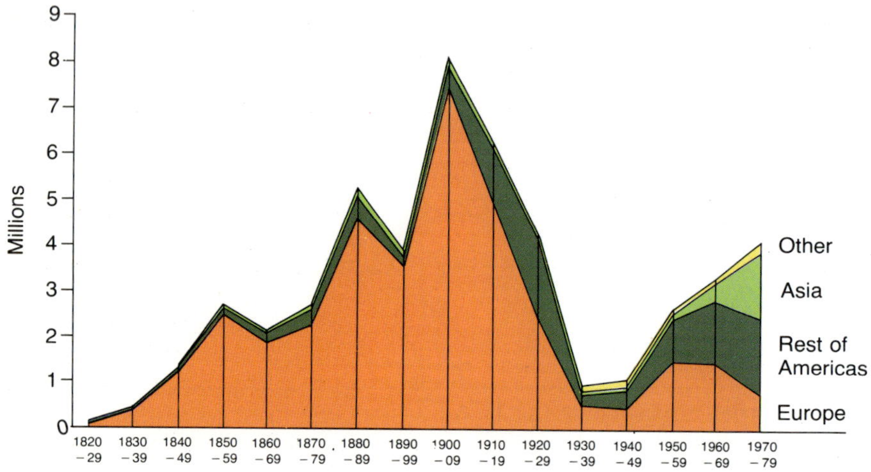


**Fig 1 Immigration into the USA by continent of origin 1820–1979.**

## Land of opportunity

The population grew relentlessly in the 19th century. North America offered fresh opportunities to millions of people (Figure 1). Most headed for the USA where prospects were perceived to be better than in Canada. Never before did people change the natural environment so quickly. Thriving cities grew rapidly. Forests were cut down as farming swept across the continent. Minerals were mined at an astonishing pace. The USA was on its way to becoming the wealthiest nation on earth.

## The Golden Age of the railways

Transport and communications are vital to economic growth. Without efficient ways of moving people and goods and exchanging information, little economic activity can take place. The spread of the frontier in North America relied heavily on the railways (Figure 2). As the network developed, people, farming and industry followed. In the USA

**Fig 2 The railway was the main form of transport in the nineteenth century. The routes chosen for railways are still in use today although now their main function is for carrying freight and tourists.**

track length grew from 14,500 kilometres in 1850 to 386,000 kilometres in 1910.

In 1869 the first transcontinental railway terminating at San Francisco was completed. By 1883 the USA had four routes to the west coast. New settlements grew up along these routes. Another year of great importance was 1861. This was when the first transcontinental telegraph service linking New York to San Francisco opened. As the Pacific ports expanded, the USA became more conscious of trading opportunities with Asia.

In Canada the frontier moved forward at a slower pace. Only 106 kilometres of railway track existed in the whole country in 1850. Nevertheless, the first Canadian transcontinental railway was completed in 1885. The cold climate of the northlands limited development in a large part of Canada. As time passed, the contrasts between the two nations were becoming clearer.

## The abolition of slavery

Black people were first brought from Africa to the USA as slaves in 1619. The slave trade was limited until the end of the 17th century. It then increased greatly as the demand for labour rose.

**Fig 3 Nineteenth century print showing the separation of a family by slave traders in America.**

Slaves were made to work mainly on large farms (plantations) in the South and generally endured a harsh life (Figure 3). After slavery was abolished in 1865 Blacks slowly began to move north to seek work in the expanding industrial cities (Figure 4). However, over 80% of the USA's Black population still lived in the South in 1910. They worked mainly as farm labourers or as sharecroppers (page 26 Unit 5.5). But migration to the north then increased substantially. Later, Blacks responded to new opportunities in the west,

Migration of USA's Black Population 1870–1980

| Period | South | North | West |
|---|---|---|---|
| 1870–80 | − 60 | + 60 | (n.a.) |
| 1880–90 | − 70 | + 70 | (n.a.) |
| 1890–1900 | − 168 | + 168 | (n.a.) |
| 1900–10 | − 170 | + 150 | + 20 |
| 1910–20 | − 454 | + 426 | + 28 |
| 1920–30 | − 749 | + 713 | + 36 |
| 1930–40 | − 347 | + 299 | + 49 |
| 1940–50 | −1599 | +1081 | +339 |
| 1950–60 | −1473 | +1037 | +293 |
| 1960–70 | −1380 | + 994 | +301 |
| 1970–80 | + 209 | − 342 | +132 |

Numbers in thousands. Plus sign (+) denotes net in-migration; minus sign (−) denotes net out-migration.

**Fig 4 The movement of blacks from the South to other regions of the USA was one of the greatest migration flows in the history of the continent.**

particularly in California. Despite the end of slavery, Blacks still remained very much second class citizens, a situation that (many people feel) still remains today.

## Immigration

Before 1890 most immigrants entering the USA came from north-west Europe (Figure 5). Britain, Germany and Ireland were the leading 'donor' countries. After 1890, this situation changed and between then and the First World War (1914–18) the majority of the new arrivals came from southern and eastern Europe.

The American government began to be concerned about two aspects of this flood of immigrants: the enormous numbers of people entering the USA, and the countries from which they had come.

In 1924 legislation was passed to reduce immigration. It was felt that if too many people were allowed to settle in the USA living standards would fall: the resources of the country might not be sufficient to share among a much larger population. The 1924 law is now seen as being racist. It favoured people from north-west Europe by making it easy for them to get into the USA. These were seen to be the most desirable immigrants. On the other hand, it was biased against people from other parts of the world and made immigration more difficult for them. Fairer legislation now exists, although immigration policy is still a major issue.

Most Canadian settlers came from Britain and France. People of French origin were greater in number at first. But by 1900 those of British extraction formed the majority. French Canadians remain in the minority today but have a strong influence on the government of the country.

**Fig 5 Emigrants leaving Belfast quay in 1851. Conditions on ships like these were harsh and thousands of emigrants did not survive the journey.**

**Q1**
**(a)** Why did the railway network spread more rapidly in the USA compared with Canada?
**(b)** With the help of an atlas show how railway routes influenced the pattern of settlement in the West.

**Q2**
**(a)** Describe the changing pattern of immigration into the USA shown by Figure 1.
**(b)** List your reasons why people leave their native countries to settle elsewhere.
**(c)** Why do you think the USA is still the country that most people around the world want to emigrate to today?

**Q3**
**(a)** Draw a line graph to show the information given in Figure 4.
**(b)** Describe the pattern of Black migration within the USA from 1870 to 1980.

**Q4**
Look at Figure 3. What does it tell you about slavery in the USA? Use your library to find out more about the lives of Black people during the slavery period.

**Fig 6 New York at the beginning of the twentieth century.**

# 4. The people of North America

# 4.1 A multiracial society

## People and place

Human geography is about people and the environments they live in. It looks at the patterns people make on the earth's surface: where they live, work, play and how they move about. As they do these things people alter the natural environment. For example, the sprawling cities and irrigated farmlands of present day southern California are very different from the semi-desert that the early settlers found there.

The geographer is equally interested in the influence nature has on people's lives. Look at an atlas to see how few people live in the cold, dry and high lands of the continent.

## Not just from Europe

In 1983 the USA was the fourth most populous country in the world with 234 million people. Canada with a population of 25 million ranked 31st. The USA in particular is a multiracial society.

USA: Population by race (and Spanish origin) 1980

| *Race* | *Millions* |
|---|---|
| White | 188.0 |
| Black | 26.5 |
| American Indian | 1.4 |
| Chinese | 0.8 |
| Filipino | 0.8 |
| Japanese | 0.7 |
| Asian Indian | 0.4 |
| Korean | 0.4 |
| Vietnamese | 0.3 |
| All other races | 7.0 |
| Total | 227.0 |
| [Spanish origin | 15.0] |

**Fig 1 Racial groups in the USA. People of Spanish origin are listed separately as they come from a number of racial groups.**

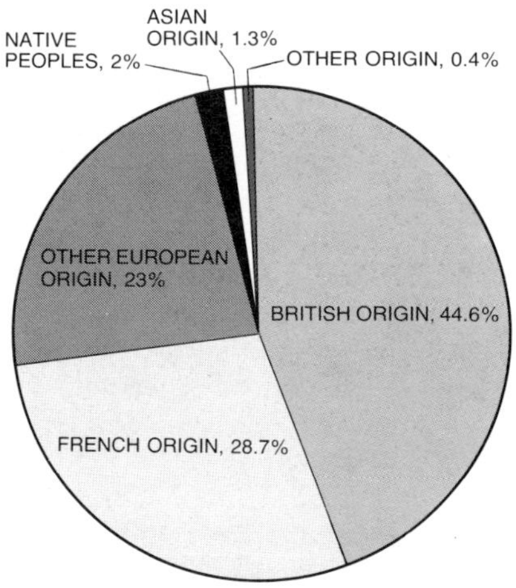


**Fig 2 Racial groups in Canada, 1981.**

Of the 49 million immigrants who arrived between 1820 and 1979, 36 million came from Europe (including the USSR), nine million from elsewhere in the Americas (north, central and south) and almost three million from Asia. A sizeable Black population already lived in the southern states at the beginning of the 19th century and it has grown steadily through natural increase.

The US Bureau of the Census also counts people originating from Spanish-speaking countries (Hispanics). They may be of any race. The Hispanic population has grown rapidly to almost fifteen million as more and more people have arrived from Mexico and other countries in Central and South America. Miami, Florida is the first US city to become officially bilingual. Twenty five states have passed laws that either mandate (make compulsory) or allow a period of bilingual education for children who cannot speak much English.

Minority groups usually have a standard of living well below the average. This has led to much frustration. At times it has exploded into violence, as in the 'race riots' of the late 1960s and early 1970s. Since then new laws have been passed to combat racism and some attempt has been made to improve the living standards of minority groups. But this is a very difficult task and great inequalities remain.

In the early part of the 20th century immigration numbers fell as the government made it more difficult for people to enter the country. More recently numbers have risen again because (i) immigration laws have been changed and (ii) illegal immigration is higher than ever before. However, this increase has caused considerable resentment (Figure 3). Some Americans feel that recent immigrants are taking scarce jobs. People who are often welcomed when their labour is needed may be made scapegoats when times are harder.

## Refugees

In the past most immigrants came from Europe. Now most arrive from South America and Asia. Many Asians came as refugees from war-torn countries such as Vietnam, Cambodia and Laos. The USA takes far more refugees than any other country.

Refugees often find it very difficult to settle. Unlike official immigrants, most of them did not leave their homelands by choice. A study of south-east Asian refugees in 1983 found:

- 76% living in poverty. The most recent arrivals were the poorest.
- Difficulty in adjusting to life in a new country with a strange culture ('exile shock').

## Will U.S. Shut The Door on Immigrants?

A flood of immigrants, only half of them legal, is bringing well over 1 million newcomers a year into the U.S.—the highest level since the mass migration of Europeans at the turn of the century. America today is accepting twice as many foreigners as all other nations combined.

While stories of individual refugees can be heartbreaking, Americans are increasingly reluctant to welcome newcomers, no matter where they come from—or why. Explains Leon Bouvier of the Washington-based Population Reference Bureau: "Your heart goes out to refugees and other immigrants. But there is a feeling across the land that enough is enough, and that we cannot continue absorbing the numbers that have been coming. America is no longer a nation of empty frontiers in need of settling."

Like it or not, demand for room in the U.S. is building day by day. By some estimates, El Salvador alone has generated as many as 500,000 U.S. bound refugees since 1980, only a handful of whom have been apprehended and sent back by overwhelmed American immigration authorities. Haiti and other nations of the Caribbean Basin yearly spawn thousands of illegal immigrants. The tide of job-seeking Mexicans flowing across U.S. borders, estimated by some at as high as 1 million annually, shows no signs of ebbing.

Millions more could soon flee Central America as violence flares in one country after another.

Yet the problem goes far beyond Central America. Tensions in Poland, Afghanistan and elsewhere could end up sending many more to U.S. shores. The world's refugee population—mostly illiterate and desperately poor—is now estimated at between 11 million and 16 million. Indo-China's refugee camps still brim with 261,000 people anxious to come to America.

**Fig 3 The high level of legal and illegal immigration is alarming some Americans. This extract is from the *US News and World Report* 12 April 1982.**

**Q1**
Look at Figures 1 and 2.
**(a)** How does the racial composition of the USA differ from that of Canada?

**Q2**
What are the advantages of a multicultural society compared with a monocultural society? Can you think of any disadvantages?

**Q3**
Why are some Americans unhappy about the large influx of immigrants and refugees?

**Q4**
**(a)** Describe the problems that refugees can face in North America.
**(b)** How might these problems be solved?

- Most people living in close-knit communities. California is the home of 40% of the USA's south-east Asians.
- Harassment from other racial groups.
- Many working in low-wage, declining industries.

## Multicultural Canada

Canada is populated mainly by people of British and French origin. But in recent times arrivals from other countries have increased. In 1980 Asians made up almost half of all Canadian immigrants. It is the large cities that are really multicultural.

Over 90% of French Canadians live in the province of Quebec where French is the main language. French Canadians have always been worried about losing their cultural identity because of the greater number of English-speaking people. To lessen this fear Canada officially became bilingual in 1975. There is a steady migration of people between the USA and Canada. For example, in 1983 7400 people left the USA to live in Canada while 11 800 left Canada for the USA.

Like the USA, Canada has a good record for taking in refugees. However, it remains to be seen whether North America can satisfy the hopes of its many different peoples in the future.

**Fig 5 An extract from *The Times* 16 January 1986.**

## Britons top European immigrant list in US

Britain was the only European country among the top 10 sending immigrants to the United States in 1984. Immigrants from Britain were the ninth largest group, numbering 13,949 out of the total legal immigration of 543,903.

The total was slightly down on the 1983 figure of 559,763, but the top four on the list remained unchanged: Mexico, with 57,557 immigrants, the Philippines, 42,768; Vietnam, 37,236; and South Korea 33,042. India came next, overtaking China, which had been in fifth place in 1983. In sixth place was the Dominican Republic, followed by Jamaica, Britain and Iran.

**Fig 4 The bodies of eighteen illegal Mexican immigrants were discovered in this freight train car at Sierra Blanca, Texas in 1987.**

# 4.2 Where do people live?

## The effect of the physical environment

North America has a low density of population compared with most other continents (Figure 1). The USA has an average of 25 persons per square kilometre, while Canada has only two. In both countries population is highly concentrated in some areas while large expanses of land elsewhere are very sparsely settled. Very few people live in the cold, dry and mountainous regions.

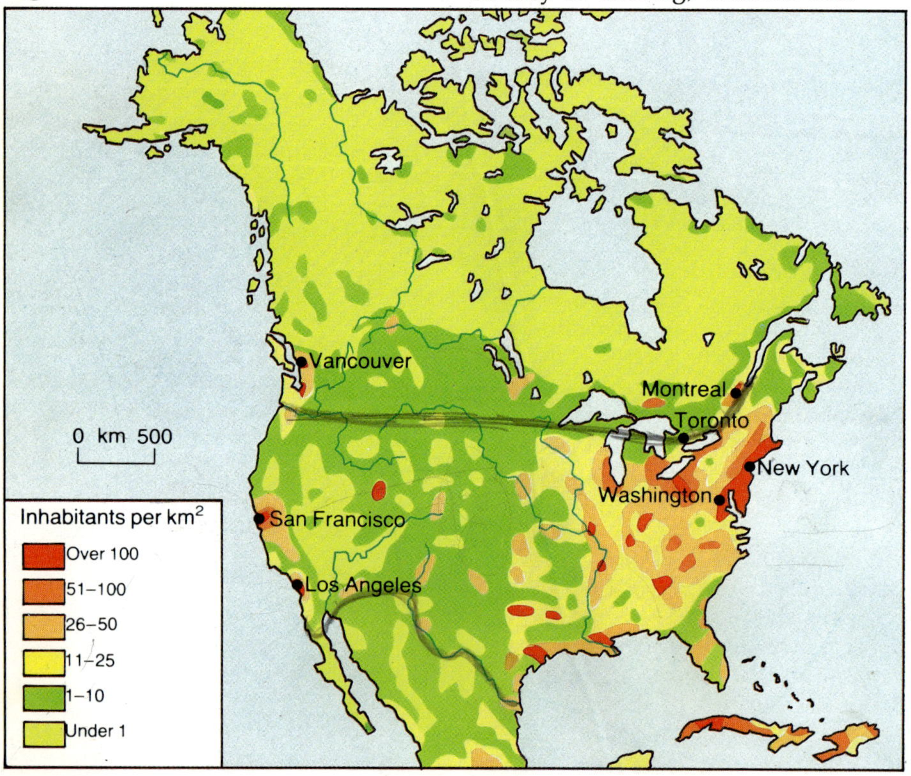


**Fig 1 The density of population in North America.**

The influence of low temperature is very clear in the north (Figure 2). This largely explains why 75% of Canada's population lives within 160 kilometres of the USA border. Over two-thirds of Canada has a mean January temperature below -20°C. The far north is affected by permafrost. Here the ground is permanently frozen to a depth of about 300 metres. In summer the top metre or so thaws out resulting in a marshy, waterlogged landscape. Life is difficult in such a cold and barren environment. Apart from the native Inuits and Indians, the few people living there are mainly involved in the exploitation of raw materials and minerals and in maintaining defence installations.

The mountain ranges of the west form imposing landscapes. But few people live in this rugged environment since opportunities for earning a living are scarce. Mountain settlements are related mainly to mining, tourism and agriculture and are small in size. For example, Cheyenne (altitude 1850 metres), the largest settlement in the state of Wyoming, has a population of only 50 000.

The Appalachian mountains in the east are both lower in height and less in land area. As Figure 1 shows, the influence of the Appalachians on population distribution is also less. However, few people live in the most isolated parts of these eastern mountains.

Much of the south-western USA is desert or semi-desert (Figure 4). But no country in the world has been more successful in watering its drylands. Expensive irrigation schemes have opened up many parts of the region to farming, settlement and industry. The rich farms of southern California and exciting cities such as Phoenix, Las Vegas and Salt Lake City, standing out like oases in the desert, are evidence of the high level of investment. Yet large parts of the south-west still remain almost empty. These areas may well stay empty in the future as water supply is now a big problem in the region.

## Where are the jobs?

In the USA the greatest concentration of people is in the north-east. This was the first region of substantial European settlement. Wealth and political power became established here as the rich natural resources were exploited. As the economy grew, more and more people from abroad were attracted here. Of course, people also settled in other parts of the country as new job opportunities were created but this settlement was on a smaller scale. By the end of the 19th century the north-east was the greatest manufacturing region in the world. However, in this century there has been a major shift of population and wealth towards the south and west.

The coastline and major river valleys are as attractive to settlement now as they have been in the past (Figure 1). The fertility of the land is another influence on population distribution. However, this was more important in the past than it is today. (Can you suggest why?)

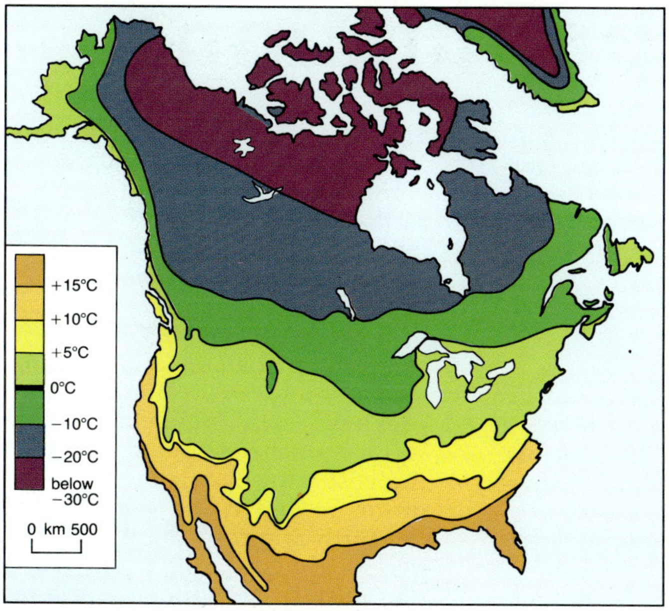


**Fig 2 Average annual January temperatures.**

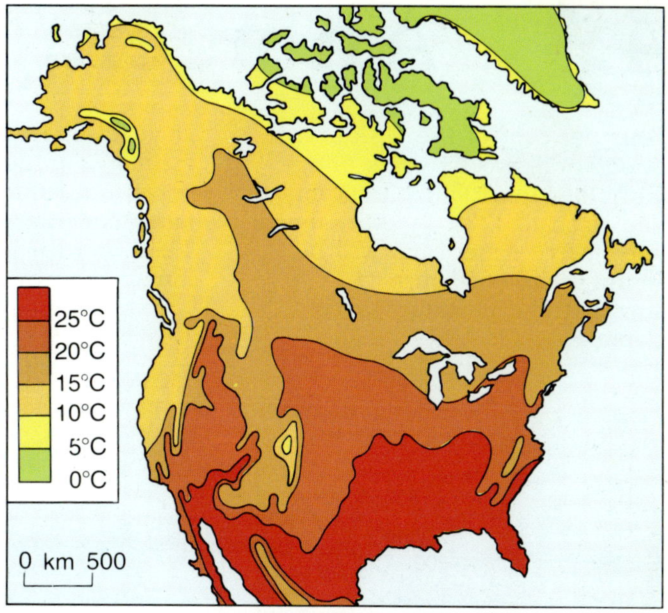


**Fig 3 Average annual July temperatures.**

The location of other natural resources such as minerals and timber also plays a part. Most Americans today live in towns and cities and work in the production of goods or the provision of services. The availability of employment in these sectors of the economy is the most important influence on the distribution of population today.

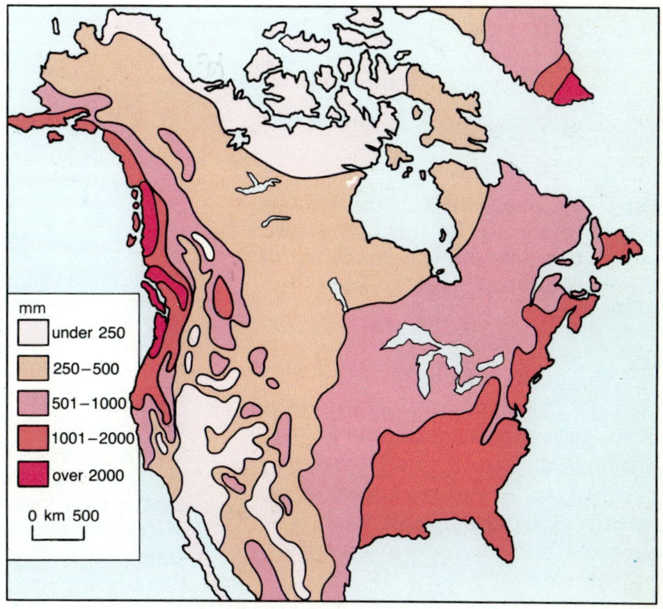


**Fig 4 Average annual precipitation.**

## People in Canada

The main concentration of population in Canada is in the southern parts of Ontario and Quebec. This region has advantages over most of the rest of the country in terms of climate, soil fertility and accessibility to the USA and Europe. Two of Canada's three 'million-size' cities, Toronto and Montreal, are located here. Canada's third largest city, Vancouver, is situated on the Pacific coast. A large area of low to moderate population density (by Canadian standards) is found in the cereal farming region of the Prairie Provinces (Alberta, Saskatchewan and Manitoba).

**Q1**

**(a)** On an outline map carefully shade in different colours the areas of North America (i) above 400 metres in height, (ii) with rainfall below 400 millimetres, and (iii) with a mean January temperature below -20°C. At regular intervals on your map write down the population density of the areas you have shaded.
**(b)** Under what circumstances might population density increase in the future in these areas?

**Q2**

**(a)** Make a list of the regions with the highest population densities.
**(b)** What are the main reasons for such high densities?
**(c)** Make lists of both the possible advantages and disadvantages of high population density.

# 4.3 An ageing population

Four per cent of the USA's population was 65 years of age and older in 1900. By 1985 this had risen to 12%. By 2030 almost one in five Americans will be senior citizens (Figure 1). A similar trend is underway in Canada.

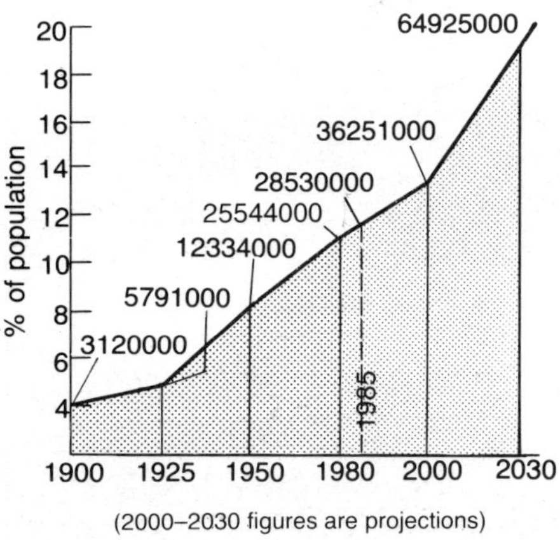


**Fig 1 The population of the USA is getting older all the time. The 1980 population over 65 was made up of fifteen million women and ten million men.**

The ageing of North America's population is an important issue. Both governments are very concerned. It will need careful planning and the reallocation of resources to cope with such a change. The average age of the population is rising. It was 23 years in 1900, 32 in 1985 and is estimated to be 36 in 2000. This is because (a) the birth rate has fallen considerably since the mid-1960s and (b) people are living longer than in the past.

## Fewer children

Figure 3 shows that four factors contribute to population change.

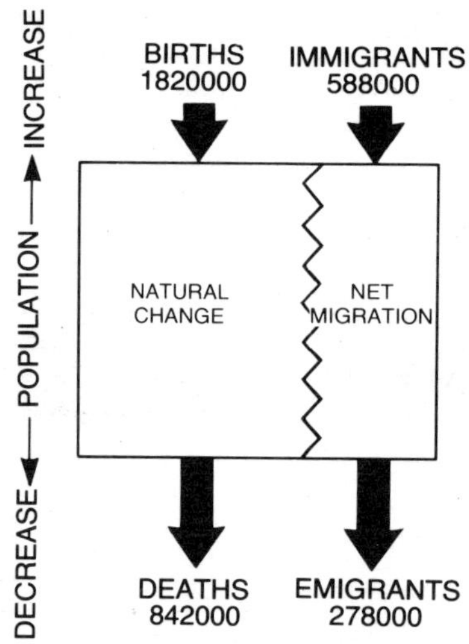


**Fig 3 A combination of natural change and net migration decides how much a population rises or falls. Natural change is the balance between the number of births and deaths in a year. Net migration is the difference between immigration and emigration. The figures are for Canada for the period 1976–81.**

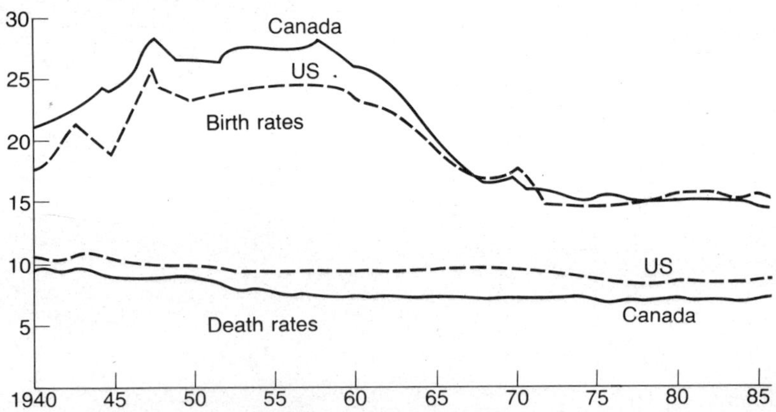


**Fig 2 The birth rate is the number of live births per 1000 of the population per year. The death rate is the number of deaths per 1000 of the population per year. In 1980 the birth rate for the world as a whole was 29/1000 and the death rate was 11/1000. How does North America compare?**

The data are for Canada for the 1976–81 period. The population of North America has risen steadily as the combination of births and immigrants has always been higher than the total of deaths and emigrants.

In the 1920s and 1930s the birth rate in both Canada and the USA was at a low level compared with previous years. In general, people wanted smaller families than in the past. However, after the end of the Second World War (1945) the birth rate rose sharply. This period of high fertility was called 'the postwar baby boom'. It lasted almost twenty years. But since the mid-1960s the birth rate has returned to a lower level. This is because:

- Children are expensive to bring up. Many couples choose to improve their standard of living instead.
- Many women see their careers as more important than starting or extending a family.
- Contraception is more reliable and more widely used than ever before.

## Living longer

Average life expectancy (longevity) continues to rise. This is due to better living standards, particularly nutritional and medical improvements. In 1920 a baby girl could expect to live on average 54.6 years and a boy 53.6 years. Today male life expectancy at birth is 71 years. Men reaching 65 can expect to live another fourteen years on average. Life expectancy still remains higher for women. At birth it is now 78 and at age 65 it is almost nineteen years. The fastest growing category among the aged are the 'old old', people who are in their 80s and beyond (5.2 million in the USA in 1980). It is the old old who need the most expensive health and home care.

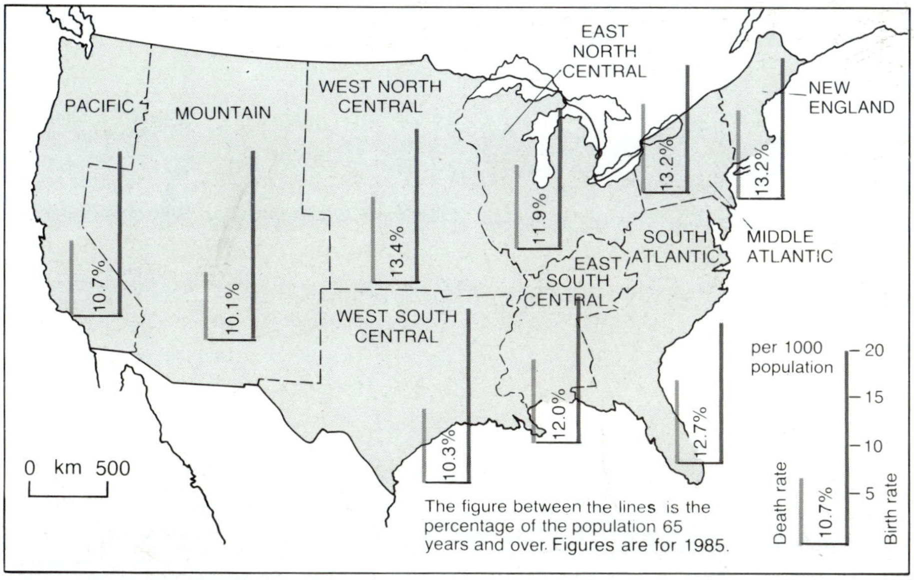


**Fig 4 Birth and death rates vary considerably between different areas of the USA. So does the proportion of old people.**

## What are the consequences?

- A steady fall in the ratio of the working to the non-working population from 5:1 in 1980 to 3:1 in 2030.
- Pressure on social security and private pension schemes as more people spend a larger part of their life in retirement.
- Greater demand for expensive medical care.
- Increased political power of the elderly.
- Greater sex imbalance. There are 131 women for every 100 men at age 65. At age 85 and over there are 224 women for every 100 men.

## What can government do?

Providing for the elderly is going to be a big problem in the future. Very few countries are generous in looking after their elderly at present. Poverty amongst the old is a world problem. New technology might provide the solution by improving living standards for everyone. But if it doesn't, what other alternatives are there? One possibility is to increase the retirement age to, say, 70. What do you think about this? Can you suggest any other ways of tackling the problem?

**Fig 6 Sun City, Florida. A growing number of people spend their retirement in specially planned retirement centres. Because of the warm climate the sunbelt states (in southern USA) are favourite locations. However, many senior citizens cannot afford to live like this.**

### Q1
Look at Figure 3. Calculate Canada's (i) natural change (ii) net migration and (iii) total population change, for the five year period.

### Q2
Look at Figure 2.
**(a)** When was the rate of natural change highest and lowest for the USA and Canada?
**(b)** Why has natural change varied so much since 1920?

### Q3
Draw a table to show the information given in Figure 1.

### Q4
**(a)** How might life expectancy be increased in the future?
**(b)** What kind of decisions might the government have to make to cope with this trend?

### Q5
Look at Figure 4.
**(a)** Describe how the following vary in the USA: (i) birth rates; (ii) death rates; (iii) population aged 65 years and over.
**(b)** Suggest reasons for these differences.

### Q6
**(a)** Draw a population pyramid for the USA for 1985.
**(b)** How would you expect a population pyramid for 1960 to be different?

**Fig 5 The numbers of people in different age groups in the USA (1985).**

| | *Total* | *Under 5 years* | *5–9 years* | *10–14 years* | *15–19 years* | *20–24 years* | *25–29 years* | *30–34 years* | *35–39 years* | *40–44 years* | *45–49 years* | *50–54 years* | *55–59 years* | *60–64 years* | *65–74 years* | *75 years and over* |
|---|---|---|---|---|---|---|---|---|---|---|---|---|---|---|---|---|
| **1985, total[1]** | **238 740** | **18 036** | **16 821** | **17 102** | **18 552** | **20 994** | **21 751** | **20 267** | **17 708** | **14 055** | **11 648** | **10 941** | **11 337** | **10 997** | **16 995** | **11 535** |
| Male | 116 161 | 9 230 | 8 608 | 8 762 | 9 445 | 10 515 | 10 886 | 10 096 | 8 741 | 6 889 | 5 679 | 5 281 | 5 380 | 5 120 | 7 466 | 4 062 |
| Female | 122 579 | 8 806 | 8 213 | 8 340 | 9 107 | 10 479 | 10 865 | 10 171 | 8 967 | 7 166 | 5 969 | 5 660 | 5 957 | 5 877 | 9 529 | 7 473 |

[[1]Figures in thousands]

# 4.4 On the move

## Going west and south

Since European settlement of North America began, enterprising people have moved out from the main centres of population in the north-east to seek fresh opportunities elsewhere. By the beginning of this century thriving business centres had been established in other parts of the continent. This trend has continued strongly.

The USA is undergoing a marked shift of population (Figure 1), wealth and political power towards the west and the south. In the USA people use the term 'sunbelt' to refer to the southern part of the country from Florida to California. This is a region of generally strong economic growth. In contrast, the 'frostbelt' states of the north-east have faced mounting problems as many of their main industries have declined. A similar east to west movement is underway in Canada (Figure 2). Here Alberta and British Columbia have been the major centres of new prosperity.

**Fig 1 Population by division in the USA 1940 and 1985. In every division, the 1985 population is greater than the 1940 population. In the Pacific division, it is more than three times as much.**

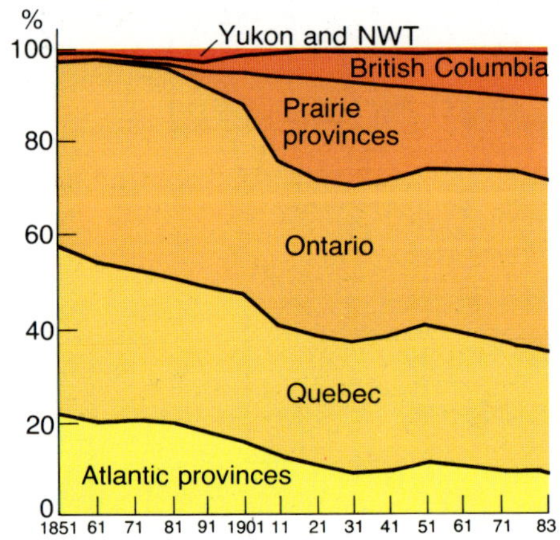


**Fig 2 The distribution of Canadian population by region 1851–1983.**

## Core and periphery

A simple model can be used to show how economic development can spread outwards from one region to other parts of a country (Figure 3). As the traditional area for industry and commerce, the north-eastern USA and the southern parts of Quebec and Ontario became the continent's 'economic core'. (The area outside the core is known as the 'periphery'.) In the early years of European settlement, industry and commerce were very limited outside the core. However, sub-cores of economic growth began

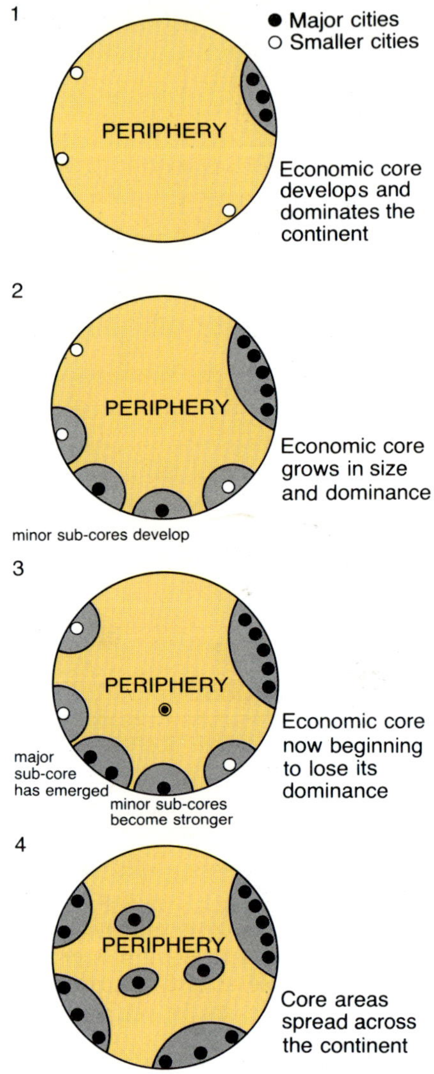


**Fig 3 A four-stage model showing the spread of economic development across the continent.**

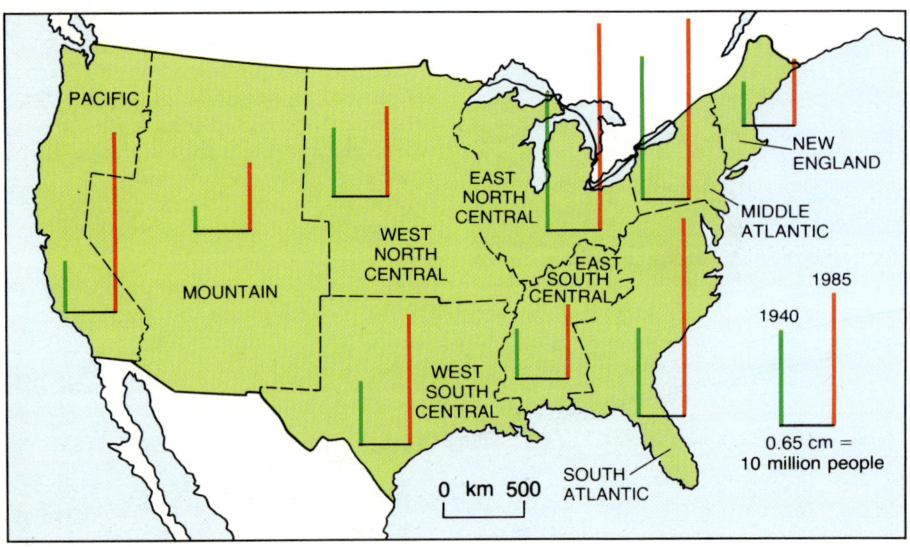


to develop strongly in the 19th century. Some have now reached a considerable size (Figure 4).

In the 1940s, California emerged as the continent's first major sub-core because of the high productivity of its agriculture and its increasing variety of manufacturing and service industries. People flocked in as new jobs were created. In 1960 California took over from New York as the most highly populated state of the USA. (In 1985, California had 26.4 million

Fig 4 **Economic growth: a winery in California.**

people and New York had 17.8 million.) Enterprise (business, commerce, retailing, etc.) is concentrated in the three large metropolitan areas of Los Angeles, San Francisco and San Diego.

Texas is another state which has grown rapidly. It is about to overtake New York and become the second most populous state. The 1990 estimated population figures are, California 27.5 million, Texas 17.5 million, New York 16.5 million. Its main business centres are Houston, Dallas, Fort Worth and San Antonio. Smaller sub-cores include Atlanta-Birmingham, New Orleans-Mobile, the Seattle region, eastern Florida and the Vancouver, Edmonton and Calgary regions of Canada.

Business has been attracted to areas outside the long-established core region for a number of reasons:

- The location of raw materials. For example, oil and gas have attracted industry to Texas, California and Alberta.
- The Interstate Highway System (USA) and the Trans-Canada Highway have increased the accessibility of the south and the west.
- The warm climate of the sunbelt makes it an attractive place for industries to locate and for workers to live.
- Generally cheaper land, lower taxes and lower trade union membership.
- The growth of Pacific and Gulf Coast ports as trade with Asia, South America and Australasia has expanded.
- Universities in the south and west are producing more highly skilled graduates than in the past.

It is likely that the spread of economic growth will continue because of the advantages now enjoyed by many parts of the south and west. The north-east still has merits of its own and it will remain important. But its days of such strong dominance over the whole continent are over. As the distribution of population changes so too do other geographical patterns.

## The future

Most countries and regions try to estimate how their populations will change in the future. This is important for planning schools, housing, jobs and many other aspects of life. The USA and Canada both have three estimates for the near future; a low projection, a medium projection and a high projection (Figure 6). Every year new information is studied carefully to try to improve these forecasts.

| | *Millions* | |
|---|---|---|
| | *1985* | *2000* |
| New England | 12.7 | 12.8 |
| Middle Atlantic | 37.2 | 33.6 |
| East North Central | 41.6 | 41.6 |
| West North Central | 17.6 | 18.1 |
| South Atlantic | 40.2 | 49.0 |
| East South Central | 15.1 | 17.2 |
| West South Central | 26.5 | 32.7 |
| Mountain | 12.8 | 20.1 |
| Pacific | 35.0 | 42.4 |
| USA | 238.7 | 267.4 |

**Fig 5 USA populations in the nine divisions, 1985, and projected figures for 2000.**

**Q1**
On a map of North America and with the help of an atlas, shade and label (i) the core, (ii) the major sub-core, (iii) minor sub-cores, (iv) the periphery.

**Q2**
How would you expect the core and sub-cores to differ from the periphery in (i) population, (ii) employment, (iii) standard of living? Give reasons for your answers.

**Q3**
Look at Figures 1 and 2.
**(a)** How has the distribution of population changed in the two countries?
**(b)** Suggest how this has affected the balance of political power in the USA and Canada.

**Q4**
Describe and account for the predicted divisional population changes in the USA between 1980 and 2000.

**Q5**
Suggest why the USA and Canada each have three population estimates for the near future.

| | *Millions* | |
|---|---|---|
| | *USA* | *Canada* |
| Present population | 234 | 25 |
| Low projection | 256 | 28 |
| Medium projection | 268 | 31 |
| High projection | 282 | 35 |

**Fig 6 Population projections for 2000 AD for the USA and Canada.**

# 5. The quality of life

# 5.1 Wealth and poverty

## The land of a million millionaires

**Washington** – Being rich is no longer a one-in-a-million occurrence in the United States.

In fact, by the end of this year, one American household in 100 will have a net worth of $1 million or more, according to *US News & World Report* – a total of a million millionaires.

Citing information from market researchers, the magazine said the route to riches is more likely to be that of an entrepreneur than of a professional. The typical US millionaire is a white male in his early 60s, still married to his first wife and with a business catering to the ordinary needs of his neighbours, it reported.

"The real way people make money is . . . hard work for 30 years, six days a week," said Professor Thomas Stanley, of the marketing department of Georgia State University who has been watching millionaires for more than a decade.

Nor does fortune always go with fame. Entertainers, athletes, writers and the like make up less than 1 per cent of the millionaire population. Eighty per cent of the elite group did not inherit their wealth, but came from middle or working-class backgrounds.

Many millionaires do not see themselves as rich.

The highest concentration of millionaires is found in Florida, where 19 out of 1,000 are in that category.

**Fig 1 An extract from *The Times* 6 January 1986.**

**Fig 2 Child poverty in the USA.**

## Congressional study finds that 22% of US children live in poverty

Twenty-two per cent of American children live in families with incomes below the poverty line.

The Congressional Research Service and the Congressional Budget Office concluded that government spending for programmes directed specifically at children had failed to keep pace with population increases and inflation since the 1970s.

The rise in single-parent families since the early 1970s is a major cause of the increase in poverty rates, the study said. It found that half of all poor children lived with a single female parent.

Nearly half of all black children, a third of all Hispanic children, and 17 per cent of white children lived in families with incomes below the poverty line in 1983. In white families headed by women the poverty rate for children was 47.6 per cent. For black families headed by women the figure was 68.5 per cent, and 70.5 per cent for Hispanic families headed by women.

It found that more than 2.5 million of the 13.8 million children below the poverty line lived in families where at least one person had a full-time job, "which belies the widespread view that a full-time job throughout the year is near insurance against poverty".

North America is the world's richest continent (Figure 1). Life is good for many people. The super-highways of Los Angeles and the casinos of Las Vegas are examples of this wealth that we often see on TV. However, there is another side to the story. Millions of people live in desperate poverty and see little chance of a better future. A recent survey in the USA found that over one in five children live in families with incomes below the poverty level (Figure 2). Homelessness is another big social problem. Over 300 000 Americans are now living rough (Figure 3). The living conditions of the poorest North Americans are little different from those found in Third World countries.

Many factors determine the quality of a person's life. Employment and wages are very important. The unemployed and low paid struggle to afford the basic necessities of life. Those on higher incomes can buy better food, clothing, housing, transport and entertainment. But other aspects of life which may not depend so much on income must also be considered. These include the standard of health care and education and the levels of pollution and crime.

In the USA poverty is most widespread in the south-east. In Canada it is the Atlantic provinces which have the lowest standard of living. However, in the large metropolitan areas such as New York, Chicago and Toronto, rich and poor districts

**Fig 3 Homelessness is a growing problem in the USA as in many other 'rich' countries.**

are often not far apart in distance. Variations in wealth happen for many reasons. Three of the most important are social injustice, geographical location, and entrepreneurial ability.

## Social injustice

Social injustice exists all over the world. In North America as elsewhere it is minority groups such as Black and Indian people who lose out the most (Figure 4). Government data shows them to be worse off for income, health, education, housing, unemployment and many other measures of well-being (Figure 5). Efforts have been made in the last twenty years to reduce discrimination and poverty. In fact, between 1965 and 1980 there was a considerable fall in poverty. However, recent spending cuts have halted this process.

Discrimination and the poverty that often results do not arise only because of race. They also occur because of gender, age and handicap.

**Fig 4 Many people in North America have housing of a very poor standard.**

## Geographical location

The quality of life of people in the same racial or social groups can vary because of where they live. Geographical location can affect prosperity in a number of ways.

- Regions with advantages such as good accessibility and valuable raw materials attract industry and commerce. Wealth is created and average living standards may rise (but think of reasons why they may not).
- The physical environment makes life difficult in parts of the continent. Today life can be made tolerable even in the harsh conditions of the Arctic but this is expensive.
- The federal government in both countries allocates more money to some regions than others (for medical funds, government contracts, road building, etc.).
- The way a region is perceived by the population in general and the business world in particular is important to its progress. The dynamic image of California shown by the cinema and TV has done much to attract people and business. In Canada, Alberta and British Columbia have a similar progressive image.

## Entrepreneurial ability

An entrepreneur is somebody who runs a business and makes decisions about what to produce and how to produce it. The entrepreneur uses resources to make money. The most successful businesses have been quick to grasp new ideas and then sell them to the public. Successful businesses create employment and wealth for the whole community. Some parts of the continent have been very good at this while others have not. Also some racial groups have been more successful entrepreneurs than others. For example, members of the Asian population in the USA have been more inclined to set up their own businesses than Black Americans.

**Q1**
How is a typical American millionaire described in Figure 1?

**Q2**
**(a)** Set up a class debate. Imagine you are members of the US government. Some of you want to spend more to help the poor. Others believe that the government has different priorities.

**Q3**
Look at Figure 5.
**(a)** How do each of the four minority groups compare with the national average?
**(b)** Make a list of five other ways that the standard of living of minority groups might be compared.

| *Percentage of:* | *All races* | *Black* | *Indian Eskimo Aleut* | *Asian & Pacific Islander* | *Spanish Origin Population* |
|---|---|---|---|---|---|
| Families with incomes over $25 000 | 35.5 | 23.1 | 20.4 | 44.6 | 27.5 |
| People below poverty level | 12.4 | 34.2 | 27.5 | 13.1 | 26.5 |
| People owning their houses | 64.4 | 47.2 | 52.5 | 51.4 | 46.5 |
| People unemployed | 4.0 | 11.3 | 7.5 | 3.1 | 8.6 |
| People over 25 who attended college | 31.9 | 22.4 | 24.2 | 50.1 | 18.7 |

**Fig 5 Some indicators of the standard of living of minority groups in the USA, 1980.**

# 5.2 Income and unemployment

In 1985 9.6 million North Americans were unemployed. The good times of the 1950s, 1960s and early 1970s seem to have passed. Then, economic growth was strong and steady and few people were out of work. Although the situation has improved recently many economists believe that relatively high unemployment is here to stay.

Some parts of the continent have been hit much worse than others. In Canada the Atlantic Provinces and Quebec have the highest unemployment rates (Figure 1). These are also the regions with the lowest average incomes. The Atlantic Provinces form Canada's poorest region because:

- There are few natural resources.
- Agriculture is hindered by cool summers while soils are of poor quality in many areas.
- More people live in the countryside than elsewhere in Canada. The scattered rural population is not attractive to business, and services are expensive to provide.
- There is little manufacturing industry because of (a) few natural resources, (b) a small population, (c) the distance from Canada's major cities.

Quebec's problems are of a different kind. Along with Ontario, Quebec has always had most of Canada's manufacturing industry. But as older industries have closed, Quebec has been slow to attract new ones. The newer and fast-growing industries have gone mainly to Ontario and the provinces further west. This is because:

- The energy resources of the west have stimulated much economic growth.
- Better transport and communications have made the west more accessible than in the past.
- Population has risen faster in Ontario and the west. So these regions have become more attractive as markets and centres of skilled labour.
- Trade across the Pacific Ocean has risen substantially.
- The western provinces now have a dynamic image of progress that is attractive to business.

Wealth and power in the USA have historically been concentrated in the three north-eastern divisions. The area became known as the 'manufacturing belt' because so much of the nation's industry was located here. The Pacific is the only other division in the USA where incomes have been higher than the national average throughout the century. Figure 2 shows that these four divisions still top the USA's wealth league table. However, the gap between rich and poor divisions has closed over the years.

**Fig 1 Per capita income and unemployment rates for Canada's provinces and territories in 1985.**

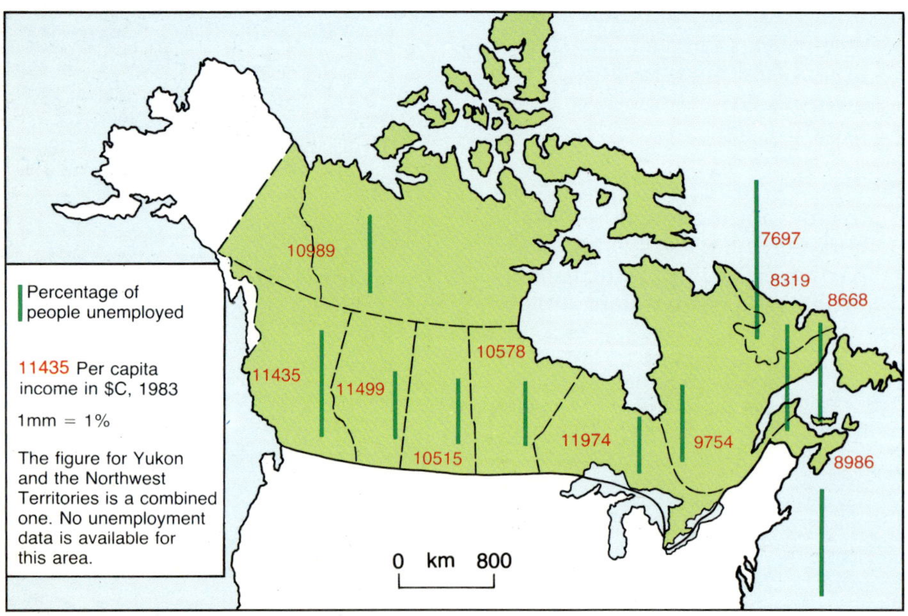


| | Income per person 1985 ($) | Rate of unemploy-ment % 1985 |
|---|---|---|
| New England | 15 914 | 4.4 |
| Middle Atlantic | 15 454 | 6.8 |
| East North Central | 13 617 | 8.8 |
| West North Central | 13 286 | 6.2 |
| South Atlantic | 13 222 | 6.1 |
| East South Central | 10 633 | 9.0 |
| West South Central | 12 686 | 7.9 |
| Mountain | 12 687 | 6.8 |
| Pacific | 15 490 | 7.4 |
| USA | 13 867 | 7.2 |

**Fig 2 Per capita income and unemployment by division in the USA.**

The three southern divisions – South Atlantic, East South Central and West South Central – have for long been the centre of poverty. In 1900 average income in the East South Central was only half the national average. By 1980 it was up to 79%. However, it remains the poorest division in the country. Mississippi is the poorest of the USA's fifty states. Its average income for 1985 was

THE IMPACT OF UNEMPLOYMENT

| *Scale* | *Impact* |
|---|---|
| Individual and family | Increase in suicide, homicide, alcoholism, admission to mental hospitals, prison entry and family break-up. Racial minorities bear brunt of unemployment. |
| Local community | Community spirit slowly declines. Housing deteriorates and local shops close because of shortage of money. Total quality of environment degenerates. |
| City region | As businesses close, the tax base falls. Public services suffer as a result. If prospects are better elsewhere people move out. Impact felt most in inner city. |
| Nation | For every one point rise in the unemployment rate sustained over a year, the USA*(a) loses $68 billion in output (GDP), (b) loses $20 billion in tax revenues, (c) must spend an additonal $3.3 billion on unemployment benefits etc. |

* Bureau of Economic Analysis, US Dept of Commerce 1981

**Fig 3 The impact of unemployment. It has a devastating effect at all scales.**

$9187. Compare this with $18 187 in Alaska and $18 089 in Connecticut, the highest in the USA.

Unemployment rates vary considerably too, although the link between income and unemployment is not so straightforward as it is in Canada. Some of the richest states in the USA have unemployment rates above the national average.

Unemployment can have a devastating effect. The costs are great to individual families and to nations (Figure 3). Unemployment is one of the main reasons why people move home. Such movement has costs and benefits for both the regions gaining and losing people (Figure 4).

**Fig 4 An extract from the *Economist*, 23 May 1981. Since then the fall in the price of oil has slowed growth in parts of the sunbelt.**

## Go South

Americans are always on the move and the sunbelt has been a magnet since the 1960s. But the flight from the north-central states to the south-west is something new and special. The signs are plain. In Michigan workers in Dearborn and Detroit line up to buy the Houston Chronicle, the Dallas Morning News and the San Antonio Light, with their pages and pages of job offers.

The reasons are plain, too. Michigan has more than 600 000 unemployed out of a workforce of just over 4 million; Ohio has half a million out of a 5 million workforce. Illinois is only slightly better off.

The stampede is viewed with concern in the states losing skilled workers. Many of the people who are leaving came originally from the south.as unskilled labourers and they are taking their skills with them. If the old heavy industries are dying out in Michigan, Ohio and Illinois, diversification into new industries must be the order of the day. But where will the skilled, educated workers be found if the present drain continues?

Immobility of labour is a bad thing. But too much mobility can be bad too. It can overwhelm the south-western states. Where will they find enough water for a burgeoning population and industry? Their finances will be strained to provide enough schools and hospitals. And northern states may be left without enough taxpayers to maintain the infrastructure in which they have invested so much.

**Q1**

**(a)** Draw a scattergraph by plotting unemployment against average income per person for the USA's nine divisions (Figure 2).
**(b)** What does your graph tell you about the relationship between the two measures?
**(c)** Using the information in Figure 1, draw a scattergraph for Canada. How much does it differ from your USA scattergraph?

**Q2**

**(a)** Suggest why few large businesses locate in the Atlantic provinces.
**(b)** How might the provinces attract more firms to the region in the future?

**Q3**

When many people move from one region to another, what problems can arise in **(a)** the donor region **(b)** the receiving region?

# 5.3 Health patterns

## How can health be measured?

'Living here can seriously damage your health!' Should some places have a government health warning like this? The chance of dying from certain diseases is much greater in some places than in others.

The two main causes of death in the USA are heart disease and cancer. The death rate for both is highest in the Middle Atlantic (Figure 1). The Mountain division has the lowest rate for these two diseases. The suicide rate though is 70% higher in the Mountain division than in the Middle Atlantic. Can you think of possible explanations for such great variation in death rates?

Health and health care can be measured in a number of ways. The data available is of two kinds:

- Direct indicators, e.g. death rate from heart disease and cancer, infant mortality and the incidence of various non-fatal illnesses. Direct indicators measure the actual well-being (or lack of it) of the population.

- Indirect indicators, e.g. the number of doctors or number of hospital beds per 100 000 people and the health care spending per person (Figure 2).

These measures show how much money is invested in health care. Where money is invested well, it should reduce the level of illness and disease. However, where money is invested unwisely it may not. Of course the general environment can make some places less healthy than others and so they need more money to achieve the same level of health.

## Infant mortality

One of the best measures of the state of health is the infant mortality rate. This is the number of children that die under the age of one year per 1000 live births. Poor health kills the very young and the very old much more easily than the age groups in between (Figure 3). Money spent on facilities to care for infants can greatly reduce deaths. The infant mortality rate in the USA fell from 20.0 in 1970 to 11.5 in 1982. There are big variations across the country. The highest rates are in the South Atlantic and East South Central (both 13.2). Infant mortality is lowest in the Pacific and Mountain divisions (both 10.0). The most striking aspect of infant mortality is the gap between the Black and White populations. There is also much greater variation in the mortality of Black infants than White infants across the USA (Figure 4).

## Medicare and Medicaid

Most Americans get medical care through either (a) insurance they pay for themselves, or (b) insurance cover provided by their employers. There is no national health system as in Britain. So what about the poor and the old in the USA? The system for looking after these groups was set up in 1965. It has two main parts:

- **Medicare** provides medical care for the elderly but does not cover long-term care in nursing homes. It only pays for up to 100 days post-hospitalisation nursing care. The total cost of Medicare has risen from $1 billion in 1966 to $66 billion in 1984.

**Fig 2 A scattergraph showing the 'best-fit line' between health care expenditure per person and the number of doctors for the nine divisions.**

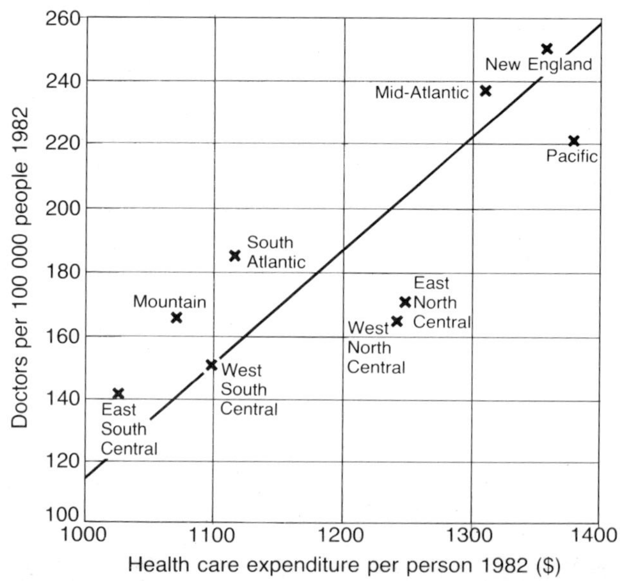


**Fig 1 Death rates by four selected causes 1982 (per 100 000 population) in the nine USA divisions.**

| *Division* | *Diseases of the heart* | *Cancer* | *Suicide* | *Chronic liver disease and cirrhosis* |
|---|---|---|---|---|
| New England | 354 | 212 | 10 | 13 |
| Middle Atlantic | 406 | 216 | 9 | 15 |
| East North Central | 345 | 191 | 11 | 11 |
| West North Central | 347 | 192 | 11 | 8 |
| South Atlantic | 322 | 194 | 14 | 12 |
| East South Central | 322 | 186 | 12 | 9 |
| West South Central | 280 | 160 | 13 | 9 |
| Mountain | 227 | 139 | 17 | 11 |
| Pacific | 268 | 171 | 15 | 15 |
| USA | 326 | 187 | 12 | 12 |

Number of deaths per 100 000 population in each age group, 1982

| *Sex/Race* | *Under 1 yr old* | *1–4 yrs old* | *5–14 yrs old* | *15–24 yrs old* | *25–34 yrs old* | *35–44 yrs old* | *45–54 yrs old* | *55–64 yrs old* | *65–74 yrs old* | *75–84 yrs old* | *85 yrs old and over* |
|---|---|---|---|---|---|---|---|---|---|---|---|
| Male – black | 2 169 | 93 | 44 | 175 | 360 | 607 | 1352 | 2 758 | 5 040 | 8 477 | 15 118 |
| Male – white | 1 136 | 58 | 33 | 146 | 159 | 239 | 660 | 1 655 | 3 860 | 8 445 | 18 123 |
| Female – black | 1 760 | 76 | 29 | 64 | 135 | 283 | 693 | 1 498 | 2 863 | 5 709 | 11 660 |
| Female – white | 895 | 47 | 21 | 50 | 61 | 128 | 355 | 860 | 2 023 | 5 101 | 14 124 |

**Fig 3 Death rates vary greatly according to age. There are also considerable differences by sex and race.**

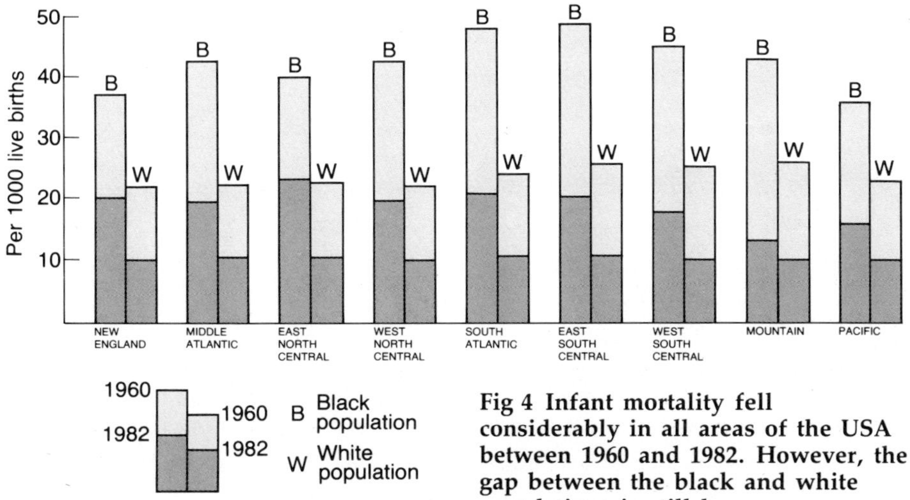


**Fig 4 Infant mortality fell considerably in all areas of the USA between 1960 and 1982. However, the gap between the black and white populations is still large.**

- **Medicaid** pays for medical care for 22 million people. It is for (a) people in receipt of government welfare and (b) poor, elderly and disabled people who need long-term care. Access to Medicaid is more restricted than in the past (Figure 5). Health experts estimate that millions of people in need are not now eligible for assisted health care.

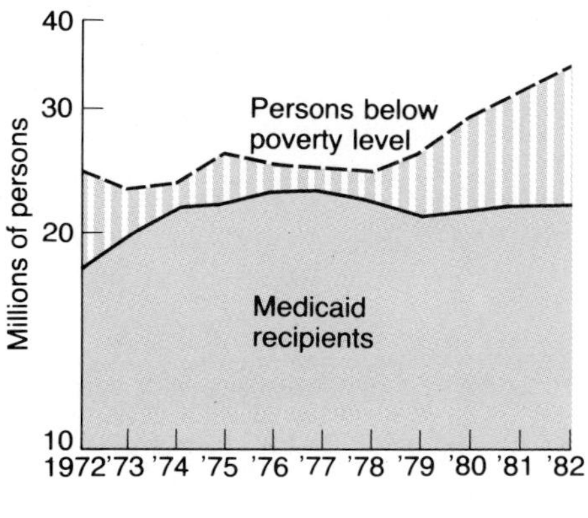


**Fig 5 The number of people entitled to Medicaid is not keeping pace with the rising population living below the poverty level.**

## Can the USA cope?

The USA spends more per person on health care than any other country. The cost has risen steeply. In 1960 it was $129 per person. By 1983 it had reached $1500 per person with a total health care bill of $355 billion (Figure 6). As the number of elderly people rises and they live even longer, the health care bill will become much higher. Where will the money come from?

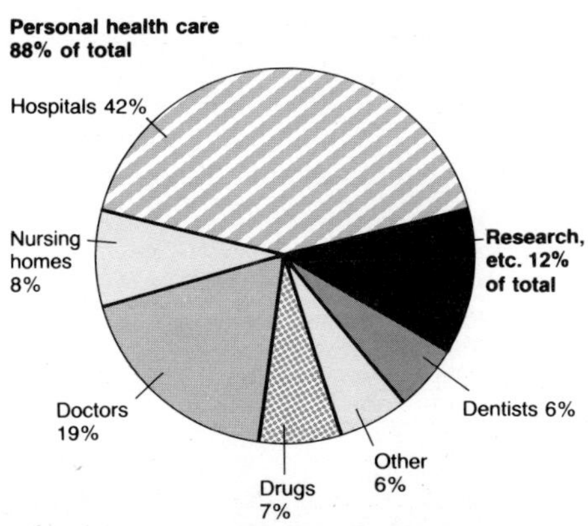


**Fig 6 Health care spending in the USA is at a record level. This is what the money was spent on in 1983.**

**Q1**

**(a)** What is the difference between direct and indirect indicators of health?
**(b)** Select what you consider to be the three most important indicators of health shown in the graphs and tables. Rank the nine divisions for each of these measures. Add your rankings together to get a composite quality of health index.
**(c)** How useful is this technique for comparing health across the USA?
**(d)** Name two other measures not considered in this unit that would help provide a more accurate picture of health in the USA.

**Q2**

Look at Figure 2.
**(a)** How strong is the relationship between the two measures of health care?
**(b)** Suggest reasons why there is not a perfect relationship (correlation) between the two measures.

**Q3**

**(a)** Suggest reasons for the big variations in the infant mortality rate and the death rate by age group shown in Figures 3 and 4.
**(b)** What do you think should be done about this?

**Q4**

Why are many health experts worried by the rise in numbers of elderly people in the USA?

# 5.4 Crime: safe and dangerous places

Where is the safest place to live in the USA? If you're worried about being murdered, then avoid Cleveland, Detroit and Houston. The murder rates in these cities are the highest in North America.

The level of different types of crime varies from region to region. New England has the lowest murder rate of all nine divisions. In the West South Central it is almost four times higher. But there is a greater likelihood of having your car stolen in New England (Figure 1). For all parts of the USA, crime rates are highest in the big cities (Figure 2). Here many people, particularly women and the elderly, are afraid to go out after dark. Almost every city has its 'no-go' areas which people avoid for fear of becoming a victim. Crime has risen alarmingly. In the last twenty years all types of crime are well up in all divisions. Figures 1, 2, 3 and 4 show that crime is not evenly spread. Instead it forms clear geographical patterns. The geography of crime is an influence on decisions that people and businesses make.

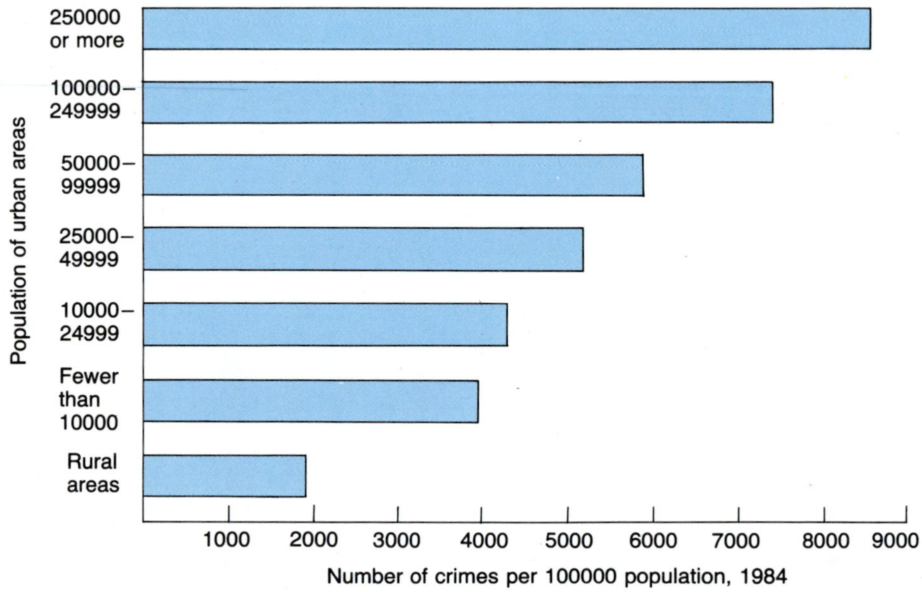


**Fig 2 Crime rate by size of urban area, USA 1984. There is a steady increase in the crime rate as settlements get bigger.**

Where people have a choice they avoid living in areas where crime is known to be high. Businesses too will avoid such areas because of:

- Fear of burglary and criminal damage
- The difficulty of attracting key employees to work in 'risky' areas
- The desire to locate in an area with a pleasant image. The image a company projects is often important to its success.

**Fig 1 The level of crime can vary greatly by type and by area.**

USA: DIVISIONAL CRIME RATES 1986

| | *Violent Crime* | | | | *Property Crime* | | |
|---|---|---|---|---|---|---|---|
| *Division* | *Murder* | *Forcible Rape* | *Robbery* | *Aggravated assault* | *Burglary* | *Larceny/theft* | *Motor vehicle theft* |
| New England | 3.5 | 25.2 | 151 | 239 | 1064 | 2398 | 622 |
| Middle Atlantic | 8.0 | 29.3 | 348 | 316 | 1035 | 2498 | 575 |
| East North Central | 7.5 | 39.4 | 213 | 316 | 1118 | 2845 | 518 |
| West North Central | 4.6 | 26.1 | 97 | 228 | 995 | 2665 | 281 |
| South Atlantic | 9.8 | 40.1 | 222 | 412 | 1473 | 3159 | 407 |
| East South Central | 9.6 | 32.5 | 127 | 280 | 1115 | 2030 | 316 |
| West South Central | 12.3 | 45.8 | 207 | 360 | 1828 | 3639 | 462 |
| Mountain | 7.4 | 38.4 | 127 | 335 | 1540 | 3911 | 366 |
| Pacific | 9.9 | 46.4 | 296 | 445 | 1719 | 3572 | 664 |

[Offences known to the police per 100 000 population]

**Fig 3 The incidence of robbery by division, USA 1950–86. Robbery, like all types of crime, has risen considerably over the years.**

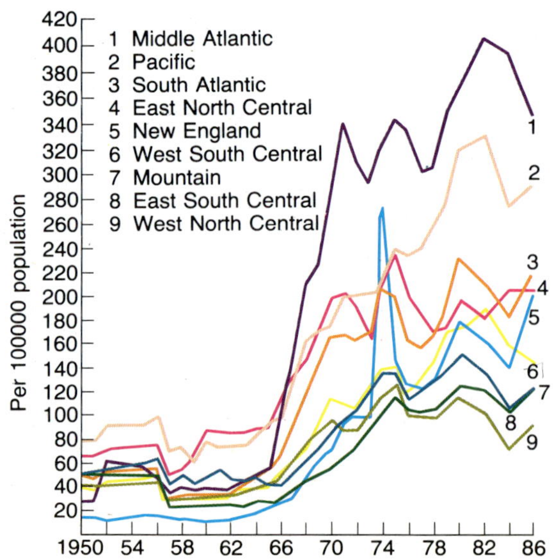

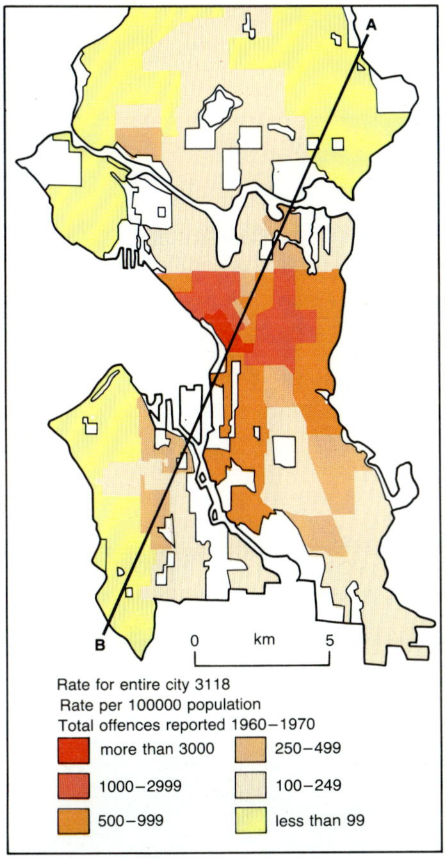


**Fig 4 Map of Seattle showing level of violent crime 1960–70. Seattle, like most North American cities, has a relatively low crime rate in the suburbs compared to the inner city and central business district.**

**Fig 5 Metro Toronto police on patrol.**

**Fig 6 The war against drug traffickers often results in gun battles and street violence.**

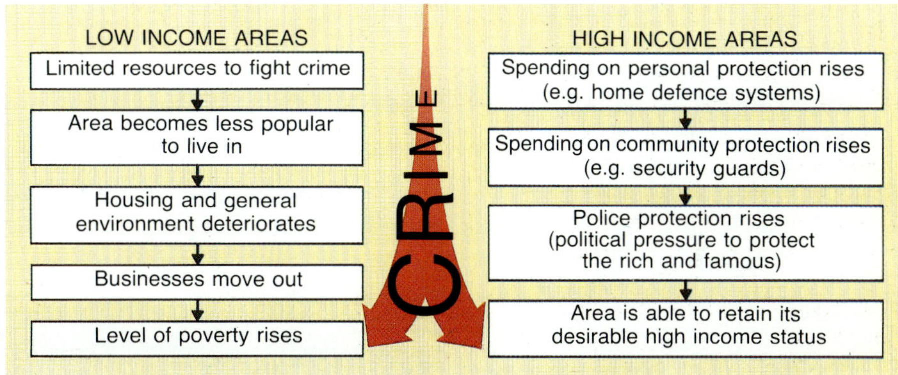


**Fig 7 The response of high and low income areas to crime. When crime increases in low income areas it can set off a chain reaction.**

The worst crime is experienced in poor inner cities. Sociologists believe that the high crime rate is directly related to crowded living conditions. It is very difficult for the poor to protect themselves. Black people are 50% more likely to be the victims of crime than Whites. In contrast, the wealthy are spending more and more money on protection (Figure 7). Many rich residential estates in Los Angeles have private security guards at each entrance. They are also surrounded by high walls monitored by the most up-to-date electronic surveillance devices. These are the 'no-go' areas of the rich suburbs. Entry is only for the wealthy. The divide between poor inner cities and rich suburbs is getting stronger.

Organised crime (e.g. the Mafia) remains strong in the USA. In recent years more and more of its money has come from drug trafficking. Miami, Florida, is one of the main entry points for drugs from South America. With such a long coastline and lengthy border with Mexico providing many unsupervised entry points, the war against drug trafficking will be a very difficult one to win.

Canada's crime rate is much lower than the USA's, and is at about the same level as in Britain. Canada also has regional variations. For example, the homicide rate in the Yukon and Northwest Territories is way above the level in the rest of the country. As in the USA, Canada's crime rate is rising. Again it is the large cities which have the worst problems.

**Q1**

**(a)** Make a copy of Figure 1 but leave out the figures. Add on an extra column at the end. Now rank the nine divisions for each type of crime. The division with the worst crime should be ranked first in each case. In the last column total the rankings for each division.
**(b)** Is there much change in ranking for different crimes?
**(c)** How good do you think this method is for comparing crime in the regions of the USA? Suggest how you might improve on it.

**Q2**

**(a)** Describe the link between crime and the size of urban areas shown by Figure 2.
**(b)** Suggest reasons for these differences.

**Q3**

Look at Figure 4.
**(a)** Draw a section diagram to show how the rate of violent crime changes along line A–B.
**(b)** Suggest why inner cities have higher crime rates than suburban areas.

# 5.5 Black America

## From slavery to Civil Rights

The Black population of North America began when twenty young people were taken in slavery from Africa to Virginia in 1619. Today over 27 million Blacks live in the USA (Figure 1). Theirs is a history of over three centuries of struggle against racial discrimination.

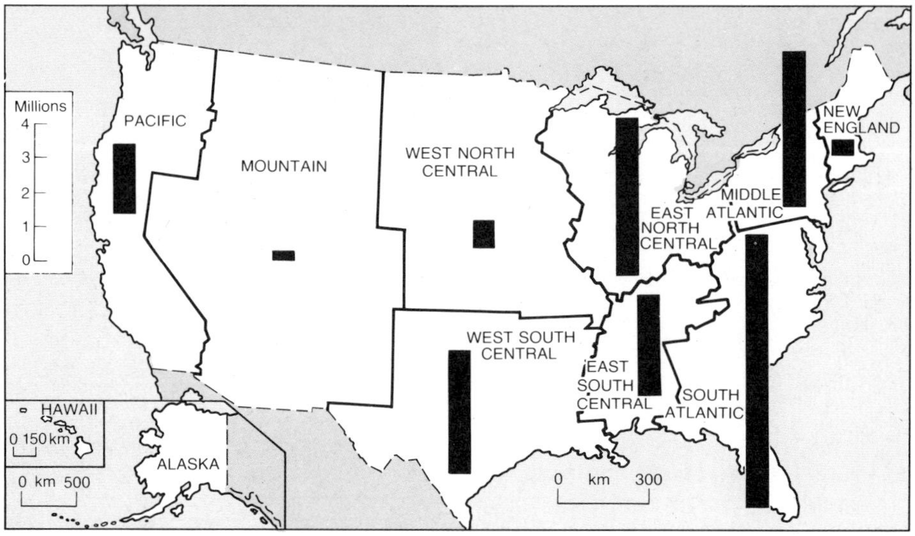


Fig 1 The Black population of the USA, 1980.

- Slavery was not abolished until 1865. At this time most Blacks worked on plantations in the south. Conditions were harsh and families were often split up. A smaller number of Blacks worked in domestic service in the north-eastern states.

- After 1865 many Blacks became sharecroppers. They rented small farms and paid the landowners a share of their crop. Incomes from these small farms were very low. The sharecropping period lasted a hundred years. During that time many farmers struggled to buy their land. In 1910 Black land ownership reached its peak at fifteen million acres.

- From 1910 many Blacks left farming for work in the cities. Their small farms could not compete with larger mechanised farms elsewhere. They migrated in large numbers from the south, mainly to the north-east.

- Open discrimination and the violation of civil rights reached a climax in 1965 in Selma, Alabama (Figure 2). Here 600 civil rights marchers were attacked with tear gas, bullwhips and club-wielding police on horseback. The American public were outraged when they saw this violence on TV. Since then legislation such as the Voting Rights Act and the Civil Rights Act has been passed to end discrimination. The law has also tried to end racially segregated schooling. As a result some children have to travel a long way to attend racially mixed schools. But while the USA is a fairer society now under law, racial discrimination continues in a range of other ways.

Fig 2 Police and state troopers break up the Selma–Montgomery protest march.

## Unemployment and low pay

The unemployment rate for Black Americans was almost 15% in 1985. This was over twice the rate for Whites. Over 40% of Black teenagers are without a job. In recent years the situation has become worse because:

- Blacks live mainly in inner cities where business closures have been very high.

- Black employment has been concentrated in industries like steel and cars where automation has replaced millions of jobs.

Most working Black Americans are in unskilled and semi-skilled jobs where wages are low, although a very small number of Blacks now have top jobs in industry and commerce. In some occupations, particularly in public services, positive discrimination is used to improve opportunities for Black people. Here preference is given to Black job applicants over Whites in order to achieve a better racial balance.

## Social deprivation

- Half of all Black children live in families below the official poverty line.
- Half of all people in prison are Black although only 12% of the USA's whole population is Black.
- The infant mortality rate is twice that for White Americans.
- 43% of Black families are single parent homes headed by a woman, compared with 12% of White families.
- Murder is the second highest cause of death among Black males aged 20 to 24 years.

These are just a few of many measures which show the poor social conditions of Black Americans. Most Black children are brought up in the ghettos of the big cities. Here the schools are short of money, housing is substandard and social services poor. In the inner cities the USA is developing an underclass of between five to seven million people where poverty is handed on from generation to generation.

## New political power

Since the success of the Civil Rights movement led by Dr Martin Luther King, Black Americans have become more aware of their political power. New leaders such as Jesse Jackson and Louis Farrakhan have emerged. Louis Farrakhan, the Black Muslim leader, is feared by many Whites because of his views (Figure 5). He wants a separate country created in the USA for Black Americans. Many Blacks see political power as the only way of improving their status.

Some large cities now have Black mayors. But will there ever be a Black President of the USA?

### Q1
Look at Figure 1.
**(a)** Describe the distribution of the Black population in 1980.
**(b)** How and why has it changed since 1910?

### Q2
**(a)** What is meant by an 'underclass'?
**(b)** Where does the USA's underclass live and why does it exist?

### Q3
If you were a major US politician what suggestions would you put forward to improve the quality of life of Black Americans?

### Q4
Make a list of the differences between Black and White America shown in Figure 3.

**Fig 4 Low income area of East Boston, Massachusetts.**

**Fig 5 Louis Farrakhan addressing a meeting.**

**Fig 3 Life expectancy, unemployment and poverty, comparisons between Blacks and Whites.**

# 5.6 Native peoples of Canada

| *Province or territory* | *Inuit* | *Status Indian* | *Non-status Indian* | *Métis* | *Total native peoples* |
|---|---|---|---|---|---|
| Newfoundland | 1 850 | 1 010 | 1 185 | 385 | 4 430 |
| Prince Edward Island | 30 | 400 | 140 | 50 | 625 |
| Nova Scotia | 130 | 5 905 | 1 155 | 605 | 7 795 |
| New Brunswick | 5 | 4 235 | 865 | 415 | 5 515 |
| Quebec | 4875 | 34 400 | 5 810 | 7 310 | 52 395 |
| Ontario | 1 095 | 70 190 | 26 090 | 12 680 | 110 060 |
| Manitoba | 230 | 39 710 | 5 855 | 20 485 | 66 280 |
| Saskatchewan | 145 | 37 470 | 4 135 | 17 455 | 59 200 |
| Alberta | 510 | 35 810 | 8 595 | 27 135 | 72 050 |
| British Columbia | 515 | 54 085 | 19 085 | 8 955 | 82 645 |
| Yukon | 95 | 2 770 | 990 | 190 | 4 045 |
| Northwest Territories | 15 910 | 6 720 | 1 205 | 2 595 | 26 430 |
| Canada | 25 390 | 292 700 | 75 110 | 98 260 | 491 460 |

**Fig 1 The native peoples of Canada, 1981 census.**

## Welfare

While the standard of living of Indian bands has improved it is still well below the Canadian average.

- Life expectancy is ten years less.
- Less than 50% of Indian homes are properly serviced compared to 95% nationally.
- Only 23% of working-age people have jobs. The national average is 57%.
- Violent deaths are three times the average.
- University entrance is half the national average.

## Location and groups

Many centuries before the first Europeans arrived Canada was settled by people from north-eastern Asia. The Inuits (Eskimos) and Indians of today are their descendants. But as a result of later immigration by other groups they now form only 2% of Canada's population. Figure 1 shows where native peoples live. Four groups are listed:

**Métis** People of mixed Indian and non-Indian blood.

**Inuit** There are about 100 000 Inuits living in the eastern tip of the USSR, Greenland, northern Alaska and northern Canada. Canada's Inuits number 25 000. Their language is Inuktitut.

**Non-Status Indians** Native by birth and heritage but not registered as members of specific bands. Most live away from Indian reserves.

**Status Indians** Registered by the Canadian government as members of specific Indian bands. Most live on Indian reserves. There are 576 bands on 2,250 reserves spread throughout Canada.

Inuit communities are sited mainly on the coast. This reflects the use of the sea for food and transport. Sites were also determined by the location of trading stores, giving Inuit hunters a local centre to trade their furs and skins. Today the Inuit depend less on hunting, trapping and fishing. Work in tourism, arts and crafts, oil exploration and municipal services is now more important. Many people now work for their own co-operatives rather than outside companies. However while the Inuit have achieved much, their standard of living is still low.

The Inuits are keen to protect their culture. In 1951 the Inuit Broadcasting Corporation was set up. It broadcasts up to six hours of Inuktitut programmes a week. Inuktitut newspapers and magazines have also been established. Schools now teach more and more in Inuktitut rather than in English.

The Inuits now have more control over local government through settlement councils. Like the Indians to the south, the Inuits have made a number of land claims. Some agreements have been reached with the Canadian government but this issue will extend well into the future.

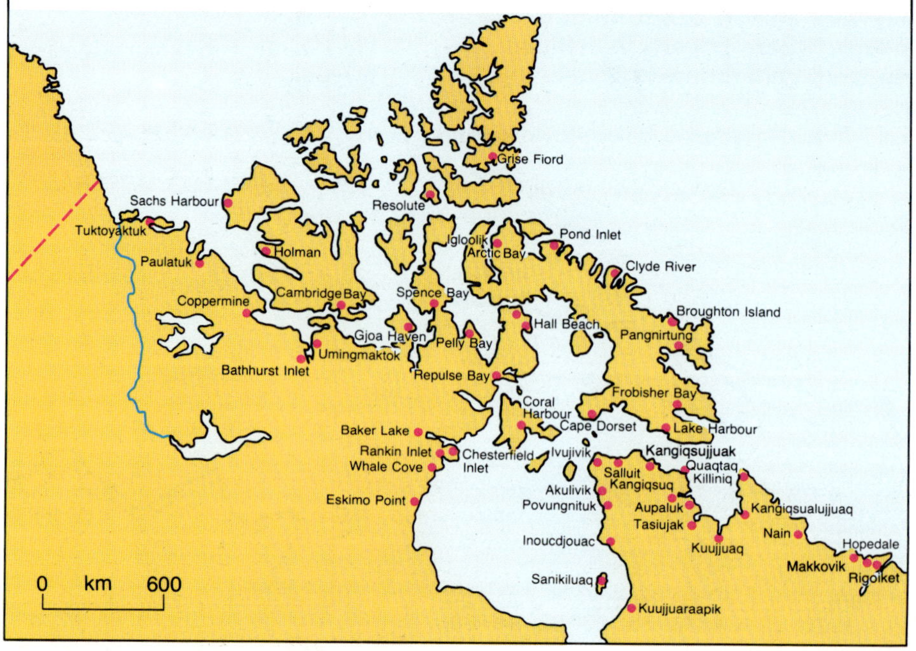


**Fig 2 Inuit communities in northern Canada.**

The Indians say that this is a result of a history of discrimination against them. They argue that:

- Much of their land was taken from them without compensation
- Many reserves have very poor quality land
- Canadian law restricts the ways reserve land can be used
- Government investment in Indian projects has been too low
- Firms are less likely to employ Indians than other Canadians.

## New political awareness

The Indians have become more aware of the need to state their case clearly (Figure 4). To do this the bands have formed associations. The most influential is the Assembly of First Nations. It talks directly to the government. In the last twenty years the Indians have assumed much greater responsibility for their own affairs.

## Land claims

In the earlier years of European settlement the Indians were compensated for the loss of their land. These agreements also set aside areas (reserves) for continuing Indian use. However, after 1921 many bands lost land without their agreement and without compensation. They are now claiming their right to these lands either in court or in negotiation with the government. For example, in 1982 the government signed an agreement with the Penticton band in British Columbia. In addition to having 4900 hectares of land returned to them, the band received $14 million in compensation. Not all land claims have been so successful and there are still many more to be settled. Some of the disputed lands are rich in minerals and other resources. Land claims are now a major issue in Canada.

**Q1**
Describe the distribution of native peoples in Canada.

**Q2**
Look at Figure 4. Why do the Micmacs want to control their children's education?

**Q3**
**(a)** Imagine you are the leader of an Indian band which lost land earlier in the century without compensation. Write a letter to the Canadian government claiming your right to this land.
**(b)** Suggest why some people in Canada are against the government settling land claims.

**Q4**
Describe and suggest reasons for the location of Inuit communities in Canada.

**Fig 3 Indian bands range in size from two members to over 10 000 (Six Nations of the Grand River, Ontario).**

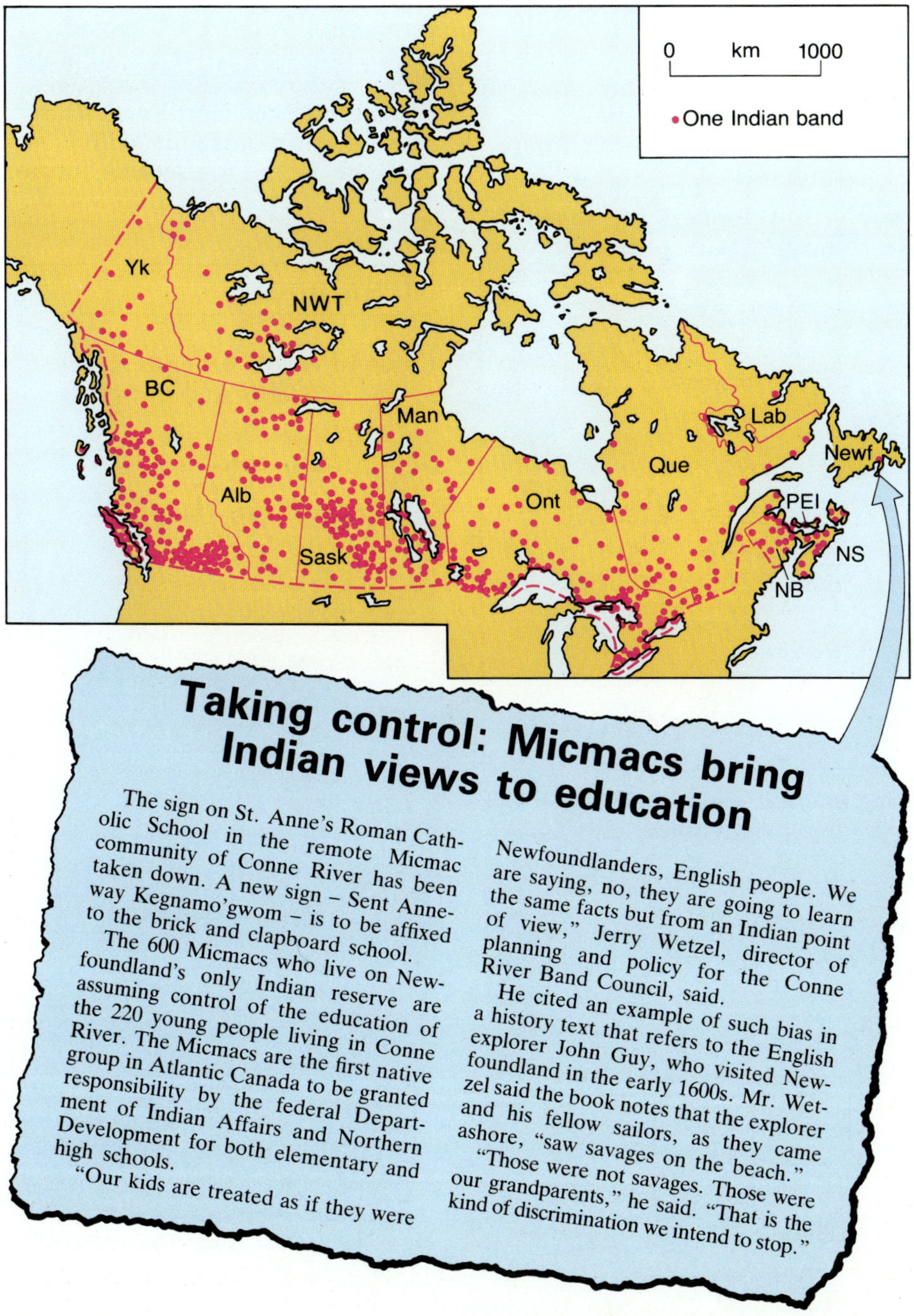


### Taking control: Micmacs bring Indian views to education

The sign on St. Anne's Roman Catholic School in the remote Micmac community of Conne River has been taken down. A new sign – Sent Anne-way Kegnamo'gwom – is to be affixed to the brick and clapboard school.

The 600 Micmacs who live on Newfoundland's only Indian reserve are assuming control of the education of the 220 young people living in Conne River. The Micmacs are the first native group in Atlantic Canada to be granted responsibility by the federal Department of Indian Affairs and Northern Development for both elementary and high schools.

"Our kids are treated as if they were Newfoundlanders, English people. We are saying, no, they are going to learn the same facts but from an Indian point of view," Jerry Wetzel, director of planning and policy for the Conne River Band Council, said.

He cited an example of such bias in a history text that refers to the English explorer John Guy, who visited Newfoundland in the early 1600s. Mr. Wetzel said the book notes that the explorer and his fellow sailors, as they came ashore, "saw savages on the beach."

"Those were not savages. Those were our grandparents," he said. "That is the kind of discrimination we intend to stop."

**Fig 4 An extract from *Toronto Globe and Mail* 8 August 1986. The Indians are concerned to preserve their culture and to fight discrimination.**

# 6. Cities

# 6.1 Urbanisation

## A global trend

More than seven in every ten Americans and Canadians live in towns and cities (Figure 1). Of the remainder of the population many live within easy reach of urban jobs and services. Urbanisation is on the increase globally (Figure 2). By 2000 it is estimated that over half of all the world's people will be urban residents.

## Why has urbanisation increased in North America?

- Farming and other traditional rural industries have either become highly mechanised or have declined. Employment in many rural areas has steadily fallen.
- Jobs today are mainly in urban areas. Work is the most important influence on where people live.
- North Americans are wealthy compared to most people elsewhere. Much of this wealth is spent on a wide variety of goods and services. These are mainly urban-based and they attract people to live in towns and cities.

The proportion of people living in urban areas has been steadily rising since the early years of European settlement. In the 1970s rural areas in the USA gained population at a faster rate (Figure 3) but this reversal of the long-term trend was short-lived. The process of urbanisation will continue in the foreseeable future.

**Fig 1 Cities with more than one million people in North America.**

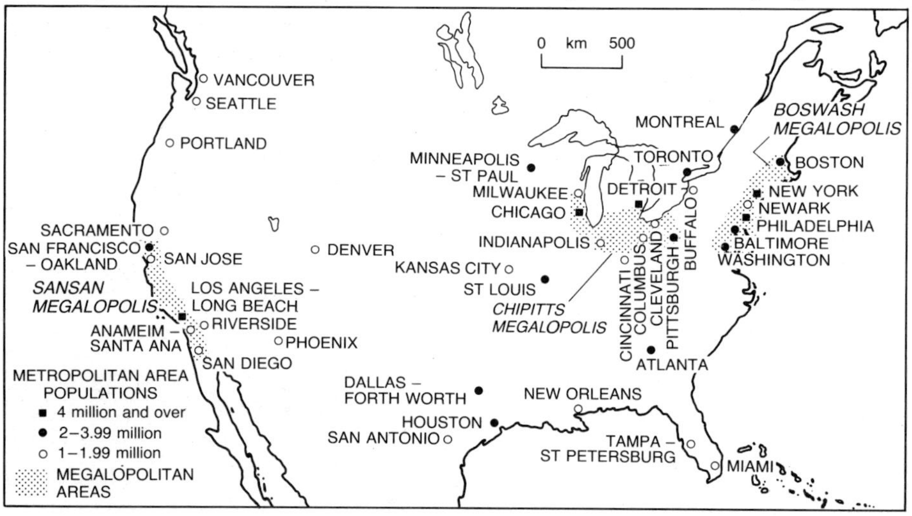


**Fig 2 The percentages of the population living in urban areas in 1960, 1980 and 2000. The proportion living in towns and cities is steadily rising.**

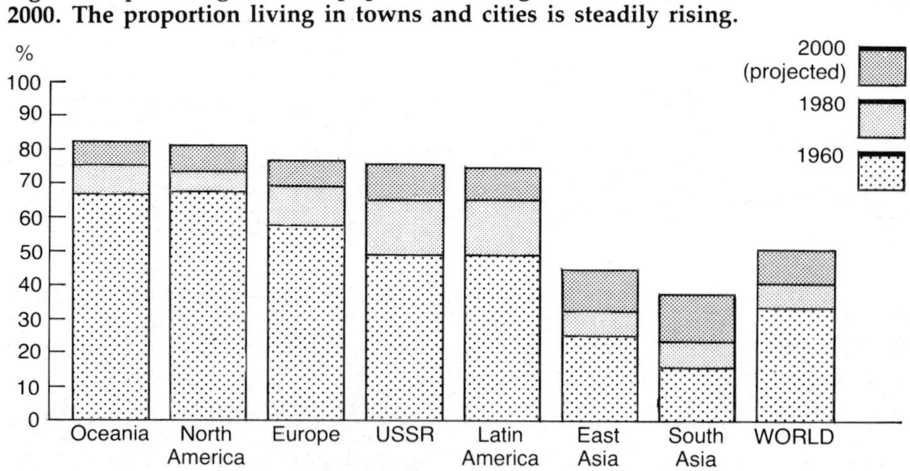


## Megalopolis

Cities in North America have spread upwards and outwards

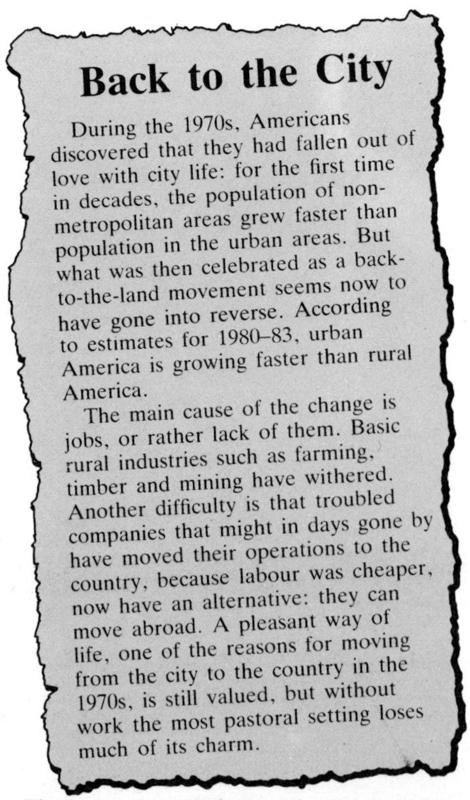

**Back to the City**

During the 1970s, Americans discovered that they had fallen out of love with city life: for the first time in decades, the population of non-metropolitan areas grew faster than population in the urban areas. But what was then celebrated as a back-to-the-land movement seems now to have gone into reverse. According to estimates for 1980–83, urban America is growing faster than rural America.

The main cause of the change is jobs, or rather lack of them. Basic rural industries such as farming, timber and mining have withered. Another difficulty is that troubled companies that might in days gone by have moved their operations to the country, because labour was cheaper, now have an alternative: they can move abroad. A pleasant way of life, one of the reasons for moving from the city to the country in the 1970s, is still valued, but without work the most pastoral setting loses much of its charm.

**Fig 3 An extract from *The Economist* 8 June 1985.**

more than anywhere else in the world (Figure 4). The steel-framed skyscrapers, first built in Chicago in the late 1800s, now mark the centre of all large cities. However, it is the outward spread of cities that has had the greatest effect on people and the landscape (Figure 5). Cities have sprawled over such vast areas because:

- The USA and Canada are big countries. Until recently land was seen as being in plentiful supply.

**Fig 4 High-rise commercial buildings, like these in Toronto, characterise the centre of all major cities in North America.**

- Planning regulations, particularly in the USA, have been weak compared with Europe. Land speculation and property developers have largely had a free hand.
- High average incomes mean that people can afford large homes.
- Car ownership is very high and the quality of roads good. This allows people to commute long distances to work.

By the early part of the century some neighbouring urban areas had merged to form **conurbations**. In the north-eastern USA in particular the conurbations came closer together as urban sprawl continued. Here the intervening countryside has been much reduced. Its character has also changed. Criss-crossed by freeways, the density of rural settlement is high. Most of these rural dwellers commute to work in the nearby towns and cities. Such a heavily urbanised area is known as a **megalopolis** (Figure 1).

One megalopolis is the region between *Bos*ton and *Wash*ington DC. It is sometimes called 'Boswash'. Its other major cities are New York, Philadelphia and Baltimore. Over 40 million people live here. The term megalopolis has also been used for two other areas in the USA, although not all geographers agree that this is correct. The areas are:
(i) 'Chipitts', the major industrial area between *Chi*cago and *Pitts*burgh.
(ii) 'Sansan', the west coast region between *San* Francisco and *San* Diego. The area between San Francisco and Los Angeles has no major cities but many smaller communities have been growing at very fast rates.

## The future

Estimates for the near future show that urbanisation will continue. However, it is unlikely that there will ever be a time when all Americans and Canadians are urbanites because:

- Farming and other rural industries will always provide some employment. And in some rural areas there is now a high rate of manufacturing and service employment.
- Where people have a choice some will prefer to live in rural areas. This is either because they appreciate the attractions of the countryside or they want to escape from the social and environmental problems of the cities.

USA: URBAN AND RURAL POPULATION BY SIZE OF PLACE

| *Size of place* | *1960 (%)* | *1980 (%)* |
|---|---|---|
| *Total urban population* | *69.9* | *73.7* |
| Places of | | |
| 1 million or more | 9.8 | 7.7 |
| 500 000–1 million | 6.2 | 4.8 |
| 250 000–500 000 | 6.0 | 5.4 |
| 100 000–250 000 | 6.5 | 7.5 |
| 50 000–100 000 | 7.7 | 8.7 |
| 25 000– 50 000 | 8.3 | 10.3 |
| 10 000– 25 000 | 9.8 | 12.2 |
| 5 000– 10 000 | 5.5 | 6.8 |
| 2 500– 5 000 | 4.2 | 4.1 |
| under 2 500 | 0.4 | 0.6 |
| other urban | 5.5 | 5.6 |
| *Total rural population* | *30.1* | *26.2* |
| Places of | | |
| 1000–2500 | 3.6 | 3.1 |
| Places under 1000 | 2.2 | 1.7 |
| Other rural | 24.3 | 21.4 |

**Fig 5 Urbanisation continues to increase but it is not the largest cities that are growing at the fastest rates.**

**Q1**

Look at Figure 1.
**(a)** How many cities have populations of (i) 1–2 million (ii) 2–4 million (iii) over 4 million?
**(b)** What happens to the number of cities as population increases? Why do you think this is so?

**Q2**

Look at Figure 1 and at an atlas.
**(a)** How many cities over 1 million population are located: (i) on the coast; (ii) beside major rivers or lakes; (iii) beyond 55° North.
**(b)** Why have (i), (ii) and (iii) influenced the location of cities? Make a list of other factors which are also important.

**Q3**

Look at Figure 2.
**(a)** In which world regions did/will urbanisation increase most (i) between 1960 and 1980 (ii) between 1980 and 2000?
**(b)** Why do so many people live in towns and cities in North America?

**Q4**

Look at Figure 5.
**(a)** How has population distribution changed by size of place?
**(b)** Suggest reasons for these changes.

# 6.2 Urban structure

## Land use models

The structure of a city is the pattern of its buildings, streets and people. It is the way land is used. It includes the location of shops, offices, factories, open space and different types of housing. No two cities are the same. What images come into your mind when you think of New York, Dallas, Los Angeles, Las Vegas and Miami? As popular TV programmes are set in these cities you might already have some idea of what they look like.

So every city is unique. However, similar land-uses often group together in cities. Because of this, basic patterns of land use are formed. In the 1920s William Burgess studied a number of cities, including Chicago. He argued that land-uses formed a circular pattern. Burgess drew a simplified diagram (or 'model') to show the main land-use zones. In the 1930s Homer Hoyt claimed from his study of American cities that land-uses tended to form wedges. Figure 1 compares the two models.

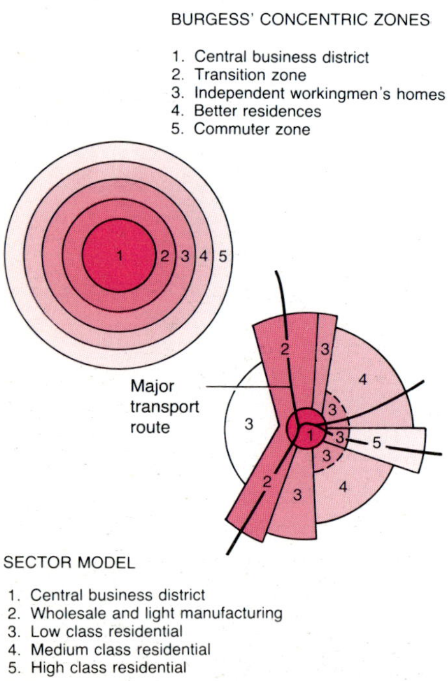


**Fig 1 The (a) concentric zone and (b) sector model of urban land.**

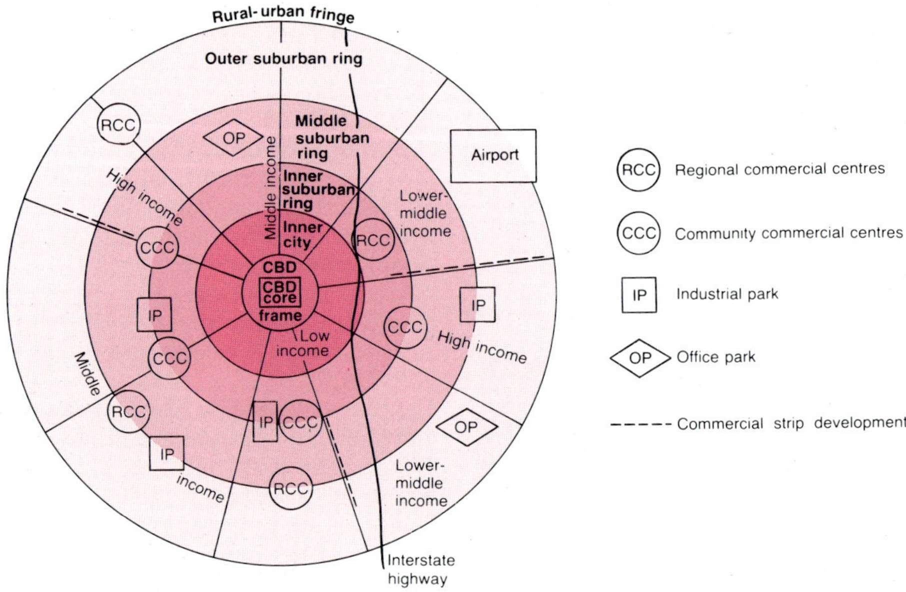


**Fig 2 A model of the modern city in North America.**

Cities today are many times bigger and more complex than they were in the 1920s and 1930s. Figure 2 is a model of the modern North American city containing a Central Business District core (CBD), a CBD frame and three suburban rings.

## The Central Business District

A cluster of skyscrapers marks the position of the CBD. Shops and personal services occupy much of the ground floor space. Upper floors are mainly offices, apartments and hotels. Much CBD retailing is now found in indoor shopping malls. These can extend over a number of floors and may be linked to each other by underground walkways. Many of the city's important public buildings are found in, or close to the CBD. Major roads converge on the CBD and it is the focus for public transport. The CBD core (its centre) is supported by the CBD frame. Here are car parks, train and bus stations, garages, open spaces and small businesses providing services for firms in the CBD core.

## The inner city

The oldest and poorest quality housing is found here. Residents are mainly on low incomes and many belong to racial minority groups. Urban renewal schemes have replaced some of the worst housing with apartment blocks, offices and other land uses. In some areas Young Urban Professionals (Yuppies) and 'empty nesters' (older couples whose children have grown up) have bought old, run-down houses and renovated them. This process is often termed 'gentrification'. Some parts of the inner city are now very fashionable. However, the economic, environmental and social problems of urban areas remain concentrated in the inner city.

## Suburban rings

The density of population and housing generally falls from the inner city to the outer suburbs. Different income areas cross all three suburban rings. High income areas are marked by large

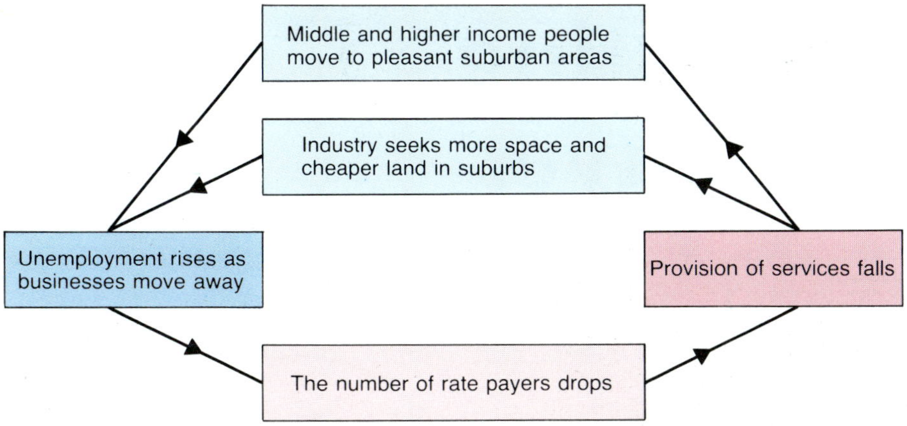


**Fig 3 Many inner city areas have been in decline for years. This is a simplified explanation of what has happened.**

detached houses and gardens. Housing is more tightly packed in middle and lower-middle income areas. But even here population density is much lower than in Europe. This is why North American cities are so large in area. For example, Atlanta with a population of two million covers the same area as London (6.7 million). Strips of fast food restaurants, garages, bars, general stores and motels have developed along some of the main radial roads. Industry is sited mainly in attractively planned industrial parks. Over the years industry has moved from the inner city to the suburbs. Office building has greatly increased in suburban areas too. Much of it is concentrated in purpose built office parks (Figure 5).

Suburban populations have increased while inner city populations have often fallen. It is not surprising then that new shopping centres have been built in key suburban locations. These are often enclosed and carefully planned to provide a wide range of goods and services.

## The rural-urban fringe

This is the boundary between city and countryside. It is often a not very distinct area, with villages, hamlets and single buildings dotted over the landscape. Much of the land is often owned by property speculators waiting for it to increase in value. Building tends to occur first along the main roads. The areas between are filled in later.

**Fig 4 Decaying inner city: Philadelphia.**

**Fig 5 Office park Harrison, Michigan**

**Q1**
Compare the two land use models shown in Figure 1.

**Q2**
**(a)** Identify two locations in Figure 2 where industry is absent which would normally be attractive to industrial development.
**(b)** Why would these locations be popular choices?

**Q3**
**(a)** Suggest why people on low incomes live mainly in the inner city.
**(b)** What is gentrification? Why does it occur?

**Q4**
Look at Figure 3. Draw a similar model to illustrate the process of gentrification in inner city areas.

**Q5**
What differences in housing might you expect to find when moving from the inner city to the outer suburban ring? Illustrate your answer with a profile drawing.

**Fig 6 Toronto middle income suburbs.**

# 6.3 The commuting problem: Vancouver

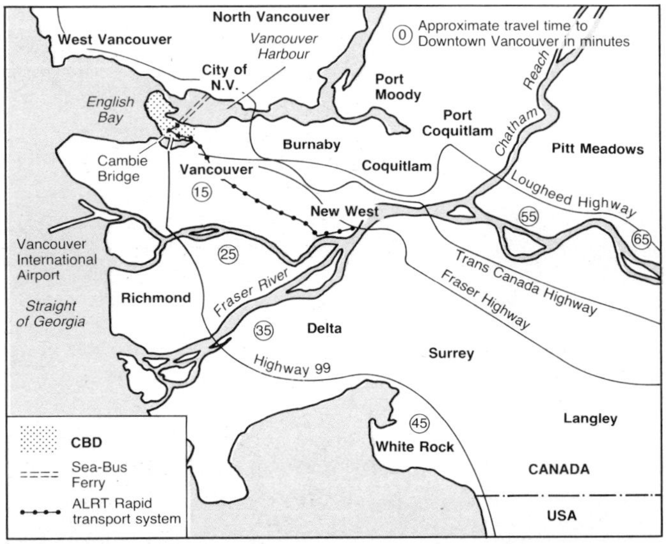


**Fig 1 This map shows the average travel time in minutes to Vancouver's CBD from major suburban areas during the morning rush hour.**

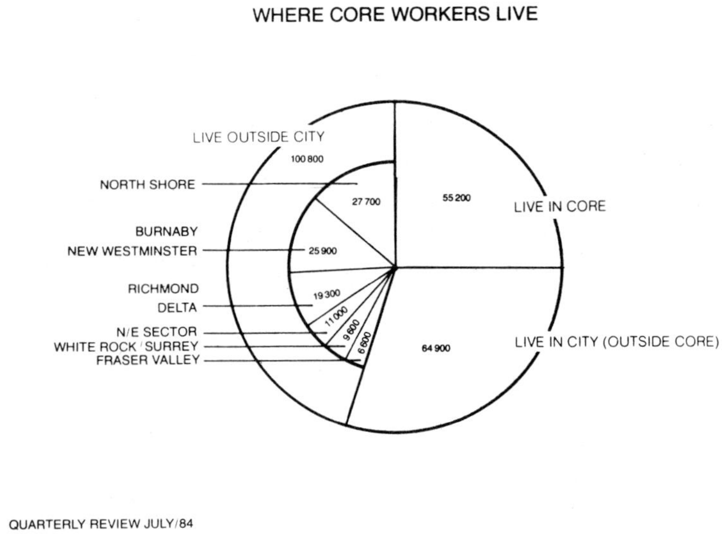


**Fig 2 The majority of people who work in Vancouver's core live elsewhere.**

## Congested roads

Every workday morning almost half a million people in the Vancouver metropolitan area leave home to go to work (Figure 1). By car or by bus they filter out of residential areas onto major roads. They are heading for Vancouver's CBD and other smaller employment centres. During the morning peak period (7–9 a.m.) the journey to work accounts for 90% of travel to the CBD. In the late afternoon (4.30–6.30 p.m.) the commuting pattern is reversed. Now tens of thousands of cars and hundreds of buses stream out of the CBD toward the suburbs. Vancouver's planners are concerned. If the volume of commuting continues to rise, the traffic saturation point will soon be reached.

Commuting creates problems in all cities. In most the situation is getting worse. This is because:

- Office and other service jobs are heavily concentrated in the CBD. The main access roads to the CBD can become heavily congested.
- The number of vehicles is steadily rising. Roads are breaking up under the strain and maintenance costs are high.
- Daytime parking needs more and more space in the CBD.
- More traffic increases air and noise pollution.
- Never before have people lived so far from their jobs. Some people commute more than 100 kilometres each way. Bottlenecks can occur in suburban areas long before drivers reach the CBD. Multi-lane highways and complex intersections are usually needed to cope with the heavy traffic.

Two hundred and twenty thousand people work in Vancouver's core (the CBD and its immediate surroundings). This is one-third of all employment in the metropolitan area. Most of these people live outside the core (Figure 2). Many travel a considerable distance. Between 1971 and 1981 employment in the core grew by 46 000 jobs. Seventy five per cent of these jobs were filled by suburban residents. Since the start of the 1980s there has been a boom in office development in the core. In addition, several big public projects including a convention centre, a stadium and Expo 86 were completed. This has generated even more traffic, particularly at peak periods.

Vancouver's suburbs have spread rapidly. In 1951 the city of Vancouver had 65% of the metropolitan area population. By 1981 it was down to 33%. The population of the city did not fall; it was the rest of the metropolitan area that grew at a rapid rate. This is a trend experienced by all North American cities. In fact, in the USA, urban areas have sprawled over a wider area than in Canada with people commuting even longer distances (Figure 3).

## Possible solutions

In the early 1970s the 'Liveable Region Program' set out two ways

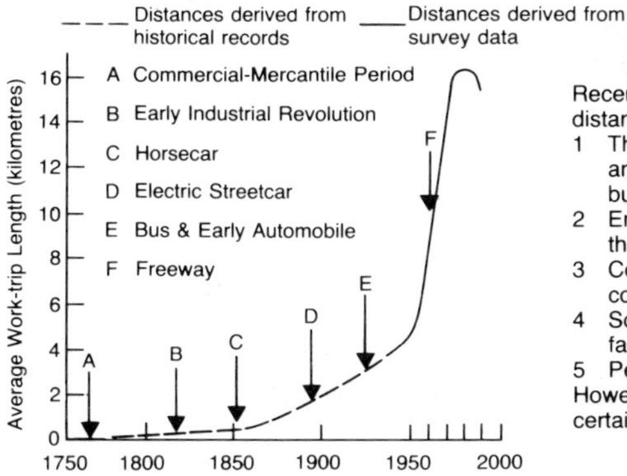


Recent studies in the USA show that commuting distances might be falling. Reasons for this include:

1 The main highway building period was in the 1960s and early 1970s. There has been much less road building since. This has slowed suburban sprawl.
2 Employment opportunities have increased outside the CBD.
3 Congestion in city centres is a disincentive to commuting.
4 Some inner city areas have become very fashionable and slowed the move to the suburbs.
5 Petrol prices are higher than in the past.

However, more evidence is needed before we can be certain that this is the start of a long-term trend.

**Fig 3 The journey-to-work distance in the USA has steadily risen for hundreds of years – until recently.**

to tackle the journey to work problem in Vancouver:

- Encourage employment growth in the suburbs. In the 1970s more than twice as many new jobs were created in the rest of the metropolitan region as in the city of Vancouver.

- Shift spending from road building to public transport. This led to a big increase in the bus fleet. In 1971, 33% of people entered the CBD during the morning peak period by bus. By 1980 this had risen to 42%.

**Fig 4 Transport planners continually struggle to improve traffic flows. However the problem of congestion is a difficult one to overcome.**

However, congestion continued to get worse (Figure 4). New measures were needed so money was invested in:

- ALRT. In 1981 construction began on the ALRT (Advanced Light Rapid Transit) railway. The 21 kilometre route was completed in 1986. ALRT has fifteen stations and links the CBD to New Westminster (Figure 6). It operates from 5 a.m. to 1 a.m. ALRT is closely linked with bus routes and with Sea-Bus (the ferry link to North Vancouver). It is designed to carry 20 000 commuters during the peak period with potential for later expansion to 50 000.

- Improving road access in the CBD. The new Cambie Bridge is a major part of this work.

Other strategies which might also be used are:

- Encouraging residential development close to the CBD. This would reduce long distance commuting.

- Putting a limit on commercial development in the CBD. Commuting is linked to the number of jobs available.

Vancouver is faced with a dilemma. On the one hand, there is potential for employment growth in the core. On the other hand, the consequence of growth will affect almost everyone who lives or works in the metropolitan region.

**Fig 5 Aerial view of Vancouver.**

## Q1

**(a)** Use Figure 2 to find out the percentage of core workers who: (i) live in the core; (ii) live in the city but outside the core; (iii) live outside the city.
**(b)** Why is it important for Vancouver's transport planners to have this information?

## Q2

Look at Figure 1.
**(a)** How does the average commuting time vary with distance from the CBD?
**(b)** Is this the pattern you would expect? Give reasons for your answer.
**(c)** What kind of transport developments might cause this pattern to alter in the future?

## Q3

Outline the advantages and disadvantages of each possible solution to the commuting problem.

## Q4

Recent evidence suggests that commuting distance in the USA may be falling. What are the possible reasons for this?

**Fig 6 Thirteen kilometres of ALRT are elevated, six kilometres are at surface level and two kilometres are underground. Two and four car trains run at intervals of not more than five minutes.**

# 6.4 The Central Business District: Houston, Texas

A cluster of skycrapers marks the position of Houston's CBD or 'Downtown', the biggest employment centre in the city. Downtown Houston covers four square kilometres. It is bordered by elevated freeways (Figure 2). Most downtown blocks are set out in a square grid pattern. Each side of a block measures 76 metres. The street right-of-way between blocks is usually 24 metres (road plus pavements). Only 2145 people live downtown, but during working days well over a quarter of a million people may be found there. The downtown area has changed much in the last twenty years. Such changes have occurred in many North American cities.

## Offices

Commercial land uses dominate downtown. These include offices, shops, hotels and off-street parking (Figure 1). Downtown is not the only large office area in Houston. Since the early 1970s suburban centres have also grown rapidly. Downtown office space rose from 8.3 to 45.8 million square feet between 1960 and 1980. This was due to (a) the expansion of existing firms and (b) new firms moving in from other cities.

Downtown's economy is based on businesses such as oil and petrochemical companies, financial institutions and other professional services. The oil companies include Shell, Texaco, Exxon, Gulf and Tenneco. The growth of energy-related companies has been responsible for much of downtown's development and redevelopment.

**Fig 2 The pattern of land use in Houston's CBD. The area is bordered by elevated highways which cope with almost 200 000 commuters every morning and evening rush period.**

| Use | *1000s of square feet* 1971 | 1982 |
|---|---|---|
| Office | 25 903 | 45 800 |
| Retail/Services | 7 142 | 4 995 |
| Hotel | 3 040 | 4 317 |
| Parking garage | 6 803 | 15 946 |
| Total | 42 888 | 71 058 |

**Fig 1 The area of commercial floorspace in Houston's CBD, 1971 and 1982.**

Energy-related firms now occupy 55% of all office space. However, the drop in oil prices in the mid-1980s has slowed development. Banks have also played a big role in Houston's changing skyline. They occupy a number of recently completed office towers. High-rise blocks often have several uses, such as parking in basement floors, shops at the pedestrian tunnel and street levels and offices above. The penthouse floor may have a restaurant or nightclub. So that aircraft can safely use Houston's two main airports, buildings can be no more than 304 metres above ground level.

## Retailing

Downtown no longer dominates retailing in Houston. Custom has shifted to suburban and out of town shopping centres. This is because:

- Many people now live far from the CBD.
- The outlying fully planned shopping centres are very popular.
- Traffic congestion and parking are big problems in the CBD.
- Few CBD shops are open late.

Downtown has responded to these changes. Retailers now cater mainly for daytime office shoppers along with business and tourist visitors, rather than family shoppers. Many older shops have been demolished in redevelopment schemes. In contrast much of the 200 000 square metres of underground retail space is recently built. Houston has five kilometres of underground tunnels linking downtown blocks and twenty skywalk connections. Downtown office employment will probably increase in the future. In turn, retailing will expand to meet the extra demand (Figure 3).

## Other land uses

These include:

- Two major hospitals, St Joseph's and Medical Arts.
- Government buildings including the Federal Building, US Post Office and City Hall.
- Sixteen major hotels; the Hyatt-Regency with 958 rooms is the largest.

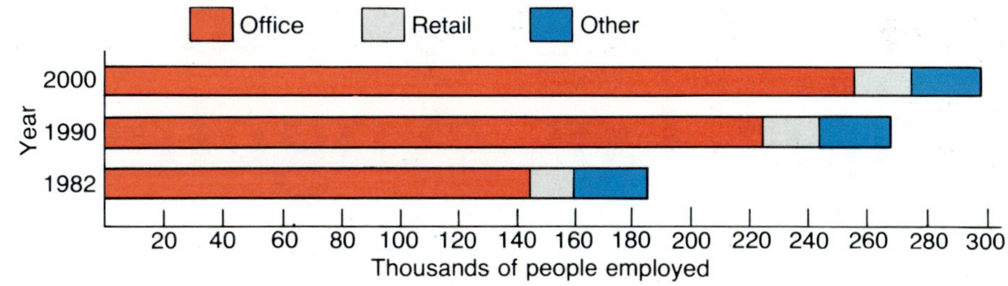


**Fig 3 Downtown employment forecasts for 1990 and 2000.**

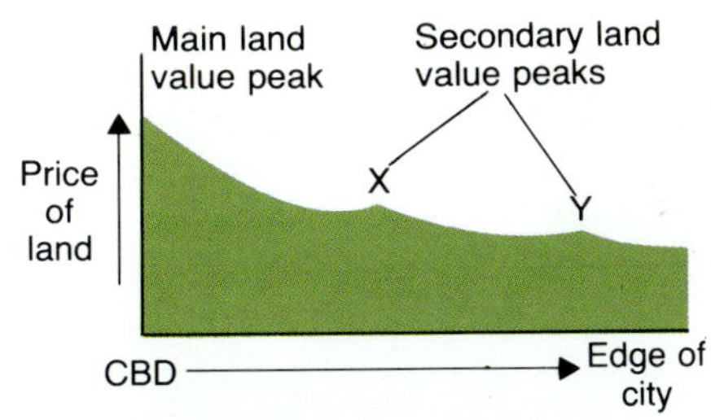


**Fig 4 The price of land varies considerably from the city centre to the rural-urban fringe.**

- Educational and cultural establishments such as the University of Houston and the Music Hall.
- Industrial land which is found mainly to the north-east.

## Accessibility

Houston has one of the most active downtowns in the USA. Its prosperity depends largely on people being able to move to, from and within downtown without too much difficulty. Over 88% of journeys are by private car and congestion can be a problem. To give the best traffic flows most streets are in one-way pairs. Downtown is the focus of bus routes, some of which have exclusive bus lanes.

An eighteen mile rail transit line is planned to link downtown with the north and south-west suburbs. This should improve accessibility and reduce traffic congestion. Passenger train services operate out of the Amtrak railway station in the northwest of downtown. A helicopter service links two downtown sites to the Intercontinental Airport.

## Outlook

- Downtown will remain the main employment centre in Houston and office jobs will increase.
- The resident population will grow as more housing is built.
- An increase in evening and weekend activities will make downtown a more attractive place outside of office hours.
- More open places and green space will make it a more people-oriented place.
- Transport improvements will improve accessibility.

**Q1**
Look at Figure 2.
**(a)** Describe the pattern of land use in the CBD.
**(b)** What evidence is there that road transport is vital to the CBD?

**Q2**
**(a)** Suggest reasons for the change in commercial floorspace shown in Figure 1.
**(b)** How might you expect commercial floorspace to change by 2000? (Use Figure 3 to help you.)

**Q3**
How does the price of land vary from the CBD to the edge of the city? Suggest reasons for the very high price in the CBD and the secondary peaks at X and Y.

# 6.5 Poverty and wealth in cities: Los Angeles

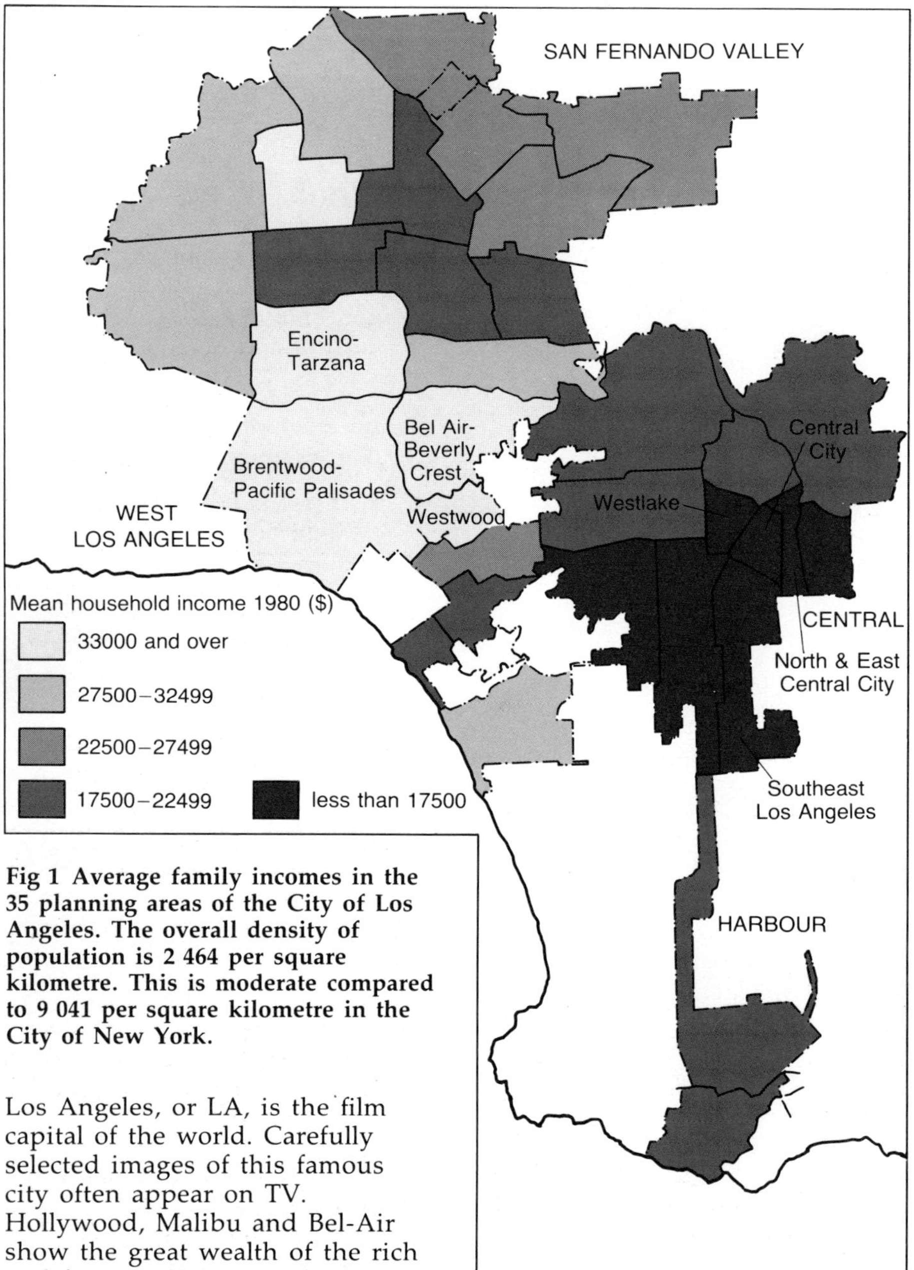


**Fig 1 Average family incomes in the 35 planning areas of the City of Los Angeles. The overall density of population is 2 464 per square kilometre. This is moderate compared to 9 041 per square kilometre in the City of New York.**

Los Angeles, or LA, is the film capital of the world. Carefully selected images of this famous city often appear on TV. Hollywood, Malibu and Bel-Air show the great wealth of the rich and famous. However, there is another side to LA that is not so familiar. This is the great poverty of tens of thousands of people. The evidence is poor housing, homelessness, unemployment, health problems and crime.

LA, with over eleven million people, is the second largest urban area in the USA. It is actually made up of a number of separate cities. The oldest and largest is the City of Los Angeles (population three million). Figure 1 shows how average family income varies in the City of Los Angeles. All cities have their rich and poor people but rarely is the gap between them so great. There are clear areas of high, middle and low income. The result is great differences in the quality of housing and of the general environment. Bel-Air and Brentwood have their large mansions, luxurious swimming pools and spacious gardens. Inner city areas like Southeast Los Angeles and Westlake suffer from decaying tenement blocks, overcrowding and a lack of basic facilities. Here are found some of the worst living conditions in North America (Figure 2).

There is a line that runs through Los Angeles roughly north to south. In places it follows the great Harbor Freeway, in others it runs along the concrete gulch of the Los Angeles river, elsewhere it snakes along broad roads such as Crenshaw Boulevard, Vermont Avenue and Main Street. It is the frontier between the success that Los Angeles so dearly loves, and the failure it despises. It is the frontier where, in the language of Hollywood, the dream ends and the nightmare begins. On one side is the fantasy of a place like Bel Air, and on the other the reality of a place like Skid Row. It is an ever-present reminder to those who live in the plush mansions of Beverly Hills and Westwood, of the proximity of poverty. The population of 'skid row' is rising steadily. There are a dozen missions operating within a few city blocks of the great banks and administration buildings of the world's wealthiest conurbation.

**Fig 2 An extract from the *Sunday Times Magazine* . . . 1986**

Segregation is not only by income but also in terms of race. As Figure 3 shows, Whites make up over 88% of residents in each of the four areas with the highest average household incomes. The situation is very different in the four poorest areas. Overall 48.3% of people in the City of Los Angeles are White, 17.0% are Black and 27.5% are Hispanic and 6.6% Asian. Hispanics are people of Spanish origin. Most came to LA from South and Central America. More than one-third of the City's population speak Spanish as a first language. This

| Planning area | Average income ($) | Percentage population: White | Black | Spanish | Asian | Persons per acre | Employment participation rate |
|---|---|---|---|---|---|---|---|
| Bel Air – Beverly Crest | 80 220 | 90.8 | 1.9 | 3.6 | 3.5 | 2.1 | 52.2 |
| Brentwood – Pacific Palisades | 48 351 | 92.4 | 0.9 | 3.4 | 3.2 | 2.1 | 54.4 |
| Encino–Tarzana | 39 475 | 90.5 | 1.2 | 5.8 | 2.1 | 5.1 | 53.2 |
| Westwood | 36 506 | 88.2 | 1.6 | 4.0 | 6.1 | 13.7 | 54.1 |
| Westlake | 11 158 | 17.0 | 3.2 | 69.7 | 9.5 | 44.5 | 45.3 |
| North and East Central City | 10 804 | 15.4 | 21.1 | 34.4 | 28.4 | 7.3 | 19.1 |
| Southeast Los Angeles | 10 655 | 0.7 | 70.2 | 28.3 | 0.6 | 18.8 | 27.1 |
| Central City | 9 015 | 25.2 | 18.3 | 48.1 | 7.2 | 13.1 | 42.6 |

**Fig 3 The four wealthiest and four poorest areas in the City of Los Angeles.**

will rise to 50% by 2000. It is interesting to remember that Los Angeles (City of the Angels) was originally founded by Spanish missionaries.

Los Angeles has taken over from New York as the main point of entry into the USA for legal and illegal immigration. It is rapidly becoming a truly inter-racial and international city. Hundreds more people arrive daily. Most have very little money. Only the worst housing is open to them. Because of the high rents, many live in very overcrowded conditions. Some will not even achieve this and will be homeless (Figure 4). The City is either unable or unwilling to provide for so many poor newcomers. Most illegal immigrants come from Mexico. The Mexican border town of Tijuana is only two hours drive down the coastal freeway. The City is also a centre of immigration from South east Asia. Vietnamese have accounted for most Asian immigrants in the last ten years.

The Black community experiences the worst quality of life of all. Black unemployment is close to 50% and is even higher for young adults. While immigrant groups often move steadily up the income ladder after they have established themselves in the USA, things have changed little for Blacks. They are little better off now than at the time of the Watts riots in 1965. Racial tension can still come violently to the surface today. In 1984 there were 850 murders in the metropolitan area. This was a 60% increase over 1974. Many of these murders were due to gang warfare involving minority groups.

A clear pattern of migration occurs within the city. Neighbourhoods are changing and entire subpopulations are relocating. For example, large numbers of Hispanics have recently moved into the southern part of the area occupied by the Black community. Those people whose incomes rise move out from the densely populated inner city areas to middle income areas in the north and west of the City (Figures 5 and 6).

**119 illegal aliens discovered living under L.A. bridge**

Government agents yesterday arrested 119 illegal aliens living in burrows under a busy road bridge in the centre of Los Angeles, an immigration spokesman said.

Agents found 40 mattresses hidden under bushes, kerosene stoves, radios and even two television sets plugged into a municipal power cable running under the bridge.

The aliens, from Mexico and other Latin American countries, had dug homes, many of them less than 1½ metres high, and were living in jungle conditions, said Immigration and Naturalization Service spokesman John Belluardo.

**Fig 4 An extract from the *Toronto Globe and Mail*, 8 August, 1986.**

**Fig 5 Wealth.** **Fig 6 Poverty.**

**Q1**

**(a)** On a copy of Figure 1 divide the City into areas of high, moderate and low household income.

**(b)** Comment on the pattern of income.

**Q2**

Look at Figure 3.

**(a)** What is the relationship between average income and racial composition?

**(b)** Use an appropriate graphical technique to show this relationship.

**(c)** Suggest how Westwood could have a higher population density than the much poorer N and E Central City.

**(d)** How do the areas differ in employment participation rates?

**Q3**

Look at Figure 4. Why do so many illegal immigrants go to LA?

# 6.6 Shopping in cities: Toronto

| Type of retailing activity | Per cent distribution | | | | | |
|---|---|---|---|---|---|---|
| | *1953* | *1966* | *1971* | *1976* | *1983* | *1986* |
| Strip Retail | 97.6 | 65.4 | 59.2 | 53.3 | 49.5 | 45.4 |
| Shopping Centres | 2.4 | 34.2 | 39.8 | 40.5 | 40.5 | 44.5 |
| Ancillary Mall | – | 0.4 | 1.0 | 6.2 | 8.6 | 8.1 |
| Individual Outlets | – | – | – | – | 1.4 | 2.0 |

**Fig 1 Retailing activity in metropolitan Toronto, 1953–1986. The relative percentages of the different types of retailing have changed considerably.**

## Trends in Toronto

A recent survey in Toronto noted four types of retail area (Figure 1).

- **Strip Retail** These are shops spread along major roads. Toronto's CBD has the greatest strip development, with Yonge Street as its focus. The older parts of the city have more strip retail than more recently built-up areas (Figure 2). Most newer strip facilities have some off-street parking space, unlike the older areas.
- **Shopping Centres** These are fully planned retail areas usually with free off-street parking. Some of those built in Toronto in the 1950s and 1960s have now been modernised. Most new centres are enclosed. The City's Eaton Centre (160 000 square metres of floor space), opened in 1977, is by far the largest (Figures 3 and 4). It attracts about one million shoppers each week and is firmly on the tourist's list of places to go. Metropolitan Toronto has six other shopping centres with a floor space of over 46 000 square metres.
- **Malls** Here retailing is built into a development in which another land use dominates. Malls are usually in the lower levels of offices, apartment blocks and hotels. They have internal access and are mostly indoor. The City of Toronto has now more floor space in malls than in shopping centres.
- **Individual outlets** These are large individual stores of over 2000 square metres. Most are in the food, furniture and DIY sectors. The size of this kind of individual store has increased considerably in recent years.

Figure 2 shows the location of all retail areas in Toronto (a) between 23 000–46 000 square metres floor space and (b) over 46 000 square metres floor space.

**Fig 2 The locations of large retail areas in Toronto.**

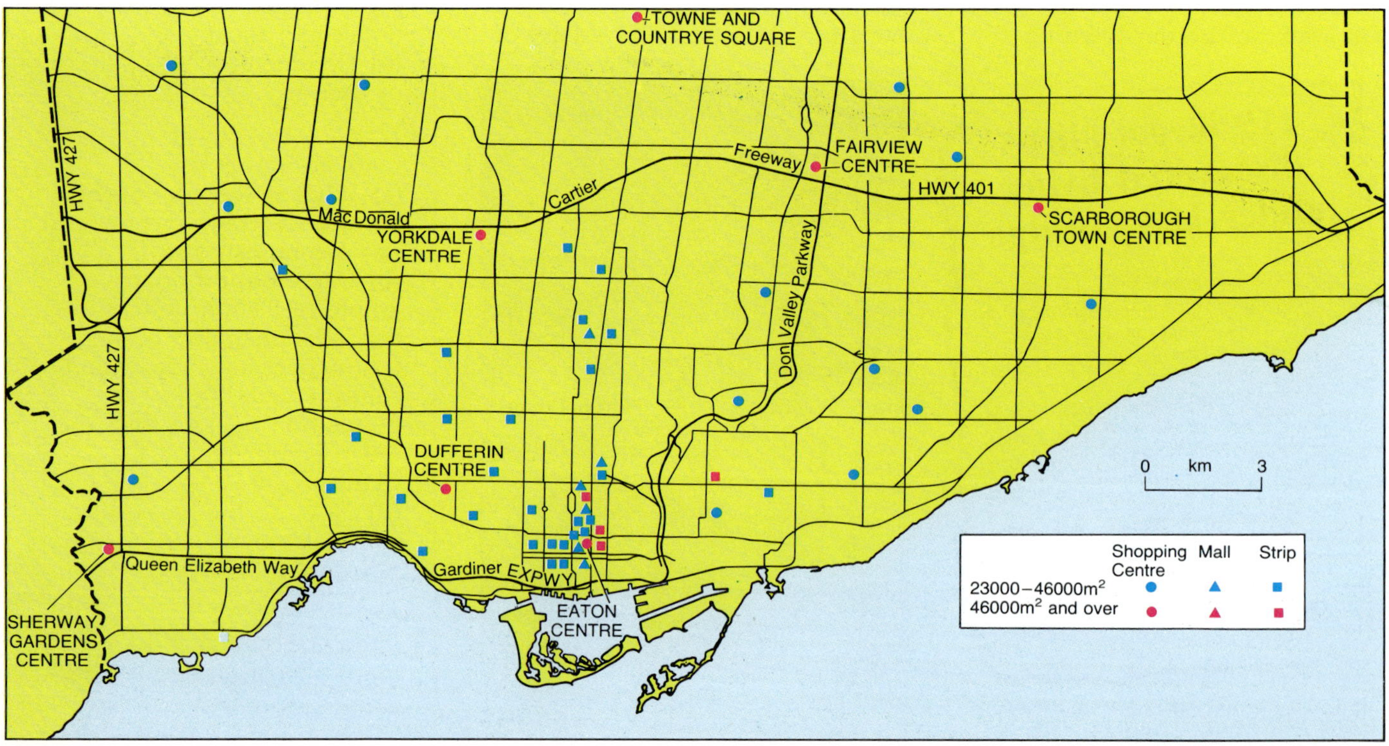

Fig 3 The interior of the Eaton Centre.

Fig 4 Eaton Centre, Toronto.

Of course, there are also very many much smaller retail areas. Retailing is a major land use in Toronto. It is an important part of the city's economy and a large employer. One-third of Canada's total buying power lives within a 160 kilometre radius of Toronto.

**Fig 5 TO Below: Toronto's system of underground pedestrian walkways.**

**Fig 6 TO Below.**

## T O Below

Toronto has a system of tunnels beneath its CBD with brightly lit sequences of stores, cafés and malls. It is almost a second city in itself. The system interconnects 30 office towers, twenty parking garages, three hotels, five subway stations, the railway station and about a thousand shops. At over five kilometres in total length it is the largest underground pedestrian walkway system in the world. T O Below (Toronto, Ontario, Below, Figures 5 and 6) has over 125 ground-level access points. Just three subway stops to the north at Bloor Street is another, smaller underground retail complex. It is possible that the two systems will be linked in the future. In the hot summer, TO Below is a cool escape; in the cold winter it is a welcome shelter from the storm.

**Q1**

**(a)** Draw a line graph to show the information in Figure 1.
**(b)** Give reasons for these changes.

**Q2**

Look at Figure 2.
**(a)** How many shopping centres are there (i) between 23 000–46 000 sq m and (ii) over 46 000 sq m.
**(b)** Suggest reasons for this difference.
**(c)** Comment on the distribution of the largest shopping centres.
**(d)** How does the balance between the different types of retail area change with distance from the centre of the city (approximately the Eaton Centre.)

**Q3**

**(a)** Give reasons for the development of T O Below.
**(b)** Suggest why some people might be unhappy about the growth of retailing underground.

# 6.7 Capital Cities: Ottawa and Washington

Ottawa and Washington are not the biggest cities in their countries. Yet as capital cities they are very important. This is where the governments of the USA and Canada work. Each day they make decisions that affect people's lives, not only in North America but also in other parts of the world. Hardly a day passes without the White House in Washington appearing on a British TV news item.

The two cities are similar in many ways:

- Their locations were carefully chosen for political reasons. Ottawa is on the boundary between Quebec and Ontario, the two most powerful provinces at the time of choice. Washington is on the banks of the Potomac River, the historic divide between the USA's northern and southern states.
- They have been carefully planned and contain many important and famous buildings.
- Many people are employed in government and other professional services.
- They have excellent transport and communications links to the rest of North America and abroad.
- They are cosmopolitan cities and big tourist attractions.

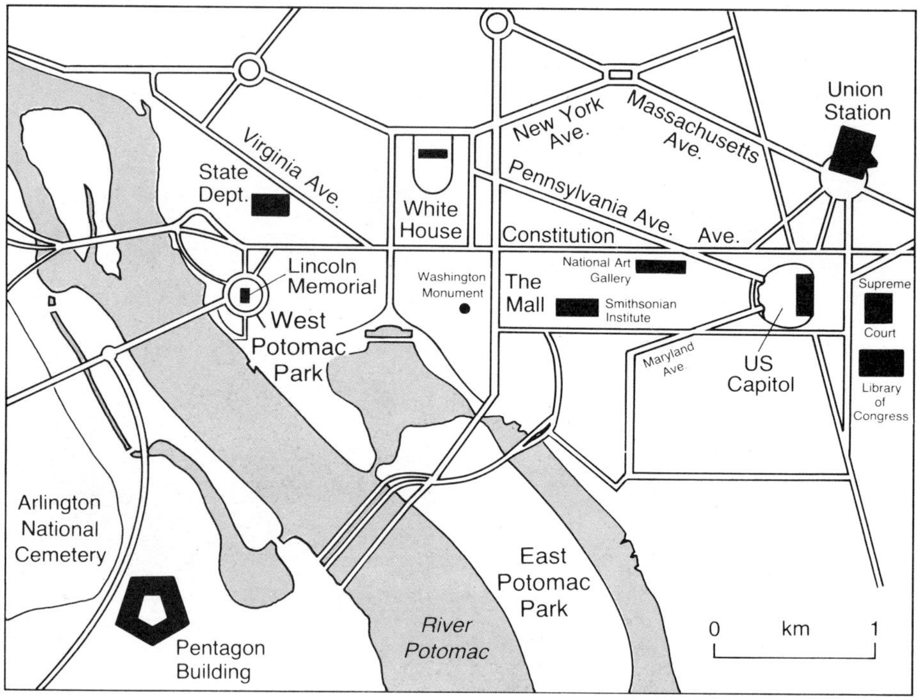


**Fig 1 Central Washington, DC capital of the USA.**

## Washington

The site of the federal District of Columbia (DC) was selected by George Washington, the USA's first president. It is now almost totally covered by the city of Washington. Washington DC has a population of 638 000. But it is at the centre of a larger metropolitan area that extends into Maryland and Virginia. The total population of the metropolitan area is 3.3 million. Washington's major buildings are world famous (Figure 2). The two best-known are the White House and the Capitol. But there are many others, including the Supreme Court Building, The Library of Congress, the National Archives Building and the National Gallery of Arts. The Library of Congress has almost twenty million books in worldwide languages.

**Fig 2 Washington, DC, showing the White House in the foreground.**

One-third of the workforce is employed by the federal government. Government functions have attracted other professional services. For example, Washington has thousands of lawyers and many people working for TV, radio and newspapers. Big decisions made in Washington are news all over the world. Financial services are also very important. This is because Washington is the home of the US Treasury, the World Bank and the International Monetary Fund. Like Ottawa, the

USA's capital city is a big education centre with universities such as Georgetown, George Washington and Howard.

However, Washington DC is not without its problems. Nearly one-fifth of the population lives below the poverty line. Most of Washington's poor are Black; a startlingly high 40% of Black males are unemployed. Housing in poor areas is overcrowded, substandard and steadily getting worse. There is a seven year waiting list for public housing. 10 000 units of subsidised housing are boarded up and abandoned. Investment in public housing is very low. In contrast, building continues at a rapid rate where profits are to be made, on offices, shopping malls and hotels. There is a fairly clear pattern of racial segregation in terms of housing. Thirty per cent of the city's population are Whites. They reside mainly to the west of Rock Creek Park. However, 'Yuppies' have 'gentrified' parts of the inner city which previously housed Black families. This has created even greater pressure on housing in Black districts. There is also a growing colony of illegal immigrants from Central America whose living conditions are even worse. This is the side of the USA's capital city that few people hear about.

## Ottawa

Ottawa (in Ontario) became Canada's capital in 1858. Before this it was a small lumber town. It is situated on the west bank of the Ottawa River. On the opposite bank (in Quebec) is the city of Hull (Figure 4). The two cities are at the centre of the National Capital Region (NCR) which covers almost 4700 square kilometres. Three-quarters of a million people live here. Of these over 300 000 are in Ottawa and 65 000 in Hull. The NCR is a cosmopolitan centre that blends Canada's two national cultures.

Ottawa is dominated by government functions and services attracted to this major decision-making centre. Most of the big public buildings are sited close to Parliament Hill, the seat of government. Some, such as the Government Printing Bureau, are located in Hull. The main shopping area is centrally located close to Parliament Hill. Ottawa is home to more than a hundred foreign diplomatic missions. Heads of government and state from all over the world visit it each year. The city also hosts many international conferences. With three universities the capital is an important centre for education. Government and education together have attracted high technology industry. Average incomes are well above the Canadian norm. Housing is generally of a high standard. The dereliction found in parts of Washington is not evident in Ottawa.

**Fig 3 The city of Ottawa, Ontario.**

**Fig 4 Map of Ottawa/Hull in the National Capital Region.**

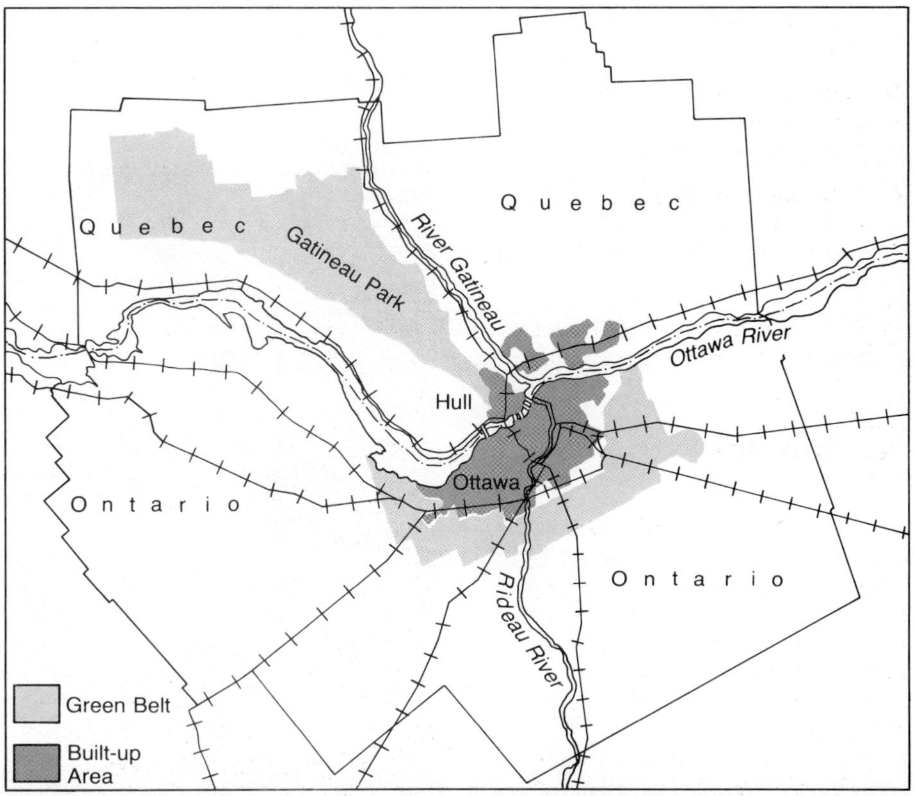

# 7. Transport

# 7.1 Railways

## The importance of transport

Transport is the movement of people and goods from one place to another. Good transportation is vital to the high standard of living enjoyed by Americans and Canadians. In no other continent do people use transport more and travel further. Transport networks (the pattern of routes and the places they connect) are highly developed due to much investment over many years. All places can be reached more easily, quickly and cheaply from other places than at any time in the past.

## Railways hit by competition

Transport is big business and there is great rivalry for custom. This is between both the different modes of transport and companies offering similar services. Figure 2 shows how inter-city passenger and freight traffic moves in the USA and its changes since 1960. The market share of the railways has been cut severely. But the problems of the railways go back much further than this. In 1916 trains carried 98% of all inter-city passenger traffic in the USA. By 1984 this was down to 0.7%. Today people prefer to travel by car over short and medium distances and by air on long journeys.

## Amtrak and Conrail

As custom fell, the financial problems of the privately-owned railways companies increased. The situation became so bad that in 1971 the government set up the Amtrak corporation to run the USA's passenger trains (Figure 1). Without this action services would have disappeared from many parts of the country. Amtrak scrapped many poorly used services but routes linking all the major cities were kept. Much of the rolling stock has been modernised but a lot of government money has been needed to keep Amtrak going ($684 million in 1985 alone). Many Republican politicians say this huge subsidy should be stopped.

Rail freight is in a better position but the impact of competition has still been strong. In 1976 the government formed Conrail (the Consolidated Rail Corporation) to run rail freight in the north-east USA because of the collapse of six railway companies. However, Conrail no longer needs

**Fig 2 US intercity passenger and freight traffic by mode of transport, 1960 and 1984.**

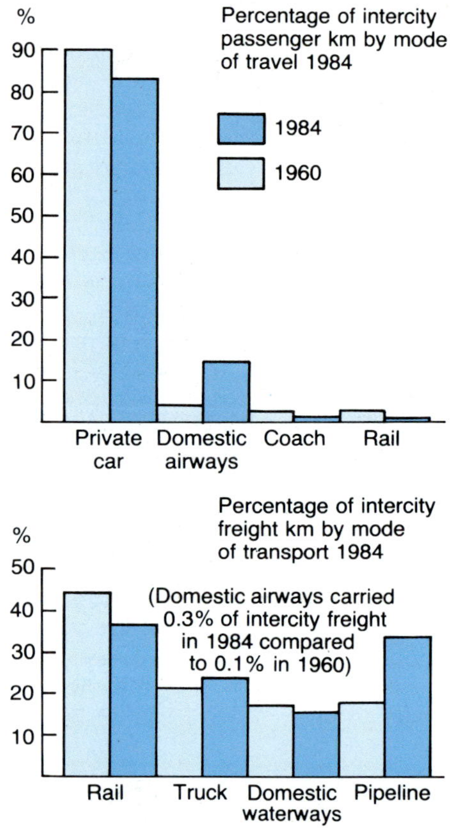


**Fig 1 The Amtrak passenger rail system in the USA. The east coast route between Boston and Washington is the busiest part of the network.**

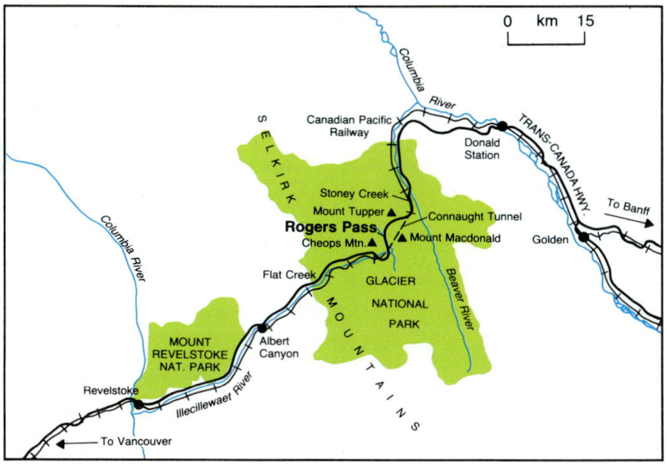


**Fig 3 Rogers Pass in the Selkirk Mountains.**

**Fig 5 The Rogers Pass Project: work on the western end of the Macdonald Tunnel.**

to be subsidised and it may be sold back to private companies now it is in a healthier position.

In Canada the railways have a larger share of traffic but face a similar challenge from road, air, water and pipeline transportation.

**Amtrak: New York to San Francisco**

| | *Time* | *Place* | *Distance (km)* |
|---|---|---|---|
| Day 1 | 2.50 pm | New York | 0 |
| | 4.22 pm | Philadelphia | 145 |
| | 11.52 pm | Pittsburg | 710 |
| Day 2 | 9.35 am | Chicago (arr) | 1463 |
| | **Change trains** | | |
| | 6.50 pm | Chicago (dep) | 1463 |
| Day 3 | 3.01 am | Omaha | 2261 |
| | 11.40 am | Denver | 3127 |
| | 11.00 pm | Ogden | 4055 |
| Day 4 | 8.10 am | Reno | 4924 |
| | 1.08 pm | Sacramento | 5171 |
| | 4.10 pm | San Francisco | 5320 |

**Fig 4 Coast to coast rail travel takes a long time. This is why most people travel by air on long journeys.**

## Rogers Pass; congestion in the mountains

The high passes of the Western Cordillera were a great challenge to the first railway engineers. That challenge has now returned. As freight traffic to the Pacific ports has increased major improvements have become necessary.

Rogers Pass crosses the Selkirk Mountains in British Columbia (Figure 3). It curves through a steep-sided valley between peaks towering 2800 metres high. The first track through Rogers Pass was laid in the 1880s. Avalanches from the snow-capped peaks were a frequent and dangerous problem. To avoid this hazard, the eight kilometre Connaught Tunnel was built 150 metres below the summit of the pass. It was opened in 1916. Now a new and longer tunnel is being built to cope with the increasing number of trains between Calgary and Vancouver.

The pass is used mainly by unit trains carrying bulk material such as coal, potash and grain. The coal trains often consist of over a hundred wagons hauling up to 10 000 tonnes. Such loads are pulled by six diesel engines over gentler gradients. But six more engines may be needed to push the load over twelve kilometres up the steepest part of the track to the Connaught Tunnel. Once the train is on a gentler gradient the pusher locomotives return downhill for the next push. This may happen up to ten times a day, causing considerable delays to traffic.

Rogers Pass has a capacity of fifteen west-bound trains a day. By the early 1980s this limit had almost been reached. The solution is to build 34 kilometres of new track for westbound traffic, including a new 14.5 kilometre tunnel, the longest in North America. This will reduce the gradient and speed the flow of traffic. Rogers Pass is the last phase of the Canadian Pacific Rail project to eliminate the steep inclines facing west-bound trains by reducing the gradient to a maximum of 1%. It was recently completed at a cost of C$ 600 million.

**Q1**
Look at Figure 1.
**(a)** Which cities in the USA have the best Amtrak route connections?
**(b)** What other information would you need to have a full picture of the inter-city rail passenger service?

**Q2**
**(a)** Imagine you are a Republican politician. (The Conservative Party is the nearest British equivalent to the Republican Party in the USA). Write a letter to the President of the USA putting the case for scraping the subsidy to Amtrak.
**(b)** Now imagine you are a member of the Democratic Party (the Liberal Democrats and SDP are the nearest British equivalents). Write a letter to the President in support of the subsidy.

**Q3**
With the help of an atlas
**(a)** Describe the routes taken by US and Canadian railways through the Western Cordillera.
**(b)** Make a list of problems that landscape and climate can present to railway routes.

# 7.2 Intermodal transportation

Fig 1 The supercontainership 'American New York' made its maiden voyage in June 1984. It is one of the first of a new size of container ships. It can only call at ports with very tall quayside gantries.

Terminals have always provided for the transfer of goods from one form of transport to another. For over a century, grain from the Canadian prairies has been hauled by train to the Great Lakes ports for movement by water to eastern North America and abroad. Oil delivered to major terminals by pipeline is distributed to customers by fleets of road tankers. Today the scale of inter-model transfer is much greater than in the past. Major terminals in North America now have the most sophisticated equipment in the world for the rapid handling of goods and their transfer between transport modes.

Fig 2 Railway companies have invested much money in container facilities. They have had to do so to compete with road haulage.

## Competition and co-operation

Although there is fierce competition between the modes of transport the links between them have steadily increased. Many journeys use more than one type of carrier: they are inter-modal. Firms always want to cut costs and will switch goods between road, rail, water, pipeline and air when savings can be made.

Fig 3 Containers can also be carried by aircraft. Why are these containers a different shape from those in Figures 1 and 2?

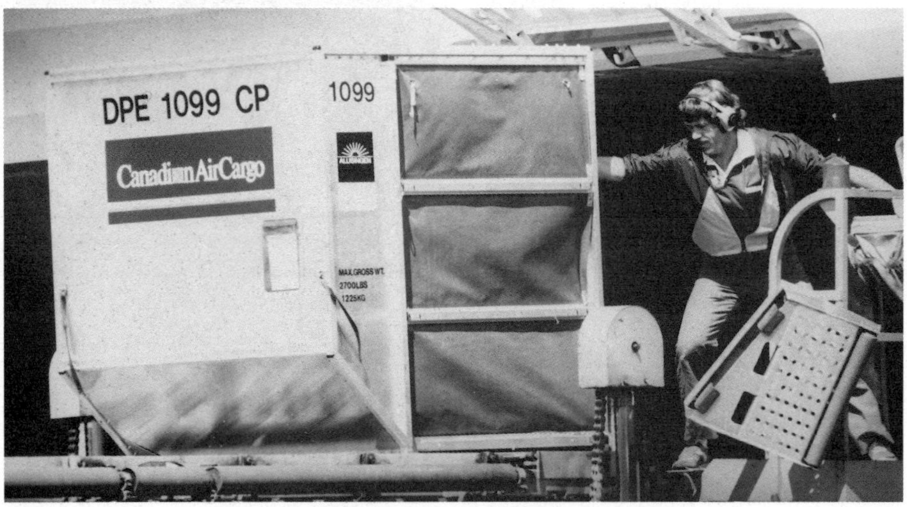


## The container revolution

The container has been the major development in inter-modal transportation. It has changed the movement of goods so much that the term 'container revolution' is often used. Containers are boxes made of steel or aluminium into which goods are packed. They are 2.4 metres high, 2.4 metres wide and can be 3, 6, 9 or 12 metres long. They can be carried on railway flat cars, lorries, aircraft, barges and ships and moved quickly from one to another. The general use of standard-sized containers began in the early 1960s and now all major transport terminals in the USA and Canada have container facilities.

The change from traditional cargo handling to containers is costly. Giant gantry cranes are needed for loading and unloading and special berths have to be built at ports. Goods packed in containers are much quicker to handle. This has greatly reduced the time that ships, trains, lorries and aircraft need to wait at terminals. They can spend more time on the move earning money. There is also less risk of damage to goods or of them being stolen.

# 7.3 Pipelines

## Increasing market share

The first major transport pipeline in North America was built in 1879 from oilfields in Titusville, Pennsylvania to the Reading Railroad 177 kilometres away. Since then, the pipeline and the oil and gas industries have developed hand in hand. By 1958 pipelines ranked third behind railways and trucks in the volume of freight carried in the USA. Twenty years later the pipeline industry was in second place. It is likely that the gap between pipelines and the market leader, the railways, will narrow in the future.

**Fig 1 Laying a gas pipeline in Saskatchewan, Canada.**

## Environmental problems

Pipelines are very different from other carriers. They just carry freight and move traffic one way only. Each pipeline carries only one product. North America has the most developed pipeline network in the world. As the network has expanded, environmental groups have become increasingly concerned. The main worries are:

- Oil spilling from a cracked pipeline could greatly damage wildlife and the countryside.
- Surface pipelines are ugly in both town and countryside. Houston, Texas has been nicknamed 'Spaghetti City' because so many pipelines come to the surface there.
- Even when pipelines are buried underground the disturbances to wildlife can be great during construction.

## The Black Mesa coal slurry pipeline

Pipelines are not just for liquids and gases. In the south-western USA a 440 kilometre coal slurry pipeline is in operation. It carries coal from the Indian reserves in Black Mesa, Arizona to a 1510 megawatt power plant in south-east Nevada. The coal is pulverised and mixed evenly with water which is pumped to its destination by engines placed along the route. This needs a continuous supply of water at the mine site at a rate of 5600 litres a minute. At the end of the line the coal and water are separated. The water is cleaned for other use and the coal is burned to generate energy. The pipeline can deliver over four million tonnes of coal a year.

The use of slurry pipelines will increase in the future. The next stages in the story of the pipeline are likely to be solids moved by air pressure instead of water, and the movement of goods in capsules along a pipeline. It may be some years though before these ideas are put into commercial practice.

**Fig 2 The environmental impact of pipelines showing the removal of tree cover to make way for the pipeline.**

# 7.4 Inland waterways

Water transport is the cheapest way of moving heavy and bulky goods such as iron ore, coal, and grain. A gallon of fuel (4.5 litres) can move a tonne of freight eight kilometres by air, 80 kilometres by truck, 290 kilometres by rail and 530 kilometres by barge. The US inland waterway system, 47 000 kilometres in length, is the second largest in the world (after the Soviet Union). Canada's inland waterway system is much smaller. Look at winter temperature and natural drainage maps to discover the main reasons why.

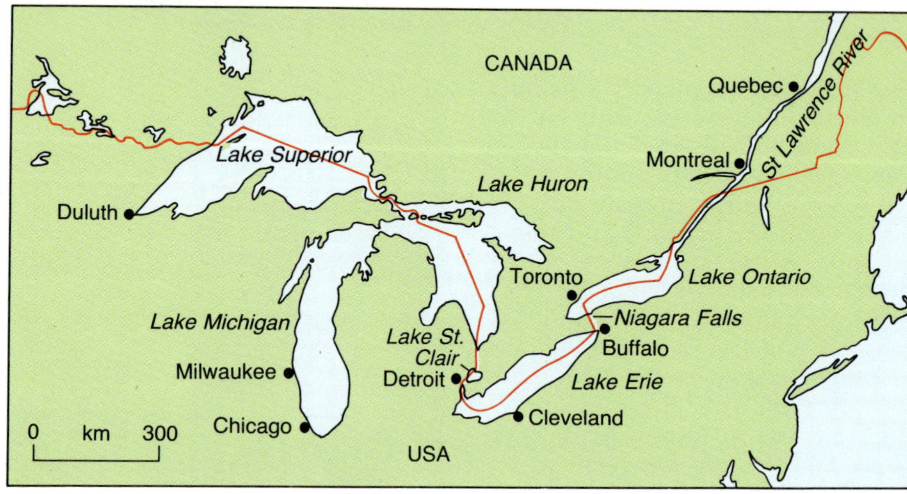


**Fig 1 The Great Lakes – St Lawrence Seaway is an important part of the freight transport system in North America.**

## The St Lawrence Seaway

The St Lawrence Seaway opened in 1959 (Figure 1). It allowed ships of ocean-going size (up to 24 000 tonnes) to travel 3700 kilometres into the interior of North America for the first time.

Early settlers found the route from the Gulf of St Lawrence to Lake Superior blocked by many obstacles. The gigantic Niagara Falls was the greatest barrier. But elsewhere treacherous rapids and thick deposition also hindered transport. Projects to improve navigation began in the late 18th century. Then the first small canals were built around the rapids of Sault Ste Marie. Larger schemes were to follow, including the Welland Canal to bypass Niagara Falls. The biggest problem remained the stretch of waterway from Montreal to Kingston. Here the narrow canal system could only take ships up to 4000 tonnes. Upstream and downstream much larger ships could be used.

The Seaway Project was a joint venture between the USA and Canada. It was a much larger scheme than either the Suez Canal (1914) or the Panama Canal (1869). Three hundred and forty million tonnes of rock were removed along the main 180 kilometre construction site. Thousands of people had to move. After five years work the new deep channel and seven locks were ready. Hydro-electric power stations were built to provide energy for both countries. The connecting channels between the Great Lakes were deepened in line with the Seaway. The total cost was over $1 billion. Ships travelling from the Gulf of St Lawrence to Lake Superior rise the height of a 60 storey building (Figure 2).

## Traffic management

Seaway traffic has greatly increased since 1959. It is now nearing capacity. Good traffic management has become more essential than ever. This is shared between the USA and Canada. Along the Seaway, Call-In Points keep regular contact with ships by radio. They give upcoming traffic patterns, directions to proceed on course, weather information and orders to pass through each lock. Computers,

**Fig 2 A profile view of the Great Lakes – St Lawrence Seaway.**

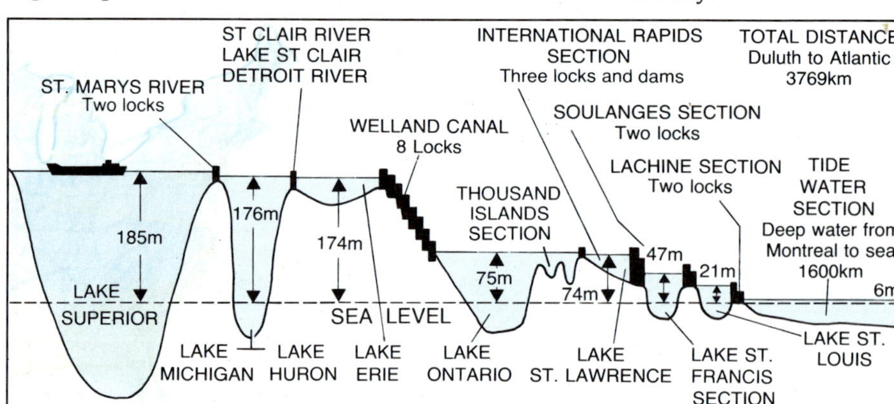


The Seaway links 56 ports and offers ships direct access to the heart of North America. The system handles about 100 million tonnes of traffic a year and collects almost $40 million in toll revenues. In 1984 the cost of moving grain from Lake Superior to the eastern end of the Seaway was $22.25 per tonne. The same journey by rail cost $36.64 per tonne.

**Fig 3 The Tennessee – Tombigbee waterway.**

The Tennessee-Tombigbee Waterway is the latest addition to the inland waterway system. The $2 billion, 377 km waterway was opened in January 1985. Its main cargo will be coal from the Appalachian mining states. Pittsburg is now 378 km nearer to the Gulf of Mexico by water and Knoxville is 1420 km closer.

The Environment Defence Fund tried and failed twice to halt the project in court. It called the waterway an environmental disaster arguing that it (a) destroyed one of the few remaining high quality rivers in the USA (b) destroyed 14165 hectares of forested wetlands (c) killed fish and other aquatic life.

television and radar are also used to guide ocean-going ships and lake barges (some are 223 metres long) through the canals and locks. Traffic is dominated by bulk cargoes, ores and grain in particular.

Freezing causes the Seaway to close during the winter. This is when the locks are overhauled. As the system gets older maintenance becomes more important. In 1984 a lift bridge jammed near Valleyfield, Quebec causing an eighteen day shipping delay. There have been a number of other stoppages in recent years due to equipment failure. However, the shipping season has been extended from early April to mid-December. This is due to the increased use of icebreakers and air pumps to control ice formation in the locks.

The Great Lakes–St Lawrence Seaway is very important to transport in North America. It has provided a fourth coastline for both countries. However, the average size of shipping has increased since the opening of the Seaway, so many modern ships are now too big to use it.

**Fig 5 The eastern end of the St. Lawrence Seaway.**

| *System* | *Billions of ton-miles* |
|---|---|
| Atlantic coast waterways | 22.5 |
| Gulf coast waterways | 32.4 |
| Pacific coast waterways | 13.2 |
| Mississippi River system | 223.0 |
| Great Lakes system | 68.0 |

**Fig 6 Freight carried by inland waterway systems, USA, 1983.**

**Fig 4 The Port of Duluth, Minnesota at the western end of the St. Lawrence Seaway.**

## Q1
**(a)** Draw a graph to show how far a gallon of fuel can move a tonne of freight by each of air, truck, rail and barge.
**(b)** How and why would you expect the types of goods carried by air and water to differ?

## Q2
Rank the inland waterway systems in the USA in order of freight carried.

## Q3
Imagine you are on a ship sailing from the Atlantic Ocean to the port of Duluth. Describe your journey.

## Q4
Why is traffic management so important on the Seaway? What does it involve?

## Q5
Look at Figure 3. Why was the controversial Tennessee–Tombigbee Waterway built?

# 7.5 Road transport

## A motor society

In the USA there are about 700 motor vehicles (cars, trucks and buses) for every 1000 people. In Canada it is slightly less. Many North American families own two or more cars. More than any other form of transport the car has changed people's lives.

The US Interstate Highway System and the Trans-Canada Highway form the basis of city to city transport (Figure 1). This motorway-class network provides fast, direct links to all of the USA and southern Canada. The highways were built because the existing main roads couldn't cope with the rising level of traffic. There were two major problems: roads were narrow and they often passed through the centre of settlements. Modern high capacity highways allow fast average speeds to be maintained and bypass settlements. The 1956 Federal Aid Highway Act gave the go-ahead for the US Interstate Highway System to be built. With the federal government paying 90% of total costs, completion was at first expected in 1971. However, some short links in and close to urban areas remain to be built. The 7535 kilometre Trans-Canada Highway was completed in 1962 (Figure 1).

**Fig 1 The USA Interstate Highway system and the Trans-Canada Highway.**

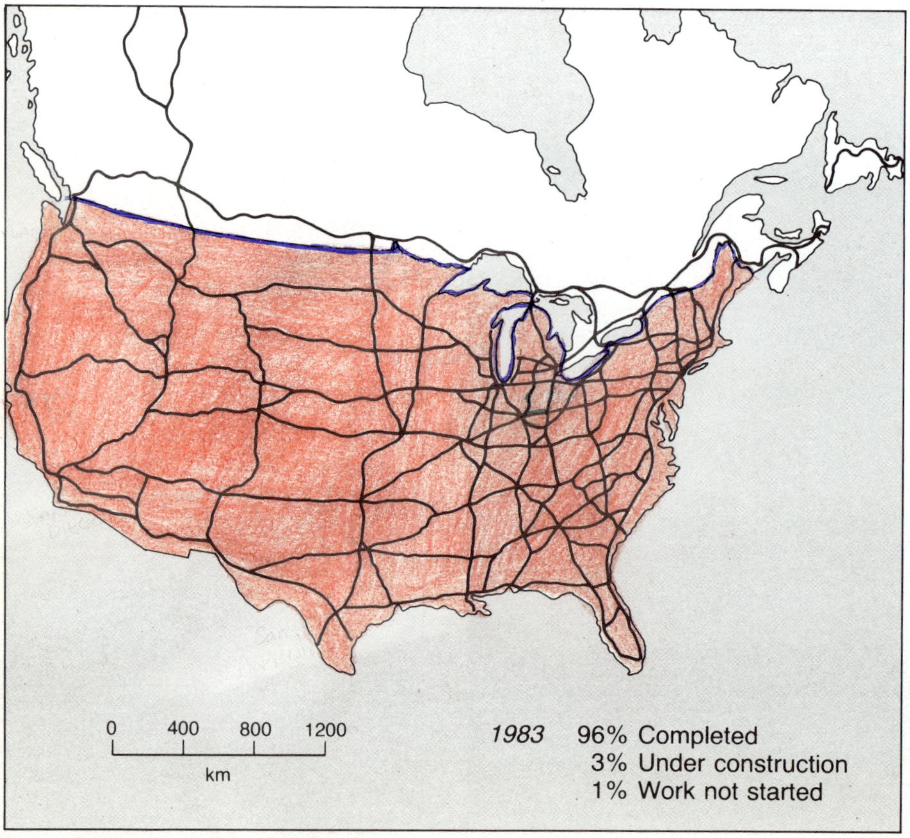


## Highways: some problems

Motorways carry much traffic but not everyone is happy with them because:

- They encourage more people to use cars because they are so quick. This means more air pollution and noise.

**Fig 2 The intersection of a busy interstate highway.**

- They take up a lot of space and greatly influence the way that land around them is used.
- They are expensive to build and maintain. North America's highways began to crack up more quickly than expected and many are now in urgent need of repair. This problem is at its worst in the north-east USA because of very heavy traffic and the effect of the cold winters on the road surfaces.
- Although accidents are fewer overall, multiple pile-ups sometimes occur in poor weather on these fast roads causing considerable loss of life. (Cutting the speed limit to 55 m.p.h. in the USA in the early 1970s has reduced accidents.)
- Road transport is a large user of the continent's resources and is not as energy-efficient as the alternatives.

Road transport has brought many benefits. Never before have people been able to get about so easily, but do the benefits outweigh the costs?

## Arctic highway

Few roads reach into the inhospitable Northlands. In Canada only three highways extend beyond 60°N, the Alaska, Mackenzie and Dempster highways. The latter is Canada's first road to cross the Arctic Circle ($66\frac{1}{2}$°N).

The $103 million highway was opened in 1979. It begins near Dawson and cuts through tundra and mountains to Inuvik (Figure 4). In winter an ice road continues the highway to Tuktoyaktuk on the Beaufort Sea. Vehicles cross the Peel and Mackenzie rivers by ferry in summer. Bridges made of ice make it possible to drive across in winter. The highway is closed during the spring break-up (April 15–May 30) and the autumn freeze-up (Oct 15–Nov 30). The times when the highway is closed roughly coincide with the yearly migration of over 100 000 caribou between the Yukon and Alaska. Even so, some people still feel that the highway will disturb the caribou's regular habits and would prefer it not to have been built.

A metre thick layer of gravel and shale insulation under the highway keeps the permafrost from melting and breaking up the surface. In winter, drifting snow is a major problem. When drifts get too high (up to six metres) the snow ploughs bypass them and make an auxiliary winter road.

Fig 3 **The Dempster Highway, through the Yukon, Canada and Northwest Territories, Canada.**

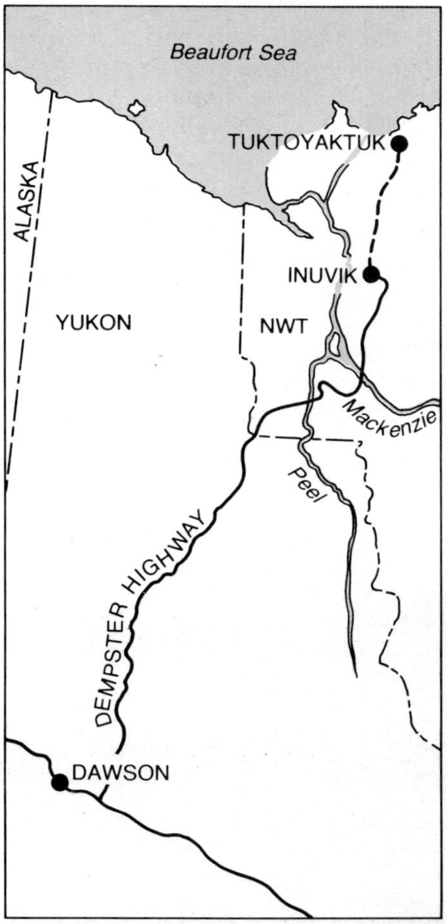

**Fig 5 Greyhound bus on the USA interstate highway system.**

## The future

The automobile dominates transport in the 20th century as the railway did before it. What will the transport scene be like in the next century? Will the automobile continue to rule or will new forms of transport revolutionise people's lives?

**Fig 4 The Dempster Highway.**

**Q1**

**(a)** Suggest why the Dempster highway was built.
**(b)** Using an atlas, draw a map to show the routes followed by the Alaska and Mackenzie highways. Label the settlements along each highway.
**(c)** Why is it likely that more highways will be built in the Northlands? Suggest two possible routes.

**Q2**

Look at Figure 1 and use an atlas.
**(a)** For the USA, make a list of all the cities where at least four highway routes meet.
**(b)** List all the main cities along the Trans-Canada highway.
**(c)** In Canada, why are the high capacity routes mainly confined to the southern part of the country?

**Q3**

Imagine you are the chairperson of an environmental group campaigning against further highway construction within a large city. Write a policy statement explaining your views.

# 7.6 Air transport

## The best way to travel?

More North Americans than ever before are using air transport. The cost of the fastest way to travel has never been so low. In contrast, air freight traffic is still small in volume compared to rail, road, water and pipeline.

Over 60% of North Americans have flown compared with less than 1% of the people in Asia. Air travel is so important because:

- Wages for those in employment are high and most people can afford to fly. Also fares are low compared with many other countries.
- The USA and Canada are huge countries and long-distance travel by car or train takes days.
- Both governments have helped air transport with generous subsidies for many years.

**Fig 1 The world's top 25 airlines in 1983 by total passenger-kilometres flown.**

| *Rank* | *Airline* | *Passenger-kilometres (100 000s)* |
|---|---|---|
| 1 | Aeroflot | 176 480 |
| 2 | United | 70 465 |
| 3 | American | 54 700 |
| 4 | Pan Am | 46 389 |
| 5 | Eastern | 45 581 |
| 6 | TWA | 43 867 |
| 7 | Delta | 43 071 |
| 8 | British Airways | 34 731 |
| 9 | Japan Air Lines | 32 237 |
| 10 | Northwest | 28 497 |
| 11 | Air France | 27 452 |
| 12 | Lufthansa | 22 875 |
| 13 | Air Canada | 20 479 |
| 14 | Singapore | 18 498 |
| 15 | All Nippon | 17 062 |
| 16 | KLM | 16 803 |
| 17 | Iberia | 15 742 |
| 18 | Republic | 15 498 |
| 19 | Western | 15 150 |
| 20 | Saudia | 14 950 |
| 21 | Continental | 14 935 |
| 22 | Qantas | 14 362 |
| 23 | Alitalia | 12 628 |
| 24 | Swissair | 12 310 |
| 25 | Korean | 12 060 |

In many parts of the Northlands aircraft are essential. They provide the only transport to and from almost a half of Canada. In Alaska one in every 40 people has a pilot's licence and there are more private planes per person than anywhere else in the world, one for every hundred people.

## Hub and spoke

Air travel is big business. American airline companies carry over two-thirds of the world's air traffic (Figure 1). The large number of advertisements in newspapers and on TV shows how competitive air travel is. To keep costs down, most big airlines operate a 'hub and spoke' system. British Airways in conjunction with Piedmont use Baltimore (BWI) as one of their connecting 'hubs' (Figure 2). Another hub and spoke system is based on Atlanta, used by Delta Airlines and Eastern Airlines as their gateway to the rest of the USA. Delta flights to the USA from Gatwick and other European airports go to Atlanta. Passengers for other destinations change onto smaller planes here. Delta estimate that as many as 80% of its passengers from Gatwick transfer to other destinations. For this the airline lays on over a hundred connecting flights. Passengers travelling with Delta out of other towns and cities in the south-east USA also change at Atlanta to go further afield. Atlanta has a population of only two million yet its airport handles 40 million passengers a year; 65% of these are purely in transit. Atlanta is the world's second busiest airport.

## Flying to work

Many Americans and Canadians go to work by air. There's no better way to beat highway traffic jams! People tend to live much

**Fig 2 The 'hub and spoke' system based on Baltimore Washington International Airport, operated by British Airways and Piedmont.**

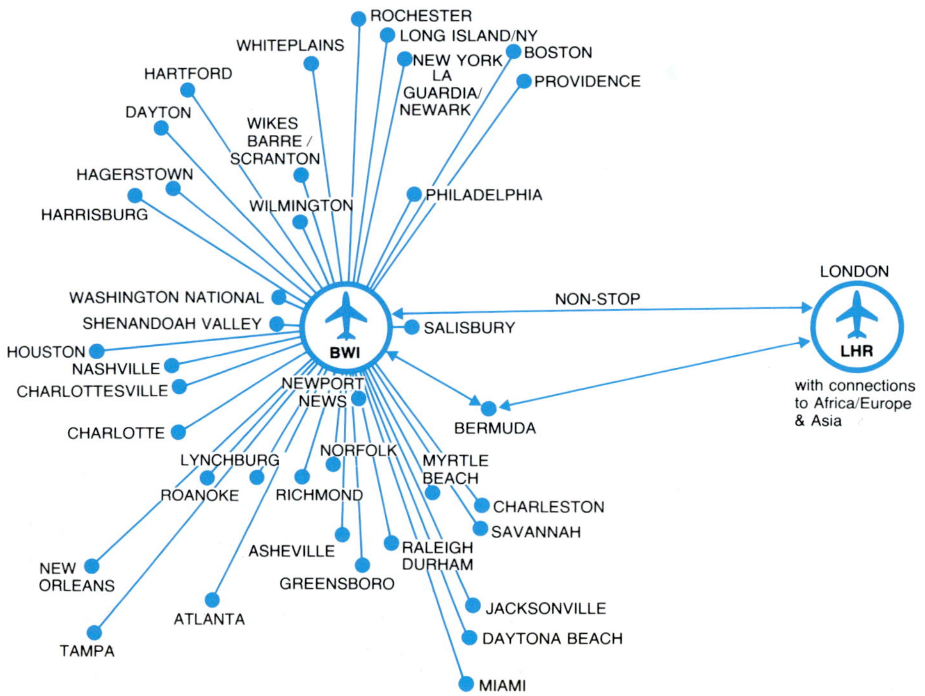

further from work than in Europe. Distance is thought of in a different way and people are prepared to travel further. Even small communities have airstrips for commuter aircraft. A short drive, park the car and then up and away to work. At the other end, cities have special airports to handle such traffic (Figure 5). This leaves large airports free to link up with the rest of North America and abroad.

## Saturation

Major airports are struggling to cope with rising traffic. This problem falls into three parts:

- **Aircraft operations** The rate of service is affected by the layout of runways, the paths through the airspace leading to and from the airport, the air traffic control rules, weather conditions and the mix of aircraft using the airport.
- **The terminal(s)** The number of passengers accommodated at any one time depends on the facilities available and their design.

**Fig 3 Getting closer in the sky. Near misses: incidents where aircraft have almost collided.**

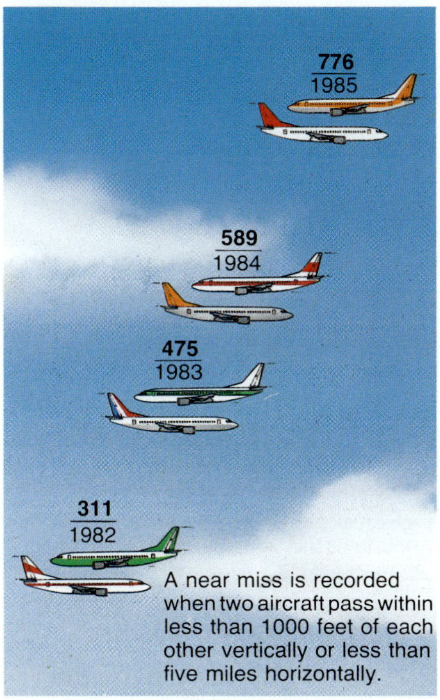

**Fig 4 Airport congestion is a growing problem.**

- **Landside** The volume of motor traffic that can be taken on access roads to the airport.

Delays can have a ripple effect throughout the system. Congestion at a few 'hub' airports causes delays in connecting flights to and from other airports. The air traffic of a whole region can be thrown into chaos.

## Alternative solutions

A number of alternatives have been suggested to ease the capacity problem.

- Build new airports.
- Expand existing airport facilities.
- Make better use of existing airport capacity. For example, improved technology could reduce the spacing between aircraft on final approach.
- Manage airport demand so that activity is more evenly distributed by time of day and among airports.

Airports and aircraft affect the environment in a big way. Airports need large areas of land. They cause high volumes of traffic on routes to city centres. People do not like to live near them because there is so much noise. We like the benefits of air travel but not the drawbacks!

**Fig 5 Toronto Island short take-off and landing airport.**

**Q1**
Look at Figure 1.
**(a)** Which of the top 25 are North American airlines?
**(b)** Which countries do the others come from?

**Q2**
Suggest why
**(a)** Air travel is cheaper in North America than elsewhere in the world.
**(b)** So little freight is carried by air.

**Q3**
**(a)** Why has the number of 'near misses' steadily increased?
**(b)** What are the advantages and disadvantages of the alternative solutions to the airport saturation problem?

**Q4**
Why do many airlines operate hub and spoke systems?

**Fig 6 O'Hare International Airport, Chicago.**

# 7.7 A world airport: Los Angeles International

## A multi-airport city

Los Angeles is the second largest metropolitan area in North America. Fast links to the rest of the continent and beyond are vital to its economy. The city has a number of airports (Figure 1). Los Angeles International (LAX) is by far the largest. But traffic is also rising sharply at Ontario, the city's other international airport. The smaller airports handle much of the regional and local traffic. More people travel to work by air in California than anywhere else in the world. Van Nuys, Long Beach and Santa Ana are the three most active general aviation airports in the USA (handling mainly business, recreation and instruction flights).

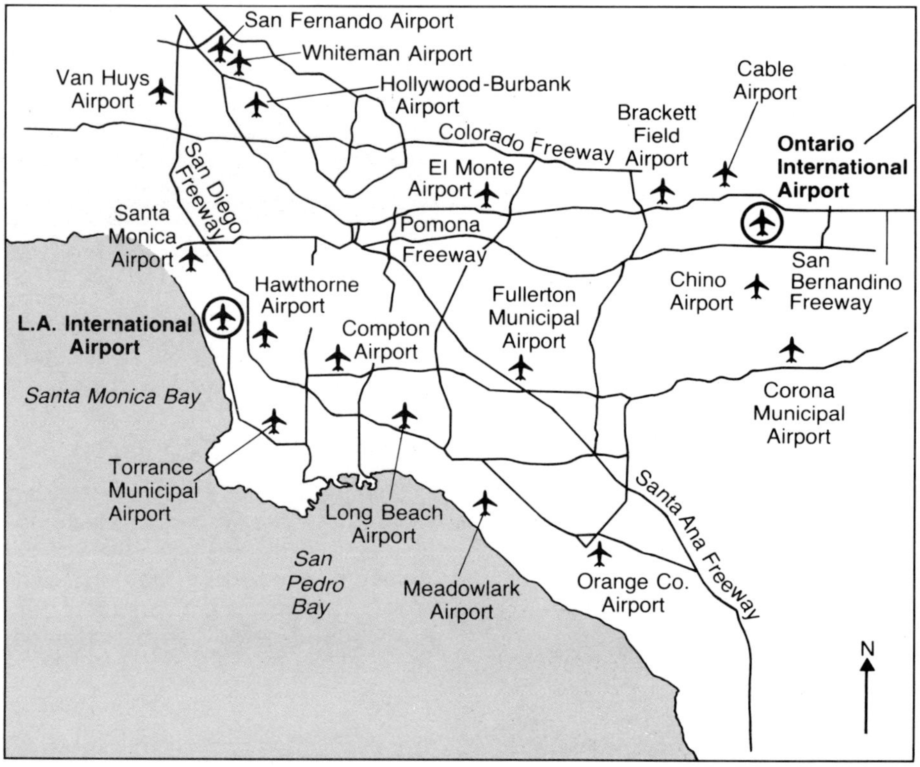


**Fig 1 Los Angeles, showing the location of international and general aviation airports.**

## LAX: a major world airport

LAX is the world's third largest airport after O'Hare (Chicago) and Hartsfield (Atlanta). The 1418 hectare site is ideally located on the coast. Aircraft can approach LAX, and take off from it, over Santa Monica Bay. This avoids flying low over the city. The airport is about eighteen kilometres from the city centre. Freeways and a well-developed grid of other roads link LAX to the city and beyond.

LAX is served by 70 airlines:

- 28 non-US airlines
- 23 US international, national and regional airlines
- 10 cargo carriers
- 8 commuter airlines
- one helicopter airline.

There are four parallel runways, two on each side of the central terminal complex. In 1983 they accommodated just over 500 000 aircraft movements (landings and take-offs). The total number of passengers using LAX is almost five times more than in 1961 (Figure 2). The growth of international traffic has been particularly strong.

**Fig 2 The numbers of passengers using LAX in 1961, 1971 and 1983.**

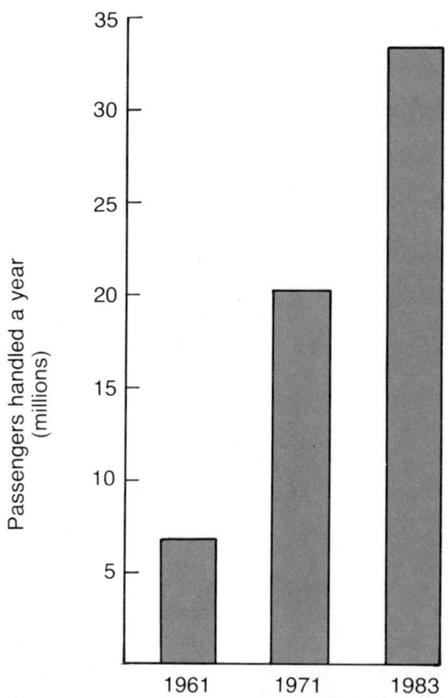


## $700 million redevelopment

LAX underwent major redevelopment between 1981 and 1984 at a cost of $700 million. No other existing world class airport has ever been given such an expensive facelift. General Manager Clifton Moore said, 'We have created a new LAX on top of the old'. Remarkably, business continued as usual during construction which included:

- A $60 million double decking

of the loop road that links the nine terminals. Departing and arriving passengers are now separated.

- A new $123 million West Terminal to house 22 international airlines with the USA's largest Customs and Immigration facility.
- A new $47 million domestic Terminal One.
- Improvements costing $100 million to Terminal Seven and $30 million to Terminal Four.
- Airfield improvements costing $76 million.
- A new 23 hectare cargo complex.
- New parking facilities and landscaping.

The improvements are designed to cope with up to 40 million passengers a year, a limit set by the capacity of the road system linking Los Angeles to its main airport. There would have to be a major shift from private to public transport to allow the airport to take more passengers.

## Environmental protest

The start of the LAX redevelopment was held up for ten years. Many people were concerned about the effect air transport has on the environment. The issue had to be decided in the courts. This has also happened with other airport developments in the USA. The Department of Airports has tried to improve conditions on the ground at LAX. It has spent $4 million on planting 1300 trees and 19 000 other plants. But it can't do much about aircraft noise and road traffic.

**Fig 3 The approach to LAX showing the double-decker loop road.**

**Fig 4 Los Angeles International Airport showing parallel runways.**

**Q1**
**(a)** How many airports are located in the Los Angeles region?
**(b)** What is their average distance apart? What are the advantages and disadvantages of having so many airports?

**Q2**
**(a)** Why was the expensive redevelopment of LAX necessary?
**(b)** Why did many people in Los Angeles object to the redevelopment?

**Q3**
Make a list of factors which have to be considered when choosing the site for a new airport.

**Fig 5 Los Angeles International Airport.**

# 8. Energy

# 8.1 Fuelling an affluent continent

## The energy crisis

North Americans use huge amounts of energy each year. Consumption per person is almost two and a half times more than in Europe, seventeen times more than in the South as a whole and 28 times more than in Africa, the least developed continent.

The USA and Canada have been fortunate in having large deposits of coal, oil, and gas. There were also many good sites for hydro-electric power plants.

| Energy source | 1950 | 1960 | 1970 | 1980 | 1985 |
|---|---|---|---|---|---|
| Coal | 38.0 | 22.7 | 18.9 | 20.3 | 23.7 |
| Oil | 39.7 | 45.0 | 43.9 | 45.0 | 41.8 |
| Natural gas | 18.1 | 28.5 | 32.8 | 26.8 | 24.1 |
| HEP | 4.2 | 3.7 | 3.9 | 4.1 | 4.6 |
| Nuclear | 0.0 | 0.0 | 0.3 | 3.6 | 5.6 |
| Other | 0.0 | 0.0 | 0.1 | 0.2 | 0.2 |

**Fig 1 The sources of energy in the USA between 1950 and 1985.**

Both countries have had the money and the technology to exploit these resources and to invest in newer forms of energy. Energy is vital for the creation of wealth by industry and commerce.

For a long time the continent was able to supply its own needs. However, by the 1950s demand for oil rose to such a high level in the USA that imports were needed. These rose rapidly to 47% of consumption in 1977 (Figure 2). By 1983 imports had fallen back to 28% of consumption. This was due to more careful use of oil because of a) higher oil prices and b) energy conservation measures.

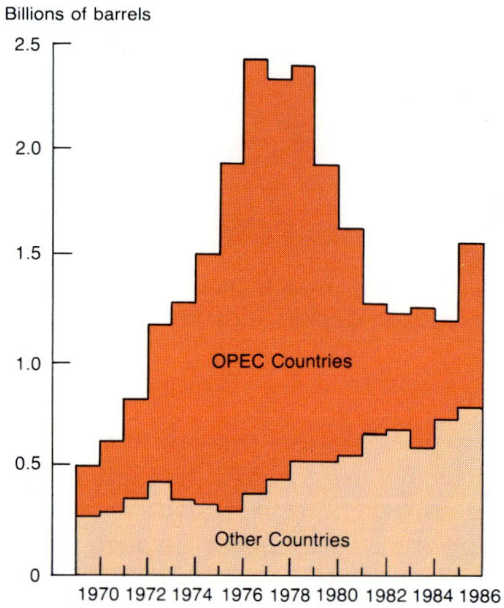


**Fig 2 Crude oil imports into the USA 1970 to 1984.**

Canada became a net importer of oil in the late 1970s. Recent discoveries have made the country self-sufficient again.

**Fig 3 Energy Crisis North. This is what happened to North America and other rich parts of the world in the 1970s. Some experts think that another energy crisis is not too far off.**

The demand for energy rose because (a) the population was increasing and (b) energy was generally cheap and people used it lavishly (Figure 3). In the 1970s North Americans had to think about using energy more carefully. In the USA many oil and gas fields were drying up. Oil production reached a peak in 1970 and natural gas in 1973. International politics made the situation worse. After the 1973 Arab–Israeli war the Arab nations (who were large-scale producers) reduced their exports of oil to the USA and other countries. This was an attempt to influence the US to reduce support for Israel. Long queues of cars and rationing at garages became commonplace. This was a clear reminder of how dependent the rich North is on resources from the rest of the world. The oil embargo was short-lived but the Organisation of Petroleum Exporting Countries (OPEC) sharply increased the price of oil on the world market. It rose from $3 to $12 per barrel in three months in 1973 (a barrel = 35 Imperial gallons). By 1980 it

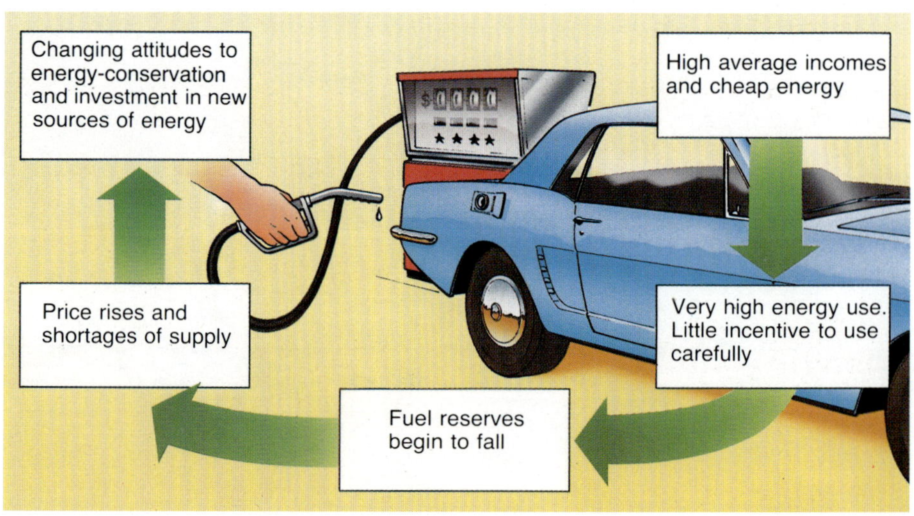

**Fig 4 To most Americans, long queues for petrol in 1973 and 1979 represented energy problems at their worst.**

was $32 per barrel. While it has fallen considerably since, there is no doubt that the age of cheap energy is over.

The energy crisis of 1973 was a warning about the need for sensible management of resources. This means using resources carefully to get the greatest benefit over the longest period of time. Fossil fuels are a non-renewable resource; once they have been used they are gone forever.

## A threat to the environment

Economic activity has had a severe impact on the environment. As the continent has grown rich the damage done has increased. Land, sea and air are heavily polluted in many areas. Energy production and use has caused much of this damage. As concern grew in the 1970s, both the USA and Canada introduced new laws to protect the environment. This has helped but the situation is still serious.

## Energy supply – a changing situation

In 1980 almost 93% of the energy used in the USA came from fossil fuels (oil, coal and natural gas). The rest was supplied by nuclear, hydro-electric and geothermal power. In Canada only 70% of consumption was met by fossil fuels. This is due mainly to the greater importance of hydro-electric power in Canada.

Both countries have invested heavily in nuclear electricity. However, it is not as important today as earlier estimates suggested it would be. This is due to (a) technical problems which have increased costs and (b) concern over the safety of nuclear power plants. Investment in other methods of producing electricity – solar, wind, geothermal, biomass, OTEC (Ocean Thermal Energy Conversion, see p. 68) and tidal – really began in the 1970s. But it has been too little to really reduce reliance on fossil fuels and nuclear power.

## The North American energy market

Both electricity and primary energy (coal, oil, gas) are transferred daily between the USA and Canada. Most of this transfer is from Canada to the USA in the form of electricity and gas. Canada used to sell big quantities of oil to the USA as well, but this stopped because of rising demand in Canada itself. In 1983 net energy exports amounted to 10% of total Canadian production. This had a value of $7.8 billion. In contrast, the USA is a large importer of energy.

| | | | | | | | | | | | | |
|---|---|---|---|---|---|---|---|---|---|---|---|---|
| G | A | S | I | F | I | C | A | T | I | O | N | N |
| R | E | L | E | C | T | R | I | C | I | T | Y | U |
| E | S | O | L | A | R | C | E | L | L | I | | C |
| E | M | E | T | H | A | N | E | S | | D | B | L |
| N | P | A | | H | F | O | O | D | U | E | R | E |
| P | R | E | N | K | E | R | O | S | E | N | E | A |
| L | O | A | H | Y | D | R | O | P | O | W | E | R |
| A | P | R | I | V | E | R | M | W | O | O | D | O |
| N | A | T | U | R | A | L | G | A | S | | E | C |
| T | N | H | U | O | I | L | S | O | L | A | R | E |
| S | E | N | | D | O | M | E | S | T | I | C | A |
| G | A | S | O | L | I | N | E | C | O | A | L | N |
| M | A | N | P | E | T | R | O | L | E | U | M | S |

**Fig 5 The energy puzzle.**

**Fig 6 Oil refinery, Edmonton, Alberta.**

**Q1**
**(a)** Draw a bar graph to show the difference between the energy used per person in North America, Europe, the South as a whole, and Africa.
**(b)** In what ways do North Americans use so much energy?

**Q2**
Why have attitudes changed towards energy in North America since the early 1970s?

**Q3**
**(a)** Suggest ways in which the US government could reduce the total amount of energy used in the country.
**(b)** How do you think people would react to these measures?

**Q4**
Make a list of the ways in which the production and use of energy can pollute the environment.

**Q5**
The puzzle (Figure 5) contains 27 words which relate to energy. Some are horizontal, some vertical and some diagonal.
**(a)** List as many as you can.
**(b)** Which are the oldest and the newest forms of energy?

# 8.2 Oil and natural gas

Fig 1 The settlement of Prudhoe Bay on the north coast of Alaska.

Oil and natural gas are the two main energy sources in North America. Both have been important to the wealth of the continent as a whole and to the regions (e.g. Texas, California, Alberta) where they are found. Because of high demand many older oil and gas fields have dried up. Now exploration is focusing on new 'frontier' and offshore areas and on deeper deposits. Drilling is more expensive in these difficult environments. But the rise in energy prices since the early 1970s has made it worthwhile.

## Prudhoe Bay: a frontier oilfield

In 1968 the largest oilfield in North America was discovered at Prudhoe Bay in the far north of Alaska (Figure 1). Alaska is the USA's largest state but it has a very small population. This cold and mountainous environment offers few opportunities to make a living. People have been attracted to the state in the past by natural resources. These include furs, seals, salmon, whales, timber and gold. There are also important military bases in Alaska. Today oil is Alaska's major resource. Developing an oilfield in such a cold desolate region is not easy.

Winter temperatures can fall below -50°C. For 56 days the sun never rises above the horizon. Northern Alaska also has permafrost. Here the ground is permanently frozen down to about 300 metres, apart from the top metre which melts during the summer. Building foundations have to extend well below the melting zone (called the active layer). The main buildings at Prudhoe Bay are on high metal stilts driven well into the frozen ground.

A major problem was how to move the oil to refineries elsewhere in the USA. Tankers were of little use as the Arctic Ocean is frozen for much of the year. The decision was to build a pipeline from Prudhoe Bay to Valdez (Figure 2). Alaska's south coast is ice-free all year round. From here oil could be taken further south by tanker.

The Trans-Alaskan Pipeline was built between 1974 and 1977. It cost $8 billion. The service road built alongside the pipeline was the first to link the north coast to the rest of Alaska. The pipeline has a diameter of 1.22 metres. Much of it is above ground to avoid the permafrost problem. The oil takes about six days to make the 1270 kilometre journey. The settlement of Prudhoe Bay did not exist before the search for oil began. It now has a workforce of about 3000 people.

Many people were opposed to the development of Prudhoe Bay

Fig 2 The trans-Alaska pipeline crosses plains, three rugged mountain ranges and several large rivers. It reaches its highest point, 1 463 metres above sea-level at Atigun Pass in the Brooks Range.

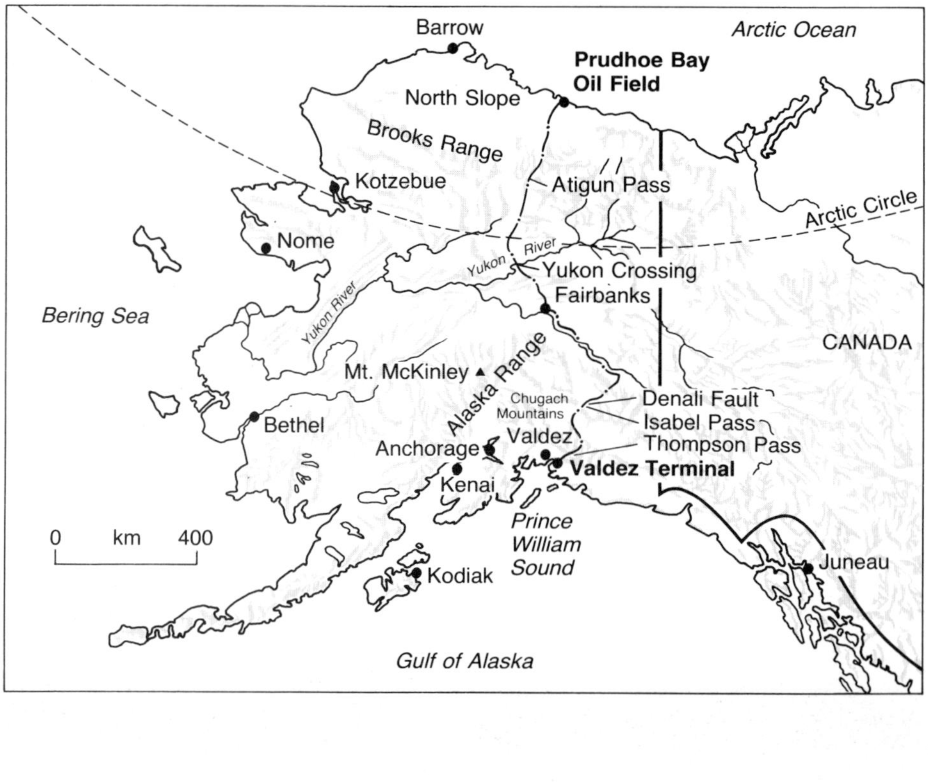

and the pipeline. Environmental groups see Alaska as the 'last wilderness'. They are concerned that it will be permanently damaged by such development. The pipeline was delayed for three years because of the strong opposition to it. But in the end the government decided that the oil was too important to the country. Many precautions were taken to protect the environment. This was clearly the result of pressure from environmentalists. Oil revenues have pushed average income in Alaska to just about the highest in the USA.

Oil and gas discoveries have also been made in other remote regions such as northern Canada. In each case, the natural environment will be damaged to some extent. In years to come many more pipelines may cross the frozen northlands.

**Fig 3 Building the pipeline in such a difficult environment was an expensive project.**

## Enhanced oil recovery

When the price of oil was lower, wells were often abandoned after all the easily extractable oil had been brought to the surface. Now oil companies often use Enhanced Oil Recovery (EOR) methods to extract more oil. Here water is pumped underground to dislodge trapped oil. The oil floats to the top of the water and is pumped up. Many abandoned oilwells in the USA have been restarted using EOR. This is often not expensive as in many cases the pumps and piping were not dismantled, the wells were just capped. Oil companies are also looking again at oilfields which were uneconomic to produce when the price of oil was lower.

## Alberta's tar sands

The rise in oil prices in the 1970s made the energy companies look closely at unconventional sources of oil and gas. One area of interest was the vast tar sands deposits in Alberta. Here the oil is mixed with sand in a tar-like form. Because the oil and sand have to be separated it is more expensive to produce than crude oil (petroleum). Production also has a greater impact on the environment. As oil prices have fallen in the 1980s, plans to develop the oil sands have been scaled down. Production in 1983 was at a rate of 157 000 barrels/ day. The sands deposits contain an estimated 250 billion barrels of recoverable oil. This compares with Alberta's crude oil reserves of 4.7 billion barrels. The further development of Alberta's tar sands and other unconventional deposits of oil and gas depends very much on world energy prices.

**Fig 4 Every day the pipeline is carefully checked by helicopter for damage. This report from the *Oil and Gas Journal*, 28th January 1985 shows one problem that can occur.**

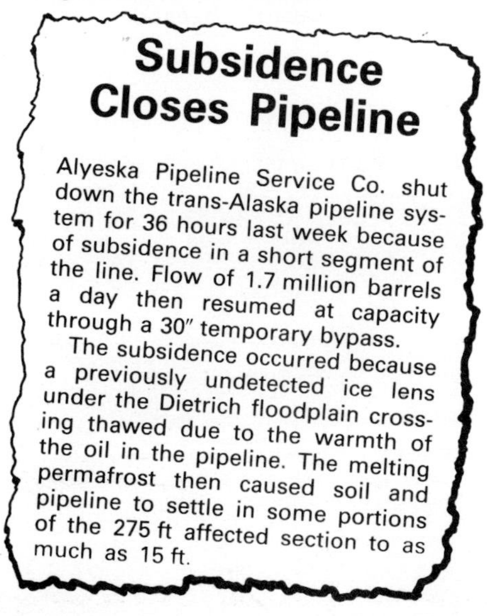

**Subsidence Closes Pipeline**

Alyeska Pipeline Service Co. shut down the trans-Alaska pipeline system for 36 hours last week because of subsidence in a short segment of the line. Flow of 1.7 million barrels a day then resumed at capacity through a 30″ temporary bypass.

The subsidence occurred because a previously undetected ice lens under the Dietrich floodplain crossing thawed due to the warmth of the oil in the pipeline. The melting permafrost then caused soil and pipeline to settle in some portions of the 275 ft affected section to as much as 15 ft.

**Fig 5 The changes in oil and gas production in the USA since 1968.**

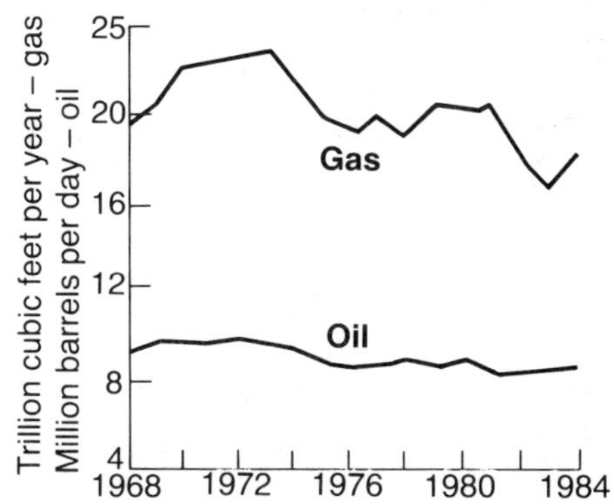


**Q1**

**(a)** Why is much oil and gas exploration now in frontier and offshore areas?

**(b)** How does the world price of oil affect the rate of exploration?

**Q2**

**(a)** Outline the reasons for and against the development of Alaska's oil resources.

**(b)** Suggest why much of the Alaskan pipeline is above ground level.

**(c)** What do you think will happen to the settlement at Prudhoe Bay when the oilfield dries up?

**Q3**

**(a)** Draw a diagram to illustrate Enhanced Oil Recovery.

**(b)** Why has the use of this technique increased?

**Q4**

What does Figure 5 tell you about oil and gas production in the USA?

# 8.3 Coal

## Huge reserves, falling popularity

The USA is the world's number one in coal mining. It produces about a quarter of the world total (Figure 1). Canada is a much smaller producer of coal.

U.S. COAL INDUSTRY: FACTFILE 1983

- World No. 1 producer: 712 million tonnes per year
- 38% from underground and 62% from opencast mines
- 73% of coal used for electricity generation
- 5800 mines operated by 3700 different companies
- World's No. 1 coal exporter: 71 million tonnes per year
- 190 000 employees: the industry has an unemployment rate of three times the national average (due to the early 1980s recession)
- Coal is transported by rail, barge, truck and slurry pipeline. It is exported from ten ports.

**Fig 1 The US coal industry.**

More coal is now mined in the USA than at any time in the past, but other energy sources have been developing at a faster rate. So coal only accounts for 23% of total energy supply today compared to 36% in 1950. Coal's share of the energy market has fallen because:

- It is a heavy and bulky solid, costly to store and transport.
- The mining and burning of coal can cause considerable environmental problems.
- Other popular fuels are available at very competitive prices.
- New technology often excludes the use of coal. In 1945 the railways bought a quarter of all coal mined in the USA. Now trains are diesel or electric powered.

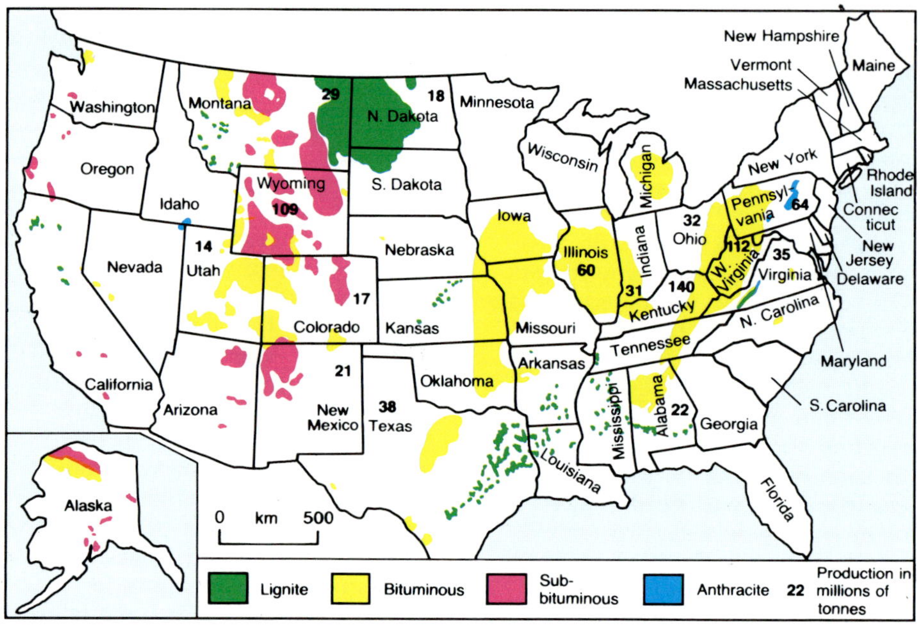


**Fig 2 The fifteen major coal- producing states of the USA, showing 1983 production.**

## Moving west

Coal is mined in over half the states of the USA (Figure 2). Five states – Kentucky, West Virginia, Wyoming, Pennsylvania and Illinois – account for over 60% of production. The Appalachian coalfield is the oldest and most important coalfield. Until recently the eastern coalfields produced nearly all of the USA's coal. Since 1970, mining in the west has expanded rapidly because:

- The Clean Air Act (1970) placed strict limits on the amount of sulphur released into the atmosphere. Most eastern coal has a high sulphur content. Expensive anti-pollution equipment has to be installed if this coal is burned. Most western coal has very little sulphur and can be burned directly without breaking the law.

**Fig 3 Loading coal at an Appalachian strip mine.**

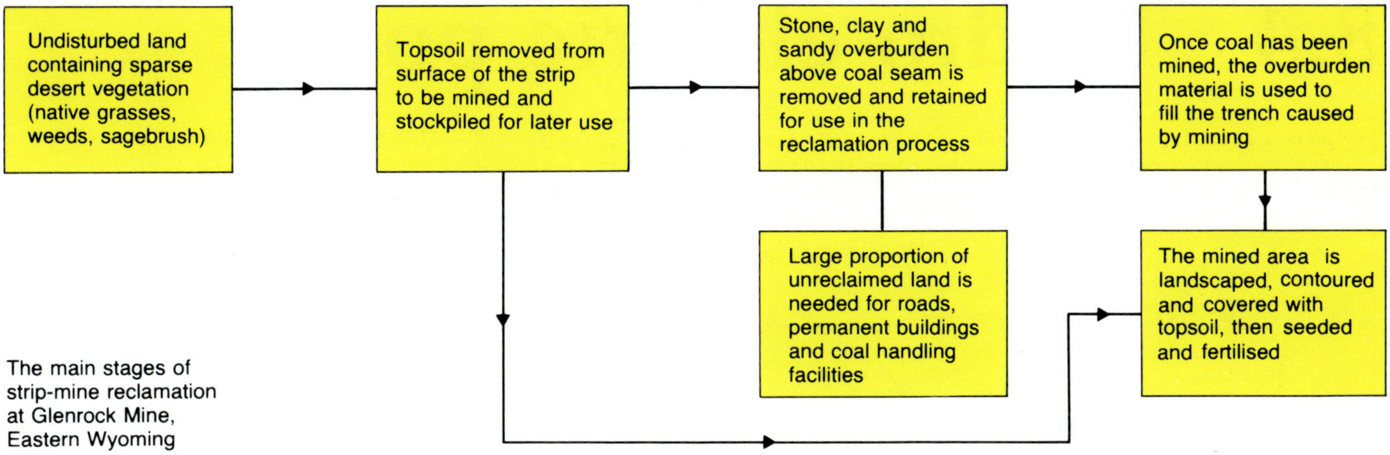


**Fig 4 Reclamation at a strip mine.**

- Most western coal is found at or near to the surface. It can be strip mined. This is much cheaper than underground mining. Less labour is required and huge coal cutting machines can be used. Many eastern mines are underground.

But the western coalfields do have some problems. The coal has a lower calorific value than coal mined in the east. This means that more is needed for the same amount of heat. It is also far away from the power stations in the east which buy most of the coal. Transport costs can add 60% to the price of coal at the mine. However, the advantages of western coal generally outweigh the disadvantages, so it is able to compete with other sources in its market area. It is likely that more of the USA's coal will be mined in the west in the future.

## Impact on the landscape

Great environmental damage was caused in the earlier years of coal mining. The evidence is widespread in the Appalachian mountains. Mountain tops were scalped of vegetation and topsoil to reach the coal below. Slopes were gouged out to build haul roads, and trees and soil were pushed over hillsides. Rain falling on exposed coal seams carried coal dust into nearby rivers. The sulphur in the coal made the water acidic.

Once the coal was mined no reclamation was attempted. The mining companies moved to other areas to repeat their havoc yet again. Strict laws have been passed to prevent this happening today. Now stripped land has to be restored to a usable condition.

## The future

The future of the coal industry is uncertain. In the 1970s it was suggested that production should be increased to between 1500 and 2000 million tonnes a year. This would greatly reduce oil imports. However, such a large rise in output would create a number of problems. It is now unlikely that coal output will rise much above its present level of 712 million tonnes.

**Q1**
Why has coal's share of the North American erergy market fallen?

**Q2**
List four differences in coal mining between the east and west of the USA.

**Q3**
Describe the distribution of coal deposits and coal production in the USA.

**Q4**
Describe the differences between stripmining in the Appalachian coalfield in earlier years and stripmining in the western coalfields today.

**Fig 5 Strip mine in Hanna, Wyoming showing the extent of the coal deposit.**

# 8.4 Hydro-electric power

The map shows the three power stations of La Grande Phase I (now completed) and the water diversion schemes. The proposed power station sites for La Grande II are also shown. If further development occurs in the future it is likely that La Grande II will be built next.

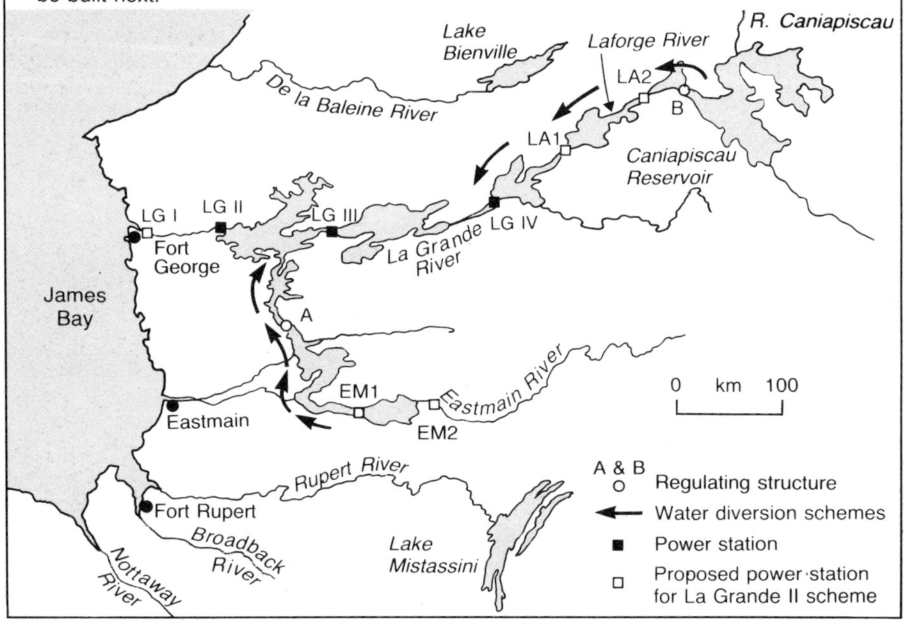


**Fig 1 The James Bay project area.**

## The James Bay Project

In 1985 the world's second largest hydro-electric power scheme was completed. Smaller only than Brazil's Itaipu project, it is in the remote James Bay region of Quebec. The James Bay Project began in 1972. Quebec called it 'the project of the century'. The aim was to use more of Quebec's abundant water resources to provide low cost power both for the province itself and for export. The total cost was a massive C$15 000 million.

The rivers flowing into James Bay (Figure 1) are powerful. This is not because of their slopes (which are gentle) but because of the large areas they drain. The biggest of the rivers is La Grande Rivière. Its drainage basin covers 98 000 square kilometres, more than twice the size of Switzerland.

The original plan was to build five hydro-electric power complexes, La Grande I, La Grande II, NBR (named after the Nottaway, Broadbeck and Rupert Rivers), Baleine and Caniapiscau. Total capacity would be 25 000 MW when completed in the mid-1990s. (By comparison, all the power stations in the UK have a combined capacity of 55 000 MW.) In 1982 it was decided to postpone the rest of the project after the completion of La Grande I. This decision was made for two reasons: (a) the estimate of future power needs made in the early 1970s proved to be too high a decade later, (b) the rising costs of the project. However, in 1985 plans to build another power-house at one of La Grande I's three sites were set in motion.

## Phase I completed

The La Grande river drops only 376 metres in its 800 kilometre course. It has no natural waterfalls. So dams and reservoirs had to be built to generate electricity. To increase the flow of water in the La Grande and so build larger power stations, water was diverted from two other rivers. Now 87% of the water from the basin of the Eastmain River and 27% of the water from the Caniapiscau basin is channelled into the La Grande. The construction of the reservoirs and the diversion schemes involved the building of eight dams and 174 dykes. The three power stations along the La Grande have a total capacity of 10 269 MW. LG2 is the largest single hydro-electric power station in North America. At its peak in 1978, 20 000 people worked on the project. The permanent workforce operating La Grande I is 500.

**Fig 2 La Grande II powerhouse, an underground area that is large enough to hold five football fields.**

## The postponed schemes

The four stages originally planned to follow Phase I have been postponed indefinitely. They are:

- **La Grande II** (3266 MW): another power station on the

La Grande (LGI) and two power stations each on the Eastmain River (EMI and EM2) and on the Laforge River (LAI and LA2).

- **NBR** (6200 MW): exploiting the waters of the Nottaway, Broadbeck and Rupert rivers which are south of the La Grande. Seven power stations on the Broadbeck were planned.
- **Baleine** (2900 MW): three power stations on the Baleine river.
- **Caniapiscau** (2240 MW): two power stations harnessing the power of three rivers, the Caniapiscau, des Mélèzes and Koksoak rivers.

**Fig 3 The spillway can handle 100m$^3$ of water per second.**

## Environmental impact

When the James Bay project began Quebec had no environmental protection laws. Many people were concerned that it could do great harm to the environment. So as the project progressed, a range of protection measures were introduced. In all, 60 square kilometres of forest were cleared of vegetation and soil. All these areas are being replanted, although it will take some time for vegetation regeneration and for fauna to find new feeding and breeding grounds. Over C$300 million has been spent on environmental studies in the area. The aim has been to keep the impact of the project to a minimum. Nevertheless, the overall change has been staggering. Maps of the James Bay Area in 1970 show nothing but string bogs, eskers, rivers, lakes and scattered Indian villages. Maps today show airports, roads, power stations, dams, reservoirs and a network of 735 -KV transmission lines, the longest on the continent.

CREE AND INUIT LAND CLAIMS

The 5000 Inuit and Cree living in the region brought a court action to try to stop the James Bay project. They wanted the government of Québec to recognise and settle their land claims. In 1975 both sides reached agreement. By signing the James Bay and Northern Quebec Agreement the native peoples gave up all claims based on aboriginal rights. In return they got among other things:

- compensation of C$ 225 million
- native land reserves and exclusive hunting, fishing and trapping rights
- a voice in approving or rejecting, on the basis of environmental impact, developments in the region

**Fig 4 Cree and Inuit land claims.**

## Hydro-electric power: location factors

Hydro-electricity supplies almost 30% of Canada's energy (69 million tons oil equivalent). In the USA it contributes less than 5% (88 million tons oil equivalent). The location of hydro-electric power plants is determined to a great extent by relief and drainage. An ideal location would have:

- A large fast flowing river
- A steep sided valley cut into hard impermeable rock
- Easy access to existing transmission corridors
- An absence of settlement
- Existing transport networks close at hand.

Few sites will combine all these factors. When a possible site is being assesssed, difficult decisions concerning costs have to be made.

**Q1**
Why is it so difficult to estimate accurately the final costs of large schemes like the James Bay project?

**Q2**
How was the flow of the La Grande river increased so that more power could be generated?

**Q3**
The native peoples were divided about signing the James Bay and Northern Quebec Agreement. Simulate a meeting of native peoples in class to discuss the Agreement. Then write down all the advantages and all the disadvantages of signing the Agreement.

**Fig 5 An aerial view of the James Bay hydro-electric power scheme.**

# 8.5 The nuclear controversy

Fig 1 Three Mile Island nuclear power plant.

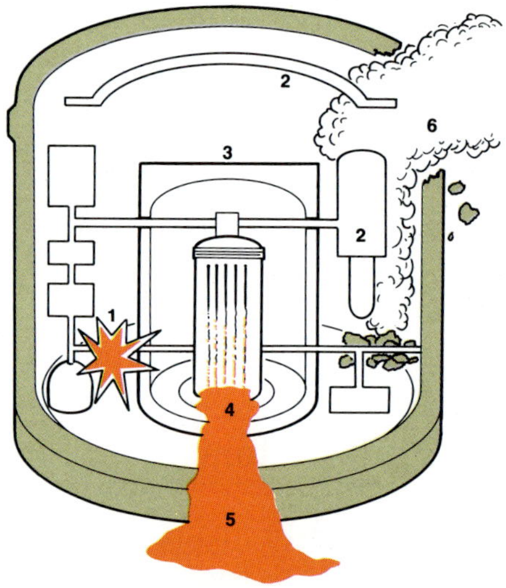


**Fig 2 The 'China Syndrome': what would happen in the event of a nuclear meltdown.**

A sequence of events that would lead to the worst accident possible – the 'China Syndrome': A break on the coolant pipe (1) and failure of emergency cooling (2) would cause the reactor vessel (3) to overheat, melting the fuel (4). This would escape through the concrete slab (5). The containment building (6) would crack, allowing more escapes.

## Three Mile Island

At 4 a.m. on 28 March 1979 the cooling system at the Three Mile Island nuclear power plant near Harrisburg, Pennsylvania broke down (Figure 1). For a while it was feared that intensely hot radioactive material would burn through its casing. This would contaminate the environment and cause a major disaster. Fortunately, engineers brought the reactor under control before this could happen. The clean-up operation inside the plant has cost millions of dollars. Such a disaster, in which many people would die, is known as the China Syndrome in the USA (Figure 2). The Three Mile Island accident has been restaged ten times at a desert testing ground in Idaho to learn more about preventing similar accidents in the future.

## Not so popular now

Since the Three Mile Island incident no new nuclear power plants have been ordered in the USA. In fact, since the early 1970s, over a hundred planned nuclear power plants have been cancelled. However, plants under construction before 1979 are still coming 'on line'. So by the mid 1990s 130 nuclear plants will be producing 20% of the nation's electricity. The USA and Canada rank first and sixth in the world nuclear power league. In 1984 the two nations together produced 36% of the world total (Figure 3).

| *Region* | *Percentage of world total nuclear power 1984* |
|---|---|
| North America | 35.9 |
| Latin America | 0.6 |
| Western Europe | 37.1 |
| Middle East | 0.0 |
| Africa | 0.4 |
| S and SE Asia | 3.7 |
| Japan | 10.8 |
| Australasia | 0.0 |
| USSR and Eastern Europe | 11.5 |
| China | 0.0 |

**Fig 3 The percentage of total world nuclear power produced in different regions.**

France, USSR, Japan and West Germany are the other leading nuclear countries. The nuclear programme in the USA is in deep trouble because of public opposition and rising costs, but other countries are still firmly committed to more nuclear electricity. For example, France already produces 60% of its electricity from nuclear power plants (Figure 4). This compares with 16% in the USA.

In North America electricity is produced and supplied by many different companies. Some were very keen on nuclear power from

**Fig 4 Nuclear energy's share of electricity production in thirteen countries. Only one of these is reducing its percentages of nuclear energy production.**

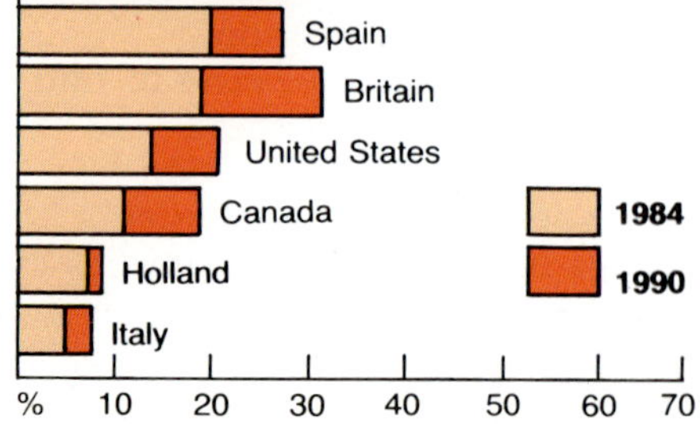

the start. Others were more cautious. In the USA the South Atlantic, East North Central and Middle Atlantic regions have the most nuclear power plants. In Canada ten of the country's eleven plants are sited in Ontario. There are three main reasons why nuclear power is not more evenly spread over the continent:

- Regions with the greatest demand for electricity and regions with limited availability of other power sources have been more attracted to nuclear power.
- Some regions calculated that nuclear power would be cheaper than the alternatives .
- In some areas opposition to nuclear power has been very strong and companies decided to produce electricity in other ways.

## Environmental groups say 'No!'

Opposition to nuclear power was already strong before the Three Mile Island accident. Many people fear a big escape of radioactive material. This would cause great loss of life and long-term environmental damage. Future generations would also have to bear the consequences. It would be impossible to live in contaminated areas for hundreds of years.

Nuclear waste is another big concern. America's 103 nuclear power plants produce about 1500 tonnes of spent fuel each year. Much of it is highly radioactive. It is kept at the power plants in water-filled pools. But this is only a temporary arrangement. The government plans to build a permanent underground store for all the USA's nuclear waste. However, none of the 50 states wants to become the USA's nuclear dustbin. What would happen if an earthquake hit such a site? What are the dangers of transporting nuclear waste from the power plants to a central site?

Organisations such as the Sierra Club, based in San Francisco, campaign strongly against nuclear power (Figure 5) and other issues which affect the environment. The Sierra Club has a more powerful voice now than in the past. This is because more people are concerned about the quality of the environment. The Sierra Club publicises its views to increase people's awareness of environmental problems.

However, the propaganda war is not all one-way. The power companies, who have invested so much money in nuclear energy, also use the media to put their views to the public (Figure 6).

**Q1**
Draw a pie graph to show the information in Figure 3.

**Q2**
Suggest why a nuclear meltdown is known as the 'China Syndrome' in the USA. (Look at a globe!)

**Q3**
**(a)** Outline the reasons why many environmental groups first believed that nuclear power was an improvement over existing ways of generating electricity.
**(b)** Environmental groups like the Sierra Club are now firmly against nuclear power. Discuss three reasons for their opposition.
**(c)** The Commonwealth Edison power company has been changing from coal-burning stations to nuclear power stations. How is the company justifying this change to its customers?

**Fig 5 The Sierra Club, one of the biggest environmental groups in the USA, is now firmly against nuclear power.**

# NUCLEAR POWER & THE SIERRA CLUB

**During the 1950s and 1960s many environmentalists looked upon nuclear power as an ally. They believed that using nuclear energy to generate electricity would bring cleaner air, reduce strip-mining for coal and offshore drilling for oil, and end plans to dam more rivers for hydro-electric power. In 1974, however, the Sierra Club's Board of Directors voted to oppose construction of more nuclear power plants. They did so because of growing concern about the long-unsolved problems of safety, waste disposal, nuclear weapons proliferation and theft of nuclear materials. In 1979, after the major reactor accident in Pennsylvania, the Board went still further and called for the phasing out of all existing nuclear power plants.**

**The events at the Three Mile Island nuclear plant reaffirm our concern about the lack of safety of nuclear plants and demonstrate that the possibility of human error dooms the nuclear fuel cycle to unacceptable risks.**

**Fig 6 This advertisement by the Commonwealth Edison Electricity Company appeared in newspapers in Illinois, USA. It argues that nuclear power plants will save people money.**

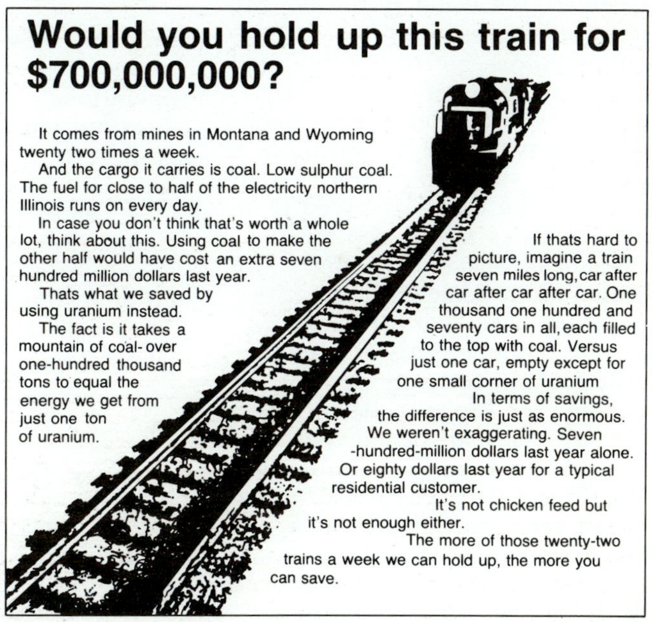

# 8.6 Power for the future

## Solar power

In 1983 Solar One became fully operational as the world's largest solar power station (Figure 1). It is sited in the Mohave desert n the south-western USA. 1818 computer-controlled mirrors (**heliostats**), each seven metres square, follow the sun across the sky. They focus its reflection on a fourteen metre high boiler. The boiler, mounted on a 73 metre high tower, is known as a central receiver. The water in the boiler is raised to very high temperatures. Steam is produced and used to generate electricity, as in power stations which burn fossil fuels. At the hottest times of day more steam is produced than needed. The excess is piped to storage tanks to be used when the sun is weaker or at night. The $140 million Solar One can generate 10 MW of electricity during daytime. This is enough only for a community of 7000 people. The Mohave desert is in the sunniest part of the continent. It has more than three hundred cloudless days a year. Solar power is not very practical in cooler, cloudy regions.

Electricity can also be produced by solar cells. Here numerous small strips of semi-conductor material, made mainly of silicon, are placed on large panels. They produce electricity when sunlight shines on them. However, many of these expensive panels are needed to produce small amounts of power. The world's first one megawatt size solar cell unit began operation in southern California in 1982. Computer control rotates the panels to receive maximum sunshine. The USA is also thinking about solar satellites (Figure 2). But it will probably be well into the 21st century before they could become operational.

At present, solar electricity is costly but as technology improves the cost will fall. It should not be long before solar power is competitive with other types of energy. It is renewable and causes no atmosphere pollution, but it does make a visual impact on the landscape.

**Fig 1 A section of the heliostats (the heat-gathering mirrors) which form part of the Solar One power plant in Barstow, California.**

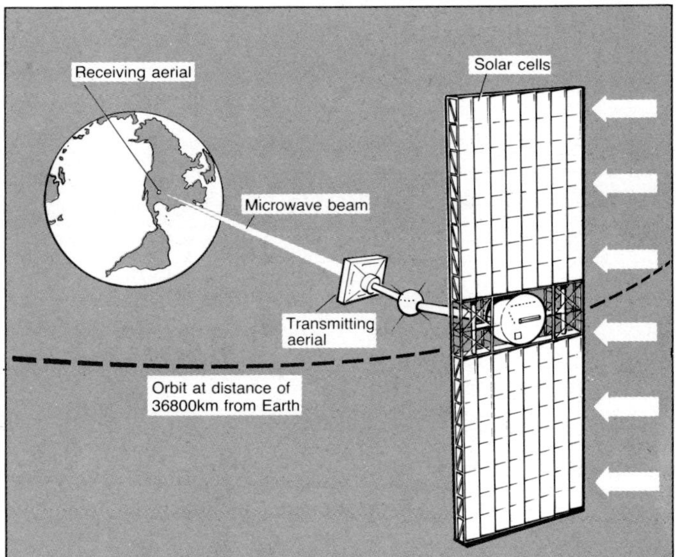


The USA hopes to develop a solar satellite. It will collect the sun's rays in space. The satellite's photocells will convert the sun's rays into electricity. This will then be changed into microwaves which will be beamed to a receiving dish on Earth where they will be converted into electricity.

**Fig 2 A solar satellite enables the energy from the sun to be converted into electricity for use on earth.**

## Power from the wind

In the early 1900s more than six million small windmills in the USA powered water pumps, grist mills and small electricity generators. By the middle of the century most had been abandoned. Now Canada and the USA are showing renewed interest in wind power to generate electricity.

A number of large single turbines operate at various sites in North America. They are located in areas of high average wind speeds. In California the 'wind farm' concept is well-developed (Figure 3). Here many turbines (over a hundred at times) operate at a single site and feed power into the local grid. There is no atmospheric pollution but the visual impact of so many turbines has to be considered.

It is unlikely that wind will ever be a major source of energy but it should make a useful contribution in some regions. Wind-powered generators could be particularly useful in isolated regions where small, electrical networks are currently fed by diesel-driven units. Wind power could greatly reduce oil consumption in such areas.

## Geothermal energy

Geothermal energy is the natural heat found in the earth's crust in the forms of steam, hot water and hot rock (Figure 4). Rain water may sink down several kilometres in permeable rocks. The water is heated due to the earth's geothermal gradient. This is the rate at which temperature rises as depth below the surface increases.

The average rise in temperature is about 30°C per kilometre but can reach 80°C in the world's volcanic regions. The Western Cordillera is one such region. Only a few nations use geothermal heat at present but more countries are now showing interest.

The USA is the world leader in the use of geothermal heat to generate electricity. The largest facility is at The Geysers, Sonoma County, California which began operation in 1960. The capacity of the field will be 2000 MW when new development is completed in the late 1980s. Half of San Francisco's electricity comes from The Geysers which is a dry steam site. There is some degree of pollution because the steam contains impurities such as hydrogen sulphide.

Research into the use of the underground hot water reservoirs in the western USA is also in progress. However, technical problems have caused delays. The hot water below the Imperial Valley in California is very briny. For every litre brought to the surface, up to a quarter may be salts and solid particles that corrode and cloy the wells' piping. In addition, there is the big problem of disposing of the waste.

It is more difficult to use the heat of the hot rock below the surface. Power companies are experimenting by pumping water several kilometres underground and then bringing it to the surface after it has been heated. It may be some time before this technique is fully developed.

The USA's Department of Energy is now looking at an even newer type of geothermal energy, magma energy extraction. This would involve drilling a hole through the earth's crust to the molten rock below, magma, at 1560°F–2000°F. A heat exchanger would be installed at the bottom. Energy could be extracted by water or another fluid that is brought to the surface to drive a heat engine. Sites must be found where molten magma is not much more than five kilometres down to keep costs at a reasonable level.

**Fig 3 These 56 kw turbine generators are among the first that were installed at a wind farm near San Francisco. There will eventually be 300 windmills which will be able to generate up to 17 000 kw.**

**Q1**

**(a)** Why is Solar One's tower known as a central receiver?

**(b)** Solar One produces 10 Mw from a 32 hectare site. How much land would be needed to produce 1000 MW (the standard capacity for a fossil fuel power station)? Why might power plants of this size be unpopular?

**Q2**

What major advantage would a solar satellite have over other methods of solar power?

**Q3**

**(a)** What is a 'wind farm'?

**(b)** If a community relied totally on wind turbines for its electricity, what problems might it have?

**(c)** How might such problems be overcome?

**Q4**

Describe the different forms of geothermal energy and identify any environmental problems which may occur.

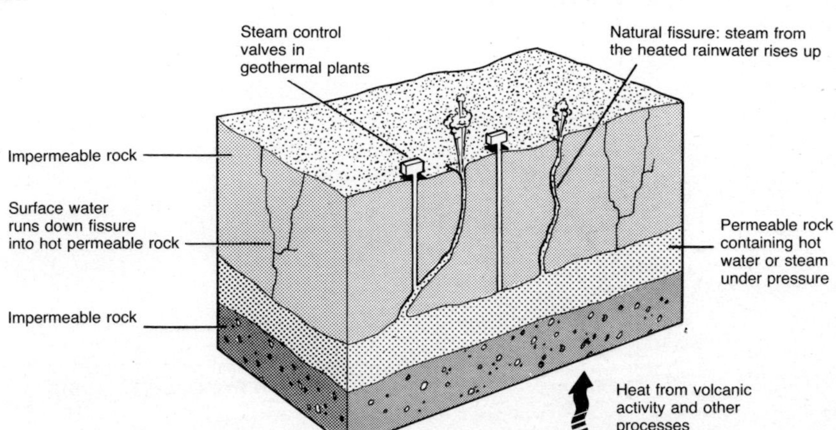


**Fig 4 Geothermal energy is produced within the earth's crust.**

The Earth's crust gets hotter the closer it is to the molten ore of the centre. For every kilometre of depth the temperature rises about 30°C. In areas with very high volcanic activity, this can rise to 80°C. Rainwater may work its way down several kilometres, where it is heated and turned into steam. The steam rises up through natural fissures in the rocks. It can be trapped and used for heating or to generate electricity.

# 8.7 Power for the future

## Tidal power

The Annapolis Tidal Power Generating Station is on the coast of Nova Scotia (Figure 1). This is one of only 40 sites worldwide which are suitable for large scale electricity generation from the tides.

Work began on the $46 million pilot project in 1980. It opened in 1983 with a capacity of 20 MW. The turbine propellor is housed on an island near the mouth of the Annapolis River which flows into the Bay of Fundy (Figure 2). The bay has a huge tidal range. At Annapolis it extends from 8.7 metres during spring tides to 4.4 metres during neap tides. At high tide, sea water passes through the sluice gates in the barrage built across the river into the reservoir behind. At low tide, the sluice gates are closed and water flows out through the turbine water passage, as the level of water in the reservoir is higher than that in the bay. The turbine generates power when the head of water between reservoir and sea exceeds 1.4 metres. Power is generated during two periods of five to six hours, each beginning two to three hours after high tide.

Fig 1 **Annapolis tidal power station.**

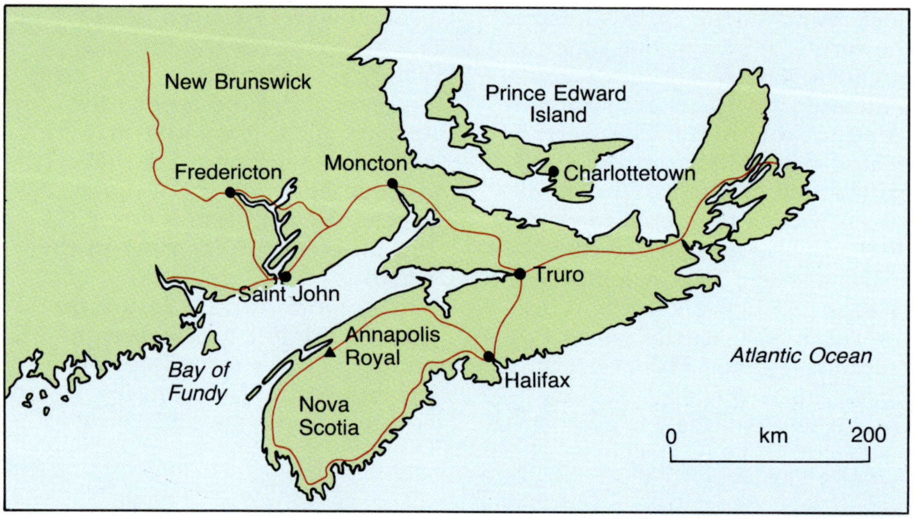


**Fig 2 Annapolis power station.**

The success of the pilot project means that further development of the Bay of Fundy may occur. The Bay has 37 possible sites, ranging in size from 50 to 10 000 MW. In theory they could all be developed without interfering with each other. Nova Scotia would hope to sell much of this extra electricity to the USA.

People have shown some concern about environmental impact. It has been argued that the barrages and other installations will spoil an area of great beauty. More drastic consequences have also been predicted. These include changes in local weather patterns, the inundation of the power site by silt within twenty years and even the flooding of Boston's Logan airport by a consequent rise in New England's tidal range. However, there is little evidence to support such claims.

## Ocean Thermal Energy Conversion [OTEC]

OTEC uses the temperature difference between the ocean's warm surface water and the cold deep waters to generate electricity. In the world's first at-sea power plant, off the coast of Hawaii, the warm surface water vapourises ammonia which is used to drive a turbine (Figure 3). The ammonia is then condensed by deep cold water and the cycle begins all over again. OTEC can only work in the tropics where the temperature difference between surface and deep water is at least 20°C.

Unlike other renewable energy sources OTEC provides 'base load' power (a continuous electricity flow). At present the costs of OTEC are high and the total electricity production small. But as technology improves it should become commercially viable. Environmental impact is very small.

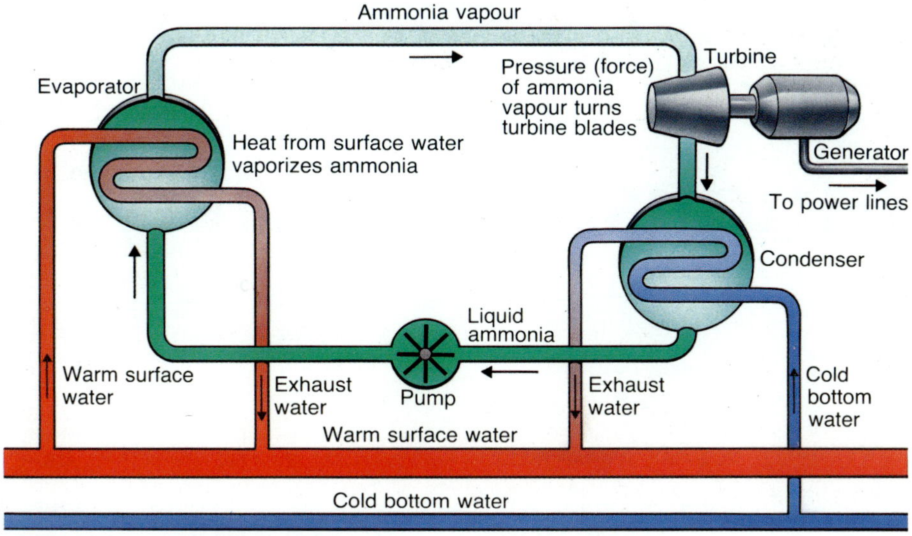


**Fig 3 Ocean Thermal Energy Conversion (OTEC). Liquid ammonia is vaporized by the heat in the surface water. The ammonia vapour is then used to drive a turbine. Then the ammonia is condensed by the deep cold water and the cycle begins again.**

- Combustible waste chippings from forestry are used as boiler fuel.
- Some types of tree can be milked of an oil-like sap which can be converted into petroleum.

## Renewable energy

Renewable sources of energy cannot run out, and they do not pollute, blow up or melt down. After the first oil shock, some optimists claimed that they could eventually meet all demand for energy. That optimism is fading. The money spent by governments on research and development into renewable energy has halved from its 1980 peak of $1.2 billion.

The reason is that the renewables have two drawbacks: they are diffuse and they are intermittent. The diffuseness means that a 1000-megawatt solar farm might occupy about 5000 acres, compared with less than 150 acres for a similar-capacity nuclear power station. A 1000-megawatt wind farm would be several times larger still. A wave-power station generating 1000-megawatts might be 30 miles long. If crops were grown for conversion to oil or gas by digestion, 1000-megawatts-worth would occupy 200 square miles.

**Fig 5 An extract from *The Economist*, 24th May 1986.**

## Biomass

Biomass is organic matter from which energy can be produced. Living plants make ten times as much energy each year as people consume. Some of the countries of the South (Africa, Asia, excluding USSR and Japan, and Latin America) get over 90% of their energy from biomass, mainly by burning firewood. In North America biomass is used for energy in more technically advanced ways:

- In the Mid-West of the USA some motorists fill their cars with gasohol. This is a mixture of 10% alcohol and 90% gasoline (petrol). The alcohol is produced by the distillation of surplus crops such as maize and sugarbeet. The government has supported the small gasohol industry by waiving the federal tax which has to be paid on every gallon of petrol.
- In some cities, such as Los Angeles, methane gas is obtained from decomposing rubbish tips.

**Fig 4 Gasohol on sale in the USA.**

These are just some of the ways in which biomass can be used to produce energy. At present, biomass energy is small in scale and it is unlikely that it will ever become very important in North America. But it is another alternative that can help meet the continent's energy needs.

**Q1**
Explain how the Annapolis tidal power station works.

**Q2**
**(a)** Why will tidal power, OTEC and biomass at best only make a small contribution to North America's energy supply in the future?
**(b)** Compare these sources of power in terms of environmental impact.

**Q3**
**(a)** Imagine you work in the nuclear power industry. In a televised debate you have to put the case for the USA investing in more nuclear power stations rather than in renewable sources of energy. Write down your main arguments for nuclear power.
**(b)** Now imagine you work for the Sierra Club. You are putting the case for investment in renewable energy. What would your main points be?

# 9. Industry

# 9.1 A post-industrial society?

## Classifying employment

In every American state or Canadian province people do hundreds of different jobs. All these jobs can be placed into broad groups:

**Primary industries** take raw materials directly from the land and the sea. Mining and quarrying, farming, fishing and forestry make up most of the jobs in this sector. Some primary products are sold directly to the consumer (ie fresh fish, potatoes) but most go to secondary industries for processing.

**Secondary industries** manufacture primary materials into finished products. Activities include the production of processed food, furniture and motor vehicles. The construction of buildings is also included in this sector. Secondary products are classed either as consumer goods (produced for sale to the consumer) or capital goods (produced for sale to other industries).

**Tertiary industries** provide services to businesses and to people. Shopworkers, drivers, architects and nurses are examples of people who work in tertiary industries.

**Quaternary industries** use high technology in providing information and expertise. Research and development is an important part of this sector. Quaternary industries have been recognised as a separate group since the late 1960s. In the past, quaternary jobs were included in the tertiary sector. Even today much of the available information on employment does not consider quaternary sector (Figure 1).

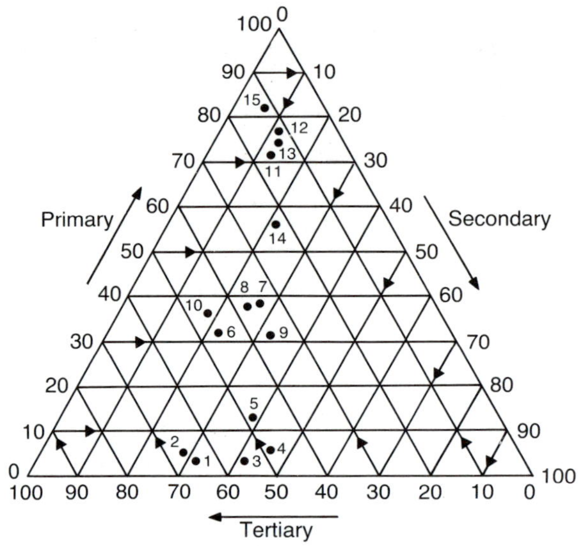


| No | Country | GNP per capita 1986 |
|---|---|---|
| 1 | USA | 17 480 |
| 2 | Canada | 14 120 |
| 3 | UK | 8 870 |
| 4 | W Germany | 12 080 |
| 5 | Japan | 12 840 |
| 6 | Brazil | 1 810 |
| 7 | Greece | 3 680 |
| 8 | Mexico | 1 860 |
| 9 | Yugoslavia | 2 300 |
| 10 | Jamaica | 840 |
| 11 | India | 290 |
| 12 | Kenya | 300 |
| 13 | China | 300 |
| 14 | Pakistan | 350 |
| 15 | Tanzania | 250 |

**Fig 1 Triangular graph showing employment structure in 15 countries (1980).**

North America is now often called a 'post-industrial society'. This means that the share of its population working in primary and manufacturing industry (the secondary sector) is falling (Figure 2). At the same time more people are working in the tertiary and quaternary sectors.

## Employment: changing all the time

Work and working conditions are constantly changing. In 1900 40% of employment in the USA was in the primary sector. However, the

**Fig 2 Employment trends in the USA, 1870–1980.**

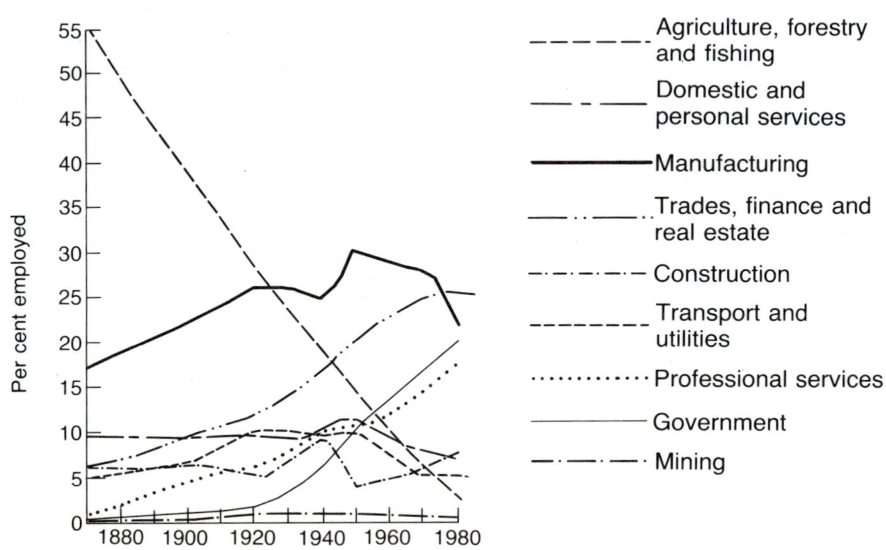

**Fig 3 A computer controlled robotic welder in operation at a car plant.**

mechanization of farming, mining, forestry and fishing means that far fewer people are now needed in these industries. Most primary employment is in rural areas. As these jobs disappeared people moved to towns and cities. This is where most secondary, tertiary and quaternary jobs are found. Only 4% of employment in the USA is now in the primary sector.

Human labour is steadily being replaced in manufacturing too. In more and more factories, robots and other advanced machinery handle assembly line jobs which once employed large numbers of people (Figures 3 and 4).

Automation is expensive to install at first. But it usually saves money for firms in the long run by reducing wage bills considerably. In 1950 the same number of Americans were employed in manufacturing as in services. By 1980 two-thirds were working in services.

The tertiary and quaternary sectors are also changing. In banking, insurance and many other types of business, word processors and computers have reduced the number of people required. But elsewhere service employment is rising. Education and health are two of these expanding areas. In 1980 over nine million Americans worked in hospitals and health services

**Fig 4 Automation in a service industry: a drive-in bank at Oshkosh, Wisconsin.**

**Fig 5 The share of manufacturing in GDP and employment for the major western economies.**

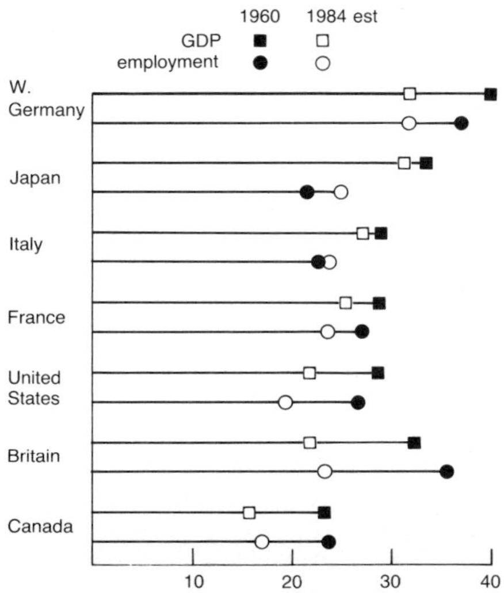


**Fig 6 An extract from the *Toronto Sunday Star*, 3rd August 1986.**

## PART-TIME WORKFORCE GROWING

One in six Canadian workers is now a part-timer, working less than 30 hours a week, usually with fewer benefits and less chance of job training and promotion than full-time colleagues.

Governments and corporations are turning to part-time workers to trim their budgets, hiring them even in years of heavy layoffs for full-time workers, and keeping them on as 'permanent' part-timers after financial recovery. Advocates of 'leaner and meaner business' argue that the world economy is going the way of part-time labor, and that the full-timers will eventually be a small elite.

while seven million were employed in education. It is easier to replace people in some jobs than in others.

## Part-time work

More North Americans are now working part-time. Some choose part-time work because they like working this way but for many people it is the only work available. The greatest proportion of part-time jobs is in the tertiary sector. Public services and private firms are turning to part-time workers to reduce their wage bills (Figure 6). This is a trend in most other developed countries too.

### Q1

**(a)** On a copy of Figure 1 put the fifteen countries into groups, based on employment structure, by drawing circles around each group.
**(b)** Explain why you have grouped them in this way.
**(c)** On a scattergraph, plot GNP per capita against the percentage of the labour force working in the tertiary sector for each country.
**(d)** How strong is the relationship (correlation) between the two measures? Why do you think this is so?

### Q2

Figure 2 divides total employment in the USA into nine groups.
**(a)** Which are (i) primary? (ii) secondary? (iii) tertiary?
**(b)** Describe and suggest reasons for the changes shown by the graph.

### Q3

Make lists of the advantages and disadvantages of part-time work for (a) employees, (b) employers.

### Q4

Describe and suggest reasons for the changes shown in Figure 5.

# 9.2 Motor vehicles: a mature industry

## Stages in development

Motor vehicle production is the world's biggest manufacturing industry. The first motor car was built in 1885; a century later almost 450 million were registered around the world. Some 160 million of these are in the USA. This means about 700 vehicles for every 1000 people. In contrast, Bangladesh has less than one vehicle per 1000 people.

Most industries go through three stages in their life cycles (Figure 1). The motor vehicle industry has followed this pattern:

**1 The Early Stage** In the 1890s and very early 1900s there were hundreds of small car-makers. Each car was seen as a separate manufacturing task. Detroit, Michigan became one of the main centres of the industry. This was where some of the first American car-makers such as Henry Ford lived. The city was also well placed for local hardwood forests (wood was used in early cars), for steel made in the region and for easy access to much of the North American market.

**2 The Growth Stage** After 1908 great changes occurred. Henry Ford introduced standardised parts and the assembly line. Mass production had arrived. Many cars makers found the competition too tough. During the growth stage General Motors, Ford and Chrysler came to dominate the industry, which became concentrated in Detroit. A motor vehicle is made up of over a thousand parts. A ring of industrial towns developed around Detroit to supply these parts to the main assembly plants. Later, assembly plants were built elsewhere in the USA. At first most were in other northern states (Figure 2).

**3 The Mature Stage** The industry entered this stage in the mid-1960s. The high growth rate of earlier years had slowed. The market now depended largely on motorists replacing their existing vehicles or purchasing second cars (or more) rather than on first-time buyers. More assembly plants were built in the south and in the west. Car sales in these regions were rising faster than in the north.

| | |
|---|---|
| California | 161 921 |
| Delaware | 416 170 |
| Georgia | 315 448 |
| Illinois | 399 074 |
| Indiana | 9 908 |
| Kansas | 229 577 |
| Kentucky | 350 092 |
| Louisiana | 137 815 |
| Maryland | 136 762 |
| Massachusetts | 51 816 |
| Michigan | 2 557 462 |
| Minnesota | 128 314 |
| Missouri | 721 544 |
| New Jersey | 261 989 |
| New York | 98 794 |
| Ohio | 1 130 480 |
| Oklahoma | 148 316 |
| Oregon | 4 000 |
| Pennsylvania | 87 964 |
| Tennessee | 24 279 |
| Texas | 225 745 |
| Utah | 750 |
| Virginia | 87 409 |
| Washington | 3 900 |
| Wisconsin | 418 702 |
| USA | 8 108 231 |

**Fig 3 The number of motor vehicles assembled in each US state, 1983.**

**Fig 2 The assembly line of the General Motors car plant, Baltimore, Maryland.**

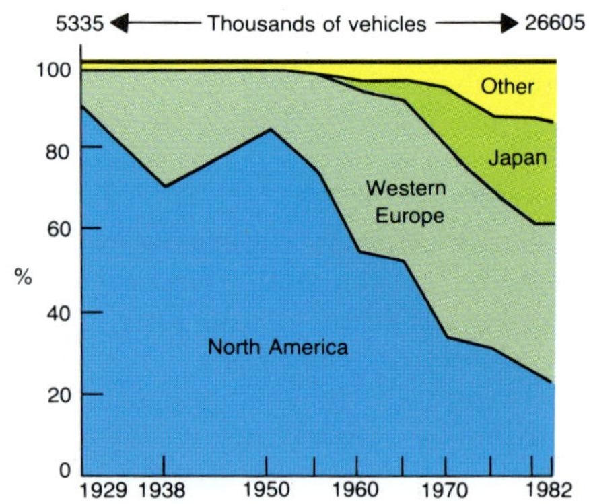


**Fig 4 World car production. As North America's share has decreased, other areas' shares have increased.**

**Fig 1 The stages of an industry's development.**

| *Early* | *Growth* | *Mature* |
|---|---|---|
| New product on the market | Product is a success. Large capital input needed for change to mass production. | Selling largely to a replacement market (ie cars, household appliances). High level of automation. |
| Limited production with small highly skilled workforce. | New factories located in same regions. | Now employing more semi-skilled and unskilled workers. |
| Located in major industrial regions – close to large markets, skilled labour and other new technology firms. | Management skills now of much greater importance. Workforce expands. | Production often moves to new markets and sources of cheaper labour (at home and abroad). |

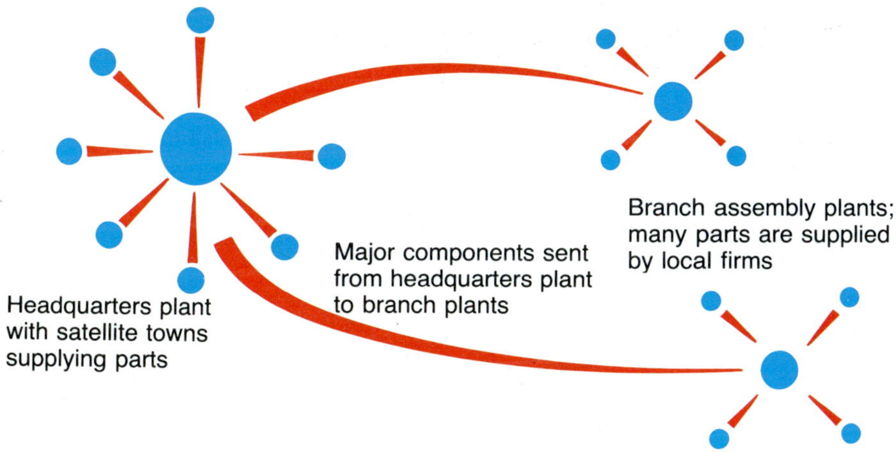


**Fig 5 A simplified model of the US car industry.**

It is much cheaper to transport parts than completed cars. The cost of building and running an assembly plant has to be weighed against this fact. Two hundred thousand vehicles a year is now thought of as the minimum production for a new assembly plant to be economical, although many older assembly plants produce much less than this. Only the essentials of the vehicles are transported from Michigan. When a new assembly plant opens, a ring of parts producers usually set up nearby to supply it (Figure 5). This cuts the cost of transport even further. However, one-third of US motor vehicles are still assembled in Michigan.

## Competition from abroad

Since the early 1960s American car makers have faced strong competition from Japan and Europe. In 1958 Japan exported 7000 cars to the USA. By 1980 this had risen to three million. 1978 was the peak of production in the USA when 12.9 million vehicles rolled off assembly lines. It is unlikely that this figure will be reached again.

The demand for cars is now rising fastest in the developing continents, particularly in South America and Asia. The world's big car makers are expanding production in these areas. At present, 85% of world motor vehicle production is in North America, Western Europe and Japan (Figure 4). This will fall in the future.

## The 'Big Three' in Canada

Vehicle production in Canada is dominated by the American 'big three'; General Motors, Ford and Chrysler. The Canadian motor industry is almost entirely located in southern Ontario. American companies operate here because of:

- The lower cost of labour in Canada compared to the USA
- The affluent Canadian market
- Proximity to major markets in the USA.

**Fig 6 The General Motors car plant at Hamtramck, Detroit.**

Also there are virtually no restrictions on the sale of motor vehicles between the two countries. In 1984 Canada produced a total of 1.5 million cars, trucks and buses (compared to 9.2 million in the USA). Canada has shown some concern about the policies of the 'big three' because (a) most research and development is done in the USA and (b) Canadian factories tend to build older models while newer and better selling models

**Q1**
**(a)** On an outline map of the USA illustrate the data given in Figure 3.
**(b)** Describe and suggest reasons for the distribution shown.

**Q2**
**(a)** Make a list of all the factors that can influence the location of manufacturing industry.
**(b)** How can the factors affecting the location of an industry change as it moves through the three stages of its life cycle?

**Q3**
Explain the model of the US car industry shown in Figure 5.

**Q4**
How has the regional distribution of world car production changed since 1929?

# 9.3 High technology: a growth industry

## What is high-tech industry?

High technology is the fastest growing industry in North America today. 'High-tech' companies use or make silicon chips, computers, robots, aerospace components and other very technically advanced products. These companies usually put much of their money into scientific research. Their aim is to develop newer, even more advanced products.

Manufacturing and service industries are becoming more and more electronics intensive. This really began in the 1950s. Then the main market was military and space equipment. At this time American firms dominated the world market. Today commercial markets are more important and other countries such as Japan, Canada, France, West Germany and Britain now compete fiercely with US firms.

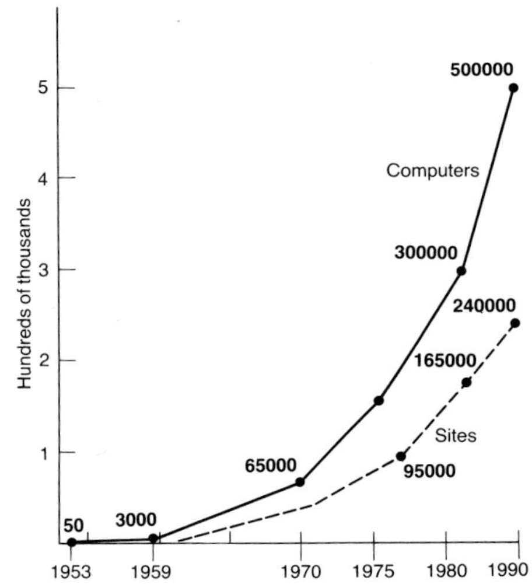


**Fig 2 The growth in the number of computers in the USA.**

Like many other industries high-tech firms concentrate in certain areas. This happens for a number of reasons.

## Silicon Valley North

Ottawa has the greatest number of electronics and computer companies in Canada. The area is known as Silicon Valley North (Figure 1). There are over a hundred high technology manufacturers and another two hundred sales, service and consulting operations. These firms employ over 20 000 people. Ottawa is a popular location for high technology because:

- It is the capital city. Decision-makers and experts of all kinds work there.
- It is close to major Canadian and US markets.
- Many high-tech companies began with the help of government grants. Many rely on government contracts for work.
- Ottawa's two universities are famous for science and engineering. There are strong formal and informal links between high-tech firms and the universities.
- High-tech companies benefit from being close together. They swap ideas, staff and equipment.
- Ottawa is a very pleasant place to live. This helps firms to attract highly skilled workers.
- The region's industrial agency, the Ottawa–Carleton Commercial and Industrial Corporation advertises the advantages of Ottawa throughout North America.

The majority of high-tech firms in Ottawa are Canadian owned.

**Fig 1 The distribution of the major high-tech companies in the Ottawa–Hull region.**

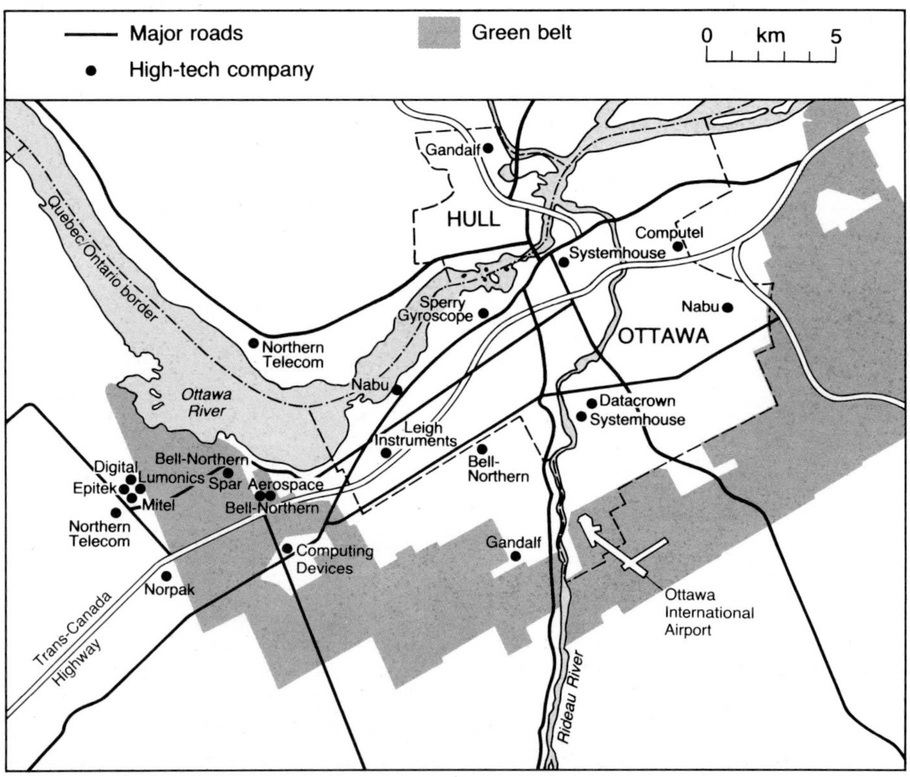

Many are small; others have grown rapidly in a very short time. Small firms though may have greater problems in the future. As electronics products become more complex they cost more to develop. This means that new firms need more money to get started than in earlier years. High technology is one of the few industries which is often short of staff. The industry needs highly skilled people. At present there are not enough of them to go round. Ottawa has to compete with other high-tech regions in North America for the best staff.

## Massachusett's Intelligence Alley

'Whole new industries spring up around university laboratories. Immediate access to new ideas and innovation is what counts', says David Birch, a US expert on job creation. California's Silicon Valley, which began its rise to fame 40 years ago, is the classic example. Its firms were fed from new ideas developed by Stanford University's engineering department.

A more recent high-tech growth area is Intelligence Alley in Cambridge, Massachusetts. The larger city of Boston is just south of Cambridge across the Charles River. Intelligence Alley covers a neighbourhood of almost two square kilometres close to the Massachusett's Institute of Technology (MIT). There are very strong links between MIT and many high-tech firms which specialise in artificial intelligence and computer software. There are also links with other institutions. In fact, the Boston–Cambridge area has the USA's largest concentration of educational institutions. These employ nearly 10% of the labour force. The region also has other attractions for high-tech firms. These include; (a) the high concentration of industry in the northeast which provides a large market for high-tech products (b) the high quality of life (c) excellent transport and communications links; (d) local

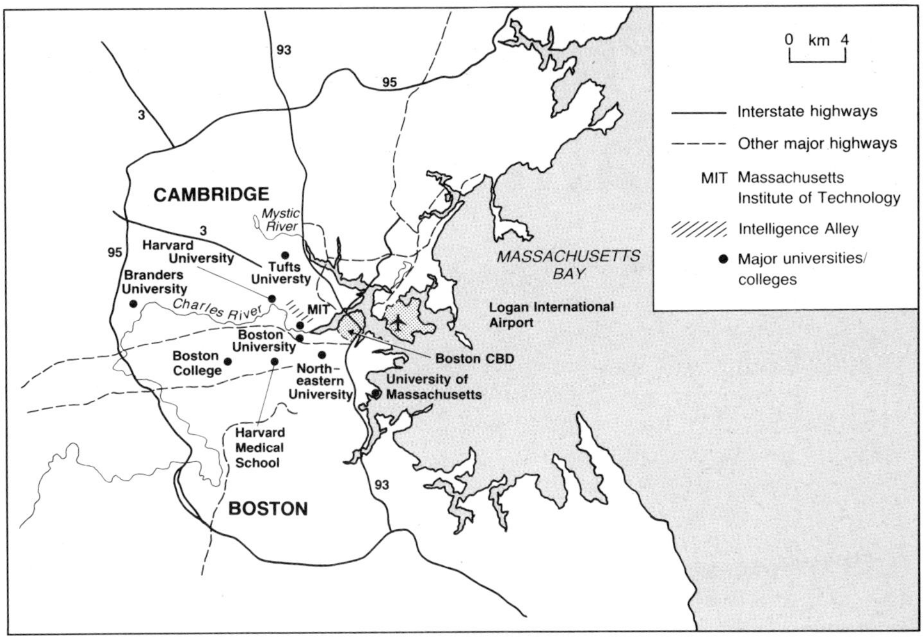


**Fig 3 Intelligence Alley, Massachusetts.**

**Fig 4 High Tech industry in the Ottawa region.**

government which is keen for the industry to expand. Twenty thousand new jobs were created in Intelligence Alley between 1980 and 1986. This should increase considerably in the future.

## A footloose industry

The high-tech industry is not really tied to any one or a small number of regions. In theory it could locate anywhere, providing the highly skilled workers it needs are prepared to live there. The term '**footloose**' is often used to describe such industries which have a wide choice of location. In contrast, many older and heavier industries like iron and steel, shipbuilding and heavy engineering can only operate economically in certain locations. These are areas where costs of production and distribution are considerably lower than elsewhere.

**Q1**
Look at Figure 2.
**(a)** Describe the growth in the number of computers in the USA.
**(b)** Suggest reasons for the trend.

**Q2**
**(a)** What is high-tech industry?
**(b)** Why do high-tech companies frequently locate close to major universities?
**(c)** What other factors influence the location of such companies?

**Q3**
Why is it now more difficult for small new companies to become established in the high-tech market?

# 9.4 The manufacturing belt: the challenge of change

## The rise and the fall

The regions of New England, Middle Atlantic and East North Central cover only one-eighth of the USA. Yet they have over 45% of all its manufacturing jobs. It had even more in the past. In 1910 68% of manufacturing employment was here. Because of this the region became known as the '**manufacturing belt**'. Industry developed here on such a large scale because:

- This was the first major centre of population. Immigrants brought industrial and business skills with them and the rising population provided both a market and a source of labour.
- Raw materials such as coal and iron ore were available locally.
- The Great Lakes, major rivers and the coast provided cheap transport for the movement of bulky goods.
- Accesss to Europe across the North Atlantic encouraged trade.
- Firms benefited from the wide variety of manufacturers in the region by using each others products and skills.
- High investment in research meant that most of the USA's new products were developed in the north.

Yet the dominance of the north was not to last as industry was increasingly attracted to other regions. The recession of the late 1970s and early 1980s also hit the north badly. During this period the level of world trade dropped considerably. Many of the manufacturing belt's older industries, such as iron and steel, heavy engineering and motor vehicles lost orders and jobs on a big scale. The region became known as the 'rustbelt'.

Within the region manufacturing industry is concentrated in ten areas (Figure 1). Some areas have coped quite well with changing economic conditions. As old industries have closed new ones have opened in their place. But other parts of the north have found it difficult to attract new industry. In a 1985 survey of manufacturing in the USA, most manufacturing belt states were shown to be high-cost locations compared to elsewhere in the country (Figure 1). The costs which concerned firms most were (in rank order) 1 Wages, 2 Unionization, 3 Energy. Overall, 22 factors were considered to get the rankings shown in Figure 1. The lower the figure, the more favourable was the area. However, it must be remembered that some industries, such as high-tech, are prepared to pay high costs for the locations which give them the conditions they need in which to flourish.

**Fig 1 Map of the USA manufacturing belt showing the ten major industrial areas and the best manufacturing climates by state and region.**

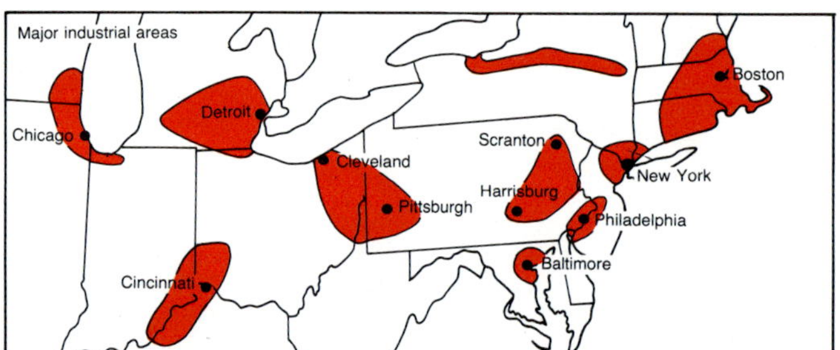


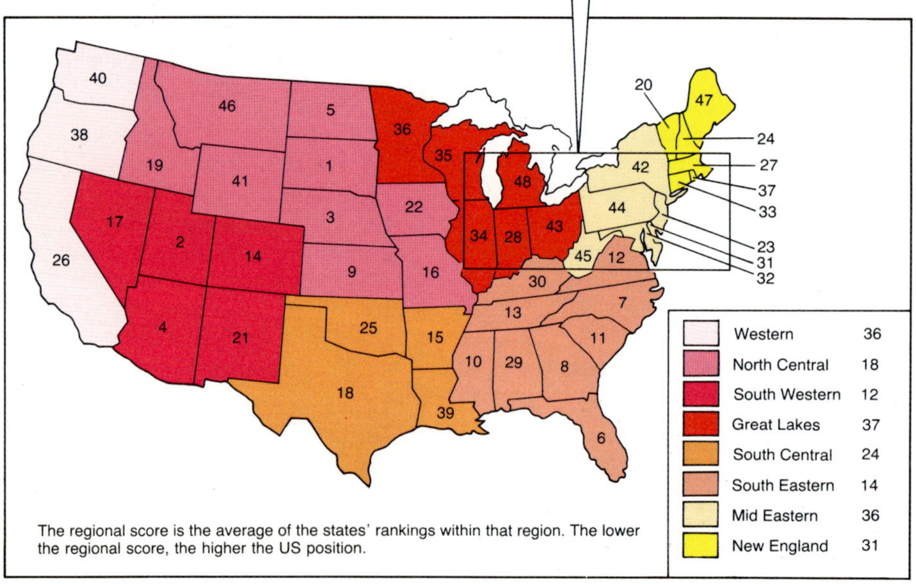


The regional score is the average of the states' rankings within that region. The lower the regional score, the higher the US position.

## East Central Pennsylvania

Iron and steel became the basis of manufacturing here in the 19th century. This was because of the local deposits of coal, iron ore and limestone. A range of other metal-working activities grew up around iron and steel. Other industries such as textiles, clothing, silk, lace and shoes also developed.

Nowadays, most of the region's traditional industries have declined. Factories have closed and many jobs have been lost. Demand for these products has either fallen or they are being

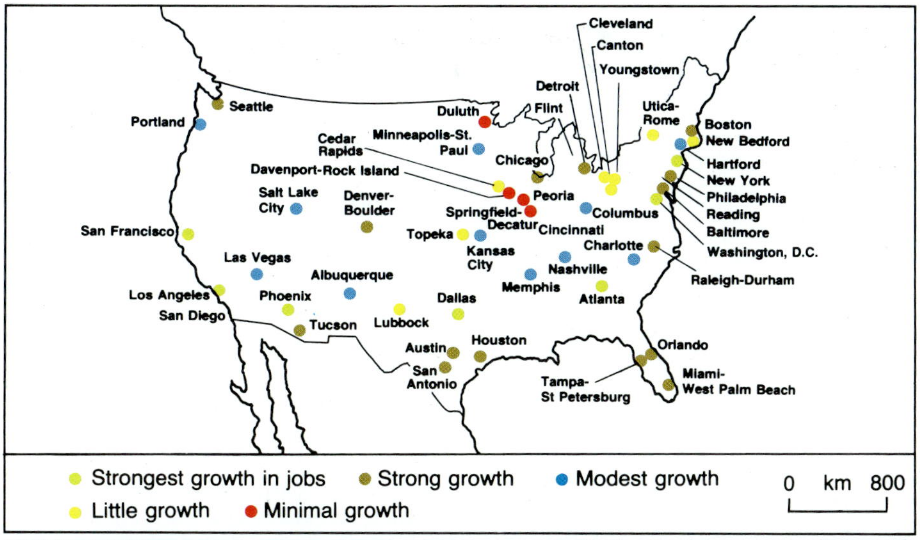


A recent study (Job Creation in America by David Birch) has predicted these employment trends in the USA's metropolitan areas for the 1990s. These predictions are based on a detailed study of job creation over many years. Birch found that every locality loses from 8% to 10% of its jobs each year. Thus, to stay even, every locality must replace about half of its jobs every five years. To stand a good chance of attracting sufficient new jobs, a locality needs at least:

- To be of a reasonable size. Small new firms need to have access to many specialists they cannot afford to hire full time.
- A major airport and good highways.
- Adequate public services, i.e. education, police, fire, environmental.
- A reasonably good overall quality of life.

**Fig 2 The best places in the USA in which to look for a job.**

produced more cheaply elsewhere. Local government has tried to attract new enterprise by offering incentives such as cheap land and tax exemptions. New roads have improved accessibility. This has helped but overall not enough new jobs have been created. Many new firms are small in size and some have not stayed in the region for long.

East Central Pennsylvania has over one million people. Most live in a line of towns stretching from Scranton to Harrisburg. Unemployment is high and wages are well below the national average. Unemployment could rise even higher in the future. For example, iron and steel is produced more cheaply in other parts of the USA. The industry only remains here because of inertia. This means that the initial reasons for its development have largely disappeared; production continues here mainly because of the high investment in plant and machinery. But as competition among steelmakers gets even sharper it is likely that only the lowest cost producers will survive.

## Southern New England

This is the oldest industrial area in the USA. Many traditional activities such as textiles, leather goods, clothing, small metal goods and jewellery are still important. Southern New England has also been successful in attracting new fast-growing industry. High-tech has grown spectacularly. Its main location is alongside Route 128 which arcs around Boston. The world-famous computer firms include Digital Equipment, Prime and Wang Laboratories. The quality of the region's universities and the excellent road, rail and air communications have been a major attraction to new high-tech firms.

There are still over 150 000 people employed in producing textiles, clothing and leather goods. Textiles and other traditional industries have survived by concentrating on up-market and more specialised products. This makes them safer from lower-priced foreign competition. Southern New England has coped with changing economic conditions better than East Central Pennsylvania because:

- It has been successful in attracting a range of new industry, particularly in the high-tech area.
- Its traditional industries have survived by producing for the higher-priced and more specialised areas of the market.
- There is a very wide range of industry in the area. This spreads the risk of unemployment and recession.

**Q1**
Look at Figure 1.
**(a)** Suggest why wages, unionization and energy were the major factors concerning manufacturers when choosing where to locate.
**(b)** List and justify five other factors which usually need to be considered when deciding to locate a factory.
**(c)** Rank the eight regions shown in Figure 1. Put the region with the best manufacturing climate first.

**Q2**
Look at Figure 2.
**(a)** Describe the predicted pattern of job creation in the USA in the 1990s.
**(b)** Suggest reasons for this pattern.

**Q3**
Why has southern New England coped better with changing economic conditions than East Central Pennsylvania?

# 9.5 The tertiary sector

## Producer and consumer services

The tertiary sector is concerned with the exchange and consumption of goods and services. It can be divided into:

**Producer services** Activities such as wholesaling, freight transport and market research consultants are used by other firms to help them run more efficiently or to distribute their goods.

**Consumer services** These serve the consumer directly. Examples are shops, public transport, hospitals, cinemas and restaurants.

| | Percentage of labour force in the Primary sector | | Secondary sector | | Tertiary sector | |
|---|---|---|---|---|---|---|
| | Canada | USA | Canada | USA | Canada | USA |
| 1951 | 19 | 12 | 36 | 34 | 45 | 54 |
| 1961 | 12 | 7 | 33 | 35 | 55 | 58 |
| 1971 | 8 | 4 | 31 | 34 | 61 | 62 |
| 1981 | 5 | 2 | 29 | 32 | 66 | 66 |

**Fig 1 The percentages of the labour force employed in the primary, secondary and tertiary sectors.**

The tertiary sector is the largest employer in North America today (Figure 1). It has become more and more important due to:

- The adoption of new technology
- Steadily rising average incomes
- Increasing leisure time
- New social values leading to, for example, more women in the labour force.

**Fig 2 The differences between the output of the goods-producing sector and that of the service-producing sector, 1959–1981.**

| Sector | 1959 | 1969 | 1981 |
|---|---|---|---|
| Goods-producing | 41.4 | 40.0 | 35.4 |
| Service-producing | 58.6 | 60.0 | 64.6 |

## Scale and location

The tertiary sector is dominated by small firms employing fewer than twenty people. Many of these firms are owned by one person and operate within one city region. There are also internationally sized firms such as the major airlines and banks.

The distribution and density of population is a major influence on services which look for highly accessible locations. Spatial variations in the age and the purchasing power of the population are also important. This is because many services are targeted at certain sections of the population. For example, a retailer of baby equipment and toys would not locate in an area where most of the population was of retirement age. Consumer services often occupy prime sites in the CBD while producer services are usually found in less expensive sites not too far away. When choosing a location, service industries must also consider how much labour they need in terms of both numbers and skills. In some locations it may be very difficult to attract highly skilled workers.

Areas where services are grouped together are called 'central places'. Places with large populations usually offer a greater variety of services than smaller places. Central places can in fact be arranged in rank order, or a hierarchy, in terms of the services they offer. Figure 4 shows the distribution of central places in Southern Saskatchewan while Figure 3 shows some of the services on offer in five of these central places.

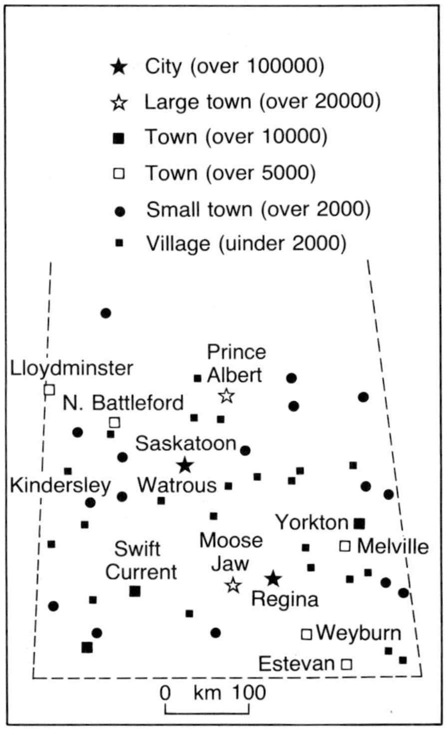


**Fig 4 The distribution of different sizes of settlements and service centres, South Saskatchewan.**

**Fig 3 Some of the services available in five population centres in South Saskatchewan.**

| Service centre | Selected services: Hospital beds | Dentists | High Schools | Eating places | Furniture shops | Car salerooms |
|---|---|---|---|---|---|---|
| Saskatoon (132 000) | 1423 | 53 | 11 | 65 | 25 | 26 |
| Prince Albert (28 500) | 350 | 12 | 6 | 28 | 11 | 9 |
| Lloydminster (7800) | 318 | 5 | 3 | 14 | 6 | 8 |
| Kindersley (3600) | 55 | 2 | 1 | 12 | 4 | 3 |
| Watrous (1650) | 35 | 1 | 1 | 6 | – | 5 |

## Offices in the CBD

Over 90% of employees in some services work in offices, although in other service occupations it may be less than 15%. In spite of increasing suburban office development the CBD remains the main location for offices. Over 60% of all office employment in New York City is in Manhattan. In Houston almost 70% of all office space is in the CBD. A Toronto business survey found that offices located in the city's CBD because of:

- The clustering of decision-makers
- The prestige of a central location
- The availability of a wide range of services
- The quality of public transport compared to other locations
- The ability to recruit staff in an accessible location.

The great demand for office space in the CBD has led to high-rise buildings and very high land values. By the turn of the century skyscrapers were commonplace in New York and Chicago. Since then they have been built in most large North American cities.

## Office parks

An office park is an area in the suburbs or the countryside where offices are grouped together. Other land uses are excluded. Buildings are usually low-rise and comfortably spread out. Carefully planned grass and wooded areas help to provide a pleasant working environment. Firms can save money on essential services and benefit in other ways by grouping together like this. Such grouping usually attracts support services such as restaurants, bars and shops to locate nearby. There are 54 office parks in Houston (Figure 5.) Most are between four and ten miles from the CBD. They range in size from less than ten acres up to 1300 acres. The largest park has 61 buildings. The office park idea which began in the USA has now spread to other countries.

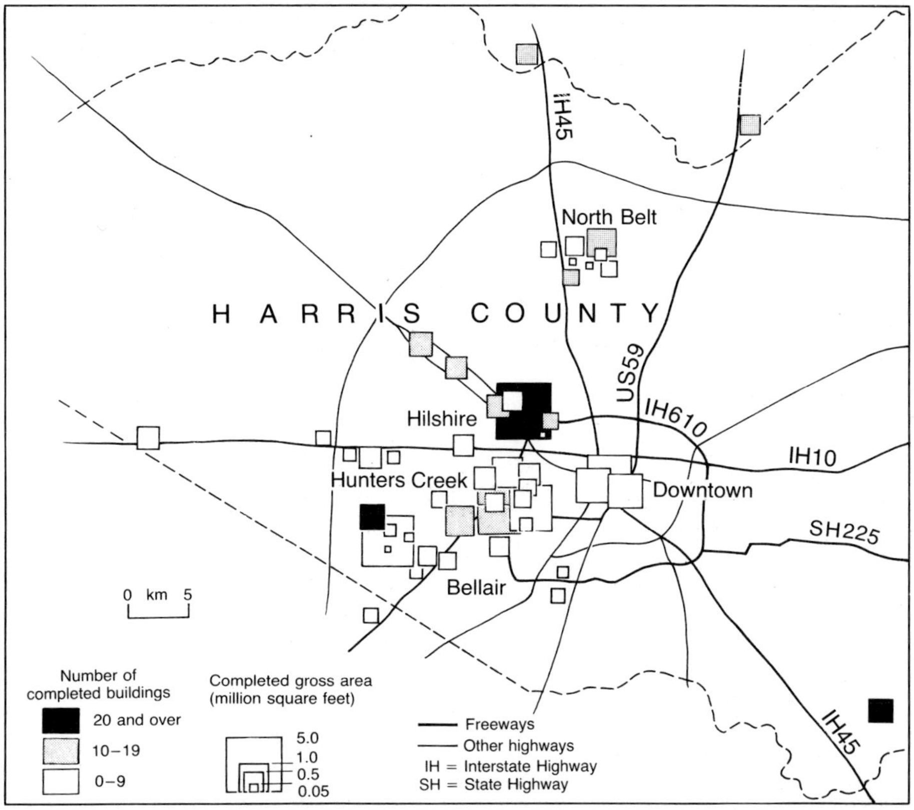


**Fig 5 The location and size of office parks in Houston.**

**Q1**
Group the following into
**(a)** producer services
**(b)** consumer services
Dentist, shopfitters, shoe shop, oil pipeline company, food and drink wholesaler, newsagent.

**Q2**
Make a list of services created by new technology in the last twenty years or so.

**Q3**
Look at Figure 4.
**(a)** Describe the spacing of central places of different sizes.
**(b)** Suggest reasons for this difference.

**Q4**
Look at Figure 3.
**(a)** How does the provision of the six services change with settlement size?
**(b)** Why does this happen?

**Q5**
Attempt to explain the distribution of office parks shown in Figure. 5.

# 9.6 California: sunbelt state

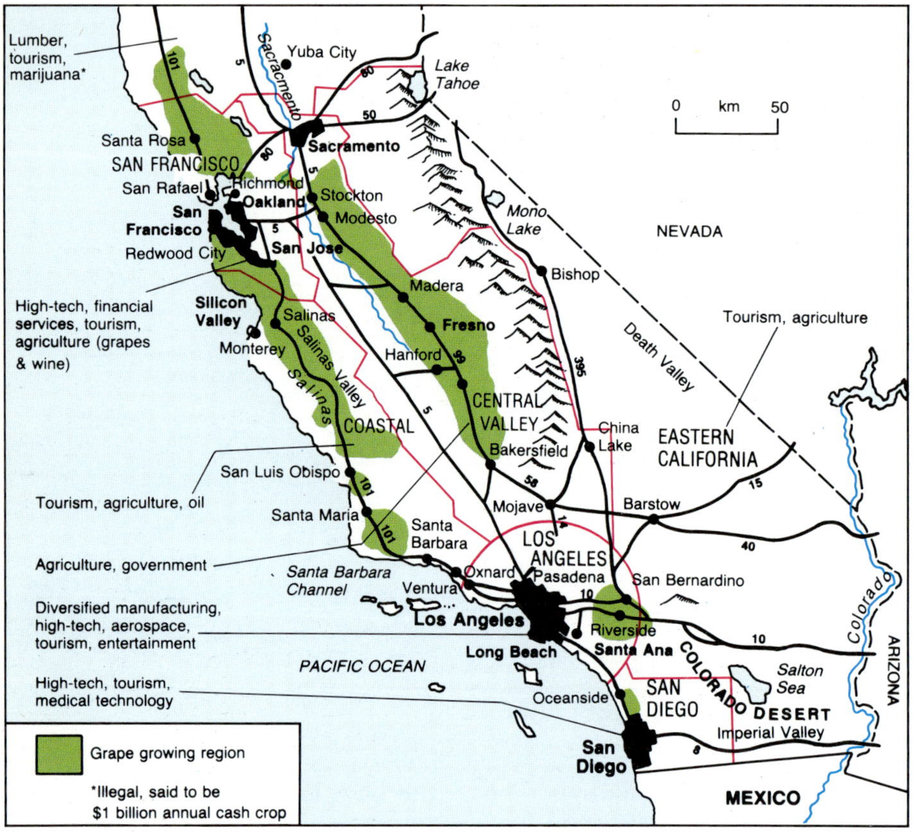


**Fig 1 Map of California showing the major activities of each region.**

## Sunbelt v frostbelt

If California was an independent country it would have the world's sixth largest gross domestic product (GDP). Its 26 million people produce about the same value of goods and services each year as Britain's 56 million. California is in the 'sunbelt' which stretches from the South Atlantic states to the Pacific coast cities of Los Angeles and San Francisco. Since the end of the Second World War (1945) the sunbelt has developed rapidly, much faster in fact than the northern states (the 'frostbelt'). The warm climate is one of a number of reasons for this (see Unit 4.4, page 16). California is the major sunbelt state in both population and wealth.

## A history of growth

The discovery of gold in 1849 set off California's first economic boom. In just two years the population rose from 10 000 to 100 000. But the gold rush did not last long. Development was then led by farming and the railways. A series of other industries have taken the lead since (Figure 2). The big one today is microelectronics. Some experts believe that biotechnology will be the next leader. The key to California's continuing success has been the ability of new industries to take over from, and grow out of, older ones.

**Fig 2 The leading California industries, from 1849 to 2000.**

| | |
|---|---|
| 1849 | Gold mining |
| | Farming |
| | Railways |
| 1900 | Oil |
| 1920 | Movies |
| 1930 | Construction |
| 1940 | Defence |
| | Aerospace |
| 1970 | Microelectronics |
| 2000 | Biotechnology? |

## A wider industrial base

California has a wide variety of industry. This is a big advantage. If some industries decline people can seek other employment.

California's high technology is world famous. However, many more people work in lower technology industries such as food processing, clothing and furniture manufacture. These industries use technology that has been developed for some time (although most take on some aspects of new technology as well). Their growth is not spectacular, but it does benefit from sales to the largest market in the USA. In some older industries, however, many jobs have been lost. For example, in the 1970s California had five car assembly plants. Only one remains today.

## Microelectronics

Most firms are located in two areas:

- The Los Angeles basin (250 000 employees)
- The Santa Clara valley, south of San Francisco (200 000

**Fig 3 High tech industry: Silicon Valley, California.**

Fig 4 Production line showing the construction of military aircraft at the Lockheed Plant, California.

employees). This area is known as Silicon Valley. Microelectronics firms here are concentrated in a much smaller area than in the Los Angeles basin.

The expertise of Stanford University was the main reason for the development of the industry in Silicon Valley. It is one of the most advanced scientific centres in the world. The 3000 high-tech firms also benefit from years of experience gained by suppliers, subcontractors, technicians and many other services. The industry's leading products are computers and semiconductors. Software production is also developing rapidly.

Almost 30% of the USA's microelectronics production comes from California. But competition is getting sharper from other areas in North America and from abroad (particularly Japan).

## Other major industries

- **Aerospace** This is concentrated in the Los Angeles basin (Figure 4). California consistently wins over 20% of the US Defence Department's contracts for research and development and for sales. The state also wins almost half of all NASA (National Aeronautics and Space Administration) contracts.
- **Tourism** There are many attractions including national parks, major cities, scenic coastline and the state's heritage. Expenditure on tourism in California in 1984 was $26 billion.
- **Agriculture** A great variety of products originate here, led by dairy products, cattle, cotton and grapes. The total value of agricultural production is by far the highest in the USA.
- **Oil** This led the state's economy early in the century. Recent large discoveries offshore have greatly increased the value of production again (Figure 5).

Fig 5 Offshore oil rigs, Santa Barbara, California.

## The problems of growth

Rapid economic development has many benefits but it can also bring problems. In California some of the main concerns are:

- **Urban sprawl.** This is the most urbanised state in the USA with 91% of the population living in cities. The Los Angeles metropolitan area alone (11 million people) covers over 88,000 square kilometres. Farmland is being lost in many areas as cities continue to spread rapidly.
- **Water supply.** Precipitation in southern California is low. Water transfer systems bring water to cities and farms from the Colorado river, the foothills of the Sierra Nevada mountains and from northern California. The high demand for water is now almost equal to the available supply.
- **Pollution.** There are so many cars on Los Angeles' highways that air pollution is a serious problem. Huge amounts of fertilizers and pesticides seep from farmland into streams. Pollution of the coastline has increased as the offshore oil industry grows.
- **The cost of living.** In 1983 the average price of a house in California was $115,000, almost 40% higher than the US average.

**Q1**
Look at Figure 2.
**(a)** How many leading industries are listed?
**(b)** Which are: (i) primary, (ii) secondary, (iii) tertiary, (iv) quaternary?
**(c)** Suggest why no one industry has remained dominant for very long.

**Q2**
**(a)** Make separate lists of the benefits and the costs of economic growth to the people of California.
**(b)** Suggest how the problems of growth might be tackled.

# 9.7 Multinational companies

## Ford: a world giant

The Ford Motor Company is a huge worldwide business. It employs almost 400 000 people in over a hundred countries. Its HQ is in Dearborn, Michigan. This is where it all began. The company was formed in 1903, seven years after Henry Ford built his first car. Ford Motors grew rapidly and its first assembly plant outside North America was opened in Britain in 1911. This was just the start of a spread around the world.

In 1984 Ford sold 5.7 million vehicles worldwide. Its Escort was the best-selling car for the fourth year in a row. Manufacturing takes place in the USA, Argentina, Australia, Belgium, Brazil, Canada, Britain, France, Germany, Mexico, The Philippines, South Africa, Spain, Taiwan and Venezuela. Also there are assembly plants in Malaysia, New Zealand, Portugal, Singapore, South Korea and Thailand. It's not surprising then, that Ford is the second largest industrial corporation in the world (Figure 1). All the other companies listed are also transnationals, that is, they operate in more than one country.

Michigan is the centre of the Ford empire in North America. It has 33 of Ford's 57 manufacturing plants and six of the twenty Ford assembly plants in the USA. Ford's main factory is at Rouge, Dearborn. Occupying 1200 acres it's the world's largest single industrial site. All the company's Canadian operations are in southern Ontario. The interests of Ford are not confined to motor vehicles. Ford companies are also established in financing, insurance, electronics, communication and space technology. Many transnational companies have wide business interests like this.

**Fig 2 One of the Ford Motor Company's 20 US assembly plants.**

**Fig 1 The world's twenty largest industrial corporations (1988).**

| Rank | Company | Headquarters | Industry | Sales ($) millions |
|---|---|---|---|---|
| 1 | General Motors | Detroit | Motor Vehicles | 121 085 |
| 2 | Ford Motor | Dearborn, Mich. | Motor Vehicles | 92 445 |
| 3 | Exxon | New York | Petroleum refining | 79 557 |
| 4 | Royal Dutch/Shell Group | London/The Hague | Petroleum refining | 78 381 |
| 5 | International Business Machines | Armonk, N.Y. | Computers | 59 681 |
| 6 | Toyota Motor | Toyota City (Japan) | Motor vehicles | 50 789 |
| 7 | General Electric | Fairfield, Conn. | Electronics | 49 414 |
| 8 | Mobil | New York | Petroleum refining | 48 198 |
| 9 | British Petroleum | London | Petroleum refining | 46 174 |
| 10 | Iri | Rome | Metals | 45 521 |
| 11 | Daimler-Benz | Stuttgart | Motor Vehicles | 41 817 |
| 12 | Hitachi | Tokyo | Electronics | 41 330 |
| 13 | Chrysler | Highland Park, Mich. | Motor Vehicles | 35 472 |
| 14 | Siemens | Munich | Electronics | 34 129 |
| 15 | Fiat | Turin | Motor Vehicles | 34 039 |
| 16 | Matsushita Electric Industrial | Osaka | Electronics | 33 922 |
| 17 | Volkswagen | Wolfsburg (W. Ger.) | Motor Vehicles | 33 696 |
| 18 | Texaco | White Plains, N.Y. | Petroleum refining | 33 544 |
| 19 | E.I. Du Pont De Nemours | Wilmington, DEL. | Chemicals | 32 514 |
| 20 | Unilever | London/Rotterdam | Food | 30 488 |

## How popular are the multinationals?

Between 1980 and 1984 Ford invested almost $14 000 million worldwide on new products, processes, machinery and equipment and another $9000 million on research and engineering development. Foreign governments usually welcome large companies like Ford. It can mean jobs for many people. In 1984 Ford of Britain paid £606 million in wages to its

**Fig 3 Ford has manufacturing or assembly plants in these Asian countries.**

| Country | Gross National Product 1986 ($) millions |
|---|---|
| Thailand | 42 606 |
| South Korea | 98 355 |
| Taiwan | 46 831 (GDP 1982) |
| Malaysia | 29 463 |
| Singapore | 19,266 |
| Philippines | 32,088 |

**Fig 4 Foreign investment by US companies. Investment in the US by foreign companies.**

employees. In addition, it spent almost £1500 million with British suppliers of materials, components and services. Many of the cars made in Britain are sold abroad. This helps Britain's balance of payments.

However, governments and trade unions are concerned at the way that production and investment can be quickly moved from one country to another. Transnational companies look closely at the differences between countries in:

- The cost of labour
- The productivity of the workforce
- Currency exchange rates
- Government incentives to manufacturers
- Environmental regulations.

Ford's British car workers have been accused of being less efficient than workers in other countries. The unions deny this vigorously. Nevertheless, at Ford's huge Dagenham works the workforce has been cut from 25 000 in 1978 to 13 000 in 1985 (because of both automation and greater investment elsewhere). In contrast, Ford's workforce in Spain has increased. Wages there are considerably lower. Ford is now expanding car production in the countries of the South. Wages here are much lower still and there is little trade union organisation.

## The world car

Whole cars are now rarely built in just one country. Different parts are made where production is cheapest. These are then sent to a Ford plant elsewhere in the world to be assembled. This is the age of the 'world car' which can be made almost anywhere. This gives Ford great power. In Ford's Asian operations no one country has a monopoly on any aspect of production. Each process is duplicated at least once.

## Returning home

American transnationals' share of overseas investment around the world is falling. A number of large US companies have sold assets overseas. At the same time, they have increased their investment in the USA. In 1965 US companies accounted for over 65% of overseas worldwide investment. Their share is now below 50%. There are a number of reasons why many American companies are now concentrating more on the US market. These include:

- The fall in the value of the dollar against other currencies, which has made overseas investment more expensive.
- American tax reform has made the US market generally more profitable than overseas markets.
- The fear that foreign competitors will grab too large a share of business in the USA.

**Fig 5 Foreign investment: the development centre in Merkenich, West Germany.**

**Q1**
**(a)** In how many countries does Ford have (i) manufacturing plants, (ii) assembly plants?
**(b)** What is the difference between a manufacturing plant and an assembly plant?
**(c)** Why does Ford have factories in so many other countries?
**(d)** Suggest why no one country is ever given a monopoly over one aspect of production in the Ford empire.

**Q2**
**(a)** In which continents are the headquarters of the world's twenty largest industrial companies?
**(b)** Suggest reasons for this pattern of location.

**Q3**
**(a)** Ford has factories in six Asian countries. Compare the GNP of these countries with the Ford Company's annual sales.
**(b)** Ford's decision to build factories in Asia was welcomed by the governments of these countries. Explain why.

**Q4**
**(a)** What does Figure 4 tell you?
**(b)** Suggest reasons for the trends shown.

**Q5**
Why are trade unions concerned about the power of multinational companies?

# 9.8 The environmental impact of industry in Ontario

## Dirty water

The pollution problem in Ontario is causing public concern. The editorial in the Toronto Star (Figure 1) shows why. Southern Ontario has Canada's greatest concentration of manufacturing industry. On the American side of the Great Lakes is another line of industrial cities. This high level of factory development has had many benefits but the impact on the environment has been considerable. Until recently many decision-makers chose to ignore the environmental costs of economic growth. But as pollution affects people's lives more directly (Figure 2) the call for action gets louder.

**'Mind-blowing' pollution report**

It's disturbing to think that nearly half of Ontario's major industries could contaminate the Great Lakes and the St. Lawrence River in violation of pollution control standards that they themselves negotiated with the province. Yet that's what has been happening in Ontario for years. A provincial survey found that 45 of 103 major industries were in 'non-compliance' with their agreed-upon pollution limits in 1984.

The levels of non-compliance are — as one American source suggests — 'mind-blowing.'

One company, for example, was found to be discharging nearly 19 kilograms (42 pounds) of lead into the St. Lawrence River a day — almost double the company's prescribed limit of 10 kilograms (22 pounds).

Another company was reported to be discharging nearly 10 tonnes of sulphuric acid *a day* into the river. The company's sewer water was so polluted that, in tests, it killed fish within five minutes of exposure.

What's worse, the ineffectiveness of pollution controls revealed in the report of this survey should come as no surprise. The information contained in the report is provided annually by the province to the International Joint Commission responsible for monitoring the Great Lakes. Its findings are, therefore, merely the latest in a string of horror stories.

Enough is enough. The pollution can't be wished away. Sooner or later, society pays the price — in dead wildlife, filthy water and threats to human health.

**Fig 1 An extract from the *Toronto Star*, 26th July 1986.**

**POLLUTED WEST BEACHES STILL CLOSED**

Metropolitan Toronto's western beaches will be off-limits to swimmers until the middle of next week. Last weekend's heavy storm caused raw sewage to discharge directly from the Humber River treatment plant into Lake Ontario. Readings near the mouth of the Humber showed a high fecal coliform count of 3178 per 100 millimetres of water. The acceptable limit is 100 fecal coliform per 100 millimetres. For up-to-date details, swimmers should call the city's Beaches Hotline at 392–7161.

**Fig 2 An extract from the *Toronto Star*, 26th July 1986.**

An Ontario Environment Ministry report highlighted a number of industries which create pollution, including:

- Paper mills: most failed to comply with limits set for oxygen-eating pollutants which threaten aquatic life.
- Steel works: a trend of decreasing outflowing water quality since 1983.
- Petroleum industry: increases in the total loads of solid pollutants, oil and grease.
- Motor industry: discharging a high level of harmful pollutants in Lake Ontario.

The province intends to strengthen its water pollution laws. The problem will not be easy to solve. An estimated 1000 chemicals are now polluting the Great Lakes from sources on both sides of the border. Much stronger joint action by the USA and Canada is needed to really improve water quality.

## Air pollution

More positive action has already been taken against air pollution. In 1968 the Ontario government assumed responsibility for air quality in the province. Since then, industry has had to spend more than C$3 billion reducing the air pollution it causes. Minimum air quality standards have been set for more than 160 pollutants. Some of these are the strictest in North America. There are 1400 air quality and precipitation monitoring instruments across the province.

Ontario operates an Air Pollution Index (API). Its job is to warn about and to prevent heavy air pollution. Weather conditions are important. The Ministry can order the reduction of factory operations which cause high pollution when weather conditions encourage the build-up of pollution. Since API began in 1970, the number of occasions on which the index has exceeded the advisory level of 32 has dropped from nineteen to three times per

**Fig 3 An extract from the *Toronto Star*, 26th July 1986.**

**OFFICIALS PROBE VAPOUR LEAK**

The Ontario environment ministry is investigating the cause of a "potentially hazardous" vapour cloud that leaked from the Polysar Ltd plant in Corunna. The cloud of butane and propane escaped into the atmosphere on Wednesday from an underground storage system, but did not drift beyond the company's property. Polysar officials said the cloud was dispersed by firefighters.

## Acid Rain Watch

A severely acidic rainfall Thursday from the Ohio industrial belt, with a pH level of 3.7, was fortunately a light one of 1 millimetre. A big rainfall of 30 millimetres last Saturday from Duluth had a relatively cleaner pH level of 4.6, according to the acid rain centre in Dorset, Muskoka, 185 kilometres (115 miles) north of downtown Toronto.

The lower the pH reading the more serious the acid content. Readings below pH 4.7 often indicate environmental damage, those below 4.0 a danger to plants and animals.

**Fig 4 The daily Acid Rain Report from the *Toronto Star*, 9th August, 1986.**

**Fig 5 Pollution has many sources such as this super stack at Sudbury.**

year in Toronto. A new air quality telemetry system is being established that will allow the index to be made public in twenty cities across the province. Since 1970 the level of sulphur dioxide in downtown Toronto has been reduced by 94%. Carbon monoxide is down by 56%. Suspended particulates and lead levels are also well down.

Acid deposition is carefully monitored. Regular reports appear in daily newspapers alongside the weather forecast (Figure 4). The province has reduced its own emissions of the pollutants that form acid rain. However, much of Ontario's acid rain comes from the USA. So far, co-operation between the USA and Canada on the acid rain problem has been limited.

## Hazardous waste dumps

There is also a land pollution problem. Hazardous chemical wastes have been dumped at a number of sites across Ontario. Some have long since been abandoned. Less attention has been given to this problem compared to air and water pollution although recently regulations on hazardous waste dumping have been improved.

## A continental problem

Pollution has affected the environment all over North America. In some regions conditions are much worse than in Ontario. Pollution is a big influence on the quality of life. Poeple want to have clean air, water and land. But most people also want a share of the wealth that industry creates. What is needed is a sensible balance between these two goals.

### Q1

**(a)** Write to the Letters Column of the Toronto Star giving your views on the four extracts from this newspaper.
**(b)** Scan your own local and national newspapers for a week for articles about pollution. Put up a class display.

### Q2

How successful has Ontario been in combating air pollution?

### Q3

Look at Figure 6.
**(a)** How does public concern vary between the USA, the EEC and Japan about the different types of pollution?
**(b)** Sugest reasons for the differences in concern.

**Fig 6 Recent public opinion polls demonstrate concern about local, national and global environmental problems.**

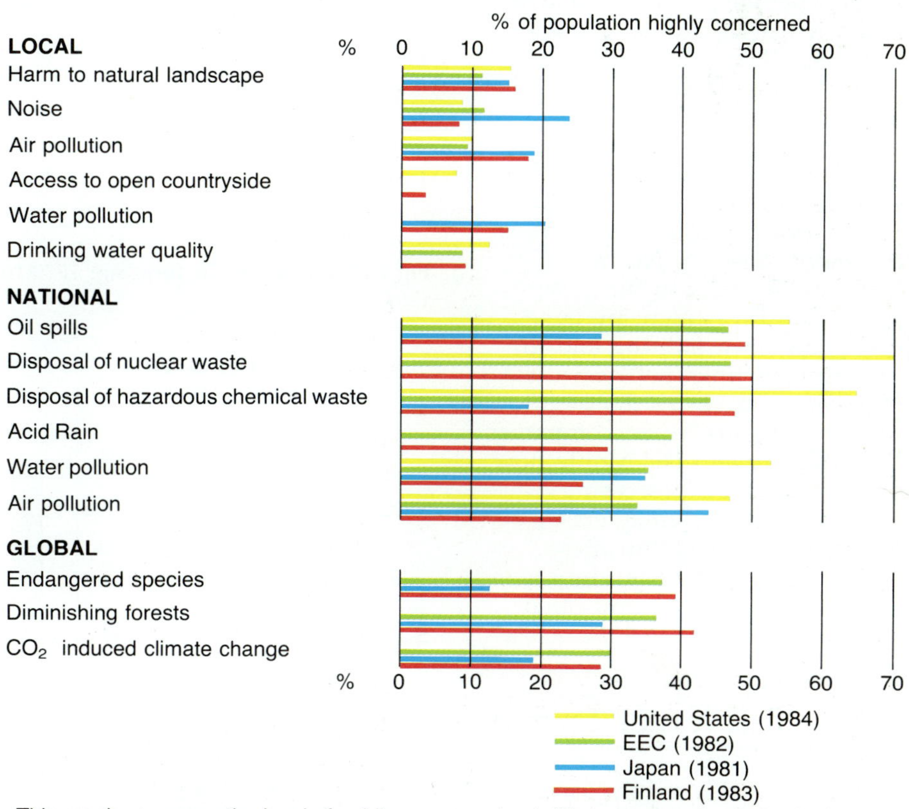


This graph compares the level of public concern about different types of pollution in the USA, the EEC and Japan. The graph is not complete for all types of pollution because the opinion polls were not exactly similar.

# 10. Agriculture

# 10.1 Challenge and change

**Fig 1 The food industry, from farm to supermarket: (a) irrigating wheat, Oregon; (b) cheese production, Oregon; (c) supermarket, Canada.**

Agriculture in North America is big business. The continent not only feeds itself but also exports much food abroad. Almost seven million people live on over two and a half million farms. They produce a fantastic variety of crops and livestock. This is possible because of the large areas of favourable climate, relief and soil and a very high level of investment.

The term 'agribusiness' is now commonly used in North America. It refers to the increasing investment by large corporations in farming and to the stronger links between the three main stages of the food industry (Figure 1). So companies like Safeway and Del Monte now own farms, food processing factories and supermarkets. Another part of agribusiness supplies farms with machinery, fertilizers, pesticides and other needs.

## Fewer but larger farms

In 1935 there were 6.8 million farms in the USA. By 1984 there were only 2.4 million, although average farm size has increased (Figure 2). Income from smaller farms is often low and very changeable. Although small farmers often have other jobs, many have been forced to sell up. Larger farms are generally more efficient. They are better able to cope with the uncertainties of farming such as poor harvests and changing food prices.

**Fig 2 The changes in farming: 1950 to 1984.**

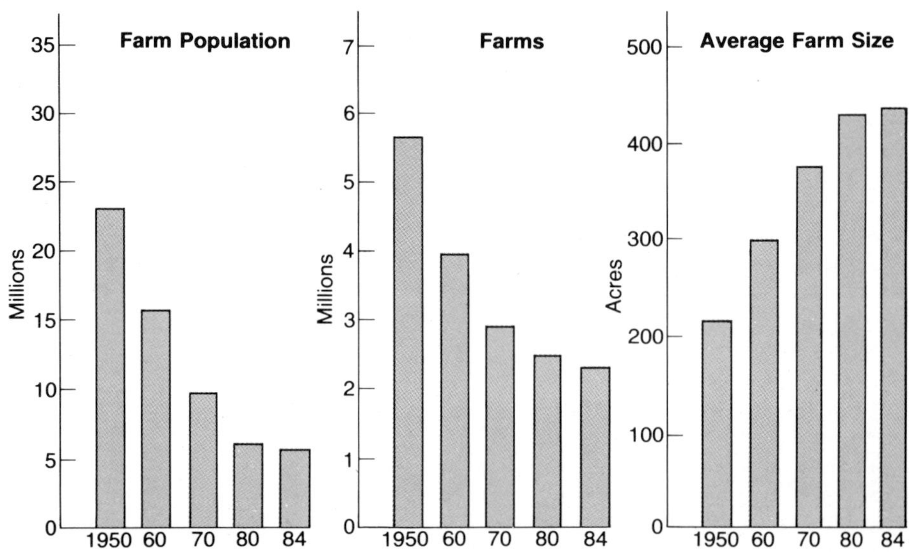


## Capital intensive farming

Labour accounted for half the cost of running a typical farm before 1940. By 1985 it was down to 12%. Giant machinery allows a single family to run a 1000 acre farm producing $400 000 worth of food a year. Use of fertilizers has greatly increased (Figure 3). Yields per agricultural worker are over seven times the average for Western Europe. In the USA the average yield of maize (corn) rose from 40 bushels per acre in 1939 to 113 bushels per acre in 1982. Highly mechanised cultivation on large farms results in huge production totals of major crops.

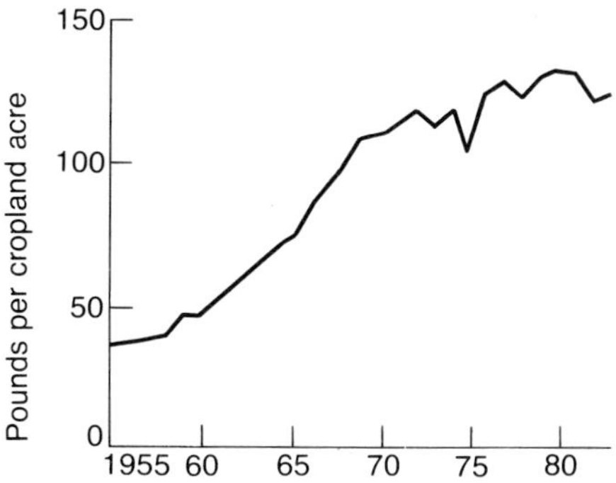


**Fig 3 The quantity of fertilizer nutrients used on cropland in the USA.**

## Competition for land

Agriculture covers a larger area than any other land use in North America. In many places it is the only profitable way to use the land. However, in some places competition for the use of land for other purposes is intense. It is greatest close to urban areas where the value of land is high. Between 1950 and 1980 in the USA over 1.2 million hectares of farmland was taken for urban development. Farmland can also face competition in rural areas.

## The debt problem

By the end of 1984 US farmers owed £190 billion, much of it to small agricultural banks. This was more than the combined foreign debts of Brazil and Mexico. The problem began in the boom years of the early 1970s. Then the USA's food exports rose rapidly. The USSR was the biggest customer. Land under the plough in the USA rose from 290 million acres to over 350 million acres between 1973 and 1980. Farmers borrowed heavily to buy more land and equipment. Land values rose sharply ($300 an acre in 1970; $1700 in 1981). Food exports fell as production continued to rise. As a result, crop prices dropped but interest payments on loans remained high. The farming community was hit badly (Figure 4). In 1983 alone nearly 13 000 farmers lost their farms. Other sectors of the agricultural industry were also affected. For example, the number of people employed in manufacturing farm equipment fell from 160 000 in 1979 to 90 000 in 1984.

**DESPAIR GROWS IN THE GRAIN BELT**

Despair is running deep across the Mid-Western grain belt, the most productive agricultural land in the world. Hundreds of thousands of farmers are in deep financial trouble. They are facing their worst economic crisis since the depression. Many of the farms will not survive.

The most severe financial crisis is being acutely felt by the 700 000 full-time family farmers who grow between $50 000 and $200 000 worth of produce a year on medium-sized farms of between 400 and 800 acres.

About a third of them are so deeply in debt that bankruptcy is a real possibility. They have difficulty in paying interest on their loans, and may have to give up their farms. Mid-Western newspapers are full of notices of farm sales and foreclosures. Despairing farmers, stretched to their credit limit, no longer able to borrow enough money to stay in business, are becoming severely depressed and breaking under the strain. Alcoholism and suicide rates are rising in the rural areas. And so is violence.

As farmers give up their land, rural towns which depend on them are facing crisis. Shops are going out of business, schools are closing. Young people are seeking work elsewhere, leaving a disproportionate number of elderly people in the towns.

**Fig 4 An extract from *The Times*, 6th November 1985.**

## Tackling overproduction

The USA produces much more than it can sell of some types of food. The Food Security Act (the 'farm bill') offers cash payments to reduce these types of farming. For example:

- Dairy farmers are compensated if they halt milk production for at least five years.
- Farms taking 25% of their cotton acreage out of production receive compensation. This reduced cotton acreage in California by 20% between 1985 and 1986.

There are similar compensation payments for a range of other surplus products.

**Q1**
Suggest why companies like Safeway own businesses in all three major stages of the food industry.

**Q2**
Look at Figure 2.
**(a)** Summarise the changes it shows.
**(b)** Give reasons for these changes.

**Q3**
Draw a table to show how the use of fertilizer has increased in the USA since 1955.

**Q4**
Look at Figure 4. How has the debt problem on farms affected rural areas in general?

**Q5**
What might happen in the future if adequate preventative measures are not taken now to combat soil erosion?

## Soil erosion

This is one of the major problems facing farmers. Average soil erosion on cropland in the USA was estimated at 3 metric tons per hectare in 1982. Forty four per cent of cropland is eroding above tolerance rates that will enable sustained, high level production in the future. As the cultivated area expanded in the 1970s much marginal land was ploughed up. This made it particularly vulnerable to erosion. Now that there is overproduction of a number of major crops a chance exists to tackle this serious problem. Many soil experts say that much more needs to be done to protect the USA's soil for the future.

# 10.2 Regions and systems

## Factors affecting farming

North America has many different physical environments. This allows a wide variety of crops to be grown and livestock kept. New technology and high investment has steadily extended farming into more difficult environments. For example, irrigation has enabled farming to flourish in the arid west while new varieties of wheat have pushed production northward into Canada. However, the physical environment remains a big influence on farming. There are certain things that technology and investment can do little to alter. So relief, climate and soils set broad limits as to what can be produced. This leaves the farmer with some choices even in difficult environments. The farmer's decisions are then influenced by:

- **Economic factors.** (a) The cost of growing different crops or keeping different livestock varies. Market prices will vary also and can change from year to year. (b) The necessary investment in buildings and machinery can mean that some changes in farming activities are very expensive. These would be more difficult to achieve than other, cheaper changes.

- **Political factors.** The influence of government has steadily increased. In the USA the main parts of federal farm policy are (a) **Price-support loans**: loans which tide farmers over until they sell their produce. The government sets a price for each farm product that it is willing to support, i.e. $3.30 a bushel for wheat. If a farmer cannot sell the wheat for at least this price, he/she can keep the loan and let the government keep the crop that secured it. (b) **Production controls**: these limit how much a farmer can produce of surplus crops, such as peanuts and tobacco. Farmers lose price-support loans and other benefits if they don't comply. (c) **Income supplements**: these are cash payments to farmers for major crops in years when market prices fail to reach certain levels.

- **Social/cultural factors** include what the farm and neighbouring farms have produced in the past. There is a tendency for farmers to stay with what they know best.

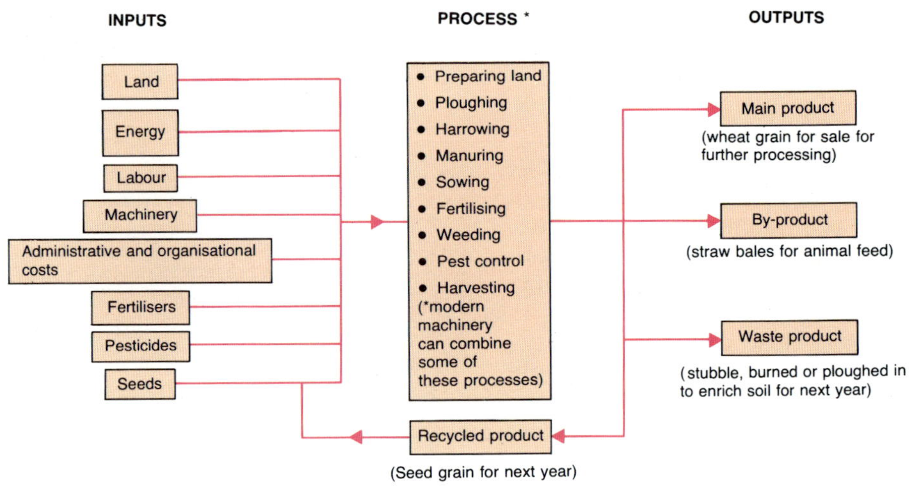


**Fig 1 An input-process-output diagram for a wheat farm.**

## Systems

A farm operates as a system (Figure 1). It requires a range of inputs so that the processes of farming can be carried out. The aim is to produce the best possible outputs. A profit will only be made if the income from selling all or part of the outputs is greater than expenditure on the inputs and processes.

## Farming regions in the USA

Although major farming zones are not as specialised as earlier in this century, different farming regions can still be identified. In the USA these include:

- **The dairying (and hay) belt.** Cool summers and long severe winters made grain growing impractical here. Dairying was the obvious alternative because of (a) the cultural traditions of the German, Swiss, Scandinavian and Dutch farmers who settled here, (b) the great cities of the north that provided a large market for dairy products.

- **The corn and livestock belt.** Corn needs a growing season of at least 130 days. For the crop to ripen properly, high summer temperatures of 21°C are needed along with warm

**Fig 2 A dairy farm in Minnesota.**

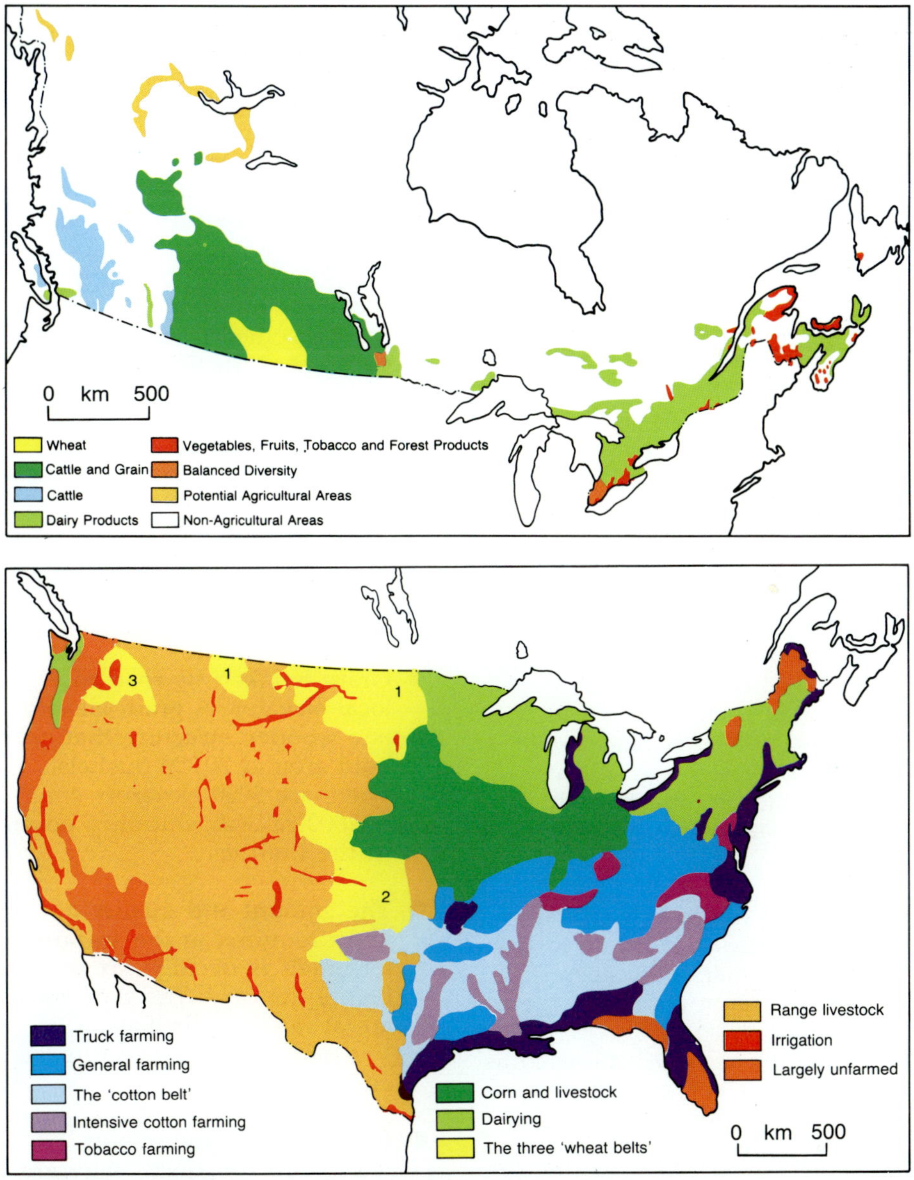


**Fig 3 The agricultural regions of Canada and the USA.**

nights. Precipitation should be over 500 mm with at least 200 mm in the three summer months. This is an area of mixed farming.

- **The wheat belts.** Wheat dominates the High Plains with winter wheat in the south and spring wheat in the Dakotas. Wheat is grown farther west than other grain crops because it can tolerate drier conditions. However, the risk of crop failure is greater in the wheat belts than in almost every other region.

**Fig 4 Harvesting soya in the USA.**

- **Ranching.** This is the most important type of farming within the area from the drier parts of the High Plains, across the mountain states, into the poorer agricultural areas of the Pacific division. Cattle are the main source of farm income in thirteen of the seventeen states (not including Alaska and Hawaii) west of Wisconsin.

- **The cotton belt.** Cotton needs a frost-free period of at least 200 days. Rainfall should be over 625 mm a year with not more than 250 mm in the autumn harvest season. Cotton production is now highly mechanised. Irrigation has allowed cotton to flourish in the drier western states of California, New Mexico and Texas. In contrast, cotton acreage has fallen considerably in the South. A crop pest called the cotton boll weevil, which caused great destruction to cotton crops in the past, has been a big factor in the diversification of agriculture in the southern states.

## Canada

Farming in Canada is severely restricted by climate. Less than 8% of the total area of the country is farmed. Seventy per cent of Canada lies north of the thermal limit for crop growth and most farms are within 500 kilometres of the US border. The largest of Canada's agricultural regions, with over three-quarters of all farmland (Figure 3), is in the southern Prairies (Alberta, Saskatchewan, Manitoba). Canada's highest quality farmland is in south-western Ontario.

**Q1**
Look at Figure 1. Now try to draw an input-process-output diagram for a dairy farm.

**Q2**
**(a)** Why is almost all of the USA's range livestock and irrigated farming in the west?
**(b)** On a copy of Figure 3 (USA) draw a line from Lake Superior to the Gulf Coast. How and why does farming change along this line?

**Q3**
**(a)** Describe the pattern of farming in Canada.
**(b)** Why is so much of the country unfarmed?

# 10.3 The Prairies

## Extensive farming

Three-quarters of Canada's farmland lies in the Prairie provinces of Alberta, Saskatchewan and Manitoba. It is an area of 'extensive' farming. Here, farms averaging 300 hectares in size stretch for almost 1500 kilometres from east to west. Two or three workers can run a farm by using a range of modern machinery. This contrasts with intensive farming, for example, fruit and vegetable growing in southern Ontario. Here there is a higher investment per hectare on smaller farms of 30–40 hectares. So labour, fertilizer and other inputs per hectare are much greater. Because there is much less farmland in southern Ontario farmers have decided to use it in a different way.

The hot, dry summers of the Prairies favour wheat. Feed grains (oats, rye, barley and corn) are also grown. There are dairy and livestock farms scattered throughout the region. Cattle ranching predominates in southern Alberta, where the Rocky Mountains produce a rain shadow and very dry conditions.

**Fig 1 Grain harvesting on the Prairies.**

Oilseed crops – rapeseed, flax and sunflowers – have also become important in recent years.

## Wheat still number one

Wheat was first grown here in the early 1600s. Since then many changes have occurred:

- The family farm has grown from a few hand-worked hectares to a large, highly mechanised unit (Figure 1).
- New strains of wheat can withstand colder temperatures and a shorter growing season. This is twenty days less than in the early 19th century.
- Today's wheat is resistant to many diseases (e.g. wheat streak mosaic disease) which once destroyed huge areas of crops.
- Inputs of fertilizer, herbicides and pesticides continue to rise. Prairie farmers now spend over $1 billion a year on them.
- Ploughing is now little used as it increases soil erosion by making the topsoil more likely to drift. Instead, cultivators cut weeds below the surface without turning the soil.
- A modern combine harvester allows one person to harvest more than 2000 bushels a day. Farmers now spend 10–15% of their income on machinery and equipment, including repairs.

## Transport to markets

Most of the food produced on Prairie farms is sold in other parts of Canada or abroad (Figure 2). The transport of grains, for example, has a set routine:

- Grain is taken by road to a local elevator. A grain elevator is a wooden structure that can hold around 70 000 bushels. There are 5000 elevators sited at 2000 railway shipping points in the Prairies.
- The amount and quality of grain required at the shipping terminals is decided six weeks before delivery. The terminals are at (a) Thunder Bay (b) Vancouver and Prince Rupert, and (c) Churchill.
- Elevator managers report weekly on the stocks they are holding.
- Shipping instructions are issued on the basis of the 48 loading zones in the Prairies.
- Trains pick up grain and deliver to port. Here it is either loaded on ship or placed in the huge terminal storage elevators.

## Soil erosion

Severe droughts in 1984 and 1985 in part of the Prairies had a great impact. Many farmers in southern Alberta suffered financial hardship through losing part or all of their crops. However, the long-term problem is even more serious, that of soil erosion

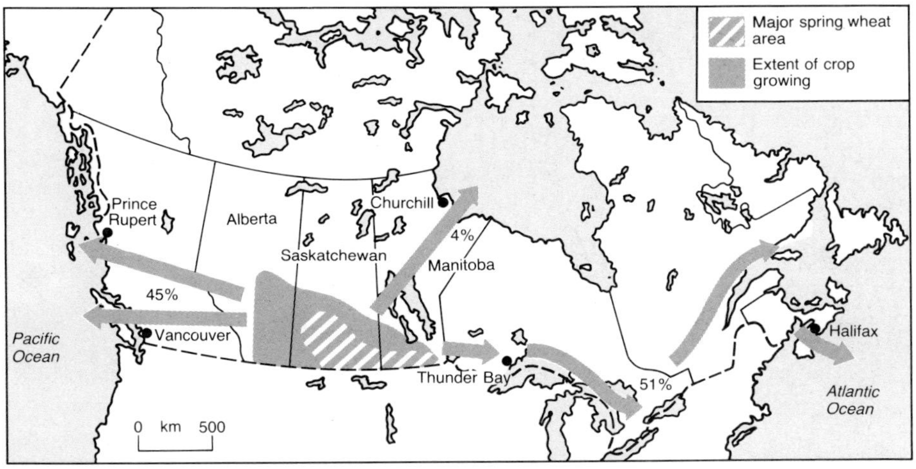


**Fig 2 The Prairies: grain export routes.**

**Fig 3 Map of Alberta and Saskatchewan showing the areas in danger of wind erosion, estimated to be a total of 60 million acres.**

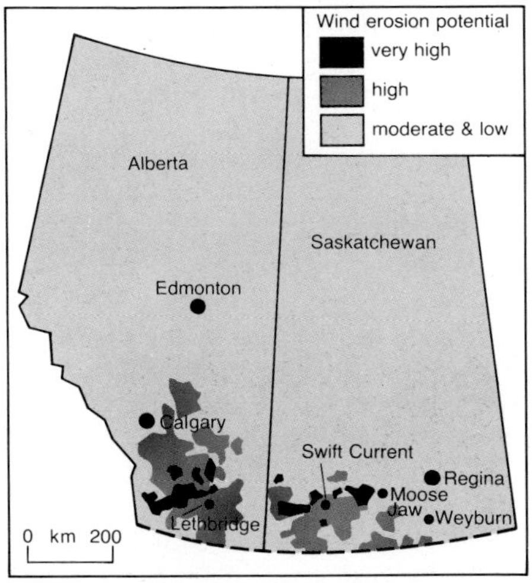


(Figure 3). In 1986 Alberta classed 3.4 million hectares of farmland at 'high' or 'very high' risk from wind erosion. Another 12 million hectares in Alberta were classed as 'vulnerable'. In Saskatchewan the problem is almost as serious. In just one windy day 7.5 million tonnes of topsoil blew off 60 000 hectares in southern Alberta. In the worst affected areas five to six centimetres of topsoil was lost between 1984–86. But it takes 25–30 years for nature to replace 2.5 centimetres of lost earth. Prairie farmers try to protect the soil by:

- **Crop-fallow rotation.** Fields are left fallow every other year to replenish soil moisture. The crop stubble is left to further reduce the effect of the wind.
- **Ripping.** A Caterpillar tractor is used in winter to cut the frozen soil and knurl it into one-third of a metre chunks. These chunks break the effect of the wind close to the soil surface.
- **Strip farming.** The farmer leaves narrow strips of fallow land, perpendicular to the prevailing wind, between seeded fields.
- **Irrigation.** While some of the dry areas of the Prairies have good irrigation systems, others are not so lucky. Dry soil crumbles into fine particles which are easily picked up by the wind.

## Export competition

Export sales of wheat are important to Prairie farmers. Without exports farm incomes would fall. There is great competition between sellers on the world food market. The USA is Canada's biggest competitor in exporting wheat. This has caused argument between the two countries. Both give subsidies to grain farmers. The subsidy is larger in the USA. In 1986 Canadian wheat farmers got C$3.50 a bushel for their produce while US farmers got C$6 a bushel. Higher subsidies in the USA allowed the Americans to sell wheat at a cheaper rate to the USSR and other buyers. Canadian farmers say this is deliberate price undercutting and is very unfair. The issue is being discussed between the two governments.

**Q1**
Give three differences between extensive and intensive farming in Canada.

**Q2**
Describe three ways in which Prairie farming has changed.

**Q3**
**(a)** How far are each of the grain shipping terminals from Regina?
**(b)** Suggest reasons for these different locations.

**Q4**
**(a)** Describe the distribution of the farmland in the Prairies which is most in danger of wind erosion.
**(b)** How bad is the situation in the worst affected areas?
**(c)** What can farmers do to reduce wind erosion?

**Fig 4 Soil erosion in the Prairies.**

# 10.4 Cotton in the USA

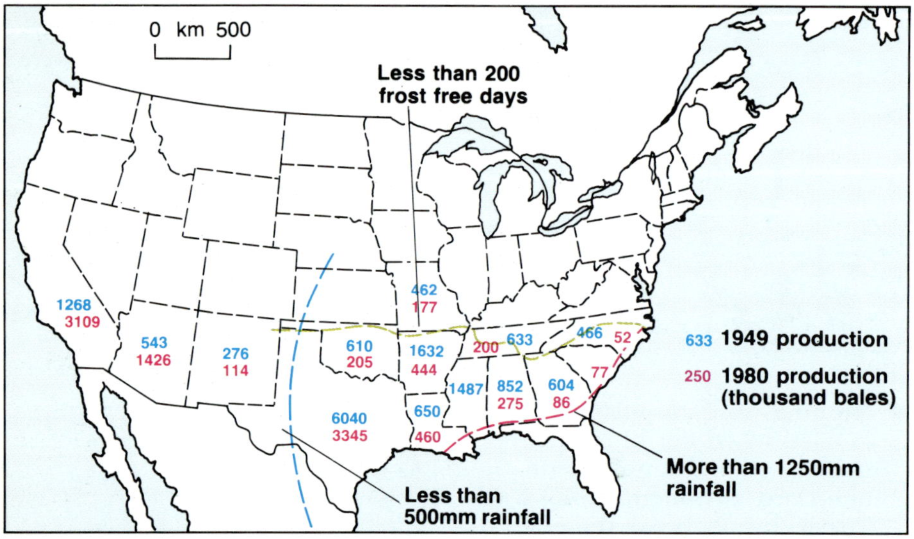


**Fig 1 The physical limits of cotton production (without irrigation) and production figures for 1949 and 1980 (thousands of bales).**

## Physical requirements

Cotton, like all crops, will only grow in certain conditions. Its northern limit is roughly the 25°C July isotherm (Figure 1). Farther north it cannot get the 200 frost-free days it needs. To the south it is confined to where autumn rainfall exceeds 250 mm. So cotton will not grow well along the middle and eastern Gulf Coast. Cotton can grow in a wide variety of soils but needs at least 500 mm of rain each year. So the 500 mm isohyet sets the far western limit of cotton which can be grown without irrigation.

## Early development

Cotton has been grown in the south-east since early settlement. In the 1800s it became the mainstay of the region's economy. 'King Cotton' was grown on plantations, which were very large farms which grew almost nothing else. Slavery provided the large amounts of labour needed.

After slavery was abolished (1865) many plantations were split into share-crop units. Tenants gave a share of their yearly crop to the landowner as rent. Many share-croppers were former slaves who now became 'economic slaves' through the harsh terms of their agreements with the landowners.

## Westward to Texas

Cotton began to move further west on a large scale in the late 19th century. It expanded mainly in Texas's Black Waxy Prairies and High Plains. At the same time many of the traditional cotton areas were declining. The main reasons for these changes were:

- Soil exhaustion. Poor methods of cultivation had caused severe soil erosion and exhaustion.
- The boll weevil. This pest which attacks cotton spread from Mexico to the USA in 1862. It destroyed large areas of cotton fields as it moved eastward, reaching the Atlantic coast in 1921. The boll weevil thrives in moist, humid conditions. It is much less of a problem in drier Texas.
- New irrigation technology was the key to much cotton farming in Texas.
- Large farms in Texas were much more profitable than the smaller cotton farms further east.

**Fig 3 Cotton: the percentage of the crop grown to the west of Texas, 1924–1980.**

| | *Percentage* |
|---|---|
| 1924 | 0.8 |
| 1934 | 3.5 |
| 1949 | 12.9 |
| 1959 | 20.3 |
| 1969 | 21.0 |
| 1980 | 41.8 |

**Fig 2 Cotton field being irrigated by sprinklers.**

## Further west to California

In the early 1920s less than 1% of the USA's cotton was grown west of Texas (Figure 1). Now it is over 40% and all of it is irrigated. Cotton production in California is now almost as great as in Texas. In California the southern part of the San Joaquin valley is the main cotton growing area. Cotton is also grown in the Imperial Valley. This further move west has been due to:

- The low cost of irrigation water.
- Good fertile soils in the valleys where cotton is grown.
- Government price supports for cotton were fixed in relation to the smaller, less efficient cotton farms of the south-east. They provided a great incentive to the larger western growers.
- The mechanisation of cotton harvesting proved to be more difficult than for most other crops. When mechanisation was established, it further increased the efficiency of larger farms.
- Intensive cotton farming was more profitable than most of the alternatives.

## Falling demand for cotton

In the USA consumption of cotton per person dropped from 14.5 kilograms in 1945 to 7.3 kilograms in 1980. This has been due mainly to competition from synthetic fibres such as terylene and nylon. US exporters have also found the world market more competitive. Although the area planted with cotton has steadily decreased (mainly in the south-east) total production has not changed so much (Figure 6). This is due to steadily rising yields. In recent years cotton goods have regained some popularity. But the textile market remains very competitive.

**Fig 4 Cotton picker in operation in Mississippi.**

## Government controls

Cotton production in the far west would be even greater but for government intervention. Only a set acreage of cotton is allowed to be grown in the USA each year. This is done to try to avoid over-production. Western growers can only expand their cotton farms when smaller, less efficient growers in the south-east leave cotton farming and give up their acreage allotments.

**Q1**
Look at Figure 1.
**(a)** How did the location of cotton production change between 1949 and 1980?
**(b)** Identify the reasons for these changes.

**Q2**
Draw a graph to compare
**(a)** the areas harvested for the principle crops and
**(b)** the value of their harvests, in the USA in 1982.

**Q3**
Look at Figure 6. Suggest why cotton production has fallen to a much lesser extent than the area harvested.

**Q4**
How does the government control the production of cotton in the USA?

**Fig 5 Principal crops; the area harvested and the value, 1982.**

| *Crop* | *Thousand hectares* | *$ million* |
|---|---|---|
| Corn | 29 429 | 22 039 |
| Wheat | 31 541 | 9 813 |
| Soybeans | 28 103 | 12 463 |
| Hay | 24 206 | 9 479 |
| Cotton | 3 939 | 3 410 |
| Sorghums | 5 721 | 2 091 |

**Fig 6 Cotton: the production and the area harvested, 1949–1980.**

| | *1949* | *1959* | *1969* | *1980* |
|---|---|---|---|---|
| Production (millions of bales) | 16.1 | 14.6 | 10.0 | 11.1 |
| Area harvested (millions of hectares) | 11.0 | 6.1 | 4.5 | 5.3 |

# 10.5 California: an agricultural giant

## Number one farming state

If California were a country it would be the world's seventh major food producer. In 1985 its farm produce was worth a staggering $13.9 billion. This was 45% more than Iowa, the next biggest farming state in the USA. Farms in California are generally large. In 1982 2400 Californian farms had annual sales of over $1 million each. Florida was second with 643 and Texas third with 618. California produces about half of the USA's fruit and vegetables and more than 10% of its milk and cream. It also provides one-tenth of US food exports. It is the main producer of about 30 crops and the only state producing some of them.

California's farm wealth is due to:

- Large areas of fertile soils, particularly in the Central, Imperial and Coachella Valleys and the coastal valleys.
- An advanced irrigation system which brings water to the drier parts of the state. Irrigation is heavily subsidised by the federal government.
- The Mediterranean type climate which favours a wide variety of crops. Sub-tropical fruits can be grown if frosts are guarded against. Temperate crops can be grown if water supply is ensured. This large, physically varied state has many different sub-climates which have helped to form distinct farming areas.
- A large 'home' market. California is the most populous state in the USA.
- Excellent processing and distribution systems which allow the rapid marketing and export of farm products.

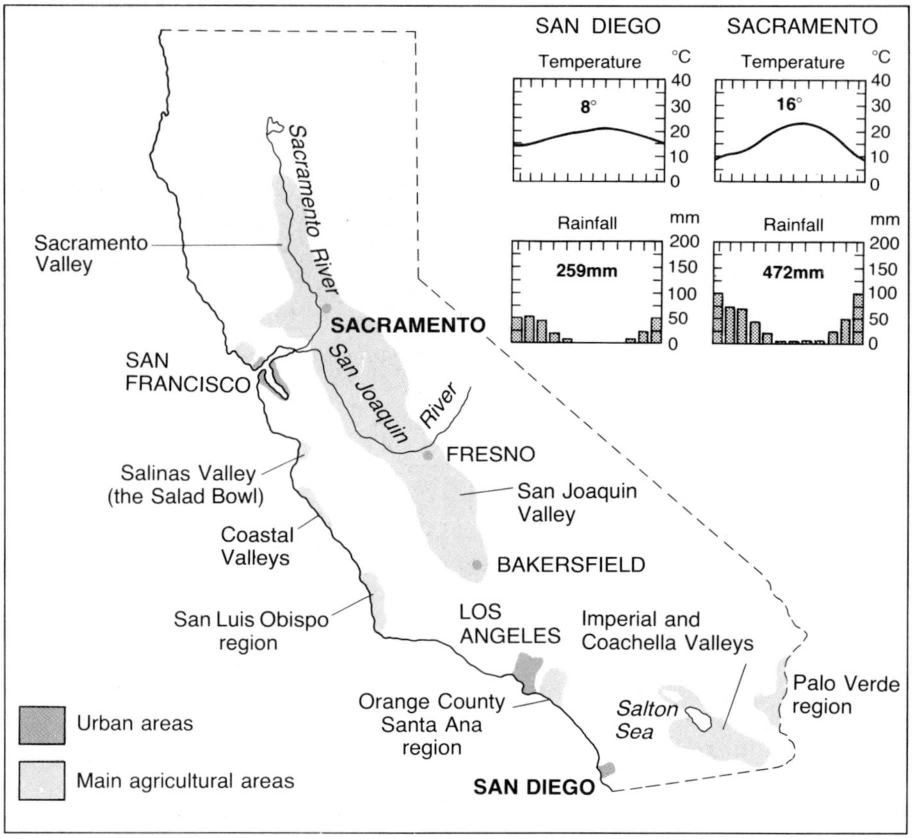


**Fig 1 The main agricultural areas of California.**

- A high level of investment. Large corporations own many farms in the state and operate with high levels of mechanisation.
- Advanced agricultural research by university departments and farm companies helps to raise output.

| *Product* | *Area (hectares)* | *Value ($M)* |
|---|---|---|
| Lettuce | 23 000 | 112 |
| Other vegetables | 30 000 | 100 |
| Strawberries | 4 000 | 100 |

**Fig 2 The main products grown in the Salad Bowl, 1980.**

## America's Salad Bowl

One of California's many areas of specialised farming is known as America's 'Salad Bowl'. It is the coastal valley area centred on the town of Salinas and extending into Monterey, San Mateo and Santa Cruz counties. Lettuce and strawberries are the main crops (Figure 2) but others include broccoli, sprouts, cauliflowers, celery, spinach, radishes, tomatoes and artichokes. The Salad Bowl has rich alluvial soils and its climate is ideal for its main crops. It is protected by coastal mountains and is close to the Pacific Ocean. These two factors give rise to mild-to-warm equable temperatures all year round. Rainfall is seasonable with 300–500 mm between November and April and very little in the summer. Wells, some more than 200 metres deep, provide an alternative water supply. Strawberries are grown on absolutely flat furrow-irrigated fields. The land must be fumigated to give a good quality strawberry crop. Other vegetables grown in rotation benefit greatly from this. Much of the production is on a share-cropping basis with small growers tending units of 1–1.5 hectares. The owner (usually a large corporation) provides housing, plants, fertilizer and other inputs. The share-cropper provides the labour. Profits are divided 60:40 in favour of the owner. Within half an hour of picking, the crop is in cooled stores. It remains cool until reaching the shops, maybe in Britain three days later. The largest area of the Salad Bowl is planted with lettuce. The newest harvesting machines span 30 rows. The crop is cut, film-wrapped and boxed in the field. It is then sped quickly to markets across America and beyond. Much of the labour for lettuces and other crops comes from Mexican and Philippino workers. The highly intensive farming of the Salad Bowl needs a very large investment per hectare but the profits make it worthwhile. Unlike some of the USA's major crops (i.e. corn, wheat, cotton) the products of this region are not in surplus. There is a ready demand both in the USA and abroad.

**Fig 3 Irrigating crops in the Salad Bowl.**

**Fig 4 Vineyards, Napa Valley, California.**

**WATER PRICES**

The fall in the water table, on which at least half of the state's farmland depends for irrigation, is almost certain to increase irrigation costs over the next few years. The state government looks likely to give in to pressure for reductions in water subsidies to farmers.

**BIOTECHNOLOGY**

Bigger, more efficient farmers have bought most of the land that formerly belonged to the 10–12% of the state's farmers who have sold up since 1984. The big farms are beginning to use biotechnology to boost yields and to reduce disease among crops. This promises to help them cut production costs and so to sharpen their competitive edge.

**FARM CHEMICALS**

Another threat is proposition 65, the Californian Clean Water Act, passed last autumn by popular vote. Officials in Sacramento, are, under the terms of the act, drawing up a list of chemicals that farmers will be banned from using in the hope of protecting drinking water from contamination. The farmers worry that basic chemicals like sulphur (a common soil additive) and chlorine (used to wash cows), plus several common pesticides, will be outlawed under the act.

**SURPLUSES**

Dairy farmers have benefited from the provision in the farm bill which compensates them for sending their herds to slaughter if they halt milk production for at least five years.

In California, about 11% of all dairy cows are thought to have been slaughtered last year in exchange for payments of nearly $300m.

The scheme has outraged cattlemen. The slaughter of dairy cows has contributed to a surplus of meat on the market.

**Fig 5 Extracts from *The Economist*, 7th March 1987 about some of the current issues in Californian agriculture.**

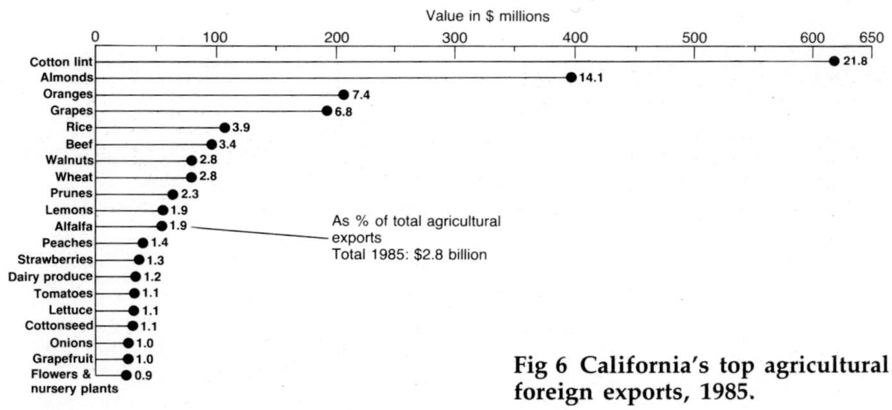


**Fig 6 California's top agricultural foreign exports, 1985.**

**Q1**
Compare the climate graphs in Figure 1.
**(a)** How is it possible to farm successfully in the dry southern part of the state?
**(b)** Suggest why the value and range of products grown in California is greater than any other state in the USA.

**Q2**
**(a)** Why are fruit and vegetables produced in the Salad Bowl rather than other farm products?
**(b)** Suggest why much of the strawberry production is organised on a share-cropping basis.

**Q3**
Look at Figure 5. Which issue do you think is the most serious for Californian farmers at present? Give reasons for your answer.

# 11. Forests, Fish and Water

# 11.1 Canada's disappearing forests

## Number one in Canada

North America has huge forest resources, an important source of wealth (Figure 1). The USA and Canada are first and third in the world for the amount of timber cut each year. However the Canadian forest industry has reached a major crisis: huge areas of forest have been lost because of poor resource management.

The forest products industry is Canada's main wealth creator and the revenue produced each year is double that from agriculture

| | Million metres, board measure 1980 | Percentage |
|---|---|---|
| Nova Scotia | 56 | 1.0 |
| New Brunswick | 144 | 2.5 |
| Quebec | 1036 | 18.1 |
| Ontario | 574 | 10.0 |
| Saskatchewan | 49 | 0.9 |
| Alberta | 190 | 3.3 |
| British Columbia | 3651 | 63.7 |
| Other regions | 28 | 0.5 |
| Total | 5728 | 100.0 |

**Fig 2 The production of Canadian sawn lumber.**

**Fig 3 The start of a forest fire in the Wasatch Mountains, Utah.**

**Fig 1 The natural vegetation of North America.**

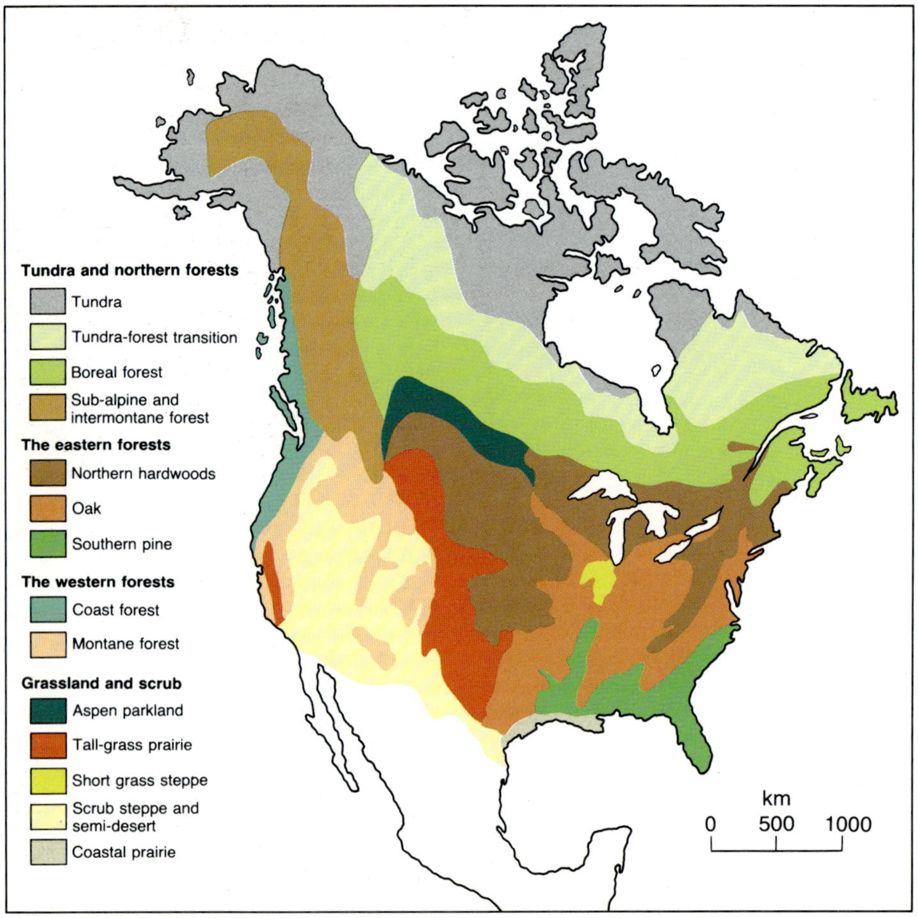


**Fig 4 Fighting forest fires.**

**FIGHTING FOREST FIRES**

Fires destroy 2 million hectares of forest a year – a loss of $100 million. The battle against fire involves:

- Computerized fire prediction based on analysis of temperature, humidity, wind and rainfall. Computers also store information on thunderstorm paths and past fires.
- Sensors in the forest to detect lightning as it hits the ground.
- Helicopter and airplane patrols. Fires can be water-bombed with 1500 gallons dropped at a time. Canada's thousands of lakes allow quick refilling in most areas.
- Fire fighters landed by helicoper to cut down burning trees to hinder the spread of flames. In most cases the flames are out in an hour. Three per cent of fires cause 95% of the damage. If a fire gets out of control it is virtually unstoppable until it burns itself out.

(Figure 2). It is the largest employer in the country with 300 000 people working as loggers, sawmill workers and in pulp and paper factories. A further 700 000 jobs are indirectly dependent on the industry. In 1985 Gerald Merrithew, the minister of state for forestry said, 'If the forest industry fails, there is hardly a community in Canada that will not be affected'.

## Various problems

The forest industry is in trouble because of:

- Forest fires. In the early 1980s fires destroyed six times more trees than the timber companies cut down.
- Pest infestations, for example, the spruce budworm which destroyed nearly 75 million hectares of timber in the Maritime Provinces, Quebec and Ontario during the 1970s.
- Acid Rain. It is thought this is the reason for dead and dying trees in a number of forests.
- Large amounts of cut timber have been left to rot in places because of miscalculation of transport costs.

  **And most seriously**:

- Scientific replanting of cleared areas has been the exception rather than the rule.

## Poor forest management

Almost 250 million trees are cut in Canada each year. But very little money has been invested in replacing them. Forested areas rarely grow back to their former state after large-scale cutting. In many areas new forest growth is so poor and patchy that it will not be economical to cut again in the future. There are now 20 to 25 million hectares of logged and unreforested land in Canada. This is increasing by almost one million hectares a year. In British Columbia, which accounts for 60% of Canada's lumber production, timber shortages of as much as 30% are predicted before 2000. What is required is carefully planned forest management. This costs money as it is very labour-intensive. The cost, however, would only be a fraction of the profits made by the industry. So why has Canada been so short-sighted compared to countries such as the USA and Sweden?

- The enormous size of the forest fostered a feeling that it would last forever.
- Arguments between the government and the timber companies as to who should pay the cost of forest management.

## What does good management involve?

- Scientific replanting: spacing seedlings to allow full growth to maturity. This varies for different species.
- Thinning and weeding during early growth to ensure survival of the maximum number of fully developed trees.
- Regular fertilization to improve growth.
- Research and action to control pest infestation.
- Strategies to prevent and contain forest fires.

**Fig 5 The lumber industry at Algonquin Provincial Park, Ontario.**

**Fig 6 Planting new trees in British Columbia.**

**Q1**
**(a)** Describe the distribution of forests in North America.
**(b)** Why is tundra rather than forest found in northern Canada?

**Q2**
**(a)** How important is the forest industry to the Canadian economy as a whole?
**(b)** Which regions depend on the industry most?

**Q3**
Make a list of the problems facing the forest industry. Now suggest a way to tackle each problem.

Good management can only be achieved by greater investment. Advanced forest management techniques practiced in Scandinavia enable growth of three to four times more wood per hectare than in Canada. Experts argue that Canada should follow a 'sustained yield' policy. This means that trees are cut only as fast as they can be replaced. If action is not taken, Canada could lose its number one resource – for ever.

# 11.2 Fishing: the battle against over-exploitation

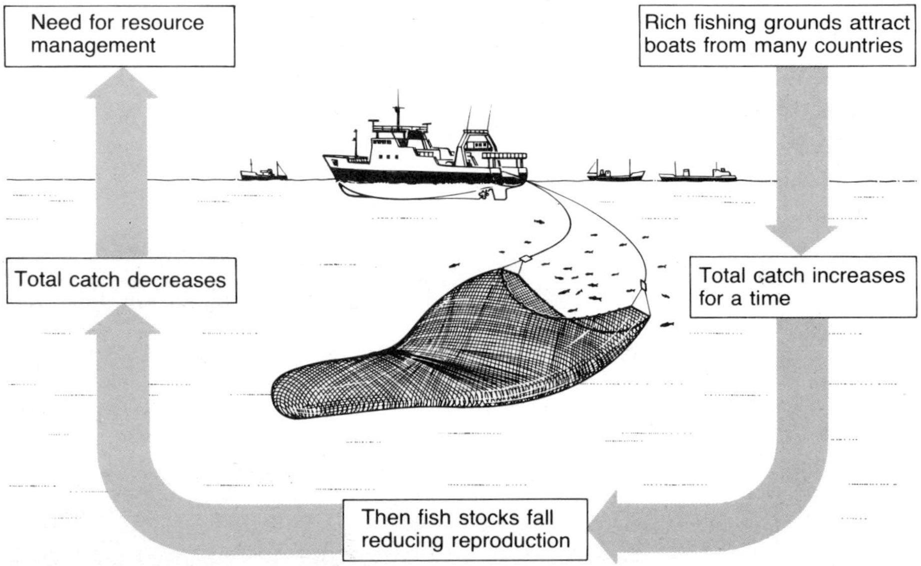


**Fig 1 This is what happens when rich fishing grounds are over-fished. The need for resource management to keep up the stocks of fish has become greater than ever.**

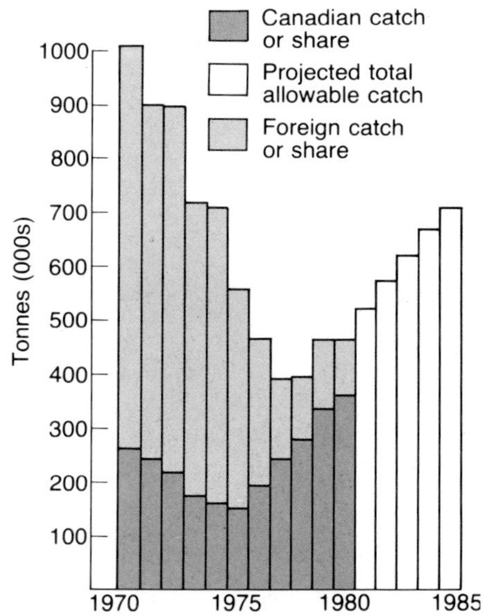


**Fig 3 Total catches of cod on the Labrador–Scotian shelf. Stocks were falling rapidly before Canada set its 200 mile fishing zone and took other resource management measures as well.**

**Fig 2 Boats from many different countries are attracted to the fishing grounds of North America's continental shelf.**

## Over-fishing

By the mid-1970s the North American fishing industry was in serious trouble. The main problem was over-fishing (Figure 1). Over the years more and more foreign fishing fleets came to the rich fishing grounds close to the Atlantic and Pacific coasts (Figure 2). Not surprisingly more fish were caught. But there is an upper limit to the exploitation of this valuable resource. Not enough fish were being left to reproduce and stocks began to fall (Figure 3). Canadian and American boats were returning to port with smaller catches. Something had to be done to prevent the industry from total collapse.

## 200 mile fishing limits

The answer was better resource management. The important first step was the introduction of new fishing limits. The USA and Canada took control of all fishing up to 200 miles from their coastlines. Foreign fleets now need licences to fish in these zones. When Canada or the USA grant a fishing licence to another country (which must be paid for) a maximum is set on the amount of fish that country can catch. The USA and Canada also set a limit on the total volume of fish caught in their 200 mile zones. They calculate how much their own industries need. Other countries are then allowed to take what is left. However, only a certain proportion of available fish must be caught each year. The aim is for fish stocks to rise to their old levels. Other nations have also extended their fishing limits to

200 miles. This is not the answer to all the problems of the world fishing industry but it has done much to improve the situation. Since Canada declared its 200 mile fishing zone in 1977 the Canadian fishing fleet has caught 50% more groundfish and 100% more cod.

## Research

Fishery management does not end with a 200 mile limit. It also involves research programmes. These study the distribution of fish, their migration patterns, stock forecasting, quality control and biological reproduction. The aim is to improve understanding of the marine world and of the way the fishing industry can best take advantage of it, without over-exploitation.

## Canada: the world's leading exporter

The USA is the fourth largest fishing nation in the world (after Japan, the USSR and China). Canada ranked sixteenth in 1980. The industry is more vital to Canada than to its southern neighbour. In the past the USA has done little to develop its fishing. Much of the fish eaten in the country is imported from abroad. Canada is its main supplier. In fact, Canada is the world's number one exporter of fish.

## A major industry in the Atlantic provinces

Fishing is essential to the Atlantic provinces. The industry there employs 40 000 people on fishing boats. Another 20 000 work in 500 fish-processing plants. This is the poorest part of Canada with the lowest incomes and the highest unemployment. Without fishing there would be little left in many areas. Nowhere is this more so than in Newfoundland, the centre of the industry.

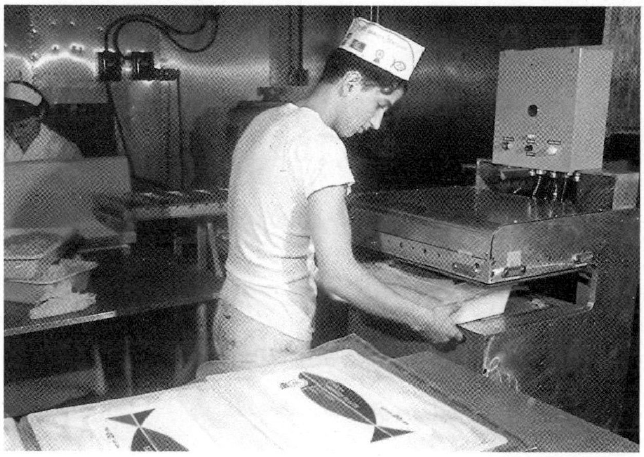

**Fig 4 A fish processing factory in Newfoundland.**

Apart from over-fishing, the industry in the Atlantic provinces has suffered from other problems. Compared to other nations, such as the USSR and Japan, much of Canada's fishing industry is small scale. It is carried out by small boats dispersed along thousands of kilometres of coast. Fish handling, processing and marketing needs to be modernised. Attempts have been made to change this situation. Newfoundland's Fisheries Household Resettlement Program, which started in 1965, aimed to persuade people to move from small isolated communities to more prosperous 'growth centres'. Apart from the fragmented nature of fishing it was very expensive to provide small remote communities with schools, medical care and other essential services. Much of the program concentrated on Placentia Bay, 60 miles west of St John's. Here 814 families from 29 isolated communities were uprooted between 1966 and 1969. The pressure to move exerted on communities by the provincial government was resented by many.

## Recent problems

The success of the 200 mile fishing limit created new problems for the industry in the early 1980s. Better fish stocks allowed the industry to expand. To do this the fishing companies borrowed money at high interest rates. Then the world market prices for fish products fell. The result was deep financial trouble and a desperate need to restructure the whole industry. This was done by co-operation between the federal government, the provinces of Newfoundland and Nova Scotia, the big banks and the troubled fishing companies. Canada's fishing industry is now in a much better position to face the future.

**Fig 5 A fishing village abandoned under Newfoundland's Fisheries Household Resettlement Program.**

**Q1**
**(a)** What is over-fishing?
**(b)** How has the Canadian government tackled this problem?

**Q2**
**(a)** Why is Newfoundland so dependent on the fishing industry?
**(b)** Put the case for and against Newfoundland's Fisheries Household Resettlement Program.

**Q3**
Summarise the information shown in Figure 3.

# 11.3 Water shortage in the American West

## The dry western states

The western half of the USA gets only 20% of the country's precipitation (Figure 1). But each day it uses as much water as the east. The west has prospered this century. Agriculture, industry and settlement have flourished due to a huge investment in water transfer schemes. Hundreds of aqueducts take water from water surplus areas to drier areas. The federal government has paid most of the bill. The demand for water is now greater than the supply. If the west is to continue to expand, a solution to the water problem must be found.

Although much of the west is desert or semi-desert, large areas of dryland have been transformed into fertile farms and sprawling cities. It all began with the Reclamation Act of 1902. This allowed the building of canals, dams and hydro-electric power systems in the states that lie, all or in part, west of the 100th meridian (Figure 1). Water supply was to be the key to general economic development. It would benefit not only the west but the country as a whole.

## Bringing water to southern California

California has benefited most from this investment in water supply. It has changed much of California's dry south into the most productive farming region in the USA. It has allowed Los Angeles and San Diego to sprawl way out into the desert. Much of the region's water is brought by canal from wetter northern California and from the Colorado river. Water is also pumped to the surface from underground aquifers (water-bearing rock strata). But water is being pumped out much faster than the aquifers naturally refill. The imbalance is so great in some areas that the land surface has subsided.

California would like to buy water from the wetter states of Washington and Oregon. But these states are against pumping their water elsewhere; they might need it themselves in the future.

## The Central Arizona Project

California is not the only state to draw water from the Colorado river, although it does take the most. Wyoming, Utah, Colorado, Nevada, New Mexico and Arizona also take a share. So does Mexico after the Colorado flows across the border. The Central Arizona Project (CAP) is the latest big money scheme to divert water from this great river (Figures 2 and 3). Each state through which it flows has a legal right to withdraw a certain amount of water. The maximum for Arizona is 2.8 million acre-feet. (An acre-foot would fill an acre of land to a depth of one foot.) In the past, Arizona has taken much less; it could not afford to build a water transfer system from the Colorado to its main cities. Most of the state's water came from aquifers. But it has been overdrawing this supply by about 2 million acre-feet a year. If thirsty Phoenix and Tucson were to remain prosperous, something had to be

**Fig 1 In general, precipitation decreases steadily from east to west in the USA.**

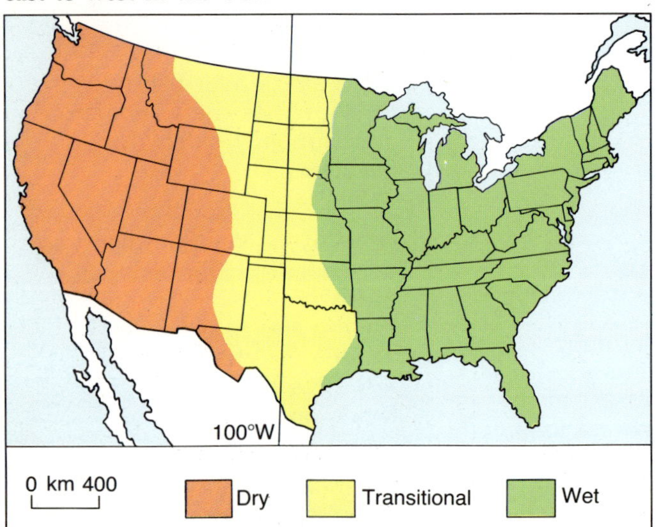


**Fig 2 The Central Arizona Project is the latest and probably the last major water transfer scheme to take water from the Colorado River.**

**Fig 3 Part of the Central Arizona Project showing a field levelled using laser equipment.**

**Fig 4 East Highline Canal, near Imperial Dam, Southern California.**

done. The answer was CAP, to be completed in 1991. Partly funded by the federal government it will carry water almost 500 kilometres.

While CAP will do much to solve Arizona's problem it creates another for California. There will be less water in the Colorado when it reaches California. California now has to find more water from elsewhere.

## The future

It seems that two things must happen. First, the west needs to use water more carefully. Most water is used for irrigated agriculture (Figure 4). This is heavily subsidised by the government so farmers often take more than they really need. Increasing the price of water should encourage more careful use. Secondly, there will be a need for new water transfer schemes. What about buying water from Canada? One scheme proposed some years ago (but never adopted) was the Grand Canal Project (Figure 6). In the past the Canadian government has not been in favour of selling water. Will it change its mind in the future?

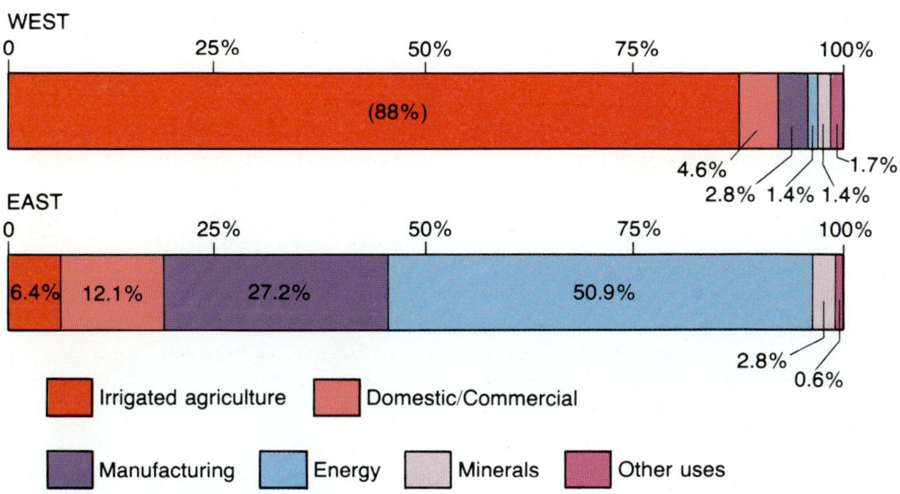


**Fig 5 Water is used very differently in the eastern and western parts of the USA.**

**Fig 6 The Grand Canal Project.**

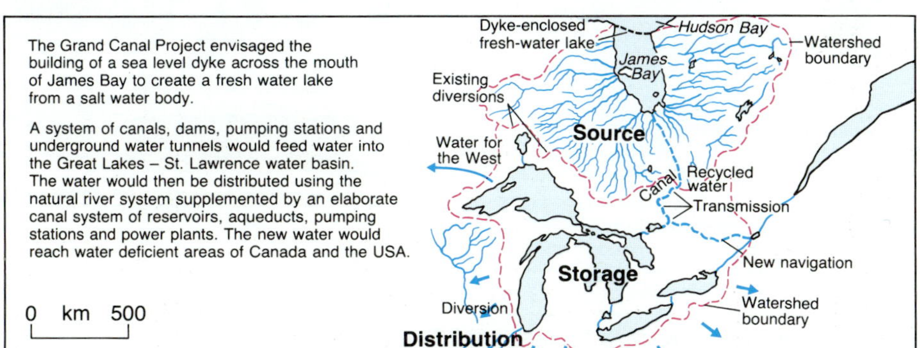


**Q1**
Look at the climatic graphs for North America in an atlas.
**(a)** Compare the precipitation each month for San Diego and New York. How do they both compare with London?
**(b)** Which part of Canada has the lowest precipitation? Why is this not a big problem?

**Q2**
Look at Figure 5. If new sources of water cannot be found for the west, how might the water supply have to be redistributed among the main users?

**Q3**
If the price of subsidised water in the west is increased, how do you think people might feel in **(a)** western USA? **(b)** eastern USA?

**Q4**
Summarise the main proposals of the Grand Canal Project.

# 12. Recreation and Tourism

# 12.1 Tourism: a major industry

## Selling Canada to the world

Tourism is growing rapidly. Some experts say it will be the world's most important industry by the year 2000. In 1981 tourism in Canada:

- Accounted for 5% of the nation's GNP
- Was the fifth most important export, earning $3.8 billion in foreign exchange
- Provided the government with $8 billion in tax revenues
- Was a big employer. Ten per cent of all jobs depend directly or indirectly on tourism.

The federal and provincial governments spend much money trying to persuade (a) Canadians to spend their holidays exploring their own country and (b) people from other countries to visit Canada. Advertising is carefully directed at certain groups of people. It is also aimed at particular countries. The USA is the main target. In 1983 Tourism Canada spent 62% of its advertising budget ($13 million) there. Some of the big tourist promotions in recent years have been:

- Quebec's 'Welcome to the Good Times'
- British Columbia's 'Super Natural'
- Ontario's 'Yours to Discover' (Figure 1).

The provinces often target their advertising on the states closest to them. For example, Ontario sees its main US market as the region

*Among the world's most celebrated lakelands, in a class with England's Lake District and the magical landscapes of Northern Italy and Switzerland, Muskoka represents a kind of perfection in a northern Canadian setting.*

*Here, in a district no more than 650 kilometres square –(250 miles square), bounded by Georgian Bay on the west and the Severn River on the south, the last ice age carved dramatic contours in the billion-plus year-old granite of the Precambrian Shield.*

*Now splashed with scores of clear, blue-black water lakes including the three largest, Muskoka, Rosseau and Joseph, Muskoka boasts lovely resorts and holiday homes nestled in pine woods along the rock-clad shores.*

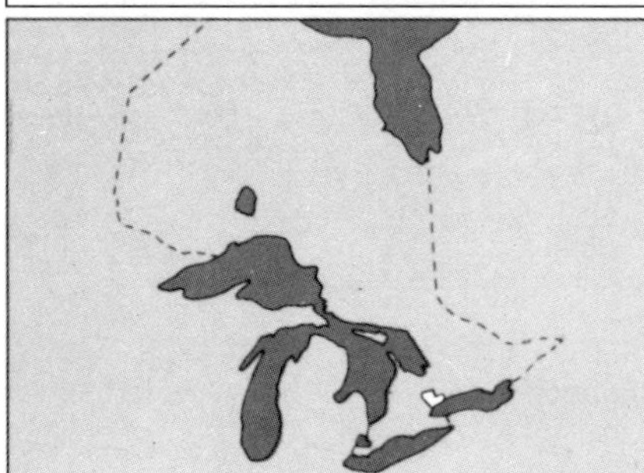

Toronto

DISCOVER THE FEELING!

Metropolitan Toronto Travel Association
Eaton Centre Galleria
Suite 110
220 Yonge Street
Telephone: (416) 979-3143 or
**1-800-387-2999**
Toll Free: Mich., N.Y., Ohio, Penn. and Ontario (excluding Thunder Bay).

- *People from everywhere in a city with everything, all living together with the greatest of ease.*
- *There are towers of gold that thrust ever skyward.*
- *There are Victorian villas under a mantle of green.*
- *There are great stores and markets, museums and galleries, first-rate live theatre and exquisite cuisine.*
- *Toronto. There's a whole world to see.*

**Fig 1 Tourist literature for Muskoka and Toronto, Ontario.**

within 350 miles of its border, from New York City in the east to Minneapolis-St Paul in the west. In contrast, British Columbia advertises mainly in the Pacific states. Canada is promoted as an all-year-round holiday destination.

Toronto is a major tourist magnet. It is seen by many Americans as a model city. In rural areas the quality of facilities is of great importance. Investment in first class facilities at Whistler Village in British Columbia has changed a sleepy settlement into a thriving tourist operation. It has become one of the most desirable ski destinations in North America.

After the USA, Europe is Canada's next major source of tourists. In recent years increasing numbers of tourists have come from countries such as Japan, Korea and Venezuela.

## Come to the USA

In 1961 the USA earned just over $1 billion from international tourism. Then almost 90% of all foreign visitors came from Canada and Mexico. The situation has changed much since then:

- The arrival of the 747 jumbo jet in 1969 reduced the time and cost of transoceanic travel.
- The use of the microcomputer since 1971 created a global reservations network which simplified foreign travel arrangements.
- Increasing competition in the tourist market has made package tours more attractive.
- More people earn higher incomes and have longer holidays.

In 1983 five states earned more than $1 billion from foreign visitors while two states, New York and California, earned more than $2.6 billion each. Spending by foreign visitors supports more than 300 000 jobs throughout the country.

**Q1**

**(a)** How important is tourism to the Canadian economy?
**(b)** Identify the major tourist related industries.

**Q2**

Look at Figure 4. Identify and explain the main changes in the origin of visitors to the USA between 1961 and 1984.

**Q3**

Look at Figure 3.
**(a)** Which US destinations are in the top ten for both European and Asian visitors?
**(b)** Suggest reasons for the differences between the two lists.

**Fig 2 The major tourist-related industries.**

| *Group* | *Examples* |
|---|---|
| Transport | Air, rail, water, bus, taxis, car hire |
| Accommodation | Hotels, motels, camp sites, trailer parks, sporting and recreational camps |
| Entertainment | Theatres, cinemas, amusement parks, arcades, racing, professional sports clubs |
| Public Facilities | Museums, art galleries, botanical and zoological gardens |
| Food and Drink | Restaurants, bars, street stands |
| Financial | Banks and foreign exchange establishments |
| Travel | Travel agents, tour operators |
| Shops | Gifts, sourvenirs, photography, etc. |

**Fig 4 The numbers of visitors to the USA, by country of origin.**

| *Country of origin* | *Arrivals in the US in 1961* | *Arrivals in the US in 1984* | *% Change* |
|---|---|---|---|
| Japan | 19 872 | 1 414 909 | 7 020 |
| Hong Kong | 1 561 | 93 426 | 5 885 |
| Spain | 4 477 | 90 946 | 1 931 |
| Brazil | 9 334 | 168 508 | 1 705 |
| Philippines | 4 732 | 83 937 | 1 674 |
| Germany, F.R. | 38 028 | 545 247 | 1 334 |
| Switzerland | 11 051 | 156 157 | 1 313 |
| France | 24 270 | 330 660 | 1 262 |
| Colombia | 11 798 | 157 896 | 1 238 |
| Italy | 16 425 | 218 379 | 1 230 |
| New Zealand | 6 570 | 86 136 | 1 211 |
| Australia | 18 897 | 231 429 | 1 125 |
| Sweden | 9 431 | 115 307 | 1 123 |
| Mexico | 197 710 | 2 300 000 | 1 063 |
| United Kingdom | 93 653 | 927 574 | 890 |
| Netherlands | 15 295 | 134 192 | 777 |
| Venezuela | 21 127 | 169 666 | 703 |
| Argentina | 18 224 | 82 579 | 353 |
| Canada | 4 680 000 | 10 981 949 | 135 |

**Fig 3 The destinations within the USA of European countries visitors and Asian visitors.**

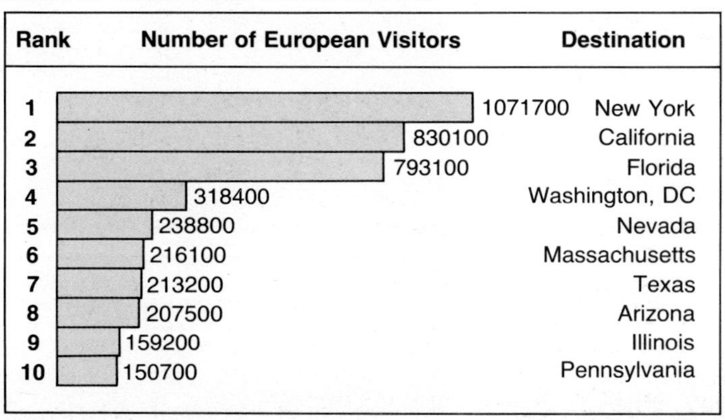


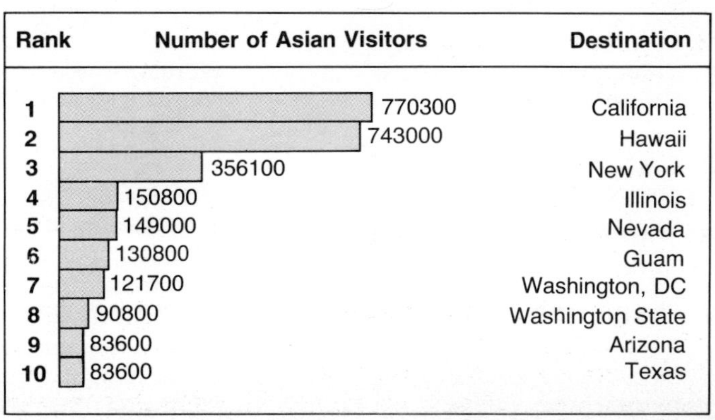

# 12.2 Recreation activities

Recreation is the use of leisure time for relaxation and enjoyment. In 1983 Americans spent $141 billion on recreation (Figure 1). It has become a more important part of life for several reasons:

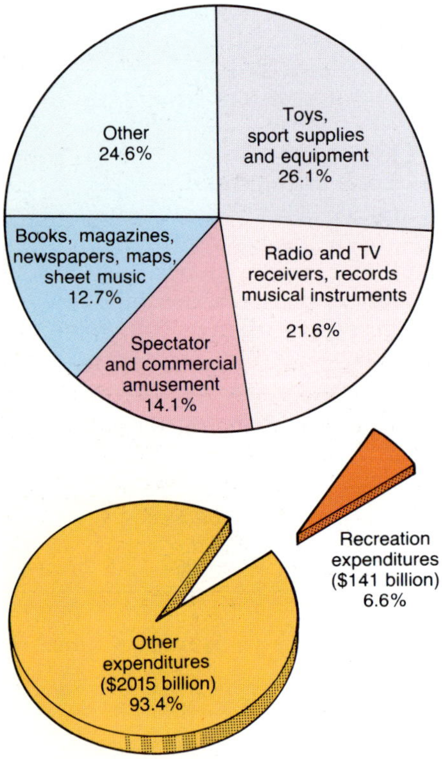


**Fig 1 How people choose to spend their money: the Personal Consumption Expenditures (PEC) for recreation in the USA, 1983.**

- Leisure time has increased as the working week has been shortened. An increasing number of people now work a four day week. This gives them a longer weekend.
- Higher average incomes leave more money for leisure activities.
- Greater personal mobility means that people can seek recreation in places that were once too far away.
- Health education has made people more aware of the importance of relaxation and regular exercise.

## Outdoor recreation increases

Some recreational activities such as reading and watching TV are passive. They involve little effort and are done mainly in the home.

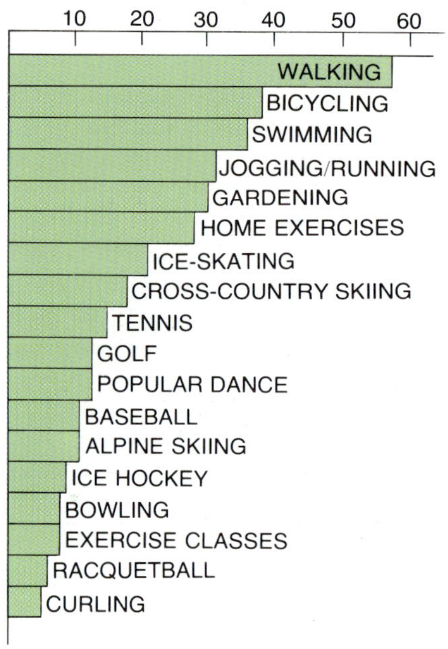


**Fig 2 The most popular recreational activities in Canada, 1981. This figure shows the percentage of people aged 10 and above who participated at least once in these activities in the 12 months preceding the survey.**

Active pastimes are now becoming more popular. These involve physical exercise. A Canadian survey of national recreational activities (Figure 2) found that walking, bicycling and swimming were top of the list. Comparison with a 1976 survey shows that participation in four activities rose by over 20%. These were cross-country skiing (142%), alpine skiing (69%), golf (32%) and tennis (23%).

Activity patterns are far from uniform. Participation is highest among (a) the young, (b) people living in western Canada, (c) people in managerial and professional jobs, (d) single people. Overall, there was no difference in degree of participation between men and women, that is, both participated equally.

A survey of outdoor recreation activities in the USA also found that participation in some activities is affected by income much more than others.

## Urban recreation

The provision of public recreation facilities has a big effect on the level of participation. In the City of Toronto provision varies considerably from region to region (Figure 4). In many North American cities there are far fewer public recreation facilities. In many inner cities lack of money and high land values makes recreation provision difficult. For the inner city poor, the continent's outstanding recreation facilities — national parks and forests, seashores, scenic rivers etc. — seem unattainable. In the USA less than 3% of public recreation lands (parks, forests etc.) are within an hour's drive of major cities. In contrast to the inner cities, most suburban communities offer good recreational opportunities. The higher income suburbs can usually afford better public facilities.

**Fig 3 Urban recreation, Canada.**

| Facility | Thousands of persons per facility North | Central | East | West | City average |
|---|---|---|---|---|---|
| Arena | 47.5 | 87.0 | 127.5 | 60.5 | 66.5 |
| Artificial ice rinks | 16.0 | 11.0 | 16.0 | 18.5 | 16.0 |
| Indoor pools | 14.5 | 6.5 | 8.0 | 10.5 | 9.5 |
| Outdoor pools | 72.0 | 43.5 | 25.5 | 48.5 | 43.0 |
| Hardball regulation | 72.0 | 29.0 | 21.0 | 30.2 | 31.5 |
| Softball regulation (lit) | 143.0 | — | 42.5 | 34.5 | 54.5 |
| Softball regulation (unlit) | 14.5 | 43.5 | 7.5 | 12.0 | 13.5 |
| Hard/softball scrub | 8.0 | 8.5 | 4.5 | 12.0 | 8.0 |
| Football regulation | 24.0 | 17.5 | 18.0 | 16.0 | 18.0 |
| Soccer regulation (lit) | — | — | 127.5 | 121.0 | — |
| Soccer regulation (unlit) | 48.0 | 43.5 | 21.0 | 24.0 | 28.5 |
| Scrub fields | 12.0 | 17.5 | 5.5 | 15.0 | 10.5 |
| Track regulation | 29.0 | 87.0 | 42.5 | 30.0 | 35.0 |
| Tennis (lit) | 2.5 | 14.5 | 9.0 | 6.5 | 5.0 |
| Tennis (unlit) | 9.0 | 12.5 | 3.5 | 5.5 | 6.0 |
| Regulation gym | 14.0 | 5.0 | 6.0 | 8.5 | 7.5 |
| General (multi-purpose room) | 2.5 | 1.5 | 1.5 | 2.0 | 1.8 |
| Auditorium/room | 16.0 | 14.5 | 21.0 | 20.0 | 18.0 |
| Natural ice rinks | 0.8 | 2.5 | 1.2 | 1.5 | 1.3 |
| Wading pools | 1.2 | 0.4 | 0.8 | 0.8 | 0.8 |
| Playgrounds1 | 0.3 | 0.1 | 0.5 | 0.5 | 0.4 |
| POPULATION | 143 010 | 87 007 | 127 475 | 241 725 | 599 217 |

1 Based on number of children aged 0–14 years

**Fig 4 Participation in recreational activities in Toronto.**

**Fig 5 The impact of recreation and tourism.**

**SPATIAL**
More space is needed as demand for facilities in both urban and rural areas increases. Land use competition in some areas is intense.

**ENVIRONMENTAL**
Some activities and the traffic they generate can do considerable harm to the environment. This is often greatest in rural areas.

**ECONOMIC**
Spending on recreation and tourism is rising steadily. This is now a major sector of the economy. The industry is a big employer but much of the work is seasonal.

**SOCIAL**
Some activities cost little or nothing. Others are only open to people on higher incomes. Public facilities are often worst in poor areas while those on low income can't afford the membership fees of private clubs.

**POLITICAL**
This growing industry looks to politicians and their parties to support it. As the industry expands it can exert more political pressure.

**Fig 6 Cross country ski-ing, Canada.**

**Fig 7 Toronto offers many different activities and facilities for recreation. The figures at the foot of the columns in Fig 4 are the populations of the four city regions.**

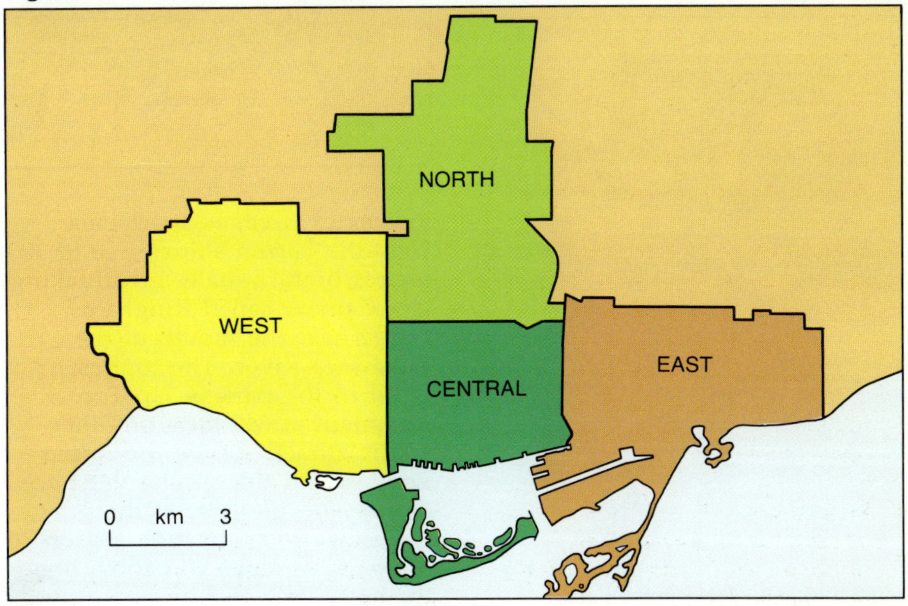


**Q1**
What is the difference between active and passive recreation?

**Q2**
Look at Figure 2.
**(a)** Suggest reasons for the differences in popularity of the 18 activities.
**(b)** Name four other recreational activities.

**Q3**
Which of the activities in Figure 2 are likely to
**(a)** need most space?
**(b)** have the greatest impact on the environment?

**Q4**
Look at Figure 4. Study the level of provision for the 21 types of facility for each of the four regions of Toronto.
**(a)** For how many facilities is provision in each region worse than the City average?
**(b)** What other information might you require for a more detailed picture of recreation provision in Toronto?

# 12.3 National Parks

## Pukaskwa

Opened to the public in July 1983, Pukaskwa (pronounced Puck-a-saw is one of Canada's newest national parks. It is located on the stormy northern shore of Lake Superior (Figures 1 and 2). Pukaskwa is 1880 square kilometres of wilderness. It was created to preserve the fragile boreal forest environment.

The only developed campground in the park is at Hattie Cove. It has a 70-site camping area, hot showers, washrooms and hook-up facilities for trailers. Access to Hattie Cove is by the only road through the park. Registration at the park HQ is compulsory for those venturing into the back country on hiking or canoe routes. For water travel the best routes are along the White and Pukaskwa rivers as well as along the coast.

The scenery along the 100 kilometre coast between Hattie Cove and the mouth of the Pukaskwa River is spectacular. Here the barren shores rise to 300 metres high. Equally breathtaking is a Canyon called Ringhams Gorge near the mouth of the Pukaskwa River. The highest point in the park is Tip Top Mountain at 640 metres. Other scenic attractions are the raised beaches and the spectacular traces of early people (e.g. at the Pukaskwa Pits). In high season the park employs 70 people but there are only twenty year-round employees. Many are hired from the nearby Pic River Indian reservation. Pukaskwa is an example of the new generation of Canadian national parks – it is well off the beaten track!

**Fig 1 Pukaskwa National Park, on the northern shore of Lake Superior.**

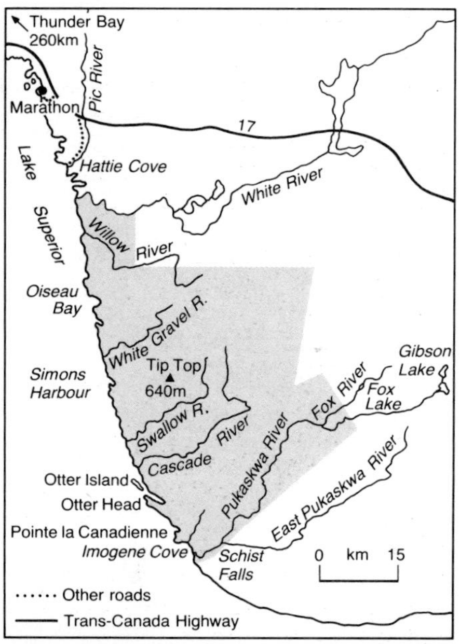

**Fig 2 Pukaskwa National Park.**

## A national system

National parks are found worldwide. The United Nations lists more than 1000 in over 100 countries. Canada, with 31 parks, has the largest system (Figure 3).

**Fig 3 Canada's National parks.**

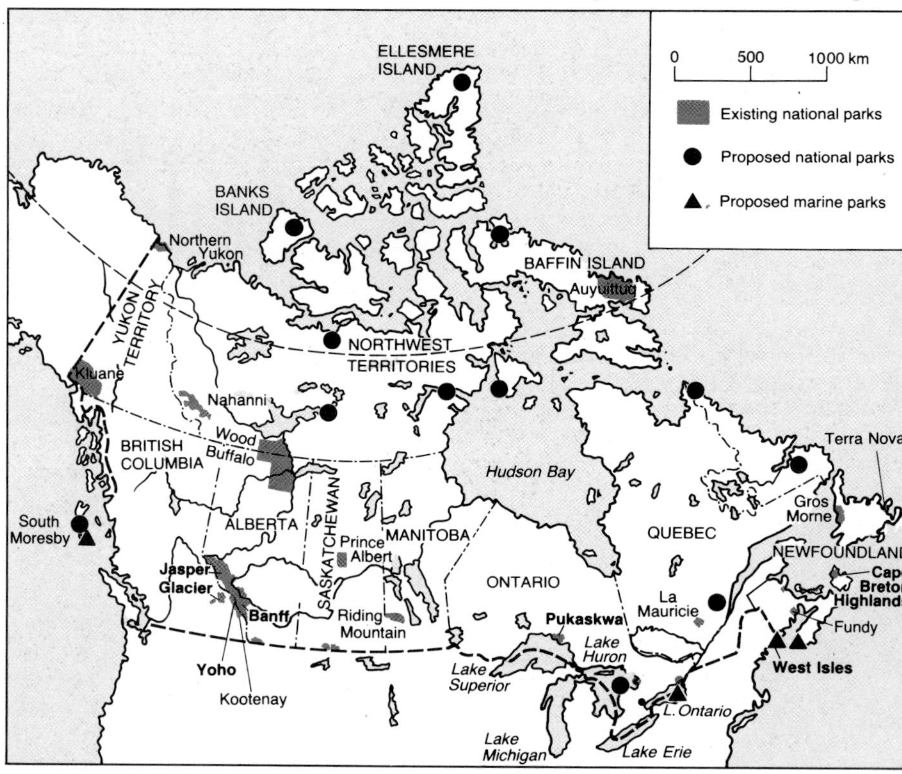


Altogether Canada's National Parks, historical sites and heritage canals cover 40 000 square kilometres, an area larger than England. New areas of unique interest will be added to Canada's park system in the future.

It all began in 1885 when ten square miles around a hot spring in Banff, Alberta were reserved for the people of Canada. The early parks (Banff, Yoho, Glacier and Jasper) were created more for the profits of the Canadian Pacific

**MARINE PARKS**

Canada has decided to protect areas of special interest in its coastal waters. These will be called marine parks. The first will be off the coast of New Brunswick. The proposed West Isles marine park (Figure 3) will take in the waters and numerous tiny islands to the east of Deer Island. The natural world of the West Isles includes:

- seals, porpoises, the occasional whale and a huge variety of fish, some very rare.
- numerous birds, including ospreys, cormorants and the bald eagle.
- fascinating island ecosystems.

Visitors to the marine park could sail on the water, explore under it and camp on its tiny islands. Regulations would be strict to ensure the conservation of this unique area.

However, local fishermen have strongly objected to the proposal. The West Isles is famous for its herring weirs. These are enclosures made of poles driven into the sea bottom. The poles support nets which trap herring as they swim along the shoreline. The fishermen fear that a large influx of visitors would drive the herring away. Catches have already fallen in recent years. The fishermen blame the increase in tourism that has already taken place. But some local people are in favour of the marine marks. Local hotels and tour boat operators would benefit. New jobs would be created and new services would be attracted to the area.

**Fig 4 Canada's marine parks.**

**Q1**
Describe the distribution of national parks in Canada (Figure 3).

**Q2**
List the different reasons for setting up national parks since the creation of Banff in 1885.

**Q3**
What are the main problems facing park managers?

**Q4**
Write/draw an advertisement for Pukaskwa national park to be placed in a tourist brochure.

**Q5**
**(a)** Why is Canada setting up a system of marine parks?
**(b)** Outline the reasons for and against the proposed West Isles marine park (Figure 4).

Railroad (CPR) than to preserve the environment. The CPR benefited not only from the fare-paying passengers visiting the parks; it was also given major commercial concessions such as long leases on hotels. However, the arrival of the motor car weakened the link between the railroads and the parks.

Other national parks were created to stimulate economic development. For example, the seven parks in the Atlantic provinces have done much to encourage tourism in the region. Cape Breton Highlands in Nova Scotia was the first to be opened in 1936. Political considerations ensured that there would be at least one park in every province and territory. Since the early 1970s the preservation of unique environments has been the main reason for the creation of new parks.

## Balancing recreation and conservation

Between 1953 and 1981 there was a sevenfold increase in the number of visitors to Canada's national parks (Figure 5). Public interest has been an important reason for the increase of these protected areas. However, it has also caused a number of problems.

*Visitors to Canada's National Parks*

| | |
|---|---|
| 1953 | 3 million |
| 1963 | 9 million |
| 1973 | 16 million |
| 1981 | 21 million |

**Fig 5 The number of visitors to the Parks has greatly increased.**

- The most popular park sites regularly have their full quota of visitors at peak holiday times.
- Traffic on access routes has risen substantially, adding to environmental pollution.
- Footpath erosion is severe in some areas. The growing use of snowmobiles has opened up areas previously too difficult to get to.
- Vegetation (including some unique species) has been destroyed because of carelessness by visitors.
- There is pressure to increase building to provide more and better facilities for tourists. Also more people want to live in those parks which are not too far from the cities.
- The risk of forest fires being started by carelessness is high.
- There are pressures from other land uses such as mining and forestry.

Park managers have the difficult job of conserving the wildlife and landscape of the parks while still offering people access to these unique areas. The two aims can only be combined through careful management.

**Fig 6 The Angel Glacier in Jasper National Park.**

# 12.4 Forest recreation

## Mainly in the west

The USA's National Forest system was started in 1891. This was when the Yellowstone Park Timber Reserve (now Shoshone National Forest) was established. The system now covers 76 million hectares. The 155 national forests are federal lands run by the Forest Service. By law the forests are used for timber, livestock grazing, watershed, wildlife preservation and outdoor recreation. The Forest Service has the difficult job of keeping a reasonable balance between the needs and the impacts of these different land uses.

Like other federal lands (i.e. national parks) much of the national forest is in the west (Figure 1). So, while most people live in the east, the greatest opportunities for outdoor recreation are elsewhere. Alaska, Idaho and California have the largest forest areas. But all the western states have substantial areas of forest lands. In the east large national forests are in the Green, White, Allegheny and Blue Ridge mountains. Although the national forests are usually less spectacular landscapes than the national parks, they are very popular. The demand for forest recreation is rising sharply and there are fewer restrictions than in the national parks. In 1983 recreation use in the forests totalled 228 million visitor-days (Figure 3). Camping and recreation travel are by far the most popular activities. But there are also many other things to do. The more adventurous might go mountain climbing or scuba diving!

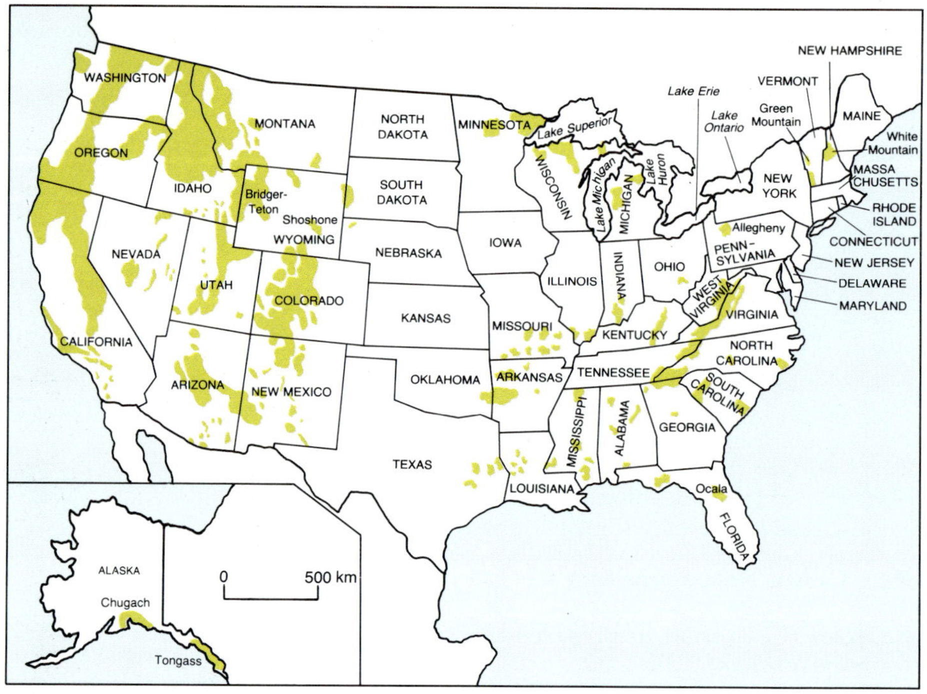


**Fig 1 Map showing the US National Forests.**

## Wilderness

Figure 4 is a profile of three contrasting national forests. Each is unique in its own way with plenty to see and to do. Both the White Mountain and Bridger-Teton forests have Wilderness areas. These are isolated virgin forest lands. Few have been penetrated by roads. There are strict regulations about access. In Wilderness areas the protection of the environment is all-important. Seventeen per cent of all national forest lands are classed as Wilderness. Environmental groups would like it to be more. However, commercial interests, particularly the forest industry, are against this. They feel that the regulations are already too strict.

Much of the USA's timber and mineral resources are in national forest and other federal lands. Therefore the government has considerable control over the rate of exploitation. For example, the Forest Service carefully calculates how much timber it will allow to be cut on its land each year.

## Access v preservation

The Forest Service is very aware of the environmental problems it faces. To manage the impact of recreation properly it studies the carrying capacity of camps and trails. This is to find the amount of use an area can take without causing real damage. The balance between the number of visitors and the impact they cause varies from place to place. Visitor impact is greatest in mountain areas where the ecosystem is very fragile.

**Fig 2 White water rafting in a National Forest.**

Some environmental groups say that not enough is being done. They see road building as the main danger. Once a road is built through an area many other changes often follow. The increasing use of all-terrain vehicles (ATVs) is causing ecological damage in areas which were previously untouched.

| *Place where use occurred* | *Visitor-days (1000s)* | *Percent* | *Activity* | *Visitor-days (1000s)* | *Percent* |
|---|---|---|---|---|---|
| **Sites and areas** | **227 708** | **100.0** | **Total** | **227 708** | **100.0** |
| **Developed sites** | **80 988** | **35.6** | Camping | 54 103 | 23.8 |
| | | | Picnicking | 8 430 | 3.7 |
| Observation sites | 1 257 | 0.6 | Recreation travel (mechanized) | 51 635 | 22.7 |
| Boating and fishing sites | 3 070 | 1.3 | Water travel | 8 814 | 3.9 |
| Swimming sites, playgrounds, etc. | 2 441 | 1.1 | Games and team sports | 1 464 | 0.6 |
| Campgrounds and trailheads | 36 673 | 16.1 | Water skiing and other water sports | 988 | 0.4 |
| Picnic grounds | 4 923 | 2.2 | Swimming and scuba diving | 5 216 | 2.3 |
| Hotels, lodges, resorts | 5 007 | 2.2 | Winter sports | 14 747 | 6.5 |
| Organization sites | 5 198 | 2.3 | Fishing | 15 567 | 6.8 |
| Recreation residence sites | 6 110 | 2.7 | Hunting | 16 129 | 7.1 |
| Ski areas and winter sports sites | 13 729 | 6.0 | Hiking and mountain climbing | 12 497 | 5.5 |
| Documentary areas, concession sites, visitor centres | 2 580 | 1.1 | Horseback riding | 3 743 | 1.6 |
| | | | Resort use | 4 579 | 2.0 |
| **Dispersed areas** | **146 720** | **64.4** | Organization camp use | 3 927 | 1.7 |
| Roads (recreation) | 52 675 | 23.1 | Recreation cabin use | 6,247 | 2.7 |
| Trails (recreation) | 12 986 | 5.7 | Gathering forest products | 5 499 | 2.4 |
| Airfields | 15 | (Z) | Nature study | 1 730 | .8 |
| Waters | 27 240 | 12.0 | Viewing scenery, sports, environment | 8 859 | 3.9 |
| General undeveloped country | 53 804 | 23.6 | Visitor information (exhibits, talks, etc.) | 3 534 | 1.6 |

Z Less than .05 percent

**Fig 3 National Forests are used for many different recreational activities.**

| **Forest, size, location** | **Facilities and services** | **Activities** | **Special attractions** | **Wildlife** |
|---|---|---|---|---|
| OCALA 382 000 acres in central Florida | Campgrounds, picnic areas, boat ramps, canoe rentals, visitors' centre | Camping, picnicking, hiking, hunting, fishing, boating, canoeing, swimming, snorkelling, scuba diving | Only entirely subtropical forest in USA; the Oklawaha wild and scenic river; freshwater springs; more than 600 lakes | Threatened red-cockaded woodpecker, bald eagle and American alligator; black bear; bobcat; great variety of birds |
| WHITE MOUNTAIN 687 000 acres in New Hampshire and Maine | Campgrounds, picnic areas, visitors' centre, backpacking shelters | Camping, picnicking, hiking, backpacking, hunting, fishing, snowshoeing, cross-country skiing, snowmobiling | Mount Washington; alpine habitats with unusual plant life; virgin stands of red spruce; unmatched autumn foliage; two wilderness areas; | Endangered American peregrine falcon; moose and black bear; several birds usually found in far northern regions |
| BRIDGER-TETON 3 440 000 acres in western Wyoming | Campgrounds, picnic areas, boat ramps, swimming beaches, horse corral | Camping, picnicking, hiking, backpacking, hunting, fishing, boating, swimming, horseback riding, nature study, winter sports | Bridger Wilderness (glaciers, over 1000 lakes), Kendall Warm Springs; Periodic Springs; Gros Ventre Slide Area; Teton Wilderness 20 peaks over 12 000 ft | Endangered or threatened bald eagle, rare trumpeter swan, grizzly bear and Kendall Warm Springs dam; moose, elk, Rocky Mountain bighorn sheep, mountain lion, bobcat |

**Fig 4 A profile of three National Forests.**

## Q1
**(a)** How are national forest lands used?
**(b)** For each use write a summary of its needs and its possible impact on other land uses.

## Q2
**(a)** Describe the distribution of national forests in the USA.
**(b)** Suggest reasons for this pattern.

## Q3
Write and/or draw a tourist advertisement for one of the forests profiled in Figure 4. Use an atlas to help you.

## Q4
Make a list of five ways the managers of national forests can reduce the environmental damage caused by recreational use.

## Q5
Use a simple graphical technique to illustrate the information in Figure 3.

## Q6
Compare the wildlife and the special attractions in the three National Forests profiled.

# 12.5 Tourist resorts

Fig 1 Las Vegas strip, Nevada, USA.

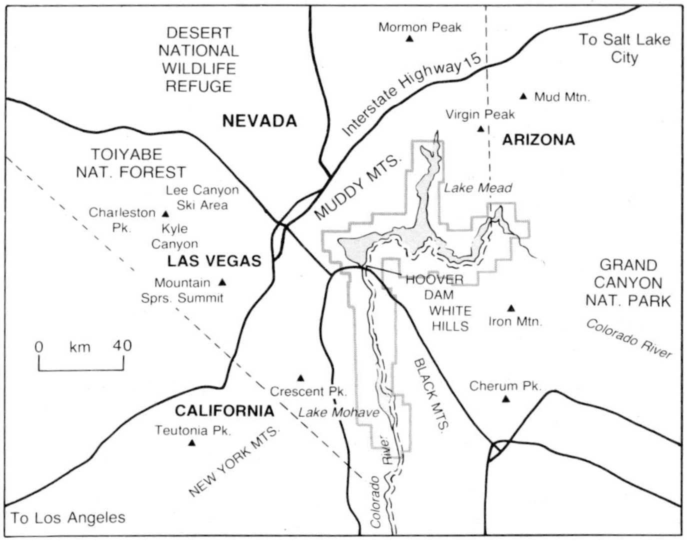


Fig 2 Location of Las Vegas.

## Las Vegas

Las Vegas is known as the 'gambling capital of the world'. Income from hotels, casinos, entertainment and other tourist services is the backbone of its economy.

Las Vegas developed as a stop-over for travellers heading for southern California. It then became a service centre for local ranches and mines. But it was gambling that made it world famous. This industry developed here because of:

- Nevada's liberal gambling regulations
- Electricity generated at Boulder Dam
- The attractive climate and landscapes of the region (e.g. Lake Mead, Kyle Canyon, Muddy Mountains)
- Large investors willing to back the entertainment potential of the city
- Accessibility; (a) regular air services to all large cities in the USA, (b) only 420 kilometres along Interstate Highway 15 from Los Angeles.

In 1984 gross gaming earnings in Las Vegas (money bet over money paid out) was over $2000 million. The big casinos have no limit: you can bet a million dollars if you wish! People typically stay four or five nights in this resort city. Hotels are reasonably priced and well below prices in, say, New York or San Francisco. The big casinos do everything they can to attract the 'high rollers', gamblers ready to risk big money. The major casinos along Las Vegas Strip rely heavily on these big money players for their profits. Lavish entertainment with the biggest names in show business attracts the wealthy from both North America and overseas. Sport has become a big part of Las Vegas's high profile image. World championship boxing is now regularly staged in the city. For the high rollers virtually the whole deal (accommodation, entertainment, etc.) is complimentary. The casino managers hope that they will pay

Fig 3 Inside a casino, Atlantic City, New Jersey.

Fig 4 Las Vegas Strip is lined with hotels and casinos.

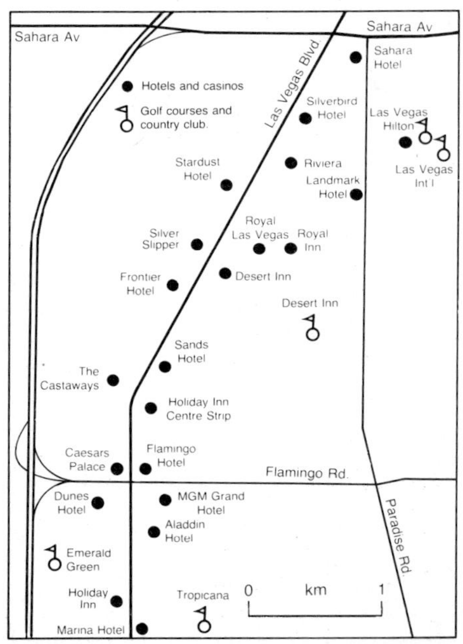

at the gaming tables. Las Vegas is not the only settlement in the USA to depend heavily on gambling. Other gambling resorts of note are Atlantic City, New Jersey and Reno, Nevada.

## Disney World

Disney World is near Orlando in central Florida. This is the USA's 'sunshine state'. Florida has long been a major tourist centre. It benefits from warm winters and hot summers with long hours of sunshine. Good quality beaches, lagoons, sandbars and warm blue seas provide an ideal coastal environment. Other natural attractions of the state include the Everglades national park, Ocala national forest and Lake Okeechobee.

The recreation industry has based a huge investment on such natural resources. Disney World is one of the major built attractions. Opened in 1971 it covers 100 square kilometres of reclaimed swamp, lake and forest. Artificial hills have been built to create a more interesting landscape. Disney World comprises hotels, campsites, a lake, top class golf courses, a marina, a natural conservation area and a car park with 12 000 places. But of course its main attraction is the Magic Kingdom Theme Park. This and some of Orlando's other famous theme parks are described in Figure 7.

**Fig 5 Many Theme Parks and attractions within driving distance of each other.**

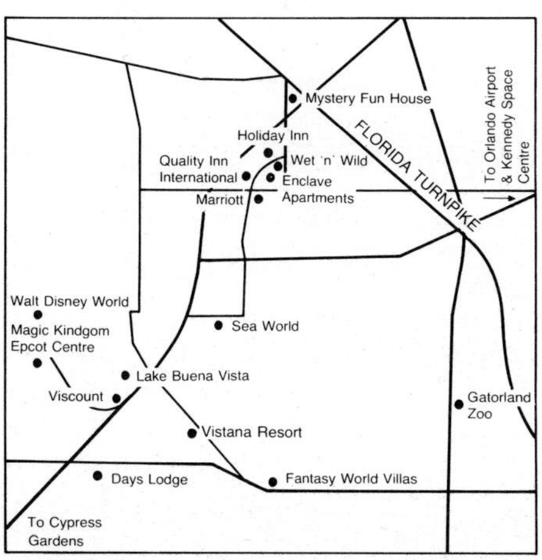


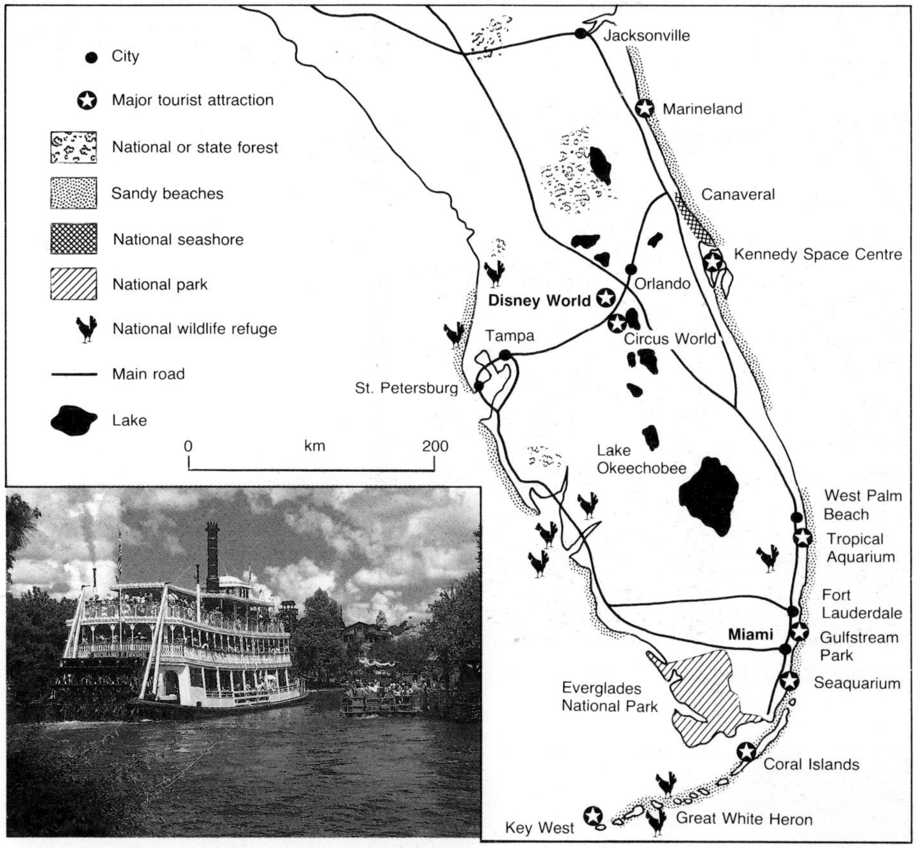


**Fig 6 Florida's Theme Parks attract visitors of all ages.**

**Fig 7 Some of Orlando's famous theme parks.**

WALT DISNEY WORLD is a collection of fantasy theme parks ranging from Adventureland's Jungle Cruise to Frontierland's steamboat rides past the haunted mansion. Disney brings alive Mickey and his pals in Fantasyland and then thrills you on The Runaway Train. See how Cinderella's Castle really looks as you stroll down 'Main Street USA' in turn-of-the-century America. Here you can take a trip to the moon from Space Mountain or plunge 20,000 leagues under the sea.

EPCOT CENTER The newest Wonder of the World is Florida's EPCOT Center—twice the size of Disney World and offering all the charms and cultures of our planet displayed around a single lake. Here you'll find Futureworld, a place to marvel at man's achievements in communications, energy and transportation by land, sea, air and, most of all, imagination. Visit the Western Entertainments Center, Discovery Island and River Country.

SEA WORLD Another 'world's largest' from Florida, Sea World is the World's largest seaquarium. The fame of its personalities, such as the performing killer whales, has grown to rival that of Mickey and Donald! Not to be missed is Shark Encounter, where you travel through a glass tunnel in the deep heart of shark infested waters. Lighter entertainment comes from the comedy Otter and Walrus shows and the Dolphinarium. A South Sea Island flavour is given by Polynesian Dancers at the Hawaiian Village and pearl-diving and the best food, drink and gifts are assembled from all over the state in the Florida Festival.

WET 'N' WILD Fun for all the family in the 15 acres of incredible watersports – waterslides, rapids, wave machines and bumper boats, known as Wet 'n' Wild. The name of this theme park says it all!

**Q1**

Study travel brochures offering holidays in Florida.

**(a)** Make lists of the locations and activities mentioned.

**(b)** To what extent and why does the price of holidays in Florida vary throughout the year?

# Index